Seventh Edition

The European Union
Economics and Policies

Edited by

Ali M. El-Agraa, PhD, DSc

Prentice Hall

FINANCIAL TIMES

An imprint of **Pearson Education**

Harlow, England • London • New York • Boston • San Francisco • Toronto • Sydney • Singapore • Hong Kong
Tokyo • Seoul • Taipei • New Delhi • Cape Town • Madrid • Mexico City • Amsterdam • Munich • Paris • Milan

Pearson Education Limited
Edinburgh Gate
Harlow
Essex CM20 2JE
England

and Associated Companies around the world

Visit us on the world wide web at:
www.pearsoned.co.uk

First published under the Philip Allan imprint in 1980
Second edition published 1983
Third edition published 1990
Fourth edition published under the Harvester Wheatsheaf imprint in 1994
Fifth edition published under the Prentice Hall Europe imprint in 1998
Sixth edition published under the Financial Times Prentice Hall imprint in 2001
Seventh edition published 2004

© Ali M. El-Agraa 1980, 2004

ISBN 0 273 67999 6

British Library Cataloguing-in-Publication Data
A CIP catalogue record for this book can be obtained from the British Library.

10 9 8 7 6 5 4 3
08 07 06 05

Typeset in 9/11.5 Sabon by 35
Produced by Ashford Colour Press, Gosport

The publisher's policy is to use paper manufactured from sustainable forests.

To all those who believe in and actively support an ever-closer unity for Europe

Lest it be forgotten, the European Union stands for the harmonized integration of some of the oldest countries in the world with very diverse cultures, languages and economic and political systems. The European Union is about unity within diversity.

Contents

Part Five EU budget and structural policies

Part Six EU external relations

Part Seven Enlargement, success and future of the EU

List of figures

List of tables

List of contributors

Brian Ardy is Research Fellow at the European Institute, London South Bank University, UK and is Visiting Lecturer in Economics at the University of Reading, UK.

Harvey W. Armstrong is Professor of Economic Geography, Department of Geography, University of Sheffield, UK.

Iain Begg is a Visiting Professor attached to the London School of Economics and Political Science, University of London, UK, and served as co-editor of the *Journal of Common Market Studies* from 1998 to 2003.

Dr Marius Brülhart is Professor of Economics, Départment d'économétrie et économie politique, Ecole des HEC, University of Lausanne, Switzerland.

Dr Kenneth Button is Professor of Public Policy, School of Public Policy, George Mason University, USA.

Dr Damian Chalmers is Reader in European Law, London School of Economics and Political Science, University of London, UK.

Dr C. Doreen E. Collins was Senior Lecturer in Social Policy and Administration, University of Leeds, UK, before taking early retirement in 1985.

Dr Victoria Curzon Price is Professor of Economics, University of Geneva, Switzerland, and former Director of the same university's European Institute.

Dr Nigel Grimwade is Principal Lecturer of Economics and Head of Economics, the Business School at London South Bank University, UK.

Dr Juha Kilponen is Economist with the Research Department of the Bank of Finland.

Dr Ulrich Koester is Professor at the Institute of Agricultural Economics, University of Kiel, Germany.

Alan Marin is Senior Lecturer in Economics, London School of Economics and Political Science, University of London, UK.

Dr Stephen Martin is Professor of Economics and Faculty Director of the Technology Transfer Initiative at the Krannert School of Management, Purdue University, USA, and is co-Managing Editor of the *International Journal of Industrial Organization*.

Alan Matthews is Jean Monnet Professor of European Agricultural Policy and Head of the Department of Economics, Trinity College Dublin, Ireland.

Dr David G. Mayes is Adviser to the Board of the Bank of Finland and Professor of Economics at London South Bank University, UK.

Dr Ella Ritchie is Jean Monnet Professor of European Integration in the School of Geography, Politics and Sociology, University of Newcastle upon Tyne, UK.

Dr Robert Salais is Professor of Economics and Director of the Research Centre IDHE, Ecole Normale Supérieure de Cachan, France.

Dr Wolf Sauter, is National Expert with the EU's Directorate General for Competition and Policy Advisor to the Independent Authority for Telecommunications and Posts (OPTA), The Hague, and was Professor of Economic Law, Groningen University, The Netherlands.

Preface

Since the first edition of this book, *The Economics of the European Community*, in 1980, it has undergone many changes. This is not the place to go through all of them, but three warrant particular mention. First, new policy areas have been added, either because they were non-existent at the beginning or have become prominent since then. Second, new contributors have joined my team, some replacing those who, for one reason or another, could no longer be with me. Third, since the fifth edition in 1998, a new title has been adopted to reflect the changes that have taken place within the Community itself as well as in the general nature and contents of the book, and for the sixth edition in 2001 the subtitle was amended.

This seventh edition maintains this tradition in all three respects. On the first count, there are two new chapters on the EMU and euro to reflect the significance of these historical EU developments and to inform about their development and operation.

On the second, Professors Iain Begg (Single European Market), Nigel Grimwade (measurement of the effects of economic integration), Ulrich Koester (Common Agricultural Policy), Stephen Martin (Energy Policy), Alan Matthews (External Trade Policy and relations with the developing countries), Ella Ritchie (Common Fisheries Policy), Robert Salais (Social Policies), and Dr Brian Ardy (tax harmonization and the general budget) have joined my team. They are all recognized experts in their respective fields and not only add freshness to the book, but also reduce my personal commitments, hence allowing me more time to devote to the entire book. I welcome all of them to my team. Dr Doreen Collins, who has been with me since the first edition, has decided to reduce her presence because she feels that she is unable to devote so much time to EU matters, especially with the demands of setting up home so far away in New Zealand. Professor Dermot McAleese, who has been a member of my team since the 1990 third edition has had to leave because of a retirement which will no doubt impose more demands on his time, given his contributions to and commitments in Ireland at both the professional and personal levels! In addition, Professor Enzo Grilli has had to leave for personal reasons. I am deeply grateful to them for their excellent contributions over the years and bid them all farewell and success with their new endeavours.

On the third count, although there is no change in either the title or subtitle, the chapters have been rearranged in a more logical fashion and now come under seven parts: EU history, institutions, legal dimension and basic statistics (four chapters); theory and measurement of economic integration (two chapters); EU monetary integration (three chapters); the single market (eight chapters); the EU budget and structural policies (five chapters); EU external relations (two chapters); and the enlargement, success and future of the EU (three chapters). I am particularly grateful to Dr Ardy for recommending the rearrangement and to Dr Adrian Gourlay of Loughborough University for his hints about them, as well as for offering a thorough report on the sixth edition. I have also split the chapter on history and institutions into two so that more guidance can be offered on the latter.

Simply updating the book is enough justification for a new edition. Adding the mentioned changes not only reinforces this, but also gives urgency to the task. However, since the publication of the sixth edition, there have been two major developments in the Union itself.

The first is the ratification of the Nice Treaty, which has enabled the 2002 Copenhagen summit to extend invitations to Cyprus, the Czech Republic, Estonia, Hungary, Latvia, Lithuania, Malta, Poland, the Slovak Republic and Slovenia to join the EU in 2004, and to Bulgaria and Romania to join in 2007, as well as recognizing Turkey as a candidate for negotiating membership at a later date. Such enlargement, the Accession Treaties for which were signed in Athens on 16 April 2003, is unique in EU history since it is set to almost double EU membership, bringing in countries very different in structure and level of development.

There are thus significant implications for almost all policy areas, especially the budget, Common Agricultural Policy, regional policy and external economic and aid relations.

The second development is related to the first, since it is about the future of the EU within the context of enlargement. The debate on this was opened by Joschka Fischer, the German Foreign Minister, but in a personal capacity, in his speech on 12 May 2000 at Humboldt University. He said, 'If we are able to meet this historic challenge and integrate the new member states without substantially denting the EU's capacity for action, we must put into place the last brick in the building of European integration, namely political integration.' The speech has attracted both positive and negative reactions from all leading EU politicians and set the scene for the Convention on the Future of Europe which has been described as a historic moment and likened to the Philadelphia Convention for America. Although the Convention is not expected to report until December 2003, it has already offered an interim constitution. Given the historic importance of enlargement, the debate on the future of Europe and the interim report, these three dramatic developments should be in any book of this nature; hence they further reinforce the need for a new edition. Therefore, they are covered in this edition, especially in the chapters where they are of direct relevance, those on history and institutions, with the final chapter being entirely devoted to them.

Again, let me thank all my contributors, not only for their excellent chapters but also for working with me under the very strict conditions (see the guide to users which follows) and bid farewell to departed members of my old team. Also, many thanks to all those who continue to use the book and send me comments on it.

Ali M. El-Agraa
Fukuoka University
Japan
September 2003

A guide to the book

The book is written in such a way that pure theory and measurement techniques are confined to separate chapters. This means that the policy chapters should be accessible to all readers. However, it also means that those who seek a rigorous, yet brief, background on international economic integration can find it handily in the same book. Moreover, as my contributors will no doubt attest, my editing style has been to ensure that the book reads as a complete whole, not as a collection of independent articles, each contributed for its own sake. This has been ensured through thorough editing and consultation with the contributors, cross-referencing, allowing repetition only where absolutely necessary, logical sequencing and a setting which begins with an introductory chapter and finishes with two on the success and future of the EU. Therefore the reader has a unique product which offers a truly single entity, yet is authored by several acknowledged authorities in the various fields.

As to the guide to users, those truly interested in the EU as a whole will have to read the entire book, if they want to understand it as a most successful scheme of international economic integration. However, those who are simply interested in the EU itself without the global context can skip Chapters 6, 7 and 8, since these are devoted to theoretical and measurement considerations which pertain to all schemes. Those interested only in the policy areas of the EU can drop Chapters 2–9, although Chapter 2 is important for a proper understanding. Those interested only in EU economic policies can drop Chapters 2–4 and 23 and, if not interested in the future of the EU, can also drop Chapter 28. Those interested only in EMU and the euro can confine themselves to Chapters 8–11, but are advised to read Chapters 2 and 28 for a proper understanding; those interested in this area with emphasis on the UK will find my 2002 book *The Euro and Britain: Implications of Moving into EMU* more appropriate. Also various combinations of chapters can be made, depending on what the user/reader has in mind. For example those interested in a very basic understanding of the EU can use Chapters 2, 3, 27 and 28.

Finally, the entire book is written with those in mind who want to pursue further study. Thus, within every chapter the reader is directed to the most relevant research publications in the field and these are fully set out in the References at the end of the book. This means that there are no guides to further reading at the end of each chapter and certainly no guides to other texts, since it is not our task to supply them, especially when this book is a pioneer in its field.

Acknowledgements

We are grateful to the following for permission to reproduce copyright material:

Table 5.16 adapted from *Atlantic Tariffs and Trade*, published by Routledge, reprinted by permission of Thomson Publishing Services (Political and Economic Planning, 1962); Figures 6.8, 6.9 and 6.10 from The UTR versus CU formation analysis and Article XXIV in *Applied Economics Letters*, Vol. 9, No. 9, reprinted by permission of Taylor & Francis, http://www.tandf.co.uk/journals/routledge/13504851.html (El-Agraa, A. M. 2002); Tables 7.1 and 7.7 from Trade creation and trade diversion in the European Common Market: An appraisal of the evidence in *The Manchester School*, Vol. 42, reprinted by permission of Blackwell Publishing Ltd. (Balassa, B. 1974); Table 7.11 adapted from The contribution of the European Community to economic growth in *Journal of Common Market Studies*, Vol. 24, No. 4, reprinted by permission of Blackwell Publishing Ltd. (Marques-Mendes, J. A. 1986); Table 13.11 from *Technology Policy in the European Union*, reprinted by permission of Palgrave Macmillan (Peterson, J. and Sharp, M. 1998); Table 14.1, Figure 25.1 and Table 25.3 from *Revenue Statistics 1965–2001*, reprinted by permission of OECD (OECD 2002); Table 14.6 from Tax policy in the European Union in *FinanzArchiv* 58/4, reprinted by permission of the author (Cnossen, S. 2001); Figures 16.1, 16.2 and 16.3 from *Energy Balances of OECD Countries, 1999–2000*, reprinted by permission of OECD (OECD 2002); Table 16.2 from *Energy Balances of the OECD Countries 1999–2000*, © OECD/IEA, 2002, reprinted by permission of OECD/IEA (IEA 2002); Tables 16.4 and 16.5 from *Annual Statistical Bulletin*, reprinted by permission of OPEC (Public Relations and Information Dept.) (OPEC 2001); Table 16.6 from *A European Market for Electricity?*, reprinted by permission of CEPR (Bergmann, L. *et al.* 1999); Table 16.7 republished with permission of Dow Jones & Co. Inc., from EU states agree to open energy markets by 2004 in *Wall Street Journal. Europe*, 18 March 2002; permission conveyed through Copyright Clearance Center, Inc. (Hofheinz, P. and Mitchener, B. 2002); Table 18.1 from Summary indicators of product market regulation with an extension of employment protection legislation in *Working Paper No. 226*, reprinted by permission of OECD (Nicoletti, G., Scarpetta, S. and Boylaud, O. 2000); Tables 18.6 and 18.8 adapted from *SOPEMI: Trends in International Migration: Annual Report 1999. Continuous reporting system on migration*, reprinted by permission of OECD (OECD 1999); Table 24.1 from *International Trade Statistics*, November, reprinted by permission of WTO (WTO 2002); Tables 24.2, 24.3 and 24.4 computed from *International Trade Statistics*, reprinted by permission of WTO (WTO 2002); Table 24.5 from *The European Union's Trade Policies and their Economic Effects*, reprinted by permission of OECD (OECD 2000); Table 25.1 republished with permission of World Bank, from *Global Economic Prospects 2003*, Copyright 2003; permission conveyed through Copyright Clearance Center, Inc. (World Bank 2003); Table 25.2 from *European Community Development Cooperation Review Series*, reprinted by permission of OECD (OECD 2002).

We are grateful to the following for permission to reproduce texts:

WTO for an extract from WTO's Article XXIV.

In some instances we have been unable to trace the owners of copyright material, and we would appreciate any information that would enable us to do so.

List of abbreviations

AAMS	Association of African and Malagasy States	BENELUX	Belgium, the Netherlands and Luxembourg Economic Union
AAU	Arab–African Union	BRAIN	Basic research in adaptive intelligence and neurocomputing
ACC	Arab Cooperation Council		
ACM	Arab Common Market		
ACP	African, Caribbean and Pacific countries party to the Lomé Convention (now the Contonou Agreement)	BRIDGE	Biotechnological Research for Innovation, Development and Growth in Europe
		BRITE/EURAM	Basic research in industrial technologies for Europe/raw materials and advanced materials
ADAPT	Community initiative concerning the adaptation of the workforce to industrial change		
AEC	Arab Economic Council	BSE	Bovine spongiform encephalopathy
AIM	Advanced informatics in medicine		
		BU	Benin Union
AL	Arab League	CAA	Civil Aviation Authority
ALADI	Association for Latin American Integration	CACM	Central American Common Market
Altener	Specific actions to promote greater penetration of renewable energy sources	CADDIA	Cooperation in automation of data and documentation for imports/exports and agriculture
AMU	Arab Maghreb Union		
ANZCERTA	Australia and New Zealand Closer Economic Relations and Trade Agreement (also CER)	CAEU	Council for Arab Economic Unity
		CAP	Common Agricultural Policy
ARION	Programme of study visits for decision makers in education	CARICOM	Caribbean Community
		CARIFTA	Caribbean Free Trade Association
ASEAN	Association of South-East Asian Nations		
		CCP	Common Commercial Policy
ASEM	Asia–Europe meeting	CCT	Common Customs Tariff
AU	The African Union	CEAO	Communauté Economique de l'Afrique de l'Ouest
BAP	Biotechnology action programme		
		CEC	Commission of the European Communities
BATNEEC	Best available technology not entailing excessive cost		
		CEDB	Component event data bank
BC-NET	Business Cooperation Network	CEDEFOP	European Centre for Development of Vocational Training
BCR	Community Bureau of References		
BEP	Biomolecular engineering programme	CEEC	Countries of Central and Eastern Europe
BEST	Business Environment Simplification Task Force	CEEP	European Centre for Population Studies

CEN	European Committee for Standardization	CU	Customs union
CENELEC	European Committee for Electrotechnical Standardization	DAC	Development Assistance Committee (OECD)
CEP	Common energy policy	DDR	German Democratic Republic (now part of Germany)
CEPGL	Economic Community of the Countries of the Great Lakes	DELTA	Developing European learning through technological advance
CER	Closer Economic Relations	DG IV	Directorate General Four
CERN	European Organization for Nuclear Research	DI	Divergence indicator
		DRIVE	Dedicated road infrastructure for vehicle safety in Europe
CET	Common external tariff		
CFP	Common Fisheries Policy	DV	Dummy variable
CFSP	Common Foreign and Security Policy	EAC	East African Community
		EAGGF	European Agricultural Guidance and Guarantee Fund
CI	Community Initiative		
CIS	Commonwealth of Independent States	EBRD	European Bank for Reconstruction and Development
CM	Common market		
CMEA	Council for Mutual Economic Assistance	EC	European Community
		ECB	European Central Bank
CN	Combined Nomenclature	ECHO	European Community Humanitarian Office
CODEST	Committee for the European Development of Science and Technology	ECIP	European Community Investment Partners
COMECON	see CMEA	ECJ	European Court of Justice
COMETT	Community programme in education and training for technology	ECLAIR	European collaborative linkage of agriculture and industry through research
CORDIS	Community research and development information service	ECMT	European Conference of Ministers of Transport
COREPER	Committee of Permanent Representatives	ECOFIN	European Council of Ministers for Financial Affairs
CORINE	Coordination of information on the environment in Europe	ECOSOC	Economic and Social Committee (also ESC)
COSINE	Cooperation for open systems interconnection networking in Europe	ECOWAS	Economic Community of West African States
		ECSC	European Coal and Steel Community
COST	European cooperation on scientific and technical research	ECU	European currency unit
CREST	Scientific and Technical Research Committee	EDC	European Defence Community
		EDF	European Development Fund
CRS	Computerised Reservation System	EDIFACT	Electronic data interchange for administration, commerce and transport
CSCE	Conference on Security and Cooperation in Europe	EEA	European Economic Area
CSF	Community support framework	EEC	European Economic Community
CSTID	Committee for Scientific and Technical Information and Documentation	EEZ	Exclusive Economic Zone
		EFTA	European Free Trade Association
CTP	Common Transport Policy	EGE	European Group on Ethics in Science and New Technologies
CTS	Conformance testing services		

EIB	European Investment Bank	FCO	Foreign and Commonwealth Office
EIF	European Investment Fund		
EMCF	European Monetary Cooperation Fund	FEER	Fundamental Equilibrium Exchange Rate
EMF	European Monetary Fund	FEOGA	European Agricultural Guidance and Guarantee Fund
EMI	European Monetary Institute		
EMS	European Monetary System	FIFG	Financial Instrument for Fisheries Guidance
EMU	European monetary union or economic and monetary union	FLAIR	Food-linked agro-industrial research
EP	European Parliament		
EPC	European political cooperation	FSU	Former Soviet Union
EPOCH	European programme on climatology and natural hazards	FTA	Free trade area
		GATS	General Agreement on Trade in Services
EQS	Environmental quality standard		
Erasmus	European Community action scheme for the mobility of university students	GATT	General Agreement on Tariffs and Trade (UN)
		GCC	Gulf Cooperation Council
		GDP	Gross domestic product
ERDF	European Regional Development Fund	GFCM	General Fisheries Council for the Mediterranean
ERM	Exchange-rate mechanism		
ESA	European Space Agency	GNI	Gross national income
ESCB	European System of Central Banks	GNP	Gross national product
		GSP	Generalized system of preferences
ESF	European Social Fund		
ESI	Electricity supply industry	HDTV	High-definition television
ESPRIT	European strategic programme for research and development in information technology	HELIOS	Action programme to promote social and economic integration and an independent way of life for disabled people
ETUC	European Trade Union Confederation	HS	Harmonized Commodity Description and Coding System
EU	European Union		
EUA	European Unit of Account	IAEA	International Atomic Energy Agency (UN)
Euratom	European Atomic Energy Commission		
		IATA	International Air Transport Association
EUREKA	European Research Co-ordinating Agency	IBRD	International Bank for Reconstruction and Development (World Bank) (UN)
EURES	European Employment Services		
EUROCONTROL	European Organization for the safety of Air Navigation		
EURONET-DIANE	Direct information access network for Europe	ICES	International Council for the Exploration of the Seas
EUROSTAT	Statistical office of the EC/EU	ICONE	Comparative index of national and European standards
EVCA	European Venture Capital Association	IDA	International Development Association (UN)
FADN	EEC farm accountancy data network	IDB	Inter-American Development Bank
FAO	Food and Agriculture Organization of the United Nations	IDO	Integrated development operation
FAST	Forecasting and assessment in the field of science and technology	IEA	International Energy Agency (OECD)

IEM	Internal energy market	MAGP	Multi-annual guidance programme
IGC	Intergovernmental conference		
IIT	Intra-industry trade	MARIE	Mass transit rail initiative for Europe
ILO	International Labour Organization		
		MAST	Marine science and technology
IMF	International Monetary Fund (UN)	MB	Marginal benefit
		MC	Marginal cost
IMP	Integrated Mediterranean programme	MCA	Monetary compensatory amount
IMPACT	Information market policy actions	MEDIA	Measures to encourage the development of the audio-visual industry
INSIS	Inter-institutional system of integrated services		
		MEP	Member of the European Parliament
INTERREG	Community initiative concerning border areas		
		MERCUSOR	Southern Cone Common Market
IRCC	International Radio Consultative Committee		
		MERM	Multilateral exchange rate model
IRIS	Network of demonstration projects on vocational training for women		
		MFA	Multifibre Arrangement (arrangement regarding international trade in textiles)
IRTE	Integrated road transport environment		
		MFN	Most-favoured nation
IPR	Intellectual Property Rights	MFP	Multiannual framework programme
ISIS	Integrated standards information system		
		MFT	Multilateral free trade
ISPA	Instrument for structural policies for pre-accession	MISEP	Mutual information system on employment policies
ITA	Information technology agreement	MONITOR	Research programme on strategic analysis, forecasting and assessment in research and technology
ITER	International thermonuclear experimental reactor		
JESSI	Joint European Submieron Silicon Initiative	MP	Marginal productivity
		MRU	Mano River Union
JET	Joint European Torus	NAFTA	North Atlantic Free Trade Agreement; New Zealand Australia Free Trade Area
JHA	Judicial and home affairs		
JOP	Joint venture programme PHARE-TACIS		
		NAIRU	Non-accelerating inflation rate of unemployment
JOULE	Joint opportunities for unconventional or long-term energy supply		
		NATO	North Atlantic Treaty Organization
JRC	Joint Research Centre	NCB	National Central Bank
KALEIDOSCOPE	Programme to support artistic and cultural activities having a European dimension	NCI	New Community Instrument
		NEAFC	North-East Atlantic Fisheries Commission
LAFTA	Latin American Free Trade Area	NET	Next European Torus
LDC	Less-developed country	NETT	Network for environmental technology transfer
LEDA	Local employment development action programme		
		NGO	Non-governmental organization
LIFE	Financial Instrument for the Environment	NIC	Newly-industrializing country
		NIE	Newly-industrializing economy

NIEO	New International Economic Order	PTC	Pacific Telecommunications Conference
NIS	Newly Independent States (of the former USSR)	PTT	Posts, Telegraphs and Telecommunications
NOHA	Network on Humanitarian Assistance	QMV	Qualified Majority Voting
NPCI	National programme of Community interest	RACE	Research and development in advanced communication technologies for Europe
NPT	Treaty on Non-proliferation of Nuclear Weapons	RARE	Réseaux associés pour la recherche européenne
NTB	Non-tariff barrier	R&TD	Research and technological development
NTM	Non-tariff measure		
NUTS	Nomenclature of Territorial Units for Statistics	RCD	Regional Cooperation for Development
OAPEC	Organization of Arab Petroleum Exporting Countries	REGIS	Community initiative concerning the most remote regions
OAU	Organization for African Unity	REIMEP	Regular European interlaboratory measurements evaluation programme
OCTs	Overseas countries and territories		
ODA	Overseas Development Aid	RENAVAL	Programme to assist the conversion of shipbuilding areas
OECD	Organization for Economic Cooperation and Development	RESIDER	Programme to assist the conversion of steel areas
OEEC	Organization for European Economic Cooperation	RIA	Regional impact assessment
OPEC	Organization of Petroleum Exporting Countries	RTA	Regional trade agreement
		RTD	Research and Technological Development
OSCE	Organization for Security and Cooperation in Europe	SACU	Southern African Customs Union
OSI	Open systems interconnection		
PAFTAD	Pacific Trade and Development Conference	SAP	Social action programme
		SAST	Strategic analysis in the field of science and technology
PBEC	Pacific Basin Economic Council		
PECC	Pacific Economic Cooperation Conference	SAVE	Specific Actions for Vigorous Energy efficiency
PEDIP	Programme to modernize Portuguese industry	SCENT	System for a customs enforcement network
PETRA	Action programme for the vocational training of young people and their preparation for adult and working life	SCIENCE	Plan to stimulate the international cooperation and interchange necessary for European researchers
		SDR	Special drawing rights
PHARE	Programme of community aid for central and eastern European countries	SEA	Single European Act
		SEDOC	Inter-state notification of job vacancies
PO	Producer Organization	SEM	Single European Market
POSEIDOM	Programme of options specific to the remote and insular nature of the overseas departments	SEM 2000	Sound and efficient management
		SFOR	Multinational stabilization force
PPP	Polluter pays principle	SLIM	Simpler Legislation for the Internal Market
PTA	Preferential trade area		

SMEs	Small- and medium-sized Enterprises	UEMOA	West African Economic and Monetary Union
SPD	Single Programme Documents	UES	Uniform emission standards
SPEAR	Support programme for a European assessment of research	UN	United Nations
		UNCLOS	United Nations Conference on the Law of the Sea
SPES	Stimulation plan for economic science	UNCTAD	United Nations Conference on Trade and Development
SPRINT	Strategic programme for innovation and technology transfer	UNECA	United Nations Economic Commission for Africa
STABEX	System for the stabilization of ACP and OCT export earnings	UNEP	United Nations Environment Programme
STAR	Community programme for the development of certain less-favoured regions of the Community by improving access to advanced telecommunications services	UNESCO	United Nations Educational, Scientific and Cultural Organization
		UNHCR	United Nations High Commissioner for Refugees
STEP	Science and technology for environmental protection	UNICE	Union of Industries of the European Community
SYNERGY	Multinational programme to promote international cooperation in the energy sector	UNIDO	United Nations Industrial Development Organization
		UNRWA	United Nations Relief and Works Agency for Palestine Refugees in the Near East
SYSMIN	Special financing facility for ACP and OCT mining products		
TAC	Total allowable catch	URAA	Uruguay Round Agreement on Agriculture
TARIC	Integrated Community tariff		
TEDIS	Trade electronic data interchange systems	URBAN	Community initiative for urban areas
TELEMAN	Research and training programme on remote handling in nuclear hazardous and disordered environments	UTR	Unilateral tariff reduction
		VALOREN	Community programme for the development of certain less-favoured regions of the Community by exploiting endogenous energy potential
TEMPUS	Trans-European cooperation scheme for higher education		
TENs	Trans-European Networks	VALUE	Programme for the dissemination and utilization of research results
TESS	Modernization of the exchange of information between national social security institutions		
		VAT	Value added tax
TEU	Treaty on European Union	VER	Voluntary export restraint
TRIPs	Trade-related aspects of intellectual property rights	VSTF	Very short-term financing facility
TSEs	Transmissible spongiform encephalopathies	WEU	Western European Union
		WFC	World Food Council (UN)
t/t	Terms of trade	WFP	World Food Programme (UN)
TVA	Tax sur la valeur ajoutée	WIPO	World Intellectual Property Organization (UN)
TUC	Trades Union Congress		
UDEAC	Union Douanière et Economique de l'Afrique Centrale	WTO	World Trade Organization
		YES	'Youth for Europe' programme (youth exchange scheme)

Chapter 1

General introduction: the EU within the global context of regional integration

ALI EL-AGRAA

The European Union (EU) is the most prominent scheme of 'international economic integration' (hereafter, simply economic integration). The aim of this chapter is to provide a precise definition of the term economic integration, to describe the various schemes that have been adopted worldwide, hence to set the EU within their broader context, and to provide a general outline of this book.

1.1   What is economic integration?

Economic integration is one aspect of 'international economics' which has been growing in importance for just over five decades. The term itself has a rather short history; indeed, Machlup (1977) was unable to find a single instance of its use prior to 1942. Since then the term has been used at various times to refer to practically any area of international economic relations. By 1950, however, the term had been given a specific definition by economists specializing in international trade to denote a state of affairs or a process which involves the amalgamation of separate economies into larger free trading regions. It is in this more limited sense that the term is used today. However, one should hasten to add that economists not familiar with this branch of international economics have for quite a while been using the term to mean simply increasing economic interdependence between nations.

More specifically, economic integration (also referred to as 'regional integration', 'preferential trading agreements' – PTAs – and trading blocs) is concerned with the discriminatory removal of all trade impediments between at least two participating nations and with the establishment of certain elements of cooperation and coordination between them. The latter depends entirely on the actual form that integration takes. Different forms of economic integration can be envisaged and many have actually been implemented (see Table 1.1 for schematic presentation):

1   *Free trade areas*, where the member nations remove all trade impediments among themselves but retain their freedom with regard to the determination of their own policies *vis-à-vis* the outside world (the non-participants). Recently, the trend has been to extend these treatments also to investment. Examples of FTAs are, the European Free Trade Association (EFTA), the defunct Latin American Free

Table 1.1 Schematic presentation of economic integration schemes

Scheme	Free intra-scheme trade	Common commercial policy	Free factor mobility	Common monetary and fiscal policy	One government
Free trade area (FTA)	Yes	No	No	No	No
Customs union (CU)	Yes	Yes	No	No	No
Common market (CM)	Yes	Yes	Yes	No	No
Economic union (EcU)	Yes	Yes	Yes	Yes	No
Political union	Yes	Yes	Yes	Yes	Yes

Trade Area (LAFTA), and the North American Free Trade Agreement (NAFTA) which explicitly covers investment.

2 *Customs unions*, which are very similar to free trade areas except that member nations must conduct and pursue common external commercial relations – for instance, they must adopt common external tariffs (CETs) on imports from the non-participants as is the case in, *inter alia*, the EU, (which is in this particular sense a customs union, but, as we shall presently see, it is more than that), the Central American Common Market (CACM) and the Caribbean Community and Common Market (CARICOM).

3 *Common markets*, which are custom unions that allow also for free factor mobility across national member frontiers, i.e. capital, labour, technology and enterprises should move unhindered between the participating countries – for example, the EU (but again it is more complex).

4 *Complete economic unions*, simply economic unions, which are common markets that ask for complete unification of monetary and fiscal policies, i.e. the participants must introduce a central authority to exercise control over these matters so that member nations effectively become regions of the same nation – the EU is close to becoming one.

5 *Complete political unions*, where the participating countries become literally one nation, i.e. the central authority needed in complete economic unions should be paralleled by a common parliament and other necessary institutions needed to guarantee the sovereignty of one state – an example of this is the unification of the two Germanys in 1990.

However, one should hasten to add that political integration need not be, and in the majority of cases will never be, part of this list. Nevertheless, it can, of course, be introduced as a form of unity and for no economic reason whatsoever, as was the case with the two Germanys and as is the case with the pursuit of the unification of the Korean Peninsula, although one should naturally be interested in its economic consequences (see below). More generally, one should indeed stress that each of these forms of economic

integration can be introduced in its own right; hence they should not be confused with *stages* in a *process* which eventually leads to either complete economic or political union although many schemes evolved in stages.

It should also be noted that there may be *sectoral* integration, as distinct from general across-the-board integration, in particular areas of the economy as was the case with the European Coal and Steel Community (ECSC, see Chapters 2 and 16), created in 1951 and valid for fifty years, but sectoral integration is a form of cooperation not only because it is inconsistent with the accepted definition of economic integration but also because it may contravene the rules of the General Agreement on Tariffs and Trade (GATT), now called the World Trade Organization (WTO) – see below. Sectoral integration may also occur within any of the mentioned schemes, as is the case with the EU Common Agricultural Policy (CAP, see Chapter 20), but then it is nothing more than a 'policy'.

One should further point out that it has been claimed that economic integration can be *negative* or *positive*. The term negative integration was coined by Tinbergen (1954) to refer to the simple act of the removal of impediments on trade between the participating nations or to the elimination of any restrictions on the process of trade liberalization. The term positive integration relates to the modification of existing instruments and institutions and, more importantly, to the creation of new ones so as to enable the market of the integrated area to function properly and effectively and also to promote other broader policy aims of the scheme. Hence, at the risk of oversimplification, according to this classification, it can be stated that sectoral integration and free trade areas are forms of economic integration which require only negative integration, while the remaining types require positive integration, since, as a minimum, they need the positive act of adopting common relations. However, in reality this distinction is oversimplistic not only because practically all existing types of economic integration have found it essential to introduce some elements of positive integration, but also because theoretical considerations clearly indicate that no scheme of economic integration is viable without certain elements of positive integration; for example, even the ECSC deemed it necessary to establish new institutions to tackle its specified tasks – see below and Chapter 2.

1.2 Economic integration and WTO rules

The rules of WTO, GATT's successor, allow the formation of economic integration schemes on the understanding that, although free trade areas, customs unions, etc. are discriminatory associations, they may not pursue policies which increase the level of their discrimination beyond that which existed prior to their formation, and that tariffs and other trade restrictions (with some exceptions) are removed on *substantially* (increasingly interpreted to mean at least 90% of intra-members' trade) all the trade among the participants. Hence, once allowance was made for the proviso regarding the external trade relations of the economic integration scheme (the CET level, or the common level of discrimination against extra-area trade, in a customs union, and the average tariff or trade discrimination level in a free trade area), it seemed to the drafters of Article XXIV (see Appendix 1.1, p. **20**) that economic integration did not contradict the basic principles of WTO – trade *liberalization* on a most-favoured-nation (MFN) basis, *non-discrimination, transparency* of instruments used to restrict trade and the promotion of *growth and stability* of the world economy – or more generally the principles of *non-discrimination, transparency* and *reciprocity.*

There are more serious arguments suggesting that Article XXIV is in direct contradiction to the spirit of WTO – see Chapter 6 and, *inter alia*, Dam (1970). However, Wolf (1983, p. 156) argues that if nations decide to treat one another as if they are part of a single economy, nothing can be done to prevent them, and that economic integration schemes, particularly like the EU at the time of its formation in 1957, have a strong impulse towards liberalization; in the case of the EU at the time mentioned, the setting of the CETs happened to coincide with GATT's Kennedy Round of tariff reductions. However, recent experience, especially in the case of the EU, has proved otherwise since there has been a proliferation of non-tariff barriers, that is why the 'single market' programme (Chapter 11) was introduced in 1992, but the point about WTO not being able to deter countries from pursuing economic integration has general validity: WTO has no means for enforcing its rules; it has no coercion powers.

Of course, these considerations are more complicated than is suggested here, particularly since there are those who would argue that nothing could be more discriminatory than for a group of nations to remove all tariffs and trade impediments on their mutual trade while *at the same time* maintaining the initial levels against outsiders. Indeed, it would be difficult to find 'clubs' which extend equal privileges to non-subscribers, although the Asia Pacific Economic Cooperation (APEC) forum aspires to 'open regionalism', one interpretation of which is the extending of the removals of restrictions on trade and investment to all countries, not just the members. This point lies behind the concern with whether economic integration hinders or enhances the prospects for the free multilateral regime that the WTO is supposed to promote (see El-Agraa, 1999, for the arguments for and against). Moreover, as we shall see in Chapter 6, economic integration schemes may lead to resource reallocation effects which are economically undesirable. However, to deny nations the right to form such associations, particularly when the main driving force may be political rather than economic, would have been a major setback for the world community. Hence, all that needs to be stated here is that as much as Article XXIV raises serious problems regarding how it fits in with the general spirit of WTO, and many proposals have been put forward for its reform, it also reflects its drafters' deep understanding of the future development of the world economy.

1.3 The global experience

Although this book is concerned with the EU, it is important to view the EU within the context of the global experience of economic integration. This section provides a brief summary of this experience – see El-Agraa (1997) for a full and detailed coverage.

Since the end of the Second World War various forms of economic integration have been proposed and numerous schemes have actually been implemented. Even though some of those introduced were later discontinued or completely reformulated, the number adopted during the decade commencing in 1957 was so great as to prompt Haberler in 1964 to describe that period as the 'age of integration'. After 1964, however, there has been such a proliferation of integration schemes that Haberler's description may be more apt for the post-1964 era.

The EU is the most significant and influential of these arrangements since it comprises some of the most advanced nations of Western Europe: Austria, Belgium, Denmark, Finland, France, Germany, Greece, Ireland, Italy, Luxembourg, the Netherlands, Portugal, Spain, Sweden and the United Kingdom (UK) – see Table 1.2 for a tabulation of integration arrangements (note that Tables 1.2–1.5 include arrangements not specified in the text but which are self-explanatory). The EU was founded by six (not quite, since Germany was then not yet united) of these nations (Belgium, France, West Germany, Italy, Luxembourg and the Netherlands, usually referred to as the *Original Six*, simply the Six hereafter) by two treaties, signed in Rome on the same day in 1957, creating the *European Economic Community* (EEC) and the *European Atomic Energy Community* (Euratom). However, the Six had then been members of the *European Coal and Steel Community* (ECSC) which was established by the Treaty of Paris in 1951 and valid for 50 years. Thus, in 1957 the Six belonged to three communities, but in 1965 it was deemed sensible to merge the three entities into one and to call it the *European Communities* (EC). Three of the remaining nine (Denmark, Ireland and the UK) joined later, in 1973. Greece became a full member in January 1981, Portugal and Spain in 1986, and Austria, Finland and Sweden in 1995.

At present, the EU is set to include another 12–15 new members. Six began full accession negotiations in 1988 and the 2002 Copenhagen summit gave them the go ahead to join in 2004: Cyprus, the Czech Republic, Estonia, Hungary, Poland and Slovenia. Also, the Helsinki summit of December 1999 ruled that six more (Bulgaria, Latvia, Lithuania, Malta, Romania and Slovakia) could commence full negotiations from February 2000, each at its own pace, and the 2002 Copenhagen summit also decided that four of the six could accede in 2004 and Bulgaria and Romania in 2007. Moreover, a change in regime brought Croatia closer to joining. Furthermore, after 36 years of temporizing, it was also agreed at the same summit that Turkey is a recognized candidate, but negotiations are unlikely to start for a long time since the EU wants to see big improvements in Turkey's political and human

rights behaviour, including the rights of Kurds and other minorities and the constitutional role of the army in political life, which might require changes in its constitution. The EU also wants the country to resolve territorial squabbles with Greece in the Aegean Sea and to help end the division of Cyprus, where a Turkish-backed regime has occupied the north of the island since 1974. However, one should add that these conditions are not new since they are consistent with those in *Agenda 2000*, the EU's official document on enlargement (CEU, 1997b). Note that most of these Central and Eastern European Countries (CEECs), had already signed *Agreements of Association* with the EU and the ten also signed accession treaties on 16 April 2003. Furthermore, the EU, Iceland, Liechtenstein and Norway belong to the *European Economic Area* (EEA), a scheme introduced in 1992 which provides Iceland and Norway with virtual membership of the EU, but without having a say in EU decisions; indeed the EEA is seen as a stepping-stone in the direction of full EU membership. Thus, if all goes according to plan, the EU is set to comprise the whole of Europe since Switzerland has not withdrawn the application it lodged several years ago.

Although the EEC Treaty relates simply to the formation of a customs union and provides the basis for a common market in terms of free factor mobility, many of the originators of the EEC saw it as a phase in a process culminating in complete economic and political union. Thus the *Treaty on European Union* (the Maastricht Treaty, later ratified and extended by the *Treaty of Amsterdam* – see Chapter 2), which transformed the EC into the EU in 1994 and which provides the EU with, *inter alia*, a single central bank, a single currency (presently for only 12 members), and common foreign and defence policies, would be regarded in some quarters as a positive step towards the attainment of the founding fathers' desired ideal.

EFTA is the other major scheme of economic integration in Europe. To understand its membership one has to know something about its history (detailed in Chapter 2). In the mid-1950s when an EEC of the Six plus the UK was being contemplated, the UK was unprepared to commit itself to some of the economic and political aims envisaged for that community. For example, the adoption of a common agricultural policy and the eventual political unity of Western Europe were seen as aims which were in direct conflict with the UK's powerful position in the world and its interests in the Commonwealth, particularly with regard

Table 1.2 Economic integration in Europe

Scheme Founded Aim	EU 1957 CM/EcU[a]	EU 2004 CM/EcU[a]	EU 2007 CM/EcU[a]	EFTA[b] 1960 FTA[a]	EEA 1992 FTA[a]	EFTA/East Europe[c] 1992 FTA[a]
Austria	x				x	
Belgium	x				x	
Denmark	x				x	
Finland	x				x	
France	x				x	
Germany	x				x	
Greece	x				x	
Ireland	x				x	
Italy	x				x	
Luxembourg	x				x	
Netherlands	x				x	
Portugal	x				x	
Spain	x				x	
Sweden	x				x	
UK	x				x	
Iceland				x	x	x
Norway				x	x	x
Switzerland and				x		x
Liechtenstein				x	x	x
Bulgaria			x			x
Cyprus		x				
Czech Rep.		x				x
Estonia		x				
Hungary		x				x
Latvia		x				
Lithuania		x				
Malta		x				
Poland		x				x
Romania			x			x
Slovak Rep.		x				
Slovenia						x
Turkey						

[a] FTA = free trade area; CU = customs union; EcU = complete economic union.
[b] Finland was an associate member until its accession in 1986, and Liechtenstein became a full member in 1991.
[c] The countries involved have agreed to examine conditions for the gradual establishment of an FTA.

to 'Commonwealth preference' which granted special access to the markets of the Commonwealth. Hence the UK favoured the idea of a Western Europe which adopted free trade in industrial products only, thus securing for itself the advantages offered by the Commonwealth as well as opening up Western Europe as a free market for its industrial goods. In short, the UK sought to achieve the best of both worlds for itself, which is, of course, quite understandable. However, it is equally understandable that such an arrangement was not acceptable to those seriously contemplating the formation of the EEC, especially France which stood to lose in an arrangement excluding a common policy for agriculture. As a result the UK approached those Western European nations which had similar interests with the purpose of forming an alternative scheme of economic integration to counteract any possible damage due to the formation of the EEC. The outcome was EFTA, which was established in 1960 by the Stockholm Convention with the object of creating a free market for industrial products only; there were some agreements on non-manufactures but these were relatively unimportant.

The membership of EFTA consisted of Austria, Denmark, Norway, Portugal, Sweden, Switzerland (and Liechtenstein) and the UK. Finland became an associate member in 1961, and Iceland joined in 1970 as a full member. But, as already stated, Denmark and the UK (together with Ireland) joined the EC in 1973; Portugal (together with Spain) joined in 1986; Austria, Finland and Sweden joined the EU in 1995. This left EFTA with a membership consisting mainly of a few and relatively smaller nations of Western Europe – see Table 1.2.

Until recently, economic integration schemes in Europe were not confined to the EU and EFTA. Indeed, before the dramatic events of 1989–1990, the socialist planned economies of Eastern Europe had their own arrangement which operated under the CMEA, or COMECON as it was generally known in the West. The CMEA was formed in 1949 by Bulgaria, Czechoslovakia, the German Democratic Republic, Hungary, Poland, Romania and the USSR; they were later joined by three non-European countries: Mongolia (1962), Cuba (1972) and Vietnam (1978). In its earlier days, before the death of Stalin, the activities of the CMEA were confined to the collation of the plans of the member states, the development of a uniform system of reporting statistical data and the recording of foreign trade statistics. However, during the 1970s a series of

measures was adopted by the CMEA to implement their 'Comprehensive Programme of Socialist Integration', hence indicating that the organization was moving towards a form of integration based principally on methods of plan coordination and joint planning activity, rather than on market levers (Smith, 1977). Finally, attention should be drawn to the fact that the CMEA comprised a group of relatively small countries and one 'super power' and that the long-term aim of the association was to achieve a highly organized and integrated bloc, without any agreement ever having been made on how or when that was to be accomplished.

The dramatic changes that have recently taken place in Eastern Europe and the former USSR have inevitably led to the demise of the CMEA. This, together with the fact that the CMEA did not really achieve much in the nature of economic integration – indeed some analysts have argued that the entire organization was simply an instrument for the USSR to dictate its wishes to the rest – are the reasons why El-Agraa's (1997) book does not contain a chapter on the CMEA; the interested reader will find a chapter in El-Agraa (1988b). However, one should hasten to add that soon after the demise of the USSR, 12 of the 15 former Soviet Republics formed the Commonwealth of Independent States (CIS) to bring them closer together in a relationship originally intended, but to no avail, to match that of the EU nations. The countries are Armenia, Azerbaijan, Belarus, Georgia, Kazakhstan, Kyrgyzstan, Moldova, Russia, Tajikistan, Turkmenistan, Ukraine and Uzbekistan; the missing three being Estonia, Latvia and Lithuania which are as mentioned set to join the EU in 2004.

Before leaving Europe it should be mentioned that there are also the Central European Free Trade Agreement (CEFTA), in force since 1993, the Baltic Free Trade Area (BFTA), in force since 1994 and the Nordic Community. The CEFTA comprises Bulgaria, the Czech Republic, Hungary, Poland, Romania, the Slovak Republic and Slovenia so it is between transition countries now set to join the EU. The Nordic Community consists of the five Nordic countries: Denmark, Finland, Iceland, Norway and Sweden. However, in spite of claims to the contrary (Sundelius and Wiklund, 1979), the Nordic scheme is one of cooperation rather than economic integration since its members belong to either the EU or EFTA, and, as we have seen, the EU and EFTA are closely linked through the EEA.

Africa has numerous schemes of economic integration, with practically all the African countries belonging to more than one scheme (Table 1.3). In West Africa, the *Union Economique et Monétaire Ouest-Africaine* (UEMOA) and *Mano River Union* (MRU) co-exist with the *Economic Community of West African States* (ECOWAS), with all members belonging to ECOWAS. In Central Africa, the *Economic Community of Central African States* (ECCAS), the *Communauté Economique et Monétaire des Etats de l'Afrique Centrale* (CEMAC) and the *Economic Community of the Countries of the Great Lakes* (CEPGL) all co-exist. In Eastern Africa, there is the *Common Market for Eastern and Southern Africa* (COMESA), with the *Inter-governmental Authority on Development* (IGAD) and *East African Community* (EAC) as smaller inner groups. In Southern Africa, there are the *Southern African Development Community* (SADC) and *Southern African Customs Union* (SACU). Northern Africa used to be the only sub-region with a single scheme, the *Arab Maghreb Union* (UMA), but the recent creation of the *Community of Sahel-Saharan States* (CENSAD) has brought it in line with the rest of Africa.

UMA, created in 1989, aimed for a CU before the end of 1995 and a CM by 2000, but has yet to achieve a mere FTA. CENSAD, established in April 1999, has no clear objectives, not even with regard to a trade liberalization strategy, but since its members belong to other blocs, the aims of these are pertinent. ECOWAS was launched in 1975, but its revised treaty envisaged a CU by 2000, now delayed to 1 January 2003 and some members do not even apply a FTA. UEMOA, created in 1994 by the francophone members of ECOWAS, is now a CU, introducing its common external tariffs (CETs) in January 2000, but applies them to the rest of ECOWAS as well, and some member nations are still not even a FTA! MRU, established in 1973, is a CU with a certain degree of cooperation in the industrial sector. ECCAS has been dormant for almost a decade, but has recently been resuscitated. CEPGL was created in 1976, but is virtually inactive due to the conflicts within the bloc. Most activity in this part of Africa is confined to CEMAC, which has a common currency and has taken steps towards a CU. COMESA, established in 1993, launched a FTA in October 2000 comprising nine of its member states. Note that of the member nations of the EAC (first established in 1967), Kenya and Uganda are also members of COMESA, while Tanzania also belongs to SADC, having earlier withdrawn from COMESA. EAC and COMESA, in their May 1997 *Memorandum of Understanding*, agreed to become a CU. SADC aims to achieve a FTA

within the next eight years. Note that IGAD (formed in 1996 to replace the equivalent association on Drought and Development of 1986) and the *Indian Ocean Commission* (IOC, set up in 1982 with vague aims and ambitions, except for concentration on some functional cooperation areas such as fisheries and tourism) have agreed to adopt the aims of COMESA.

Hence, a unique characteristic of economic integration in Africa is the multiplicity and overlapping of its schemes, both made more complicated by the coexistence of inter-governmental cooperation organizations. For example, in the West alone, in 1984 there was a total of 33 schemes and inter-governmental cooperation organizations, and by the late 1980s, about 130 inter-governmental, multi-sectoral economic organizations existed simultaneously with all the mentioned economic integration schemes (Adedeji, 2002, p. 6). That is why the United Nations Economic Commission for Africa (UNECA) recommended in 1984 that there should be some rationalization in the economic cooperation attempts in West Africa. Therefore, some would claim that the creation, by all the African nations except Morocco, of the *African Economic Community* (AEC) in 1991, and the *African Union* (AU) in 2001 by the Constitutive Act, are the appropriate response; the AU replaced the *Organization for African Unity* (OAU). However, that is not the case, since the AEC not only officially endorses all the existing African economic integration schemes, but also encourages the creation of new ones while remaining silent on how they can all co-exist (El-Agraa, 2004). When this uniqueness is combined with proliferation in schemes, one cannot disagree with Robson (1997) when he declares that:

> *Reculer pour mieux sauter* is not a dictum that seems to carry much weight among African governments involved in regional integration. On the contrary, if a certain level of integration cannot be made to work, the reaction of policy makers has typically been to embark on something more elaborate, more advanced and more demanding in terms of administrative requirements and political commitment.

Economic integration in Latin America has been too volatile to describe in simple terms, since the post-1985 experience has been very different from that in the 1960s and 1970s. At the risk of misleading, one can state that there are four schemes of economic integration in this region – see Table 1.4. Under the

Table 1.3 Regional trade arrangements in Africa

Country	UMA	CENSAD	ECOWAS	UEMOA	CEMAC	ECCAS	CEPGL	MRU	COMESA	EAC	IGAD	IOC	SADC	SACU	AEC	AU
Algeria	×														×	×
Angola									×				×		×	×
Benin			×	×											×	×
Botswana													×	×	×	×
Burkina Faso			×	×											×	×
Burundi						×	×		×						×	×
Cameroon					×	×									×	×
Cape Verde			×												×	×
CAR		×			×	×									×	×
Chad		×			×	×									×	×
Comoros									×			×			×	×
Congo, Rep.					×	×									×	×
Côte d'Ivoire			×	×											×	×
Djibouti		×							×		×				×	×
D. R. Congo						×	×		×				×		×	×
Egypt		×							×						×	×
Eq. Guinea					×	×									×	×
Ethiopia									×		×				×	×
Gabon					×	×									×	×
Gambia			×												×	×
Ghana			×												×	×
Guinea			×					×							×	×
Guinea-Bissau			×	×											×	×
Kenya									×	×	×				×	×
Lesotho													×	×	×	×

Liberia
Libya
Madagascar
Malawi
Mali
Mauritania
Mauritius
Morocco
Mozambique
Namibia
Niger
Nigeria
Réunion
Rwanda
Sao Tome and P.
Senegal
Seychelles
Sierra Leone
Somalia
South Africa
Sudan
Swaziland
Tanzania
Togo
Tunisia
Uganda
Zambia
Zimbabwe

Table 1.4 Regional trade arrangements in the western hemisphere[a]

Scheme	NA-FTA[b]	CACM[b]	LAFTA-LAIA	CARICOM[c]	Andean Pact[d]	US-Canada	MER-COSUR[e]	OECS[f]	US-Israel	Argentina-Brazil	Chile-Mexico	El Salvador-Guatemala[g]	EAI (US)[h]	Mexico-Central America[i]	Chile-Colombia-Venezuela	Colombia-Mexico-Venezuela[j]	Venezuela-Central America[k]	RIO Group
Founded	1993	1961	1960/80	1973	1969	1988	1991	1991	1989	1990	1991	1991	1991					
Aim	FTA	FTA	FTA	CU	FTA	FTA	FTA	CU	FTA	FTA	FTA	FTA	FTA					
Canada	X					X												
Mexico	X		X			X					X					X		X
USA	X					X			X									
Belize			X								X							
Costa Rica		X											X	X			X	
El Salvador		X										X	X	X			X	
Guatemala		X										X	X	X			X	
Honduras		X											X	X			X	
Nicaragua		X											X	X			X	
Panama[l]		X											X	X			X	
Antigua/Bermuda				X				X					X					
Bahamas				X									X					
Barbados				X									X					
Dominica				X				X					X					
Grenada				X				X					X					
Jamaica				X									X					
Montserrat				X				X					X					
St Kitts/Nevis				X				X					X					

St Lucia				x	x				x
St Vincent				x	x				x
Trinidad/Tobago				x					x
Argentina	x						x		x
Bolivia	x	x							x
Brazil	x						x		x
Chile	x							x	x
Colombia	x	x				x			x
Ecuador	x	x							x
Guyana				x					x
Paraguay	x						x		x
Peru	x	x							x
Uruguay	x						x		x
Venezuela	x	x				x			x
Israel								x	

a Does not include unilateral trade preferences and exclusive countries with no arrangements.
b Revived in 1990; aimed to establish a common market by 1992.
c Aimed to achieve a common external tariff by 1994.
d Efforts were being made to revive the AP and to create a common market by 1994.
e Aimed to achieve a common market by 1995.
f Organization of East Caribbean States.
g Effective in October 1991.
h The Enterprise of the Americas Initiative aims to achieve a hemisphere free trade zone. By October 1991, the USA had signed framework agreements with 29 countries, including: the 13 CARICOM nations; the 4 MERCOSUR states, Chile, Colombia, Costa Rica, Ecuador, El Salvador, Honduras, Panama, Peru, Nicaragua and Venezuela.
i These countries aimed to form a Central America–Mexican free trade zone by 1996.
j Signature of the trade and investment agreement occurred in 1991 and trilateral limited free trade was supposed to happen by the end of 1993.
k The agreement aims to phase out tariffs on trade in the area.
l Panama participates in summits but is not ready to participate fully in regional integration.

1960 Treaty of Montevideo, the *Latin American Free Trade Association* (LAFTA) was formed between Mexico and all the countries of South America except for Guyana and Surinam. LAFTA came to an end in the late 1970s but was promptly succeeded by the *Association for Latin American Integration* (ALADI or LAIA) in 1980. The Managua Treaty of 1960 established the *Central American Common Market* (CACM) between Costa Rica, El Salvador, Guatemala, Honduras and Nicaragua. In 1969 the *Andean Pact* (AP) was established under the Cartegena Agreement between Bolivia, Chile, Colombia, Ecuador, Peru and Venezuela; the AP forms a closer link between some of the least developed nations of LAFTA, now LAIA.

Since the debt crisis in the 1980s, economic integration in Latin America has taken a new turn with Mexico joining Canada and the US (see below) and Argentina, Brazil, Paraguay and Uruguay, the more developed nations of LAIA, creating MERCOSUR in 1991. MERCOSUR became a customs union by 1 January 1995 and aimed to become a common market by 1995, but is yet to arrive. Bolivia and Chile became associate members in mid-1995, a move which Brazil sees as merely a first step towards the creation of a *South American Free Trade Area* (SAFTA), a counterweight to the efforts in the north (see below). In June 1999 MERCOSUR reached agreement with the EU to start negotiations in November 1999 on an arrangement for free trade and investment between them, which is yet to be concluded.

There is one scheme of economic integration in the Caribbean. In 1973 the *Caribbean Community* (CARICOM) was formed between Antigua, Barbados, Belize, Dominica, Grenada, Guyana, Jamaica, Montserrat, St Kitts–Nevis–Anguila, St Lucia, St Vincent, and Trinidad and Tobago. CARICOM replaced the *Caribbean Free Trade Association* (CARIFTA) which was established in 1968.

In 1988 Canada and the United States established the *Canada–US Free Trade Agreement* (CUFTA), and, together with Mexico, they formed the *North American Free Trade Agreement* (NAFTA) in 1993 which started to operate from 1 January 1994. Despite its name, NAFTA also covers investment. The enlargement of NAFTA to include the rest of the western hemisphere was suggested by George Bush while US president. He hoped to construct what is now referred to as the *Free Trade Area of the Americas* (FTAA) which is under negotiation, aiming for a conclusion by 2005. Chile has been negotiating membership of NAFTA.

Asia does not figure prominently in the league of economic integration schemes, but this is not surprising given the existence of such large (if only in terms of population) countries as China and India. *The Regional Cooperation for Development* (RCD) was a very limited arrangement for sectoral integration between Iran, Pakistan and Turkey. The Association for *South-East Asian Nations* (ASEAN) comprises 10 nations: Brunei, Cambodia, Indonesia, Laos, Malaysia, Myanmar, the Philippines, Singapore, Thailand and Vietnam. ASEAN was founded in 1967 by seven of these countries. Brunei joined in 1984, Vietnam in July 1995, Laos and Myanmar in July 1997 and Cambodia in December 1998. After almost a decade of inactivity ASEAN 'was galvanized into renewed vigour in 1976 by the security problems which the reunification of Vietnam seemed to present to its membership' (Arndt and Garnaut, 1979). The drive for the establishment of ASEAN and for its vigorous reactivation in 1976 was both political and strategic. However, right from the start, economic cooperation was one of the most important aims of ASEAN, indeed most of the vigorous activities of the group since 1976 have been predominantly in the economic field, and the admission of Vietnam in 1995 is a clear manifestation of this. Moreover, ASEAN has recently agreed to accelerate its own plan for a free trade area to the year 2002 from 2003, itself an advance on the original target of 2008, agreed in 1992.

In 1965 Australia and New Zealand entered into a free trade arrangement called the *New Zealand Australia Free Trade Area*. This was replaced in 1983 by the more important *Australia New Zealand Closer Economic Relations and Trade Agreement* (CER, for short): not only have major trade barriers been removed, but significant effects on the New Zealand economy have been experienced as a result.

A scheme for the Pacific Basin integration-cum-cooperation was being hotly discussed during the 1980s. In the late 1980s I argued (El-Agraa, 1988a, 1988b) that 'given the diversity of countries within the Pacific region, it would seem highly unlikely that a very involved scheme of integration would evolve over the next decade or so'. This was in spite of the fact that there already existed:

1 the *Pacific Economic Cooperation Conference* (PECC) which is a tripartite structured organization with representatives from governments, business and academic circles and

with the secretariat work being handled between general meetings by the country next hosting a meeting;

2 the *Pacific Trade and Development Centre* (PAFTAD) which is an academically oriented organization;

3 the *Pacific Basin Economic Council* (PBEC) which is a private-sector business organization for regional cooperation; and

4 the *Pacific Telecommunications Conference* (PTC) which is a specialized organization for regional cooperation in this particular field.

The reason for the pessimism was that the:

region under consideration covers the whole of North America and Southeast Asia, with Pacific South America, the People's Republic of China and the USSR all claiming interest since they are all on the Pacific. Even if one were to exclude this latter group, there still remains the cultural diversity of such countries as Australia, Canada, Japan, New Zealand and the USA, plus the diversity that already exists within ASEAN. It would seem that unless the group of participants is severely limited, Pacific Basin *cooperation* would be the logical outcome. (El-Agraa, 1988a, p. 8)

However, in an attempt to provide a rational basis for resolving Japan's trade frictions, I may appear to have contradicted myself:

it may be concluded that . . . Pacific Basin cooperation-cum-integration is the only genuine solution to the problems of Japan and the USA (as well as the other nations in this area). Given what is stated above about the nature of the nations of the Pacific Basin, that would be a broad generalisation: what is needed is a very strong relationship between Japan and the USA within a much looser association with the rest of SE Asia. Hence, what is being advocated is a form of involved economic integration between Japan and the USA (and Canada, if the present negotiations for a free trade area of Canada and the USA lead to that outcome), within the broad context of 'Pacific Basin Cooperation', or, more likely, within a free trade area with the most advanced nations of SE Asia: Australia, New Zealand, South Korea, the nations of ASEAN, etc. (El-Agraa, 1988b, pp. 203–4)

I added that the proposed scheme should not be a protectionist one. Members of such a scheme should promote cooperation with the rest of the world through their membership of GATT (now WTO) and should coordinate their policies with regard to overseas development assistance, both financially and in terms of the transfer of technology, for the benefit not only of the poorer nations of SE Asia, but also for the whole developing world.

Thus the *Asia Pacific Economic Cooperation* (APEC) forum can be considered as the appropriate response to my suggestion. It was established in 1989 by ASEAN plus Australia, Canada, Japan, New Zealand, South Korea, the USA. These were joined by China, Hong Kong and Taiwan in 1991. In 1993 President Clinton galvanized it into its present form and increased its membership to 18 nations. In Bogor, Indonesia, in 1994 APEC declared its intention (vision) to create a free trade and investment area by the year 2010 embracing its advanced members, with the rest to follow suit ten years later. APEC tried to chart the route for realizing this vision in Osaka, Japan, in November 1995, and came up with the interesting resolution that each member nation should unilaterally declare its own measures for freeing trade and investment, with agriculture completely left out of the reckoning. In November 1998 Peru, Russia and Vietnam joined the APEC forum, increasing its total membership to 21 nations – see Table 1.5.

There are several schemes in the Middle East, but some of them extend beyond the geographical area traditionally designated as such. This is natural since there are nations with Middle Eastern characteristics in parts of Africa. The *Arab League* (AL) clearly demonstrates this reality since it comprises 22 nations, extending from the Gulf in the East to Mauritania and Morocco in the West. Hence the geographical area covered by the scheme includes the whole of North Africa, a large part of the Middle East, plus Djibouti and Somalia. The purpose of the AL is to strengthen the close ties linking Arab states, to coordinate their policies and activities and to direct them to their common good and to mediate in disputes between them. These are vague terms of reference, which remain so even when other schemes are mentioned. For example, the *Arab Economic Council*, whose membership consists of all Arab Ministers of Economic Affairs, was entrusted with suggesting ways for economic development, cooperation, organization and coordination. The *Council for Arab Economic Unity* (CAEU), which

Table 1.5 Regional trade arrangements in Asia–Pacific and the Middle East

Scheme Founded Aim	CER 1983 FTA	ASEAN 1967 FTA	ACM 1964 CU	ECO[a] 1985	GCC 1981 CU	AFTA[b]	APEC[c]	EAEC[d]
Australia	x						x	
Brunei Darusslam		x				x	x	x
Cambodia		x						
Chile							x	
China							x	x
Hong Kong							x	x
Indonesia		x				x	x	x
Japan							x	x
Laos		x						
Malaysia		x				x	x	x
Myanmar		x						
New Zealand	x						x	
Papua New Guinea							x	
Philippines		x				x	x	x
Singapore		x				x	x	x
South Korea							x	x
Taiwan							x	x
Thailand		x				x	x	x
Vietnam		x					x	
Bahrain					x			
Egypt			x					
Iran				x				
Iraq			x					
Jordan			x					
Kuwait					x			
Libya			x					
Oman					x			
Qatar					x			
Saudi Arabia					x			
Syria			x					
UAE					x			
Yemen			x					

Table 1.5 (continued)

Scheme Founded Aim	CER 1983 FTA	ASEAN 1967 FTA	ACM 1964 CU	ECO[a] 1985	GCC 1981 CU	AFTA[b]	APEC[c]	EAEC[d]
Canada							x	
Mauritania					x			
Mexico							x	
Pakistan						x		
Peru							x	
Russia							x	
Turkey						x		
USA							x	

[a] The purpose of this group is bilateral trade promotion and cooperation in industrial planning.
[b] Thailand proposal endorsed by ASEAN Ministers in 1991.
[c] Originally a regional grouping to represent members' views in multilateral negotiating fora, now committed to freeing trade and investment among its richer members by 2010 and by 2020 by the rest.
[d] This grouping was initially proposed by Malaysia in 1990.

was formed in 1957, had the aim of establishing an integrated economy of all AL states. Moreover, in 1964 the *Arab Common Market* was formed by Egypt, Iraq, Jordan and Syria, but practically never got off the ground. The exception seems to be the 1981 *Gulf Cooperation Council* (GCC), established between Bahrain, Kuwait, Oman, Qatar, Saudi Arabia and United Arab Emirates to bring together the Gulf states and to prepare the ground for them to join forces in the economic, political and military spheres.

The latest schemes of economic integration in the Middle East have already been mentioned, but only in passing in the context of Africa. The ACC was founded on 16 February 1989 by Egypt, Iraq, Jordan and the Arab Yemen Republic with the aim of boosting Arab solidarity and acting as 'yet another link in the chain of Arab efforts towards integration'. Moreover, on 18 February 1989 the AMU was formed by Algeria, Libya, Mauritania, Morocco and Tunisia. The AMU aims to create an organization similar to the EU.

All these schemes are connected by an increasing number of PTAs between them. This had resulted in an intricate web of interrelationships, clearly depicted by Figure 1.1 even though the EEA and some minor schemes have been left out to avoid a further cluttering of the picture. Considering the EU alone, since it is the

main protagonist of PTAs, and adding to the picture the 77 APC nations and the EEA, one can imagine why the term spaghetti bowl has been used to describe this intricate web.

Moreover, there are two schemes of sectoral economic integration which are not based on geographical proximity. The first is the *Organization for Petroleum Exporting Countries* (OPEC), founded in 1960 with a truly international membership. Its aim was to protect the main interest of its member nations: petroleum. The second is the *Organization for Arab Petroleum Exporting Countries* (OAPEC), established in January 1968 by Kuwait, Libya and Saudi Arabia. These were joined in May 1970 by Algeria, and the four Arab Gulf Emirates: Abu Dhabi, Bahrain, Dubai and Qatar. In March 1972 Iraq and Syria became members and Egypt followed them in 1973. Tunisia joined in 1982, but withdrew in 1986. OAPEC was temporarily liquidated in June 1971.

Finally, there are also the *Organization for Economic Cooperation and Development* (OECD) and the *World Trade Organization* (WTO). However, these and the above are schemes for intergovernmental cooperation rather than for economic integration. Therefore, except where appropriate, nothing more shall be said about them.

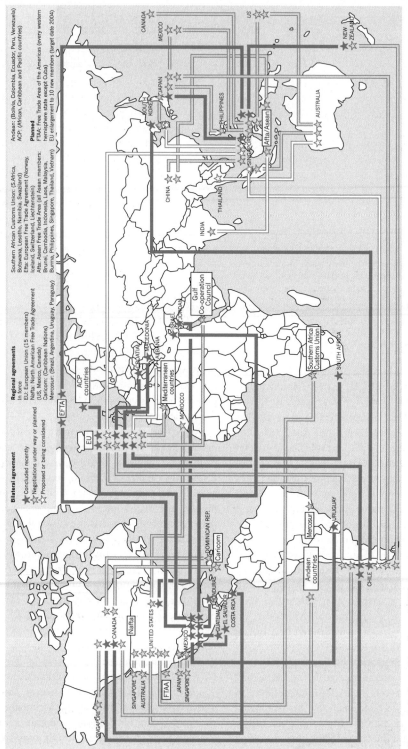

Figure 1.1 A proliferation of PTAs

Note: To reduce clutter on the chart, some arrangements have been omitted, among them are the European Economic Area (EEA) between the EU and the EFTA minus Switzerland, the 77 member nations of the ACP and the Central European Free Trade Area (CEFTA).

Source: Financial Times, 19 November 2002

1.4   The EU

Since this book is devoted to the EU, it is important to establish the nature of the EU within the context of the different types of economic integration discussed at the beginning of the chapter – readers interested in the other schemes will find a full discussion of them in El-Agraa (1997).

Article 2 of the treaty establishing the EEC, now incorporated in the Amsterdam Treaty, pronounces that:

> The Community shall have as its task, by setting up a common market and progressively approximating the economic policies of Member States, to promote throughout the Community an harmonious development of economic activities, a continuous and balanced expansion, an increase in stability, an accelerated raising of the standard of living and closer relations between the Member States belonging to it. (Treaty of Rome, Article 2, p. 3)

Article 3 then states that for the purposes set out in Article 2:

> The activities of the Community shall include, on the conditions and in accordance with the time-table provided in this Treaty:
>
> (a) the elimination, as between Member States, of customs duties and of quantitative restrictions in regard to the import and export of goods, as well as of all other measures having equivalent effect;
>
> (b) the establishment of a common customs tariff and a common commercial policy towards third countries;
>
> (c) the abolition, as between Member States, of obstacles to the freedom of movement for persons, services and capital;
>
> (d) the establishment of a common policy in the sphere of agriculture;
>
> (e) the adoption of a common policy in the sphere of transport;
>
> (f) the establishment of a system ensuring that competition in the common market is not distorted;
>
> (g) the application of procedures by which the economic policies of Member States can be co-ordinated and disequilibria in their balances of payments can be remedied;

> (h) the approximation of the laws of Member States to the extent required for proper functioning of the common market;
>
> (i) the creation of a European Social Fund in order to improve the possibilities of employment for workers and to contribute to the raising of their standard of living;
>
> (j) the establishment of a European Investment Bank to facilitate the economic expansion of the Community by opening up fresh resources; and
>
> (k) the association of overseas countries and territories with a view to increasing trade and to promoting jointly economic and social development. (Treaty of Rome, pp. 3–4)

These elements are stated more elaborately in later articles. For instance, Article 9(1) states:

> The Community shall be based upon a customs union which shall cover all trade in goods and which shall involve the prohibition between Member States of customs duties on imports and exports and of all charges having equivalent effect, and the adoption of a common customs tariff in their relation with third countries. (Treaty of Rome, p. 6)

Articles 35–7 elaborate on the common agricultural policy (CAP), Articles 48–73 on the conditions for freedom of movement of factors of production, Articles 74–84 on the common transport policy (CTP) and Articles 99 and 100 on the harmonization of certain taxes.

The Treaty of Rome provisions are only a starting point since they should be augmented by aims added later on. These are incorporated into the Single European Act (SEA), the creation of a true single market by the end of 1992 and the Maastricht/Amsterdam treaties which led to the realization of the 'European Union', with a single currency (the euro) for 12 of its 15 members, a common central bank, a common monetary policy, a common defence policy and rudiments of a common foreign policy, beginning in 1999 – these are fully discussed in Chapter 2. It can thus be categorically stated that the EU is at present certainly much more than a common market but in some respects falls a bit short of being a complete economic union yet in others goes beyond it. Moreover, at least some members would like to go even further, edging closer to a political union (see Chapters 2 and 28).

1.5   The possible gains from economic integration

We shall see in Chapters 2 and 9 that the driving force behind the formation of the EU, the earliest and most influential of all existing integration schemes, was the political unity of Europe with the aim of realizing eternal peace in the continent. Some analysts would also argue that the recent attempts by the EU for more intensive economic integration can be cast in the same vein, especially since they are accompanied by one currency, the euro, and by common foreign and defence policies. At the same time, during the late 1950s and early 1960s economic integration among developing nations was perceived as the only viable way for them to make some real economic progress; indeed that was the rationale behind the United Nations' encouragement and support of such efforts. More recently, frustrations with the GATT's slowness in reaching agreement, due to its many participants and their variable interests, have led some to the conclusion that economic integration would result in a quicker pace for negotiations since, by definition, it would reduce the number of parties involved. There are also practical considerations and countries may feel that economic integration would provide security of markets among the participants. However, no matter what the motives for economic integration may be, it is still necessary to analyse the economic implications of such geographically discriminatory associations; that is one of the reasons why I have included political unification as one of the possible schemes.

At the customs union (CU) and free trade area (FTA) levels, the possible sources of economic gain from economic integration can be attributed to:

1 enhanced efficiency in production made possible by increased specialization in accordance with the law of comparative advantage, due to the liberalized market of the participating nations;
2 increased production levels due to better exploitation of economies of scale made possible by the increased size of the market;
3 an improved international bargaining position, made possible by the larger size, leading to better terms of trade (cheaper imports from the outside world and higher prices for exports to them);
4 enforced changes in efficiency brought about by intensified competition between firms;

5 changes affecting both the amount and quality of the factors of production due to technological advances, themselves encouraged by (4).

If the level of economic integration is to go beyond the free trade area and customs union levels, then further sources of economic gain also become possible:

6 factor mobility across the borders of the member nations will materialize only if there is a net economic incentive for them, thus leading to higher national incomes;
7 the coordination of monetary and fiscal policies may result in cost reductions since the pooling of efforts may enable the achievement of economies of scale; and
8 the unification of efforts to achieve better employment levels, lower inflation rates, balanced trade, higher rates of economic growth and better income distribution may make it cheaper to attain these targets.

It should be apparent that some of these possible gains relate to static resource reallocation effects while the rest relate to long-term or dynamic effects. It should also be emphasized that these are *possible* economic gains, i.e. there is no guarantee that they can ever be achieved; everything would depend on the nature of the particular scheme and the type of competitive behaviour prevailing prior to integration. Indeed, it is quite feasible that in the absence of 'appropriate' competitive behaviour, economic integration may worsen the situation. Thus the possible attainment of these benefits must be considered with great caution:

> Membership of an economic grouping cannot of itself guarantee to a member state or the group a satisfactory economic performance, or even a better performance than in the past. The static gains from integration, although significant, can be – and often are – swamped by the influence of factors of domestic or international origin that have nothing to do with integration. The more fundamental factors influencing a country's economic performance (the dynamic factors) are unlikely to be affected by integration except in the long run. It is clearly not a necessary condition for economic success that a country should be a member of an economic community as the

experience of several small countries confirms, although such countries might have done better as members of a suitable group. Equally, a large integrated market is in itself no guarantee of performance, as the experience of India suggests. However, although integration is clearly no panacea for all economic ills, nor indispensable to success, there are many convincing reasons for supposing that significant economic benefits may be derived from properly conceived arrangements for economic integration. (Robson, 1980/1985)

However, in the case of the EU, one should always keep in mind that the 'founding fathers' had the formation of a United States of Western (hopefully all) Europe as the ultimate goal and that economic integration became the immediate objective so as to facilitate the attainment of political unity via the back door (see Chapter 2). Those who fail to appreciate this will always undermine the EU's serious attempts at the achievement of economic and monetary union via the Maastricht Treaty as the ongoing discussion clearly demonstrates – see Chapter 6.

1.6   Areas of enquiry

The necessary areas of enquiry, emphasizing the economic and social aspects, are quite apparent now that we have established the nature of the EU. It is necessary to analyse the effects and consequences of the removal of trade impediments between the participating nations and to make an equivalent study of the establishment of the common external relations; these are tackled in Chapters 6 and 7. It is also extremely important to discuss the role of competition and industrial policies and the presence of multinational firms; these are covered in Chapters 12 and 13. Moreover, it is vital to analyse the implications and consequences of the single market (Chapter 11), the special provisions for agriculture (Chapter 20), fisheries (Chapter 21), transport (Chapter 15), EMU (Chapters 8–10), tax harmonization and general budget (Chapters 14 and 19), regional disparity (Chapter 22), energy (Chapter 16), social dimensions (Chapter 23), factor mobility (Chapter 18), environmental considerations (Chapter 17) and external relations (Chapters 24 and 25). The book also contains chapters on the history and institutions of the EU (Chapters 2 and 3), the legal dimension of European integration (Chapter 4), the basic statistics

(Chapter 5), enlargement (Chapter 26), and the success and future of the EU (Chapters 27 and 28).

These chapters come under seven coherent parts. Part One deals with the history, institutions, legal dimension and basic statistics of the EU; hence it offers in four chapters, the general background to the EU. Part Two, consisting of two chapters, is concerned with the theory and measurement of economic integration. Part Three, comprising three chapters, is devoted to the theoretical and operational aspects of EMU. Part Four deals with various areas dealing with the creation of a single EU market and does this in eight chapters on the single market itself, competition and industrial policies, tax harmonization, transport, energy and environmental policies and factor mobility. Part Five tackles budgetary and structural policies in five chapters on the budget, common agricultural and fisheries policies, and regional and social policies. Part Six deals with EU external affairs in two chapters on trade policy and relations with the developing countries. The final part, comprising three chapters, deals with enlargement and the success and future of the EU.

1.7   About this book

This book offers, more or less, a comprehensive but brief coverage of the theoretical issues: trade creation, trade diversion and the Cooper–Massell criticism; the domestic distortions argument; the terms of trade effects; the economies of scale argument. It also offers a fresh look at the different attempts at the economic justification of customs union formation. A full chapter deals with the methodology and results of the measurements of the

effects of the EU formation on the member states and the outside world. These are discussed briefly since a comprehensive book on them is available – see El-Agraa (1989a and 1999). There is also a full treatment of all major policy considerations – see previous section.

Although chapters on EU political cooperation, distributional problems and political and legal considerations may seem to be absent, these aspects have not been omitted: some elements of political coopera- tion are discussed in Chapters 2, 27 and 28, while some of the most significant elements of the distribu- tion problem are tackled in the chapters on the role of the EU budget, social policies and regional policies. This does not imply that these aspects are not worthy of separate chapters, as one could in fact argue that these are the most important issues facing the EU. The

treatment given to them in this book is such that the significant aspects of these policies are tackled where they are particularly relevant. Moreover, with regard to some of these policies, the EU is not yet certain in which direction it is heading, and this in spite of the adoption and endorsement of the Maastricht Treaty, which specifies certain details. The wider political considerations lie outside our scope.

Appendix 1.1 WTO's Article XXIV

Territorial application – frontier traffic – customs unions and free trade areas

1 The provisions of this Agreement shall apply to the metropolitan customs territories of the contract- ing parties and to any other customs territories in respect of which this Agreement has been accepted under Article XXVI or is being applied under Article XXXIII or pursuant to the Protocol of Pro- visional Application. Each such customs territory shall, exclusively for the purposes of the territorial application of this Agreement, be treated as though it were a contracting party; *provided* that the pro- visions of this paragraph shall not be construed to create any rights or obligations as between two or more customs territories in respect of which this Agreement has been accepted under Article XXVI or is being applied under Article XXXIII or pur- suant to the Protocol of Provisional Application by a single contracting party.

2 For the purposes of this Agreement a customs ter- ritory shall be understood to mean any territory with respect to which separate tariffs or other regulations of commerce are maintained for a substantial part of the trade of such territory with other territories.

3 The provisions of this Agreement shall not be construed to prevent:

(a) advantages accorded by any contracting party to adjacent countries in order to facilitate frontier traffic;

(b) advantages accorded to the trade with the Free Territory of Trieste by countries con- tiguous to that territory, provided that such advantages are not in conflict with the Treaties of Peace arising out of the Second World War.

4 The contracting parties recognize the desirability of increasing freedom of trade by the development, through voluntary agreements, of closer integration between the economies of the countries parties to such agreements. They also recognize that the pur- pose of a customs union or of a free-trade area should be to facilitate trade between the constituent territories and not to raise barriers to the trade of other contracting parties with such territories.

5 Accordingly, the provisions of this Agreement shall not prevent, as between the territories of con- tracting parties, the formation of a customs union or of a free-trade area of the adoption of an interim agreement necessary for the formation of a customs union or of a free-trade area; *provided* that:

(a) with respect to a customs union, or an interim agreement leading to the formation of a customs union, the duties and other regula- tions of commerce imposed at the institution of any such union or interim agreement in respect of trade with contracting parties not parties to such union or agreement shall not on the whole be higher or more restrictive than the general incidence of the duties and regulations of commerce applicable in the con- stituent territories prior to the formation of such union or the adoption of such interim agreement, as the case may be;

(b) with respect to a free-trade area, or an interim agreement leading to the formation of a free- trade area, the duties and other regulations of commerce maintained in each of the con- stituent territories and applicable at the formation of such free-trade area or the adop- tion of such interim agreement to the trade of contracting parties not included in such area or not parties to such agreement shall not be higher or more restrictive than the corresponding duties and other regulations of commerce existing in the same constituent territories prior to the formation of the free-trade area, or interim agreement, as the case may be; and

(c) any interim agreement referred to in sub-paragraphs (a) and (b) shall include a plan and schedule for the formation of such a customs union or of such a free-trade area within a reasonable length of time.

6 If, in fulfilling the requirements of sub-paragraph 5(a), a contracting party proposes to increase any rate of duty inconsistently with the provisions of Article II, the procedure set forth in Article XXVIII shall apply. In providing for compensatory adjustment, due account shall be taken of the compensation already afforded by the reductions brought about in the corresponding duty of the other constituents of the union.

7 (a) Any contracting party deciding to enter into a customs union or free-trade area, or an interim agreement leading to the formation of such a union or area, shall promptly notify the CONTRACTING PARTIES and shall make available to them such information regarding the proposed union or area as will enable them to make such reports and recommendations to contracting parties as they may deem appropriate.

(b) If, after having studied the plan and schedule included in an interim agreement referred to in paragraph 5 in consultation with the parties to that agreement and taking due account of the information made available in accordance with the provisions of sub-paragraph (a), the CONTRACTING PARTIES find that such agreement is not likely to result in the formation of a customs union or of a free-trade area within the period contemplated by the parties to the agreement or that such period is not a reasonable one, the CONTRACTING PARTIES shall make recommendations to the parties to the agreement. The parties shall not maintain or put into force, as the case may be, such agreement if they are not prepared to modify it in accordance with these recommendations.

(c) Any substantial change in the plan or schedule referred to in paragraph 5(c) shall be communicated to the CONTRACTING PARTIES,

which may request the contracting parties concerned to consult with them if the change seems likely to jeopardize or delay unduly the formation of the customs union or of the free-trade area.

8 For the purposes of this Agreement:

(a) A customs union shall be understood to mean the substitution of a single customs territory for two or more customs territories, so that

(i) duties and other restrictive regulations of commerce (except, where necessary, those permitted under Articles XI, XII, XIII, XIV, XV and XX) are eliminated with respect to substantially all the trade between the constituent territories of the union or at least with respect to substantially all the trade in products originating in such territories, and,

(ii) subject to the provisions of paragraph 9, substantially the same duties and other regulations of commerce are applied by each of the members of the union to the trade territories not included in the union.

(b) A free-trade area shall be understood to mean a group of two or more customs territories in which the duties and other restrictive regulations of commerce (except, where necessary, those permitted under Articles XI, XII, XIII, XIV, XV and XX) are eliminated on substantially all the trade between the constituent territories in products originating in such territories.

9 The preferences referred to in paragraph 2 of Article I shall not be affected by the formation of a customs union or of a free-trade area but may be eliminated or adjusted by means of negotiations with contracting parties affected. This procedure of negotiations with affected contracting parties shall, in particular, apply to the elimination of preferences required to conform with the provisions of paragraph 8(a)(i) and paragraph 8(b).

10 The CONTRACTING PARTIES may by a two-thirds majority approve proposals which do not fully comply with the requirements of paragraphs 5 to 9 inclusive, provided that such proposals lead to the formation of a customs union or a free-trade area in the sense of this Article.

11 Taking into account the exceptional circumstances arising out of the establishment of India and Pakistan as independent States and recognizing the fact that they have long constituted an economic unit, the contracting parties agree that the provisions of this Agreement shall not prevent the two countries from entering into special arrangements with respect to the trade between them, pending the establishment of their mutual trade relations on a definitive basis.

12 Each contracting party shall take such reasonable measures as may be available to it to ensure observance of the provisions of this Agreement by the regional and local governments and authorities within its territory.

Source: WTO Article XXIV. Reprinted by permission of WTO.

Part One EU history, institutions, legal dimension and basic statistics

The aim of this part of the book is to provide the reader with a general background to the EU. Chapter 2 gives a short account of the history of European integration and development of the EU. Chapter 3 provides a bare description of the EU institutions and their functioning. Chapter 4 explores the legal dimension in EU integration. Chapter 5 offers a general statistical survey of the major economic indicators for the present 15 member nations of the EU as well as for those involved in the imminent enlargement and, to enable comparison, also for Canada, Japan, the Russian Federation and the United States.

Chapter 2

A history of European integration and evolution of the EU

ALI EL-AGRAA*

This book contains a full and detailed coverage of all the significant facets of the EU as well as the international contexts and constraints within which they operate, with specific chapters devoted to each. There is therefore a need for a chapter providing an overall perspective of the EU. Also, a proper appreciation of why the EU has been created and how it has evolved would not be possible without an understanding of the history of European unity. This is because in a world presently dominated by immediate considerations, recently bordering on the purely economic, the driving force behind European integration is often forgotten and attempts to reform existing policies and to steer the EU in new directions seem to be frustrating. Thus the overall perspective must not only include this wider historical dimension, but history must also colour the entirety of its exposition. This chapter is therefore devoted to these considerations and comes in two main sections. The first provides a very brief history of European unity; brief since otherwise this book would become a real tome and those interested in a detailed and comprehensive coverage can always consult the voluminous literature on the subject, including, *inter alia*, Haas (1958), Palmer and Lambert (1968), Lipgens (1982) and, for modern aspects, Wallace (1990). The second offers a bird's eye view of the evolution of the EU.

2.1   A short history of European unity

Most, if not all, actual steps taken to achieve economic and political unity in Europe originated after 1945. However, the idea of European unity is deeply rooted in European thinking. History shows that there have been a number of proposals and arrangements designed to create it. In the fourteenth century, the idea of a united Christendom inspired Pierre Dubois to propose a *European Confederation* to be ruled by a *European Council* of wise, expert and faithful men. In the seventeenth century, Sully desired to keep peace in Europe by means of a *European Army*. In 1693, William Penn, the English Quaker, then the eponymous governor of Pennsylvania, wanted the creation of *An Imperial Dyet, Parliament or State of Europe* in his *Essay Towards the Present and Future Peace of Europe*. In the nineteenth century, Proudhon was strongly in favour of the formation of a *European Federation* and predicted that the twentieth century would witness an era of federations, forecasting disaster in the absence of such a development.

However, immediately after the First World War, politicians began to give serious consideration to the concept of European unity. For example, in 1923 Count Coudenhove Kalergi, the Austrian founder-leader of the *Pan-European Movement*, called for the formation of a *United States of Europe*, his reason being the successful assertion of Swiss unity in 1848, the forging of the German Empire in 1871 and, most significantly, the independence of the United States in 1776. And on 5 September 1929, in a renowed speech, delivered to the *League of Nations Assembly* in Geneva, the French foreign minister, Aristide Briand, with the backing of his German counterpart, Gustav Stresemann, proposed the creation of a *European Union* within the framework of the League of Nations, and reiterated this later, when prime minister, by declaring that part

---

* The second half of this chapter is an amended/updated version of the first part of the History and Institutions chapter contributed by Doreen Collins since the first edition in 1980.

of his political manifesto was the building of a *United States of Europe*.

The main reason for the pursuit of European unity was the achievement of lasting peace in Europe. It was realized that there was no other means of putting an end to the continent's woeful history of conflict, bloodshed, suffering and destruction. However, economic reasons were also a contributing factor. These were influenced by the tradition of free trade and Adam Smith's argument, in his *An Inquiry into the Nature and Causes of the Wealth of Nations* (1776), that 'the division of labour is limited by the extent of the market', which the German philosopher Freidrich Naumann utilized to propose in 1915 that European nation states were no longer large enough to compete on their own in world markets, therefore, they had to unite in order to guarantee their survival.

Despite the fact that there was no shortage of plans for creating a united Europe, nevertheless it was not until 1945 that a combination of new forces and an intensification of old ones that prompted action. First, Europe had been at the centre of yet another devastating war, caused by the ambitions of nation states. Those who sought and some of those who still seek a united Europe have always had at the forefront of their minds the desire to prevent any further outbreak of war in Europe. It was believed that if the nations of Europe could be brought closer together, such war would become unthinkable. Second, the Second World War left Europe economically exhausted, and this led to the view that if Europe were to recover, it would require a concerted effort on the part of European states. Third, the Second World War also soon revealed that for a long time Western Europe would have to face not only a powerful and politically alien USSR, but also a group of European nations firmly fixed within the Eastern European bloc. It was felt that an exhausted and divided Europe (since the war embraced co-belligerents) presented both a power vacuum and a temptation to the USSR to fill it. Fourth, the ending of the war soon revealed that the wartime allies were, in fact, divided, with the two major powers, the USA and USSR, confronting each other in a bid for world supremacy. Hence, it should come as no surprise to learn that members of the *European Movement*, who wanted to get away from intergovernmental cooperation by creating institutions leading to a *Federal Europe*, felt the need for a third world force: 'the voice of Europe'. This force would represent the Western European viewpoint and

could also act as a bridge between the Eastern and Western extremities.

2.1.1 Concrete unity efforts

The first concrete move for regional integration in Europe was made in 1947 with the establishment of the *Economic Commission for Europe* (ECE), which was set up in Geneva as a regional organization of the United Nations (UN). Its objective was to initiate and participate in concerted measures aimed at securing the economic restructuring of the *whole* of Europe. A year later, the *Brussels Treaty Organization* (BTO) was founded by the UK, France, Belgium, the Netherlands and Luxembourg. In recognition of the newer threat of the USSR, it was designed to create a system of mutual assistance in times of attack on Europe, but it simultaneously perpetuated the wartime alliance against Germany. The BTO took an Atlantic form in 1949 when the five nations, together with the USA and Canada as well as Denmark, Iceland, Italy (significantly, since it had been an Axis power), Norway and Portugal founded the *North Atlantic Treaty Organization* (NATO). The aim of NATO was, and continues to be, to provide military defence against attack on any of its members. Greece and Turkey joined NATO in 1952, West Germany became a member in 1955, and Spain was added in 1982, after the disappearance of General Franco from the political scene. After the collapse of communism in Eastern Europe, not only were the Czech Republic, Hungary and Poland added in 1997 to give NATO 19 members, but, vitally, NATO and Russia signed the *Act on Mutual Relations, Cooperation and Security*, and during the meetings in Prague on 21 and 22 November 2002, NATO invited Bulgaria, Latvia, Lithuania, Romania, Slovakia and Slovenia to start negotiations with a view to becoming members in 2004.

Also, in 1948 the *Organization for European Economic Cooperation* (OEEC) was formed and was followed a year later by the *Council of Europe*. These marked the beginning of the division of Western Europe into two camps, with, on the one hand, the UK and some of the countries that later formed the *European Free Trade Association* (EFTA), and, on the other, Belgium, France, West Germany, Italy, Luxembourg and the Netherlands, usually referred to as the Original Six (hereafter, simply the Six) who subsequently established the *European Economic Community* (EEC). The main reason for this division was that the UK was less committed to Europe as the main policy area than the Six. This was because until the second half of the 1950s, the UK was still a world power which had been on the victorious side and a major participant in some of the fateful geo-political decision making at the time, and it still had the Empire to dispose of. Therefore, British policy was bound to incorporate this wider dimension: relations with Europe had to compete with Empire (later, Commonwealth) ties and with the *special relationship* with the USA. In addition, the idea of a politically united Europe (as we have seen, in some quarters this meant a United States of Europe) was strongly held by the other countries, particularly by France and BENELUX; *Be*lgium, the *Ne*therlands and *Lux*embourg agreed in 1944 to form a customs union (for a technical definition, see Chapter 1), which did not become effective until 1948. But, despite the encouraging noises made by Winston Churchill, the British Prime Minister at the time, both during the Second World War and after, this was not a concept that thrilled British hearts (see Young, 1998, for an excellent exposition of the British attitude towards European unification).

The different thinking between the UK and the Six about the political nature of European institutions was revealed in the discussions leading up to the establishment of the OEEC and the Council of Europe. The Second World War had left Europe devastated. The year 1947 was particularly bleak: bad harvests in the previous summer led to rising food prices; the severe winter of 1946–1947 led to a fuel crisis; and the continental countries were producing very little, and what was produced tended to be retained rather than exported, while imports were booming, hence foreign exchange reserves were running out. It was at this junction that the USA entered the scene to present the *Marshall Plan*. General George Marshall proposed that the USA make aid available to help the European economy find its feet and that European governments 'should get together' to decide how much assistance was needed. In short, the USA did not feel it appropriate that it should unilaterally decide on the programme necessary to achieve this result. Although it seemed possible that this aid programme could be elaborated within the ECE framework, the USSR felt otherwise. Soviet reluctance was no doubt due to the fear that if its satellites participated, this would open the door to Western influence. Therefore,

a conference was convened without the USSR, and the *Committee for European Economic Cooperation* (CEEC) was established.

The attitude of the USA was that the CEEC should not just provide it with a list of needs. The USA perceived that the aid it was to give should be linked with progress towards European unification. This is an extremely important point since it shows that right from the very beginning, the *European Movement* enjoyed the encouragement and support of the USA. Of course, the driving force behind the USA's insistence on European unity was its desire to establish a solid defence against any western advance by the USSR, i.e. the US did not insist on unity for unity's sake. Indeed, the USA also asked that its multinational companies should have free access to European markets. The CEEC led in turn to the creation of an aid agency: the OEEC. Here, the conflict between the UK and the Six, especially France, came to a head over the issue of *supranationalism*. France in particular (and it was supported by the USA) wanted to introduce a supranational element into the new organization. But what is supranationalism? It can mean a situation in which international administrative institutions exercise power over, for example, the economies of the member states; or ministerial bodies, when taking decisions (to be implemented by international organizations) work on a majority voting system rather than insisting on unanimity.

The French view was not shared by the British since they favoured a body which was to be under the control of a ministerial council in which decisions should be taken on a unanimity basis. The French, on the other hand, preferred an arrangement in which an international secretariat would be presided over by a secretary-general who would be empowered to take policy initiatives on major issues. Significantly, the organization which emerged was substantially in line with the British wish for unanimity rule. This was undoubtedly a reflection of the UK's relatively powerful position in the world at the time.

In the light of subsequent events, it is also interesting to note that the USA encouraged the European nations to consider the creation of a customs union. Although this was of considerable interest to some continental countries, it did not appeal to the UK. In the end the OEEC convention merely recorded the intention to continue the study of this proposal. For a variety of reasons, one of which was the opposition of the UK, the matter was not pursued further.

The creation of the Council of Europe, with broad political and cultural objectives, including the notable contribution of protecting the individual through the *Convention for the Protection of Human Rights and Fundamental Freedoms* (its statute expresses a belief in a common political heritage based on accepted spiritual and moral values, political liberty, the rule of law and the maintenance of democratic forms of government), also highlighted the fundamental differences in approach between the countries who later founded the EEC, on the one hand, and the British and Scandinavians, on the other. The establishment of the Council of Europe was preceded by the *Congress of Europe* at The Hague in May 1948. This was a grand rally of 'Europeans' which was attended by leading European statesmen, including Winston Churchill. The Congress adopted a resolution which called for the giving up of some national sovereignty before the accomplishment of economic and political union in Europe. Subsequently, a proposal was put forward, with the support of the Belgian and French governments, calling for the creation of a *European Parliamentary Assembly* in which resolutions would be passed by majority vote. A *Committee of Ministers* was to prepare and implement these resolutions.

Needless to add, the UK was opposed to this form of supranationalism and in the end the British view largely prevailed. The Committee of Ministers, which was the executive organ of the Council of Europe, alone had power of decision and generally these were taken on the unanimity principle. The *Consultative Assembly* which came into existence was a forum (its critics called it a debating society), not a European legislative body. In short, the British and Scandinavian *functionalists*, those who believed that European unity, in so far as it was to be achieved, was to be attained by *intergovernmental cooperation*, triumphed over the *federalists*, those who sought unity by the radical method of creating European institutions to which national governments would surrender some of their sovereignty. The final disillusionment of the federalists was almost certainly marked by the resignation of Paul-Henri Spaak (see below), a devoted European federalist, from the presidency of the Consultative Assembly in 1951.

The next step in the economic and political unification of Western Europe was taken without the British and Scandinavians. It took the creation in 1951 of the *European Coal and Steel Community* (ECSC) by the Six, and marked the parting of ways in post-war Western Europe. The immediate factor in these developments was the revival of the West German economy. The passage of time, the efforts of the German people and the aid made available by the USA through the Marshall Plan all contributed to this recovery. Indeed, the West German *economic miracle* was about to unfold.

It was recognized that the German economy would have to be allowed to regain its position in the world, and that the Allied control of coal and steel under the *International Ruhr Authority* could not last indefinitely. The fundamental question was how the German economy in the sectors of iron, coal and steel (the basic materials of a war effort) could be allowed to regain its former powerful position without endangering the future peace of Europe. The answer was a French plan, elaborated by Jean Monnet, a French businessman turned adviser, but put forward by Robert Schuman, French minister of foreign affairs, in May 1950. The *Schuman Plan* was essentially political in character. It was brilliant since it sought to end the historic rivalry of France and Germany by making a war between the two nations not only unthinkable but also materially impossible. This was to be achieved in a manner which ultimately would have the result of bringing about that European federation which is indispensable to peace. The answer was not to nationalize or indeed to internationalize the ownership of the means of production in coal, iron and steel, but to create, by the removal of customs duties, import quota restrictions and similar impediments on trade and factors of production, a common market (for a technical definition, see Chapter 1) in these products. Every participating nation in such a common market would have equal access to the products of these industries wherever they might be located, and, to reinforce this, discrimination on the grounds of nationality was to be forbidden.

The plan had a number of attractive features. First, it provided an excellent basis for solving the 'Saar problem': the handing back of the Saar region to West Germany was more likely to be acceptable to the French if Germany was firmly locked in such a coal and steel community. Second, the plan was extremely attractive to Germany since membership of the community was a passport to international respectability; it was the best way of speeding up the end of occupation and avoiding the imposition of dampers on the expansion of the German economy. Third, the plan was also attractive to the federalists who had found the OEEC far short of their aspirations for the Council of Europe (its unanimity rule and that no powers could be delegated to an independent commission or

Commissariat were extremely frustrating for them), and, in any case, the prospects for the OEEC were not very good since by 1952 the four-year period of the Marshall Plan would be over, and the UK attitude was that thereafter the OEEC budget should be cut and some of its functions passed over to NATO.

As it turned out, however, the ECSC was much more to the federalists' taste since its executive body, the *High Authority*, was given substantial direct powers which could be exercised without the prior approval of the *Council of Ministers* (the ECSC's second institution; it also had a *Parliamentary Assembly* and a *Court of Justice*).

The plan received favourable responses from the Six. The UK was invited to join but refused. Clement Attlee, British Prime Minister at the time, told the House of Commons: 'We on this side [of the House] are not prepared to accept that the most vital economic forces of this country should be handed over to an authority that is utterly undemocratic and is responsible to nobody.' However, the Six were not to be deterred, and in April 1951 the *Treaty of Paris*, valid for fifty years, was signed. The ECSC was born and it embarked on an experiment in limited economic integration, albeit a sectoral one, on 1 January 1952.

The next stage in the development of European unity was also concerned with Germany. When the Korean War broke out in 1950, the USA, faced with the need to reduce its forces in Europe for deployment in Korea, put pressure on the Western European nations to do more to defend themselves against possible attack by the USSR. This raised the issue of a military contribution from West Germany, the implication being that Germany should be rearmed. However, this proposal was opposed by France, which was equally against Germany becoming a member of NATO. This was not a purely negative attitude. Indeed, René Pleven, French Prime Minister at the time, put forward a plan which envisaged that there would be no German army as such, but that there would be a *European Army* to which each participating nation, including Germany, could contribute.

Britain was not against this idea but did not herself wish to be involved. The Six were positively enthusiastic and discussion began in 1951 with a view to creating a *European Defence Community* (EDC). It was envisaged that there would be a *Joint Defence Commission*, a *Council of Ministers*, a *Parliamentary Assembly* and a *Court of Justice*. In other words, the institutions of the EDC were to parallel those created for the ECSC. The Six made rapid progress in the negotiations and the *EDC Treaty* was signed in May 1952.

Having gone so far, there were a number of reasons for further integrative efforts. First, the pooling of both defensive and offensive capabilities inevitably reduced the possibility of independent foreign policies. It was logical to follow integration in defence with measures which served to achieve political integration as well. Second, it was also desirable to establish a system whereby effective control could be exercised over the proposed European army. Third, there was also the Dutch desire that progress in the military field should be paralleled by more integration in the economic sphere as well. Therefore, the foreign ministers of the Six asked the ECSC Assembly, together with co-opted members from the Consultative Assembly of the Council of Europe, to study the possibilities of creating a *European Political Authority*.

In 1953, a draft of a *European Political Community* (EPC) was produced in which it was proposed that, after a period of transition, the political institutions of the ECSC and the proposed EDC be subsumed within a new framework. There would then be a *European Executive* responsible to a *European Parliament* (which would consist of a *People's Chamber* elected by direct universal suffrage, and a *Senate* elected by national parliaments), a *Council of Ministers* and a *European Court* to replace the parallel bodies created under the ECSC and EDC treaties.

This was a watershed in the history of the European movement. The Six had already successfully experimented in limited economic integration in the fields of iron, coal and steel; had now signed a treaty to integrate defence; and were about to proceed further by creating a community for the purposes of securing political unity. Moreover, the draft treaty proposed to push economic integration still further by calling for the establishment of a general common market based on the free movement of commodities and factors of production.

However, on this occasion the success that had attended the Six in the case of iron, coal and steel was not to be repeated. Five national parliaments approved the EDC treaty, but successive French governments felt unable to guarantee success in asking the *French Assembly* to ratify. Finally, the Mendès-France government attempted to water down the treaty but failed to persuade the other five nations. The treaty as it stood was therefore submitted to the French Assembly, which refused to consider it, and in so doing killed the EPC too.

There were a number of reasons for the refusal of the French Assembly to consider the treaty. First, there was opposition to the supranational elements which it contained. Second, the French 'left' refused to consider the possibility of the rearmament of Germany. Third, the French 'right' refused to have the French army placed under foreign control. Fourth, British aloofness was also a contributing factor: one of the arguments employed by those who were opposed to the treaty was that France, fearing German domination, could not participate in the formation of a European army with Germany if the UK was not a member.

It is perhaps worth noting that the failure of the EDC was followed by a British initiative also aimed at dealing with the problem of rearming Germany in a way acceptable to the French. A series of agreements was reached in 1954 between the USA, the UK, Canada and the Six under which the BTO was modified and extended: Germany and Italy were brought in and a new intergovernmental organization was formed – the *Western European Union* (WEU). These agreements also related to the termination of the occupation of Germany and its admission into NATO. As a counterbalance to the German army, the UK agreed to maintain specified forces on the Continent. In short, the gist of the agreements was to provide a European framework within which Germany could be rearmed and become a member of NATO, while providing also for British participation to relieve French fears that there would be no possible German predominance. It should be pointed out that the response of Eastern Europe to these agreements was a further hardening of the East/West division in the shape of the formation of the *Warsaw Pact*.

2.1.2 Unity via the back door

The year 1954 was a bad year for European unity since those advocating the creation of supranational bodies had suffered a reverse and the establishment of the WEU, an organization cast more in the traditional intergovernmental mould, had thereafter held the centre of the stage. However, such was the strength then of the European Movement that by 1955 new ideas were being put forward. The relaunching initiative came from the BENELUX countries. They produced a memorandum calling for the establishment of a general common market and for specific action in the fields of energy and transport.

The basic idea behind the BENELUX approach was that political unity in Europe was likely to prove difficult to achieve. It was the ultimate objective but it was one which could be realized in the longer run. In the short and medium terms the goal should be overall

economic integration. Experience gained in working together would then pave the way for the achievement of political unity, i.e. *political unity should be introduced through the 'back door'*. The memorandum called for the creation of institutions which would enable the establishment of a *European Economic Community* (EEC).

These ideas were considered at the meeting of the foreign ministers of the Six at Messina, Italy, in June 1955. They met with favourable response. The governments of the Six resolved that work should begin with a view to establishing a general common market and an atomic energy pool. Moreover, a committee should be formed which would not merely study the problems involved but should also prepare the texts of the treaties necessary in order to carry out the agreed objectives. An inter-governmental committee was therefore created, and significantly enough, Paul-Henri Spaak (see above), by then foreign minister of Belgium, was made its president; what a triumph for members of the European Movement.

The Messina resolution recorded that since the UK was a member of the WEU and had been linked with the ECSC, through an *Agreement of Association* in 1954, she should be invited to participate in the work of the committee. The position of the other OEEC countries was not so clear. In fact, the question of whether they should be allowed to participate was left for later decision by the foreign ministers of the Six.

The *Spaak Committee* held its first meeting in July 1955. British representatives were present and then and subsequently played an active role in the committee's deliberations. However, as the discussions continued, differences between the Six and the UK became evident. The UK was in favour of a free trade area (for a technical definition, see Chapter 1) arrangement, while the Six were agreed upon the formation of a customs union; the Messina resolution had explicitly called for this type of arrangement. Moreover, the UK felt that only a little extra machinery was needed to put the new arrangement into effect: the OEEC, perhaps somewhat strengthened, would suffice. This view was bound to anger the federalists who put emphasis on the creation of supranational institutions which should help achieve more than just economic integration. These differences culminated in the withdrawal of the UK representatives from the discussions in November 1955 (for a detailed exposition, see Young, 1998).

Meanwhile, the Spaak Committee forged ahead, although not without internal differences. For example, the French had apprehensions about the transition period allowed for the dismantling of the intra-member tariffs, escape clauses, the harmonization of social charges and the height of the common external tariffs (CETs); they wanted high CETs while the BENELUX nations desired low ones.

The Spaak Committee reported in April 1956 and its conclusions were considered by the foreign ministers of the Six in Venice in May of the same year. However, the attitudes amongst the Six were not uniform. On the one hand, the French naturally liked the idea of an atomic energy community, given that they were the only one of the Six to have it then, but were not keen on the proposition for a general common market, while, on the other, the remaining five had reverse preferences. Nevertheless, in the end the Six agreed that the drafting of two treaties, one to create a general common market and another to establish an atomic energy community, should begin. Treaties were subsequently signed in Rome on 25 March 1957. These were duly ratified by the national parliaments of the Six. The *EEC* and *Euratom* came into being on 1 January 1958. Thus, in 1958 the Six belonged to three separate entities: the ECSC, EEC and Euratom.

But what are the aims set out in these treaties? The overall guiding light is the achievement of an 'ever closer union' of Europe. The aims of the EEC are stated in article 3 of its treaty and can be summarized as:

(a)   The establishment of free trade between the member nations such that *all* impediments on intra-union trade are eliminated. The impediments included tariffs, import quota restrictions and export subsidies as well as all measures which had an equivalent or similar effect (now generally referred to as *non-tariff trade barriers* – NTBs). Moreover, that treaty called for the creation of genuine free trade and therefore specified rudiments of common competition and industrial policies.

(b)   The creation of an intra-EEC free market for all factors of production by providing the necessary prerequisites for ensuring factor mobility. These included taxes on, and subsidies to, capital, labour and enterprise.

(c)   The formation of common policies with regard to particular industries which the members deemed it necessary to single out for special treatment, namely, agriculture (hence the *Common Agricultural Policy* – CAP) and transport (hence the *Common Transport Policy* – CTP).

(d)   The application of procedures by which the economic policies of the member nations could be coordinated and disequilibria in their balances of payments remedied.

(e)   The creation of a *European Social Fund* (ESF) to improve the possibilities of employment for workers and to contribute to the raising of their standard of living.

(f)   The establishment of a *European Investment Bank* (EIB) to facilitate the economic expansion of the EEC by opening up fresh resources.

(g)   The establishment of a common commercial policy vis-à-vis the outside world, i.e. the creation and management of the CETs, the adoption of a common stance in multinational and multilateral trade negotiations, the granting of a *Generalized System of Preferences* (GSP) treatment to imports of certain manufactured and semi-manufactured products coming from the least developed countries (LDCs) and the reaching of trade pacts with associated nations.

It should be noted that a period of transition of twelve years, divided into three four-year stages, was granted for the elimination of intra-EEC trade barriers and for the establishment of the CETs.

Euratom asked for (h) a common approach to atomic energy, although at the time only France had such capabilities. We have already seen that the ECSC created (i) a common market for, and equitable access to, iron, coal and steel. Thus the totality of all these aims (a–i) depicted the aspirations of the Six at the time.

2.2   The evolution of the EU

2.2.1 The EC

Each one of the three entities had its own institutions. These centred on a *Council of Ministers* (Council, hereafter) and a *Commission* (*High Authority* in the case of the ECSC, see above), backed by a *European Parliament* (*Assembly* in the case of the ECSC) and a *Court of Justice*. Although there were some differences of legal competences, it later became convenient to consider the three entities as branches of the same whole and, in this, the EEC became the dominant partner. When the *Merger Treaty* was passed in 1965, it seemed more logical to refer to the whole structure as the European Communities (EC), or European Community, whose main constitutional base was the Treaty of Rome creating the EEC.

By the 1970s, however, it was clear that the EC needed institutional strengthening. Having completed the early tasks laid down in the treaties (see Chapter 27), further internal objectives had to be formulated and a way found to ensure that the EC could act more effectively on the international stage. The result was to bring national political leaders more closely into EC affairs by the introduction of summit meetings. These were formalized under the name of the *European Council* in 1974, but the first summit was held in 1969 (the end of the transition period), in The Hague, when the member states agreed that they were then so interdependent that they had no choice but to continue with the EC. That decision provided the necessary political will to reach agreement on the development of the CAP (see Chapter 20), on budgetary changes (see Chapter 19), on embarking on *economic and monetary union* (EMU, to be achieved in three stages, beginning in 1970 and completed in 1980 – see the Werner Report (CEC, 1970a) – and Part Three) and, most importantly, on the need to work on enlargement. At that time, this meant settling the teasing question of relations with the UK, which, as we have seen, had vexed the EC from the very beginning.

Moreover, it was recognized that the EC needed institutional development to match its growing international stature. Its existing international responsibilities neither matched its economic weight nor allowed effective consideration of the political dimensions of its external economic relations. Individual members still conducted most of their external affairs themselves and could easily cut across EC interests, and this was apart from the issue of whether the EC should begin to move into the field of wider foreign affairs. Since the member states had very different interests and, often, conflicting views on relations with the USA, with the USSR and on defence, it was clear that the EC was not ready to take over full competences. However, the foreign ministers were asked to study the means of achieving further political integration, on the assumption of enlargement, and to present a report. Consequently, the EC began, in a gingerly fashion, to move into political cooperation with an emphasis on foreign affairs. This did not result in a common foreign policy, but it did mean that efforts were to be exerted to identify common aims and it led to further institutional innovation alongside the institutions of the EC rather than as part of them, although the new and the old gradually came together.

A second landmark summit was held in 1972 (in Paris) and was attended by the three countries set to join in 1973: Denmark, Ireland and the UK. It devoted considerable attention to internal affairs and notably to the need to strengthen the social and regional aims of the EC as part of an ambitious programme designed to lead to EMU, thus to a full 'European Union'. It also saw a continuous need to act externally to maintain a constructive dialogue with the USA, Canada and Japan and for member states to make a concerted contribution to the *Conference on Security and Cooperation in Europe*. Foreign ministers were to meet more frequently to discuss this last issue. This meeting marked the realization that the heads of governments would have to meet more frequently than in the past. At first sight this seemed to strengthen the intergovernmental structure of the EC at the expense of the supranational element, but this was not really the case. Rather it showed that the future was a joint one, that the international climate was changing and often bleak and that if the members dealt with their internal economic difficulties alone then this could undermine the efforts of the EC to strengthen its economies. Informal discussion of general issues, whether economic or political, domestic or worldwide, was a necessary preliminary to action which often seemed stronger if it were to be EC-based. Through the summit meetings and the *Political Cooperation Procedure* (ECP) the subject matter coming to the EC steadily enlarged.

Indeed, the 1969–1972 period can be described as one of great activity. Apart from what has just been mentioned, in 1970, the Six reached a common position on the development of a *Common Fisheries Policy* (CFP, see Chapter 21), although total agreement was not to be achieved until 1982. Also, at another Paris summit in 1973, agreement was reached on the development of new policies in relation to industry and science and research (see Chapter 13). Moreover, the summit envisaged a more active role for the EC in the area of regional policy (see Chapter 22) and decided that a *European Regional Development Fund* (ERDF) should be created to channel EC resources into the development of the backward EC regions; the UK demanded such a fund during the accession negotiations, expecting to get most of it. Furthermore, later in the 1970s, the relationship between the EC and its ex-colonies was significantly reshaped in the form of the *Lomé Convention*, which became the EU-ACP agreements when the Caribbean and Pacific ex-colonies were later added (see Chapter 25).

It was obvious from all these developments that the EC needed financial resources not only to pay for the day-to-day running of the EC but also to feed the various funds that were established: the ESF, ERDF and, most important of all, the *European Guidance and Guarantee Fund* (EAGGF; see Chapter 20), to finance the CAP. In 1970, the EC took the important step of agreeing to introduce a system that would provide the EC, and specifically the EC general budget, with its 'own resources' (see Chapter 19), thus relieving it of the uncertainty of annual decisions on national contributions for its finances as well as endorsing its political autonomy in this respect. Another step of great importance was the decision that the European Parliament (EP, discussed in Chapter 3) should be elected directly by the people, not by national parliaments. In addition, the EC decided to grant the EP certain powers over the EC general budget, which proved to be a very significant development. Finally, but by no means least, was the development of the political cooperation mechanism. It is important not to forget that the dedicated members of the European Movement had always hoped that the habit of cooperation in the economic field would spill over into the political arena, one aspect of which is foreign policy matters.

By the 1980s, it was clear that the political and economic environment in which the EC operated was changing fast. Tumultuous events in the former USSR and the countries of the *Warsaw Pact* threw the institutional arrangements of Western Europe into disarray and brought the need to reassess defence requirements, the role of NATO and the continuance of the US defence presence. The unresolved issue of whether the EC needed a foreign policy, or at least some halfway house towards one, was bound to be raised once more. Meanwhile, the economic base upon which the EC had been able to develop became much more uncertain. Recession, industrial change, higher unemployment, slower growth and worries about European competitiveness undermined previous confidence.

The twin issues of constitutional development and institutional reform continued to exercise EC circles but little progress was possible and the EC seemed to be running out of steam. The deepening of the integrative process required action which governments found

controversial, the new members, now including Greece (1981), Spain (1986) and Portugal (1986), inevitably made for a less coherent group, while the recession hardened national attitudes towards the necessary compromise required for cooperative solutions. EC finances were constrained such that new policies could not be developed and this, in turn, led to bitter arguments about the resources devoted to the CAP and its inequitable impact, especially on the UK. Internal divisions were compounded by fears of a lack of dynamism in the EC economy, threatening a relative decline in world terms. Such worries suggested that a significant leap forward was required to ensure a real common market, to encourage new growth and at the same time to modernize EC institutions.

2.2.2 The single European market

As the debate progressed, a major division emerged between those who were primarily interested in the political ideal of political union and who wished to develop the EC institutions accordingly and those, more pragmatic in approach, who stressed the need for new policies. It was not until 1985 that the lines of agreement could be settled. These were brought together in the *Single European Act* (SEA) which became operative on 1 July 1987.

The SEA contained policy development which was based upon the intention of creating a true single market (usually referred to as the single European market – SEM – and '*internal market*'), by the end of 1992 (hence, the popular term *EC92*) with free movement of goods, services, capital and labour (the so-called '*four freedoms*') rather than the patchy arrangements of the past. The SEA also introduced, or strengthened, other policy fields. These included: responsibilities towards the environment; the encouragement of further action to promote health and safety at work; the promotion of technological research and development (R&D); work to strengthen economic and social cohesion so that weaker member nations may participate fully in the freer market; and cooperation in economic and monetary policy. In addition, the SEA brought foreign policy cooperation into scope and provided it with a more effective support than it had in the past, including its own secretariat, housed in the Council building in Brussels. Institutionally, it was agreed that the Council would take decisions on a qualified majority vote (QMV, see

Chapter 3) in relation to the internal market, research, cohesion and improved working conditions and that, in such cases, the EP should share in decision making (see Chapter 3). These developments were followed later by agreement regarding the control of expenditure on the CAP, which, as we have seen, had been a source of heated argument for a number of years and, most importantly, a fundamental change in the EC general budget.

The single market (see Chapter 11) provided a goal for the next few years and the EC became preoccupied with the necessary preparations (300 directives – see Chapter 3 – had to be passed and then incorporated into national law for this purpose), giving evidence of its ability to work together as one unit. However, it also brought new complications. It raised the question of how much power should be held by the EC institutions, presented member states with heavy internal programmes to complete the changes necessary for the single market, and exposed the very different economic conditions in member states which were bound to affect their fortunes in the single market. Meanwhile, the unification of Germany in 1990 fundamentally changed its position within the EC by giving it more political and economic weight, but at the same time it required it to expend considerable effort eastwards.

A further challenge at the time came from new bids for membership (so far there has been one withdrawal: the position of Greenland was renegotiated in 1984, but it remains associated and has a special agreement to regulate mutual fishing interests). The single market finally convinced the doubters in Western Europe that they should try to join. This was both a triumph and an embarrassment for the EC in that it was preoccupied with its own internal changes and a belief that it had not yet fully come to terms with the southern enlargement which had brought in Greece, Portugal and Spain. An uncertain reaction was shown in that some member states wished to press on with enlargement as a priority, while others wished to complete the single market and tighten internal policies before opening the doors. A closer economic relationship was negotiated between the EC and the EFTA countries, except for Switzerland, to form the *European Economic Area* (EEA), on 2 May 1992, which was widely assumed to be a preliminary step towards membership since it extended all the privileges of the EC except in agriculture to these countries, but without giving them voting rights.

Austria, Finland, Sweden and Switzerland all formally applied between 1989 and 1992 and Norway shortly followed them; Switzerland's application remains on the table, which is odd, given its snub of the EEA. Hungary, Poland and Czechoslovakia signed association agreements and hoped that they might join in a few years' time. Turkey and Morocco applied in 1987, although the former application was laid aside and the latter rejected. Cyprus and Malta applied in 1990. Later, most states in Central and Eastern Europe expressed their desire to join and formal negotiations were opened in 1998 with those most likely to succeed: Cyprus, the Czech Republic, Estonia, Hungary, Poland and Slovenia. However, the instability in the Balkans and the war in Kosovo showed the need to hasten the process and, at Helsinki in December 1999, it was agreed to open accession talks with Bulgaria, Latvia, Lithuania, Malta, Romania and Slovakia. Moreover, after 36 years of temporizing, it was also agreed at the same summit that Turkey is a recognized candidate, but negotiations were unlikely to start for a very long time since the EU wanted to see big improvements in Turkey's political and human rights behaviour, including the rights of Kurds and other minorities and the constitutional role of the army in political life, which might require changes in her constitution (these are known as the *Copenhagen criteria*, introduced in June 1993 at the Copenhagen summit; see below). Therefore, there was then an active list of the 13 candidates, which included Turkey, and a change in regime brought Croatia closer to joining this group (for the latest on this, see the section below on the Copenhagen 2002 summit).

It did not seem easy to generalize about the issues involved in admitting such a variety of countries for membership, but the brief history shows that integration was always meant to apply to all of Europe. However, the EC already had a series of agreements with the applicants through which it provided aid and advice on development and reform; these are set out in *Agenda 2000* (CEU, 1997b) and discussed in detail in Chapters 19, 22 and 26. In particular, the EC was looking for economic reform, the development of democratic political institutions and the protection of minority and human rights as necessary preconditions for closer relationships before full membership (the Copenhagen criteria). Partnership and cooperation agreements with Russia and the newly independent states also existed, but they did not aspire to join.

Clearly, an organization with such a large and varied membership would be very different from the original EEC of the Six, and the application challenged received wisdom as to its nature. This is one reason why pursuing the question of enlargement was made consequent upon the finalizing of the Maastricht Treaty (see below) and agreement upon new financial and budgetary arrangements for the existing member states. Continuing issues about defence and the appropriate reaction to conditions in Central and Eastern Europe, the Gulf War and the collapse of Yugoslavia all suggested further considerations to foreign and defence capabilities were important.

2.2.3 The Treaty on European Union

It was therefore against a troubled background that the EC set up two *Inter-governmental Conferences* (IGCs; see Chapter 3) to prepare the way for a meeting of the European Council in Maastricht in December 1991 which produced a new blueprint for the future. It aimed to integrate the EC further through setting out a timetable for full EMU, introducing institutional changes and developing political competences, the whole being brought together in the *Treaty on European Union* (popularly known as the Maastricht treaty) of which the EC should form a part of a wider European Union. Since this treaty was later added to and adapted as the 1997 *Amsterdam Treaty*, we shall discuss its details in the next section.

It is not surprising that the Maastricht treaty's ratification process, for which some have argued not a great deal of time was allowed, produced furious argument across Western Europe after Denmark, the first to begin the ratification process, rejected it in a referendum on 2 May 1992. Although each nation had its own peculiar worries, a general characteristic which the treaty made obvious was the width of the gap between political elites and the voters in modern society. Even though political leaders rapidly expressed contrition that they had failed to provide adequate explanation for their moves, they seemed less able to accept that there were strong doubts about many of the proposed new arrangements as being the best way forward, and that a period of calm reflection, with less frenetic development, might in the end serve the EC and its people better.

2.2.4 The Amsterdam Treaty

Maastricht left contentious problems for the Amsterdam conference to tackle. Although the hard core, comprising changes to the voting system in the Council and the size of the Commission, was not tackled (but the 2000 *Nice Treaty* does so – see below), the 1997 Amsterdam Treaty was useful in updating aims and policies, in clarifying the position regarding foreign and defence policies and justice and home affairs, and in strengthening the social side. The treaty itself modified the existing treaties, notably those on the EEC and Union, and these, together with the *acquis communitaire* (legislation deriving from the treaties), can be considered as the constitution of the EU (see below). Supplementary treaties must be used when developments go beyond the existing ones. Past examples include changes in budget procedures, agreements to admit new members and the single market (see above). In addition, a unique arrangement was attached to the Maastricht treaty in 1991: an agreement and protocol were annexed because the UK could not accept changes in the social field endorsed by the other members. The EC, i.e. EEC, ECSC and Euratom, forms the most developed section (or, in current jargon, one of three pillars of the EU, the other two being 'foreign and defence policies' and 'justice and home affairs') of the Union and its legislation takes precedence over national decisions in the appropriate field. A moment's reflection will show that this is a necessary precondition for the EC to work at all; it would otherwise be impossible to create a single economic unit, to establish the confidence needed between members or to handle external relations.

The Amsterdam treaty gives the EU a more coherent structure, a modern statement of its aims and policies, and brings some necessary improvements in the working of the institutions. Naturally, it highlights the new aspects, but these are not necessarily more important than more long-standing policies, for example, publicity is given to provisions on foreign and defence policy, yet they remain far less developed than arrangements in the economic sphere. Despite being thought of as a tidying up of the Maastricht loose ends, the treaty is a substantial document, but naturally greatly overlaps with Maastricht. Thus, it has three parts on substantive amendments to previous treaties, their simplification and modernization and their renumbering, ratification procedures and official language versions. In addition, there are an annexe, 13 protocols, often dealing with very difficult issues, 51 declarations and 8 declarations by individual member states.

The post-Amsterdam EU has broad objectives, but again these naturally overlap with those in the Maastricht treaty. The classic aim, set out long ago, is to lay the foundations of, and subsequently develop, the 'ever closer union'. It promotes economic and social progress, an aim which includes the abolition of internal frontiers, better economic and social cohesion to assist the less-developed members to catch up with the EU average (facilitated by the creation in 1993 of a *Cohesion Fund*) and an EMU, complete with a single currency (see Chapter 9). It wishes to assert an international identity through a common security and defence policy and new provisions designed to enhance this and to draw closer to the WEU (see above), which has been dormant since it was launched in 1954, and will become the equivalent an EU defence force. Thus for the first time the EU is set to have a common defence policy with the implication that the WEU will eventually be responsible for implementing decisions of an inevitable political union. Appreciation for (or is it accommodation of?) NATO was reiterated by stating that the revival of the WEU is to be linked to NATO, thus ensuring a continued alliance with the USA and Canada for the defence of Europe. It has not only introduced a formal Union citizenship, but also taken steps to strengthen the commitment to democracy, to individual rights, to promote equality and to combat discrimination. It has a procedure to be followed should a member state appear to breach human rights. The treaty has also established the EU as an area of free movement, security and justice and is attempting to establish clearer and more uniform rules in these fields. These goals should be complemented by those in the EEC treaty (see last part of Section 2.1.2). Internally, the EU has general economic objectives relating to the single market (Chapter 11), agriculture (Chapter 20) and transport (Chapter 15), the aim of economic and social cohesion and a new emphasis on policy making in employment (Chapters 5, 9, 10 and 23), social (Chapter 23) and environmental matters (Chapter 17). The need for enhanced competitiveness for EU industry (Chapters 12 and 13), the promotion of R&D, the construction of trans-European infrastructure, the attainment of a high-level of health protection, better education, training and cultural development all find their place (Chapters 12, 13 and 23). Recognition is given to development policies (Chapter 25), consumer protection (Chapter 23) and to measures in energy policy (Chapter 16) and tourism. There are, of course, a host of subsidiary and supporting objectives.

After many arguments, the concept of flexible integration has been brought out in the open. Articles 40, 43 and 44 (EU) allow some member states to establish closer cooperation between themselves with the aim of developing EU policies which not all members wish to pursue, but subject to veto by dissenting members. This was fully endorsed in the 2000 Nice Treaty by stating that groups of eight or more member countries may pursue greater integration in certain areas. Such a move must be supported by a majority of members, must not harm the interests of others and must allow the non-participating members to be involved in the discussion of developments, but without voting on them. There are some important examples of policies which are less than fully inclusive, amongst them are membership of the single currency, the Danish opt-outs from the free movement provisions although accepting the *Schengen Principle* dictating it, and from decisions with defence implications, and the British and Irish non-acceptance of the abolition of border controls.

The Maastricht conference touched fears of the creation of a superstate. In an attempt to counter this, the *subsidiarity principle* was agreed during the Edinburgh summit in December 1992 and the Amsterdam treaty tried to clarify it further. Article 5 (EC) explains that, where the EU does not have exclusive competence, it may proceed only if the member states cannot pursue the action themselves, or it is an objective better achieved by EU action. A protocol attached to the treaty has tried to clarify how this concept should be applied and, in particular, insists that the reasons for action must be stated, EU action must be simple and limited and a report given to EU institutions on what has been done. These provisions are meant as a check on an insidious growth of EU power, allowing it to slip in a direction which has never been agreed. This brake is supported by the right of member states to bring a case in the Court of Justice arguing that the EU is extending its powers unjustifiably.

An element in the debate about subsidiarity is doubt concerning the remoteness of decision making in Brussels. There is a need to make the EU more responsive to the needs of the general public and more sensitive to the effects of the intrusiveness that EU legislation appears to bring. The 'democratic deficit' is an issue that has long been discussed and there are several ways of addressing it, of which greater powers to the EP is one (see the section below on the constitutional convention and Chapter 3). Individuals have long had the right to petition the EP and this has been supported by the appointment of an *ombudsman*, chosen by the EP but independent of it.

A particular issue is the undermining of national parliaments, especially those that have an important legislative function and that have found it hard to find ways of exercising control over the EU. In practice, they have been limited to scrutiny of proposals which, once they are in the advanced stage, are very difficult to change. Some efforts have also been made, through scrutiny committees, to discuss general issues, thus helping to suggest policy positions for the future, while Denmark, in particular, has tried to define the parameters within which ministers may negotiate. A protocol of the Amsterdam treaty tries to increase the influence of national parliaments. It requires that all Commission consultation papers be forwarded promptly, that proposed legislation should be made available in time for parliaments to consider it and that there should be a six-week gap between a legislative proposal being submitted to the EP and the date it is sent to the Council (see Chapter 3). A great deal is, of course, up to national parliaments to keep abreast of events and to improve contacts with the EP. Associated with this was the general acceptance of the need to keep the public better informed and to provide access to EU documentation. A declaration attached to the treaty stresses the importance of transparency, access to documents and the fight against fraud, Article 255 (EC) giving citizens a right to access official documents. A further declaration accepts the importance of improving the quality of drafting in legislation. Over the years, efforts have been made, too, to help individuals question the EU. The right to petition the EP was buttressed by the establishment of the ombudsman (see above). A further change, directly affecting individuals, was to confer the citizenship of the EU on the nationals of member states. Although such changes are intended to encourage a greater openness in decision making, their implementation will take time. Actual decision making in the Council remains private.

Flexible policies and subsidiarity have been tackled together, although they deal with very different circumstances, because they both suggest that the EU is still uneasily balanced between the two opposing views on how to organize Western Europe which have been so eloquently expressed since the end of the Second World War. To some observers, the Amsterdam treaty is one more step towards a federal Europe, but to others, it is a means of keeping a check upon this drive and retaining a degree of national governmental control. The final outcome remains uncertain.

2.2.5 Nice Treaty

Hammered out over four bitter days and nights on the French Riviera, the Nice Treaty of 11 December 2000 is both complex and insubstantial; one of its authors even called it 'lousy'. The treaty's main concern is with EU enlargement, especially with the institutional changes that would be needed to accommodate 12–15 new members (see above). Since its provisions will not make sense until we have discussed the EU institutions, they will be dealt with in Chapter 3. Here, it suffices to state that the treaty both amends QMV and extends it to new areas, including trade in services; asks the larger member nations to drop their second commissioner after 2005; limits the total number of commissioners to 20 after 2007; and proclaims the Charter of Rights, but without legal force.

Also, it is vital to add that at the Nice meetings, it was decided to 'engage in a broader and more detailed analysis of the future of the EU, with a view to making it more democratic, more transparent and more efficient'. The ensuing debate culminated at the December 2001 Laeken summit when, on 12 December, it was decided to create a convention for the purpose. On 28 February 2002, the *Convention for the Future of Europe* was set up under the chairmanship of ex-French President Valéry Giscard d'Estaing, with ex-Italian Prime Minister Giuliano Amato and ex-Belgian Prime Minister Jean-Luc Dehaene as vice-chairpersons, to discuss the matter further and then report to an IGC in mid-2003. The convention has 105 delegates, representing EU governments, parliaments and institutions and is set two tasks: to propose a set of arrangements to enable the EU to work when it has 25–30 member nations; and to express the purpose of the EU, so that the citizens whom it is meant to serve will understand its relevance to their lives and, with luck, feel some enthusiasm for its activities.

Surprisingly, the Convention issued a draft of a constitution for the EU on 6 February 2003. The contents are mainly about the consolidation of the various EU treaties, but they include proposals for the reform of existing EU institutions and on the future of the EU. Since the final, but not complete, draft adopted on 20 June 2003 at the Thessaloniki Greece summit not only contained changes to the original draft, but is most likely to undergo further change before the inter-governmental conference scheduled for the end of the first half of 2004 gives final approval, it would be pointless to waste space on it here, but the institutional changes being proposed are dealt with in Chapter 3 and the draft's proposals for the future of the EU in Chapter 28.

One should add that the ratification of the treaty followed almost the same path as Maastricht's. The Irish, whose constitution demands a referendum on such issues, were the first to kick off the process and shocked all by rejecting it on 7 June 2001 by 54% to 46%. Although technically that meant the death of the treaty, the other member nations stubbornly went ahead with ratification, leading to a dramatic situation in 2002 when all but Ireland had ratified.

However, in a second referendum on 20 October 2002, Ireland recorded an emphatic 'yes' (by 62.9% against 37.1%). This then set the tone for the Copenhagen summit of 12–13 December 2002 when it was agreed that: (a united) Cyprus, the Czech Republic, Estonia, Hungary, Latvia, Lithuania, Malta, Poland, the Slovak Republic and Slovenia can join the EU on 1 May 2004; Bulgaria and Romania can join in 2007, provided they met the necessary criteria; and Turkey can open accession negotiations immediately after the December 2004 summit pending a favourable report by the Commission on its status on the Copenhagen criteria. Indeed, the ten countries signed accession treaties with the EU on 16 April 2003 at the Athens summit, and have since then ratified their accession treaties, nine through popular referendums, with Cyprus not needing one – see Table 2.1 below for details on the outcome of the referendums.

Table 2.1 Results of the referendums on EU membership

Country	Date	Turnout (%)	Yes (%)	No (%)
Malta	8 March 2003	91.00	53.6	46.4
Slovenia	23 March 2003	99.97	89.61	10.39
Hungary	12 April 2003	99.44	83.76	16.24
Lithuania	10–11 May 2003	63.37	89.95	8.82
Slovakia	16–17 May 2003	52.15	92.46	6.20
Poland	7–8 June 2003	58.85	77.45	22.55
Czech Republic	13–14 June 2003	55.21	77.33	22.67
Estonia	14 September 2003	64.06	66.83	33.17
Latvia	20 September 2003	72.53	67.00	32.30

2.3 Conclusion

The adherents to the original ideal for European unity would stress that from what has been stated in this chapter, one cannot escape the conclusion that although the EU has not yet arrived, it has gone a long way towards achieving the dream of its founding fathers: the creation of a United States of Europe. They would add that the long march is easily explicable in terms of the difficulties inherent in securing the necessary compromises needed for going forward while accommodating new members, and the tackling of unforeseen economic and political problems, from both within and without. They would concede that it would, of course, require a big leap from the present 'union' to a full state of Europe, but would insist that it did not really matter when, or if ever, the EU realized that dream, especially when there are more ways than one to achieving a federation and some members do not share it, since what is important is that one should never forget that this vision has been the guiding light without which disaster might have struck at any time, and it remains so for at least France and Germany (see Chapter 28). They would also add that it behoves all those who would like to think of the EU as, or dearly want to reduce it to, a mere trading bloc to think twice. However, several member nations, especially the new ones and most definitely the UK and many EU citizens do not share this view and insist that the EU has more or less reached the pinnacle of what they have aspired for it, and would add that even though the creation of a powerful united European economy with most of its members using the same currency is an historic achievement, nothing further should ensue, least of all political unity.

I shall leave it there since my own position, if it is not yet apparent, should not matter; it is what you believe in the light of the facts and your own deep reflection that really matters. I shall, however, return to this issue in the final chapter on the future of European integration.

Chapter 3

EU institutions

ALI EL-AGRAA*

The EU has a unique institutional structure. EU member nations delegate sovereignty in specific areas to independent institutions, entrusting them with defending the interests of the EU as a whole as well as of both its member states and citizens. The *European Commission* (Commission, hereafter) upholds the interests of the whole EU. The *Council of the European Union* (Council, hereafter) upholds those of the governments of the member nations through their ministerial representatives. And the *European Parliament* (EP) upholds those of the EU citizens, who directly elect its members.

The Commission, Council and EP, known as the 'institutional triangle', are flanked by the *European Court of Justice* (ECJ) and *Court of Auditors* as well as by five other bodies: the *European Central Bank* (ECB), the *Economic and Social Committee* (ESC), the *Committee of the Regions*, the *European Investment Bank* (EIB) and the *European Ombudsman*. There are also thirteen agencies taking care of specialized concerns, which are basically of a technical, scientific or managerial nature (see Appendix 3.1, p. 55).

This chapter provides a basic coverage of these institutions, but does so more adequately for the institutional triangle. This is due not only to the fact that the Commission, Council and EP between them initiate and finalize most new EU legislation, hence

constitute the core of the EU legislative process, but also because the others are dealt with in some detail in the chapters where they are most relevant, for example, the ECB operations are fully covered in Chapter 10, the EIB's in Chapters 13 and 22 and the Ombudsman's in Chapter 23.

Before explaining these institutions, one should recall from Chapter 2 that the EU also has the *European Council*, which is a summit meeting of heads of state or government and generally meets twice a year. As mentioned in that chapter, although the European Council was formalized in 1974 and given a formal status in the Maastricht treaty, summit meetings were introduced during 1957–1969, with the first formal one being held in 1969 in The Hague at the end of the 12-year transition period for the EEC. No more needs to be mentioned on this since it is not an institution except to add that it simply offers general guidelines, blueprints, providing impetus for the development and political guidance of the EU as a whole, which the Commission then studies carefully before it lodges a proposal for legislation with the Council and EP – see below. One should also add that occasionally special summit meetings are held under the title of *Inter-Governmental Conferences* (IGCs), called to order for specific issues of major importance.

3.1 The Commission

The EU treaties assign the Commission a wide range of tasks, but these can be narrowed down to four major roles. It initiates EU policy by proposing new legislation to the Council and EP. It serves as the executive arm of the EU by administering and implementing EU policies. Jointly with the ECJ, it acts as the guardian of the EU treaties by enforcing EU law. And it acts as the EU spokesperson and negotiator of international

agreements, especially in relation to trade and co-operation, such as the Lomé Convention, which links the EU with 77 African, Caribbean and Pacific nations (see Chapter 25). It may prove helpful to elaborate somewhat on some of these roles.

As the initiator of EU policies, the Commission formulates proposals in areas defined by the treaties. These areas cover a wide spectrum and particularly

* I wish to express my thanks to Doreen Collins for her constructive comments on the first draft of this chapter.

relate to agriculture, development cooperation, energy, the environment, industry, regional development, social policy, trade relations and transport. Due to the 'subsidiarity principle' (Chapter 2), such proposals should be confined to those where action at the EU level would be more productive than at the national, regional or local level. However, once the Commission has lodged a proposal with the Council and EP, the three institutions collaborate together to ensure an agreed outcome for it. Note that the Council generally reaches its decision by qualified majority voting (QMV, see Section 3.2), needing unanimity only when it rejects a proposal. Also, the Commission carefully scrutinizes amendments by the EP (Section 3.3) before offering, where deemed appropriate, an amended proposal.

As the EU Executive, the Commission is involved in all the areas in which the EU is concerned. However, the role it plays assumes particular significance in certain fields. These include: 'competition policy', where it monitors cartels and mergers and disposes of or monitors discriminatory state aid (Section 3.4 and Chapter 12); agriculture, where it drafts regulations (see Chapter 20); and technical R&D, where it promotes and coordinates through EU framework programmes (see Chapter 13). The Commission is also entrusted with the management of the EU general budget, and for this purpose it is supervised by the Court of Auditors, whose annual reports are relied upon by the EP for granting the Commission discharge for their implementation of the budget.

As the joint guardian of the EU treaties, the Commission has to see to it that EU legislation is properly implemented in the member nations. In doing so, it is hoped that it would be able to maintain a climate of mutual confidence so that all concerned, be they the member nations, economic operators or private citizens, can carry out their obligations to the full. If any member state is in breach, say by failing to apply a EU directive (Section 3.4), the Commission, as an impartial authority, should investigate, issue an objective ruling and notify the government concerned, subject to review by the ECJ, of the action needed to rectify such infringement of EU obligations. If the matter cannot be dealt with through the infringement procedure, the Commission has then to refer it to the ECJ, whose decision is binding. Likewise, with the supervision of the ECJ, the Commission monitors companies for their respect of EU competition rules.

The Commission consists of 20 members, one of whom is president and two are vice-presidents. Two commissioners come from each of the five large member nations and one from each of the remaining ten, i.e. the number of commissioners is determined, very roughly, by population size (see Table 5.1). However, the Nice Treaty asks that the larger member nations should drop their second commissioner after 2005 and that the total number of commissioners should be limited to 20 after 2007, when the EU is expected to comprise at least 27 members.

All commissioners are appointed for five-years (4 until 1994) and have renewable terms. They are chosen for their *competence and capacity to act independently in the interest of the EU itself*, not of their own countries. They have all been prominent politicians in their own countries, often having held ministerial positions. That is because they need to be people familiar with the political scene, able to meet senior politicians on equal terms, for without this stature and ability to understand political pressures they would lose the senses of touch and timing which are essential for effective functioning.

The commissioners' appointment process begins within six months of the elections to the EP. This is to allow time for the necessary procedure taken by the EP to approve the Commission. This procedure commences with the appointment of the president, who is nominated by the member states and has to be approved by the EP. Once confirmed, the president, with the collaboration of the governments of the member states, nominates the remaining 19 commissioners. The EP then gives its opinion on the entire college of 20 through an approval process. Once the college is approved by the EP, the new Commission assumes its official responsibilities in the following January.

It is pertinent to add here that following the exposure of the ineptness and laxity of some parts of the Commission, the EP has taken the question of approval even more seriously and has subjected nominees to detailed scrutiny including their suitability for their intended posts. It has also been made clear that the commissioners must work under the political guidance of the president (Article 219 EC) while the present commissioners have had to agree to resign if asked to do so by the president. The procedures have enhanced the EP powers considerably since it can satisfy itself about the Commission's programme and intended initiatives before giving its approval.

While these moves are intended to ensure a more efficient Commission, the episode has brought a latent contradiction to the surface. The Commission was

Table 3.1 EU Directorates General and services

Policies	External relations
Agriculture	Development
Competition	Enlargement
Economic and Financial Affairs	Europe Aid-Cooperation Office
Education and Culture	External Relations
Employment and Social Affairs	Humanitarian Aid Office – ECHO
Energy and Transport	Trade
Enterprise	***General services***
Environment	European Anti-Fraud Office
Fisheries	Eurostat
Freedom, Security and Justice	Budget
Health and Consumer Protection	Press and Communication
Information Society	Publications Office
Internal Market	Secretariat General
Joint Research Centre	***Internal services***
Regional Policy	Financial Control
Research	Group of Policy Advisers
Taxation and Customs Union	Internal Audit Service
	Joint Interpreting and Conference Service
	Legal Service
	Personnel and Administration
	Translation Service

designed as the powerhouse of political momentum for the EU, although, as we have seen, this function is to some extent now shared with the European Council and the EP, it has been less effective in administrative and managerial functions where its weakness has been exposed. This has led some critics to argue that reform should include a shift of responsibility away from policy towards execution so that the Commission becomes more like a national civil service.

Each commissioner is responsible for a portfolio, which in many cases is a mixture of policy areas and administrative responsibilities, generally referred to as *Directorates General* (DGs). However, since there are 36 DGs (Table 3.1), some commissioners have more than one portfolio, but that does not mean that they are busier since the workload for each DG depends on its relative weight within the EU. The DGs used to be numbered in roman style (e.g. DG I, DG II), but the numbers have now been dropped, so Table 3.1 gives the latest designations and Appendix 3.2 provides the previous system so as to facilitate comparison and to assist the reader when encountering them elsewhere.

A *director general* is in charge of a DG, under him/her is a *director*, followed by *head of division*. Each commissioner has a private office or *cabinet*, the staff to which is selected by the commissioner and has traditionally come from the same member nation, for ease of communication, but see next paragraph. When the commissioner is away, the head of his/her private office, the *chef de cabinet*, will act on his/her behalf at the weekly meetings, held on Wednesdays in Brussels, but in Strasbourg during the plenary sessions of the EP.

One should add that over time, some directorates have acquired greater prestige than others; not surprisingly, those that deal with core EU policies are most prominent and, as the EU has developed, so the possibility for conflict between directorates over policy matters has arisen. Agricultural, competition and regional and external trade policies, especially imports from the LDCs are obvious examples. A new development brought in with the 1999 Commission is to have a senior commissioner responsible for an oversight of external affairs whether of an economic or political nature. The reform of the Commission has therefore begun. The personal cabinets of the commissioners are being opened to wider recruitment so that they are less obviously national enclaves attached to a particular commissioner; reform of financial controls and stronger management systems are being put into place and merit is to account for more and nationality less for promotion to senior posts. Personnel are to receive more training and be subject to tighter controls. These reforms are the remit of Neil Kinnock, an energetic vice-president, who is trying to lift the Commission to modern standards of public administration, but as expected, he has been meeting with strong resistance, as union control of internal staff matters has traditionally been very tight.

Once the Commission has reached a decision on a matter presented by the commissioner concerned, the decision becomes an integral part of its policy and will have the unconditional backing of the entire college even if simple majority voting led to its adoption. In a sense, the Commission follows the British practice of 'collective responsibility', i.e. it acts as a collegiate body accepting responsibility as a group, but in practice policy rests mainly with the responsible commissioner, perhaps in association with two or more colleagues.

In carrying out its responsibilities, the Commission seeks the opinions of national parliaments, administrations and professional and trade union organizations. For the technical details of its legislative provisions or proposals, it consults the experts meeting in the committees and working groups that it organizes. In carrying out implementing measures, the Commission is assisted by committees of representatives of the member nations. Also, it works closely with the ESC and the Committee of the Regions since it has to consult them on many proposed legislative acts. The Commission also attends all the sessions of the EP, where it must clarify and justify its policies, and regularly replies to both written and oral questions posed by members of the EP (MEPs).

One should point out that in some ways, both for interest groups and for the man or woman in the street who wishes to make the effort, the Commission is more accessible than national administrations. This is in part because the consultation processes, although clumsy, do bring a wide range of people into touch with EU affairs. The danger of this web of machinery and consultation is indecision and slowness of action. At the same time it puts a premium on the views of those who are effectively organized. Additionally, there is a well-established Commission policy of informing and educating the public in order to mobilize public opinion behind the integration process. Unfortunately, this policy often fails to reach its target, so that considerable unease remains and its relative success in establishing relations with bankers, organizational representatives, industrialists and other power groups has contributed to a widespread belief that the EU is an elitist institution far away from the ordinary citizen. Hence a new drive towards better information, and public access to it was promised in the Maastricht Treaty and is continuing.

Finally, one should add that it is natural that the term Commission may be confusing. This is because it is used to refer to both the college of 20 commissioners as well as to the entire institution with approximately 24 000 staff, most of them in Brussels, but about 2 000 are in Luxembourg, and there are representatives in every EU nation as well as in delegations in almost all other countries. However, one should encounter no major difficulties since it is easy to judge from the context. Note that although the number of people working for the Commission may seem excessive, it is actually less than that employed by most of the councils of medium-sized EU cities.

3.2   The Council

As mentioned in Chapter 2, the three Councils of Ministers, one for each of the ECSC, EEC and Euratom, were merged in 1965. With the adoption of the Treaty on European Union (the Maastricht treaty) in 1992, the name was changed in 1993 to the Council of the European Union (hereafter, simply the Council; see above) to reflect the three pillars of the EU. Recall that the pillars are based on 'community' action in the case of the 'EC' and on 'inter-governmental cooperation' in the two cases of 'common foreign and security policy' (CFSP) and 'home and judicial affairs' (JHA). Hence, the field of Council activities covers all three pillars, but in this context the precise term for the third should be 'police and judicial cooperation in criminal matters'.

The Council consists of representatives of the governments of the member states, who are accountable to their national parliaments and citizens, hence it is the embodiment of national interests, but representatives of the Commission always attend its meetings. Note that although the Commission has no voting rights, it plays an active role in helping to reach a decision, and that it is here that it can perform an important mediator function between national viewpoints and its own, which, as we have seen, is intended to represent the general EU interest. Who constitutes the Council would depend upon the matter under consideration: if the matter were about finance, it would be the ministers of finance of the member nations; if the matter concerned agriculture, it would be the ministers of agriculture; and so on and so forth. Thus, unlike the Commission, the Council is not made up of a fixed body of people. The Council is seated in Brussels and most of its meetings are held there except during April, June and October when they take place in Luxembourg.

Since membership of the Council varies according to the subject matter under review, this has led to problems for the member states. Because EU issues are handled by various ministers, briefed by their own civil servants, it becomes harder for any government to see its EU policy as a coherent whole. In turn, coordination within the government machine becomes important. For the EU too, the greater specialization of business creates difficulties, for it has become far harder to negotiate a package deal whereby a set of decisions can be agreed, and each member nation has gains to set off against its losses although, in the long run, governments need to show the benefits they have won.

The presidency of the Council rotates, with each member nation holding it in turn for a period of six months, and the chairmanship of the many committees alters correspondingly. The president plays an active role as the organizer of Council's work and as the chairperson of its meetings; as the promoter of legislative and political decisions; and as an arbiter between the member states in brokering compromises between them. It has become the practice for each member state to try to establish a particular style of working and to single out certain matters to which it wishes to give priority. Since any chairperson can influence business significantly, the president may occupy an important, albeit temporary, role. The president also fulfils some representational functions both towards other EC institutions, notably the EP, and in external negotiations where the presidents of the Council and Commission may act in association. However, discussions are now underway (see Section 3.11) for limiting the presidency to the larger nations, due to its international importance and the ability of the assuming nation to cope with the extra costs involved in preparing for and hosting the meetings. Naturally, the general secretariat assists the presidency.

The Council has five major responsibilities. It is the main EU legislative body, but in many areas, it exercises this prerogative jointly with the EP, through the 'co-decision procedure' (*see* Section 3.3). The Council co-ordinates the broad economic policies of the member states. Together with the EP, it has authority on the EU general budget. On the basis of general guidelines from the European Council, it takes the necessary decisions for framing and implementing the CFSP. And, it coordinates the activities of the member nations as well as adopts measures in the area of JHA.

It may prove helpful to elaborate on three of these roles. With regard to its decision-making powers, generally speaking, the Council only acts on a proposal from the Commission (see above) and in most cases acts jointly with the EP in the context of a co-decision, consultation or assent procedure (*see* Section 3.3). Under the co-decision procedure, originally, the Council and EP shared legislation in the general areas, which included the completion of the internal market, the environment and consumer protection, but with the ratification of the Amsterdam Treaty, new areas were added in 1999, such as non-discrimination, free movement and residence and combating social exclusion. However, the Council plays a dominant role when it comes to the CFSP and JHA when they relate to essential components of national policy since both the EP and Commission have more limited says in these areas. Also, although the Commission is entrusted with the enforcement of EU legislation, the Council may reserve the right for it to perform executive functions.

The Maastricht treaty calls for an economic policy that closely coordinates those of the individual EU member nations. In order to achieve this task, each year the Council adopts draft guidelines for the economic policies of the member countries, which are then incorporated into the conclusions of the European Council. They are then converted into a Council recommendation and accompanied by a multilateral surveillance mechanism. This coordination is performed entirely in the context of EMU, where the Economic and Financial Affairs (ECOFIN) Council plays a leading role (Chapter 10).

Finally, with regard to the joint responsibility of the Council and EP for the EU general budget, each year the Commission submits a preliminary draft budget to the Council for approval. Then two successive readings allow the EP to negotiate with the Council the modification of certain items of expenditure and to ensure that budgetary revenues are allocated appropriately. In the case of disagreement with the EP, the Council is entrusted with making the final decision on the so-called 'compulsory expenditures' (Chapter 19), relating mainly to agriculture and financial commitments emanating from EU agreements with non-member nations. However, with regard to 'non-compulsory expenditures' and the final adoption of the whole budget, the EP has the final say.

Council decisions are taken by unanimous, simple or qualified majority voting (QMV), with QMV being the most common. When QMV is used, each member nation is endowed with a number of votes. The votes are weighted so that at least some of the smaller member nations must assent. For the EU of 12, the total number of votes was 76 (France, Germany, Italy and the UK 10 each; Spain 8; Belgium, Greece, the Netherlands and Portugal 5 each; Denmark and Ireland 3 each; and 2 for Luxembourg), with 54 votes needed for a decision. Thus the large countries could not impose their wishes on the rest.

For the EU of 15, it was agreed that 62 votes, out of a total of 87 (France, Germany, Italy and the UK 10 each; Spain 8; Belgium, Greece, the Netherlands and Portugal 5 each; Austria and Sweden 4 each; Denmark, Finland and Ireland 3 each; and 2 for Luxembourg), will be needed for a decision, but if 26 votes are recorded against a decision, 'reasonable time' should be allowed for further discussion. The UK suggested that it should be indefinite, but the others believe it to be no more than three months.

This general picture remains basically true after the Nice Treaty in spite of increased votes for the larger member nations (29 for each of France, Germany, Italy and the UK; 27 for Spain; 13 for the Netherlands; 12 for each of Belgium, Greece and Portugal; 10 each of Austria and Sweden; 7 for each of Denmark, Finland and Ireland; and 4 for Luxembourg), with 169 out of the total 237 votes needed for a decision. The proviso is added that a member of Council can request verification on whether the member nations constituting the 169 votes represented at least 62% of total EU population; if not, the decision cannot be adopted.

As a final word on QMV, one should add that its proponents often claim that it is *a device meant to ensure that the large countries cannot impose their wishes on the smaller member nations* since the largest four countries need another four to secure the 169 votes. However, it can equally be claimed that it is a system which prevents majority opinion from being stymied by a few smaller nations, which is what could happen in the case of a decision requiring a simple majority of the EU nations, i.e. eight out of fifteen; hence the intricate play with figures.

The Council is served by its own secretariat and is supported by an important body called the *Committee of Permanent Representatives* (COREPER). The membership of COREPER comprises senior representatives from the member nations, holding ambassadorial ranks. This body prepares the work of the Council, except for agricultural matters since these are entrusted to the *Special Committee on Agriculture*. The Council is also assisted by working groups, which consist of officials from the national administrations.

In 1966, it was agreed that it would be desirable for the Commission to contact national governments via COREPER before deciding on the form of an intended proposal. As a result of its links with both the Council and Commission, COREPER is involved in all major stages of EU policy making. Many matters of policy are in fact agreed by COREPER and reach the Council only in a formal sense. While this is one way of keeping business down to manageable proportions, it has meant that the Council itself has become concerned only with the most important matters or those which may not be of great substance but which are nevertheless politically sensitive. This has encouraged domestic media to present Council meetings as national battles in which there has to be victory or defeat and politicians, too, have become extremely adept at using publicity to rally support to their point of view. As a result, the effect has become the opposite of that originally intended when it was thought that the experience of working together would make it progressively easier to find an answer expressive of the general good and for which majority voting would be a suitable tool. Instead, conflict of national interests is often a better description. The Council also encounters practical problems. The great press of business, the fact that ministers can only attend to Council business part time, the highly sensitive nature of their activities and the larger number of members all contribute to a grave time-lag in reaching policy decisions and the move towards QMV was one measure designed to overcome this difficulty.

The General Affairs, ECOFIN and Agriculture Councils meet once a month, whilst the others meet between two and four times a year, the frequency depending on the number and urgency of the issues under consideration. Because the ministers of finance and foreign affairs also meet in other capacities, due to the nature of EU activities, their meetings have attracted the term 'Senior Council'.

3.3   The European Parliament

Originally, the European Parliament (EP) was a consultative rather than a legislative body, since the Council (of Ministers) had to seek its opinion, but without obligation, before deciding on a Commission proposal. It did have the power to dismiss the entire Commission, but because it did not possess the right to appoint commissioners, many analysts did not attach much significance to this. However, as mentioned in Chapter 2 and above, the EP acquired budgetary powers in 1970 and financial provisions powers in 1975. The SEA gave it more powers in 1986. And the Maastricht (1992) and Amsterdam (1997) treaties have turned the EP into a true legislative body as well as strengthened its role as the democratic overseer of the EU. Some elaboration on this is warranted.

The EP acts together with the Council in formulating and adopting certain legislation emanating from the Commission. Here, the most common path is through the *co-decision procedure*, which gives equal weight to both and results in the adoption of joint acts (see Figure 3.1). In the case of disagreements between the two, *conciliation committees* would be convened to find a common ground. The co-decision procedure applies particularly in the case of: the management of the single market; freedom of movement of workers; technological research and development; the environment; consumer protection; education; culture; and public health.

Also, the EP's approval is needed in certain areas. These include the accession by new member nations, association agreements with non-members, notably in the Mediterranean, the conclusion of international agreements, decisions affecting the right of residence for EU citizens, its own electoral procedures and the task and powers of the ECB.

Moreover, although the Commission remains the main proposer of new legislation, the EP also provides significant political momentum, especially through its examination of the annual programme for the Commission and asking it to submit appropriate proposals.

With regard to the EU general budget (see Chapter 19), as we have seen, the EP and Council are the key players. Each year, the Commission has to prepare a *preliminary draft budget*, which has to be approved by the Council. Then two *readings* ensue, providing the EP with the occasion to negotiate with the Council the amendment of certain items of expenditure, although such amendments are generally subject to the financial constraints of the budget, and to ensure that the budgetary resources are appropriately allocated. Finally, it is the EP that has the right to adopt the final budget, which needs the signature of the president of the EP before it can come into force. Also, the EP's Committee on Budgetary Control is entrusted with monitoring the implementation of the budget, and each year the EP grants a discharge to the Commission for the implementation of the budget for the previous year.

The cooperation procedure was established following the SEA. It was the testing ground for the co-decision procedure. The implementation and management of the internal market was one of the main areas, but this is now under the co-decision procedure. However, under the Maastricht Treaty, the cooperation procedure now includes: social policy; education and training; the environment; legislation for EMU and implementing measures for the EU structural funds, the trans-European infrastructure networks, etc.

Thus the EP of today performs three important functions: together with the Council, it legislates; together with the Council, it shares authority on the EU general budget and its adoption of the budget is the end of the budgetary procedure; and it approves the nominations of commissioners, has the right to censure the Commission, forcing its resignation, and exercises political supervision over all the institutions.

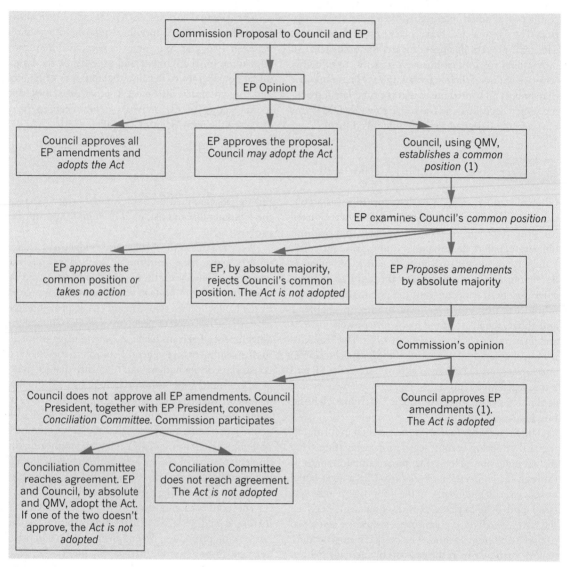

Figure 3.1 The co-decision procedure

The EP operates in three different places. It meets in Strasbourg, where it is seated, for its plenary sessions, which all members must attend. Its Parliamentary Committees (see Table 3.2) hold their meetings in Brussels and additional plenary sessions are held there too. Its secretariat is located in Luxembourg. This set up has attracted harsh criticism not only for its inconvenience and money and time wasting, due to the travel involved, but more importantly for making it difficult for the EP to become a more coherent and effective organization. It is often claimed that the reasons for these locations are mainly historical going back to the creation of the ECSC, EEC and Euratom, but the history was no accident, given the prestige it extends to the countries where they are located and the economic value of the assets.

The EP is still in an evolutionary stage and cannot be expected to follow the path of national parliaments which, in any case, differ among themselves. It operates in a different environment and its power struggles, so far, have been with the Council and Commission rather than with national parliaments.

Table 3.2 Committees of the European Parliament

Parliamentary committees	On
AFET	Foreign Affairs, Human Rights, Common Security and Defence Policy
BUDG	Budgets
CONT	Budgetary Control
LIBE	Citizens' Freedoms and Rights, Justice and Home Affairs
ECON	Economic and Monetary Affairs
JURI	Legal Affairs and the Internal Market
ITRE	Industry, External Trade, Research and Energy
EMPL	Employment and Social Affairs
ENVI	The Environment, Public Health and Consumer Policy
AGRI	Agriculture and Rural Development
PECH	Fisheries
RETT	Regional Policy, Transport and Tourism
CULT	Culture, Youth, Education, the Media and Sport
DEVE	Development and Cooperation
AFCO	Constitutional Affairs
FEMM	Women's Rights and Equal Opportunities
PETI	Petitions
Temporary committees	*On*
FIAP	Foot and mouth disease
GENE	Human genetics and other new technologies of modern medicine
ECHE	The ECHELON interception system
ESB1	Enquiring into BSE (bovine spongiform encephalopathy)
ESB2	Monitoring action taken on BSE recommendations
TRAN	Enquiring into EU transit regime
CONV	EP's Delegation to the Convention of the Future of Europe

The EP had its first elections by direct universal suffrage on 7 and 10 June 1979 and elections are based on a system of proportional representation and are held either on a regional basis (e.g., Belgium, Italy and UK) or on a national basis. It has 626 members (see Table 3.3), elected for a term of five years. Once elected, members are organized in political rather than national groups although, in some cases, national identity remains very strong.

Its present membership of 626, given in national terms, is such that: Germany has 99 members; France, Italy and the UK have 87 each; Spain has 64; the Netherlands has 31; Belgium, Greece and Portugal have 25 each; Sweden has 22; Austria has 21; Denmark and Finland have 16 each; Ireland has 15; and Luxembourg has 6.

In terms of party distribution, the EP elected in 1999 consists of: 232 from the group of European People's

Table 3.3 Members of the European Parliament, 1999–2004

	PPE-DE	PSE	ELDER	GUE/NGL	Verts/ALE	UEN	EDD	NI	*Total*
Austria	7	7			2			5	21
Belgium	5	5	6		7			2	25
Denmark	1	2	6	4		1	2		16
Finland	5	3	5	1	2				16
France	21	18		15	9	3	9	12	87
Germany	53	35		7	4				99
Greece	9	9		7					25
Ireland	5	1	1	2	6				15
Italy	35	16	8	6	2	10		10	87
Luxembourg	2	2	1		1				6
Netherlands	9	6	8	1	4		3		31
Portugal	9	12		2		2			25
Spain	28	24	3	4	4			1	64
Sweden	7	6	4	3	2				22
UK	37	29	11		6		2	2	87
Total	232	175	54	50	45	22	17	31	626

Note: PPE-DE is a group of European People's Party (Christian Democrats) and European Democrats; PSE is a group of the Party of European Socialist; ELDER is a group of European Liberal, Democrat and Reform Party; GUE/NGL is a Confederal group of European United Left and Nordic Green Left; Verts/ALE is a group of the Greens and European Free Alliance; UEN is the group of the Union for Europe of Nations; EDO is a group of Europe of Democracies and Diversities; and members of NI are unattached, i.e. independents.

Party (Christian Democrats) and European Democrats (PPE-DE); 175 from the Party of European Socialists (PSE); 54 from the group of European Liberal, Democrat and Reform Party (ELDER); 50 from the Confederal group of European United Left and Nordic Green Left (GUE/NGL); 45 from the group of the Greens and European Free Alliance (Verts/ALE); 22 from the Union for Europe of Nations (UEN); 17 from the group of Europe of Democracies and Diversities (EDO); and 31 are unattached (NI), i.e. independents. Since the ideologies of the different factions in a group are not identical, one may wonder how such motley collections ever get anything useful done. The response would be that in reality they do agree on many issues, but, of course, the pace at which they do so is dictated by the time needed to reach consensus.

3.4   Types of EU decision

It will become clear later that all EU institutions have a part to play in the decision-making process, depending on a *modus vivendi* existing between them to allow the process to operate. However, now that the three institutions most directly involved in EU decision making have been introduced, it is appropriate to specify the nature of decisions taken before going on to consider the remaining institutions and bodies. Formally, a EU decision results in: (a) a *Regulation*, (b) a *Directive*, (c) a *Decision*, (d) a *Recommendation*, or (e) an *Opinion* (Article 249 EC). A Regulation is directly applicable and binding in its entirety in all the member states without the need for any national implementing legislation decision; hence it is automatic EU law. A Directive binds the member states to the objectives to be achieved within a certain period of time while leaving the national authorities the choice of form and means to be used; thus directives have to be implemented by national legislation in accordance with the procedures of the individual member states. A Decision, which is a more specific act and often administrative in nature, is binding in all its facets only for the party it is addressed to, be it all the member states, any member state, an enterprise, an individual or individuals. Recommendations have no binding force, but they express detailed EU preferences on an issue. Finally, Opinions are neither binding in force nor have direct effect. The formal acts, notably recommendations and directives, are constantly adding to EU law (Chapter 4).

3.5   The Economic and Social Committee (ESC)

Two ESCs were established in 1957 in the Rome treaties, one for each of the EEC and Euratom, following the lines of that for the ECSC of 1951. Thus in 1957, there were three such committees, but as mentioned in the previous chapter and above, these were merged into one ESC in 1965.

The ESC is a forum for organized EU civil society. It comprises the various categories of economic and social activity such as employers, unions and the self-employed together with representatives from community and social organizations (in particular, producers, farmers, carriers, workers, dealers, craftsmen, professional occupations, consumers and the general interest). These are considered as three groups: Group I, which consists of employers' representatives from both the private and public sectors; Group II, the vast majority of which come from national trade union organisations; and Group III, which is a miscellaneous group, including members from farmers' organizations, small and medium-sized enterprises (SMEs), various NGOs, etc.

The ESC plays an important role of a general consultative and informative nature. Its opinions have to be sought by the Commission, Council and EP (since the Amsterdam Treaty), on all matters under its jurisdiction. Also, since 1972 the ESC itself can also formulate its own opinions on issues it deems important. It also offers 'exploratory opinions' when approached by the Commission or EP to discuss and make suggestions on an issue which could lead to a Commission proposal.

The Maastricht treaty endowed the ESC with a status akin to that of the other EU institutions, especially in terms of its procedural rules, budget, the reinforcement of its right of initiative and the management of its staff with the Secretariat General. The committee saw a broadening in its field of action, notably in social matters, in 1997 as per the Amsterdam treaty.

It has 222 members, appointed by the Council by lists forwarded by the governments of the member nations. Each member is appointed for four years and acts independently in a personal capacity. The national distribution of the 222 members is as follows: France, Germany, Italy and the UK have 24 members each; Spain has 21; Austria, Belgium, Greece, the Netherlands, Portugal and Sweden have 12 each; Denmark, Finland and Ireland have 9 each; and Luxembourg has 6.

The Committee is housed in Brussels, but although most of its meetings and plenary sessions are held there, meetings are also scheduled in other locations. It has a plenary assembly, a bureau, the three groups just mentioned, six sections and a secretariat-general. It elects its own president and two vice-presidents who hold office for two-year terms. The president acts as its external representative.

The six sections deal with the main activities of the EU: (i) agriculture, rural development and the environment; (ii) EMU and economic and social cohesion; (iii) employment, social affairs and citizenship; (iv) external relations; (v) the single market, production and consumption; and (vi) transport, energy, infrastructure and the information society.

In reaching its opinion, the ESC follows a certain procedure. When the president receives a request for an opinion from the Council, Commission or EP, the Bureau lodges it with the appropriate section. The section then sets up a study group, consisting of about nine persons, and appoints a 'rapporteur' assisted by about four experts in the field. Based on the recommendations of the group, the section adopts its opinion on the basis of simple majority and this is then considered in the plenary session, which decides likewise before addressing it to the requesting institution.

3.6   The Committee of the Regions

The Committee of the Regions was set up in 1994, following the Maastricht Treaty, in response to demands by several member nations that regional and local authorities should be directly involved in deliberations at the EU level. In many countries these authorities enjoy wide-ranging powers, either because of the federal structure of the country concerned or by virtue of legislative or constitutional measures adopted over the past few decades. The treaty specifies that the Committee members must hold a regional or local authority electoral mandate or be politically accountable to an elected assembly.

The Committee is an advisory body to the Council, Commission and EP and its main work entails advancing its own opinions on Commission proposals. It also ensures that the subsidiarity principle is safeguarded. Moreover, the Council and Commission must consult it on any issue of direct relevance to local and regional authorities, and it can initiate its own opinions on matters of particular concern to itself and lodge them with either, or the EP.

The structure and procedures of the Committee resemble those of the ESC in practically every respect. The exceptions are four. First, for every one of the 222 members, there is an alternate. Second, all the members are mainly politicians. Third, the members are assigned to six specialist commissions whose job is to prepare for the five annual plenary sessions: Commission for Territorial Cohesion Policy (COTER); Commission for Economic and Social Policy (ECOS); Commission for Sustainable Development (DEVE); Commission for Culture and Education (EDUC); Commission for Constitutional Affairs and European Governance (CONST); and Commission for External Relations (RELEX). Fourth, its bureau consists of a president, 35 members and the leaders of its political groups.

3.7   The European Central Bank (ECB)

The ECB was established on 1 June 1998 and is located in Frankfurt, but its foundations were laid through the European Monetary Institute (EMI), introduced on 1 January 1994, during the second stage of EMU (Chapter 10). It is given total independence to carry out its mandate.

The ECB and the 12 central banks of the euro adopting nations are known as the *Eurosystem*, which distinguishes them from the *European System of Central Banks* (ESCB) since the latter includes the central banks of all 15 EU nations. The ECB lies at the very heart of the Eurosystem whose primary task is to ensure price stability in the euro zone; price stability has been defined to be an annual increase in the consumer price index of less than 2%. To achieve this, a so-called two-pillar strategy is followed: (i) setting a target for the growth of money supply, defined in the broadest sense; and (ii) assessing future price trends and risks to price stability by examining trends in wages, exchange rates, long-term interest rates, various measures of economic activity and the like. It is also responsible for collecting all necessary statistical information, from both the national authorities and economic agents, e.g. financial institutions, and for following developments in the banking and financial sectors and promoting the exchange of information between the ESCB and banking authorities.

In executing its task, the ECB defines and implements the monetary policy of the euro zone; holds and manages the foreign exchange reserves of the euro zone and conducts foreign exchange operations; issues euro notes and coins; and promotes the smooth operation of the payment systems.

The head of the ECB is its *Executive Board*, which is responsible for the daily running of the bank, implementation of its monetary policy and transmitting the necessary instructions to the national central banks. It comprises the president, vice-president and four other members, all six being appointed on the agreement of the heads of state or government of the nations in the euro zone. All six hold non-renewable eight-year terms.

The top decision-making body of the ECB is the *Governing Council*, which comprises the six members of the executive board and the 12 governors of the euro zone banks. The president of the ECB acts as its chairperson.

There is also the *General Council* consisting of the president and vice-president of the ECB as well as the governors of the national central banks of all 15 EU nations. Its task is to contribute to the advisory and coordinating work of the bank and to assist with the future enlargement of the euro zone.

3.8   The European Investment Bank (EIB)

The EIB was set up in 1958 in Luxembourg, following from the 1957 Treaty of Rome (EEC), to fund both private and public investment projects that enhance economic integration. Its capital is provided by the member states, each contributing according to its relative GNP standing within the league of EU nations, and it is empowered to make its own decisions on the projects to finance.

The bank has a *board of governors*, a *board of directors*, a *management committee* and an *audit committee*. The board of governors, consisting of ministers appointed by the member states, usually the finance ministers, defines the general guidelines for lending, approves the balance sheet and annual report, decides on the funding of projects outside the EU (see below) and further capital generation and appoints the members of the other three. The board of directors, comprising 25 members, 24 appointed by the member states and one by the Commission, and headed by the bank's president, ensures that the bank is run properly and approves its borrowing and lending operations. The management committee is the full-time executive and consists of the president and seven vice-presidents. The audit committee not only overseas the proper management of the bank's operations and financial resources, but also cooperates with the Court of Auditors for the external auditing of the bank.

The bank is usually invited by the EP to participate in the committees concerned with the banks' operations. It also has an input in preparing the work of the Council, hence the bank's president may be asked to attend some meetings of the Council, and it cooperates with other institutions concerned with its activities.

The bank finances its activities by borrowing on the financial markets, thus does not receive any EU budgetary contribution, and is run as a non-profit making entity. It is, however, different from traditional banks since it does not offer current and savings accounts. It follows three criteria in deciding which investment projects it should fund. First, the investment must be instrumental in enticing other sources of funding. Second, it must be in specified fields. Third, it must be in the most disadvantaged regions. It has steadily grown in stature and is now ranked AAA, the highest credit rating on the capital markets, and this enables it to raise funds on the most competitive of terms. It is also a majority shareholder in the European Investment Fund (EIF), created in 1994, and located in Luxembourg, to assist with the financing of investments in SMEs. The bank deals directly with those promoting large-scale projects, worth at least 25 million euro, but cooperates with about 180 banks and specialist European financial intermediaries in the case of SMEs and local authorities.

The bank's activities promote EU integration in a wider sense. This is because about 10% of its funding goes to projects in applicant countries (Chapters 22 and 26), Mediterranean nations (Chapter 22) and the ACP countries (Chapter 25) as well as to some Asian and Latin American nations for ventures of common interest.

3.9   The Courts

3.9.1 The European Court of Justice

There are three reasons why the ECJ is needed. First, a body of legal experts is indispensable for ensuring that the EU institutions act in a constitutional manner, fulfilling the obligations laid on them by the treaties. Second, a court is essential for seeing to it that the member states, firms and individual citizens observe the (increasing number of) EU rules. And, a court at the EU level is vital for guiding national courts in their interpretation of EU law, hence for ensuring that EU legislation is uniformly applied.

The ECJ is seated in Luxembourg. It has 15 judges, appointed on the joint agreement of the member states for 6-year renewable terms, with partial reappointment every three years. The judges are selected from persons from the member nations whose *independence is beyond doubt*, thus they come from the highest national judiciary or are 'juriconsults' of recognized competence. Hence, the treaties do not lay down any rules on the nationality of the judges, since this might compromise this condition, but in reality there is one judge from each of the present 15 member states.

The ECJ has a president whose term of office is three years. There are also 8 *Advocates-General*, who are responsible for (a) the preliminary investigation of a matter and (b) presenting publicly and impartially *reasoned opinions* on the cases brought before the ECJ to help the judges in reaching their decisions (more on this at the end of this section). Each judge has a cabinet to take care of administrative responsibilities and its members are recruited directly by the judge. A cabinet comprises three law clerks to the ECJ and two to the Court of First Instance – see below. The clerks help the judges draw up their reports and draft their rulings. The administrative service of the ECJ is led by the Registrar, who is also responsible for following the cases procedurally – see below.

In carrying out its responsibilities, the ECJ has a wide jurisdiction that it exercises in the context of various categories, the most common of which being four: preliminary rulings, failure to fulfil an obligation, annulment and failure to act. Preliminary rulings were introduced in the treaties to institutionalize cooperation between the ECJ and national courts, thus ensuring that the latter are also upholders of EU law. When the national courts receive cases involving EU law, they will ask the ECJ for the interpretation or validity of the law when in doubt, and sometimes they are obliged to consult the ECJ. The proceedings for failure to fulfil an obligation endow the ECJ with the power to monitor the member nations for their carrying out EU law. Such a process is commonly initiated by the Commission and sometimes by a member state, and if the offending party is proven guilty, it must rectify the situation with immediate effect. Proceedings for annulment allow the member nations, Council, Commission and, under certain conditions, EP to request the annulment of a EU provision and private citizens to request the annulment of certain acts that affect them directly and individually. They also provide the ECJ with the opportunity to examine the legality of acts adopted by the EU institutions. When the proceedings are found to be legitimate, the act in dispute may be declared null and void. Finally, proceedings for failure to act apply where the EP, Council or Commission fails to take a decision when the treaties stipulate it should. Under such circumstances, member states, and other EU institutions and, under certain conditions, natural or legal persons can lodge a complaint with the ECJ requesting that the violation be officially recorded.

A few words on how business is handled by the ECJ may be in order. After cases are lodged with the registry, they are distributed among the judges. A specific judge and advocate general assume responsibility for each case. A judge, appointed as 'judge rapporteur', has to write a report for the hearing, providing a summary of the legal background to the case and the observations of the parties to the case submitted in the first written phase of the procedure. In the light of the reasoned opinion of the responsible advocate general, the judge rapporteur writes a draft ruling, which is then submitted to the other members of the ECJ for examination. Thus, the procedure has both a written and an oral phase. The written consists of the statements exchanged between the parties concerned and the report by the judge rapporteur. The oral is the public hearing where the lawyers for the parties involved are invited to argue their case before the judges and advocates general, who have the right to question them. The advocate general then submits his/her conclusion, i.e. reasoned opinion, before the judges deliberate and deliver their judgment on the case.

In general, the ECJ meets in plenary session, but it can also establish chambers of between three and five judges, depending on the complexity or importance of the case. ECJ judgment is reached by majority decisions and is pronounced at public hearings. There is no expression of 'dissenting opinions' and all the judges partaking in the deliberations must sign the judgment.

3.9.2 The Court of First Instance

Because the ECJ has had several thousands of cases submitted to it since its creation as an ECSC institution in 1952, it had been too busy to reach quick decisions; essential for a smooth operation of the integration process. To cater for this, the SEA introduced a *Court of First Instance* in 1989 to deal with: (a) matters relating to the ECSC treaty, (b) the enforcement of competition rules, (c) disputes between the EU institutions, and (d) from June 1993, actions brought by individuals against EU institutions and agencies, except in cases concerning trade protection. The Court has the same number of judges as the ECJ, who are subject to precisely the same conditions, and has a three-year President.

3.9.3 The Court of Auditors

The *Court of Auditors* was introduced in 1977 when the EC budgetary arrangements were revised. It became an independent institution in 1993 when the Maastricht treaty became operative. It was given further responsibilities in 1999, following the Amsterdam Treaty.

The main function of the Court is to ensure that the EU budget is properly implemented, i.e. it is entrusted with the external monitoring of EU revenues and expenditures. In exercising this role, it also tries to secure sound financial management and to enhance the effectiveness and transparency of the whole system.

To carry out these responsibilities, the Court needs to be independent, and indeed it is. However, the Court does communicate and collaborate with other institutions. It assists the EP and Council, the joint budgetary authority, by presenting them each year with observations on the annual report for the previous year. These observations are taken seriously by the EP and influence its decision on the granting or otherwise of the implementation of the budget. It also submits to them statements of assurance regarding the proper use of EU revenues. Moreover, it gives its opinion on the adoption of financial regulations; it can submit observations on specific issues and respond

with opinions to any request from any EU institution. Furthermore, in the reports issued by the Court, based on its investigation of documents and where necessary of organizations managing revenues and expenditures on behalf of the EU, it draws the attention of both the Commission and the member nations to any outstanding problems.

The Court has 15 members, appointed by the Council, but Council must first consult the EP before doing so, and must decide on unanimous agreement. The appointees are chosen from those who have worked for auditing institutions in their member states or are specifically qualified for the job, and must meet the requirements of independence and full-time work. They elect one of them to be president for three years.

The Court has a staff of about 550. Of these, 250 are qualified auditors who are divided into 'audit groups' according to the nature of their work and who prepare reports for the Court to help it reach its decisions.

3.10   The Ombudsman

Following the Maastricht treaty's call for the establishment of a European Ombudsman to deal with complaints raised by EU citizens, the post was created in July 1995, when its first occupant commenced work. The appointment, which is for five years and renewable, is the prerogative of each new EP, hence it coincides with the life of each EP. The office is located in Strasbourg where there is a Secretariat whose principal administrator is appointed by the Ombudsman.

Being authorized to act independently as a full-time intermediary between EU citizens and authorities (only the ECJ and Court of First Instance, in their judicial roles, do not come under the Office's jurisdiction), the Ombudsman uncovers malpractices in EU institutions and bodies and makes recommendations for their elimination. The Ombudsman can also investigate on his own initiative. Issues are referred to the EP to act

on them. The Ombudsman also presents an annual report on its investigation to the EP.

Complaints to the Ombudsman must be submitted within two years of their being brought to the attention of the offending party, provided that the administrative procedures had already been undertaken and no legal proceedings have been initiated. When the Ombudsman has lodged his comments on an issue with the institution or body concerned, it can respond to them and it is also obliged to provide the Ombudsman with any solicited information or access to relevant files, except where there are justifiable confidentiality grounds. If a case of malpractice has been established, the Ombudsman notifies the institution or body involved and the latter must respond in three months with a detailed opinion. The Ombudsman then lodges a report with both the EP and the institution or body involved and notifies the complainant of the outcome of the investigations.

3.11   Institutional reform

There are obvious questions for the immediate future relating to EU institutions. Finding a satisfactory voting system for the Council of the European Union,

which allows for reaching decisions and at the same time effectively represents the forces at work in the EU, is one of the hardest. Reforming the Commission to become an efficient machine and clarifying its role comes close to that. The interrelationship between the EU institutions with national systems of government receives less publicity, but also requires attention. With the growth in importance of the EU and the loss of national power, the question must arise whether national parliaments can still perform a democratic role satisfactorily. It is clear that the EU has not been able to exert adequate control over the application of its policies within member states. The EU writ does not always run to achieve a uniform application of a regulation, an effective interpretation of a directive or even the proper use of EU funds. National parliaments have not shown much interest in controlling these matters on behalf of the Union, and it remains primarily up to the Commission to ensure the smooth running of policies on the ground. 'To do less, but do it better' remains a valid goal.

Substantive policy issues are looming (see Chapters 2 and 28). Political events in the world change quickly, so that the foreign policy role of the EU and its corresponding security and defence policy, including the complications in the NATO relationship, are sure to be tested – witness the Iraq war situation at the time of writing. Many practical difficulties must arise consequent upon the greater mobility of people both internally and would-be migrants from the rest of the world, so it is indeed essential that the institutional structure is adequate. However, no matter how good reform may be in itself, the changes will not endure if they are not supported by public opinion – and this has shown itself to be somewhat uncertain about the developments of recent years. The Maastricht Treaty was greeted with widespread hostility and was nearly lost in referendums in Denmark and France, and the same applied to the Nice Treaty when the Irish initial vote rejected it. The Commission has recently made efforts (of variable quality and accessibility) to counter public ignorance, and less has been done to improve awareness of the EP and the Council of the European Union. A major criticism of the latter remains its lack of openness and the failure of existing democratic institutions to control decisions taken. No obvious remedy exists. National Parliaments have perhaps too often allowed decisions and developments to pass them by, displaying little, or only a desultory, interest in the work of the European institutions. At the same time the institutions themselves have been too absorbed in the excitements of creating a political first to remember that time is needed for the general public

to come to terms with these changes. All in all, there is indeed a democratic deficit in the EU, but this is not to be solved simply by increasing the powers of the EP – which is often put forward as the solution.

Understanding and support of the EU is not a question of reform of the institutions alone but of long years of hard grind and painstaking effort on everyone's part to ensure that the EU commands support.

The reaction to these points would be that the *Convention on the Future of Europe* has been asked to cater for them. After all, it has been entrusted with making the EU more effective and more accountable and, above all, to bring European institutions closer to the citizens (see Chapters 2 and 28). Yet the draft constitution offered by the Convention on 6 February 2003 seems to indicate nothing of a dramatic nature since it is basically about unifying the EU treaties. However, it would be premature to dwell on this since the final, but not complete, draft adopted on 20 June 2003 at the Thessaloniki Greek summit introduced major changes, but these may be watered down before the constitution is finalized at the Intergovernmental Conference to be held towards the end of the first half of 2004 (see Chapter 28 for details).

What is pertinent is what is precisely expected of it. For example, given that the 'European Council has suffered from inconsistent leadership, wrangling at ill-prepared summits with over-detailed agendas and poor follow-through', and the Commission being 'a shadow of the body that once led the drive to the single market and a single currency' (*Financial Times*, 12 November 2002), Britain, France and Spain have come up with a proposal which is expected to appear in the final draft. The proposal is to appoint a full-time chairperson or president of the European Council who would champion the EU's internal agenda and represent it to the outside world. Those who support it insist that it makes sense only if the Commission itself is also strengthened at the same time, with its president elected directly by the EP. The president of the Commission, Romano Prodi, however, believes that this solution has a number of drawbacks. It needs to ensure that rivalry between the presidents of the Commission and European Council does not become a divisive factor; it must avoid any risk of creating a second administration; it must make sure that reforms actually improve the quality of work in the European Council and the various council configurations; and it must settle satisfactorily the issue of the accountability of the presidents of the European Council and

General Affairs Council (speech delivered by Romano Prodi to the French National Assembly in Paris on 12 March 2003). He urged for a clarification of: how competences should be shared by the two presidents and how long their terms of office should be; who the president of the European Council should be accountable to; how to avoid duplicating the administration; and how should the work of the Council, and in particular the presidency of General Affairs Council, be organized.

Appendix 3.1 Agencies of the European Union

A EU agency is a different animal from a EU institution. It is governed by European public law and has its own legal personality. It is created by an act of secondary legislation (see Chapter 4) to carry out a narrowly defined technical, scientific or managerial assignment specified in the relevant EU Act. In 2003, there are fifteen – see Table A3.1 – agencies, although some carry different tags such as Authority, Centre, Foundation and Office or Observatory. One should take special care when referring to the agencies since the same terms may be used in other contexts, easily creating confusion, and this also applies even to acronyms: as we have seen in Chapters 2 and 3, EEA also stands for 'European Economic Area'.

Table A3.1 Agencies of the European Union

Cedefop	European Centre for the Development of Vocational Training
EUROFOUND	European Foundation for the Improvement of Living and Working Conditions
EEA	European Environmental Agency
ETF	European Training Foundation
EMCDDA	European Monitoring Centre for Drugs and Drug Addiction
EMEA	European Agency for the Evaluation of Medical Products
OHIM	Office for Harmonization in the Internal Market (Trade Marks and Designs)
EU-OSHA	European Agency for Safety and Health at Work
CPVO	Community Plant Variety Office
CdT	Translation Centre for the Bodies of the European Union
EUMC	European monitoring Centre for Racism and Xenophobia
EAR	European Agency for Reconstruction
EFSA	European Food and Safety Authority
EMSA	European Maritime Safety Agency
EASA	European Aviation Safety Agency

Appendix 3.2 The previous policy/administrative areas of the European Union

The Commission
Secretariat General of the Commission
Forward Studies Unit
Inspectorate General
Legal Service
Spokesman's Service
Joint Interpreting and Conference Service
Statistical Office
Translation Service
Informatics Directorate
Security Office

Directorates General:

DG I	External Relations: Commercial Policy and relations with North America, the Far East, Australia and New Zealand
DG IA	External Relations: Europe and the Newly Independent States, Common Foreign and Security Policy and External Missions
DG IB	External Relations: Southern Mediterranean, Middle East, Latin America, South and South-East Asia and North–South Cooperation
DG II	Economic and Financial Affairs
DG III	Industry
DG IV	Competition
DG V	Employment, Industrial Relations and Social Affairs
DG VI	Agriculture
DG VII	Transport
DG VIII	Development
DG IX	Personnel and Administration
DG X	Information, Communication, Culture and Audiovisual Media
DG XI	Environment, Nuclear Safety and Civil Protection
DG XII	Science, Research and Development and Joint Research Centres
DG XIII	Telecommunications, Information Market and Exploitation Research
DG XIV	Fisheries
DG XV	Internal Market and Financial Services
DG XVI	Regional Policy and Cohesion
DG XVII	Energy
DG XIX	Budgets
DG XX	Financial control
DG XXI	Customs and Indirect Taxation
DG XXII	Education, Training and Youth
DG XXIII	Enterprises Policy, Distributive Trade, Tourism and Cooperatives
DG XXIV	Consumer Policy Service

European Community Humanitarian Office

Euratom Supply Agency

Office of Official Publications of the European Communities

Notes: (i) The missing DG XVIII used to be on Credit and Investment, but was merged into DG II in 1995.
(ii) The Informatics Directorate is one of the Directorates of DG XIII.

Chapter 4

The legal dimension in EU integration

DAMIAN CHALMERS

In one sense, it should not be difficult to pinpoint the legal dimension to EU integration. As a political system, the EU has been constituted through a legal instrument, the Treaty on European Union (TEU); it has its own system of administration of justice; and its output has traditionally been measured in terms of the number of legally binding acts it has adopted (Majone, 1994; Wessels, 1997). Viewed through these lenses, the contribution of law to European integration seems considerable (on 'legalization' see Abbott *et al.*, 2000). Few systems, either national or transnational, have given the judiciary such a pre-eminent role and the measure of EC (one of the three EU pillars – see Chapters 2 and 3) legislative outputs alone can be gauged by estimates which suggested that 53% of legislation adopted in France in 1991 emanated from the EC and that 30% of all legislation in the Netherlands comprises provisions implementing EC Directives (on this see Mancini, 1998, p. 40).[1] Yet to stop there is to beg the question how does EU law act upon and reconfigure the behaviour of the actors that invoke it and are subject to it? Instead of attempting the impossible task of trying to recount the contents of all this legislation, this chapter addresses this latter question, considering in particular how the use of law steers the integration process.

'Integration through law' pulls this process in three broad directions. The first direction is an actor-interest based one. This considers the opportunity structures provided through the creation of specifically legal institutions (see Chapter 3), in the form of the European Court of Justice (ECJ) and the Court of First Instance (CFI), and of specifically 'legal relations' between these and national courts, most notably in the form of the Article 234 EC reference procedure, but more generally in the authority conferred on the formers' judgments by the latter. This leads not merely, in crude policy terms,

to both national and EC courts becoming significant players and agenda setters, with the Article 234 EC reference procedure having to be considered as influential a relationship in its own way as that of the Commission and Council (for a particularly important early analysis of this see Volcansek, 1986). It also leads to fresh opportunities for new types of actor, in the shape of litigants and lawyers, and for new forms of knowledge, in the form of EC law, at the expense of other actors and forms of knowledge.

Many EU legal scholars, by contrast, look not so much at the opportunities provided by EU law, but at its mapping functions, namely how it shapes expectations and understandings of the integration process, which in turn influences how parties act within that process. They thus note how debates about the values and directions of the EU, its legitimacy and the patterns of inclusion and exclusion established by it invariably involve, first and foremost, debates about the contours of EU law (on an informative discussion about these two approaches see Alter, Dehousse and Vanberg, 2002).

The third direction in which EU law pulls the integration process is in its communicative functions. The establishment of a series of networks by EU legal instruments creates a series of new interrelationships and modifies existing relations between parties across a variety of fields. Parties have to adapt to and communicate with each other through and within these legal relationships. This process not only generates new forms of power, practices, understandings and identities, but in so far as these relationships are generated in a 'transnational' manner, contributes to the emergence of a transnational society. It is in this that EU law is perhaps broadest in its embrace and most sweeping in its ambition.

4.1 Actor-interest based approaches

The capacity to determine the content of a legal provision is a cherished prize within any communal arrangement, be it an international, national or subnational one. For a legal provision will do a number of things. It will stabilize expectations as to what is required of parties and provide a benchmark by which each party judges the behaviour of the other. In addition, in so far as any legal provision must allow for the possibility that it will be obeyed out of a sense of duty, legal provisions can induce more wide-ranging assumptions over what constitutes appropriate behaviour. The ability to influence the content of norms occurs at a variety of points in their life cycle, be it in their formulation, enactment, application or enforcement. Within classic international treaty regimes, national governments, as both authors and addressees of the international treaty in question, preserve a monopoly over this capability through the device of autointerpretation, namely their ability to interpret the substantive content of the norms to which they are subject (Gross, 1984). This has been only marginally disturbed through the increasing resort, since the Second World War, to judicial or quasi-judicial decision-making bodies in both regional human rights and regional and global trade treaties (Merrills, 1998). Access to such bodies is limited and they do not disturb the national governments' monopoly of violence over their territories as no sanctions are provided for in the event of non-compliance with these bodies' rulings. The central actors brought into play by these instruments, therefore, continue to be bureaucrats, be they national civil servants or the international organizations or secretariats set up by the treaties.

The legal arrangements of the TEU, particularly those of the EC pillar, stand in marked contrast to this. The public spheres surrounding most EC legislative and quasi-legislative procedures involve a wide variety of actors beside national governments. Most explicitly, these procedures provide for the participation of a whole series of supranational institutions, depending upon the field in question. These can take the form of a wide array of bureaucratic interests, be they the Commission, the European Central Bank (ECB, see Chapter 9), scientific committees or euro agencies; representative institutions in the form of the Economic and Social Committee (ESC) and the Committee of the Regions; and, finally, directly elected interests in the shape of the European Parliament (EP). Even in those areas, such as Common Foreign and Security Policy

(CFSP), which are characterized by limited supranational institutional influence and national government vetoes, the requirement to carry out measures through the Union's institutional procedures generates structures and dialectics which constrain and shift preferences and curb unilateralism (Hill, 1997).

An even more potent feature of the EU than the pluralism surrounding its law making is that national governments have lost their monopoly over the application and enforcement of law in the EC pillar and, since the Treaty of Amsterdam, over certain areas of EU law in the Justice and Home Affairs (JHA) pillar. This has had particularly disempowering consequences for national governments as the legislative dynamics of the EU render unexpected interpretations or applications particularly difficult to remedy. Interpretations of the Treaties themselves can only be rectified through the unanimous agreement of the national governments (Article 48 TEU). Pressures militate against even amendment of secondary legislation. Most EC legislative procedures require a national government to negotiate amendments with a number of actors, notably the Commission and the Parliament, both of which, depending upon the legislative procedure deployed, may be able to veto any proposed amendments. In addition, the voting thresholds within the Council of Ministers will, depending upon the area in question, require the national government to co-opt either all or a qualified majority of its fellow governments into agreeing to its amendments. Within even highly rationalist accounts, which place national governments at the centre of the EU integration, these features grant those actors responsible for the application and enforcement of EC law a considerable degree of autonomy and power (Alter, 1998b; Garrett and Tsebelis, 1999). This autonomy has allowed these actors to develop autonomous dynamics and agenda-setting powers of their own (Armstrong, 1998; Armstrong and Bulmer, 1998, pp. 263–9).

4.1.1 The European Court of Justice

The organization of the work of the European Court of Justice

The most salient of these actors is the ECJ. At the centre of the Court sit 15 judges, one from each member state (Article 221 EC). Judges do not need to have held prior national judicial office, but are to be chosen 'from persons whose independence is beyond doubt and who possess the qualifications required for appointment to the highest judicial offices in their respective countries or who are jurisconsults of recognised competence' (Article 223 EC). They are appointed for a renewable term of six years by the common accord of the national governments. To ensure continuity, half the Court is appointed or reappointed every three years (Article 223(3) EC). The Court works on the principle of collegiality. Drafted in the first place by a single judge, a *juge rapporteur*, and then negotiated between the different judges and their offices, a single judgment is given with no possibility for dissenting opinions. This, together with the relatively remote location of the Court in a rather drab Luxembourg suburb and the similar social backgrounds of the judges, is credited with giving it a certain *esprit de corps* which contributes to its collective autonomy (Kenny, 1998).

The Court is assisted in its work by eight advocates-general. The conditions for office and length of term for these is the same as for judges of the Court. There is a convention that one is taken from each of the five larger member states and the other three are rotated among the smaller member states. The duty of the advocate general is to present in open court 'with complete impartiality and independence . . . reasoned submissions on cases before the court' (Article 222 EC). The opinions of the advocate-general are in no way binding upon the Court.

The workload of the Court is considerable. Up until the end of 2001 it had given 5513 judgments (ECJ, 2002, Table 16). Despite this, since the late 1970s, backlog has been a recurring feature of the caseload. This combination of workload and backlog has given rise to a number of problems. The most practical of these is obviously delay to individual litigants, which, in turn, provides incentives for national courts not to refer matters to the Court, irrespective of the wider importance of the legal questions raised. The workload has also affected the quality of judgments, partly, by placing the Court under considerable time constraints. The large number of judgments also gives national legal communities little time to digest EC law. This both contributes to the unfamiliarity of many national lawyers with important areas of EC law and prevents quick feedback on judgments, with unforeseen or unfortunate results (Jacqué and Weiler, 1990).

The ECJ made attempts to address this, first, by expanding the Chamber System. Unless a member state or EC institution is one of the parties, the case need not be heard by the full Court, but by a Chamber of three or five judges. The full Court will also hear cases that involve difficult or important points of EU law. Yet the influence of the Chamber system is illustrated by its enabling the Court to decide 244 cases in 2001, as compared with an average of 133 cases per annum in the period 1979–1981, with 196 of those decisions being made in Chambers (ECJ, 2002, Table 5).

The second innovation was the establishment of a Court of First Instance (CFI) in 1988.[2] The CFI is essentially an 'administrative court' (Dehousse, 1998, p. 28) which has jurisdiction for all direct actions brought by individuals reviewing the action or inaction of the EC institutions. Like the ECJ, it has 15 judges whose terms of office are of the same length as those of the ECJ judges, and, as with the ECJ, it operates a Chamber system. In 2001 it gave 340 judgments (Court of First Instance, 2002, Table 10).

Third, the ECJ has developed a system of docket-control (Strasser, 1995; Barnard and Sharpston, 1997). It has refused to accept references where a dispute is not pending before a national court or where it considers there is no genuine dispute at hand and the questions referred are merely hypothetical in nature.[3] It will also refuse to answer references where it considers insufficient information is provided about the factual and national legal context to the dispute (ECJ, 1996). Yet such docket-control has proved to be controversial on the grounds both that it might lead to a 'denial of justice' in individual cases and that, through its second-guessing of national courts, the ECJ is introducing unwarranted hierarchies between it and national courts (O'Keeffe, 1998). In any case, it has led to the ECJ refusing to rule in less than 30 cases in the 1990s.

These largely internal developments have had little long-term impact on the problem of backlog. In 2001 the length of proceedings before the ECJ averaged, depending upon the procedure, between 16.3 and 23.1 months, and, at the end of 2001, 839 cases were still pending (ECJ, 2002, Table 8 and Table 1 respectively). Matters were equally bad for the CFI, which had 501 cases pending at the end of 2001 (CFI, 2002, Table 1). This situation had led to a number of difficulties. The most obvious is that of *bottlenecking*. The delays incurred are in addition to those incurred before national courts. A reference not only affects the ability of parties to secure a timely securing of their rights. It also provides opportunities for parties to abuse the litigation process through using threat of a reference to pressurize the other party into accepting claims they would otherwise not accept (Chalmers, 2000b). A second difficulty is that of *expertise*: the sheer breadth of subject-matter upon which the ECJ is called to adjudicate requires it to pronounce on many areas (e.g. tax, competition, anti-dumping, intellectual property) in which it does not have a specialized knowledge. Finally, the structure of the reference system leads to the ECJ being used as a forum for 'outsider Elites'. The unwieldy nature of the process leads to relatively few litigants coming before the ECJ who are interested in simple monetary compensation. Instead, an ECJ judgment is an important vehicle through which national or EC law can be changed. Typically, groups will use such an avenue where they doubt they will be able to achieve their goals through administrative or legislative procedures, and where their policy goals are sufficiently narrow that they can be met by a judgment (Alter, 2000). The consequence is that there is an asymmetry in the type of claims coming before the ECJ. The vast majority seek revision of the domestic settlement. The ECJ need only adjudicate in favour of a few to be seen as a revisionary, supranational institution unsympathetic to established domestic interests.

The problems threatened to be exacerbated by a number of developments. It is impossible to predict the pattern of references from the 10 new member states entering the Union in 2004. It is certain that they will increase the workload of the ECJ. An expansion of workload is also likely as a consequence of the expansion of the EC into new domains. Single market legislation, the development of a considerable corpus of intellectual property law in the late 1990s and the emergence of EC law on asylum and migration of non-EU nationals will all increase the docket of the ECJ. Finally, ECJ decisions have created more, not less, work for the institution. A feature of the case law before national courts is its very narrow remit. Some 61% of all reported litigation within the United Kingdom has been found to occur within five very narrow areas – taxation, sex discrimination, free movement of goods, free movement of persons and intellectual property (Chalmers, 2000b, pp. 179–180). This suggests not only that the judicial contribution to the EU is narrowly focused, but also that it is intensely focused with litigants seeking to challenge, explore, expand and qualify any new ruling by the ECJ.

Attempts to reform the system were brought in by the Treaty of Nice. A first part of the response was to improve the efficiency of the working of the ECJ through expanding the Chambers System. The Statute of the Court of Justice has been amended so that it

will be very rare for the Court to meet in plenary session. Instead, the normal procedure will be for cases to be heard by Chambers of either three or five judges. If a member state or Community Institution that is party to proceedings requests, a Grand Chamber of 11 judges will be formed. Otherwise the ECJ will sit in plenary session in only cases of 'exceptional importance' or where an offence holder (e.g. Commissioner, ECJ judge or member of the Executive Board of the ECB) is to be disciplined (article 16, Statute of the ECJ). Second, the workload of the CFI is to be expanded. Provision is made for it to hear preliminary references in certain areas (Article 225(2) EC). While these areas are yet to be determined, the Working Party set up by the Commission to consider the question of judicial reform suggested that five areas are susceptible to this. These are: competition; private international law; trademarks; migration of non-EU nationals and asylum; and policing and judicial cooperation (CEU, 2000b). Finally, the CFI will be facilitated in doing this in two ways. There is the possibility of expansion of the CFI, so that it includes more than one judge from each member state (Article 224 EC). Provision is also made for the creation of Judicial Panels by the Council to ease the workload of the CFI through deciding areas that are less central to the development of EC law (Article 225a EC). The member states have already indicated that one such area is disputes between the EC Institutions and their staff (Declaration to Article 225a EC).

The ethos behind these reforms is that the crisis in the EC judicial system can be managed through the EC judiciary maximizing output, and deciding more cases for discussion of these reforms (see Rasmussen, 2000; Meij, 2000; Craig, 2001; Johnston, 2001; Dashwood and Johnston, 2001; Weiler, 2001). Reforms that have tried to limit the flow of references to the ECJ through creating a system of intermediary regional courts similar to the US Courts of Appeal (Jacqué and Weiler, 1990) or through the provision of guidelines that would enable national courts to refer less (CEU, 2000b)[4] were rejected. It is not clear how effective such an approach will be. The Chamber system was already heavily utilized and the CFI has a considerable backlog of its own. It seems highly unlikely that resort to either of these devices alone will resolve the question of backlog. The reforms threaten, furthermore, to generate other problems. Increasing reliance upon Chambers or the CFI will raise questions about the variable quality of judgments and the influence of individual judges. Questions of expertise and specialization are unaddressed. If there is a perception that the ECJ is already deciding too many cases for the good of EC legal doctrine, then the Treaty of Nice simply contributes to a deterioration of the status quo.

The jurisdiction of the European Court of Justice

The only parts of the TEU that the ECJ is now fully excluded from ruling upon are the opening Common Provisions and the Title on CFSP (Article 46 TEU). Since the Treaty of Amsterdam it is now possible for it to rule on the third pillar of the TEU – on police and judicial cooperation. This possibility is substantially reduced by its having no jurisdiction to review the validity of police or law enforcement agency operations or the exercise of member state responsibilities with regard to the maintenance of law and order and the safeguarding of internal security (Article 35(5) TEU).

The ECJ has contributed to this wide remit by bestowing upon itself a unique authority to comment upon the quality of EC law. In its judgments of *Van Gend en Loos* and *Costa* in 1963 and 1964, it began its 'constitutionalizing' jurisprudence which bestowed attributes upon EC law that are not possessed by any other international legal order.[5] In these judgments, the ECJ distinguished the EC Treaty from other international treaties, which it characterized as compacts between sovereign states. By contrast, in the EC Treaty the member states had transferred sovereignty to a new legal order which acted for the benefit not just of national governments and individuals. The immediate practical effects of this were that the ECJ considered in *Van Gend en Loos* that EC law contained provisions which could be invoked directly in national law and that, in *Costa*, in the instance of conflicts between EC law and national law the national courts should give precedence to EC law.

These judgments and the subsequent line of case law also had important institutional implications for the ECJ. It gave it a capacity to adjudicate upon conflicts between national law and EC law and upon the effects of provisions of EC law in national courts. This capacity has not really been questioned by national courts. The ECJ has also interpreted this as granting it the exclusive capacity both to adjudicate upon the boundaries between EC and national competencies[6] and to declare EC acts illegal.[7] This has been challenged

by national courts. Stated most aggressively by the Germans and Danish Constitutional Courts,[8] a number of courts from other States, notably Belgium,[9] Spain,[10] France,[11] the United Kingdom[12] and Italy,[13] have asserted that the sovereignty of the EC has a limited material remit and cannot be extended beyond the powers, as they see it, conferred by the Treaty. Secondly, EC law must not violate fundamental rights recognised in the national constitutions. Notwithstanding the development of EC law on fundamental rights, national courts will disregard EC law if they see it as violating national fundamental rights, and have guarded this power jealously for themselves. There has been well-noted resistance to intervention by EC law and the ECJ in Italy,[14] Germany,[15] Sweden[16] and Ireland[17] on this point. Such decisions suggest that there are national constitutional sanctuaries which must not be violated by the ECJ if there is not to be national judicial resistance. Yet, for all this, they still allow a considerable *de facto* hegemony for the ECJ to delimit the boundaries of national and EC jurisdiction. So much so in fact, that, although the *Kompetenz-Kompetenz* debate attracted considerable academic attention (Arnull, 1990; Schilling, 1996; Weiler and Haltern, 1998; Eleftheriadis, 1998; Kumm, 1999), there is no example of a judgment of the ECJ being actively challenged in these jurisdictions in recent years.

The sweeping material jurisdiction of the ECJ is limited by the circumstances in which actions can be brought before it. There are four routes. The first is an appeal from the CFI. Appeals accounted for 19 judgments in 2001 (ECJ, 2002, Table 3). Second, a variety of enforcement actions can be brought before the ECJ. These accounted for 111 of its judgments in 2001. There are enforcement actions against individual EC institutions. Within the EC pillar a distinction is made between acts which breach EC law and failures to act. The former can be brought by any member state, the Commission and the Council (Article 230(1) EC). They can also be brought by the ECB, the Court of Auditors and the EP where the measure touches on their institutional prerogatives (Article 230(2) EC). The jurisdiction for failures to act is more sweeping, as actions can be brought by the member states or any other institution (Article 232 EC). In the case of policing and judicial cooperation under the third pillar, enforcement actions can only be brought against the Council, and only by member states or the Commission (Article 35(6) TEU). More common than enforcement actions against the EC institutions are enforcement actions against the member states. In theory, these can be brought by other member states or the Commission (Articles 227 and 226 EC respectively). Only once in the history of the ECJ has an action, however, been brought against one member state by another. It is more usual for them to co-opt the Commission into action. That said, the central dynamic of enforcement actions brought by the Commission against member states is negotiation in the shadow of litigation. In 1998 it commenced 1101 proceedings but referred only 153 to the ECJ.[18] Since the Maastricht Treaty the possibility has existed for the Commission to bring member states back to the ECJ to be fined if they failed to comply with ECJ judgments. The flat rate for the fine is 500 euros per day. This rate will be multiplied by two coefficients which reflect the seriousness and duration of the offence, which will increase the penalty substantially (OJ 1997, C 63/2). The procedure has proved unwieldy. The Commission did not instigate the proceedings until January 1997 when it brought a series of actions against Italy and Germany. These were settled and it was not until July 2000 that the first Government, the Greek Government, was fined.[19] Third, member states, the Commission and the Council can ask the ECJ to rule on the EC's competence to sign an international agreement (Article 300(6) EC). In the 1980s and 1990s perhaps one ruling every two years was given on average under this heading. Fourth, the Treaty of Amsterdam provides that the ECJ shall rule on disputes between member states about the interpretation and application of any measures adopted under police and judicial cooperation where the matter has not been resolved by the Council within six months of its being referred to the Council by one of its members (Article 35(7) TEU). The same provision also allows for disputes between the Commission and any member state about the interpretation or application of any of the conventions adopted under the pillar to be brought before the ECJ. No case has yet been brought under this heading.

Finally, questions of EC law can be referred by national courts to the ECJ. Prior to the Treaty of Amsterdam the position was relatively simple. National courts against whose decisions there is no judicial remedy were required to refer those matters of EC law that were necessary to enable them to decide the dispute before them (Article 234(3) EC). Other courts had a discretion whether to refer (Article 234(2) EC).

The matter was blurred both formally and in practice. In formal terms, all national courts were obliged to refer a matter if they considered a piece of EC secondary legislation might be invalid.[20] Conversely, higher courts were not obliged to refer where a materially identical question of EC law had already been resolved by the ECJ or where the interpretation of the provision is so clear as to 'leave no scope for any reasonable doubt'.[21] The matter is obscured in practice by there being no effective remedy against national courts of last resort that do not refer.

Undoubtedly facilitated by the ECJ's case law stating that some provisions of EC law generate rights that individuals may invoke in national courts, the preliminary reference procedure has been the ECJ's principal source of work. In 2001 it accounted for 113 out of the 244 cases decided by the ECJ (ECJ, 2002, Table 2). The matter was complicated by the Treaty of Amsterdam in two respects. Only national courts against whose decisions there is no judicial remedy in national matters may refer questions on the interpretation and application of the new Title in the EC Treaty on Visas, Asylum, Immigration and Other Provisions Relating to the Free Movement of Persons (Article 68(1) EC). In addition, non-judicial bodies, namely the Council, the Commission or a member state, may refer question on interpretation of this Title or acts adopted under it to the ECJ. The reason for barring lower courts from referring was, allegedly, that it would lead to the ECJ being swamped with references over asylum and other immigration related matters. The Treaty of Amsterdam also allowed member states to make a declaration stating whether they would allow national courts to refer questions to the ECJ about EC secondary legislation adopted under policing and judicial cooperation (Article 35(2) TEU). Those adopting this path had two options (Article 35(3) TEU). They could choose to allow any national court to refer, with courts of last resort being obliged to refer. This path has been adopted by Austria, Belgium, Germany and Luxembourg. They could alternatively allow courts of last resort a discretion as to referral – a route chosen by Greece. The Netherlands has stated that it will make provision for the possibility of national judicial referral, but has not yet decided which option to adopt.[22] It is not clear whether those member states who have not given their courts the possibility to refer will be bound by judgments of the ECJ given in response to referrals from other jurisdictions.

Explaining the powers of the European Court of Justice

The institutional design and jurisdiction of the ECJ raises interesting questions about its role in the integration process and the motivations behind its establishment. The most complete research on the historical background to the development of the ECJ (Alter, 1998a; Alter, 2001, pp. 5–11) suggests that the member states intended three roles for it. The first of these was to prevent the other EC institutions from exceeding their powers. Second, the ECJ was to solve the 'incomplete contract problem' by being a forum for dispute resolution where EC laws were vague. Third, while responsibility for monitoring compliance lay with the Commission, the enforcement action mechanisms allowed the ECJ to 'mediate Commission charges and member state defences regarding alleged treaty breaches' (Alter, 1998a, p. 125). A similar pattern emerges with regard to the jurisdiction of the ECJ over policing and judicial cooperation except that the Commission is deprived of its monitoring role: national governments take that responsibility upon themselves. Central to this paradigm was a perception amongst participants that the preliminary reference was not to be used as a mechanism for reviewing national laws but more as a vessel for advice over EU law. This was certainly the view of the EEC Treaty negotiators in 1957, and a not dissimilar view is apparent in the Treaty of Amsterdam negotiations, where the possibility of references from national courts is left to the national government's discretion.

Notwithstanding this, a variety of writers have argued that a number of mechanisms exist at the disposal of the national governments which severely curtail the autonomy of the ECJ (Garrett, 1992, 1995; Garrett and Weingast, 1993; Garrett, Keleman and Schulz, 1998). These mechanisms include non-compliance with ECJ judgments; replacement of judges at the end of their term; and amendment of legislation to circumvent unfavourable judgments. Non-compliance with any unfavourable judgment would lead to a breakdown in the credibility of the rules underpinning the single market, which the authors argue is in the social and economic interests of the national governments to promote. As a strategic actor, however (so the argument goes), the ECJ is aware that it cannot diverge over a long period from the preferences of the central member states and a *de facto* principal–agent relationship emerges between it and the national governments.

If this was so, it was a foolish hope. As Bzdera has observed, central judicial institutions almost invariably have centralizing rather than particularist tendencies, and are therefore rarely sensitive to locally specific concerns of constituent states (Bzdera, 1992, pp. 133–4). There is little evidence, moreover, that the ECJ systematically behaves in a strategic manner, free from the arguments and legal reasoning presented to it in each individual case. It has taken decisions, for example, that were clearly against the interests of virtually all the national governments, such as declaring the European Economic Area (EEA; see Chapter 1) agreement void[23] and holding national governments to be liable to individuals for loss suffered as a result of their failure to comply with EC law.[24]

Such principal–agent accounts suffer from two further structural weaknesses. The first is why, as principals, the national governments should, in these terms, allow such an inefficient agent to endure. The ECJ's inefficiencies lie not just in its backlog. The wide array of matters upon which it is called to adjudicate ranges from constitutional theory through to environmental science, questions of economics, fiscal arrangements and accounting. The ECJ being a collection of generalists, its expertise is obviously found wanting in some of these specializations, the most commented upon being competition (e.g. Bishop, 1981, pp. 294–5; Korah, 2000, pp. 347–357). As an agent it is also inefficient in its inability to generate feelings of wider identification with and support for its behaviour. Studies have shown that while there is reasonable voter satisfaction with the behaviour of the ECJ, it was the least salient of the institutions and enjoyed low diffuse support (Gibson and Caldeira, 1995, 1998). This lack of any reservoir of goodwill renders it particularly vulnerable to attacks where it makes decisions deviating from short-term public opinion.

The second weakness of this account is that it gives an impression which differs so radically from that of the lawyers who work in the field. There is considerable consensus that the judgments of the ECJ follow highly idiosyncratic paths, which appear simultaneously bereft of any long-term strategic vision and highly individualistic. Differences among legal scholars congregate rather around the normative characterization of this. To some, it is positive evidence of the upholding of judicial autonomy and the rule of law (Arnull, 1996; Tridimas, 1996) or the upholding of important liberal ideals (Cappelletti, 1987). To others, it smacks of a lack of judicial objectivity (Hartley, 1996, 1999) or unattractive centralizing activism (European Research Group, 1997; Neill, 1996; Rasmussen, 1986, 1998). Yet the bedrock of all this debate is a shared agreement that the ECJ has behaved in such a highly autonomous manner that it is difficult to either explain or predict its case law on the basis of a relationship or series of relationships that it has with a group of other institutional actors.

4.1.2 The national courts

The constitutional case law of the ECJ has resulted in the emergence of three discrete doctrines which allow EC law to be invoked before national courts, and thereby bring them into play in the integration process.

The oldest is that of *direct effect*. This allows a provision, which is sufficiently clear and precise, to be invoked before a national court. It does not prescribe the remedy that must be applied if the provision is breached other than to stipulate the remedy should be effective and should not be less favourable than those remedies applying to similar domestic claims.[25] Typically, there are two forms of direct effect. Vertical direct effect is where a provision may be invoked against state or public bodies. It is particularly important in fields of market liberalization where a trader is normally arguing that a law, regulation or administrative measure be disapplied. Horizontal direct effect, by contrast, allows individuals to invoke an EC provision against other private individuals. It is central to fields that rely upon associative obligations such as labour law, consumer law and environmental law where, in the vast majority of cases, it will be a private party that is being sued. Depending upon the wording of the provision, EC Treaty provisions, provisions of regulations and provisions of certain international agreements entered into by the EC can be vertically and horizontally directly effective (for more on this see Weatherill and Beaumont, 1999, pp. 392–413). Directives, by contrast, are only vertically directly effective. They cannot generate a cause of action against private parties[26] although this has been tempered by their being allowed to be used as a defence against actions brought in national law by private parties.[27] As Directives are the central instruments used in the fields of the single market, the environment, social policy and consumer protection, this diminished judicial protection in these fields. It also gave rise to inequalities

where the capacity of parties performing identical functions to sue depended on the wholly extraneous circumstance of the status of the defendant, namely whether it was a private or public body.[28]

A second doctrine emerged, that of *indirect effect*. This requires national courts to interpret all national law so as to conform with EC law in so far as it is given discretion to do so under national law. A strong interpretive duty is thereby placed on national courts which applies whether or not the national legislation was intended to implement EC law and whether or not the national precedes the EC provision in question.[29] The effect of this was to allow all binding EC law, including Directives, to be invoked, albeit indirectly, in disputes between private parties. Nevertheless, the results were unsatisfactory. Apart from the uncertainty and instability this doctrine brings to national law (De Búrca, 1992), there are circumstances where it will not guarantee the judicial application of EC law. The doctrine is of little effect where either the national provision explicitly or implicitly contradicts the EC provision or there is no national provision to interpret. There is a further exception which prevents this doctrine being applied to Directives where the effect would be to aggravate criminal liability.[30]

The third doctrine that seeks to compensate for this is that of *state liability*. Individuals can sue the state for compensation where an EC provision grants them individual rights and they have suffered loss as a consequence of the state's illegal conduct. While the doctrine provided strong incentives for national governments to implement and apply EC law, it met strong opposition from national administrations which, in the light of the inherent uncertainties in EC law, saw it as imposing open-ended, financially onerous duties upon them (United Kingdom Government, 1996, paras. 8–10). The doctrine was thus mitigated so that a breach of EC law by a member state, *simpliciter*, was insufficient to ground liability. It was necessary that the breach be serious. While the full doctrinal implications of this are still being probed, it appears there are three scenarios which justify liability. These are a failure to transpose a directive;[31] a failure to follow settled case law;[32] and a failure to follow EC law where there is no reasonable doubt about the application of the provision.[33]

While these doctrines still leave gaps where individuals will be unable to invoke EC provisions before national courts, their sweep is still considerable. The Registrar of the ECJ estimated therefore that it has, on its records, 30 000 instances of EC law being considered by national courts (conversation with author, 9 July 1999). In this, the importance of national courts is threefold.

First, they act as gatekeepers to the preliminary reference procedure. Enabling EC law to be invoked in national courts transformed the preliminary reference procedure into the central source of jurisdiction for the ECJ. This is not simply a quantitative process. In qualitative terms, in all areas other than the institutional prerogatives of the EU institutions the most difficult and path-breaking questions upon which the ECJ has had to adjudicate have come via this procedure. This is, in itself, hardly surprising given the heterogeneity of courts and litigants who contribute to this procedure and the legal training and resources that these collectively can put into the formulation of questions of EC law.

Second, national courts have become important interlocutors of EC law. Only a small proportion of cases go to the ECJ. In the UK, for example, it is estimated that about one in six of the recorded judgments in which EC law is considered in any depth by the national court results in a reference to the ECJ (Chalmers, 2000b). A similar study in Spain found an even lower proportion of references, with 90.1% of cases not referred (Rameu, 2002, pp. 23–24). Yet the disciplines of EC law have been generally accepted by national courts (Slaughter, Stone Sweet and Weiler, 1998). This entails a transformation of the national legal system, so that, in Weiler's words, national courts 'render Community law not as a counter-system to national law, but as part of the national legal order to which attaches "the habit of obedience" and the general respect, at least of public authority, to the "law" ' (Weiler, 1994, p. 519). At its narrowest, the assertion that an EC provision can be invoked before a national court will involve the tailoring of surrounding national procedures and remedies. More far-reaching, however, it often involves substantial administrative reorganization. This can take the form of the creation of new powers of judicial review not previously available to the courts or the widening of those courts which are to have powers of judicial review. It can also mean that areas such as competition policy and environmental law, which traditionally were not dealt with in a substantial way previously in the judicial arena, have increasingly to be decided by judges. Matters previously dealt with through the language of collective goods now have to be considered in terms of individual rights.

There is, however, another aspect to national courts' roles as interlocutors of EC law. They act, in many ways, as laboratories for the understanding of and experimentation in EC law. National courts provide arenas for the testing, debating and refining of EC norms. Furthermore, the preliminary reference procedure allows the experiences of one national court and the responses of it and the ECJ to be communicated across the Union (de la Mare, 1999). This results in national courts acting, in many areas of EC law, as important dynamos for the transformation not just of national law but also of EC law.

National courts have a final role as enforcers of EC law. The application of EC law by national courts necessarily involves its enforcement against those against whom it is invoked. In this, their involvement significantly enhanced the formal effectiveness of EC law in a number of ways. The institutional position of national courts within national constitutional settlements resolves the compliance problems that have traditionally bedevilled judgments of international judicial bodies. For failure to comply with a judgment of a national court is seen as a breakdown in the rule of law in all EU jurisdictions. Application of EC law by national courts also allows for a wider interpretation of EC norms than would be likely to be the case if they were merely subject to the auto-interpretation of national ministries. Enforcement of EC law through national courts brings other benefits. It decentralizes the system of enforcement, thereby reducing costs and barriers to enforcement. By enabling private parties, through litigation, to become involved in the process of enforcement, it also provides incentives for more effective enforcement by attaching the power of initiative, in the form of the grant of individual rights to those whose property or interests are impaired.

That said, this system of decentralized judicial enforcement is not without its limits. By only allowing those who can show infringement of their individual rights to bring a matter before a national court, the constitutionalizing case law of the ECJ privileges private interests over collective goods, such as the protection of the environment, public health, social cohesion and prevention of regional disparities (Harlow, 1996). For a feature of the latter is that their 'public' nature prevents any one individual being able to appropriate and thereby assert an individual interest in them. The result is that legislation protecting the latter has generally been less fully applied and subject to more individual complaints about non-compliance by national governments than EC law asserting market or other private rights (CEU, 1996e).

In their capacity as gatekeepers, interlocutors and enforcers, national courts act as the fulcrum of the ECJ's power. This has prompted debate as to why they have been generally ready to accept EC law. Undoubtedly, such acceptance has been facilitated by the ECJ being sensitive to the arguments of higher national courts. Thus, it has responded to prompts from national courts that it develop a fundamental rights doctrine; not accord the EC unlimited powers; nor allow Directives to impose duties on individuals by tailoring EC law accordingly (Chalmers, 1997a). Yet these, by their nature are high profile and occasional. They cannot explain the structural conditions that might induce national courts more generally to apply EC law.

A variety of theories has emerged in this regard. There are, on the one hand, theories that cast national courts as strategic actors who apply EC law because it allows them to maximize their interests or preferences. It has been argued that acceptance of EC law was prompted by courts wishing to acquire or exercise powers of judicial review at the expense of other arms of government (Weiler, 1993; Burley and Mattli, 1993; Mattli and Slaughter, 1998); lower courts wishing not merely to acquire new powers of review, but also to escape existing judicial hierarchies (Alter, 1996, 1998b, 2001; Mattli and Slaughter, 1998); and courts wishing to exercise their own policy preferences at the expense of national legislatures (Golub, 1996a). While such analyses may have some force in some cases, they make highly contestable assumptions about the motivation for judicial decisions and disregard any impact that the surrounding legal context or legal reasoning will exert upon the decision. They are unable to explain why national courts should behave in this manner when, traditionally, there has been resistance to the application of international legal norms (Benvenisti, 1993). Empirical studies therefore suggest little general support for any of these theses (Stone Sweet and Brunell, 1997). Other arguments rely more upon courts acting as socialized institutions. It is therefore argued that they are induced to accept EC law by the formal pull of legal language (Weiler, 1993) or because it fits with their perception of this being the appropriate judicial thing to do either because this was being done by their peers or because EC law asserted rights-based discourses and notions of judicial autonomy (Chalmers, 1997a; Plötner, 1998; Rameu, 2002).

Others have observed that its incorporation into national legal orders results in a transmutation of EC law, with its becoming tailored to the culture and context of these legal orders, with a corollary limiting of its ability to bring about substantial change (Conant, 2002). These theories are more case sensitive and bring questions of identity and context more to the fore. Yet, by relying on existing identities, they suffer from being unable to explain transformation other than to rationalize it, unconvincingly, as being some form of extension of existing processes.

The limitations of these respective accounts has led some authors to amalgamate them in a manner that weight is given to all of the above factors (Slaughter, Stone Sweet and Weiler, 1998; Alter, 1998b, 2001, pp. 45–52). Such amalgamations probably give a more complete list of the motives that are likely to lead national courts to accept EC law. Yet, in their inability to explain how competing variables should be weighed against each other, the last paradigms hint at the difficulties in this area of providing a single explanation across such a wide field where individual courts will be subject to varying institutional, cultural and sectoral contexts.

4.1.3 Litigants and other players

Most actor-based theories of EC law acknowledge that national courts, while important, act only as intermediaries. The opportunity structures they provide lead to their being surrounded by networks of actors and interests. They serve not merely to inform these interests of EC law and resolve disputes between them. As reactive bodies which must respond to the arguments and interests that appear before them, they enjoy a dialectical relationship with the former. These articulate, refract and test their judgments as well as provide the legal disputes and legal arguments that constitute the raw material of litigation. Attention has focused on a variety of groups.

Materialist analyses argue that the growth of transnational exchange within the EU has generated a demand for a supranational organization in order to reduce transaction costs. Part of any such organization must include a system of legal rules and a system of dispute resolution. Such analyses therefore draw a causal link between the degree of intra-EC trade and the quantity of litigation of EC law (Stone Sweet and Caporaso, 1998; Stone Sweet and Brunell, 1998). They infer this from two features. On the one hand, the increase in preliminary references over the long term mirrors the increase in intra-EC trade. In addition, fewer references have come from those jurisdictions where intra-EC trade constitutes a lower proportion of national GDP. Such analyses see the transnational merchant as someone who not only is the central motor behind the development of EC litigation, but has used the opportunities created by the EC court structure to develop a governance regime outwith the nation-state. Yet such actors have traditionally developed private legal regimes, such as the *lex mercatoria*, outside the court system altogether (Teubner, 1997). This transnationalization of exchange, combined with the restructuring and internationalization of the European legal profession, has led increasingly to large law firms and arbitrators acting as important additional generators of rules of the game for the single market (Dezalay, 1992; Trubek *et al.*, 1994).

As a paradigm, materialist analyses treat as unproblematic the processes which lead parties to go to court and which they use in going to court. There has been criticism of analyses which focus predominantly on transnational exchange. It has been argued that the time it takes for new transnational alliances to emerge is so great that they arrive on the 'scene too late to play the game' (Conant, 2001). Instead, on the basis of a comparative analysis of references from France, Germany and the UK, she argues that the extent to which EC law is invoked will depend far more upon pre-existing domestic institutions. They will be affected, on the one hand, by the extent to which they are able to adjust to and 'fit' with substantive EC law. Conant argues that equally important are pre-existing patterns of civil litigation and the presence of resources or public institutions that facilitate access to the courts. The high number of referrals in the UK, by contrast to the other two, in areas such as social security, labour law (and one could add VAT) is thus influenced by a system of accessible, low-cost tribunals and public support in the form of Citizens' Advice Bureaux.

Other commentators have noticed a division within domestic structures between 'one-shotters' and 'repeat players' (Mattli and Slaughter, 1998, pp. 186–92). The former are litigants merely interested in winning the particular case in hand. Repeat players, by contrast, treat litigation as part of a two-level game (on this more generally within the EU see Anderson and Liefferink, 1997). EC law and courts are used as a counterweight

by parties where they have been unable to attain their objectives through local law or in national administrative and legislative arenas. They take a more prospective view of law in which the gains they seek are modifications of the rules of the game. As a consequence, they are less inclined to settle out of court and more likely to engage in repeated litigation, 'forum-shopping' before a number of tribunals. In a limited number of instances, such actors come directly before the ECJ (Harding, 1992). This institution's restrictive standing requirements and the proximity of the national courts have meant that, more frequently, they come before the latter. Such actors can be commercial groups of actors, as was the case in the Sunday trading saga, where a series of DIY stores engaged in repeated litigation under EC law to bring about a change in the legislation in Britain on trading hours (Rawlings, 1993). They can also be non-governmental organizations which seek to further certain post-material values and may seek to do this either by litigating directly or by providing support for litigants in areas of strategic interest – the latter tactic was pursued by the Equal Opportunities Commission in the UK (Barnard, 1995; Alter and Vargas, 2000). Repeat actors not only influence some areas of EC law – notably free movement of goods, gender discrimination and some areas of environmental law – disproportionately more than others, although their effects ripple out across the Union; their incidence is unevenly distributed across the different member states. Alter and Vargas have noted that a number of conditions normally have to inure for such groups to take action (Alter and Vargas, 2000). As litigation is an avenue of last resort, there have to be strong patterns of institutional exclusion from other arenas for such groups. It would appear to be an advantage that such groups have a narrow mandate and constituency. More dispersed groups may not have the concentration of expertise, and internal conflicts of interest might arise that will prevent litigation and provide incentives to spend resources elsewhere. Furthermore, such groups will seek narrowly focused policy gains, the costs for which may be widely distributed and therefore not strongly opposed.

All interest-group theories acknowledge that interest groups cannot, alone, engineer EC legal change. They point, in particular, to the importance of sympathetic judiciaries (Mattli and Slaughter, 1998; Alter and Vargas, 2000). Yet there is another group of actors who are important to the development of EC law and that is the EC legal community.

It was widely acknowledged that, certainly in the first 30 years, the capacity of the ECJ to establish EC law doctrine was dependent upon a community of lawyers and academics, specialists in EC law, who could provide new arguments for the fleshing out and development of EC law, analogize it to national legal systems and doctrines, and disseminate and advocate it amongst both lay and legal communities (Stein, 1981). This community was, certainly in each member state, relatively small and many of the high-profile writers had strong institutional links with either the Commission or the ECJ. It is also not unfair to suggest that most of the early writing was sympathetic both to the general idea of EC integration and to the process of integration being done through legal instruments and judicial interpretation (Schepel and Wesseling,

1997). The unfolding of EC law over time and its expansion into new areas have destroyed this cohesion. New academics, with axes to grind and totems to smash, have emerged on the one hand (for a discussion of this see Shaw, 1999), and academics and professionals from other fields, reticent about the destabilizing effects of EC law on those fields, have begun to discuss EC law (e.g. Teubner, 1998). This is not leading to legal communities ceasing to have influence over the integration process. It is probably more accurate to suggest a recasting of this influence within which specialized legal communities, increasingly brought together by the function of the law in which they specialize rather than its designation, have a heightened influence over narrow areas of expertise (on trade marks see Chalmers, 1997b).

| 4.2 | The structuring of EU integration through EU law |

All actor-interest theories of EU law conceive of EU law in relatively passive terms. It is something used by particular actors to prosecute particular advantages. Its enabling qualities are confined to the creation of particular legal institutions, notably courts, which provide opportunity structures for additional actors. Yet law is not infinitely malleable. Even as an agent of national preferences the ECJ can only express national preferences in terms of individual rights and win-lose (as opposed to mediated) scenarios and act on the basis of the limited information that parties, constrained by processes of standing and intervention, can put before it. The relationship is therefore a dialectic one, in which the very features of EU law that make it attractive to actors to be involved in its formulation and application also configure those and other actors' actions.

4.2.1 The symbolic effects of EU law

Giving legal value to certain arrangements carries with it certain symbolic effects (Dehousse and Weiler, 1990, p. 244). The formality of legal texts confers greater weight to commitments. Even instruments such as Recommendations, which do not formally oblige parties to do anything, nevertheless indicate a description of good practice agreed by all the parties who adopted the instrument. Yet, it is nevertheless true that the degree

of commitment, in symbolic terms at least, is often reflected in the prescriptive terms of the instrument used. The increasing commitment to integrate environmental concerns into other EC policies was therefore reflected in the manner in which it started as an undertaking in the Third Action Plan on the Environment in 1983 (see Chapter 17); was made a Treaty commitment (Article 130r(4) EC in 1986 by the SEA); was placed at the Head of the Title on the Environment by the Maastricht Treaty in 1991 (Article 130r(2) EC); and was then placed as one of the Principles of the Treaty by the Treaty of Amsterdam in 1996 (Article 6 EC). While the commitment was not actively pursued in a general manner until the mid-1990s (Wilkinson, 1997), this intensification made it increasingly difficult for the principle to be contested at the policy-making level, with debate focusing far more on the modalities of operation.

Translating a matter into law also confers a recognition upon it, which gives it both a greater importance and greater priority. Dehousse and Weiler therefore mention how it was the legal nature of the Elysée Treaty between France and Germany in 1963 on military cooperation that caused controversy. For it suggested a prioritization of defence links between these states over commitments to other states, despite the agreement being relatively empty of substantial commitments (Dehousse and Weiler, 1990, pp. 244–5). More recently, the European citizenship provisions introduced into the EC Treaty by the TEU conferred few new rights upon individuals. The provisions provoked such backlash, however, that the member states felt, at the Edinburgh European Council in 1992, that, to enable the second Danish referendum on Maastricht to be successful, the provision had to be revised to indicate explicitly that it did not encroach upon national citizenship. In symbolic terms, the adoption of laws at a EU level has a tri-dimensional quality.

As EU law signifies law beyond the nation-state, it relativizes national law, irrespective of the form it takes. EU law, whether intended to supplant or supplement national measures, exposes the functional limits of nation-state legal structures and pluralizes legal authority within the territory of any state. Legal authority becomes something constructed from a variety of sources rather than simply the national constitution (MacCormick, 1993, 1999). The opposition between EU law and national law leads to further dichotomies. At its crassest, the justifications for EU law residing in the limitations of national law create a characterization within which the EU acts as a form of enlightened, cosmopolitan counterweight to the atavistic qualities of the nation-state (Fitzpatrick, 1997); some even urge this (e.g. Weiler, 1997a). Others have noted an oppositionality within which EU law may justify itself by reason of arguments of rationalization, efficiency and integration, but the pluralization of its implementation creates new schisms and dislocations within the national legal system (Wilhelmsson, 1995; Schepel, 1997; Teubner, 1998).

Second, the 'Euro-centrism' of EU law lies also in its signifying an intensification of cooperation and integration between certain polities and societies to the exclusion of others. Numerous commentators have therefore pointed to its creating new insider/outsider pathologies (Geddes, 1995; Hervey, 1995; Ward, 1996, pp. 147–52). This dichotomy does not simply run along crude EU/non-EU lines. All legal instruments, in so far as they generate their own processes of bounding, will contain elements of integration/inclusion and elements of exclusion/disintegration. For any legislation will empower or disempower, impose duties or rights selectively (Shaw, 1996). As a text, it will, furthermore, translate roles, identities, etc. in a manner where only facets are recognized, to the exclusion of other aspects.

The third symbolic quality of EU law derives from the interaction between it and the policy domain it governs. EU law enlarges understanding of a policy domain, not through creating that policy domain for the first time – be it environment, health and safety, etc.

– but by giving it a European dimension. The policy domain can no longer be understood without taking account of this dimension. A new horizon is added which might include new networks, technologies, instruments or values (Barry, 1993). In this manner, EU law is a practical manifestation of the way in which 'Europe' transforms understandings and expectations of a particular field, irrespective of questions of fact, interests and preferences (Christiansen, 1997).

4.2.2 The stabilization of expectations about EU government

A feature of EU law is its normativity. This normativity provides that EU law cannot be falsified by subsequent conduct. That is to say, where conduct deviates from the norm, it will be the conduct rather than the norm that will be considered deviant (i.e. illegal). This results in EU law being the central instrument through which expectations are stabilized about the distribution, reach and modalities of power within the EU system of government. It is the legal instruments which detail what powers the EU enjoys and how it empowers and restricts those within its embrace.

At the very least, therefore, EU law sets out the rules of the game, which, there is an expectation, will be habitually obeyed. Rational choice institutionalists qualify this by claiming that while such rules may not affect parties' deep-seated preferences, they do, by forestalling certain options, determine the strategies adopted by the parties (e.g. Pollack, 1997; Tsebelis and Kreppel, 1998; Tsebelis and Garrett, 2000). Classically, therefore, legal constraints on national governments' ability to curb the Commission's exercise of its powers may lead to their trying to secure influence within the Commission. Even within the parameters of this analysis, the influence of EU law is considerable.

It prevents certain outcomes being achieved, irrespective of the preferences of the parties. The decision of the ECJ in 1975 that the Community enjoyed exclusive competence in the field of external trade did not bring about a uniform commercial policy.[34] Yet it forestalled national government unilateralism, by requiring any autonomous measure to be first approved by either the Council or the Commission, with the consequence that any unilateral measure had to illustrate that it did not impinge excessively on other national or Community interests.

EU law also challenges existing asymmetries of power. In the case of the legislative influence of the EP, not only do legal provisions 'constitute' the Parliament through providing for its existence, but it is the legal peculiarities of the cooperation and co-decision procedures which enable the Parliament to act, in many circumstances, as a 'conditional agenda-setter' (Tsebelis, 1994; Scully, 1997; Tsebelis and Garrett, 1997). For they make it easier for the Council to accept Parliamentary amendments (which with Commission agreement can be approved by qualified majority voting (QMV) in the Council) than to introduce its own (which require unanimity). The consequence of this is an increased propensity on the part of member states to accept Parliament's amendments. For the test is no longer whether this is an 'ideal' amendment, but, *faute de mieux*, becomes whether this is an improvement on the original proposal. In such circumstances, the legal procedures have resulted in the preferences of a player other than the national governments becoming important, and inevitably require that national governments realign their behaviour, and, to some degree, thereby adjust their preferences, if legislation contrary to their interests is not to be passed.

Legal structures determine outcomes in another way. As outcomes have to be translated into legal structures, actors are able to use prior legal structures to pattern outcomes and negotiations. Most famously, the Commission exploited the *Cassis de Dijon* judgment to provide the basis for its New Approach to Harmonization which lay at the heart of the 1992 programme (Alter and Meunier-Aitsahalia, 1994). This judgment stated that Article 28 EC, on the provision on free movement of goods, required member states, in the absence of a compelling public interest, to grant market access to products lawfully marketed or manufactured in another member state.[35] Undoubtedly, it shifted Article 28 EC away from being an instrument that exclusively tackled discriminatory, protectionist measures to one that was essentially deregulatory in nature, which was concerned with sweeping away measures that had unnecessarily restrictive effects upon inter-state trade. Beyond that, the parameters of the judgment were inconclusive (Barents, 1982; Chalmers, 1993). The Commission argued, however, that the judgment entrenched the principle of mutual recognition, whereby a member state should accept that the regulatory requirements of the member state where the good (or service) was produced were, in principle, equivalent to its own ([1980] OJ C256/2).

This alleviated the need for total harmonization of regulatory requirements by the Community. Instead, an approach based on mutual recognition transformed the role of the EC legislature into that of providing minimum guarantees. It would harmonize only those essential health and safety standards that were necessary to prevent member states claiming that trade infringed some essential public interest ([1985] OJ C136/1). This governance structure was conceived as placing limits on EC legislative output, preserving national regulatory traditions and increasing consumer choice. To be sure, it allowed different interests to be reconciled in a manner which had not previously been possible. It also structured future relations and provided the source of future tensions. These included doubts about the standardization bodies' capacity to develop standards quickly enough or in a sufficiently pluralist manner (Vos, 1998, pp. 281–308); and breakdowns in the mutual trust and national internal administrative organization required to bring about mutual recognition (CEU, 1999b, pp. 4–5).

While the autonomy given to actors by EU legal structures affords them the possibility to use these strategically, a feature of legal autonomy is that it always gives actors the possibility of complying with the law for no ground other than simple legal obedience. Others have observed that in so far as EU law allows, there exists the possibility of inculcating certain patterns of obedience and behaviour. In this manner, it is argued, EU law not only stabilizes patterns of behaviour, but also produces socializing effects which transform and adapt expectations and preferences (Armstrong and Bulmer, 1998; Armstrong, 1998; Shaw and Wiener, 1999). The general force of this argument is not undermined by such effects being difficult to prove or disprove in any one instance. It is also not necessarily incompatible with the argument that actors also use law strategically. In both instances, the law in question 'frames' the action in question. It influences the modalities of behaviour of the actor by simultaneously enabling and foreclosing certain courses of action. Thus, the legal structure of subsidiarity came to frame and emasculate debates about the intensity and breadth of EC law making in the post-Maastricht era, so that protagonists of all sides couched their arguments in terms of that structure (Maher, 1995). The question of whether an actor responds strategically to this frame is both largely a matter of degree and one of *ex post facto* rationalization. The degree to which legal or other structures condition actions will vary according to the dynamics of the relations entered into at the time (Granovetter, 1985). No actor is ever completely conditioned by any one structure, but analysis of the level of conditioning will be assessed by reference to the extent of determined calculation on the part of that actor; that is to say to what extent the actor uses other recognizable structures in interactions with legal instruments (Callon, 1998). In the *Cassis de Dijon* example, therefore, the Commission was taken to be acting strategically because it used the judgment as the basis for a series of political structures which distributed governmental power. Nevertheless, a degree of framing was present as it perceived these in terms of an overarching principle, namely free movement of goods. It will be obvious from this that not only may EU law appear to socialize some actors more heavily than others, but a condition of law is that it allows for the possibility of strategic and socialized interaction with all actors. The degree to which particular players act strategically will therefore vary across context.

4.3   Law as the cipher for the legitimacy of the EU

One corollary to the normativity of law is that law always has the ability to acquire different meanings. A bald legal statement that 'theft is wrong' would transmutate, to prevent falsification, when confronted with the situation of the person who steals to survive, either by providing a justification or by modifying the definition of theft. This means that an invocation of law involves not merely its application to a particular situation but also an 'idealising moment of unconditionality that takes it beyond its immediate context' (Rehg, 1996, p. xiii). A legal interpretation is thus never just a description of the political settlement or social interaction it regulates, but also a prescriptive assertion of what it ought to be. Law is distinguished from morality or ethics in that it only governs social interaction and does not purport to regulate or judge behaviour that falls outside this interaction. Yet it is their shared features of normativity – namely that both prescribe norms which enjoy a priority to any subsequent conduct and which are never fully directly observable in that their meaning can never be derived from any single context – that allow government framed by law or enacted through legislation to describe itself as value oriented (Chalmers, 2000b). It also leads to EU law being seen as the central cipher through which the values of the EU are to be understood. Most notably, therefore, debates about legitimacy and reform of the EU revolve around legal reform, as law is premised, perhaps falsely, as the enabling medium through which these questions can be gauged and re-established.

In this context legal integration, within the EC pillar of the TEU at least, has been seen as being characterized by a series of liberal attributes (Slaughter, 1995, pp. 510–14). These include the assurance of peaceful relations between member states; the assurance of some degree of civil and political rights, now brought together under the umbrella of 'European citizenship'; and the protection of transnational transactions and cross-boundary property rights. It also includes the emergence of transgovernmental communications, which not only involve ties between national administrations but collapse traditional foreign/domestic distinctions through the 'recognition of multiple actors exercising different types and modes of governmental authority' (Slaughter, 1995, p. 513) in increasingly pluralistic and heterarchical patterns (MacCormick, 1993, 1996, 1999).

The liberal paradigm draws a nexus between legal integration and achievement of these values (Reich, 1997). Within this understanding, the broader the reach of EC legal integration and the more intensely it is pursued, the greater the likelihood that these values will be achieved. These attributes provide the source for much of the criticism of EU law. Thus, EC law is castigated for not going far enough to afford judicial protection to rights granted under EC law (Szyszczak, 1996); not extending market freedoms sufficiently widely (Arnull, 1991; Gormley, 1994); failing to extend its fundamental rights competence sufficiently broadly (Alston and Weiler, 1999); and not affecting third country nationals the same market rights as EU citizens (Hedemann-Robinson, 1996). Within the liberal paradigm, individual autonomy, protected through the grant of certain liberal rights, is to be complemented by the notion of public autonomy within which each individual agrees to limit his or her freedoms so as to ensure the freedom of others. The right to an equal distribution of liberties and constraints can only be given concrete shape, however, through the exercise of legislation in which all have the right to participate (Habermas, 1996, p. 125). It is possible, therefore, to argue that a similar line of liberal reasoning underpins those 'republican' theories which push for a broadening of participatory and dialogic opportunities for private parties in EC law making and administration (Craig, 1997; Weiler, 1997b; Scott, 1998; Bellamy and Warleigh, 1998). All the above suggest that all that is needed to remedy the 'legitimacy deficit' of the Union is for the reforms they suggest to be adopted. This legal vision of integration posits this deficit as simply residing in the Union not being sufficiently ideological.

This view has been criticized on the ground that there is an inevitable 'integration/disintegration' nexus to any liberal paradigm of law. Within this it is argued that, within the EU, any system of law inevitably generates new patterns not merely of inclusion but also of exclusion and alienation (Shaw, 1996). This is likely to be particularly the case with the liberal paradigm. By seeking to enhance the autonomy of the Imaginary Subject this rewards the attributes of the competitive and the efficient and those with the resources to translate their autonomy into substantive rewards at the expense of those without these capacities.

Others have also observed that it is too simplistic to attribute a single set of values to an organization such as the EU, and that within any legal instrument a plurality of values is present (Joerges, 1996). Thus,

it has been argued that central structures within much of EC regulation are knowledge based, with EC regulation acting to secure the primacy of certain forms of knowledge over other forms (Sand, 1998). It has been noted in the field of policing that the principal values are those of 'securitization', the central pathologies of which are surveillance and re-establishing or consolidating certain territorial patterns of control (Chalmers, 1998). Within this mêlée, EU law acts more as an arena for bringing to the fore and institutionalizing conflicts between values. In so far as particular values are recognized, conflicts become patterned, recurrent and routinized (e.g. trade versus the environment, freedom versus security, etc.). Within such an environment it becomes increasingly difficult to argue for the priority of particular values. Instead, legitimization becomes centred around the perfection of dispute-resolution processes that seek to rationalize or mediate between these interests or values. This might be through seeking to optimize a set of outcomes having regard to a set of pre-given preferences (Majone, 1998) or through exclusively processual means, such as requiring all decision makers either to recognize (Shaw, 1999) or to enter into dialogue with and be accountable to certain interests or identities (Joerges, 1996; Shapiro, 1996).

4.4   Actor network theories

Like the two sides of a coin, structural accounts of EU law encounter the reverse objections to those made against actor-interest accounts. By failing to consider the contexts in which EU law is invoked, which actors invoke EU law and which frames are adopted by actors when considering EU law, they are criticized for treating EU law in too isolated a manner. Nuances are, thus, drawn over and contingencies dismissed. Centrally, as they have no theory of agency, they struggle to explain how EU law is transformed over time or even adopted in the first place.

While both actor-interest and structural accounts present valuable insights into how EU law contributes to the integration process, it is the dichotomy that they draw which leads to the failings of each. More generally, they tend to centre upon law's contribution to EU government and administration. A feature of law, however, is that it transcends the political system. On the one hand, it is through law that claims are made against or to the political system. Conversely, a feature

of law is that it communicates a vision of governance to social, economic and cultural arenas outside the political system (within the EU context see Chalmers, 1999; Zürn and Wolf, 1999; Shaw and Wiener, 1999). EC environmental, labour and health and safety legislation all structure how the workplace is organized, and can be used as instruments in negotiations, for example, between management and labour. EU law also serves to restructure expectations in these arenas. Thus, in its first significant review of the Single European Market in 1996 the Commission observed that a perennial complaint of traders was patchy transposition of EC Directives and uneven enforcement of EC law (CEU, 1996f, p. 20). Nevertheless, after the enactment of the programme, while there were mixed views on whether restrictions on trade had been removed, 29% of small and medium-sized enterprises (SMEs) and 7% of large firms felt that the process, necessarily a legal one, had encouraged them to export (CEU, 1996f, pp. 12–13).

A paradigm that seeks to capture these features, as well as the mutually transformative qualities of agency and structure, is actor network theory. This conceives of EU law as being both implicated in and generating a series of networks (Ladeur, 1997). These are:

> . . . the process of co-operation itself which furnishes solutions to complex problems via joint problem definition and the drafting of a possible decision, which is then subject to ongoing evaluation on the basis of 'new' knowledge (that is new technology, new management forms, the definition of new social risks and so forth). . . . Networks do not merely consist in the identification of stable and pre-existing interests; rather they themselves generate new operating knowledge. (Ladeur, 1997, p. 46)

Such networks straddle any form of political/economic or public/private delimitation. As the network defines the mode of participation of actors and the attributes through which others recognize them, it is the network that serves to reconfigure actors' identities. It will also be clear that at any one time any single actor will be participating in multiple networks. The model is not without its disadvantages. It is elusive on how networks emerge or terminate. In addition, while it emphasizes the interplay of relationships, as high levels of interdependence can stretch on indefinitely, it is obtuse about how networks bound themselves, so as to enable one network to start and another to stop. Yet it points to EU law contributing in a central manner to a transnational society through the putting in place of a series of interlocking, interdependent relationships which serve to reforge functions and identities around new axes.

In this, legal networks are differentiated from other networks by their relatively high levels of formalization and textual dependencies. A feature of any legislation is that it sets in place in a relatively immutable manner who may and who may not participate in a network and the forms of relationship participants may enjoy with others. While such relationships are not so rigid that transformation cannot take place, this feature contributes to legal networks having a high propensity for path dependency. The tracks down which the initial relationships are channelled cannot be changed. As time passes these routines become central to the constitution of the network, with the result that legal networks tend to be more stabilized and patterned than other forms. Through patterning and stabilization of transnational society, EU law performs another function, in that it allows this society to generate securities and routines which act as artifices for participants to look to, in an otherwise unstable and fast-moving world.

The second feature of legal networks is that they revolve around interpretation of a legal text. They are thus distinct from epistemic communities, which are centred around some form of prized, shared knowledge, and economic networks, which are centred around some form of material exchange. As actors configure their actions around interpretation of this text, the text has the power to bring actors into mutually transformative relations not just with other actors but also with non-human objects (Callon, 1986; Latour, 1993). As others adapt their behaviour to the articulated qualities of these objects, EU law allows these to acquire a status and a power within the integration process.

For example, the qualities ascribed to Special Areas of Conservation (SAC) by the Habitats Directive (see Chapter 17), namely their high conservation status, and the need for their status to be restored or for them to maintain that status has shaped a number of policies.[36] The establishment of both the specific guidelines on TRENS and proposals for individual networks must take account of the needs of these areas.[37] They are eligible for specific funding under the funds earmarked for the environment[38] and grants under the Cohesion Fund will be influenced by whether a project contributes to a SAC.[39] The need for a development project to undergo an environment impact assessment will also depend upon whether it impairs a SAC.[40]

4.5 Conclusion

From all this, it will be clear that it is better to conceive of EU law as bringing a variety of new dimensions to the integration process. How central does all this render EU law to the integration process? All the above perspectives agree upon the quintessentially formal nature of EU law. This formality establishes very clear limits for its contribution to governance. The only opportunities, values, behaviour and relationships that can be influenced by EU law are ones that respond to formal structures, typically those centred around economic transactions or political opportunities. There are plenty of forms of interaction that operate outside of and that are largely unresponsive to these structures (Snyder, 1990a; 1999b) – be they economic networks, the dissemination of cultural images or various forms of communication. It is also dangerous to view those that do respond purely through the prism of the legal instruments to which they respond (Chalmers, 1999). Such confining analysis can obscure the variety of other structures and tensions that act upon these actors. Notwithstanding this, the sheer intensity and breadth of

EU law renders it an important point of organization within Europe. The formality of EU law contributes to this power by emphasizing the saliencies and certainties of EU law. In EU law, one finds a vision both for integration within Europe – set out clearly in the primary texts – and for management of various policy sectors – explored in the secondary legislation. Even if actors choose not to respond to this vision – either positively or negatively – it inevitably forms a backdrop which casts a shadow over almost any form of participation in or resistance to transnational interaction.

NOTES

1. The EC pillar is distinguished at various points throughout this chapter, as it involves a more intense form of 'legalization' in terms of the laws made and the actors implicated than the other two pillars.
2. Decision 88/591/EEC, OJ 1988, L319/1.
3. E.g. Case C-153/00 *Weduwe*, Judgment of 10 December 2002.
4. A particularly important reiteration of this view is that of Advocate General Jacobs in Case C-338/95 *Wiener* v *Hauptzollamt Emmerich* [1997] ECR I-6495.
5. Case 26/62 *Van Gend en Loos* v *Nederlandse Administratie der Belastingen* [1963] ECR 1; Case 6/64 *Costa* v *ENEL* [1964] ECR 585.
6. *Opinion 1/91 on the Draft Agreement on a European Economic Area* [1991] ECR I-6079.
7. Case 314/85 *Firma Fotofrost* v *HZA Lubeck Ost* [1987] ECR 4199.
8. *Brunner* v *European Union Treaty* [1994] 1 CMLR 57; *Carlsen* v *Rasmussen*, Judgment of the Danish Constitutional Court of 6 April 1998, available at www.um.dk/udenrigspolitik/europa/domeng
9. CA, 3 February 1994, *Ecole Européenne*, Case No. 12/94, B6.
10. *Re Treaty on European Union*, Judgment of 1 July 1992 of Spanish Constitutional Court [1994] 3 CMLR 101.
11. *Re Treaty on European Union*, Decision 92-308 of the Constitutional Council, Journal Officiel de la République Française 1992, No. 5354.
12. *R* v *MAFF exparte First City Trading* [1997] 1 CMLR 250; *Marks & Spencer* v *CCE* [1999] 1 CMLR 1152.

13. *Granital Foro*, it. 1984, I, 2064.
14. *Frontini* v *Ministero delle Finanze* [1974] 2 CMLR 372.
15. The current German position is that the German Constitutional Court will not review individual EC acts for their compliance with fundamental rights norms but reserves the right to do so if the general level of protection is not assured. *Bundesverfassungsgericht* 7 June 2000, (2000) *EuZW* 702.
16. The amendment to the Swedish Constitution, Chapter 10 Section 5, that paved the way for accession provides for supremacy of EC law on the condition that it complies with the European Convention on Human Rights, U. Bernitz, 'Sweden and the European Union: On Sweden's Implementation and Application of European Law' (2001) 38 *CMLRev* 903, 910–911.
17. *Attorney General* v *X* [1992] 2 CMLR 277.
18. http://europa.eu.int/comm/secretariat_general/sgb/droit_com/index_en.htm (Accessed 27 December 2002).
19. Case C-387/97 *Commission* v *Greece* [2000] ECR I-5047.
20. Case 314/85 *Firma Fotofrost* v *HZA Lubeck Ost* [1987] ECR 4199.
21. Case 283/81 *CILFIT* [1982] ECR 3415.
22. [1997] OJ, C340/308.
23. *Opinion 1/91 on the Draft Agreement on a European Economic Area* [1991] ECR I-6079.
24. Joined Cases C-6 and 9/90 and C-9/90 *Francovich and Others* v *Italy* [1991] ECR I-5357.
25. Case 45/76 *Comet* v *Produktschap* [1976] ECR 2043.

26. Case 125/84 *Marshall* v *Southampton and South-West AHA* [1986] ECR 723.

27. Case 194/94 *CIA Security International* v *Signalson* [1996] ECR I-2201.

28. See the Opinion of Advocate-General Jacobs in Case C-316/93 *Vaneetveld* v *Le Foyer* [1994] ECR I-763.

29. Case C-106/89 *Marleasing* v *La Comercial* [1990] ECR I-4135.

30. Joined Cases C-58, 75, 112, 119, 123, 135, 140-1, 154 and 157/95 *Gallotti* [1996] ECR I-4345.

31. Joined Cases C 178, 179, 188-190/94 *Dillenkofer* v *Germany* [1996] ECR I-4845.

32. Case C-46/93 *Brasserie du Pêcheur* v *Germany* [1996] ECR I-1029.

33. Case C-5/94 *R* v *MAFF ex parte Lomas* [1996] ECR I-2553.

34. Opinion 1/75 *Local Cost Standard Opinion* [1975] ECR 1355.

35. Case 120/78 *Rewe* v *Bundesmonopolverwaltung für Branntwein* [1979] ECR 649.

36. Directive 92/43/EC, [1992] OJ, L206/7, Articles 3 and 4(4).

37. Decision 1692/96/EC, [1996] OJ, L228/1, Article 6.

38. Regulation 1404/96/EC, [1996] OJ, L181/1, Article 2(1)(a) (LIFE).

39. E.g. Decision 93/707/EC on the grant of aid to the Closa rising bog in Ireland, [1993] OJ, L331/20; Decision 93/714/EC on the restoration of natural resources in natural parks in Spain, [1993] OJ, L331/83.

40. Directive 97/11/EC, [1997] OJ, L73/5, Annex III, 2(e).

Chapter 5

The basic statistics

ALI EL-AGRAA

This chapter provides the reader with a brief summary of the basic statistics of the EU and its candidates. For comparative purposes and in order to preserve a general sense of perspective, similar information is given for Canada, Japan, the United States, the Russian Federation and for the member nations of EFTA, since, except for Switzerland, they are members of the European Economic Area (EEA), which is considered as a stepping-stone to full EU membership (see Chapters 1 and 2).

The main purpose of this chapter is to provide the latest information since the analysis of longer-term statistics and the economic forces that determine them is one of the main tasks of the rest of this book. For example, the analysis of the composition and pattern of trade prior to the inception of the EU and subsequent to its formation is the basic aim of Part Two on the theory and measurement of economic integration. Moreover, all the policy chapters are concerned with the analysis of particular areas of interest, such as the social policies, especially the problem of unemployment, the Common Agricultural Policy (CAP), the role of the EU general budget, competition and industrial policies, EU regional policy, etc., and these specialist chapters contain further detailed and pertinent information.

5.1 Area and population concerns

Table A5.1 (the tables may be found in Appendix 5.1, p. 79) gives information on area, population and its growth and life expectancy at birth. Tables A5.2 and A5.3 provide supporting data on various aspects of health and education. Table A5.4 offers data on the sectoral distribution of the labour force in terms of the broad categories of agriculture, industry and services, and on unemployment. The data are self-explanatory but a few points warrant particular attention.

The EU of 15 has a larger population (about 378 million) than any country in the advanced Western world. This population exceeds that of the United States (about 285 million) by about a third, is about 2.6 times that of the Russian Federation (about 145 million) and is just over three times that of Japan. It falls short of the combined population of the United States, Canada and Mexico (member nations of the North American Free Trade Agreement, NAFTA) by about 37 million (Mexico has a population of about 99 million) and that of the United States and Japan, the world's two largest economies, by about 34 million. This picture will change dramatically when the over 100 million in the candidate countries join the EU and more so if Turkey ever succeeds in acceding.

The average annual rate of population growth during 1980–2001 is between 0.1 and 1.4 for the EU, the highest being recorded for Luxembourg, which is not surprising, given its administrative significance within the EU. It is 1.1 for Canada and 1.2 for the United States, both with high immigration rates. Thus, Turkey with 1.9 is the truly exceptional case within the sample.

Life expectancy at birth in 2001 is 76–80 years for the EU and 78–81 for Canada, Japan and the United States, hence there is not much difference between them. In 2000, it is 79–83 years for females and 72–77 for males in the EU and these are close to those for Canada, Japan and the United States. For the potential EU nations, the respective figures are 72–78 and 64–74 and are therefore much lower.

One should note the high unemployment rates in the EU and its candidates. Unemployment has become such an important issue for the EU that it is now developing into a policy area of its own. Although this book does not contain a chapter on it, unemployment concerns form a large section of Chapter 23 on EU social policies and is also touched on in various chapters, especially in Chapters 9 and 10 since EMU impinges on it.

One should also note the dominance of the services sector in total employment. Services is mainly the tertiary sector, comprising such divergent items as banking, distribution, insurance, transport, catering and hotels, laundries and hairdressers, professional services of a more varied kind, publicly and privately provided, and so on and so forth. For the countries in the sample, it is in excess of 50% in the majority of them. Indeed, in terms of both sexes (not in the table), for seven of the EU nations it is 68–72% and 60–66%

for the rest. The US records 71% and Japan 66%. This is significant, particularly since it has frequently been alleged in the past that the size of this sector was the cause of the slow rate of growth of the UK economy; there is nothing in the data to suggest that the UK is unique in this respect. Moreover, the increasing size of this sector over time has led to the doctrine of 'deindustrialization': as this sector grows in percentage terms, it automatically follows that the other sectors, especially industry, must decline in relative terms.

5.2   GNI per capita and GDP

Table A5.5 gives per capita GNI in 2001, using both exchange rate conversion and 'purchasing power parity' (PPP). The table also provides the ranking of nations in terms of both measures. Total GNI and GDP structure are provided in Table A5.6 and the average annual rate of GDP growth for 1980–1990 and 1990–2000 is given in Table A5.7.

One of the salient features is the disparity between the member nations of the EU in terms of per capita GNI: the rank ranges from 1 to 51 and 1 and 47 for

the respective measures, with Portugal and Greece exchanging the bottom position. All three member countries of EFTA have per capita incomes exceeding the average for the EU, while all the EU potential partners, with the exception of Cyprus, Malta and Slovenia, have per capita GNPs in the range of 15%– 49% that of Portugal. Note that one should not read too much in Luxembourg's number one ranking, given the dominance of high ranking and well paid EU officials.

5.3   Demand

The structure of demand is given in Table A5.8. It is about the distribution of GDP between household final consumption expenditure (private consumption), general government final consumption expenditure (public consumption), gross capital formation (investment expenditure), gross domestic savings and the export/import of goods and services. Tables A5.9 and A5.10 then provide detailed information on the government, export and import sectors as well as on gross international reserves, and Table A5.11 completes the picture by offering information on official development assistance (ODA) and gross foreign direct investment (FDI).

With regard to private consumption in the EU, Greece records a high 70%, Italy, Portugal and the UK fall in the 60%–66% range, the rest in the 50%– 59% except for Denmark and Ireland with 47% and 48%, respectively. As to gross capital formation, the lowest percentage belongs to United Kingdom (17%) and the highest to Portugal (28%), with Spain not far behind. The percentage on gross domestic savings shows a larger divergence between the lowest (15%

for Greece and the United Kingdom) and the highest (38% for Ireland). Note that of the EU nations, only Austria has equality between the percentages devoted to gross savings and capital formation. Exports of goods and services loom large in the case of Ireland (95%) and Belgium (84%), but vary between 25% and 65% for the rest. Imports of goods and services behave likewise with Belgium (81%) and Ireland (80%) at the top and the rest between 26% and 60%. Norway and Switzerland fit into the general picture for the EU, but the divergence is somewhat wider for the remaining nations, with the United States being almost in a league of its own in terms of gross domestic savings, exports and imports, and Japan with high gross domestic savings and capital formation and low export/import rates.

There is dissimilarity between the EU member nations with respect to both their total government expenditure and current revenue as percentages of GDP in 2000. In terms of total expenditure, the range is between 30.7% for Greece and 45.9% for the Netherlands. This is in stark contrast to Japan (15.3%), the United States (19.30%), Canada (20.3%) and Switzerland (26.7%). For the EU candidates, the range (27.6%–46.2%) resembles that for the EU nations. A proper and detailed discussion of the role played by the government budget is provided in Chapter 19.

Of particular interest for the EU is the 2000 figure for the overall budget balance since it is one of the five Maastricht criteria for EMU membership, which specifies 3% of GDP as the maximum permitted. It has now become one of the rules of the Growth and Stability Pact (GSP), governing euro membership; those interested should turn to Chapter 10.

A particularly interesting feature is the percentage of GDP spent on ODA extended to developing countries and multilateral agents, given in Table A5.11. Denmark (1.03%), Norway (0.83%), Luxembourg (0.82%), the Netherlands (0.82%) and Sweden (0.81%) come at the top of the league while the United States (0.11%) and Japan (0.23%) come at the bottom. One does not want to dwell too much on this, but the information suggests that the advanced world, in resisting the demands made by the developing world and endorsed by the UN, is more concerned with absolute figures than with percentages. The latter clearly indicate the significant implications for ODA of the developing countries' plea (through UNCTAD) that this figure should be raised to 0.5% (originally 1.0%) of the major donor countries' GDP: Germany, Japan, the United Kingdom and the United States. Therefore, as far as developing countries are concerned, only Denmark, Luxembourg, the Netherlands, Norway and Sweden will be applauded.

5.4　Money, consumer price index and interest rates

Table A5.12 provides information on the annual growth rate of money and quasi money (M2) and consumer prices as well as on the interest rates. Note the absence of the money data for the 12 euro nations, due to its being controlled by the European Central Bank with a set inflation target (see Chapter 10); there are data for Denmark, Sweden and the UK because they have not adopted the euro. Note also the close similarity in the EU interest rates, and for the same reason; Greece is out of line and that is why it was not a euro nation then. Note further how out of line Greece is from the rest of the EU nations in terms of its high level of consumer price index and for the same reason.

5.5　Direction of trade

Tables A5.13 and A5.14 warrant particular attention. They should be considered together since they give the percentages for the share of imports of the importing country coming from the EU and the share of exports of the exporting country going to the EU. The reader should be warned that these percentages are not strictly comparable, because for the year 1957 the EU refers to the original Six, while for 1974 it refers to the nine, for 1981 to the 10, for 1986 and 1990 to the 12, and for 1995 and 2000 to the 15. For an analysis of the proper trends, the reader should consult Chapter 7, and for a full analysis consult El-Agraa (1989a and 1999).

The tables show that, in 2000, EU member nations' imports from each other vary from about 49% for the United Kingdom to about 74% for Portugal. The percentages for exports vary likewise, with the lowest being over 43% for Greece and the highest over 80% for Portugal. Thus, Portugal comes at the top on both counts. Of the potential EU partners, all the three member nations of EFTA conduct more than half of their total trade (both exports and imports) with the EU, with Norway, for exports, and Switzerland, for imports, exceeding 70%. Note, however, that except for Denmark in the case of exports and Portugal for imports, these percentages have declined relative to 1995, but the overall trend is upwards.

5.6	Income/consumption distribution

Table A5.15 gives some information on the distribution of income and consumption, but note that the survey years vary greatly, 1987 for the earliest and 2000 for the latest. The table shows that for all the countries under consideration the highest 10% received between 20.1% (Sweden) and 36.7% (Russian Federation) of income-consumption, while the lowest 10% received between 1.8% (Russian Federation and United States) and 4.8% (Japan). It is interesting to note that the disparity is widest for both the United States and Russia.

5.7	Tariffs

Table A5.16 provides the average tariff levels by industry classification for the original six plus Denmark, the United Kingdom, Canada and the United States. To compare them with present levels, one should turn to Chapter 24.

Appendix 5.1 The statistical tables

In all tables, *na* means not available. Unless otherwise stated, the sources for all the tables are the World Bank's *World Development Report* and *World Development Indicators*, Eurostat's *Basic Statistics of the EU*, *Statistical Review* and *Eurostat Yearbook*, and OECD publications for various years. The data are subject to technical explanations as well as to some critical qualifications; hence the reader is strongly advised to turn to the original sources for these.

Table A5.1 Area, population and life expectancy

	Area (000 km²)	Population (m)	Average annual growth of population (%)		Life expectancy at birth (years)		
					Both	Male	Female
	2001	**2001**	**1965–80**	**1980–2001**	**2001**	**2000**	**2000**
EU countries							
Austria	84	8.1	0.3	0.4	78	75	81
Belgium	30	10.3	0.3	0.2	78	75	81
Denmark	43	5.4	0.5	0.2	76	74	79
Finland	338	5.2	0.3	0.4	78	74	81
France	552	59.2	0.7	0.4	79	75	83
Germany	357	82.3	0.2	0.2	78	74	81
Greece	132	10.6	0.7	0.4	78	75	81
Ireland	70	3.8	1.2	0.6	77	74	79
Italy	301	57.9	0.5	0.1	79	76	82
Luxembourg	2.6	0.4	*na*	1.4[a]	77	74	81[b]
Netherlands	42	16.0	0.9	0.6	78	75	81
Portugal	92	10.0	0.4	0.1	76	71	79

▶

Table A5.1 (*continued*)

	Area (000 km²)	Population (m)	Average annual growth of population (%)		Life expectancy at birth (years)		
					Both	Male	Female
		2001	1965–80	1980–2001	2001	2000	2000
Spain	506	41.1	1.0	0.5	78	75	82
Sweden	450	8.9	0.5	0.3	80	77	83
United Kingdom	243	58.8	0.2	0.2	77	75	80
EU (15)	3 242.6	378.0					
EU candidates							
Bulgaria	111	8.0	0.4[c]	−0.5	72	68	75
Cyprus	9.3	0.8	na	1.0[a]	78	78[b]	78[b]
Czech Republic	79	10.2	0.5[c]	0.0	75	74	79
Estonia	45	1.4	0.8[c]	−0.4	71	65	76
Hungary	93	10.2	0.4[c]	−0.2	72	67	76
Latvia	65	2.4	0.4	−0.4	70	65	76
Lithuania	65	3.5	na	0.1	73	68	78
Malta	0.3	0.4	na	0.8[a]	78	77[b]	77[b]
Poland	323	38.6	0.8	0.4	74	69	78
Romania	238	22.4	na	0.0	70	66	74
Slovak Republic	49	5.4	0.9[c]	0.4	73	69	77
Slovenia	20	2.0	0.9[c]	0.2	76	72	79
Turkey	775	66.2	2.4	1.9	70	67	72
EFTA countries							
Iceland	103	0.3	na	1.0	80	80	82
Norway	324	4.5	0.6	0.5	79	76	81
Switzerland	41	7.2	0.6	0.6	80	77	83
Other countries							
Canada	9 971	31.0	1.3	1.1	79	76	82
Japan	378	127.0	1.2	0.4	81	78	84
Russian Federation	17 075	144.8	0.6[c]	0.2	66	59	72
United States	9 629	285.3	1.0	1.2	78	74	80

[a] The rate is for 1990–2001.
[b] The figure is for 1999.
[c] The rate is for 1970–1980.

Table A5.2 Health expenditure, mortality and fertility

	Public expenditure on health, % of GDP	Percentage of total population with access to		Infant mortality rate (per 1000 live births)		Total fertility rate (births per woman)	
		Safe water	Sanitation				
	1997–2000	2000	2000	1980	2001	1980	2001
EU countries							
Austria	8.0	100	100	14	5	1.6	1.3
Belgium[b]	8.7	100[a]	100[a]	12	5	1.7	1.6
Denmark	8.3	100	100[a]	8	4	1.5	1.8
Finland	6.6	100	100	8	4	1.6	1.7
France	9.5	100[a]	96[a]	10	4	1.9	1.9
Germany	10.6	100[a]	100[a]	12	4	1.4	1.4
Greece	8.3	100[a]	96[a]	18	5	2.2	1.3
Ireland	6.7	100[a]	100[a]	11	6	3.2	1.9
Italy	8.1	100[a]	100[a]	15	4	1.6	1.2
Netherlands	8.1	100	100	9	5	1.6	1.7
Portugal	8.2	82[a]	100[a]	24	5	2.2	1.5
Spain	7.7	99[a]	97[a]	12	4	2.2	1.2
Sweden	8.4	100	100	7	3	1.7	1.6
United Kingdom	7.3	100	100	12	6	1.9	1.7
EU candidates							
Bulgaria	3.9	100[a]	99[a]	20	14	2.0	1.3
Cyprus	na	na	na	na	na	na	na
Czech Republic	7.2	na	na	16	4	2.1	1.2
Estonia	6.1	na	na	17	11	2.0	1.2
Hungary	6.8	99	99	23	8	1.9	1.3
Latvia	5.9	na	na	20	17	2.0	1.2
Lithuania	6.0	na	na	20	8	2.0	1.3
Malta	na	na	na	na	na	na	na
Poland	6.0	100[a]	100[a]	26	8	2.3	1.4
Romania	2.9	58	53	29	19	2.4	1.3
Slovak Republic	5.9	100	100	21	8	2.3	1.3
Slovenia	8.6	100	98[a]	15	4	2.1	1.2
Turkey	5.0	83	91	109	36	4.3	2.4
EFTA countries							
Iceland	na	na	na	na	na	na	na
Norway	7.8	100	100[a]	8	4	1.7	1.8
Switzerland	10.7	100	100	9	5	1.5	1.4
Other countries							
Canada	9.1	100	95	10	5	1.7	1.5
Japan	7.8	96[a]	100[a]	8	3	1.8	1.4
Russian Federation	5.3	99	na	22	18	1.9	1.2
United States	13.0	100	100	13	7	1.8	2.1

[a] The figure is for other years.
[b] Includes Luxembourg.

Table A5.3 Expenditure on education, 2000[a]

	Public expenditure per student (percentage of GDP per capita)		
	Primary	Secondary	Tertiary
EU countries			
Austria	15.9	13.9	24.9
Belgium[b]	17.0	13.5[c]	17.6[c]
Denmark	23.4	37.2	65.1
Finland	17.3	25.5	39.1
France	18.0	29.3	30.0
Germany	17.8	20.5	42.5
Greece	16.0	17.9	26.1
Ireland	13.3	15.2	27.8
Italy	21.2	27.1	26.0
Netherlands	15.4	21.8	43.0
Portugal	20.5	29.4	28.2
Spain	18.8	25.5	19.8
Sweden	23.5	28.3	53.5
United Kingdom	14.0	14.9	26.3
EU candidates			
Bulgaria	15.2	17.1	14.5
Cyprus	na	na	na
Czech Republic	12.5	23.2	33.9
Estonia	24.5	30.8	33.0
Hungary	17.7	18.7	30.5
Latvia	32.6	25.2	22.5
Lithuania	61.4	27.8[c]	40.4
Malta	na	na	na
Poland	26.5	12.0	20.2
Romania	19.9[c]	8.7[c]	31.3[c]
Slovak Republic	10.8	19.2	29.3
Slovenia	20.6[c]	24.6[c]	37.9[c]
Turkey	17.6	11.8	72.1
EFTA countries			
Iceland	na	na	na
Norway	29.2	18.7[c]	46.5
Switzerland	23.2	28.2	55.8
Other countries			
Canada	na	na	na
Japan	21.3	16.4[d]	20.7[d]
Russian Federation	19.9[d]	20.5	15.8
United States	17.9	22.4	47.8[d]

[a] Provisional.   [c] The figure is for 1980.
[b] Includes Luxembourg. [d] The figure is for 1997.

Table A5.4 Labour force and unemployment

	Labour force (1998–2001)[a] in						Unemployment (percentage of total labour force)
	Agriculture		Industry		Services		
	Male[c]	Female[d]	Male[c]	Female[d]	Male[c]	Female[d]	1998–2001[b]
EU countries							
Austria	6	7	43	14	52	79	4.7
Belgium	3	2	37	13	60	86	7.0
Denmark	5	2	37	15	58	83	5.4
Finland	8	4	40	14	52	82	9.8
France	2	1	35	13	63	86	10.0
Germany	3	2	46	19	50	79	8.1
Greece	16	20	29	12	54	67	10.8
Ireland	12	2	38	15	50	83	4.7
Italy	6	5	39	21	55	74	8.3
Luxembourg	na	na	na	na	na	na	2.4
Netherlands	4	2	31	9	63	84	3.6
Portugal	11	14	44	24	45	62	3.8
Spain	8	5	41	14	51	81	14.1
Sweden	4	1	38	12	59	87	5.1
United Kingdom	2	1	36	12	61	87	5.3
EU candidates							
Bulgaria	na	na	na	na	na	na	14.1
Cyprus	na	na	na	na	na	na	na
Czech Republic	6	4	49	28	48	69	8.8
Estonia	11	7	40	23	49	70	14.8
Hungary	9	4	42	25	48	71	6.5
Latvia	17	14	35	18	49	69	8.4
Lithuania	24	16	33	40	43	63	16.6
Malta	na	na	na	na	na	na	na
Poland	19	19	41	21	39	60	16.7
Romania	39	45	33	22	29	33	10.8
Slovak Republic	10	5	49	26	42	69	18.9
Slovenia	11	11	46	28	42	61	7.5
Turkey	34	72	25	10	41	18	8.3
EFTA countries							
Iceland	na	na	na	na	na	na	na
Norway	6	2	33	9	61	88	3.4
Switzerland	5	4	36	13	59	83	2.7
Other countries							
Canada	5	2	32	11	63	87	6.8
Japan	5	6	38	22	57	73	4.8
Russian Federation	15	8	36	23	49	69	11.4
United States	4	1	32	12	64	86	4.1

[a] Data may not sum to 100 due to workers not being classified by sector.
[b] Data are for the most recent years available.
[c] % of male labour force.
[d] % of female labour force.

Table A5.5 GNI per capita, 2001

	GNI per capita US$		Rank	
	Exchange rate conversion (1)	PPP (2)	(1)	(2)
EU countries				
Austria	23 940	26 380	17	17
Belgium	23 850	26 150	18	18
Denmark	30 600	28 490	8	9
Finland	23 780	24 030	19	28
France	22 730	24 080	23	27
Germany	23 560	25 240	20	21
Greece	11 430	17 520	47	47
Ireland	22 850	27 170	22	14
Italy	19 390	24 530	30	25
Luxembourg	39 840	48 560	1	1
Netherlands	24 330	27 390	16	13
Portugal	10 900	17 710	51	46
Spain	14 300	19 860	41	38
Sweden	25 400	23 800	12	29
United Kingdom	25 120	24 330	14	26
EU candidates				
Bulgaria	1 650	6 740	114	89
Cyprus	12 320	21 110		
Czech Republic	5 310	14 320	70	55
Estonia	3 870	9 650	79	71
Hungary	4 830	11 990	71	59
Latvia	3 230	7 760	86	82
Lithuania	3 350	8 350	83	78
Malta	9 210	13 140		
Poland	4 230	9 370	75	73
Romania	1 720	· 5 780	110	101
Slovak Republic	3 760	11 780	81	60
Slovenia	9 760	17 060	52	49
Turkey	2 530	5 830	95	100
EFTA countries				
Iceland	29 810	28 850		
Norway	35 630	29 340	4	7
Switzerland	38 330	30 970	3	5
Other countries				
Canada	21 930	26 530	25	15
Japan	36 610	25 550	5	20
Russian Federation	1 750	6 880	108	87
United States	34 280	34 280	7	3

Table A5.6 Structure of output, 2001

	GNI (US$ bn)		Value added as % of GDP			
	Exchange rate conversion	PPP	Agriculture	Industry	Manufacturing	Services
EU countries						
Austria	194.7	215	2	33	22	65
Belgium	245.3	269	2	27	20	71
Denmark	164.0	153	3	26	17	71
Finland	123.4	125	3	33	26	63
France	1380.7	1425	3	26	18	72
Germany	1939.6	2078	1	31	24	68
Greece	121.0	186	8	21	12	71
Ireland	87.7	104	4	42	33	55
Italy	1123.8	1422	3	29	21	68
Luxembourg	17.6	21.4	2[a]	36[a]	na	62[a]
Netherlands	390.3	439	3	27	17	70
Portugal	109.3	178	4	30	19	66
Spain	558.0	816	4	30	19	66
Sweden	225.9	212	2	27	na	71
United Kingdom	1476.8	1431	1	27	19	72
EU (15)	7836.2	8388				
EU candidates						
Bulgaria	13.2	54	14	29	18	57
Cyprus	9.4	16.1	na	na	na	na
Czech Republic	54.3	146	4	41	na	55
Estonia	5.3	13	6	29	19	65
Hungary	49.2	122	6[b]	34[b]	25[b]	61[b]
Latvia	7.6	18	5	26	15	69
Lithuania	11.7	29	7	35	23	58
Malta	3.6	5.2	na	na	na	na
Poland	163.6	362	4	37	20	59
Romania	38.6	130	15	35	27[b]	50
Slovak Republic	20.3	64	4	29	21	67
Slovenia	19.4	34	3	38	28	58
Turkey	167.3	386	14	25	15	61
EFTA countries						
Iceland	8.2	8.1	na	na	na	na
Norway	160.8	132	2	43	na	55
Switzerland	227.2	224	2[b]	30[b]	na	68[b]
Other countries						
Canada	681.6	825	3[a]	40[a]	na	57[a]
Japan	4523.3	3246	1	32	22	67
Russian Federation	253.4	995	7	37	na	56
United States	9780.8	9781	2[b]	25	17	73

[a] The rate is for 1992.　　[b] The rate is for 2000.

Table A5.7 Growth of output

	Average annual percentage growth							
	GDP		Agriculture		Industry		Services	
	1980–1990	1990–2001	1980–1990	1990–2001	1980–1990	1990–2001	1980–1990	1990–2001
EU countries								
Austria	2.3	2.2	1.4	3.7	1.8	2.8	2.8	1.9
Belgium[a]	2.1	2.2	2.2	2.3	2.4	2.0	1.8	2.0
Denmark	2.0	2.4	2.6	2.7	2.0	2.2	1.9	2.5
Finland	3.3	2.9	−0.4	1.2	3.3	4.8	3.6	2.5
France	2.4	1.9	1.3	1.9	1.4	1.5	3.0	2.0
Germany	2.3	1.5	1.7	1.7	1.1	0.0	3.1	2.4
Greece	0.9	2.4	−0.1	0.7	1.3	1.0	0.9	2.8
Ireland	3.2	7.7	na	na	na	na	na	na
Italy	2.5	1.6	−0.5	1.4	1.8	1.2	3.0	1.8
Netherlands	2.4	2.9	3.6	2.0	1.6	1.7	2.6	3.2
Portugal	3.2	2.7	1.5	−0.2	3.4	3.0	2.5	2.2
Spain	3.1	2.7	3.1	1.0	2.7	2.3	3.3	2.9
Sweden	2.5	2.1	1.4	0.0	2.8	3.6	2.4	1.8
United Kingdom	3.2	2.7	2.4	−0.1	3.3	1.3	3.1	3.4
EU candidates								
Bulgaria	3.4	−1.2	−2.1	3.0	5.2	−4.0	4.7	−3.9
Cyprus	na	na	na	na	na	na	na	na
Czech Republic	na	1.2	na	3.5	na	−0.3	na	1.8
Estonia	2.2	0.2	na	−2.8	na	−1.9	na	2.2
Hungary	1.3	1.9	1.7	−2.2	0.2	3.8	2.1	1.4
Latvia	3.5	−2.2	2.3	−5.9	4.3	−6.7	3.3	3.1
Lithuania	na	−2.2	na	−0.3	na	2.8	na	4.3
Malta	na	na	na	na	na	na	na	na
Poland	na	4.5	na	−0.2	na	4.2	na	4.2
Romania	1.0	−0.4	na	−0.6[b]	na	−0.8[b]	na	−0.5[b]
Slovak Republic	2.0	2.1	1.6	1.6	2.0	−2.1	0.9	5.6
Slovenia	na	2.9	na	−0.1	na	2.9	na	3.9
Turkey	5.3	3.3	1.2	1.1	7.7	3.1	4.5	3.5
EFTA countries								
Iceland	na	na	na	na	na	na	na	na
Norway	2.8	3.5	0.1	2.4	4.0	3.9	2.9	3.4
Switzerland	2.0	1.0	na	na	na	na	na	na
Other countries								
Canada	3.2	3.1	2.3	1.1	2.9	3.1	3.2	2.9
Japan	4.1	1.3	1.3	−3.1	4.1	−0.2	4.2	2.3
Russian Federation	na	−3.7	na	−4.5	na	−6.1	na	−0.3
United States	3.5	3.4	3.2	3.5	3.0	3.7	3.4	3.7

[a] Includes Luxembourg.　　[b] The figure is for 1990–2000.

Table A5.8 Structure of demand, 2001

	Distribution of gross domestic product (%)					
	Household final consumption expenditure	General government final consumption	Gross capital formation	Exports of goods and services	Imports of goods and services	Gross domestic savings
EU countries						
Austria	58	19	23	52	53	23
Belgium[a]	54	22	21	84	81	24
Denmark	47	26	21	46	39	28
Finland	50	21	20	40	32	29
France	55	23	20	28	26	22
Germany	59	19	20	35	33	22
Greece	70	15	23	25	33	15
Ireland	48	13	24	95	80	38
Italy	60	18	20	28	27	21
Netherlands	50	23	22	65	60	27
Portugal	61	21	28	32	41	18
Spain	59	17	25	30	31	24
Sweden	50	27	18	46	41	24
United Kingdom	66	19	17	27	29	15
EU candidates						
Bulgaria	71	16	20	56	63	13
Cyprus	na	na	na	na	na	na
Czech Republic	53	20	30	71	74	27
Estonia	56	20	28	91	94	24
Hungary	64	11	27	60	63	25
Latvia	59	22	28	46	54	19
Lithuania	68	16	22	50	56	16
Malta	na	na	na	na	na	na
Poland	66	17	22	29	33	18
Romania	80	6	22	34	42	14
Slovak Republic	56	21	32	74	82	23
Slovenia	55	21	28	59	63	24
Turkey	67	14	16	34	31	19
EFTA countries						
Iceland	na	na	na	na	na	na
Norway	43	19	22	47	30	38
Switzerland	61	13	22	45	41	26
Other countries						
Canada	56	19	20	44	39	25
Japan	56	18	25	10	10	26
Russian Federation	51	14	22	37	24	35
United States	69	14	21	11	15	17

[a] Includes Luxembourg.

Table A5.9 Central government budget, 2000

	Total expenditure (% of GDP)	Current revenue (% of GDP)	Overall budget balance[a] (% of GDP)
EU countries			
Austria	40.4	37.3	−3.1
Belgium	45.6	43.6	−1.8
Denmark	34.9	36.2	1.6
Finland	33.4	32.0	−0.3
France	46.2[b]	41.4[b]	−3.5[b]
Germany	32.7	31.3	−0.9
Greece	30.7	23.4	−4.4
Ireland	33.0[c]	31.9[b]	0.7[b]
Italy	41.9[c]	41.3[b]	−1.6[b]
Luxembourg	42.8	46.4	na
Netherlands	45.9[b]	44.1[b]	−1.6[b]
Portugal	38.5	34.2	−1.2
Spain	32.8[b]	28.7[b]	−2.9[b]
Sweden	39.3	39.4	0.1
United Kingdom	36.0	36.0	0.0
EU candidates			
Bulgaria	35.3	33.7	0.6
Cyprus	na	na	na
Czech Republic	36.8	32.7	−3.0
Estonia	31.4	30.1	−0.2
Hungary	40.2	36.0	−3.5
Latvia	31.6	28.6	−2.7
Lithuania	27.6	24.6	−1.3
Malta	na	na	na
Poland	34.6	31.3	−0.3
Romania	34.2	29.6	−4.0
Slovak Republic	40.5	35.6	−3.0
Slovenia	40.2	38.6	−1.3
Turkey	39.4	28.1	−11.4
EFTA countries			
Iceland	na	na	na
Norway	36.5	41.3	−3.9
Switzerland	26.7	25.4	3.0
Other countries			
Canada	20.3	21.8	1.3
Japan	15.3[b]	14.0[b]	−1.5[b]
Russian Federation	22.9	24.6	3.9
United States	19.2	21.5	2.4

[a] Includes grants.
[b] The figure is for 1999.

Table A5.10 Exports and imports of goods and services, current account balance and international reserves (US$ bn)

	Exports		Imports		Current account balance		Gross international reserves	
	1980	2001	1980	2001	1980	2001	1980	2001
EU countries								
Austria	26.7	99.8	29.9	99.8	−3.9	−4.1	17.7	15.6
Belgium[a]	70.5	213.8	74.3	203.1	−4.9	9.4	28.0	15.6
Denmark	220.0	77.9	21.7	67.5	−1.9	4.1	4.4	17.7
Finland	16.8	48.8	17.3	38.4	−1.4	8.6	2.5	8.4
France	153.2	371.8	156.0	351.0	−4.2	21.4	75.6	58.6
Germany[b]	224.2	657.5	226.0	619.9	−13.3	2.4	104.7	82.0
Greece	8.1	30.1	11.1	41.3	−2.2	−9.4	3.6	6.2
Ireland	9.6	95.6	12.0	83.2	−2.1	−1.0	3071	5.6
Italy	97 298	300.0	110.3	283.9	−10.9	−0.2	62.4	46.2
Netherlands	90.4	255.9	91.6	238.0	−0.9	3.7	37.6	16.9
Portugal	6.7	34.6	10.1	45.0	−1.1	−10.0	13.9	15.1
Spain	32.2	175.3	38.0	182.6	−5.9	−15.1	20.5	34.2
Sweden	38.2	98.2	39.9	85.4	−4.3	6.7	7.0	15.6
United Kingdom	146.1	385.8	134.2	418.0	6.9	−30.3	31.8	40.4
EU candidates								
Bulgaria	9.3	7.5	8.0	8.6	1.0	−0.9	na	3.7
Cyprus	na	na	na	na	na	na	na	na
Czech Republic	na	40.5	na	42.1	na	−2.6	na	14.5
Estonia	0.7[c]	5.0	0.7[c]	5.2	na	−0.4	0.2[c]	0.8
Hungary	9.7	35.8	9.2	35.6	−0.5	−1.1	1.2[c]	10.8
Latvia	1.1[c]	3.4	1.0[c]	4.3	na	−0.7	na	1.2
Lithuania	na	6.1	na	6.7	na	−0.6	0.1[c]	1.7
Malta	na	na	na	na	na	na	na	na
Poland	16.1	51.4	17.8	58.3	−3.4	−5.4	0.6	26.6
Romania	12.1	13.4	13.7	14.1	−2.4	−2.3	2.5	6.4
Slovak Republic	na	15.1	na	16.8	na	−0.7	na	4.5
Slovenia	7.9[c]	11.3	6.9[c]	11.4	na	0.0	0.1[c]	4.4
Turkey	3.6	50.4	8.1	45.9	−3.4	3.4	3.3	19.9
EFTA countries								
Iceland	na	na	na	na	na	na	na	na
Norway	27.3	77.7	23.8	49.1	1.1	26.0	6.8	15.8
Switzerland	48.6	123.6	51.8	109.5	−0.2	22.6	64.8	51.5
Other countries								
Canada	75.0	304.5	70.3	268.5	−6.1	19.5	15.5	34.3
Japan	147.0	448.1	157.0	421.6	−10.8	187.8	39.0	402.0
Russian Federation[c]	53.9[c]	112.5	48.9[c]	73.2	na	34.6	na	36.3
United States	271.8	998.0	290.7	1356.3	2.2	−393.4	171.4	131.1

[a] Includes Luxembourg.   [b] Data prior to 1990 refer to West Germany before unification.   [c] Data is for 1990.

Table A5.11 Official development assistance and gross foreign direct investment

	Net official development assistance						Gross foreign direct investment in US$ bn	
	Amount in US$ m[a]			Percentage of donor country GNI				
	1975	1985	2001	1975	1985	2001	1990	2001
EU countries								
Austria	79	248	533	0.21	0.38	0.29	0.7	5.9
Belgium	378	440	867	0.59	0.55	0.37	na	73.6
Denmark	205	440	1 634	0.58	0.80	1.03	1.1	7.2
Finland	48	211	389	0.18	0.40	0.32	0.8	3.7
France	2 093	3 995	4 198	0.62	0.78	0.32	13.2	52.5
Germany	1 689[a]	2 942[a]	4 990	0.40[a]	0.47[a]	0.27	2.5	31.5
Greece	na	−11	202	na	0.10	0.17	1.0	1.6
Ireland	8	39	287	0.09	0.24	0.33	0.6	22.8[b]
Italy	182	1 098	1 627	0.11	0.26	0.15	6.4	14.9
Luxembourg	na	na	141	na	na	0.82	na	na
Netherlands	608	1 136	3 172	0.75	0.91	0.82	12.4	51.2
Portugal	na	−101	268	na	0.50	0.25	2.6	5.9
Spain	na	0	1 737	na	0.00	0.30	14.0	21.5
Sweden	566	840	1 666	0.82	0.86	0.81	2.0	13.1
United Kingdom	904	1 530	4 579	0.39	0.33	0.32	32.5	63.1
EU candidates								
Bulgaria	na	na	na	na	na	na	0.0	0.7
Cyprus	na	na	na	na	na	na	na	na
Czech Republic	na	na	na	na	na	na	0.2	4.9
Estonia	na	na	na	na	na	na	0.1	0.5
Hungary	na	na	na	na	na	na	0.0	2.4
Latvia	na	na	na	na	na	na	0.0	0.2
Lithuania	na	na	na	na	na	na	0.0	0.5
Malta	na	na	na	na	na	na	na	na
Poland	na	na	na	na	na	na	0.1	5.7
Romania	na	na	na	na	na	na	0.0	1.2
Slovak Republic	na	na	na	na	na	na	0.0	1.5
Slovenia	na	na	na	na	na	na	na	0.5
Turkey	na	−175	na	na	0.60	na	684	3.3
EFTA countries								
Iceland	na	na	na	na	na	na	na	na
Norway	184	574	1 346	0.66	1.01	0.80	1 003	2.2
Switzerland	104	302	908	0.19	0.31	0.34	4 961	8.6
Other countries								
Canada	880	1 631	1 533	0.54	0.49	0.22	7.6	27.4
Japan	1 148	3 797	9 847	0.23	0.49	0.23	1.8	6.2
Russian Federation	na	na	na	na	na	na	0.0	2.5
United States	4 161	9 403	11 429	0.27	0.24	0.11	47.9	130.8

[a] Data refer to West Germany before unification.   [b] The figure is for 2000.

Table A5.12 Money and consumer price index

	Money and quasi money (annual % growth of M2)		Consumer price index (average annual % growth)		Interest rates (2000)	
	1990	2001	1990	2001	Short term	Long term
EU countries					4.5	5.4
Austria	a	a	3.2	2.2	3.3[b]	5.6
Belgium	a	a	2.9	1.9	3.5[b]	5.6
Denmark	6.5	3.6	5.6	2.1	4.4	5.6
Finland	a	a	6.2	1.6	3.2[b]	5.5
France	a	a	5.8	1.6	3.3[b]	5.4
Germany	a	a	2.2	2.2	3.4	5.3
Greece	a	a	18.7	8.3	8.24	6.1
Ireland	a	a	6.8	2.4	5.8[b]	5.5
Italy	a	a	9.1	3.5	5.2[b]	5.6
Luxembourg	a	a			na	5.5
Netherlands	a	a	2.0	2.4	3.2[b]	5.4
Portugal	a	a	17.1	4.3	4.3[b]	5.6
Spain	a	a	9.0	3.7	4.3[b]	5.5
Sweden	0.8	1.9	7.0	1.8	3.8	5.4
United Kingdom	10.5	8.6	5.8	2.8	5.9	5.3
EU candidates						
Bulgaria	53.8	26.7	6.3	105.3	na	na
Cyprus	na	na	na	na	na	na
Czech Republic	na	11.2	na	7.3	na	na
Estonia	76.5	23.0	na	18.9	na	na
Hungary	29.2	16.6	9.6	19.2	na	na
Latvia	na	19.8	na	25.0	na	na
Lithuania	na	21.4	na	27.0	na	na
Malta	na	na	na	na	na	na
Poland	160.1	15.0	50.9	23.1	na	na
Romania	26.4	46.2	na	92.8	na	na
Slovak Republic	na	11.9	na	8.5	na	na
Slovenia	123.0	30.4	na	22.0	na	na
Turkey	53.2	86.2	44.9	77.9	na	na
EFTA countries						
Iceland	na	na	na	na	12.0	na
Norway	5.6	8.7	7.4	2.2	6.6	na
Switzerland	0.8	3.9	2.9	1.5	2.8	na
Other countries						
Canada	7.8	6.5	5.3	1.7	5.5	na
Japan	8.2	2.2	1.7	0.6	0.1	na
Russian Federation	na	36.1	na	85.9	na	na
United States	4.9	14.0	4.2	2.7	6.2	na

[a] Member of the euro (see text and chapter).   [b] The figure is for 1998.

Table A5.13 Exports to EU (12, 15) countries (except for Turkey, data for the candidates is too meagre to warrant inclusion)

Exporting country	Percentage share of total exports of exporting country						
	1957	1974	1981	1986	1990	1995	2000
EU countries							62.3
Austria	na	na	na	60.1	65.2	65.5	61.7
Belgium[a]	46.1	69.9	70.0	72.9	75.1	76.5	75.0
Denmark	31.2	43.1	46.7	46.8	52.1	66.7	67.2
Finland	na	na	na	38.3	46.9	57.5	55.7
France	25.1	53.2	48.2	57.8	62.7	63.0	61.4
Germany	29.2	53.2	46.9	50.8	53.6	57.1	56.5
Greece	52.5	50.1	43.3	63.5	64.0	59.1	43.4
Ireland	na	74.1	69.9	71.9	74.8	73.4	62.9
Italy	24.9	45.4	43.2	53.5	58.2	56.8	54.9
Luxembourg							83.9
Netherlands	41.6	70.8	71.2	75.7	76.5	79.9	78.7
Portugal	22.2	48.2	53.7	68.0	73.5	80.1	79.4
Spain	29.8	47.4	43.0	60.9	64.9	67.2	69.4
Sweden	na	na	na	50.0	54.3	59.3	55.9
United Kingdom	14.6	33.4	41.3	47.9	52.6	59.8	56.9
EU candidate							
Turkey	na	na	47.3[b]	44.0	53.3	51.3	na
EFTA countries							
Iceland	na	na	52.2[b]	na	na	62.7	67.2
Norway	na	na	83.5	65.1	64.9	77.9	76.5
Switzerland	na	na	60.9	54.9	58.1	62.1	56.8
Other countries							
Canada	9.3	12.6	10.7	6.8	8.1	5.9	4.1
Japan	na	10.7	12.4	14.8	18.8	15.9	15.2
Russian Federation	na	na	na	na	na	33.7	na
United States	15.3	21.9	22.4	24.5	25.0	21.2	20.0[c]

[a] Except for 2000, includes Luxembourg.
[b] The figure is for 1980.
[c] The figure is for 1999.

Table A5.14 Imports from EU (12, 15) countries (except for Turkey, data for the candidates is too meagre to warrant inclusion)

Importing country	Percentage share of total imports of importing country						
	1957	1974	1981	1986	1990	1995	2000
EU countries							**58.8**
Austria	na	na	na	66.9	68.6	75.9	68.5
Belgium[a]	43.5	66.1	59.3	69.9	70.7	72.2	69.3
Denmark	31.2	45.5	47.9	53.2	53.7	71.0	68.5
Finland	na	na	na	43.1	46.3	65.0	61.9
France	21.4	47.6	48.2	64.4	64.8	68.5	64.7
Germany	23.5	48.1	48.2	54.2	54.1	58.6	55.4
Greece	40.8	43.3	50.0	58.3	64.1	68.8	58.7
Ireland	na	68.3	74.7	73.0	70.8	63.9	61.3
Italy	21.4	42.4	40.7	55.4	57.4	60.5	56.3
Luxembourg							82.9
Netherlands	41.1	57.4	52.4	61.0	59.9	63.2	51.3
Portugal	37.1	43.5	38.0	58.8	69.1	73.9	74.0
Spain	21.3	35.8	29.0	51.3	59.1	67.5	64.6
Sweden	na	na	na	57.2	55.3	68.6	64.1
United Kingdom	12.1	30.0	39.4	50.4	51.0	55.3	49.3
EU candidate							
Turkey	na	na	33.8[b]	41.0	41.9	47.9	na
EFTA countries							
Iceland	na	na	51.7[b]	na	na	58.3	56.3
Norway	na	na	70.8[b]	50.1	45.8	71.7	63.6
Switzerland	na	na	74.5[b]	73.0	71.7	79.7	71.3
Other countries							
Canada	4.2	6.9	8.0	11.3	11.5	11.0	10.0
Japan	na	6.4	6.0	11.1	15.0	14.7	11.8
Russian Federation	na	na	na	na	na	38.8	na
United States	11.7	9.0	16.0	20.5	18.6	17.8	18.1[d]

[a] Except for 2000, includes Luxembourg.
[b] The figure is for 1980.
[c] The figure is for 1994.
[d] The figure is for 1999.

Table A5.15 Distribution of income or consumption[a]

| | Survey year | Percentage share of income or consumption | | |
		Gini index	Lowest 10%	Highest 10%
EU countries				
Austria	1995	30.5	2.3	22.4
Belgium	1996	25.0	2.9	22.6
Denmark	1997	24.7	2.6	21.3
Finland	1995	25.6	4.1	20.9
France	1995	32.7	2.8	25.1
Germany	1998	38.2	2.0	28.0
Greece	1998	35.4	2.9	28.5
Ireland	1987	35.9	2.5	27.4
Italy	1998	36.0	1.9	27.4
Luxembourg	1998	30.8	3.2	24.7
Netherlands	1994	32.6	2.8	25.1
Portugal	1997	38.5	2.0	29.8
Spain	1990	32.5	2.8	25.2
Sweden	1995	25.0	3.4	20.1
United Kingdom	1995	36.0	2.1	27.5
EU candidates				
Bulgaria	2001	31.9	2.4	23.7
Cyprus	na	na	na	na
Czech Republic	1996	25.4	4.3	22.4
Estonia	1998	37.6	3.0	29.8
Hungary	1998	24.4	4.1	20.5
Latvia	1998	32.4	2.9	25.9
Lithuania	2000	36.3	3.2	24.9
Malta	na	na	na	na
Poland	1998	31.6	3.2	24.7
Romania	2000	30.3	3.3	23.6
Slovak Republic	1996	25.8	3.1	20.9
Slovenia	1998	28.4	3.9	23.0
Turkey	2000	40.0	2.3	30.7
EFTA countries				
Iceland	na	na	na	na
Norway	1995	25.8	4.1	21.8
Switzerland	1992	33.1	2.6	25.2
Other countries				
Canada	1997	31.5	2.7	23.9
Japan	1993	24.9	4.8	21.7
Russian Federation	2000	45.6	1.8	36.0
United States	1997	40.8	1.8	30.5

[a] The data refer to income shares by percentiles of population and are ranked by per capita income.

Table A5.16 Average tariffs (%), 1958[a]

	Benelux	France	West Germany	Italy	EC (six)	Denmark	United Kingdom	Canada	United States
Instruments (86)	13	22	8	17	16	3	27	19	29
Footwear (851)	20	21	10	21	19	19	25	24	19
Clothing (84)	20	26	13	25	21	19	26	25	$32^{1}/_{2}$
Furniture (821)	13	23	8	21	17	11	20	25	24
Building parts and fittings (81)	15	19	8	25	17	8	15	16	20
Transport equipment (73)	17	29	12	34	22	8	25	17	13
Electric machinery, etc. (72)	11	19	6	21	15	8	23	18	20
Machinery other than electric (71)	8	18	5	20	13	6	17	9	12
Manufactures of metals (699)	11	20	10	23	16	6	21	18	23
Ordnance (691)	9	14	7	17	11	1	22	13	26
Iron and steel (681)	5	13	7	17	10	1	14	12	13
Silver, platinum, gems, jewellery (67)	5	13	3	7	6	5	11	13	29
Non-metallic mineral manufactures (66)	12	16	6	21	13	5	17	21	13
Textiles, etc. except clothing (65)	14	19	11	20	16	9	23	21	26
Paper, paperboard, etc. (64)	14	16	8	18	15	6	13	17	$10^{1}/_{2}$
Wood manufactures, etc. except furniture (63)	11	19	7	22	16	4	15	12	18
Rubber manufactures (62)	17	17	10	19	18	8	21	18	18
Leather, etc. (61)	11	11	12	18	12	11	16	17	17
Chemicals (59)	7	16	8	17	12	4	15	11	24

[a] The figures are subject to the reservations stated in the source. The figures in parentheses refer to SITC classification.
Source: Adapted from Political and Economic Planning (1962) *Atlantic Tariffs and Trade*, Routledge. Reprinted by permission of Thomson Publishing Services

Theory and measurement of economic integration

Part Two of this book is devoted to the discussion of the theoretical aspects of the EU and to the measurement of the impact of the formation of the EU on trade, production and factor mobility (the policy aspects of this are discussed in Chapter 18).

The whole part is basically concerned with three concepts: 'trade creation', 'trade diversion' and 'unilateral tariff reduction'. These can be illustrated rather simplistically as follows. In Table II.1 the cost of beef per kg is given in pence for the United Kingdom, France and New Zealand. With a 50% non-discriminatory tariff rate the cheapest source of supply of beef for the United Kingdom consumer is the home producer. When the United Kingdom and France form a customs union, the cheapest source of supply becomes France. Hence the United Kingdom saves 10p per kg of beef, making a total saving of £1 million for ten million kg (obviously an arbitrarily chosen quantity). This is 'trade creation': *the replacement of expensive domestic production by cheaper imports from the partner.*

In Table II.2 the situation is different for butter as a result of a lower initial non-discriminatory tariff rate (25%) by the United Kingdom. Before the customs union, New Zealand is the cheapest source of supply for the UK consumer. After the customs union, France becomes the cheapest source. There is a total loss to the United Kingdom of £1 million, since the tariff revenue is claimed by the government. This is 'trade diversion': *the replacement of cheaper initial imports from the outside world by expensive imports from the partner.*

In Tables II.3 and II.4 there are two commodities: beef and butter. The cost of beef per kg is the same as in the previous example and so is the cost of butter per kg. Note that Table II.3 starts from the same position as Table II.1 and Table II.4 from the same position as Table II.2. Here the United Kingdom does not form a customs union with France; rather, it reduces its tariff rate by 80% on a non-discriminatory basis, i.e. it adopts a policy of unilateral tariff reduction.

Now consider Tables II.3 and II.4 in comparison with Tables II.1 and II.2. The total cost for Tables II.1 and II.2 before the customs union = £9 million + £7 million = £16 million.

Table II.1 Beef

	United Kingdom	France	New Zealand
The cost per unit (p)	90	80	70
UK domestic price with a 50% tariff rate (p)	90	120	105
UK domestic price when the UK and France form a customs union (p)	90	80	105

Total cost before the customs union = 90p × 10 million kg = £9 million.
Total cost after the customs union = 80p × 10 million kg = £8 million.
Total savings for the UK consumer = £1 million.

Table II.2 Butter

	United Kingdom	France	New Zealand
The cost per unit (p)	90	80	70
UK domestic price with a 25% tariff rate (p)	90	100	87½
UK domestic price when the UK and France form a customs union (p)	90	80	87½

Total cost to the UK government before the customs union = 70p × 10 million kg = £7 million.
Total cost to the UK after the customs union = 80p × 10 million kg = £8 million.
Total loss to the UK government = £1 million.

Table II.3 Beef

	United Kingdom	France	New Zealand
The cost per unit (p)	90	80	70
UK domestic price with a 50% tariff rate (p)	90	120	105
UK domestic price with a non-discriminatory tariff reduction of 80% (i.e. tariff rate becomes 10%) (p)	90	88	77

Total cost to the UK before the tariff reduction = 90p × 10 million kg = £9 million.
Total cost to the UK after tariff reduction = 70p × 10 million kg = £7 million.
Total savings for the UK = £2 million.

Table II.4 Butter

	United Kingdom	France	New Zealand
The cost per unit (p)	90	80	70
UK domestic price with a 25% tariff rate (p)	90	100	87½
UK domestic price with a non-discriminatory tariff reduction of 80% (i.e. tariff rate becomes 5%) (p)	90	84	73½

Total cost to the UK before the tariff reduction = 70p × 10 million kg = £7 million.
Total cost to the UK after the tariff reduction = 70p × 10 million kg = £7 million.
Total savings for the UK = nil.

The total cost for Tables II.1 and II.2 after the customs union = £8 million + £8 million = £16 million.

The total cost for Tables II.3 and II.4 after the customs union = £7 million + £7 million = £14 million.

This gives a saving of £2 million in comparison with the customs union situation. Hence, a non-discriminatory tariff reduction is more economical for the United Kingdom than the formation of a customs union with France. Therefore, *unilateral tariff reduction is superior to customs union formation.*

This dangerously simple analysis (since a number of simplistic assumptions are implicit in the analysis and all the data are chosen to prove the point) has been the inspiration of a massive literature on customs union theory. Admittedly, some of the contributions are misguided in that they concentrate on a non-problem due to definitional mis-specification, as explained in the following chapter.

Chapter 6 tackles the basic concepts of trade creation, trade diversion and unilateral tariff reduction, considers the implications of domestic distortions and scale economies for the basic analysis and discusses the terms of trade effects. Chapter 7 discusses the measurement of the theoretical concepts discussed in Chapter 6.

Chapter 6   The theory of economic integration

ALI EL-AGRAA

In reality, some existing schemes of economic integration, especially the EU, were either proposed or formed for political reasons even though the arguments popularly put forward in their favour were expressed in terms of possible economic gains. However, no matter what the motives for economic integration are, it is still necessary to analyse the economic implications of such geographically discriminatory groupings.

As mentioned in Chapter 1, at the customs union (CU) and free trade area (FTA) level, the *possible* sources of economic gain can be attributed to the following:

1 Enhanced efficiency in production made possible by increased specialization in accordance with the law of comparative advantage.
2 Increased production level due to better exploitation of economies of scale made possible by the increased size of the market.

3 An improved international bargaining position, made possible by the larger size, leading to better terms of trade.
4 Enforced changes in economic efficiency brought about by enhanced competition.
5 Changes affecting both the amount and quality of the factors of production arising from technological advances.

If the level of economic integration is to proceed beyond the CU level, to the economic union level, then further sources of gain become *possible* as a result of:

6 Factor mobility across the borders of member nations.
7 The coordination of monetary and fiscal policies.
8 The goals of near-full employment, higher rates of economic growth and better income distribution becoming unified targets.

I shall now discuss these considerations in some detail.

6.1   The customs union aspects

6.1.1 The basic concepts

Before the theory of second best was introduced, it used to be the accepted tradition that CU formation should be encouraged. The rationale for this was that since free trade maximized world welfare and since CU formation was a move towards free trade, CUs increased welfare even though they did not maximize it. This rationale certainly lies behind the guidelines of the GATT–WTO Article XXIV (see Appendix 1.1, p. 20) which permits the formation of CUs and FTAs as the special exceptions to the rules against international discrimination.

Viner (1950) and Byé (1950) challenged this proposition by stressing the point that CU formation is by no means equivalent to a move to free trade since it amounts to free trade *between* the members and

protection *vis-à-vis* the outside world. This combination of free trade and protectionism could result in trade creation and/or trade diversion. Trade creation (TC) is the replacement of expensive domestic production by cheaper imports from a partner and trade diversion (TD) is the replacement of cheaper initial imports from the outside world by more expensive imports from a partner. Viner and Byé stressed the point that trade creation is beneficial since it does not affect the rest of the world, while trade diversion is harmful; it is the relative strength of these two effects that determines whether or not CU formation should be advocated. It is therefore important to understand the implications of these concepts.

Assuming perfect competition in both the commodity and factor markets, automatic full employment of all resources, costless adjustment procedures,

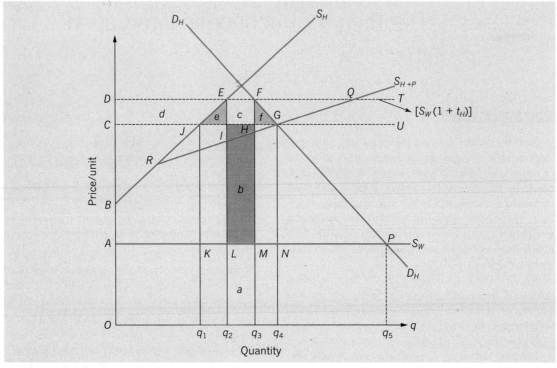

Figure 6.1 Trade creation and trade diversion

perfect factor mobility nationally but perfect immobility across national boundaries, prices determined by cost, three countries H (the home country), P (the potential CU partner) and W (the outside world), plus all the traditional assumptions employed in tariff theory, we can use a simple diagram to illustrate these two concepts.

In Figure 6.1, I use partial-equilibrium diagrams because it has been demonstrated that partial- and general-equilibrium analyses are, under certain circumstances, equivalent – see El-Agraa and Jones (1981). S_W is W's perfectly elastic tariff-free supply curve for this commodity; S_H is H's supply curve while S_{H+P} is the joint H and P tariff-free supply curve. With a non-discriminatory tariff (t) imposition by H of AD ($= t_H$), the effective supply curve facing H is $BREFQT$, i.e. its own supply curve up to E and W's, subject to the tariff $[S_W(1 + t_H)]$ after that. The domestic price is therefore OD, which gives domestic production of Oq_2, domestic consumption of Oq_3 and imports of q_2q_3. H pays q_2LMq_3 ($= a$) for the imports while the domestic consumer pays q_2EFq_3 ($a + b + c$) with the difference ($LEFM = b + c$) being the tariff revenue

which accrues to the H government. This government revenue can be viewed as a transfer from the consumers to the government with the implication that, when the government spends it, the marginal valuation of that expenditure should be exactly equal to its valuation by the private consumers so that no distortions should occur.

If H and W form a CU, the free trade position will be restored so that Oq_5 will be consumed in H and this amount will be imported from W. Hence free trade is obviously the ideal situation. But if H and P form a CU, the tariff imposition will still apply to W while it is removed from P. The effective supply curve in this case is $BRGQT$. The union price falls to OC resulting in a fall in domestic production to Oq_1, an increase in consumption to Oq_4 and an increase in imports to q_1q_4. These imports now come from P.

The welfare implications of these changes can be examined by employing the concepts of consumers' and producers' surpluses. As a result of increased consumption, consumers' surplus rises by $CDFG$ ($= d + e + c + f$). Part of this (d) is a fall in producers' surplus due to the decline in domestic production and another part (c) is a portion of the tariff revenue now transferred back to the consumer subject to the same condition of equal marginal valuation. This leaves e and f as gains from CU formation. However, before we conclude whether or not these triangles represent net gains we need to consider the overall effects more carefully.

The fall in domestic production from Oq_2 to Oq_1 leads to increased imports of q_1q_2. These cost q_1JIq_2 to import from P while they originally cost q_1JEq_2 to produce domestically. (Note that these resources are assumed to be employed elsewhere in the economy without any adjustment costs or redundancies.) There is therefore a saving of e. The increase in consumption from Oq_3 to Oq_4 leads to new imports of q_3q_4 which cost q_3HGq_4 to import from P. These give a welfare satisfaction to the consumer equal to q_3FGq_4. There is therefore an increase in satisfaction of f. However, the *initial* imports of q_2q_3 cost the country a, but these imports now come from P costing $a + b$. Therefore these imports lead to a loss in government revenue of b (c being a retransfer). It follows that the triangle gains $(e + f)$ have to be compared with the loss of tariff revenue (b) before a definite conclusion can be made regarding whether or not the net effect of CU formation has been one of gain or loss.

It should be apparent that q_2q_3 represents, in terms of our definition, trade diversion, and $q_1q_2 + q_3q_4$ represents trade creation, or alternatively that areas $e + f$ are trade creation (benefits) while area b is trade diversion (loss). (The reader should note that I am using Johnson's 1974 definition so as to avoid the unnecessary literature relating to a trade-diverting welfare-improving CU promoted by Gehrels (1956–1957), Lipsey (1960) and Bhagwati (1971).) It is, then, obvious that trade creation is economically desirable while trade diversion is undesirable: hence Viner and Byé's conclusion that it is the relative strength of these two effects which should determine whether or not CU formation is beneficial or harmful.

The reader should note that if the initial price is that given by the intersection of D_H and S_H (due to a higher tariff rate), the CU would result in pure trade creation since the tariff rate is prohibitive. If the price is initially OC (due to a lower tariff rate), then CU formation would result in pure trade diversion. It should also be apparent that the size of the gains and losses depends on the price elasticities of S_H, S_{H+P} and D_H and on the divergence between S_W and S_{H+P}, i.e. cost differences.

6.1.2 The Cooper–Massell criticism

Viner and Byé's conclusion was challenged by Cooper and Massell (1965a). They suggested that the reduction in price from OD to OC should be considered in two stages: first, reduce the tariff level indiscriminately (i.e. for both W and P) to AC which gives the same union price and production, consumption and import changes; second, introduce the CU starting from the new price OC. The effect of these two steps is that the gains from the trade creation $(e + f)$ still accrue while the losses from trade diversion (b) no longer apply since the new effective supply curve facing H is BJGU which ensures that imports continue to come from W at the cost of a. In addition, the new imports due to trade creation $(q_1q_2 + q_3q_4)$ now cost less, leading to a further gain of KJIL plus MHGN. Cooper and Massell then conclude that *a policy of unilateral tariff reduction (UTR) is superior to customs union formation*. This criticism was challenged by Wonnacott and Wonnacott (1981), but their position was questioned by El-Agraa and Jones (2000a, b), although El-Agraa (2002a) demonstrates that it can be validated when WTO's Article XXIV rules were incorporated into the analysis; I shall return to these considerations in Section 6.1.7 since a different theoretical model is needed for these analyses.

6.1.3 Further contributions

Immediately following the Cooper–Massell criticism came two independent but somewhat similar contributions to the theory of CUs. The first development is by Cooper and Massell (1965b) themselves, the essence of which is that two countries acting together can do better than each acting in isolation. The second is by Johnson (1965b) which is a private plus social costs and benefits analysis expressed in political economy terms. Both contributions utilize a 'public good' argument, with Cooper and Massell's expressed in practical terms and Johnson's in theoretical terms. However, since the Johnson approach is expressed in familiar terms this section is devoted to it – space limitations do not permit a consideration of both.

Johnson's method is based on four major assumptions:

1 Governments use tariffs to achieve certain non-economic (political, etc.) objectives.

2 Actions taken by governments are aimed at offsetting differences between private and social costs. They are, therefore, rational efforts.
3 Government policy is a rational response to the demands of the electorate.
4 Countries have a preference for industrial production.

In addition to these assumptions, Johnson makes a distinction between private and public consumption goods, real income (utility enjoyed from both private and public consumption, where consumption is the sum of planned consumption expenditure and planned investment expenditure) and real product (defined as total production of privately appropriable goods and services).

These assumptions have important implications. First, competition among political parties will make the government adopt policies that will tend to maximize consumer satisfaction from both 'private' and 'collective' consumption goods. Satisfaction is obviously maximized when the *rate of satisfaction per unit of resources is the same in both types of consumption goods*. Second, 'collective preference' for industrial production implies that consumers are willing to expand industrial production (and industrial employment) beyond what it would be under free international trade.

Tariffs are the main source of financing this policy simply because GATT–WTO regulations rule out the use of export subsidies, and domestic political considerations make tariffs, rather than the more efficient production subsidies, the usual instruments of protection.

Protection will be carried to the point where the *value of the marginal utility derived from collective consumption of domestic and industrial activity is just equal to the marginal excess private cost of protected industrial production.*

The marginal excess cost of protected industrial production consists of two parts: the marginal production cost and the marginal private consumption cost. The marginal production cost is equal to the proportion by which domestic cost exceeds world market costs. In a very simple model this is equal to the tariff rate. The marginal private consumption cost is equal to the loss of consumer surplus due to the fall in consumption brought about by the tariff rate which is necessary to induce the marginal unit of domestic production. This depends on the tariff rate and the price elasticities of supply and demand.

In equilibrium, the proportional marginal excess private cost of protected production measures the marginal 'degree of preference' for industrial production. This is illustrated in Figure 6.2 where S_W is the world supply curve at world market prices; D_H is the constant-utility demand curve (at free trade private utility level); S_H is the domestic supply curve; S_{H+u} is the marginal private cost curve of protected industrial production, including the excess private consumption cost (*FE* is the first component of marginal excess cost – determined by the excess marginal cost of domestic production in relation to the free trade situation due to the tariff imposition (*AB*) – and the area *GED* (= *IHJ*) is the second component which is the dead loss in consumer surplus due to the tariff imposition); the height of *vv* above S_W represents the marginal value of industrial production in collective consumption and *vv* represents the preference for industrial production which is assumed to yield a diminishing marginal rate of satisfaction.

The maximization of *real* income is achieved at the intersection of *vv* with S_{H+u} requiring the use of tariff rate *AB/OA* to increase industrial production from Oq_1 to Oq_2 and involving the marginal degree of preference for industrial production *v*. Note that the higher the value of *v*, the higher the tariff rate, and that the degree of protection will tend to vary inversely with the ability to compete with foreign industrial producers. It is also important to note that, in equilibrium, the government is maximizing real income, not real product: maximization of real income makes it necessary to sacrifice real product in order to gratify the preference for collective consumption of industrial production. It is also important to note that this analysis is not confined to net importing countries. It is equally applicable to net exporters, but lack of space prevents such elaboration – see El-Agraa (1984b) for a detailed explanation.

The above model helps to explain the significance of Johnson's assumptions. It does not, however, throw any light on the CU issue. To make the model useful for this purpose it is necessary to alter some of the assumptions. Let us assume that industrial production is not one aggregate but a variety of products in which countries have varying degrees of comparative advantage, that countries differ in their overall comparative advantage in industry as compared with non-industrial production, that no country has monopoly–monopsony power (conditions for optimum tariffs do not exist) and that no export subsidies are allowed (GATT–WTO).

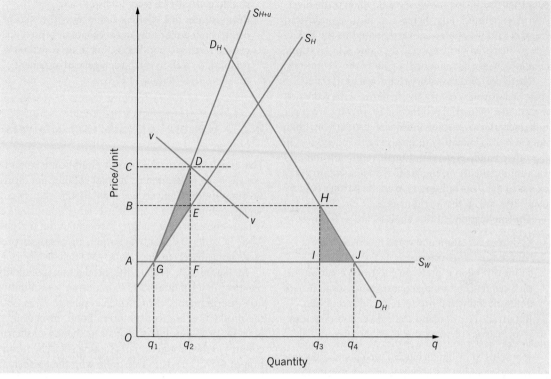

Figure 6.2 Marginal 'degree of preference' for industrial production

The variety of industrial production allows countries to be both importers and exporters of industrial products. This, in combination with the 'preference for industrial production', will motivate each country to practise some degree of protection.

Given the third assumption, a country can gratify its preference for industrial production only by protecting the domestic producers of the commodities it imports (import-competing industries). Hence the condition for equilibrium remains the same: $vv = S_{H+u}$. The condition must now be reckoned differently, however: S_{H+u} is slightly different because, first, the protection of import-competing industries will reduce exports of both industrial and non-industrial products (for balance of payments purposes). Hence, in order to increase total industrial production by one unit it will be necessary to increase protected industrial production by more than one unit so as to compensate for the induced loss of industrial exports. Second, the protection of import-competing industries reduces industrial exports by raising their production costs (because of perfect factor mobility). The stronger this effect, *ceteris paribus*, the higher the marginal excess cost of industrial production. This will be greater the larger the industrial sector compared with the non-industrial sector and the larger the protected industrial sector relative to the exporting industrial sector.

If the world consists of two countries, one must be a net exporter and the other necessarily a net importer of industrial products and the balance of payments is settled in terms of the non-industrial sector. Therefore for each country the prospective gain from reciprocal tariff reduction must lie in the expansion of exports of industrial products. The reduction of a country's own tariff rate is therefore a source of loss which can be compensated for only by a reduction of the other country's tariff rate (for an alternative, orthodox, explanation see El-Agraa, 1979b; 1979c).

What if there are more than two countries? If reciprocal tariff reductions are arrived at on a 'most-favoured nation' basis, then the reduction of a country's tariff rate will increase imports from *all* the other countries. If the tariff rate reduction is, however, discriminatory (starting from a position of non-discrimination), then there are two advantages: first, a country can offer its partner an increase in exports of industrial products without any loss of its own industrial production by diverting imports from third countries (trade diversion); second, when trade diversion is exhausted, any increase in partner industrial exports to this country is exactly equal to the reduction in industrial production in the same country (trade creation), hence eliminating the gain to third countries.

Therefore, discriminatory reciprocal tariff reduction costs each partner country less, in terms of the reduction in domestic industrial production (if any) incurred per unit increase in partner industrial production, than does non-discriminatory reciprocal tariff reduction. On the other hand, preferential tariff reduction imposes an additional cost on the tariff-reducing country: the excess of the costs of imports from the partner country over their cost in the world market.

The implications of this analysis are as follows:

1 Both trade creation and trade diversion yield a gain to the CU partners.
2 Trade diversion is preferable to trade creation for the preference-granting country since a sacrifice of domestic industrial production is not required.
3 Both trade creation and trade diversion may lead to increased efficiency due to economies of scale.

Johnson's contribution has not been popular because of the nature of his assumptions. For example, an:

economic rationale for customs unions on public goods grounds can only be established if for political or some such reasons governments are denied the use of direct production subsidies – and while this may be the case in certain countries at certain periods in their economic evolution, there would appear to be no acceptable reason why this

should generally be true. Johnson's analysis demonstrates that customs union and other acts of commercial policy may make economic sense under certain restricted conditions, but in no way does it establish or seek to establish a general argument for these acts. (Krauss, 1972)

6.1.4 General equilibrium analysis

The conclusions of the partial equilibrium analysis can easily be illustrated in general equilibrium terms. To simplify the analysis we shall assume that H is a 'small' country while P and W are 'large' countries, i.e. H faces constant t/t (t_p and t_w) throughout the analysis. Also, in order to avoid repetition, the analysis proceeds immediately to the Cooper–Massell proposition.

In Figure 6.3, HH is the production possibility frontier for H. Initially, H is imposing a prohibitive non-discriminatory tariff which results in P_1 as both the production and consumption point, given that t_w is the most favourable t/t, i.e. W is the most efficient country in the production of clothing (C). The formation of the CU leads to free trade with the partner, P, hence production moves to P_2 where t_p is at a tangent to HH, and consumption to C_3 where CIC_5 is at a tangent to t_p. A unilateral tariff reduction (UTR) which results in P_2 as the production point results in consumption at C_4 on CIC_6 (if the tariff revenue is returned to the consumers as a lump sum) or at C_3 (if the tariff is retained by the government). Note that at C_4 trade is with W only.

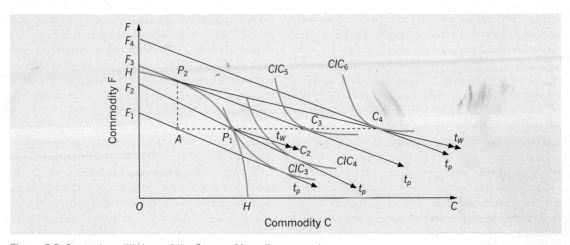

Figure 6.3 General equilibrium of the Cooper–Massell argument

Given standard analysis, it should be apparent that the situation of UTR and trade with W results in exports of AP_2 which are exchanged for imports of AC_4 of which C_3C_4 is the tariff revenue. In terms of Johnson's distinction between consumption and production gains and his method of calculating them (see El-Agraa, 1983b, Chapters 4 and 10), these effects can be expressed in relation to food (F) only. Given a Hicksian income compensation variation, it should be clear that: (i) F_1F_2 is the positive consumption effect; (ii) F_2F_3 is the production effect (positive due to curtailing production of the protected commodity); and (iii) F_3F_4 is the tariff revenue effect. Hence the difference between CU formation and a UTR (with the tariff revenue returned to the consumer) is the loss of tariff revenue F_3F_4 (C_4 compared with C_3). In other words, the consumption gain F_1F_2 is positive and applies in both cases but in the Cooper–Massell analysis the production effect comprises two parts: (i) a *pure* TC effect equal to F_2F_4; and (ii) a *pure* TD effect equal to F_3F_4. Hence F_2F_3 is the difference between these two effects and is, therefore, rightly termed the *net* TC effect.

Of course, the above analysis falls short of a general equilibrium one since the model does not endogenously determine the t/t (El-Agraa, 1983b, Chapter 5). However, as suggested above, such analysis would require the use of offer curves for all three countries both with and without tariffs. Unfortunately such an analysis is still awaited – the attempt by Vanek (1965) to derive an 'excess offer curve' for the potential union partners leads to no more than a specification of various possibilities; and the contention of Wonnacott and Wonnacott (1981) to have provided an analysis incorporating a tariff by W is unsatisfactory since they assume that W's offer curve is perfectly elastic – see Chapter 4 of El-Agraa (1999) and Section 6.1.7.

6.1.5 Dynamic effects

The so-called dynamic effects (Balassa, 1961) relate to the numerous means by which economic integration may influence the rate of growth of GNP of the participating nations. These ways include the following:

1 Scale economies made possible by the increased size of the market for both firms and industries operating below optimum capacity before integration occurs.

2 Economies external to the firm and industry which may have a downward influence on both specific and general cost structures.

3 The polarization effect, by which is meant the cumulative decline either in relative or absolute terms of the economic situation of a particular participating nation or of a specific region within it due either to the benefits of trade creation becoming concentrated in one region or to the fact that an area may develop a tendency to attract factors of production.

4 The influence on the location and volume of real investment.

5 The effect on economic efficiency and the smoothness with which trade transactions are carried out due to enhanced competition and changes in uncertainty.

Hence these dynamic effects include various and completely different phenomena. Apart from economies of scale, the possible gains are extremely long term and cannot be tackled in orthodox economic terms: for example, intensified competition leading to the adoption of best business practices and to an American type of attitude, etc. (Scitovsky, 1958), seems like a naïve sociopsychological abstraction that has no solid foundation with regard to either the aspirations of those countries contemplating economic integration or to its actually materializing.

Economies of scale can, however, be analysed in orthodox economic terms. In a highly simplistic model, like that depicted in Figure 6.4 where scale economies are internal to the industry, their effects can easily be demonstrated – a mathematical discussion can be found in, *inter alia*, Choi and Yu (1984), but the reader must be warned that the assumptions made about the nature of the economies concerned are extremely limited, e.g. H and P are 'similar'. $D_{H,P}$ is the identical demand curve for this commodity in both H and P and D_{H+P} is their joint demand curve; S_W is the world supply curve; AC_P and AC_H are the average cost curves for this commodity in P and H respectively. Note that the diagram is drawn in such a manner that W has constant average costs and is the most efficient supplier of this commodity. Hence free trade is the best policy resulting in price OA with consumption that is satisfied entirely by imports of Oq_4 in each of H and P giving a total of Oq_6.

If H and P impose tariffs, the only justification for this is that uncorrected distortions exist between the

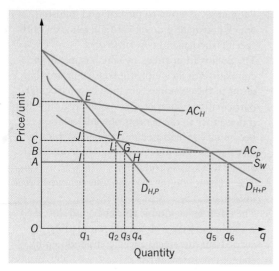

Figure 6.4 Internal economies of scale

privately and socially valued costs in these countries – see Jones (1979) and El-Agraa and Jones (1981). The best tariff rates to impose are Corden's (1972a) made-to-measure tariffs which can be defined as those that encourage domestic production to a level that just satisfies domestic consumption without giving rise to monopoly profits. These tariffs are equal to AD and AC for H and P respectively, resulting in Oq_1 and Oq_2 production in H and P respectively.

When H and P enter into a CU, P, being the cheaper producer, will produce the entire union output – Oq_5 – at a price OB. This gives rise to consumption in each of H and P of Oq_3 with gains of $BDEG$ and $BCFG$ for H and P respectively. Parts of these gains, $BDEI$ for H and $BCFL$ for P, are 'cost-reduction' effects. There is also a production gain for P and a production loss in H due to abandoning production altogether.

Whether or not CU formation can be justified in terms of the existence of economies of scale will depend on whether or not the net effect is a gain or a loss, since in this example P gains and H loses, as the loss from abandoning production in H must outweigh the consumption gain in order for the tariff to have been imposed in the first place. If the overall result is net gain, then the distribution of these gains becomes an important consideration. Alternatively, if economies of scale accrue to an integrated industry, then the locational distribution of the production units becomes an essential issue.

6.1.6 Domestic distortions

A substantial literature has tried to tackle the important question of whether or not the formation of a CU may be economically desirable when there are domestic distortions. Such distortions could be attributed to the presence of trade unions which negotiate wage rates in excess of the equilibrium rates or to governments introducing minimum wage legislation – both of which are widespread activities in most countries. It is usually assumed that the domestic distortion results in a *social* average cost curve which lies below the private one. Hence, in Figure 6.5, which is adapted from Figure 6.4, I have incorporated AC_H^s and AC_P^s as the *social* curves in the context of economies of scale and a separate representation of countries H and P.

Note that AC_H^s is drawn to be consistently above AP_W, while AC_P^s is below it for higher levels of output. Before the formation of a CU, H may have been adopting a made-to-measure tariff to protect its industry, but the first best policy would have been one of free trade, as argued in the previous section. The formation of the CU will therefore lead to the same effects as in the previous section, with the exception that the cost-reduction effect (Figure 5.5(a)) will be less by DD' times Oq_1. For P, the effects will be as follows:

1   As before, a consumption gain of area c.
2   A cost-reduction effect of area e due to calculations relating to social rather than private costs.
3   Gains from sales to H of areas d_1 and d_2, with d_1 being an income transfer from H to P, and d_2 the difference between domestic social costs in P and P_W – the world price.
4   The social benefits accruing from extra production made possible by the CU – area f – which is measured by the extra consumption multiplied by the difference between P_W and the domestic social costs.

However, this analysis does not lead to an economic rationale for the formation of CUs, since P could have used first best policy instruments to eliminate the divergence between private and social cost. This would have made AC_P^s the operative cost curve, and, assuming that D_{H+P+W} is the world demand curve, this would have led to a world price of OF and exports of q_3q_5 and q_5q_6 to H and W respectively, with obviously greater benefits than those offered by the

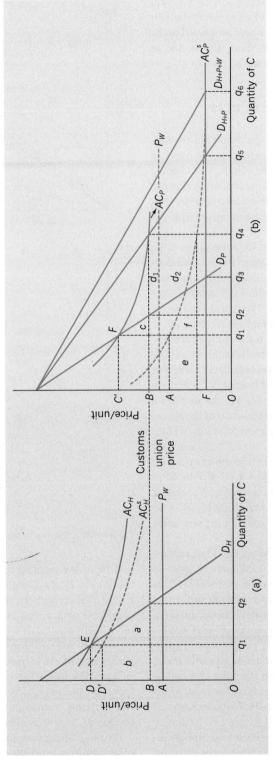

Figure 6.5 Social costs and economies of scale: (a) the home country; (b) the partner country

CU. Hence the economic rationale for the CU will have to depend on factors that can explain why first best instruments could not have been employed in the first instance (Jones, 1980). In short, this is not an absolute argument for CU formation.

6.1.7 Terms of trade effects

So far the analysis has been conducted on the assumption that CU formation has no effect on the terms of trade (t/t). This implies that the countries concerned are too insignificant to have any appreciable influence on the international economy. Particularly in the context of the EU and groupings of a similar size, this is a very unrealistic assumption.

The analysis of the effects of CU formation on the t/t is not only extremely complicated but is also unsatisfactory since a convincing model incorporating tariffs by all three areas of the world is still awaited – see Mundell (1964), Arndt (1968, 1969) and Wonnacott and Wonnacott (1981). To demonstrate this, let us consider Arndt's analysis, which is directly concerned with this issue, and the Wonnacotts' analysis, whose main concern is the Cooper–Massell criticism but which has some bearing on this matter.

In Figure 6.6, O_H, O_P and O_W are the respective offer curves of H, P and W. In section (a) of the figure, H is assumed to be the most efficient producer of commodity Y, while in section (b), H and P are assumed to be equally efficient. Assuming that the free trade t/t are given by OT_O, H will export q_6h_1 of Y to W in exchange for Oq_6 imports of commodity X, while P will export q_1p_1 of Y in exchange for Oq_1 of commodity X, with the sum of H and P's exports being exactly equal to OX_3.

When H imposes an *ad valorem* tariff (percentage tariff), its tariff revenue-distributed curve is assumed to be displaced to O'_H altering the t/t to OT'_1. This leads to a contraction of H's trade with W and, at the same time, increases P's trade with W. In section (a) of the figure, it is assumed that the net effect of H and P's trade changes (contraction in H's exports and expansion in P's) will result in a contraction in world trade. It should be apparent that, from H's point of view, the competition of P in its exports market has reduced the appropriateness of the Cooper–Massell alternative of a (non-discriminatory) UTR.

Note, however, that H's welfare may still be increased in these unfavourable circumstances, provided

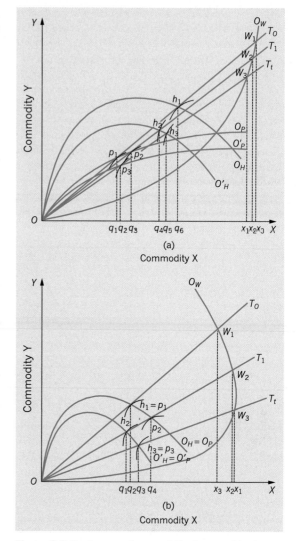

Figure 6.6 Customs unions and the terms of trade

that the move from h_1 to h_2 is accompanied by two conditions. It should be apparent that the larger the size of P relative to H and the more elastic the two countries' offer curves over the relevant ranges, the more likely it is that H will lose as a result of the tariff imposition. Moreover, given the various offer curves and H's tariff, H is more likely to sustain a loss in welfare, the lower her own marginal propensity to spend on her export commodity, X. If, in terms of consumption, commodity Y is a 'Giffen' good in country H, h_2 will be inferior to h_1.

In this illustration, country H experiences a loss of welfare in case (a) but an increase in case (b), while country P experiences a welfare improvement in both cases. Hence, it is to H's advantage to persuade P to adopt restrictive trade practices. For example, let P impose an *ad valorem* tariff and, in order to simplify the analysis, assume that in section (b) H and P are identical in all respects such that their revenue-redistributed offer curves completely coincide. In both sections of the figure, the t/t will shift to OT_t, with h_3, P_3 and W_2 being the equilibrium trading points. In both cases, P's tariff improves H's welfare but P gains only in case (b), and is better off with unrestricted trade in case (a) in the presence of tariff imposition by H.

The situation depicted in Figure 6.6 illustrates the fundamental problem that the interests, and hence the policies, of H and P may be incompatible:

Country [H] stands to gain from restrictive trade practices in [P], but the latter is better off without restrictions – provided that [H] maintains its tariff. The dilemma in which [H] finds itself in trying to improve its terms of trade is brought about by its inadequate control of the market for its export commodity. Its optimum trade policies and their effects are functions not only of the demand elasticity in [W] but also of supply conditions in [P] and of the latter's reaction to a given policy in [H].

Country [H] will attempt to influence policy making in [P]. In view of the fact that the latter may have considerable inducement to pursue independent policies, country [H] may encounter formidable difficulties in this respect. It could attempt to handle this problem in a relatively loose arrangement along the lines of international commodity agreements, or in a tightly controlled and more restrictive set-up involving an international cartel. The difficulty is that neither alternative may provide effective control over the maverick who stands to gain from independent policies. In that case a [CU] with common tariff and sufficient incentives may work where other arrangements do not. (Arndt, 1968, p. 978)

Of course, the above analysis relates to potential partners who have similar economies and who trade with W, with no trading relationships between them. Hence, it could be argued that such countries are ruled out, by definition, from forming a CU. Such an argument would be misleading since this analysis is not concerned with the static concepts of TC and TD; the concern is entirely with t/t effects, and a joint trade policy aimed at achieving an advantage in this regard

is perfectly within the realm of international economic integration.

One could ask about the nature of this conclusion in a model which depicts the potential CU partners in a different light. Here, Wonnacott and Wonnacott's (1981) analysis may be useful, even though the aim of their paper was to question the general validity of the Cooper–Massell criticism (see below), when the t/t remain unaltered as a result of CU formation. However, this is precisely why it is useful to explain the Wonnacotts' analysis at this juncture: it has some bearing on the t/t effects and it questions the Cooper–Massell criticism.

The main point of the Wonnacotts' paper was to contest the proposition that UTR is superior to the formation of a CU; hence the t/t argument was a side issue. They argued that this proposition does not hold generally if the following assumptions are rejected:

1 That the tariff imposed by a partner (P) can be ignored.
2 That W has no tariffs.
3 That there are no transport costs between members of the CU (P and H) and W.

Their approach was not based on t/t effects or economies of scale and, except for their rejection of these three assumptions, their argument is also set entirely in the context of the standard two-commodity, three-country framework of CU theory.

The basic framework of their analysis is set out in Figure 6.7. O_H and O_P are the free trade offer curves of the potential partners while O_H^t and O_P^t are their initial tariff-inclusive offer curves. O_W^1 and O_W^2 are W's offer curves depending on whether the prospective partners wish to import commodity X (O_W^1) or to export it (O_W^2). The inclusion of both O_H^t and O_P^t meets the Wonnacott's desire to reject assumption (1) while the gap between O_W^1 and O_W^2 may be interpreted as the rejection of (2) and/or (3) – see Wonnacott and Wonnacott (1981, pp. 708–9).

In addition to these offer curves, I have inserted in Figure 6.7 various trade indifference curves for countries H and P ($T_{H...}$ and $T_{P...}$ respectively) and the pre-CU domestic t/t in H (O_t). $O_W^{2'}$ is drawn parallel to O_W^2 from the point c where O_P intersects O_t.

The diagram is drawn to illustrate the case where a CU is formed between H and P with the CET set at the same rate as H's initial tariff on imports of X and where the domestic t/t in H remain unaltered so that trade with W continues after the formation of the CU.

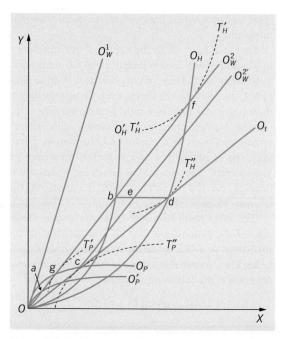

Figure 6.7 UTR versus customs unions

With its initial non-discriminatory tariff, H will trade along O_W^2 with both P (Oa) and with W (ab). The formation of the CU means that H and P's trade is determined by where O_p intersects O_t (i.e. at c) and that H will trade with W along cO_W^2 (drawn parallel to OO_W^2). The final outcome for H will depend on the choice of assumptions about what happens to the tariff revenue generated by the remaining external trade. If there is no redistribution of tariff revenue in H, then traders in that country will remain at point d. The tariff revenue generated by the external trade of the CU with W is then shown to be equal to ed (measured in units of commodity X) which represents a reduction of be compared with the pre-CU tariff revenue in H. Further, if procedures similar to those of the European Union were adopted, the revenue ed would be used as an 'own resource' (see Chapter 19) to be spent or distributed for the benefit of both members of the CU whereas the pre-union tariff (bd) would be kept by country H.

It can be seen that country P will benefit from the formation of the CU even if it receives none of this revenue, but that H will undoubtedly lose even if it keeps all the post-union tariff revenue. This is the case of pure TD (trade diversion) and, in the absence of additional income transfers from P, H clearly cannot

be expected to join the CU even if it considers that this is the only alternative to its initial tariff policy. There is no rationale, however, for so restricting the choice of policy alternatives. UTR is unambiguously superior to the initial tariff policy for both H and P and, compared with the non-discriminatory free trade policies available to both countries (which take country H to T_H' at f and country P to T_P' at g), there is no possible system of income transfers from P to H which can make the formation of a CU Pareto-superior to free trade for both countries. It remains true, of course, that country P would gain more from membership of a CU with H than it could achieve by UTR but, provided that H pursues its optimal strategy, which is UTR, country P itself can do no better than follow suit so that the optimal outcome for both countries is multilateral free trade (MFT).

Of course, there is no *a priori* reason why the CU, if created, should set its CET at the level of country H's initial tariff. Indeed, it is instructive to consider the consequences of forming a CU with a lower CET. The implications of this can be seen by considering the effect of rotating O_t anticlockwise towards O_W^2. In this context, the moving O_t line will show the post-union t/t in countries H and P. Clearly, the lowering of the CET will improve the domestic t/t for H compared with the original form of the CU and it will have a trade-creating effect as the external trade of the CU will increase more rapidly than the decline in intra-union trade. Compared with the original CU, H would gain and P would lose. Indeed, the lower the level of the CET, the more likely is H to gain from the formation of the CU *compared with the initial non-discriminatory tariff*. As long as the CET remains positive, however, H would be unambiguously worse off from membership of the CU than from UTR and, although P would gain from such a CU compared with any initial tariff policy it may adopt, it remains true that there is no conceivable set of income transfers associated with the formation of the CU which would make both H and P simultaneously better off than they would be if, after H's UTR, P also pursued the optimal unilateral action available – the move to free trade.

It is of course true that, if the CET is set to zero, so that the rotated O_t coincides with O_W^2 then the outcome is identical with that for the unilateral adoption of free trade for both countries. This, however, merely illustrates how misleading it would be to describe such a policy as 'the formation of a CU'; a CU with a zero CET is indistinguishable from a free-trade policy by both countries and should surely be described solely in the latter terms.

One can extend and generalize this approach beyond what has been done here – see El-Agraa (1989b) and Berglas (1983). The important point, however, is what the analysis clearly demonstrates: the assumption that the t/t should remain constant for members of a CU, even if both countries are 'small', leaves a lot to be desired. But it should also be stressed that the Wonnacotts' analysis does not take into consideration the tariffs of H and P on trade with W nor does it deal with a genuine three-country model since W is assumed to be very large: W has constant t/t.

Back to the Cooper–Massell criticism

Before finishing this section, it is important to address the question regarding what would happen to the Cooper–Massell criticism when WTO's Article XXIV is catered for within the context of the orthodox offer-curve analysis. Such an analysis is fully set out in El-Agraa (2002a) so here is a brief taste of it.

The clearest way to demonstrate how the incorporation of the requirements of Article XXIV into the analysis would impact on the Cooper–Massell criticism is by adapting the very case which the Wonnacotts use to illustrate its validity. Here, W is 'very large' and has no tariffs or transportation costs and the potential CU partners H and P are 'very small'. Hence, in Figure 6.8, W's offer curve (O_W) is a straight line: H and P being very small can trade with W without in any way influencing the prices of commodities X and Y. Before the formation of the CU, O_H^t and O_P^t are the respective H and P tariff-inclusive offer curves. H trades at A, exporting X in exchange for imports of Y while P trades at C, exporting Y in exchange for imports of X, the relevant distances along O_W determining the volume of trade. When H and P form a CU with a prohibitive common external tariff (CET) – the Wonnacotts' assumption (p. 707) – the respective offer curves for H and P become their tariff-ridden ones, i.e. their free-trade offer curves O_H and O_P, and the equilibrium trading point becomes E since W is excluded from trade by assumption.

The Wonnacotts stress that the move from A to E represents an improvement for H (they afford it better terms of trade) and that E is also superior for H in comparison with the position it can achieve by UTR (point B). However, not only is E inferior to C for P, but also P can reach a superior position (point D) by

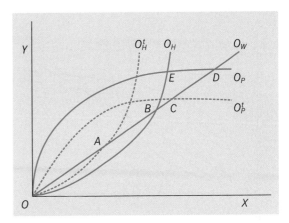

Figure 6.8 Vindicating the Cooper–Massell criticism when dominant W has no tariffs/transport costs
Source: El-Agraa (2002a), Fig. 1. Reprinted by permission of Taylor & Francis

simply adopting UTR policy. Hence, the formation of the CU will depend on whether H can persuade P to join: H will have to compensate P for the loss of welfare, measured by the difference between E and D. This compensation cannot be met by H since, given standard assumptions, P's loss at E (*vis-à-vis* D) exceeds H's gain at E (*vis-à-vis* B). Hence, 'UTR dominates CU' and both H and P are better off adopting UTR. The Cooper–Massell criticism is therefore vindicated.

We have just seen that it is essential for the Wonnacotts' to resort to their assumption of the CU needing a prohibitive CET in order to justify the only case they have that negates the Cooper–Massell criticism. Yet, such an assumption is not only puzzling, but is also in direct contradiction to WTO's Article XXIV which clearly specifies that the CET must not exceed the (weighted) average of the pre-CU tariffs – see Section 1.2 and Appendix 1.1. If WTO rules were to be adhered to, at least one of the CU partners would continue to trade with W (and at an expanded rate) since the CET must be lower for that country than its pre-CU tariff rate.

To put it differently, the analysis illustrated in Figure 6.8 can be true only if the *non-discriminatory* tariffs imposed by H and P prohibited trade *between* them. This can be so only if W is both 'large' and the most efficient producer of the three countries while H and P are small, otherwise the Wonnacotts' reference to a country being 'dominant' has no theoretical meaning. However, such an interpretation does not dispose of the problem altogether since the formation

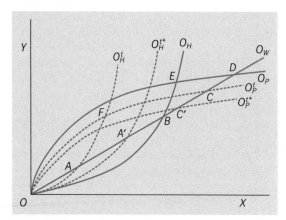

Figure 6.9 Dominant *W* has no tariffs/transport costs – non-discriminatory tariffs by *H/P* and a CET consistent with WTO rules: case I

Source: El-Agraa (2002a), Fig. 2. Reprinted by permission of Taylor & Francis

of the CU need not result in a CET which is prohibitive of trade between *H* and *P and W*: as long as the CET is a (weighted) average of the initial tariffs, either *H* or *P* must end up with a lower tariff after the formation of the CU (unless their tariffs were initially equal, but as will be shown below the inferences are similar) and this *may* open up trade between the relevant CU partner and *W*.

Hence, Figure 6.8 needs to be adapted to cater for Article XXIV's requirements. Assuming that *H*'s initial tariff is higher than *P*'s, the CET will ensure that *H*'s tariff must be reduced, hence *H* must continue to trade with *W* after the formation of the CU. Moreover, the elimination of *H* and *P*'s mutual tariffs may open up trade between them. Hence, in Figure 6.9, *H* and *P* initially have the same (tariff-inclusive) offer curves for trade with all countries, but after the formation of the CU have in effect two offer curves each, one, tariff-free, for mutual trade and another, CET-inclusive, for trade with *W*, with O_H and O_P defined as before. O_H^{t*} and O_P^{t*} are *H* and *P*'s respective offer curves when a CET consistent with WTO rules is adopted. Since after the formation of the CU *W* faces a lower *H* tariff, *H* and *W* will trade at *A′* and since *H* and *P* have no mutual tariffs, *H* will want to trade with *P* at *E*: the vector *OE* (not drawn) indicates better terms of trade for *H* in comparison with vector OO_W. Note that both the movement from *A* to *A′* and from *A′* to *E* indicate welfare improvement for *H*.

Taking these considerations into account, it should be apparent that the Wonnacotts' analysis of this 'most general' case does not necessarily vindicate the Cooper–Massell criticism of UTR dominating a CU. One needs to evaluate not only *E* and *D* and *E* and *B* (an evaluation which leads to the conclusion that UTR dominates a CU since *H* cannot bribe *P* into joining the CU and still be better off – see the analysis illustrated by Figure 6.8), but also *AA′* (which is a gain for *H*) and *CC′* (which is a loss for *P*). Since *AA′* may be equal to, longer or shorter than *CC′*, it follows that if *AA′* is either equal to or shorter than *CC′*, UTR must dominate a CU. However, if *AA′* is longer than *CC′*, the difference may enable *H* to bribe *P* into joining the CU and still become better off. Therefore, UTR need not dominate a CU.

This is a significant conclusion, given that this case is conceded by the Wonnacotts as vindicating the Cooper–Massell criticism. Surprisingly, it turns out that a world trade rule consistent, as opposed to a 'prohibitive', specification of the CET provides a clearer and more general case supporting a negation of the criticism. However, theoretical completeness necessitates that one should consider the alternative situation where the initial *H* tariff is lower than *P*'s before dwelling on this conclusion. Hence, in Figure 6.10, after the formation of the CU, *H* would be interested in trading with *P* only (at *E*) since trade with *W* (at *A″*) would not be desirable: *A″* indicates a lower level of welfare relative to *A* while *E* indicates better terms of trade and a higher level of welfare. However, *P* will want to trade at *C″* since it gives a higher level of welfare relative to *C*, but will have no interest in trading with *H* since *OE* are worse terms of trade relative OO_W. Therefore, it should be evident that since UTR takes *P* to *D* (giving a higher level of welfare relative to *C″*), *P* would have no interest in the CU. Whether *H* can bribe *P* to join the CU would depend on the relative lengths of *A″A* and *CC″*, more precisely, on *A″A* being shorter than *CC″* by a distance sufficient to make *BE* exceed *CD*. Hence, again, UTR need not dominate a CU and, therefore, the conclusion reached here reinforces that arrived at in the previous case.

Note that in both cases, initially *H* would have been interested in trading with *P* rather than *W* since trade with *P* offers better terms of trade (*OF* relative to OO_W in both Figures 6.9 and 6.10). However, *H*'s desires are frustrated simply because *P* chooses to trade with *W* at better terms of trade for itself; once *P*

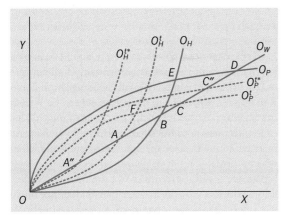

Figure 6.10 Dominant *W* has no tariffs/transport costs – non-discriminatory tariffs by *H/P* and a CET consistent with WTO rules: case II

Source: El-Agraa (2002a), Fig. 3. Reprinted by permission of Taylor & Francis

chooses to trade with *W*, *H* has no alternative but to follow suit.

Analytical completeness requires a discussion of the two alternatives where the offer curves for *H* intersect O_W to the northeast of all the points where *P*'s offer curves intersect it. However, it should be obvious that under such circumstances the same conclusions would be reached. Hence, UTR need not dominate CU formation.

A final question remains: would the assumption of equal initial *H* and *P* tariff rates nullify this generalization? The answer is in the negative and can be explained in the following way. If they were equal, the CET would also be equal to them. Hence, O^t_H and O^t_P will continue to be the respective *H* and *P* offer curves for trade with *W*. Therefore, in Figure 6.8 trade with *W* would continue at the initial level: *OA* trade between *H* and *W* and *OC* trade between *P* and *W*. It follows that the evaluation of the CU formation versus UTR must lead to the same conclusion as that reached in the case illustrated by Figure 6.8. However, there would be one significant difference: in the Wonnacotts' analysis, the conclusion reached from Figure 6.8 rests entirely on the CET being prohibitive of trade between the CU partners and *W*, while in this (generalized) case trade between the CU partners and *W* would continue on the same basis and to the same extent as before the CU formation. The implication of this result is that the outright vindication of the Cooper–Massell criticism would depend on assuming that the *H* and *P* tariffs being equal rather than on the CET being prohibitive. This implication is consistent not only with some of the literature on the subject, but also with practical notions: in the real world, the formation of CUs has never completely eliminated trade with the non-members, *W* – see, *inter alia*, El-Agraa (1999).

6.2 Customs unions versus free trade areas

The analysis so far has been conducted on the premise that differences between CUs and FTAs can be ignored. However, the ability of the member nations of FTAs to decide their own commercial policies *vis-à-vis* the outside world raises certain issues. Balassa (1961) pointed out that free trade areas may result in deflection of trade, production and investment. Deflection of trade occurs when imports from *W* (the cheapest source of supply) come via the member country with the lower tariff rate, assuming that transport and administrative costs do not outweigh the tariff differential. Deflection of production and investment occur in commodities whose production requires a substantial quantity of raw materials imported from *W* – the tariff differential regarding these materials might distort the true comparative advantage in domestic materials, therefore resulting in resource allocations according to overall comparative disadvantage.

If deflection of trade does occur, then the free trade area effectively becomes a CU with a CET equal to the lowest tariff rate which is obviously beneficial for the world – see Curzon Price (1974). However, most free trade areas seem to adopt 'rules of origin' so that only those commodities which originate in a member state are exempt from tariff imposition. If deflection of production and investment does take place, we have the case of the so-called tariff factories; but the necessary conditions for this to occur are extremely limited – see El-Agraa in El-Agraa and Jones (1981, Chapter 3) and El-Agraa (1984b, 1989a).

6.3   Economic unions

The analysis of CUs needs drastic extension when applied to economic unions. First, the introduction of free factor mobility may enhance efficiency through a more rational reallocation of resources but it may also result in depressed areas, therefore creating or aggravating regional problems and imbalances – see Mayes (1983) and Robson (1985). Second, fiscal harmonization may also improve efficiency by eliminating non-tariff barriers (NTBs) and distortions and by equalizing their effective protective rates – see Chapter 14. Third, the co-ordination of monetary and fiscal policies which is implied by monetary integration may ease unnecessarily severe imbalances, hence resulting in the promotion of the right atmosphere for stability in the economies of the member nations.

These economic union elements must be tackled *simultaneously* with trade creation and diversion as well as economies of scale and market distortions. However, such interactions are too complicated to consider here: the interested reader should consult El-Agraa (1983a, 1983b, 1984a, 1989a). This section will be devoted to a brief discussion of factor mobility. Since monetary integration is probably the most crucial of commitments for a regional grouping and because it is one of the immediate aspirations of the EU, the following chapter is devoted to it.

With regard to *factor mobility*, it should be apparent that the removal (or harmonization) of all barriers to labour (L) and capital (K) will encourage both L and K to move. L will move to those areas where it can fetch the highest possible reward, i.e. 'net advantage'. This encouragement need not necessarily lead to an increase in actual mobility since there are socio-political factors which normally result in people remaining near their birthplace – social proximity is a dominant consideration, which is why the average person does not move (Chapter 18). If the reward to K is not equalized, i.e. differences in marginal productivities (MPs) exist before the formation of an economic union, K will move until the MPs are equalized. This will result in benefits which can be clearly described in terms of Figure 6.11, which depicts the production characteristics in H and P. M_H and M_P are the schedules which relate the K stocks to their MPs in H and P respectively, given the quantity of L in each country (assuming two factors of production only).

Prior to formation of an economic union, the K stock (which is assumed to remain constant throughout the analysis) is Oq_2 in H and Oq_1^* in P. Assuming that K is immobile internationally, all K stocks must be nationally owned and, ignoring taxation, profit per unit of K will be equal to its MP, given conditions of

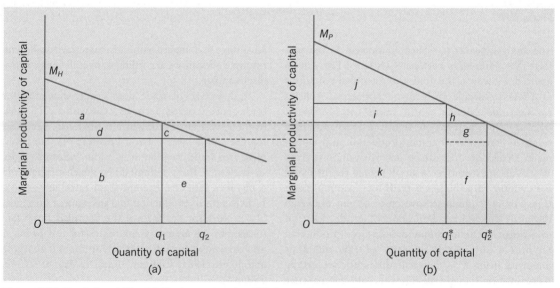

Figure 6.11 Capital mobility: (a) the home country; (b) the partner country

perfect competition. Hence the total profit in H is equal to $b + e$ and $i + k$ in P. Total output is, of course, the whole area below the M_P curve but within Oq_2 in H and Oq_1^* in P, i.e. areas $a + b + c + d + e$ in H and $j + i + k$ in P. Therefore, L's share is $a + c + d$ in H and j in P.

Since the MP in P exceeds that in H, the removal of barriers to K mobility or the harmonization of such barriers will induce K to move away from H and into P. This is because nothing has happened to affect K in W. Such movement will continue until the MP of K is the same in both H and P. This results in q_1q_2 ($= q_1^*q_2^*$) of K moving from H to P. Hence the output of H falls to $a + b + d$ while its *national* product including the return of the profit earned on K in P ($= g + f$) increases by ($g - c$). In P, *domestic* product rises by ($f + g + h$) while *national* product (excluding the remittance of profits to H) increases by area h only. Both H and P experience a change in the relative share of L and K in national product, with K owners being favourably disposed in H and unfavourably disposed in P.

Of course, the analysis is too simplistic since, apart from the fact that K and L are never perfectly immobile at the international level and multinational corporations have their own ways of transferring K (see McManus, 1972; Buckley and Casson, 1976; Dunning, 1977), the analysis does not take into account the fact that K may actually move to areas with low wages after the formation of an economic union. Moreover, if K moves predominantly in only one direction, one country may become a depressed area; hence the 'social' costs and benefits of such an occurrence need to be taken into consideration, particularly if the economic union deems it important that the economies of both H and P should be balanced. Therefore, the above gains have to be discounted or supplemented by such costs and benefits.

6.4   Macroeconomics of integration

We have seen that trade creation and trade diversion are the two concepts most widely used in international economic integration. We have also seen that their economic implications for resource reallocation are usually tackled in terms of particular commodities under conditions of global full employment. However, the economic consequences for the outside world and their repercussions on the integrated area are usually left to intuition. Moreover, their implications for employment are usually ruled out by assumption.

In an effort to rectify these serious shortcomings, I have used a macroeconomic model (see Chapters 6–8 of El-Agraa and Jones, 1981, and El-Agraa, 1989a) with the purpose of investigating these aspects; the model has been refined (see A. J. Jones, 1983). However, even the crude model indicates that the advantages of using a macro model are that it clearly demonstrates the once and for all nature of trade creation and trade diversion. It also shows the insignificance of their overall impact given realistic values of the relevant coefficients: marginal propensities to import, marginal propensities to consume, tariff rates, etc. The model also demonstrates that trade creation is beneficial for the partner gaining the new output and exports but is detrimental to the other partner and the outside world and that trade diversion is beneficial for the partner now exporting the commodity but is detrimental for the other partner and the outside world.

6.5   Economic integration in developing countries

It has been claimed that the body of economic integration theory as so far developed has no relevance for the Third World. This is because the theory suggests that there would be more scope for trade creation if the countries concerned were initially very competitive in production but potentially very complementary and that a CU would be more likely to be trade creating if the partners conducted most of their foreign trade among themselves – see Lipsey (1960) and Mcade (1980). These conditions are unlikely to be satisfied in the majority of the developing nations. Moreover, most of the effects of integration are initially bound to be trade diverting, particularly since most of the Third World seeks to industrialize.

On the other hand, it was also realized that an important obstacle to the development of industry in these countries is the inadequate size of their individual markets – see Brown (1961), Hazlewood (1967, 1975) and Robson (1980, 1983, 1997). It is therefore necessary to increase the market size so as to encourage optimum plant installations: hence the need for economic integration. This would, however, result in industries clustering together in the relatively more advanced of these nations – those that have already commenced the process of industrialization.

I have demonstrated elsewhere (El-Agraa, 1979a) that there is essentially *no theoretical difference* between economic integration in the advanced world and the Third World but that there is a major difference in terms of the *type* of economic integration that suits the particular *circumstances* of developing

countries and that is politically feasible: the need for an equitable distribution of the gains from industrialization and the location of industries is an important issue (see above). This suggests that any type of economic integration that is being contemplated must incorporate as an essential element a common fiscal authority and some coordination of economic policies. But then one could equally well argue that *some degree* of these elements is necessary in *any* type of integration – see the Raisman Committee recommendations for the EAC (1961).

6.6   Economic integration among communist countries

The only example of economic integration among communist countries was the CMEA. However, there the economic system perpetuated a fundamental lack of interest of domestic producers in becoming integrated with both consumers and producers in other member countries. As Marer and Montias (1988) emphasize, the integration policies of member nations must focus on the mechanism of state-to-state relations rather than on domestic economic policies which would make CMEA integration more attractive to producers and consumers alike. That is, integration must be planned by the state at the highest possible level and imposed on ministries, trusts and enter-

prises. It should also be stated that the CMEA operated different pricing mechanisms for intra- and extra-area trade. Moreover, the attitude of the former USSR was extremely important since the policies of the East European members of the CMEA were somewhat constrained by the policies adopted by the organization's most powerful member, for economic as well as political reasons. CMEA integration, therefore, had to be approached within an entirely different framework but this is not the appropriate place for discussing it, especially since the CMEA met its demise soon after the collapse of socialism in the former USSR and Eastern Europe.

6.7   New theoretical developments

There are many new developments in the analysis of economic integration, but they do not have a consensus, hence do not amount to a body coherent enough to be briefly explained and discussed within the general introductory nature of this chapter. To mention but one, Schiff and Winters (1998) examine regional integration as diplomacy. They do this by analysing a model of a scheme motivated by security concerns. Assuming that trade can help reduce frictions among antagonistic neighbouring nations by raising trust between them, they show that: a regional bloc is optimum or first-best under traditional static welfare

terms; optimum CETs fall over time; the CETs fall in the aftermath of deep integration which includes such NTBs as harmonization and mutual recognition of standards, investment codes and the like (see Chapter 1); and enlargement enhances the welfare of the members of the bloc, with optimum CETs likely to rise. Their general conclusion being that the optimum intervention under these circumstances is a subsidy on imports from the neighbour and the equivalent solution is for the neighbouring countries to tax imports from the rest of the world, i.e. to form a trading bloc, as well as to have domestic taxes.

6.8   Conclusions

The conclusions reached here are consistent with my 1979a, b and 1989a conclusions and with those of Jones in El-Agraa and Jones (1981). They are as follows.

First, the rationale for regional economic integration rests upon the existence of constraints on the use of first best policy instruments. Economic analysis has had little to say about the nature of these constraints, and presumably the evaluation of any regional scheme of economic integration should incorporate a consideration of the validity of the view that such constraints do exist to justify the pursuit of second rather than first best solutions.

Second, even when the existence of constraints on superior policy instruments is acknowledged, it is misleading to identify the results of regional economic integration by comparing an arbitrarily chosen common policy with an arbitrarily chosen national policy. Of course, ignorance and inertia provide sufficient reasons why existing policies may be non-optimal; but it is clearly wrong to attribute gains which would have been achieved by appropriate unilateral action to a policy of regional integration. Equally, although it is appropriate to use the optimal common policy as a point of reference, it must be recognized that this may overstate the gains to be achieved if, as seems highly likely, constraints and inefficiencies in the political processes by which policies are agreed prove to be greater among a group of countries than within any individual country.

Although the first two conclusions raise doubts about the case for regional economic integration, in principle at least, a strong general case for economic integration does exist. In unions where economies of scale may be in part external to national industries, the rationale for unions rests essentially upon the recognition of the externalities and market imperfections which extend beyond the boundaries of national states. In such circumstances, unilateral national action will not be optimal while integrated action offers the scope for potential gain.

As with the solution to most problems of externalities and market imperfections, however, customs union theory frequently illustrates the proposition that a major stumbling block to obtaining the gains from joint optimal action lies in agreeing an acceptable distribution of such gains. Thus the fourth conclusion is that the achievement of the potential gains from economic integration will be limited to countries able and willing to cooperate to distribute the gains from integration so that all partners may benefit compared with the results achieved by independent action. It is easy to argue from this that regional economic integration may be more readily achieved than global solutions but, as the debate about monetary integration in the EU illustrates (see Chapters 8 and 9), the chances of obtaining potential mutual gain may well founder in the presence of disparate views about the distribution of such gains and weak arrangements for redistribution.

Chapter 7

Measuring the impact of economic integration

NIGEL GRIMWADE

7.1   Introduction

Chapter 6 discussed the theory of economic integration in an attempt to see how different forms of integration impacted on both the member states and rest of the world. We now need to turn to a consideration of the extent to which these theoretical expectations were born out by the experience of integration in Europe. What were the effects of the formation and subsequent enlargement of the European Community/ European Union on the allocation of resources? Was the net effect trade creating or trade diverting? By how much was the economic welfare of the member states increased as a result of integration? Also, how significant were the longer-run, dynamic effects, as opposed to the purely static, resource-reallocation effects? Did integration have any impact on the rate of economic growth in the countries involved? Finally, were the rest of the world harmed by the process of integration taking place in Europe or did it share in the gains?

The major problem that researchers face when seeking to find answers to these questions is the classic, counterfactual problem common to all areas of research of a similar kind. We simply do not know what would have happened to Europe or the rest of the world if European integration had not taken place. This means that we can never know for sure the precise impact of integration. We should, therefore, treat all attempts to estimate these effects with a high degree of caution. At best, they are 'estimated guesses' concerning their broad direction and magnitude. It is just as important to appreciate the limitations of studies carried out to measure these effects, as to know the results that were obtained. In this chapter, we begin with a brief review of the main kind of effects that it is important to consider. This is followed with a survey of the different types of studies carried out to estimate these effects. We finish with a discussion of the strengths and weaknesses of different approaches and appraisal of the results obtained.

7.2   The effects of economic integration

Economic integration has a number of different effects on the countries participating and on the rest of the world as described in the following sections.

7.2.1 Trade effects

A major concern of the orthodox theory of free trade areas (FTAs) and customs unions (CUs) is with the impact of integration on trade. The simple theory of FTAs and CUs distinguishes between two effects – trade creation and trade diversion. *Trade creation* is defined as the displacement of high cost domestic production of a product in one member state by lower cost

imports from another member state. This improves the allocation of global resources and represents a step in the direction of free trade. *Trade diversion* is defined as the displacement of lower cost imports of a product from a non-member state by higher cost imports from a member state. This results from the discriminatory nature of the tariff. As it worsens the global allocation of resource, it represents a step towards protectionism.

However, it has long been recognized that economic integration may have other effects on trade. Where a FTA or CU results in a lower level of external tariffs or other restrictions compared with the situation before integration, the result may be *external trade creation*. The same may result if faster economic growth inside the area or union due to integration leads to the member states importing more from the rest of the world.

Another effect is that of *trade suppression*. This is like trade diversion, but different. In this case, the production of a particular good in one of the member states disappears altogether following the formation of the union. Instead, production shifts to another member state where costs are lower. However, prior to the formation of the union, the latter imported the product from the rest of the world. The reason, of course, for this situation is that a high tariff in the former country before the formation of the union made it profitable to produce the good, but import nothing at all. In the latter country, however, the tariff was low, discouraging domestic production and resulting in the good being imported. As the resource reallocation effects are the same as with trade diversion, trade suppression may be regarded as a special form of trade diversion.

Finally, integration may result in *supply-side diversion*. This will take place when, due to a supply-side constraint (e.g. shortage of capacity), increased exports of a product to a member state following integration result in reduced exports of the product to a non-member state. However, such an effect is likely to be of a short-term nature only, as, given time, producers will expand their capacity to meet the greater demand for their product. This effect may, therefore, be regarded as being of trivial importance only.

As we have seen, these effects on trade can only be measured if we know, for sure, what the level of imports (or exports) would have been had integration not happened. As this cannot be known, we have to find a way of estimating what the level of imports (or exports) might have been. We shall see later a variety of approaches have been used in studies of this kind to estimate the so-called *anti-monde*. Whatever method is used, several requirements must be satisfied. First, the *anti-monde* must be constructed for a time period that is sufficiently long for the various integration effects to have taken place. Second, in doing so, a distinction must be made between different trading partners, in particular between those that are members of the union and those that are not. Finally, account must be taken of the effects of other influences on trade flows both before and after integration. For example, any tariff cuts made as a result of multilateral trading agreements entered into will have affected the actual level of trade flows. Changes in the real exchange rate

will also be important, as these affect the prices of tradable relative to non-tradable goods.

7.2.2 Income effects

Trade effects are not of themselves very interesting. More important is the effect that changes in trade patterns have on *economic welfare*. In the orthodox theory, different trade effects have different impacts on economic welfare. From a *global* point of view, trade creation is welfare enhancing, while trade diversion is welfare decreasing. However, for *members of the union*, trade diversion will raise the real incomes of the exporting countries, while lowering the welfare of importing countries. The accurate estimation of these income effects, however, is difficult even for the members of the union alone. If the amount of trade creation is known, the welfare gain from tariff elimination can be estimated in the conventional manner by multiplying half the tariff reduction by the volume of extra trade generated. The loss of economic welfare from trade diversion can be measured by multiplying the volume of trade diverted by the difference between the world, free-trade price and the union price. For exports, the welfare gain is half the increase in price, following the adoption of the common external tariff, multiplied by the increase in the volume of exports following integration.

Although such a *partial equilibrium* approach is acceptable when estimating the gain from a tariff cut in a single sector, the procedure is less than satisfactory when considered across the whole economy. This is because it ignores the feedback effects of a tariff cut on a single product on other parts of the economy. These effects are better captured using a *general equilibrium* model that shows the interrelationships between different sectors of the economy. We discuss this further below. Another difficulty arises when measuring the impact of a tariff reduction on a product that is a differentiated good. In this case, imports and importables are not perfect substitutes. This means that the prices of importables fall by less than the price of imports after liberalization, resulting in a smaller welfare gain than where imports and importables are perfect substitutes. However, tariff liberalization in differentiated goods industries also tends to result in more intra-industry trade (IIT) – two way trade in different varieties of the same product. This makes possible further gains to consumers from having a wider variety of goods to choose from. The gains from increased choice, however, are clearly more difficult to quantify than those resulting from lower prices.

IIT in differentiated goods is also more likely to yield dynamic welfare gain from decreasing average cost and increasing competition. Both inter- and intra-industry trade may have other positive, long-run effects on output in the union/area. For example, output may be increased as a result of firms investing more both to take advantage of the wider market and to cope with increased competition. Increased competition may also spur firms to engage in more technological innovation. These dynamic gains are often more difficult to quantify, but must be included in any comprehensive estimate of the true welfare gain from integration. Most of the early studies of integration were concerned with the static welfare gain only, making no attempt to quantify the dynamic gains. This accounts for the small size of the gain that they estimated. More recently, however, trade economists have developed general equilibrium models that incorporate dynamic effects of this kind.

7.2.3 The balance of payments effect

Economic integration may also have an effect on the balance of payments of individual countries. This could be favourable (if exports increase by more than imports) or unfavourable (if imports expand more than exports). At the time when the EC was set up, there was some concern that Italy would experience an adverse balance of payments effect because of a lower degree of industrial competitiveness. It is clear, however, that these concerns proved unwarranted, as the Italian economy thrived after the formation of the EC. Likewise, there was a concern when the UK joined the EC in 1973 that the effect on the balance of payments would be adverse. UK tariffs on industrial goods imported from the EC were slightly higher than on such goods when exported to the EC, so British imports from the EC could be expected to rise by more than British exports to the EC. Also, UK exports would suffer from the loss of tariff preferences in the EFTA and Commonwealth. Added to that, the need to make large net contributions to the EC budget was expected to have a harmful effect on the balance of payments.

An adverse balance of payments effect, however, need not be a matter of concern, providing the country is prepared to allow the real exchange rate to fall. This can happen either by lowering the nominal exchange rate or by reducing the country's price level relative to that of the rest of the world. Where the exchange rate is floating, the nominal rate may well fall anyhow if the balance of payments deteriorates, although this may not be the case if large inflows of capital from abroad create greater demand for the currency on foreign exchange markets. Reducing the price level may be more difficult to achieve, if prices are slow to fall in response to a tightening of monetary and fiscal policy. Both measures, however, will entail a resource cost for the country. Where the exchange rate bears the brunt of the adjustment, the cost is measured by the deterioration in the terms of trade necessitated by integration. Where, instead adjustment is achieved by domestic deflation, the resource cost could be measured by the loss of output and employment in the short run that is necessitated by the fall in aggregate demand. In practice, both are likely to prove difficult to measure, as there is no way of distinguishing between those effects that are the result of integration and those which are due to extraneous factors. Nevertheless, these effects are potentially very important for individual countries, especially countries that are contemplating joining a regional trading bloc such as the EC.

7.2.4 Economic growth

In addition to the effects on income, economic integration can be expected to affect the rate of growth in GDP in individual countries. The relationship between trade liberalization and economic growth is a complex one. The explanation for how integration will affect growth depends on the model of growth that is used. In the *neo-classical theory of growth*, economic integration could bring about an increase in the growth rate through an increase in the rate of capital accumulation in the economy. Improvements in economic efficiency brought about by integration may induce more investment in the region. With a fixed capital–output ratio, the result will be a faster rise in output, which, in turn, will bring a further increase in savings and, hence, investment. However, as the stock of capital relative to labour is rising, the marginal productivity of capital will fall, reducing the incentive to invest more. Eventually, it will fall to a level where it is no longer profitable for firms to undertake any more new investment. As the rate of capital accumulation approaches zero, the growth rate declines, until it eventually returns to its former level. This is known in neo-classical growth theory as the 'steady state'. A number of EU countries experienced such a boost to their growth rates following entry (e.g. Spain after 1986). Such effects may take time to work their way through the economy, so that the boost to economic growth may be sustained for a considerable period of time.

In neo-classical growth theory, a permanent, long-run boost to economic growth is not possible, as this would require ceaseless accumulation. The rate of capital accumulation would have to continue growing at the higher rate. However, in *new growth theory*, this is possible, because capital accumulation is treated as an endogenous variable in the growth process. Capital accumulation can refer to investment in physical capital, human capital or knowledge capital. Firms are motivated by the *private* rate of return on investment, which they perceive to diminish as the stock of capital increases. However, the *public* rate of return from new investment, which determines the total amount of investment undertaken by firms as a whole, need not fall. In effect, a wedge is created between the private and public rates of return on investment.

One reason is that knowledge accumulation is, itself, an endogenous variable. As firms invest in knowledge capital, there occur technological spillovers to other firms, which offsets any tendency towards diminishing returns. Integration may play a positive role in stimulating continuous accumulation of knowledge capital, making possible sustained GDP growth. By widening the market for new products, trade boosts the profitability of investment in R&D. At the same time, by lowering import barriers, trade stimulates competition. Although competition may reduce the profitability from investing in R&D, it forces domestic firms to step up the rate of their innovation in order not to lose market share to foreign rivals. Capital market integration may also stimulate greater investment in R&D by eliminating imperfections in capital markets and reducing the costs of borrowed funds.

7.3   Estimating the trade effects – different approaches

The starting point of any attempt to quantify the effects of economic integration must be the trade effects. This exercise may be carried out as an *ex ante* or as an *ex post* study. *Ex ante* studies are, generally, more problematic, as they are trying to find out in advance what the effects of integration might be. This is impossible to do, as we have no idea of knowing how the future might turn out if integration did not take place. Estimating the income effect will also be more difficult, as the effects of tariff reductions on imports will have to be determined using historical estimates of the elasticity of demand for and supply of different goods. *Ex post* estimation is somewhat less hazardous, as we are looking back at what has taken place. There is still the difficulty of constructing a suitable *anti-monde*, but, as we shall see, techniques are available whereby economists can make a moderately intelligent guess at this. Not surprisingly, the greater number of studies conducted have been of the *ex post* variety. *Ex ante* studies are used where economists want to make predictions about the likely effects of integration, often the result of an individual country joining, or wanting to join, the EU.

A number of different approaches have been used in the construction of the anti-monde. Broadly speaking, these fit into one of three broad categories:

1 *Residual models.* The commonest approach has been to use a residual model, in which hypothetical trade flows are imputed from existing trade flows, making plausible assumptions about demand-size variables such as GDP/GNP, consumption, economic growth and possibly some supply-side variables. The integration effect is then treated as being the difference between these imputed flows and actual trade flows. Some studies have used the trade flows of some third country as a normalizing factor.

2 *Econometric models.* An alternative approach is to use a formal econometric model that isolates the influence of different variables on trade, including economic integration, and, then, estimates the explanatory power of each. In this way, we can, directly, see how much of any increase (or decrease) in trade has been due to integration and how much to other factors. Such

an approach has the advantage that all of the determinants of trade (including changes in relative prices, demand-side and supply-side factors, economic growth, multilateral trade liberalization) are taken into account rather than just some. The important question then becomes what type of model should be used for this purpose. Econometric models are, especially, useful when making *ex-ante* estimates of the effects of integration. Once, the coefficients have been estimated for the different variables in the equation, these may be used to project trade flows, providing that plausible assumptions can be made about the values of the exogenous variables.

3 *Computable general equilibrium models.* More recently, economists have shown an interest in using general equilibrium models that are capable of being run on a computer to estimate the effects of integration. Such models have been widely used in estimating the probable impact of different multilateral trade liberalization scenarios on different countries and regions of the world. In this case, the models used are multi-country and multi-regional models, as well as being multi-sectoral. The advantage of such models is that they can estimate how the various effects of liberalization feed back into different sectors of the economy and how such effects are transmitted from different countries and regions to each other. The approach is to construct a model that sets out the conditions that are required for equilibrium to exist simultaneously in all sectors and all markets. Once constructed, the model can then be calibrated, usually for a single year as close as possible to the period under investigation. The model may then be used to simulate various policy scenarios, such as a reduction in tariffs and other trade costs. In the main, CGE models are used to make *ex-ante* estimations of the likely effects of trade liberalization. However, they may be used to study the effects of integration, beginning from either an *ex-ante* or *ex-post* premise.

7.3.1 Residual models

A number of different approaches have been used for the construction of the *anti-monde* in residual modelling as described under the following three headings.

Simple extrapolation

The simplest approach of all is to assume that the value of imports coming from partner countries would have continued to grow at the same rate after integration as before, had integration not taken place. Then, the difference between this figure and actual imports could be regarded as being the integration effect. Clearly, however, such an assumption is fatally flawed. There are no grounds for supposing that the growth in imports that has taken place in previous years would have been repeated. The volume of imports in any given year is highly sensitive to the particular point reached in the business cycle, so that the pre- and post-integration periods would, at the very least, have to cover the full length of the cycle. However, these will be different for different countries. Changes in relative prices, including changes in the exchange rate, can also be expected to affect the growth of import volume. Any fall in the price of domestic goods relative to imports, including any fall brought about by a decline in the real exchange rate, might be expected to result in a slower growth in import volume. Structural changes within the country affecting both the composition of demand and output might also impact on the demand for imports, if some sectors or products have greater propensity to import than others. Finally, reductions in multilaterally negotiated tariffs either in the pre- or post-integration period could be expected to cause imports to grow at different rates in the two periods.

A slightly, more sophisticated approach is to extrapolate import *shares*. One possibility is to assume that the share of intra- and extra-area imports in total imports would have been unchanged had integration not taken place. However, such a procedure is subject to much the same objections as the linear approach discussed above. There is no reason to assume that these shares would have remained the same, as different factors can be expected to have affected these shares in the post- rather than in the pre-integration period. A further problem with this method is that it provides no way in which a distinction can be made between trade creation and trade diversion. An increase in the intra-area trade share (and decrease in the extra-area trade share) could be due to either imports from partner countries displacing high-cost domestic production or imports from partner countries displacing lower cost imports from third countries.

The alternative is to extrapolate the share of imports to GNP/GDP or to the share of imports in apparent consumption, defined as domestic consumption less exports plus imports. Of these, apparent consumption is the preferred measure. One possibility is to assume that the share of imports from domestic sources, partner sources and the rest of the world would have remained constant, had integration not taken place. Then, any decrease in the share of imports coming from domestic sources is evidence for gross trade creation. An increase in the share of imports coming from partner countries is evidence for net trade creation (gross trade creation less trade diversion) and any decrease in the share of imports coming from the rest of the world is evidence for trade diversion. In this way, the different effects of integration on trade can be identified and measured. The first study to use such an approach was Truman (1969). He found that, by 1968, the amount of new trade created in manufactured goods was $9.2 billion (or 26% of trade), while external trade creation (negative trade diversion) of $1.0 billion (or 7% of trade) took place.

However, a more realistic approach is to allow for *changes* in the share of imports from different sources in apparent consumption over time. The simplest way of handling this is to assume that the change in the share of imports from different sources in apparent consumption in a suitable pre-integration period would have continued in the post-integration period. Such an approach was used by the EFTA Secretariat (1969, 1972) to estimate the trade effects of both the EC and EFTA. They estimated trade creation for EFTA at $2.3 billion and trade diversion at $1.1 billion respectively. In a later study, Truman (1975) allowed for increases in the share of imports in apparent consumption over time. This resulted in an estimate for trade creation of $2.5 billion (or 7% of trade) and trade-diversion of $0.5 billion (or 4% of trade) for 1968.

One of the difficulties with this approach is that the trend extrapolated into the post-integration period is highly dependent on the years chosen for estimating the trend in the pre-integration period. A further difficulty concerns the assumptions made, namely, that import shares would have continued rising in the same way as they did in the pre-integration period had integration not taken place. This is simply not tenable, as many factors may have caused changes in the share of imports coming from different countries in the pre-integration period. Although the use of import shares makes it possible to incorporate economic growth, changes in import shares may still be affected by changes in relative prices, changes in real exchange rates and tariff reductions. Furthermore, the more disaggregated the data that is used (and disaggregation is desirable to capture the full effects of integration), the less tenable is the assumption of a linear trend in import shares. A further problem is that the GNP of the member states is, itself, affected by the process of integration. Using import shares will mean that these effects will not be fully captured in the estimation and, hence, the integration effect will be underestimated.

Changes in the income elasticity of demand for imports

An alternative solution to the problem of how to separate the trade creation and trade diversion effects was proposed by Balassa (1967, 1974a). He suggested basing the *anti-monde* on the estimated *ex-post* income elasticity of demand for imports in the pre-integration period. The income elasticity of import demand was defined as the average annual rate of change of imports divided by that of GNP, both being expressed at constant prices. A rise in the income elasticity of demand for intra-area imports following integration was, then, defined as gross trade creation. However, as this may have resulted from either imports displacing domestic production (trade creation proper) or imports from other member states displacing imports from the rest of the world (trade diversion), only a rise in the income elasticity of demand for imports from *all* sources taken together would constitute trade creation proper. A fall in the income elasticity of demand for extra-area imports would indicate that trade diversion had taken place. On the other hand, a rise in this ratio would be evidence for external trade creation. The *anti-monde* was determined in this way for seven separate commodity groups for the pre-integration period from 1953 to 1959. In his initial study (Balassa, 1967), the post-integration period was from 1959 to 1965, but, in a later study, this was extended to 1970 (Balassa, 1974a).

Balassa's results are summarized in Table 7.1. The results for *total imports* show that trade creation occurred in all product groups, except temperate-zone food, beverages and tobacco and other manufactures. Account must be taken of the fact that the income elasticity of demand for food was falling over time. If consumption or industrial production is used instead of GNP as the denominator, trade creation is found to have taken place. Other manufactured goods

Table 7.1   Changes in *ex-post* income elasticities of import demand in the EC

Product group	*Ex-post* income elasticity of import demand		Difference, 1959–1970/ 1953–1959
	1953–1959	1959–1970	
Total imports			
Non-tropical food, beverages, tobacco	1.7	1.5	−0.2
Raw materials	1.1	1.1	0
Fuels	1.6	2.0	+0.4
Chemicals	3.0	3.2	+0.2
Machinery	1.5	2.6	+1.1
Transport equipment	2.6	3.2	+0.6
Other manufactured goods	2.6	2.5	−0.1
Total of above	1.8	2.0	+0.2
Intra-area imports			
Non-tropical food, beverages, tobacco	2.5	2.5	0
Raw materials	1.9	1.8	−0.1
Fuels	1.1	1.6	+0.5
Chemicals	3.0	3.7	+0.7
Machinery	2.1	2.8	+0.7
Transport equipment	2.9	3.5	+0.6
Other manufactured goods	2.8	2.7	−0.1
Total of above	2.4	2.7	+0.3
Extra-area imports			
Non-tropical food, beverages, tobacco	1.4	1.0	−0.4
Raw materials	1.0	1.0	0
Fuels	1.8	2.1	+0.3
Chemicals	3.0	2.6	−0.4
Machinery	0.9	2.4	+1.5
Transport equipment	2.2	2.5	+0.3
Other manufactured goods	2.5	2.1	−0.4
Total of above	1.6	1.6	0

Source: Balassa (1974a). Reprinted by permission of Blackwell Publishing Ltd

consisted of intermediate products and non-durable consumer goods. The absence of trade creation in this category may have been due to the rapid expansion of trade in the 1950s, which could not be replicated in subsequent years. The results for *extra-area imports* show trade diversion as occurring in temperate-zone food, beverages and tobacco, chemicals and other manufactured goods. Trade diversion in foodstuffs was, undoubtedly, due to the effects of the Common Agricultural Policy, which increased levels of external protection (see Chapter 20). However, in several other categories (fuels, machinery and transport equipment), substantial external trade creation took place. In the case of fuels, this reflected the switch away from indigenous coal to imported oil during this period. In the case of machinery, the trend reflected, in part, the big increase in investment that took place following the establishment of the EC. Expressed in absolute terms, trade creation amounted to an estimated $11.3 billion (or 21% of trade) and trade diversion at $0.3 billion (or 1%).

Balassa's approach, however, is subject to much the same objections as the import share approach discussed above. First, it cannot be assumed that income elasticities of import demand would have remained unchanged in the absence of integration. To do so is to disregard entirely the effects of price changes and changes in real exchange rates that took place in the two periods. Second, the results are highly dependent on the precise years chosen for the pre-integration period. If they do not represent equivalent years in the business cycle, the trend in the income elasticity of import demand will be a distorted one. Third, there is a further possibility that the trend in the pre-integration period could have been affected by special factors. Trade liberalization by the EC countries in their trade with non-EC countries in the 1950s may mean that trade diversion after integration was overestimated. Equally, it may mean that the extent of trade creation after integration was underestimated. Finally, the method is unable to take into account any effects that the establishment of the EC may have had on economic growth and any possible pro-trade or anti-trade bias that they may have given rise to.

Normalizing trade shares

One way of getting round the problems involved in constructing the *anti-monde* from data drawn from the period before integration (that might be wholly uncomparable with the period after) is to use data *for the same period* drawn from some third country. The third country or group of countries, then, acts as a 'normalizer' or control group. One possibility is to normalize changes in the imports/apparent consumption ratio for the EC for the post integration period by using changes in the same ratio for some other country as the normalizer. Kreinin (1972) used the United States as the normalizing country, but made additional adjustments for differences in the rate of growth of incomes and prices. He estimated trade creation in manufactured goods and processed foods at $7.3 billion, compared with trade diversion at $2.4 billion. Using the United Kingdom as the normalizing country, trade creation was estimated to amount to $9.3 billion and trade diversion at $0.4 billion .

The choice of the normalizer is, clearly, of major importance. This must be a country that has experienced similar changes to the integrating countries, but was not itself affected by the process of integration under investigation. Thus, for the purposes of measuring the effects of European integration, it should be a non-European country, as European countries that were not part of the EC would still have been affected by the integration process taking place in the EC. This, therefore, may be a good reason for not using the United Kingdom since it belonged to EFTA. Other requirements for a good normalizer are that the country or group of countries should have growth and inflation rates similar to those of the EC over the period covered, as income and relative prices are known to be the major determinants of import demand. In a later study covering the two stages of integration in Western Europe involving both the EC and EFTA countries, Kreinin (1979) used industrialized countries outside Europe, namely, the United States, Canada and Japan as the normalizer. He estimated the trade creation for the EC and EFTA countries from both stages of integration (1959/60 to 1977) at $20–$31 billion and trade diversion at $5–$8 billion. These results are summarized in Table 7.2.

Row A shows Kreinin's own estimates for the two stages of integration. Row B shows the range of estimates of other studies for the first stage of integration (up to 1969/70). Row C shows the results of the adaptation of an earlier study of Kreinin (1973) for the period from 1970/71 to 1977.

Much earlier, Lamfalussy (1963) had suggested comparing changes in the share of trade of EC and EFTA members in the rest of the world as indicative

Table 7.2 Estimated annual effects of European integration on trade flows in manufactured products (US$ bn)

		Annual trade creation	Annual trade diversion
A	Two stages of integration combined (independent estimate)	20–31	5–8
B	First stage integration:		
	EEC	9–11	1–2
	EFTA	2–4	1
	EEC plus EFTA	11–15	2–3
C	Second stage integration	11–17	2
D	Two stages added up	22–32	4–5

Source: Kreinin, M. E. (1979). Reprinted by permission of the author.

of what would have happened had integration not taken place. In other words, changes in the share of EC and EFTA countries in non-European markets is taken as indicative of how they would have performed if integration had not taken place. There are obvious disadvantages to this approach. First, no account is taken of changes taking place in the importing country that might have altered the share of imports coming from an individual partner country. Second, as with extrapolation based on the share of intra-area imports in total imports, the method cannot distinguish between trade creation and trade diversion, without introducing information from other sources. Nevertheless, Williamson and Bottrill (1971) used this method in an early study of the effects of integration on trade flows in manufactures. They found that, in 1969, intra-EC trade was roughly 50% greater than it would otherwise have been. By inserting estimates of trade creation and trade diversion from other studies, they estimated trade creation and trade diversion together at $12.4 billion.

7.3.2 Econometric models

The problem with using any of the residual models discussed above is that the construction of the *anti-monde* is based, purely, on assumptions about what would have happened had integration not taken place. Although refinements can be made by including adjustments to take account of special factors, there can be no certainty about the extent to which these factors have affected the result. A better approach is to construct a model that incorporates all of the determinants of trade flows and use the model to estimate the effect of integration on trade. Such an approach is essential when it comes to *ex ante* prediction of the likely effects of integration yet to take place.

Two types of econometric model have been used to estimate the effects of European integration as described under the following headings.

Gravity models

These were among the first type of model to be used in empirical work concerned with the effects of European integration. A gravity model is a model that seeks to explain trade flows between pairs of countries (bilateral trade flows) by variables drawn from both the importing and the exporting country. Such models were pioneered by Tinbergen (1952, 1962), but developed later by Linnemann (1966) and others. The major variables in a conventional gravity equation are the GNP/GDP of the two countries, their populations and the distance between them. Such an equation has the attraction that it incorporates both supply- and demand-side determinants of trade. While the GNP/GDP of the importing country will exert a positive influence on trade flows, the GNP/GDP of the exporting country will also do so. The *population* of the importing country can also be expected to increase the demand for imports. However, the population of the exporting country is, generally, considered as having a negative relationship with exports. This is because population is a proxy for size and size results in greater self-sufficiency. *Distance* exerts, of course, a negative effect on trade flows. Additional dummy variables may be added for countries that are *adjacent* to one another and to capture the effect of any *preferential trading agreement* existing between the two countries. Such models have been found to be capable of explaining a significant proportion of the bilateral trade flows taking place between countries in the world. Despite this, they have often been criticized for lacking any robust theoretical basis. In particular, prices are excluded entirely from the model, it being assumed that markets adjust to equate demand and supply. It is possible, however, to modify the gravity equation to incorporate both prices and exchange rates. If this is done, Bergstrand (1985) has shown that gravity models are consistent with trade theory. (Frankel (1997) provides a useful discussion of the contribution of the 'new' international economics to giving gravity modelling a solid theoretical foundation.)

Verdoorn and Schwartz (1972) were the first to use a gravity model to explain bilateral trade flows between countries in manufactured goods. The main variables were the growth rate of GNP in the importing country, the growth of manufacturing production in the exporting country, distances, changes in relative prices (including the effect of tariff change) and tariff reductions in intra-area trade. They estimated trade creation at $10.1 billion ($10.4 billion including EFTA) in 1969 and trade diversion at $1.1 billion ($1.9 billion including EFTA). Aitken (1973) used a conventional gravity equation, with GNP and population in the importing and exporting countries, distance between commercial centres and dummy variables for adjacency and for trade among the partner countries of the EC and EFTA as the explanatory variables. The model was estimated annually for the period from 1951 to 1967. The equation for 1958 was used to represent the pre-integration situation. The study estimated trade creation in the EC as reaching $9.2 billion in 1967 or 1.4% of trade. However, the method used only permitted the measurement of EC trade diversion against EFTA countries, which was estimated at $0.6 billion or 2% of trade. In using 1958 trade flows as the normalizer, however, trade creation was overstated and trade diversion understated, as no allowance was made for a continuing upward trend in intra-trade that would have happened had integration not taken place.

Prewo (1974) is another example of a study that used a gravity approach to estimate the trade effect. A special feature of this approach was the use of an input–output framework, which helped capture the effects of trade creation and trade diversion on intermediate products that other studies largely omitted. Using a share approach, he compared the actual level of intra- and extra-area imports of the EC for 1970 with the hypothetical level estimated using the gravity equation. The exercise was carried out for eleven product groups. He found that the formation of the EC has resulted in both internal and external trade creation in agriculture, fishing and forestry. This was explained in terms of increased demand for feeding stuffs required for expanded meat production and the need to import more forestry products that the EC lacked (see Chapter 20). In processed food, beverages and tobacco, however, the expected trade diversion resulting from the CAP was recorded. Some trade diversion was found for minerals and metals, but external trade creation took place in fuels due to the switch from coal to oil. Trade creation was found for all six manufactured product groups, with trade diversion occurring only in the case of textiles, leather, shoes and clothing. Trade creation was greatest in chemicals, metal products, machinery and transport equipment.

Recently, there has been a renewed interest in the use of gravity models to estimate the determinants of bilateral trade flows, including the influence of regional trading arrangements. Frankel (1997) used a gravity model to estimate the explanatory power of all the conventional variables determining a comprehensive cross-section of data covering the period from 1965 to 1992. Ordinary least squares was used to estimate a gravity equation that included total bilateral exports and imports as the dependent variable and GNP, per capita GNP, distance, adjacency, language and membership of a regional trading arrangement as the independent variables. Five separate trading blocs were included in the equation – EU 15, NAFTA, Mercosur, Andean Pact, ASEAN, AUS–NZ. Bilateral trade flows from the United Nations trade matrix covering some 63 countries were included. An estimated 75% of all bilateral trade flows were explained by the model. With regard to European integration, Frankel found evidence that European integration had a positive effect on trade flows between member states, although much depended on whether the EU Fifteen or the EC Twelve was taken as the relevant trading bloc. In the case of the EU, there was no statistically significant effect until after 1985, which is not surprising given that the EU did not come into being until the end of the period covered. By 1990, trade between members of the EU was found to be 35% more than trade between two similar countries, allowing for all the other factors determining trade between them. The EC bloc effect was stronger, but not statistically significant until 1980. Again, however, membership of the EC was not complete until 1986, with the accession of Spain and Portugal. Frankel's results showed that, by 1992, bilateral trade between any two EC member states was 65% higher than it would have been had the EC not existed. Both of the two enlargements in 1973 and 1985 were found to have contributed about one half of the increase.

Gravity models have also been used to analyse the effects of increased integration between Western and Eastern Europe, following the collapse of Communism and the break up of COMECON. Wang and Winters (1991) provided one of the first examples of such studies. They used a gravity model to estimate bilateral trade flows between some 76 countries over the period 1984–86, excluding the Central and East European countries (CEECs) and former Soviet Republic (FSR) countries. The reason for excluding the CEEC and FSR countries was to determine the relationship between bilateral trade flows and variables such as GDP, population and distance for 'normal' countries, defined as countries that are properly integrated into the world trading system, which the CEECs were not. Their equation predicted 70% of all the observed bilateral trade flows, with the expected signs for the major variables. Next, data for GDP, population and distance for the CEEC countries were inserted into the equations to estimate the 'potential' trade flows for the base year 1985 if these countries were to become fully integrated. These *potential* trade flows were then compared with *actual* trade flows to determine how trade patterns could be affected if these countries were integrated with those of Western Europe. Their results predicted a big boost in trade between the two blocs, but decline in trade between the CEECs.

Baldwin (1994) also used a gravity model to estimate the effects of increased integration between the two halves of Europe. The model was estimated using trade flows between EC and EFTA countries and between these countries and the United States, Japan, Canada and Turkey for the period 1979 to 1988. Ordinary least squares were then used to estimate the coefficients in an equation with all the standard variables, including a dummy variable for adjacency and membership of the European Economic Area (EEA) (see Chapters 1 and 2). Using a random-effects estimator with a maximum likelihood correction for first-order autocorrelation, the equation was able to predict as much as 99% of all bilateral trade flows. In a similar manner to Wang and Winters, data for GDP, population and distance for the base year 1989 were used to predict potential trade flows between the EFTA countries, EU member states, CEECs and FSR countries. The results showed a very large medium term potential for export growth from Western to Eastern Europe, with Germany being the largest potential beneficiary. CEECs and FSR countries also enjoyed scope for increased exports to the EU and EFTA countries, although exports to other CEECs and FSR countries could be expected to fall. The latter, however, was a case of reversed trade diversion, caused, in the past, by COMECON. In a second scenario, allowance was made for a rise in the per capita incomes of the CEECs and former Soviet Republic as they caught up with the levels of poorer West European countries. This paints an even rosier picture for the exports of the West European countries spread over several decades, with exports to Eastern Europe growing by between 10% and 15% per annum.

Very recently, Rose (1999) used an augmented gravity model to evaluate the effects of European Monetary Union (EMU) on trade. In addition to the standard GDP, population and distance variables, the model included adjacency, common language, regional trading arrangements, common nationality and colonial relationship variables, as well as a variable for using the same currency and for volatility of bilateral exchange rates. The equation was estimated for 186 countries for five different years – 1970, 1975, 1980, 1985 and 1990. The model was found to explain 63% of trade flows, with all the expected results. More importantly, exchange rate volatility (measured by the standard deviation of bilateral nominal exchanges in the preceding five years) was found to have a strong negative effect on trade and the effect of a common currency an even larger positive impact. Frankel (1997) also found that exchange rate volatility exerted a strong negative effect on worldwide bilateral trade flows. For the member states of the EC, he found that, if the level of exchange rate variability that prevailed in 1980 was eliminated, intra-EC trade would have been increased by 14.2%.

Analytic models

As we have seen, a criticism of gravity models is that they lack an adequate theoretical foundation. In particular, most versions exclude relative prices and real exchange rates as variables. An alternative approach would be to find a model that includes the full range of variables that are capable of explaining trade flows between countries. An analytic model has been defined as a model that 'provides a direct economic explanation of the value of trade flows after economic integration' (Mayes, 1978). Such a model is, especially, necessary where the need is to make an *ex ante* prediction of the effects of integration. However, an analytic model may be equally useful in *ex post* estimation as a way of isolating the integration effect from all the others influencing trade during the integration period.

At a simple level, the main determinants of *total* imports in any year are the level of economic activity (with GNP or GDP or apparent consumption as the most suitable proxy) and the prices of domestic products relative to the price of imports. The relationship between GNP/GDP and imports is given by the income elasticity of demand for imports and between relative prices and imports by the price elasticity of demand for imports. However, in order to measure the impact of integration on imports, it is necessary to distinguish between *total*, *intra-area* and *extra-area* imports. Intra- and extra-imports will be determined by the relationship between the prices of imports from partner countries and the price of imports in non-partner countries. This will depend on the elasticity of substitution of imports with respect to price changes between partner and non-partner countries. We may summarize these relationships as follows:

$$M_T = á + â_1 GNP + â_2 Pd/Pw$$

$$M_I = á + â_1 GNP + â_2 Pd/Pw - â_3 Pp/Pw$$

$$M_E = á + â_1 GNP + â_2 Pd/Pw + â_3 Pp/Pw$$

Where M_T, M_I and M_E stand for total, intra-area and extra-area imports respectively, GNP for gross national product in the importing country, Pd/Pw for domestic prices relative to prices in the rest of the world and Pp/Pw for prices in partner countries and prices in the rest of the world. The coefficients measure income elasticity of import demand, price elasticity of import demand and the elasticity of substitution of import demand with respect to partner and non-partner countries.

The integration effect may be assumed to work though changes in relative prices. Multilateral tariff reductions work through raising Pd/Pw and preferential tariff reductions through lowering Pp/Pw. How-

ever, this assumes that tariff changes are fully passed onto prices. Such an assumption may be tenable where goods are homogeneous and sold in perfectly competitive markets. However, where goods are differentiated and/or markets less than perfectly competitive, price changes may not equate with tariff changes. A further difficulty is that tariff changes may have an effect on imports other than through changes in relative prices. Balassa (1974a) and others have drawn attention to the possible 'promotional effects' of integration, whereby integration stimulates imports through increased information flows, direct investment by firms in sales and distribution outlets and a reduction of risk and uncertainty. For this reason, some models have preferred to include a separate variable for tariff changes.

Once a suitable model has been decided upon, the task is to estimate the coefficients in the equation for a suitable period of time and, then, to use the completed equation to estimate what trade would have been had integration not taken place. Actual trade flows may, then, be compared with flows predicted by the model and the residual treated as the integration effect. In this case, the *anti-monde* is based on actual estimates of how income and relative prices have affected trade flows over the integration period. If the purpose is to make an *ex ante* prediction as to how integration will affect trade flows in the future, the coefficients in the equation may be used to compare the effects with and without integration. For this purpose, integration may be treated as a separate dummy variable taking the value of one or zero according to the simulation. Rather than estimating the model for the EC for a different period of time to that during which integration took place, an alternative might be to estimate the equation for a comparable country or group of countries for the same period of time. This is the equivalent of using a normalizer in residual models. Whatever the procedure, the estimation should be done at as disaggregated a level as possible, as individual countries and products do not behave in the same fashion.

Resnick and Truman (1975) used a regression model of the kind described above to measure the impact of European integration on trade in manufactured goods. Major variables in the model were real income, relative prices and a separate variable designed to capture the effects of greater pressure of demand. Coefficients were obtained by estimating the equations for EC trade for the period from 1953 to

1968. The model was then simulated to estimate the impact of integration by altering the 1968 values of the relative price variables for tariff changes in the EC and EFTA. Trade creation was estimated at $1.2 billion ($1.4 billion including EFTA) and trade diversion at $2.7 billion ($3.6 billion including EFTA). These figures were much lower than the estimates obtained by other studies, with trade diversion actually exceeding trade creation. Several reasons were given for this (see Balassa, 1974a). First, Resnick and Truman used export price indices with respect to foreign products and the GNP deflator for domestic products to capture the relative price effect. However, as the GNP deflator included non-traded as well as traded goods, the estimated price elasticities of import demand may have been biased downwards and, hence, trade creation underestimated. This was borne out by separate tests for bias carried out by Resnick and Truman. The use of ordinary least squares in the trade creation equations was also criticized as imparting a downward estimate to the calculations. Finally, the use of price equations was criticized for failing to capture the so-called 'promotional effects' of integration. Indeed, as Balassa argues, the difference between Resnick and Truman's estimates and those of other studies suggests that these promotional effects were quite important.

More recent econometric work has made use of a methodology based on consumer demand theory known as the Almost Ideal Demand System (AIDS), developed by Deaton and Muellbauer (1980). Winters (1984, 1985) used this approach to model the effects on the UK of accession to the EC (see below). For each industry, the share of the market taken by individual supplier may be denoted by s_{ik} where i denotes the ith supplier's share of the kth country's market for a particular industry. This is given by the following equation:

$$S_{ik} = á + Ó ë_{ij} \ln p_{jk} + â \ln Y_k / P_k$$

Where p_{jk} is the price of the jth country supplier into the kth country market, Y_k is total nominal expenditure by k residents and P_k is a price index covering supplies from all sources. The set of equations are concerned with showing how consumers allocate their spending over different sources that is both rational and consistent with their aim of maximizing their utility. Behaviour of consumers is constrained by a set of parameters designed to ensure that this happens. The attraction of this model is that it accounts for the allocation of consumer expenditure on manufactures

among all suppliers, not just between domestic suppliers and foreign suppliers. The effects of tariff reductions on intra-area imports are incorporated into the model through the use of dummy variables. This may be preferable to doing so through alterations in relative prices in order to capture non-price as well as price effects and to overcome data constraints regarding prices.

CEPR/EU Commission (1997) used a similar approach to estimate the effects of the creation of the single market (see Chapter 11). They used three demand equations for fifteen three-digit sensitive goods sectors for four principal countries, namely, Germany, France, Italy and the UK. The equations estimated the share of nominal sectoral expenditure accounted for by domestically produced goods, intra-EU imports and extra-EU imports. A separate dummy variable was included to capture the effect of the creation of the single market. The single market was expected to affect trade flows not only through the *direct* effects of reductions in trade costs on demand, but also through the *indirect* effects of increased competition and reductions in price–cost margins. Separate price equations for each of the sectors covered were used to estimate these indirect, supply-side effects. The estimated impact of the single market on price–cost margins were, then, used to simulate the impact of price reductions on trade flows using the estimated demand equations. They found that the overall impact of the Single Market Programme was to cause a decrease in the domestic producers' share in the fifteen sectors covered of 4.2% and a rise in the share of EU producers of 2.1% and of the rest of the world of 2%. A similar exercise was carried out for the manufacturing sectors as a whole in order to be able to examine the effects of the single market on other manufacturing sectors. For manufacturing as a whole, the fall in the domestic producers' share was 2.3%, with EU producers increasing their share by 0.5% and the rest of the world by 1.8%. In other words, the impact of the single market was, overwhelmingly, one of both internal and external trade creation. These results are summarized in Table 7.3.

7.3.3 Computable general equilibrium models

Econometric models are essentially *partial equilibrium* models. That is to say, they seek to show the immediate effects only of tariff changes on imports by

Table 7.3 Estimated impact of the single market on market shares

| | Percentage change in market share | | | | | | | |
| | demand | | Price competition | | | Overall impact | | |
	U	RoW	Home	EU	RoW	Home	EU	RoW
Glasswar	1	+1.4	+0.7	−0.1	−0.5	−0.7	−0.2	+0.9
Ceramic		+2.4	−0.2	+0.3	−0.1	−4.4	+2.0	+2.4
Basic i		+1.8	+1.1	−0.7	−0.3	−3.3	+1.8	+1.5
Pharr		+1.5	−0.1	+0.2	−0.1	−2.0	+0.5	+1.4
Boil		+0.9	+0.9	−0.9	+0.0	−4.4	+3.5	+0.9
Ma		+4.2	−0.6	+0.2	+0.4	−2.6	−2.0	+4.6
M		+4.4	+0.5	−0.4	−0.1	−6.9	+2.6	+4.3
F		0.7	+1.1	−0.6	−0.5	−0.6	+0.4	+0.2
		5.0	+1.1	+0.1	−1.2	−6.7	+3.0	+3.8
		.0	+1.0	−1.5	−0.5	−1.7	+0.2	+1.5
		1	+4.0	−2.2	−1.8	−11.7	+2.2	+9.5
		2	+0.3	−0.7	+0.3	−4.6	+3.0	+1.5
			+7.0	−2.5	−4.4	−8.3	+12.0	−3.8
			+1.5	−1.4	−0.1	−4.8	+4.5	+0.3
			+0.7	−0.5	−0.2	−2.1	−3.1	+5.2
			+1.2	−0.8	−0.4	−4.2	+2.1	+2.0
			−0.8	+0.4	+0.4	−1.2	−0.4	+1.7
			−0.1	+0.0	+0.1	−2.3	+0.5	+1.8

...ted by permission of the European Communities.

such models are highly complex and require a computer program to be designed both to solve the equations in the model and to simulate the policy changes being investigated.

CGE modelling is a comparatively recent development in the empirical estimation of the effects of trade liberalization. Partly, this is because the construction of a CGE model is a complex and time-consuming exercise. Partly, too, it is because the possibilities that such a model opens up have not been fully understood until now. Most applications of CGE modelling have been concerned with simulating the effects of various *multilateral* trade liberalization scenarios, such as the effects of cuts in tariffs and non-tariff barriers agreed through the GATT/WTO. However, CGE models have also been used to analyse the effects of *regional* trade liberalization, including the likely effects of further European integration. CEPR/EU Commission (1997) attempted to use a CGE model to simulate the effects of the Single Market Programme. The model was a 12-country model with 118 manufacturing industries. A particular attraction of the model was that it contained both a perfectly competitive, non-agricultural sector and an imperfectly competitive manufacturing sector, in which products are differentiated and produced under conditions of increasing returns to scale

CGE modelling involves a two-stage approach. First, the model must be calibrated for a base year. This involves estimating the equations making up the model for a particular year using a data set containing values for all the variables in the model. However, not all parameters are estimated; of necessity, some are imposed using estimates taken from the literature. Second, the model is then subjected to a series of external shocks that simulate the effects of the liberalization process that is being analysed. This is then compared with what would have happened had no

change taken place. In the case of the CEPR/EU Commission model, both *ex-ante* and *ex-post* simulations were undertaken. The *ex-ante* exercise simulated the likely effects of the single market on intra-EU trade costs, by using sectoral estimates taken from an earlier study by Buigues, Ilzkovitz and Lebrun (1990). These estimates were imposed on the model for 1990 and the effects on the equilibrium were re-computed. The results showed the share of domestic producers in home consumption falling by just over 2% in most member states, while the share of EU producers increased by roughly 3% and the rest of the world declined by less than 1%. Thus, about two-thirds of the effect of the single market on intra-EU trade was trade creation and about one-third trade diversion. Table 7.4 below summarizes the results of the *ex-ante* simulation.

The *ex-post* simulation involved performing the same exercise in reverse. The changes in trade costs needed to reproduce the equilibrium in import penetration that actually took place between 1988 and 1994 was estimated. It is assumed that during this period, producers only had time to make limited adjustments to the changes taking place. In the long run, however,

Table 7.4 Changes in trade patterns in manufacturing resulting from the single market – an *ex-ante* simulation by EU Commission and CEPR

	Base shares (%)			Changes in shares (%)			Percentage change in EU share
	Home	EU	Row	Home	EU	RoW	
France	76.75	16.05	7.19	−2.55	2.99	0.44	1.19
Germany	75.6	13.58	10.82	−2.28	2.83	−0.55	1.21
Italy	79.53	13.41	7.07	−2.15	2.5	−0.35	1.19
United Kingdom	74.19	14.48	11.32	−2.25	2.88	−0.63	1.2
Netherlands	62.63	25.7	11.67	−2.32	3.42	−1.1	1.13
Belgium–Luxembourg	58.34	31.21	10.45	−2.47	3.59	−1.11	1.11
Denmark	63.75	21.69	14.55	−1.85	3.05	−1.21	1.14
Ireland	71.53	20.34	8.13	−2.04	2.72	−0.68	1.13
Greece	73.29	18.47	8.24	−1.4	2.13	−0.73	1.12
Spain	77.55	16.45	6	−2.35	2.78	−0.43	1.17
Portugal	72.54	21.74	5.71	−1.6	2.29	−0.69	1.11

Source: CEPR/European Commission (1997), Table 5.3. Reprinted by permission of the European Communities.

Table 7.5 Changes in trade patterns in manufactures resulting from the single market – an *ex-post* simulation by the EU Commission

	Changes in shares: base (%)			Percentage change in EU share	Changes in shares: competition effect (%)			Percentage change in EU share
	Home	EU	RoW		Home	EU	RoW	
France	−3.22	2.12	1.11	1.13	0.08	−0.04	−0.02	1.13
Germany	−2.78	1.63	1.14	1.12	0.04	−0.02	−0.03	1.12
Italy	−2.7	1.82	0.88	1.14	0.1	−0.07	−0.03	1.14
United Kingdom	−2.79	1.7	1.08	1.12	0.08	−0.05	−0.04	1.12
Netherlands	−2.8	1.78	1.02	1.07	0.19	−0.12	−0.06	1.07
Belgium–Luxembourg	−2.76	1.98	0.77	1.06	0.22	−0.16	−0.07	1.07
Denmark	−2.36	1.4	0.96	1.06	0.55	−0.34	−0.21	1.08
Ireland	−2.58	1.74	0.84	1.09	0.48	−0.34	−0.15	1.1
Greece	−1.46	0.92	0.54	1.05	0.61	−0.4	−0.21	1.07
Spain	−2.41	1.74	0.67	1.11	0.21	−0.16	−0.05	1.12
Portugal	−1.31	1.03	0.28	1.05	0.3	−0.24	−0.06	1.06

Source: CEPR/European Commission (1997), Table 5.5. Reprinted by permission of the European Communities.

full adjustment is assumed to take place. Two simulations were then carried out, one in which price-cost margins were fixed (i.e. no competition effects were assumed) and one in which the full effects of the single market were assumed to take place. By comparing the actual changes in trade shares with those resulting from the simulation, the single market effect was determined. These showed that, for manufacturing as a whole, the share of domestic producers fell by roughly 1.5%, whereas that of EU producers rose by 2% and that of the rest of the world fell by roughly 0.5%. However, this takes no account of the fall in extra-EU trade costs that the single market brought. In a second simulation, the results of a fall in extra-EU trade costs were estimated. They are summarized in Table 7.5.

7.3.4 Summary of the trade effects of integration

Table 7.6 summarizes the results obtained by different studies of the effects of the first and second stages of European integration on trade flows.

For the *first stage* of economic integration, trade creation for all goods was estimated at between $9.2 and $19.8 billion and trade diversion at between –$2.5 billion (i.e. external trade creation) and $0.5 billion. For manufactures, only, trade creation ranges from $1.2 to $18 billion, while trade diversion lies between –$3.1 billion and $2.7 billion. Subsequent enlargements of the EC have added to these effects. Estimates for the second stage of integration suggest that enlargement of the EC after 1973 resulted in further trade creation of $11–$17 billion and trade diversion of $2 billion. For *both stages* of integration, Kreinin (1979) has estimated the combined effects of EEC and EFTA for manufactures only as trade creation of between $20–$31 billion and trade diversion as between $5 – 8 billion. To these gains should be added the gains from subsequent enlargements of the EC, including the admission of Greece in 1981 and of Spain and Portugal in 1986 and, finally, of Sweden, Austria and Finland in 1995. No estimates have been made of the effects of these later enlargements. Finally, as we have seen above, the establishment of the single market in 1992 appears to have resulted in further net trade creation.

Table 7.6 A summary of the results of attempts to estimate trade creation and trade diversion in the EC, US$ billion

Author/study	Period studied	Trade created		Trade diverted	
		All goods $ billion	Manufactures $ billion	All goods $ billion	Manufactures $ billion
Balassa	1967	1.9		0.1	
	1974a	11.3	11.4	0.3	0.1
Prewo	1974b	19.8	18.0	−2.5	−3.1
Truman					
(unadjusted)	1969		9.2		−1.0
(adjusted)	1969		2.5		0.5
Kreinin	1979b		20–31		5.8
Williamson and Bottrill	1971		11.2		0
Verdoorn and Schwartz	1972		10.1		−1.1
Aitken	1973	9.2		−0.6	
Resnick and Truman	1975		1.2		2.7

7.4   The nature of European specialization

One important aspect of the trade effects is the evidence showing that trade creation mainly took the form of *intra-* rather than *inter-*industry specialization. That is to say, individual member states have tended to increase their specialization in a narrow range of products within a given industry, rather than in the industry *per se*. Orthodox trade theory predicts that tariff liberalization will lead to countries specializing in those industries or activities in which they have a comparative cost advantage. This leads to industries being relocated in countries where relative costs are lowest. Although this will leave the member states as a whole better off as resources are being used more efficiently than before, there may be considerable adjustment costs for particular groups of workers whose jobs disappear as a consequence and who must move to where new jobs are available and/or re-train. Where markets are imperfectly competitive, however, the effects of trade barriers disappearing may be for the number of varieties of a product to increase and for individual producers to specialize in particular varieties. This can be expected to result in fewer adjustment difficulties, as the geographical pattern of activity is not affected, only the nature of what is produced in each country.

Balassa (1974a) used a representative ratio, showing trade imbalances for individual product groups divided by the sum of exports and imports of products belonging to the group, to estimate the extent of intra-industry trade. The formula was as follows:

$$E_j = 1/n \sum |X_i - M_i| / (X_i + M_i)$$

where j stands for country j and i for product group i out of n industries and X and M for exports and imports respectively. A movement in the ratio towards unity was taken as evidence for inter-industry specialization and towards zero as evidence for intra-industry specialization. The ratios were calculated for 91 separate product groups at two-, three- and four-digit levels of aggregation and for bilateral trade flows in manufactured goods between the six member states for the period 1958–70. Balassa's results are shown in Table 7.7.

In all cases, the ratio was found to fall over the period covered, confirming that intra- rather than inter-industry specialization was taking place.

Balassa's results were confirmed by subsequent studies using different measures for the level of intra-industry trade. Grubel and Lloyd (1975) used a formula, in which the trade imbalance for an individual

Table 7.7 Representative ratios of trade balances for 91 product groups for EEC member states, 1958–1970

	1958	1963	1970
Belgium	0.458	0.401	0.339
France	0.394	0.323	0.273
Germany	0.531	0.433	0.331
Italy	0.582	0.521	0.410
Netherlands	0.495	0.431	0.357

Source: Balassa (1974a). Reprinted by permission of Blackwell Publishing Ltd

product group was deducted from total exports and imports before being divided by total exports and imports. The summary measure for all of a country's trade was as follows:

$$B_j = \sum (X_{ij} + M_{ij}) - \sum |X_{ij} - M_{ij}| / \sum (X_{ij} + M_{ij}) \times 100$$

The summary measure had the further attraction that the individual intra-industry trade ratio for each product group was weighted according to the importance of each product group in total trade. Their estimates showed the EC member states have among the highest levels of intra-industry trade of all OECD countries. The intra-industry trade ratio increased in all member states over the period from 1964 to 1974, with the single exception of the Netherlands. The highest levels of intra-industry trade were found for France, Belgium–Luxembourg and the Netherlands, with lower levels for Italy and West Germany.

Greenaway and Hine (1991) used the GL index to show that the level of intra-industry trade has continued to increase since 1970. Their results for the EC member states are summarized in the Table 7.8. However, there is some evidence that, in the 1980s, the increase in intra-industry trade may have weakened in some countries (France, Germany and the Netherlands).

On the other hand, CEPII/EU Commission (1997) showed that, following the launch of the single market, the importance of intra-industry trade has increased further. Using a Grubel–Lloyd index, they measured both vertical and horizontal intra-industry trade and inter-industry trade for bilateral trade flows in no fewer than 10 000 different products over the period from 1980 to 1994. The Grubel–Lloyd index showed rising intra-industry trade during this period, but, mainly, this took the form of vertical rather than horizontal intra-industry trade. That is to say, countries specialized in product groups ranked according to quality differences, rather than products differentiated purely by branding and advertising. Table 7.9 below summarizes their results.

Important country differences are apparent. France, Belgium–Luxembourg and Germany have high levels of horizontal IIT, while the UK, France and Germany have high levels of vertical IIT. By way of contrast, Greece, Portugal and Spain, all countries at a lower stage of development have high levels of inter-industry trade, as does Denmark. Although Spain and Portugal enjoyed the largest rise in IIT over the period of the single market programme, it is apparent that the overall rise in IIT in the EC could not be attributed to this. IIT increased in all countries, except Ireland and Denmark.

Table 7.8 Estimates of intra-industry trade for EC member states, 1970–1985

Country	1970	1978	1980	1983	1985
Belgium	0.800	0.835	0.841	0.875	0.867
Denmark	0.630	0.679	0.674	0.721	0.726
France	0.814	0.828	0.861	0.855	0.855
Germany	0.607	0.641	0.554	0.687	0.682
Ireland	0.444	0.600	0.685	0.723	0.703
Italy	0.617	0.614	0.696	0.662	0.695
Netherlands	0.741	0.759	0.779	0.776	0.763
United Kingdom	0.620	0.807	0.808	0.832	0.843

Source: Summarized from Greenaway and Hine (1991)

Table 7.9 Share of inter-industry and intra-industry trade in intra-EC trade 1987–1994 (percentage change)

Country	Shares in 1994 (%)			Variation, 1987–1994 (%)		
	Inter-industry trade	Horizontal intra-industry trade	Vertical intra-industry trade	Inter-industry trade	Horizontal intra-industry trade	Vertical intra-industry trade
France	31.6	24.1	44.3	−6.4	2.8	3.6
Germany	32.6	20.5	46.9	−5.4	1.9	3.4
Belgium–Luxembourg	34.8	23.2	42.0	−3.8	1.6	2.2
United Kingdom	35.6	16.5	47.9	−7.0	−1.9	8.9
Netherlands	39.3	18.9	41.9	−4.8	−0.3	5.1
Spain	45.9	18.9	35.2	−12.0	8.7	3.3
Italy	46.9	16.2	36.9	−2.8	5.8	−3.1
Ireland	57.7	7.9	34.4	2.2	−0.9	−1.3
Denmark	60.0	8.1	31.9	1.1	−1.1	0.0
Portugal	68.6	7.5	23.9	−8.6	3.9	4.8
Greece	86.0	3.7	10.3	−0.2	0.8	−0.6
EC Twelve	38.5	19.2	42.3	−5.1	2.0	3.1
EC without Spain and Portugal	37.4	19.5	43.1	−5.0	1.7	3.3

Source: CEPII/European Commission (1997), Table 1.1. Reprinted by permission of the European Communities.

7.5   Estimating the income effects

Most studies of the effects of integration have been concerned purely and simply with measuring the *trade* impact of integration. However, these trade effects are of little interest *per se*. More important is the extent to which real *incomes* were raised or lowered by integration. As we have seen, these involve an additional stage of calculation. In the orthodox theory of customs unions, the increase in economic welfare brought about by trade creation is measured by the value of trade created multiplied by half the reduction in tariffs on intra-area trade. The loss from trade diversion is the value of trade diverted multiplied by the difference between EC prices and world prices. Applying this approach, Balassa (1974a) estimated the welfare gain from trade creation in manufactured goods at $0.7 billion in 1970, by multiplying increased trade in

manufactures of $11.4 billion by an average tariff of 12%. As the loss from trade diversion in manufactures was negligible, the welfare gain from trade creation was equivalent to 0.15% of GNP, a surprisingly small amount. With trade diversion in agriculture of $1.3 billion and an average external rate of protection of 47%, the loss from trade diversion was estimated at $0.3 billion.

In fact, most studies of the welfare gain from tariff liberalization have found it be quite small when expressed as a percentage of GDP/GNP. One reason for this is that trade typically accounts for a small proportion of total output, so that, when gains are expressed in relation to national output, they appear quite low. A further reason is that the tariff reduction that resulted from integration was small, as tariffs in several member states were already quite low by the time the EEC came into being. Another consideration is that most studies have been concerned purely and simply with the effects of *tariff* liberalization. No account is taken of the effects of the removal of *non-tariff* barriers, although most of this did not take place until the launching of the Internal Market Programme in 1987. A more important consideration concerns the nature of the expansion of intra-European trade that took place following integration. As we have seen, this mainly took the form of *intra-industry specialization*. Although intra-industry specialization still benefits consumers at least as much as inter-industry specialization, the gain comes mainly from increased choice as more varieties of the product become available. Consumer welfare is increased both as they can choose a variety that is closer to their preference and because they can maximize their utility by consuming more varieties of the same good.

However, intra-industry specialization may also bring further, long run gains for consumers that will not be fully captured by conventional measures of welfare gain from lower tariffs. Where producers specialize in particular products or processes, average costs are often lowered as the scale of production can be increased. It will be the cost savings that come from increased plant specialization and longer production runs, rather than plant size, which will result from greater IIT. By expanding the number of varieties available, IIT will also increase the degree of competition facing individual producers, which may bring further benefits from the elimination of X-inefficiency (managerial slack). If producers are forced by this process to cut prices, consumers will enjoy a further increase in their real incomes. As these gains will accrue more in the long run, they constitute the *dynamic* effects of integration. Arguably, however, they may be the more important type of gains. One reason is that reductions in unit costs resulting from greater plant specialization and increased competition affect the full range of the output produced, not just the part that is traded. Another reason is that they are ongoing, not once-and-for-all, effects, which continue being enjoyed for several years after the integration process is complete. The dynamic gains are not confined to industries in which intra-industry specialization takes place. They may also occur in industries where conventional *inter-industry specialization* occurs. Where an industry enjoys a relative cost advantage in a particular industry, increased specialization after integration

will enable producers to expand the scale of their production and enjoy economies of plant size. These are different from the economies resulting from increased plant specialization and long production runs that result where intra-industry specialization is the outcome. Both forms of specialization are also likely to stimulate greater competition, which should lead to further efficiency gains as producers are forced to cut costs and rationalize their production operations.

Few of the early studies of the effects of integration tried to quantify these effects. Any attempt to do so confronts even bigger counterfactual problems than estimating the static effects alone. Balassa (1974a) used estimates of the efficiency gains from increasing the scale of production in manufacturing to make a guess at the possible magnitude of the gain. According to a study by Walters (1963), a doubling of inputs in United States non-agricultural production led to a 130% increase in output. Applying this to the amount of trade created by integration, Balassa estimated a gain in GNP for 1970 of slightly over 0.5%, sufficient to add 0.1% to the EC's actual growth rate. However, the gain might be greater if the cost reduction were applied to all intra-area trade in manufactures or to the entire manufacturing sector. One difficulty, however, with an exercise of this sort is that of knowing the extent to which producers in the individual member states were constrained before integration by the size of their domestic markets from operating at an optimum scale. Moreover, firms might have been able to achieve these scale economies through an expansion of their exports to the rest of the world without integration taking place. On the other hand, as Balassa argued, the fact that the elimination of tariffs between EC member states was irreversible reduced the risk for producers from investing in large-scale production methods.

One later attempt to estimate these effects of integration on manufacturing was a study by Owen (1983). He argued that, potentially, the gains from integration were quite large, because of the effects that integration had on both the scale of production and competition. As tariff barriers are lowered, Owen argued that firms are forced to rationalize their operations, closing small, high-cost plants and concentrating production in large, low cost plants. Using detailed estimates of the efficiency gains in three branches of manufacturing industry – namely, washing machines and refrigerators, trucks and cars – Owen calculated the cost reductions resulting from intra-EC trade creation. The gains were put at 54% for washing machines, 135% for refrigerators, 53% for cars and 4% for trucks. Added to these gains from an increased scale of production were the cost savings from the elimination of high-cost marginal producers in importing countries. In total, the welfare gain to the original six EC members from these dynamic effects was estimated at between 3% and 6% of the combined GNP. By way of contrast, the pure static welfare gains, amounted to only 2/3%. However, Owen has been criticized for deducing a very large welfare gain from a comparatively, narrowly focused study.

To the welfare gains from the first two stages of European integration must be added those resulting from the creation of the single market. The most comprehensive attempt at estimating the potential to the EC from the realization of the single market was a study carried out on behalf of the European Commission by a committee chaired by Paulo Cecchini. The Cecchini Report (1988) was, in fact, the popular version of a more definitive piece of technical work carried out by Emerson (1988). This sought to estimate the welfare gain from removing a wide range of non-tariff barriers by estimating the costs to the EC of having these barriers. It included both the static welfare gains from trade creation as these barriers were

removed *and* the longer-run dynamic gains that were expected to result from increased competition and the exploitation of economies of scale.

These gains were estimated at between ECU 70 and 190 billion or between 2.5% and 6.5% of EC GDP with the gain spread over a period of five years or more. In a separate macroeconomic exercise, the effect of these costs savings on the whole economy were simulated on different assumptions about the stance of macroeconomic policy. Assuming passive macroeconomic policies, an increase in real GDP of 4.5% was predicted over a period of between 5 and 6 years. With more active macroeconomic policies, an increase in real GDP of roughly 7% was predicted.

However, Emerson was essentially an *ex-ante* study of the likely effects of the single market. Subsequently, as part of the Single Market Review, the Commission has sought to estimate the actual effect of the single market on EC GDP. As part of this study, the EU Commission/CEPR (1997) used the CGE model designed to estimate the effects of the single market on trade to estimate the welfare gain from the single market for the period from 1991 to 1994. If reductions in trade costs for extra- as well as for intra-EC trade are included, the gains range from 2% to 10% of GDP. These are summarized in Table 7.10.

Table 7.10 Changes in GDP and welfare resulting from trade creation and trade diversion in the single market

Country	Percentage change in GDP	Change in welfare as percentage of GDP	Change in welfare as percentage of manufacturing value added
France	2	2.27	8.72
Germany	2.2	2.47	2.22
Italy	1.9	2.22	7.33
United Kingdom	2.4	2.8	9.9
Netherlands	3.2	3.74	14.34
Belgium–Luxembourg	4	4.55	16.59
Denmark	2	2.36	11.68
Ireland	3.3	3.96	12.03
Greece	4.2	5.04	19.59
Spain	2.8	3.35	11.05
Portugal	8.6	10.02	27.49

Source: CEPR/European Commission (1997), Table 5.6. Reprinted by permission of the European Communities.

7.6   Economic growth

An increase in real income due to the static and dynamic effects of integration is not the same as increase in the rate of economic growth. An increase in the growth rate is the result of an increase in a country's potential to go on producing more every year. Few of the early attempts to estimate the impact of integration had much to say about the effect of integration on growth. Balassa (1974a) estimated that the formation of the EC added a further 1% increase in GNP due to increased savings and investment. This was sufficient to raise the growth rate by 0.05%. This occurred through higher incomes, leading to higher savings and higher investment. However, the exploitation of economies of scale and rationalization of production might be expected to lead to further new investment. Indeed, the share of fixed investment in GNP in the Six rose from 21% in 1958 to 25% in 1970. Suggesting that this share might have been about 1% smaller than if integration had not taken place, Balassa estimated that the rate of economic growth was increased by a further 0.2% as a result of integration.

Marques-Mendes (1986) proposed a simple balance of payments constrained growth model, based on the work of Thirlwall (1979, 1982) for analysing the effects of integration on growth. The model makes use of the concept of the foreign trade multiplier whereby an increase in export volume causes an increase in output, not only in the exporting country but also in trading partners through an increase in imports. Some of the increase in output in trading partners returns to the country that experiences the initial export expansion through increased imports by trading partners. The size of the foreign trade multiplier depends on the income elasticity of demand for imports in both countries. However, the extent to which output can grow is constrained by the need to achieve balance of payments equilibrium.

The model has the advantage that it can break down the integration impact on economic growth into a variety of different factors. In addition to increased exports, integration may affect a country's growth through a change in the trade balance and through any change in the terms of trade required to adjust for any change in the trade balance. Integration will have a negative effect on a country's growth if it leads to an increased propensity to import. Other negative effects

will include the need to make net budget payments to the EC and/or to make net transfers to other member states under the CAP. Factor flows, such as net inward investment and/or labour remittances from abroad, will have a positive effect on the growth rate. Thus, the model makes possible the construction of a broader framework for analysing the effects of integration on GDP, than reliance purely and simply on net trade creation effects. Using this framework, Marques-Mendes estimated the impact of integration on economic growth for the two phases of integration – 1961 to 1972 and 1974 to 1981. Table 7.11 below summarizes the results he obtained.

For the first period of integration, despite the fact that France and, to a lesser extent, Germany experienced negative effects, integration appears to have had a sizeable positive effect on economic growth. For the second period, all countries, except Denmark, enjoyed faster growth as a result of integration. Taking the figures as a whole, Marques-Mendes found that the GDP of the EC was 2.2% higher than it would have been had integration not taken place and, by 1981, 5.9% higher.

With regard to the single market, Baldwin (1989) showed how increased integration results in a permanently higher growth rate in the member states and not just a higher level of output. He argued that conventional estimates of the impact of the single market (see Cecchini, 1988 and Emerson *et al.*, 1988) underestimated the potential gain from integration because they were based on once-and-for-all gains only. He drew a distinction between two effects on economic growth – a *medium-term* acceleration as higher incomes boost savings and investment and a *long-term* effect as an increased rate of investment induces still further increases in investment in other parts of the economy. To begin with, integration raises incomes by increasing efficiency. However, if we assume that the share of savings and investment in national income is constant, higher incomes will lead to more saving and investment. As a result, the stock of capital will rise, leading to a further increase in output and further rise in savings and investment. A virtuous cycle of growth takes place. However, as we have seen, in a neo-classical growth model, this growth would eventually come to an end. This is because, with a constant supply of labour, increases in

Table 7.11 The effects of economic integration on the growth rate of member states, 1961–1972 and 1974–1981

	1961–1972		1974–1981	
	Actual growth rate (%)	Growth rate due to EC	Actual growth rate (%)	Growth rate due to EC
Germany	4.39	−0.02	2.65	0.91
France	5.40	−2.71	2.66	1.57
Italy	4.97	1.04	2.74	0.42
Netherlands	5.17	2.94	1.99	0.53
Belgium–Luxembourg	4.56	2.45	2.03	0.71
United Kingdom	–	–	1.24	0.37
Ireland	–	–	3.84	0.31
Denmark	–	–	1.98	−0.64

Source: summarized from Marques-Mendes (1986), Table 1 (extract). Reprinted by permission of Blackwell Publishing Ltd

the capital stock will eventually result in diminishing returns. At this point, new investment will fall until eventually all investment will be devoted to replacing capital stock that has worn out during the course of the year. With a constant capital stock, output will cease growing. During the time that it takes for this process to work itself out, the EC would enjoy faster growth than before, but the growth rate would eventually settle back at the steady rate. Even this effect alone, however, is sufficient to add significantly to the gains from integration. Baldwin estimated a gain in the medium term at between 3.5% and 9% in GDP might be achieved, which compares favourably with Cecchini's estimate of 2.5% to 7%.

However, if instead of a neo-classical growth model, an endogenous growth model is used, it is

entirely possible that growth might continue at a *permanently* higher rate than before. As we have seen, in new growth theory, knowledge accumulation is treated as an endogenous rather than exogenous variable. Faster growth creates a wedge between the private and public rates of return on capital. Instead of growth returning to a steady state, a process of ceaseless accumulation takes place, in which higher investment by individual firms increases the return to investment for firms taken as a whole. This offsets any tendency towards diminishing returns that result from increased capital accumulation. Using an endogenous growth model, Baldwin estimated the potential gains from the single market at between 11% and 35% of GDP, substantially more than the gains predicted by Cecchini.

7.7   Conclusion

In this chapter, we have surveyed the various attempts made by researchers to measure the impact of economic integration. We have seen that the major problem of all of these studies is that we do not know what would have happened had European integration not taken place. The major task for researchers is one of constructing as accurately as possible an *anti-monde*

so that the effects of integration on trade can be approximated. Methods for resolving the counterfactual problem range from the simplistic to the sophisticated. At the simplistic end of the spectrum are the residual models that extrapolate pre-integration trends into the post-integration period, on the assumption that the post-integration period was no different to the period preceding. At the sophisticated end, economists seek to use models of import demand to estimate the impact of integration. Although the latter approach is preferable, it should be borne in mind that the results obtained are only as good as the model that is used. Partial equilibrium models seek to identify and isolate the impact of integration on trade flows, but are unable to capture the different ways in which effects in one sector or country feedback into other sectors or countries. Although CGE models overcome these problems by stipulating the conditions for equilibrium to exist simultaneously in markets, too much should never be claimed for the results obtained.

What is clear from the range of estimates available is that the net effect of integration on trade appears to have been positive. Most studies show that integration resulted in significant net internal trade creation in manufactures and many show external trade creation resulting also. Although the Common Agricultural Policy has resulted in net trade diversion in agricultural goods, this is much less than the trade creation occurring in manufactures. Economic welfare has, therefore, risen as a result of the establishment of both the EC and EFTA and from their subsequent enlargements. However, when trade effects are translated into income effects, the benefit to the citizens of the EC appears surprisingly small. One reason is that the effects are being measured in relation to the GNP/GDP of the member states, which appears small because trade is only one component of national income.

The effects are larger if account is taken of the gains from removing non-tariff barriers rather than tariffs alone. This is born out by the studies carried out to estimate the gains from the completion of the internal market. Some further efficiency gains are expected to have resulted also from the adoption of the common currency. Furthermore, the gains appear much larger if account is taken of the dynamic, not just the static, effects. Attempts to measure these effects appear to show a sizeable gain to the EC, which is quantitatively more significant than the resource allocation effects. Cost savings from an enlarged scale of production affect the entire output of the firms producing the goods, not just the proportion of trade. Likewise, efficiency gains brought about as a result of increased competition affect a potentially much larger share of the output base than just the share that is traded. Integration appears also to result in firms restructuring their production to take advantage of the opportunities created by the larger market and in order to cope with the challenge posed by new competition.

However, integration does not affect just the level of national income. It has a positive effect on the rate at which income grows. At the very least, integration is likely to lead to faster growth in the medium term, as higher incomes lead to higher savings and investment and an enlarged capital stock. Recent developments in growth theory suggest that there might be more lasting effects, which enable all the member states participating in the integration process to grow at a permanently faster rate. Although the precise relationship between integration and growth has yet to be established, recent developments in growth theory suggest that the impact may be considerably greater than what has, in the past, been supposed. The modelling of these growth effects is, clearly, the major challenge for researchers of the future.

EU monetary integration

Part Three of this book covers all aspects of that far-reaching and most demanding element of integration: monetary unification, including the adoption of a single currency. The three chapters cover the theoretical analysis of the gains and losses from EMU, the EU developments that have led to the present situation where twelve of the fifteen EU member nations are using the euro as their only currency and the management of the euro by the European Central Bank and how the euro is operated.

Chapter 8

The theory of monetary integration

DAVID MAYES AND ALI EL-AGRAA

Chapter 6 was devoted mainly to a discussion of the economic consequences of tariff removal and the establishment of the common external tariff (CET). However, it is now well recognized that economic and monetary union (EMU), is by far the most challenging feature of the EU, or any scheme of economic integration that may decide to embrace it. Therefore in this and the two subsequent chapters we deal in turn with: the theoretical context of economic and monetary integration (this chapter); the current and planned development of EMU (Chapter 9); and an appraisal of the operation of EMU (Chapter 10). Between them, these chapters explain the reasons for the challenge as well as trace the EU's endeavours in this respect. First, however, we need to explain what economic and monetary integration means in this context.

8.1 Disentangling the concepts

One of the problems with EMU is that a large number of people think that the abbreviation stands for European Monetary Union. This is understandable because the largest element of EMU (economic and monetary union) has been the setting up of monetary union, with the establishment of a single currency, the euro, and the new central banking system to run it. The provisions of the treaty setting up EMU are heavily dominated by the monetary aspect and it is this which forms the heart of the present chapter.

However, in a unitary country or even a fairly weakly federal one, economic *and* monetary integration would involve having a countrywide fiscal policy as well as a single monetary policy for the whole country. Arrangements vary as to how much of fiscal policy is handled at the country/federal level and how much at lower state or regional levels. However, the norm is that the federal level imposes some limitations on what the states and regions can do even in very loose federations. The EU, however, has not attempted this level of integration. The centralized budget amounts to only around 1% of the GDP of the EU (see Chapter 19) and at this level cannot constitute a real macroeconomic policy instrument. It is a structural budget whose form is largely set for periods of around five years. It is thus both too small and too inflexible to be used in any sense to manage the path of the EU economy in either real or nominal terms.

The EU adopts a different approach, which is to constrain the ability of the member states to run independent fiscal policies. These constraints have three characteristics. The first are laid down in the Treaty, as part of the conditions for membership of EMU – the so-called Maastricht criteria. We return to these in detail in the next chapter but in the present context they can be regarded as constraints designed to impose prudence on fiscal policy so that no one country's debt can start to raise the interest rates/lower the credit ratings of the other EMU countries. The constraints relate to the ratio of debt to GDP as a measure of long-run sustainability and to the ratio of the government deficit to GDP in the short term.

The second set of constraints operationalize the membership requirements for continuing behaviour of the member states inside EMU – this is known as the Stability and Growth Pact (SGP). This we also deal with in Chapter 10. The coordination among the member states takes place through the framework of ECOFIN assisted by the Commission and includes the ability to impose financial penalties on member states that do not adhere to the prudent limits.

However, even though the SGP has the effect of coordinating fiscal policy to some extent through its constraints, the third aspect of policy among the member states is a more positive form of cooperation. This occurs through the annual setting of Broad Economic Policy Guidelines. Here there is not only discussion among the member states to try to set a framework for policy consistent with the longer-term objectives of the EU, but there is an informal dialogue between the fiscal and monetary authorities.

The ability to levy taxation is normally one of the key elements of economic independence and the EU countries have only agreed fairly limited constraints on their individual behaviour. These relate to the nature of indirect taxation (VAT and specific duties), which is largely a facet of the treatment of trade and the internal market discussed in Chapter 11. It is proving very difficult to get agreements on the nature of the taxation of income from capital and on the taxation of company profits. Discussion of agreements on the levels of taxation of personal incomes is even

further from practical realization, as the range between the highest and lowest is very large (Chapter 14). It has, however, been possible to get agreement that reductions in the level of non-wage taxes on labour would assist the overall economic strategy of the EU.

Taken together these measures represent rather soft and limited coordination, which affects the nature of the theoretical discussion we can have about monetary integration. Fiscal policy in the EU is neither a single coordinated policy nor a set of uncoordinated national policies run for the individual benefit of each member state. Indeed the degree of automatic or discretionary coordination is difficult to estimate before the event. This makes the assessment of the impact of monetary integration a somewhat uncertain exercise.

8.2   What is monetary integration?

Monetary integration has two essential components: an exchange-rate union and capital (K) market integration. An exchange-rate union is established when member countries have what is in effect one currency. The actual existence of one currency is not necessary, however, because, if member countries have *permanently* and *irrevocably* fixed exchange rates among themselves with currencies costlessly exchangeable at par, the result is effectively the same. Having a single currency makes the aspect of permanence and irrevocability more plausible as there would be severe repercussions from exit, not least the need to produce new coins and notes. But one could equally well argue that if a member nation decided to opt out of a monetary union, it would do so irrespective of whether or not the union entailed the use of a single currency. Giving the impression of permanence is a crucial ingredient for such fixed exchange rate regimes. Hence those, like currency boards, which permit the continuation of more than one currency, tend to back one currency with the other. This then offers full adoption of the backing currency as the likely way out of a crisis rather than a breaking of the union. In the same way exchange-rate unions between more equal partners have tended to back the two currencies by a common medium, such as silver or gold. Again this offers a more rather than a less unifying way forward.

Exchange rate integration requires convertibility, the *permanent* absence of all exchange controls for both current and K transactions, including interest and dividend payments (and the harmonization of

relevant taxes and measures affecting the K market) within the union. It is, of course, absolutely necessary to have complete convertibility for trade transactions, otherwise an important requirement of CU formation is threatened, namely the promotion of free trade among members of the CU, which is an integral part of an economic union – see Chapter 1. That is why this aspect of monetary integration does not need any discussion; it applies even in the case of a free trade area (FTA). Convertibility for K transactions is related to free factor mobility and is therefore an important aspect of K market integration which is necessary in common markets (CMs), not in simple CUs or FTAs. Nevertheless the pattern of both trade and production will be affected if there are controls on capital transactions.

In practice, monetary integration should specifically include the following if it is to qualify under this definition:

1   An explicit harmonization of monetary policies.
2   A common pool of foreign exchange reserves.
3   A single central bank or monetary authority.

There are important reasons for including these elements. Suppose union members decide either that one of their currencies will be a reference currency or that a new unit of account will be established. Also assume that each member country has its own foreign exchange reserves and conducts its own monetary and fiscal policies. If a member finds itself running out of reserves, it will want to engage in a monetary and fiscal contraction sufficient to restore the reserve position. Both these actions and the failure to undertake them could put pressure on the exchange rate. This will necessitate the fairly frequent meeting of the finance ministers or central bank governors, to consider whether or not to change the parity of the reference currency. If they do decide to change it, then all the member currencies will have to move with it (and with any consequent shifts compared to other currencies). Such a situation could create the sorts of difficulty which plagued the Bretton Woods System:

1   Each finance minister might fight for the rate of exchange that was most suitable for his/her country. Any such rate would be conceived relative to the others. If they also want to move then this becomes a rather involved set of contingent positions. This might make bargaining hard; agreement might become difficult to reach and the whole system might be subject to continuous strain.

2   Each meeting might be accompanied by speculation about its outcome. This might result in destabilizing speculative private K movements into or out of the union.

3   The difficulties that might be created by (1) and (2) might result in the reference currency being permanently fixed relative to outside currencies, e.g. the US dollar.

4   However, the system does allow for the possibility of the reference currency floating relative to non-member currencies or floating within a band. If the reference currency does float, it might do so in response to conditions in its own market. This would be the case, however, only if the union required the monetary authorities in the partner countries to vary their exchange rates so as to maintain constant parities relative to the reference currency. They would then have to buy and sell the reserve currency so as to maintain or bring about the necessary exchange-rate alteration. Therefore, the monetary authorities of the reference currency would, in fact, be able to determine the exchange rate for the whole union. (Except insofar as the other members can also deal in third currencies.)

5   Such a system does not guarantee the permanence of the parities between the union currencies that is required by the appropriate specification of monetary integration. There is the possibility that

the delegates will not reach agreement, or that one of the partners might finally choose not to deflate to the extent necessary to maintain its rate at the required parity or that a partner in surplus might choose neither to build up its reserves nor to inflate as required and so might allow its rate to rise above the agreed level.

In order to avoid such difficulties, it is necessary to include in monetary integration the three elements specified. The central bank (or monetary authority) would operate in the market so that the exchange parities were permanently maintained among the union currencies and, at the same time, it would allow the rate of the reference currency to fluctuate, or to alter intermittently, relative to the outside reserve currency. For instance, if the foreign exchange reserves in the common pool were running down, the common central bank could allow the reference currency, and with it all the partner currencies, to depreciate. This would have the advantage of economizing in the use of foreign exchange reserves, since all partners would not tend to be in deficit or surplus at the same time. Also surplus countries would automatically be helping deficit countries inside the exchange rate area.

However, without explicit policy coordination, a monetary union would not be effective. If each country conducted its own monetary policy, and hence could engage in as much domestic credit as it wished, surplus countries would be financing deficit nations without any incentives for the deficit countries to restore equilibrium. If one country ran a large deficit, the union exchange rate would depreciate, but this might put some partner countries into surplus. If wage rates were rising in the member countries at different rates, while productivity growth did not differ in such a way as to offset the effects on relative prices, those partners with the lower inflation rates would be permanently financing the other partners.

In short,

Monetary integration, in the sense defined, requires the unification and joint management both of monetary policy and of the external exchange-rate policy of the union. This in turn entails further consequences. First, in the monetary field the rate of increase of the money supply must be decided jointly. Beyond an agreed amount of credit expansion, which is allocated to each member state's central bank, a member state would have to finance any budget deficit in the union's capital market at the ruling rate of interest. A unified monetary policy would remove one of the main reasons for disparate movements in members' price levels, and thus one of the main reasons for the existence of intra-union payment imbalances prior to monetary union. Second, the balance of payments of the entire union with the rest of the world must be regulated at union level. For this purpose the monetary authority must dispose of a common pool of exchange reserves, and the union exchange rates with other currencies must be regulated at the union level. (Robson, 1980)

Monetary integration which explicitly includes the three requirements specified will therefore enable the partners to do away with all these problems right from the start. Incidentally, this also suggests the advantages of having a single currency. With a single currency, the members can all have a say in the setting of policy. With a reference currency, the tendency will always be for the country whose currency it is to dominate the decision-making, as the others will have to follow or leave the arrangement. A tighter arrangement is likely to give them explicit rights in decision making, perhaps even including a veto.

8.3   The gains and losses

The gains due to membership of a monetary union could be both economic and non-economic, e.g. political. Some of the non-economic benefits are obvious. For example, it is difficult to imagine that a complete political union could become a reality without the establishment of a monetary union. However, it is not our intention to discuss security and other issues. The discussion will be confined to the economic benefits, which can be briefly summarized as follows:

1 The common pool of foreign exchange reserves already discussed has the incidental advantage of economizing in the use of foreign exchange reserves, since member nations may well not go into deficit *simultaneously* so one country's surplus can offset another's deficit. Intra-union trade transactions will no longer be financed by foreign exchange, so the need for foreign exchange is reduced for any given trade pattern. Frankel and Rose (2002) argue that having a currency union will itself lead to an increase in intra-trade at the expense of trade with other countries outside the area. In the context of the EU this will reduce the role of the US dollar or reduce the EU's dependence on the dollar.

2 In the case of forms of economic integration like the EU, the adoption of the common currency (the euro) would transform that currency into a major world medium able to compete with the US dollar or Japanese yen. The advantages of such a currency from seignorage are well established. An external rôle for the euro outside the member countries seems likely, especially among the accession countries.

Supplanting much of the rôle of the US dollar as an international vehicle currency could take much longer.

One facet of having a second major currency to compete with the US dollar is that international market conditions can become more, or less, stable depending upon whether the two authorities decide to cooperate or permit major swings. Since, for a large currency bloc, foreign trade forms a small proportion of total transactions, wide swings in exchange rates can be accommodated with limited impact on the overall economy. These swings can have more striking effects on smaller countries, so large currency areas normally feel an obligation to consider the wider implications. Indeed, the group of seven (G7) was created in 1986 to establish a system of international coordination between the most advanced nations in the world for precisely such a reason.

3 Another source of gain could be a reduction in the cost of financial management. Monetary integration should enable the spreading of overhead costs of financial transactions more widely. Also, some of the activities of the institutions dealing in foreign exchanges might be discontinued, leading to a saving in the use of resources. These gains are, however, thought to bea fraction of a percentage point of GDP, but there is normally a clear interest rate gain for the smallerand previously high inflation countries without any noticeable downside for the larger, if the area as a whole has credible institutions and policies.

4 There are also the classical advantages of having permanently fixed exchange rates (or one currency) among members of a monetary union for free trade and factor movements. Stability of exchange rates enhances trade, encourages K to move to where it is most productively rewarded and ensures that labour (L) will move to where the highest rewards prevail. It seems unnecessary to emphasize that this does not mean that *all L* and *all K* should be mobile, but simply enough of each to generate the necessary adjustment to any situation. Nor is it necessary to stress that hedging can tackle the problem of exchange-rate fluctuations only at a cost, no matter how low that cost may be. Here again, however, the evidence suggests that hedging costs and penalties from uncertainty are relatively small, except for smaller companies that tend to be unhedged. The much greater advantage is that it seems to cement integration, encouraging greater trade and FDI than would be expected just from all the other economic variables; this is shown very clearly in the gravity model literature (see Mélitz, 2001).

5 The integration of the K market has a further advantage. If a member country of a monetary union is in deficit (assuming that countries can be recognized within such a union), it can borrow directly on the union market or raise its rate of interest to attract K inflow and therefore ease the situation. However, the integration of economic policies within the union ensures that this help will occur automatically under the auspices of the common central bank. Fiscal transfers and continuing private sector transfers, as with retirement areas, can support indefinite deficits with no strain on the system.

6 When a monetary union establishes a central fiscal authority with its own budget, then the larger the size of this budget, the higher the scope for fiscal harmonization (the *MacDougall Report*, CEC, 1977). This has some advantages: regional deviations from internal balance can be financed from the centre and the centralization of social security payments financed by contributions or taxes on a progressive basis would have some stabilizing and compensating effects, modifying the harmful effects of monetary integration (see Chapter 19).

There are negative advantages in the case of the EU in the sense that monetary integration is helpful for maintaining the EU as it exists; for example, realizing the 'single market' would become more difficult to achieve and the common agricultural prices enshrined in the *Common Agricultural Policy* (CAP – see Chapter 20) are complicated when exchange rates are flexible. These benefits of monetary integration are clear and there are few economists who would question them. However, there is no consensus of opinion with regard to its costs.

The losses from membership of a monetary union are emphasized by Fleming (1971) and Corden (1972a). Assume that the world consists of three countries: the home country (H), the potential partner country (P) and the rest of the world (W). Also assume that, in order to maintain both internal and external equilibrium, one country (H) needs to devalue its currency relative to W, while P needs to revalue *vis-à-vis* W. Moreover, assume that H and P use fiscal and monetary policies for achieving internal equilibrium. If H and P were partners in an exchange-rate union, they would devalue together – which is consistent with H's policy requirements in isolation – or revalue together – which is consistent with P's requirements in isolation – but they would not be able to alter the rate of exchange in a way that was consistent with both. Under such circumstances, the alteration in the exchange rate could leave H with an external deficit, forcing it to deflate its economy and to increase/create unemployment, or it could leave it with a surplus, forcing it into accumulating foreign reserves or allowing its prices and wages to rise. If countries deprive themselves of rates of exchange (or trade impediments) as policy instruments, they impose on themselves losses that are essentially the losses emanating from *enforced departure from internal balance* (Cordon, 1972a). In short, the rationale for retaining flexibility in the rates of exchange rests on the assumption that governments aim to achieve both internal and external balance, and, as Tinbergen (1952) has shown, to achieve these *simultaneously* at least an equal number of instruments is needed. This can be explained in the following manner, taking the standard assumption that there are two macro-economic policy targets and two policy instruments. Internal equilibrium is tackled via financial instruments, which have their greatest impact on the level of aggregate demand, and the exchange rate is used to achieve external equilibrium. Of course, financial instruments can be activated via both monetary and fiscal policies and may have a varied impact on both internal and external equilibria. Given this understanding, the case for maintaining flexibility in exchange rates depends entirely on the presumption that the loss of one of the two policy instruments will conflict with the achievement of both internal and external equilibria.

With this background in mind, it is vital to follow the Corden–Fleming explanation of the enforced departure from internal equilibrium. Suppose a country is initially in internal equilibrium but has a deficit in its external account. If the country were free to vary its rate of exchange, the appropriate policy for it to adopt to achieve overall balance would be a combination of devaluation and expenditure reduction. When the rate of exchange is not available as a policy instrument, it is necessary to reduce expenditure by more than is required in the optimal situation, with the result of extra unemployment. The *excess* unemployment, which can be valued in terms of output or some more direct measure of welfare, is the cost to that country of depriving itself of the exchange rate as a policy instrument. The extent of this loss is determined, *ceteris paribus*, by the marginal propensity to import and to consume exportables, or, more generally, by the marginal propensity to consume tradables relative to non-tradables. (Supply-side responses can, of course, mitigate any losses.)

The expenditure reduction which is required for eliminating the initial external account deficit will be smaller the higher the marginal propensity to import. Moreover, the higher the marginal propensity to import, the less the effect of that reduction in expenditure on demand for domestically produced commodities. For both reasons, therefore, the higher the marginal propensity to import, the less domestic unemployment will result from abandoning the devaluation of the rate of exchange as a policy instrument. If the logic of this explanation is correct, it follows that as long as the marginal propensity to consume domestic goods is greater than zero, there will be some cost due to fixing the rate of exchange. A similar argument applies to a country which cannot use the exchange-rate instrument when it has a surplus in its external account and internal equilibrium: the required excess expenditure will have little effect on demand for domestically produced goods and will therefore exert little inflationary pressure if the country's marginal propensity to import is high. This analysis is based on

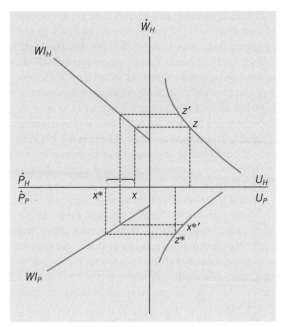

Figure 8.1 The Fleming–Corden analysis of monetary integration

the assumption that there exists a trade-off between rates of change in costs and levels of unemployment – the Phillips curve. Assuming that there is a Phillips (1958) curve relationship (a negative response of rates of change in money wages – $\dot{W}$ – and the level of unemployment – U), Fleming (1971) and Corden's (1972a) analysis can be explained by using a simple diagram devised by de Grauwe (1975). Hence, in Figure 8.1, the top half depicts the position of H while the lower half depicts that of P. The top right and the lower right corners represent the two countries' Phillips curves, while the remaining quadrants show their inflation rates corresponding to the rates of change in wages – $\dot{P}$. WI_H (which stands for *wage-rate change* and corresponding *inflation*) and WI_P are, of course, determined by the share of L in total GNP, the rate of change in the productivity of L and the degree of competition in both the factor and the commodity markets, with perfect competition resulting in the WIs being straight lines. Note that the intersection of the WIs with the vertical axes will be determined by rates of change of L's share in GNP and its rate of productivity change. The diagram has been drawn on the presumption that the L productivity changes are positive.

The diagram is drawn in such a way that countries H and P differ in all respects: the positions of their Phillips curves, their preferred trade-offs between $\dot{W}$ and $\dot{P}$, and their rates of productivity growth. H has a lower rate of inflation, x, than P, x^* (equilibria being at z and z^*); hence, without monetary integration, P's currency should depreciate relative to H's; note that there is only a minute chance that the two countries' inflation rates would coincide. Altering the exchange rates would then enable each country to maintain its preferred internal equilibrium: z and z^* for countries H and P, respectively.

When H and P enter into an exchange-rate union, i.e. have irrevocably fixed exchange rates *vis-à-vis* each other, their inflation rates cannot differ from each other, given a model without traded goods. Each country will therefore have to settle for a combination of U and $\dot{P}$ which is different from what it would have liked. The Fleming–Corden conclusion is thus vindicated.

However, this analysis rests entirely on the acceptance of the Phillips curve. The continuing controversy over the Keynesian position, although still far from being resolved, has at least led to the consensus that the form of the Phillips curve just presented is too crude. This is because many economists no longer believe that there is a fundamental trade-off between unemployment and inflation; if there is any relationship at all, it must be a short-term one such that the rate of unemployment is in the long term independent of the rate of inflation: there is a 'natural rate' of unemployment which is determined by rigidities in the market for L. Alternatively, at any particular time, there is a level of unemployment that is consistent with constant inflation. The simple version of the Phillips curve has been replaced by an expectations-adjusted one along the lines suggested by Phelps (1968) and Friedman (1975), i.e. the Phillips curves become vertical in the long run. This position can be explained with reference to Figure 8.2 which depicts three Phillips curves for one of the two countries. Assume that unemployment is initially at point U_2, i.e. the rate of inflation is equal to zero, given the short-term Phillips curve indicated by ST_1. The expectations-augmented Phillips curve suggests that, if the government tries to lower unemployment by the use of monetary policy, the short-term effect would be to move to point a, with positive inflation and lower unemployment. However, in the long term, people would adjust their expectations, causing an upward shift of the Phillips curve to ST_2

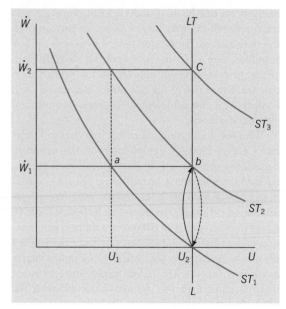

Figure 8.2 The expectations-augmented Phillips curve

which leads to equilibrium at point b. The initial level of unemployment is thus restored but with a higher rate of inflation. A repetition of this process gives the vertical long-term curve labelled LT.

If both partners H and P have vertical LT curves, Figure 8.1 will have to be adjusted to give Figure 8.3. The implications of this are that:

1 Monetary integration will have no long-term effect on either partner's rate of unemployment since this will be fixed at the appropriate NAIRU for each country – U_H, U_P.
2 If monetary integration is adopted to bring about balanced growth as well as equal the natural rate of unemployment, this can be achieved only if *inter alia* other policy instruments are introduced to bring about uniformity in the two L markets. This is, however, only a necessary condition; other aspects of similarity in tastes and production structures would be necessary to make it a sufficient condition.

Therefore, this alternative interpretation of the Phillips curve renders the Fleming–Corden conclusion invalid.

Be that as it may, it should be noted that Allen and Kenen (1980) and P. R. Allen (1983) have demonstrated, using a sophisticated and elaborate

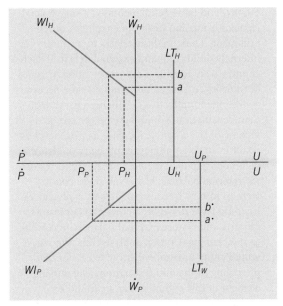

Figure 8.3 Monetary integration with expectations-augmented Phillips curves

model with financial assets, that, although monetary policy has severe drawbacks as an instrument for adjusting cyclical imbalances within a monetary union, it may be able to influence the demand for the goods produced by member countries in a differential manner within the short term, provided that the markets of the member nations are not too closely integrated. Their model indicates that economic integration, in this sense, can come about as a consequence of the substitutability between nations' commodities, especially their financial assets, and of country biases in the purchase of commodities and financial assets. The moral of this is that the central bank of a monetary union can operate monetary policies in such a manner as to have differing impacts on the various partner countries and thus achieve real effects without compromising their internal and external equilibria – a severe blow to those who stress the costs from monetary integration. Moreover, once non-traded goods are incorporated into the model and/or K and L mobility is allowed for, it follows that the losses due to deviating from internal equilibrium vanish, a point which Corden (1972a, 1977) readily accedes to. Finally, this model does not allow for the fact that monetary integration involves at least three countries; hence W has to be explicitly included in the model. Allen and Kenen (1980) tried to develop a model along

these lines, but their model is not a straightforward extension of that depicted in Figure 8.1.

In concluding this section, it may be appropriate to highlight the limitations in the argument put forward by Fleming and Corden:

1. It is clearly stated in the definition of monetary integration that the fixity of exchange-rate parities within a monetary union (or the adoption of one currency) does not mean that the different member currencies cannot vary in unison relative to extra-union currencies. Hence the monetary union is not forgoing the availability of exchange rate variations relative to the outside world.

2. In a proper monetary union, an extra deficit for one region can come about only as a result of a revaluation of the union currency – the union as a whole has an external surplus *vis-à-vis* the outside world. Such an act would increase the foreign exchange earnings of the surplus region, and therefore of the union as a whole, provided that the conditions for a successful revaluation existed. The common central bank and the integration of monetary policies will ensure that the extra burden on the first region is alleviated: the overall extra earnings will be used to help the region with the extra deficit. Needless to say, such a situation does not lead to surplus regions financing deficit regions indefinitely because no single region is likely to be in deficit or surplus permanently and because the policy coordination will not allow one region to behave in such a manner unless there are reasons of a different nature which permit a situation to be sustained.

3. Even if one accepts the Fleming–Corden argument at its face value, the assumptions are extremely controversial. For instance, devaluation can work effectively only when there is 'money illusion'; otherwise it would be pointless since it would not work. Is it really permissible to assume that trade unionists, wherever they may be, suffer from money illusion? Many authors have disputed this assumption, but Corden's response has been to suggest that exchange-rate alterations may work if money wages are forced up because the catching-up process is never complete. Such an argument is far from convincing simply because the catching-up process has no validity as a true adjustment; it cannot be maintained

indefinitely because, sooner or later, trade unions will allow for it when negotiating money wage increases.

4   One must remember that in practice there would never be a separation between the exchange-rate union and K market integration. Once one allows for the role of convertibility for K transactions, K will always come to the rescue. Corden has reservations about this too since he argues that K integration can help in the short run, but, in the long term, while it has its own advantages, it cannot solve the problem. The rationale for this is that no region can borrow indefinitely on a private market, no matter how efficient and open the market is, to sustain levels of real wages, and hence real consumption levels, which are too high, given the productivity level in the region. Clearly, this is a switching of grounds: devaluation is nothing but a temporary adjustment device as the discussion of the monetary approach to the balance of payments has shown. Why then should devaluation be more desirable than short-term K adjustment? Moreover, for a region that is permanently in deficit, all economists would agree that devaluation is no panacea.

5   We have seen that monetary integration can be contemplated when the countries concerned have an economic union in mind. In such conditions, the mobility of L will also help in the adjustment process. This point is conceded by Corden, but he believes that L mobility may help only marginally since it would take prolonged unemployment to induce people to emigrate, and, if monetary integration proceeded far in advance of 'psychological integration' (defined as the suppression of existing nationalisms and a sense of attachment to place in favour of an integrated community nationalism and an American-style geographic rootlessness), nationalistic reactions to any nation's depopulation may become very intense. This reasoning is similar to that in the previous case since it presupposes that the problem region is a *permanently* depressed area. Since regions in the union are not likely to experience chronic maladjustments, L mobility needs only to be marginal and not national depopulation. Distortionary circumstances, such as Southern Italy, have their impact independent of the existence of EMU.

6   Finally, and more fundamentally, a very crucial element is missing from the Fleming–Corden argument. Their analysis relates to a country in internal equilibrium and external deficit. If such a country were outside a monetary union, it could devalue its currency. Assuming that the necessary conditions for effective devaluation prevailed, then devaluation would increase the national income of the country, increase its price level or result in some combination of the two. Hence a deflationary policy would be required to restore the internal balance. However, if the country were to lose its freedom to alter its exchange rate, it would have to deflate in order to depress its imports and restore external balance. According to the Fleming–Corden analysis, this alternative would entail unemployment in excess of that prevailing in the initial situation. The missing element in this argument can be found by specifying how devaluation actually works. Devaluation of a country's currency results in changes in relative price levels and is price inflationary for, at least, both exportables and importables. These relative price changes, given the necessary stability conditions, will depress imports and (perhaps) increase exports. The deflationary policy which is required (to accompany devaluation) in order to restore internal balance should therefore eliminate the *newly injected* inflation as well as the *extra* national income. By disregarding the 'inflationary' implications of devaluation, Fleming and Corden reach the unjustifiable *a priori* conclusion that membership of a monetary union would necessitate extra sacrifice of employment in order to achieve the same target. A comparison of the two situations indicates that no such *a priori* conclusion can be reached – one must compare like with like. Exchange rate changes following windfall gains or losses, such as a natural disaster, would not fit under this heading.

There will be a limit to how far the argument of costs of forgoing the ability to have one's own exchange rate and monetary policy can go even in a purely economic context. The whole net benefit of the increased integration has to be taken into account. Hence, even if the rates of inflation and unemployment may differ from those that would be preferred without union, when combined with other benefits to real incomes and wealth. Similar agreements with parts of *W* may not be politically superior even if they might be economically so. Similarly, monetary integration may reinforce the barriers to reversion to less desired examples of economic dominance – a point emphasized by some of the accession countries.

A further justification that can be advanced is that monetary independence offers an element of contingency planning. Sweden explicitly and Denmark implicitly have argued that even though they may wish to shadow EMU very closely, maintaining a separate currency gives them the opportunity to respond rather better to a very large adverse shock. Thus with care they can manage to secure most of the gains from a monetary union and yet retain an element of flexibility.

We can perhaps think of the reservations in terms of Tinbergen's criterion of an equal number of policy instruments and objectives. Although a country may lose an instrument individually it is gaining other instruments from other aspects of the economic union. The union as a whole does not lose the exchange rate route of adjustment. A voluntary economic union of this depth is likely to offer a sufficient degree of 'political' union that unacceptably adverse effects on a particular country or part of it will be recognized and acted upon. When countries are in a voluntary union they will be prepared, within limits, to act in favour of other members, even when it is not in their immediate economic interest. Next time it may be they who would benefit from the voluntary assistance of others. Taking either a legalistic view of what actions union agreements compel or a relatively short-run perspective of economic gains can be misleading. Ultimately the alternative would be that the member would leave, which could also harm the other members and threaten the credibility of the union thereafter. Relevance to reality therefore requires taking a somewhat broader view of the policy problem.

8.4   A 'popular' cost approach

As we have seen, the purely economic costs of EMU are technical. Fortunately, a simpler version of their presentation, made popular in the context of the discussions concerning the euro as the single currency for the EU is available. We use the term 'purely economic' since the literature under consideration deals with only the economic conditions necessary for countries to adopt permanently fixed exchange rates – the 'optimum currency areas' in the terminology of (Mundell, 1961; Fleming, 1971), some implications of which are known within the EU as the 'impossible trilogy' or 'inconsistent trinity' principle.

The principle states that only two out of the following three are mutually compatible:

1   completely free capital mobility;
2   an independent monetary policy; and
3   a fixed exchange rate.

This is because with full capital mobility, a nation's own interest rate is tied to the world interest rate, at least for a country too small to influence global financial markets. More precisely, any difference between the domestic and world interest rates must be matched by an expected rate of depreciation of the exchange rate. For example, if the interest rate is 6% in the domestic market, but 4% in the world market, the global market must expect the currency to depreciate by 2% this year. This is known as the 'interest parity condition', which implies that integrated financial markets equalize expected asset returns; hence assets denominated in a currency expected to depreciate must offer an exactly compensating higher yield for the expected depreciation.

Under such circumstances, a country that wants to conduct an independent monetary policy, raising or lowering its interest rate to control its level of employment or unemployment, must allow its exchange rate to fluctuate in the market. Conversely, a country confronted with full capital mobility, which wants to fix its exchange rate, must set its domestic interest rate to be exactly equal to the rate in the country to which it pegs its currency. Since monetary policy is then determined abroad, the country has effectively lost its monetary independence.

The loss from EMU membership can be calculated in terms of the employment sacrificed, or increased unemployment due to fixing the exchange rate between EMU members – see the previous section. The extent of this loss is evaluated relative to the three criteria, known as the Mundell–McKinnon–Kenen (respectively, 1961, 1963 and 1969) criteria, under which two or more countries can adopt a common currency without subjecting themselves to serious adverse economic consequences. These criteria relate to elements which render price adjustments through exchange rate changes less effective or less compelling. They are:

(a) openness to mutual trade;
(b) diverse economies; and
(c) mobility of factors of production, especially of labour.

Greater openness to mutual trade implies that most prices would be determined at the union level, which means that relative prices would be less susceptible to being influenced by changes in the exchange rate. An economy more diverse in terms of production would be less likely to suffer from country-specific shocks, reducing the need for the exchange rate as a policy tool. Greater factor mobility enables the economy to tackle *asymmetric shocks* via migration; hence reducing the need for adjustment through the exchange rate.

The EU nations score well on the first criterion since the ratio of their exports to their GDP is 20% to 70% while that for the USA and Japan is, respectively, 11% and 7%; although just because the USA is the preferred reference nation that does not mean that it is an optimum currency area! They also score well in terms of the second criterion, even though they are not all as well endowed with oil or gas resources as the Netherlands and Britain. As to the third criterion, they score badly in comparison with the USA since EU labour mobility is rather low due to the Europeans' tendency to stick to their place of birth, not only nationally but also regionally. Indeed, while in the USA an employee who moves to San Francisco after being made redundant in Nashville enters the national statistics as a welcome example of internal mobility, an Italian who moves to Munich after losing a job in Milan is seen in a different light. To the Italian government, emigration would have overtones of domestic policy failure, and to the German government the inflow of Italian workers might be seen as exacerbating Germany's unemployment problem. In the EU there is also the language factor, but Europeans are increasingly becoming bilingual, with English being the dominant second language. Moreover, in the EU, casual observation reveals that it is the unskilled from the 'south' who tend to be relatively less immobile in terms of moving north in search of jobs, i.e. they move because they have no other choice. (There is also a tendency for migration to be temporary and only involve part of a larger family, see Chapter 18.)

Although there is no definitive estimate of the costs due to the relative lack of labour mobility, it is generally thought to be considerable. However, it would have to be very large to offset the gains from monetary union. In any case much of the problem from lack of mobility is as relevant within the member states as between them. It therefore requires addressing through structural policy in each member state regardless of monetary union or indeed of membership of the EU for that matter. Tackling the problem has become more important since the late 1960s and will remain so in the face of faster rates of technical change in products and production methods. (In part it is a consequence of globalization but that is an aspect of economic integration.)

Nonetheless, even on purely economic grounds alone, the longer-term perspective will not lend support to some of the more pessimistic assessments. Consider, for example, Krugman's (1990) model, which utilizes such a perspective when examining the costs and benefits of EMU. In Figure 8.4, the costs are represented by *CC* and the benefits by *BB*, and both costs and benefits are expressed in relation to GDP. The benefits from the single currency are shown to rise with integration, since, for example, intra-EU trade, which is expected to increase, and has been doing so for a long time (El-Agraa, 1989a and Tables 2.9a and 2.9b therein), with integration over time, will be conducted with lesser costs, while the losses from giving up the exchange rate as a policy variable decline with time. To put it in modern economic jargon, as we have seen, changes in the exchange rate are needed to absorb asymmetric shocks but these will

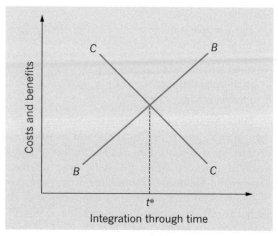

Figure 8.4 Krugman's (1990) cost–benefits of EMU

decline with time owing to the shocks becoming less asymmetric as integration proceeds and becomes more intensive. In short, the essence of Krugman's analysis is that as the member economies become more integrated, the use of the exchange rate instrument for variations against member nations' currencies would become less and less desirable. Thus, for countries seriously and permanently involved in an EMU, sooner or later a time is likely to come when the benefits will exceed the costs and this balance will be maintained thereafter. All this is tantamount to stating that the optimum currency area concept is non-operational; indeed, a very long time ago, Corden (1972b) castigated it as one of 'feasibility', rather than 'optimality', and although Bayoumi and Eichengreen (1996) developed methods for identifying the suitability of various EU nations for EMU, their method only succeeds in ranking suitability rather than actual cost–benefit measures which would indicate where the line separating included from excluded countries should be (see Capie and Wood in El-Agraa, 2002b).

One could add that those who ignore the other features of integration and regard the net outcome being a negative sum are ignoring the EU 'structural funds' aimed at assisting the poorer regions and member nations. Admittedly, these funds are presently small relative to EU GDP but as economic integration becomes well established, the EU general budget may increase and local deviations from the desirable levels of economic activity could be addressed centrally.

In many respects the key issue in the policy choice relates to uncertainty about the future. If a prospective member of a monetary union could be certain that the economies would grow more closely together in the sense of becoming more economically similar and that the chance of having a serious external shock that affects only one of them or both of them in opposite directions then worries about a single monetary policy being inappropriate would be reduced. Such shocks are normally labelled 'asymmetric' as described above.

However, in advance, such developments can only be assessed, they cannot be known. The traditional Mundell–Fleming analysis tends to ignore the fact that behaviour is likely to change after the event and assesses the net benefits of monetary union on the basis of *ex ante* behaviour. Mayes and Suvanto (2002) take this even further and argue that in the case of Finland, for example, one of the factors swaying the authorities in favour of membership of monetary union was that it would force generally favourable changes in labour market behaviour. In other words, knowing that the exchange rate mechanism is not available to accommodate asymmetric shocks may actually cause people to change their behaviour so that the impact of the shocks is reduced to acceptable levels.

Furthermore, there is a tendency to ignore positive asymmetric shocks. In such cases the impact of the favourable shock will be magnified by membership of a monetary union. Out of the union such a shock would increase the demand for the currency as investors from other countries seek to join in the benefits. The surge in demand would be likely to push the domestic central bank into raising interest rates to head off any inflationary pressure thereby also raising the exchange rate and reducing the expected rate of growth. Inside monetary union the capital inflow will have a much more limited impact on the exchange rate as it relates only to a part of the union. Similarly the response of monetary policy will be negligible. Knowing that there will be no offsetting policy changes will in turn help keep down inflationary pressures. Such an experience seems to have occurred with the favourable technology shock or 'Nokia phenomenon' in Finland. The growth, inflation combination that occurred in the early years of monetary union was considerably more favourable than that which prevailed in earlier decades. Other factors such as the continuing impact of the collapse of the former Soviet Union and banking crisis in the early 1990s may no doubt have also been influential but the evidence is at the very least suggestive.

8.5   A concluding remark

We have gone to some lengths in this chapter to emphasize three facets of EMU – the wider process of economic and monetary integration that has been dominating the integration process in Europe over the last decade and more. These are:

1 The rationale for current steps in EMU has to be seen in the light of both the longer term and the wider political context. Narrow short-run economic assessments can make the decisions that have been taken look illogical.

2 EMU is expected to change the behaviour and
   structure of the European economy. Assessment
   of the likely impact therefore has to include these
   structural changes. Many traditional models that
   have been used to assess the impact of integration
   either do not take this into account adequately or
   have sometimes been used in ways that ignore
   these essential structural components of the
   process of change.
3 While the focus on the monetary aspect of
   EMU is understandable in the context of the

major institutional changes that have taken
place since the Maastricht Treaty, it is the
'economic' E in EMU that is both the more
complex issue and the key to the ultimate
success of the enterprise.

Hence, in the next two chapters, we appraise both the
development of EMU over the last 35 years and the
way in which it is currently operating and will develop
as the accession countries join, in the light of these
three observations.

Chapter 9

The development of EU economic and monetary integration

DAVID MAYES AND ALI EL-AGRAA

The aim of achieving EMU, although enshrined in the Maastricht treaty, is not a new phenomenon for the EU – see Chapters 2 and 27. This chapter provides a historical perspective by travelling on the route taken by the EU in this direction. The actual route followed has been the combination of the objectives for increasing economic integration, paving the way for the political unity of Europe (Chapter 2, Section 2.1.2), and the more immediate economic needs and shocks along that path. While there is a danger, with the benefit of knowledge of the current outcome, of setting out the particular route that has been travelled as if that were the precise plan from the beginning; realizing the Benelux vision of political unity via the back door depended precisely on waiting for and then seizing the right opportunities when they arose. Nevertheless, the initial ideas, sketched out as early as 1970, bear striking similarities to what has eventually been accomplished.

9.1   The Werner Report

From 1967, the prevailing world order for exchange rates, established as part of the Bretton Woods agreement in 1944, began to fall apart. Until that point the system of having exchange rates that were 'fixed' but adjustable occasionally when the existing rate was shown to be unsustainable had worked rather well. Fixity permitted fluctuations within 1% of a peg with the US dollar, which in turn was convertible for gold at 35$ per ounce. Despite some initial repositioning after the war, the number of occasions on which pegs had been changed meant that the system had seemed credible. The contrast with problems after the First World War with hyperinflation in Germany and then the deflationary impact of trying to return to the gold standard was striking. However, while the early problems lay with other countries trying to stabilize themselves with respect to the United States, the problem in the 1960s was that the US, hindered by the cost of the Vietnam war, was no longer able to act as the anchor for the international system.

Other countries therefore had to look elsewhere for stability. While the main initial thrust was towards a reform of the Bretton Woods system, the EC looked at the possibility of trying to create a locally stable system with the same sort of architecture for itself. In 1969, during The Hague summit (see Chapters 2 and 27), the Six decided that the EC should pro-gressively transform itself into an EMU, and set up a committee, led by Pierre Werner, then Prime Minister of Luxembourg, to consider the issues involved. The Werner Committee presented an interim report in June 1970 and a final report in October of the same year. The latter became generally known as the 'Werner Report', and was endorsed by the Council in February 1971.

According to the Council resolution, the EC would:

1 Constitute a zone where persons, goods, services and capital would move freely – but without distorting competition, or creating structural and regional imbalances – and where economic undertakings could develop their activities on a Community scale;

2 Form a single monetary entity within the international monetary system, characterised by the total and irreversible convertibility of currencies; the elimination of fluctuation margins of exchange rates between the [members]; the irrevocable fixing of their parity relationships. These steps would be essential for the creation of a single currency, and they would involve a Community-level organisation of central banks;

3 Hold the powers and responsibilities in the economic and monetary field that would enable its institutions to ensure the administration of the economic union. To this end, the necessary economic policy decisions would be taken at Community level and the necessary powers would be attributed to community institutions.

The Community organisation of central banks would assist, in the framework of its own responsibilities, in achieving the objectives of stability and growth in the Community.

These three principles would apply to:

(a) The internal monetary and credit policies of the union;

(b) Monetary policy *vis-à-vis* the rest of the world;

(c) Policy on a unified capital market and capital movements to and from non-member countries;

(d) Budgetary and taxation policies, as related to the policy for stability and growth . . . ;

(e) Structural and regional action needed to contribute to the balanced development of the Community.

As progress was made in moving closer to the final objectives, Community instruments would be created whenever they seemed necessary to replace or complement the action of national instruments. All actions would be interdependent; in particular, the development of monetary unification would be backed by parallel progress in the convergence, and then the unification of economic policies.

The Council decided that EMU could be attained during that decade, if the plan had the permanent political support of the member governments. Implementation was envisaged to be in three stages, with the first beginning in 1971 and the third completed by 1980. The Council made quite clear how it envisaged the process leading to full EMU (emphasis added):

(a) The first phase should begin on January 1, 1971, and could technically be completed within three years. This phase would be used to make the Community instruments more operational and to mark the beginnings of the Community's individuality within the international monetary system;

(b) The first phase should not be considered as an objective in itself; it should be associated with the complete process of economic and monetary integration. *It should therefore be launched with the determination to arrive at the final goal*;

(c) In the first phase consultation procedures should be strengthened; the budgetary policies of the member states should accord with Community objectives; some taxes should be harmonised; monetary and credit policies should be coordinated; and integration of financial markets should be intensified.

The EMU launched by the EC in 1971 was thus consistent with the requirements for a full EMU discussed in the previous chapter. While the problems of integrating product markets may not have been clear then, the intention to have the free flow of capital and labour rather than just free trade and ordered payments is set out, foreshadowing the later developments.

Although the 1971 venture did fail after an earlier than expected successful negotiation of the first phase and some progress during the second, the failure was not due to lack of commitment, determination or both. The Nixon shock, the first oil shock and the enlargement shock (the admission of three new members, each bringing with it its own unique problems) were the real culprits. The first step in coordinated monetary management had been that the EC countries, including the UK, Denmark and the Irish Republic that were joining at the time, would keep all their bilateral exchange rates within $2\frac{1}{4}\%$ of each other. Their joint rates would therefore move quite closely together in a 'snake' round the US dollar, which was still treated as the numeraire of the system. (The Smithsonian Agreement that was in force at the time would have limited each currency's fluctuation with respect to the US dollar to $2\frac{1}{4}\%$. Thus without the 'snake' the EC currencies could have moved up to $4\frac{1}{2}\%$ from each other. This would have been clearly more than is acceptable without renegotiating prices and hence would have violated the degree of stability required within the EC.) Not only were the lira, sterling and the French franc unable to hold their parity within the first year or so but the Smithsonian Agreement itself had collapsed into generalized floating by 1973.

9.2   The EMS

In some quarters, the European Monetary System (EMS) has been considered as the next EC attempt at EMU, but it was really little more than a mechanism devised to check the monetary upheavals of the 1970s by creating a 'zone of monetary stability'. The route to EMS was a fairly short one. The idea was floated, not by the EC Commission but by German Chancellor, Helmut Schmidt and French President, Valery Giscard d'Estaing and was discussed in the Council of Ministers in Copenhagen in April 1978. Roy Jenkins, the Commission President, had called for such a corrective initiative in a speech in Florence the previous October. By 5 December the Council had adopted the idea, in the form of a resolution 'on the establishment of the European Monetary System (EMS) and related matters', after a period of intensive discussion (Ludlow, 1982, gives a full account of the negotiations involved).

The EMS was introduced with the immediate support of six of the EC nations at the time. Ireland, Italy and the United Kingdom adopted a wait-and-see attitude; 'time for reflection' was needed by Ireland and Italy, who required a broader band of permitted fluctuation of ±6% when they did enter, and a definite reservation was expressed by the United Kingdom. Later, Ireland and Italy joined the system, while the United Kingdom expressed a 'spirit of sympathetic cooperation'. The EMS was to start operating on 1 January 1979, but France, which wanted assurances regarding the MCA system (see Chapter 20), delayed that start to 13 March 1979.

The main features of the EMS are given in the annex to the conclusions of the EC presidency (*Bulletin of the European Communities*, no. 6, 1978, pp. 20–21) set out in the box.

In essence, the EMS is concerned with the creation of an EC currency zone within which there is discipline for managing exchange rates. This discipline is known as the 'exchange rate mechanism' (ERM), which asks a member nation to intervene to reverse a trend when 75% of the allowed exchange rate variation

Provisions of the EMS

1 In terms of exchange rate management, the... (EMS) will be at least as strict as the 'snake'. In the initial stages of its operation and for a limited period of time, member countries currently not participating in the 'snake' may opt for somewhat wider margins around central rates. In principle, intervention will be in the currencies of participating countries. Changes in central rates will be subject to mutual consent. Non-member countries with particularly strong economic and financial ties with the Community may become associate members of the system. The European Currency Unit (ECU) will be at the centre of the system; in particular, it will be used as a means of settlement between EEC monetary authorities.

2 An initial supply of ECUs (for use among Community central banks) will be created against deposit of US dollars and gold on the one hand (e.g. 20% of the stock currently held by member central banks) and member currencies on the other hand in an amount of a comparable order of magnitude.

The use of ECUs created against member currencies will be subject to conditions varying with the amount and the maturity; due account will be given to the need for substantial short-term facilities (up to 1 year).

3 Participating countries will coordinate their exchange rates policies *vis-à-vis* third countries. To this end, they will intensify the consultations in the appropriate bodies and between central banks participating in the scheme. Ways to coordinate dollar interventions should be sought which avoid simultaneous reserve interventions. Central banks buying dollars will deposit a fraction (say 20%) and receive ECUs in return; likewise, central banks selling dollars will receive a fraction (say 20%) against ECUs.

4 Not later than two years after the start of the scheme, the existing arrangements and institutions will be consolidated in a European Monetary Fund.

5 A system of closer monetary cooperation will only be successful if participating countries pursue policies conducive to greater stability at home and abroad; this applies to deficit and surplus countries alike

of ±2.25% is reached; this is similar to that which was practised within the preceding 'snake' arrangements. The crucial differences were, however, twofold. First was the creation the European Currency Unit (ECU) as the centre of the system against which divergence of the exchange rate was to be measured. (The ECU followed on directly from the European Unit of Account as a basket of *all* the EC currencies, not just those participating in the ERM. Weights in the basket, based on economic importance in the system were revised every five years.[1] It was the means of settlement between the EC central banks.) Second, the EMS was to be supported by a European Monetary Fund (EMF) which (supposedly within two years) was to absorb the short-term financing arrangements operating within the snake, the short-term monetary support agreement which was managed by the European Monetary Cooperation Fund (EMCF) and the medium-term loan facilities for balance of payments assistance (*Bulletin of the European Communities*, no. 12, 1978). The EMF was to be backed by approximately 20% of national gold and US dollar reserves and by a similar percentage in national currencies. The EMF was to issue ECUs to be used as new reserve assets. An exchange-stabilization fund able to issue about 50 billion US dollars was to be created (*Bulletin of the European Communities* no. 12, 1978).

It is clear from the above that the EMS asks neither for permanently and irrevocably fixed exchange rates between the member nations nor for complete capital convertibility. Moreover, it does not mention the creation of a common central bank to be put in charge of the member nations' foreign exchange reserves and to be vested with the appropriate powers. Hence, the EMS was not EMU, although it could be seen as paving the way for one.

9.2.1 The success of the EMS

The survival of the EMS belied the early scepticism and there is little dispute that the EMS was something of a success. There was, however, a period from 1992 onwards when it looked as if the EMS might collapse altogether, just at the time that the final push to EMU was being agreed upon (see below). This success can be seen as embodied in three principal achievements.

First, despite occasional realignments and fluctuations of currencies within their pre-set bands, it seems that the EMS succeeded in its proximate objective of

stabilizing exchange rates – not in the absolute sense but in the relevant and realistic sense of appearing to have brought about more stability than would have been enjoyed without it. Moreover, up to 1992 this was done without provoking periodic speculative crises such as marred the demise of the Bretton Woods system. This stability had two elements. Not only did the number of realignments in the central rates fall (with one minor exception there were none in the five years following 1987), but the variation of exchange rates between the ERM countries fell much faster than that of those outside even in the early period up to 1985 (Ungerer *et al.*, 1986). Just having scope for realignments meant that unlike the 'snake' a parity change did not entail a confidence-shaking exit from the system.

Second, the claim is made for the EMS that it provided a framework within which member countries were able to pursue counterinflationary policies at a lesser cost in terms of unemployment and lost output than would have been possible otherwise. The basis of the claim is that the structure of the EMS began to attach a measure of 'reputation' to countries that managed to avoid inflation and hence depreciating their exchange rate. This element of loss of reputation through 'failure' may have reduced the expectation of inflation and hence made counterinflationary policy less 'costly'. However, estimates of the change in the 'sacrifice ratio' (ratio of the rise in unemployment to the fall in inflation in a period) made in the previous edition of this book (Table 17.4) do not indicate any improvements compared to countries outside the ERM (which were also successful in lowering inflation). Although, as generally expected, sacrifice ratios observed did rise as inflation fell.

Third, while it is claimed that nominal exchange rate stability was secured, it is also argued that the operation of the EMS prevented drastic changes in *real* exchange rates (or 'competitiveness'). This is contrasted with the damaging experience in this respect of both the United Kingdom and the United States over the same period. However, in one sense it may merely have encouraged countries to put off necessary realignments, leading ultimately to the drastic changes and crisis in 1992/3 (see below and Section 9.4).

Finally, while not an immediate objective of the EMS as such, it is well worth mentioning that the ECU became established as a significant currency of denomination of bond issues, which can be viewed as some testimony to the credibility of the EMS and the successful projection of its identity. In part, the use of the ECU in international bond issues may have reflected its role as a hedge by being a currency 'cocktail'. It also provided a means of getting round some of the currency restrictions in force, particularly in France and Italy. The high point for new ECU issues was 1991 and external issues never recovered after the 1992/3 crisis (see below).

These achievements have not been without some qualifications. The 'divergence indicator' mechanism for triggering intervention before the limits of the band was reached did not withstand the test of time, for example, while sceptics would charge that the counterinflationary achievements of the EMS in fact amounted to little more than a bias against growth and expansion.

The enforced changes to parities in and after September 1992 considerably reduced the credibility of the system and called into question the validity of the idea of approaching monetary union through increasingly fixed exchange rates while having no controls over capital flows. Although the widening of the bands to ±15% in August 1993 appeared to remove much of the effective distinction between the ERM and freely floating exchange rates, the practice was for very considerable convergence and for a system which took only limited advantage of the flexibility available.

What we saw after 1993 was effectively pressure on member states through the convergence criteria for EMU, as discussed in the next section. The requirement to keep inflation close to that of the least inflationary member states, the need to follow a prudent fiscal policy and the requirement for longer-term interest rates to converge will also tend to lead towards exchange rate stability. As a result the goal of EMU gained increasing credibility and took over as the anchor of the system.

9.3　The Delors Report and the Maastricht Treaty

As we have noted, by 1987 the EMS and the ERM within it appeared to have achieved considerable success in stabilizing exchange rates. This coincided with legislative progress towards EMU on other fronts. The EC summit held in Hanover on 27 and 28 June 1988 decided that, in adopting the Single Act, the EC member states had confirmed the objective of 'progressive realisation of economic and monetary union'. The heads of state agreed to discuss the means of achieving this in their meeting in Madrid in June of the following year, and to help them in their deliberations then they entrusted to a committee composed of the central banker governors and two other experts, chaired by Jacques Delors, then president of the EC Commission, the 'task of studying and proposing concrete stages leading towards this union'. The committee reported just before the Madrid summit and its report is referred to as the Delors Report on EMU.

The committee was of the opinion that the creation of the EMU must be seen as a single process, but that this process should be in stages, which progressively led to the ultimate goal. Thus the decision to enter upon the first stage should commit a member state to the entire process. Emphasizing that the creation of the EMU would necessitate a common monetary policy and require a high degree of compatibility of economic policies and consistency in a number of other policy areas, particularly in the fiscal field, the Report pointed out that the realization of the EMU would require new arrangements which could be established only on the basis of a change in the Treaty of Rome and consequent changes in national legislation.

According to the Report, the first stage should be concerned with the initiation of the process of creating the EMU. During this stage there would be a greater convergence of economic performance through the strengthening of economic and monetary policy coordination within the existing institutional framework. The economic measures would be concerned with the completion of the internal market and the reduction of existing disparities through programmes of budgetary consolidation in the member states involved and more effective structural and regional policies. In the monetary field the emphasis would be on the removal of all obstacles to financial integration and on the intensification of cooperation and coordination of monetary policies. Realignment of exchange rates was seen to be possible, but efforts would be made by every member state to make the functioning of other adjustment mechanisms more effective. The committee was of the opinion that it would be important to include all EC currencies in the exchange rate mechanism of the EMS during this stage. The 1974 Council decision defining the mandate of central bank governors would be replaced by a new decision indicating that the committee itself should formulate opinions on the overall orientation of monetary and exchange rate policy.

In the second stage, which would commence only when the Treaty had been amended, the basic organs and structure of the EMU would be set up. The committee stressed that this stage should be seen as a transition period leading to the final stage; thus it should constitute a 'training process leading to collective decision-making', but the ultimate responsibility for policy decisions would remain with national authorities during this stage. The procedure established during the first stage would be further strengthened and extended on the basis of the amended Treaty, and policy guidelines would be adopted on a majority basis. Given this understanding, the EC would achieve the following:

1 Establish 'a medium-term framework for key economic objectives aimed at achieving stable growth, with a follow-up procedure for monitoring performances and intervening when significant deviations occurred'.
2 'Set precise, although not yet binding, rules relating to the size of annual budget deficits and their financing.'
3 'Assume a more active role as a single entity in the discussions of questions arising in the economic and exchange rate field.'

In the monetary field, the most significant feature of this stage would be the establishment of the European System of Central Banks (ESCB) to absorb the previous institutional monetary arrangements. The ESCB would start the transition with a first stage in which the coordination of independent monetary policies would be carried out by the Committee of Central Bank Governors. It was envisaged that the formulation and implementation of a common monetary policy would take place in the final stage; during this stage exchange rate realignments would not be allowed barring exceptional circumstances.

The Report stresses that the nature of the second stage would require a number of actions, e.g.:

1 National monetary policy would be executed in accordance with the general monetary orientations set up for the EC as a whole.
2 A certain amount of foreign exchange reserves would be pooled and used to conduct interventions in accordance with the guidelines established by the ESCB.

3 The ESCB would have to regulate the monetary and banking system to achieve a minimum harmonization of provisions (such as reserve requirements or payment arrangements) necessary for the future conduct of a common monetary policy.

The final stage would begin with the irrevocable fixing of member states' exchange rates and the attribution to the EC institutions of the full monetary and economic consequences. It is envisaged that during this stage the national currencies would eventually be replaced by a single EC currency. In the economic field, the transition to this stage is seen to be marked by three developments:

1 EC structural and regional policies may have to be further strengthened.
2 EC macroeconomic and budgetary rules and procedures would have to become binding.
3 The EC role in the process of international policy cooperation would have to become fuller and more positive.

In the monetary field, the irrevocable fixing of exchange rates would come into effect and the transition to a single monetary policy and a single currency would be made. The ESCB would assume full responsibilities, especially in four specific areas:

1 The formulation and implementation of monetary policy.
2 Exchange-market intervention in third currencies.
3 The pooling and management of all foreign exchange reserves.
4 Technical and regulatory preparations necessary for the transition to a single EC currency.

As agreed, the Report was the main item for discussion in the EC summit which opened in Madrid on 24 June 1989. In that meeting member nations agreed to call a conference which would decide the route to be taken to EMU. This agreement was facilitated by a surprisingly conciliatory Margaret Thatcher, the British Prime Minister, on the opening day of the summit. Instead of insisting (as was expected) that the United Kingdom would join the exchange rate mechanism of the EC 'when the time is ripe', she set out five conditions for joining:

1 A lower inflation rate in the United Kingdom, and in the EC as a whole.
2 Abolition of all exchange controls (at the time

and for two years after, Italy, France and Spain
had them).

3 Progress towards the single EC market.
4 Liberalization of financial services.
5 Agreement on competition policy.

Since these were minor conditions relative to the
demands for creating the EMU, all member nations
endorsed the Report and agreed on 1 July 1990 as the
deadline for the commencement of the first stage.
Indeed, the economic and finance ministers of the EC
at a meeting on 10 July 1989 agreed to complete the
preparatory work for the first stage by December,
thus giving themselves six months to accommodate
the adjustments that would be needed before the
beginning of the first stage.

The three-stage timetable for EMU did start on
1 July 1990 with the launching of the first phase of
intensified economic cooperation during which all the
member states were to submit their currencies to the
EMS's ERM (see above and below). The main target of
this activity was the United Kingdom whose currency
was not subject to the ERM discipline; the United
Kingdom joined in 1991 while Margaret Thatcher was
still in office, but withdrew from it in 1992, as did Italy.

The second stage is clarified in the Maastricht
Treaty. It was to start in 1994. During this stage the
EU was to create the *European Monetary Institute*
(EMI) to prepare the way for a European Central
Bank (ECB) which would start operating on 1 January
1997. Although this was upset by the 1992 turmoil in
the EMS, the compromises reached in the Edinburgh
summit of December 1992 (deemed necessary for creating the conditions which resulted in a successful second referendum on the Treaty in Denmark and hence
in ratification by the United Kingdom – see Chapter 2)
did not water down the Treaty too much. Be that as it
may, the Treaty already allowed Denmark and the
United Kingdom to opt out of the final stage when the
EU currency rates would be permanently and irrevocably fixed and a single currency floated. However,
in a separate protocol, all the then 12 EC nations
declared that the drive to a single currency in the
1990s was 'irreversible'. Denmark, which supported
the decision, was an exception because its constitution
demands the holding of a referendum on this issue;
the United Kingdom, because of very specific problems
(see El-Agraa, 2002b).

A single currency (the euro), to be managed by an
independent ECB, was to be introduced as early as

1997 if seven of the then 12 EC nations passed the
strict economic criteria required for its successful
operation, and in 1999 at the very latest. These conditions are as follows:

1 *Price stability*. Membership required 'a price
performance that is sustainable and an average
rate of inflation, observed over a period of one
year before the examination, that does not exceed
by more than [1.5] percentage points that of, at
most, the three best performing' EC member
countries. Inflation 'shall be measured by means
of the consumer price index on a comparable
basis, taking into account differences in national
definitions'.

2 *Interest rates*. Membership required that,

> observed over a period of one year before the
> examination, a Member State has had an
> average nominal long-term interest rate that
> does not exceed by more than two percentage
> points that of, at most, the three best
> performing Member States in terms of price
> stability. Interest rates shall be measured on
> the basis of long-term government bonds or
> comparable securities, taking into account
> differences in national definitions.

3 *Budget deficits*. Membership required that a
member country 'has achieved a government
budgetary position without a deficit that is
excessive' (Article 109j). However, what is to
be considered excessive is determined in Article
104c(6) which simply states the Council shall
decide after an overall assessment 'whether an
excessive deficit exists'. The Protocol sets the
criterion for an excessive deficit as being 3% of
GDP. However, there are provisos if 'either the
ratio has declined substantially and continuously
and reached a level that comes close to the
reference value; or . . . the excess over the
reference value is only exceptional and
temporary and the ratio remained close to the
reference value.'

4 *Public debt*. Here the requirement in the Protocol
is that the ratio of government debt should not
exceed 60% of GDP. But again there is an
important proviso 'unless the ratio is sufficiently
diminishing and approaching the reference value
at a satisfactory pace.' Whether such an excessive
deficit exists is open to interpretation and is

decided by the Council under qualified majority. In helping the Council decide, the Commission is to look at the medium term and quite explicitly can have the opinion that there is an excessive deficit if there is risk, 'notwithstanding the fulfilment of the requirements under the criteria'.

5 *Currency stability*. Membership required that a member country

> has respected the normal fluctuation margin provided for by the exchange-rate mechanism of the [EMS] without severe tensions for at least two years before the examination. In particular, [it] shall not have devalued its currency's bilateral central rate against any other Member State's currency on its own initiative for the same period.

One is, of course, perfectly justified in asking about the theoretical rationale for these convergence criteria. The answer is simply that there is not one; for example, the inflation criterion is not even based on NAIRUs (i.e. inflation could be convergent simply because the economy is out of internal equilibrium over the examination period) and there is no way to evaluate whether or not a 60% of GDP public debt is better or worse than, say, a 65% of GDP rate. Normally the criterion used for assessing the debt position of a country in rating its debt is 'sustainability', which is subject to a wide range of considerations. One easy rationalization that could be applied is that 3% of GDP happened to be the average level of public investment at that time, and the member nations deemed this percentage acceptable. Given this, it is often also accepted that investment – provided it has an equivalent financial rate of return – can be sustainably financed by a budget deficit. Calculating this at the steady state of equilibrium and a compound rate of interest of 5% per annum results in a public borrowing of 60% of GDP (see Buiter, Corsetti and Roubini, 1993), which also happened to be the average at the time.

The important requirements for a stable system are that no member should be able to run their economy in a way that increases the cost for the others. Provided that the minimum standard set is high enough then the euro area as a whole will get the finest credit ratings/lowest interest costs. Unless there is some means of differentiation, then the single exchange and interest rate for the EMU will reflect the aggregate behaviour. In a more developed federal system it

becomes possible to have two sorts of public debt, as in the US, for example. Then the states (or whatever lower level authorities exist) have the ability to raise their own debt but subject to limits and very explicitly without a guarantee from the federal authorities. The US therefore shows noticeable spreads for local and state debt and some have indeed got into difficulty as the Orange County case illustrated.

It is interesting to note that the timing of these convergence tests has been crucial. If they had occurred in 1992, only France and Luxembourg would have scored full marks, i.e. five points. The others would have scored as follows: Denmark and the United Kingdom four points each; Belgium, Germany and Ireland three points each; the Netherlands two points; Italy and Spain one point each; Greece and Portugal zero points each. Hence, the EMU could not have been introduced since seven countries would have needed to score full marks for this purpose. The position at the end of 1996 was even worse since only Luxembourg qualified – see Figure 9.1. Hence the third stage of EMU did not begin by the earlier date of 1997. What is extraordinary is the turnaround by the final qualifying date of 1998. Then, only one country was deemed not to qualify, Greece, and even Greece was able to qualify at the first subsequent reassessment in 2000. However, one should hasten to add the proviso regarding this test, that the text permitted the exercise of considerable discretion, reinforced by Article 6 of the Protocol which states that the

> Council shall, acting unanimously on a proposal from the Commission and after consulting the European Parliament, the EMI or the ECB as the case may be, and the Committee referred to in Article 109c, adopt appropriate provisions to lay down the details of the convergence criteria referred to in Article 109j of the Treaty, which shall then replace this Protocol.

The data on which the decision on 2 May 1998 was based – see Table 9.1 – was deemed, in the opinion of the EU Commission, to indicate that 11 nations had passed the test. Of the remaining four, three (Denmark, the UK and Sweden) had already decided not to join in the first wave, and Greece was not in the running. The Commission's interpretation of the member states' performance was clearly 'flexible' (the EMI, which was also charged with issuing a convergence report, was of exactly the same opinion as the Commission (EMI, 1998)):

Table 9.1 EU member states' performance to convergence criteria

	Inflation		Government budgetary position					Exchange rates	Long-term interest rates[d]
	HICP[a]	Existence of an excessive deficit[b]	Deficit (per cent of GDP)[c]	Debt (per cent of GDP)				ERM participation	
	January 1998		1997	1997	Change from previous year			March 1998	January 1998
					1997	1996	1995		
Reference Value	2.7[e]		3	60					7.8[f]
Austria	1.1	yes[g]	2.5	66.1	−3.4	0.3	3.8	yes	5.6
Belgium	1.4	yes[g]	2.1	122.2	−4.7	−4.3	−2.2	yes	5.7
Denmark	1.9	no	−0.7	65.1	−5.5	−2.7	−4.9	yes	6.2
Finland	1.3	no	0.9	55.8	−1.8	−0.4	−1.5	yes[k]	5.9
France	1.2	yes[g]	3.0	58.0	2.4	2.9	4.2	yes	5.5
Germany	1.4	yes[g]	2.7	61.3	0.8	2.4	7.8	yes	5.6
Greece	5.2	yes	4.0	108.7	−2.9	1.5	0.7	yes[h]	9.8[i]
Ireland	1.2	no	−0.9	66.3	−6.4	−9.6	−6.8	yes	6.2
Italy	1.8	yes[g]	2.7	121.6	−2.4	−0.2	−0.7	yes[j]	6.7
Luxembourg	1.4	no	−1.7	6.7	0.1	0.7	0.2	yes	5.6
Netherlands	1.8	no	1.4	72.1	−5.0	−1.9	1.2	yes	5.5
Portugal	1.8	yes[g]	2.5	62.0	−3.0	−0.9	2.1	yes	6.2
Spain	1.8	yes[g]	2.6	68.8	−1.3	4.6	2.9	yes	6.3
Sweden	1.9	yes[g]	0.8	76.6	−0.1	−0.9	−1.4	no	6.5
United Kingdom	1.8	yes[g]	1.9	53.4	−1.3	0.8	3.5	no	7.0
EU (15)	1.6		2.4	72.1	−0.9	2.0	3.0		6.1

[a] Percentage change in arithmetic average of the latest 12 monthly-harmonized indices of consumer prices (HICP) relative to the arithmetic average of the 12 HICP of the previous period.
[b] Council decisions of 26.09.94, 10.07.95, 27.06.96 and 30.06.97.
[c] A negative sign for the government deficit indicates a surplus.
[d] Average maturity 10 years; average of the last 12 months.
[e] Definition adopted in this report: simple arithmetic average of the inflation rates of the three best performing member states in terms of price stability plus 1.5 percentage points.
[f] Definition adopted in this report: simple arithmetic average of the 12-month average of interest rates of the three best performing member states in terms of price stability plus two percentage points.
[g] Commission recommended abrogation.
[h] Since March 1998.
[i] Average of the available data during the past 12 months.
[j] Since November 1996.
[k] Since October 1996.
Source: EU Commission Services

Well, inflation's on target . . .
Inflation and government bond yields,* latest

Source: National statistics, J.P. Morgan; ABN AMRO; Hoare Govett.
* n.a. for Portugal and Greece.

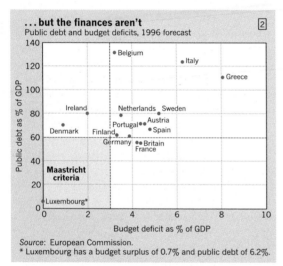

. . . but the finances aren't
Public debt and budget deficits, 1996 forecast

Source: European Commission.
* Luxembourg has a budget surplus of 0.7% and public debt of 6.2%.

Figure 9.1 Performing to the convergence
criteria, 1996

Fourteen Member States had government deficits
of three per cent of GDP or less in 1997: Belgium,
Denmark, Germany, Spain, France, Ireland, Italy,

Luxembourg, the Netherlands, Austria, Portugal,
Finland, Sweden and the United Kingdom. Member
States had achieved significant reductions in the
level of government borrowing, in particular in
1997. This remarkable outcome was the result of
national governments' determined efforts to tackle
excessive deficits combined with the effects of
lower interest rates and stronger growth in the
European economy. The Commission's report
critically examined one-off measures which have
contributed to some Member States' 1997 figures.
In particular it analysed Budget measures for 1998
and other factors to assess whether the budgetary
situation was sustainable. *The report concluded
that the major part of the deficit reductions were
structural.*

In 1997 government debt was below the
Treaty reference value of 60% of GDP in four
Member States – France, Luxembourg, Finland
and the United Kingdom. According to the
Treaty, countries may exceed this value as long
as the debt ratio is 'sufficiently diminishing and
approaching the reference value at a satisfactory
pace'. This was deemed to be the case in almost
all Member States with debt ratios above 60% in
1997. Only in Germany, where the ratio was just
above 60% of GDP and the exceptional costs of
unification continued to bear heavily, was there a
small rise in 1997. All countries above the 60%
ratio were expected to see reductions in their
debt levels. *The Commission concluded that the
conditions were in place for the continuation
of a sustained decline in debt ratio in future
years.* (EU Commission Services, 1998,
italics added)

Thus, it should be clear that the EMU envisaged in
the Delors Report and detailed and endorsed in the
Maastricht Treaty is consistent with and satisfies all
the requirements of a full economic and monetary
union in the sense described in Chapter 8.

9.4   The transition to EMU

As the EU progressed towards EMU it was opening
itself up to the possibility of severe strains through the
EMS as exchange controls were removed as part of
Stage 1. The removal posed two problems for the
EMS. First, a protection against speculation was lost.

Second, because interest parity was no longer prevented, interest rates everywhere were tightly linked
as the amount of expected depreciation was confined
by the bands of permissible fluctuations of the currencies against one another. Because Germany was by

far the largest economy in the EMS, this meant that interest rates, and hence monetary policy, everywhere in the system were dominated by Germany. Unless Germany in turn tempered its monetary policy by concern for the economic situation in other countries this could turn out to be an unacceptable state of affairs, as indeed proved to be the case in 1992–1993.

These problems were realized and various solutions proposed. First, as regards the problem of speculation, the mechanisms of the EMS were improved by measures to accommodate automatic lending by a strong-currency country to a weak-currency country in the event of need; whereas previously this automaticity applied only when intervention was taking place at the edge of the band, since the deliberations of the EMS finance ministers in Nyborg in September 1987, it applied also to so-called intra-marginal intervention, i.e. foreign exchange operations taking place to support a currency before it has reached its limit. These new provisions were tested by a speculative run on the French franc in the autumn of 1987 and proved successful; the Bundesbank lent heavily to the Banque de France but the lending was rapidly repaid once the speculation subsided and confidence returned. The second problem – that of excessive German dominance – was only resolved by moving on to full EMU. The Nyborg provisions called for much closer monetary cooperation, implying more continuous exchange of information, and interest rate movements within the EMS after that time displayed a high degree of synchronization. However, the cooperation called for also seemed to imply a degree of common decision making going beyond simply following a German lead in a prompt and well-prepared way. Progress on this front is less evident. The anxiety of France on this score, however, led to important initiatives. First, France called upon Germany to discuss economic policy on a regular basis and an economic council was set up for this purpose. Second, it was on French initiatives that the EC was led to call for an investigation into the requirements of full monetary union, an investigation subsequently carried out by the Delors Committee, the recommendations of whose report were endorsed by all 12 nations of the EC in June 1989, leading to the Maastricht Treaty on European Union (see above).

The path which the EMS participants agreed to follow thus called for increasing intervention resources and other devices to combat the threat of speculation and for increased economic and monetary cooperation between member countries, eventually leading to the creation of the European Central Bank. But we should note that there were alternative short-run solutions. One way in which countries can recover a greater measure of independence from the dominant power is to enlarge the bands of exchange rate fluctuation, which is what they did in 1993; another would have been to compromise on the single market by retaining a measure of exchange control. Either device has obvious counterspeculative advantages too. If maintained over the long term, these alternative solutions would have been in effect a defeat for the higher aspirations of the EMS. But either one could, in principle, have been adopted on a purely monetary basis until such time as the political prerequisites for greater cooperation were met. The second mechanism was not used but it is not difficult to think of circumstances in which it might have been, given the increasing popularity in the late 1990s of the idea of putting 'sand in the wheels' of international financial transactions in order to limit their volatility.

The removal of exchange controls undoubtedly posed problems for the future of the EMS. Following the delicate path to which the member countries agreed, exposed the system to the hazards of speculation and posed political problems relating to the acceptance of German dominance in monetary affairs. The alternative short-run solutions had the disadvantage of taking the pressure off the search for a solution to the political problem, or perpetuating an obstacle to the integration of the European financial area.

The forecast threat to the system duly occurred in September 1992. Uncertainty about the outcome of the French referendum on the Maastricht Treaty contributed to speculation against the weakest currencies in the ERM, sterling and the lira. Both were unable to resist the pressure despite substantial increases in interest rates. By the summer of 1993 not even the French franc could survive the pressure and the bands had to be widened to ±15% to allow it to devalue without realigning within the system.

Other currencies also came under pressure, such as the Irish punt and the Swedish krone (which was shadowing the ERM), and were forced to devalue. There was considerable pressure on the French franc in September 1992 but it survived, aided by substantial intervention by the Bundesbank on its behalf. It is arguable that all the currencies which were devalued were in some sense overvalued in terms of their long-term sustainable values. (One interpretation of this is the Fundamental Equilibrium Exchange Rate, FEER, the rate at which the balance of payments is sustainable in the long run.) However, the problem was not merely one of great domestic inflation by the devaluing countries but of the special problems of the dominant German economy leading to a divergence from the domestic objectives of the other countries.[2] German interest rates were driven up by the need to finance unification over and above the willingness to raise taxes. With the tight linkage of EMS interest rates other states also had to have rates that were high in real terms.

In the case of the United Kingdom it was clearly a relief that the constraints of the ERM could be broken. Interest rates had already been progressively cut to the point that sterling was close to its lower bound. A domestic recession was being exacerbated by the inability to use monetary policy to alleviate it. On exit, interest rates were lowered by four percentage points in virtually as many months. There was no immediate prospect of sterling re-entering the ERM and indeed its fall of over 15% is no larger than that suggested by the FEER, and its subsequent rise as the economy recovered was predictable.

The EMS suffered considerably through being unable to organize an orderly realignment of exchange rates. The mechanisms existed but political pressures meant that the member states could not agree among themselves. Blame has been placed in a number of quarters – on the Bundesbank for not taking greater account of the impact of its policy on other countries and on the United Kingdom for not being sincere in trying to maintain parity within the bounds – but the basic weakness of the system remained: that trying to have narrow bands without exchange controls is really not sustainable when there are substantial shocks to the system. This was admitted in practice by widening the bands.

The EMS took a back seat after the devaluations of September 1992 and the widening of the band to ±15% in August 1993. However, the system remained intact and slowly regained credibility. Despite three devaluations of the peseta and the escudo between November 1992 and March 1995 the participating currencies moved back into closer alignment. At the end of 1996 all bar the Irish punt were within the ±2.25% band. Although sterling and the drachma remained outside the ERM and the Swedish krone did not join, Italy rejoined in November 1996 and Finland (October 1996) and Austria (January 1995) also became participants.

As we have noted, the EMS survived through to its replacement by the Eurosystem at the start of 1999 primarily because of the determination of EU governments to qualify for EMU under the Maastricht criteria. The restraints on fiscal policy from needing to keep deficits below 3% of GDP and debt below 60% (or make credible progress towards 60%) simultaneously helped inflation to converge and the member states to get their business cycles in line. The steady development of the internal market has integrated them further.

In part the reason why Stage 3 of EMU did not begin in 1997 was simply that the convergence period after the shocks of 1992–1993 was just too short, particularly for countries like Sweden and especially Finland for which the shocks were greatest, but the evolution of the general economic cycles was not favourable. From then onwards, however, convergence was easier. Yet, just as the adverse circumstances in the mid-1990s were bad luck so the EU was extremely lucky that 1996–1998 was a period of very considerable stability. Even the Asian crisis did not have a marked effect and decreased the chance of importing inflation from the rest of the world.

Once financial markets felt that fiscal convergence and EMU were likely, this expectation brought the required convergence in real interest rates. Had it not been possible for some of the countries that had experienced the greatest difficulty in converging to join then, it is likely that they would have experienced considerable pressures in the period immediately after the decision. The loss of credibility involved would then have made joining at a subsequent date much more expensive than it was for those who were successful earlier on.

The creation of the Eurosystem has established three groups of countries within the EU: those who are in the euro area, those who are outside but hope to join in the reasonably near future and those who are outside but have no immediate plans. This third group, Denmark and the UK, are free to pursue their own independent monetary policies just as they could outside the ERM of the previous EMS. The second 'group' is simply Sweden at present but the signs are that all the ten new members set to join the EU in 2004 and the two set for 2007 also want to move to membership of the euro area as soon as possible. Indeed it is not at all clear whether the third group will have any members after 2003 if the planned referenda in Denmark and the UK resulted in a majority in favour. (Given history, this is by no means a foregone conclusion. Indeed, at the time of writing it is still a very open question which way the referendum in Sweden will go despite the enthusiasm of the government for membership. However, the outcome of the referendum was euro non-adoption.) The Eurosystem has, however, created an extension of the ERM labelled ERM2 for those countries that wish to try to converge. Currently only Denmark is participating in ERM2 but this mechanism remains open for all those who wish to be considered for membership of Stage 3. The rules are similar to those that faced the new members, Austria, Finland and Sweden under the original ERM. Their currencies did not form part of the ECU basket and hence if their exchange rate moved with respect to the other members it did not affect the value of the ECU itself.

A central value is agreed between the ECB and the member state for the exchange rate with the euro. The intention then appears to be for the rate to remain within the same 2.25% range that prevailed within ERM. Realignments are possible and indeed have already happened for Greece (upwards). However, in its latest Convergence Report, the ECB (2002) remains rather more vague. Having outlined history with the ±2.25%, ±6% and ±15% bands it goes on to conclude: 'Against this background, in the assessment of exchange rate developments the emphasis is placed on exchange rates being close to the ERM II central rates.' Indeed they go further and explain that this needs to have been achieved without 'severe tensions' in the sense of requiring interventions or wide interest rate spreads.

The reason for the vagueness is obvious, as the new system has to cope with a variety of arrangements. Some countries like Estonia already have a much tighter arrangement with the euro, through having a currency board. There is therefore no variation at all with respect to the euro. It would clearly make no sense for them to have to float their exchange rate in the last two years of the run up to hoped-for convergence. That would just open them up to risks they do not need to run. Indeed their exit route from pressure would be more likely to be unilateral adoption of the euro than floating. In their case therefore the assessment would be on the basis of the absence of 'severe tensions' alone.

ERM2 is thus a rather one-sided affair, very much reminiscent of the early days of the original ERM. It is for the applicants to adjust to the behaviour of the euro area. Euro monetary policy is run without regard to their problems, it is the ECB that determines the parities. The ECB (and the Commission) will offer an opinion on whether convergence has occurred. In the case of Greece, the government was keen to go ahead with membership of the euro area as soon as possible. It was accepted for membership in June 2000 and joined the Eurosystem at the beginning of 2001. Even if all of the 10 new EU members were to join ERM2, the system would be highly unbalanced in favour of the Eurosystem in terms of relative economic size. In some ways dependency will actually be a strength to the system, as it makes stable alternatives substantially more costly for the applicants. Thus not only will they have a strong incentive to try to remain in the system and not follow policies that are likely to lead to downward realignments, but the existence of these incentives will be obvious to everybody else as well, thereby increasing the credibility of the commitment.

However, the new members are likely to find ERM2 a much more difficult proposition than their predecessors had it or ERM(1), as they are still undergoing a major process of structural change and have not in some cases achieved sustainably low inflation. It is therefore likely that, as with the original ERM, the weaker members will experience real exchange rate increases that will ultimately force them into realignments. Adopting a currency board based on the euro may offer greater credibility. Ironically, one element of convergence to the behaviour of the Eurosystem may be easier than for some of the existing ESCB members as the applicants are in the main heavily integrated with the euro economy already, even though geography might have led one to expect closer links with third countries. Particularly in the case of the former Soviet bloc countries, the economic ties further east have been thoroughly broken. It is thus the problems of transition that are likely to present the greatest strains rather than worries about asymmetric shocks that have affected countries like the UK with substantial economic linkages outside the euro area.

Transition is likely to be slow in some cases, particularly for those countries that have not yet been accepted for membership of the EU, so ERM2 is also likely to be a relatively long-lived arrangement. However, in many cases the new members will feel that they would rather complete the process of adjustment within EMU than outside. The credibility and hence much lower real interest rates offered by membership may very well be thought to outweigh the gains from exchange rate flexibility. Massive changes in their labour markets are known to be inevitable, so there may be a willingness to accept the pressures on non-monetary and non-fiscal routes to adjustment, a process that has presented considerable difficulties for many of the current EU members.

The combination of the single market and the absence of exchange controls clearly added to the risk from speculative pressures for the EMS. It is not surprising therefore that there was very strong pressure to move to Stage 3 of EMU despite the costs of transition. This will still apply.

9.5   The position of the United Kingdom, Sweden and Denmark

It might appear, prima facie, odd in purely economic terms that the UK, Sweden and Denmark have chosen to stay out of Stage 3 of EMU, while other countries that seem less convergent on standard optimum currency area (OCA) criteria, such as the Irish Republic, Finland and Greece have chosen to join. Setting aside the political issues, there are three simple economic reasons that help explain the decisions, but the case of the UK stands out for a further reason. The UK is larger in economic terms than the other five countries mentioned above taken together. It is the only EU member with a world scale financial market although Frankfurt has been improving its relative position. We therefore spend rather more time on the UK in the rest of this section.

The simple economic reasons are:

1 Life on the outside has been successful. It is very difficult in the case of Denmark, for example, to point to the extra costs from staying outside, but shadowing the euro very closely, except in terms of foregoing a seat at the table (both in the ECB and the Euro Group). With little right of veto, the impact of a single small country is rarely going to be decisive.
2 Some of the joining countries, particularly Finland (see Mayes and Suvanto, 2002) have put a much higher weight on the expectation that membership would change behaviour for the better. Furthermore, in the case of both Finland and the Irish Republic the expectation has been that membership would support their propensity for faster than average growth by offering lower real interest rates and dampening inflationary pressures through the threat of competition.
3 It is better to adjust first, making use of the extra flexibility available, and join second. This has been very much the view in Sweden, set out at

length in the report of the Calmfors Commision that was appointed by the Swedish government to assess the costs and benefits of full EMU participation (Calmfors *et al.*, 1997). This caution, particularly about being able to cushion the impact of shocks on employment and unemployment, remains in the more recent 'Committee on Stabilization Policy for full Employment if Sweden joins the Monetary Union' (Johansson *et al.*, 2002). The Committee concludes 'Our view is that changes in the degree of nominal wage flexibility are likely to compensate only to a minor extent for the loss of national monetary policy as an instrument of stabilization policy' (p. 3). Indeed they see that wages in Sweden might themselves be a source of shocks. This reaction reflects a general expectation that flexibility will not work. The same argument is applied to fluctuations in working hours. Because so much of working hours are statutorily controlled, the Committee (pp. 5–6) did not see them as being able to act as a shock absorber. If rules were changed they would apply to all sectors. The rigidities imposed on the labour market mean that it is necessary to look elsewhere for offsetting fluctuations in the system. This implies that much of the successful readjustment of the Swedish economy to the crisis at the beginning of the 1990s can be attributed to the operation of monetary policy and to the movement in the exchange rate.

One might wish to add two further reasons. The first is a much more pessimistic view of the secondary benefits that could accrue under a more complete EMU than in the partial or 'pseudo' union envisaged in the Corden–Fleming model (see Chapter 8). This would be particularly true for countries that expect to be net payers rather than net recipients. The second is that, if a country feels that it is already more flexible than its potential partners, membership and a tendency towards common behaviour might actually be retrogressive and result in a structure that generates slower growth. Some of this flavour emerges from the discussion of the UK.

9.5.1 The UK

The United Kingdom declined to participate in the operation of the EMS, to begin with, out of a belief that the system would be operated in a rigid way which would threaten the UK, with its high 'propensity to inflate', with a decline in its competitiveness, especially *vis-à-vis* Germany. This concern for the UK's freedom to determine or preserve its competitiveness still marks one strand of oppositional thinking on the question of British membership of EMU today. The problems of September 1992 in many ways served to reinforce the views that had led to the initial reluctance to join the ERM and hence were not wholly uncongenial.

While opposition to full membership of the EMS was voiced on these grounds by the Labour government of James Callaghan, opposition on different grounds was propounded by the incoming Conservative government headed by Margaret Thatcher. The Thatcher government wished to run an experiment in monetary policy in order to bring inflation down and reasoned, correctly, that if the instruments of monetary policy (principally interest rates) were to be directed at reducing the rate of growth of the money supply, they could not simultaneously be used to target the exchange rate. Technically, this dilemma could be avoided by maintaining a suitably strong set of exchange controls; such controls would allow a government some freedom to maintain two different targets for monetary policy, but the Thatcher government was keen to remove these controls in any case and did so not long after taking office.

Events were to turn out somewhat paradoxically. The first phase of the Conservative government's monetary experiment was associated with a very marked *appreciation* of the exchange rate – so competitiveness would have been *better* preserved inside the EMS – and the deep recession that soon set in was attributed by many observers to this cause. The view took root that while the Thatcher government was correct to say that membership of the EMS was

incompatible with pursuit of an independent monetary policy and would involve a loss of sovereignty in this respect, better results would nevertheless be attained by adhering to the EMS. In particular, the exchange rate would be steadier and competitiveness more assured, while inflation would be dragged towards the modest German level (we have already described the claims made for the EMS as a counter-inflationary framework).

This view gained momentum as official British policy towards the exchange rate as a target changed and as it became clear that monetary policy was no longer aimed in single-minded fashion solely at controlling the supply of money. In fact, with practice preceding the public statement, the Chancellor of the Exchequer made this very clear in his 1983 budget speech. A House of Lords report on the question of entry into the EMS, published a little later in the same year, favoured 'early, though not necessarily immediate' entry into the system.

That report referred to four problems that the United Kingdom had had in relation to the EMS and noted that in each case events had moved in a favourable fashion. The first problem was the apprehension that the EMS would prove rigid and inflexible: the committee noted that the EMS had allowed a number of realignments. The second problem was that the United Kingdom had wanted to put the control of the money supply ahead of the goal of stabilizing the exchange rate – where, as described, policy had already retreated somewhat. The third problem was related to the UK position as an oil exporter, with sterling subject to quite a different response from that of the EMS currencies to oil price shocks. The committee saw this as less problematic as the oil market had become less disturbed. The fourth problem arose from sterling's still persistent role as a vehicle currency, i.e. one widely held by agents other than those solely concerned with UK trade. The committee acknowledged that this might mean that it would not be so easy to stabilize sterling in the ERM.

The viewpoint of the House of Lords report appears to have been representative of a wide range of opinion. Although the later report of a subcommittee of the House of Commons Select Committee on the Treasury and Civil Service revived some of the earlier arguments against entry, the general climate of opinion had changed markedly in a favourable direction by the early 1980s. With the passage of time, the lingering reservations over the exposure of sterling to oil shocks and over the problem of speculation diminished still further, while the case for exchange-rate management became more widely and firmly accepted. The initiative launched by the United States in 1985 to secure the coordinated actions of its major partners to bring the dollar down substantially reinforced the latter process.

In September 1986, at the meetings of the IMF, the Chancellor of the Exchequer advertised the non-speculative realignment process of the EMS and not long afterwards followed this up with a policy of 'shadowing the EMS', keeping the sterling exchange rate closely in line with the deutschmark. This policy initiative lasted for just over a year; by the end of February 1988, following a well-publicized exchange of views between the Chancellor and the Prime Minister, sterling was uncapped. Higher interest rates, invoked as a means of dampening monetary growth and in response to forecasts of inflation, caused the exchange rate to appreciate through its previous working ceiling. The incident underlined the inconsistency between an independent monetary policy and an exchange-rate policy and at the same time served to confirm that sterling was unlikely to participate in the ERM during the prime ministership of Margaret Thatcher. Even when sterling ultimately went into the ERM in October 1990, it appeared to be with considerable reluctance.

Membership of the ERM only lasted until September 1992, when markets pushed sterling out of the system. It did not rejoin, even when a government with a more favourable attitude was elected in May 1997. The issue has now been overtaken by whether the UK should join EMU. While a close shadowing of the euro, as has been followed by Denmark, could make sense in its own right to help acquire greater stability, the main reason for such a policy would be as part of the preconditions for membership of the Eurosystem. UK monetary policy was immediately focused on an explicit inflation target of 2.5% a year in May 1997. Pursuit of this target with only narrow bands of 1% either side almost inevitably means that UK monetary policy will vary from that of the ECB, with its medium-term target of inflation being less than 2% (see Chapter 10).

As just mentioned, and also in Chapter 2, the present UK government has turned to a serious consideration of euro membership. It has decided that it would recommend in a referendum to the British people the adoption of the euro provided five tests, set by Chancellor Gordon Brown in October 1997, are met. The performance of the UK against these tests was evaluated during the summer of 2003 and gave a negative result, but the government said it would try again.

What are the five Brown economic tests? The first is about business cycles and economic structures being compatible 'so that we and others could live comfortably with euro interest rates on a permanent basis'. The second relates to whether there would be 'sufficient flexibility to deal with' any problems if they emerge. The third concerns whether the adoption of the euro would 'create better conditions for firms making long-term decisions to invest in Britain'. The fourth is about what the impact of euro adoption would be 'on the competitive position of the UK's financial services industry, particularly the City's wholesale markets'. The final sums up the other four since it is about whether the adoption of the euro would 'promote higher growth, stability and a lasting increase in jobs'. The Treasury report tries to knit the tests together:

> Sustainable and durable convergence is the touchstone and without it we cannot reap the benefits of a successful EMU. It means that the British economy:
> - has converged with Europe;
> - can demonstrably be shown to have converged;
> - that this convergence is capable of being sustained; and
> - that there is sufficient flexibility to adapt to change and unexpected economic events.
> (UK Treasury, 1997, p. 2)

However, when announcing these tests in October 1997, Brown added that the Treasury must decide that there is a 'clear and unambiguous' economic case for recommending British adoption of the euro, but can one seriously establish that within the context of economics, let alone political economy? In other words, it would seem that this addition has been made to ensure that any decision on the matter would be based on purely political grounds.

We should add that it is now generally agreed that it is also vital to include an economic test omitted by Brown. It is the testing of a factor, which would determine the economic performance of the UK for years to come: the value at which sterling would enter the euro. Contrary to popular perception, this need not be the present market exchange rate. This raises the question regarding how much lower should sterling be relative to the euro at the appropriate time. Many commentators have suggested that a rate of between 1.25 to 1.45 euros to £1 sterling would be about right.

Since the decision on euro entry rests on the Treasury's own assessment of the performance of the British economy against its own tests, we do not advance our own. However, several such assessments have already been published (see, *inter alia*, NIESR and UBS Warburg, latest available, or Barrell, 2001) and all agree that the British economy has been converging with the euro zone area; indeed, even the Treasury's own evaluation is expected to concur with this view. Yet, the expectation at the time of writing is that the Chancellor will announce that convergence has not been sufficient, i.e. not enough to make a 'clear and unambiguous' case for entry. The relative success of the UK economy in recent years can be expected to influence the economic judgement over the appropriate timing of entry. While this book was in production, the Chancellor announced (on 9 June 2003) that Britain failed to meet the tests, but the government promised to review the position in 2004. The Treasury's assessment (see their website), backed by 2000 pages of supporting analysis, confirms our prediction: that convergence has improved but a 'clear and unambiguous case' has yet to be established. There is, however, no need to go through the details of the assessment here since a clear and unambiguous case can never be made, as the result depends on a comparison of two hypothetical futures that are unknowable by definition and cannot even be validated after the event. Moreover, even if the economic case can be established, it will ebb and flow as the performances of the EU economies move relative to each other. This would be so, even though the next target for the Bank of England will be the HICP with a centre point and range, which will make the UK consistent with the ECB target and enhance economic convergence. The final decision is, therefore, bound to be a political rather than an economic one.

9.6 Conclusions

Even a few years ago, conclusions on the prospects for EMU in the EU were cautious. In 1996 when the time for assessing whether Stage 3 could start at the beginning of 1997 it was not even worth looking as only one country, the smallest, qualified under the Maastricht criteria. Only two years later the ECB was up and running and 11 member states had both qualified and decided upon membership. By 2002 the notes and coins of the euro currency were in circulation and the national currencies of member states, by then increased to 12, had been withdrawn. There was a large element of luck in the specific timing but nevertheless one must conclude that the process to EMU has been a remarkable success. It is difficult to tell whether those framing the Maastricht Treaty a decade earlier really believed their efforts would turn out so well. Previous attempts had run into difficulty.

It will be some time before it is possible to estimate the degree of success of EMU in economic terms. In any case any such assessment will always be highly contested, as it rests on comparison with a hypothetical alternative that did not occur. The years 1999 and 2000 were good years not just in the euro area but also more generally. While 2001 and 2002 saw a serious setback. Public support for EMU has risen and fallen with the general economic climate, irrelevant of whether EMU was actually causal. Now, 2003 and 2004 will be equally important in the popular success of the enterprise as a serious recovery in the world economy and the euro area within it is yet to emerge. It is, however, difficult to gainsay the beneficial impact on those countries that previously faced problems of credibility in their macroeconomic policy. The enthusiasm by the accession countries for moving on to membership of Stage 3 of EMU as soon as possible after they join the EU itself in 2004 shows that this expectation is widely shared.

In this chapter we have deliberately concentrated on the 'M' in EMU leaving the 'E' for the discussion in Chapter 10 – not because it is less important but because the main developments have occurred more recently as the euro area became a reality. This emphasis on the monetary side is strongly reflected in the literature and may help explain some of the emphasis on the potential difficulties stemming from adverse asymmetric shocks within an EMU. The monetary side of EMU in Europe involves new institutions and a strong legal basis for a single monetary policy. The economic side on the other hand relies on relatively soft coordination among the member states through a series of 'processes' regulated by the Stability and Growth Pact (see Chapter 10). As soon as the constraints of the SGP have started to bind, those affected have tended to complain and seek for ways round the restrictions. This has led to both popular scepticism and academic criticism because the terms of the pact are rather simplistic and pragmatic and not founded on clear economic principles.

The reality, however, has been a major turnaround in the macroeconomic behaviour of many of the EU economies, particularly those that were facing the greater inflationary and budgetary problems. This change has been perpetuated after the initial convergence conditions for membership of Stage 3 were met and has resulted in a much more prudent fiscal basis for the EU. As noted elsewhere (Chapters 10 and 23) this process is by no means completed, given the challenges from ageing and the continuing problems of adjustment caused by increasing competition and the more rapid change in products and technology. It has, however, achieved a degree of success well beyond what many expected.

A key feature of this success is that assessments of the potential benefits of EMU based on pre-existing structures of behaviour have proven mistaken. The economies have become more symmetric. Thus, not only has the chance of adverse asymmetric shocks fallen, but also the automatic response of other countries (through the 'automatic stabilizers') has helped to offset some of the anticipated loss of flexibility from having a single monetary and exchange rate policy. Furthermore there is evidence that bargaining and other structures have themselves responded, irrespective of regulatory reform, to offer more flexibility and hence reduce the real impact of shocks.

Lastly, countries such as Finland and the Irish Republic have demonstrated that in EMU favourable asymmetric shocks are also amplified, resulting in faster growth and less inflation than would otherwise have been possible.

In the next chapter we look at the operation of EMU in more detail.

NOTES

1. These revisions ended in 1989 when Portugal and Spain were added and the same weight continued until the ECU was replaced by the euro. Thus when Austria, Finland and Sweden joined the EU in 1995, their currencies did not become components of the ECU, even though the first two later joined the ERM.

2. Cobham (1996) provides a helpful exposition of the different possible explanations of the crisis.

Chapter 10 — The operation of EMU

DAVID MAYES

Economic and monetary union has four broad ingredients: the euro and the single European monetary policy; the coordination of European macroeconomic policies through the *Stability and Growth Pact* (SGP), the Broad Economic Policy Guidelines (BEPG) and related processes; the completion of the internal market; and the operation of the structural funds and other cohesion measures. In this chapter we will look only at the first two as the others are dealt with in Chapters 11 and 22.

Although the euro did not come into existence until 1 January 1999 and then only in financial markets, most of the characteristics of Stage 3 of EMU (Chapter 9) were operating once the European Central Bank (ECB) opened in June 1998. The ECB in the form of the European Monetary Institute (EMI) had been preparing for the day since 1994 with all of the EU national central banks (NCBs). The form of the coming single monetary policy was known already by 1998, both in framework and instruments. In the same way much of the framework for the operation of the economic coordination among the member states had been developed with the SGP of July 1997 and the BEPG that commenced in 1998. The generalized framework was incorporated in the Treaty of Amsterdam (October 1997). There was thus no great break in behaviour at the beginning of 1999, especially since the main qualification period under the convergence criteria had related to 1997.

In what follows we look first at the provisions for the single monetary policy and second at those for policy coordination and then explore how they have worked.

10.1 The Eurosystem and the euro

The institutional system behind the single monetary policy is quite complex because it has to deal with the fact that some EU members are not participants in Stage 3 of EMU (yet). The Treaty sets up the *European System of Central Banks* (ESCB), which is composed of all the national central banks and the ECB, which is sited in Frankfurt. The ECB and the participating NCBs form the *Eurosystem*, which is what is running the monetary side of the euro area. The term 'Eurosystem' has, however, only been coined by its members, in order to make the set up clearer. It does not occur in the Treaty. The body responsible for the ECB and its decisions is the *Governing Council*, which is composed of the governors of the NCBs and the six members of the *Executive Board*, who provide the executive management of the ECB in Frankfurt. The Executive Board is composed of the *President* and *Vice-president* and four other members, responsible for the various parts of the ECB, which are labelled Directorates General in the same manner as the Commission. If that were not enough the ECB also has a *General Council*, which is composed of the president, vice-president and the governors of *all* the NCBs whether participating in the euro area or not (i.e. it includes the governors of the Danish, Swedish and UK central banks as well). Thus the *General Council* will have 29 members in 2004, once the 10 new member states join the EU (27 governors + 2) but the *Governing Council* will continue to have 18 members (12 governors + 6) until such time as more member states join the euro area. (Fortunately there are many books on the institutional organization so we shall not pursue it further. The book by the ECB itself, *The Monetary Policy of the ECB* (2001) is one of the most comprehensive and straightforward.)

The Eurosystem is relatively decentralized compared to the Federal Reserve System in the United States, although the names for the various institutions imply the opposite relative structures. The central institution in the US, the Board of Governors of the Federal Reserve System, which is the controlling body, having powers over the budgets over the twelve

Federal Reserve Banks, does not have another label for its staff and administrative operations. The seven governors of the Federal Reserve Board hold a voting majority on the monetary policy-making body, the Federal Open Market Committee (FOMC), where only the president of the New York Fed and five of the presidents of the other Fed Banks, by rotation, can vote (although all are present at each meeting).

The Eurosystem on the other hand operates through a network of committees, where each NCB and the ECB has a member. The ECB normally provides the chairman and the secretariat. It is the Governing Council which takes the decisions but the executive board coordinates the work of the committees and prepares the agenda for the Governing Council.

To complete the confusion over labels, the Eurosystem has a *Monetary Policy Committee*, but unlike the UK and many other central banks round the world, this is not the decision-making body on monetary policy. It organizes and discusses the main evidence and discussion papers to be put before the Governing Council on monetary matters.

There are, however, some key characteristics of this structure and other elements of the institutional set up of the Eurosystem which have important implications for policy. As the Delors Committee (Chapter 9), which designed the set up for the Eurosystem, was composed almost entirely of central banks' governors it is not surprising that it is very well adjusted to the current views about the needs of monetary policy. First of all, although the Treaty sets down the objective of monetary policy (maintaining price stability) – in general terms – the Eurosystem bank has a high degree of independence from political influence in exercising their responsibility. Not only is the taking or seeking of such advice explicitly prohibited but the Governing Council members are protected in a number of ways in order to shield them from interest group pressures. First of all they have long terms of office, eight years in the case of the Executive Board – and not renewable – so that they are less likely to have any regard for their prospects for their next job while setting monetary policy. Secondly, the proceedings are secret so that people cannot find out how they voted. Each member is supposed to act purely in a personal capacity and solely with the aims of price stability at the euro area level in mind and without regard to national interests. No system can ensure this but a well-designed one increases the chance of this happening substantially. More import-

antly it can reduce any belief that the members will act with national or other interests in mind. Thirdly, the Eurosystem is explicitly prohibited from 'monetizing' government deficits.

The point of trying to achieve this independence is simply 'credibility' – to try to maximize the belief that the Eurosystem will actually do just what it has been asked to do – namely maintain price stability. The stronger that belief can be then the less 'costly' monetary policy will be. If people do not believe that the ECB will be successful they will base their behaviour on that belief. Hence price and wage setters who believe that there will be increases in inflation substantially beyond what the ECB says it will deliver will set their prices with that higher outcome in mind. That means that the ECB then has to struggle against that belief, thereby entailing high interest rates. Thus even though the ECB may intend exactly the same outcomes in both cases it does not have to run such high interest rates to achieve them if it is 'credible'.

This credibility comes from other sources than independence. The structure of the Governing Council is strongly reminiscent of that of the Bundesbank. The Bundesbank was highly successful in maintaining low inflation. By having a similar structure (probably assisted by the Frankfurt location just a few kilometres down the road) the Eurosystem can hope to 'borrow' much of the Bundesbank's credibility.

10.1.1 The monetary policy of the Eurosystem

The Eurosystem is further assisted in the inherent credibility of its policy by having a simple single objective of price stability laid down by the Treaty. If a central bank has multiple objectives then it will have difficulty explaining the balance between them, especially when they conflict. There was, for example, a short period of confusion at the outset over exchange rate policy, as the Eurosystem is not responsible for the regime, only the execution. However, it rapidly became clear that since exchange rate policy and the objective of monetary policy are inextricably linked, one of the two must have primacy and ministers made it clear that it was going to be price stability that was going to be the driving force. The other common objectives for a central bank of maximizing employment and the rate of growth – in this case expressed as 'without prejudice to the objective of price stability, the ESCB shall support the general economic policies of the Community . . .' – are clearly subservient.

However, for monetary policy to be credible it is necessary that the objective should be clear enough for people to act on and that the central bank's behaviour in trying to achieve that objective should be both observable and understandable as a feasible approach to success. Here the ECB had to define the objective since the Treaty's concept of price stability is far too vague to be workable. They opted for inflation over the medium term of less than 2%. They also defined the inflation they were talking about as that in the Harmonized Index of Consumer Prices. After a swift clarification that this meant that zero inflation was the lower bound, the specification was widely criticized for being too inexact (compared with other central banks). Not only is the length of the medium term not spelt out but it is not clear how much and for how long prices can deviate from the target. Nor is there indication of how fast inflation should be brought back to the target after a shock hits.

This means that a wide range of policy settings would be consistent with such a generalized target. Policy is thus not very predictable – something the Governing Council has sought to offset by trying to give clear signals about interest rate changes. The inevitably diffused structure of decision making with 18 independent decision makers means that the Eurosystem cannot offer a single and closely argued explanation of how it regards the working of the economy. The Bank of England, with a committee half the size is pushing the limits of what can be agreed. Even then dissenting views are expressed from time to time. This is reflected in a further facet of the Eurosystem strategy that has come in for criticism, namely what is known as the two 'pillars'. Rather than adhering to any specific model or suite of models the Eurosystem announced that it would base its decision on a wide range of indicators under two pillars. The first of these assigns a prominent role to money and has included a 'reference value' for the growth of broad money (M3). The second is a broadly based assessment of the outlook for price developments (Chapter 3, Section 3.7).

Assigning money such an important role by at least some of the members of the Governing Council was inevitable, given that this was the policy of the Bundesbank and some other successful predecessor NCBs. The particular reference value of 4.5% growth (based on the sum of the expected medium-term infla-

tion around 1.5%, the expected rate of growth around 2% and the drift in the velocity of circulation around 1%) has proved a bit of a problem, as it has been exceeded almost all of the time and a lot of effort has had to be spent explaining the discrepancies. Similarly the price assessment has been rather more a story in prose than a firmly based discussion of options and their possible outcomes. Although the Eurosystem does publish its forecasts twice a year these are 'staff' forecasts and do not necessarily represent the views of any one member of the Governing Council, still less the Governing Council as a body. Again the decentralized structure of the Eurosystem would make any closer 'ownership' of the forecasts by decision makers impossible – hence the character of the explanations of monetary policy decisions.

The Eurosystem is, of course, in good company. The Federal Reserve in the US has multiple objectives and offers no quantification at all for its target for the price level/inflation. It only publishes the staff forecasts by the Board of Governors with a lag.

Thus far policy has been fairly successful, but since mid-2000 inflation has been stubbornly above 2%. Although it has been possible to blame the rapid rise in oil prices and some other shocks, the deviation is getting to the stage where it could have an effect on expectations. Until now price inflation expectations have remained a little below 2% (as calculated from French index linked bonds).

One concern, which does not seem to have proved relevant was the fear that NCB governors and Executive Board members for that matter would, either explicitly or unconsciously as a result of their backgrounds, tend to promote monetary policy decisions that supported the particular economic conditions in their country of origin rather than in the euro area as a whole. As a result complex models of coalitions have been developed and there have been worries about whether those voting in favour are sufficiently representative of the euro area as a whole. The first reason why this is not relevant is that the Governing Council has not been voting on these issues. It has operated by consensus, in the sense that decisions are taken when the majority in favour is such that the minority withdraws its objection and does not feel the need to register dissent in some public manner.

The possible objection to that form of behaviour is not some form of country bias but that it might engender conservatism in policy making. Since the records of the debates are not published there is no way of finding out whether the particular structure has inhibited or delayed action. The simplest way of judging the issue, however, is to look at the voting records in the FOMC, where the results are published with a lag. Here it is immediately clear that deep divisions over what to do are relatively unusual. Most of the time there is not only no division at all, but also no proposal to change policy. When there are divisions the number of dissenters, even before the vote in the debate, tends to be quite small. The problem is thus predicated on a much more random and indeed contentious approach to policy making than is actually the case.

There has been strong pressure for the Governing Council to be more open and publish minutes of its discussions, as this would inhibit the members from following obviously national interests. However, it is not at all clear what the impact would be. Publishing minutes or resolutions leads to more formal proceedings or taking positions for the sake of having them recorded if the US and Japanese experiences are anything to go by (Pollard, 2003). If the real discussion is pushed outside the meeting into informal subgroups and consultations the result can be counter productive and it will be even more difficult to sort out what opinions were responsible for what decisions.

10.2   The coordination of fiscal and other macroeconomic policies

Operating a single monetary policy for a diverse area has proved quite tricky. Policy which is well suited to some economies has been rather ill-suited to others. It is important to be clear about the extent of the differences. Mayes and Virén (2000, 2002c) have shown that in some member states the exchange rate is at least twice as important as a determinant of inflation (as compared with interest rates). Similarly the length of time it takes for the impact of policy on inflation to take its full effect also varies by a factor of two. Thus if the main problem lies in a region where policy has both a relatively small and a relatively slow effect, a policy based on the average experience of the euro area would not be very efficient.

The problem is further complicated because the main economic relationships involved such as the Phillips curve are nonlinear and asymmetric. To spell this out a little: whereas a low unemployment/positive output gap has quite a strong upward pressure on inflation, high unemployment and a negative output gap has a considerably smaller downward impact for the same sized difference. This means that simply adding up inflation rates and growth across the euro area and exploring aggregate relationships will be misleading. The analysis needs to be at the disaggregated level and then summed using the appropriate estimates of the effect in each region/member state.

However, once we look at fiscal and structural policy then these differences become even more important because they have to offset the differential impact of monetary policy. The coordination of fiscal and other policies therefore needs not merely to permit different policy settings by each member state, subject to the constraints of prudence, but to expect it.

10.2.1 The coordination processes for macroeconomic policies

The structure of the 'economic' side of macroeconomic policy making thus involves constraints from following policies that could harm the system as a whole – the Excessive Deficit Procedure (EDP) with the SGP and system of enhanced policy learning or soft-coordination under the Broad Economic Policy Guidelines. The annual Broad Economic Policy Guidelines are the framework that brings together three main elements:

- the orientation of general fiscal policy – (EDP, SGP and multilateral surveillance);
- the European Employment Strategy – (the Luxembourg process); and
- the actions on structural reforms – (the Cardiff process).

There is actually a fourth process – the Cologne process – which involves an informal exchange of views twice a year between *inter alia* the current, past and future presidents of ECOFIN, the Employment and Social Affairs Councils, the ECB, the Commission and the social partners. These processes are named after the location of the meeting places at which they were agreed. The coordination is somewhat broader than this as the annual reviews of the single market are also taken into account by the Economic Policy

Committee (EPC); the committee of officials responsible for overseeing the Cardiff process. This is not to be confused with the EFC, Economic and Financial Committee, also composed of officials, which undertakes the preparation and offers advice for ECOFIN – the decision making Council of Economics and Finance Ministers.

The general approach, spelt out in some detail in the Conclusions of the Lisbon Council in 2000, was to set

> . . . a *new strategic goal* for the next decade: *to become the most competitive and dynamic knowledge-based economy in the world, capable of sustainable economic growth with more and better jobs and greater social cohesion.*

This involves aiming to change the structure of development of the EU so that it can achieve a rate of growth of 3% a year (without inflationary pressure), which should be enough to bring down unemployment/increase employment to acceptable levels over the course of a decade. The key ingredients in this are continuing structural reform – overseen by the Cardiff process – a labour market strategy (Luxembourg) and the development of the appropriate fiscal incentives through a sound budgetary system within the member states. (It was amended at the end of 2002, at the Laeken Council, by the addition of a social policy strategy, which follows the same form of process as for the labour market.)

These processes do not compel, but by agreeing objectives, setting out how each member state intends to achieve the objectives and evaluating progress, particularly through annual reports by the Commission, they act as considerable moral suasion. The meetings and the annual round of plans and evaluations enable the member states to learn from each other and encourage a search for best practice. These plans can be quite detailed. The annual National Action Plans under the Employment Strategy have for example covered over 20 Guidelines grouped under four pillars: employability, entrepreneurship, adaptability and equal opportunities. Although the Commission produces assessments much of the point of the arrangement is that it involves *multilateral surveillance*, so that each country is looking at the successes and failure of the others.

While there are obvious opportunities for window dressing, this process, labelled 'the Open Method of Coordination', appears to have worked remarkably well. This does not, of course, mean that the objectives set out by the Lisbon Council will be achieved. Indeed since the EU economy has experienced a downturn in the growth process in the first two years of the next decade there are obvious worries that there will be inadequate recovery thereafter to set the strategy back on track. It may nevertheless be the case that the practical ability to reform and introduce the flexibility required may be insufficient.

The key feature of the Open Method is that it does not compel specific actions but allows each member state and indeed the regions within to respond to the challenges in the manner that best meets their local conditions, institutions and structures. Given that the whole structure of social welfare varies across the EU (Mayes *et al.*, 2001, distinguish four different sorts of regime, for example) any given measure will have different outcomes in different member states. In a sense this is an example of the operation of the subsidiarity principle (Chapter 2, Section 2.2.4).

10.2.2 The Stability and Growth Pact and Excessive Deficit Procedure

As was argued above, the SGP and the EDP have two features: a general orientation to ensure a policy that is sustainable over the longer term and a constraint on short-term actions – the excessive deficits – to ensure that the process is not derailed on the way. This general orientation is to achieve budgets that are 'in surplus or near balance'. This orientation will actually result in a continuing reduction in debt ratios. While this is necessary anyway for the member states exceeding the 60% limit, it has been thought generally more desirable because of the expected strains on the system that are expected to occur with the ageing of the population. In any case it makes sense to have sufficient headroom to meet shocks. This headroom is required in two respects. First of all, given the structure of automatic stabilizers, each member state needs to be far enough away from the 3% deficit ratio limit that the normal sorts of adverse economic shock will not drive them over that limit. If that threatens to happen then the member state would need to take contractionary fiscal action when the economy is performing weakly. This is precisely the problem facing the German authorities in 2003. The combination of being too close to the limit and lower than expected growth will probably force them a little over the limit. Needing to raise taxes and restrain expenditure is proving politically difficult.

The extent to which a member state needs to be inside the 3% boundary depends on the extent of the automatic stabilizers and the distribution of expected shocks. Thus a country like Finland, which has fairly large stabilizers and seems prone to above average shocks, would need to run a small surplus if it is to avoid hitting the 3% boundary. (In fact Finland is running a much larger surplus and is deliberately trying to take the opportunity of relatively favourable economic developments to move well away from the 60% debt limit.)

There is a danger (noted by von Hagen and Mundschenk, 2002) that having the 3% deficit boundary will have a deflationary longer-term bias on the EU if member states compete too strongly to have very strong stabilizers. Sweden might be regarded as a case in point as its reaction to the pressures from membership has been to advocate the establishment of a substantial buffer fund (Johansson et al., 2002). These funds, if they are implemented, will be far larger than the Finnish buffer funds, which were put in place when Finland joined the euro area. However, Ricardian equivalence would suggest that simply repaying debt should have no longer run influence on longer-term growth, it is simply having a higher tax burden today at the benefit of a lower burden in the future.

From time to time the SGP has come under pressure, the greatest pressure not surprisingly coming in 2002 and 2003 when the EU economy was not performing well. France, Germany and Portugal all triggered the first steps in the EDP. However, while the second two countries have shown some embarrassment and regret and have tried to implement remedial measures, France refused to alter its stance on the grounds that it was not actually exceeding the 3% deficit, its debt ratio would remain inside 60% and the results would be good for growth and the achievement of the longer-term objectives of the EU[1]. While breaches of the target ratios are unfortunate, the SGP is actually strengthened when the penalty system is seen to come into operation and have an effect. Refusal to follow the requirement of the Pact, even while inside the limits, weakens the credibility of the system. It is clear that for Germany and France, the euro area has reached the point for the first time

where appropriate monetary policy for those countries on their own differs from that for the area as a whole. It is thus an unusual experience for what thought itself the core of the system to have to adjust to match the needs of the whole.

Various proposals have been put forward for reforming the SGP and indeed the Commission has itself advanced proposals (Buti et al., 2002; CEU, 2002a). These can be classified under three main headings but they all relate to means of easing the constraints somewhat without altering the overall principles. The first set of proposals relate to *symmetry*. Member state behaviour is constrained when deficits are in danger of becoming too large. There is no such restraint on surpluses. However, if we look at issues of macroeconomic management a switch from a 2% surplus to balance can have just as much impact on aggregate demand as a switch from balance to a 2% deficit. Hence countries which notch up major surpluses could destabilize the system somewhat simply by switching rapidly to a modest deficit well within the permissible limit. (The Commission in particular is suggesting enhancing the ability to affect fiscal policy in 'good times'.) The second set of proposals seeks to differentiate between member states more according to whether they are well inside, near or above the 60% limit for the debt ratio. Here the argument is simply that countries with no sustainability problem should be allowed more licence in the short run over deficits. This line of argument, of course, runs against that in the first group as such licence could easily result in much bigger swings in fiscal policy that will affect the overall level of inflationary pressure in the euro area if we are talking about larger countries. Pisani-Ferry (2002) suggests that countries could choose to be in a Debt Stability Pact rather than the SGP if they keep their debt ratios below, say 50%.[2] The third group of suggestions relate to measurement issues.[3] In the traditional literature the concern is with 'cyclically adjusted' deficits

There is a fourth set of suggestions that look for a more market-based solution to the question of fiscal discipline. One of the big advantages of EMU has been that interest rates on sovereign debt in the previously more inflation prone and more indebted parts of the euro area have converged on the lowest. Credit ratings have similarly increased. Although there is explicitly no agreement to bail out member states across the euro area, the market is behaving as if there were. Or at least it is behaving as if the EDP will restrain member states from running policies that will ever get them near default. This means that there is not so much pressure on marginal borrowing by those states that have debt or deficit ratio problems. The response of euro area interest rates as a whole to their difficulties will be muted. If on the other hand sovereign debt were specifically to be in different tiers then there would be much more pressure on the marginal borrowers. The member states in a strong position would not be so adversely affected by their weaker colleagues and would get an interest rate reduction. The simplest way to introduce at least one tier might be for a EU guarantee to be offered for it. Since there are differences, even at present, the ECB could have an impact by not treating debt from all members identically and limiting the extent that it could hold debt from the lower tier countries in its financing operations.

The difficulty with any such proposals is that they would involve an element of penalizing the countries with the less sustainable position compared to the current arrangements. It is not clear that they would be prepared to vote for such a proposal even under QMV (Chapter 3, Section 3.2). Furthermore, raising marginal interest rates makes the position of countries wanting to correct their budgetary balances even more difficult as their servicing costs rise. This could place a greater procyclical pressure on the financial economy.

Mayes and Virén (2002a, b) show that there are considerable spillover benefits to the member states if they can become more coordinated. As a generality, the effectiveness of fiscal policy is doubled if countries moved together than if they moved differently. However, the biggest gain is for the smaller countries, because fiscal policy is less effective in a more open economy. Without coordination the impact of fiscal policy in small countries is about half that in the larger. With coordination the effects become much more similar.[4]

A different and more fundamental concern for coordination is that currently the SGP relates to each member state individually. The normal concern for an EMU should be with the combined budgets of the member states. In that case the 3% rule could be applied more leniently if some other states had much smaller deficits/larger surpluses. (The same could be applied to the structural requirement to be in surplus or near balance.) However, to run such a system, the sanctions would have to be much more effective and there would be a danger of a competition to be in the

leniently treated group, which would tend to frustrate the overall criterion.

10.2.3 Policy coordination

The type of coordination described thus far differs from that normally discussed in the literature where much of the point is the coordination of monetary and fiscal policy. The argument is that there are some choices that can be made over how much to use fiscal policy rather than monetary policy to smooth fluctuations in the real economy or maintain price stability. The set up within EMU rests upon a fairly simple economic model. The first side of it is that monetary policy cannot be used effectively to achieve longer-term real objectives, except in two senses:

- first, that having higher rates of inflation beyond levels near zero will tend to result in reductions in the overall rate of growth of the economy and indeed having falls in the price level may also be damaging; and
- second, that inept policy that does not generate credibility will also impose a cost on society.

In general, taking these together the argument is in effect that the long-run Phillips curve is vertical and monetary policy *per se* will not have adverse effects on the longer-term level of unemployment. Monetary policy can therefore be targeted appropriately at the stabilization of the price level rather than real concerns. The scope for using monetary policy for smoothing real behaviour beyond that point is limited. As Thornton (2002) puts it, in general, the impact of monetary policy on inflation variation and output gap variation should be regarded as one of complements rather than tradeoffs. A credible monetary policy aimed at restricting inflation to a fairly narrow range in a smooth manner should *ipso facto* also restrain the fluctuations in output round the sustainable path.

Similarly in this simple paradigm, fiscal policy can affect the rate of growth in terms of how funds are raised and spent. For example, one can view this in terms of incentives. Moreover, as discussed above, for fiscal policy to be consistent with price stability over the medium term it has to be sustainable (and believed to be such by markets). But discretionary fiscal policy, beyond the automatic stabilizers, is unlikely to be of much value, except to help exit the deflationary spiral as Keynes identified in the 1930s (Feldstein, 2002, offers a clear exposition of this view). One of the main reasons for avoiding discretionary fiscal policy to address fluctuations in the economy is that policy operates with a lag, and there is a danger that by the time the problem is identified, the necessary measures agreed by the legislature and implemented, by the time the impact occurs it may destabilize what is then going on.

In these circumstances there is no need for much policy coordination between the monetary and fiscal authorities beyond transparency. The monetary authorities need to be able to make a reasonable assessment of the inflationary pressure likely to stem from fiscal policy and the fiscal authorities need to know what to expect from monetary policy when setting their fiscal objectives. The potential conflict comes from the fact that unlike fiscal policy, monetary policy can be changed quickly and substantially and indeed with fairly limited transactions costs. In the EU framework the coordination works because the monetary authorities are predictable. If they do react quickly it is to specific crisis signals like the September 11th 2001 shock. Given the time lag for fiscal changes the fiscal authorities need to be confident that their monetary counterparts will not do anything in the intervening period that will render their policy stance inappropriate.

Pinning the ECB down to a single objective helps achieve this predictability. In the same way the rules of the SGP and macroeconomic coordination ensure that the ECB has good warning about the way in which fiscal policy is likely to develop and hence is less likely to set inappropriate levels for interest rates. The EMU coordination will not work if the Eurosystem always believes that the fiscal authorities will always be too inflationary and/or ECOFIN always believes that the Eurosystem will set interest rates that are too high. In these circumstances the problem will be self-fulfilling and monetary policy and fiscal policy will tend to push against each other. The resulting bias will be a cost. Fiscal policy needs to be credible to the monetary authority and vice versa. There is a danger of paying too much attention to the rhetoric in this regard. One of the strongest themes in the ECB Monthly Bulletin is the advocacy of fiscal prudence by the member states. It could be argued that if the ECB sees the need to make these remarks at that frequency then there must be a problem. This does not follow. The problem only has to be in prospect. Exhortation can fulfil an important role in reinforcement.

The final part of the simple model which underlies the coordination mechanism, is the belief that it is structural policies that will change the underlying rate of economic growth. Hence these form a key part of the continuing annual policy discussion. Once fiscal policy is largely automatic with respect to shocks, the surveillance mechanisms can focus on sustainability and on whether the size of budgetary swings that the automatic processes deliver are appropriate. If there were little concern for fine-tuning then having more than the current six-monthly informal dialogue laid down by the Cologne process would seem unnecessary.

10.2.5 Asymmetry

Traditionally the focus on the *suitability and sustainability of EMU* has been on asymmetry in the sense of the differences between the member states, as discussed at the beginning of Section 10.2. However, a different asymmetry is also present in the behaviour of the member states, namely asymmetry over the cycle. We can take both the deficit to GDP ratio and its revenue and expenditure components and see whether they respond in the same way to changes in GDP when it is in the 'up' phase of the cycle as they do changes in GDP when it is in the 'down' phase (Mayes and Virén, 2002a).[5]

As far as the total deficit is concerned, it is clear that it is much more responsive in the down than the up phase. While responsiveness over the cycle as a whole is of the order of 0.2 to 0.3 (a 1% increase in real GDP lowers the deficit ratio by 0.2–0.3%) in the first year, it is five times as large in the downturn as the upturn. This bundles together all the influences – automatic stabilizers, discretionary policy changes, interest rate changes and any special factors. On unbundling, we can see that the automatic or cyclical part of the deficit behaves in a fairly symmetric manner. It is what governments choose to do with the structural part of the deficit which causes the asymmetry – stripping out the interest expenses element has little effect on the picture, although both the level of the interest rate and the level of the debt ratio tend to put downward pressure on deficits. What has happened is that governments increased the structural deficit in both downturns and upturns. Thus in good times governments tend to allow the system to ratchet up. The effect is split between revenues and expenditures but the asymmetry is more prominent on the revenue side. Tax rates are cut in upturns so that revenue GDP ratios do not rise (they fall, of course, in recessions) while expenditures show milder asymmetry and are not 'perverse' in the sense of moving in a counter-intuitive direction.

The SGP, EDP and the other components of macroeconomic coordination in EMU would have to lean against this tendency for asymmetric behaviour to reduce the pressures it generates. In practice the pressure is placed somewhat more on the downside, the area where governments have themselves responded more effectively in the past. Tackling this asymmetry and 'procyclicality in good times' forms one of the five areas for action in the Commission's 2002 proposals for reforming the SGP (CEU, 2002a).

10.3   Completing EMU

It has to be said that the earlier discussion of coordination leaves a lot to the credibility of the process. Institutional credibility would be much greater if the degree of control over fiscal actions at the EU level were larger and there were some parallel institution to the ECB on the fiscal side. While this is not on the political agenda, its relevance would be much greater if one further plank were in place, which characterizes most economic and monetary unions, namely a significant revenue raising and spending capability at the EU level. This does not have to take the form of a larger budget *per se* (see Chapter 19) as transfers from one region or member state to another in a form of fiscal federalism would also suffice. Currently stabilization takes place automatically within the member states. It only takes place between them to the extent that their agreed and automatic actions spill over from one to another because of their economic interdependence. The actual size of such a budget – around $2\frac{1}{2}$ to 7% of Community GDP – to be highly effective (MacDougall Report, 1977; Mayes *et al.*, 1992; Chapter 19) is quite small compared to many existing federal states. It is, however, rather large compared to the structural funds and the current budgetary limit.

With the enlargement of the EU that is in progress the need will increase. However, the current small economic size of the new members keeps the scale of any transfers needed down in the short term at any rate (see Chapter 26). We are, of course, concerned here with cross-border fiscal flows to help balance out the effect of asymmetric shocks; dealing with income inequality is a problem of a very different order. Nevertheless, given the persistence of shocks, particularly with respect to their impact on the labour market, if fiscal flows do not ease the pressure then other changes will result to compensate. The most obvious would be an increase in migration. That is also not politically attractive at present. It remains to be seen whether some greater integration on the macroeconomic side of EMU may not be preferred to increasing flexibility through cross-border migration. The relative attraction of stabilizing flows is that according to their definition they should be temporary. However, the shape of economic cycles does vary across the EU.

10.3.1 Enlargement

It seems likely, however, that before EMU moves further towards 'completion', it will be expanded by the addition of new members. Adding Denmark and Sweden would make little difference to the structure of the euro zone or the issues that have been raised in this chapter. If the UK were to join the position would be different, as the country is large enough to alter the balance of the single monetary policy. Also since the UK is somewhat different both in its flexibility of response and its symmetry with the other member states, the consequences could be measurable. Whether it would affect the decision making is a different matter. However, the bigger concern is the new members of the EU, set to join in 2004. Several of them have expressed a desire to move to euro zone membership as soon as possible. If that implies simply adhering to the present criteria, then it may be possible for some of these countries to join within quite a short number of years. While the technical minimum of two years seems rather unlikely it is still probable that such membership would take place with a level of income per head well below the average of the existing members, as convergence in these real terms is not one of the criteria. This could alter the character of the zone.

We have already noted that in the run up to membership there was greater convergence of the member states than there has been in the period afterwards. This was because they had to run their monetary and fiscal policies individually to converge to quite a narrow band. Once inside the SGP, EDP and the rest of coordination under the BEPG apply, but the single monetary policy is no longer related to the inflation concerns of each country, just the total, so more inflation and indeed growth variation is possible and likely. This experience is likely to be reflected even more strongly by the new members, as they are generally expected to 'catch up' quite rapidly with the existing members in real terms. This means that they will have faster rates of growth than the existing members, driven primarily by productivity. It has also been pointed out that this may have implications for inflation and monetary policy. While the price of tradeable goods and services may be reasonably similar across the EU, the same is not the case for non-tradeables. Large portions of non-tradeables are public and private services, where their principal input is labour. As productivity grows in the tradeable industries so wages are likely to rise with it. In turn, in a competitive economy, this is likely to result in wage increases in the non-tradeables sector. There it will not be so easy to find productivity growth to offset it and prices will tend to rise. Insofar as there are no offsets elsewhere this will result in a rise in the general price level, faster than in the rest of the euro area.

This process, known as the Balassa–Samuelson effect, will probably not be substantial by the time the new members join the euro area, perhaps of the order of 1% a year (Björksten, 1999). Given that the new members, taken together, will only contribute a fraction of the euro area GDP, this implies that the total effect on inflation would be of the order of 0.2% a year. That may seem very small but with a medium-term target of inflation below 2% it could represent an increase in the rate of interest. An increase would in any case be expected if the euro zone's growth prospects and hence rates of return increased. The actual impact is speculative and could vary from the disastrous to the trivial. It would be disastrous if some countries cannot cope with the increase in the real exchange rate that this relative inflation might imply. The problems of asymmetry that have worried some of the existing members of the EU could be much larger for the new members, yet the drive for locking in credibility and buying lower interest rates by euro zone membership may be sufficient to play down the worries about sustainability at the time of joining. Too rapid expansion of EMU could actually harm the prospects of the enterprise as a whole. It is therefore not surprising that the ECB has already blown relatively cold on some of the ideas implying early membership and has sought to toughen the interpretation of the convergence criteria.

NOTES

1. More recently France has passed the threshold and has deliberately planned to prolong that excess by cutting taxes in the hope of generating longer-term growth.

2. Calmfors and Corsetti (2002) suggest allowing more deficit flexibility as the debt ratio falls below 60% in a series of steps.

3. There are other proposals and concerns. For example, one concern is the unspecific nature of the requirement for the debt ratio to be diminishing and approaching the reference value 'at a satisfactory pace'. Some logical basis for defining 'satisfactory' would be helpful.

4. These results are derived using the NIESR NiGEM model. They are higher than those achieved from SVAR models with a similar dataset so some caution in interpretation is merited. Mayes and Virén (2002b) use panel data for 16 West European countries for the period 1960–2000 to estimate spillover equations and also obtain somewhat higher estimates of the benefit than traditionally estimated.

5. The study uses annual data for the period 1960–1999 for the 2002 members of the EU excluding Luxembourg and treats them as a panel. The structural deficit are as defined by the Commission.

Part Four of this book covers all aspects of the single European market. Hence it tackles all the policy areas which have an impact on the free movement of goods, services, labour, capital and enterprises, with Chapter 11 providing an overall perspective, hence setting the scene for the other seven.

The economics of the single market

IAIN BEGG AND ALI EL-AGRAA

The single market, declared to have been completed at the end of 1992, celebrated its tenth birthday at the beginning of 2003, amid the customary fanfare and claims about its success. Unlike many areas of EU policy making, it is almost universally seen in a positive light and can, moreover, be regarded as a natural, but significant extension of the idea of the 'common market'. Put another way, the single market is an important stepping stone on the route from the customs union to the development of a fully-fledged economic union (see Chapter 1), and many regard monetary union as the last stage in creating an open market and thus final piece in the jigsaw of 'negative' integration. Therefore, the reader who is interested in the details of the Single European Act (SEA) (see Chapter 2) and the internal

market, and their implications for both the EU and the rest of the world, will have to go through virtually every chapter of the book for information; the implications of the single market are too wide and far reaching to be tackled in a vacuum. This approach may offend those who believe that the future should be highlighted and the past forgotten; but the emphasis in this book is on the evolution and dynamism of the EU. To follow the bandwagon by concentrating entirely on the economics of the single market or economic and monetary union (EMU) would be to negate the very foundations of our approach. However, it is appropriate to devote a chapter to the internal market, emphasizing its key characteristics and the continuing debates about how to measure its benefits.

11.1   Why 'the single market'?

The Commission that took office in 1984, presided over by Jacques Delors, arrived at a time of pessimism about a European economy that was struggling to emerge from the recession of the early 1980s and sought to reinvigorate integration as a way of countering the gloom. According to Lord Cockfield (1994), the Vice-President of the Commission responsible for the internal market, the completion of the single market was the first priority of the new Commission. He went so far as to state that its accomplishment would be the greatest achievement of the Commission during its term of office. This was put succinctly in the *Bulletin of the European Communities* (no. 6, 1985, p. 18):

> From the words of the Treaties themselves
> through successive declarations by the European
> Council since 1982, the need to complete the
> internal market has been confirmed at the highest
> level. What have been missing have been an agreed
> target date and a detailed programme for meeting
> it. The Commission has welcomed the challenge of
> providing the missing piece. It has interpreted the

challenge in the most comprehensive way possible: the creation by 1992 of a genuine common market without internal frontiers.

Cockfield's great contribution was to draw up a White Paper – at the time a novel approach for the Community – setting out an ambitious, but feasible legislative programme designed to sweep away cross-border restrictions and to restore the momentum of economic integration. The Commission stressed three main features that would characterize the single market programme:

(i) there are to be no more attempts to harmonize or standardize at any price – a method originating in too rigid an interpretation of the Treaty; in most cases, an 'approximation' of the parameters is sufficient to reduce differences in rates or technical specifications to an acceptable level [see Chapter 15];

(ii) the programme will propose no measures which, while supposedly facilitating trade or travel, in fact maintain checks at internal frontiers and

therefore the frontiers themselves, the symbol of the Community's fragmentation; their disappearance will have immense psychological and practical importance; [and]
(iii) a major factor for the success of the programme is its two-stage, binding timetable, with relatively short deadlines, relying as far as possible on built-on mechanisms; the programme is a comprehensive one, which means that it has the balance needed if general agreement is to be forthcoming. (*Bulletin of the European Communities*, no. 6, 1985, p. 18)

The aim was to eliminate borders and other obstacles to the free movement of goods, services, labour and capital – collectively known as the four freedoms – altogether, not just to reduce them, so that the EU would become a single economic space in which common rules applied. What was remarkable about the internal market programme (IMP) was its broad aims and ambitions and the fact that a clear approach to achieving these aims was developed. It embraced measures as diverse as animal health controls and licensing of banks; public procurement and standards for catalytic converters. The key to progress was a range of innovations introduced in the SEA, most notably the use of qualified majority voting as a means of countering the legislative gridlock that resulted from the unanimity principle.

Alternative ways of achieving regulatory aims without obliging stops at border crossing-points were sought. For example, with regard to health protection, the Commission suggested that checks on veterinary and plant health should be limited to destination points, the implication being that 'national standards be as far as possible aligned on common standards'. With regard to transport, quotas had to be progressively relaxed and eliminated, and common safety standards introduced for vehicles so that systematic controls could be dispensed with.

The principle of mutual recognition was another important plank in the edifice. Provided that certain health and safety-related constraints and safeguards are met, goods which are 'lawfully' made and sold in one EU member nation should be able to move freely and go on sale *anywhere* within the EU, and the same was true of potentially traded services such as banking or insurance. The Commission recognized that there had been much slower progress in opening-up markets for services than was the case for goods, but claimed that the distinction between goods and services had never been a valid one, and that the EU had undermined its own economic potential by retaining it (see Chapter 4). This was because the services sector not only was growing fast as a 'value-adding provider of employment in its own right', but also gave vital support and back-up for the manufacturing sector.

For this reason, the scope of the IMP measures covered not just traditionally tradeable services such as banking, insurance and transport, but also the new areas of information, marketing and audiovisual services. Thus the White Paper put forward proposals and a timetable for action covering all these services until 1992. With regard to transport, the agenda included the 'phasing out of all quantitative restrictions (quotas) on road haulage', further liberalization of road, sea and air passenger services through the fostering of increased competition (see Chapter 15). The aim for audiovisual services was to create a single EU-wide broadcasting area.

Factor mobility was to be stimulated both by the progressive reduction in currency control measures applied at borders and, despite the fact that freedom of movement of labour was already almost entirely complete, dealing with remaining restrictions. Already, the rulings of the Court of Justice had restricted the right of public authorities in the EU member states to reserve jobs for their own nationals. Further measures to eliminate the cumbersome administrative procedures relating to residence permits or to assure the right of establishment for the self-employed, were, however, deemed to be necessary, especially in relation to professional qualifications. For example, in professions such as accounting and auditing, practitioners perform completely different jobs and receive completely different training in the different EU member states and hence harmonization implies a drastic change in both education and training before the profession can hope to be seen as performing the same task.

Indirect taxation was one of the more intractable challenges the single market had to face, because rates were, in some cases, so divergent that they would no doubt create trade distortions, leading to loss of revenue to the exchequers of the member states (see Chapter 14). The White Paper concluded that, if frontiers and associated controls were to be eliminated, 'it will be necessary not only to set up a Community clearing system for VAT and a linkage system of bonded warehouses for excised products, but also to introduce a considerable measure of approximation of indirect taxes'. This raised the question of how close the approximation should be, recognizing that as in the US, sufficient competition could remain without a complete equalization of rates. Although there was uncertainty about how big a disparity would be tolerable, agreement was reached on a 'standstill clause' to guarantee that prevailing variations in the number and levels of VAT rates would not be widened. Approximation of indirect taxation would, nevertheless result in a number of problems for some of the EU member nations, and derogations were therefore countenanced. Nevertheless, the discussion in Chapter 14 clearly shows that the Commission has delivered these proposals as promised.

11.2   An evolving programme

The details of the actual proposals put forward by the Commission to enable the creation of the single market are by now not only common knowledge (the original White Paper is still posted on the Commission website and Cockfield himself has written a history, published in 1994), but can be found in a number of academic books and papers (see, *inter alia*, Emerson *et al.*, 1988; Pelkmans and Winters, 1988; Sapir, 1995; Mayes, 1997b; Fielder, 1997; and Lucarelli, 1999) as well as in the majority of the chapters in this book. They therefore need not detain us here. Although the end of December 1992 was set as a target date for completion of the internal market, only 95% of the 300 directives had actually been launched, but all internal EU border checks were abolished by then. Jacques Delors, then President of the EU Commission, stated that as a gradual process the single market project was never supposed to end with a 'big bang' on 1 January 1993 and, as the discussion in Chapter 3 makes clear, directives also have to be incorporated into national law before they are put into practice (transposition) and further delays or distortions can arise in implementation.

Despite transposition and implementation problems and lags, the original legal process is now effectively complete. To keep the pressure on, the Commission introduced a regular publication, the *Single Market Scoreboard*, which reported on the progress made and difficulties encountered in the various sectors of the internal market, and the latest issue shows only a tiny proportion of unfinished business in terms of transposition (see Figure 11.1). On the other hand, problems can arise with infringements and the focus has in many sectors, shifted to monitoring of these implementation problems.

Overall, the IMP can be regarded as a considerable achievement, but it is also important to recognize that the single market is not static and that there are further areas that were either considered 'too difficult' in 1985, or have since come to be regarded as vital to deepen market integration, where complementary action was desirable. Following the launch by the Commission, in 1997, of an *Action Plan for the Single Market* (1997h) which sought to plug the gaps from the original '1992' programme and to restore the impetus of market integration, the main thrust today is on two areas: financial services and network industries. Creating a fully integrated European financial area is a long-standing ambition. It was present in the Werner Plan for monetary union launched in 1970 (see Chapter 9), a key part of the IMP from 1985 onwards and is manifestly associated with monetary union. Building on the 1996/7 Action Plan, the Commission brought forward two further action plans: the *Financial Services Action Plan* (FSAP) and the *Risk Capital Action Plan* (RCAP) designed to achieve financial integration. Their underlying function is to improve the efficiency of financial intermediation in the European Financial Area, and especially on lowering the costs of cross-border flows of financing.

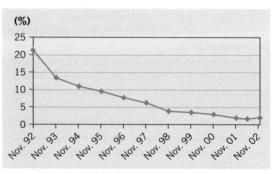

Figure 11.1 Transposition deficit, 1992–2002 (percentage of directives not transposed)

The FSAP, launched in 1999 with a deadline of 2005 for completion, has a number of clearly specified aims. These were grouped under four broad headings:

- Completing a single wholesale market.
- Developing open and secure markets for retail financial services.
- Ensuring the continued stability of EU financial markets.
- Eliminating tax obstacles to financial market integration.

Regular progress reports have been produced by the Commission which show that although there is always foot-dragging and a need for compromise, member states have been willing to countenance difficult changes, especially to their respective regulatory styles.

Network industries, which might also be labelled 'utilities', are a cross between unfinished business, in so far as some of them were a target of the 1985 White Paper, and a broadening of the scope of the internal market to confront new areas, especially the principal energy and transport network industries. The common ground of the various industries – gas, electricity, water, post, telecommunications and transport services – is that they are a basic input into all other economic activities, so that efficiency in their operation can contribute to greater productivity in downstream economic activities as well as providing benefits to consumers. In this sense, the extension of the internal market to these network industries (arguably also the case for financial services) can be seen as a means of improving the business environment within which export-orientated firms operate.

11.2.1 The impact of financial integration

The 'Costs of non-Europe' studies summarized in the Cecchini Report (1988), attributed as much as a quarter of the potential gains for EU GDP from the single market to the liberalization of financial services. These gains were projected to arise from competitive pressures that would reduce intermediation margins, thereby lowering the cost of capital to investors; from opportunities to procure services from other member states; lower regulatory costs; and an impetus to financial innovation. Both microeconomic and macroeconomic benefits were expected.

The review of the internal market conducted in the mid-1990s (see the Monti Report, 1996) was markedly less optimistic about the benefits that would flow from the internal market, largely because remaining regulatory and other barriers had inhibited the emergence of genuine pan-EU provision of services. This was especially true of retail financial services, but some barriers also remained in other areas, and it has been observed that there are few moves as yet towards the cross-border consolidation of the financial services industry that would be expected as a concomitant of integration. Indeed, one of the reasons for the FSAP was to restore the impetus towards integration, not least because of the perception that potential gains from greater capital market efficiency were being lost.

There are several possible channels through which undeveloped financial markets hold back growth. Financial weakness is also seen as an obstacle to exploiting new technologies where a different approach is needed to justify the more risky investments implicit in innovative products and services. A strong argument for financial integration is that it will allow such innovative investment to occur more readily, thereby promoting overall growth. A study for the Commission by Giannetti et al. (2002) maintains that despite the progress in financial integration in the early 1990s there is still plenty of potential for further integration of financial markets to enhance economic growth.

In more detail, the key mechanisms through which financial integration translates into improved economic performance can be summarized as follows:

- Improvements in the 'x-efficiency' of financial intermediaries as competitive pressures oblige them to adopt new technologies, to pare operating costs and to restructure to more optimal sizes.
- A second competitive effect is that lower cost or more innovative provision (such as electronic trading) may lead to increases in, especially, retail demand for financial services.
- Pooling of liquidity that deepens the supply of finance, an effect estimated by a London Economics study to be capable of lowering the cost of capital by an average of 40 basis points. The same study suggests that the cost of capital to firms will also be lowered if trading costs fall and that there will be a narrowing of bond spreads calibrated at 40 basis points reduction in the cost of bond financing.

- In macroeconomic terms, the gains from a truly integrated financial market are projected to be of the order of 0.5% of GDP (in the short term, according to European Financial Services Roundtable, 2002) to 1% (London Economics, 2002, in the long run). The latter increase in GDP would result – on typical elasticities – in around 0.5% more jobs. Not surprisingly, it is the member states with the least developed financial markets that stand to gain most from accelerated integration (Giannetti *et al.*, 2002). In sum, the potential benefits from integration of financial markets are considerable.

11.2.2 Network industries

Network industries, also known as utilities, pose particular challenges for a number of reasons. First, many have long been predominantly under state ownership (Pelkmans, 2001, p. 17), and often have stronger than average unions which are able to resist change. Natural monopoly may inhibit the introduction of competition, while the perception that so many network industries are 'services of general economic interest' that should not be subject to the same rigours of competition (a formal derogation under article 86 of the Treaty) as other industries. Nevertheless, as Pelkmans (2001) notes, there has been considerable progress in liberalizing network industries and they are now firmly in the sights of the custodians of the internal market.

The industries in question (gas, electricity, water, telecommunications, post, rail and air, and possibly also broadcasting) have been subject to a range of opening-up measures, some dating from the 1980s. A recent Commission review (CEU, 2003a) suggests that there is general progress in liberalizing network industry markets, but that national incumbents continue to hold very high market shares. This is true even of telecommunications where technological developments might have been expected to have accentuated competitive pressures.

11.3   The benefits of the single market

The rationale for the single market is that it reinforces the market opening principle of the common market by focusing not just on existing trade flows, but also on subjecting hitherto protected sectors to greater competition and the prospect of cross-border exchanges. In so doing, it establishes a number of channels for improved resource allocation and efficiency gains that, in turn, offer the promise of improved economic performance. The prospective economic gains can be summarized under five broad headings: four distinct sets of microeconomic benefits can be envisaged and there are also macroeconomic gains to be had. Some accounts of the benefits can come close to displaying missionary zeal and it is important to recognize that, as with any supply-side change, there can be dislocations resulting from the changes needed to achieve the goals. The principal categories of benefits are:

- price reductions that provide benefits to consumers and businesses alike;
- increased competition that not only lessens producer power in imperfectly competitive markets, but also stimulates more rapid innovation and product development;

- opportunities to realize economies of scale by concentrating production, and of scope by broadening producers' markets and allowing sunk costs to be more broadly spread; and
- a recasting and focusing of regulatory interventions, both to eliminate unnecessary duplication and to modernize processes.
- In aggregate, the prospective improvements in resource allocation make it possible for the aggregate output of the economy to be increased, provided always that factors of production are fully employed.

All five of these benefits can be assessed in comparative static terms, that is by comparing 'before' and 'after'. In addition, there are important dynamic effects to consider and it is likely to be the case that successful transformation of the supply-side will allow a higher sustainable growth rate without triggering either inflationary pressures or supply bottlenecks. Strong advocates of the single market argue that the real gains are to be had from these dynamic effects, even if they welcome the static changes.

Structural reforms can, however, hurt and may, collectively, have adverse short-term effects on output and employment. Indeed, one can postulate a form of 'j-curve' – similar to that used to analyse devaluations[1] – through which the initial impact is depressing to growth or employment, but provides a platform for subsequent improvement. Figure 11.2 portrays a possible trajectory. Without reform, the economy would be locked into a trajectory of sluggish performance and might even see a tailing off as weaknesses on the supply side became progressively more debilitating.

As an illustration, consider a hypothetical economy that fails to renew its capital stock sufficiently rapidly. Over time, its capacity to compete with other economies that have been investing steadily will erode, undermining its overall performance. Persevering with an outdated regulatory framework or labour market practices could have similar effects. When structural reforms are introduced, it is probable that the initial dislocations will result in a loss of performance. Under the single market programme, for instance, the elimination of excess capacity in industries that were opened up to more intense competition inevitably saw job losses that resulted in unemployment. These processes are captured in the downward movement along the j-curve in the early stages. Subsequently, however, the improve-

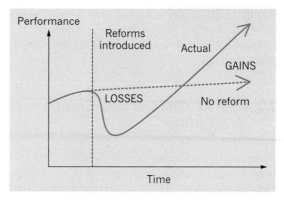

Figure 11.2 The structural reform 'j'-curve (trajectory of the economy)

ments in aggregate efficiency that result from the structural reforms offer the prospect of higher productivity leading to improved competitiveness and thus a better trajectory for performance: this is the upward slope of the j-curve. A study by Notaro found that the internal market had boosted productivity in the most sensitive industrial sectors by 2% during the years 1992 and 1993 (Notaro, 2002).

11.4   Empirical research on the single market

Empirical work on the benefits of the single market has, on the whole, concentrated on the static effects, partly because they are, methodologically, easier to estimate and measure, but partly also because the dynamic effects are less easy to theorize. This section reviews a number of substantial empirical exercises that have been conducted to measure the impact of the single market, starting with a major research programme conducted in the second half of the 1980s that sought to measure the 'Costs of non-Europe' (see next section) under a steering group headed by a senior Commission official, Paolo Cecchini. Its findings were published in sixteen volumes (CEC, 1988a). Although the methodology of the research programme as a whole was one which sought to compare the effects of the single market with no change, the novelty in the approach was to reverse the burden of proof by assuming an integrated market to be the null hypothesis and fragmentation to be the counterfactual. It also entailed working out how the many different measures would affect sectors, and involved techniques as diverse as surveys of price differences (for financial

services), estimations of surplus capacity (public procurement industries), and use of computable general equilibrium models (macroeconomic effects).

A second major empirical exercise was conducted in the mid-1990s, again under the auspices of the Commission, with Italian Internal Market Commissioner Mario Monti most associated with the exercise, and culminated in a series of forty volumes, the first of which summarized the findings (Monti, 1996). In contrast to the 'Costs of non-Europe' studies, this second exercise was able to draw on the experience of the early years of the single market and on the transition to it. Thus, rather than being an *ex-ante* appraisal, it allowed the claims for what the single market was expected to achieve to be put to the test. The 'Monti' results are much less sanguine about the benefits of the single market, although it is worth noting that the early 1990s saw a sharp cyclical downturn in the EU economy.

To mark the tenth anniversary of the single market, the Commission published a much shorter review, this time largely drawing on other work, rather than another dedicated research programme. It showed that the single market was continuing to yield overall dividends, but put more effort into identifying the mechanisms and how they impinge on the functioning of the economy.

11.4.1 The costs of non-Europe studies

According to the Cecchini Report, which summarizes in an accessible, popular form the costs of non-Europe research (Cecchini, 1988), the completion of the internal market will regenerate both the goods and services sectors of the EU. The study estimated the total potential gain for the EC (the 12) as a whole to be in the region of 200 billion ECU, at constant 1988 prices. This would increase EC gross domestic product (GDP) by 4%–6% or more. The gains would come not only from the elimination of the costs of barriers to intra-EC trade, but also from the exploitation of economies of scale which were expected to lower costs by about 2% of EC GDP. The medium-term impact of this on employment was expected to be an increase of about two million jobs. These estimates were considered to be minimal since, as the study points out, if the governments of the member nations of the EU pursue macroeconomic policies that recognize this potential for faster economic growth, the total gains could reach 7% of EC GDP and increase employment by about five million jobs.

The summary of the Cecchini Report given in Cecchini (1988) is written for the general public. The definitive technical work is that by Emerson *et al.* (1988) which presents the official Commission analysis; hence the interested reader is advised to consult this work. Here it should be asked why the elimination of the various barriers mentioned above should lead to economic benefits for the EU. To answer this question meaningfully, one needs to specify the barriers, which are all of the non-tariff type, slightly differently and in a more general context:

1   Differences in the technical regulations adopted in the various member nations which tend to increase the cost of intra-EU trade transactions.
2   Delays in the customs procedures at border crossing points and related extra administrative tasks on both private firms and public organizations which further increase the costs of intra-EU trade transactions.

3   Public procurement procedures which effectively limit if not completely eliminate competition for public purchases to own member nation suppliers, a procedure often claimed to raise the price of such purchases.
4   Curtailment of one's ability either to transact freely in certain services, especially finance and transport, where barriers to entry are supposedly great, or to get established in them in another EU member nation.

No claim has been made to suggest that the benefits of eliminating each of these barrier categories is substantial, but Emerson *et al.* (1988) have argued that the combination of these barriers, in an EU dominated by oligopolistic market structures, amounts to 'a considerable degree of non-competitive segmentation of the market', with the implication that the cost of not eliminating all the barrier categories then becomes considerable. Since the emphasis is on costs (the Cecchini Report stresses them as the 'cost of non-Europe' – see above and Chapter 7), it follows that the elimination of these barriers will reduce the costs, i.e. increase the benefits; these are two sides of the same coin.

Here, it may be appropriate to provide a brief explanation of this methodology. Recall that the majority of the 300 or so areas of barrier identified with the cost of Europe related to differences in technical requirements, whether product standards, required qualifications for workers, location for financial services or domestic ownership for public procurement. The remainder were labelled as fiscal barriers, through the differential operation of tax systems (see Chapter 14), or physical, such as border controls. Identifying these areas was a major challenge, and trying to quantify their importance was even more so. Instead of carrying out a microeconomic exercise of assessing the degree to which each measure could be translated into a value equivalent (see Chapter 7), an almost impossible task, Cecchini (or the EU Commission in disguise) opted for this novel approach to examining the impact of economic integration by measuring departures from it. This inverted the procedure of trying to explain what the counterfactual might have been had economic integration not taken place. Instead the comparison became one with a specified view of what the integrated economy might have looked like. In such an economy there would be little price dispersion and firms would have operated on a EU-wide level. Thus, in setting out the potential impact, the Cecchini study looked at the extent of departures from the lowest prices and the extent to which economies of scale had not been exploited. Thus, this approach did not estimate the likely impact of economic integration; rather, it provided an estimate of the scope for gains (Mayes, 1997d).

These benefits can also be expressed forthrightly. The elimination of the costs of non-Europe is tantamount to the removal of constraints which 'today prevent enterprises from being as efficient as they could be and from employing their resources to the full' (Emerson *et al.*, 1988, p. 2). They go on to argue that since these are constraints, their removal will 'establish a more competitive environment which will incite [the enterprises] to exploit new opportunities' (p. 2). They were quick to add that these processes free resources for alternative productive uses, and, when they are so utilized, the total sustainable level of consumption and investment in the EU economy will be increased. They stressed that this was their fundamental criterion of economic gain.

The sheer difficulty in calibrating the gains in an *ex-ante* evaluation of this sort is demonstrated by the ranges that Emerson *et al.* (1988) felt obliged to report. Their estimates range from 70 billion ECU (2.5% of EC GDP) for 'a rather narrow conception of the benefits' of eliminating the remaining barriers to the single market, to about 125–190 billion ECUs (4.5%–6.5% of EC GDP) in the case of a more competitive and integrated market. Also, 'there would be good prospects that longer-run dynamic effects could sustain a buoyant growth rate further into the 1990s' (p. 5).

Actually realizing these potential gains would take time (following the j-curve logic set out above) and it was anticipated by Emerson *et al.* (1988) that it might take five or more years for the upper limits to be achieved and that policies at both the microeconomic and the macroeconomic level would have to ensure that the resources (basically labour) released by the savings in costs would be fully and effectively utilized elsewhere in the EC.

Greater rigour was introduced by using the microeconomic estimates to generate macroeconomic simulations from macrodynamic models (see Chapter 7). The results of the simulations are then presented according to whether or not passive macroeconomic policies are pursued. In the case of passive macroeconomic policies, the overall impact of the measures is felt most sharply in the earlier years in reduced prices and costs; but after a modest time lag output begins to increase.

The major impact was expected in the medium term (five to six years) by when a cumulative impact of 4.5% increase in GDP and a 6% reduction in the price level were expected. The effect on employment is slightly negative at the beginning, but increases by two million jobs (almost 2% of the initial level of employment) by the medium term. Moreover, there is a marked improvement in the budget balance and a significant improvement in the current account.

In the case of more active macroeconomic policies, it was argued that since the main indicators of monetary and financial equilibrium would then be improved, it would be perfectly in order to 'consider adjusting medium-term macroeconomic strategy onto a somewhat more expansionary trajectory' (Emerson *et al.*, 1988, p. 6). This yielded a central case in which the level of GDP is 2.5% higher after the medium term. Since this is additional to the 4.5% boost obtained with passive macroeconomic policies, the total effect is therefore 7%, yet inflation would still be below its projected value in the absence of the single market, the budget balance would also be improved and the balance of payments might be worsened by a 'moderate but sustainable amount'.

Although these estimates depend largely on a number of crucial qualifications, Emerson *et al.* (1988) state that, irrespective of these qualifications, the upper limits to the gains are unlikely to be overestimates of the potential benefits of a fully integrated EC market. This is because

> . . . the figures exclude some important categories of dynamic impact on economic performance. Three examples may be mentioned. Firstly, there is increasing evidence that the trend rate of technological innovation in the economy depends upon the presence of competition; only an integrated market can offer the benefits both of scale of operation and competition. Secondly, there is evidence in fast-growing high technology industries of dynamic or learning economies of scale, whereby costs decline as the total accumulated production of certain goods and services increase[s]; market segmentation greatly limits the scope of these benefits and damages performance in key high-growth industries of the future. Thirdly, the business strategies of European enterprises are likely to be greatly affected in the event of a rapid and extensive implementation of the internal market programme; a full integration

of the internal market will foster the emergence of truly European companies, with structures and strategies that are better suited to securing a strong place in world market competition. (Emerson *et al.*, 1988, pp. 6–7)

11.4.2 The 'Monti' mid-term review

Compared with the very optimistic picture of the 'Costs of non-Europe' studies, the findings of the second major exercise conducted by the Commission in the mid-1990s have to be regarded as a disappointment. The effort put into the research which comprised some 38 studies, plus a business survey (CEU, 1997g) was enormous. Yet the headline figure this time was that the single market had raised EU GDP by just over 1% by 1994 and had increased employment by about half a million.

Why was there such a difference not only in the measured aggregate impact but also in the 'spin' put on it? The Commission[2] identified three main problems.

First, it argued that it was just too soon to observe the medium-term effects of the single market. Not only were some measures not even implemented until 1994 or 1995, but also economic agents had not yet had time to adjust – the downward slope of the j-curve. The Commission also argued that, at the macroeconomic level, there has been insufficient time for the effects of regulatory change to work through to any great extent.

A second 'defence' is one which bedevils many exercises in applied economics, namely that the data that could be used were, at best, only up to 1994 and thus only allowed a very short assessment from the time when the internal market measures – even if they had been fully implemented – were introduced.

Third, in a context in which many other important influences are simultaneously affecting the economy, separating out the effects of a relatively small and incremental effect such as market integration is difficult. In fact, revisions to GDP data – quite reasonably made as national statisticians obtain further information about the output of the economy – can be as great as the effects in question. In addition, the problems include cyclical effects, and the impact of technological or structural change.

In spite of these difficulties (and it is worth recalling that the equally daunting methodological challenges of the 'Cecchini' estimates were rather glossed-over),

it is instructive how much the tone of the 1996 review differs from the optimism of the 1980s. Thus, in the Working Paper, the Commission report starts by stressing that it 'expected that the Review would not show very much change'.

Strong survey evidence is presented on the perceived benefits to business of the single market, with respondents representative of companies accounting for nearly half of all output and employment reporting a strong or significant impact of the SEM. Yet the more detailed responses have to do with the protection the internal market programme provides 'against the introduction of new barriers and the refragmentation of the market'. The report provides solid evidence about the detailed challenges and successes of the single market, demonstrating that the internal market changes are a long haul, rather than the somewhat misleading impression of the 'Costs of non-Europe' studies that it would provide instant benefits. Obstacles such as the slow pace of adoption and transposition of measures are discussed and analysed, and shortcomings in the legislation itself are highlighted.

The report also provides valuable additional insights into the economic processes and what has to be done to achieve the desired outcomes. For example, it notes that 'differences in market structure from country to country may deter new entry, even where this is legally feasible'. The impact of innovations and market-driven changes are also mentioned, and the fact that regulation has continually to adapt to these is salient: financial markets in particular have exhibited a capacity to evolve faster than their regulatory frameworks, and the incidence of environmental measures emerges as a phenomenon of growing importance. Another important factor mentioned as affecting the economic impact is the costs of compliance which mean that companies often incur heavy costs before they achieve benefits.

11.4.3 Ten years of the single market

Ten years after the conclusion of the '1992' programme, the Commission, not surprisingly, was keen to celebrate the achievements of the single market. The Commission estimates that EU GDP in 2002 is 1.8% or 164.5 billion euros higher thanks to the internal market, and that employment is 1.46% higher which means that around 2.5 million extra jobs have been created. The Commission review also shows that there is still momentum behind the legislative process. By 2002 the total number of internal market directives had risen to 1475, with one eighth of these having been agreed between 1995 and 2002, that is in a period *starting* two years after the original end 1992 target date.

Table 11.1, drawn from the ten-year review of the internal market and the latest 'Cardiff' report summarizes the Commission's assessments of some of the principal benefits of the internal market.

Benefits from providing companies access to liquid markets throughout the EU have been estimated at between 0.74% and 0.92% of the value added of the manufacturing industry, with smaller firms expected to benefit significantly. Moreover, the potential savings from the elimination of inefficiencies in the financial sector caused by lack of integration are far from negligible. In the EU banking segment they can be estimated to total between 1.4% and 1.6% of GDP.

The Commission estimates that a mere 1% of savings as a result of more competition in public procurement 'would have released 14 billion euros in 2001 to be spent more efficiently or to allow reductions in the tax bill'. When countries are struggling to conform to the terms of the Stability and Growth Pact (see Chapter 10), such savings would be especially welcome.

One, admittedly crude, indicator used by the Commission is comparisons between convergence in unit export prices of trade in harmonized and non-harmonized products. The review finds that 'between 1993 and 2002, the dispersion of export unit values has been on average lower in the EU than in OECD countries. Over 80% of the sample products exhibit lower dispersion in the EU than in the OECD at the end of the period. Export unit values inside the EU have converged more intensively than in the OECD as a whole. For the vast majority of EU countries, more than 50% of export goods show converging unit values.'

In public procurement, by contrast, the Commission's evidence is not very encouraging. Although it is clear that the obligation to publish invitations to tender in the *Official Journal* has resulted in a growing number of such invitations, the number of contracts awarded to tenderers from other countries has not increased commensurately. Direct cross-border procurement accounted for just 1.26% of award notices in 2001 (1.5% in 2000). This figure does not capture indirect procurement through affiliates in foreign countries, so the real level of cross-border procurement is greater than the figures suggest. Nonetheless, direct cross-border procurement is abysmally low and has not increased in recent years. The Commission is concerned that because little information is published on the outcomes of procurement competitions, market transparency is deficient.

Retail financial services seem to be especially resistant to integration and the Commission cites the virtual absence of convergence of interest rates on consumer loans. It also argues that even though there are signs that mortgage rates are converging, this is less the result of intensified competition than of the impact of common monetary policy on money market rates.

11.4.4 Dynamic effects of the single market

Although the static gains from the internal market have been seen as welcome, even if the optimistic scenario of the 'Costs of non-Europe' research subsequently had to be scaled down, it is argued that because they do not take account of dynamic effects, they do not fully capture the potential benefits. In addition to the allocation effects, key dynamic processes include accumulation and location effects and there has been extensive theoretical and empirical work – especially drawing on the 'new economic geography' approaches pioneered by Paul Krugman and Tony Venables (Krugman and Venables, 1990; Krugman, 1991). A number of studies have, therefore, tried to look beyond the largely comparative static approach.

An early study by Baldwin (1989) suggested that the dynamic gains may be about five times those given in Cecchini. His approach differs from that of Cecchini in one significant respect. He challenges the lack of allowance for an increase in the long-term rate of growth. He contends that the methodological background to the estimates in Cecchini is based on traditional growth theory which assumes that countries become wealthier because of technological change, and that the dismantling of barriers to trade and increasing the size of markets will not permanently raise the rate of technological progress. Thus, both Cecchini and the traditional methodology are built on the premise that the liberalization of markets cannot permanently raise the rates of growth of the participating countries. In this respect, the Baldwin approach can be portrayed as consistent with endogenous growth theory.

Table 11.1 Benefits of the internal market after ten years

Effect on:	Actual or potential gains	Explanation
GNP	Higher by 1.8% than 'counterfactual' from 1992–2002, the internal market has increased the Union's GDP by 877 billion euros, an average of 5700 euros of extra income per household	Mainly static, reallocation benefits
Employment	Raised by 2.5 million, 1992–2002	Job gains in services offset by losses in manufacturing
Export competitiveness	EU exports of goods up from 6.9% of GDP to 10.2% of GDP	Direct impact of internal market open to question
Impact on intra-EU and inward investment	Intra-EU FDI flows increased by a factor of 15 between 1995 and 2000, but were hit by the downturn in 2001, falling below 1999 levels. FDI inflows from third countries have increased fourfold	Progressive easing of controls and administrative obstacles to cross-border investment Incentives to firms to concentrate production The growing gap between intra- and third country inflows testifies to a single market effect
Intensification of competition	Steady downward price convergence – down 3.6% by 1996 in 'sensitive' sectors Greater choice of products and services Lower margins Impact of competitive threats on productivity trends – up 2% in 1992 and 1993	Market opening raises the threat of market entry and obliges incumbents to improve their efficiency and quality of products and services Gains to consumers from greater rivalry and to businesses from pressures to innovate
Public procurement	Increase in share of cross-border procurement from 6% in 1987 to 10% in 1998 More competitive pricing	Obligation to advertise contracts and to solicit tenders from across the EU. Clearly, however, it remains rather low Lessens tendency to favour national champions
Network industries	Progressive opening of markets, leading to lower overall costs for consumers and businesses alike Possible threats to universal service	Breaking of national monopolies and encouragement of new entrants Spur to innovation and business restructuring
Financial markets	Increase of 1% in EU GDP Growth in jobs of 0.5% Lower costs of investment 40–80 basis points	Progressive reductions of regulatory constraints Increased liquidity

Source: Based on European Commission, *The Internal Market – Ten years without frontiers*, 8 January 2003 (http://www.europa.eu.int/comm/internal_market/10years/docs/workingdoc/workingdoc_en.pdf)

Baldwin's claim that the static approach under-estimates the gains rests on two distinct arguments. The first endorses the traditional approach, but asks about what the expected rise in output will do to savings and investment. He argues that, if savings and investment stay as constant percentages of national income, they will both rise in absolute terms. Consequently, the stock of physical capital will also increase, leading to a further rise in output which will raise savings and investment again; hence a virtuous cycle will set in. Thus the expected rise in GDP identified by Cecchini will raise the levels of savings and investment and increase the capital stock, making the EU grow faster while this process continues. Baldwin anticipated that half of this adjustment – which he labels a 'medium-term growth bonus' – might take about ten years. Converting this into an equivalent change in the level of output, and relying on conservative assumptions, Baldwin concludes that the gains from the internal market will be in the region of 3.5%–9%, as against the 2.5%–7% predicted by Cecchini.

However, Baldwin is not content with this. He declares that the medium-term bonus may be augmented by a permanent rise in growth, giving a 'long-term growth bonus'. This is because, unlike orthodox theory (which argues that there is a 'steady state' in which the capital stock grows at the same rate as the labour force, thus with the constant labour force assumed by Cecchini there will be a constant capital stock), he follows the model proposed by Romer (1986) which is built on the premise that the capital stock can rise indefinitely. This leads him to believe that the increase in EU investment after 1992 will

raise the growth rate for the EU permanently by something in the range of a quarter to three-quarters of a percentage point. Expressed as an equivalent increase in the level of output, the total bonus (the combined bonuses from the medium and long terms) would be about 9%–29% of GDP. Adding this estimate to that by Cecchini, one gets an overall figure of 11%–35% increase in GDP.

Much subsequent work on the dynamic impact of the single market has focused on its impact on location (examples of studies include Amiti, 1998; Midelfart-Knarvik *et al.*, 2000; and Aiginger and Pfaffermayr, 2000). New economic geography contains conflicting propositions about how market integration will affect location. The pursuit of economies of scale will induce concentration, whereas congestion costs have a centrifugal effect. Midelfart-Knarvik *et al.* (2000) suggest that the completion of the single market had not had much impact on patterns of location and specialization, whereas Aiginger and Pfaffermayr (2000) found that spatial concentration decreased in the 1990s. The differences in findings depend partly on the methodologies employed and partly on the sheer complexity of the processes at work. New economic geography theories offer an analytic approach with a greater degree of formal modelling than much conventional regional analysis (Krugman and Venables, 1996). They do not, however, yield unambiguous predictions about the *ex-ante* effects of integration on the core and the periphery. Instead, the outcome will depend on the relative strengths of different mechanisms and the impact on them of different policy choices.

11.5   Conclusion

In both political and economic terms, the single market must be regarded as a success. Despite some foot-dragging in the implementation of key measures, the strategic aim of opening-up markets has been consistently advanced and has retained wide political support. Although, in a sense, the internal market will never be fully completed, because there will always be formal or informal barriers that give some advantage to indigenous economic actors, there can be little doubt that the EU has moved a long way since the White Paper was launched nearly twenty years ago. It is also undeniable that member states continue to abide by the spirit of the single market and will tend

to accept proposed measures to further the internal market. Yet it is equally clear that there is unfinished business, with a number of business services and network industries to the fore. Further initiatives to complete the internal market must, consequently, be envisaged, especially following the launch of the euro. Indeed, many commentators regard monetary union as a critical step in fostering a genuinely integrated market in the EU. More attention to the implementation and enforcement is also warranted.

Although much of the rhetoric surrounding the single market has been about liberalization and deregulation, with the implication that it is principally concerned with *negative* integration (as explained in Chapter 1), the reality is more complex. In a number of areas, the outcome has been more a recasting of the regulatory framework than its dismantling, and the resulting regulatory style is one that reflects European values.

Quantitatively, the gains from the single market revealed by the Commission's ten-year review might be regarded as rather slender. But it can also be argued that the indicators only provide a limited and possibly rather misleading perspective on the impact of market integration. Not only is there still considerable scope for the dynamic impact of the SEM to come through, but also it is, by now, an unanswerable question what would have happened without it.

NOTES

1. An initial 'terms of trade loss' gives rise to a worsening trade balance, but improved price competitiveness eventually facilitates improvement. The difficulty with devaluation, however, is that it risks higher inflation that leads to a further loss of competitiveness. There is no reason to expect such a third phase with supply-side reforms, unless their momentum is lost.

2. The 1996 single market review: background information for the report to the Council and European Parliament, SEC(1996) 2378.

Chapter 12

Competition policy

WOLF SAUTER

12.1 Introduction

The main purpose of competition policy is generally seen as protecting the market mechanism from breaking down by promoting competitive market structures and policing anti-competitive behaviour, thereby enhancing both the efficiency of the economy as a whole and consumer welfare. In the EU this objective is pursued by means of enforcing prohibitions against (1) anti-competitive agreements between different companies, as well as against (2) anti-competitive behaviour by companies that are large enough – either individually or jointly – to harm competition, and (3) by vetting mergers between companies to verify whether these are likely to result in non-competitive market structures. These are features that the EU shares with numerous countries, including the EU member states that have all implemented national competition policies.

However, EU competition policy also has three important characteristics that are not commonly found elsewhere. First, it does not only aim to protect the competitive process as such, but also aims to promote and protect market integration between the member states of the EU. Second, apart from addressing private distortions of competition, it also curbs distortions of the market process by these member states. Both result from the third distinguishing feature of EU competition policy: it is implemented in a multi-level political system, that of the European Union and its member states. In this context, it is worth noting that although until recently the application of the EU competition rules was highly centralized in the hands of the European Commission, this will change in May 2004. All these aspects are examined further below.

This chapter first discusses in greater detail the rationale for competition policy generally, and of EU competition policy in particular. Next, it sets out the basic instruments of the EU competition policy, its rules and procedures, and the manner in which they are implemented. Finally, three important developments in EU competition policy are addressed: the focus on public intervention; its shift to a more economic approach; and, most recently, toward decentralization.

12.2 The rationale for EU competition policy

The reasons for introducing competition rules have varied, both between different jurisdictions, and over time. Although it is possible to draw up a long pedigree for competition law by pointing to Roman law, the Magna Carta, common law or the statutes of medieval city states, the first set of competition rules that are clearly related to the EU rules is contained in the US Sherman Act (1890). They were adopted as the result of political concern over the railroad, oil and financial 'trusts' emerging in the United States at the end of the nineteenth century, an economic concentration of power that threatened to upset the popular consensus underpinning the economic as well as the political system of that country. In various European states from the early twentieth century onward, national competition rules typically sought to balance the perceived benefits of economic collaboration between undertakings – cartels – against their acknowledged political and economic dangers (Gerber, 1998). Such competition policies often sought to provide protection against the socially and therefore politically undesirable results of 'unfair' competition, and aimed to ensure the survival of established undertakings by foreclosing markets from unregulated entry. In some cases, the legislation concerned enabled public authorities to impose the terms of existing private cartel agreements on entire economic sectors, as an alternative for state-designed market regulation, e.g. in the interest of price control. American ideas about competition policy were exported both to Germany and Japan after the Second World War, when the allied occupation forces imposed new anti-monopoly legislation to curb the power of the financial–industrial combines that were widely seen as having powered the war effort of these two countries. For similar reasons antitrust provisions were introduced into the 1951 Paris Treaty on Coal and Steel (ECSC), that consequently, unlike the EC Treaty, included control of concentrations from the outset.

For the European Community beyond coal and steel, competition rules were introduced in the 1957 EEC Treaty, albeit for a different reason. In this case, the competition rules served primarily to ensure that restrictions on trade between member states – tariff and non-tariff barriers – that the member states' governments agreed to remove under this Treaty, would not be replaced by cartels between undertakings following national lines (Goyder, 1999). Hence, remarkably, competition rules addressed to undertakings were introduced into what at the time of its conclusion was otherwise still widely seen as an international Treaty between, and addressed to, independent states.

Initially, therefore, the EU competition rules essentially served to complement an inter-state trade policy of reducing trade barriers and promoting market integration. From this starting-point, promoting market integration has developed into the overriding rationale of EU competition policy, alongside that of maintaining 'effective competition' (Bishop and Walker, 1999). This integration rationale has had a profound impact on the orientation of EU competition policy that has at times led it into conflict with the emerging economic consensus favouring efficiency considerations. For example, the integration rationale tended to lead to a negative view of vertical agreements with territorial effects.

In spite of these varied origins, and while it is difficult to find a case where pure economic reasoning motivated the introduction of competition rules, the rationale of competition policy is increasingly defined in economic terms. Evidently, the relevant economic theory has evolved over time as well.

The economic reasoning concerning the goals and limits of competition policy has been developed in particular in the United States, where an early willingness of courts to entertain economic arguments was subsequently stimulated by the appointment of law and economics scholars to the bench and to influential regulatory positions alike (including, for example, justices Easterbrook and Posner). Over the past century, the resulting debate has had a profound impact on the way competition policy is applied both in the USA and beyond. Originally, competition policy focused on the results of market structure and the behaviour of market participants associated with the 'Harvard School'. Increasingly, the so-called 'Chicago School' of antitrust economics, focusing on efficiency, price effects, and the self-policing nature of the market (Posner, 1976), has become the new mainstream of industrial organization, and hence of much analysis underlying competition policy (Scherer and Ross, 1990). In addition, game theoretic approaches are increasingly used to deal with, for example, problems of collusion and joint dominance in oligopolistic markets (Phlips, 1995). EU competition policy has followed these trends to varying degrees, modified in particular by the intervening variable of its overriding integration objective (Mehta and Peeperkorn, 1999).

Today, the market is generally seen as the most efficient instrument to set prices and thereby allocate resources. To a large extent, however, the success of markets at doing this is determined by the degree of competition in the market involved. Economists have traditionally illustrated this argument by analysing 'ideal types' of the two theoretical extremes: contrasting, on the one hand, the maximum imaginable number of competitors in a given market, and, on the other hand, the least possible number. 'Perfect competition' in fully contestable markets can be demonstrated to lead to Pareto-optimal, or maximal allocative efficiency: a situation in which the welfare of any single participant cannot be increased without another participant being disproportionately worse off. Conversely, monopoly markets can be demonstrated to lead to monopoly rents and net welfare losses, further aggravated by technical developments and efficiencies forgone, and with further losses caused by attempts to lock in monopoly advantage by political 'rent seeking'. However, 'perfect competition', which presupposes homogeneous products, and full transparency of prices and costs, as well as the absence of market barriers, economies of scale and scope, and learning effects, is not a real-world phenomenon. Instead, market imperfections, or market failures, are likely to lead to restrictions of competition that produce sub-optimal results. Firms also have economic incentives to collude and to exclude competitors. Consequently, the role of competition policy is to substitute for competitive pressure by ensuring that restrictions on competition between undertakings that are harmful to the competitive process (rather than to individual competitors) are prevented or removed.

Because pure market outcomes are likely to be theoretically sub-optimal in many cases, this leaves ample room for disagreement on what amounts to a restriction of competition that merits policy intervention. For example, views vary on whether vertical restraints, pricing below cost, or even the effects of mergers on market structure and degree of concentration as such – the number of firms present, and their relative size – form appropriate targets of competition policy.

In the context of EU competition policy, the key concept in this regard is that of maintaining 'effective competition' or 'workable competition'. Here again there is debate about whether effective competition concerns the process of competition as such, or the outcome that markets produce in terms of improving consumer welfare – generally equated with efficiency. In any event, it is by now well established that effective competition is seen in terms of preventing harm to competition as such, not to particular competitors (Bishop and Walker, 1999). Whether there is effective competition has to be determined in relation to a specific 'relevant market' that is defined both in terms of the product concerned, and geographically. Factors taken into account such as the existence of market power, the number of competitors, relative market share and degree of concentration, demand and supply substitution, the existence of barriers to market entry and exit, and potential competition, affect both the evaluation of the degree of effective competition in the relevant market and market definition itself (CEU, 1997e).

The result is an approach that considers both market structure and the efficiency of market outcomes, although the emphasis assigned between these two may be shifting towards efficiency, as is emphasized in particular by the new policy on vertical restraints that has emerged in recent years (CEU, 1999e; 2000f).

12.3 Legal framework

Although EU competition policy is increasingly driven by economic considerations, its origins are found in European law, and it must evidently operate within the constraints of its legal framework. This legal framework consists of the substantive, procedural and institutional rules that govern EU competition policy (see Chapter 3).

The legal basis of EU competition policy is found, first of all, in the EU Treaty itself (Articles 3, 10, 81–6 and 87–9). Second, it is found in implementing legislation adopted by the Council and Commission in the form of Regulations and Directives, which develop in particular the wide-ranging powers of the European Commission in this field (notably, Council Regulation 17 of 1962, recently reformed by Regulation 1 of 2004). Council Regulation 4064 of 1989 provides the framework for merger control by the Commission (European Council, 1989, 1997). In addition, an increasing number of notices and guidelines that are not formally binding provide essential information on the manner in which the Commission intends to apply EU competition policy. An example is the Commission notice on the definition of the relevant market referred to above (CEU, 1997e). By issuing such guidance both on how it interprets the binding rules of EU law, and on how it intends to use the margin of discretion inherent in its policy powers, the Commission increases the predictability of its policy – and thereby facilitates the enforcement of EU competition law between private parties and at national level.

The ultimate arbiter of the various rules, and on whether Commission policy remains within the bound of its powers, is the European Court of Justice (ECJ). The ECJ is seized either directly on a 'pre-judicial' reference by a national court, or in judicial review proceedings following a first appeal against Commission Decisions to the EU Court of First Instance (CFI). In principle, the standards applied are those of administrative review of policy: i.e., they focus on formal competence to act, controlling respect for the rights of the defence and enforcing minimum standards of reasoned rationality. The ECJ has nevertheless on a number of occasions led the way in demanding higher standards of economic argument, rather than more formal reasoning, from the Commission (Korah, 1997).

The European Commission is the institution that is responsible at EU level for the implementation of EU competition law and policy. It takes most formal decisions by simple majority, as a collegiate body. These decisions are prepared by the Directorate General for Competition, DG COMP (formerly known as DG IV), which reports to the commissioner responsible for competition policy, since September 1999, Mario Monti. Competition commissioners have often lasted more than a single four-year term and carried considerable clout within their respective Commissions, adding to the stature of the office. The Commission can be apprised of a competition problem by notification, following a complaint by an undertaking or member state, and act on its own initiative ('*ex officio*') to investigate either specific cases, or entire economic sectors ('sector inquiries'). It has considerable powers to require undertakings to collaborate in its investigations, backed up by fines, including the right to obtain evidence by unannounced inspections of company offices ('dawn raids'). In addition, the Commission can penalize all infringements of the competition rules, including the cartel prohibition, with significant financial penalties, including fines of up to 10% of the (global) group turnover of the companies involved, without any absolute upper limit. Fines of well over a hundred million euros have already been imposed in a number of cases.

Apart from the Commission, most national competition authorities in the member states now have powers to apply the EU rules where there is an effect on trade between the member states. Under the modernization and decentralization of EU competition law that was introduced by Regulation 1 or 2003 (European Council, 2003) however, the importance of the national competition authorities' role in enforcing the EU competition rules is scheduled to increase significantly from 1 May 2004 onward.

Finally, because the Treaty prohibitions on restrictions of competition are directly effective, parties may choose to invoke these rules in procedures before national courts of all levels in the EU member states. This in turn gives rise to requests by such national courts for the pre-judicial rulings on points of law by the ECJ that are an important mechanism to ensure the coherent application of EU competition law and policy. It is expected that private enforcement, and therefore the role of the ECJ as supreme legal arbiter, will increase as a result of modernization.

There are three core substantive norms of EU competition law that are addressed to undertakings:

1 the prohibition of agreements and concerted practices between firms restricting competition;
2 the prohibition of abuse of (single firm or joint) dominance;
3 the obligation to submit mergers and acquisitions for prior clearance under the merger control rules.

In addition there are specific competition rules that apply to aid by the member states, and to companies privileged in their relation to public authority.

The prohibition of collusion restricting competition (cartels) is found in Article 81(1) EC. Prohibited cartel agreements cover, e.g., price fixing, market sharing, tying, and discrimination. By force of Article 81(2), infringement of the prohibition of Article 81(1) triggers the nullity of the restrictive clauses of the agreements involved, which can lead to civil law liability and hence to claims for damages under national law. As mentioned, the Commission can in addition penalize infringements by means of fines. Certain national systems may in addition provide for penal sanctions. Article 81(3), however, provides for the possibility of exemptions from the Article 81(1) prohibition. Under the present system of Council Regulation 17/62, such exemptions can only be awarded by the Commission, and only following mandatory notification of the agreements involved to the Commission. Exemptions are given for a limited period of time and may be subject to conditions, obligations and reporting requirements. As a result of modernization this highly centralized system will be phased out in May 2004, when the notification system and the exemption monopoly of the Commission will be abolished.

The prohibition of abuses of dominant position (monopolies and oligopolies) in Article 82 EC focuses on abusive anti-competitive behaviour associated with market power rather than on the acquisition of high market shares as such. Although, therefore, it is not illegal to be dominant, provided dominance is achieved based on legitimate commercial advantage won in the market, there are evidently no exemptions for abuse of such dominance. Like the restrictions of competition covered by the cartel prohibition, possible abuses of dominance include unfair (e.g. excessive or predatory) pricing, discrimination and tying. However, unlike the cartel prohibition, which in principle applies to all undertakings, the prohibition of abuse of dominance is asymmetrical in nature: it only applies to those firms that can afford to behave – and price – independently of their competitors, suppliers and customers. The prohibition on abuse of dominance is intended to force such firms to behave as if they were subject to effective competition by abstaining from anti-competitive behaviour. In order to establish a breach of Article 82, first the relevant (product and geographic) market must be established, second, the existence of dominance in that relevant market, and finally, the existence of an abuse must be shown, as well as an effect on trade between member states. It would be possible to examine mergers under Article 82, as they may affect the market structure in a manner constituting abuse. However, it is generally not attractive to address mergers possibly years after they have taken place, because following the consumation of a merger remedies such as the forced divestiture of assets may become disproportionately burdensome on the undertakings involved. Moreover, merger control by means of Article 82 could not be systematic, and is therefore likely to be unpredictable and at odds with requirements of legal certainty. These drawbacks have stimulated the introduction of a separate system of prior merger control in 1989.

Unlike the prohibitions on cartels and abuse of dominance, which are normally enforced after the alleged infringement occurs (or *ex post*), EU merger control is based on a system of pre-notification (or *ex ante* control) that is elaborated in the Merger Control Regulation. This system is intended to provide legal certainty to firms before they consume their transaction, and to allow the Commission to vet all such transactions of a certain size (or Community dimension), based on a complex system of turnover thresholds. Merger control aims at preserving 'effective' or workable competition, based on an assessment of the structural characteristics of the relevant product and geographical markets. The relevant test is whether a merger is likely to create or strengthen a dominant position as a result of which effective competition in the internal market would be significantly impeded. As elsewhere in EU competition policy, market definitions are essential here: if wide product and geographical market definitions are used, mergers are evidently less likely to be considered problematic than if narrower markets are concerned: size, and the effects of size, are relative to a specific factual context. In principle, mergers are considered useful to allow undertakings to realize potential efficiencies of scale and scope in contestable markets. Mergers cannot normally be executed until they have been formally approved. Such approval may be given subject to structural remedies (e.g. divestiture of assets such as brands and intellectual property rights, as well as production facilities), and frequently is. In addition, behavioural remedies such as non-discrimination obligations are sometimes considered (Jones and Gonzalez-Diaz, 1992). The latter type of remedy is, however, difficult to monitor and enforce effectively, and is generally avoided whenever possible.

The EU was long denied merger policy powers, because its member states preferred to vet themselves (or indeed promote) the creation of national 'industrial champions', in particular in a wide and often ill-defined set of industries considered to be of strategic or political importance. The failure of such mutually exclusive national strategies, the increasing desire of businesses to merge across national borders without engaging in multiple notifications subject to different rules, and the merger boom triggered by the 1985 internal market initiative, were all instrumental in finally convincing the member states to adopt the Merger Control Regulation in 1989 (Neven, Nutall and Seabright, 1993a). Since then, merger control has become widely acclaimed as a model for EU competition policy generally. The main reasons for this success are strict rules and deadlines that force the Commission to produce binding decisions within a limited time frame, and undertakings to collaborate fully in the process of preparing these decisions. The scope of Community competence in this area – determined by the turnover thresholds in the Regulation – remains politically sensitive: the member states are reluctant to agree to extend it further. In 1997, the Merger Control Regulation was nevertheless amended to lower the turnover thresholds above which it applies, bringing a larger number of mergers within its scope, and to apply to cooperative joint ventures (European Council, 1997). In the case of cooperative joint ventures, the Article 81(3) test is applied to decide whether they are likely to give rise to unacceptable anti-competitive economic effects, in particular in adjacent upstream or downstream markets where both parents remain present. Recent proposals for reform of the Merger Control Regulation set out to improve the system of referrals between the EU and national jurisdictions, to clarify the concept of dominance – i.e. the substantive test applied – as including collective dominance in tight oligopoly situations, and to introduce a number of procedural changes (CEU, 2003e).

In addition to the rules that apply to undertakings in general, the EU Treaty includes specific provisions governing the application of competition rules for undertakings that are controlled, favoured or charged with executing key economic tasks by public authorities.

Article 86 EC provides rules concerning state-owned undertakings, undertakings that benefit from certain legal advantages assigned in an arbitrary manner or from legal monopoly rights and undertakings charged with tasks in the general economic interest, such as utilities (e.g. in the energy, transport and communications sectors). Article 86 states that, in principle, the competition rules apply to such companies without limitation, unless this makes it impossible for undertakings charged with services in the general economic interest to carry out their duties. The Commission can address secondary rules based on Article 86 to undertakings as well as member states. Exceptionally, it does not require permission from the European Parliament or the Council to adopt such rules. The importance of Article 86, long a dormant provision of the Treaty, has increased markedly since 1988, when it was applied to the telecommunications sector. This is because 'natural monopoly' arguments that were long held to apply to public utilities have become contested, and public ownership is increasingly unpopular. Consequently, the application of the competition rules has worked in favour of the spread of independent private enterprise in sectors traditionally controlled by the state. The Treaty itself, however, remains formally neutral concerning public and private ownership, by force of its Article 295.

Finally, in its Articles 87–9, the Treaty contains rules on restrictions of effective competition that result from member states' authorities at any level favouring some companies over others by means of subsidies: state aid (Hancher, Ottervanger and Slot, 1999; see also Chapter 10). Illegal state aid covers subsidies in any form, including outright financial subsidies as well as tax advantages or exceptions, favourable loan terms, credit guarantees, the sale or lease of goods and real estate below market prices, and many other forms of discrimination by public authorities between undertakings. Some types of state aid are, however, acceptable. Hence, state aid is governed by a rule in Article 87(1) prohibiting aid that distorts competition, and two possible exceptions to this rule: first, aid that is by definition considered compatible with the internal market, as listed in Article 87(2) (e.g. social aid to consumers and disaster relief); and, second, aid that the Commission may clear by decision, following mandatory notification, as listed in Article 87(3) (e.g. certain regional and sectoral aid). Commission findings of illegal aid can in theory be overruled by the Council, although in practice this rarely occurs (Ehlermann, 1995). Although they are also applied by DG COMP, the state aid rules constitute a separate system under which the Commission is attributed powers that are considerably less significant than those it enjoys in relation to private undertakings, in particular because the Council was long unable to agree on any secondary implementing legislation for state aid. As will be discussed below, this has changed over recent years.

Whether directed at private undertakings or member states, the EU competition norms are triggered only if constraints on competition are both appreciable, and have the effect of distorting trade between the member states (CEU, 1997f). This is consistent with the integration rationale of EU competition policy: unless they distort trade flows, restrictions of competition do not hamper integration, and consequently do not concern the EU. However, the integration rationale also means that certain types of territorial protection are prohibited that might not otherwise be particularly objectionable from an economic perspective, if they have the effect of reinforcing trade barriers along national lines. This still leaves EU competition policy a broad scope, which has often made it difficult to enforce effectively.

12.4   Enforcement

The Commission's relatively limited human resources have long been dedicated largely to the enforcement of the prohibition of anticompetitive agreements contained in Article 81 (although, more recently, the relative weight of state aid policy has increased). This is the result of interrelated systemic, political and practical constraints.

Article 82 decisions remain relatively rare. This is in large part due to the high burden of proof the European courts have imposed on the Commission, given the inherently intrusive nature of this prohibition, which bars individual behaviour by companies based on their size, that would otherwise be acceptable business practice. A clear indication of the difficulties involved is that over the period of almost 40 years that the Commission has actively applied the competition rules, it has adopted only around 40 such decisions: evidently, it is likely that in reality over this period significantly higher numbers of grave abuses of dominance occurred. Since 1989, however, effective EU merger control may also have played a role in preventing dominant positions from emerging in the first place. Due to political resistance, cases involving public authorities (including state aid) and public undertakings have also traditionally been difficult to pursue. The manner in which the system of Article 81 was implemented so far, on the other hand, was clearly biased in favour of attracting cases to the Commission.

Article 81(1) EC prohibits agreements and parallel behaviour that restrict or distort competition within the common market. However, it is not always clear whether restrictions capable of affecting trade are involved, and in any event the benefits of such restrictions may be more significant than their negative effects. In practice, there are therefore many agreements, which are on their face restrictive, that ought not to be prohibited, and are not. Because under Article 81(2) EC agreements that infringe the prohibition of Article 81(1) EC are automatically void, it was long held that undertakings require prior assurances that their prospective agreements are not caught by this prohibition. Under the key implementing Regulation 17/62 (European Council, 1962) only the Commission can provide exemptions of the prohibition on policy grounds and because notification to the Commission of the agreements involved is a precondition for obtaining an exemption. However, this has resulted in a flood of thousands of notifications from the first day this system entered into force. Due to the capacity constraints imposed on DG COMP (even today, only about 150 'A-grade' Commission officials are responsible for dealing with the enforcement of the rules on merger control, cartel infringements and dominance abuse), a timely handling of all of these notifications has eluded the Commission from the outset. Moreover, the effectiveness of this system is by no means self-evident in terms of measurable results: harmful cartels are rarely caught in this manner, as clearly illegal cartels are more likely to be carefully kept secret, than notified. In over 35 years, the Commission has adopted only nine decisions prohibiting agreements based on notifications, without in addition a complaint having been lodged against them (CEU, 1999f).

Over time, the Commission has developed a number of different ways of dealing with the problem of its antitrust notification overload. These solutions share the common feature of increasing reliance on instruments that allow the Commission to provide collective rather than individual clearances and exemptions, and to employ informal administrative solutions (so-called 'comfort' and 'discomfort' letters), rather than fully reasoned formal decisions that are subject to judicial appeal. Both the instruments defined by the Treaty and those developed under secondary legislation or in administrative practice are categorized as based either on clearances, or on exemptions.

Clearances concern cases in which the Commission considers that an agreement does not restrict competition or does not affect trade between the member states, and is therefore not caught by the prohibition of Article 81(1). They are rarely awarded on a formal basis: when addressed to individual undertakings, clearances are usually based on informal administrative letters instead (in fact, over 90% of all notifications are closed informally, including informal clearances and informal exemptions). At present the most important instrument providing a collective negative clearance is the new *de minimis* notice (see Chapter 13, Section 13.3), concerning agreements of minor importance, i.e., with negligible effects on trade between the member states or on competition (CEU, 2001k). This concerns primarily agreements between small and medium-sized enterprises (SMEs), that do not affect goods and services representing more than 10% of the relevant market, where the agreement is made between undertakings that are actual or potential competitors; or 15% of the relevant market, where the agreement is made between undertakings that are not actual or potential competitors. In such cases restrictions of competition between the undertakings involved are assumed sufficiently unlikely to result in uncompetitive markets to merit a contestable presumption of legality.

Aside from agreements covered by the *de minimis* notice, few agreements benefit from a negative clearance, largely because the Commission has traditionally preferred to perform its antitrust analysis under Article 81(3) EC. This approach has been consistently criticized by advocates of a 'rule of reason' approach under Article 81(1). Under Article 81(3), an agreement that is in principle prohibited under Article 81(1) may, if its effects are on balance considered beneficial to competition, obtain a waiver, or 'exemption' from this prohibition. Such waivers or exemptions can be subject to structural and behavioural conditions, and are limited in time. They include the following categories:

- formal individual exemption decisions under Article 81(3) EC;
- informal individual exemptions by means of administrative 'comfort letters';
- general block exemptions covering certain types of agreements found across different sectors (concerning exclusive distribution, exclusive purchasing, franchising, specialization, technology transfer and R&D agreements);
- sector-specific block exemptions for agreements prevalent in particular sectors (e.g. air and sea transport, insurance, motor vehicle and beer distribution).

In order to be eligible for an exemption, agreements must make a contribution to production, distribution or technical or economic progress, and allow consumers a fair share of the resulting benefits (generally seen in terms of price and availability of new products). Moreover, the particular restraints of competition involved must be indispensable for achieving these benefits, and may not eliminate competition completely, for example by foreclosing market entry. In determining whether any competition remains, 'potential competitors', and hence barriers to entry, are taken into account.

Formal individual exemptions are relatively rare because the Commission is not required to respond to a notification within a specific deadline, and due to its limited resources it could not, in any event, in this way address the numerous agreements that might qualify. Alongside administrative 'comfort letters', block exemptions have become the main solution to the problem of providing legal certainty to business, while reducing the overwhelming numbers of notifications for the Commission. The system of block exemptions as originally designed allows large numbers of agreements to be cleared, based on 'white' lists of admissible restrictions and 'black' lists of strictly prohibited restrictions: if agreements contain only white-listed restrictions and no black-listed ones, they need not be notified. This had the disadvantage that businesses were forced to design their agreements to fit the template of an individual block exemption (as the benefits of several block exemptions cannot be applied to a single agreement), leading to a 'strait-jacket effect' that was unlikely always to coincide with the optimal

business case. Moreover, undertakings often sought to structure transactions so as to fall within the merger control regime, which provided the certainty of obtaining decisions within strict deadlines. This in turn added to the rapidly growing merger caseload, in effect shifting rather than resolving the notification problem. As is discussed below, more recent block exemptions no longer contain 'white lists', are less specific to certain types of agreement, focus on situations of 'market power', and are accompanied by interpretative notices that better enable undertakings to make their own assessment.

Its monopoly on exemptions from the prohibition on restrictive agreements set out in Article 81(1) gives the Commission sole control of key levers of competition policy. Although the direct effect of the EU competition prohibitions means that undertakings and individuals can invoke these norms in legal proceedings before national courts, the possibility that the Commission could still act to exempt the agreements involved tied the hands of the national authorities involved. The resulting centralization of EU competition law enforcement in the hands of the Commission has considerable benefits in terms of consistency and credibility, and was probably indispensable in order to allow a fully-fledged EU competition policy to develop. With few exceptions (notably Germany), in the EU a true competition policy was long pursued only at Community level, and even there it was constructed step by step.

Over recent years, however, this situation has changed fundamentally. All member states now accept, at least in principle, that state intervention and tolerance or promotion of private cartel arrangements cannot efficiently substitute for the market allocation of resources. Hence, in a process of 'spontaneous harmonization' most member states have adopted national competition rules based on the EU model, and work toward their increasingly effective enforcement. At the same time, it is clear that in order to advance the development of competition policy further, the Commission would have to focus on new problems such as those which arise in recently liberalized markets, in oligopolistic markets and in markets that extend beyond the EU. Likewise, to ensure proactive enforcement, it would have to focus more on complaints, and on (time-consuming) own-initiative action to pursue the gravest cartels and dominance abuses. Moreover the adoption of a 'leniency notice' (CEU, 2002l) has led to a steep increase in the number of applications for a reduction of fines in cartel cases by undertakings 'coming clean' about cartel abuses in which they were involved, and providing the evidence against their co-conspirators. Following up these cases in a timely and effective manner now requires increased resources.

This means that many of the initial arguments to concentrate policy competence on the application of Article 81(3) at EU level in the hands of the Commission no longer hold, or at least no longer outweigh the negative effects of centralization, given the capacity constraints as sketched above.

Hence, at the time of writing, the centralization resulting from the Article 81(3) EC notification and exemption system has just been fundamentally reviewed and a new system based on decentralized and private enforcement will come into force on 1 May 2004. Already at an earlier stage the Commission has started rationalizing its existing Article 85(3) practice by streamlining and consolidating its block exemptions, and by moving toward an approach that relies more on economic insights, in particular in the area of vertical restraints. Already at an earlier stage, following the momentum generated by the internal market programme, the Commission had started focusing its competition policy more on public undertakings and state intervention. These three developments are each in turn discussed below, in rough chronological order.

12.5   The public turn

During the first three decades of its competition policy, the Commission focused on the basic task of enforcing the Article 81 EC and Article 82 EC prohibitions against private undertakings. This required it to elaborate implementing rules (the procedural Regulations and group exemption Regulations discussed above) and to develop its practice concerning a range of standard competition policy problems in this area. After consolidating this part of its competencies, the Commission started expanding the scope of its enforcement efforts to cover the politically more delicate areas of the public sector and state aid over the course of the 1980s and 1990s. This trend has been defined as the 'public turn' of EU competition law (Gerber, 1998).

In the first place, the Commission has begun more active enforcement of the competition rules against public undertakings, and undertakings that enjoy special and exclusive rights, such as legal monopolies, as well as licences or concessions limited in number and awarded on discretionary grounds. In doing so, it had begun to address not only the undertakings benefiting from such privileges, but also the member states responsible for awarding them. In some previously sheltered sectors, notably that of telecommunications, the Commission actually abolished such exclusive and special rights by means of competition law Directives. In a number of other sectors concerned, such as posts, energy and transport, it relied more heavily on Treaty infringement actions and sector-specific harmonization legislation adopted by the Council and European Parliament, albeit inspired by the drive to create competitive conditions, and fuelled by (potential) competitors' complaints under the competition rules. Once statutory prerogatives are removed, the competition rules come to play a key role in ensuring the markets involved are contestable. This means that there are no longer any economic sectors that are completely immune from the competition rules, although significant differences in the degree to which they are subject to effective competition are likely to persist for some time.

The Commission's policy on state aid has matured, in particular following the completion of the internal market programme (Ehlermann, 1995). This policy has included: targeting aid to public enterprises; the elaboration of the 'market investor test', which means aid is not acceptable unless private investors might have taken similar investment decisions; and enforcing the repayment of illegal aid. At the same time, the conviction that state control over the economy is inversely related to its performance is now widely shared by policy makers at national level. This realization has been reinforced by the move to Economic and Monetary Union (EMU), which imposes budgetary constraints that make member states reluctant to expose themselves to the significant potential liabilities represented by public investment that is not guided by efficiency considerations, and indeed by public ownership as such (Devroe, 1997).

An indication of the fundamental change in the attitude of the member states is that the Council has at last introduced secondary legislation implementing the state aid provisions of the Treaty. In the past few years it adopted both a Regulation concerning the conditions under which horizontal state aid may be acceptable (European Council, 1998), and a Regulation concerning procedural rules for state aid (European Council, 1999a) that also delegates new rule-making powers to the Commission. These implementation measures not only provide the Commission with improved enforcement instruments, but also increase the transparency of state aid policy, and therefore offer greater legal certainty to undertakings and national authorities.

Although the developments that constitute the 'public turn' of EU competition policy can certainly also be seen as a form of modernization and rationalization, they still remain distinct from the changes to its traditional core, antitrust enforcement (discussed below). In the utilities sectors, where traditional monopoly markets must be opened up to competitive entry, sector specific competition rules enforced by independent sector regulators will continue to play an important role at least in the medium term, until competition becomes sufficiently effective for application of the general (or horizontal) competition rules to suffice. Meanwhile, the existence of such sector-specific national regulators helps to relieve the burden on the competition services of the Commission, and to spread an understanding of how the process of competition may be protected in technically often complex fields, such as telecommunications. A similar phasing

out of the rules on state aid is, of course, not contemplated, as the need to distinguish legitimate public measures from illegal aid will persist as long as public authorities are tempted to interfere in markets. Moreover, because, unlike the antitrust provisions, the state aid rules are by definition not suited to decentralized application, and no such rules exist at national level, they must be enforced in a centralized manner.

Hence, there is a clear case for the Commission services to focus on state aid, mergers and other cases with a significant Community interest due to the size, trans-national nature and precedent value of the problems involved, while leaving the large majority of competition cases to national competition authorities and, at least until effective competition in previously monopolized utility sectors takes off, to sector-specific regulators. As a significant Community interest or dimension is arguably not involved in the bulk of competition cases currently examined under Article 81, this would require the empowering of national authorities to deal with such cases. In addition, limiting the scope of the prohibitions to cases where economically significant effects are concerned would help to allow a clearer focus on more serious competition problems both at national and at EU level. Recent developments in the area of vertical restraints, and toward modernization, clearly indicate a policy trend in this direction.

12.6   Rationalization

Many commentators have criticized EU competition policy for its lack of economic analysis, in particular in relation to restraints on competition under Article 81 (Korah, 1998). In part, the Commission's approach was a logical consequence of the integration objective, with its focus on formal and territorial restraints. The system of parallel block exemption regulations for similar types of agreements led to inconsistencies, and the practice of identifying exempted restrictions rather than just those restrictions held illegal led to the 'straitjacket' effects mentioned above. Moves toward consolidation and reform started in 1996, when the Commission adopted a single block exemption for technology transfer agreements, replacing previously separate Regulations concerning patent and know-how licences. Since then EU competition policy has shifted away from an approach based on legal form, toward an approach based on economic effects.

The most important examples so far concern the Commission's approach to vertical and horizontal restraints. In 1999, it adopted a single block exemption Regulation for vertical restraints, replacing the formerly separate legal instruments concerning exclusive distribution, exclusive purchasing and franchising agreements. In addition, the new block exemption covers selective distribution agreements, which were previously dealt with under individual decisions (CEU, 1999e). The verticals' block exemption is accompanied by extensive guidelines that aim to enable undertakings to make their own assessment of the applicability of the relevant rules (CEU, 2000f). In 2000, the Commission adopted 'horizontal' block exemption Regulations respectively for specialization agreements and research and development agreements (CEU, 2000g, 2000h), followed by a notice on horizontal cooperation agreements (CEU, 2001l).

Both as regards vertical and horizontal agreements the emphasis is now on undertakings with some significant measure of market power. Only the verticals' block exemption regulation is discussed in more detail here.

Vertical agreements are entered into between undertakings operating at different levels of the production or distribution chain that relate to the purchasing, sale or resale of certain goods and services. The restraints involved in such agreements typically cover various forms of exclusivity, non-competition clauses, branding and pricing constraints that may foreclose market entry, reduce, in particular, intra-brand competition and create obstacles to market integration. Especially for the latter reason, they have generally been frowned upon in EU competition law and a systematic policy based on the potential benefits of vertical agreements has been slow to develop. However, as the various specific block exemptions recognized, these potential benefits can be significant: vertical agreements can improve economic efficiency by reducing the transaction and distribution costs of the parties involved, and lead to an optimization of their respective sales and investment levels, in particular where there is effective competition between brands. Moreover, and most important from an integration perspective, vertical agreements offer particularly effective ways of opening up or entering new markets. The objective of the new block exemption is to secure these positive effects in a turning away from EU competition law's earlier focus on integration through protecting inter-brand competition (Peeperkorn, 1998).

In a first important move going beyond past practice, the block exemption for vertical restraints is no longer based on exemptions for specifically listed agreements: instead, there is a general exemption, subject only to a prohibition of a limited number of black-listed clauses (such as resale price maintenance, and most territorial constraints), leaving broader freedom for commercial contracts. As the efficiency-enhancing effects of vertical agreements are likely to outweigh the anti-competitive effects of restrictions they may contain, unless the undertakings involved enjoy market power, the block exemption creates a presumption of legality for vertical agreements concerning the sale of goods and services which are concluded by companies with less than 30% market share. Only cases involving undertakings that fall above this threshold have to be notified to the Commission for exemption. However, if cumulative effects occur in markets that are in large part covered by networks of agreements imposing similar vertical restraints, the Commission can decide the block exemption no longer applies, requiring individual notifications. In a move toward decentralization, national authorities are authorized to withdraw the benefits of the block exemption if vertical agreements have effects incompatible with Article 81(3) EC on a geographically distinct market within their jurisdiction. Guidelines will serve to inform undertakings of the way the block exemption is applied.

12.7 Modernization

For more than 35 years, following the Council's adoption of the key procedural Regulation 17 in 1962, the Commission has been responsible for the administration of a highly centralized authorization system for exemptions to the cartel prohibition of Article 81(1). This system rests on the notification requirement and exemption monopoly introduced by Regulation 17. Over time, it has served the uniform application of EU competition law, which in turn fostered a 'culture of competition' now shared with national competition authorities in all 15 member states, a majority of which have authority to apply both Community and national competition law (Temple Lang, 1998). However, as described earlier in this chapter, this success has come at significant cost to effective enforcement: mass notifications overburden the Commission services, leading to administrative solutions that do not provide adequate legal certainty for undertakings, and which can be used strategically to trump national courts and competition authorities in their own enforcement of the directly effective cartel prohibition (Wils, 1999).

Over time, many elements of the widespread criticism of this system (Forrester and Norall, 1984; Bright, 1995; Neven, Papandropoulos and Seabright, 1998) have come to be shared by the Commission itself. In addition, it has identified the impending further enlargement of the EU, the effects of economic restructuring following EMU, and the need to reallocate resources to respond adequately to the broadening geographic scope of various anti-competitive practices as the result of economic globalization, as reasons to adopt a programme of far-reaching modernization and reform of the manner in which Article 81 is applied. In its modernization White Paper of 1999 (CEU, 1999f), the Commission set three objectives for this exercise: ensuring effective supervision, simplifying administration and easing the constraints on undertakings while providing them with a sufficient degree of legal certainty (Rodger, 1999; Wesseling, 2000). Meanwhile the Commission's proposals have resulted in the adoption of a new Council regulation on the implementation of Articles 81 and 82 (European Council, 2003), which is to enter into force on 1 May 2004 (coinciding with enlargement).

The key element of modernization is replacing the mandatory notification and authorization system by a directly applicable legal exception system. This constitutes a shift from a system of *ex ante* control to a system of *ex post* supervision that relies more on direct effect, and hence on enforcement by national authorities and in private court actions by the undertakings concerned. Undertakings will now be required to assess themselves whether their contemplated agreements are likely to infringe the prohibition of Article 81(1), and, if they do, whether they remain within the scope of the legal exception of Article 81(3), because the restrictions involved are the minimum necessary to realize legitimate economic benefits shared with consumers, consistent with established EU competition policy practice. This assessment remains subject to challenge before national courts and by the competition authorities both at national and at Community level. It is intended that enforcement at national level will be facilitated by Commission guidance, both in the form of general notices, block exemptions, and by providing 'amicus curiae' input directly to national courts at their request. In its own handling of such cases, the Commission has announced that it will limit the scope of its review to undertakings with market power. Hence, as with the approach adopted to vertical restraints, market shares will come to play a key role.

All national competition authorities are not only to be empowered but also obligated to apply Articles 81 and 82 in cases where there is an appreciable effect on trade between the member states. This considerably reinforces decentralized application of EU competition law. However, because the national competition authorities have to keep the Commission informed of their intentions in such cases, and must submit substantive decisions to prior Commission scrutiny, while the Commission retains the right to take over cases where this is deemed in the Community interest, there will also be an increase in coordination at Community level. The ambition is that DG COMP will become the lynchpin of a seamless network of closely cooperating competition authorities at national and EU level.

This fundamental reform still requires important changes that remain to be worked out. Procedures to facilitate coordination between national authorities require new structures and additional practical and legal measures at both Community and national level, and new mechanisms to ensure consistent application of the competition rules by national courts will have to be elaborated. Criteria and methods for effective case allocation must be defined. Perhaps most important, if decentralization of EU competition policy is to be implemented with minimal inconsistencies, a more concentrated focus on a limited number of – predominantly economic – objectives appears to be required.

However, it is true that because giving up formal centralization will give rise to an increased need for coordination, it is by no means certain that the Commission's ambitions to refocus its own enforcement activities on intensified *ex post* control – including that against the gravest cartels – can be realized without additional resources. Whether sharing responsibility for competition law enforcement more broadly will create momentum in favour of providing the necessary means, remains an open question. At a minimum, it will provide the Commission with increased flexibility in reordering its priorities.

12.8   Conclusion

Following its initial system-building efforts, EU competition policy became increasingly hampered by a mismatch between the scope of the European Commission's powers and its capacity for effective enforcement. To some extent the Commission has

been the victim of its own success at centralizing its competence in order to secure its key mission of promoting market integration. Nevertheless, its efforts have spawned the spontaneous harmonization of competition policy and an increasingly effective enforcement culture at national level that are now considered the key to modernization.

EU competition policy is in a process of rationalization and modernization that involves imposing increasingly stringent curbs on public intervention, and moving away from its former primary focus on the integration objective, toward increasing reliance on economic logic and on enforcement at national level.

Although significant advances have already been made concerning previously privileged economic sectors, state aid, revising the block exemptions, the ongoing review of EU competition policy instruments is not complete: a review of policy on market power and dominance, including approaches to dominance and collusion in oligopolistic markets, remains to be worked out. The Commission will have to strengthen the proactive enforcement of its anti-cartel policy. The process of decentralizing the enforcement of the principles established so far forms a precondition for such further modernization that has only recently begun. Methods and principles for case allocation and cooperation within the fledgling network of European competition authorities must be developed further. In a next round, the state aid and merger control machinery are likely to be reformed further. Priorities may have to be established in relation to a growing flow of leniency applications. Nevertheless, the contours of a fully-fledged 'second generation' system of EU competition law are emerging.

Chapter 13

Industrial policy

VICTORIA CURZON PRICE

This chapter is divided into four sections. Section 13.1 briefly defines industrial policy and discusses its intellectual foundations. Sections 13.2 and 13.3 describe and analyse the two main areas where the EU has an active industrial policy: the control of state aid and support for research and development. The final section (13.4) attempts an evaluation.

13.1   What is industrial policy?

It is important to define what we mean by industrial policy before proceeding to discuss the EU approach to the issue. Industrial policy has several dimensions of interest to us. If we adopt the broadest possible definition, '[industrial policy] embraces all acts and policies of the state in relation to industry' (Bayliss and El-Agraa, 1990), it is clear that *no industrial policy at all* could be an industrial policy by default. This policy option, while not central to our story, should be kept in mind.

Second, while it is conventional to speak of 'industrial' policy, it is clear that we do not intend to limit our domain to policies directed only at manufacturing. The term 'industrial' is retained only because it has entered into common usage. It goes without saying that a policy to support a service activity, like a bank or an airline, qualifies as 'industrial' policy. For the same reason, one should include agricultural policy (although we shall not do so in this chapter), for the simple reason that it also affects the allocation of resources, not only within the agricultural sector itself, but also between agriculture and other activities. Indeed, a broad *economic* definition of industrial policy might be 'all acts and policies of the state to alter the allocation of resources between and within sectors'.

The *level of generality* of the 'acts and policies' is an issue in deciding what to include in a definition of industrial policy. Thus, while it is true that the rate of interest affects investment, hence industry, few people would hold that monetary policy is part of industrial policy. In fact, broad general policies which do not discriminate between economic activities, and therefore do not affect the inter-sectoral allocation of resources, are often defined as lying outside the boundary of industrial policy. The EU refers to these as 'horizontal' policies (fiscal, competition, regional, social, labour, environmental policies, etc.) and generally allows them if they do not discriminate between sectors. However, some general policies can fit a broad definition of industrial policy (see above). Thus, 'completing the internal market' was for many years considered to be a EU industrial policy in its own right. Geroski and Jacquemin (1989) had this in mind when they adopted the following broad definition: 'in our view, [industrial policy] should be designed not to specify and enforce particular *outcomes* but to alter market *processes* by attacking the rigidities which impede . . . the force of market selection' (p. 298). They specify their preference for an industrial policy which provides 'a framework in which private sector flexibility is encouraged and adjustment to shocks is facilitated' (p. 305) and express disapproval of industrial policy which 'might try to lead the private sector through a more or less explicit planning procedure' because it would take the form of ' "picking winners", predicting the emergence of "sunrise" sectors, and charting the rationalization of "sunset" sectors' (p. 305).

Geroski and Jacquemin's (normative) definition of industrial policy thus includes horizontal policies at a high level of generality, designed to improve the natural forces of the market. It is clear, however, that any practical definition of industrial policy must *also* allow for policies which target a sector of economic activity, or a type of product (even if one does not, like Geroski and Jacquemin, approve of them), and which therefore affect the inter-sectoral and inter-firm allocation of resources. In its most specific form, industrial policy supports a firm in particular (and discriminates against other firms in the same sector), clearly a very distorting version of industrial policy.

There has been an evolution in the philosophy underlying government intervention in economic affairs in the last forty years or so. Thus, in the 1960s and 1970s people approached microeconomic intervention (and hence specific industrial policies) with enthusiasm, convinced that government should and could correct market failures of various kinds. For instance, according to Geroski and Jacquemin, European industrial policies 'aimed to create European super-firms to compete with the US giants' (p. 299). By the 1990s, however, the tide had turned. We had become less convinced that government action was effective, even in the presence of market failures, and respect for market forces had increased. For instance, Martin Bangemann (1994), Commissioner for Industry from 1989 to 1999, endorsed the by-then fashionable general definition of industrial policy and proclaimed that 'it should promote adaptation to industrial change in an open and competitive market'. This gives us a benchmark for the Commission's views.

Thus the Commission, along with mainstream academic opinion, treats firm and sector-specific policies with suspicion but approves of 'horizontal' or general policies to support market activity in general. It is clear that these two aspects of industrial policy are not easy to reconcile. I propose to resolve this difficulty by retaining the distinctions between 'firm-specific industrial policy', 'sector-specific industrial policy' and 'general industrial policy'. Another semantic way of distinguishing between these concepts might be to refer respectively to 'micro-microeconomic', 'microeconomic' and 'general' industrial policy, and I shall sometimes do so in what follows.

Competition policy is a special case, and in another context would have had to be included in our discussion of industrial policy. It is general in intent, but is often specific in application. Thus the EU Commission's Directorate General for Competition (DG COMP, formerly known as DG IV – see Table 3.1 for the renaming of DGs) affects the internal structure of industries by controlling mergers, joint ventures and minority acquisitions, and by attempting to prevent cartels. It can support or discourage certain types of agreement between firms (for instance, collaborative R&D arrangements). It possesses considerable

administrative discretion, and can even allow a 'restructuring cartel' to ease the burden of adjustment in a declining sector (see below). Since these aspects are covered in Chapter 12, they will only be touched upon here. However, Section 13.3 discusses the role of DG Comp in monitoring state aid to industry and services, since these are potentially a major source of distortions of competition.

Fourth, it is a matter of empirical observation that microeconomic industrial policy is often dualistic and contradictory. Governments tend to simultaneously support 'sunrise' and 'sunset' industries, an apparently irrational approach, which encourages economists, when they come across the phenomenon, to use the theory of public choice to explain it (see below), since little can be said to justify it.

It is worth noting that in the examples just given, the policy is assumed to be pro-active: its aim is to *help* a targeted activity, whatever one might think about the wisdom of such an approach. In fact, there are very few examples of state interventions which explicitly penalize or run down an industry (this is understandable from a political point of view). However, one should bear in mind that a decision to *remove* a life-support machine, or to cut off a past stream of subsidies (as the UK has done with its coal mines and France with its shipyards), is indeed part of industrial policy as well (see the very first point, above, that having no industrial policy is an industrial policy by default).

The opportunity cost of specific industrial policy should also not be forgotten. Thus sums which are devoted to support A, B and C must come from somewhere, and will penalize all non-supported activities from D to Z. No government, as far as I know, has ever attempted to evaluate this hidden cost of industrial policy, and the public are certainly not aware of it.

A brief word is needed on the *instruments* of specific industrial policy. The favoured instruments of microeconomic or micro-microeconomic intervention, whether forward or backward looking, are subsidies, tax breaks and protection from foreign competition. These instruments are easy to aim at the desired target – the sector or firm selected for preferential treatment, but consolidation of international rules governing trade and investment makes it increasingly difficult for modern governments to adopt overtly protectionist measures. For this reason, tariff protection has gradually been replaced by non-tariff barriers (NTBs); and non-tariff barriers are being replaced by sector- or firm-specific subsidies or tax breaks. But the purpose remains the same: to encourage this or that economic activity. For instance, a public procurement policy to 'buy national' at twice the price and half the quality of a foreign competitor is both a form of hidden subsidy and a clear non-tariff barrier against foreign competition. Any protective barrier, whether tariff or non-tariff in nature, against foreign competition permits local firms to raise their prices, which means that they enjoy a hidden subsidy which does not appear in any accounts, but is transferred directly from consumers to producers. Regulations can also be implicit or explicit instruments of industrial policy, since they can shape a sector (see, for instance, the furore over the regulatory environment for High Definition TV (HDTV) in the mid-1990s, or the GSM standard which

excludes all cell phones manufactured to different specifications). Targeted tax breaks also qualify as instruments of industrial policy and are particularly hard to detect and monitor.

The EU is present in all areas. It has exclusive competence over external trade policy (see Chapters 2 and 24), shared (but growing) competence over regulatory policy, a duty to supervise member states' subsidies to industry, and small (but growing) subsidy policy of its own – not to speak of competition policy, just mentioned. Space and time constraints compel us to restrict this chapter to the supervision of member states' aid to industry on the one hand (traditional microeconomic industrial policy) and the encouragement of pre-competitive scientific and technological R&D (new 'general' industrial policy) on the other.

13.2   Industrial policy: for and against

International trade theorists have long asked why, as a matter of empirical observation, discriminatory protection (favouring some industries and penalizing others) is so prevalent. Most of the work on why governments practise *specific* industrial policy has therefore already been done by trade theorists. It just needs transposing to the slightly broader framework of industrial policy. Since the arguments are familiar, I shall simply mention them, without going into great detail. The case for *general* industrial policy, however, is based simply on improving the competitive functioning of markets.

13.2.1 Market failure in general

An economic case for government action can be made whenever an instance of general market failure can be spotted. For example, firms are naturally inclined to form cartels to reduce competition if the cost of forming the arrangement is lower than the expected benefit (often the case when a small number of firms is involved). For this reason antitrust policies are devised to improve the competitive functioning of markets. The failure of the market to account properly for damage to the environment is another well-known and widely acknowledged reason for government action. Finally, it is often claimed that the market will under-supply useful scientific and industrial knowledge because of the public-goods aspect of information. It is on this

that public funding of R&D is based. We shall return to this question below.

In the area of specific industrial policy, however, the case for market failure is much harder to make, because the underlying assumption is that the government is better at allocating resources than the market, or at any rate can improve substantially upon it. This is increasingly questioned and has led to growing scepticism regarding selective industrial policy.

Several different types of market failure arise under this head which are discussed below.

13.2.2 Infant industries

This is the oldest and most popular of the (economic) arguments for subsidization and/or protection. Even in its traditional formulation, it appeals to the notion of economies of scale. It asserts that an 'infant' industry operating below optimum size will never achieve the low costs associated with large-scale production of established firms, because the latter possess a 'first mover advantage' that the newcomer simply cannot overcome. For this reason, it needs a start-up subsidy. Once it is up and running it will become competitive, in theory at least. In practice, many infants never grow up. The art is in selecting the right sector – in 'picking the winners'. This is not easy, even for entrepreneurs investing their own money. It is much harder for public officials, investing other people's money. The process tends to become politicized, of which more below.

13.2.3 Strategic industrial policy

In the 1980s, under the leadership of Paul Krugman (1979), trade theory turned to models of imperfect competition to explain phenomena such as intra-industry trade between developed countries. From this exercise there emerged not only an explanation for certain empirical observations in terms of oligopolistic rivalry, but also some policy prescriptions (see, in particular, Brander and Spencer, 1983).

For many observers, however, the policy prescriptions looked remarkably like the old infant-industry argument, dressed up in modern clothes. What is perhaps new is the idea that comparative advantage is no longer a matter of traditional factor endowments, but can be *consciously shaped* by judicious industrial policy. This at any rate is the claim of the new trade theory.

In a world where *technology* determines the competitiveness of firms and where location is no longer a question of hard geographic facts, but rather proximity to other firms in the same sector, economic activity can become (fairly) 'footloose'. Attracting specific sectors to particular locations therefore becomes a feasible, and potentially profitable, object of public policy. The market-failure reasons why markets need a helping hand are the same as before: first-mover advantages, barriers to entry due to economies of scale and perhaps lack of appropriate general infrastructure (high-speed communication networks, universities, publicly funded research laboratories, etc.). The problem, as always, lies in whether the response to the observed market failure is to be selective or general.

13.2.4 Industrial agglomerations

The idea that economies of scale are paramount, that geographic location is no longer an issue and that comparative advantage can be 'shaped', has led to some spectacular failures when, combining industrial with regional policy, governments erected 'cathedrals in the desert' (such as huge steel and chemical complexes in Italy's Mezzogiorno). Clearly, something was missing from the recipe. Geography matters – but what kind? The failure of old-style regional policy to create viable industries in blighted areas, as well as the astonishing success of Silicon Valley, has led to a renewed interest in the economics of agglomeration (Fujita and Thisse, 1996). The notion that people following the same skilled trade derive advantages from proximity to each other goes back to Alfred Marshall, who noted that they gained from lower factor prices and economies of scale (Marshall, 1920).

The 'pull' factors which reduce costs for members of an agglomeration include: positive externalities based on mass production of specialized inputs (i.e. access to lower costs from efficient suppliers), access to specialized labour, specialized services, shared consumers, shared infrastructure (especially universities), flow of information (especially tacit information and informal gossip) and the sheer efficiency of markets as coordinating agents (as compared with the corresponding inefficiency of hierarchical management as a method of coordination beyond a certain degree of complexity). An agglomeration reduces costs by allowing firms to contract out all but their very core activities, but this is only efficient if the specialized suppliers can themselves operate on a large enough scale, thus offsetting market transaction costs.

For instance, some hospitals no longer employ nurses directly, but contract out this seemingly core activity to a nursing-services agency.[1] However, such a practice will only get good results if there are many hospitals and many service providers, offering similar (but often subtly differentiated) specialized nursing services. The truly spectacular benefits will come when specialization and economies of scale, in turn, hit the nursing services supply industry as well, spreading pecuniary externalities (Scitovsky, 1954) throughout the agglomeration and creating a Silicon Valley for health care. At one point, the hospital might become just a Coasian locus for a multitude of contracts (Coase, 1937).

One important implication for industrial policy is that while the agglomeration may be very large, most of the firms which compose it will be very small, at least relative to the traditional multinational corporation or national champion. In fact, the economies of agglomeration can be interpreted as being both substitutes for and complements of technical economies of scale. Thus an agglomeration of small-specialized firms might compete head-on with a large, vertically integrated corporation, each being equally efficient. On the other hand, a complementary structure would involve large firms capturing the available technical economies of scale, surrounded by a dense network of suppliers and subcontractors, all working to keep costs and prices down, and variety and innovation up.

This means that industrial policy can no longer simply target large firms and hope for the best. Support for small and medium-size enterprises (SMEs) is (perhaps) needed too. But we are far from understanding industrial agglomerations and even further from knowing how to create them. This is not an argument for an industrial policy based on market failure, but rather one based on mysterious market success, which we would dearly like to duplicate.

13.2.5 Domestic distortions

In a world of political and social constraints, with numerous public policies affecting every aspect of business life, it might be efficient to adopt an industrial policy to offset some of the unintended consequences of other types of policies. For instance, it is often claimed that Europe's expensive social welfare system, the cost of which appears to fall mostly on firms, discourages them from hiring extra employees, creating new enterprises or investing in R&D. Rather than dismantle the entire welfare system (which would anyway be politically impossible) it might be preferable to adopt an industrial policy to offset some of the negative side-effects. Here the argument for industrial policy is based on policy, rather than market failures.

13.2.6 Support for research and development

The importance of technological change in explaining economic growth has long been recognized (Solow, 1957; Denison, 1974). Furthermore, it has long been acknowledged that firms will only invest heavily in research and development (R&D) if they can appropriate for themselves the new knowledge they have created. However, since much scientific knowledge, once discovered, is freely available for anyone to use, firms have little incentive to produce it (the free-rider problem). This market failure (due to the public-goods nature of knowledge) gives rise to two broad policy responses: the patent system on the one hand, giving inventors a temporary and exclusive right to exploit the new knowledge they have created; and public funding of basic research at universities and technical

laboratories on the other. The question is whether firms need *more* than the patent system to encourage them to create new knowledge. For instance, should the government offer to defray part of the cost of R&D? Irrespective of the answer to this question (which indeed remains open) most developed countries do actually devote substantial public funds to financing R&D in private industry. The argument in favour of doing so must rest on something more than the free-rider problem, since this could be remedied by strengthening and, above all, lengthening the time of protection under the patent system.

Public funding of R&D, however, allows governments to be selective up to a point, in other words, to adopt a microeconomic industrial policy under the banner of a well-recognized general market failure in the area of knowledge creation. Governments can promote *indirectly* those industries which they wish to support (see the infant industry and strategic arguments outlined above) by sponsoring R&D in selected areas. This is less risky than 'picking the winners' directly (by supporting investment in new production facilities, for instance) since the new knowledge thus created might 'spill over' into other areas and be generally useful. For instance, the Apollo space programme is often credited with having developed the transistor, the grandfather of the silicon chip.

These technological loops, linkages, feedbacks and spillovers (all terms frequently used by true believers) are in fact at the heart of the argument. They help to translate scientific knowledge into commercially useful innovations, and vice versa. Industrial research by one firm takes known science, applies it to solving a particular problem and, in the course of this work, adds to general scientific knowledge which can be exploited by other firms and perhaps find its way back to the universities. Thus the creation of new knowledge by one firm is assumed to generate positive externalities for other firms, both in the form of better and cheaper products, and in the form of new scientific (non-patented) information, as well as ensuring the firm's own longer-term survival through the development of patented information (Grossman and Helpman, 1991).

A further point made by Grossman and Helpman is that the ability to assimilate existing technologies and generate new ones is by no means universal, but has to be cultivated. Countries in which technological research is carried out acquire a *comparative advantage in the form of human capital resource endowments that may persist for some time* (Ruttan, 1998). It is also a plausible hypothesis that pure science will remain economically inert unless society possesses a steady supply of entrepreneurs operating through markets to convert it into something useful for everyday life. For example, the USSR could put a man into orbit, but could not provide its population with a high standard of living. The link between pure science and economic growth is therefore complex.

Efforts to include technology in standard economics are beginning. When successful, the implications are staggering. Thus Romer (1994) argues that if, when tariffs come down, firms do not choose simply between known goods X and Y, but include in their choice set the as-yet-undiscovered sector Z, the cost of protection is very high – namely, a lack of dynamism and innovation. Standard neoclassical economics cannot capture these effects because it assumes perfect knowledge (Hayek, 1945). In the real world markets reward the search for useful knowledge, whose stock increases day by day, adding to our set of entrepreneurial options.

13.2.7 The innovation 'pipeline'

The main question for policy makers is not so much whether R&D needs public support (there seems little doubt, even in the minds of many sceptical academics), but how and at what stage. The process of transforming general scientific knowledge into useful commercial applications can be viewed as a kind of pipeline, running from academic institutions as far from the business world as is possible to imagine, with links to general industrial research laboratories, where much scientific knowledge is created, but few innovations emerge, to the more focused development of prototype products or processes in an engineering laboratory, on to the testing of innovations on a small scale and finally, after much trial and error, if successful, to their full-scale commercial development and marketing on a broad scale. New knowledge is created at each stage in the process. But which stage is the most deserving of public support? Generally speaking, the further away from 'the market place' and the more general the type of research, the more appropriate it is for public funding. In this way, one can avoid targeting public funds to particular firms which, as we have already seen, is a particularly degenerate form of industrial policy. For this reason, as we shall see, the EU promotes 'pre-competitive' R&D, i.e. in principle

it does not fund the development of prototypes or anything 'too close' to the market.

Agglomerations, discussed above, are also conducive to technological change. Information and ideas circulate informally within an agglomeration, speeding up the process of product development (Lucas, 1988). Thus, support for agglomerations, if such could be devised, might be an indirect way of promoting innovation. This may be the thinking behind the EU recent attempts to aim more R&D support at SMEs.

13.2.8 Attracting foreign direct investment

Many governments adopt policies to attract foreign direct investment (FDI). The reasons are obvious: to promote employment, 'help' the balance of payments, increase the level of economic activity, benefit from new technologies, enhance exports, expand the tax base – the list is endless. The problem with such policies, however, is that they discriminate between local and foreign investors. From an economic point of view, it is no more acceptable to give an artificial advantage to foreign investors over local investors, just because they are foreign, than it is to give local producers an artificial advantage over foreign producers, just because they are local. Discrimination on these grounds will simply produce wasteful distortions and ultimately too much FDI as governments compete with each other to attract it. Discriminatory pro-FDI policies are quite different from structural reforms aimed at making a country more attractive to investors *in general*. Such policies do not distort the economy, but promote investment, growth and healthy institutional competition between countries.

13.2.9 Problems with industrial policy

The principal problem with industrial policy is the fact that it often implies selectivity *in practice*. As we saw in Section 13.1, if a policy is general and 'horizontal', it does not distinguish between sectors and it avoids all the problems of 'picking the winners'. But support for R&D, for instance, often ends up targeting particular sectors. *Someone* must do the selecting. If not the market, then who? Are public officials so wise and far-seeing that they can really do better?

Second, if all governments enter the industrial policy game, each supporting the sectors they think are promising or in need of help, there is a fair chance that they will all choose the same sectors and collectively spend too much on them. Their efforts will cancel out and much misallocation of resources will occur.

Third, the process of allocating industrial policy funds is bound to become ever more politicized with time. Once 'hooked' on industrial policy funds, sectors grow beyond their market-determined size and hence enjoy more political support than is their due. Industrial policies become 'path dependent' and self-perpetuating.

If industrial policy is hijacked by rent-seekers, as is likely (see Tullock, 1967; Kreuger, 1974 for seminal articles on 'public choice'), it will end up reducing rather than improving welfare. Its ostensible purpose is to improve markets by offsetting market or policy failures, but in reality it will have been captured by special interest groups. The latter have a direct interest in the creation of public support programmes and in their expansion over time. Lobbying public authorities for privileges of one kind or another diverts resources from producing real goods and services of marketable value. The loss to society is thus twofold: not only do lobbies extract rents from the less well organized members of society, generating the usual opportunity costs, but they also waste real resources to obtain them. Furthermore, the whole process can become dynamic (Olson, 1982) as more and more firms try to join the gravy train. According to Olson, there is no end to this process (except long-term decline in growth as firms invest more and more in rent-seeking and less and less in production). The principal victims (consumers and taxpayers) remain 'rationally ignorant', allowing themselves to be regularly fleeced by rationally knowledgeable and politically active interest groups. And the public choice school does not even discuss the problem of outright corruption, favouritism and nepotism, which nowadays surfaces regularly at Commission level.

Finally, one does not need the apparatus of public choice theory to spot the occasions when industrial policy degenerates into pure political opportunism, as when subsidies are given to loss-making firms to 'save jobs' (especially politicians' jobs). The urge to save bankrupt firms is strong in every country. The status quo has huge political value. But it is impossible to save bankrupt firms without destroying the pattern of rewards and penalties which fuels the market system. Every corporate rescue undertaken at tax-payers' expense sends the message 'forget the market: *we* reward inefficiency'. A sure recipe for low growth and high unemployment.

13.2.10 Conclusion

If any general conclusion is to be drawn from this brief summary of the intellectual case for state intervention it is this: it should not target specific firms or sectors, but aim at improving the general functioning of markets. Another point is that it is not enough to demonstrate the existence of a market failure to justify government intervention. Government action is costly in its own right and if selective, quickly becomes politicized. In fact, the direct and indirect costs of selective government action over time are probably far greater than the original market imperfection, if such can be demonstrated. This is not to say that no industrial policy is the best policy, but to make a plea for very close scrutiny of what is advanced under this banner and to use the level of generality as the guiding principle for forming an opinion.

| 13.3 | Industrial policy in the EC: the control of state aid |

The Treaty of Rome does not provide for a 'Common Industrial Policy' in the same way as it provides, for instance, for a Common Agricultural Policy, a Common Transport Policy and a Common Social Policy (see Chapters 2, 20, 15 and 23). It did not even provide for a Common Regional Policy until 1987 (see Chapters 2 and 22). This is no accident. Common policies were necessary in areas where government intervention at member-state level was so extensive that freeing markets could only produce a distorted outcome and policy competition. Where these loomed, and the political will was present, the problem was elevated to Community level and a 'common' policy was born. Sometimes (as in the case of road transport) the problem was never dealt with and remains a source of tension to this day.

In the case of industrial policies, the founding fathers deemed it sufficient to grant the Commission powers of supervision to ensure that state aid did not distort conditions of competition in the common market. Articles 87–9 (formerly Articles 92–4) set forth the general rules.

Article 87(1) states that:

> Save as otherwise provided in this Treaty, any aid granted by a Member State or through State resources in any form whatsoever which distorts or threatens to distort competition by favouring certain undertakings or the production of certain goods shall, in so far as it affects trade between Member States, be incompatible with the common market.

Apart from the introductory caveat (see next paragraph), this is an extremely sweeping prohibition. It covers aid in 'any form whatsoever', targeted either at the level of individual firms ('favouring certain undertakings'), or at the level of an entire sector ('the production of certain goods'), including services. Its purpose is to prevent member states' industrial policies from undermining the common market by distorting the allocation of resources.

However, some industrial policies may be deemed compatible with the common market. Article 87(3) lists in this regard aid to promote development of depressed or backward areas, aid for 'important projects of common European interest', aid for 'certain economic activities' or 'certain economic areas' (aid granted to shipyards is expressly mentioned) and 'such other categories of aid as may be specified by decisions of the Council'. These are known in Community-speak as 'horizontal' aids. In 1992 the Maastricht Treaty introduced a specific derogation for State aid to culture and heritage conservation (Article 87(3)(d)). In fact, Article 87(3) allows the Commission considerable leeway in developing a policy with regard to state aid.

Article 88 empowers the Commission to 'keep under constant review all systems of aid' in member states and Article 89 allows the Commission to propose appropriate regulations to ensure the proper application of Articles 87 and 88.

It was some time before the Commission developed these powers into a 'policy', since the role of *gendarme* was not an easy one to assume when the miscreants were member states. On the whole, however, the 1960s and early 1970s were good years and there was little excuse, or perceived need, for state intervention in industry. According to the Commission's *First Report on Competition Policy* (published in 1972) the only sectors in trouble were shipbuilding, textiles and film production, and the Commission limited itself to exhortations to keep national aid within rather vague 'guidelines'. General aid schemes to promote investment were approved, and even dowries for industrial weddings in the French electronics industry (Machines Bull and CII) were passed without difficulty.

In fact, during this period, the term 'industrial policy' was either not in use at all, or subsumed under the generic term 'completion of the internal market' (see, for instance, the Commission's 'Colonna Report', CEC, 1970c). It covered the elimination of NTBs, the regulation of public procurement to avoid hidden subsidies, and the creation of a single regulatory environment for European industry. In a word, Community industrial policy at that time took the form of a *withdrawal* of the state from the market place, in order to create the 'common' market, while specific industrial policy remained the province of member states and was not seen to be much of a problem.

The 1970s and early 1980s, were much more turbulent. Two successive oil price increases plunged Europe into a prolonged recession, characterized by high rates of inflation and unemployment. Traditional macroeconomic policies were powerless to cope with this hitherto unprecedented combination. Firms continued to fail, unemployment continued to rise, exchange rates gyrated. Many EC members resorted to the direct subsidization of loss-making firms.

To begin with, the Commission did not appreciate the danger. It found that 'Member States, in an attempt to protect employment, were justified in boosting investment by granting firms financial benefits . . . it agreed to financial aid being granted to ensure the survival of firms which have run into difficulties, thereby avoiding redundancies' (CEC, 1976, para. 133). The list of sectors 'in difficulty' expanded to include automobiles, paper, machine tools, steel, synthetic fibres, clocks and watches and chemicals. The number of subsidy schemes notified to the Commission rose from a mere handful in the early 1970s to well over one hundred by the end of the decade.

Finally waking up to the danger, the Commission decided to take a less lenient view of subsidies to preserve employment (CEC, 1979a, paras 173, 174), putting more emphasis on the 'need to restore competitiveness' and to 'face up to worldwide competition'. The change in policy and circumstance emerges quite clearly from Table 13.1, which shows that while the total number of cases trebled from 1976 to 1978, the ratio of 'objections' to 'total decisions' halved to only 12%–14%. This period of excessive leniency

Table 13.1 Accumulated data on state subsidies, 1970–2001

(1) Year	(2) Total decisions	(3) No objection	(4) Objection	(5) Of which final negative decision	(6) Objections/total (col. 4/col. 2)
1970	21	15	6	1	0.29
1971	18	11	7	3	0.39
1972	35	24	11	3	0.31
1973	22	15	7	4	0.32
1974	35	20	15	0	0.43
1975	45	29	16	2	0.36
1976	47	33	14	2	0.30
1977	112	99	13	1	0.12
1978	137	118	19	0	0.14
1979	133	79	54	3	0.41
1980	105	72	33	2	0.31
1981	141	79	62	14	0.44
1982	233	104	129	13	0.55
1983	195	101	94	21	0.48
1984	314	201	113	21	0.36
1985	178	102	76	7	0.43
1986	181	98	83	10	0.46
1987	274	205	69	10	0.25
1988	410	303	107	14	0.26
1989	343	259	84	16	0.24
1990	492	415	77	14	0.16
1991	597	493	104	7	0.17
1992	552	473	79	8	0.14
1993	467	399	68	6	0.15
1994	527	440	87	3	0.17
1995	619	504	115	9	0.19
1996	474	373	101	23	0.21
1997	502	385	117	9	0.23
1998	460	413	47	–	0.09
1999	460	393	67	26	0.05
2000	475	409	66	31	0.16
2001	451				

Source: Compiled from Commission of the European Union, Annual Competition Reports

was succeeded by one (1979–1986) where the rate of 'objections' rose again to between 30% and 55% – evidence of a battle royal between the Commission and the member states. From 1987 onwards, not only did the economy pick up somewhat, but one may also assume that member states had learned to avoid, as much as possible, the inconvenience and embarrassment of going through the Commission's 'objection' process. The rate of 'objections' thus fell back to very low levels (5% in 2001). This ratio is, however, clearly related to the business cycle, rising when the economy slows and falling again during expansionary phases.

Another problem which developed during those dark years was an open conflict between DG III (Industrial Affairs) and DG IV (Competition). Etienne Davignon, Commissioner for Industrial Affairs, sponsored 'temporary crisis cartels' in two stricken industries – steel and synthetic fibres. They were plagued by over-capacity, chaotic price-cutting and huge losses. Viscount Davignon offered an 'orderly' way out, which involved all producers bearing equal shares of the agony of cutting back capacity. However, while the steel cartel was in accordance with the Treaty of Paris, the synthetic fibre cartel was not compatible with the Treaty of Rome, and DG IV duly condemned it (CEC, 1979a, para. 42).

What was the industry to do? One Commissioner told them to set up a cartel, the other told them to dismantle it! In fact, DG IV did not pursue the matter, and the synthetic fibre agreement continued in a kind of legal twilight until 1982, when the Commission published its 'policy' on the matter.

The statement on the application of competition rules to agreements aimed at reducing 'structural over-capacity', still applicable today, reads as follows:

> The Commission may be able to condone agreements in restraint of competition which relate to a sector as a whole, provided they are aimed solely at achieving a coordinated reduction of overcapacity and do not otherwise restrict free decision-making by the firms involved. The necessary structural reorganization must not be achieved by unsuitable means such as price-fixing or quota agreements, nor should it be hampered by State aids which lead to artificial preservation of surplus capacity. (CEC, 1983, para. 39)

The synthetic fibre producers duly amended their agreement and obtained an exemption in 1984 (CEC, 1985b, paras 81–2).

Without being exhaustive, it is not difficult for an economist to pick holes in this policy statement. There is a world of difference between reductions in capacity that market competition would have produced (the weakest firms would have collapsed) and the 'coordinated reduction of overcapacity' by agreement between firms (each firm, irrespective of its efficiency, reduces capacity by an agreed amount). The latter process guarantees the survival of the un-fittest. So *why* the Commission believed that it would 'restore competitiveness' is not clear.

In the meantime, the Commission did not prosecute, but permitted, under supervision, the continuing subsidization by member states of 'sectors in difficulty' (coal-mines, shipyards, textiles, etc.). It was easier to supervise help for stricken industries than to condemn it outright – and to enforce its abolition.

The latter 1980s were marked by a spectacular renewal of the European Community: the adoption in 1985 of the Commission's White Paper on completing the internal market, the entry into force in 1987 of the Single European Act (SEA; see Chapter 2), and the launching of Economic and Monetary Union (EMU; see Chapters 9 and 10) were huge steps undertaken, in part, as a response to the terrible decline into which the oil-price induced recession had thrown all European countries. The creation of a genuine single market made it more important than ever that member states should not thwart the competitive process by extensive use of state aid. It was therefore agreed in 1985 that the Commission should issue a general report on the subject every three years. At the time of writing (2003) there have been nine of these reports, which give a good idea of the evolution of state aid over time (see Tables 13.2 to 13.7).

The rescue and restructuring of East German industry after reunification, under the guiding hand of the Treuhand, gave rise to a large number of firm-specific subsidies subjected to evaluation by DG Comp. Other members also indulged in a growing number of 'ad hoc' aids to rescue companies in difficulty (see Tables 13.5, 13.6). These were recognized as being particularly distortive and damaging both to the single market and to the Commission's reputation for maintaining fair competition at Community level. In 1999 the Commission published a set of guidelines in an attempt to contain the problem (OJ C 288, p. 2). *Rescue* aid must be given on a 'one time, last time' basis; it must be no more than a short-term holding operation and must take the form of transparent loans or loan guarantees. *Restructuring* aid

Table 13.2 State aid as a percentage of GDP

	1981–86	1986–88	1988–90	1990–92	1992–94	1994–96	1996–98	1998–2000
Austria						0.6	1.24	1.06
Belgium	4.1	3.2	2.8	2.3	1.7	1.3	1.49	1.38
Denmark	1.3	1	1.1	1	1.1	1	1.08	1.77
Finland						0.5	1.89	1.60
France	2.7	2	2.1	1.8	1.4	1.1	1.5	1.25
Germany	2.5	2.5	2.5	2.4	2.5	1.9	1.57	1.31
Greece	2.5	4.5	3.1	2.2	1.3	1.2	1.39	0.99
Ireland	5.3	2.7	1.9	1.5	1	0.8	0.98	1.32
Italy	5.7	3.1	2.8	2.8	2.1	2	1.53	1.06
Luxembourg	6	4	3.9	3.9	2.4	1	1.18	1.35
Netherlands	1.5	1.3	1.1	0.9	0.7	0.7	0.86	0.94
Portugal		1.5	2	1.4	1	0.9	1.72	1.28
Spain		2.7	1.8	1.3	1.1	1.2	1.27	1.07
Sweden						0.8	0.92	0.81
United Kingdom	1.8	1.1	1.2	0.6	0.4	0.5	0.7	0.53
EU average	**3**	**2.2**	**2.1**	**1.9**	**1.6**	**1.3**	**1.32**	**1.08**

Source: Compiled from Commission of the European Union, Surveys of State Aid in the European Union (1st to 9th surveys). Includes aid to agriculture

Table 13.3 State aid to manufacturing by objectives (%)

	1981–86	1986–88	1988–90	1990–92	1992–94	1994–96	1996–98	1998–2000
Horizontal objectives	22	40	42	38	30	30	26	39
of which R&D	4	9	10	10	7	9	8	10
Regional objectives	14	34	38	50	53	57	37	29
Sectoral objectives and coal	63	26	20	12	17	13	37	32

Source: Compiled from Commission of the European Union, Surveys of State Aid in the European Union (1st to 9th surveys). See also *Tableau de bord des aides d'état*, Commission of the European Union (2002e) COM (2002) 242 final pp. 44–45

must be justified by a detailed corporate plan to restore commercial viability. It is, however, very odd that the Commission should classify rescue and restructuring (R&R) aid as 'horizontal', along with help for the environment and R&D (see XXXI Report on Competition policy 2001, paragraphs 389–393). It would be difficult to imagine anything *less* 'horizontal', or general, than emergency aid to bankrupt firms. It is difficult to believe that R&R aid is available on demand without any selectivity.

The French and Italian banking crises of the 1990s (Crédit Lyonnais, Banco di Napoli), coinciding with

Table 13.4 State aid to the manufacturing sector (million ECU, million euro since 1999)

	EUR 10	EUR 12	EUR 15
1981–1986 annual average	42 161		
1986		35 580	
1987		32 620	
1988		37 690	
1989		30 253	
1990		42 059	
1991		35 734	
1992		39 062	
1993		44 057	
1994		41 198	
1995		37 386	38 591
1996			35 163
1997			33 385
1998			28 471
1999			25 027
2000			23 844

Source: Based on Commission of the European Union, Surveys of State Aid in the European Union (1st to 9th surveys). See also *Tableau de bord des aides d'état*, Commission of the European Union (2002e) COM (2002) 242 final, Table 7, p. 42

the liberalization of capital movements and the beginnings of a single European financial market (see Chapter 11), directed the Commission's attention to a new and highly controversial area. Bank rescues are always expensive, but are undertaken in order to protect the public from a large-scale banking crisis, as healthy banks weaken and perhaps fail from 'contagion'. Viable banks, however, complain of unfair competition. Why should a failed bank be rescued by taxpayers? It could just as well be taken over by its more successful rivals. Why are the normal rules of market selection suspended for the banking sector? So go the arguments.

In practice, the Commission also applies its rules on rescue and restructuring to this sector, and has registered some success. For example, following a complaint by the European Banking Federation in 1999, state guarantees for Germany's public *Länder* banks, worth an estimated 1 billion euro a year (Moser and Pesaresi, 2002, p. 3), were condemned by the Commission because they were granted on a regular basis, thus leading to a long-term distortion of competition in the commercial banking sector. In March 2002 the German government agreed to isolate commercial activities from public tasks assigned to state banks, and to confine all subsidies to the latter (Moser and Pesaresi, 2002, p. 11).

State aid to R&D received special attention in 1986, when the Commission adopted its first 'Framework on State Aid for Research and Development'. The Commission emphasized its favourable attitude to this type of aid, warned of the dangers of fruitless duplication of effort and hence pointed to the need for proper coordination by the Commission (see below). It called for the notification of all R&D subsidies in excess of 20 million ECU. A good part of the increase in the number of cases investigated by the Commission from 1987 onwards (see Table 13.1) was due to the adoption of this new framework. Other reasons include the increase in membership from 1970 to 1997, and, according to the Commission, the growing efficiency with which it tracks such aid (CEC, 1987a, para. 174), but not an increase in the total volume of state aid in euro terms, or as a proportion of GDP, which has been declining (see Tables 13.2 and 13.4).

The adoption of the framework on state aid for R&D in 1986 was no accident. In 1985 President Mitterrand launched his Eureka initiative (see Section 13.4.3) to counter President Reagan's 'Star Wars' programme, and since this involved large sums of money being channelled towards national champions (a typical 'picking the winners' industrial policy), the French government wanted some kind of recognition at Community level that the Eureka programme would not be thwarted by Brussels.

Because of the growing caseload, the Commission proposed a regulation to grant group exemptions for certain categories of state aid, which was adopted by the Council in 1998.[2] The types of state aid which are deemed to be compatible with the Treaties are: horizontal aid (in particular, aid to SMEs, R&D, environmental protection, employment and training), regional aid and *de minimis* aid (aid so small as to be deemed to have no discernable effect on competition). This list is indicative of the Commission's own policy towards industrial policy, already suggested in the

Table 13.5 *Ad hoc* aid to individual enterprises, 1992–2000 (million ECU, million euro since 1999)

	Total *ad hoc* aid	Of which Treuhand aid	Non-Treuhand *Ad hoc* aid	Total aid to industry	Total *ad hoc* aid as % of total aid to industry	*Ad hoc* aid excluding Treuhand (% of total)
1992	7 583	5 161	2 422	39 062	19	6
1993	14 596	8 854	5 742	44 057	33	13
1994	18 319	11 013	6 922	41 198	41	16
1995	13 389	6 550	5 776	38 386	30	14
1996	14 210	4 742	5 888	35 163	28	16
1997	11 721	3 554	8 167	33 385	35	24
1998	9 037	2 346	6 691	28 471	32	23
1999	1 939	637	1 302	25 027	8	5
2000				23 844		

Source: Compiled from Commission of the European Union, Sixth and Ninth Surveys of State Aid, 1998, 2001

Table 13.6 *Ad hoc* aid to individual enterprises: country breakdown (million euro)

	1993–95		1997–99	
	Value	%	Value	%
Austria	–*		14	0.2
Belgium	30		8	0.1
Denmark	0	0.0	0	0.0
Germany	9 865	64.0	2 396	31.7
Greece	100	1.0	152	2.0
Finland	–*		1	
France	2 538	16.0	3 512	46.4
Ireland	75	0.7	0	
Italy	1 813	12.0	836	11.0
Luxembourg	0	0	0	0.0
Netherlands	40	0.4	75	1.0
Portugal	299	2.0	89	1.2
Spain	726	5.0	483	8.5
Sweden	–*		0	0.0
United Kingdom	0	0	0	0.0
EU	15 487	100	7 566	100

* Not then members.
Source: Compiled from Commission of the European Union, Seventh and Ninth Surveys of State Aid, 1999 and 2001

Table 13.7 State subsidy decisions by member state, 1997 and average 1999/2001

		(1) Total decisions	(2) Of which final negative	(3) Negative % total (col. 2/col. 1)	(4) Breakdown by country % (col. 1, %)
Austria	1997	32	1	3.1	6.4
	1999/2001	31	1	3.2	5.4
Belgium	1997	11	0	0.00	2.2
	1999/2001	30	3	10	5.3
Denmark	1997	16	1	6.2	3.2
	1999/2001	16	0	0.00	2.8
Finland	1997	8	0	0.00	1.6
	1999/2001	14	0	0.00	2.5
France	1997	38	1	2.6	7.6
	1999/2001	49	4	8.1	8.6
Germany	1997	194	4	2.1	38.6
	1999/2001	104	13	12.5	18.3
Greece	1997	5	0	0.0	1.0
	1999/2001	12	1	8.3	2.1
Ireland	1997	2	0	0.00	0.4
	1999/2001	18	0	0.00	0.00
Italy	1997	63	1	1.5	12.5
	1999/2001	88	12	13.6	15.5
Luxembourg	1997	1	0	0.00	0.2
	1999/2001	3	0	0.00	0.00
Netherlands	1997	33	0	0.0	6.6
	1999/2001	42	3	7.1	7.4
Portugal	1997	15	0	0.00	3.0
	1999/2001	16	1	6.2	2.8
Spain	1997	53	1	1.9	10.6
	1999/2001	102	8	7.8	18.0
Sweden	1997	10	0	0.00	2.0
	1999/2001	9	0	0.00	1.5
United Kingdom	1997	21	0	0.00	4.2
	1999/2001	33	0	0.00	5.8
Total or average	**1997**	**502**	**9**	**1.7**	**100.0**
	1999/2001	**567**	**46**	**8.0**	**100.0**

Source: Compiled from Commission of the European Union, 27th and 31st Reports on Competition Policy and Tableau de bord des aides d'état, Commission of the European Union (2002e) COM (2002) 242 final, p. 47

way the statistical surveys of state aid are structured (see below). We can see that it follows current thinking in allowing general aid and, in particular, aid to SMEs and R&D, although R&R and *ad hoc* aid remains a problem.

Tables 13.2 and 13.4 show that state aid has fallen steadily from 1981 to 2000 as a proportion of GDP (from 3% to 1.08% on average). All countries have participated in this trend, the most spectacular declines being registered by Italy (from 5.7% to 1.06%), Ireland (5.3% to 1.32%) and Belgium (4.1% to 1.38%), with most of the reductions taking place in the 1990s. This trend is doubtless due partly to the need for these countries to meet the public sector debt and deficit criteria for euro members, partly to the realization that public handouts often miss their mark, and partly to Commission and peer pressure. In any event, by 2000 all members had cut subsidies to well below 2% of GDP, and subsidies to manufacturing and service activities only (excluding agriculture and primary production) had fallen to 0.7%. This is a dramatic turnaround by comparison with the 1980s, but only time will tell if this downward trend will survive a major recession.

Another trend is to be found in the breakdown of state aid to manufacturing by objective (see Table 13.3). In its statistical surveys of state aid, the Commission distinguishes between 'horizontal' aid programmes, regional aid and 'sectoral' aid programmes (mainly aimed at traditional sectors in difficulty, such as steel, coal, shipyards, automobiles, etc.). Regional objectives, after rising to over 50% of total state aid have returned to 30% (see Chapter 22). Regional aid, as we have seen, is permitted under Article 87(c), and the Treaty of Rome as amended by the SEA in 1987. The Treaty of Amsterdam (1999) provides explicitly in Title XVII, Articles 158–162, for regional policies to promote social and economic cohesion throughout the Union. It is therefore logical that state spending should reflect this emphasis.

'Horizontal' aid has stabilized at between 30% and 40% of the total, while sectoral aid, which started with a very high share in 1980 (63%), fell to only 12% in the early 1990s, only to rise again to over 30% by 1998–2000. This suggests that traditional failing sectors can basically obtain government support on demand, under Commission supervision (see discussion on R&R aid above).

Table 13.4 charts the trend of state aid to the manufacturing sector on an annual basis from 1981

to 2000, for the EU as a whole. Although a direct comparison over time is to be avoided (for reasons such as inflation, changing EU membership, etc.), it is clear that the 23 billion euro spent on aid to manufacturing by 15 member states in 2000 represented much less than the annual average of 42 billion ECU spent by 10 member states in the period 1981–1986. This is amply borne out by the trend of subsidies as a whole, as a percentage of GDP, already noted in Table 13.2.

However, there is a tendency for member states to grant *ad hoc* aid outside any structured programme or authorized scheme (see Tables 13.5, 13.6). As the official publication *European Economy* puts it: 'Because such aids are concentrated on a small number of firms, often operating in oligopolistic markets, they present a danger of significant distortions of competition through rent shifting' (Vanhalewyn, 1999). A significant proportion of this *ad hoc* aid relates to the restructuring of East German industry ('Treuhand' aid) but this proportion is gradually falling. However, *ad hoc* aid *excluding* 'Treuhand' aid rose from 6% in 1992 to 24% of total aid in 1997, before falling back again in 1999. This aid, usually given to bankrupt firms in an emergency, lately in the banking, air transport and telecommunications sectors, is in principle incompatible with the competition rules of the EU and falls into the aforementioned category of micro-microeconomic industrial policy. These troubled service sectors are, in some countries, replacing steel, textiles and shipyards as the new 'lame ducks'.

This type of aid is particularly sensitive to the business cycle, and country shares vary accordingly. Germany seems to be finally emerging from a decade of massive 'Treuhand' aid. After spending an average of 6 billion euro a year on restructuring East German industry, the amount spent in 1999 was only 600 million euro. As a result, Germany's share of *ad hoc* aid fell from 64% in 1993–1995 to 46% in 1997–1999, while France's share rose from 16% to 46%. Italy and Spain remained steady at 12% and 8% respectively. During the years 1992 to 1999, of the five large economies in the Community, only the UK offered no *ad hoc* aid at all, in company with Denmark, Sweden and Luxembourg. All other members, at one time or another, had indulged in this type of micro-micro emergency aid.

Table 13.7 looks at the number of state subsidy *cases*, by country, for 1999–2001. These data are published annually in the Commission's *Reports on Competition Policy* and appear also in greater detail in the semestrial *Tableau de Bord des Aides d'Etat*. The

Table 13.8 Instruments of state aids, 1998–2000

	Average 1998–2000 (euros)	Percentage of total
Total aids to manufacturing sector	25 780.6	
Subsidies	16 271.4	63.1
Tax breaks	6 442.8	25.0
Re-capitalization	166.4	0.6
Subsidized loans	2 015.2	7.8
Tax deferral	157.7	0.6
Guarantees	726.9	2.8

Source: Compiled from Commission of the European Union, *Tableau de bord des aides d'état*, Commission of the European Union (2002e) COM (2002) 242 final, p. 47

'objections', to see which countries get into the most trouble with the Commission. There has been a clear upward trend in the rate of objections, from 2% in 1997 to 8% in 2001. Perhaps the Commission is getting tougher.

Table 13.8 looks at the instruments of state aid, from which it can be seen that subsidies are the preferred form (63%). Tax breaks account for 25%, and subsidized loans, loan guarantees and re-capitalization make up the remainder. Ireland stands out as giving most of its aid (75%) in the form of corporate tax breaks. The Commission has only recently attempted to discipline member states' in this area. In 2001 it launched a series of investigations into tax breaks for inward investment offered by Belgium, Ireland, Luxembourg, Portugal and the Netherlands. According to press reports, DG Comp agreed in 2003 to drop these investigations in exchange for (unanimous) agreement on common rules on the taxation of interest on savings, an interesting insight into how the Commission manages to optimize its different objectives (*Financial Times*, 14 February 2003, p. 1).

Table 13.9 looks at reimbursements of illegal state aid (requested, effectively reimbursed and outstanding) from 1982 to 1993. This is the final test of the effectiveness of the Commission in disciplining member

same countries crop up as being the sources of most of the cases examined by the Commission (Germany, Spain, Italy, France – and now Austria, which is not doing badly for its size). Column 3 looks at the rate of

Table 13.9 Reimbursements demanded by the Commission, 1982–1993 (million ECU)

	Amount	Reimbursed	Outstanding	Percentage reimbursed
Italy	566.46	0.00	566.46	0.00
Belgium	403.16	292.00	111.16	72.43
France	180.24	98.74	81.50	54.78
Netherlands	136.84	0.00	136.84	0.00
Spain	113.90	0.00	113.90	0.00
Germany	108.06	17.70	90.36	16.38
United Kingdom	59.39	57.89	1.50	97.47
Denmark	–	–	–	–
Greece	–	–	–	–
Ireland	–	–	–	–
Luxembourg	–	–	–	–
Portugal	–	–	–	–
EU	1568.05	466.33	1101.72	29.74

Source: Compiled from Commission of the European Communities, 23rd Report on Competition Policy, 1993, Annex II, pp. 484–6

Table 13.10 Outstanding demands for reimbursements, as of 2001 (inclusive)

	Amount (m euros)	No. of cases	Percentage amount
Germany	1156	30	46.15
Italy	1084	5	43.27
Spain	145	16	5.79
France	71	6	2.83
Belgium	40	6	1.60
Greece	8	1	0.32
United Kingdom	1	1	0.04
Total	2505	65	100.00

Source: Compiled from Table F (State Aids), 31st Report on Competition Policy (2001)

governments, and their willingness to submit to its authority. How successful has it been? We note that Italy is the main culprit: it not only heads the list of reimbursements demanded, but had (at the time of the survey) not enforced the reimbursement of any of the illegal aid given. The Netherlands and Spain were also noteworthy for not clawing back any of the aid which the Commission had determined was illegal. Belgium had given plenty of illegal aid, but had enforced reimbursement of 72% by the end of the period under consideration. Denmark, Greece, Ireland, Luxembourg and Portugal were all 'clean', having given no illegal aid at all. The UK had clawed back 97%.

Unfortunately, this information does not appear in subsequent reports, but a less detailed table can be derived from the cases listed at the end of the 31st Report on Competition Policy (2001) – see Table 13.10. Italy once more stands out as a major miscreant, but is joined this time by Germany. The Italian case is exceptional in that a single case (bank rescues) accounts

for 1 billion euros worth of aid deemed to be illegal by the Commission. The German cases almost all involve aid to individual firms in Eastern Germany. The total amount of outstanding reimbursements demanded by the Commission has risen from 1568 billion euros in 1993 to 2502 billion euros in 2001, which suggests that cases simply add up and seldom get resolved. Germany, Italy, France and Spain accounted for 98% of the sums due in 2001, and for 88% of the cases. Is it a coincidence that these are all large countries which the Commission finds hard to 'discipline'?

Conclusion

In conclusion, it may be said that state aid is gradually being brought under control, but most governments find it difficult to relinquish this instrument of policy. That France, Italy and Spain should appear at the head of the list is of no surprise, given their tradition of state intervention and 'indicative' planning, but they have radically reduced the absolute level of public aid. That Germany should frequently appear heading the same group is more surprising. Much of this is due to the reunification process, which has turned Germany into a more interventionist state. Thus, while France, Italy and Spain radically reduced their levels of intervention from a high initial starting point in 1981 (see Table 13.2), Germany started from a comparatively low point, maintained it through 1992–1994, dropping only towards the year 2000. The end result is that Germany now stands out as an interventionist member state, with one of the highest subsidization rates. The Commission still has problems enforcing discipline on member states, as Tables 10.8 and 10.9 suggest, but the overall level of state aid is declining. Time will tell whether this is a permanent improvement, or whether it will unravel in an economic downturn.

Or perhaps, to some extent, it may be that state aid at member state level has been replaced by aid at Community level. To this question we now turn.

13.4   Industrial policy in the EU: research and technological development

EU policy towards Research and Technological Development (R&TD) is inspired by the idea that Europe fails to realize its full scientific and technological potential because its research efforts are dispersed, expensive and given to wasteful duplication. Much is

made of the 'technology gap' which separates Europe from the United States and Japan, and the EU Commission regularly publishes depressing statistics on all aspects of this problem (CEC, 1994a, 1997a; CEU, 2002f). The answer, in the view of the Commission, is to create a 'European research area' by fostering long-term collaborative ventures between Community firms; between European firms and publicly funded research institutions; and between universities themselves, at a European level.

To this end, the EU uses two broad policy instruments: a dispensation from Article 81 (formerly Article 85) for R&TD collaborative agreements between large firms, and direct subsidies to encourage such agreements.

13.4.1 Competition aspects of policy on research and technological development

The Treaty of Rome makes express provision for cooperative R&TD within the private sector which 'contributes to improving the production or distribution of goods or to promoting technical or economic progress' (Article 81(3)). This is one of the principal exceptions to the blanket prohibition of agreements between undertakings laid down in Article 81(1). As early as 1968, the Commission established guidelines for the application of Article 81, which permitted agreements between firms (even large ones) for the exclusive purpose of developing joint R&D, provided the cooperation remained 'pre-competitive' (i.e. did not extend to actual production), and on condition that the results of the R&D were freely available to the members of the consortium, and preferably also to outsiders on a licensing basis (CEC, 1972, paras 31–32).

In December 1984 the Commission adopted a 'block exemption' for R&D agreements between firms which established a new, more favourable policy. Cooperative R&D schemes no longer had to be individually notified and could extend downstream to the joint exploitation of the results. This represented a considerable shift in policy for which European industry had been asking for some time, on the grounds that it made little sense to pool R&D efforts if, once they were successful, competition between the members of the pool wiped out all the potential monopolistic rents: under such circumstances, firms would prefer not to pool R&D resources at all, but take the risk of going it alone.

We saw earlier (in Sections 13.1 and 13.2) that the level of generality of industrial policy is an issue. We come across the problem again here. Thus, giving all firms, large and small, special dispensation from normal antitrust rules to permit long-term collaborative research agreements does not pre-judge the sectors which will avail themselves of the opportunity. It is therefore a truly *general* or macroeconomic industrial policy. Because it is so general, the EU, as we have just seen, after some arm-twisting, now allows the anti-trust dispensation to cover not only pre-competitive research, but also *technological development and marketing* of actual products. The general industrial policy thus risks becoming *specific* in its effect as the Commission exercises its discretion. Attentive readers will also have noted the innovation in terminology, from old-fashioned R&D to a more trendy 'R&TD'. Quite why the adjective 'technological' was thought useful has never been explained.

In terms of the policy pipeline described earlier, the competition policy arm of the EU R&TD policy goes all the way to the market place, and it can do so without attracting criticism as long as it is seen to act impartially.

However, the subsidy arm of the R&TD policy only goes as far as the 'pre-competitive' (i.e. pre-market) stage because, by its very nature, it is selective to start with. It cannot go all the way to supporting the market-based stage of developing prototypes without laying itself open to accusations that it is 'picking the winners'. These two branches of Community policy (antitrust dispensation and direct subsidies) enable a third, non-Community instrument of joint industrial policy – the 'Eureka' initiative – to flourish under the benign dispensation from the European antitrust authorities, *and with financial support from member states*, which is the level at which 'picking the winners' takes place (see Table 13.3, Section 13.3 above and the discussion of 'sectoral' subsidies). Thus selective support for R&TD at national level is permitted by the Commission as long as it involves agreements between firms from two or more member countries. As such, it promotes the 'ever-closer union among the peoples of Europe' which is the over-riding political objective of the EU.

13.4.2 European subsidies to research and technological development

Despite the obvious advantages of pooling R&D efforts at a European level (as compared with strictly national support for R&D), the Treaty of Rome does not mention joint European technology policy and it has taken many years to develop one.

Member states have long been hesitant to relinquish their prerogatives. Industrial policy based on subsidizing 'sunrise' sectors, after all, was the last remaining area in which they might still exercise some national policy of their own. However, their experience at pooling research efforts in the nuclear field have not been happy (Guzzetti, 1995). France under President de Gaulle was not inclined to share the results of French nuclear research, so Germany, Italy and the Netherlands used American technology when developing their nuclear reactors. By 2000, all that remained was a recognized European presence in nuclear fission research and a distant (and very expensive) experimental technology aimed at producing pollution-free energy from smashing atoms in huge cyclotrons (CERN).

However, this had very little to do with what, over the years, has become a major worry: Europe's declining 'competitiveness' in commercially useful high technology.

The origins of EU technology policy lie in the disastrous state of the European economy after the two oil price increases of the 1970s. By contrast, both the United States and Japan shook off the negative effects quickly. At the same time that Viscount Davignon was organizing 'crisis cartels' in declining industries (see Section 13.3), he also was trying to drum up support for a programme to help 'sunrise' industries. He believed that there was a case for European high-technology firms to pool their R&D efforts, to avoid useless duplication and to benefit from trans-European synergies. Following Servan-Schreiber (1967), he and others were upset by the tendency of European firms to form technological alliances, if at all, with American or Japanese partners, rather than with fellow Europeans.

During 1979–1980 Davignon invited the heads of Europe's biggest electronics and information technology companies[3] to participate in a set of 'round table' discussions to see if there was any appetite for joint R&D projects among them. The response was not overwhelming, but gradually a strategy emerged which involved linking universities, research institutes, the major European companies and some SMEs in an effort to narrow the 'technology gap' which had opened up between Europe and the United States in the area of electronics and information technology. A pilot proposal was prepared in 1980, approved by the Council in 1981 and given funding of 11.5 million ECU in 1982 (Peterson and Sharp, 1998, pp. 70–71). Davignon's strategy of involving from the very start 12 major European firms, which then lobbied their respective

governments to support the scheme, had paid off. The rest, as the saying goes, is history. Today, 20 years later, the EU spends approximately 4.5 million euros a year on R&TD.

The ESPRIT programme (acronym for European Programme for Research in Information Technology), proposed by the Commission in May 1983 and adopted unanimously by the Council in February 1984, proved hugely popular with industry. It provided 750 million ECU of Community funding over the period 1984–1988, matched ECU for ECU by private funding from the participating companies. Calls for research proposals produced over 900 projects, only 240 of which were finally approved, after consultation with the round table representatives.

Other sectoral support programmes soon followed. Davignon and his advisers had noticed that the European telecommunications industry was in danger of slipping well behind that of the USA and Japan. Not only did both these countries offer a far larger domestic market to their telecoms hardware producers, but the United States was in the process of deregulating AT&T, introducing competition and new electronic technologies into an industry which, in Europe, was dominated by entrenched public monopolies, the famous PTTs (combined postal, telegraph and telephone services). Each country's market was, in fact, a bilateral monopoly: a single public-sector buyer (not accountable to shareholders in a competitive capital market), and a single (highly protected) private-sector supplier. Breaking this system up and forging a 'single market' in telecommunications, with firms accountable in the normal way to market-based shareholders, is one of the Commission's major achievements.

The pilot phase of Research in Advanced Communications for Europe (RACE) was launched in 1985 with a small budget of 21 million ECU, and a much larger programme followed in 1989: RACE I ran from 1990 to 1994 with a budget of 460 million ECU; RACE II ran from 1992 to 1994 with a budget of 489 million ECU. In the meantime, the Commission sponsored research in developing European standards in the area of telecommunications (establishing the European Telecommunications Standards Institute – ETSI) and broke open the old PTT monopolies with the 'open network provision' as part of the single market programme. The PTTs and their local suppliers viewed all this activism with little enthusiasm and the Commission, in desperation at the foot-dragging it encountered, in 1988 declared that

PTTs were subject to Article 86 (formerly Article 90). This Article states:

> In the case of public undertakings and undertakings to which Member States grant special or exclusive rights, Member States shall neither enact nor maintain in force any measure contrary to the rules contained in this Treaty.

After a protracted battle, the European Court of Justice agreed that Article 86 was directly applicable and endorsed the Commission's directive on opening up members' markets for telecommunication terminal equipment.[4]

Other important sectors were targeted in the same way. Thus Basic Research in Technologies/Advanced Materials for Europe (BRITE/EURAM) was launched with a 100 million ECU pilot phase in 1985–1988, followed by two major programmes with budgets of 450 million ECU and 660 million ECU running from 1986 to 1992.

Smaller programmes can only be mentioned by their acronyms (see Table 13.11 and List of abbreviations on pp. xxi and xxiv).

In short, by the late 1980s European technology policy had been well and truly launched. In this it was helped by the Single European Act (1987) which for the first time gave the Community a legal basis for all these schemes. A new title VI entitled 'Research and technological development' (R&TD) was added (Articles 163–173 – formerly 130(F) – 130(Q)) gave the Community a new aim: 'to strengthen the scientific and technological bases of Community industry and to encourage it to become more competitive at international level'. To achieve this end, the

Community decided to 'adopt a multiannual framework programme setting out all its activities' (Article 166). While decisions relating to establishing the budget of the multiannual framework programme (MFP) were to be taken unanimously by the Council on a proposal from the Commission and after consulting the European Parliament (EP), decisions on its implementation through specific programmes and detailed arrangements were to be taken by the Council by qualified majority voting in cooperation with the EP. The provisions requiring both unanimity in the Council *and* consultation of the EP in the first phase of the MFP, as well as the need, in the second stage, to obtain Council *and* EP approval for individual research projects, proved to be politically fraught, contentious and time consuming (Peterson and Sharp, 1998, pp. 172–173). For this reason the Treaty of Nice provides for qualified majority voting and consultation of the EP under Article 251 for the first and subsequent stages of the decision-making process (Article 166).

Another Maastricht Treaty innovation was to add a qualifying phrase to Article 163 to the effect that Community R&TD policies, besides strengthening the scientific and technological bases of Community industry and encouraging it to become more competitive at international level, should also promote 'all the research activities deemed necessary by virtue of other Chapters of this Treaty'. This allows for R&TD which is not directly concerned with competitiveness of European industry, such as basic science, or research connected with social objectives. This modification, though modest in appearance, in fact represents a very great shift in Community R&TD policy. Whereas before it was focused entirely on making European industry more competitive, it is now diffused across the entire range of Community objectives, such as regional and social cohesion, quality of life, the environment, etc. This is clear from the evolution of the 5th and 6th framework programmes by comparison with previous ones (see Table 13.12). Not only has the share devoted to industrial technologies dropped spectacularly, but also even the 'user-friendly information society' has suffered a cut from almost 40% to only 20% of the budget, while 'energy, environment and sustainable growth' has dropped from 50% to only 12% (despite the expansion of the category to include the ever-fashionable 'sustainable growth'). On the other hand, 'other' programmes have risen from 2% to over 30%. The 6th MFP contains some 30 headings which it would be tedious to reproduce,

Table 13.11 Various R&TD programmes subsequently integrated into the multiannual framework programmes

	Budget (million ECU)	Years
BAP	75	1985–1989
BRIDGE	100	1989–1993
ÉCLAIR	80	1989–1994
FLAIR	25	1989–1994
COMETT	230	1987–1994

Source: Peterson and Sharp (1998), pp. 74–75. Reproduced with permission of Palgrave Macmillan

Table 13.12 Aims of EU R&TD multiannual framework programmes: trends from 1984 to 2006 (%)

	MFP 1 1984–1987	MFP 2 1987–1991	MFP 3 1990–1994	MFP 4 1994–1998	MFP 5 1998–2002	MFP 6 2002–2006
Information and communications (*Now* 'User-friendly information society')	25	42	38	28	24	20.7
Industrial technologies (*Now* 'Competitive and sustainable growth')	11	16	15	16	18.1	6.2
Environment (*Now* included under Energy)	7	6	9	9		
Life sciences (*Now* 'Quality of life and management of living resources')	5	7	10	13	16.1	16.8
Energy (*Now* 'Energy, environment and sustainable growth')	50	22	16	18	22.6	12.1
New						
Training, mobility, human capital				6	8.6	9.0
Governance, SMEs				2.4	2.4	3.7
Other	2	7	12	16	24.3	31.4
Total (million ECU/euro)	3 750	5 396	6 600	13 100	14 960	17 500
Share of total EU government appropriations for RD	2.5	3.7	4.8	5.5	5.4	

Sources: Compiled from Commission of the European Communities, *The European Report on Science and Technology Indicators 1994* (DGXII, Luxembourg, 1994); Commission of the European Union, *Annual Report on Research and Technological Development Activities of the European Union 1999* COM (99) 284 final. For 6th MFP see Decision no. 1513/2002/CE of the European Parliament and OJ L 232 29/08/02. Last line: Commission of the European Union (2002f), *Towards a European Research Area, Science, Technology and Innovation, Key Figures 2002*, Official publications of the European Communities, Luxembourg, p. 20

but a few examples may provide the flavour: 'Policy support and anticipating scientific and technological needs' sounds promising, as do 'Citizens and governance in a knowledge-based society', 'Specific actions covering a wider field of research' and 'Sustainable surface transport', among many others. SMEs receive special attention, possibly in response to a desire to foster industrial agglomerations (see Section 13.2.4). Attentive readers will note the proliferation of trendy titles under whichever larger sums of money are devoted to deserving projects and may be forgiven for wondering if this is not a gravy train in full flood.

The Maastricht Treaty added a new title called 'Industry' (Article 157, formerly 130), in which the Community was given a broad mandate to promote the competitiveness of European industry by improving its ability to adjust to structural change, encourage SMEs, favour cooperation between enterprises and increase the effectiveness of the Community's R&TD policies by promoting their dissemination. Decisions, if any, were to be taken unanimously. This Article was the result of a compromise between those countries which wanted the EU to possess a clear mandate to develop a fully-fledged industrial policy, and those which did not. The Treaty of Nice submits 'Industry' to the 'Article 251 procedure', namely the complicated shuttle between Council, Commission and Parliament, based on qualified majority voting (see Chapter 3). It is too soon to tell whether the Commission will use this article to promote a European industrial policy. For the time being the Commission finds it more convenient to pursue these aims under the more familiar R&TD Title, but it will surely respond in due course to the invitation contained in Article 157.2 to 'take any useful initiative to promote such coordination' in order to promote 'the competitiveness of the Community's industry', in line with the much-trumpeted 'Lisbon objective' to make Europe 'the most competitive and dynamic knowledge-based economy in the world' by 2010. One could say that with the Treaty of Nice, industrial policy at Community level has finally 'arrived'.

Tables 13.12 and 13.13 chart the evolution of the MFPs from their inception. Over the years total EU funding of R&TD has risen from zero in 1982 to over 4% of the budget for the 6th MFP, which runs from 2002 to 2006. The annual sums involved, currently some 4 500 million euro a year, are 5.4% of national state R&D expenditure (see Table 13.12), which itself is running at 164 billion euros, or 2% of EU GDP (Commission of the European Union (2002f), *Key Figures 2002*, p. 15). This is a big change from the first MFP, when Community expenditure on R&TD represented only 2.5% of national R&D budgets, and 2.4% of the Community budget. The trend is something of a political triumph for the Commission, given the great opposition on the part of many member states to transferring any industrial policy mandate to Brussels whatsoever.

This expenditure growth on R&D has gone hand in hand with a decline in selective state aid (see Tables 13.2 and 13.3), from which we can conclude that there has been a shift of emphasis away from supporting 'sunset' industries and firms, to supporting 'sunrise' sectors. Where the balance actually lies, however, is impossible to determine without much greater statistical detail than is provided by official EU data.

13.4.3 Non-EU technological cooperation

No account of European industrial policy would be complete without a brief description of the Eureka (European Research Co-ordinating Agency) programme. Variable geometry applies in the field of industrial policy. In 1985 President Mitterrand of France launched the Eureka programme. He was clearly frustrated with the lack of anything resembling EU industrial policy, and alarmed at the implications of President Reagan's 'Star Wars' or Strategic Defence Initiative (SDI). This was scheduled to spend $26 billion on advanced electronic, nuclear and space technology, and threatened to siphon off the best European intellectual talent in these areas. President Mitterrand gathered together the then 12 members of the European Community, plus Spain, Portugal, Turkey, the EFTA countries and the European Commission, and founded an intergovernmental organization with a secretariat in Paris. Today Eureka has 34 members and sponsors some 700 projects, involving 1.3 billion euros of R&D effort, not all of it state-funded (see Eureka website).

Its purpose is to promote, through public subsidies, any 'near market' R&D project involving firms in more than one member country. It possesses no central allocative function. Projects are generated in member states and circulated among members to see if other firms or governments might like to join. The Eureka secretariat simply keeps track of what is going on. It has no 'policy' as such and therefore fits the definition of a general or macroeconomic industrial policy (although individual projects are obviously the outcome of individual governments' different industrial policies). Any attempt to define an overall objective would have foundered anyway, given Eureka's intergovernmental structure and the fact that member states are free to give the Eureka 'label' to whatever project they consider fits the bill (Peterson and Sharp, 1998, p. 92). The only organizing principle is that projects must involve more than one country and in principle should promote the *development* phase of R&D

Table 13.13 Annual R&TD expenditures at Community level, 1984–2006 (million ECU and million euro, current prices)

Year	Annual expenditure						
1984	593.0	MFP 1					
1985	735.0	MFP 1					
1986	874.0	MFP 1					
1987	939.3	MFP 1	MFP 2				
1988	1 128.0	MFP 1	MFP 2				
1989	1 412.2		MFP 2				
1990	1 784.4		MFP 2	MFP 3			
1991	1 887.4		MFP 2	MFP 3			
1992	2 863.2			MFP 3			
1993	2 691.2			MFP 3			
1994	2 753.5			MFP 3	MFP 4		
1995	2 985.8				MFP 4		
1996	3 153.5				MFP 4		
1997	3 485.6				MFP 4		
1998	3 499.3				MFP 4	MFP 5	
1999	3 450.0					MFP 5	
2000	3 600.0					MFP 5	
2001	3 900.0					MFP 5	
2002	4 010.0					MFP 5	MFP 6
2002–2006	4 × 4 375						MFP 6
Grand total 1984–2006	63 245						
Community budget %		2.42	3.18	4.05	4.00	3.73	4.0–4.3

Source: Compiled from Commission of the European Union, *Annual Report on Research and Technological Development Activities of the European Union 1999*, Brussels, COM (99) 284 final, Table 10 and Commission of the European Union (2002f), *Towards a European Research Area, Science, Technology and Innovation, Key Figures 2002*, Official publications of the European Communities, Luxembourg, p. 20

(so as to comply with EU competition rules – see Section 13.4.1 above). According to Peterson and Sharp, Eureka in the early 1990s represented 'a total research effort only marginally smaller than the Framework programme' (p. 90). This is no longer true today, partly because of the expansion of the MFPs, but also because the Eureka projects also seem to attract less attention. Unlike the EU itself, Eureka opened its arms to Central and Eastern Europe and beyond to Russia, in the 1990s. It has welcomed non-member observers, from the US government to the Vatican City.

After starting off with two *grands projets* which absorbed large amounts of public money (the ill-fated HDTV project and the more successful Joint European Submicron Silicon Initiative – JESSI), Eureka has settled down to sponsoring an ever-larger number of smaller research projects.[5] By so doing, it substantially increases the chances of 'stumbling on winners', and decreases the incidence of R&D disasters, but it no longer hits the headlines.

Eureka coincided with the launching of the Commission's own proposal for an expanded role in R&D

(see above) and was viewed with deep suspicion in Brussels. Meanwhile, Germany under Chancellor Kohl was torn between accepting participation in the American SDI programme and teaming up with France and President Mitterrand. In the end, the Franco-German axis withstood the strain and Eureka survived.

The ostensible division of labour between the two was that the EU should devote its energies to 'precompetitive' R&TD (essentially research and technology), while Eureka should sponsor 'near-market' development (R&D). The Commission retains its overarching supervisory function. As we have already seen, it has long taken a favourable view of state aid to R&D, but in 1986 insisted on the 'notification' of any aid in excess of 20 million ECU (see Section 13.2 above), the timing of which suggested a negative institutional reaction to the Eureka programme. In 1996 the Commission issued a new set of guidelines for state aid to R&D[6] to bring Community practice into line with new WTO obligations. In particular, the Commission highlighted the distinction between WTO-compatible support for R&D (squarely in the pre-competitive box) and illegal R&D support (aid to the commercial introduction of industrial innovations or the marketing of new products). This left very little space between the Commission's own 'pre-competitive' MFPs, and the 'near-market' Eureka projects. The battle for turf continues. The only concession to Eureka projects made by the Commission was to increase the notification threshold to 40 million ECU in 1996 (but it has never challenged a Eureka project in practice).

The Commission, overwhelmed by the caseload all this had generated, made a strategic withdrawal in 1998 when it decided to sponsor a new Council regulation to grant group exemptions, *inter alia*, for R&D state aid.[7]

While there is clearly some overlap between Eureka and the EU MFPs, there is also plenty of complementarity. At least theoretically, a project sponsored by the EU at the top end of the R&TD pipeline could be taken up by a Eureka project at the lower end of the process. But one sees little or no mention of Eureka in the official Commission literature. In short, Mitterrand's Eureka failed to become the spearhead for massive government-sponsored R&D projects in clear opposition to the EU attempts to coordinate R&D at a European level.

The Lisbon European Council in 2000 set the goal to make Europe 'the most competitive and dynamic knowledge-based-economy in the world' by 2010 – a laudable but unverifiable and probably unattainable objective. Obtaining more funds to spend for the 6th MFP was one result. Another was the creation of the 'European Research Area', or ERA, which aims at a better coordination of European research efforts. The Commission's contribution to this effort is 'benchmarking of national research polices', which studies, compares and evaluates individual member state R&D policies, in an elusive search for 'best practices'. Ultimately the aim is

> . . . a range of linked policies that attempt to coordinate European research and facilitate the research policies of the individual Member States . . . The combination of national research and Community-level collaborative work should improve European research capabilities and overall make research more strategic.
> (*Key Figures CEU 2002f*, p. 8)

Coordinating research in order to prevent overlap is a favourite rationalist panacea to make limited research funds go further. It overlooks the paradoxical fact that independent, non-coordinated research scans a far broader area of the unknown and is more likely to stumble on solutions than so-called 'strategic' approaches. However, if spending more money on trying to make national R&D policies 'strategic' is difficult to justify in terms of generating extra innovation, one can quite understand why the Commission should be making a bid to supervise and coordinate the 164 billion euros a year spent on R&D by member states in terms of public choice theory.

13.5   Conclusion

The EU industrial policy has come a long way since the Commission first sponsored 'crisis cartels' in the 1970s. Thanks to the Commission's policies, the EU has shifted, slowly but surely, away from supporting 'sunset' sectors to sponsoring 'sunrise' industries. The Commission has been unfailingly critical of member states' *ad hoc* subsidies to individual firms and is managing to claw back a certain proportion of illegal aid. It is correct in preferring 'horizontal' to 'sectoral' aid. However, while its battle to contain selective state aid has been commendable, and at least partly successful, it is not clear that the same can be said of its own programme for R&TD. That it has launched this programme successfully in the teeth of member state opposition is incontrovertible. It has tried hard to avoid the trap of 'picking the winners' by supporting only 'pre-competitive' R&TD. But the fact remains that firms are the principal beneficiaries of these projects and that micro-micro selection is inevitable. Such huge sums of money being managed by even the most honest bureaucracy are bound to end up being poorly allocated.

There are by now countless evaluations of all these efforts to support innovation in Europe, all of which are globally positive while pointing out some of the obvious deficiencies. Academic sources are naturally more critical, and emphasize problems such as the eternal *juste retour*, the inevitable politicization of the R&TD funding process,[8] holding private beneficiaries to account,[9] and so on. Looking back over the last 15 years, with an accumulated R&TD expenditure of 63 billion euros at EU level, and much more at member state level, who can tell where European industry would have been today without it? The HDTV experiment was a fiasco,[10] but clearly support for telecommunications research has paid off, since the European global mobile telephone system (GSM) has proved to be a huge commercial success, and some of this success is perhaps attributable to the ESPRIT and BRITE programmes (and their successors). The fact is that no one will ever know what the anti-monde would have looked like. If half the effort that went into R&TD had been devoted to creating pro-entrepreneurial and pro-market *institutions*, the European economy might today be more dynamic. But who can tell? One can only say that the sums are huge, the opportunity costs are enormous, and the probability of a massive improvement on what markets would have achieved is small. It is possible that it is all a great waste of money.

Looking to the future, it is clear that support for R&TD at European level (and perhaps also at member state level) will become more and more involved with aims which have nothing to do with the competitiveness of European firms. Since the Maastricht Treaty, R&TD is supposed to serve any and all of the EU many objectives. Is this to be welcomed or deplored? One suspects that the lack of focus will open the doors to plenty of nonsense.

Some obvious improvements can be suggested. First, the EU lacks a common 'European Institute of Technology', like MIT or Imperial College. It needs a post-graduate European institute of higher scientific learning, in order to promote basic research, to attract the best of its young graduates and provide an extra tier to the European academic career ladder. At present, far too many young Europeans go to the United States for their doctoral and post-doctoral research, never to return. Money spent at the top end of the R&TD pipeline, farthest away from the market place, is probably by far the most effective in the long run.

Second, the multi-annual framework programmes must encourage links with firms from non-EU countries, not only current applicants and future candidates as is already the case, but also with American, Japanese or *any* firms, from any country at all. There should be an end to the idea that R&D should carry the burden of 'building Europe'. Europe is pretty well 'built' by now, and can well afford to set its technological community free to seek partnerships wherever they happen to be the most fruitful. Discriminating between European and non-European firms cannot possibly promote efficiency.

Third, given that R&D resources managed at Community level are likely to become increasingly misallocated and wasted, the steady growth of the MFP budget over time (see Table 13.13) should be halted and probably reversed.

Finally, the Commission, as guardian of the competition rules, cannot allow member states to get away with flouting its guidelines and decisions. As the Community enlarges to 25 members (see Chapter 26), of which none of the new members has a free market tradition, its task will increase enormously. Each country, individually, would like to break the rules – providing all other countries abide by them. If all follow their inclinations, the Economic Community will collapse. The battles ahead are likely to be interesting.

1. An astonishing example along the same lines was provided by the *Financial Times* in a story entitled 'Police to hire investigators for company fraud cases' (1 March 2000, p. 7). After contracting out the task of running prisons, the British police are now extending the concept to detective work. What next? Presumably the taxpayer benefits from unbundling police work and using markets instead of hierarchies to deliver this complex set of services.

2. Council Regulation (EC) 994/98 on the application of Articles 87 and 88 of the EC Treaty to certain categories of horizontal state aid.

3. The Round Table of industrialists (also known as the 'Big 12') brought together by Viscount Davignon in 1982 was composed of the chief executives of the following companies: for Germany: AEG, Nixdorf and Siemens; for France: Bull, CGE-Alcatel and Thomson; for the UK: GEC, ICL and Plessey; for Italy: Olivetti and STET; and for the Netherlands: Philips. This influential group is credited not only with supporting the EU R&TD policy, but also with backing Eureka (see Section 13.4.3) and with shaping much official policy in this area. In turn the group is suspected of being among the principal beneficiaries.

4. *France* v. *Commission*, Case C-202/88, ECJ decision of 19 March 1991.

5. See *Eureka News* and consult the Eureka website for information.

6. 'Community framework for state aid for research and development', OJ C 405 17/2/96, pp. 0005–0014.

7. Council Regulation 994/98 on the application of Articles 87 and 88 of the EC Treaty to certain categories of horizontal state aid [1998] OJ L142, 14/5/1998.

8. Peterson and Sharp, 1998, provide an excellent and balanced account.

9. The European Court of Auditors (Annual Report, 1995) C 340 12/11/96, Chapter 12, complained that the Commission audited only 60 contracts out of 13 500 in 1995 (recovering 9 million ECU in the process), while its own audit of eight projects revealed 'grave anomalies' in each and every one! The problems became public in 2002 with the dismissal of Ms Marta Andreasen, chief accountant, who tried to alert the public to faulty accounting practices in the Commission.

10. See Court of Auditors, *op. cit.*, paras 9.12–9.49.

Chapter 14

Tax harmonization

BRIAN ARDY AND ALI EL-AGRAA

Tax harmonization has turned out to be a very thorny issue for the EU: witness the vehement utterances during 1988 and 1989 by Margaret Thatcher, the British Prime Minister, and by both Helmut Kohl, the German Chancellor, and Jacques Delors, President of the Commission, when she flatly declared that tax harmonization was not EU business, only to hear the other two announce that it was indispensable for EU integration. Such a bold statement cannot be treated lightly since tax harmonization remains one of the few areas where new EU legislation requires unanimity; hence a single EU member nation can frustrate any new initiatives within this domain. The purpose of this chapter is to clarify what tax harmonization means, to consider to what extent it is necessary for the EU, before going on to assess the progress the EU has achieved in this field.

14.1 Why is tax harmonization necessary?

The Government plays a very important role in modern economies: in 2000 tax revenue accounted for 41.6% of EU GDP.[1] Usually tax and government expenditure is primarily the responsibility of the highest tier of government, the federal or central government. As is demonstrated in Chapter 19, this is not the case in the EU, since the member states control most tax revenue and are responsible for most government expenditure. This makes the EU unusual because there is a large variation of taxes and government expenditure in a single market.[2]

There are two basic types of taxation: direct and indirect. Direct taxes, such as income and corporation taxes, are levied on wages and salaries (income taxes), or on the profits of industrial or professional businesses (corporation taxes). Direct taxes are not intended to affect the price of commodities or professional services.[3] Indirect taxes are levied specifically on consumption and are, therefore, in a simplistic model, significant in determining the pricing of commodities, given their real costs of production.

Taxes (and equivalent instruments) have similar effects to tariffs on the international flow of goods and services – they are non-tariff distortions of international trade (generally referred to as non-tariff trade barriers, NTBs – see Baldwin (1971) and Chapter 8). Other elements have also been recognized as operating similar distortions on the international flow of factors of production (Bhagwati, 1969; Johnson, 1965a, 1973). In the particular context of the EU, it should be remembered that its formation, at least from the economic viewpoint, was meant to facilitate the free and unimpeded flow between the member nations of goods, persons, services, and capital, the four freedoms, and the other elements discussed in Chapter 1. Since tariffs are not the only distorting factor in this respect, the proper establishment of intra-EU free trade necessitates the removal of all non-tariff distortions that have an equivalent effect. The removal of tariffs does not even establish free trade inside the EU, since the existence of sales taxes, excise duties, corporation taxes, income taxes, etc. may impede this freedom. Similarly, the free movement of persons, services and capital can be influenced by differences in tax systems.

The other reason for tax harmonization is that the ability of national tax systems to raise revenues, and the efficiency effects which they have, are affected by the tax regimes in the other member states of the single market. For example, the revenue from tobacco taxation will depend upon the rates of taxation in neighbouring countries. Thus there can be positive or negative spillovers/externalities between member states' tax systems. The movement of factors of production can be influenced by government tax and expenditure policies. The administrative and compliance costs for the government and taxpayers may be affected, and the ability of national governments to pursue redistributive policies is constrained. Tax harmonization in the EU is the alignment of tax bases, rules and rates to reduce the harmful interactions between different member states tax systems.[4]

14.2 The principles of tax harmonization

Three criteria should inform tax harmonization: *jurisdiction, distortion* and *enforcement*.

Jurisdiction relates to the determination of who should receive the revenue from a particular tax. With EU taxation tightly controlled, member states are the jurisdiction for the overwhelming majority of tax revenue, but this sovereignty has to be pooled for the effective operation of national tax systems in a single market. Transparency is required with clear definitions of tax bases and regulations. The operational independence of national tax systems should be possible within agreed rules; cooperation and information exchange should not be part of the day-to-day operation of the tax system. The clearest example of the jurisdictional principle applies to consumption taxes and the choice between the destination and origin principles. With the *destination principle* the revenue goes to the country of final sale. To achieve this, exports are tax free and imports are taxed at the local rate; this was achieved before the single market with customs borders between member states. Under the *origin principle* revenue is received by each state involved in proportion to its share of value added; roughly speaking exports are taxed but imports are not. Labour taxes are usually paid in the country of *residence*, which is normally the same as the *source* country where the income is earned. Income from capital is taxed at source as in the case of corporation tax, but investment income is also subject to residence-based tax. Where more than one tax jurisdiction is involved the interaction between national tax systems becomes important.

Distortion concerns the avoidance of tax-induced inefficiency in the operation of the internal market. Spillover/externalities can occur as a result of the operation of tax systems. The most common externality is the result of tax competition, which will tend to lead to lower tax rates, because governments fear the loss of the tax base to countries with lower rates. This will reduce tax revenues overall and increase the marginal cost of public funds.[5] Tax competition encourages the taxation of less mobile tax bases and may cause lower provision of government services. Whether this is a problem is debatable; it can be argued that tax competition acts as a necessary discipline on government fiscal profligacy.

The extent of the problem of distortion depends upon the type and rate of tax. It is possible to argue that with a general consumption tax, the use of the origin or destination principle has no effect on real trade and investment, because of the equivalence theorem (Tinbergen, 1953). The requirements for equivalence are onerous: the consumption tax must be comprehensive, at a uniform rate and trade must initially be balanced (Lockwood *et al.*, 1994). Differences in tax bases and rates can distort consumer and producer choices; thus reduce market efficiency. There are particular problems with excises on products such as alcohol and tobacco with enormous differences in rates. Tax competition is not a significant problem with labour taxation because of the very low degree of international mobility in the EU[6] (Braunerhjelm *et al.*, 2000, pp. 46–59). High tax countries would also tend to offer a higher provision of public services, offsetting the higher taxes. The high mobility of capital, especially in a monetary union, means that owners of capital will move theirs to where taxation is lowest. This process will continue until differences in the return on capital offset differences in taxation and returns on immovable factors, labour and land are accordingly depressed.

Enforcement is about the ability to ensure that the agreed rules apply in practice. Large differences in excise taxes on cigarettes are difficult to enforce in the absence of borders. Taxes on labour are usually withheld by employers at source and so are relatively easy to enforce. Capital income taxation poses particular enforcement problems. If the tax is based on the source of the income, this requires separate national accounting for each member state, but this is not possible for multinational corporations, so unsatisfactory *ad hoc* arrangements are necessary. The location of profits can also be shifted by the manipulation of transfer prices.[7] Taxes based on residence also face problems associated with the need to allow for taxes paid elsewhere.

Tax independence within the EU necessitates a significant degree of tax coordination to ensure the effective operation of tax systems. The analysis now turns to the development of the EU's tax harmonization policies.

14.3   The EU's experience of tax harmonization

At the inception of the EEC in 1957, there were wide differences in tax levels and tax rates, a problem particularly acute in relation to consumption taxes. Four types of sales, or turnover, taxes operated in Western Europe (Dosser, 1973; Paxton, 1976): the *cumulative multi-stage cascade system* (operated in West Germany, Luxembourg and the Netherlands) in which the tax was levied on the gross value of the commodity at each and every stage of production without any rebate on taxes paid at earlier stages; *value added tax* (VAT), which has operated in France since 1954 where it is known as TVA – *Taxe sur la Valeur Ajoutée* – the tax is levied at each stage of production as the value of sales as a percentage of the selling price less tax levied at earlier stages of production;[8] *mixed* systems (operated in Belgium and Italy) were cumulative multi-stage systems down to the wholesale stage, but taxes which applied to a single stage of production were applied to certain products; finally, *purchase tax* (operated in the United Kingdom) was a single-stage tax normally charged at the wholesale stage by registered manufacturers or wholesalers, which meant that manufacturers could trade with each other without paying tax.

Although all these tax systems had a common treatment of trade with no tax paid on exports, and tax levied on imports at the point of entry, the cumulative systems involved distortions. Since the amount of tax in cumulative systems varied with the number of transactions in the supply chain, the precise amount of tax to be remitted on exports could not be calculated accurately, nor could the tax on imports; this meant these taxes could be used as NTBs.[9]

A variety of taxes also existed in the form of excise duties, justified by information failures[10] or externalities,[11] but their main purpose is to raise revenue for the government by taxing goods with inelastic demand. The number of commodities subjected to these duties ranged from the usual (or 'classical') five: tobacco products, hydrocarbon oils, beer, wine and spirits; to an extensive number of other products including coffee, sugar, salt, matches, etc. The means by which the governments collected revenue from excise duties ranged from government-controlled manufacturing, e.g. tobacco goods in France and Italy, to fiscal imposts based on value, weight, strength, quality, etc. (Dosser, 1973, p. 2).

For the taxation of company profits, three basic schemes of corporation tax existed, and still exist in a slightly disguised form today. The first is the *separate* system, which was used in the United Kingdom; this calls for the complete separation of corporation tax from personal income tax and is usually referred to as the 'classical' system. The second is the *two-rate* or *split-rate* system that was the German practice. The third is the *credit* or *imputation* system which gives shareholders credit for tax paid by the company, the part of the company's tax liability 'imputed' to the shareholders is regarded as a prepayment of their income tax on dividends; this was the French system and was adopted in the United Kingdom in 1973 (Kay and King, 1996).

14.3.1 From the EEC Treaty (1958) to the internal market (1985)

In the EEC Treaty Articles 95–99 tax harmonization is solely concerned with indirect taxes. Harmonization here was seen as vital, to prevent indirect taxes acting as NTBs on intra-EU trade. However, the Treaty only required harmonization necessary to ensure the establishment and functioning of the internal market and put very little stress on the harmonization of the EEC's initial tax diversity. Thus the Treaty is rather vague about what it means by harmonization; this is the norm however: the Treaty lays down the objective but further negotiations lead to detailed legislation. Given the technical nature of the issues, the whole development of tax harmonization during this period was influenced by the work of special committees, informal discussions, etc., i.e. the procedure detailed in Chapter 2. This, however, should not be interpreted as a criticism of those who drafted the Treaty. On the contrary, given the very complex nature of the subject and its closeness to the issue of national sovereignty, it would have been shortsighted to do otherwise.

In the area of indirect taxation, most of the developments were in terms of VAT, which the EU adopted as its turnover tax following the recommendations of the Neumark Committee in 1963, which was in turn based on the Tinbergen study of 1953 (Tinbergen, 1953). Between 1967 and 1977, six directives were issued with the aim of achieving conformity between the different practices of the member countries. These related to: the adoption of VAT as the EU sales tax; the use of VAT for the EU general budget (see Chapter 19); the achievement of a harmonized VAT base.[12]

Having chosen the tax and the tax base, the EEC had to decide on the tax jurisdiction; it had to opt for either the 'destination' or 'origin' principle. Taxation under the destination principle specifies that tax revenue would be attributable to the country of their final purchase. For example, if the UK levies VAT at 8% and France a similar tax at 16%, a commodity exported from the United Kingdom to France would be exempt from the United Kingdom's 8% tax but would be subjected to France's 16% tax. Hence, France would collect the tax revenue and the UK's export commodity would compete on equal terms with French commodities sold in the French market. VAT under the origin principle would distribute taxation according to the value added in each country. Hence, a commodity exported by the UK to France would pay the UK tax (8%) and in France additional tax would be levied to bring the overall tax on the commodity to (16%). Under strict conditions equivalence would apply: tax revenue and its distribution would be the same under the destination and origin principles. These conditions are that the tax systems in both countries must be exactly the same in terms of base, rules and rates, and trade should be balanced. In this situation the tax collected from foreign countries on exports would be the same as the tax paid to foreign countries on imports. In the absence of these conditions the destination and origin principles will lead to an uneven distribution of the tax burden among countries. The destination principle, however, would require the retention of fiscal frontiers for border tax adjustments, so the EU should shift to the origin principle (Shibata, 1967). In the absence of the equivalence conditions both systems involve potential jurisdiction and distortion problems, so it is practical issues that will decide the choice of system (Bovenberg, 1994; Lockwood *et al.*, 1994).

The EEC decided to remain with the destination principle, which is consistent with undistorted intra-EU trade, provided that customs controls remain in place. So this decision ensured that the EEC would remain as separate national markets divided by physical borders. It was agreed by all the member states that the coverage of VAT should be the same and should encompass all the stages of production including the retail stage. Although there was agreement about the general principles of VAT there was no agreement on exemptions and rates, with significant variations from one member country to another.

As far as excise duties were concerned, progress was rather slow, and this can be attributed to the large differences in rates between member states and the different attitudes these represent. Thus Northern Europe would object to lowering rates because of a loss of revenue and adverse effects on health, whereas Southern Europeans would object to the implications for their life style of raising rates. The greatest progress was achieved in tobacco, where a new harmonized system was adopted in January 1978. The essential elements of this system were the abolition of any duties on raw tobacco leaf and the adoption of a new sales tax at the manufacturing level, combined with a specific tax per cigarette and VAT. Prest (1979) argues that the overall effect of this was to push up the relative prices of the cheaper brands of cigarettes.

With respect to corporation tax, there was little consistency in the Commissions position. The Neumark Report of 1963 (CEC, 1963) recommended a split-rate system, the van den Tempel Report of 1970 (CEC, 1970b) preferred the adoption of the separate or classical system, and the draft directive of 1975 went for the imputation system. Hence, all systems were entertained at some time or another and all that can be categorically stated is that by 1986 the EU limited its choice to the separate and imputation systems. Moreover, the method of tax harmonization, which was accepted, was not a single EU corporation tax and a single rate, but rather a unified EU corporation tax accompanied by freedom of tax rates. It is not surprising, therefore, that there was little convergence of corporation tax systems.

Some progress was achieved with regard to stamp duties, which are taxes on capital transactions. Harmonization here was necessary for promoting the freedom of intra-EU capital flows. The 1976 draft directive recommended a compromise between the systems existing in the member countries. This recommendation was accepted, with the proviso that time would be allowed for adjustment to the new system.

Nothing was attempted in the area of personal income taxation and very slight progress was achieved in social security payments, unemployment benefits, etc.; the only exception was the draft directive of 1979, which dealt with equity in the taxation of migrant workers (see Chapter 23).

There was, therefore, very limited progress on tax harmonization over this period and, with the exception of the use of VAT, member states continued to operate largely independent national tax systems. This was made possible by the retention of the fiscal frontiers, limited capital and labour mobility, and the relatively insubstantial degree of intra-European multinational company activity. All this was, however, to change with the single market.

14.3.2 From the internal market to the single market

The SEA aim was to transform the EC into a single internal market by the end of 1992, i.e. 'an area without internal frontiers in which the free movement of goods, persons, services and capital is ensured' (see Chapter 11). The continuing existence of customs and immigration frontiers were the clearest symbol of divisions within the EU, permitting the continuation of protectionist measures.

The most significant feature of frontiers is the customs posts, which limited the need for tax harmonization.[13] Customs controls protected the indirect taxes of one EU member state from tax bargains that were obtainable elsewhere within the EU. Moreover, customs controls guaranteed that governments could collect the VAT and excise duties on goods sold in their country. A frontier-free EU would potentially cause problems of jurisdiction, distortion and enforcement unless there was a greater degree of tax harmonization. Tax rates did not have to be equalized; the experience of the United States indicates that contiguous states can maintain differentials in sales taxes of up to about 5 percentage points without the tax leakage becoming significant.

In the 1985 Internal Market White Paper (CEC, 1985a), the Commission reached the conclusion that for the single market, tax harmonization was essential for the elimination of internal frontiers. Thus the White Paper made the following proposals for VAT and excise duties. For VAT, these were as follows:

1   Moving from the destination to the origin system of tax collection.
2   The introduction of an EC clearing mechanism, to ensure that revenues would continue to accrue to the EU member nation where consumption

took place, so that the destination principle would remain intact.
3   The narrowing of the differentials in national VAT rates so as to lessen the risks of fraud, tax evasion and distortions in competition.

With regard to excise duties, three reforms were deemed necessary:

1   An interlinkage of the bonded warehouse system (created to defer the payment of duty since, as long as the goods remain in these warehouses, duties on them do not have to be paid; recall that excise duties are levied only once on manufacture or importation).
2   Upholding the destination principle.
3   An approximation of the national excise duty rates and regimes.

The ability to achieve this harmonization was, however, constrained by the fact that fiscal provisions remained subject to unanimity in decision making. This has remained a factor hindering progress on tax harmonization in the face of very different tax systems and the various national interests associated with them. Agreement was reached on a transitional VAT regime in 1991,[14] a VAT Information Exchange System (VEIS) was established to monitor VAT on trade in goods, and rate approximation with a minimum standard rate of 15% and minimum reduced rate of 5%.[15]

The internal market had fundamental implications for capital markets and, therefore, for capital taxation. Freedom of movement of capital meant that national differences in capital taxation would be more likely to affect international capital flows. Abandoning capital controls also meant that it would be more difficult to tax the income from capital via the personal tax system. The single market was also to lead to the development of pan-European multinational companies, capable of competing in the world market with US and Japanese corporations. The variations in Corporation Tax regimes could both create difficulties for the development of such corporations and distort their choice of locations for their activities. Despite these problems the harmonization of capital income taxation has made little progress, with a failure to finalize definitive proposals in relation to Corporation Tax, and inability to agree on proposals for a withholding tax[16] on capital income.

14.4 Tax harmonization today

The extent to which member states have retained sovereignty over their tax systems is indicated by the very wide differences in total taxation and the structure of taxes between member states (Table 14.1). The lion's share of taxes in all countries is collected by personal income tax and social security payments, and as argued above differences in these taxes can persist without distorting the single market or giving rise to problems from tax competition.[17] Corporation tax,[18] VAT and excises remain very differentiated despite the drive for harmonization and it is the nature and effects of these differences that are considered in this section.

14.4.1 Value added tax

There are three fundamental problems that remain with regard to VAT: first, the ageing definition of the tax base provided by the Sixth Directive; second, the widespread use of multiple rate VAT; third, the treatment of cross-border trade.

Under the Sixth Directive, exemptions from VAT include: health care, education, social services, cultural services, public broadcasting, postal services, immovable property, insurance, financial transactions and gambling. There are also exemptions for public bodies, small business and farmers. Public bodies are exempt

Table 14.1 EU 15 tax structure, 2000

	Personal income tax	Corporation tax	Social security payments	VAT	Excises	Total tax revenue
	Percentage of total tax revenue					Percentage of GDP
Belgium	31.0	8.1	30.9	16.3	7.1	45.6
Denmark	52.6	4.9	4.6	19.6	11.3	48.8
Germany	25.3	4.8	39.0	18.4	8.8	37.9
Greece	13.5	11.6	30.1	22.7	11.7	37.8
Spain	18.7	8.6	35.1	17.6	9.8	35.2
France	18.0	7.0	36.1	16.9	8.2	45.3
Ireland	30.8	12.1	13.6	21.5	14.1	31.1
Italy	25.7	7.5	28.5	15.8	10.0	42
Luxembourg	18.3	17.7	25.6	14.3	12.7	41.7
Netherlands	14.9	10.1	38.9	17.3	8.9	41.4
Austria	22.1	4.7	34.2	19.0	7.7	43.7
Portugal	17.5	12.2	25.7	24.2	15.2	34.5
Finland	30.8	11.8	25.6	18.0	10.4	46.9
Sweden	35.6	7.5	28.1	13.4	6.7	54.2
UK	29.2	9.8	16.4	18.4	12.4	37.4
EU 15 average	**25.6**	**9.2**	**27.5**	**18.2**	**10.3**	**41.6**

Source: OECD (2002b). OECD©, 2002

because it seems strange for the government to tax itself but recent experience, of privatization and contracting out, has indicated that there is no clear division between public and private activities. The exemption of small business is the result of the high largely fixed cost of operating VAT, which would function as a regressive tax on small business.[19] The compliance costs of VAT are estimated to be 2% of turnover for small businesses (turnover below 60,000 euros) but only 0.3% for large companies (turnover greater than 1 million euros) (Sandford *et al.*, 1989). The problem with exemptions is that they can lead to distortions in prices, reduce the efficiency of tax collection and increase compliance and administration costs. A wider tax base with fewer exemptions is called for, but would be very difficult to achieve given the need for unanimity. A possible way forward would be to allow countries to use a VAT base that extends beyond the definition in the Sixth Directive.

The EU is still a long way from achieving the approximation of VAT rates envisaged in the Internal Market White Paper. All countries respect the minimum standard rate of 15% with a range from 15% in Luxembourg to 25% in Denmark and Sweden (see Table 14.2). Lower rates vary between 0 and 8% with the majority of countries operating multiple rate VAT. As can be seen from the notes to Table 14.2, with a long list of exceptions, that considerably complicates the system.

The extent to which the variation in rates represents a problem with regard to cross-border shopping is arguable. Evidence suggests that the magnitude of cross-border shopping diminishes rapidly with the distance that needs to be covered to exploit tax differences. In addition, on a net basis, differences in excises are responsible for two thirds of the value of cross-border shopping (Bode *et al.*, 1994; Bygrä *et al.*, 1987; Fitzgerald *et al.*, 1988). Similarly, European Commission studies find that the abolition of border controls has not led to significant changes in cross-border shopping patterns, distortions of competition or changes in trade, due to differences in VAT rates (European Parliament, 2001b). So there does not seem to be any great need to further harmonize VAT rates to reduce distortions caused by cross-border shopping.[20]

The existence of multiple rates is much more questionable. The major reasons for special exemptions and reduced rates is social, to reduce their regressive impact, but as is usual the major beneficiaries of such exemptions are not the poor. The conclusion of a 1988 study

which has been supported by more modern evidence,[21] was that the distribution of the tax burden was not very different if products were zero rated (UK), taxed at a reduced rate (Netherlands) or even at the same rate as other goods and services (Denmark) (OECD, 1988b). Thus, although expenditure on food is proportionally higher for poorer groups, the better off spend more in absolute terms, thus the improvement in the progressivity of the tax system is minor (Cnossen, 1999). 'Differentiated VAT rates are an ineffective, ill targeted instrument for eliminating the impact of the tax on the poor' (Cnossen, 2001; p. 492).

Multiple rates are also not without cost since they increase the administrative complexity of the system and cause problems for compliance. One study suggested that UK firms found that having multiple rather than single rate output, doubled compliance costs (Hemming and Kay, 1981). Imposing an additional VAT rate reduces the compliance rate by 7% (Agha and Houghton, 1996). This is not surprising when one realizes that the following factors need to be considered in applying the zero rate to food in the UK: 'place of consumption, timing of consumption, temperature, saltiness, number, volume, concentration, sugar content, use of fingers in consumption and alcoholic content.' (Cnossen, 2001; p. 493). There is, therefore, no economic or social justification for the continued use of multiple rates.

The EU responded to the abolition of fiscal borders with a transitional regime of cross-border trade on a deferred payment or postponed accounting basis. Under this system exports are free of VAT but the exporter must inform the fiscal authorities in the country it is exporting to. Importers must declare imports and pay VAT at the local rate on them. A VAT Information Exchange System (VEIS) reinforces checks within the system; this requires registered businesses to file quarterly reports of exports and imports. The European Commission has in the past argued that the deferred payment system is bureaucratic and creates additional administrative burdens for companies and is subject to fraud. The European Parliament (2001b; p. 44) suggests that the identified 1300 million euros of VAT fraud, is merely 'the tip of the iceberg'. Accordingly, the Commission has consistently recommended that the system should be reformed to the origin system, with exports becoming subject to VAT of the member state of sale.

Whether such a change is desirable is, however, questionable. The evidence of fraud under the systems

Table 14.2 VAT in EU member states, 2002

	VAT rates %		VAT revenue %	
	Standard	Other	Total tax revenue	GDP
Single rate				
Denmark	25	–[a]	19.2	9.7
Dual rate				
Austria	20	10[b]	19.0	8.4
Germany	16	7	18.4	6.9
Netherlands	19	6	16.9	7.1
United Kingdom	17.5	0[c]	18.8	6.8
Multiple rate				
Belgium	21	6 / 12[d]	16.0	7.3
Finland	22	6 / 17[e]	18.8	8.7
France	19.6	2.1 / 5.5	17.3	8.0
Greece	18	4 / 8	21.7	8.0
Ireland	20	0 / 12.5[f]	22.0	7.1
Luxembourg	15	3 / 6 / 12	15.0	6.3
Italy	20	4 / 10[g]	13.7	5.9
Portugal	17	5 / 12	13.8	7.2
Spain	16	4 / 7	17.5	6.1
Sweden	25	6 / 12[h]	18.1	7.4
Unweighted average	**19.4**		**18.1**	**7.4**
Minimum rates	**15.0**	**5.0**[i]		

[a] Newspapers are taxed at 0%.
[b] Wine supplied by farmers and electrically driven vehicles are taxed at 12%.
[c] Certain 'energy saving materials' are taxed at 5%. An effective rate of 5% is also applied to some imported works of art, collectors items and antiques.
[d] Newspapers, magazines and waste products are taxed at 0%.
[e] Newspapers and magazines are taxed at 0%.
[f] Livestock and greyhounds are taxed at 4.3%.
[g] Waste paper and scrap iron are taxed at 0%.
[h] Prescribed medicines are taxed at 0%.
[i] Reduced rate to apply only to specified categories of goods.
Source: European Commission (2002) Excise Duty Tables, REF 1.015, August, DG Taxation and Customs Union. Reprinted by permission of the European Communities.

is limited, with few complaints from the member states. Indeed it is the system that has operated satisfactorily in the Benelux countries ever since they introduced VAT. A more sensible approach might be to improve the transitional regime, and since 2000 this has been the strategy of the European Commission (CEU 2000d). The major problem that needs to be resolved is the compliance costs for firms with limited imports (Verwaal and Cnossen, 2002).

This analysis leads to the conclusion that the major benefits from VAT reform would stem from an extension of the tax base and the elimination of multiple rates, rather than the harmonization of rates and the move to the origin system as have been emphasized in the past.

Table 14.3 Cigarette taxation in EU member states 2002 (per pack of 20 cigarettes)

	Specific excise euro	Ad valorem excise %[a]	VAT %[a]	Total tax euro[b]
Belgium	0.3	45.8	17.4	2.1
Denmark	1.6	21.2	20.0	3.3
Germany	1.1	23.3	13.8	2.3
Greece	0.1	53.9	15.3	1.7
Spain	0.1	54.0	13.8	1.3
France	0.1	55.2	16.4	2.7
Ireland	2.2	18.7	17.4	4.0
Italy	0.1	54.3	16.7	1.5
Luxembourg	0.2	46.8	10.7	1.4
Netherlands	1.1	20.5	16.0	2.1
Austria	0.4	42.0	16.7	2.0
Portugal	0.8	23.0	16.0	1.5
Finland	0.3	50.0	18.0	3.0
Sweden	0.4	39.2	20.0	2.7
United Kingdom	3.1	22.0	14.9	5.6
Average	**0.8**	**38.0**	**16.2**	**2.5**

[a] Per cent of retail selling price including all taxes.
[b] Tax on the best selling brand.
Source: European Commission (2002) Excise Duty Tables, REF 1.015, August, DG Taxation and Customs Union. Reprinted by permission of the European Communities.

14.4.2 Excise duties

Excise duties are an important tax for EU governments, being the fourth most important source of revenue after social security contributions, VAT and income tax (Table 14.1). The importance of excises varies substantially among the member states from 15.1% of tax revenue in Portugal to 6.6% in Sweden.[22] This reflects the very wide variations in rates, which have been subject to only very limited harmonization, mainly the result of the tax competition. The major problem with excise duties is the large variation in tax between member states and the impact of this differential on legal and illegal cross-border movement of goods.

The EU position on tobacco duties is a compromise between the southern and northern member states. The south favours taxation based on the value of the product to protect their cheap homegrown tobacco. The north prefers specific taxes based on volume rather than value to discourage tobacco smoking. This has led to wide discretion in rates and wide variation in the total tax burden on cigarettes,[23] which is permitted by current EU regulations.[24] These require that the specific and *ad valorem* excises plus VAT must not be less than 57% of the retail price. The average total tax on a pack of 20 cigarettes varies between 1.3 euros in Spain to 5.64 euros in the UK (Table 14.3). With such a disparity of tax and consequent variation in prices, it is not surprising that high tax countries such as the UK are suffering a substantial loss of revenue, as a result of personal purchases overseas, and small and large scale smuggling. It is estimated that 25% of the cigarettes smoked in the UK are smuggled (Public Accounts Committee, 2002). As a result the rules have been tightened so that the total excise should not be less than 60 euros per thousand cigarettes (or 95 euros if the member state does not comply with the 57% rule).[25] This increase in specific taxation may, however, simply increase the

Table 14.4 Alcohol taxation in EU member states 2002 (per litre)

	Still wine	Beer	Spirits	
	Specific excise euro[a]	VAT %[b]	Specific excise euro[c]	VAT %[b]
Belgium	0.47	0.02	6.64	21.0
Denmark	0.95	0.62	14.79	25.0
Germany	0.00	0.01	5.21	16.0
Greece	0.00	0.01	3.63	18.0
Spain	0.00	0.01	2.96	16.0
France	0.03	0.03	5.80	19.6
Ireland	2.73	0.19*	11.05	21.0
Italy	0.00	0.01	2.58	20.0
Luxembourg	0.00	0.01	4.16	15.0
Netherlands	0.59	0.25	6.02	19.0
Austria	0.00	0.02	4.00	20.0
Portugal	0.00	0.17	3.34	5.0[d]/19.0
Finland	2.35	0.29*	20.18	22.0
Sweden	2.27	0.15*	20.61	25.0
United Kingdom	2.50	0.19*	12.67	17.5
Average	**0.79**	**0.13**	**8.4**	**19.5**
EU minima	**0.00**	**0.01**[e]	**2.2**	

[a] Tax per litre of wine.
[b] Per cent of retail selling price excluding VAT.
[c] Tax per litre of 40% alcohol.
[d] Lower rate of VAT for wine.
[e] Except for countries marked * where it is €0.0187 per litre per degree of alcohol in finished product.
Source: European Commission (2002) Excise Duty Tables, REF 1.015, August, DG Taxation and Customs Union. Reprinted by permission of the European Communities.

volume of smuggling from outside the EU, with which it has been suggested the tobacco companies have cooperated (Public Accounts Committee, 2002). With internal harmonization of tobacco duties problematic and the threat of external smuggling, governments in high tax countries are faced with a difficult choice between lower duties or revenue loss.

The situation is similar for alcohol taxation where the EU is very far from the harmonization of rates. A judgment of the European Court of Justice (1983) has indicated that excises based on relative alcohol content provide for equality of competitive conditions within member states. Thus the most flagrant discrimination in favour of local producers has been eliminated (Cnossen, 1987), but national beverages

are still protected by, for example, applying different excises to still and sparkling wine. Some convergence of rates has occurred as member states have moved towards the lowest rate, so seven member states levy no excises on wine and in France it is only 3 euro cents a litre. Some high rates persist so large differentials remain, thus the excises on wine vary from 0 to 2.73 euros a litre and on spirits from 6.45 to 15.45 euros (Table 14.4). Thus substantial smuggling still occurs; it is estimated that about a quarter of the spirits consumed in Denmark and Sweden are purchased outside the consumers' own member state (European Parliament, 2001b; p. 39). A directive on minimum rates was agreed in 1992[26] but the minimum was very low and has not been revised since.

The differences in alcohol and tobacco taxation are causing significant problems of smuggling and revenue loss for the member states, and there is a strong case for EU action. In these cases a harmonization of rates is required with reduced rates in northern Europe leading to some increase in consumption and higher rates in the South causing some inflation.[27] These, largely transitional problems, are a price worth paying to eliminate the difficulties caused by current large differences in rates.

It is convenient to consider the taxation of private and commercial road users separately (see Chapter 15). Although there are large variations in the taxation of private road users (Table 14.5), this does not raise tax harmonization problems. Taxes on car ownership are based on residence, which presumably is where the vehicle is used. Although the tax on unleaded gasoline varies between 0.32 euros in Greece to 0.79 euros in the UK, there is little possibility of cross-border shopping or smuggling.[28]

Differences in the excise duties on commercial diesel fuel can affect competition in road transport where goods in one country can be transported by lorries buying their fuel in another. The extent of such problems have been limited by a reasonable degree of similarity of rates; ten member states have rates between 3 and 4.55 euros per litre of normal diesel fuel (Table 14.5). The UK is way out of line, with a rate of 8.69 euros per litre. Since the UK is such an exception the solution seems to lie in its own hands.[29]

This survey indicates that further reform of indirect taxes in the EU is desirable. With VAT the problems lie not with differences in rates but with the complications caused by multiple rates, which seem to have little merit. The transitional regime for the collection of VAT is working reasonably well and some administrative

Table 14.5 Taxes on petrol and diesel fuel

	Unleaded petrol	Diesel fuel	Diesel and gasoline
	Excise duty (euros per litre)	Excise duty (euros per litre)	VAT %
Belgium	0.49	0.29	21
Denmark	0.62	0.41	25
Germany	0.64	0.46	16
Greece	0.30	0.25	18
Spain	0.43	0.29	16
France	0.57	0.39	19.6
Ireland	0.51	0.35	21
Italy	0.52	0.40	20
Luxembourg	0.37	0.25	12
Netherlands	0.61	0.34	19
Austria	0.41	0.28	20
Portugal	0.48	0.27	19
Finland	0.56	0.33	22
Sweden	0.48	0.32	25
United Kingdom	0.79	0.84	17.5
Average	**0.51**	**0.37**	**19.4**
Agreed minima	**0.34**	**0.25**	

Source: European Commission (2002) Excise Duty Tables, REF 1.015, August, DG Taxation and Customs Union. Reprinted by permission of the European Communities.

reform could remove the problems it causes for small businesses with few intra-EU transactions. Differences in excise rates are a cause of substantial smuggling both from within and from without the EU. Further harmonizations with, in particular, reductions in the highest rates seem the only answer here.

14.4.3 Capital income taxation

There are four sets of interrelated issues pertaining to capital income taxation potentially affecting the operation of the single market. First, is the way in which dividends and retained earnings of corporations are treated for tax purposes. Second, is the rate at which corporation tax is levied, which is dependent not only on the rate but also upon allowances. Third, is the taxation of income on equity as compared with income on debt. Fourth, is the way in which personal income tax is levied on interest payments. This section accordingly considers these issues in turn.

Corporation taxes (CTs) vary in the extent to which the personal income tax liability on dividend income (distributed profits) makes allowance for them. There are two extreme systems of corporation tax: the classical and imputation systems. Under the classical system corporations pay tax on their profits but there is no allowance for this tax against personal taxation (PT). Under the imputation system the whole or part of the CT can be used to offset PT liability on dividends. Another possibility is the subjecting of dividend income to a separate lower rate of PT. At present CT systems in the EU run the whole gamut with four different systems in operation and a range of rates from 16% to 41% (Table 14.6).

The imputation system is used by six member states, with tax credits varying from full credit to one-ninth of net dividend. A separate usually flat rate of PT on dividend income is used in another six countries. Dividend income received by individual shareholders is exempt from tax in two countries. One of these countries, the Netherlands, has a net wealth tax instead and five other countries have wealth taxes. Ireland operates the classical system with dividends being fully subject to CT and PT, but the rate of CT is very low so total tax on dividends is low. The trend in the EU has been to replace imputation systems with schedular taxes on dividends, because of the cross-border complications and distortions imputation causes. Retained profits are taxed indirectly by taxation of capital gains.

Six member states do not tax capital gains on ordinary shares but all except Belgium tax substantial holdings (i.e. controlling interests). This all adds up to a very complex system as indicated by the length of notes to Table 14.6. CT is an important source of tax revenue accounting in 2000 for 9.2% of the total taxation in the EU. The considerable variation[30] in the importance of CT revenue indicates that tax competition has not been that serious. Statutory rates have been lowered (Cnossen and Bovenberg, 1997) but the tax base has been broadened (Gorter and de Mooij, 2001).

These variations in tax allowances for dividends when combined with PT leads to widely varying rates of tax on dividends (Table 14.6). There are also substantial differences within countries between the tax on distributed and retained profits. In member states except Finland, Greece and the Netherlands the tax on dividends is greater than the tax on retained profits. There are two views on the effect of differential taxation: the 'traditional' and the 'new' (Sinn, 1991). The traditional view argues that dividends offer benefits, which can at least partially offset tax disadvantages. These advantages of distribution include the signalling to shareholders that the corporate performance is good and the limitation of management financial discretion and thus of potential misuse of retained profits.[31] The corporation would equalize the tax disadvantages with these nontax advantages of distributing profits, thus tax discrimination distorts the choice between retaining and distributing profits. This distortion is effectively a decrease in the return on corporate investment, the overall level of which will be depressed. The new view suggests that there are no nontax advantages to dividend distribution: the shareholders enjoy their return in the form of tax efficient capital gains rather than dividends. The higher tax on dividends does not, therefore, involve any diminution in the level of investment. Empirical studies support the traditional rather than the new view (Cnossen, 2001, p. 523). Whichever view is correct, encouraging the retention of profits reduces the capital available for new share issues to the detriment of new and fast expanding firms, which will adversely affect the dynamism of the economy.

Corporate tax regimes not only favour profit retention but also the use of debt rather than equity for finance. This is particularly the case since financial innovation is blurring the distinction between equity and debt. Again this will tend to make it more difficult for new firms to raise capital, because of their limited

Table 14.6 EU taxes on company earnings in 2002 (%)

CT system	CT (on retained profits)[a,b]	Dividend relief	PT on capital gains[c,d]		Net wealth tax	CT + top PT on distributed profits[e]	PT on interest[f]
Imputation		Tax credit	Ordinary shares	Substantial holdings			
Finland	29	29/71	29	29	0.9[i]	29	29**
France	34$^{1}/_{3}$	1/2 (basic CT)[j]	26[k]	26[k]	0.55–1.8	65.2	26**
Italy[g]	36[l]	36/64	12.5	27	–	44	27**
Portugal	33	3/5 of CT[k]	3.6–12	3.6–12	–	49	20**
Spain	35	2/5	18	18	0.2–2.5	52.7	48*
United Kingdom	30	1/9	6–24	6–24	–	53.3	40*
Special PT rate		*PT rate*[m]					
Austria[h]	34	25*	–	half of PT	–	50.5	25**
Belgium[h]	40.2	15*	–	–	–	49.1	15**
Denmark	30	43[n]	43[n]	43[n]	–	60.1	47.6
Germany	41.1	half of PT	–	half of PT	–	56.2	36.9**
Luxembourg	37.4	half of PT	–	half of PT	0.5	50.9	43
Sweden	28	30	30	30	1.5	49.6	30
Dividend exemption		*No tax*					
Greece	35[o]	Exempt	–[p]	25	1.2	35	10**
Netherlands	35	Exempt	–	25	1.2	35	None
Classical system		*No relief*					
Ireland	16(10)[q]	None	20	20	–	51.3	20**

Abbreviations have the following meaning: CT = company income tax; PT = personal income tax.
Some information may be incomplete or out of date.
Percentages have been rounded to one decimal place.
[a] CT Rates include the following:
  - Surcharges in Belgium (3%), France (3%), Germany 5.5%, Luxembourg (4%), Portugal (10%) and Spain (0.75%–0.01%); and
  - local taxes (deductible from corporate profits) in Germany (18%) and Luxembourg (10%); Spain levies a local tax based on the type of business activity and the surface area of the premises.
[b] Flat minimum taxes, creditable against the final CT are levied in Austria, France and Luxembourg (in the form of a net wealth tax). Lower or graduated CT rates apply to lower amounts of profits or to small businesses in Belgium, France, Ireland, Luxembourg, the Netherlands, Portugal, Spain and the UK.
[c] Capital gains realized by companies are usually subject to CT at the normal rate, generally the gains can be rolled over.
[d] Capital gains are adjusted for inflation in Ireland and Luxembourg. Alternatively, short-term and long-term gains are taxed at different rates in Denmark, Portugal, Spain and the UK. PT rates shown are for the long-term capital gains. Various member states exempt small amounts of capital gains. Italy levies the tax on accrued gains.
[e] Calculated as CT + [(1 – CT)PT] *minus* any tax credit available.
[f] An asterisk (*) means that interest payments are subject to a withholding tax: a double asterisk means that the withholding tax is final on option. Generally, royalty payments to residents are not subject to withholding tax except in France (26% – final), Spain (18%) and the UK (22%).
[g] Italy levies a regional tax on productive activities (IRAP), in fact an income-type VAT at 4.25%.
[h] Austria and Belgium permit a limit deduction from individual income of expenditure on the purchase of newly issued shares.
[i] In addition, non-resident companies and domestic legal entities other than corporations are subject to a 1% net wealth tax.
[j] France provides a 25% tax credit for the subscription to shares in specified companies.
[k] French PT on capital gains of 16% plus full social taxes.
[l] Italy levies a reduced rate of 19% on profits attributable to increases in equity capital (retained profits and newly issued shares).
[m] An asterisk (*) indicates that the special PT rate is final without the withholding tax option.
[n] In Denmark, share income not exceeding DKr 39 700 is taxed at 28%.
[o] The CT rate is 37.5% for Greek companies with bearer shares not quoted on the Athens Stock Exchange and on non-resident companies.
[p] In Greece, shares in unquoted corporations are taxed at 5% of the sale price.
[q] The rate given in parenthesis applies to profits of qualifying manufacturing and processing companies.
Source: Cnossen, 2001; Tables 8 and 9. Reprinted by permission of the author

Table 14.7 EU 15: effective average corporation tax rates (EATR)[a] (percentage)

	Statutory tax rate 2001	Micro forward EATRs 2001			Statutory tax rate 1998	Micro backward EATR 1995–1999
		Overall	Retained earnings	Debt		
Italy	40.25	27.6	28.7	25.5	37.0	21.8
Belgium	40.17	34.5	39.1	25.8	40.2	12.1
Germany	39.40	34.9	38.7	27.7	47.5	20.6
Greece	37.50	28.0	32.4	19.7		–
Luxembourg	37.45	32.2	36.6	24.0		–
France	36.43	34.7	39.0	26.8	41.6	13.5
Portugal	35.20	30.7	34.8	23.0	37.4	13.3
Netherlands	35.00	31.0	35.2	23.3	35.0	19.1
Spain	35.00	31.0	35.2	23.3	35.0	13.5
Austria	34.00	27.9	30.7	22.6	34.0	10.7
United Kingdom	30.00	28.3	31.8	21.7		–
Denmark	30.00	27.3	30.7	21.0	34.0	18.3
Finland	29.00	26.6	30.0	20.2	28.0	15.5
Sweden	28.00	22.9	26.0	17.1	28.0	10.4
Ireland	10.00	10.5	11.7	8.2		–
EU 15 average	**32.9**	**28.5**	**32.0**	**22.0**		**15.5**
Pearson coefficient	**33.16**	**0.92**	**0.91**	**0.93**		**0.35**

[a] All effective tax rates relate to CT only. PT on dividends and interest have not been taken into account.
[b] Ranked in order of statutory rate.
[c] Calculated on actual corporate profits inclusive of depreciation.
Source: Devereux and Griffith, 2001; Nicodème, 2001

credit history and asset bases for collateral. The bias in favour of debt finance is shown by studies for the European Commission (Devereux and Griffith, 2001) who calculate effective average CT rates on hypothetical investment projects using the rates and rules in current legislation. This indicates that although high tax rates are associated with narrower bases, effective tax rates are correlated with nominal rates (Table 14.7). Retained earnings have an effective CT rate on average 10% higher than that on debt. Such studies cannot capture the complexities of the operation of the system; for this analysis of data on corporate profits and corporation tax is needed (Nicodème, 2001). This study indicates that there are substantial differences between the statutory and effective rates within as well as between companies for different sectors and company

sizes. There is little association between the actual and effective rates of the member states, and this is not the result of differences in tax bases.[32] These variations in effective corporation tax rates are likely to affect the distribution of footloose economic activities between countries (Gorter and de Mooij, 2001). One estimate suggests that for every 1% increase in effective CT foreign investors reduce their investment in that state by 4.3%, indicating the importance of CT in investment decisions.

This analysis of the effects of CT suggests that the distortions caused can extend across EU borders. The bias in favour of retained earnings favours incumbent as opposed to new firms limiting competition and reducing the dynamism of the single market. It also favours markets where shareholder involvement in the company is more direct, such as in Germany where banks typically have large holdings and where the need to satisfy shareholders with dividends is lower. Differences in effective CT bias the choice of location for foreign investment to which intra-EU investment is particularly sensitive (Cnossen, 2002, p. 62; CEU, 2001g) – see Chapter 18. The lower taxation of debt finance is to the advantage of member states with large firms that are creditworthy; where there are close links between banks and companies it can protect against foreign takeovers, because foreign firms do not have the same access to local bank finance. The favourable tax treatment of debt finance is reinforced by internationalization and liberalization of capital markets. With withholding tax on cross-border interest payments very low (Table 14.6), a large part of internal interest income escapes taxation (Huizinga, 1994). Thus companies are encouraged to finance their activities with international debt affecting member states tax bases.

The requirement that profits for CT should be calculated separately for each member state creates problems for pan-European business. This means that tax losses in one member state cannot be offset against profits in another and assets transferred between member states may be subject to capital gains tax. This discourages cross-border mergers and takeovers and constrains the operation of multinational companies within the EU. The administrative costs of complying with different CT regimes can also be high.

The European Commission (CEU, 2001g) in the Bolkestein Report scrutinizes two approaches to these problems: first, piecemeal changes to legislation to correct particular distortions, e.g. improving double taxation conventions; second, general measures to establish a common tax base for EU activities. There are three possibilities for a common tax base: a EU CT, common base taxation (CBT) and home state taxation (HST). A EU-wide CT would be difficult to agree, given the requirement for unanimity, so the Commission is less concerned with this option. CBT would harmonize rules for calculating taxable profits on cross-border operations (national rules would remain for domestic operations). HST means that multinational businesses would only be taxed in the member state in which their headquarters is located. With both systems one set of consolidated accounts would be produced, and a formula using shares of sales, payroll and property, would be used to apportion profit,[33] to which member states would apply their tax rates.

These proposals are not without problems; they would tend to increase tax competition due to greater transparency, because differences in tax paid would depend solely upon rates. Distortions between states caused by national distortions such as the favouring of debt over equity finance are not dealt with, 'the elimination of in-state distortions is a prerequisite to the elimination of interstate distortions' (Cnossen, 2001, p. 531). Although part of the purpose of the proposals is to make cross-border mergers easier, tax considerations will become a factor influencing such mergers. Formula apportionment of profit would lead to further distortions of the location of production. The problems are such that some commentators doubt whether CBT or CHT is worth the effort (Mintz, 2002).

Harmonization of CT remains an attractive objective. Cnossen (2001) suggests a five stage process: first, the introduction of dual income taxation (DIT); second, the levying of a EU wide interest withholding tax; third, capital is taxed by the proportional CT. With these changes, further steps become possible: fourth, the introduction of common base taxation with formula apportionment; finally, the creation of an EU CT. DIT, which is operated in Scandinavia, involves separating capital from labour income, capital is taxed at the proportional CT. Labour income is taxed progressively, with the first income tax bracket rate set at the CT rate. Double taxation of dividends is avoided by full imputation of CT payments against capital income taxation. This avoids the bias in the system in favour of retained profits.

This still leaves the problem of interest payments to foreign debt holders, who can avoid income taxation, but this problem can be dealt with by an interest withholding tax at the CT rate. This tax would have to be accepted to offset income tax liability in the member state of residence. Appealing as the potential benefits of these suggestions are, they do have the potential to raise the cost of capital to the detriment of investment. The cost of capital could rise because of the ability to utilize lower tax debt financing, so some reduction in overall rates would be required to compensate. In addition there is the 'London' problem that withholding taxes in the EU would encourage an outflow of funds from the EU and the City in particular. The current approach is to require the exchange of information on assets held by residents of other member states, so as to enforce residence based taxation. This approach also suffers from the 'London' problem, so progress in this area is dependent upon cooperation with other countries particularly Switzerland and the USA.

14.5   Conclusion

It should not come as a surprise that tax harmonization remains a difficult issue for the EU: a sensitive area of national sovereignty that remains the prerogative of the member states, collides with the need to avoid distortions to trade and investment in an increasingly integrated single market. It is clear from the foregoing that reform of member states' tax systems would benefit the domestic economy, as well as reduce cross-border distortions. The needs for these adjustments and for tax harmonization are principally in relation to taxes on consumption and on capital.[34]

Of the consumption taxes, VAT and excise duties, VAT presents limited problems. The tax base of consumption is relatively immobile and consumers are not very sensitive to differences in rates. The tax is relatively cheap to collect and it is difficult to evade. The principal difficulties with VAT are associated with exemptions, multiple rates and the administrative costs that they incur. There seems to be little need for further harmonization of rates. There is a good case, however, for making the tax base as wide as possible and for the abolition of multiple rates. The transitional regime on cross-border trade is working satisfactorily, but attention should be given to reducing the administrative burden on small business.

Excise duties on cigarettes and alcohol do present substantial problems because of the high rates in some countries and the enormous differences of rates that persist. This encourages a substantial illegal market, with suppliers ranging from small-scale smuggling to organized crime, operating in some cases with cooperation from multinational corporations. These problems can, probably, only be dealt with effectively by harmonization of rates. By contrast the taxation of motor vehicles and fuel presents few cross-border problems.

Taxation of capital presents problems because of the mobility of the tax base and the spread of corporate activities across states. This means that the taxation jurisdiction is somewhat arbitrary and the taxes levied will have considerable cross-border effects. Corporation tax is also notable for its complexity, which is not helped within the EU by differences in its bases, rules and rates. The system at the moment distorts the choices of retaining and distributing profits and encourages financing by debt rather than equity. These within member state distortions also have cross-border effects on investment and business restructuring. Commission proposals of Home State Taxation or Common Base Taxation do not appear to solve these problems. The Dual Income Tax system operated by Nordic countries seems worth further investigation as a practical way forward for capital taxation.

This analysis indicates that tax harmonization involves a trade off between national sovereignty over tax and the difficulties caused by variations in rates and systems. The limited degree of tax convergence achieved so far indicates that tax competition cannot be relied on to achieve spontaneous harmonization. Tax competition moves rates to lower levels, but such a race to the bottom is not always undesirable, it may act as a restraining influence on taxation. For example, lower rates of taxation on corporations could be a way of stimulating investment (Berglöf *et al.*, 2003). Tax harmonization may, therefore, be regarded as a way of maintaining the level of taxation. There are some areas, however, where harmonization could achieve significant potential benefits (excise duties), but given the law of unintended consequences, which seems to hold sway in tax matters, a gradualist approach to harmonization is both practical and preferable.

NOTES

1. Compared to only 29.6% in the USA (OECD, 2002a; p. 74).
2. Lower tiers of government within nation states have independent tax revenue and expenditure, but the amounts involved are normally much smaller than those of federal/central governments within the EU. There are also constraints on the taxes and expenditure of lower levels of government in national systems.
3. In competitive markets labour taxes will tend to be paid by workers as reductions in their real incomes.
4. Different systems of government expenditure can cause analogous effects to differences in taxes.

These effects are dealt with by internal market legislation (Chapter 11) and for industrial subsidies by competition policy (Chapter 12).

5. Tax competition means that a higher rate of tax is needed to raise funds, increasing tax-induced inefficiency.

6. The main people affected will be very high-income earners, who would in any case be attracted by tax havens, which offer extremely low rates of tax.

7. The intra-company price for international trade which takes place within the company.

8. Thus the tax paid equals the rate of tax times the value added at that stage of production.

9. Such taxes also had variable effects on prices and encouraged the vertical integration of companies.

10. Tobacco taxation is justified by ignorance of the health risks of smoking. In reality there seems to be little information failure because 90% of smokers are aware of these risks (Cnossen, 2001, p. 501).

11. Petrol taxes are supposed to reduce congestion and the production of greenhouse gases by reducing the number of car journeys undertaken.

12. Sixth Council Directive 77/388/EEC of 17 May 1977 on the harmonization of the laws of the member states relating to turnover taxes – common system of value added tax: uniform basis of assessment, *Official Journal L 145*, 13/06/1977, pp. 1–40, is still the harmonized base and rules under which the EU operates.

13. Internal EU frontiers are also seen to be important in the UK for the control of immigration, terrorists and drug trafficking.

14. Council Directive 91/680/EEC of 16 December 1991 supplementing the common system of value added tax and amending Directive 77/388/EEC with a view to the abolition of fiscal frontiers, *Official Journal L 376*, 31/12/1991, pp. 1–19.

15. Council Directive 92/77/EEC of 19 October 1992 supplementing the common system of value added tax and amending Directive 77/388/EEC (approximation of VAT rates) *Official Journal L 316*, 31/10/1992, pp. 1–4.

16. A withholding tax is a tax directly on interest payments before they are distributed to owners of the debt.

17. They may, however, have other economic effects, for example on the level of employment.

18. Including personal taxes on capital income and gains.

19. This is the reason for the exemption of farmers, although they receive flat rate compensation for tax on agricultural inputs.

20. There are problems associated with e-commerce where consumers buy electronic products paid for and delivered over the Internet. The problem here is likely to come from beyond the EU and so is not amenable to solution by EU tax harmonization.

21. For example, Australian Society of CPAs (1998) estimated that only 15% of the benefit of a zero rate on food in New Zealand would go to households with the lowest 20% of income.

22. The difference in the excise taxes share of GDP is much narrower from 5.5% in Denmark to 3.2% in Belgium.

23. 95% of total tobacco consumption.

24. Council Directive 95/59/EC of 27 November 1995 on taxes other than turnover taxes which affect the consumption of manufactured tobacco, *Official Journal L 291*, 06/12/1995, pp. 40–45. Council Directive 92/79/EEC of 19 October 1992 on the approximation of taxes on cigarettes, *Official Journal L 316*, 31/10/1992, pp. 8–9.

25. Council Directive 2002/10/EC of 12 February 2002 amending Directives 92/79/EEC, 92/80/EEC and 95/59/EC as regards the structure and rates of excise duty applied on manufactured tobacco, *Official Journal L 046*, 16/02/2002, pp. 26–28.

26. Council Directive 92/84/EEC of 19 October 1992 on the approximation of the rates of excise duty on alcohol and alcoholic beverages, *Official Journal L 316*, 31/10/1992, pp. 29–31.

27. Although additional revenue could be used to lower other indirect taxes eliminating the inflationary effect.

28. There is the possibility of other distortions, e.g. the fact that taxation of diesel fuel is much lower than that of petrol in France, gives manufacturers of diesel engine cars an advantage. French manufacturers have traditional strength in the manufacture of diesel cars.

29. Part of the justification for high vehicle taxes is to reduce emissions for environmental reasons. The European Commission's (1991) proposal for a

carbon tax was not approved but some member states have introduced carbon taxes.

30. Besides variations in the tax rate and base, other factors influence CT revenue, such as the proportion of businesses that are incorporated (only 15% in Germany), revenue from natural gas in the Netherlands, and the presence of holding companies in Luxembourg.

31. An advantage considerably enhanced by recent corporate scandals.

32. Care needs to be taken in interpreting the results, because these are model specific.

33. This is the system widely used in the US and Canada.

34. Since income taxes present few independent cross-border problems; they are not considered here.

Chapter 15 Transport policy

KENNETH BUTTON

Introduction

Transport has exerted important influences in shaping the human geography of Europe. Military conquests in the past were largely along well-defined transport corridors and the growth of cities has mainly been at important junctions in transport networks. Technology advances and changes in political ambition, as well as new economic conditions and institutional developments, have altered the nature of this link but its fundamental importance remains. The role of transport as a lubricator of economic reconstruction was appreciated in the post-Second World War period. Institutions such as the European Conference of Ministers of Transport (ECMT) were set up under the Marshall Plan to assist in reconstructing transport infrastructure while the European Coal and Steel Community (ECSC) devoted energies to improving the efficiency of the European rail transport system (Meade *et al.*, 1962). It was even more transparent in the formation of the European Economic Community (EEC) whereby the explicit creation of a Common Transport Policy (CTP) was mandated (see Chapter 1).

Transport is a major industry in its own right. It directly employs about 7% of the European Union (EU – the term largely used throughout this chapter for simplicity although the title has changed over the years; see Chapter 2) workforce, accounts for 7% of total EU GDP and for about 30% of final energy consumption. But this is perhaps not really the important point. The crucial thing about transport from an economic perspective is its role in facilitating trade and in allowing individuals, companies, regions and nation states to exploit their various comparative advantages. Early debates concerning the merits of free trade tended to assume away the friction associated with moving goods to markets, and the analysis of migration patterns exhibited similar tendencies to assume transport costs to be negligible. Some economists, such as von Thünen (1826), did take account of transport costs when trying to explain land use patterns but such explicit consideration of space and the problems of trasversing it

was exceptional. The situation changed with the advent of new transport technologies in the mid-nineteenth century and as countries appreciated that manipulation of the transport system could influence their economic conditions. Manipulation of transport rates and the strategic design of infrastructure networks were used to protect domestic industries in ways akin to tariff and non-tariff trade barriers (NTBs; see Chapter 6). Individual states sought to develop transport policies that were to their short-term benefit irrespective of their consequences for overall trade.

The contemporary upsurge of interest in supply chain management, just-in-time production and the like has led to a wider appreciation of the general need to enhance the efficiency of European transport if the region as a whole is to compete successfully in the global economy. The concern is that the effectiveness of transport logistics in the EU are at least comparable with those elsewhere to ensure that the labour, capital and natural resources of member states can be exploited in a fully efficient manner.

It was against this broad background that the EU initially sought to develop a transport policy, of which the CTP has been but one element, designed to reduce artificial friction. It has taken time for the CTP and other elements of policy to come together to represent anything like a coherent strategy. There have been shifts of emphasis since the signing of the EEC Treaty and frequent changes in the types of policy deemed appropriate to meet these moving objectives. This chapter provides details of the underlying issues that have been central to these efforts and charts out some of the paths that have been pursued to confront them. The process has not been smooth and has involved a number of discrete phases. To pre-empt the conclusions, it can be said that ultimately, and after many tribulations, the EU has emerged with a relatively coherent approach to transport that has removed many of the potential bottlenecks to economic integration that dogged the early development of the Union.

15.2 The European transport system

Problems with the creation of a transport policy began early. The EEC Treaty contained an entire chapter on transport, although apparently limiting itself to movement of freight by road, rail and inland waterways. Strictly the treaty said, 'The Council may, acting unanimously, decide whether, to what extent and by what procedure appropriate provisions may be laid down for sea and air transport'. It is thus not clear whether these modes were excluded only from the transport clauses or from the treaty as a whole, including its competition provisions. The Netherlands, having considerable maritime interests, was particularly concerned about retaining autonomy in these areas, and this concern contributed to the ambiguity.

While the treaty gave indications of what national obligations should be, it was not until 1961 that a memorandum appeared setting out clear objectives (CEC, 1961) and not until the following year that an Action Programme was published. The emphasis of these initiatives was to seek means to remove obstacles to trade posed by the institutional structures governing transport and to foster competition once a level playing field of harmonized fiscal, social and technical conditions had been established. That it has subsequently taken over forty years to make significant progress towards a CTP is in part due to the nature of European geography and the underlying transport market, although continued insistence on nation states pursuing their individual agendas was also a causal factor.

Examination of a map of the EU provides information on some of the problems of devising a common transport policy. Even when the Community consisted of only six members, the economic space involved hardly represented a natural market. Ideally transport functions most effectively on a hub and spoke basis with large concentrations of population and economic activity located at corners and in the centre and with the various transport networks (roads, railways and the like) linking them. The central locations act as markets for transport services in their own rights but also as interchange and consolidation points for traffic between the corner nodes. In many ways the US fits this model rather well but the EU never has. When there were six members the bulk of economic activity was at the core, with limited growth at the periphery. The joining of such states as Ireland, Greece, Portugal, Finland and Sweden added to the problems of serving peripheral and often sparsely populated areas. The geographical separation of some states and the logical routeing of traffic through non-member countries, together with the island nature of others, posed further problems.

The CTP also was not initiated with a clean slate – member states had established transport networks and institutional structures that could not rapidly be changed even if a common set of principles could have been established. At the outset countries such as France and West Germany carried a significant amount of their freight traffic by rail (34% and 27% by tonne–kilometres respectively). Others, such as Italy and the Benelux nations, relied much more on road transport; the average length of domestic hauls being an important determining feature. The resultant differences were also not simply physical (including variations in railway gauges, vehicle weight limits and different electricity currents). They also reflected fundamental differences in the ways transport was viewed.

At a macro, political-economy level there were two broad views on the way transport should be treated. Following the Continental philosophy, the objective was to meet wide social goals that require interventions in the market involving regulations, public ownership and direction. This approach particularly dominated much of twentieth-century transport policy thinking in Continental Europe and has its genesis in the Code Napoléon with its focus on centralism. Its place has been taken in recent years by a wider acceptance of the Anglo-Saxon approach to transport policy. This treats the transport sector as little different to other economic activities. Transport provision and use should be efficient in its own right. Efficiency is normally best attained by making the maximum use of market forces. Of course, the extremes of the Continental approach never existed and nowhere has the strict Anglo-Saxon philosophy been fully applied; it has been a matter of degree. Even in countries such as the UK that had in the past been seen as a bastion of the Anglo-Saxon ideology there existed extensive regimes of regulation and control and large parts of the transport system were in state or local government ownership.

The periodic enlargements of the EU, together with broader shifts in the way that transport is viewed that transcended the narrow European situation, have resulted in a move away from the Continental way of thinking to a more market-based approach to a CTP.

The interventionist positions of Germany and France were initially set against the more liberal approach of the Netherlands. With the accession of the UK and Denmark in 1973 the more interventionist approach was now in the minority. Subsequent enlargements added to the impetus for less regulation of transport markets.

The situation can also be looked at from a more analytical perspective over time. This is in terms of the ways that efficiency is viewed. The approach until the 1970s was to treat efficiency in transport largely in terms of maximizing scale efficiency while limiting any deadweight losses associated with monopoly power. Most transport infrastructure was seen as enjoying economies of scale that could only be exploited by coordinated and, *ipso facto*, regulated and often subsidized, development. State ownership, the extreme of regulation, was also often adopted. Many aspects of operations were also seen as potentially open to monopoly exploitation and hence in need of oversight. This situation has changed since the late 1970s. From a pragmatic perspective, the high levels of subsidies enjoyed by many elements of the transport sector became politically unsustainable. Economists began to question whether the regulations deployed were actually achieving their stated aims. They may, for example, have been captured by those that are intended to be the regulated or have been manipulated to the benefit of individuals responsible for administering the regime. Government failures, it was argued, were larger than the market failures they were trying to correct.

New elements also came into play in the 1970s, and especially concern about the wider environmental implications of transport. Attitudes towards the environmental intrusion associated with transport vary between member states as well as having changed more generally over time. To some extent this has been part of a wider effort within the Union to improve the overall environment (see Chapter 17) and to fulfil larger, global commitments on such matters as reducing emissions of global warming gases (CEC, 1992b). Transport impacts the environment at the local level (noise, lead, carbon monoxide, and so on), at the regional level (e.g. nitrogen oxide emissions and maritime pollution) and at the global level (carbon dioxide). It is this diversity of implications and the trade-offs between them, as well as the absolute scale of some of the individual environmental intrusions, that make policy formulation difficult. Local effects have largely been left to the individual countries but as the implications of regional and global environmental intrusions have become more widely appreciated so EU transport policy has become proactive in these areas. The main problem with these types of environmental issue is that their effects are often trans-boundary and thus give little incentive for individual action by governments.

15.3 The initial development of a CTP

As we have seen, the past forty years have seen important changes in the ways in which transport is viewed. There have always been periodic swings in transport policy but the period since the late 1970s provides a classic watershed (Button and Gillingwater, 1986) that has permeated EU thinking. The change has been a dramatic one that transcends national boundaries and modes. The liberalization of transport markets throughout the world and the extension of private sector ownership have also had the wider influence of providing important demonstration effects to other sectors that in turn have also been liberalized (Button and Keeler, 1993).

The early thinking regarding the CTP centred on harmonization so that a level playing field could ultimately be created on which competition would be equitable. The ECSC had initiated this approach in the early 1950s and it continued as EU interest moved away from primary products. The ECSC had removed some artificial tariff barriers relating to rail movements of primary products and the CTP initially attempted to expand this idea in the 1960s to cover the general carriage of goods and especially those moved on roads. Road transport was viewed rather differently to railways. It was perceived that the demand and supply features of road haulage markets could lead to excessive competition and supply uncertainties.

The early efforts involved such actions as seeking to initiate common operating practices (e.g. relating to driving hours and vehicle weights), common accounting procedures and standardizing methods of charging. A forked tariff regime for trucking, with rates only allowed between officially determined

Table 15.1 Summary of the policy of EC 9

Emphasis on

Links between transport and: regional; social; fiscal; industrial; environmental and energy affairs

Intervention with transport within a Community-led framework

The joint movement forward on consistency of regulations and liberalization

The increasing importance attached to coordination of infrastructure investment

Policy

Infrastructure coordination

(Important in the Action Programme, 1974–1976)

– New consultation procedure with a Transport Infrastructure Committee (1978)

– Oort's study of infrastructure pricing (Oort and Maaskant, 1976)

(Contained in the 'Green Paper' of 1979)

– Creation of an Infrastructure Fund

– Extension of interest in the infrastructure of non-members (e.g. Austria and Yugoslavia) where it affects links between members

Liberalization

– Reference tariff system (1978)

– Permanent quota system (1976)

– Common method for determining bilateral quotas (1980)

maxima and minima, was aimed at meeting the dual problems of possible monopoly exploitation in some circumstances and of possible inadequate capacity due to excess competition in others. Maximum and minimum rates on international movements within the EU were stipulated and statutory charges established on this basis. Practically, there were problems in setting the cost-based rates but beside that, questions must be raised concerning a policy that was aimed at simultaneously tackling monopoly and excess competition (Munby, 1962). Limitations on the number of international truck movements across borders were marginally reduced by the introduction of a small number of Community Quota licences – authorizing the free movement of holders over the entire EU road network (Button, 1984).

The 1973 enlargement of the Union to nine members stimulated a renewed interest in transport policy. The new members – the UK, Ireland and Denmark – tended to be more market oriented in their transport policy objectives. Also, there was inevitable horse-trading

across policy areas and with the enlargement came the opportunity to review a whole range of policy areas. At about the same time, the Commission raised legal questions concerning the inertia of the Council of Ministers to move on creating a genuine CTP. It also followed a period of rapid growth in trade within the Union, with a shift towards greater trade in manufactures. As a result infrastructure capacity issues were coming to the fore and the case for more flexible regulation of road freight transport was being argued (Button, 1990).

The outcome was not dramatic although new sectors entered the debates, most notably maritime transport, and wider objectives concerning environmental protection and energy policy played a role (Table 15.1). Overall, the actions in this period were a gentle move to liberalization by making the Quota system permanent and expanding the number of licences increased international intra-EU road freight capacity. The option of using reference tariffs rather than forked tariffs was a reflection of the inherent problems with the latter.

A major element of the measures involved transport infrastructure in terms of improving decision making regarding its provision and with regard to consideration of the way that charges should be levied for its use. The importance of transport links outside of the EU, but part of a natural European network, also began to play a part in policy formulation with the Union beginning to develop mechanisms for financing investment in such infrastructure.

The enlargements of the Union as Greece, and then Spain and Portugal, joined had little impact on the CTP. It still essentially remained piecemeal. The only significant change prior to major developments in the early 1990s was the gradual widening of the modes covered. There were, for example, moves to bring maritime and air transport policy in line with Union competition policy.

Efforts to develop a common policy on maritime transport represent one of the spheres in which there was a broadening out of EU transport policy (Brooks and Button, 1992) from the mid-1980s. Since 35% of the international, non-intra EU trade of member states involves maritime transport (some 90% of the Union's aggregate imports and outputs) it may seem surprising that it took so long for this mode to come within the CTP. The reason for this, as we have seen, was that the EEC Treaty required unanimous decisions regarding the extent to which sea transport was to be included in EU policy – although it was unclear whether this applied to EU policy as a whole or purely to the CTP.

The accession to membership in the 1970s and early 1980s of countries such as the UK and Greece with established shipping traditions brought maritime issues to the table and then the Single European Act (SEA) of 1987 provided a catalyst for initiating a maritime policy (Erdmenger and Stasinopoulos, 1988). A series of measures were introduced aimed at bringing shipping within the Union's competition policy framework. This came at a time when major changes were beginning to permeate the way in which maritime services were provided. Technical shifts, such as the widespread adoption of containerization, had begun to influence the established cartel arrangements that had characterized scheduled maritime services. (These initial arrangements were 'conferences' that coordinated fares and sailings but later were more integrated 'consortia'.) The ability to discriminate in relation to price that these cartels enjoyed was beginning to be eroded as it became more difficult to isolate cargoes. Conferences had been permitted in most European countries since the late nineteenth century because they were seen as a way to offer scheduled services of less than a shipload at relatively stable rates to shippers. Action by the United Nations to limit the power of these cartels in the 1970s was largely aimed at protecting developing countries but was in conflict with national policies of some EU members while others ratified it. A need for a more coordinated EU maritime policy emerged.

This view was reinforced in the 1980s as the size of the EU shipping sector declined significantly. The relative size of the sector had been falling for many years but accelerated in the face of competition from Far East and Communist bloc fleets. Taxation and policies on such matters as wages and technical standards were adding to the problem by stimulating operators to 'flag out' and register in non-member states.

The 'First Package' in 1985 sought to improve the competitive structure of the European shipping industry and its ability to combat unfair competition from third countries (CEC, 1985c). It gave the Commission power to react to predatory behaviour by third party ship owners which when initially applied (e.g. the *Hyundai* case) exerted a demonstration effect, especially on Eastern bloc ship owners. The measures also set out an interpretation of competition policy that allowed block exemptions for shipping cartels (shipping conferences), albeit with safeguards to ensure the exemption was not exploited (see Chapter 12).

In 1986 a 'Second Package' – the Positive Measures Package – was initiated by the Commission and was aimed at addressing the decline in the competitiveness of the EU's fleets as well as covering safety and pollution issues. Greater coordination of fleets was seen as important and to stimulate this a common registry was proposed (CEC, 1991c). It has not, however, proved a success, and fleet sizes have continued to decline, bringing forth new ideas for capacity reduction from the EU Commission. Also as part of the general effort to liberalize the European market and enhance the efficiency of the industry, agreement on cabotage (the provision of a domestic service within a country by a carrier from another nation) was reached but with exceptions in some markets, e.g. the Greek Islands.

Compared to shipping, ports policy can best be described as *ad hoc* (Chlomoudis and Pallis, 2002). Initial concerns in the early 1990s centred around modernizing European ports, and in particular to ensure that they could handle the large ships that were being introduced. Progress was relatively slow until 2000 when sea and inland ports were incorporated into the Trans-European Networks (TENs) initiative with the objective of integrating and prioritizing investment in transport infrastructure.

Air transport in general, since the initiatives of the USA in the late 1970s that had liberalized its domestic passenger and freight markets and fostered an Open Skies policy for international aviation, was moving away from a tradition of strict regulation that had pertained since the pioneering days (Button *et al.*, 1998). Until the early 1980s, however, it had also generally been thought that aviation policy was outside of the jurisdiction of the EU Commission and a matter for national governments. This changed, following a number of legal decisions by the European Court of Justice (ECJ) (e.g. *Nouvelles Frontières* and *Ahmed Saeed* cases) regarding the applicability of various aspects of EU competition rules to air transport.

The European bilateral system of air service agreements covering scheduled air transport between member states was, like those in other parts of the world, tightly regulated. Typical features of a bilateral agreement meant that: only one airline from each country was allowed to fly on a particular route with the capacity offered by each bilateral partner also often restricted; revenues were pooled; fares were approved by the regulatory bodies of the bilateral partners; and the designated airlines were substantially state owned and enjoyed state aid. Domestic air markets were also highly controlled. The charter market, largely catering for holiday traffic from northern Europe to southern destinations, represented about 50% of the revenue seat miles within the EU and was less strictly regulated but the regulations were such that services seldom met the needs of business travellers.

A change in the policy climate began in 1979 when the Commission put forward general ideas for regulatory reform (CEC, 1984). The push for change came from the ECJ's verdict in the *Nouvelles Frontières* case concerning the cutting of airfares. This encouraged the Commission to adopt the view that its powers to attack fare-fixing activities were greater than the implementing regulation suggested. The Council subsequently decided that the best way to regain control was to agree to introduce deregulation but of a kind, and at a pace, of its own choosing. Hence the 1987 'First Package'.

The basic philosophy was that deregulation would take place in stages, with workable competition being the objective. A regulation was adopted that enabled the Commission to apply the antitrust rules directly to airline operations. Only interstate operations were covered; intrastate services and services to countries outside the EU were not at this stage affected. Certain technical agreements were left untouched. The Council also adopted a Directive designed to provide airlines with greater pricing freedom. While airlines could collude, the hope was that they would increasingly act individually. The authorities of the states approved applications for airfare changes. Also the new arrangements did not constitute free competition since an element of regulation remained. While conditions were laid down that reduced the national authorities' room for manoeuvre in rejecting changes in airfares, they could still reject them. However, if there was disagreement on a fare the disagreeing party lost the right of veto under arbitration.

The 1987 package also made a start on liberalizing access to the market. To this end the Council of Ministers adopted a decision in 1987 that provided for a deviation from the traditional air services agreement which set a 50/50 split. The capacity shares related to total traffic between the two countries. Member states were required to allow competition to change the shares up to 55/45 in the period to 30 September 1989 and thereafter to allow it to change to 60/40. Normally they could only take action if capacity shares threatened to move beyond such limits. Fifth freedom traffic[1] was not included in these ratios but was additional. There was also a provision in which serious financial damage to an air carrier could constitute grounds for the Commission to modify the shift to the 60/40 limit.

The decision also required member states to accept multiple designations on a country-pair basis by another member. A member state was not obliged to accept the designation of more than one air carrier on a route by the other state (that is, a city-pair basis) unless certain conditions were satisfied. These conditions were to become less restrictive over time. The decision also made a limited attempt to open up the market to fifth freedom competition.

The 1989 'Second Package' involved more deregulation. From the beginning of 1993 a system of double disapproval was accepted. Only if both civil aviation authorities refused to sanction a fare application could an airline be precluded from offering it to its passengers. From the same date the old system of setting limits to the division of traffic between the bilateral partners was to disappear totally in a phased manner. Member states also endorsed the vital principle that governments should not discriminate against airlines provided they meet safety criteria and address the problem of ownership rules. In the past, an airline had typically to be substantially owned by a European state before it could fly from that country, but the Council abolished this rule over a two-year period.

Air cargo services were liberalized so that a carrier operating from its home state to another member country could take cargo into a third member state or fly from one member state to another and then to its home state. Cabotage and operations between two freestanding states were not liberalized.

The most recent initiatives of the Union have involved the move to a 'Single Sky' over Europe and to the Union taking responsibility for the negotiation of external air traffic rights. The notion of a Single Sky is that air traffic control should be reorganized to reduce the excessive fragmentation of the current system, up-date the technology used and be operated under common EU rules. The aim is to achieve this by 2004 (CEU, 2001e). A ruling by the ECJ in 2001 has been interpreted to imply that de facto the Commission has power over negotiating external air service agreements between members of the Union and third parties. This has brought into question some existing bilateral agreements between individual members and third parties and raises longer-term issues, yet to be resolved, about how the Commission will go about this task and what the reaction of third party countries, that may not recognize EU jurisdiction, will be.

15.4 The CTP and other aspects of policy in the 1990s

The creation of the Single European Market in 1992 (see Chapters 2 and 11), and subsequent moves towards greater political integration, brought important changes to the CTP and related transport policies (Button, 1992). Broadly, the 1987 SEA stimulated a concerted effort to remove institutional barriers to the free trade in transport services. At about the same time, efforts at further political integration led to major new initiatives to provide an integrated European transport infrastructure – e.g. the TENs (CEC, 1989b). These strategic networks were aimed at facilitating higher levels of social and political integration at the national and regional levels. They also had purely economic objectives.

While there were moves to liberalize industries such as air transport from the late 1980s, the broad basis of the current phase of EU transport policy was established in the Commission's White Paper on *The Future Development of the Common Transport Policy* (CEC, 1992b). This set out as a guiding principle the need to balance an effective transport system for the EU with a commitment to the protection of the environment. The environmental theme was expanded subsequently (CEC, 1992a). This was to be set in the context of defending the needs and interests of individual citizens as consumers, transport users and people living and working in areas of transport activity.

Even if these effects were not present, questions arose at the time regarding the ability of regulators to serve the public interest with the information that they had at hand. The development of economic theories involving such concepts as contestable markets (where potential competition could be as effective as actual competition in blunting the power of monopoly suppliers), although subsequently the centre of intellectual and empirical debate, provided new ways of thinking about transport markets and were central to several EU initiatives. There was also a switch away from concern about problems of optimal scale and monopoly power that had been the intellectual justification for state ownership and regulation of such industries as railways and air transport, to attempts at seeking to create conditions favourable to X-efficiency and dynamic efficiency. Technically, this was largely but not exclusively a concern with reducing costs replacing that of containing consumer exploitation. In particular, there was mounting concern about the costs of regulated transport that had macroeconomic implications for inflation and also often led to the need for high levels of public subsidy. These undertakings were neither producing at the lowest possible costs for the technology they were using at the time nor moving forward to adopt lower-cost technologies.

One can also look at the situation in the much wider context of the past thirty years being a period of important economic change as the information age has gradually taken over. Improved new forms of communication of all types have come to the fore that affect both production and consumption activities. Transport is part of the supply side in that it involves the facilitation of personal and commercial interactions but it is also part of the demand side, being a major user of information services. Modern aviation services, for example, could not operate without this technology and innovations in freight transport such as just-in-time management would hardly be possible on the scale on which they are now practised without it. As the structure of production has changed, not only in the EU but throughout the world, and as social changes have taken place it would have been almost impossible for the institutional structure of a key industry such as transport to have been unaltered. In this sense EU policy in the 1990s must be seen as partly flowing with much stronger international tides.

The nature of the policy changes, however interpreted, has not been uniform in either time or space. Countries and regional groupings have differed in their approach. The USA tended to lead the way as it deregulated its domestic transport markets between 1977 and 1982. Demonstration effects resulted in other countries following. The reforms in the USA were, however, only partly copied elsewhere. There were different starting points but also later reformers benefited from the experiences of the first-time movers. Transport systems differ across countries. In the USA, for instance, the average car is driven about 12 500 miles a year whereas in Europe the figure is less than 9000. Western Europe has only about 30% of the freeway mileage of the USA. Similarly, the demands placed on transport systems vary according to such things as the goods produced and the physical structure of the area. There are, however, common lessons to be learned, but they need to be taken in the context of the geography of the countries involved, the individual details of the reforms, their wider institutional context and their particular timing (Button, 1998). In some senses the EU benefited from the experiences of pre-1990s reforms when devising its current transport priorities and strategies.

Although terms such as multi-modalism abound in the official literature and, indeed, some initiatives have transcended the conventional bounds of modal-based actions, a useful and pragmatic way of treating these recent developments is by mode.

15.4.1 Road transport

Road transport is the dominant mode of both freight and passenger transport in the EU. The share of freight going by rail, for example, has fallen from 32% of the EU total in 1970 to about 14% today. Over the period, the total freight tonnage in Europe has increased 2.5 times and the share of this going by road has risen from 48% to 74%. The initial efforts to develop a common policy regarding road transport, however, as we have seen, proved problematic. Technical matters were more easily solved than those of creating a common economic framework of supply although even here issues concerning such matters as maximum weight limits for trucks have tended to be fudged. Economic controls lingered on as countries with less efficient road haulage industries sought to shelter themselves from the more competitive fleets of countries such as the UK and the Netherlands. There were also more legitimate efficiency concerns throughout the EU over the wider social costs of road transport, regarding both environmental matters and narrower questions of infrastructure utilization.

The single market initiative, also later influenced by the potential of new trade with the post-Communist states of Eastern and Central Europe (Button, 1993), has resulted in significant reforms to economic regulation in recent years. From the industrial perspective, road freight transport offers the flexibility that is required by modern, just-in-time production management, but from the social perspective it can be environmentally intrusive and, in the absence of appropriate infrastructure pricing, can contribute to excessive congestion costs.

Earlier measures had helped expand the supply of international permits in Europe, the EU quota complementing bilateral arrangements, and reference tariffs had introduced a basis for more efficient rate determination. The 1990s were concerned with building on this rather fragile foundation. In particular, as part of the 1992 single market initiative, a phased liberalization was initiated that both gradually removed restrictions on trucking movements across national boundaries and phased in cabotage that had hitherto not been permitted by member states.

The long-standing bilateral arrangements for international licensing led to high levels of economic inefficiency. This was not only because the system imposed an absolute constraint on the number of movements but also because cabotage was not permitted, and combinations of bilateral licences permitting trucks to make complex international movements were difficult to obtain – trucks had to travel long distances without cargo. The system also added to delays at borders as documents were checked. Besides leading to the gradual phasing out of bilateral controls and the phasing in of cabotage rights, the 1992 initiative also led to considerable reductions in cross-border documentation.

Passenger road transport policy has largely been left to individual member states, although in the late 1990s the Commission began to advocate the development of a 'citizens' network' and more rational road-charging policies (notably systems of congestion pricing). Perhaps the greatest progress has been made regarding social regulations on such matters as the adoption of catalytic converters in efforts to limit the environmental intrusion of motor vehicles. It has taken time to develop a common policy regarding public transport despite efforts in the 1970s to facilitate easier cross-border coach and bus operations.

15.4.2 Railways

Rail transport, while largely filling a niche market in many countries, is an important freight mode in much of continental Europe and provides important passenger services along several major corridors. At the local level, it serves as a key mode for commuter traffic in larger cities. Much of the important economic reform of European railways was undertaken in the early phase of integration by the ECSC, with actions on such matters as the removal of discriminatory freight rates. The recent phase has been concerned less with issues of economic regulation and with operations and more with widening access to networks and with technological developments, especially regarding the development of a high-speed rail network as part of the TENs initiative.

The earlier phase had initially sought to remove deliberate distortions to the market that favoured national carriers but from the late 1960s and 1970s had shifted to the rationalization of the subsidized networks through more effective and transparent cost accountancy. However, the exact incidence of subsidies still often remained uncertain. The Union has also instigated measures aimed at allowing the trains of one member to use the track of another with charges based upon economic costs. The aim of EU Directive 91/440 (CEU, 1995a) was to develop truly European networks but at the time of writing the open access rules explicitly do not apply to the new high-speed rail lines such as the French and Belgian Lignes à Grande

Vitesse and the German Neubaustrecken networks. The implementation of the open access strategy has been slow and has had limited impact (CEU, 1998b).

The EU has traditionally found it difficult to devise practical and economically sound common pricing principles to apply to transport infrastructure despite the proposals of the Oort Report (Oort and Maaskant, 1976). With regard to railways, the gist of the overall proposals is for short-run marginal costs (which are to include environmental and congestion costs as well as wear on the infrastructure) to be recovered. Long-run elements of cost are only to be recovered in narrowly defined circumstances and in relation only to passenger services. This clearly has implications, especially on the freight side, if genuine full cost-based competition is to be permitted with other transport modes.

Rail transport has also received considerable support from the Commission as an integral part of making greater use of integrated, multi-modal transport systems. Such systems would largely rely upon rail (including piggy-back systems and kangaroo trains) or waterborne modes for trunk haulage, with road transport used as the feeder mode. This is seen as environmentally desirable and as contributing to containing rising levels of road traffic congestion in Europe.

The success of some of the French TGV services, and especially that between Paris and Lyon, where full cost recovery has been attained, has led to a significant interest in this mode. In 1990 the Commission set up a high-level working group to help push forward a common approach to high-speed railway development. A master plan for 2010 was produced. The EU's efforts to harmonize the development of high-speed rail has not been entirely successful and there are significant technical differences, for example between the French and German systems. Indeed, both countries actively market their technologies as superior (Viegas and Blum, 1993).

The difficulties that still remain with rail transport reflect technical variations in the infrastructure and working practices of individual states that are only slowly being coordinated. Some countries, such as the Netherlands, Sweden and the UK, have pursued the broad liberalization philosophy of the EU and gone beyond the minimal requirements of the CTP, but in others rigidities remain and the rail network still largely lacks the integration required for full economies of scope, density and market presence to be reaped.

15.4.3 Inland waterway transport

Inland waterway transport was already an issue in the early days of the EU. This is mainly because it is a primary concern of two founder member countries, the Netherlands and Germany, which in 1992 accounted for 73.1% of EU traffic. France and Belgium also had some interest in this mode of transport. Progress in formulating a policy has tended to be slow, in part because of historical agreements covering navigation on the Rhine (e.g. the Mannheim Convention), but mainly because the major economic concern has been that of over-capacity. In 1998 over-capacity was estimated at between 20% and 40% at the prevailing freight rates. Retraction of supply is almost always inevitably difficult to manage, both because few countries are willing to pursue a contraction policy in isolation and because of the resistance of barge owners and labour.

As in other areas of transport, the EU began by seeking technical standardization, and principles for social harmonization were set out by the Commission in 1975 and 1979 (CEC, 1975; 1979b), but economic concerns have taken over in the 1990s. In 1990 the EC initiated the adoption of a system of subsidies designed to stimulate scrappage of vessels. Subsequent measures only permitted the introduction of new vessels into the inland fleet on a replacement basis. Labour subsidies operated in the Netherlands, Belgium and France (the rota system that provides minimum wages for bargemen) have also been cut back in stages. They were removed entirely in 2000.

These measures were coupled with an initiative in 1995 to coordinate investment in inland waterway infrastructure (the Trans-European Waterway Network), designed to encourage, for environmental reasons, the greater use of waterborne transport. More recently, in *European Transport Policy for 2010: Time to Decide* (CEU, 2001e), the Commission has put emphasis in its Marco Polo programme on integrating inland waterways transport with rail and maritime transport for the movement of bulk consignments within an intermodal chain.

15.4.4 Maritime transport

Much of the emphasis of the EU maritime policy in the late 1990s has been on the shipping market rather than on protecting the Union's fleet. In other words, it is user rather than supplier driven. In the 1990s the sector became increasingly concentrated as, first, consortia grew in importance, mergers took place (e.g. P&O and Nedlloyd in 1997) and then the resultant large companies formed strategic alliances. (In 1999 all shipping companies, with the exception of two of the world's largest, were part of alliances.) An extension of the 1985 rules to cover consortia and other forms of market sharing was initiated in 1992 and subsequently extended as the nature of maritime alliances has become more complex (CEU, 1995a).

The Commission also initiated a number of actions supporting this position. In 1994 it acted to ban the Transatlantic Agreement reached the preceding year by the major shipping companies to gain tighter control over the loss-making North Atlantic routes. It did so on the grounds of capacity and rate manipulations and because it contained agreements over pre- and on-carriage over land. In the same year it also fined 14 shipping companies that were members of the Far East Freight Conference for price fixing. The main point at issue was that these prices embodied multi-modal carriage and while shipping *per se* enjoyed a block exemption on price agreements, multi-modal services did not.

Ports also attracted the attention of the EU in the 1990s. Ports are major transport interchange points and in 1994 handled about 24% of the world's ton equivalent units. Advances in technology have led to important changes in the ways in which ports operate, and there has been a significant concentration in activities as shipping companies have moved towards hub-and-spoke operations. The main EU ports have capacity utilization levels of well over 80% and some are at or near their design capacity. Whether this is a function of a genuine capacity deficiency or reflects inappropriate port pricing charges that do not contain congestion cost elements is debatable. The Commission has produced further proposals for coordinating investment in port facilities (CEU, 1997d).

In 2001 the Commission launched an initiative to improve the quality of services offered by ports. This involves tightening access standards for pilotage, cargo handling, etc. and to make more transparent the rules of procedure at ports with the particular aim of bringing ports more fully into an integrated transport structure (CEU, 2001f).

15.4.5 Air transport policy

While liberalization of EU air transport may be considered one of the successes of the CTP, in the late 1980s the air market was still heavily regulated at the time of the Cockfield Report that heralded the single market. The final reform – the 'Third Package' – came in 1992 and was phased in from the following year. The programme aimed for a regulatory framework for the EU by 1997 similar to that for US domestic aviation (Button and Swann, 1992). The measures removed significant barriers to entry by setting common rules governing safety and financial requirements for new airlines. Since January 1993, EU airlines have been able to fly between member states without restriction and within member states (other than their own) subject to some controls on fares and capacity. National restrictions on ticket prices were removed; the only safeguards related to excessive falls or increases in fares.

From 1997, full cabotage has been permitted, and fares are generally unregulated. Additionally, foreign ownership among Union carriers is permitted, and these carriers have, for EU internal purposes, become European airlines. One result has been an increase in cross-share holdings and a rapidly expanding number of alliances among airlines within the Union. This change did not initially apply to extra-Union agreements where national bilateral arrangements still dominate the market. A ruling by the ECJ in November 2002, however, gives power to the Commission to undertake such negotiations. In 2003 the Council gave powers to the Commission to proceed with negotiations with the US to liberalize the transatlantic market.

Early analysis of reforms by the UK Civil Aviation Authority (1993) and the Commission indicated that the reforms of the 1990s produced, in terms of multiple airlines serving various market areas, greater competition on both EU domestic routes and international routes within the EU. The changes varied but countries such as Greece and Portugal increased the number of competitive international services considerably. Many routes, however, either because multiple services are simply not technically sustainable or institutional impediments still limited market entry, remained monopolies in 1994.

More recently, the Commission, in examining the impact of the Third Package, reported important consumer benefits (CEU, 1996c). It found that the number of routes flown within the EU rose from 490 to 520 between 1993 and 1995, that 30% of Union routes are now served by two operators and 6% by three operators or more, that 80 new airlines have been created while only 60 have disappeared, that fares have fallen on routes where there are at least three operators and that overall, when allowance is made for charter operations, 90–95% of passengers on intra-EU routes are travelling at reduced fares. One caveat is that there have been quite significant variations in the patterns of fares charged across routes.

There was little initial change in fares on routes that remain monopolies or duopolies. The number of fifth freedom routes doubled to 30 between 1993 and 1996, although this type of operation remains a relatively small feature of the market, and seventh freedoms[2] have been little used. Indeed, much of the new competition was on domestic routes where those routes operated by two or more carriers rose from 65 in January 1963 to 114 in January 1996, with the largest expansions being in France, Spain and Germany. The charter market continued to grow and in some countries accounted for more than 80% of traffic.

More recently (BAE Systems, 2000) while promotional fares fell between 1992 and 2000 (−15%) there were rises in business (+45%) and economy fares (+14%) in nominal terms. There were regional differences in the patterns of fare changes with business fares increasing relatively more for northern European Economic Area (EEA; see Chapters 1 and 2) routes (+6.5%) than for southern routes where they fell (−2.1). The converse was true for both economy and promotional fares.

This was accompanied by an increase in the number of scheduled carriers within the EEA from 77 in 1992 to 140 in 2000. The conditions since September 2001 have led to volatility in the market that extends beyond the demise of Sabena and Swissair in 2002. In terms of the scheduled market, from September 2001 to May 2002 17 airlines withdrew and there were 14 start-ups. In the French market the number of airlines fell from a peak of 26 in 1996 to 12 at the end of 2000 to 6 by mid-2002. There were also significant turnovers in Sweden and Greece. The traditional full cost, flag carriers have been forced to restructure their operations as new low cost carriers (such have Ryanair and easyJet) have taken over 10% of the intra-European market.

15.5	The 2004 enlargement

The move towards the phased enlargement of the EU envisaged under the Treaties of Nice and Madrid has implications for transport. The enlargement will affect the demands placed on the existing transport systems of present member states and those that are acceding. Changes will perhaps be less dramatic than some suppose in that trade has already expanded considerably between the accession states and the EU of the 15 over the last decade. The accession states have also considerably reformed their economic structures – important for influencing what is transported and where – and their transport systems. Nevertheless, the difficulties to be overcome are unlikely to be trivial, especially since enlargement comes as part of a wider set of developments:

- *Geographical.* Enlargement will have implications for the economics of the operation of long haul transport as well as necessitating investment in infrastructure. It will open up new markets for trade and with this will come new demands for transport services internal to all members as well as between them. The scale effects and the ability to reap the benefits of comparative advantage will increase incomes and with this the demand for person movements. What the enlargement will not do is to create a 'natural' transport market. The spatial distribution of economic activities still does not for example have the structure of the US market. In the latter, the overall physical market is essentially rectangular with centres of population and economic activities at the corners and in the centre. This allows exploitation of efficiency benefits from long-haul carriage and hub-and-spoke structures. In the EU economic activity is dichotomously distributed and enlargement will add to the central/peripheral nature of the Union.
- *Legal.* The Constitutional Convention is seeking to develop a longer-term basis for the EU (see Chapters 2, 3 and 28). Issues concerning the nature of central legal responsibilities and the degree of local national autonomy will inevitably arise. This will shape the wider legal structure in which macroeconomic policies regarding transport will be formulated. It will also influence the external policies of the Union – important for transport in a world of global economies and global trade.
- *Economic.* In 2002 the EU Commission President raised the issue of the need for a common fiscal policy within the EU, or at least that part of it in the euro zone. Economists have long understood that a common currency requires a common fiscal policy as a concomitant (see Chapters 8, 9 and 10). This involves the centre having responsibility for fiscal transfers above that now controlled by Brussels. While the exact amount is debated, and depends on the extent to which the centre considers distribution as well as macroeconomic stabilization as part of its function, it may well be considerable. This would take away much national autonomy over major infrastructure works and influence short-term public expenditure patterns.

These are not trivial changes. In most senses it is impossible to talk about any one in isolation from the others, or without considering the background and the current state of existing Union transport policy. The countries gaining membership in 2004 (Poland, the Czech Republic, Hungary, Slovakia, Lithuania, Latvia, Slovenia, Estonia, Cyprus and Malta) also offer a variety of different challenges from a transport perspective. Adding Bulgaria and Romania later compounds the diversity.

The situation is also not one of combining two static blocks but rather of bringing together two units that have started from different places and are moving forward at different speeds. The nature of the economies of the transition states, and their relationships to the EU has already changed considerably since 1989. European Agreements have fostered trade and provided various aid. The EU and some member states unilaterally, have been involved in improving the communications systems within transition states. The EU *Agenda 2000* (CEU, 1997b) identified key links in their transport networks – some 19 000 kilometres of road, 21 000 of rail, and 4000 of inland waterway, 40 airports, 20 seaports and 58 inland ports. With the exception of Bulgaria, all accession states experienced increases in the value of their euro trade between 1989 and 1999. Their industrial structures are changing gradually in light of domestic reforms and exposure to international markets. Nevertheless, there are numerous ways in which their transport systems differ from much of the existing EU. The accession countries are largely distant from the core of the Union. Their remoteness means that railways become a potentially viable mode for long distance freight transport. Indeed, the physical area of an enlarged EU offers the prospects of haul lengths comparable with those in the US where deregulated railways have at least been maintaining their market share. However, the rail networks that currently carry 40% of freight by ton–kilometre within transition economies are largely based on dated technologies and are not oriented to meeting transport demands for movements to/from the EU. They are excessively labour intensive and serve as job creators rather than transport suppliers.

Car ownership is considerably lower in the accession countries than in the existing EU. This is changing. While several of the national markets within the present 15 members are reaching maturity, markets are expanding rapidly in the accession states. This is putting strains on urban infrastructure and poses mounting environmental problems. Smaller states, and some regions within the larger ones, will find themselves subjected to significant transit traffic flows. This raises issues of infrastructure capacity and environmental degradation but also matters of charging and pricing – a subject the EU itself has been singularly poor at addressing. The transition economies also have poorly maintained transport networks largely directed to moving bulk, raw materials to Russia. The road freight sector has begun to develop in response to the needs of modern just-in-time production and some countries are making use of the limited infrastructure links to the west.

Transition economies with maritime access and inland waterways make considerable use of them with about 40% of tonnage moves by water. The island accession states inevitably do the same. Enlargement comes at a time of technical change in maritime transport with the increasing deployment of a post-panamax fleet exploiting scale economies and putting pressures for more hub-and-spoke operations and fleet rationalization.

The transition countries are unlikely to generate a sufficient flow of resources to enhance their networks in line with anticipated demands resulting from EU membership. The EU has provided some resources to supplement those of the accession states

– pre-accession sums of 520 million euros per annum (see Chapters 19 and 22). But these are relatively small. Loan finance has been suggested and discussed in *European Transport Policy for 2010: Time to Decide* (CEU, 2001e). Essentially, the loans would be financed from user charges. A difficulty is that this is not the way most transport infrastructure has been financed elsewhere in the EU. The majority of networks have been constructed from non-dedicated general taxation revenues and direct subsidies. Measures to make transport users more aware of their costs have been discussed, and limited efforts to introduce them made but the situation is not one of a user pay principle along the lines that seem to be suggested for the transition countries.

Transport is also hardly at the forefront of accession negotiations. Direct payments and agricultural subsidies inevitably dominate. The former because of the need to transfer resources to the new member states. The latter to satisfy the essentially soviet style of agricultural policy sanctioned by both those giving and those taking, since the inception of the EEC in the late 1950s, and which politicians seem incapable either of confronting head-on or of finding an inventive path around (see Chapters 20 and 26).

The accession will inevitably, however, involve some transition period and transport will be included within this. This may be seen as reflecting the time needed for the accession countries to adjust their transport system, if not completely, at least largely to the needs of an integrated Union-wide single market. In practice, this would seem to be much less of a physical problem than one of psychology. There have already been major shifts in the way goods are transported in the transition countries as new entrepreneurial talent has come, in particular, into the trucking sector. There has also been some consolidation in rail networks, albeit not large by the scale of the likely cuts required.

Transitions inevitably pose problems. They are often used as an excuse for inertia and for extracting subsidies and grants to sustain stranded capital (infrastructure of no or little use in a new market environment). The EU has used transitions mechanisms in the past to ease change – this was the initial justification for massive agricultural subsidies – but once in place they tend to take on permanency. But even if they are removed, the incumbent pre-reform actors have enjoyed a period in which to adjust their position and to capture the new institutional structure.

The EU's White Paper on transport policy offers a potpourri of ideas on what the future may look like for the larger accession countries and the transition economies in particular. The concern is very much to make use of the 'extensive, dense network and of significant know-how' in these countries to rebalance the transport modes in Europe. In other words, to maintain the modal share of the railways in the accession states and to have 35% of freight moved on rail by 2010.

15.6 Conclusions

Papers written in the early 1990s were extremely pessimistic about the prospects for any viable transport policy being initiated within the EU. That transport was important was seldom questioned, but prior attempts to do anything other than tinker with the prevailing, largely national driven, transport policies had proved disappointing. Early efforts in the 1960s to draw up what essentially amounted to a master plan or blueprint policy had failed. The problems of continued enlargement of the Union, coupled with fresh, often radical thinking on how transport as a sector should be treated, seemed to pose almost insurmountable problems for policy makers in the 1970s and 1980s. These problems were not helped by mounting concerns over physical and institutional bottlenecks in the transport system of Europe that were manifestly an impediment to any radical shift towards a more rapid phase of economic integration.

At the time of writing the picture is entirely different. Certainly many issues remain to be resolved, such as the initiation of more rational pricing for most modes, but by and large transport inadequacies are no longer seen as a major threat to further economic and political integration within the EU. There is broad agreement that transparency and market-based systems afford an efficient way to meet the EU transport needs. While there has been much wasted time and effort, and significant economic, social and political costs are inevitably associated with this, the current phase of transport policy formulation can be seen as one of the important recent successes of the EU.

NOTES

1. The right of an airline of one country to carry traffic between two countries outside its country of registry as long as the flight originates or terminates in its country of registry.

2. The right of an airline to operate standalone services entirely outside the territory of its home state, that is, to carry traffic between two foreign states.

Chapter 16

Energy policy and energy markets

STEPHEN MARTIN AND ALI EL-AGRAA

16.1 Introduction

A full discussion of the EU Common Energy Policy (CEP) should cover a number of topics. It should give a full account of the policies pursued by the individual member nations of the EU; assess the energy balances for various years, including the latest available; describe the EU institutions which are particularly concerned with energy matters; and document the history of EU energy efforts and proposals. Such a comprehensive coverage is not attempted here simply because the diversity of policies pursued by the individual nations precludes a discussion of these aspects, and also because all the relevant EU institutions are presented and discussed in Chapter 3. In any case, such a comprehensive coverage would in effect require a whole book; hence this chapter concentrates mainly on the objectives of and recent developments in the CEP and energy markets.

This chapter considers the EU role in energy policy, notes past attempts to create a CEP, assesses the factors behind their failure and examines why the Union has been able to influence national policies more successfully during the past few years. After discussing the current policy proposals and their context, the situation in the different EU energy industries is reviewed, noting their main characteristics and the balance of past and present EU policy towards them. Finally, some of the difficulties the Commission faces both in developing a credible CEP and in addressing the energy industries within such a framework are assessed. Before carrying out all these tasks, however, it is necessary to consider the rationale for a EU energy policy.

16.2 The need for a EU energy policy

It is important to ask what the economic rationale is for a CEP. The primary energy sector comprises several major industries, including coal, natural gas, nuclear energy, and petroleum. These industries account for substantial employment in their own right, produce collectively an essential input for productive activity throughout the economy, and, at the primary level, are a sector for which the EU is increasingly dependent on external sources of supply.

Moreover, since the oil crises of the 1970s another, overlapping, set of industries has emerged. These industries produce goods and services aimed at reducing both industrial and domestic heating consumption (conserving resources) and emerging sectors supplying alternative energy sources, including solar, tidal and wave energy.

Each of these industries has its own general characteristics and problems. They interact with secondary energy industries: electricity generation and distribution; oil refining and distribution of oil products; gas collection and distribution, etc. These various and diverse industries have different market structures, ranging from large-numbers oligopoly to publicly owned monopoly; some suppliers are small private firms, others are multinational corporations. They are also subject to government policies driven by often contradictory domestic political pressures from producers, consumers, environmentalist lobbies, trade unionists and other interest groups.

If the ongoing process of EU economic, monetary and political union (EMU; see Chapters 1 and 9) is to have its full effect, market forces must be allowed to influence resource allocation in the energy sector, as in other key parts of the economy. Anything less would amount to a significant non-tariff barrier to free trade.

As the role of market forces in the energy sector increases, it should be expected that energy market performance will come under the purview of the same competition policy rules that apply to other sectors of the economy (see Chapter 12). Industrial (Chapter 13) and trade rules (Chapter 11) will apply as well. Such developments have already begun to take place, as an internal energy market begins to take shape. This does not preclude a specific policy to promote and protect the internal energy market in its early stages, and to ensure effective market performance along the way.

It must be admitted, however, that if by a policy one means a combination of a clear vision of the future, a coherent set of principles, a range of policy instruments adequate to the objectives that are set, and the existence of sufficient legitimacy and authority to carry the measures through, many analysts would argue that the EU does not have a CEP.[1]

Be that as it may, the idea of a CEP for the EU is almost as old as the Union itself. In the years since the EEC was founded in 1957, numerous policy proposals have been made by the Commission or by its predecessor. Those proposals were marked by a shifting balance of priorities and a range of proposed mechanisms, depending on the conditions in the energy markets and the influence of the Commission. For the most part, however, these attempts came to nothing, with member states either rejecting or ignoring them. Since the early 1980s the Commission has again been active in the energy sector, as the momentum of the single market debate has gathered pace and environmental concerns have intensified.[2]

16.3   Past attempts and present successes

16.3.1 The treaties and energy

That the EC attached great importance to the energy sector is demonstrated by the fact that two of the three treaties on which the EC is based are specifically concerned with energy: the 1951 Treaty of Paris creating the European Coal and Steel Community (ECSC) and the 1957 Treaty of Rome establishing Euratom were devoted to the coal and nuclear sectors, respectively. The details of these treaties (and their rationale) are covered in Chapter 2, but their significance for energy policy is clear enough. The 1951 ECSC treaty reflected the dominance of coal in the energy balance of member states (as well as its role in the steel industry); by tackling coal, most EC energy supply and demand issues were addressed. The 1957 Euratom treaty sought to foster cooperation in the development of civil nuclear power, then perceived as the main source of future energy requirements (Lucas, 1977). Both treaties, moreover, were in principle geared towards the creation of free and integrated markets in these sectors: the ECSC sought to abolish all barriers to trade between member states while controlling subsidies and cartel-like behaviour amongst producers;[3] Euratom also paid lip service to the idea of a common market in nuclear products.

A common market for other energy sectors was addressed in the EEC Rome Treaty. While the EEC was orientated towards more or less competitively structured sectors, it was also intended to cover the more oligopolistic or monopolistic sectors such as oil, gas and electricity. Accordingly, in addition to being subject to the EEC Treaty's general provisions on opening up markets, these energy industries' special characteristics were covered by the Treaty's provisions on state enterprises and their conduct.

16.3.2 Policy efforts, 1951–1973

The gap between intentions expressed in the Treaties and the outcomes, however, has been a large one for energy, more so than for most other parts of the economy. The Commission's attempts to develop an energy policy of any sort, let alone one reflecting the ideals of the treaties, have proved to be of only limited success.

From the 1950s on, the Commission or its equivalents sought to develop a policy first for coal and then for energy more broadly (see El-Agraa and Hu, 1984). On coal, the High Authority was unable to impose the spirit of the Paris Treaty on national industries; it was mainly involved in tackling the crises which beset the European coal industry from the mid-1950s onward (Lindberg and Scheingold, 1970). In the sphere of energy generally, initial efforts were made as the negotiations for the EEC were progressing. The Messina conference recommended that the potential for coordinated energy policy be considered, but the Spaak Committee determined that this would not be necessary (von Geusau, 1975).

Following the establishment of the new Communities, there was a renewed attempt to develop a CEP. The formation of an inter-executive Committee on energy in 1959 sought to develop a policy focusing on the creation of a common energy market. The main concerns of the Committee were with the effect of energy prices on industrial competitiveness and, to a lesser extent, with the security of energy supply (Political and Economic Planning, 1963). However, governments largely rejected the Committee's attempts to gain access to energy policy; instead they exercised benign neglect towards the energy sector. This inertia on energy policy reflected the largely untroubled energy markets of the period. However, when there was concern over supply in the 1950s and 1960s (such as in the wake of the Suez crisis), governments were keen to retain their autonomy.

The merger of the Communities in 1968 saw the Commission renew its efforts to develop a CEP. In its document 'First Guidelines Towards a EC Energy Policy' (CEC, 1968), the Commission noted that barriers to trade in energy persisted and stressed the necessity of a common energy market. Such a market, based on the needs of consumers and competitive pressures, would help obtain security of energy supplies at the lowest cost. To this end the Commission suggested three broad objectives: a plan for the sector involving data collection and forecasting as a means of influencing members' investment strategies; measures to bring about a common energy market (tackling issues such as tax harmonization, technical barriers, state monopolies, etc.); measures to ensure security of supply at lowest cost.

The proposals proved difficult to put into practice, partly because of the scale of objectives and contradictions between the substance of different goals, but mainly because of the resistance of member states to the goals. Even though the Council approved the strategy, it ignored most of the Commission's subsequent attempts to enact the proposals. The principal measures adopted in the wake of the Commission's proposals concerned oil stocks (following OECD initiatives) and some requirements for energy investment notification. These actions owed more to growing concern about security of supply than to the creation of a common energy market, and presaged a wider shift in Commission and member state perceptions of the priorities of energy policy. The reaction to the 1973–1974 oil crisis confirmed the change in orientation of energy policy proposals away from markets and towards security.

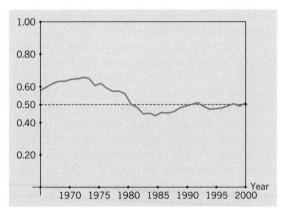

Figure 16.1 Share of net energy imports in total primary energy supply, 1966–2000

Source: OECD, *Energy Balances of OECD Countries, 1999–2000*, 2002. OECD©, 2002

16.3.3 Energy crises, 1973–1986

The backdrop for the new emphasis on security of supply was the development of the Community's energy balances and the changes in global energy markets generally. Since the 1950s, the member states had become less reliant upon domestically produced coal and more reliant on imported resources, primarily oil. This shift in demand reflected the growth in overall energy demand, but also a gradual but absolute decline in energy resources among the then member states. By 1970, over 60% of the EC's needs were imported, leaving it highly vulnerable to the supply disruptions and price increases of 1973–1974 (see Figure 16.1).

In the midst of the first oil shock, the EC attempted a crisis management role but failed even to provide a united front *vis-à-vis* the OAPEC oil embargo of the Netherlands (Daintith and Hancher, 1986). Member states pursued their own policies or worked through the International Energy Agency (IEA). Formed in 1974, the IEA overshadowed the EC both in breadth of membership (covering all the OECD countries except France) and in terms of its powers on oil sharing in a new crisis (van der Linde and Lefeber, 1988).

Even so, the shock of oil price increases reinforced the reassessment of energy policies in member states and the Commission. The Commission attempted to develop a more strategic approach to the management of energy supply and demand. The 'New Strategy' (*Bulletin of the European Communities, Supplement 4/1974*), which was only agreed to after much wrangling and dilution (a proposal for a European energy agency was abandoned after member state opposition – see Lucas, 1977), envisaged a number of targets to be met by 1985 (COM (74) 1960). These included the reduction of oil imports, the development of domestic energy capabilities (notably nuclear power) and the rational use of energy (see Table 16.1). The policy, while only indicative, mobilized resources for R&D and promotional programmes on energy, covering conventional and nuclear technologies, but also (albeit to a limited extent) renewables and energy efficiency technologies. The new strategy also provided the basis for a handful of directives designed to restrict the use of oil and gas.

The new strategy clearly entailed a shift in emphasis. The goal of a common energy market was demoted, although it was alluded to in areas such as pricing policies and some measures directed at the oil sector (see below). Overall, policy was concerned with changing the structure of energy balances rather than the structure of energy markets. The condition of energy markets (notably after the second oil shock) and concern over energy prices and security in the early 1980s were such that the policy was sustained into the decade. Further rounds of energy policy objectives were agreed in 1979 (to be met by 1990) and 1986 (for 1995). The 1995 objectives included a number of 'horizontal' objectives, aimed at more general energy policy concerns, such as its relationship with other EC policies. Each round sought to build on the previous one, and although in general the goals appeared to be on target, in some cases they reflected a degree of failure either across the EC or in certain member states, and subsequent rounds would adopt a rather less ambitious agenda (COM (84) 88 and COM (88) 174). The objectives approach reappeared as part of more recent EU energy strategy (COM (96) 431).

By the mid-1980s, therefore, the Commission had succeeded in establishing a place in energy policy making, but it was far from being central to member states' energy policy agendas, let alone one being sufficiently influential to dictate the development of a common energy market. Instead, its role consisted of information gathering, target setting and enabling activities (the latter had a substantial budget for energy R&D and promotion). While these measures ensured that the Commission had an influence on policy, they were not without problems – some of the objectives showed few signs of achievement, while aspects of the Commission's funding strategies were also open to

criticism (Cruickshank and Walker, 1981). Moreover, aside from a few legislative measures, the Commission's policy had few teeth. The locus of power remained with national governments, which generally chose to follow their own energy policies, resisting too strong a Commission role.

16.3.4 The new energy policy agenda: competition and the environment

In the course of the 1980s, however, the agenda for energy policy began to change. Developments in energy markets, the attitudes of governments towards the energy industries and the overall position of the Commission in policy making contributed to a turnaround in the concerns of EC energy policy. The new agenda rests on two broader objectives: the creation of a competition-oriented single energy market and the pursuit of environmental protection (see Chapters 12 and 17).

A key factor in the changed regime was the shift in energy markets. Prices stabilized and faltered in the early 1980s and continued to weaken until the 1986 oil price collapse. The reasons for this were more fundamental than the rows within OPEC which precipitated the fall in prices. The price increases of the early 1980s had had the effect of boosting output in OPEC countries, as well as fostering exploration and production in the rest of world. Furthermore, many countries had sought to improve energy efficiency and diversify sources of energy (if not to the levels sought by the Commission). The economic recession of the 1980s also dampened demand. The combined effect of these factors was a massive over-capacity in supply and minimal demand growth (see Figure 16.2) which forced down prices. The effects were not only confined to oil: gas and coal were in equally plentiful supply, while the consequences of past over-investment in electricity capacity also boosted the energy surplus.

The combined effect of these developments was to weaken the scarcity culture which had prevailed among suppliers, consumers, governments and the Commission. As prices fell and markets appeared well supplied so the concerns of policy focused less on energy supply *per se* and more on the price and the existence of obstacles to good market performance.

Table 16.1 The EU energy objectives for 1985, 1990, 1995 and 2010

1985 objectives

To increase nuclear power capacity to 200 GW

To increase Community production of oil and natural gas to 180 million tonnes oil equivalent

To maintain production of coal in the Community at 180 million tonnes oil equivalent

To keep imports to no more than 40% of consumption

To reduce projected demand for 1985 by 15%

To raise electricity contribution to final energy consumption to 35%

1990 objectives

To reduce to 0.7 or less the average ratio between the rate of growth in gross primary energy demand and the rate of growth of gross domestic product

To reduce oil consumption to a level of 40% of primary energy consumption

To cover 70–75% of primary energy requirements for electricity production by means of solid fuels and nuclear energy

To encourage the use of renewable energy sources so as to increase their contribution to the Community's energy supplies

To pursue energy pricing policies geared to attaining the energy objectives

1995 objectives

To improve the efficiency of final energy demand by 20%

To maintain oil consumption at around 40% of energy consumption and to maintain net oil imports at less than one-third of total energy consumption

To maintain the share of natural gas in the energy balance on the basis of a policy aimed at ensuring stable and diversified supplies

To increase the share of solid fuels in energy consumption

To pursue efforts to promote consumption of solid fuels and to improve the competitiveness of their production capacities in the Community

To reduce the proportion of electricity generated by hydrocarbons to less than 15%

To increase the share of renewables in energy balances

To ensure more secure conditions of supply and to reduce risks of energy price fluctuations

To apply Community price formation principles to all sectors

To balance energy and environmental concerns through the use of best available technologies

To implement measures to improve energy balance in less-developed regions of the Community

To develop a single energy market

To coordinate external relations in the energy sector

2010 objectives

To meet Treaty objectives, notably market integration, sustainable development, environmental protection and supply security

To integrate energy and environmental objectives and to incorporate the full cost of energy in the price

To strengthen security of supply through improved diversification and flexibility of domestic and imported supplies on the one hand and by ensuring flexible responses to supply emergencies on the other

To develop a coordinated approach to external energy relations to ensure free and open trade and to secure investment framework

To promote renewable energy resources with the aim of achieving a significant share of primary energy production by 2010

To improve energy efficiency by 2010 through better coordination of both national and Community measures

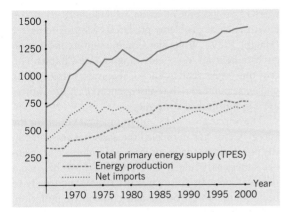

Figure 16.2 EU energy balances, 1966–2000 (millions of tonnes of oil equivalent; TPES = energy production plus net imports minus stock increases)

Source: OECD, *Energy Balances of OECD Countries, 1999–2000*, 2002

This change in market conditions made many energy policies, especially those fostering conservation or diversification from high-price fuels, hard to justify or sustain. In some countries, governments abandoned traditional approaches to energy policy. The United Kingdom was the most notable example, making an explicit move to rely on market forces for determining supply and demand. A major plank of that policy was deregulation, with attempts to introduce competition to gas and power, and privatization, with the sale of oil interests and then the gas and electricity industries (Helm *et al.*, 1989). Shifts in policies were under review in other parts of the EC (Helm and McGowan, 1989), although these were often conceived at a less ambitious level or pursued for rather different reasons.

The deregulatory thrust was not confined to the energy sector – indeed it was probably initially more widely spread in other areas of the economy. It was, for example, to the fore in the Commission's plans for the Single European Market (SEM; see Chapters 2 and 11) as covered in the White Paper (CEC, 1985a). Partly as a reflection of past energy policy failures, the Commission did not include energy in the initial agenda for the SEM. However, areas where energy was affected indirectly by more general SEM measures (such as indirect taxation and procurement policies) meant that the sector was not untouched by the proposals.

Indeed, there were already some signs of a different policy towards energy. The issue of price transparency was extended across the energy industries with attempts to agree a directive on the issue. While

the moves failed, they indicated a greater interest in the issue by the Commission. The Commission was also taking a greater interest in energy subsidies (as in the case of Dutch support to its horticultural industry through the provision of cheap gas). Other indications of change included moves to tackle state oil monopolies and the types of support given to the coal industry in a number of member states.

The potential for more radical action was indicated by a number of moves taken by the Competition Directorate of the Commission towards other 'utility' industries. It sought the introduction of more competitive arrangements in the civil aviation industry and was able to threaten use of legal powers to this end. In the field of telecommunications, it sought to open access for equipment and service sales, using powers under Article 90 to do so (see Chapter 13). These moves demonstrated not only a willingness to act but also a range of mechanisms which could be used in other sectors. The further the policy went in one industry the more likely that it would be applied to others.

This changing agenda meant that the idea of an internal energy market (IEM) was once again an issue for the EC. While the 1995 goals were largely flavoured by energy security concerns, one of the 'horizontal' objectives was the creation of an IEM. As the prospect of a SEM became realizable with the '1992' campaign, the idea of extending it to energy took root, and in 1987 the Energy Commissioner, Nicolas Mosar, announced a study of the barriers to an IEM.

The Commission's thinking was revealed in 'The Internal Energy Market' (COM (88) 238), a review which set out the potential benefits of an IEM and the obstacles that faced it. The IEM would cut costs to consumers (particularly to energy-intensive industries), thereby making European industry as a whole more competitive; it would increase security of supply by improving integration of the energy industries; it would rationalize the structure of the energy industries and allow for greater complementarity among the different supply and demand profiles of member states. The benefits would stem from a mixture of cost-reducing competition and the achievement of scale economies in a number of industries. Taken together these would more than recover the 0.5% of EC GDP which the Commission claimed was the 'cost of non-Europe' in the energy sector (although, as noted, energy was not part of the original SEM debate nor of the 'cost of non-Europe' exercise which assessed the benefits of the SEM – see Cecchini (1988) and Emerson *et al.* (1988) and Chapter 11).

According to the Commission, the obstacles to the IEM were to be found in the structures and practices of the energy industries. These ranged from different taxation and financial regimes to restrictive measures which protected energy industries in particular countries and conditions which prevented full coordination of supplies at the most efficient level (the latter applying to the gas and electricity industries). However, as the Commission admitted, the effects of particular practices were difficult to assess given the special nature of the energy industries. Indeed, in certain cases, the Commission appeared hesitant over the extent of the IEM. Nonetheless, the document demonstrated that the Commission was committed to implement an IEM and would examine all barriers to its development. It has followed up that commitment with measures to implement the White Paper proposals (on taxation and procurement) and to apply EC law to the sector.

In the period since the IEM document was published, the Commission has completed the programme of measures liberalizing the energy industries' procurement practices, but has been unable to achieve an effective harmonization of indirect taxation (see Chapter 14). It has also made considerable progress on liberalizing the electricity and gas supply markets and the offshore exploration industry. Less has been achieved by way of coal industry reform. To the extent that the policy has been successful, it has been aided not only by changes in EC decision-making procedures, notably the majority voting conditions allowed under the Single European Act (SEA), but also by the prospect of the Commission using its powers to investigate the energy sector from a Treaty of Rome perspective. However, there remain many aspects of the policy to be implemented, where the Commission will have to overcome the opposition of member states.

Since 1988, the IEM has played a major role in Commission proposals on energy policy. It has, for all its problems, shifted the emphasis in Community policy towards the energy sector. Over the same period, however, another element has also gained a higher profile in deliberations on the sector: the environment.

The Commission's interest in environmental issues is not new. The formal commitment of the EC to environmental policy dates from early 1972 when, in the wake of the Stockholm conference, the Council

agreed a programme of action, while some measures on environmental problems predated even this initiative (Haigh, 1989). While the Commission's concerns on environment are very wide ranging (see Chapter 17), covering issues such as chemical wastes, water quality and noise pollution, the consequences of energy choices are a major part of the policy.

The importance of EC environmental policy for the energy sector has paralleled the ascent of the issue up the political agenda in an increasing number of member states, particularly as the Greens have become a political force. In those cases where governments have been obliged to introduce new controls on pollution, they have sought to have them accepted across the EC so as not to lose competitiveness. The best example has been the acid rain debate where the German government, forced to introduce major controls on domestic emissions from industrial and electricity plants, has pressed for similar controls in all member states (Boehmer-Christiansen and Skea, 1990). These were agreed in 1988, setting targets for emission reduction into the next century.

The emergence of the environment has given the Commission a higher profile in energy matters and another, more robust, lever on energy policy (Owens and Hope, 1989). The importance of the issue to energy policy was demonstrated in the 1995 objectives where environmental concerns were identified as a major consideration in policy. The status of environmental issues overall was confirmed in the SEA where it was given its own provisions (allowing it to enforce decisions on a majority vote). The SEM proposals also identify the need for high standards of environmental protection in the EC and this has impacted on the IEM debate.

Integrating environment and energy has not been easy for the Commission; a document on the issue was apparently the focus for considerable dispute within the Commission because of the different perspectives of the Directorates for Energy and for the Environment (COM (89) 369). However, the issue which has both brought the environment to the centre of Community energy policy making and exposed the tensions between the two policies most starkly has been the greenhouse effect.

The Commission has sought to coordinate a common European response to the threat of global warming. In 1991 the member states, with the exception of the United Kingdom, agreed to stabilize emissions of CO_2 by the year 2000. In the following year it produced proposals for decreasing emissions of greenhouse gases, particularly CO_2 (COM (92) 246). These comprised four elements: programmes to encourage the development of renewable energy sources (which have zero or very low carbon dioxide emissions) and of energy efficiency, a monitoring system and a carbon-energy tax to discourage use of fossil fuels.

While much has been achieved by the Commission in incorporating conservation and renewables into a strategy for tackling global warming, the carbon tax has all but been abandoned. The proposed tax consists of two elements, one related to the energy used and the other to the carbon emitted by the fuel in question. The tax therefore penalizes coal use most strongly but not as much as if it were a pure carbon tax. Small renewable-based energy sources are not covered by the proposal. More importantly, large industrial consumers are also exempt from it, and the proposal will not be put into effect unless equivalent steps were undertaken by other industrialized countries (Pearson and Smith, 1991). Despite these conditions, which were included after considerable lobbying of the Commission, the proposal has drawn a good deal of criticism from industries and governments, and, although modifications have been made, the chances of an agreement in the Council appear slim. Subsequent attempts to use taxation as an instrument of environmental policy in the energy sector have also been opposed (Finon and Surrey, 1996).

Although the single market and the environment dominate energy policy, the Commission continues to pursue a variety of other energy policy objectives. It continues with its support for energy efficiency and renewables through research budgets and other measures designed to encourage their use (such as recommendations for preferential terms for renewable sources of supply). It has developed policies for supporting energy infrastructures primarily in less-developed areas of the Community, although this goal has been broadened in the light of attempts to increase integration of gas and electricity supply, through the initiative on fostering 'trans-EC networks' (McGowan, 1993).

The Commission has sought to develop a role in the traditionally difficult area of security of supply. The policy it has proposed addresses two aspects of the problem: the development of indigenous energy resources and the management of Community activities in the event of supply disruption. The first element, which was developed in response to the British government's desire to protect the nuclear industry after privatization, allows authorities to subsidize up to 20% of their energy requirements on the grounds that, while subsidization may infringe the Treaty's free market provisions, it also supports the Community's own energy resources (Brittan, 1992). The second element of the policy comprises a variety of measures designed to establish a clearer role for the Commission in energy crisis management and diplomacy.

It is largely for securing supplies that an increasingly important part of the Community's energy policy activities is the links with the rest of the world. These are focused on immediate neighbours to the north, east and south of the EU. The principal element of these links has been its efforts to draw Eastern Europe into secure energy links through the European Energy Charter (COM (91) 36). This was the initiative of the Dutch Prime Minister, Ruud Lubbers, who sought to use an agreement on energy, symbolically echoing the ECSC in ending the cold war, and, more importantly, acting as a framework for closer energy links between the Community and the East. An agreement on a basic charter was reached at the end of 1991 and an Energy Charter Treaty signed at the end of 1994 (see Sodupe and Benito, 2001).

The Energy Charter Treaty and the protocol on energy efficiency and related environmental aspects became effective on 16 April 1998, but was not fully ratified until 1999 when the remaining two EU nations, France and Ireland, did so. With the approval in December 1999 of the Altener (promotion of renewable energy sources) and SAVE (promotion of energy efficiency) programmes, the European Parliament and the Council put the finishing touches on a 1997 multi-annual framework programme for action in the energy sector (1998–2000) and its six specific programmes. The framework programme itself and the four specific programmes designated as ETAP (studies, analyses, forecasts and related work), SYNERGY (international cooperation), CARNOT (clean and efficient use of solid fuels) and SURE (nuclear transport safety and international cooperation) were adopted in 1998. These developments have kept the Commission busy. For example, on 8 November 1999, after a lengthy screening of the energy sector in the new applicants, it adopted a communication on strengthening the northern dimension of the CEP, which the Council endorsed a month later; it signed a memorandum of understanding on industrial cooperation with Russia, which included energy; on 4 May 1999, it adopted its second report on the state of liberalization of the energy markets, which it found to be 'highly satisfactory'; etc.

In financial terms, the SAVE II programme adopted in December 1999 is allocated a budget of 66 million euro. This is hardly a sum to be elated about, but it is an improvement on the 7.4 million euro for the original SAVE programme, under which 52 projects benefited in 1999.

16.3.5 The prospects for a common energy policy

Such a variety of activities, along with the increased recourse to the Community institutions by member states and pressure groups on energy matters, would suggest that the Commission anticipated the Community finally taking responsibility for energy policy. However, attempts to formalize its role in the Maastricht Treaty were unsuccessful. While the Commission was able to insert a relatively weak commitment to a Community role, which was kept in the draft treaty up to the very last negotiations, a number of member states indicated their objections to it and obtained its removal at the last stage in the negotiations. The Commission subsequently embarked on an extensive consultation exercise in order to clarify its role in energy policy making. A Green Paper was published at the end of 1994 with a White Paper following at the end of 1995. Both documents stressed the importance of energy matters by drawing attention to the prospect of increased energy dependence: Commission forecasts suggested that imported energy would account for as much as 70% of energy needs by 2020 (CEU, 1995a). The documents reiterated the need for a Community energy policy on the basis of reconciling the objectives of supply security, environmental protection and an internal market (see previous section); a Community dimension was justified on the basis of existing treaty powers (particularly in competition policy and the internal market), the international nature of energy markets and problems and existing policy and budgetary commitments (CEC, 1995c). The White Paper established an Energy Consultative Committee to ensure transparency and set out an extensive work programme for the Community in the energy sphere (although interestingly the Commission has also been willing to review, and where necessary to discard, existing policies). Since the White Paper the Commission has conducted two reviews of energy legislation and recommended the rescinding of some measures (including those affecting oil and gas use in such sectors as power generation).

Despite its ambitious scale, the White Paper did not seek to justify the inclusion of energy in the next round of treaty negotiations. However, the Maastricht Treaty had included a condition that the status of energy – along with some other policies – be reviewed as part of those discussions. In its report the Commission, while being careful not to call explicitly for a chapter on energy, indicated that inclusion was desirable given the various goals of Community energy policy and the need to rationalize the coverage of the energy sectors across the treaties. The Commission followed this up since the latter part of 1996 with documents designed to justify a Community role: although these documents spelled out a range of recommendations (including a new set of energy policy objectives) they were clearly designed to strengthen the case for a formal CEP (COM (96) 431).

The Commission's (CEU, 2001h) *Green Paper on Energy Security* laid out four principles of EU energy policy: security of supply, completion of the internal market (to which we turn our attention in the next section), environmental measures, and the promotion of renewable energy sources and demand management. The Commission has proposed a Community Framework for security of energy supplies.[4] Elements of the proposal include coordinating management of reserves at the EC level and supplementing strategic oil reserves with reserves of natural gas.[5]

16.4   Energy markets

A common element to the past energy policies of EU member states (and the policies of most other countries) seems to have been the belief that energy is too important to be left to markets. In retrospect, however, it appears that government intervention in the energy sector has often made market performance worse rather than better.

Government intervention in markets may be justified on grounds of market failure. In the energy supply chain, market failure seems present in the oil tanker industry, where the (sometimes difficult to identify) owners of rust-bucket tankers have little incentive to internalize the social cost of oil spills. The failure to internalize environmental costs of consuming carbon-based fuels is a general market failure in the energy sector. Market failure is also present in that the incentives delivered by the market for the private development of alternative energy sources do not fully reflect their expected social benefits.[6]

Government intervention may also be justified for natural monopoly markets, on the grounds that performance of such markets will be unacceptable. There have been times and segments of energy markets where firms have exercised control over prices. But in many segments of the energy sector, the belief in supply-side market power has been much more enduring than the actual exercise of market power. Where market power has endured, it has been rooted in the control of essential facilities in distribution, and in ill-founded policies that supported the extension of that market power to vertically related segments of the energy supply chain.

In many energy markets, market forces could deliver acceptable market performance, given the opportunity to do so. The recognition of this fact has triggered a policy shift that sets that stage for energy market liberalization. Actual energy market liberalization has gone forward by fits and starts, hampered by the occasional reluctance of governments to rely on the market mechanism.

16.4.1 Demand

Figure 16.2 illustrates the time path of overall EU energy use. Energy demand responds to price changes, but with a lag, reflecting the time needed to develop energy-efficient production techniques and install the physical capital required to put those techniques into effect. Thus the absolute decline in energy use in the mid-1970s is a reaction to the 1973 oil shock.

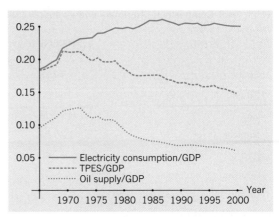

Figure 16.3 EU energy demand indicators, 1966–2000 (TPES = total primary energy supply (millions of tonnes of oil equivalent); electricity consumption measured in kilowatt hours; oil supply measured in tonnes of oil equivalent; GDP measured in 1000 1995 US$)

Source: OECD, Energy Balances of OECD Countries, 1999–2000, 2002

Similarly, the decline in the first half of the 1980s is a reaction to the 1979 oil shock.

Despite these blips, the trend in energy use is steadily upward. This trend is expected to continue. European Commission projections are that EU energy consumption in 2020 will be 22% greater than EU energy consumption in 1990 (CEU, 2001h, p. 46).

As EU energy use has increased, it has also become more efficient. Figure 16.3 shows that the intensity of use of primary energy – primary energy consumption per unit of gross domestic product – is steadily downward. So is consumption of crude oil per unit of gross domestic product.

16.5   Primary energy

Table 16.2 gives a breakdown of EU primary energy sources for the year 2000. Oil is the leading source of EU energy, and by far the largest part of that oil is imported. Figure 16.2 shows that imports generally account for about half of the EU's primary energy supply. This level is down from the mid-1970s, but above the low reached in the mid-1980s.

The prognosis is that oil and gas will continue to supply the lion's share of EU energy needs (Table 16.2). The share of natural gas is expected to rise (Kemp and

Stephen, 2001). Russia will be a major supplier of natural gas to the EU in the 21st century.

The share of imported energy in overall EU energy use is projected to rise from the current near-50% to 70% (EU 15; see Table 16.3). The anticipated increasing share of oil imports reflects in part the expected decline in output of North Sea oil. This decline has often been predicted, and often postponed by technological advance,[7] but it will eventually materialize. It follows that long-run EU energy security lies in the

Table 16.2 Composition of primary energy supply (millions of tons of oil equivalent), EU, 2000

	Production	Imports	Exports	Net supply	% TPES
Coal	99.35	117.08	9.82	212.23	14.53
Oil and oil products	164.36	799.74	325.54	592.80	40.59
Gas	190.52	204.02	49.27	338.74	23.20
Nuclear	225.14	–	–	225.14	15.42
Hydro	27.40	–	–	27.40	1.88
Geothermal and solar, etc.	5.67	–	–	5.67	0.39
Combustible, renewable, waste	53.73	0.74	0.16	54.31	3.72
Electricity		18.97	15.33	3.64	0.25
Heat	0.37	0	0	0.37	0.03
Total	766.53	1140.56	400.12	1460.28	100.00

Source: IEA (2002), p. II.47. ©OECD/IEA, 2002. Net supply of oil and gas allows for stock and other changes

Table 16.3 Projected oil and gas consumption, share of imported energy in EU energy consumption, 1998–2030

	Projected share of oil and gas in total EU energy consumption (%)		Projected import dependence (%)	
	EU	EU 30	EU	EU 30
1998	64	61	49	36
2010	66	63	54	42
2020	66	65	62	51
2030	67	66	71	60

Source: Adapted from European Commission (2001). Reprinted by permission of the European Communities.

smooth functioning of energy markets, and in particular the oil market.

The market for crude oil is in fact a world market. Before 1973, it was a large-numbers oligopoly, the most important operators on the supply side being the eight 'Seven Sisters'.[8] The rise of OPEC, itself a large-numbers oligopoly, cut the vertically integrated majors loose from their crude supplies. The majors' distribution networks remained valuable assets, and oil provinces outside OPEC proved only too willing to hire the majors to develop their own oilfields. The majors thus integrated backwards, by ownership or contact, into production, and developed new oil suppliers.

As the shares of output and proven reserves outside OPEC control rose, OPEC members learned the hard lesson that a business' most important asset are its customers. OPEC national oil companies integrated forward into refining and distribution. The world oil market continues to be a large-numbers oligopoly, and the numbers are larger than they were in 1973.

Table 16.4 shows regional data on production and proven reserves of crude oil for the year 2001. Table 16.5 shows similar data for natural gas. The figures for proven reserves should be interpreted with caution, for at least three reasons. The first reason is that reported figures for proven reserves in the Middle East are widely believed to be understated. The second reason is that not all proven reserves are created equal: what one would really like, for each region, are not figures for total supply, but rather a kind of cumulative marginal cost curve: how much could be extracted at a cost less than x per barrel (per million BTUs, in the case of natural gas), how much at a price of $x + 1$ per barrel, and so on. The third reason, related to the

Table 16.4 World crude oil proven reserves, production by region, 2001

	Production		Proven reserves	
	1000 b/d	% World total	Million barrels	% World total
Middle East	20 772.9	31.7	694 754	64.6
Latin America	9 318.1	14.2	123 780	11.5
Eastern Europe	8 245.3	12.6	67 160	6.2
Asia and Pacific	7 208.0	11.0	44 391	4.1
North America	7 181.3	11.0	33 066	3.1
Africa	6 625.4	10.1	90 004	8.4
Western Europe	6 147.7	9.4	18 033	1.7
Total world	65 498.7	100.0	1 074 850	100.0
OPEC	26 872.5	41.0	845 412	78.7

Source: OPEC, 2001 Annual Statistical Bulletin, p. 10, p. 14. Reprinted by permission of OPEC

Table 16.5 World natural gas proven reserves and marketed production, by region, 2001

	Production		Proven reserves	
	Million standard m^3	% World total	Billion standard m^3	% World total
Eastern Europe	740 290	28.9	56 377	31.6
North America	737 194	28.7	7 042	4.0
Asia and Pacific	289 670	11.3	15 225	8.5
Western Europe	285 060	11.1	7 028	3.9
Middle East	241 245	9.4	71 356	40.0
Latin America	137 390	5.4	8 082	4.5
Africa	133 386	5.2	13 107	7.4
Total world	2 564 235	100.0	178 216	100.0
OPEC	419 141	16.3	87 853	49.3

Source: OPEC, 2001 Annual Statistical Bulletin, p. 12, p. 16. Reprinted by permission of OPEC

second, is that the march of technological progress continually expands the amount of crude oil and natural gas that it is profitable to extract from known oil fields. Even if no new fields are developed, proven reserves next year are not proven reserves today minus production during the year. Proven reserves next year are proven reserves today, minus production during

the year, plus the additional deposits that it becomes profitable to produce from known oilfields as extraction technology improves.

By luck of geology, most of the world's crude oil reserves are located in the Middle East. All evidence is that these deposits are much less costly to extract than oil deposits located elsewhere in the world.

Production of crude oil is much less geographically concentrated than are proven reserves. Middle Eastern producers – more generally, OPEC member states – could easily supply most of the world's oil, at a lower price than they would like. By attempting to restrict their own output, OPEC member states (through their national oil companies) set two forces in motion.

First, OPEC as a group creates incentives for each individual OPEC member state, acting in its own immediate interest, to produce more than its OPEC quota output. Indeed, OPEC member states consistently produce more than they have agreed to produce. The interests of the various OPEC member states, not only those in the Middle East and those located elsewhere, but also those located in the Middle East taken as a group, are simply too diverse to expect most OPEC members to pay more than lip service to agreed output levels.

Second, to the extent that OPEC succeeds in raising the price of crude oil, it makes it economic to exploit deposits which would otherwise remain in the ground for decades. This second effect works with long lags, and it is to those lags that OPEC owed the momentary market control it enjoyed in the 1970s. The effects of induced entry are also long lasting. Given the high ratio of fixed to marginal cost

in developing oil fields, and the fact that fixed investments are also largely sunk,[9] once higher-average-cost oilfields come on line they tend to produce as long as price remains above a level of marginal cost that is far lower than average cost.

Thus, from Table 16.4, North America's share of world oil production in 2001 was 3.5 times its share of proven oil reserves. Western Europe's share of world oil production in 2001 was 5.5 times its share of proven oil reserves. It would be easy, and simplistic, to conclude that at 2001 production rates, Western Europe will have completely exhausted its oil supplies in eight years, North America in 12.5, at which point OPEC will have those regions over a barrel. Long before physical supplies are exhausted in the old oil provinces of North America and Western Europe, indeed, long before the world price of crude oil would make it profitable to exhaust those supplies, new oil provinces will come on line.[10] Supplies from those provinces will be available in North America and Western Europe, not out of goodwill but because international trade based on comparative advantage is mutually beneficial.

Neither OPEC nor the core of Middle Eastern OPEC members were able to stop the rise in crude oil prices in the run-up to the Gulf War of 2003. They will not be able to hold prices up in post-war periods.

16.6   The internal market in energy

The historical choice for organization of electricity and natural gas supply has been the vertically integrated, often publicly owned, regional monopolist, with the regional monopoly covering part or all of the member state. Vertical integration was justified, if it was not simply regarded as the obvious choice, on the grounds that transmission was a natural monopoly (more on this below) and that (particularly in the case of electricity), the precise coordination between supply and demand required to make the system work made integration the only practical option.

The consensus behind the public firm/public utility model was unravelled in the 1980s.[11] One contributing factor was the oil shocks of the early and late 1970s, which rendered invalid the projected increases in demand upon which energy-sector capacity plans had been based. Nuclear power turned out to be more expensive than anticipated. Heightened public awareness of the environmental implications of

nuclear and carbon-based power generation effectively internalized some costs that had hitherto been ignored or treated as external in energy-sector planning. In some EU member states, public firms had been directed to alter business behaviour in order to meet policy goals (hold down rates to fight inflation; maintain coal-fired generators to support the coal sector), with the effect of raising costs and, directly or indirectly, imposing burdens on the national budget. While the UK under Margaret Thatcher led the way (Newbery, 1999a, pp. 6–24), the Single European Act of 1986 inevitably called the position of energy sector member state monopolists into question. Further, the macroeconomic constraints adopted by the member states in connection with the introduction of the euro created incentives to balance energy-sector operating accounts and get them off government budgets.[12]

The supply-side structures of all industries are shaped by the technologies they employ. However, the impact of the laws of nature on the organization of the electricity industry is distinctive, and on the natural gas industry only slightly less so.

The electricity supply chain can be broken down into generation, transmission, and distribution. Transmission takes place over a grid. Electricity cannot be stored in a cost-effective way, and the electrons delivered to the grid by one generator are indistinguishable from those delivered to any other. The physical task of grid management is a daunting one (Green, 2001, p. 330):

> Power flows from generators to consumers cannot be directed, but will be distributed along every line in the network, according to physical laws. If too much power attempts to pass along a given line, or through a particular transformer, that component of the network will fail. Following a failure in the network, the power flows will instantaneously redistribute themselves across the remaining circuits. If any of these are now overloaded, they in turn will fail. Millions of consumers can be blacked out in seconds. To minimize the risk of this, the grid controllers must run the system in such a way that power flows will be within safe limits, not just given the present state of the network, but if any link in it suddenly fails. This implies leaving a margin of spare capacity on every part of the network . . .

To these physical challenges are added economic challenges. To achieve good economic performance, lower-cost generators should be used before higher-cost generators. The price received by generators should reflect the marginal cost of production, to give proper signals about the nature of maintenance and new capital investment needed for the future. At the same time, price must cover the average cost of suppliers efficient enough to stay in business over the long run. Further, the prices paid by final consumers should reflect the marginal cost of production, to give proper signals about the scarcity of electricity relative to other energy sources and about the overall cost of energy, and thereby to encourage efficient consumption of energy.

Taking into account that operation involves large and sunk investment, it is not surprising that the electricity sector has long been regarded as a natural monopoly. For example, Weiss (1971, pp. 89–90) writes:

> Electric power involves three major processes: (1) production . . . ; transmission . . . ; and distribution and sales. The economies of scale in distribution seem obvious . . . The presence of two or more sets of poles, wires, transformers, and meter readers would almost always imply so much unnecessary capacity that almost all observers accept the need for monopoly in the 'retailing' of electricity. . . . Transmission from the power plant to the consuming centers also involves very large economies of scale. When transmission capacity over a given distance is doubled, investment in transmission lines increases by only about 2/3. . . . There are also economies of large scale in generation, but they do reach a limit.

In markets of reasonable size – and this includes both the EU and most individual EU member states – electric power generation is not a natural monopoly. Table 16.6 gives descriptive statistics for supply-side market structures in selected EU member states.[13] The Herfindahl index[14] ranges from low (Netherlands, Germany) to the maximum possible value (1; Greece and Ireland).

The inverse of the Herfindahl index is the number of equally-sized firms that, if supplying a market, would produce the observed H-index. The numbers-equivalent concentration measure ranges from 5 to 10, for less concentrated member states, to 1 for more concentrated member states. The fourth column of Table 16.6 gives the market share of the leading firm (the one-firm seller concentration ratio), and these also show substantial variation across member states.[15] These differences in supplier concentration in the generation of electricity across member states reflect different policy choices by member state governments, not technological imperatives. Different policy choices also drive the differences in the extent of public ownership across member states shown in the final column of Table 16.6.[16]

Technological progress has made it possible to organize distribution in ways that permit rivalry, if not perfect competition in the classroom sense. The critical element in the introduction of an element of rivalry to electricity supply is organization of access to the transmission grid, which is an essential facility standing between generation and distribution. Much the same role is played by the pipeline grid in the market for natural gas. We examine the main institutional set-ups that have been used for grid management in liberalized electricity (and gas) markets.

Table 16.6 Herfindahl index (H), numbers equivalent ($1/H$), market share of leading supplier ($CR1$), and share of public ownership (%), EU electric power generation, selected member states, 1999

	H-index	1/H	CR1	Public ownership share
Netherlands	0.0938	10.6610	0.20	100
Germany	≈0.1500	6.6667	0.29	≈35
Finland	0.1682	5.9453	0.28	50
England and Wales	0.2008	4.9801	0.32	4.5
Sweden	0.3160	3.1646	0.51	
Belgium	0.8125	1.2308	0.90	11
France			0.94	100
Greece	1.0000	1.0000	1.00	100
Ireland	1.0000	1.0000	1.00	100

Source: Bergmann *et al.* (1999, pp. 37–8). Reprinted by permission of CEPR

16.6.1 England and Wales[17]

For much of the post-Second World War period, the electric power industry in England and Wales was a vertically integrated monopoly public utility. This regime came to an end in 1990, when the industry was vertically and horizontally disintegrated. The restructuring created two companies with conventional fuel generating capacity, one with nuclear generating capacity, and one to manage the transmission grid. It also reconstituted the legal status of the 12 regional distributors. Along with this supply-side restructuring, the policy change mandated a phased transition to customer freedom of choice, with very large consumers of electricity granted the right to choose their supplier immediately and successively smaller cohorts of consumers later given the same option.

Intermediation between generators and final demand took place by means of a pool designed to promote competition among generators (Glachant, 1998, p. 64):[18]

> The competitive price mechanism consists of a daily auction involving all Pool producer members. The auction covers 48 distinct half-hours of electricity for each day. For each half hour, the producers' offers are initially ranked by increasing order of offered price (or 'merit order'). Next, the production volumes offered by the producers are added together in strict compliance with the merit-order ranking until the aggregate supply matches the volume of [projected] demand for that half hour. The asking price on the final bid needed to establish the volume equilibrium gives the marginal price of the entire bid for the half-hour. This marginal supply price – . . . 'the system marginal price' or SMP – becomes the basis for settlements to all successful bidders.

The price paid by retailers was the system marginal price, increased by a margin to reflect the cost of possible supply disruptions and by another margin to cover the cost of managing the grid. The matching of supply and demand in the pool paired actual offers to supply different quantities at different prices with demand projections. There was no direct contracting between generators and retail distributors.[19]

The pool received credit (deservedly or not) for the sharp decline in the UK coal sector that followed a substitution of gas-fired for coal-fired generating capacity.[20] It also seemed subject to the strategic exercise of market power (Green, 2001, p. 336):[21]

> The Pool was . . . prone to price spikes, when a high bid set the [system marginal price]. At times, this is an appropriate price signal for an electricity market, but the Pool also suffered from glitches in its rules that made it more susceptible to spikes than was strictly necessary. Once such a problem

was identified, the next step might seem obvious: change the rules to get rid of it. Unfortunately, the Pool's decision-making procedures were designed to protect minority interests against exploitation by a majority. Since most potential rule changes will be against the interests of at least some companies, those affected have been able to delay changes, sometimes for years.

In March 2001, the pool was replaced with the New Electricity Trading Arrangement, intended to facilitate the direct interaction of demand and supply (Ofgem, 2000, p. 18):

> One of the basic principles of the New Electricity Trading Arrangements [NETA] is that those wishing to buy and sell electricity should be able to enter into any freely negotiated contacts to do so. It is expected that under the new trading arrangements, bulk electricity will be traded on one or more exchanges and through a variety of bilateral and multilateral contracts. Those buying and selling electricity on exchanges and through bilateral contracts are likely to include not only generators and suppliers (who produce or consume physical quantities of electrical energy), but non-physical traders as well.

The National Grid Company makes its own contracts to balance physical demand and supply. Settlement of financial obligations arising out of discrepancies between quantities contracted and quantities supplied or taken are handled by a separate company.

There is as yet insufficient experience with NETA to evaluate its impact on market performance. Wholesale electricity prices did fall 20% to 25% during the first three months of NETA operation. The UK Office of Gas and Electricity Markets has put forward proposals (Ofgem, 2002) to revise terms of access to the transmission grid. One motive for the proposal is the belief that current arrangements do not provide effective signals to guide location decisions of generators and of large customers.

16.6.2 The rest of Europe

The efficiency gains hoped for from the single market programme could never be completely realized in the face of intra-EU prices differences for an essential input of the kind reported in Table 16.7 (Newbery, 2001, p. 85):

Table 16.7 1998 prices per kilowatt hour (ECU cents)

Portugal	8.06
Austria	6.98
Italy	6.64
Germany	5.99
United Kingdom	5.78
Netherlands	5.56
Ireland	5.30
Denmark	5.03
Belgium	4.65
Spain	4.49
Greece	4.43
France	4.16
Finland	4.09
USA	3.58

Source: Hofheinz and Mitchener (2002), based on data from the Department of Trade and Industry. Copyright 2003 by Dow Jones & Co. Inc. Reproduced with permission of Dow Jones & Co. Inc. in the format Textbook via Copyright Clearance Centre

The underlying case for liberalising network industries is that it allows competition to put pressure on sleepy monopolies, and restricts cross-subsidies that frequently take the form of a tax on competitive medium-sized industry to subsidize domestic consumers (and sometimes politically powerful large business).

With this in mind, the European Commission issued draft directives for the completion of the internal market in electricity and gas in 1992.[22] The Commission sought (Argyris, 1993, p. 34):

> to introduce competition in the generation of electricity, the possibility to construct transmission and distribution lines (and the right to hook these up to the network) and third-party access to the network. These three measures effectively eliminate the exclusive rights which currently exist in each of these areas.

The means by which these goals were to be accomplished included (Johnston, 1999):

- a transparent and nondiscriminatory system for granting licenses for generating stations;

- unbundling the management of and the accounting for production, transmission, and distribution activities of vertically integrated operators;
- Third Party Access to transmission and distribution facilities.

The question of access to transmission facilities proved to be a thorny one. The Commission first proposed a system of regulated third party access, under which generators and retail distributors could use the grid to carry out contracts, subject to capacity constraints, at public and regulated rates. The idea of regulated third party access was criticized by industry groups (Argyris, 1993, p. 39) and in the European Parliament (Hancher, 1997, p. 94). In later proposals, the Commission added the option of *negotiated* third-party access to transmission facilities, under which generators and retail distributors would work out contracts directly and the generator would negotiate the rate to be paid for use of the grid with the grid manager.

At the insistence of France, an insistence that was widely interpreted as reflecting a reluctance to expose Electricité de France to competition, the electricity internal market directive that was eventually adopted[23] included as well the Single Buyer model for managing grid access. The Single Buyer model mandated use of the grid (Whitwill, 2000):

> . . . eligible consumers are free . . . to contract with independent (or foreign) suppliers but all energy is supplied through the Single Buyer, which in turn buys electricity from the contracted supplier at the agreed price (less any network access tariffs).

The Single Buyer model evoked considerable discussion. We need not review the terms of this discussion in detail, since in the event the Single Buyer model was not adopted in its pure form by any member state. Most member states opted for regulated third party access. Germany, which at the time of writing does not have a regulatory authority for energy sectors, chose negotiated third party access. Italy and Portugal have chosen a combination of regulated third party access and the Single Buyer model.[24]

Article 19 of the Electricity Directive included a detailed specification of the pace of liberalization. It also included a reciprocity clause: member states could block access to their market of firms from other member states that had liberalized to a lesser degree (Pelkmans, 2001, p. 445, footnote omitted):

> The political background of this provision is the monopoly of Electricité de France (EdF), a fully integrated company, also fully state-owned. . . . The reciprocity clause follows from the disparate progress in electricity liberalization among the member states: with a range of countries going faster than the EU calendar . . . the fear was that some countries, but in particular France, would stick to the minimum obligations, and otherwise exploit the many loopholes in the 1996 directives.

As things developed, the reciprocity clause did not have the desired effect of ensuring that market-opening went forward at a comparable rate across member states. EdF made acquisitions in 11 other EU member states, two of the EU candidate countries, and in South America (CEU, 2001h, p. 75), while the French market remained essentially closed to generators located in other member states.

Figure 16.4 gives a qualitative indication of progress in developing a single EU market in electricity generation. The vertical axis shows the share of cross-border capacity for different member states. Physical constraints imposed by limited electricity (and gas)

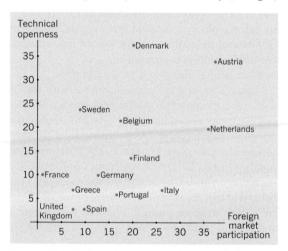

Figure 16.4 Technical openness (percentage share of interconnector capacity in total national installed capacity, summer 2001) and percentage of imported capacity in total electricity supplied (1999), selected EU member states

Source: Adapted from European Communities, Energy and Transport DG (2001), Figure 5. Reprinted by permission of the European Communities.

transmission capacity across national boundaries are a major constraint on economic integration as well, and one which the Commission proposes to relax (CEU, 2001d).

The horizontal axis in Figure 16.4 shows the actual share of electricity by foreign suppliers in different member states. Figure 16.4 shows that (CEU, 2001h, p. 149) 'the European electricity market has not yet reached the stage of being an integrated market' and also that 'the degree of technical openness and the extent of foreign market participation seem to be highly correlated in most European countries.'

In 2001, the Commission returned to the charge and put forward suggested modifications of the gas and electricity directives, modifications that would largely implement the Commission's original vision for gas and electricity (Newbery, 2001, p. 92):

> The main changes proposed were to require *regulated* Third Party Access (TPA) for both gas and electricity (denying the former option of negotiated TPA), to strengthen the requirements for unbundling to legal (but not necessarily

ownership) separation of generation and transmission, to remove the option of the Single Buyer Model, and to allow all gas and electricity customers freedom to choose their supplier by 1 January 2005 . . . require all countries to establish independent regulators . . .

In March 2002, after initial resistance from France, member states agreed to allow, by 2004, industrial consumers in one member state the option of taking electric supplies from generators located in other member states (Hofheinz and Mitchener, 2002). In November 2002, this was followed by a further agreement to extend choice of supplier to all users by 2007 (*The Economist*, 28 November 2002).

A normal result of market integration, particularly in high fixed-cost industries, is supply-side consolidation and a reduction in the number of firms (Martin, 2001, Chapter 10). It should be expected that EU energy-market integration will bring with it mergers among EU energy firms. Suppliers of the liberalized EU energy market will, of course, be subject to the provisions of EU merger policy.[25]

16.7 Conclusion

The European Union will increasingly rely on sources of primary energy located outside its borders. Efficient energy use, the development of alternative energy sources, and the geographic diversification of sources of supply can ensure long-run energy security. Strategic reserves are a way to insure against short-run disruptions of primary energy supplies.

Market integration is a process that brings short-run adjustment costs and promises long-run benefits. EU energy-sector integration will bring greater efficiency and reduced costs of what is an essential input to

virtually all EU economic activity. The long-run benefits of energy-sector integration are immense. Political pressures rooted in the short-run adjustment costs that come with market integration slow the process down. European Commission proposals for energy integration date to 1992; full freedom of choice of supplier will come into effect in 2007. The realization of the internal energy market will come after that. The internal EU energy market is not yet complete; that it will be completed is not in doubt.

NOTES

1. Even a full political and economic union like the United States does not have an energy policy in this sense.

2. With the Treaty of Nice, the Council is given the right to adopt 'measures significantly affecting a Member State's choice between different energy sources and the general structure of its energy supply' (consolidated Treaty of European Union Article 175(2)(c)).

3. ECSC prohibitions against price discrimination were initially interpreted in a way that had the effect of shackling competition; see Phlips (1993). The pertinent terms of the ECSC Treaty were interpreted in a different way after the 1967 merging of the three (ECSC, Euratom, EEC) communities.

4. COM(2002) 488 final, 11.9.2002. For current EU rules, see Council Directive 68/414 of 20 December 1968, as amended by Directive 98/93 of 14 December 1998.

5. By selling oil stocks when world crude prices reach high trigger price levels, and replenishing stocks when world crude prices fall to low trigger price levels, governments can moderate short-run price fluctuations and avoid disruptions in economic activity. International Energy Agency members are obliged to maintain reserves sufficient to cover at least 90 days of net crude oil imports. Actual reserve stocks early in 2003 were sufficient to cover 114 days. See, generally, International Energy Agency (2001). The proposed Community Framework is intended to go beyond IEA measures. Governments have tended to base decisions on the release of strategic oil supplies on indicators of physical shortage, not price triggers, an approach that is consistent with the general failure of governments to understand how markets work or to appreciate the information about scarcity conveyed by prices.

6. One can make the case that markets generally fail to deliver adequate incentives for firms to invest in innovation; see Martin and Scott (2000).

7. Although North Sea oil is relatively expensive to extract, it has the advantage of being located in a politically stable area.

8. Five US-based firms (Exxon, Gulf, Texaco, Mobil, Socal), British Petroleum, Royal Dutch/Shell and Compagnie Française des Petroles (later Total and later still TotalFinaElf).

9. Literally as well as financially.

10. British Petroleum's February 2003 investment of $6.75 billion to form a joint venture with several Russian oil companies, a joint venture that will become Russia's third-largest oil company, is a leading indicator of the commercial development of oil supplies outside the Middle East. See, more generally, Sodupe and Benito (2001).

11. See Doyle and Siner (1999, pp. 1–3); Newbery (1999a, Chapter 1); Johnston (1999).

12. It is also fair to note that the one-time injections of cash resulting from privatization were a welcome element to member state governments.

13. Jumping ahead to the topic of the following section, to the extent that there is a single market in electricity, the member state boundaries are not the geographic boundaries of economic markets. Concentration figures should in principle be calculated for economic markets. It seems clear that, at the time of writing, the geographic scope of EU electricity markets is greater than any one member state, but less than the EU as a whole.

14. The Herfindahl index is the sum of squares of market shares of all firms in the market. For discussion, see Martin (2001, pp. 6–8). On the numbers-equivalent property of the inverse of the H-index, see Adelman (1969).

15. Bergmann *et al.* (1999, p. 37) write that 'In France, the state-owned [Electricité de France] controls 94% of generation and 95% of distribution, with the rest owned by other state and municipal companies.' In Table 2.1 (p. 38) they report a two-firm seller concentration ratio for France of 0.94.

16. The Treaty of European Union is neutral regarding public vs. private ownership (Article 295). Publicly owned firms are, in general, subject to EU competition policy (see Chapter 12). An exception from this general rule is possible if it can be shown that application of the usual rules of competition policy would 'obstruct the performance' of undertakings given the responsibility by a member state of supplying services of general economic interest (Article 86).

17. See Yarrow (1991, pp. 44–47), Green and Newbery (1992), US Department of Energy (1997, pp. 13–38), Glachant (1998), Newbery (1999a, 1999b), and Green (2001). For discussions of the English gas sector, see Yarrow (1991, pp. 41–440, Waddams Price (1997), Doyle and Siner (1999, pp. 11–12), Kemp and Stephen (2001).

18. For theoretical analysis of this 'supply function oligopoly' institutional arrangement, see Klemperer and Meyer (1989).

19. Financial contracts and a futures market permitted generators to hedge against the risk that their actual output might differ from the amount they had bid to supply; see Newbery (1999a, p. 211), Green (2001, p. 334).

20. During the period of public ownership, coal was purchased for generation at prices above world levels, as a way of supporting the UK coal industry (US Department of Energy, 1997, p. 15, p. 29).

21. See also Wolfram (1999).

22. COM(91)548 final (Argyris, 1993, p. 34). The Transit Directive of 1990, Council Directive 90/547/EEC 29 October 1990, sought to promote the construction of electricity and gas networks linking member state networks, a matter that remains on the front burner.

23. EC Directive 96/92 concerning common rules for the internal market in electricity. OJ L 27/20, 30.1.1997, adopted 19 December 1996, with effect from 19 February 1997 (and with delays for Belgium, Ireland, and Greece). The Gas Directive is EC Directive 98/30 concerning common rules for the internal market in natural gas OJ L 207 21.7.1998, adopted 22 June 1998 and with effect from 10 August 1998.

24. On the Italian case, see Valbonesi (1998).

25. For the Commissions treatment of a merger by two German energy concerns, see European Commission (CEU, 2001i).

Chapter 17 Environmental policy

ALAN MARIN

17.1   Background

For a long time it was not clear whether there was any legitimate basis at all for an EC policy on the environment. In the 1950s there was no influential generalized concern for the environment. Occasionally, a specific particularly harmful episode of pollution would give rise to remedial action to deal with the specific problem, but no more. For example, in the winter of 1952–53 there was an even denser than usual smog in London, which led to a dramatic increase in mortality among the elderly and bronchitic. As a result, following an inquiry, new laws were introduced to allow the control of domestic coal fires. But the episode did not lead to a more widespread concern with air pollution generally. The same attitude was prevalent in other countries at that time. Hence, the Treaty of Rome made no provision for any joint EU policy on controlling pollution, let alone more general environmental conservation.

By the end of the 1960s, however, a new attitude, which led to demands for new policies, had become widespread. Although, perhaps, not initially as strongly as their counterparts in the United States, noticeable numbers of people in Western Europe had begun to express concern over degradation of the environment. There were various strands, not always compatible, within the burgeoning 'environmentalist' movement, in terms both of the issues of concern and of the political outlooks of those most prominent.

There were various organized groups who had an effect on EC environmental policy, especially where they gave a stronger crusading force to the aspects of environmental concern which had most influence on policy. Some were the groups who stressed ecology and preservation. It is not simply that they have eventually succeeded in getting enough votes to have some 'Green Party' members in the European Parliament (MEPs), as well as representatives at national and lower levels; some national governments felt obliged to be seen to be responsive to public opinion on environmental issues, in order to try to keep the Greens from gaining enough seats to be a threat to the government majorities. These governments, initially primarily the German and Dutch, have an extra incentive to support EU environmental policies. (The Greens have now attracted enough votes to be part of the German governing coalition.)

The areas which seem to be of general concern to the wider public (and where the Green movements have sometimes provided the impetus) are partly the preservation of natural amenity and wildlife, and, more importantly for EU policy, pollution. The change from 1957 is that pollution is seen to be a general, ongoing, problem. Concern may still be heightened by particularly harmful and/or well-publicized cases, but it is now considered that action should not be limited to reacting to such cases but should be introduced to control harm before blatantly dangerous situations occur. Even uncertain but potential harm is to be controlled, according to the 'precautionary principle'.

As a result of the changes in attitudes just outlined, in October 1972 the heads of government (prompted by a report from the Commission earlier that year) called for an EC environmental programme, which led to approval in November 1973 of the First Environmental Programme 1973–78.[1] This has been followed by subsequent programmes. The current one is the Sixth Environmental Action Programme. Originally proposed by the Commission for 2001–2010, under the title Our Future Our Choice, it was finally passed in July 2002 for a period of 10 years.

Despite the agreement of the heads of government to an EC programme, and thus to a commitment to joint policies, for some years there was doubt as to whether there really was a legal basis for issuing directives in this area. The doubts were particularly strongly expressed within the United Kingdom.[2] On several issues (as will be detailed later), the UK approach to pollution control differed sharply (or so it seemed in public statements) from the majority view among the other member states. There were some who proposed a challenge to the legality of the directives – although a recourse to the European Court of Justice (ECJ) was never, in fact, pursued.

The official basis for actions that were clearly not foreseen in the Treaty of Rome was twofold. First, a few of the types of pollution dealt with could result from the use of goods, for example noise and exhaust emissions from vehicles, packaging and labelling of solvents or foaming and bio-degradability of detergents. In these cases, joint EC standards could clearly be justified as part of product harmonization to prevent different national standards acting as a non-tariff barrier to inter-state trade.[3] However, many of the directives concerned types of pollution and environmental standards that could not constitute a hindrance to interstate trade on any reasonable criterion, such as the quality of bathing (i.e. swimming) water or the hunting of wild birds.

The second basis claimed for EC environmental policies would justify joint policies on all types of environmental concern, even where trade is unaffected. Article 2 of the Treaty of Rome stated that 'The Community shall . . . promote throughout the Community a harmonious development of economic activities, a continuous and balanced expansion . . . an accelerated raising of the standard of living.' It was claimed that measures to protect the environment could be considered to further a balanced expansion and raised standard of living, given the importance now attached to the environment by public opinion and the extent to which people's sense of well-being was threatened by pollution and environmental degradation.

No legal challenge was ever mounted to the Community's right to make decisions on the environment; the matter is now beyond dispute. In 1986, Articles 130R–130T were inserted into the Treaty by the SEA (Articles 174–176 of the Consolidated Treaty (CT)). These Articles are explicitly devoted to the environment; see Chapter 2 for more on this and other developments. Furthermore, according to Article 100A (95 (CT)), actions taken to further the 'completion of the internal market' are supposed to take as their base a high level of environmental protection. In addition, allowance is made for individual member states to set higher environmental standards, provided that these do not constitute barriers to trade – though the acceptable boundaries can be contentious.[4]

The SEA, Maastricht and, especially, Amsterdam treaties increased the power of the European Parliament. This increase in power can also lead to stronger EU policies on the environment and the adoption of stricter standards. The European Parliament is generally considered to be more concerned about environmental issues than the Council. This is partly because of the presence of the Green MEPs, but MEPs of other parties also seem to be more affected by environmental concerns. One early case where pressure from Parliament clearly helped to push the Council to take stronger action was Parliament's amendment in April 1989 of the Council's proposal on exhaust emissions, which resulted in more stringent limits that could be met only by using catalytic converters on all cars. Given the general movement towards environmental consciousness in the preceding year, the previous opponents of stringent limits (especially the United Kingdom) were not prepared to face the odium of no action at all as a result of rejecting the Parliament's amendment.[5]

Whatever the legality according to the unamended Treaty of Rome of EC directives on issues affecting the environment, there still remains the question of why the governments of the member states wanted a *joint* environmental policy at all, on those aspects where individual national policies would not be a barrier to trade and where transfrontier flows of pollution were not a problem. (As already indicated, the small group which could lead to barriers could be dealt with under the procedures on product harmonization.) It is never possible to be completely sure what is in people's minds, but discussions at the time and subsequently suggest two primary motivations.

First, statements by EC leaders often stressed that it was felt to be important that, if there were to be public support for the European ideal, the EC should be identified in the minds of the public with issues with which they were concerned. It should not be thought to be limited to 'boring' technical issues, whether product standard harmonization or the minutiae of calculating transport costs between Rotterdam and Duisberg. Joint EC policies on an issue which had recently become the focus of much media discussion and campaigning would help to convince the public that the Community was relevant to them and responsive to their worries.

Second, it was clear to governments in member states that they would have to respond to public pressures over pollution and environmental preservation. As already mentioned, this was especially true of the German and Dutch governments among the original six, but the others were not immune either. Many of the measures which would be required were likely to raise production costs. For example, firms would have to install new equipment rather than just pouring noxious waste into rivers or sewers, or would have to buy the more expensive low-sulphur fuels to limit emissions of sulphur dioxide. If some countries were to have tighter standards than others, then their firms would face 'unfair competition' from firms that had lower production costs just because they were located in countries that had laxer requirements on pollution abatement.[6] Uniform emission standards (referred to as UES in the literature) would prevent this threat to competitiveness. Hence the desire of governments for joint EC environmental policies which would affect all member states equally.

<hr>

17.2   Economic (or economists') assessment of environmental policies

In order to judge the appropriateness of EU environmental policies, it is necessary to have criteria. The criteria used elsewhere in this book are primarily (although not exclusively) those of standard neoclassical welfare economics.

For the policies examined in this chapter, equity – at least in terms of income distribution – has not been a major consideration.[7] However, it is worth noting that one difference between the approach of many environmentalists and that of many economists is related to the standard assumptions of welfare economics. Economists tend to judge policies and institutions by their effects on the welfare of individuals.[8]

Environmentalists, however, often feel that some things are worth while even if no humans are affected. They place a value on the diversity of natural habitats and the continuation of species, even where there is no benefit to humans. By their training, many (although not all) economists are resistant to such a view.[9]

There have been few binding EU policies which deal with protection of species *per se*.[10] One exception was the 1979 directive on the conservation of wild birds, augmented by a 1992 directive on habitat protection and a 1999 directive on zoos, the purpose of which is to protect wild fauna and conserve biodiversity. The Habitat Directive is supposed to lead to a wider network of conservation sites, known as the Natura 2000 programme, but progress has been slow with many member states minimizing their designation. Some have argued that the directives on water quality for rivers and estuaries containing fish or shellfish are not just to protect human health, but also to protect the fish *per se*. Another, limited, exception is the 1985 (amended 1997) directive requiring an environmental impact assessment before certain large development projects are undertaken. This exception is limited, both because the types of project requiring the assessment are largely left to national governments and because, once the assessment has been made, there is no requirement for any particular weighting to be given to adverse environmental effects in deciding whether the project should proceed. There are also EU directives concerning other endangered species (e.g. seals and whales), but, although motivated by environmental concerns (and the repugnance at the methods of killing seal pups), these formally deal with trade in the products of the species – often as a result of international agreements.

17.2.1 Externalities

Most of the EC environmental polices have concerned pollution in some form. For economists, pollution is a problem that cannot be solved by the market mechanism because it is an externality. Indeed, most textbooks on microeconomics use pollution as the classic example of an externality. One way of viewing externalities is that they are cases where the actions taken by one economic agent (individual or firm) affect others, but where there is no feedback mechanism leading the agent to take correct account of the effects on others. It is not the existence of an effect on others that constitutes an externality, but the lack of incentive to take full account of it. Every economic action may affect others, but in a well-functioning system the price mechanism provides incentives to take account of the effects.

For example, when deciding whether to drive my car to the shops or walk, in reaching my decision I use my car only if the benefit is greater than the price I have to pay for the petrol. If the price equals the marginal cost (the usual criterion for Pareto optimality), then I will use my car only if the benefit is greater than the cost to society of the scarce resources used up in providing me with the petrol. Hence the price system provides me with the correct incentive to take account of the effects of my action (driving my car) on others (using up scarce resources, which are therefore not available to provide somebody else with that petrol). However, if the use of my car pollutes the air and causes annoyance, or more serious harm, to others, there is no incentive for me to allow for this. I could be said to be using up another scarce resource (quiet and clean air), but I do not have to pay for it. Hence, there will be times when I use my car even though the benefit to me is less than the true cost to society, i.e. the sum of the costs of which I take account (the petrol) plus those of which I do not (the pollution); the result is therefore not optimal. Thus another, exactly equivalent, way of expressing an externality is to define it as when the marginal private cost is not equal to the marginal social cost.[11]

There are two diagrams which are often used to analyse the problem of pollution and to indicate possible policy solutions.[12] The first one concentrates on the divergence between social and private cost, usually in the context of a competitive industry which causes pollution during the production of some good. In Figure 17.1 the supply curve of the industry is, as always, equal to the sum of the marginal (private) costs (MPC) of the firms. Given the demand curve, Q_0 is produced and sold at a price of P_0. This is not optimal. If the pollution emitted during production is allowed for, the true sum of marginal social costs for the firms is given by MSC, and the optimal output is where $P = MSC$, i.e. at Q_1 and P_1.

Figure 17.1 has the advantage of stressing that part of the result of pollution in production is that the price to consumers is too low, and therefore consumption is

too high. Conversely, any policy to achieve efficiency will involve a higher price and less output and consumption. It is therefore not surprising that both employers and trade unions in the industries affected are sometimes among those opposing particular EU policies to control pollution. Nor is it surprising that, in some countries of the EU, the importance attached to environmental policies declined in the second half of the 1970s and early 1980s, while the same was even true of Germany in the mid-1990s. The rise in unemployment led to more stress on the reduction in output that might result from pollution control measures; an example of the more general point that if displaced workers are not confident of finding alternative jobs easily, then employment becomes an aim in its own right and policies are not judged solely by the total consumption of goods (even allowing for the 'consumption' of 'bads' involved in pollution).[13]

As a means of analysing policies to control pollution, Figure 17.1 has the disadvantage of neither explicitly showing what happens to pollution nor showing whether pollution can be reduced by means other than a drop in production of the final output of the industry. For these reasons, an alternative diagram is now often used, which draws attention to these aspects, although it has the disadvantage that the implications of Figure 17.1 to which we have drawn attention are left implicit, and may therefore be inadvertently downplayed.

In Figure 17.2, the pollution is measured explicitly. For convenience, we have drawn the diagram with the abscissa measuring pollution abatement from the

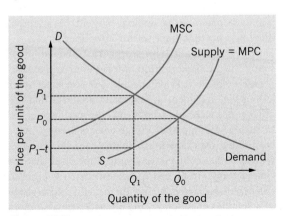

Figure 17.1 Social and private costs of pollution

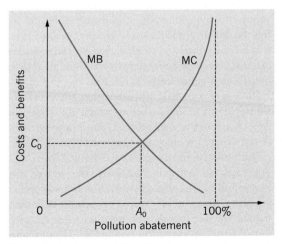

Figure 17.2 Costs and benefits of pollution abatement

level that would occur with no policy controls. Some authors use pollution emissions instead. This is equivalent to Figure 17.2 working leftwards from the 100% abatement (zero remaining pollution) point. The diagram shows the abatement of some particular form of pollution for some particular industry. The marginal benefits (MB) of pollution abatement are the avoidance of the external costs placed on others – health, annoyance at noise, loss of amenity, etc. The marginal costs (MC) of pollution abatement to the firms in the industry are the costs associated with various abatement techniques, such as the treatment plant for noxious effluents in our earlier example, as well as the loss of profits if emissions are reduced by cutting back on the level of output of the final product sold. The approach in Figure 17.2 draws explicit attention to the possibilities of using other resources (labour, capital) to reduce emissions (unlike Figure 17.1 which is usually drawn on the assumption that the externalities associated with each level of output are fixed).

The shapes of the marginal benefit and cost curves in Figure 17.2 follow from what is known for many types of pollution – some abatement is often easy but, when 95% of potential emissions have already been removed, removal of the remaining 5% is usually much more expensive. On the benefit side, the marginal curve is usually drawn downward sloping, although the justification is less well founded and there may be some forms of pollution (especially affecting amenity) where the downward slope is not correct; for example, once a line of pylons has been put over a previously unspoiled mountain range, any further developments do less marginal harm. However, most of the EU pollution policies deal with worries about effects of pollution on human health, and for this the downward MB curve is usually reasonable (as it is for the policies on sulphur dioxide and some car exhaust emissions where the motivation is also partly human, partly the effects on forests).

In some cases it is suspected that there may be thresholds of pollution below which the body can cope, but above which harm may start. In these cases, the MB curve may have the shape in Figure 17.3.

Returning to the more general case of Figure 17.2, one important policy implication of this way of analysing pollution is that there is an optimum level of pollution. Except in very special cases, it is not optimal to aim for the complete elimination of pollution.[14] Less than 100% abatement is desirable. The optimum level, which maximizes welfare, is where the marginal

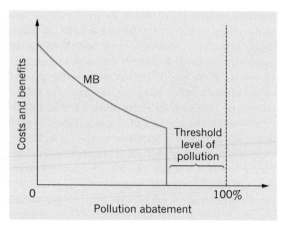

Figure 17.3 Pollution threshold

costs of further abatement just equal the marginal benefits, level A_0 in Figure 17.2. This is an implication of the economists' approach which is uncongenial to some in the Green movement.

EU policies have followed the economists' approach on the whole. In the early years of EC action there were some clashes between member states. The United Kingdom, in particular, advocated its traditional policies, summed up in such expressions as 'best *practicable* means' of pollution control. The notion of 'practicable' involves a weighing up of costs and benefits – although this balancing seems always to be implicit rather than explicit and to rely on the intuition of the relevant inspectorates. The United Kingdom feared that at times the other member states were proposing the approach of best *available* technology, i.e. pushing as far as technically feasible towards 100% abatement, irrespective of costs. Ultimately, although some directives still mentioned that best available technology should be adopted, there was no time limit set for adoption, or else the phrase was qualified by saying that the adoption should be provided if it did 'not entail excessive cost' – which reduces it to practicable – or else some other let-out was included. It is actually doubtful that the other states were completely unconcerned with costs. In reality, the apparent disagreements seem to have been rather over how much abatement was desirable, with the other countries saying in some cases that the United Kingdom tended to overestimate the costs of abatement, to underestimate the benefits and urgency of reductions in pollution, and often to claim that more evidence was needed before action should be taken.

One example is the UK position on sulphur dioxide, where for a long time the United Kingdom delayed reductions, partly because of claims that the evidence failed to show that UK emissions contributed significantly to forest damage elsewhere in West Europe. The 'Environment' title inserted by the SEA specifically refers to the need to take account of 'the potential benefits and costs of action or lack of action' (Article 130R (174 (CT)), 3). From the other side, in an attempt to appear to bridge the gap, at least superficially, UK legislation has now adopted the principle of 'BAT-NEEC', which stands for 'best available technology not entailing excessive cost'. But the 'NEEC' implies that there has been no real change in the approach.

17.2.2 Control of pollution by regulations or taxes

If the problem is that of externality, the 'obvious' solution might seem to be to 'internalise the externality'. It is often suggested that an implication of the economists' analysis is that polluters should have to pay a tax equal to the external costs imposed on others. In terms of Figure 17.2, if a tax equal to C_0 were levied for each unit of pollution emitted, firms would abate up to level A_0. At abatement levels less than A_0, it is less costly for them to abate than to pay a tax of C_0. From A_0 onwards, the marginal cost of further abatement is higher than the tax, and hence it will be more profitable to continue to pollute and pay the tax. A tax will therefore achieve the optimum. The idea of controlling pollution by taxation, rather than by quantitative regulations imposed on firms, also seems to fit economists' predilection for relying on price (here the 'price' of using up clean air, etc.) rather than on quantitative controls. The latter are supposed to require information rarely possessed by the central authorities.

In the early 1990s it became popular to argue that there is another advantage of taxes to control pollution. This argument is often called the 'double dividend' advantage. The first 'dividend' is the benefit from the reduction in pollution that is induced by the tax. The second 'dividend' is that the revenue from the pollution taxes can be used to reduce other taxes in the economy that are themselves distortionary from a welfare economics viewpoint, e.g. income tax (distorting the choice between working and leisure) or employers' taxes (distorting labour demand choices).[15] An alternative jargon was that pollution taxes were thus 'win-win'.

A particularly strong version of the 'double dividend' was sometimes advocated: a pollution tax would be desirable because of the second dividend even if it turned out there were no net benefits to reducing the pollution *per se*. For example, at the time of the proposed EU carbon tax discussed below, there was some residual scepticism over whether global warming was really occurring at all and even if it were occurring, whether the results would be harmful enough to justify the sacrifices required to have a noticeable effect on the warming. Some of the statements in favour of the carbon tax said that even if the doubts were eventually proved correct, the tax would still be worth while because of the second dividend from the use of the revenue.

However, the double-dividend argument came under attack from other economists.[16] The essence of the attack is that the idea of the double dividend inherently relies on a 'second-best world' with existing distortions, in addition to the distortion of possibly uncorrected externalities. However, the existing distortions are likely to mean that there is too little paid work (too much leisure) because of taxes that impinge on labour supply and demand. Any imposition of a pollution tax will raise the price of some products (those whose output or use involves the pollution), and thus further reduce the real return to working. This increased disincentive to employment will reduce welfare. It is quite possible to find situations where this second effect could outweigh the second dividend of using the revenue to reduce distortionary taxes – thus pollution taxes would reduce welfare if there is no 'first dividend' and possibly reduce it even if there is a 'first dividend'.

Another way of putting this is that, because of existing distortions, there is too little of most goods being produced, including too little of some goods which also cause pollution.

As often in 'second-best' analyses, all sorts of things could happen, depending on particular combinations of substitution/complementarity links. However, there is probably a consensus emerging (see the summaries referred to in note 16) that in many of the cases investigated, both theoretically and empirically, the following results are typical:

1 If the question is whether a particular level of pollution emissions should be reached via quantitative regulations or taxes, the second dividend of using the tax revenue to reduce other

distortionary taxes is a reason for pollution taxes rather than regulation.

2 When there are other distortionary taxes, the optimum level of pollution taxation is higher when the revenue is used to reduce those distortionary taxes than when the revenue is used in a lump-sum way.

3 Even if the revenue is used to reduce other taxes, the optimum level of a pollution tax is often lower in a second-best world of distortionary taxes than the level of the Pigovian tax ($P = MSC$, or $MB = MC$ of abatement) that would result if there were no other distortions in the economy; but this optimal level is still often positive (i.e. some abatement is desirable) if there are benefits to the abatement.

4 The strong double-dividend argument outlined above is generally wrong – i.e. if there are no net benefits at all from 'pollution' abatement, then the second dividend does not give a valid reason to impose a 'pollution' tax.

Despite the common view that analyses such as Figure 17.2 show the desirability of controlling pollution by taxes, even if we abstract from the second 'dividend' of the use of the revenue,[17] and that all (respectable?) economists agree, there is a serious flaw in the argument.[18] To achieve the optimum level of pollution, a government needs to know the size of the correct tax, C_0. But to know C_0 requires knowing the marginal costs and benefits of abatement and where the curves intersect. But this information is the same as is required to know, and directly to impose, A_0. Hence a government that can achieve optimality via taxes can achieve it via regulation as well.

Although it is easy to draw diagrams for hypothetical cases of unspecified pollutants and industries, to estimate reliable MB and MC curves quantitatively in real-life cases is much more difficult.[19] Very often the MB curves are little more than guesses. There is a two-stage problem:

1 Working out the physical relationship between varying levels of the pollutant and the harm caused (the dose–response relationship).

2 Putting a monetary valuation on the harm.

It is not just the economic problem of the latter stage – although that is often contentious enough – but that scientists usually have only sketchy and controversial evidence on the first stage, i.e. the way that the damage changes with different levels of the pollutant. The experts sometimes disagree over whether a substance is harmful at all, and often disagree over whether there is a safe threshold or whether even the minutest dose has some small chance of doing some harm to somebody; for example, whether there are any safe levels of lead absorption or nuclear radiation.

As a result, the level of pollution aimed at – often called the 'standard' in the EU literature – is often at best a very rough guess. However, perhaps surprisingly, once it is accepted that the aim is not an optimal level of pollution, there is then a strong argument for achieving the fairly arbitrary standard by the use of taxes, rather than by simply telling all firms contributing to the pollution to abate by some particular percentage, or telling all firms that they can each emit only some particular amount of pollution. The reason is that typically some polluters have lower abatement costs than others. To minimize the costs of achieving any given arbitrary level of aggregate abatement, more of the abatement should be done by firms which can abate more cheaply. Normally, the abatement should be spread between firms in such a way that the *marginal* cost of abatement is equal for each firm. But the argument given above as to how firms will react to a pollution tax shows that, in response to a given tax, each firm will abate up to the point where the tax equals its marginal cost of abatement. Since each firm faces the same tax, they will all end up where they have equal marginal costs of abatement. Hence taxes will minimize the cost of abatement.

Despite this cost-minimization argument, until recently pollution taxes have hardly been used in most EU countries, although their use has been increasing somewhat in recent years (Denmark is probably the EU country with most use).[20] Among the minor exceptions was the reduced tax in some countries on lead-free petrol as compared with leaded petrol, during the period when both were available. In terms of Figure 17.1, a tax differential equal to t was imposed on petrol containing lead.[21] In many of those cases where pollution charges are used in the EU they are part of a package of measures, not the sole instrument. For example, in the UK Climate Change Levy, firms which meet particular emissions reductions receive a discount of 80%.

However, the EU itself has tried taking pollution taxes more seriously. In 1989 the Council of Environmental Ministers requested the Commission to draft proposals on environmental taxation. Specific proposals by the Commission emerged with the debate on global warming, and the need to reduce emissions of carbon dioxide.[22]

In 1991 the Commission proposed an energy tax in two parts: one part related to the carbon content of fossil fuels and the other part on all non-renewable energy. Thus, for example, nuclear power might be taxed at a rate which would be about half that levied on electricity from oil-burning power stations. The proposal also allowed for possible exemptions for some industries which are particularly energy intensive, such as steel, in order to preserve international competitiveness – such exemptions could be removed if other competitor countries agreed to tax such industries in a similar way.

The proposals aroused considerable opposition, especially from fuel producers and many industrial groups. The result was that the Commission effectively agreed to make implementation contingent on the acceptance of carbon taxes in the major competitors, especially Japan and the United States. At the Earth Summit in Rio de Janeiro in June 1992, US opposition ensured that no binding international agreement was reached on controlling carbon dioxide emissions (at that time the US government claimed that lack of evidence on carbon dioxide emissions and global warming meant that the costs of controlling the emissions were unjustified – a position it later modified, then returned to under President George W. Bush). As a result, the Commission did not push its energy tax proposal with much urgency, and the Council could not come to an agreement on the tax. Eventually, UK refusal to agree to directives which could be seen as giving the EU power over member states' taxation forced the abandonment of any EU-wide carbon tax, irrespective of its other merits or drawbacks. The Commission put forward new energy tax proposals in 1997, but no action has been taken. Currently, EU directives merely 'encourage' member states to use environmental taxes.

Some interesting economic issues are raised by the episode as it developed. One is the justification for the non-carbon part of the energy tax. The Commission mentioned the encouragement of energy efficiency. This is only justifiable if there are other externalities which are due to the use of energy, which are not fuel specific and which cannot be taxed directly; but the case has not been made. It is probable that the aim was really to avoid substitution by nuclear power, because of its own risks, but that it was considered

politically more acceptable to achieve this as part of a new tax ostensibly aimed at global warming rather than as a control of nuclear power in its own right. The general economic issue is the interrelatedness of environmental impacts – as with any other aspect of resource allocation (e.g. the discussion above of the double dividend), affecting one input or output will have repercussions on others, and an overly partial analysis will miss these interconnections. The EU is now explicitly attempting to deal with such inter-relatedness by its 1996 directive (96/61) on Integrated Pollution Prevention and Control, which is applicable to some heavily polluting installations.

17.2.3 Competitiveness and pollution policy

Another issue raised by the EU energy tax proposals is that of international competitiveness and distortion of trade, as exemplified both by the initial exemptions on energy-intensive industries and by the reluctance to impose carbon-content taxes unless competitor nations do the same. From an economic efficiency perspective, it is precisely the most energy-intensive industries that should either be induced to substitute other inputs for energy usage or else raise their prices and cut back production the most, as they are the heavy users of a resource with what is now considered to be a high social cost. As seen in Figure 17.1, the relative prices of their products should rise and their outputs should therefore fall. Furthermore, if there are any possibilities for a move away from energy use in production, then the cost-minimization argument implies that they should not be exempt from the tax, at least at the margin.[23]

The reluctance to impose any carbon-related tax unless other countries do confuses a valid and an invalid argument. Since the benefits of any reduction in carbon dioxide emissions in the EU would accrue globally, it is reasonable to argue that the EU should not abate at all unless other countries do the same – it is a classic free-rider problem, since the pollution is a public bad at the global level. This was the argument for the Kyoto Agreement on reductions in emissions and why some people have objected to the EU and other countries going ahead in the absence of US participation. However, if other countries were to agree to cut back their emissions, but decide to do so by means other than economic incentives, this should not affect the EU's decision on using taxes. For any cut-back that the EU wishes to achieve, it will be better off if it achieves that cutback at the minimum cost – precisely the argument in favour of pollution taxes that has been outlined above. As always in arguments over international trade, there is a conflict between the employment impacts of changes that alter the pattern of production, and the efficient allocation once employment has adjusted to the new pattern.[24]

The issue of competitiveness brings us back to the underlying justification of having any *joint* EU policy at all. As mentioned above, a major (in my judgement, *the* major) reason was because otherwise some member states might suffer a loss of competitiveness *vis-à-vis* other member states with laxer controls on pollution. This was, and is, considered to be unfair, or distorted, competition.

Although the avoidance of 'unfair' competition (and subsequent loss of sales and employment) has always been a fundamental principle of the EU (e.g. Articles 92–93 of the Treaty of Rome (87–88 (CT)), standard economic analysis generally implies that this principle may be unnecessary. In the case of imposing uniformity of environmental standards, it may even reduce social welfare in the long run.

Left to themselves, different countries may well want different levels of environmental purity and exposure to pollutants. These choices could result from differences in culture, 'tastes' or income levels. For example, it might be expected that those with a higher level of income will demand (and be prepared to pay more for) higher levels of amenity and health.

Living standards fully defined will comprise both goods and services bought by individuals and also those provided publicly but not paid for by individual consumers. The latter include environmental quality. At any given level of national productivity and resources (i.e. a given production possibility frontier), if more publicly provided goods are consumed then less privately purchased ones can be consumed, and vice versa. Conventional measures of net real wages and real personal incomes only account for privately purchased consumption possibilities. Thus if a country wishes to have a higher standard of environmental quality, the level of real wages (as conventionally measured) will have to be below that possible with lower environmental standards.

If a country raises its environmental standards, one path that could lead to the fall in real wages is that, at existing initial levels of real wages, but with higher costs of meeting the more stringent pollution controls, firms will try to raise prices and thus become uncompetitive. They would then have to lay off workers.[25] As unemployment begins to rise, wage reductions will be needed to restore full employment. Wage cuts will enable firms to cut prices and to compete again. The final equilibrium will be one of full employment and capacity output. Although there will be lower incomes than initially when defined in terms of privately purchased goods, there should be higher living standards when these are viewed as including enjoyment of environmental amenities and reduced pollution.

In general, since not all industries pollute equally, a country which wants less pollution will also need an industrial structure which comprises less production in industries which are heavily polluting per unit value of output, and more of its production in industries which emit less pollution. Again, a path by which the reallocation could occur would be the changes in relative prices of goods that result from the more heavily polluting industries being uncompetitive at the initial prices (plus more stringent pollution controls), as well as the direct closing down of some of the now uncompetitive polluting firms. In order for those who were employed in the more heavily polluting industries to be deployed into other industries, their wages may have to fall, which should happen as a reaction to their temporary unemployment.

In the process that has been indicated here, the interim period of 'unfair competition' is part of the market mechanism leading to the correct result. The problem is that if (as some believe) wages in EU countries are rigid downwards even in the face of protracted high unemployment, the unemployment may last a long time, together with its attendant social and economic troubles.[26] Hence the pressure for common EU emission standards.

The analysis in this section applies both to the issue of unfair or distorted competition between EU states and to international competitiveness between the EU as a whole and the rest of the world. As indicated, the problems arise because the 'short run' during which wages would be too high, and thus unemployment also be too high, might last a long time. The long-run result of differing national environmental standards (where each country chooses the levels that reflect its own wishes) would eventually be higher social welfare, but it may take too long to be waited for passively. In Keynes' famous phrase, '*In the long run* we are all dead.' [Italics in the original.]

17.2.4 Tradable permits and the EU position on global warming

As stated in Section 17.2.2, one advantage of taxes over regulations is that they achieve the minimization of the aggregate cost of reaching any particular pollution reduction, even when governments are ignorant of firms' abatement cost functions. However, this same attribute can lead to what may be a major drawback. If the government does not know the firms' marginal costs of abatement, it cannot be sure what aggregate level of abatement will be induced by any particular tax level. The tax it chooses may lead to more or to less abatement than it expects.

For some pollutants the failure to hit the standard exactly is not crucial – the target itself is only a rough guess. In other cases, however, this can be a major disadvantage. This is especially in cases (like Figure 17.3) where there is thought to be a threshold of pollution above which serious effects become apparent. For example, no government is likely to use taxes to control radioactive emissions, because over-shooting the target would be unacceptable.

There is an instrument that ensures that the target is met, and yet minimizes the aggregate cost of abatement. This instrument is the use of tradable emission permits (or quotas). The aggregate volume of permits equals the maximum pollution target, but the permits can be bought or sold by firms. Trading will establish a market price per permit. Each firm will abate up to the point where its marginal cost of abatement equals the price of a permit. For example, if initially it is at a point where its marginal cost of abatement is less than the price, it would be profitable to abate more and sell its surplus permits. Conversely, if its marginal cost is above the price, it would be cheaper to buy permits and to abate less (pollute more). Since each firm sets its marginal cost equal to the same (market) price of a permit, all will have equal marginal costs – which is the condition for minimizing the cost of abatement. (There may be other problems with permits; for example, if permits are initially 'grandfathered', i.e. handed out to firms, rather than being auctioned, there is no government revenue to provide the 'double dividend'.)

Tradable pollution permits are currently under appraisal within several EU countries, including some small scale trial schemes, but are not yet really functioning in the EU, although they are in the USA.[27]

Table 17.1 Greenhouse gas emission changes from 1990 to 2010

Country	%
Austria	−13
Belgium	−7.5
Denmark	−21
Finland	0
France	0
Germany	−21
Greece	+25
Ireland	+13
Italy	−6.5
Luxembourg	−28
Netherlands	−6
Portugal	+27
Spain	+15
Sweden	+4
United Kingdom	−12.5

Source: EU press document 9402/98 (Presse 205), C–98/205

They have, however, become of practical importance in one EU pollution policy issue – global warming. In 1997, an international agreement was reached in Kyoto, Japan, on controlling emissions of 'greenhouse gases' (primarily, but not exclusively, carbon dioxide). The EU has agreed that by 2010–2012 its emissions will fall to 8% below those in 1990. The EU is to be a 'bubble', i.e. the reduction applies to the EU as a whole, not to individual countries. Within the total EU reduction, the Council agreed on an allocation in which the poorer member states (which currently emit less *per capita*) will actually be allowed to increase their emissions, in order not to inhibit their economic growth (see Table 17.1).

One of the bitterly contested issues in the negotiations leading to the Kyoto agreement was US insistence that internationally traded permits should be incorporated. Countries which emitted less than their targets would be allowed to sell their excess to other nations, which could then emit more than their targets. The EU was among those opposed to such trading, though eventually trading was conceded in order to obtain US participation in the agreement (the US later withdrew anyway, despite the concession).

There were various reasons why the EU and some others opposed pollution trading. One was the fear that because the ex-Communist countries had suffered a large drop in their industrial production after 1990, they would automatically undershoot their targets. If they then sold their surplus allowances to others who thereby did not have to meet their own targets, the aggregate cutback would be less than would otherwise be achieved.

EU-wide pollution permit trading

In March 2000, the Commission issued its 'Green Paper on greenhouse gas emissions trading within the EU', COM(2000)87, leading in October 2001 to proposals for a Directive, COM(2001)581.

The background was the EU attempt, under the Kyoto agreements, to meet its target, for the reduction in the emissions of gases that are considered to contribute to global warming, combined with the allocation of the abatement between member states (see Table 17.1). Implicitly, one reason for the Commission's proposals was that the allocation between member states had not been decided on criteria relating to the relative marginal costs of abatement. It was therefore very likely the overall EU reduction would not be the least cost pattern.

The Commission proposed to remedy the defect by allowing firms across the EU to trade emission allowances. The firms involved would initially be those in a specific set of industrial sectors, accounting for about 45% of EU emissions.

After a preliminary phase starting in 2005, the real scheme would commence from 2008 onward, coinciding with the starting date for implementing Kyoto commitments. If production facilities end up trading emission allowances, rather than just limiting their emissions to their initial allowances, this means that their actual emissions differ from their initial allowances. Correspondingly, if the trading is between facilities located in different member states, the member states in which they are situated, will be allowed to overshoot, or required to undershoot, their national targets in Table 17.1.

The aggregate cost savings of an emissions trading scheme were estimated from an energy forecasting model. The savings vary according to the number of sectors to be covered and which 'greenhouse gases' are included. For the sectors included in the 2001 Proposal, which only deal with carbon dioxide, the Commission has estimated an annual saving of 1.3 billion euros, as compared to each member state implementing its own cutback, with no trans-frontier trading. This saving is equivalent to 35% of the estimated abatement costs for those sectors if there were purely national abatement. Of course, it will never be possible to validate or to disprove the accuracy of such quantitative estimates, as we will not experience the counter-factual state of the world with which to directly compare the actual outcome.

As discussed elsewhere in this chapter, the desirability of decentralization to member states can clash with fears about unfairly distorted competition between firms in different countries. These fears similarly motivate proposed uniformity in some aspects of the Commissions emissions trading scheme. For example, states will be required to allocate initial allowances between emitters according to harmonized criteria – in particular they may not allocate higher allowances to any producer than it is likely to need (though how this might be judged is unspecified). The rationale, presumably, is that the revenue from the sale of unused excess allowances would be equivalent to giving the firm a subsidy, and hence 'distort' competition.

On 13 September 2002, the European Parliament replied to the Commission's proposals agreeing to the idea. Its Report comprised a long list of detailed amendments and comments. Some have been accepted by the Commission, others rejected (see COM(2002)680). The Council of Environmental Ministers meeting on 9 December 2002 also agreed to a scheme (but only an outline of the Council's own amendments are available at the time of writing). Thus, unless there is an unexpected hitch during the final stages of the co-decision procedure (see Chapter 3), the first EU-wide scheme of trading pollution permits will start in 2005.

Another basis of opposition was almost a moral one. It was considered wrong that the USA would be able to use its wealth to buy permits, and thus continue to use energy profligately and not share in the 'pain' of controlling its energy use or of constraining its economic growth.[28]

The distrust of international trading continued. In May 1999 (to the disapproval of the USA) the Commission proposed that at least half of the EU's target reduction of 8% must be achieved by internal abatement. The accompanying press release by the Environment Commissioner included the statement, 'Everybody needs to contribute ... We must reduce our carbon dependency.'

However, the same Commission proposal also advocated serious consideration of emissions trading by firms *within* the internal market of the EU. The Commission has since sponsored a series of studies, and put forward more detailed proposals for EU-wide trading (COM(2001)581) in greenhouse gases. Some member states, are already favourably inclined to the use of tradable permits – US experience shows

that they can achieve large savings in aggregate abatement costs.[29] It is therefore possible that tradable pollution permits will become an acceptable instrument of pollution control within the EU.

However, there is a problem with a tradable permits scheme for dealing with greenhouse gases. The costs of monitoring emissions and the transactions costs of trading mean that the permits scheme has to exclude the millions of sources emitting carbon dioxide through driving vehicles or heating buildings. This is in contrast to using taxation to induce the reduction of carbon dioxide. Because there is a unique relationship between the carbon content of fuels and the emission of carbon dioxide when they are burned, the tax can be levied on the production or sale of the fuel. It does not need to be levied on the emitters at the point of emission, and this cuts the transactions costs and monitoring to manageable levels even though the tax gives *all* emitters an incentive to reduce emissions. For this reason, tradable permits are inferior to a carbon tax as a way of reducing carbon dioxide within the EU at the minimum aggregate cost.[30]

17.3   Further implications for EU policies

Despite the cost-minimization argument discussed in Section 17.2.2, as stated above, pollution taxes are currently rare in the EU. Nevertheless, the theory outlined in Section 17.2 does have important implications for some other controversies over EU environmental policies.

In the course of the discussion of the standard economic analysis of pollution control, we have already noted in passing a few of the implications for EU policies. There are other important aspects of the policies which can also be usefully examined in the light of the analysis.

17.3.1 Polluter pays principle (PPP)

The EU has followed the rest of the OECD in accepting the polluter pays principle (now incorporated in Article 130R (174 (CT)), 2 by the Maastricht Treaty). At first, many commentators mistakenly thought that the PPP was an acceptance of the taxation approach ascribed to economists, in which polluters pay taxes on unabated pollution. However, this was not the meaning of the PPP. It was instead an agreement that

governments should not subsidize firms for the costs imposed upon them by anti-pollution regulations. The PPP is satisfied if the polluters bear the cost of achieving the prescribed standards.

The PPP is thus a way of making firms 'internalize the externality'. If the standards they have to meet are correctly chosen, then, given the constraints placed on them, individual firms' own choices of abatement techniques and of output will be correct from a social standpoint.

It might also be noted that from the point of view of the first-order conditions for achieving efficiency, a subsidy per unit abated would achieve the same result as a tax per unit emitted (though in the long run the size of the industry might differ because of the different profitability). The opportunity cost to the firm of continuing to pollute would include subsidy forgone. Thus the rationale for PPP is not to enforce efficiency, but rather fears of 'unfair competition', as discussed above.

Within the EU, although PPP (as well as the general limits to state aid in Articles 92 and 93 of the Treaty of Rome (87 and 88 (CT); see Chapter 13) has meant that subsidies for pollution abatement are generally forbidden, this has been applied very strictly only for the higher running costs associated with operating equipment to reduce emissions. The rules have changed slightly over time.[31] The Commission's 2001 Guidelines allow for temporary help with operating costs for energy saving and for some waste management schemes, where these exceed EU standards and could harm competitiveness. States may also help some firms' operating costs by granting them partial or full exemptions from environmental taxes, especially where this is necessary to avoid harming their competitiveness. (The discussion earlier in this chapter on competitiveness is relevant here.) Similarly, in 1998 when car emission limits were tightened (Directive 98/69), tax concessions on purchases of new cars were allowed for, in order to expedite the purchase of new cars meeting the revised standard and the scrapping of older, more polluting cars.

At times the Commission has allowed some help with the initial investment costs of installing abatement equipment in order to adapt to new mandatory standards, but this is now only allowed for SMEs. However, help with investment costs is still allowed to encourage firms to go beyond mandatory standards, or if national standards are stricter than the EU ones, as well as for encouragement of energy saving or use of renewable energy. In the latter case the maximum limits are higher at 40% of extra investment costs, as compared with 30% for exceeding EU standards (10% more in each case for SMEs or in assisted regions).

17.3.2 Thresholds and standards

As stated above, it is very difficult to get convincing evidence about the dose–response relationships of pollutants. The problems of obtaining evidence make the techniques used much closer to those of econometricians than those of laboratory-based science testing.[32] Where human health is concerned, it is simply unethical to conduct laboratory tests, for example taking very young babies and giving them feeds containing different levels of nitrates to observe the level which causes serious damage. Most EU policies are concerned with potential health effects. But even where only amenity is at stake, the number of possible interactions and natural variations in them still make it difficult to gather conclusive evidence. The arguments over the cause of forest die-back are a case in point. There are various possible pollutants which may interact in causing damage, damage may

depend on soil and weather, and the route taken between emissions of sulphur dioxide and nitrogen oxides on the one hand and the precipitation of acid rain on the other is difficult to forecast.

One result of this is that it is important to try to obtain reliable data on a range of pollutants, over many years and at a sufficient number of locations, so as to enable statistical studies relating various aspects of health to pollution to be based on enough observations to be significant (in a statistical sense). One of the focuses of EU environmental policy has been to require monitoring of pollutants. The earliest requirements were for smoke and sulphur dioxide (from 1975 onwards), water pollution (from 1977 onwards) and, more recently (from 1987), there has been an attempt to gather systematic data on damage to trees. The European Environment Agency, established by the EU in 1993, is similarly concerned with collecting and assessing data.

More fundamentally, the lack of definitive knowledge on the damage caused by different levels of pollution means that any standards adopted are done so largely by a political process disguised as a scientific one. Different groups put pressure on governments to be more or less lax, and the governments then take stands in the Council according to the balance of their feelings; often, possibly the position they have previously taken domestically is then taken with respect to EU policy. Each government will claim scientific backing for its stand, usually refusing to admit the uncertainty. Those pushing for the laxest standard will tend to claim that there is no conclusive evidence of harm, while not admitting that there is no conclusive evidence of lack of harm either; the UK position on sulphur dioxide mentioned above is one example. Others will mention the studies which suggest that there could well be serious damage caused by the current levels of pollution. As part of the process, there is the temptation to look for a threshold, as in Figure 17.3, even where there are no strong grounds for expecting one. If a threshold did exist, it would often make sense to adopt it as the standard – the marginal cost curve would have to cut the marginal benefit curve to the left of the threshold to justify less abatement (higher pollution).

A large number of medical scientists are doubtful that overall thresholds exist for many pollutants. The levels of a pollutant, such as smoke, that may be harmless to a healthy person may be deleterious to somebody already vulnerable, such as a bronchitic old-age pensioner living in a damp flat. Thus, a threshold which would be applicable to all might well be at so low a level of pollution as to be useless for policy.

Once a standard has been decided upon, by whatever process of bargaining based on whatever motives and justifications, it is then too often treated as though the agreed standard were really a well-defined threshold.[33] On the one hand, governments may use the fact that an EU standard exists to try to allay public anxiety over the potential harm from some pollutant and to claim that because levels are below the accepted standard there is nothing at all to worry about – even if new evidence has since emerged to suggest that low levels are more harmful than was thought before. On the other hand, environmentalists and other pressure groups may use the breach of a standard as an indication that the health of the public is being seriously damaged and argue that pollution must be immediately reduced to the standard, whatever the cost.

In most cases, the EU has laid down that member states must notify the Commission if they cannot reach the agreed standard by the required date. The Commission then has to decide whether the failure can be condoned or not. At this stage, the pressures mentioned in the previous paragraph come into play again: is the standard just a rough guess at the level at which marginal costs equal marginal benefits, so that less abatement is justified if a particular country can plausibly claim that its costs are especially high, or is it a well-defined threshold of pollution above which completely unacceptable harm is caused? The decision is complicated by the worry that, if some member states are granted exemptions too readily, others will in future not comply because of fears of 'unfair competition' from those given exemptions.

17.3.3 Emission versus ambient standards

In Figures 17.1, 17.2 and 17.3 we followed most of the literature in simply linking pollution to damage. However, on closer examination it becomes apparent that there are various stages of pollution. There is the initial emission at the point where the pollution is produced, such as the factory chimney or waste pipe outlet. The pollution may then flow through various media; for example, it may be carried by wind through air, then deposited on plants, then eaten by animals

which are then slaughtered. During the processes, the pollution from any one source is added to by pollution from other sources and simultaneously diluted by fresh air, water, etc. mixing with the carrying medium, and much of the substance may be deposited where it does no harm. The ultimate stage to be considered is where the pollution finally directly affects humans.

From the economist's, anthropocentric, viewpoint, the pollution that matters is that which affects human beings. Typically, therefore, we are concerned with the ambient levels of pollution – i.e. the concentration in the medium which affects health, such as micrograms per cubic metre of lead particles in the air or milligrams per litre of nitrates in drinking water.

In setting standards for pollution, a standard could be applied at any of the stages of the process. At the final stage, one could set standards of acceptable levels of absorption of pollution by people; for example, there was at one time a Commission proposal to set a maximum limit for the level of lead in people's blood. Obviously one would hardly fine or imprison people with more lead in their blood than the standard. Instead, the idea was that if tests showed that anybody was above the limit, then the government of their country should take agreed action to reduce their lead intake. In fact, governments do use monitoring of human exposure or absorption as a trigger for action, and occasionally set standards in this form, such as radiation exposure limits for workers. In the EC case, partly as a result of UK pressure, the directive on blood lead levels was watered down somewhat and became one for an EC-wide screening programme, primarily for information gathering and with a member state required to take only such actions as the government itself thought were appropriate measures if too many people were above the specified values.[34]

The next stage back is that mentioned above, i.e. the concentration in the medium that directly affects people. In the EU standards defined for this stage are sometimes called 'exposure standards' or 'primary protection standards'. Another example of such standards, in addition to those for drinking water or air, would be the bacteria content of bathing water.

Sometimes the standards are somewhat further back in the process, but still concern ambient levels. These are often called 'environmental quality standards'. The standards applying to water, in rivers or lakes, which could be taken for drinking, or those applying to water with shellfish, are examples.

Standards may also be set at the initial emission stage. These are usually called 'emission standards'. A similar stage is when the pollution is caused by the use of products which are sold, such as car exhaust pollution or noise from lawnmowers. A somewhat similar stage is where the EC mandates labelling or other aspects of products to avoid *potential* danger from misuse, for example the controls on the shipment of toxic waste.

As already stated, from an economist's viewpoint it would seem that, if the standards are to be used at all, the relevant standard should be as far down the chain as is technically possible – exposure standards where possible or at least environmental quality standards. The only cases for EU standards on emissions would be either where they were also product standards (to allow unhindered trade) or where there was some reason why even environmental quality standards were not feasible. Otherwise, it should be up to the relevant government inspectorate/agency to find the least-cost way of achieving the environmental quality or exposure standard. If pollution taxes (or tradable permits) were not used, then the requirement for pollution abatement should be shared between the various sources of emissions in the most efficient way possible.[35] As explained earlier, the aim would be (subject to information/enforcement limitations) to require abatement by each polluter up to the point where the marginal cost of abatement was equal.

In the 1970s there was a heated controversy over whether the EC should define its policies by environmental quality standards (EQS) or by UES, with the latter defined as maximum 'limit values' so that member states could have stricter emission limits if they wished. The issue arose over a linked series of directives on water quality aimed at rivers and estuaries – there was a framework directive, finally passed in 1976, on the approach to 'Dangerous substances discharged into the aquatic environment', followed by subsequent directives on specific pollutants/industries.[36] The contestants were the UK on the side of EQS and the other member states, plus the Commission, on the side of UES.

The reasons for the attachment of the Commission and other member states to UES were partly explicable in terms of one of the motivations for having a joint EC policy at all: the fear of 'unfair competition' if different countries had different emission standards for a set of pollutants which were primarily industrial effluents. Countries such as the UK, which has a long coastline with relatively fast-flowing estuaries and rivers, would be able to achieve any given EQS with much

higher emissions than their trade partners (rivals?). In addition, countries which shared river systems (as along the Rhine) would find it difficult to allocate individual polluters' emission levels to achieve an EQS: upstream countries would have little incentive to impose severe cutbacks on their industries. The issue of trans-frontier pollution is of less importance for the UK, which not only is primarily an island (ignoring Northern Ireland and its border) but has the fortune to be mainly upwind of its nearest neighbours. The other member states felt that the cooperation that should underlie the Community ought to lead to policies in a form which would help, not hinder, the solution of joint problems, including trans-frontier pollution.[37]

On the other side of the debate, the UK put views which are close to part of the approach taken by most economists and outlined above. Since it is the damage to humans that is the problem, an EQS is what matters, not emissions *per se*. Emissions need only be limited to the extent that they lead to unacceptable damage. In terms of a traditional British statement: 'There are no harmful substances, only harmful concentrations.' On the question of unfair competition, the UK government said that it was no more unfair that the United Kingdom should benefit from its coastline and estuaries than that Italy could benefit from its sunshine: it would be absurd to require the Italians to grow tomatoes in greenhouses just to stop them having an 'unfair' advantage over the Dutch. Although not stated in those terms, this was an application of the theory of comparative advantage, applied to polluting industries.

In the end, a typical EC compromise was reached. Countries could choose *either* to accept UES in the form of limit values *or* to establish EQS, provided that they could show the Commission that the quality standard was being met. Only the UK chose the latter. The subsequent directives for particular dangerous and persistent water pollutants followed the same compromise of a choice of either approach.

Despite the strong disagreements over UES or EQS, it could be argued that neither side was really consistent. The UK, despite the type of statement mentioned above, had in many cases applied UES to whole industries (in some cases only to new pollutants, but the EC also made a similar distinction). For example, the old Alkali Inspectorate typically applied its notion of best practicable means to the whole of an industry it supervised and the same applies to the new Pollution Inspectorate (now part of the UK's Environment Agency) and BATNEEC. Conversely, other EU policies set EQS without any fuss from the member states, for example the air quality standards for nitrogen dioxide, sulphur dioxide and particulates. It could also be argued that the dispute forced the UK to be much more rigorous about the EQS than were needed.

In view of the economic assessment of 'unfair competition' discussed in Section 17.2.3, one could go even further than the UK argument that unfair competition considerations should not impose UES. In the absence of trans-frontier effects of pollution, there may not even be a case for an EU-level EQS. As noted, however, the strong dismissal of the 'unfair competition' criterion would completely undermine not only much of EU environmental policy (e.g. on drinking water standards, where typically there are virtually no transfrontier effects), but many other EU policies as well.

17.3.4 Damage and designated areas

One last issue in EU environmental policy that we shall examine is also linked to the economic analysis. The stress on the costs and benefits of abatement implies that it is not merely the dumping itself of something into water, air or earth that matters, but the harm done relative to the benefits from the activity. The harm done will depend on the potential use by people (directly or indirectly) of the medium. It therefore makes sense to vary the desired standard of pollution according to its use. Water used for drinking could well require stricter standards on its nitrate concentration than water used only for boating. The EU has followed such a policy.

In some cases the use of the medium is obvious; in other cases, less so. In the latter cases there may be some decentralization so that countries are allowed to designate particular areas for the application of particular standards. For example, the standards for bathing water apply to stretches of water where bathing is traditionally practised by large numbers of people. Similarly, member states can designate areas where water standards need to be set to protect shellfish.

Although the approach seems sensible, the application has not always been so. In particular, in so far as governments have discretion over the areas designated, they can use this as a way of avoiding the effective implementation of EU policies that they feel are unnecessary. This has indeed happened. In the case of standards for water supporting different sorts of freshwater fish, and for the shellfish case already mentioned, some member states simply did not designate any waters at all. Similarly, those readers who are familiar with English seaside resorts might be interested to know that the UK government originally used its discretion over how to assess where 'large numbers' traditionally bathed to exclude both Blackpool and Brighton. At that time the UK government was worried about public expenditure, and any improvement in water quality of beaches would require new sewerage works. Later on though, in 1987, in response to threats from the Commission over infringement, as well as strongly adverse comments from the Royal Commission on Environmental Pollution (and the beginning of a changed attitude by the UK government to its poor reputation on environmental issues), many more beaches were added to the list.[38]

A final example is a 1975 directive on the sulphur contents of gas/diesel oil, which is a medium-grade oil used for heating of commercial, light industrial and domestic buildings, as well as for diesel fuel for vehicles. The directive is interesting partly because it was a mixture of UES and EQS, although it is also concerned with product harmonization. It set two limits on the sulphur content of the oil, and the higher sulphur type could be used only in areas designated by member states. The aim was that the higher-sulphur-content oil should only be used where air pollution from sulphur dioxide was not a problem. In the event, the UK government decided that the whole of the United Kingdom was to be designated for the use of the higher-sulphur-content oil *except for roads*. The road network would therefore be designated for the lower-sulphur-content oil – since diesel for vehicles was already low sulphur compared with other gas/diesel oil.[39]

17.4 Conclusions

In some ways the EU policies on the environment can be counted as a success story. Despite the fact that it may not be clear that common policies are required

at all in many cases, nevertheless a set of policies has emerged. Furthermore, despite some of the problems mentioned above and despite the failure to move quickly on some other policies because of the conflicting interests of the member states, as compared with other common policies (such as for transport or agriculture), progress has been fairly steady and not too divisive, acrimonious or blatantly inefficient.

From the 1990s there has been a revival of public interest in the environment, even in those member states where interest waned in the decade after 1974. Those in favour of stronger environmental policies may well feel divided about EU actions. Those who live in those member states where Green pressures are strong will feel that they are held back, as compared with what their governments could achieve (or be pressured into achieving) without the requirement to carry other member countries with them. There are limits as to how far member states can take advantage of the permission, in the treaties and in some directives, for higher standards where these do not conflict with EU policies.[40]

Conversely, environmentalists who live in those countries whose governments tend only to move on these issues when really compelled can be grateful both for the more stringent standards set by EU policies and for the possibility that the Commission will enforce compliance.[41] In particular, following a European Agency Report in 1999 claiming that too many EU environmental decisions were not fully implemented by member states, in recent years the Commission has intensified its compliance efforts. For example, the first ever fine on a member state under Article 228, for not complying with an ECJ judgement, was on an environmental case. In July 2000 Greece was ordered to pay a daily fine for as long as it did not fulfil the Directive on safe disposal of waste.[42]

In the second half of 1992 it seemed as though EU environmental policy might be put into reverse. Following problems with ratification of the Maastricht Agreements, the UK (especially) stressed the notion of subsidiarity that had been incorporated into the proposed treaty amendments. To various extents, the other member states, and even the chastened Commission, also said that subsidiarity should be taken seriously, and that EU policies should be scrutinized to see whether joint action was really necessary. As indicated at various points in this chapter, the justification of EU-level environmental policies is often debatable. It was possible, therefore, that the movement on subsidiarity might lead to the reconsideration of some existing EU environmental directives. Starting with a European Council meeting in 2000, there has also been an increased stress on reducing burdensome regulations.

However, neither subsidiarity nor deregulation has made a major difference as far as existing policies are concerned. It is difficult to judge whether new EU-level joint actions on the environment have been as readily adopted as previously, even where there is no strong reason for an EU, rather than a national, policy. My own subjective judgement is that any diminution has been minimal or even non-existent.[43] Not only do the Articles on subsidiarity include trans-national problems as a reason for joint actions, but they also include the correction of 'distorted competition'. As explained above, however misguided it may be from an economist's viewpoint, the standard interpretation of 'distorted competition' has always been a prime reason for EU-level environmental policy.

NOTES

1. For earlier years, references to the Official Journals (OJ) for the environmental programmes and various directives can be found in the Economic and Social Committee (CEC, 1987b) outline, Haigh (1989), or Press and Taylor (1990). Many of the documents up to 1994 have been reprinted in the seven volume *European Environmental Legislation* published by DGXI (updated edition, 1996 – CEU 1996k). The annual *Reports* and *Monthly Bulletins* by the Commission have brief sections on the Environment. A useful summary is in the semi-annual series of UK Government Reports, *Recent Developments in the EU*. Recent documents are also on the Europa website (http://europa.eu.int/), while European Environment Agency Reports are on www.eea.eu.int. The *Sixth Environmental Programme* is in OJL 242, 10.9.2002. The Commission's proposals and background are in COM(2001)31.

2. Including reports during 1977–1980 by the House of Lords Select Committee on the European Communities.

3. Some of these directives predate the proposal for an EC Environmental Programme.

4. See Kramer (2000) for thorough discussions of the limits on member states' ability to set higher environmental standards, and of whether it still matters whether decisions are made using Article 100A (product harmonization under the internal market) or Article 130S (environmental protection).

5. It is not always the case that MEPs are inevitably more environmentalist than the Council. For example, in debates on a tough new proposal for recycling cars in late 1999, it seemed very likely that the EP would relax the Council and Commission decision (*Financial Times*, 22 November 1999). This may be due to the more conservative political composition of the EP following the 1999 elections and/or the vulnerability of some MEPs to sophisticated lobbying by producers (though in the end the attempted weakening was not carried through). General histories of EU environmental policies and politics can be found in Weale *et al.* (2000).

6. As in other applications of this notion of 'unfair competition', or 'distortion of competition' as it is often called in EU documents, this contains implicit assumptions about the fixity of wages, prices and exchange rates. These assumptions are often not realized and their validity may or may not be dubious. This point will be amplified in Section 17.2.3 and will also be relevant to controversies discussed later in this chapter.

7. Although some of those opposed to action on the environment have alleged that concern about environmental issues is a middle-class luxury, which is not shared by the working class or the poorer members of society. Also, see note 30 below on regressivity and pollution taxes. The agreement on sharing the burden of carbon dioxide reduction within the EU 'bubble' does make special provision for poorer EU member states. See Section 17.2.4.

8. Formally, the arguments in the social welfare function are the individual welfares or utilities, even if the functional form (weighting of individual welfares) may reflect egalitarianism or some other values.

9. Theoretically, in formal treatments, there would be no obstacle to putting concern for endangered species into somebody's utility function, even where the person does not know of the existence of some of the species. Conversely, environmentalists sometimes appeal to the possible future uses to man of endangered species of plants, which would be forgone if the species were destroyed before the discovery of their uses.

10. The EU environmental policies primarily comprise regulations and directives imposing implementation requirements on member states. Unlike some other policy areas (e.g. the CAP, regional policy) there is little spending on the environment out of the EU's own budget. The only EU spending specifically on the environment (though funds in the Cohesion part of regional spending can be spent on the environment) is the LIFE programme. The priority in this programme is the protection of habitats and preservation of nature, rather than simply control of pollution. However, compared to other EU spending, the amounts are trivial: the current LIFE3 programme covering 2000–2004 has a budget of 640 million euros.

11. An externality also occurs when marginal private benefit is not equal to marginal social benefit. Pollution is a negative externality, i.e. private cost is less than social cost. Some older microeconomic textbooks sometimes use the term 'social cost' to refer only to the *excess* cost imposed on others, which is a different usage from that followed here.

12. For further detailed discussion, there is now a wide range of textbooks on the economics of pollution control, e.g. Baumol and Oates (1988) or Perman *et al.* (1999) for more advanced treatment.

13. Another way of putting the same point is to say that the MPC curve in Figure 17.1 is too high because the true opportunity cost of labour is below the wage rate. Hence the MSC, which should measure the cost of resources by the value of their alternative use, includes some components which make it lower than the MPC – see Chapter 6. Note also that if the industry is not perfectly competitive, the output may be too low for the usual reasons, despite the externality – it depends on the balance between the strength of the externality (output too high) and the imperfection (output too low).

14. A possible exception is the case of pollutants which are cumulative (non-degradable) and highly toxic – see Chapter 11 in Perman *et al.* (1999).

15. For example, in the UK, the expected revenue from the Climate Change Levy introduced in 2001 was explicitly used as the financing for a cut in employers' National Insurance contributions.

16. Many of the articles are technically advanced, especially for those who have not studied public finance. A less technical useful summary is Goulder (1997), with even more accessible accounts in Parry (1997) and Parry and Oates (1998).

17. That is, even if the revenue is not used to reduce distortionary taxation elsewhere.

18. A more detailed discussion of this and other problems of using pollution taxes is in Marin (1979) or, in a US context, in Arnold (1994), Chapter 11. Also see Kelman (1981) for a study of some other reasons for the hostility of non-economists to the idea of pollution taxes, and various articles by Frey, e.g. Weck-Hannemann and Frey (1997).

19. For a (rare) EU attempt at using a cost–benefit study, but to find the desirable *maximum* level of pollution concentrations, see COM(97)500.

20. A summary of EU countries' pollution charges can be found in OECD (2001) and European Environmental Agency (2000). The OECD data are kept up to date, and in more detail, on their website. It is not always straightforward to judge the extent of the use of pollution taxes. In particular, taxes imposed primarily for revenue raising purposes may have some anti-pollution side effects. For example, in these publications, there are tables on proportions of tax revenue raised by environmental taxes. Greece shows up as the leading EU user in the 1990s. However, this reflects its use of fuel and vehicle taxes as revenue raisers. These were not aimed at reducing pollution, and were not structured to encourage use of less polluting vehicles and fuels.

21. This case is suitable for Figure 17.1, as once the leaded petrol has been put into the fuel tank, the motorist has no realistic options for varying the total emissions of lead for each gallon bought. The same applies to the carbon content fuel tax discussed below.

22. A brief account and assessment of the Commission's proposals can be found in Pearson and Smith (1991). More detailed analyses are in the papers in Carraco and Sinisalco (1993). The EC had already agreed to aim at stabilizing CO_2 emissions at the 1990 level by the year 2000.

23. If we concentrate on the cost-minimization argument only, and (for the reasons already discussed) ignore overall optimality, imposing the pollution tax but giving lump-sum subsidies to these industries (to avoid a large rise in their average costs) might be acceptable.

24. The argument here and in the remainder of this section is made within a framework which assumes perfect competition inside countries. To what extent it still holds within the framework of the 'New Trade Theory' of oligopolistic competition is currently the subject of research.

25. Firms may also have to accept lower profits. Whether or not this happens depends on how internationally mobile capital is. In the EU now, it may well be that profit rates cannot be forced down.

26. If the country is one of those EU member states not in EMU, the change in the aggregate real wage could be hastened by changes in nominal exchange rates, provided that money wages do not respond fully to the changes in the price of imports – the usual 'money illusion' condition for devaluations to have any real effects. However, the relative sectoral reallocations of resources cannot generally just be achieved by this route (the exception would be if all traded goods were uniformly more polluting than non-traded goods).

27. There has even been one swap between firms in two EU countries – a Danish electricity generator had some unused permits in a limited Danish trial due to finish in 2003, and swapped them for some permits in the voluntary British scheme, which lasts till 2006, from Shell which wanted more emissions in Denmark. From the report (*Financial Times*, 7 May 2002), it seems that this was a straight swap: no monetary trade was involved.

28. This objection parallels some of the early popular opposition to economists' advocacy of pollution taxes. Many felt it wrong that firms or wealthy consumers could continue to pollute if they were prepared to pay. See the Kelman and Frey references in note 18.

29. See, for example, 'Symposium on SO_2 Trading', *Journal of Economic Perspectives* 12(3), Summer 1998.

30. The issue of monitoring is discussed further in the Marin and Arnold references in note 18. In its comments and amendments on the Commission's proposals in September 2002, the European Parliament worried about the distortionary effects of the partial coverage of permit trading, but its amendments do not really deal with the issue.

It should also be noticed that although a full carbon tax avoids the problem with permits, i.e. of only requiring abatement from some emitters but not from all, energy taxes are also sometimes only applied to particular groups. For example, the UK Climate Change Levy is not applied to households and small businesses, probably because of the regressivity of a tax on household fuel use (poorer households spend a higher proportion of their income on heating) – of course regressivity could have been avoided had the revenue from the tax been used for income redistribution programs rather than for reducing employment taxes.

31. The Commission's original position is briefly restated in CEC (1991a), paragraph 284, and given in greater detail in CEC (1987b), paragraph 159. Revised guidelines were published in OJ C72, 10.3.94 and summarized in CEU (1996h). The current guidelines were published in OJC 37, 3.2.2001.

32. The examples in this and the following paragraphs are taken from EU environmental policies.

33. Jordan (1999) shows in the context of water purity the way that, once a standard has been agreed, it can inhibit further adjustment.

34. The debates over this directive (77/312) illustrate not only the monitoring function of the EC mentioned above, but also the sensitivity to thresholds. Part of the objection to the original proposal was that it would suggest that the standard was a threshold which, if exceeded by anybody, would mean they were in danger.

35. Whether quantitative regulations or pollution taxes are used to apportion the necessary abatement between emitters, allowance should be made for the different contributions of emissions in different places to the pollution measured as environmental quality, e.g. because of prevailing wind or tide patterns. Tradable pollution permits should similarly allow for differential contributions (which is one practical difficulty of using them for pollutants for which the location of emissions matters).

36. An excellent detailed account of the controversies is given in Guruswamy et al. (1983). As pointed out in this article, although originally the term 'environmental quality objective' meant something else, the EQS is now sometimes referred to as a 'quality objective'.

37. The well-known 'Coase Theorem', Coase (1960), implies that optimum levels of pollution can be achieved by bargaining between the polluter (upstream country here) and the pollutee (downstream). If the polluter would otherwise have the right to pollute, then the pollutee will have to pay compensation to the polluter for the abatement. Since EU countries bargain over a wide range of issues, concessions by the pollutee country on other issues of interest to the polluter may enable an optimal level of pollution to be reached in circumstances where direct pecuniary payments would be unacceptable.

38. Though even in 2001 the ECJ found against the UK for not remedying an earlier adverse decision over bathing water. The Commission alleges that most other member states also breach this Directive, suggesting that the UK's scepticism over the scientific justification for this Directive is more widely shared.

39. In 1992 the Council agreed on a new directive setting a uniform limit on the sulphur content of all gas/oils. More recently, diesel fuels for road transport have been included in the same directives as petrol.

40. See the reference in note 4. Weale et al. (2000) discuss differences in member states' national policies and their influence on EU decisions. For a discussion of how little environmental quality has converged across EU member states, despite a trend improvement overall, see Neumayer (2001).

41. A politically important example in the UK was the Commission's threat to prosecute over the failure to meet the standards for nitrates in water (other countries besides the UK were also threatened). In the absence of these threats, especially given UK official scepticism over the levels of the EQS actually laid down in the directive, there would have been an even greater lack of

urgency over an issue which was so adverse for the privatization process. (In 1992 both the UK and Germany were found by the ECJ to be in breach of the directive, and subsequently other countries also. In 2002, according to the *Financial Times* 28 May 2002, the UK government, threatened by fines under Article 228, agreed to extend areas covered by the Directive from 8% to 80% of England – the increase will still only be to 55% according DEFRA (2002)).

42. Details of enforcement can be found in the series of Annual Surveys on the Implementation and Enforcement of Community Environmental Law, e.g. Third Annual Survey SEC(2002)1041.

43. Jeppson (2002) Chapter 3 comes to a similar conclusion, based on counting various types of decisions. Others may disagree, e.g. Golub (1996b) states that there was a fall in the number of Commission environmental proposals during the period 1992–1995.

Chapter 18 Factor mobility

DAVID MAYES AND JUHA KILPONEN

Although the freedom of mobility of labour and capital were objectives enshrined in the Treaty of Rome itself, only fairly limited progress had been made by the early 1980s in turning this into a reality. Most countries had capital controls of one form or another and labour faced considerable constraints on movement through lack of recognition of qualifications and other problems over establishment and transfer of benefits. The slow progress stemmed from two sources. In the case of capital, member states were worried that having free movements would lead to destabilizing flows that would disturb the running of the domestic economy. The main fear was a capital outflow that would depreciate the currency, drive up the rate of inflation and require monetary and fiscal contraction to offset it. Labour controls, on the other hand, were more concerned with inflows. Employees in the domestic economy feared that an inflow from other countries would lose them their jobs – countries would export their unemployment. Much of this was dressed up as a need to have certain skills, standards and local knowledge for the protection of consumers. Much of the fear stemmed from ignorance of what others' qualifications meant and overcoming this required a long and tedious process of determination and negotiation.

The 1985 White Paper on completing the internal market and the 1986 Single European Act (SEA) signalled the determination to break through this complex of restrictions and move to a much more open market, with freedom of movement of capital and labour being two of four basic 'freedoms' set out as the objective of the market (the other two being freedom of movement of goods and of services). In the case of capital, this was to be achieved by 1 July 1990. This target was largely not met for the EC of 9 and Portugal and Spain managed to participate in 1992 only for the ERM crisis of September 1992 (see Chapter 9) to require some controls to be reintroduced by member states in the hope of stabilizing their exchange rates. The setback proved to be short-lived. The Maastricht Treaty, which came into force in 1993, had advanced progress further and capital markets have become even more open with the introduction of the euro at the beginning of 1999.

The legislative programme for the single market measures was intended to be complete by the end of 1992. While this was largely achieved, some of the labour mobility measures are still to have their full effect (see Chapter 11). However, it has since become evident that these measures were by no means ambitious enough to achieve anything like a single capital market and this problem is still being tackled. This lack of completion of the single market by the legislative was clarified by the White Paper on Growth, Employment and Competitiveness in 1993, which stressed labour market inadequacies and a need to improve the efficiency of product markets.

At the end of the millennium, attention turned to the various problems in the capital markets, including rigidities in capital movements across EU borders. Consequently, the European Commission undertook an important political initiative aimed at enhancing the development of the risk capital markets and, more generally, to dealing with related problems in the financial markets. The rationale being that Europe had lost opportunities to create jobs and increase investment because its risk capital markets were underdeveloped, mainly due to the fragmentation of the regulation of the securities market (CEU, 1998d). Following the Lamfalussy Report (2001), a new Financial Services Action Plan is being implemented. This has been given special 'fast track' procedures to try to drive it through more rapidly (despite some reservations by the European Parliament). If the plan is completed on schedule in 2004 then this may bring cross-border capital movement noticeably closer to that within individual nations.

The Growth and Stability Pact (see Chapter 9), agreed on 7 July 1997, created even more pressure for the liberalization and restructuring of the factor markets. In particular, it further strengthened the need for promoting labour mobility both within and across the European countries due to current inter-regional fiscal transfers being modest in comparison to those in most federal systems, such as the US.

Finally, in Lisbon in 2001, the EU heads of state and government agreed to a political commitment to a longer-term strategy aimed at making Europe the most dynamic and competitive knowledge-based economy in the world by 2010. The target is to achieve economic growth of 3% per annum and to raise the employment rate to 70% from around 2.5% and 65% respectively by 2010. This is a very challenging task and involves even further integration of product and factor markets within Europe. In particular, different aspects related to the accumulation of human capital, skills and technology transfer have assumed crucial importance for the EU member countries. The logic behind achieving 'free movement' of capital and labour, including human capital, is that it is crucial for the full exploitation of efficiency gains within the EU and for meeting the 2001 Lisbon summit's goal of making Europe the most competitive knowledge-based society in the world.

There are some contradictions in these approaches. The logic behind the EU itself and the four freedoms is largely built on the neo-classical paradigm of perfect competition and its advantages. Yet the new development in the field with its associated knowledge-based economies is founded on notions based on new growth theory, increasing returns to scale and monopolistic competition. This means that earlier models on international factor mobility, basically static in character, are no longer useful for analysing international factor mobility since they consider the optimal allocation of given factors of production. In the new 'endogenous growth' literature, a country or region's factor endowments, hence its factor ratios, are allowed to change over time under conditions of balanced growth. Growth is endogenous in the sense that it depends on the amount of resources allocated to accumulating production factors, such as human capital. Consequently, factor mobility can have an important influence on *growth* and convergence of growth rates between the countries. In the earlier literature, per capita output grows in accordance with the exogenous growth rate of technology, with policies that affect savings only altering the *level* of per capita income. Hence, countries that have the same long-run growth rate in technology should have the same long-run growth rate in their per capita incomes, irrespective of their prevailing technology size or level.

For new growth theories, the accumulation of knowledge, generation of ideas, development of human capital and capacity to absorb new technologies are of the essence in explaining the forces underlying economic growth and determining the competitive position of individual countries. Thus, the long-term growth prospects of the EU countries importantly depend upon the flexibility and efficiency of the EU's own internal factor markets. Ongoing reallocation of production factors should transfer resources to those industries and sectors with comparative advantage and ability to achieve increasing returns to scale in the generation and application of new technology.

Moreover, according to the recent economic geography models, foreign direct investment is not simply determined by relative costs of production or national tax structures. Firms may be drawn to particular regions due to the possibility of obtaining 'agglomeration economies'. The idea is that growth can be faster if competitors, suppliers, customers and related services are all close together in dynamic interaction. Agglomeration effects can be compounded by the wider impact of inward investment. While this has certainly been beneficial for large multinational companies, the problem for economic development is that it leads to greater spatial polarization. Not surprisingly, regions do not want to be without such poles.

Globalization has turned physical capital into a much more mobile factor of production. Due to foreign investment, firms may own the export sector of another nation, and these foreign owners may repatriate most of their profits (Gill and Law, 1988). In such a case, the eventual problem from the point of view of economic development is the hierarchical and possibly exploitative character of transnational firms in a global economy: growth may be achieved, but only at the cost of international inequalities, combined with dependence on financial headquarters elsewhere. This may also apply to the eastern enlargement of the EU, if increasing flows of profit repatriation eventually outweigh the inward flows of foreign direct investment (FDI) to new member countries. It is thus not surprising to see that at the same time that the existing member states have been pulling down the barriers to the free movement of capital and labour, they have been cautious in both fields, increasing the protection of labour through the social chapter in the Maastricht Treaty and seeking to limit the powers of company takeover.

18.1   Single market

Although the single market programme will remove many of the remaining restrictions on factor movements, it is unlikely that capital, let alone labour, will be as mobile as it is within individual member countries. Factors reducing mobility include differences in tastes and customs, and variations in risk. Having a single currency is an important step in removing one source of risk and reducing transition costs.

The 1992 programme enables integration; it does not compel it. Thus, in the same way that the idealized total specialization of trade in economic theory is rarely realized, we would not expect total perfection in capital markets and nothing like it in labour markets where many other factors lead to continuing segmentation. To quite some extent this is affected by the nature and treatment of the services in which labour is embodied, which have national diversity, in the same way as there is diversity in the demand for goods.

If factors and products can move between countries freely, then, neglecting any transport or transfer costs, the whole trading area can be treated as a single market with a uniform reward right across the area to each factor as well as uniform product prices. However, such a system is not only very far from a description of the reality of the EU after 1992, but is also indeterminate and does not tell us the extent to which the products rather than the factors move – a typical problem of underidentification (see Mayes, 1988). The imperfections of the real world, however, are actually an aid in this case as they increase the chance of being able to identify the determinants of the various movements.

There is a basic distinction between direct investment, which involves the setting up or acquisition of a 'subsidiary' in a foreign country, and portfolio investment, involving the purchase of shares and bonds or the making of other forms of loan to a company in a foreign country.[1] In the case of labour movement, individuals physically move from one country to another and then provide their labour services in the second country. Capital, on the other hand, in the sense usually considered, involves the transfer of claims through a financial transaction and not the transfer of capital goods themselves in the form of plant, machinery and vehicles. If existing physical capital is exported, then the financial transfer is lowered. If new physical capital is purchased from the home country, there is an additional export but the net inflow of physical capital is smaller. The net flow is largest when the new physical capital is all produced in the country where the new plant is set up.[2]

Some of the distinctions between types of capital movement may not be very important from the point of view of actual output and trade patterns. Portfolio investment resulting in control of the foreign enterprise may be largely indistinguishable from direct investment, for example. However, the major distinction normally lies in the type of investor. Direct investment is undertaken by firms on their own behalf (or by governments). Portfolio investment, on the other hand, is more usually undertaken by financial companies of one form or another, although cross-share holdings by commercial companies are common in some parts of the EU. Much of this latter investment may therefore not seem particularly relevant to the problem in hand as it relates to a change in the ownership of existing assets rather than the direct financing of the creation of new physical assets used for the production of goods and services. However, this is mistaken from two points of view: direct investment may also be purely a change in ownership, this time involving control; second, we need to enquire what subsequent use the funds released to the seller were put to. The ability to exchange domestic debt for foreign equity can affect the range of options open to a firm. Moreover, even if the purpose of capital inflows into a country is to 'enable' the foreign government to run a deficit which cannot be financed fully by its private domestic sector, such lending may permit a higher level of investment in physical capital in that country than would otherwise be the case.

Clearly, the latter form of capital flow is of more than passing interest in a group of countries that are attempting some coordination of their economic actions. When exchange rates are fixed between member countries balance of payments surpluses/ deficits on current account may open up rather wider than would otherwise be the case. In so far as these imbalances are not met by official movements (or reserves), they must be eliminated by countervailing capital movements, encouraged in the main by differences in covered interest rates.[3,4] With freely floating exchange rates, the exchange rate can take rather more of the burden of adjustment between countries and capital flows rather less. Coordination of fiscal or monetary policies between countries will also affect the ways in which capital flows have to balance the remaining transactions.[5] Now with the euro, there is no more concern about the private financial flows between the participating countries than there is about the flows between regions of the same member state. The burden of adjustment falls largely on the labour market (see Chapter 10).

These considerations raise many issues which lie outside the scope of this chapter; but it must be borne in mind that capital transfers take place between countries for reasons that are not necessarily related to the essentially microeconomic decisions of the individual firm. To invert the argument, wider issues influence the values of the macroeconomic variables which affect firms' decisions over their overseas investment and these wider issues themselves form part of the way in which the members of the EU choose to conduct the handling of economic policy, both jointly and independently. Since direct investment abroad and borrowing of foreign funds by enterprises in foreign countries may both involve not just the same size capital inflow but also the same increase in capital formation within the country, it is not possible to set aside either long-term or short-term portfolio investment as being irrelevant to the purpose in hand.

18.2   Capital movements

Exchange controls were eliminated in the UK in October 1979, but the reasons for that move had little to do with membership of the EU. At that stage, the remaining Community countries all had restrictions on capital flows, although these varied in their degree of tightness. After the start of the single market programme, these restrictions were steadily removed and there has been effective freedom of capital movements since the start of stage 2 of EMU. With the exception of the new members, freedom throughout the Community was in place by July 1990, the start of stage 1 of EMU. In most cases there was a distinction between controls applied to residents and those applied to non-residents, with the restrictions being lighter in the latter case. However, interestingly enough, such restrictions as did apply to non-residents usually applied equally to all such non-residents, regardless of whether they were residents of another EC country or of a third country. There is thus no counterpart to the preference system applied to trade through differential tariffs as far as capital movements are concerned, nor, it seems, was there any intention of taking the opportunity of introducing discrimination against third countries by making this freedom of movement only in respect of fellow members.[6] To a large extent this is a practical matter, because it is difficult to control some transactions when others do not have to be vetted. However, 'reciprocity' is an argument which has been used in other parts of the single market programme in order to obtain concessions for the EU in third-country markets. In one sense, therefore, this simplifies the analysis, as one potential source of substitution and encouragement of capital flows does not in the main exist.

In general, the movement of financial capital among financial centres now entails only minimal intrinsic costs, due to the liberalization and development of information technology. Foreign direct investment and the (re-)establishment of productive capacity are neither costless nor prohibitively costly in terms of time and financial effort. The GATT and WTO rounds aiming at liberalization in world trade have also lowered customs duties (see Chapter 24) and enhanced direct investments. Barriers to the trade of goods are nowadays based on dumping accusations and voluntary export restrictions, rather than inefficient tariffs.

However, the restrictions that matter are not in the capital movements themselves but in how those funds can be used to purchase physical assets. Constraints, or indeed incentives, apply to inward investment, to mergers and acquisitions and to the operation of multinational companies. Thus, freedom of capital movements is to some extent a myth if there are further constraints on how the funds can be used. Nevertheless, it is clear that restrictions are being progressively eliminated.

OECD has collected a useful indicator, which provides us with information on the current state of the regulations that may hinder capital flows between different European countries. It is based on restrictions on the rights of foreign citizens to own shares, discriminatory provision concerning international trade and competition policies, average tariffs, and regulatory barriers affecting trade and investment (*see* Table 18.1).

According to this indicator, barriers to trade are now fairly low in all EU countries, in some cases

Table 18.1 Barriers to trade and investment

Country	Ownership barriers	Discriminatory barriers	Discriminatory procedures	Regulatory barriers	Overall indicator
Greece	1.0	1.0	2.0	0.7	1.3
Portugal	1.3	1.3	1.3	0.0	1.1
France	1.8	1.8	0.5	0.0	1.0
Sweden	0.0	0.0	2.0	0.0	0.8
Spain	0.0	0.0	0.3	0.7	0.7
Belgium	0.0	0.0	0.0	0.7	0.6
Finland	0.0	0.0	0.0	0.7	0.6
Italy	0.0	0.0	0.3	0.0	0.5
Austria	0.0	0.0	0.5	0.0	0.5
Germany	0.0	0.0	0.5	0.0	0.5
Denmark	0.0	0.0	0.5	0.0	0.5
Netherlands	0.0	0.0	0.5	0.0	0.5
Ireland	0.0	0.0	0.0	0.0	0.4
United Kingdom	0.0	0.0	0.0	0.0	0.4
USA	2.2	2.2	0.3	0.0	0.9

Source: Nicoletti *et al.* (2000). OECD©, 2000

even lower than in the US. There are, however, still quite large differences across countries, in particular, indicators are the highest in Greece, Portugal and France.

Like trade flows, we would expect to observe a more rapid increase in direct investment abroad than in GDP itself. This duly occurred in the second half of the 1980s, but was not confined to the EU. However, the distribution of that investment by country of investor is unlikely to have been affected by any changes relative to the EU as such because liberalization has almost entirely been non-discriminatory. The influence of the EU on capital flows is as a result likely to be in changes in discrimination in the traded goods and services market. Increased trade flows are likely to involve changes in capital flows – to set up distribution networks and to establish local production as market penetration increases – although the direction of the change is still problematic as we cannot tell *a priori* the extent to which trade and direct investment might be substitutes rather than complements.

Nevertheless, recent trends of capital movements in Europe give a clear message about the importance of capital flows in open economies. Gross flows of capital are of immense magnitude, many of the flows representing offsetting movements through which financial and other institutions achieve portfolio diversification and protection against exchange rate and other financial risks. FDIs are naturally smaller but since the second half of the 1990s they have continued to surge and have become substantially more important in the process of capital formation as well (Table 18.2). This, in part, reflects the globalization process, which has entailed the rapid expansion of the number and coverage of multinational corporations in Europe. The overall scale of FDI began to increase strikingly during recent decades as countries began to locate portions of their manufacturing, sales and service enterprises in many other countries. For example, the sum of outward and inward FDI as a share of total 1997 investment exceeded 20% for 10 of the 14 European countries. The corresponding figure was less than 10% for all but the UK and the Netherlands in 1975.

Table 18.2 Direct investment flows of EU countries, 1987–2000 (ECU/euro million)

	1987			1990			1993			1998			2000		
	Intra	Extra	Total	Intra	Extra	Total	Intra	Extra	Total	Intra	Extra	Total	Intra	Extra	Total
Outward															
BLEU	−1 655	−545	−2 200	−3 077	−1 175	−4 252	−2 698	−1 469	−4 167	na	na	−23 742	na	na	−49 133
Denmark	−278	−219	−497	−649	−415	−1 064	15	−1 234	−1 219	−3 734	−240	−4 054	−20 182	−9 701	−29 985
Germany	−1 610	−5 266	−6 876	−9 577	−5 369	−14 946	−8 869	−4 440	−13 309	−24 246	−55 130	−79 376	−7 867	−46 178	−54 045
Greece	−1	−9	−10	−16	−3	−19	−3	−4	−7	na	na	130	na	na	−517
Spain	−270	−227	−497	−1 023	−733	−1 756	−836	−796	−1 632	na	na	−6 307	na	na	−24 670
France	−3 639	−3 483	−7 122	−11 409	−6 864	−18 373	−4 575	−4 644	−9 219	−26 101	−17 344	−43 443	−108 752	−81 740	−190 492
Irish Republic	−65	−86	−151	−548	−22	−570	−353	32	−321	−1 126	−2 363	−3 489	23	−5 047	−5 024
Italy	−998	−495	−1 493	−3 250	−1 031	−4 281	−3 316	−1 530	−4 846	na	na	−8 707	−8 985	−4 424	−13 410
Netherlands	−1 998	−3 607	−5 605	−6 459	−4 497	−10 956	−4 118	−3 155	−7 273	−18 724	−15 985	−34 718	−29 076	−47 664	−76 728
Portugal	8	−6	2	−83	−26	−109	−151	−3	−154	−1 160	−1 483	−2 643	−3 056	−5 254	−8 309
United Kingdom	−1 730	−16 728	−18 458	−3 100	−392	−3 492	−5 935	−4 609	−10 544	−16 940	−91 777	−108 716	−210 661	−64 693	−275 354
Austria										−1 329	−1 036	−2 452	−3 068	−3 162	−6 230
Finland										−15 411	−1 245	−16 656	−12 849	−13 233	−26 082
Sweden										na	na	−20 053	−29 290	na	−42 030
EU12/15	−12 344	−30 670	−43 014	−39 295	−20 527	−59 822	−30 844	−21 854	−52 698	−149 443	−218 754	−368 197	−619 225	−408 925	−1 028 150

Inward

BLEU	1 265	693	1 958	6 454	1 355	7 809	5 749	3 343	9 092	na	na	20 473	na	na	119 756
Denmark	2 127	151	24	269	567	836	308	911	1 219	1 053	4 640	5 747	27 924	9 930	37 854
Germany	250	215	465	4 235	2 187	6 422	2 181	1 410	3 591	19 610	2 367	21 977	206 100	5 685	211 786
Greece	102	87	189	229	79	308	300	60	360	na	na	10	na	na	200
Spain	1 976	1 338	3 314	6 062	2 956	9 018	4 028	1 846	5 874	na	na	1 816	na	na	5 855
France	1 654	2 056	3 710	4 009	3 365	7 374	5 652	2 929	8 581	22 458	5 226	27 685	41 215	5 383	46 598
Irish Republic	160	327	487	2 233	964	3 197	1 804	1 291	3 095	4 647	3 271	7 919	40 936	-12 230	28 706
Italy	1 310	1 745	3 055	2 085	3 020	5 105	2 266	1 410	3 676	na	na	5 276	10 346	4 181	14 529
Netherlands	1 315	664	1 979	4 542	3 013	7 555	4 977	809	5 786	8 637	20 662	33 915	35 237	27 766	63 042
Portugal	230	97	327	1 135	586	1 721	758	284	1 042	1 672	1 597	2 807	6 714	285	6 998
United Kingdom	4 085	5 619	9 704	8 327	14 661	22 988	2 825	7 260	10 085	16 863	46 146	63 010	84 981	41 404	126 385
Austria										4 342	-184	4 050	7 747	1 848	9 595
Finland										10 332	516	10 848	12 849	358	9 588
Sweden										na	na	16 610	15 243	na	25 252
EU12/15	12 344	12 991	25 335	39 295	32 753	72 048	30 844	21 090	51 934	135 847	96 432	232 279	727 796	150 407	878 203

'Intra' refers to flows to or from other EU countries. 'Extra' refers to flows to or from the rest of the world.
Source: Adapted from Eurostat, European Union Direct Investment yearbooks 1984–93 and 2001

Traditionally, the main net outward investors include Germany, Japan and the UK. The Netherlands, Switzerland and Sweden also rank high as net outward investors. One of the main reasons is that in these countries reside several multinational corporations that invest extensively abroad. On the contrary, other countries receive more foreign capital than they invest abroad. These include countries like Hungary and Poland, as well as Australia and Spain. Recently, however, the picture has changed. Ranking the EU member states according to the size of their respective cumulative inflows over the 1992–2000 period, it appears that Germany has changed its position. In 2000, Germany became a net recipient of EU FDI, while the Netherlands switched to a position of net supplier (Table 18.2) (Eurostat, 2001).

18.3   On the determinants of direct investment

Investment flows between countries cannot really be treated in the same manner as investment within the economy because, although total investment can be explained through well-known relationships, the split between home and foreign expenditure, on an economy-wide basis, is not so clear. We are concerned in this case not just with what resources firms are prepared to put into capital for future production but with where they are going to site it. Most consideration, therefore, has been devoted to the problem at the level of the firm itself, rather than through modelling of the components of the capital account of the balance of payments. Even within the confines of aggregate explanation there has been a tendency to avoid modelling direct investment flows directly, modelling them indirectly through the determination of the exchange rate as a sort of reduced-growth approach (see Cuthbertson *et al.* (1980) for a discussion of this work.)

Such an approach may be appropriate for the explanation of portfolio investment, in particular, since much short-term portfolio investment is usually described as speculative in nature. It is much less useful for direct investment, because of the degree of permanence embodied in the existence of physical capital held abroad and changes in the logic in which multinational firms organize their production.[7]

Nowadays a large proportion of trade is accounted for by large MNEs, and a significant proportion of global trade – estimates are between 30% and 40% – runs through the international production and distribution networks of MNEs as *intra-company trade*. Increase in intra-company trade reflects the motives of multinationals for diversifying risk and deepening economies of scope in the world market.

This internationalization strategy can be inspired by various motives such as market extension, efficiency seeking, resource seeking and strategic asset seeking.

Whatever the motive of the investment, the transfer of resources and production capabilities, and therefore FDI, contribute to the industrial base of host country. The increasing information content in nearly all products requires experts of various fields to participate in the design and development of almost every commodity. Consequently, many global companies seek to establish both production and research and development activities in different locations all over the world, providing them with either cost effective production or an abundance of educated people and information infrastructure.

An illustrative example comes from the experience of Finland, a country that has recently been ranked as one of the most attractive targets for high-technology FDI. Due to intensive knowledge and technology investment in Finland many asset-seeking multinationals have acquired promising technology-based Finnish firms, for example in electrical engineering. In the IT sector, foreign companies have acquired innovative firms, which have advanced knowledge in some technology or business area. In knowledge-intensive sectors, asset-seeking FDI is motivated by tacit knowledge that comes in the form of know-how or competence and therefore cannot be separated from the person or organization containing it.

Another factor that may have affected the upsurge of FDI is related to changes in the production model of the multinational corporations. In the typical 'Fordist' production model, MNEs seek growth by expanding into new sectors and connected horizontal integration with diversification. Vertical integration, which was the characteristic of the Fordist production model, was a means of internalizing possible market risks in different phases of the value chains.

Globalization, however, had drastically changed the Fordist production model. In recent years, an increasing number of companies have chosen to narrow their segment of products and services and of the value chain, to concentrate on accumulating and developing core competencies. Such horizontal disintegration has become possible because companies can now balance their cash flow through differences in regional markets, which is again, largely due to integration of the product and factor markets in Europe. For instance, Finnish companies have sold divisions for strategic purposes to release resources for most promising niche markets. Recently the potential new owners have often been foreign firms. Foreign firms and small Finnish technology oriented firms have also sought to forge 'strategic alliances' to strengthen their competitive advantage and secure rapid internationalization. Traditionally, the behaviour of multinational companies has been considered as only reflecting the variations in costs of inputs in various locations and the structure of markets they wish to serve.

Moreover, due to the more open international competition and complexity of the products, companies find it harder to achieve and maintain competitive advantage in several sectors or product and service segments at once. This has affected the factor flows across territorial boundaries, in particular, FDI and reinforced the development of a more concentrated economy.

This multinational structure of production and pressures to expand it also have consequences for trade. In the case of vertical FDI, where companies allocate different parts of their production chain to those countries where production costs are lower, FDI typically boosts international trade. In the case of horizontal FDI, a company places its production close to foreign markets. In this case, FDI acts as a substitute to trade, and provides strategic market access for the investor.

18.4 Capital movements in Europe

Most early empirical work on direct investment flows in the EU concentrated on inflows from the US, partly because of the quality of data available. Later on, attention turned towards Japan, whose direct investment increased dramatically in the second half of the 1980s. Japan replaced the US as an investment 'threat', with a heavier political overtone, as the US economy has always been fairly open to return investments and acquisitions. Indeed, the level of recent direct investment in the US has been so great that concern is being expressed, while Japan is a much more difficult economy to enter through either export or investment.

Traditionally, US investment in Europe had a strong element of takeover of existing enterprises. Japanese investment, on the other hand, tended to be greenfield. Arrangements with existing European firms tended to be joint ventures without Japanese majority control. This generated worries about technology transfer, the greenfield sites often being assembly operations of established products, while the joint ventures were sometimes accused of being more effective in transferring technology to Japan. However, with the collapse of Japanese asset prices in the mid-1990s the pressure has changed. It has been outward investment by the EU in the US as well as an upsurge in intra-EU investment flows that has caught the headlines.

It is noticeable that most modelling of inward investment relates to flows into the EU from outside, not to the flows within the EU itself. Yet it is these internal flows that should be of prime interest in the case of the single market and the development of knowledge-based society. The studies of external flows suggest that there are three basic mechanisms at work. First, investment tends to increase with sales to the EU, i.e. supporting trade rather than substituting for it (Scaperlanda and Balough, 1983). Barrell and Pain (1993) suggest, following Vernon (1966), that there is an initial level of exports that is required before it becomes worth while setting up dealer networks and other downstream services. Second, investment takes place to overcome trade barriers (Culem, 1988; Heitger and Stehn, 1990) or anti-dumping duties (Barrell and Pain, 1993). However, overseas investors with a choice of locations and flows are also affected by relative costs and relative barriers. Thus, when anti-dumping actions were at their height in the US in the mid-1980s, this acted as a spur to Japanese investment there. Finally, investment flows are crucially affected by the availability of funds in the investing country.

As is clear from Table 18.2, the UK has been the largest investor overseas in the EU and is the second largest in the world after the US.[8] Only the Netherlands among other EU countries has been a net direct capital exporter over the last ten years, although West

Germany had substantial net exports between 1975 and 1990. More recently, there are striking year to year variations as the data for 2000 show, with strong outward investment by France and strong inward investment in Germany. Large parts of EU outward FDI flows are accounted for by the United Kingdom, France, the Netherlands and Germany towards the end of the millennium. In 2000 they made up 60% of outward flows outside the EU (excluding the USA) and 73% of flows to USA. At the same time, these four countries accounted for 55% of intra-EU flows.

More generally, Europe participated in the strong worldwide FDI activity in 2000, that has been closely related with re-organization of the telecommunications sector, and thus may not be indicative of the longer run. At the other end of the scale is the very low level of direct investment in Greece and Italy. Thus, despite any attractiveness which may have existed from surplus and cheaper labour in those countries, this factor advantage has been met by labour outflow rather than capital inflow. Italy similarly has a low level of direct investment abroad, although it is still sufficiently large to show net capital exports over the last four years.

Compared to the US, outward direct investment has been rising considerably faster than in the US, while inward investment has risen more slowly. Thus, while in 1981 and 1982 the US was a net capital importer, the EU was a substantial exporter. Much of EU direct investment must therefore be 'directed' outside the EU rather than to other EU countries, as is clearly the case for the UK.

Direct investment abroad, like domestic investment, has traditionally been affected by trade cycles. Thus the peak in 1973–1974 coincided with the peak of a cycle and the sharp fall in 1975 with the consequence of the first oil crisis. Of course, 1980 is an exception, for although there was a sharp downturn in UK activity (preceding that of the world in general), it coincided with the removal of exchange controls, the effect of which we have already discussed. Accession to the EC may thus have its effects obscured by the trade cycle, as total direct investment could have been expected to increase at the same time as the transition period, purely because of the trade cycle. Looking at proportions may help to reduce this confusion. The most striking facets are, first, that there is no proportionate surge of investment by the other EU countries in the UK immediately following accession. There is some increase in 1976–1978, but it is by

no means clear that this represents any particular change in behaviour as wide year-to-year fluctuations have been observed earlier. Recently, the relationship between trade cycles and FDI investment seems to have loosened somewhat.

Outward investment by the UK in the EU, on the other hand, shows a very considerable surge *before* accession, in 1971–1972, a process which ended by 1974. Since the benefits from investment are usually not immediate, some anticipatory investment might have been expected to take full advantage of membership when it occurred. There is thus some change which could be viewed as evidence of an initial investment effect of membership in this one respect. Since we are dealing with proportions, changes in one area necessarily entail relative changes elsewhere. In the case of outward investment, the short-run decline was taken by the residual (non-EC, non-US) category – the same category that absorbed much of the surge in UK investment in the US after 1977.

It is also not realistic to treat the EU as a largely homogeneous unit from the point of view of direct investment. For example, direct investment flows between the UK and the Netherlands were far larger than relative economic size would suggest both before and after accession to the EU. This presumably reflects, among other things, the number of Anglo-Dutch multinational companies.

Other differences between EU countries can readily be observed. Although Germany is economically larger than France and the UK, outward investment has followed that relation and inward investment has followed a different pattern, with French investment tending to be the larger. However, in both cases UK investment has been larger than the reverse flow. Irish investment in the UK, which was negligible before accession to the EU, has picked up substantially since. This is perhaps more difficult to explain than geographical nearness might imply, as the easy movement of funds was possible prior to accession. The total picture is thus rather confused, but it suggests that there has been no dramatic switch in the nature of direct investment in the UK as a result of its accession to the EU. In more recent years there has been a similar debate about whether non-membership of the euro area is having much effect on the pattern of direct investment.

As noted earlier, between one-half and three-quarters of net investment abroad by the UK is composed of profits by overseas subsidiaries and associated companies which are not remitted to the UK. Net acquisition of overseas companies' share and loan capital is, partly by consequence, around one-sixth to one-third of the total, except for the two years 1970 and 1980 when it was about half. Unfortunately, these same figures are only available for EC countries for the period 1975–1980, so we cannot make any contrast of the position 'before' and 'after' accession to the EU.[9]

The scale of net inward investment has meant that over the period 1973–1979 there was a steady increase in foreign ownership of UK firms, from 15% to 20% of net output in manufacturing. Not surprisingly, direct investment tends to be concentrated on larger firms, for reasons of information if for no other, and this 20% of output was produced by 2.5% of the total number of establishments in the UK. These firms also have a below average labour intensity (14% of total employment) and about average investment flow (21.5% of the total). This, however, gives us little indication about the nature of changes in investment flows which could be expected, although it does suggest that foreign-owned firms make an important contribution to productivity and investment for future growth, thus emphasizing the role that freedom of capital movement can play in increasing EU competitiveness.

It seems likely, therefore, that if we were to apply the same form of analysis as Scaperlanda and Balough (1983) to other flows of direct investment among the EU countries which involve the UK, we would not find any strong effect from changes in relative trade restrictions. Thus, while there may be some short-run effects, it does not appear likely that there are major changes in capital movements in the EU which involve the UK as there have been in trade patterns, as shown in Mayes (1983), for example.

As mentioned earlier, figures on US direct investment are rather more detailed and hence we can get some idea of whether the US changed either the extent of its investment in the EC relative to other areas, after the expansion of the EU in 1973, or the pattern of it among the member countries.

Prior to accession, the UK had a much larger proportion of US direct investment (Table 18.3) than its economic size alone would suggest. In the first few years after accession, although investment was still large in comparative terms, it was sufficiently lower to allow the UK's share of the existing stock of US investment in the EU to fall by nearly 4%. However, since 1977 the share of investment has been running

ahead of the stock share again: hence the stock share has more than recovered its previous loss. The shares of other EU countries in the total stock have also changed only slowly. This is partly because of the scale of the change in the flow (investment) required to make any substantial change in the capital stock over a short period. Nevertheless, Germany and France have seen a substantial change in share, the Netherlands being the main 'gainer'. Changes are nothing like as striking as for trade flows. Again, it must be remembered that this evidence is very limited in itself, but it contributes to the overall picture.

Now that the single market is well developed, one might have expected to see a change in behaviour. There has been no major diversion of US FDI to the EU. In fact, the share has remained remarkably stable. Expansion of the EC 9 to EC 12 and to EU 15 shows relatively little impact, investment flowing to traditional destinations. Yet, the volumes have increased during the latter half of the 1990s. During the period of 1996–2000, the share of the US hovered between 53%–74% of total FDI inflows to EU member countries. In the case of bilateral EU–US FDI, the latter half of the 1990s is characterized by substantial net outflows from the EU to US in the manufacturing sector.

More recently the European Commission has put together a database called AMDATA that provides a rather detailed list of merger and acquisitions (M&As) activity involving EU enterprises. For 2001 AMDATA records a total of 12 557 M&As involving EU enterprises. This represents a decrease of 25% by comparison with 2000, yet there has been a marked increase in M&A activity in Europe since the early 1990s. On the one hand, there has been a strong upward trend in international operations since 1992. On the other hand, cross-border M&A inside the EC started to increase steadily only after 1996 (Table 18.4). National operations account for more than half of total, but showing a decline trend since 1987.

It appears also that the evolution of M&As is linked to the evolution of the economy. The low economic growth rates and uncertainties surrounding the future development of the EU economies during 1992–1993, 1996 and 2001 are reflected in the declines in M&A activity in those years. During 1998–2000 there was another boom in M&As, particularly in the financial and other services sector. Some transactions were extremely large, making the use of counts of numbers of transactions a very misleading indicator of activity.

Table 18.3 US direct investment in the EU[a], 1980–2001

	1980	1984	1987	1993	1995	1998	2000[b]	2001[b]
Total stock ($ million) percentage of total stock in individual countries	41 476	69 500	118 614	564 283	711 621	980 565	1 293 431	1 381 674
United Kingdom	33.9	41.2	38.0	45.42	39.95	41.78	39.98	38.89
Belgium and Luxembourg	8.6	7.2	6.6	7.20	8.47	7.92	7.46	7.87
Denmark	0.5	1.7	0.9	0.72	0.75	0.61	0.89	1.02
France	14.3	9.3	9.8	10.11	10.87	9.16	6.41	6.00
West Germany	23.3	21.4	20.8	15.31	14.32	10.02	8.43	9.59
Greece	–	–	–	0.17	0.15	0.15	0.11	0.10
Ireland	3.9	4.2	4.7	3.75	3.65	3.73	5.59	5.38
Italy	8.0	6.6	7.2	5.30	5.57	3.42	3.70	3.73
Netherlands	7.5	8.4	12.0	8.70	12.46	18.57	19.45	20.58
Portugal	–	–	–	0.53	0.57	0.34	0.31	0.30
Spain	–	–	–	2.78	3.23	3.00	3.28	3.03
Austria	–	–	–	–	–	–	0.44	0.53
Finland	–	–	–	–	–	–	0.18	0.18
Sweden	–	–	–	–	–	–	3.75	2.80
US investment in EC as a percentage of total US direct investment abroad	51.7	0.0	46.1	42.61	42.91	43.61	46.73	46.38
US investment in UK as a percentage of US investment in the EC	58.5	[c]	17.6	–	–	–	18.68	18.0

[a] EC 9.
[b] Figures for 2000 and 2001 refer to EU 15.
[c] Total investment in EC, $8 million; investment in UK, $891 million.
Source: US Department of Commerce, Survey of Current Business, Department of Industry, US Bureau of Economic Analysis

Intra-EU FDI flows have been expanding during the second half of the 1990s confirming the importance of deepening integration of the product and factor markets in Europe. In particular, during 1999 and 2000, intra-EU FDI has shown a significant increase in volume relative to GDP and trade. One of the reasons behind this upsurge has been associated with re-orientation in the UK. FDI flows in favour of EU member countries. This in turn has been largely due to few huge cross-border mergers, in particular acquisition of Mannesmann by Vodafone Air Touch and successive ownership changes in two of the most important Telecom businesses (CEU, 2001j). Table 18.5 shows the 10 largest deals for 2000 and 2001 involving EU enterprises. The main targeted sectors were telecommunications, pharmaceuticals and financial services.

Table 18.4 Mergers and acquisitions involving EU firms

Year	Total (no.)	National (%)	EC (%)	International (%)
1987	2 775	71.6	9.6	18.8
1988	4 242	65.9	13.5	20.6
1989	6 945	63.2	19.1	17.7
1990	7 003	60.7	21.5	17.8
1991	10 657	54.3	11.9	14.5
1992	10 074	58.1	11.6	14.2
1993	8 759	57.4	11.7	18.8
1994	9 050	58.7	12.9	20.5
1995	9 854	57.4	12.9	22.8
1996	8 975	54.8	12.6	26.0
1997	9 784	56.0	14.0	26.0
1998	11 300	53.5	14.1	28.4
1999	14 335	55.7	14.2	26.4
2000	16 750	54.7	15.2	25.4
2001	12 557	54.1	14.9	24.1

(a) Figures do not necessarily add up to 100% since in some cases bidder is unknown. (b) Figures from 1991–2001 are based on the recent revisions of the AMDATA, while figures from 1987–1990 are based on 1999 revisions. *Source*: Figures for 1987–1990 from European Economy, European Commission, Directorate-General for Economic and Financial Affairs, Supplement A, *Economic Trends*, No. 2, February 1999 and figures for 1991–2001 from European Economy, European Commission, Directorate–General for Economic and Financial Affairs, Supplement A, *Economic Trends*, No. 12, December 2001. Reprinted by permission of the European Communities.

There have been major changes in the sectoral composition of intra-EU flows during the last few years. While in 1999, manufacturing still attracted 49% of all intra-EU FDI flows, this collapsed to 5% in 2000. The Transport and Communication sector gained the dominant position with 40% by 2000. Yet, these figures reflect the re-organization of a relatively new industry, namely telecommunications. Its consequential effects on future intra-FDI flows are highly uncertain. According to the European Commission (2001j) FDI flows may have reached a relative peak at the end of the millennium.

In summary, there has certainly been an increase in the cross-border movement of capital since the start of the 1992 programme. In particular towards the end of the millennium, there has been a substantial increase in both intra- and extra-EU FDI flows. Intra-EU FDI transactions more than quadrupled during the last years of the millennium, reflecting, at least partially, the deepening of the single EU market. In 1999–2000, intra-EU FDI amounted on average to 80% of total direct investment inflows into the EU. In the previous years, it remained around 50%.[10]

18.5   Labour movements

Often, labour mobility is assumed to be a substitute for capital mobility. However, this is quite misleading, given that labour migration is in many ways a much more complex process than international capital flows. Simply put, because the migration of labour

necessarily requires the movement of a person(s), such a move involves more than just the labour market and income considerations. Capital may be allocated internationally without requiring the movement of the capital owner. Moreover, there are many situations

Table 18.5 The ten largest deals involving EC enterprises in 2000 and 2001

Target full name	Bidder	Bid value (bn euro)	Sector	Year
SmithKline Beecham PLC (UK)	Glaxo Wellcome PLC (UK)	74.9	Manufacturing	2001
Orange PLC (Mannesman AG)	France Telecom SA (FRA)	50.8	Transportation, communication and utilities	2001
Seagram Co Ltd (CAN)	Vivendi SA (FRA)	42.2	Service industries	2001
VoiceStream Wireless Corp (USA)	Deutsche Telekom AG (GER)	30.8	Transportation, communication and utilities	2001
Bestfoods (USA)	Unilever PLC (UK)	27.6	Food and kindred products	2001
Dresdner Bank AG (GER)	Allianz AG (GER)	22.5	Finance, insurance, and real estate	2000
Allied Zurich PLC (UK)	Zurich Allied AG (SWI)	20.4	Finance, insurance, and real estate	2001
Granada Compass PLC (UK)	Shareholders (UK)	19.1	Service industries	2001
Seat Pagine Gialle SPA (ITA)	Tin.it (ITA)	18.8	Manufacturing	2001
Bank of Scotland PLC (UK)	Halifax Group PLC (UK)	16.7	Finance, insurance, and real estate	2000

Source: Adapted from European Economy, European Commission, Directorate-General for Economic and Financial Affairs, Supplement A *Economic Trends*, No. 12, December 2001. Reprinted by permission of the European Communities.

where the movements of capital and labour do not substitute but rather complement each other (Fischer, 1999). Such differences in behaviour are enormous from a practical and policy point of view.

On the one hand, total FDI statistics are sometimes affected by the behaviour of a single or very few large MNEs in a particular country. (For flows between any particular pair of countries, a single company can dominate the total effect.) Labour flows, on the other hand, are the result of the decisions of a large number of independent households (although actions by companies and communities can have a strong influence on these decisions). With some limited exceptions involving transient staff and actions in border areas, movement of labour simply involves a person shifting his residence from one country to another to take up a job in the second country. There is not the same range of possible variations as in the case of capital movements. There is also the great simplification that there is not the equivalent problem of the relation

between the financial flows (or retained earnings) and the physical capital stock. The number of foreign nationals employed will be the sum of the net inflows, without any revaluation problems and only a relatively limited difficulty for 'retirements' (through age, naturalization, etc.).

On the other hand, early theories of migration argued that a major incentive to move is an income differential in real terms. However, it is not merely that the same job will be better paid in the second country; it may be that the person moving will be able to get a 'better' job in the second country (in the sense of a different job with higher pay). There are severe empirical problems in establishing what relative real incomes are, not just in the simple sense of purchasing-power parities, but in trying to assess how much one can change one's tastes to adapt to the new country's customs and price patterns and what extra costs would be involved if, for example, the household had to be divided and so on. This is difficult to measure, not just in precise terms for the outside observer, but even in rough terms for the individual involved.

This sort of uncertainty for the individual is typical of the large range of barriers that impede the movement of labour, in addition to the wide range of official barriers that inhibit movement. Ignorance of job opportunities abroad, living conditions, costs, ease of overcoming language difficulties, how to deal with regulations, etc., is reduced as more people move from one country to another and are able to exchange experiences. Firms can reduce the level of misinformation by recruiting directly in foreign countries.

Even if it were possible to sort out what the official barriers are and to establish the relative real costs, there would still be a multitude of factors which could not be quantified but perhaps given implicit values. These other factors involve differences in language, and customs, problems of transferring assets (both physical and financial), disruptions to family life, changing of schooling, loss of friends, etc.

These considerations have led to the development of so called micro-economic behavioural models of labour mobility or immobility. These theories argue, quite convincingly, that migration decisions are made in a complex environment, where the decisions are influenced by family or group considerations as well as by time and life-course events. In some of these approaches, location-specific information and the ability to make use of insider advantage play an important role in the decision to move (Fischer, 1999). Gaining knowledge about location-specific economic, social and cultural opportunities, building up a social network or getting involved in activities of various interest groups all require a certain time of immobility. Thus immobility has a value and in moving, investment in gaining such insider advantage represents a sunk cost that needs to be covered by expected utility gains in the receiving region.

Of course, some of these factors could work in a favourable direction: it might be easier to find accommodation abroad and setting up a new household and finding new friends might be an attractive prospect. Moreover, the development of information technologies and consequential reduction in communication and organizational costs across territorial borders help in solving at least some of the problems associated with insider advantage. Nevertheless, all this suggests that margins in labour rewards between countries may be considerable in practice, even if free movement of labour is theoretically permitted. It should thus be no surprise to find that many differences in labour rewards exist among the EC countries. However, it would also be a mistake to think that there are no barriers in practice to employment in other EU countries, as is clear from the next section.

18.6 Labour flows in the EU

The official position in the EU is straightforward. Freedom of movement of labour was part of the framework of the Treaty of Rome itself. However, the original six EU member nations had to start from a position of considerable restrictions of labour movement, and it was not until 1968 that work permits were abolished and preferences for home country workers no longer permitted. The single market programme involved a range of measures to try to eliminate those fiscal barriers, not just for the worker but for the accompanying family as well. Merely permitting geographic labour mobility does not in itself either facilitate or encourage it. It is readily possible to make mobility difficult through measures relating to taxes and benefits, which make a period of previous residence or contribution necessary for benefit.

Labour markets in the EU are in general characterized by relatively low levels of geographic mobility; EU citizens have about half the mobility rate of US citizens. According to Eurobarometer, 38% of EU citizens changed residence, the majority of which moved within the same town or village (68%) and 36% moved to another town in the same region during the last 10 years. However, only 4.4% moved across national borders into another member state. Furthermore, it has been estimated that annual migration between member states amounts to around 0.75% of the resident population and perhaps only 0.4% of resident EU nationals. In the US, these figures appear about six times larger. Moreover, occupational or professional reasons account for only a small proportion of the house moves; when people move it is mainly for family and housing reasons.

Of course, these relatively low labour mobility figures reflect cultural and institutional heterogeneity in Europe but may also be due to a more systematic

Table 18.6 Inflows of foreign workers ('000) in European countries

	1988	1990	1992	1994	1996	1997
Belgium	2.8		4.4	4.1	2.2	2.5
Denmark	3.1	2.8	2.4	2.1	2.8	3.1
Germany	60.4	138.6	408.9	221.2	262.5	258.4
Spain	9.6	16	48.2	15.6	31	23.2
France	12.7	22.4	42.3	18.3	11.5	11
Ireland		1.4	3.6	4.3	3.8	4.5
Italy			123.7	99.8	129.2	166.3
Luxembourg	12.6	16.9	15.9	16.2	18.3	18.6
United Kingdom	26	34.6	30.1	30.1	37.7	42.4
Austria	17.4	103.4	57.9	27.1	16.3	15.2

Source: Adapted from OECD (1999), p. 328. OECD©, 1999

failure in the functioning of factor markets. In particular, it has been argued that real wage unresponsiveness to regional labour demand fluctuations and wage compression policies have hindered the functioning of internal labour markets.

The principal concern raised in Europe recently is that various barriers still exist and continue to keep labour mobility within the EU at a low level. Given the political commitment to enhance European competitiveness and growth in the global economy by establishing a 'knowledge-based economy', the EU has taken a look at the impediments on mobility of skills and labour.

The potential barriers to mobility in the EU can be roughly divided into 'man-made' and natural barriers. Man-made barriers include inconsistent labour market institutions, problems in the portability of pensions and social security rights, the lack of full mutual recognition of qualifications and experience. 'Natural' barriers include a range of social, cultural and language barriers and also ageing of the labour force. Given that the young tend to be more mobile than the old, demographic change will imply that there will be considerably less potential movers among the working-age population. Many empirical studies have found that both in Europe and the US, moving declines sharply after the age of 30–35.

The actual path of labour migration is, of course, heavily affected by the cyclical fluctuation of the economy. If an economy is growing and able to maintain 'full employment', it is likely to attract more labour from abroad for two reasons: first, because there are more job opportunities; and second, because there is less domestic opposition to immigration. In the period after the first oil crisis, when unemployment rose sharply and the EU economies moved into recession, there was much more resistance to the flow of labour between countries and encouragement for reversing the flow.

The clearest feature of the development of the permitted mobility of labour among the EU countries was that restrictions were lifted on workers from other member countries rather than non-members. Nevertheless, as is clear from Table 18.6, only Belgium and Luxembourg have had a higher proportion of their foreign workers coming from within the EU than from outside it. The position has changed relatively little in recent years (see Table 18.7) with the exception of Germany, where there has been a small rise, and Luxembourg, where there has been a small fall in the number of non-nationals in the workforce. Looking at it from the point of view of country of origin, Table 18.8 shows that, in all cases except Ireland, only a very small percentage of the labour force had moved to other countries. (Those who have moved and changed their nationality will be excluded, but that is unlikely to make more than a marginal difference to the total.) With the exception of Denmark and Italy,

Table 18.7 Stock of foreign labour by nationality ('000)

A Belgium	1995	1996	1997
Italy	90.5	107.8	96.9
France	37.2	40.2	40.4
Morocco	44.7	36.2	38.5
Netherlands	32.6	34.5	35.8
Spain	23.3	19.8	20.9
Turkey	19.6	22.3	19.1
Others	80.4	80.9	81.4
Total	**328.3**	**341.7**	**333**
of which: EU	225.7	254.2	249.5

B France	1985	1990	1995	1998
Portugal	456.8	428.5	375	316
Algeria	279	248.5	245.6	241.6
Morocco	186.4	168.1	197.5	229.6
Spain	117.8	108.5	82.1	88.2
Tunisia	75.1	74.7	81	84.4
Turkey	41.6	53.9	66.4	79
Italy	125.9	96.9	76.6	72.9
Former Yugoslavia	44.1	29.6	32.3	30
Poland	14.2	15.1	7.1	12.6
Other countries	308.3	325.6	409.6	432.5
Total	**1649.2**	**1549.5**	**1573.3**	**1586.7**
of which: EU	771.6	716.2	629.1	575.5

C United Kingdom	1985	1990	1995	1998
Ireland	269	268	216	221
Africa	51	59	83	108
India	66	84	60	71
US	37	50	49	63
Italy	56	48	43	52
France	17	24	34	49
Germany	18	22	27	39
Caribbean and Guyana	77	48	17	35
Central and Eastern Europe	25	20	23	32
Australia	23	39	34	31
New Zealand	na	na	19	30
Portugal	na	11	18	23
Pakistan	27	27	20	20
Spain	14	16	17	18
Bangladesh	na	na	na	16
Other countries	128	166	239	231
Total	**808**	**882**	**899**	**1039**
of which: EU	382	419	441	454

Table 18.8 Labour force by nationality in EU member states, 1990, 1995 and 1997 (% share of total labour force)

	National			Other EU			Non-EU		
	1990	1995	1997[a]	1990	1995	1997[a]	1990	1995	1997[a]
Belgium	94.6	92.2	92.2	5.2	5.4	5.8	0.2	2.5	2.0
Denmark	98.0	98.1	96.9	0.5	0.8	0.8	1.5	1.1	2.3
Germany	91.5	91.0	90.9	2.8	2.8	3.1	5.7	6.2	6.0
Greece	99.3	98.3	–	0.2	0.2	–	0.5	1.5	–
Spain	99.8	99.2	98.9	0.1	0.3	–	0.1	0.5	–
France	93.5	93.7	93.9	3.0	2.5	2.2	3.5	3.7	3.9
Ireland	97.4	97.0	96.6	2.1	2.4	–	0.5	0.6	–
Italy	98.7	99.6	100	0.38	0.1	–	0.92	0.4	–
Luxembourg	66.6	61.0	44.9	31.5	36.2	52.10	1.9	2.8	3.0
Netherlands	96.3	96.1	97.1	1.4	1.7	1.3	2.3	2.2	1.6
Portugal	99.4	99.6	98.2	0.1	0.2	–	0.5	0.2	–
United Kingdom	96.6	96.4	96.4	1.6	1.6	1.6	1.8	2.0	2.0
Austria	–	90.4	90.1	–	1.1	3.4	–	8.5	6.5
Finland	–	99.3	–	–	0.2	–	–	0.5	–
Sweden	–	95.9	94.8	–	2.0	2.4	–	2.1	2.8
EU	95.2	95.3	–	2.0	1.7	–	2.8	2.9	–

[a] Last column refers to 1997 or to the closest available year.
Source: Adapted from OECD (1999), p. 328, and own Calculations. OECD©, 1999

it appears that size and percentage of working population abroad have an inverse relation. Looking at the same figures from a different point of view, with the exception of Luxembourg, it is the EU countries with the lowest incomes that had the highest outward mobility. Greece, Spain and Portugal alter the picture fairly considerably. They all had above average numbers of people working elsewhere in the EU even before they joined, particularly Portugal. Thus, it might be expected that as restrictions were removed there would have been some expansion in movement. However, despite high levels of unemployment, there are no obvious signs of this.

The picture is a little more complex for inward flows. Luxembourg stands out with around a third of the working population coming from foreign countries. France, Germany and Belgium form a second group with a little less than 10% of their workforce from abroad; and the remaining countries have smaller proportions, down to negligible numbers in the case of Italy. Since Italy is a major exporter of labour to West Germany, France and Belgium, it is not surprising to find that it is a negligible importer since these flows do not represent an exchange of *special* skills but a movement of workers with *some* skills towards countries with greater manufacturing employment opportunities.

As only principal flows are shown in Table 18.6, it is difficult to make any generalizations across the whole range of behaviour. Some special relationships are apparent which relate to previous history rather than the EC as a determinant of the pattern of flows: former colonies in the case of France and the UK and, to a lesser extent, in the case of Belgium and the Netherlands; and the relationship between the UK and Ireland. The West German policy of encouraging foreign workers is clearly shown with the large numbers coming from Turkey and (the former) Yugoslavia.

What is perhaps surprising is that despite the recruitment ban on countries outside the EU in 1973 the shares of member and non-member countries in the number of foreign nationals employed in West Germany remained at approximately the same levels after 1974, the share of non-members falling only as some of the countries joined the EC. The more recent data, provided in Table 18.8, show a fall in foreign labour in most countries by 1990 and stabilization thereafter. However, the switch is much larger for those from non-member states than for those from the other members.

At first glance it appears that labour, in proportionate terms, is rather less mobile than capital, particularly if one takes the UK as an example. The balance of labour and capital flows tends to be in opposite directions according to the development of the various economies. However, there are many specific factors overriding this general relation. The wealthier countries have attracted labour and invested overseas at the same time, thus helping to equilibrate the system from both directions. Yet there is little evidence inside the EU that there are large labour movements purely as a result of the existence of the EU. Some movement between contiguous countries is to be expected, especially where they are small, and also movements from those countries with considerable differences in income, primarily Greece, Italy, Ireland, Portugal and, to a lesser extent, Spain. However, the major movements have been the inflow of workers from outside the EU, primarily into Germany and France. Thus, despite discrimination in favour of nationals of member countries, the relative benefits to employers (the ability to offer worse conditions, readier dismissal, lower benefits, etc.) and to employees (the size of the income gain and the improvement in living standards for their families) make flows from the lower income countries more attractive to both parties.

Worries about competitive exploitation of employees through reducing social protection (known colloquially as 'social dumping') have led the Community to develop the social dimension of the single market programme, expressed through the Charter of Fundamental Rights for Workers and the action programme for its implementation (see Chapter 23). The measures are specifically designed to ensure a 'single market' for labour in the EC. This does not necessarily mean that labour will be more mobile or labour markets more flexible as a consequence. Indeed, the UK government has argued forcefully that these actions might make it more difficult to eliminate pockets of unemployment and hence harm some of these workers whom it is designed to protect. As a consequence, the UK did not initially sign the Social Charter nor accept the Social Chapter proposed for the Maastricht Treaty. In practice the 'social dimension' has led to relatively limited changes in labour market legislation and the Social Charter has not yet been fully adopted. Even the Working Time Directive, which caused a major debate, was ultimately watered down to the point where it did not change much existing behaviour (see Chapter 23).

It should be no surprise that international mobility is limited when one sees the extent of reluctance to respond to economic stimuli for movement within countries. The existence of sharply different regional unemployment levels and regional wage differentials reveals the reluctance. In the UK the system of public sector housing is thought to aid labour rigidity. Possession of a council house in one district does not give any entitlement to one elsewhere. However, even for private sector house owners, negative equity and the very considerable transaction costs of sale and purchase act as a substantial restriction on mobility.

Idiosyncratic, region specific, shocks also importantly shape the flows of skills and labour and are related to the institutional aspects of the labour markets. Idiosyncratic employment fluctuations interact with the development of the aggregate economy and institutional differences across labour markets can steer the labour movements due to the adjustment of different sectors to idiosyncratic shocks. Decressin and Fatás (1995) suggest that economic shocks are increasingly less national and more regional in nature.

Yet, regional and industrial data in the European countries reveal only moderate differences in wages across sectors for homogenous labour. These moderate wage differentials more likely reflect the institutional rigidity of wages *per se*, rather than the efficient functioning of the factor markets. This is evident from the fact that regional unemployment rates are widely dispersed. Unemployment differentials across sectors are also fairly persistent in many European countries. European countries exhibit bigger variations across regional migration flows between the corresponding states in the US.

Decressin and Fatás (1995) note that in Europe region-specific shocks in the demand for labour are reflected in changes in regional participation rates, while unemployment rates react to a small extent during the first three years. Migration, in turn, plays a substantial role in the adjustment process only after three years. A large part of the changes in labour demand is met by people moving in and out of the labour force, instead of migrating or experiencing short unemployment spells. However, more recent evidence suggests that Europeans may be significantly more mobile than previously thought. Based on a panel of 166 regions for the period 1988–1997, Tani (2002) shows that labour demand shocks trigger fairly similar responses in local labour markets across the EU and the US. According to his study, the absorber of a labour demand shock is net migration, accounting for around 50% of the response in the first year and about 80% during the next. In the US, the corresponding numbers are about 40% and 50%.

18.7   Capital and labour movements combined

Recent trends indicate that labour and capital are neither perfectly mobile nor perfectly immobile but rather adjust gradually to market conditions and economic policies. EU member countries do experience inter-regional movements of labour and capital that are of significant magnitude. Yet, these movements are far from instantaneous. Labour and capital are clearly linked across regions but there are still some obstacles to rapid adjustments of labour and capital stocks. At the same time, liberalized immigration policies, EU enlargement and other steps that promote integration of the factor markets of Western Europe with those of surrounding regions present a challenge to policy makers to maintain social cohesion and stable development across different regions in Europe.

As noted at the outset, factor movements cannot legitimately be examined without looking at the behaviour of the markets for internationally traded goods and services at the same time. Nor are the two factor markets independent. While the capital market has little of the characteristics of discrimination in favour of fellow members of the EU that form the basis of trading relationships between the countries, the decision over whether to invest abroad or at home is related to decisions over whether or not to export from the domestic market. Other things being equal, investment at home will generate more domestic employment and indeed it may encourage an inflow of labour from abroad. Investment abroad, on the other hand, will tend to encourage employment in that country and a transfer of labour abroad as well.

The final outcome will depend very much upon whether there is full employment. When there is a shortage of skilled employees, or indeed a shortage of unskilled employees, at wages consistent with successful international competition, investment abroad, especially where costs are lower, may be a preferable substitute for labour-saving investment at home.

Clearly, within the EU there is less incentive to invest abroad, where product prices are not subject to tariffs and hence no big gains in competitiveness can be made. Indeed, one would expect investment from non-members to increase because of the increased size of the internal market. Thus, capital flows could be expected to change in the opposite direction to trade flows, with both an investment-reducing equivalent of trade creation and an investment-increasing switch from third countries as an equivalent to trade diversion. Controls on labour movements have been removed in a manner that favours inflows from EU members rather than non-members.

Running across these considerations are two other factors. Labour can be expected to move from where rewards are lower to where they are substantially higher (to cover the costs of moving), as is evidenced by the outflow from Italy. Second, capital investment could be expected to move to areas where labour costs are much lower but this movement has been much less marked. Instead, capital movements have tended to follow sales opportunities and other locational advantages rather than just labour cost. In so far as labour and capital movements do not take place, factor price differentials will continue to persist, assuming they are not eliminated by trade flows, and the allocation of resources among the EU countries, and indeed between them and non-members, will be inefficient.

In recent years Krugman and Venables (1996) *inter alia* have argued that the pattern of location of industry will be rather different from that initially expected, as there are several factors that lead to increasing economies of scale and agglomeration, at least over a range above the position applying in the early 1990s. Proximity to the main markets, networks of suppliers, skilled labour, etc. may actually attract firms to the main centres of existing industry even though costs may be higher, thus encouraging labour and capital to move in the same direction and exacerbate rather than ease existing disparities.

This idea of clustering of activity both in terms of location and in range of industrial activity has a long history, although it has been popularized by Porter (1990) more recently. Porter offers not so much an explanation of why activity concentrates, as an encouragement to governments to reorient their policies to encourage the process so that they can reap a competitive advantage. The key to this comes from the exploitation of the immobile and less mobile factors of production such as land, physical and business infrastructure and services and, particularly in the case of the EU, highly skilled labour. The increasing returns occur because the process feeds on itself – endogenous growth.

EU structural policy has followed this line of argument (see Chapters 22 and 23) using this policy as a means of helping disadvantaged regions compete through improving public and private infrastructure and human skills. Thus there have been counter-forces to those of increasing concentration in existing centres that market forces alone might have fostered.

This process of concentration has clearly been followed in practice in the EU but it is by no means the only force for development, as the Irish economy demonstrates. Here high technology and IT-based industries have been able to flourish where their location was not very important, aided by favourable macroeconomic, wage bargaining and other direct incentives. High-value, low-weight items, with a worldwide market are not so dependent on location but do require skilled labour. Similarly call centres, internet services and computer software can be located in any lower-cost region and their results transmitted electronically immediately. The 'new economy', widely talked about for the US, enables a society to change much more rapidly and hence grow faster without hitting traditional inflationary pressures from the labour market. While there are only limited signs that the 'new economy' has taken hold in the EU, except perhaps in Ireland and Finland (with the phenomenal development of Nokia), there is the potential for it to do so. If it does we can expect that there will be a further reason for labour to remain fairly immobile.

Until the downturn in the European economy, inefficiency would have been expected to take the form of insufficiently capital-sensitive investment, with a labour inflow being used to avoid restructuring. This would shift some more labour-intensive processes abroad to more labour-intensive EU members, or even outside the EU. Limits on labour mobility decrease this tendency but, with high levels of unemployment currently and for much of the foreseeable future in the EU, it seems unlikely that much further encouragement to move will take place. Indeed, the pressures are the other way round. There is a danger that protectionism will apply not just to goods but to factor movements as well. The difficulties over the new round of multilateral negotiations on reducing protection may be indicative of a gap between the liberalizing rhetoric and the more restrictive actions. In so far as the EU increased the ease of factor mobility, it may be able to maintain a competitive advantage over other countries which resort to this form of protection. It is not surprising, therefore, that third countries have been keen to operate inside the EU and are using just that freedom of capital movement to achieve it.

The experience with migration from Central and Eastern Europe since 1989 has increased the caution over opening up the labour market more widely. It reinforces the suspicion that labour movement has been widely regarded as a key ingredient of the EU largely because it has not occurred on a substantial scale. Labour markets and capital markets once again complement and importantly interact with each other and factor endowments can no longer be taken as given. Regions that are open to factor flows have additional means of adjusting to external shocks and the changing economic and political environment. Factor flows, however, are not instantaneous, but proceed at a rate that reflects economic incentives, intrinsic costs of adjustment, economic policy, institutional settings, as well as the re-organization of industrial production structures. In this sense, factor flows reflect a continuous process of adjustment towards equilibrium. What is crucial to the rate of integration in the internal market is whether differences in factor rewards persist across territorial boundaries of Europe.

NOTES

1. It is the concept of control that distinguishes direct from portfolio investment. The technical definition adopted by the IMF (Balance of Payments Manual, fourth edition, 1977) is 'Direct Investment refers to investment that adds to, deducts from or acquires a lasting interest in an enterprise operating in an economy other than that of the investor, the investor's purpose being to have an effective voice in the management of the enterprise'. Clearly, this distinction can be made only by asking companies themselves about their overseas investment.

2. Other, more complicated, arrangements exist which involve the effective transfer of capital between countries even if not recorded as such in the statistics on capital movements. 'Back-to-back' loans are a simple example whereby exchange controls can be evaded. In such a case, although the parent company can use only the domestic currency when investing in the foreign country, it can make the domestic funds available to a firm based in that same foreign country who wishes to undertake the same transaction but in the opposite direction – their funds are in their own currency while they wish to use the currency of the parent company's country.

3. 'Covered' in the sense that the forward exchange rate premium or discount is taken into account in the computation of the difference in interest rates between countries.

4. This description of capital flows 'balancing' trade flows could equally be phrased as trade flows 'balancing' capital flows. They are two sides of the same coin. If there is a differential in rates of return, capital will be attracted into a country and this will raise the exchange rate, thereby tending to encourage imports and lower exports, hence balancing the capital movement.

5. As was pointed out by Padoa-Schioppa (1987), it is not possible to run a stable system with fixed exchange rates, free capital movements, free trade and independent fiscal policies. One or other of these must be constrained (the last in the case of an integrated single market).

6. There are, of course, differential restraints on the activities of financial institutions depending upon whether or not they are registered within the EU.

7. It is interesting to note that the pressure for the European single market came just as strongly from European multinationals as it did from political sources. Wisse Dekker, then head of Philips and the European Round Table of major companies, put forward a plan in January 1985 to achieve a single market in five years, i.e. by 1990, thus anticipating the White Paper.

8. On an annual basis, the UK was overtaken by Japan, but the UK's outstanding stock of foreign direct investment was still larger.

9. Unremitted profits as a percentage of total net outward investment by the UK in the EU (all countries) were in 1975 74 (40)%, 1979 112 (71)%, 1982 40 (80)% and 1985 122 (55)% (*Business Monitor*).

10. However, not all is due to that programme. Research by Molle and Morsink (1991) shows that foreign direct investment does respond to exchange rate changes, while the dramatic fall in share prices in Japan has led to a substantial reduction in the pace of their investment throughout the world including the EU. The pattern of this investment still strongly reflects the traditional pattern of ease of entry. It is by no means clear that entry by acquisition has become particularly harmonized or, indeed, greatly eased thus far.

Part Five

EU budget and structural policies

Part Five of this book covers all EU policies which address certain structural aspects of the EU economy and society. The EU affords special treatment to those in the agricultural sector, fishing industry and depressed regions as well as dealing with the EU-wide social problems, including unemployment, equal treatment of men and women and migration. These areas are not only financed by the EU general budget, but also claim the bulk of its general budgetary resources. Thus, this Part begins with the chapter on the general budget and follows on with chapters on each of the mentioned areas.

Chapter 19

The general budget

BRIAN ARDY AND ALI EL-AGRAA

The general budget of the EU[1] (budget, hereafter) has always been an issue of high political salience. Member states are naturally concerned with how much they are contributing to and receiving from the budget, the most easily available measure of the costs and benefits of membership.[2] Until 1988 the political significance of the budget was also heightened by inter-institutional rivalry within the EC. The power to approve the budget, one of the more significant powers of the European Parliament was used as a lever to force concessions from the Council (see Chapter 3). This problem has been resolved by the gradually increasing powers to the Parliament and its more direct involvement in budgetary planning.

The budget is also a window on the nature of the EU as a political and economic institution, so a comparison can be made between the tax and expenditure of the EU and that of federal and national governments of nation states. The development of the budget parallels the development of the EU. The budget in the early years was very small and financed from national contributions. With the development EU policies, in particular the Common Agricultural Policy (CAP), expenditure rose and the growing maturity of the EU permitted the introduction of 'own resources' in 1970. There followed a period of continued growth of expenditure, principally on agriculture. The late 1970s and early 1980s were a period of disagreements over the budget between the institutions and in relation to the British contribution. The resolution of this British problem was accompanied by measures to control agricultural expenditure, and was one of the factors that facilitated the development of the Internal Market Programme and the Single European Act. The single market and the Mediterranean enlargement of the EU led in 1988 to the *Delors I* budgetary package. This resulted in a comprehensive revision of the EU budgetary arrangements which expanded the budget: modified 'own resources', expanded and concentrated structural expenditure, tightened control of agricultural expenditure and modified the system of budgetary decision making (European Council, 1988). Following on the agreement on the Treaty on European Union, the budget was further modified by the Edinburgh Agreement (European Council, 1992b) on the *Delors II* package. This accompanied a radical reform of the CAP and further expanded budgetary resources to accommodate more expenditure on structural policies, internal policies (particularly research) and on external action, recognizing the impact of the changes in Central and Eastern Europe (CEE). The reduced dynamism in the EU in the second half of the 1990s is reflected in budgetary developments. *Agenda 2000* (CEU, 1997b) proposed to finance CEE enlargement within the existing budgetary envelope with relatively modest policy reform. Even these proposals were further watered down by the agreement in Berlin in 1999, but this proved inadequate and required further modification in Brussels in 2002. This agreement avoided difficult decisions only resolving the situation up to the end of the current budgetary framework in 2006.

This chapter commences with a short survey of the economic theory of the state (Section 19.1), which examines why governments provide services and intervene in the economy. Section 19.2 considers fiscal federalism: the economic explanation of the assignment of policies between tiers of government. The application of fiscal federalism theory to the EU is examined in Section 19.3. The tackling of the actual budgetary system of the EU begins in Section 19.4, which considers the rules under which the budget operates and the procedure for the adoption of annual budgets. The revenue of the EU is the subject of Section 19.5, which covers the requirements of tax systems, the EU sources of finance and how these compare with those of national federal states. The uses to which this finance is put, EU expenditure, is analysed in Section 19.6. Then the problems facing the Budget are examined: net contributions and equity in Section 19.7; EMU considerations in Section 19.8; and enlargement provisions in Section 19.9.

19.1 The economic theory of the state

In his classic public finance text Richard Musgrave (1959) delineates the role of the state into three branches: allocation, distribution and stabilization. These days the regulatory role of the government would also be stressed (Bailey, 2002).

The government's role in allocation is the result of externalities causing market failure. Externalities are costs and benefits that arise in production but which do not directly affect either the producer or consumer, i.e. they are suffered without compensation or enjoyed free of charge by third parties. Air pollution is an obvious example of an externality, when coal was the major source of energy; households and firms burnt coal without thinking of its effects on the atmosphere. In the UK it took government intervention in the form of Clean Air Acts, to encourage the burning of smokeless fuel to solve this problem of urban air pollution. The crucial thing about externalities is that in the absence of government intervention their costs/benefits are non-rival and non-excludable. Non-rivalry occurs where one person's benefit/cost from a service does not limit other peoples' enjoyment/suffering. Such non-rivalry for a good implies that access should not be limited by price or other means. If it is not possible to prevent access to a service to individuals who have not paid, then the service is non-excludable. Where non-excludability is important it is not possible to finance the service privately because it cannot be charged for, the free-rider problem. With public goods such as defence, all the benefits are non-rival and non-excludable, so governments finance the provision of defence from general taxation. The allocative role of government involves the provision or subsidization of services where externalities are significant.[3]

The regulatory role of the state overlaps with that of allocation; regulation is concerned with setting rules in markets to make them work to society's interest. So regulation encompasses competition policy (see Chapter, 12), the rules for natural monopolies (see Chapter 16), the safety of products, financial services, etc. The reason for government regulation is either that there are problems with competition in the market or that there are informational problems. For example, with financial services there is a case for regulation because of systemic risk; the government has to ensure the viability of key financial institutions in a crisis, while avoiding moral hazard[4] in its underwriting of banks in difficulties. Financial services also need to be regulated because of information problems for the consumer related to the complexity of the product, so consumers need to be protected from fraud and misrepresentation.

The distributive role of government recognizes the fact that markets are compatible with very unequal distributions of individual income levels, which are unacceptable to modern societies. Redistribution occurs as a result of equity, insurance and special interest. Equity justifies the redistribution of income from rich to poor in accordance with society's views on fairness. Insurance is a payment to people with particular adverse circumstances: unemployment, sickness and retirement. The political power of special groups may also enable them to obtain redistribution in their favour, which is the case with farmers in the EU. Redistribution takes place via a progressive tax system, a progressive benefit system and the provision of public services that are subsidized or free of charge. Central governments also redistribute income among regions, part of this is explicit through grants and transfer mechanisms, but most occurs via the operation of national taxation, social security systems and the provision of government services (MacDougall Report, 1977, Sala-i-Martin and Sachs, 1992). There is a presumption that governments provide insurance against unemployment, sickness and pensions for the elderly. Insurance against these eventualities can, of course, be purchased privately, but market provision is unlikely to cover all eventualities (e.g. long-term unemployment) and many individuals particularly those at greatest risk would be unable to pay the necessary premiums. Thus the government provides social insurance partly as an allocative measure because of gaps in the market, but largely for redistributive reasons.[5]

Government's stabilization role is the use of monetary and fiscal policy to try to achieve the objectives of full employment, price stability, economic growth and balance of payments equilibrium. Today there is much less confidence in government's ability to stabilize the economy than there was when Musgrave's book was published. Many governments[6] have delegated authority over monetary policy to independent central banks, because it is believed that better decisions will result from technocratically driven decisions freed from inevitable short-term political considerations. Similarly difficulties with the accurate timing and magnitude of discretionary fiscal policy, has led governments to rely on automatic stabilization to achieve appropriate short-term stabilization, within a budget that is balanced over the long term (see Chapter 10).

Although these arguments provide a clear justification for state intervention in the economy, the extent of this intervention is subject to clear discretion, with the size of the public expenditure and the extent of public services varying widely among nation states. While part of this variation is due to differences in the level of development, much is the result of history, national values and institutions.

19.2   Fiscal federalism

There is a choice to be made not only about the extent of the public sector but also the level of government at which the activity takes place. The traditional theory of fiscal federalism (Oates, 1999) examines the factors that will determine the choice of which level of government will undertake the various economic tasks of the state.[7] The theory begins with the assumption that each level of government cares exclusively about the welfare of its constituents. An efficient system of fiscal federalism would then balance the advantages and disadvantages of provision at various levels of government, and then allocate competences accordingly.

The principal advantage of decentralization is that the lower the level of government the easier it is to assess the preferences of local residents, so the provision of services can be better tailored to their requirements. The existence of different sub-national units of government (regions) mean levels of taxation and public services can be varied. Central government not only has informational problems, it also has a limited ability to differentiate policies across jurisdictions.[8] Democratic accountability is also best achieved with decentralized government where the connection between costs and public provision is most apparent. It is possible to argue further that correspondence between those who benefit from public expenditure and the taxpayers who fund it is most apparent with local provision (Oates, 1977).

Centralized public service provision may offer benefits provided the preferences of citizens in different jurisdictions are similar, i.e. everyone wants roughly the same thing. The policies of one region may have effects on other regions (spillovers) only central government can take account of these interactions. Central government provision may also be more efficient when there are economies of scale, i.e. where the cost per unit diminishes with the volume of the service produced.[9] Centralization can be used to

achieve uniformity in public provision, which may be regarded as important for equity reasons in health, or for equity and efficiency reasons in the case of education. There are also advantages of centralization in relation to taxation; generally, immobile tax bases should finance state/local government. Since mobility is potentially a problem with the major sources of taxation, personal income, corporate profits, social security and to an extent the taxation of consumption (see Chapter 14), state/local government financial autonomy is limited. Local variation in taxation is, however, possible provided differences in rates are not too great and where sub-national jurisdictions are large. The ability to finance public services will, therefore, vary across jurisdictions; the national government can reduce these inequalities to acceptable levels. Redistribution is difficult to achieve at the local level because the rich would tend to migrate to low tax jurisdictions (the poor might migrate to high benefit level localities).

If the assumption of a benevolent government is relaxed then governments may also pursue their own ends, which will not always coincide with those of society. Governments have considerable discretion because parliamentary oversight is imperfect and elections infrequent. If this is the case, decentralization may be advantageous because it increases the options available to citizens (moving to a different jurisdiction), promoting competition between jurisdictions, providing an additional mechanism for achieving efficiency in the provision of public services. This argument is particularly strong in relation to the EU because of the strength of national democracy and concerns over the democratic deficit of the EU.

The Commission has examined the implications of fiscal federalism for the EU on three occasions all related to the issue of economic and monetary union (EMU; see Chapters 8, 9 and 10): the MacDougall

Report (1977); the Padoa-Schioppa Report (1987); and the European Commission (CEC, 1993). These reports mark a gradual retreat from a significant public finance role for the EU, with the extent of redistribution and the size of the Budget diminishing. In its latest assessment, *Sound Money: Stable Finances* (CEC, 1993), the Commission downgrades the importance of redistribution, emphasizes decentralization and subsidiarity and suggests a budget of 2% is sufficient for EMU. The report also points out that much of the fiscal federalism literature concerned as it is with mature federations, is of limited relevance to the EU and does not provide a blueprint for the evolution of its financial constitution.

The large gap between public finances in the EU and existing federations is indicated by a comparison of EU and federal expenditure and revenue. Even in the leanest federation, Switzerland, the federal government expenditure amounts to 10% of GDP compared with just 1.1% in the EU (see Table 19.1). So the EU is a very long way from fulfilling the 'normal' economic role of a federal government in an industrial country.

The EU does not have significant responsibilities in relation to any of the services that dominate federal government expenditure: defence, education, health and social security (see Table 19.2). The two largest categories of federal government expenditure, social security and health, are functions where the EU has very little role. Interest payments do not arise for the EU; since the EU cannot run deficits (see Section 19.4) it does not have debt to service. Defence expenditure has diminished in importance in most countries, with

the US an important exception, and again the EU currently has a very limited involvement and expenditure. Education is primarily the responsibility of lower tiers of government, so it is not surprising that the EU has few responsibilities here.

These comparisons indicate that the EU is currently very far from even a decentralized federation like Switzerland. What role should the EU have in the provision of public services? Given the crucial differences between the EU and other federations they are unlikely to provide an appropriate template. The next section considers the characteristics of the EU that will effect its economic role and what that role should be.

Table 19.1 Expenditure at different levels of government in federal states (percentage of GDP)

	Level of government			
	Federal	State	Local	Total
Australia[a]	15.7	15.6	1.9	**33.2**
Canada[b]	13.3	17.0	7.2	**37.5**
Germany[a]	30.1	8.6	7.4	**46.0**
Switzerland[c]	9.9	12.3	8.5	**30.7**
USA[d]	15.9	7.0	7.2	**30.1**
EU 15[c]	1.1	44.7		**45.8**

[a] 1998; [b] 2000; [c] 1999; [d] state and local.
Sources: Based on IMF (2001); European Commission (CEU, 2000d)

Table 19.2 Federal government expenditure by main function (percentage of total federal expenditure)

	Defence	Education	Health	Social security and welfare	Debt interest	Other functions
Australia[a]	7.0	7.6	14.8	35.5	6.1	29.0
Canada[b]	5.6	2.3	1.4	44.6	15.1	31.0
Germany[c]	3.9	0.5	18.9	50.0	7.1	19.5
Switzerland[d]	4.6	2.4	19.6	49.1	3.5	20.7
USA[b]	15.4	1.8	20.5	28.2	12.6	21.5
EU 15[b]	0.0	1.0	0.0	0.0	–	99.0

[a] 1998; [b] 2000; [c] 1996; [d] 1999.
Sources: Based on IMF (2001); European Commission (CEU, 2002h)

19.3   The EU and fiscal federalism

The EU is not a nation state, it is made up of 15 nation states, with their own institutions, history, culture and languages. Thus the evolving EU constitution is very different from that of national federal states and it is probable that the economic role and budget of the EU will remain distinct. One aspect of distinctness of the EU is the differences in income levels between EU member states, which are important for provision of public services, especially social security. The non-economic differences between member states present problems for common policies in other areas such as defence/security and education.

The dispersion of income levels is wider in the EU than in the US and this dispersion will widen considerably with enlargement (Table 19.3). This heterogeneity of income levels makes it unlikely and undesirable that the EU could have a significant distribution role.[10] It is unlikely because redistribution would involve taxpayers in one country supplementing the income of citizens of another country. Besides the questionable political acceptability, the practical difficulties are immense, e.g. how much should differences in income

be reduced? The undesirability of EU redistribution is shown in an extreme form by the problems of East Germany, which are a powerful lesson in the economic problems of trying to impose a common redistributional policy on very different economies.[11]

Where does this leave the EU's current redistributional role in the structural policies? The political stability of the EU in general, and EMU in particular, is dependent upon a reasonable degree of cohesion in the EU. While this probably does not require equality of income levels,[12] what is needed is that the poorer countries are at least converging on the rich. Convergence in income levels is not automatic (Ardy *et al.*, 2002; pp. 46–50) and so some effective aid policy can be justified.[13]

There is no compelling externality or economies of scale arguments for a significant EU involvement in health and education. With regard to defence a more compelling case can be made for a larger role for the EU. Defence is the classic public good and with war in the EU increasingly unlikely, defence is against external threats to the EU as a whole, or is related

Table 19.3 The distribution of GDP per capita in the EU and GSP per capita in the USA, 2000

GDP pc %	EU 15 member states		US States		EU 25 member states	
EU/US average	Number	% of total	number	% of total	number	% of total
190+	1	6.7	1	2.0	1	4.0
170–189	0	0.0	0	0.0	0	0.0
150–169	0	0.0	0	0.0	1	4.0
130–149	1	6.7	2	3.9	3	12.0
110–129	6	40.0	7	13.7	5	20.0
90–109	3	20.0	19	37.3	2	8.0
70–89	1	6.7	19	37.3	1	4.0
50–69	2	13.3	3	5.9	5	20.0
30–49	1	6.7	0	0.0	1	4.0
10–29	0	0	0	0	6	24
Standard deviation	38.4		32.2		57.6	

Sources: European Commission (CEU, 2002g); European Parliament (2001a); US Bureau of Economic Analysis (2003); US Census Bureau (2003).

to peacekeeping/making beyond the EU. There is public support for the development of a EU policy (CEU, 2003d). There are a number of obvious difficulties, such as the reluctance of governments to cede sovereignty over such a sensitive area, whether the public would be supportive of European armed forces and neutral countries.[14] Similarly, there are strong reasons for an important EU role in internal security, where there is again public support (CEU, 2003d).

Beyond these areas,[15] the EU economic role would seem to be confined to competences that are already part of its responsibilities such as overseeing the single market, operating competition policy and regulation more generally, and also research and development policy where EU programmes are justified because there are potentially important economies of scale.

External action is really part of foreign policy and related increasingly to defence. The EU current role in agricultural policy is more questionable; there seems little reason for the EU to be paying direct agricultural subsidies (see Section 16.6 and Chapter 20), so agricultural expenditure could shrink and the EU role be confined largely to regulation and trade policy. These arguments tend to suggest that there is a case for some limited expansion of the budget, if it were to acquire a significant defence role. It would, however, remain small, much smaller than that of existing federations. The conclusion must be that at the present stage of development, a limited budget seems well suited to the EU requirements. The EU has still to ensure that the operation of this limited budget is fair and efficient. These are the issues to which this chapter now turns.

19.4   Budget rules and procedure

There are five basic principles derived from the Treaties under which the budget operates:

1 *Annuality*, which means that the budget is only for the one year, so authorization cannot be given beyond that year. This prevents the build up of long-term commitments, but has caused some problems because much EU expenditure is now on multi-annual programmes. The practical resolution of this problem has been the use of commitments for future years, which strictly do not have to be honoured, but which in practice usually are.
2 *Balance*, or equilibrium, which means that revenues must cover expenditure and deficit financing is not possible. If expenditure is going to exceed revenue, additional resources have to be raised by supplementary or amending budgets in the current year. Surpluses at the end of the year are carried over to the next year as revenue.[16] The EU is not allowed to borrow to finance its own expenditure but can use its triple-A credit rating to borrow for loans.[17] Most of these loans take place via the European Investment Bank (EIB, see Chapter 3), which is an independent EU development bank, borrowing on international capital markets and making loans for projects in the EU and beyond (Laffan, 1997, chapter 8). These capital

transactions are financially self-supporting and do not breach the principle of EU budgetary balance.
3 *Unity*, that is, all expenditure is brought together in a single budget document.
4 *Universality*, which demands that all EU revenue and expenditure be included in the Budget, there are to be no self-cancelling items.
5 *Specification*, meaning that expenditure is allocated to a particular objective to ensure that it is used for the purposes the budgetary authority intended. There is some possibility for transfers between categories for the effective execution of the Budget.

These rules indicate very clearly the extent to which member states wanted to limit EU competence in this sensitive area of government activity. So they ensure maximum control by member states and minimum discretion for the EU.

The budgetary procedure laid out in the 1975 Budget Treaty[18] contained the seeds of discord in decision making. This Treaty granted the European Parliament (EP) the responsibility for the final approval of the budget[19] (see Chapter 3), a power the EP was determined to use. So in the early 1980s the annual budgetary cycle was one of frequent disputes between the institutions (Nicholl, 1994; p. 18). Two developments resolved this situation: first, the increase in powers of the EP which commenced with the Single European Act (SEA) in 1987; second, new budgetary procedures introduced with the 1988 *Delors I* package. This contained two innovations that continue to this day: a multi-annual financial perspective and an interinstitutional agreement on budgetary procedure.

The latest financial perspective covers the seven years 2000–2006 (European Council, 1999b, 2000), it consists of agreed ceilings on broad categories of expenditure and for the budget overall. Each financial perspective is accompanied by an inter-institutional agreement under which the Commission, the Council and the EP agree to respect the agreed ceilings. Actual levels of expenditure are set by the annual budget, which must be within the limits set by the financial perspective. This budget has to be agreed by the procedure laid down in the Treaties: preliminary draft budget from the Commission, establishment of draft budget by the Council, first reading by the Parliament, second reading by the Council and, finally, second reading by the Parliament and the adoption of the budget. With the broad parameters by the financial perspective, and trialogue meetings of the three institutions throughout this procedure, the agreement of the annual budgets since 1998 has been straightforward. The decisions on the financial perspective are, however, far more hard fought.

19.5 EU budget revenue

Tax systems should be fair, efficient and transparent. Fairness can only be evaluated on the basis of consistent principles to decide tax liability.[20] There are two dimensions of fairness or equity – horizontal equity and vertical equity. Horizontal equity, the identical treatment of people in equivalent positions, implies that those with the same level of income and similar circumstances should pay the same amount of tax. Vertical equity requires the consistent treatment of people in different circumstances. In general, equity is taken to imply a progressive tax system; the wealthy should pay proportionately more tax. Depending upon how the EU raises its revenues this could apply to taxes on individuals or it could apply to member states.

Efficiency requires that the tax system should minimize harmful market distortions. Low collection and compliance costs are important additional aspects of tax efficiency. Transparency requires that the tax system should be simple to understand, so that taxpayers are aware of their tax liability and how this is determined. This requirement of transparency is essential for democratic accountability. This section will consider development of the EU revenue system and how it matches up to these requirements, but first a comparison will be made between the EU revenue system and those of federal governments.

As Tables 19.4 and 19.5 clearly demonstrate, the EU does not have a financing system like that of other federal states. The amount of truly independent tax revenue is extremely low and taxation remains predominantly under the control of nation states in the EU 15. Federal governments typically raise a large

Table 19.4 Tax revenue of different levels of government in federal states (percentage of GDP)

	Level of government			
	Federal	**State**	**Local**	**Total**
Australia[a]	17.9	4.5	8.4	30.7
Canada[b]	19.0	13.7	3.0	35.8
Germany[c]	26.1	8.0	2.9	37.1
Switzerland[a]	22.4	7.1	5.0	34.5
USA[d]	19.8	5.6	3.5	28.9
EU 15[b]	0.2[b]	41.5[e]		**41.7**

[a] 1999; [b] 2000; [c] 1998; [d] Traditional own resources agricultural and customs duties; [e] State and local.

Sources: IMF (2001); OECD (2002b); European Commission (CEU, 2002h)

part of their revenue from taxation of income directly through the personal income tax system or indirectly through the social security system (Table 19.5). Corporation tax, VAT/general sales taxes and excises are other important sources of tax revenue for federal government. None of these revenue sources is available to the EU.

The EEC was initially financed like other international organizations by fixed national shares, but the EEC Treaty provided for the development of a system of 'own resources'. The significance of this move was

Table 19.5 Tax systems: federal states and the EU (percentage of GDP)

	Personal income tax	Corporation tax	Social security	VAT[a]	Excises	Total
Australia[b]	9.7	3.2	0.0	1.9	1.9	**17.9**
Canada[c]	8.1	2.6	4.3	2.6	0.8	**19.0**
Germany[b]	3.9	0.6	14.9	3.4	2.5	**26.1**
Switzerland[d]	2.0	1.1	12.3	3.9	1.8	**22.4**
USA[c]	10.1	2.1	6.5	0.7	0.5	**19.8**
EU 15[d]	–	–	–	–	–	**0.2[d]**

[a] general sales taxes or VAT; [b] 1998; [c] 2000; [d] agricultural and customs duties excluding VAT and the fourth resource.
Sources: IMF (2001); OECD (2002b); European Commission (CEU, 2002b)

that the EEC would have financial autonomy, by acquiring financial resources distinct from those of the member states. This proved controversial and it was not until April 1970, just before negotiations opened for the first enlargement, that agreement was reached. This provided for the EU to be financed by duties on agricultural imports and sugar production, revenue from the Common Customs Tariff (CCT) and VAT up to 1% of the harmonized base (see Chapter 14). The 'Traditional Own Resources' (TOR), agricultural levies and customs duties, are naturally EU revenue because they arise from EU policies: the Common Agricultural Policy (CAP) and Common Commercial Policy (CCP; see Chapters 6 and 24). In a common market, it is difficult to assign these revenues to individual member states because goods imported through one where the duties are paid, may then be sold in another member state where the actual burden or incidence of the tax occurs.[21] As member states have not used the harmonized base, the VAT contribution has always rested on 'artificial' calculation (Begg and Grimwade, 1998; pp. 41–2), so it amounts to being just a particular way of calculating a national contribution.

The original own resources system had a number of problems as a system of finance for the EC. At first, revenue expanded as the call up rate of VAT increased, but once the 1% limit was reached, revenue grew comparatively slowly (Figure 19.1). TOR revenue was constrained by falling agricultural imports as EC food self-sufficiency levels increased (see Chapter 20), decreasing level of tariffs, the expanding of EC membership and the extension of preferential trade agreements to third countries (see Chapter 24). The VAT

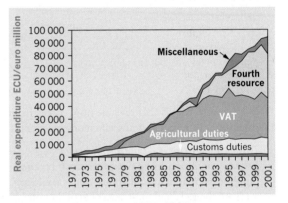

Figure 19.1 EU revenue, 1971–2001
Sources: European Commission (CEU, 2000d); ECA (various)

base also grew slowly because it excluded government expenditure and savings which tend to expand over time. It was regressive because these elements tend to increase as income levels increase. So the system was not equitable; contributions to the budget were not related to GNP per capita. The UK in particular seemed to be contributing more than its fair share, because of its high level of imports from outside the EU, and a relatively low level of government expenditure and savings.[22] Raising the VAT limit to 1.4% in 1984[23] increased revenue but this was only a temporary solution, which did not address the problems of lack of buoyancy or of equity in contributions.

The own resources system was made more equitable and more buoyant by the introduction in 1988 of the fourth resource based on GNP. The base for own resources was now expressed as a percentage of EU

Table 19.6 Sources of EU revenue, 2000 and 2001

	2000		2001	
	€ million	%	€ million	%
Traditional own resources	15 267.1	16.5	14 589.2	15.5
Agricultural duties	1 198.4	1.3	1 132.9	1.2
Sugar and isoglucose levies	1 196.8	1.3	840	0.9
Customs duties	14 568.3	15.7	14 237.4	15.1
Collection expenses	−1 696.3	−1.8	−1 621	−1.7
VAT resources	35 192.5	38.0	31 320.3	33.2
GNP resources	37 580.5	40.5	34 878.8	37.0
Other revenue	4 755.3	5.1	13 571.2	14.4
Surplus from previous financial year	3 209.1	3.5	11 612.7	12.3
Miscellaneous revenue	1 546.1	1.7	1 958.5	2.1
Total	**92 724.4**	**100.0**	**94 289.3**	**100.0**

Source: ECA (2002). Reprinted by permission of the European Communities.

GNP, currently 1.24%. EU revenue now comes from the four own resources and miscellaneous revenue:

1 *Duties on agricultural imports and sugar production*. Agricultural duties are tariff revenue on imports of agricultural goods. Sugar levies are a tax on the production of sugar beyond quota limits and on the production of isoglucose.[24]
2 *Common Customs Tariff* (CCT). The revenue from EU taxes on non-agricultural imports. The importance of these TOR was diminished by the decision, taken at Berlin in 1999, to increase the share of TOR retained by national governments to cover the cost of collection, from 10 to 25% (European Council, 2000).
3 *VAT* revenue of 0.5% of VAT on the harmonized base. VAT as a consumption tax tends to bear most heavily on poorer countries, so the VAT base has been capped at 50% of GNP since 1992, for member states whose per capita GDP is less than 90% of the EU average.
4 *The Fourth resource*. In the annual budget the revenue raised from TOR and VAT is subtracted from total EU expenditure, this amount is expressed as a percentage of EU 15 GNP and each member state contributes an amount equal to this percentage of its GNP. With the revenue

from other sources diminishing as a percentage of GNP, the fourth resource is becoming the dominant source of EU revenue (Figure 19.1 and Table 19.6).

This system of finance has given the EU revenue which grows in line with GNP and which is reasonably fair because contributions are proportional to GNP for high and low income countries (Figure 19.2).[25] Countries with between 100% and 120% of EU average GNP per head can, however, pay very different

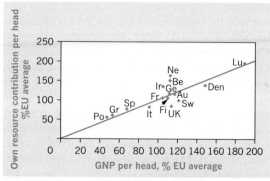

Figure 19.2 EU 15 own resource contributions and GNP per head

Sources: ECA (various); European Commission (CEU, 2002g)

contributions unrelated to their GNP levels. Although the situations of Belgium and the Netherlands (the Rotterdam Problem) and the UK (due to its correction mechanism, see Section 19.6) can be explained, for the other countries the variation represents the

continued failure of the system to relate contributions to ability to pay. The dependence on VAT and GNP contributions means that the EU has largely gone back to a system of national contributions calculated in a particular way.

19.6 EU budget expenditure

The development of budgetary expenditure traces the development of EU policies. For a long time the budget was dominated by agricultural expenditure, partly because other policies were underdeveloped but also because the CAP became expensive to operate. Up until the late 1980s, agricultural expenditure grew rapidly, since then however real budgetary expenditure has been stabilized (Figure 19.3). This was the result of production control measures (such as milk quotas) and limits being placed on agricultural expenditure, initially in 1984 but more effectively since 1988. Since when agricultural expenditure may not rise each year by more than 74% of the annual growth rate of GNP (European Council, 1998); this implied that agricultural expenditure would be a diminishing proportion of EU expenditure.[26] As enlargement increased the heterogeneity of the Community, it was felt necessary to introduce a greater redistributive element into the budget, by expanding and concentrating expenditure on structural operations. Part of this additional expenditure was financed by an expansion of the revenue base of the budget, but the stabilization of agricultural expenditure freed resources for structural policies. Expenditure on research has increased as a result of concerns over EC competitiveness. The

ending of the Cold War, has also led to increased expenditure on external action, as the EU has sought to bring stability to Central and Eastern Europe.[27] Agriculture and structural expenditure continue, however, to dominate the budget (Table 19.7).

19.6.1 CAP guarantee expenditure

Initially the CAP maintained high EC agricultural prices by protection from imports. As surpluses began to develop, support buying and dumping of surpluses on the world market, led to increased agricultural expenditure. This form of CAP, where the EU rapidly expanded its share of world agricultural trade on the basis of subsidized exports, began to wane as a result of budgetary pressures in the 1980s and trade negotiations (the Uruguay Round of the GATT) in the 1990s (see Chapter 20). The EU switched support for farmers to direct subsidies, with production restrained by lower prices and production controls. In 2001, 68% of agricultural guarantee expenditure was on direct subsidies (ECA, 2002). This change in the pattern of expenditure has substantially enhanced budgetary planning and control, because direct subsidies are much more stable and predictable than price support expenditure. It does, however, call into question the EU role in agricultural policy. Price support in a single market requires EU finance because the EU price is maintained by support buying wherever this takes place. But there seems no good reason for the EU financing direct subsidies to farmers, however, the EU should retain a regulatory role, to ensure fair competition between farmers from different countries.

Differences in the composition and volume of agricultural production mean that there are substantial variations in CAP guarantee expenditure among member states, which bear no relation to their GNP per head. In Figure 19.4 the member states are arranged in order of their GNP per head, with the lowest to the left. CAP expenditure does not diminish

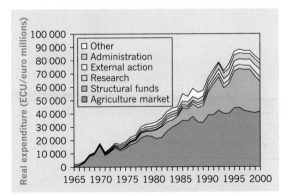

Figure 19.3 EU budget expenditure, 1965–2001
Sources: European Commission (CEU, 2000d); ECA (various)

Table 19.7 EU expenditure, 2000 and 2001

	2000		2001	
	€ million	%	€ million	%
Common Agricultural Policy	40 505.9	48.6	41 533.9	51.9
CAP markets	3 629.4	43.5	37 170.1	46.5
Rural development	4 176.4	5.0	4 363.8	5.5
Structural operations	27 590.8	33.1	22 455.8	28.1
Internal policies	5 360.8	6.4	5 303.1	6.6
Research and development	3 404	4.1	3 195.9	4.0
External action	3 841	4.6	4 230.6	5.3
Administration	4 643	5.6	4 855.1	6.1
Reserves	186.3	0.2	207.2	0.3
Pre-accession aid	1 203.4	1.4	1 401.7	1.8
Total	**83 331.2**	**100.0**	**79 987.4**	**100.0**
% EU GNP		**1.0**		**0.9**

Source: ECA (2001) and ECA (2002). Reprinted by permission of the European Communities.

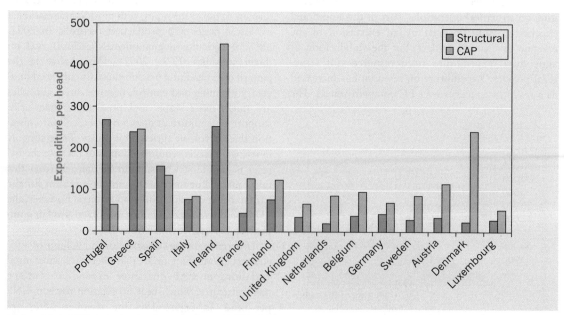

Figure 19.4 CAP and structural expenditure, 1999–2000
Source: ECA (various)

as GNP per capita increases, Ireland, Greece and Denmark receive substantial payments: Ireland has an average income level, Greece is one of the poorest EU countries and Denmark one of the richest. Countries receiving less than the average CAP expenditure are similarly diverse, ranging from the poorest, Portugal, to the richest, Luxembourg. With around half of the budget spent on agriculture it is difficult to achieve an equitable budget with such random distribution of CAP expenditure.

For farmers, landowners and industries associated with agriculture, EU support of prices and direct subsidies provide substantial benefits.[28] For taxpayers and consumers the CAP imposes substantial costs in two ways. First, the taxation paid to finance the budgetary expenditure. Second, the additional expenditure on food caused by the EU price being above the world market prices. With the reformed CAP, and the high world prices of recent years, the gaps between EU and world prices have narrowed substantially. For most agricultural products, EU prices are near to world levels, so the additional costs to the consumer are minor. This is not the case for milk products, beef and sugar. Here, in addition to the budgetary cost of financing the CAP, there is a consumer cost involved in paying in excess of the price for which the product could be imported from outside the EU. This effect is relatively minor nowadays (Ardy, 2002a; pp. 96–97) so measured CAP expenditure provides a reasonable approximation of national benefits from the CAP.

19.6.2 Structural policy expenditure

The structural funds, comprising the European Social Fund (ESF), European Agricultural Guidance Fund (EAAGF), the European Regional Development Fund (ERDF) and the Cohesion Fund, were developed to try to achieve greater solidarity within the Union. They were justified, therefore, as a redistributive policy, to encourage political solidarity within the Union. Structural expenditure has also been useful as side payments to facilitate agreement between member states. The expansion of the structural funds and their concentration on poorer regions since 1988 was part of the bargain to achieve agreement on the Single European Act (SEA). This concentration of expenditure on poorer regions redistributes income to poorer countries.[29] The highest levels of expenditure are in the poorest member states: Portugal, Greece, Spain and Ireland.[30] Italy and Finland have average structural spending, while in other member states structural expenditure per head is below average. With structural spending aimed at regional rather than national redistribution, other objectives being pursued and political factors affecting its distribution, its redistributive effect is somewhat uneven. With CAP and structural spending accounting for 80% of EU expenditure it is their distribution which largely determines the distribution of expenditure among EU member states.

19.6.3 Internal policies

Internal policies cover a range of expenditure programmes in the EU, the largest element of internal policy expenditure is research and technological development (see Chapter 13), which tries to enhance the competitiveness of the EU. Also significant under this heading are education, vocational training and youth, and Trans-European networks (TENs). Education expenditure is mainly used to finance grants for study in other European countries. This expenditure should help forge a greater sense of EU identity and could have beneficial effects on the single market by encouraging labour mobility. Expenditure on TENs is very similar to ERDF expenditure, financing cross-border networks of roads, railways, energy and telecommunications grids. Such networks are important in fostering competition in the single market, and since they are cross border, EU involvement is probably desirable to encourage the development of such networks.

19.6.4 External action

EU external expenditure is concentrated on three groups of countries:[31] Central and Eastern Europe (CEE), the Mediterranean and the Middle East and the African, Caribbean and Pacific. The first two groups represent the EU geographical neighbours and the third group is less developed former colonies. The largest component of external aid expenditure is concentrated on CEE, because with the collapse of Communism, this area represented a zone of potential instability within Europe. The EU programmes in these countries have facilitated transition. Pre-accession aid for the ten countries joining the EU in 2004 has been separated in the budget to protect this expenditure if there is pressure on the budget. In addition it under-lines the passage of relations with these countries from external to internal (see Chapter 26). Russia and the former CIS countries have not been offered EU membership, but the development of a closer political and economic relationship and economic aid is an important part of this process.

Aid to the Mediterranean and the Middle East again tries to increase the stability of another volatile region close to the EU. Economic development in this area would also help to reduce the pressure for migra-tion to the EU. Aid to the ACP reflects obligations and ties to former colonies. The EU channels aid both via the budget and by a separately financed European Development Fund (EDF), which is responsible for most aid to ACP countries. Expenditure under the EDF is decided separately from the budget by the Council and is financed by fixed national shares (CEU, 2000d; p. 19). There are concerns about the effectiveness of aid programmes (see Chapter 25), as well as about individual elements of aid. For example, Food Aid accounts for around 20% of budget expenditure on aid; this has sometimes been little more than an exten-sion of the CAP facilitating the disposal of surpluses, with problematic consequences for recipient nations (Cathie, 2001).

Although there is public support for foreign aid, the EU role is not well understood, nor is it differ-entiated from national government aid programmes. The EU has developed a clear role in relation to CEE, preparing these countries for membership. The neces-sary scale of the operations, and the need to avoid wasteful duplication justifies EU aid beyond this area, but the continuance of national government pro-grammes undermines the development of a clear role for the EU.

19.6.5 Administration

The least understood element of EU expenditure is that on administration. Constant references in the press to the Brussels bureaucracy, their gravy train lifestyle, and pictures of enormous edifices in Brussels and Strasbourg, suggest a vast and expensive bureau-cracy. Thus paying for officials, meetings and build-ings, was the category selected by the public as the area on which most of the budget is spent (CEU, 1999g; p. 16). This is a very distorted picture, the number of people employed by the European institutions is

relatively small 33 438 in 2001, 24 087 in the Commis-sion (CEU, 2002b; p. 125). This is modest compared to national and local governments. Thus in 2001 the Federal Government of the USA employed 2 596 990 people, with over 1 million of these being office and administrative staff (BLS, 2003). So the idea of the Commission as a vast and unwieldy bureaucracy is completely false. The small size of the Commission is the result of the limited policies for which the EU is responsible, and the way in which these policies are operated. Government policies with large numbers of employees, such as health, remain the responsibility of national governments. National governments and their employees largely operate EU policies. Thus for the CAP it is national officials who carry out support buying, supervise storage and disposal of surpluses and monitor the payment of subsidies. Administration has remained a small and stable proportion of total EU expenditure as a result of the continued limitation of the EU powers and responsibilities.

Concerns over administration also relate to issues about administrative competence and corruption high-lighted by the resignation of the Santer Commission in 1999. Three aspects of the EU and its administration are important in this respect. First, the multinational character of the administration makes it difficult to devise suitable codes of conduct, because different countries have different ideas of what is acceptable. Thus, the employment of relatives and friends by government and officials is normal in some countries but not in others. Second, the small size of the Com-mission, in relation to its responsibilities, has made it difficult to keep track of expenditure. There have been difficulties with the employment of contract workers, and the supervision of EU programmes is hampered by a shortage of staff. The Commission budget depart-ment has particular problems, with the European Court of Auditors only being able to provide assur-ance of the reliability and legality of administrative expenditure, around 5% of the total (ECA, 2002). Third, the member states have the primary responsibil-ity for monitoring most programmes. The Commission has a rather ambiguous managerial and supervisory role, but generally no powers to carry out investiga-tions in the member states. Proposals by Neil Kinnock, Commission Vice President for Administrative Reform, aimed to tackle the internal problems of the Commis-sion (CEU, 2000a), but progress has been slow and the problem of monitoring and the operation of the policies in the member states remains.

Administrative expenditure is heavily concentrated in Belgium and Luxembourg, but the extent of the benefits this confers on these countries is limited. With other areas of expenditure, it is possible to argue that EU expenditure is largely for activities that would have occurred anyway, and so it is a net addition to GNP. Administrative expenditure either involves the use of resources such as labour, capital and land, or is pay for individuals who are citizens of other member states. While undoubtedly Belgium and Luxembourg enjoy multiplier and balance of payments effects, this benefit is far less than the total amount of administrative expenditure in their countries.

19.7 Net contributions to the EU budget

A member state's net contribution (NC) to the budget is the difference between the amount it pays in own resource revenue and the amount its receives from allocated expenditure.[32] The Commission has often argued (CEU, 1998c) that national concerns with NCs are mistaken, the EU brings a great many benefits to member states, so the narrow budgetary costs and bene-fits are an inaccurate measure of the costs and benefits of membership.[33] While this is true, it is irrel-evant; whatever the overall costs and benefits of membership, the public finances of the EU should be arranged in an equitable manner. Another frequent observation is that the budget is too small to matter. The amounts involved are very large, not much less than the GDP of the smaller EC states, Greece, Portugal, Ireland,[34] and greater than the GDP of all ten new member states except Poland. Unlike national budgets, which are largely transfers from one group within the national economy to another, payments to the EU represent invisible imports and reductions in GNP, and receipts from the EU invisible exports additions to GNP.

Figure 19.5 plots NCs averaged for 1999–2000 against GNP per head. There is a negative relationship between net contributions and GNP per head: the NCs are equivalent to a proportional tax, for every 1% rise in GNP relative to the EU average, the NC rises by 0.03% of GNP.[35] Portugal, Greece and Spain, the poorest member states, receive net benefits equal to 3.4, 2.3 and 1.1% of GNP respectively, with Greece and Portugal treated generously relative to their income, and Spain's net benefit is what would be predicted from the estimated relationship. Ireland withan average income receives substantial net benefits of 2.1% of GNP.[36] Denmark, the second wealthiest member state, is a marginal beneficiary from the budget. Seven member states with GNP between 104 and 118% of the EU average have net contributions between 0.0% and −0.5% of GNP. The budget thus has a rather haphazard impact; overall it is redistributive, but there are large deviations in NCs from what would be expected from the fitted relationship (Domenesh *et al.*, 2001; de la Fuente and Domenesh, 2001).

National governments are very aware of their situation with regard to the budget and if they think they are being treated unfairly, they will demand that the situation be resolved. The most infamous example of this is the British Problem, a recurrent problem dating from 1973 when the UK joined the EEC until its resolution in 1984, unfortunately with a rebate specific to the UK. The UK correction for budgetary imbalances is calculated as follows (European Council, 2000): in the current year, the correction is calculated on the basis of the imbalance in the previous year, equal to the percentage share of the UK in VAT minus the percentage share in total allocated expenditure, multiplied first by total allocated expenditure and then by 0.66.[37] The correction is financed by increasing the own resource contributions by other member states, and it is not surprising that this is strongly resented by them. The fact that the UK NC with the rebate is on the regression line indicates that the correction is still justified.[38]

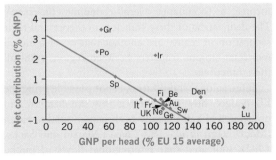

Figure 19.5 Net contribution to the EU budget and GNP per head, 1999–2000

Source: European Commission 2003. Reprinted by permission of the European Communities.

There has been a hardening of attitudes towards net contributions to the budget in other countries. Two developments have been crucial: the changing situation of Germany and EMU. German unification has both put tremendous pressure on the Federal Government's budget with a net transfer of 4% of GDP from West to East Germany (CEU, 2002c; p. 2). This burden has been made worse by the related poor performance of the German economy with low growth and high unemployment. Germany is, therefore, no longer willing or able to act as the paymaster for Europe, indeed it wants to reduce its net contribution to the budget. The change in German attitudes has been mirrored by the Netherlands, Austria and Sweden calling for reductions in their net contribution to the budget. The major factor here appears to be the process of budgetary consolidation required to meet the Maastricht convergence requirements, together with the budgetary restraint under the Stability and Growth Pact (SGP) (see Chapter 10). NCs to the budget of 0.5% of GNP do not seem very significant compared to federal/central government budgets of 10% to 30%. These EU budgetary contributions loom much larger in relation to the SGP's upper limit for public sector deficits of 3% of GDP and the medium-term requirement for the budget to be close to balance or in surplus. With monetary policy determined by the ECB on the basis of the conditions of the euro area as a whole, national fiscal policy remains the one flexible short-term element of macroeconomic policy in national governments' hands. NCs to the budget eat into this national margin for flexibility and so have become a much more salient political issue.

With the current range of revenue resources and policies, it is difficult to achieve a fair distribution of budgetary costs and benefits and thus of NCs. Policy reform could achieve a fairer outcome, but to conflate reform and equity could compromise the objectives of policy reform. In the absence of reform, NCs can be restricted by limiting budgetary expenditure and this is what has happened. Far more satisfactory would be a redistribution mechanism, which would ensure a fair distribution of net contributions (de la Fuente and Domenesh, 2001). Such a system would have the enormous advantage that each member state would feel the effects of new expenditure commitments on its net contribution.[39]

19.8 The EU budget and EMU[40]

There are two macroeconomic roles for the budget in a federation: fiscal policy and transfers between regions. Fiscal policy is the manipulation of the balance between government expenditure and revenue so as to influence aggregate demand in the economy. The small size and requirement for balance mean that the budget cannot have a role in fiscal policy. Regions within a monetary union that face asymmetric shocks can no longer use the exchange rate as a shock absorbing mechanism. With automatic transfers from the central/federal budget, fiscal policy will act as a means of interregional risk sharing by transferring resources between regions. These transfers perform three types of function (Fatás, 1998): intertemporal stabilization, interregional insurance and interregional redistribution. The first two stabilize regional income, the third reduces inequalities in income levels between regions. Intertemporal stabilization smoothes fluctuations in regional income levels due to the stabilization of the national economy by movements in the national public sector deficits; the Keynesian stabilization function. Interregional insurance, tax revenue from fast growing regions can be transferred to slow growing ones when economic cycles are imperfectly correlated between regions. Interregional redistribution involves the transfer of resources from more to less prosperous regions, so it is related to levels of rather than changes in income. Such redistribution might be justified in terms of the solidarity of the nation state, to achieve a fairer individual distribution of income, or to enhance overall economic efficiency.[41] The delineation of these transfers in theory and their separation in reality are another matter; in national monetary unions transfers between regions fulfil all three functions.

Interregional stabilization is not possible using the EU budget; how important is this stabilization and how much of a problem is its absence? Initial research (MacDougall et al., 1977; Sala-i-Martin and Sachs, 1992), indicated that interregional flows of public finance were important in reducing fluctuations in regional income. Gradually more refined research techniques have whittled away at the estimated effects and the latest research suggests that federal taxes and transfers only reduce regional income fluctuations by 10% (Obstfeld and Peri, 1998; Fatás, 1998; Asdrubali *et al.*, 2002; Mélitz and Zumer, 1998). These estimates of stabilization are for the USA, a monetary union comparable in size to EMU. Whether it is a good basis for comparison with EMU could be questioned because of the difference between US States and EU countries. The national economies[42] of EMU remain diversified so their vulnerability to asymmetric shocks

and, consequently, the need for interregional stabilization is less. The greater separation of EU nation states may also enhance the potential for differences in rates of wage and price inflation; an effective alternative adjustment mechanism. Thus, by comparison with the USA, European national economies lack adjustment mechanisms such as labour mobility and cross-border capital holdings and flows but are perhaps less vulnerable to asymmetric shocks than US States.

19.9   The EU budget and enlargement

The coming enlargement places large potential demands upon the budget because of three characteristics of the Central and Eastern European Countries[43] (CEECs): low income levels, the large total size of their populations and the importance of agriculture (see Chapter 26). Since contributions to the budget are roughly related to GNP (see Section 19.4) this would lead to the CEECs only adding a small amount to EU own resource income. The CEECs would, however, add significantly to EU expenditure because of their demands on the structural policy and agricultural budgets.

The Commission proposals for budgetary and policy reform in response to enlargement were contained in *Agenda 2000* (CEU, 1997b). The CAP was to be reformed by reducing agricultural prices for cereals and beef, partially compensating farmers by means of increased subsidies. This would reduce the cost of applying the CAP[44] to the CEECs because it was proposed not to provide direct subsidies to the new member states. Increased subsidy levels did, however, increase the cost of applying the policy in the EU 15 and this, together with the additional expenditure in the new member states, meant that proposed CAP expenditure rose substantially. With structural policies there was to be significant expenditure in the CEECs,[45] but again this was to be restricted, to a ceiling of 4% of GDP. Expenditure in the EU 15 was to be reduced in real terms after 2001, by restricting areas eligible to receive regional specific aid. Even with these changes, a large increase in structural expenditure was planned. Expenditure in other areas was to be tightly controlled, so that the overall budgetary costs of enlargement were to remain within the existing own resources revenue and expenditure ceiling of 1.27% of GNP. This was very stringent, given the difficulties of enlargement in general and this

enlargement in particular. Other enlargements had been accompanied with or followed by expansions in the budgetary resources available to the EU.

In February 1999, when the European Council met in Berlin, it was obvious that member states were not prepared to finance even the modest increase in expenditure envisaged in *Agenda 2000*. One approach was radical reform of the CAP, but France in particular was not prepared to accept this, so agricultural price reductions were cut back and this, together with other reforms, were delayed by the Berlin Agreement (European Council, 1999b). This reduced the cost of subsidies to compensate farmers, thereby reducing the overall cost of the package. Direct payments were not to apply in the new member states during a transitional period, but production quotas and set asides were to be applied.

The reforms to the structural funds agreed at Berlin were in line with *Agenda 2000* but there were two groups of concession. First, it was agreed that the Cohesion Fund could continue to apply to states that were members of the euro area. Second, there was a list of what were called 'particular situations': exceptional treatment for existing member states to partially compensate for the effects of the structural policy reform. The extent to which these particular situations are simply a mechanism for buying countries off is illustrated by the concession to the Netherlands: 'In order to take account of the particular characteristics of labour market participation in the Netherlands, an additional amount of 500 million euros are allocated to Objective 3'. Since the Netherlands has one of the lowest unemployment rates in the EU 15, it is difficult to understand the nature of these particular problems. The overall effect of these concessions is to raise structural expenditure marginally above the *Agenda 2000* proposals. The decision to raise the proportion of customs revenues retained to cover the cost of collection from 10 to 25% was designed specifically to reduce the Netherlands net budgetary contribution. The Netherlands, as well as Austria, Germany and Sweden, also benefited from reductions in their contributions to finance the UK budget rebate. Thus the combination of a lower overall level of expenditure and these side payments were sufficient to satisfy those countries demanding a reduction in their NCs.

The decision not to make direct payments to the CEECs came to be seen as untenable, so the whole issue of the budget and agriculture was on the agenda again. In January 2002, the Commission brought forward new proposals (CEU, 2002h) financing enlargement for ten new member states rather than the five envisaged at Berlin, and extending direct payments to the new member states. With the Berlin Agreement providing for a mid-term review of the CAP, the Brussels Summit of October 2002 was seen as another opportunity for significant CAP reform. These hopes were again dashed by French[46] intransigence and the vital need for an agreement if the scheduled date for enlargement was not to be missed. There were five principal elements of the Brussels Agreement (European Council, 2002).

First, there was to be no extra expenditure for enlargement; the ceiling agreed at Berlin is to be respected. Second, direct payments are to be extended to new member states at the rate of 25% in 2004, rising to 100% in 2013. Third, there is to be financial stability for the CAP: guaranteed expenditure from 2007–2013 cannot exceed the real terms expenditure in 2006. Overall expenditure that is agricultural market related and direct payment expenditure during 2007–2013 shall be kept below that for 2006 plus 1% per annum. Fourth, this is without prejudice to provisions on the reform of the CAP in the Berlin Agreement and the international commitments of the EU including the Doha round. Fifth, if forecast cash flow under the budget is less than 2003 for any new member state compensation will be offered.[47]

The EU has agreed finances up to 2006, covering only the first three years of enlargement. During this period expenditure in the CEECs will be limited by the phasing in of direct payments and the gradual build up of rural development and structural fund projects. Enlargement can take place within this financial framework but what will happen after 2006? Recent analyses (Silvis et al., 2001; Frohberg and Weber, 2001; Weise, 2002) suggest that the full application of

Table 19.8 EU financial perspective for 2000–2006 (1999 prices)

	2000	2001	2002	2003	2004	2005	2006
Agriculture	40 920	42 800	43 900	43 770	42 760	41 930	41 660
Structural operations	32 045	31 455	30 865	30 285	29 595	29 595	29 170
Internal policies	5 930	6 040	6 150	6 260	6 370	6 480	6 600
External action	4 550	4 560	4 570	4 580	4 590	4 600	4 610
Administration	4 560	4 600	4 700	4 800	4 900	5 000	5 100
Reserves	900	900	650	400	400	400	400
Pre-accession aid	3 120	3 120	3 120	3 120	3 120	3 120	3 120
Enlargement			6 450	9 030	11 610	14 200	16 780
Total commitments	91 995	93 385	100 255	102 035	103 075	104 995	107 040
Total payments	89 950	91 070	98 270	101 450	100 610	101 350	103 530
Ceiling for payments, % GNP	1.13%	1.14%	1.15%	1.11%	1.09%	1.09%	1.09%
Own resources ceiling	1.27%	1.27%	1.27%	1.27%	1.27%	1.27%	1.27%

Source: European Council (1999) and European Council (2002). Reprinted by permission of the European Communities.

the current CAP to CEEC 8 will add 6% to the agreed level of expenditure in 2007. This is well within the own resources ceiling of 1.27% because the planned payments in 2006 are 1.09% of GNP, i.e. 16.5% below the expenditure limit (Table 19.8). Expenditure could, however, be further increased by reform of the dairy and sugar sectors, as a result of the current WTO Doha Round (Swinnen, 2002, p. 11). With these reforms total additional expenditure would rise to 10.5% of the overall budget for the enlarged EU,

well beyond the Brussels limit.[48] Structural expenditure is predicted to expand in the medium term, as the new member states per capita GDP grows, but most of their regions remain within the Objective 1 limit. This could possibly add another 5% to the budget pushing expenditure near to the limit in the long term. So enlargement on unchanged policies can be financed within the existing budget ceiling but whether the EU 15 want to finance expenditure at these levels is another matter.

19.10 Conclusion

The EU budget, therefore, faces the challenges of equity, enlargement and EMU, and the future development of EU policies depends upon a successful resolution of these problems. The problem of equity is vital because member states will block future developments with budgetary implications unless the financing and expenditure system of the EU is fair. Inequality in the current budgetary arrangements is the result of the Common Agricultural Policy. It is difficult to see why the EU should continue to finance open ended subsidies to farmers; these subsidies should be phased out, which would release funds for the expansion of other policies and for expenditure in the new member states. Structural operations can be justified as facilitating convergence, providing a visible EU presence throughout the EU. Generally, the concentration of funds should be enhanced but all member states should continue to receive some structural funding; it would be undesirable to create a sub-group of client and donor states within the EU. These changes would make the budget fairer but with the EU likely to continue with a narrow range of financial resources and expenditure policies, equity in the budget can only be achieved with a generalized redistribution mechanism. This would ensure that net contributions were related to GNP per head in a consistent and equitable manner. Enlargement poses significant budgetary challenges for the EU; equitable finance and policies, which facilitate the convergence of the new member states are essential for the future development of the EU.

EMU has moved economic policy making to the EU level, but this does not seem to require the replication of a federal budget for the EU. The member states are not prepared to transfer responsibility for fiscal policy and the case for a common policy is not strong. The retention of large national budgets remains one possible adjustment to asymmetric shocks, although there are problems with the Stability and Growth Pact and the coordination of national fiscal and monetary policy is far from perfect.

That the EU does not have a budget comparable with existing federations is both unarguable and unsurprising. It is unarguable because of the requirement of balance, its small size, the composition of expenditure and the fact that it is financed largely by national contributions, not its own taxes. It is unsurprising because the EU is very far from a political federation, made up as it is of mature nation states determined to preserve a significant degree of national sovereignty. Thus the expenditure and revenues of the EU tier of government will continue to develop slowly. The most important areas of federal government activity will remain national because there are no clear advantages and many problems in moving provision to the EU tier. This is not to suggest that there should be no for further EU level development of policies, the strongest arguments here relate to internal security and Common Foreign and Security Policy. The likelihood is, therefore, that the EU budgetary responsibilities will remain limited in keeping with its status as a loose confederation.

NOTES

1. The general budget of the EU excludes the European Development Fund (see Section 19.6.4).

2. But not the most accurate, see Ardy (1988).

3. The allocative role also includes limiting the supply of goods and services, which impose external costs.

4. Moral hazard is the problem that if the government guarantees the financial viability of banks in a crisis, it may encourage greater risk taking by banks, which in turn could lead to a crisis.

5. There is again a moral hazard problem here, if the government provides adequate pensions this reduces the incentive, particularly among the less well off, to purchase private pensions.

6. Including all EU 15 member states.

7. In practice many services are shared responsibilities of different levels of government. This may allow some of the benefits of centralization and decentralization to be achieved. It may also blur responsibilities and be associated with problems of administration.

8. It would be difficult to justify such variation for policies funded from national taxation; the call is usually for equality of provision.

9. Externalities and economies of scale do not necessarily require central government provision; cooperation among local governments may be sufficient, but this can be problematic (Berglöf et al., 2003; p. 9)

10. Political support also seems lacking for substantial redistribution within the EU.

11. West German social security provided a wage floor in East Germany that was too high for the productivity levels in industry.

12. Comparisons of income are probably made within rather than between countries, even with the euro.

13. For a different view see Berglöf et al., 2003.

14. Allowing opt outs could cause free-rider problems.

15. For a discussion of the EU's stabilization role see Section 19.8.

16. Deficits would be carried over as expenditure, but surpluses are normal because planned expenditure (commitment appropriations) is usually under spent, so actual expenditure (payment appropriations) is usually lower.

17. It also guarantees loans.

18. Treaty amending Certain Financial Provisions of the Treaty establishing the European Communities, *Official Journal L*, 359, 31 December 1977.

19. If the Budget is not approved the EU works with the previous year's Budget.

20. The same principles should apply to benefit systems.

21. This is the 'Rotterdam Problem', so called because Rotterdam is the port of entry for many goods that are then sold in other countries, notably Germany.

22. The Netherlands also seemed to be making excessive contributions but this was largely because of the Rotterdam Problem.

23. It was reduced to 1% in 1988 and 0.5% in 2002.

24. A sugar substitute made from other agricultural products.

25. Shown by the fact that they are near or on the 45% line indicating that their income relative to the EU average is the same as their contribution.

26. Which could rise at 100% of the rate of increase of the annual growth rate of EU GNP.

27. Pre-accession aid is included in external expenditure for 2000 and 2001.

28. But not in an efficient manner: of the cost of farm support to taxpayers and consumers only 20%–50% (depending upon the measure) ends up as an increase in farm household incomes (OECD, 2003; pp. 54–75).

29. 68% of structural spending is on Objective 1 regions defined as having GDP per capita less than 75% of the EU average. This concentrates structural spending in poorer countries because this is where most of these regions are located.

30. Ireland's high structural receipts reflect its previous status as one of the EU's poorer states; levels of structural expenditure in Ireland are gradually being curtailed.

31. A small element of the external action is operational expenditure on joint actions decided under the Common Foreign and Security Policy.

32. Not all expenditure can be allocated to individual member states; the categories not allocated are administration for the reasons given (in

Section 19.6.5), external action and pre-accession aid, 13.3% of expenditure in 2001.

33. There are in addition methodological problems with the measurement of net contributions (CEU, 1998c, pp. 17–20).

34. The Budget is more than four times the size of Luxembourg's GDP.

35. The equation fitted by weighted OLS is NC = $3.09 - 0.03Y$, $R^2 = 0.58$, where NC is measured as a percentage of GNP and Y GNP as a percentage of the EU average.

36. This is due to delayed adjustment to Ireland's improved economic circumstances, and substantial CAP benefits.

37. Further adjustments are made for the capping of VAT, the increase in the member states collection costs from 2001 and enlargement.

38. The UK's position is less favourable than indicated here because GNP per capita in euros is inflated by the high value of Sterling.

39. At present a member state's net contribution can improve significantly as a result of new expenditure commitments because it may only bear a small part of the costs.

40. See Ardy (2002b) for a fuller discussion of these issues.

41. By utilizing unemployed factors or by spreading economic activity more evenly allowing a higher overall level of output without inflation.

42. It is national economies that are important here because the persistence of large national budgets means that interregional transfers can continue within nation states, albeit constrained by the requirement of the Stability and Growth Pact.

43. This analysis concentrates on the CEECs because Cyprus and Malta are so small that their impact on the budget is minor.

44. It would also have reduced potential WTO problems, associated with Uruguay Round limits on agricultural policy.

45. Virtually all their regions had GDP per capita less than 75% of the EU average and are, therefore, eligible for the highest level of aid.

46. With the support of Greece, Ireland, Portugal and Spain.

47. This possibility arises because the new member states will start making contributions to the budget and may find it difficult initially to generate projects for structural funding.

48. Far beyond the agricultural expenditure restraints, agreed at Brussels 2002.

Chapter 20

The Common Agricultural Policy

ULRICH KOESTER AND ALI EL-AGRAA

Unlike EFTA, the EU extends its free trade arrangements between member states to agriculture and agricultural products. The term 'agricultural products' is defined as 'the products of the soil, of stockfarming and of fisheries and products of first-state processing directly related to the foregoing' (Article 32.1, Amsterdam Treaty, to which all the articles in this chapter refer), although fisheries has developed into a policy of its own – see Chapter 21. Moreover, in 1957, the EEC Treaty dictated that the operation and development of the common market for agricultural products should be accompanied by the establishment of a 'common agricultural policy' among the member states (Article 32.4).

One could ask: why were the common market arrangements extended to agriculture? or why was agriculture (together with transport) singled out for special treatment? Such questions are to some extent irrelevant. According to the General Agreement on Tariffs and Trade (GATT, now WTO, the World Trade Organization – see Appendix 1.1, p. 20):

> a customs union shall be understood to mean the substitution of a single customs union territory for two or more territories, so that . . . duties and other restrictive regulations of commerce are eliminated with respect to substantially all the trade between the constituent territories of the union. (Dam, 1970)

Since agricultural trade constituted a substantial part of the total trade of the founding members, especially so in the case of France, it should be quite obvious that excluding agriculture from the EEC arrangements would have been in direct contradiction of this requirement (see next section). Moreover, free agricultural trade would have been to no avail if each member nation continued to protect agriculture in its own way (see Section 20.3) since that would have likely amounted to the replacing of tariffs with non-tariff trade barriers (NTBs) and might also have conflicted with EC competition rules (see Chapter 12). In any case:

> a programme of economic integration which excluded agriculture stood no chance of success. It is important to appreciate that the Rome Treaty was a delicate balance of national interests of the contracting parties. Let us consider West Germany and France in terms of trade outlets. In the case of West Germany the prospect of free trade in industrial goods, and free access to the French market in particular, was extremely inviting. In the case of France the relative efficiency of her agriculture . . . as compared with West Germany held out the prospect that in a free Community agricultural market she would make substantial inroads into the West German market . . . Agriculture had therefore to be included. (Swann, 1973, p. 82)

The purpose of this chapter is to discuss the need for singling out agriculture as one of the earliest targets for a common policy; to specify the objectives of the Common Agricultural Policy (CAP); to explain the mechanisms of the CAP and their development to date; to make an economic evaluation of its implications and to assess the performance of the policy in terms of its practical achievements (or lack of achievements) and in terms of its theoretical viability.

Before tackling these points, it is necessary to give some general background information about agriculture in the EU at the time of the formation of the EC and at a more recent date.

20.1   General background

The economic significance of agriculture in the economies of member states can be demonstrated in terms of its share in the total labour force and in the GNP. Table 20.1 gives this information. The most significant observations are as follows:

1   At the time of the signing of the treaty many people in the original six were dependent on farming as their main source of income; indeed, 25% of the total labour force was employed in agriculture – the equivalent for the United Kingdom was less than 5% and for Denmark was about 9%.

2   The agricultural labour force was worse off than most people in the rest of the EC: for example, in France about 26% of the labour force was engaged in agriculture, but for the same year the contribution of this sector to French GDP was about 12%.[1]

3   A rapid fall in both the agricultural labour force and in the share of agriculture in GNP occurred between 1955 and 1995,[2] and this trend is being maintained, albeit at a slower pace.

It is also important to have some information about the area and size distribution of agricultural holdings. This is given in Table 20.2. The most significant factor to note is that in the original six, at the time of the formation of the EC, approximately two-thirds of farm holdings were between 1 and 10 hectares in size. At about the same time, the equivalent figure for the United Kingdom was about two-fifths. Since then there has been a steady increase in the percentage of larger size holdings.

A final piece of important background information that one needs to bear in mind is that, except for Belgium, Germany, Italy, Sweden and the United Kingdom, the EU farming system is one of owner occupiers rather than of tenant farming. However, tenant shareholding increases with growth in the economy as farms expand mainly on the basis of rented land. Hence, farmers who have been expanding in the past and who want to enlarge their farm are not interested in policy measures which push up land prices.

20.2   The problems of agriculture

Although economists praise the advantages of a free market economy, the agricultural sector in most countries has been more or less regulated by specific policies for centuries. Something seems to be special with agriculture. In this section we analyse six reasons for this special treatment: food security concerns, agricultural income, efficiency concerns, stability of markets, food safety concerns and environmental concerns.

20.2.1 Food security concerns

It is well known that there are significant fluctuations in food supply at the regional level. If markets were to function perfectly, fluctuations in regional production would cause no concern as long as the world supply was stable. Regional trade and stockpiling could easily stabilize regional food consumption. However, markets are not perfect. Interregional trade may not stabilize consumption, as markets are not perfectly integrated due to high transaction costs. Moreover, specific policies may hinder interregional trade flows.

Private stockholders may not hold high enough stocks in order to stabilize consumption on the regional level, making stockpiling a risky investment, as the outcome of future harvests and future prices are not known. Market failure and policy intervention may also lead to food security concerns by other nations. Thus, most countries have food security included in the list of their agricultural policy objectives. Of course, how governments should intervene in order to achieve the objective would depend very much on the size of market failure and on available policy alternatives. The more integrated are the markets, the better the flow of information and the lower transport costs. Regional integration schemes with trading agreements mitigate food security concerns on the regional level. Markets in the EU are more integrated than in insulated countries with protectionist policies. The WTO has also helped to integrate agricultural markets by setting rules for trade. Private stockpiling is more effective in stabilizing food consumption if stockholders are not exposed to unpredictable interventions by governments. As far as the EU is concerned, markets are

Table 20.1 Share of agriculture in total labour force and GDP (%)

		Belgium	France	Germany	Italy	Luxembourg	Netherlands	Denmark	Ireland	United Kingdom	Greece	Portugal	Spain	Austria	Finland	Sweden
Labour force	1955	9.3	25.9	18.9	39.5	25	13.7	25.4	38.8	4.8	–	–	–	–	–	–
	1970	5	13.5	8.6	20.2	9.7	–	11.5	27.1	–	40.8	–	29.5	18.7	24.4	8.1
	1975	3.4	10.9	7.1	15.5	6.1	6.5	9.3	23.8	2.7	33.2	–	–	–	–	–
	1980	3.2	8.5	5.3	14.3	5.5	4.9	8.1	18.3	2.4	30.3	28.6	19.3	10.6	13.5	5.1
	1985	3.2	7.3	5.3	10.9	4	4.8	6.2	15.8	2.3	28.5	21.9	16.1	–	–	–
	1990	2.7	5.6	3.7	8.8	3.3	4.6	5.7	15	2.2	23.9	18	11.8	7.9	8.4	3.4
	1995	2.7	4.9	3.2	7.5	3.7	3.7	4.3	12	2.1	20.4	14.1	9.3	7.3	7.7	3.7
	2000	1.9	4.2	2.6	5.2	2.4	3.3	3.7	7.9	1.5	17	12.5	6.9	6.1	6.2	2.9
	2001	1.4	4.1	2.6	5.2	1.5	3.1	3.5	7	1.4	16	12.9	6.5	5.8	5.8	2.6
National output	1955	8.1	12.3	8.5	21.6	9	12	19.2	29.6	5	–	–	–	–	–	–
	1970	4.2	6.6	3	8	3.3	6	7	17	3	–	–	8.9	7	12	–
	1975	3.2	5.6	2.9	8.7	3.5	4.7	7.4	18.1	1.9	19	7.3	–	–	–	–
	1980	2	4	1.9	6	2.8	3	5	11.3	2	14	–	–	4	10	4
	1985	2	4	2	5	–	4	6	14	2	17	10	6	–	–	–
	1990	2	4	1.7	4	2.4	4	5	10.5	1.5	17	5.5	4.7	3	6	3
	1995	1.6	2	0.8	2.6	0.9	3.2	2.5	5.4	0.9	7.5	2	2.7	2.2	1.8	1
	2001	1.1	2.2	0.9	2.4	0.6	2.2	2.3	2.5	0.6	6.7	2.4	3.6	1.3	0.9	0.6

Sources: Various issues of The Agricultural Situation in The Community, European Union (EU Brussels) and World Bank's World Development Report

Table 20.2 Size distribution of agricultural holdings (% of total)

	Belgium	France	Germany	Italy	Luxembourg	Netherlands	Denmark	Ireland	United Kingdom	Greece	Portugal	Spain	Austria	Finland	Sweden
1960															
0–<5	48.5	26	45	68	32	38	18	20	29.5	na	na	na	na	na	na
5–<10	26.5	21	25	19	18	27	28	24	13	na	na	na	na	na	na
10–<20	18	27	21	8.5	26	23	28	30	16	na	na	na	na	na	na
20–<50	6	21	8	3	22	11	23	21	22.5	na	na	na	na	na	na
50+	1	5	1	1.5	2	1	3	5	19	na	na	na	na	na	na
1973															
0–<5	31	22	36	68	21	25	12	15	16	72	78	56	na	na	na
5–<10	23	16	20	17.5	13	22	20	16.5	13	20.5	12.5	18	na	na	na
10–<20	27	24	24	8.5	20	31	29	31	16	6	5	12	na	na	na
20–<50	16	28	18	4	41	20	32	29	26	1.5	2.5	8.5	na	na	na
50+	1	10	2	2	7	2	7	8.5	29	0	2	5.5	na	na	na
1980															
0–<5	28.4	20.4	34.5	68.1	19.1	24	11.1	15.2	11.8	72	77.9	55.8	na	na	na
5–<10	19.8	14.6	18.6	16.7	10.6	20.2	17.6	11.9	12.5	19.9	12.6	18	na	na	na
10–<20	26.6	21.1	22.7	8.7	14.9	28.9	26.5	30.3	16	6.2	5.2	12	na	na	na
20–<50	20.9	30.4	20.3	4.5	38.3	23.9	34.7	29.8	27.1	1.6	2.5	8.7	na	na	na
50+	4.2	13.3	3.9	2	17	2.9	10.1	8.8	32.6	0.2	1.8	5.5	na	na	na
1987															
0–<5	27.7	18.2	29.4	67.9	18.9	24.9	1.7	16.1	13.5	69.4	72.5	53.3	na	na	na
5–<10	18.1	11.7	17.6	16.9	9.9	18.4	16.3	15.2	12.4	20	15	19	na	na	na
10–<20	24.5	19.1	22.1	8.7	12.4	25	25.3	29.2	15.3	7.6	7.2	12.3	na	na	na
20–<50	23.9	32.8	24.8	4.6	32.5	27.3	39.4	30.5	25.4	2.5	3.4	9.4	na	na	na
50+	5.8	18.1	6.1	1.9	26.2	4.4	17.2	9	33.3	0.5	1.9	6	na	na	na

Table 20.2 (continued)

	Belgium	France	Germany	Italy	Luxembourg	Netherlands	Denmark	Ireland	United Kingdom	Greece	Portugal	Spain	Austria	Finland	Sweden
1995															
0–<5	31.1	26.7	31.2	77.9	24.5	31.3	2.7	9.3	13	74.8	76.4	54.3	28.1	10	11.9
5–<10	14.4	9.5	14.8	10.4	8.8	16	16.5	13.4	12.6	14.9	11.5	16.6	18.8	17.8	17.5
10–<20	17.9	12.1	17.6	5.6	7.9	18.3	21.7	26.5	15.4	6.7	6.3	11.5	22.1	30.1	21.4
20–<50	25.8	24.1	23.3	4.2	20.8	26.3	33.8	37.3	24.1	2.7	3.3	9	16.1	34.9	27.8
50+	8.4	27	12.6	1.6	37.4	6.3	24.9	13.2	34.2	0.4	2.2	7.6	3.6	6.8	21
1997															
0–<5	32.2	26.8	31.5	75.7	24.2	32	3.5	7.5	15.5	76.3	76.1	53.6	37.9	8.6	14.3
5–<10	14.2	9.1	14.6	11.8	8.6	16	16.3	12.4	12.2	14.1	11.7	16.4	18.7	15.8	17.7
10–<20	17.1	11	16.9	6.5	7.9	17.9	21.3	27.1	14.9	6.6	6.4	12.4	22.3	30	20.3
20–<50	26.5	23.4	22.9	4.1	19.7	27	31	38.8	23.8	2.6	3.6	9.5	17	36.8	26.4
50+	10	29.7	14.2	1.8	39.7	7.1	27.8	14.1	33.6	0.4	2.3	8.2	4.1	8.8	21.3
2000															
0–<5	30.8	29.1	24.9	78.3	22.4	31.2	3.4	8.2	23.1	76.7	78.8	57.5	36.4	10.5	12
5–<10	13.4	9.1	15.7	10.1	9.4	15.5	16.4	11.8	11	13.4	10.1	14.9	19.1	13.7	17.1
10–<20	16.5	10.7	18.5	6	7.6	17.2	20	24.2	13	6.5	5.5	11	22.4	24.9	20.9
20–<50	27.1	20.8	24.2	3.8	18.8	27.8	29.7	38.6	20.5	2.9	3.1	8.9	17.6	37.4	26.6
50+	12.2	30.3	16.7	1.7	41.9	8.2	30.6	17.1	32.4	0.5	2.4	7.8	4.5	13.5	23.3

na = not available

Sources: Calculated from various issues of The Agricultural Situation in The Community, European Union, Eurostat Review 1977–1986 and Eurostat Yearbook 1998/1999, all published by EU Commission, Brussels

fairly well integrated regionally, thus regional fluctuations in production should not lead to food security concerns. Nevertheless, most countries pretend that price support policies are also needed to secure food, but it is highly questionable whether protectionist policies really contribute to the achievement of food security. Food security is mainly related to income and availability of food. Poor people may not have the income to buy food. High food prices lower their purchasing power, thus lead to food insecurity for vulnerable households. Hence, an efficient food security policy should focus on the poor and not just on available supplies on the markets. The latter is a necessary condition to secure food, but it is not sufficient.

20.2.2 Agricultural income

There is a widely held perception that income from farming does not increase as much as non-agricultural income in a growing economy. The argument is based on a closed economy and limited mobility of labour. The relationship can be clarified by using a simple model, where demand is assumed to depend on income and prices:

$$q^D = q^D(Y, B, p) \qquad (20.1)$$

where q^D = quantity demanded of the agricultural product, Y = income, p = price of the agricultural product, and B = population size.

Supply is assumed to depend on prices and a supply shifter, which stands for the effect of technological change:

$$q^S = q^S(p, a) \qquad (20.2)$$

where q^S = quantity supplied of the agricultural product and a = supply, higher due to technical change.

It is assumed that demand and supply are equated by the prevailing price. Hence:

$$q^D = q^S \qquad (20.3)$$

From equations (20.1) and (20.2) one gets:

$$\frac{dq^D}{q^D} = \eta \cdot \frac{dy}{y} + \varepsilon_{q,p}^D \frac{dP}{P} + \frac{dB}{B} \qquad (20.4)$$

and

$$\frac{dq^S}{q^S} = \varepsilon_{q,p}^S \cdot \frac{dP}{P} + \frac{da}{a} \qquad (20.5)$$

where $\varepsilon_{q,p}^D$ = price elasticity of demand, $\varepsilon_{q,p}^S$ = price elasticity of supply.

Equating equation (20.4) and (20.5) and solving for the relative change in P results in

$$\frac{dP}{P} = \frac{1}{\varepsilon_{q,p}^D - \varepsilon_{q,p}^S} \left(\frac{da}{a} - \eta \frac{dy}{y} + \frac{dB}{B} \right) \qquad (20.6)$$

From equation (20.6), one draws certain conclusions. Prices will decline if the value in the bracket is positive. It will be positive if the rate of technical change da/a is larger than the product from the rate of change of per capita income in the economy times the elasticity of income plus the rate of change in population. Hence, technical change in agriculture is price depressing, but only under certain conditions. If there were no technical change, but high population growth without economic growth in the economy ($dY/Y = 0$) prices would go up as predicted by Malthus. The reality of the last 50 years shows that technical change in agriculture has been large enough to offset the price increasing effects of income and population growth. Indeed, as the elasticity of income declined with higher income and population growth somewhat flattened, technological progress in agriculture tended to lower food prices even more.

However, even if there were technological progress, farm prices may not have fallen. For example, if the elasticity of demand were infinite, prices would remain unchanged. This situation may materialize for a small open country[3] such as New Zealand. The shift in the domestic supply curve due to technical change will not alter prices, as the country is a marginal supplier of food products on the world market. However, for the world as a whole the price elasticity is fairly small and therefore prices come under pressure. Yet, even if prices did fall, labour income in agriculture may not decline. If labour input in agriculture were completely determined by opportunity costs, i.e. income which could be earned in alternative occupations, the price elasticity would be high, leading to a lower decline in prices. Hence, price elasticities of supply and demand are crucial for the effects of technical change on agricultural prices and incomes. If sectoral labour markets are not well integrated, labour income in one sector may deviate from that in others, but if they are integrated, differences in labour income will reflect preferences for work, living in the countryside, qualifications, preferences for the environment, etc.

The current situation concerning labour market integration certainly differs across countries. It can be shown that labour markets are more integrated in developed market economies where information is available and transaction costs are low. Hence, it was no surprise that Gardner (1992) in his seminal article proved that there was no income disparity in the US, i.e. farmers' total income from farm and non-farm activities was about the same as that of other people in the society.

If policy makers nevertheless assume that there is a need to support farm incomes by politically setting prices above market equilibrium, they will affect the number of people engaged in agriculture, but not necessarily their income per work unit. Yet, in spite of this reasoning, policy makers in most countries intervene in order to affect farm incomes.

20.2.3 Efficiency in agriculture

As already mentioned, agriculture in most countries consists of family-owned farms. The farm operator is in most cases one of the heirs of the preceding farm manager. It can be assumed that not all farm managers are well qualified and lack information about new technologies. Hence, the efficiency of resources use can be increased by giving advice to farmers, thus most governments intervene in order to provide information to farmers speeding up the use of new technologies.

Optimal use of land is given if its marginal product is the same in all uses. The optimum situation will change from time to time as factor prices change in the economy and new technologies can be introduced in agriculture. Consequently, there is a tendency for the marginal product of land to differ across farms. The problem can be illustrated with Figure 20.1,

where it is assumed that in the initial situation the marginal product of land is higher on farm A than on farm B. A transfer of land from farm B to A up to the quantity where the marginal value of land is the same on both farms will increase the value of total production. The decline in production on farm B is smaller than the increase in production on farm A. Hence, the total gain in welfare is equal to area *a*.

The optimal allocation of land will materialize only if land markets function perfectly. However, land markets are property intensive and the transfer of land may incur high transaction costs. The prospective buyer and seller of land have to find out the likely future returns of the land and the likely interest rates. Hence, there is high uncertainty on both sides of the market. There may even be an outcome where there are no transactions on the market. The suppliers may have a high reservation price for land, possibly because they consider land ownership as a hedge against risk or because they value land ownership more than the ownership of other assets, hence ask for a high price. The demander may be only willing to offer a low price because of uncertainty of future returns. The result can be that there is no intersection of the supply and demand curves since the former lies consistently above the latter. Actually, such a situation seems to prevail in some regional markets in transition countries.

In short, market failure on land, labour markets and markets for rural finance provide rationales for government intervention in order to improve the efficiency of agriculture. Promotion of research and extension as well as measures to increase the mobility of land and labour are most often incorporated in the policy package.

20.2.4 Stability of markets

Agricultural markets tend to be volatile. The basic reasoning has already been offered by Gregory King, an English scientist living from 1648 to 1712. He found out that a one percentage change in grain production resulted in a more than 1% change in grain prices. This finding says implicitly that the price elasticity of demand for grain is less than 1.

The reasoning can easily be illustrated with the help of some algebra. Assume that there is a demand function where demand only depends on the price of the product:

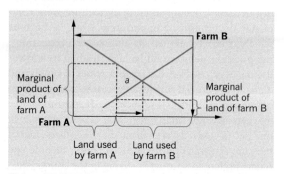

Figure 20.1 Welfare effects of suboptimal use of land. If farm A increases use of land and farm B reduces use of land, aggregate welfare will increase by the area *a*

$$q^D = q^D(p) \qquad (20.7)$$

and assume that supply is completely price inelastic, i.e. a vertical line in the diagram. Assume further that there is no storage and all that is produced has to be consumed in the same period:

$$q^S = \bar{q}^S \qquad (20.8)$$

and

$$q^D = q^S \qquad (20.9)$$

Solving this system with respect to the relative change in p results in:

$$\frac{dp}{p} = \frac{1}{\varepsilon_{q,p}} \frac{dq^S}{q^S} \qquad (20.10)$$

According to equation (20.10) the percentage changes in price resulting from a 1% change in supply will be larger, the lower the price elasticity of demand in absolute terms. It is often argued that the price elasticities for agricultural products decline with growing income and, hence, fluctuations in prices may become even more pronounced in a developed economy. However, it has to be kept in mind that the model derived above was based on the assumption that total production in a given period of time had to be consumed in the same period. If one allows for storage, market demand in a specific period will depend on demand for consumption purposes in that period and of demand for storage. The latter takes into account expected prices in future periods and storage costs. Hence, storage leads to an intertemporal integration of markets. If expectations are correct, price differences between two points in time should not be higher than storage costs and a reasonable profit to cover risk and interest. As storage costs have significantly decreased over time, the intertemporal price integration should have become stronger.

In the same direction points the impact of inter-regional trade on the price elasticity of demand. If there were fluctuation in regional production, exporters or importers would step in and link regional prices to those in other regions. Hence, the blessing of a good harvest would be spread over to other regions and the curse of a bad harvest would be mitigated by imports from other regions. Thus, the regional price elasticity of demand does not only depend on demand for consumption purposes in the region, but also on prices in other regions and on transport costs. Transport costs

have significantly declined over the last fifty years, in particular for shipping. It is cheaper to transport grain from the US Gulf to Rotterdam by ship than from Munich to Hamburg by train or lorry. Hence, an open trading economy would help mitigate fluctuations in regional production. Domestic market policies to stabilize price fluctuations are less needed nowadays than in past centuries.

20.2.5 Food safety concerns

Food safety has become a more important element in agricultural policy for many countries. This development may be seen as a surprise for an outside observer. It is questionable whether food has really become less safe over time, the opposite is more likely. Animals are healthier nowadays than fifty years ago and new technologies in food conservation and preparation have lowered food risk. Nevertheless, there are new developments which have led to food safety concerns. New technologies which are based on biotechnology have created new production processes and new products which are not always safe. Hence, control of the food chain is needed. People are aware that food is not a search good where one knows the quality of the product. Instead, many food products are credence goods. The consumer neither knows the quality of the product nor the production process, so has to trust quality. However, trust will only be sustainable if food scandals are prevented. Of course, producers and traders have a genuine interest to create and to preserve trust, but the individual producer or trader cannot control the complete marketing chain. Moreover, new products, such as genetically modified organisms in food and feed products as well as chemical and biological fertilizer and pesticides, have to be tested before they are allowed to enter the market. Hence, it is a genuine task for a government to take care of this type of market failure.

20.2.6 Environmental concerns

In general, the awareness for the environment has increased in most countries over time. Hence, the impact of agricultural production on the environment has become of higher interest. Some countries, in particular the EU nations, Japan, North Korea, Norway and Switzerland, emphasize the multifunctionality of agriculture. Agriculture produces not only the typical agricultural products like food, feed and renewable primary products, but also by-products. By-products can be 'bads', which are non-marketed goods that lower the population's welfare, or 'goods', which are non-marketed goods that increase welfare. Hence, policies have to be defined to take care of these by-products. Of course, the policy instruments used have to be different from those utilized in the past to raise agricultural income.

The arguments presented may justify governmental interference in agricultural markets. As the importance of individual justifications for intervention has been changed over time policies should also have changed. However, the change in policies in most countries is not in line with the changes in their rationale. Policies have pronounced path dependencies. Policy instruments which have been introduced in the past cannot easily be removed as any policy change leads to winners and losers. The loss often materializes in the short or medium term, whereas the gain arises in the long term. Take, for example, a reduction in politically set grain prices. Grain producers will see immediately a loss and lobby against it. Consumers may gain, if bread prices eventually decline. However, that will take time and the gain for the individual consumer is quite small as compared to the loss to the individual grain producer. Hence, it is much easier to organize producers and to lobby against price reduction than to organize consumers. This fact helps to explain why governments in democratic countries tend to be more producer than consumer friendly. It also explains why polices are as they are and that present policies are often not in line with economic reasoning. They are constrained by the past. What has been decided in the past is relevant for today even if not justified on economic grounds. The agricultural polices which were introduced in the 1930s at the time of the depression, often determined the main policy instruments of recent times. Changes will mainly occur if there are binding budgets or external constraints such as those of the WTO.

20.3　Objectives of the CAP

Owing to the variety of agricultural support policies that existed in Western Europe at the time of the formation of the EC, it was necessary, for the reasons given at the beginning, especially French insistence, to subject agriculture to equal treatment in all member states. Equal treatment of coal and steel (both necessary inputs for industry and therefore of the same significance as agriculture) was already under way through the ECSC and the importance of agriculture meant that equal treatment here was vital.

The objectives of the CAP are clearly defined in Article 33. They are as follows:

1　To increase agricultural productivity by promoting technical progress and by ensuring the rational development of agricultural production and the optimum utilization of all factors of production, in particular labour.
2　To ensure thereby 'a fair standard of living for the agricultural community, in particular by increasing the individual earnings of persons engaged in agriculture'.
3　To stabilize markets.
4　To provide certainty of supplies.
5　To ensure supplies to consumers at reasonable prices.

The Treaty also specifies that in

> working out the Common Agricultural Policy, and any special methods which this may involve, account shall be taken of:
> (i)　the particular nature of agricultural activity, which results from agriculture's social structure and from structural and natural disparities between the various agricultural regions;
> (ii)　the need to effect the appropriate adjustments by degrees;
> (iii)　the fact that, in the member states, agriculture constitutes a sector closely linked with the economy as a whole.

The Treaty further specifies that in order to attain the objectives set out above a common organization of agricultural markets shall be formed:

> This organisation shall take one of the following forms depending on the product concerned:
> (a)　common rules as regards competition;
> (b)　compulsory co-ordination of the various national marketing organisations; or
> (c)　a European organisation of the market.

Moreover, the common organization so established:

> may include all measures required to achieve the objectives set out . . . in particular price controls, subsidies for the production and distribution of the various products, stock-piling and carry-over systems and common arrangements for stabilisation of imports and exports.
>
> The common organisation shall confine itself to pursuing the objectives set out . . . and shall exclude any discrimination between producers and consumers within the Community.
>
> Any common policy shall be based on common criteria and uniform methods of calculation.

Finally, in order to enable the common organization to achieve its objectives, 'one or more agricultural orientation and guarantee funds may be set up'.

The remaining articles (34–38) deal with some detailed considerations relating to the objectives and the common organization.

The true objectives of the CAP were established after the Stresa conference in 1958 which was convened in accordance with the Treaty. The objectives were in the spirit of the Treaty:

(i) to increase farm incomes not only by a system of transfers from the non-farm population through a price support policy, but also by the encouragement of rural industrialisation to give alternative opportunities to farm labour;

(ii) to contribute to overall economic growth by allowing specialisation within the Community and eliminating artificial market distortions;

(iii) preserving the family farm and . . . ensuring that structural and price policies go hand in hand.

It can be seen, therefore, that the CAP was not preoccupied simply with the implementation of common prices and market supports; it also included a commitment to encourage the structural improvement of farming, particularly when the former measures did not show much success (see the later section on assessment). However, the focus of the CAP so far was on market organizations for individual agricultural commodities. Hence, market and price policy is discussed first in detail followed by a section on structural policy.

Before looking into how the EC went about trying to fulfil these aims, it is vital to understand the role played by the EC institutions directly involved with the CAP as well as by those institutions specifically created for CAP.

20.4   The birth of the CAP and the institutional setting

At the time of its inception, the CAP was supposed to be a major engine of European market integration; there was a widely held hope that positive integration in agriculture would force other sectors to follow the same route. However, such expectations have not materialized; the annual price negotiations for agricultural products made evident the divergence in the national interests of EU member states, with decisions being dominated by compromises between them rather than by EU-wide interests.

Agriculture is a special case in the integration process. As most countries had more or less strong national agricultural policies in the pre-integration phase, they were not willing to let market forces play freely in an integrated economy. Hence, positive integration was needed, i.e. specific policies for agricultural and food markets were needed at the Community level. In markets for industrial products a major policy decision was made at the beginning of the integration process to dismantle trade barriers without increasing the external level of protection (see Chapters 1, 24 and 27). In contrast, agricultural policy has been regulated through fundamental policy decisions made both at the beginning, and throughout this period. Consequently, one can assume that agricultural markets in the Union have been more affected by policy decisions than by pure market forces.

It is argued below that the institutional and organizational conception of the CAP was misconceived from the very beginning. Due to this, market forces have played a minor role relative to political decisions in determining the development of agricultural policy in the Community.

20.4.1 The foundation of the CAP: a crucial policy failure[4]

It is likely that European integration was only possible on a political level because the main countries leading the integration process (France and Germany) finally agreed on some form of CAP. However, that does not imply that without the specifics of the then created CAP, European integration would not have happened. If so, there would hardly be any reason to discuss the 'misconception' of the CAP. This hypothesis can be denied, as the Treaty of Rome cannot support it. The Constitution of the European Community – the Treaty – foresaw alternatives for integrating agricultural policy. The Treaty remained vague as to the nature of the common agricultural policy. It could consist of common rules of competition or of coordination of national market organizations or of a 'European' market organization. It was to take nearly three-and-a-half years of argument to settle the basic principles of a common policy after the Treaty was signed. It took another three years, from 1962 through 1964, to agree on one of the key questions, a common level of cereal prices. The second key question, to find a long-term agreement for financing the CAP, was solved after a further one-and-a-half years.

The fact that agreement was reached reflects a strong political commitment in favour of a Common Europe by all members. National interests diverged considerably. Possibly owing to Hallstein, the first president of the European Commission, the price agreement was finally settled in 1964. When the Commission submitted the proposal for the unification of cereal prices to the Council of Agricultural Ministers (Council, hereafter), at first, the Council rejected the proposal and asked for a modified version, which would more closely match individual national interests. Hallstein, a strong personality, resubmitted the original proposal after only half-an-hour arguing in favour of the unification of Europe. He asked the Council to either endorse the proposal unanimously or accept the resignation of the Commission. This contributed to the sense that a Common Europe dominated national interests. Since then, the Commission has never again fought national interests in favour of Community interests so convincingly and so crucially.

It seems justified to investigate how the organizational and institutional setting created in the first years of the CAP has affected the evolution of the CAP. The purpose is to draw lessons for the prospective design of the CAP. Moreover, it should be kept in mind that at the time of designing the CAP, the importance of organizations and institutions was less obvious than it is today.

20.4.2 A model of the decision-making process

Prescriptive policy decision models assume that policy makers try to maximize a well-defined objective function taking economic conditions as a given (Streit, 1991, p. 316). It would follow that policies change because objectives and/or economic conditions change. This prescriptive decision-making model does not reflect reality in a reasonable way, particularly as it does not take into account that present choices greatly depend on past decisions. In actuality there is a certain degree of path dependency in policies – see Figure 20.2. Path dependency explains why economic policies change only gradually over time, 'ratcheting' their effects, unless significant shocks in the economic environment force massive adjustments (like the Great Depression in the 1930s).

Following this basic idea, the status quo of a given set of policies determines the policy decisions in the next period. This assumption is in contrast to the prescriptive policy approach where policy makers are seen as newly born in each period and not bound by past decisions or conditions on the political market. According to the underlying assumption in this section, the specific economic and political environment at the birth of the CAP affects the evolution of the policy in the following years and also determines the influence of member countries.

20.4.3 The main players in European agricultural policy

Market and price policies, which have been the main determinants of developments of agricultural policy, have been in the domain of European decision makers from the very beginning of the CAP. Hence, it makes sense to base the analysis on the players foremost at the EU level. Moreover, only those players coming into existence with the foundation of the CAP (the Council) or derive their power in the field of agricultural policy from the existence of the specifics of agricultural policies (the Commission) will be considered; thus nothing shall be said about the European Parliament (see Chapter 3).

The role of the Council

We begin with the Council of the European Union since it is the ultimate EC legislative body.

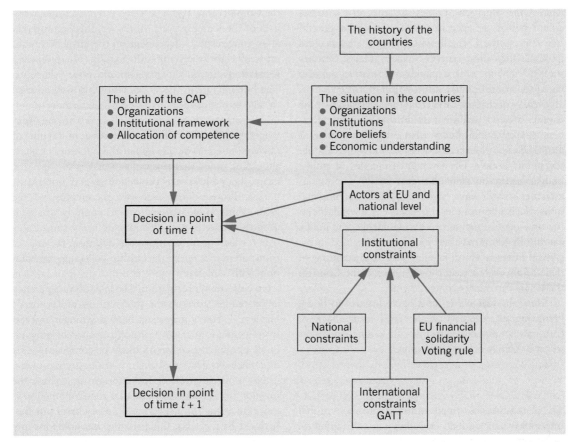

Figure 20.2 The decision-making process: a stylized model

It could have been predicted that the legislative machinery at the Community level would lead to policy failure. The ministers in the Council are in most cases more interested in the welfare of the farming population and less in that of society at large. It is true that the farm minister, like any other minister, has to swear to serve the public interest. However, who can expect that someone will be impartial when his/her main political support comes from a special interest group? Of course, there are always conflicts among interest groups that have to be settled, leading to compromises. But will someone who has strong vested interests be an unbiased arbiter? Hence, it can be concluded that the creation of the main player at the Community level provoked policy failure.

It might be argued that the Commission, as expected, might balance the 'power' of the Council (see Chapter 3). Unfortunately, the development of the CAP proves that the Commission was not in a position to serve the interest of the general public. The specifics of the CAP demand regular legislative decisions by the Council, the most important of which have been the annual price decisions. The pressure to come to an agreement in the Council placed significant constraints on the Commission. Proposals had to be submitted which could eventually be accepted by the Council. Hence, the final proposal was generally less a reflection of the interests of the society at large and more of a compromise between divergent interests of farmers or groups of farmers in the Community.

The role given to the Council violates one important principle of good governance:[5] accountability. Those who make the decisions in the Council can hardly be made accountable for the negative effects. First, due to lack of transparency – (another violation of the principles for good governance), it is not clearly known to the public who in the Council voted for what. Other legislative bodies in democratic societies accept public presence in the meetings as a general rule. Not so the Council, which nevertheless decides on highly important issues for society at large. Second, transparency not only demands information on who voted for what, but also information on the effects of alternative decisions. Concerning the decisions of the Council, there is sufficient doubt that even the members of the Council know what effects may arise as a consequence of a specific decision. How then should the public know? The German principles of public budget legislation demand a cost–benefit analysis of activities, which have 'significant' financial implications. Such information is generally not available at the time the Council has to decide. Hence, the public can hardly know whether the Council decided in the general interest. Third, as the voters in the country of their origin do not elect the members of the Council, the voters can hardly control them.

Thus, the Council is most likely a partisan body, favouring the interests of the farm lobby: lack of transparency and control allows the Council members to act in favour of interest groups.[6]

The role of the Commission

The Commission is supposed to balance the national interests in the Council (see above and Chapter 3). However, the Commission is a bureaucracy, so it is most likely to follow the general behaviour of a bureaucratic organization. According to the findings of the 'New political economy' (Downs, 1957; Buchanan and Tullock, 1962), the individual members pursue their own objectives taking into account the constraints imposed on them. It is generally accepted that bureaucrats prefer policy decisions, which lead to more regulations and higher budget expenditure.

Of course, the Commission's bureaucrats are constrained in their behaviour. First, they are bound by past policy decisions. Policies usually evolve over time, and significant changes are only undertaken if the environment has changed drastically.[7] Second, the Commission is constrained by the budget and by some control. Concerning the latter, the Commission is most likely even less controlled than national bureaucratic organizations. The general public is not well informed on what happens in the Commission, and the individual Community voter hardly has a personal interest in controlling the Commission. The farmers' union will most likely be the one to watch closely over the Commission, as it has vested interests in the activities of the Commission. Moreover, the Commission is in some respects dependent on the farmers' union, especially for receiving information for preparing legislation and implementing specific policy elements. The bureaucrats in the Commission are well advised to take into account the interest of the farmers' union in carrying out their activities. There is a strong argument that the Commission is biased in favour of farmers' interests at the cost of the public at large. It should be noted that this built-in bias is stronger the more the policies are protectionist and not transparent. Protectionism increases the interest of the farmers' union to collect information on the activities of the bureaucrats in the Commission. The same holds true for lack of transparency. In addition, the lack of transparency increases the cost for collecting information. This will divert more non-farmers than farmers from collecting information. The lack of transparency is related to government intervention in favour of farmers. Farmers may even have a stronger interest in collecting information of non-transparent policies. Higher collecting costs will likely be compensated by direct benefits accruing from non-transparent policies. There is no such effect for non-farmers. Thus, the presumption is well founded that the Commission is more interested in protection than in liberal policies. It might be true that this presumption holds for any bureaucracy, but it is most likely stronger for the Commission than for national bureaucracies. Costs for collecting information for non-farmers are certainly higher at the EU than at the national level. Hence, the Commission is more prone to neglecting general welfare effects relative to national bureaucracies. Of course, there are some institutionalized controlling organizations set into place, such as the Court of Auditors, the European Court of Justice (ECJ) and, to some extent the European Parliament. The first two can be quite effective. However, they are only supposed to check whether the activities of the Commission are in line with the law. It is beyond the tasks of the ECJ to investigate whether the Commission or the Council have taken adequately into account the interests of the public at large in carrying out their activities. It is debatable if the Court of Auditors is supposed to accept these duties. It is strongly opposed by the Commission. Anyway, the Court of Auditors has not been very effective in opposing protectionist tendencies in the Commission and the Council.

20.4.4 Institutions affecting the CAP

The evolution of the CAP is not only a consequence of the Council and Commission (players); it is even more dependent on the institutions set into place. According to North, 'institutions are the rules of the game in a society, or more formally, are the humanly devised constraints that shape human interactions' (North, 1990, p. 3). It is obvious that the outcome of the game (the shape and performance of the CAP in our case) not only depends on the organizations, but also on the allocation of competence among the players and the rules they have to follow. It will be shown that the main institutions set into force at the inception of the common market support the protectionist bias of CAP decisions.

The principle of financial solidarity

The principle of solidarity is considered to be one of the three pillars of the common agricultural market organizations (Tracy, 1989, p. 255). Indeed, it makes sense to finance common activities – such as the CAP – in solidarity, i.e. out of a common budget. However, such a financial scheme may create additional divergences in national interests. Indeed, the past and present pattern of financing the Community budget and enjoying the benefits of Community expenditure creates significant divergences in national interests (Koester, 1977, pp. 328–345). First, the welfare of individual countries is affected differently by increases in common prices for individual products. Second, individual countries may have interests which depart from those of the Community for promoting production growth. Third, countries may be more or less inclined to implement Community policies.[8] It should be noted that the integration of countries might generally have distributional implications for individual countries. Such effects just follow from differences in the countries' production and consumption patterns. However, the distributional effects of the financial system of the CAP are policy-made. Any collective that creates institutions increasing the divergence of interests of the individual members weakens the viability of the collective.

The principle of 'preference for agricultural products'

It seemed to make sense to the founders of the agricultural product market organizations to formulate the 'preference for agricultural products' as one of their basic tenets. Domestic users should first of all consume domestically produced products before relying on imported food. In reality, domestic consumers could do this on their own free will, as they do in many countries for specific food items. However, the founders of the common market organizations seemed not to believe in freedom of consumer choice. Instead, external protection has been accepted as the main instrument to achieve the principle of 'preference'. Making foreign supply more expensive does increase consumption of domestic products. Of course, the consumers have a higher preference for buying domestically produced goods, largely because they are forced to do so. Therefore, 'preference for agricultural products' is another way of saying 'external protection of domestic producers'.

The realization of this principle was most important for the evolution of agricultural policy in the Community. First, in connection with the principle of 'financial solidarity', it created additional divergences of interests among the countries as it gave rise to invisible transfers of income among the member countries. Second, the implementation of this principle created great pressure on the Council and gave it much more political power than existed in other sectors. It was accepted from the inception of the market organizations that the principle of preference for agricultural products would be enforced by a system of variable levies for the main agricultural products. Strangely enough, the Council was allowed to decide annually about the magnitude of preference given to domestic products, thus on the magnitude of the external rate of protection.

Having discussed the interests of the Council members and the distributional effects of the common financial system, it is understandable that annual decisions on the rate of external protection placed on the one hand great pressure on the Council to secure agreement, especially because of the divergent interests of the various countries. On the other hand, the Council had enormous discretionary powers, which could be exerted in favour of farmers. It goes without saying, that such a system opens the door for strong lobbying efforts. Hence, it should not be surprising that the Council could hardly resist responding to the interests of the farm lobby. It is true that the overall prices for farm products did fall over time (see Figure 20.3), but less than the aggregate level of world market prices. It should be noted that external rates of

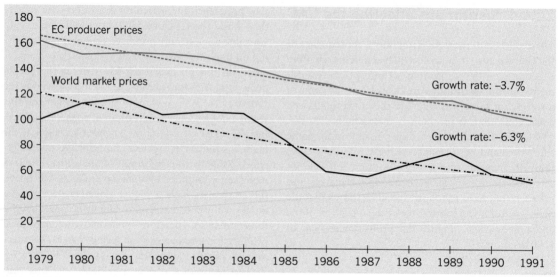

Figure 20.3 Development of EU and world market prices for agricultural prices
Source: E U Commission (1994), p. 17. Reprinted by permission of the European Communities.

protection have even been increased for products for which there was already a surplus in the Community. External protection could hardly have been justified for securing preference for domestically produced products. Indeed, the principle of 'preference for agricultural products' played hardly any role in the justification of price proposals and price decisions. Much more important was the income objective. This leads to a discussion of the misconceived CAP, the allocation of competence between national member countries and Community organizations.

20.4.5 The allocation of competence between member countries and the EC

It is well known that the EU is in charge of market and price policy, whereas structural policy is more in the domain of the member countries. Indeed, such an allocation of competence makes sense. Market and price policies rely heavily on the rate of external protection, and there are good arguments for having a common degree of external protection for all member countries. However, supranationalizing market and price policies can cause problems for the Community if

the decision-making body is allowed to set the external rate of protection annually and if the members of the decision-making body, the Council, bias their decisions in favour of farmers. Even if not supported by the Treaty of Rome, market and price policy has been used as a means to achieve the income objective.[9]

It is obvious that national interests diverge significantly on the price changes needed to achieve the national income objective. First, the need to increase national agricultural income is more related to income changes in the national economies and less so to farmers' incomes in other countries. Hence, differing growth rates in overall national income may result in divergent needs for increasing agricultural income. Second, an increase in institutional prices in EU currency leads to divergent increases in actual farm gate prices among member countries (Coleman, 1985, pp. 171–187), as the transmission coefficient between institutionalized prices and farm-gate prices varies significantly across countries. Allocating the responsibility for the income objective to the Community and accepting price support as the main instrument to achieving it necessarily enlarges the divergences in national interests with respect to price policy. It could have been expected that price changes would generally be at the cost of those parties, which had no voice in the negotiations, i.e. the consumers, taxpayers and foreign trading partners. However, the European policy makers could not externalize the costs of their decision without any constraints, and it is to these we turn next.

The importance of voting rules

Voting rules can be quite important for the behaviour of a collective. The founders of the Community had foreseen in Article 148 of the Treaty that the Council should generally decide by majority rule. Indeed, this seems to correspond with a democratic system where majority votes are normally accepted. However, the majority voting rule is more questionable if voters differ significantly in their preferences and if the individuals are affected to a different extent by the decision of a collective. Accepting majority rule for every decision would give rise to significant divergences in national interest concerning the CAP. Therefore, it is not surprising that two years after the first price decision was made, France demanded that decisions be unanimous in cases which could be considered of vital interest for any single country, hence the 'Luxembourg compromise' (see Chapters 2 and 3). Thus, the Commission made decisions only by unanimity rule up to 1982/1983. The unanimous voting rule is mainly attractive when there is significant heterogeneity among the voters. This avoids exploitation of a minority. However, it is well known that groups are well advised to apply this rule only for cases which are of utmost importance, because the 'expected external costs'[10] for such decisions are high. Unfortunately, the design of the CAP implied that policy decisions would have quite different effects on the individual countries. Hence, it might have been impossible to reach an agreement on the individual elements of a proposal presented by the Commission. There always has been at least one loser, possibly the European paymaster, who would have voted against the proposal. However, due to the specifics of the CAP, a mechanism for discretionary decisions was built into the system, and it was only feasible to decide on packages. The outcome was certainly a compromise among the Council members and their decisions were generally not in the interest of the Community at large. The move to majority voting in the 1980s has contributed to the ability of the Community to change its agricultural policy. However, the tendency to externalize the costs of the decision is still prevalent.

20.4.6 Constraints on CAP policy makers

Foreign trade restrictions

From the very beginning, agricultural policy makers had to take into account restrictions imposed by international trade agreements, principally by the GATT. The external rate of protection could not be increased for some feed imports. This constraint had significant implications for the other constraints, i.e. budget outlays (CEC, 1988b), which will be discussed below. Growth of expenditure for the market organizations for grain and milk depended directly on the constraints imposed by GATT.

Actually, GATT could have posed a much more binding constraint on CAP policy makers had its Article XVI:3 been taken literally. It states that subsidies to agricultural exports (and other primary commodities) are only allowed provided the exporting country does not capture more than an equitable share of world export trade (see, *inter alia*, Tangermann, 1991, pp. 50–61). However, it was never agreed on a clear definition of the term 'equitable share'. After the EC had passed self-sufficiency for individual products one after another, exports increased more than world trade, leading to an increase in the share in world trade.[11]

Foreign trade constraints became more binding after GATT's Uruguay Round (1986–1994) was finalized. Until the late 1970s, the EU and USA had opposing trade interests. The USA, as the main exporter of temperate zone agricultural products, was from the very beginning interested in high world market prices for them. In contrast, the EU as an importing region preferred low prices. However, in the late 1970s, the EU turned into an exporter of most of these products. Low world market prices led to negative terms of trade effects and boosted export subsidies, which in turn resulted in complaints by trading partners. Therefore, the EU agreed to open a new trade round with the focus on agricultural trade. The outcome of the negotiations was that the EU, like other GATT members, had to accept some significant constraints in its foreign trade regime, the details of which are analysed below.

These restrictions also obliged the EC to change its domestic policies for most agricultural products (see below). Further reforms can be expected after agreement is reached on the ongoing WTO Doha Round. CAP experience indicates that the driving force behind policy changes is neither rational economi/

considerations nor internal budgetary constraints, but rather external trade restrictions.[12]

One may wonder whether these trade constraints may have guided the CAP in a more welfare-maximizing direction had they been there at the time of CAP's inception. The answer would most likely be in the negative. The constraint has contributed to non-uniform rates of protection, thus increasing the overall welfare loss incurred from securing for farmers the given income level. The EC, and its main trading partner/opponent, the United States, could have enjoyed higher welfare had EC protection rates been more even (Koester and Tangermann, 1990). It is true that the restrictions on the import side for feed and some vegetable oils made protection for grain and milk more costly in economic terms. However, it is doubtful whether this had a more than marginal effect on the decisions of policy makers.

Past experience does not support the expectation that the main driving force of domestic policy changes, the foreign trade constraint, more specifically the pressure of trading partners, would eventually lead the CAP to adopt a superior resource allocation policy. Understandably, the CAP has been criticized more by countries which are exporters rather than importers of agricultural commodities. There is good reason to assume that the USA was the driving force behind demands for CAP change. However, agricultural exporters are not so much concerned about the deadweight losses caused internally by the CAP since they are harmed by lower world market prices consequent on the CAP. Hence, it was expected that international trade negotiations would focus mainly on the world market price effect. Any commitment by the EC to reduce export quantities would be welcome by exporting countries, independent of how this reduction would be achieved. Hence, although the Uruguay Round has certainly led to higher world market prices due to agreements on export constraints; it has not induced a move to improved allocation of resources internally. As countries had freedom on how to implement the export constraint, they turned to domestic supply management, instead of granting market forces a greater role.

The budget constraint

One of the main domestic constraints faced by agricultural policy makers is the budget. Even if governmental expenditure is not an adequate indicator for costs and benefits of any policy activity, expenditure plays an important role. First, most governments are restricted in their total outlays due to limited access to tax revenue. Therefore, the individual expenditure items compete with each other. The minister of agriculture has to compete with other government ministers for additional spending. Second, budget outlays are a visible indicator of governmental activity. Increasing expenditure on agriculture seems to convey to the public that the government is more strongly intervening in favour of farmers. Of course, this indicator is not at all adequate for mirroring the total transfer accruing to agriculture. It is well known that the European policy makers relied more on invisible than on visible transfers before the CAP reform of 1992.[13] Nevertheless, the general public is more informed on the visible transfer, and hence constrains the policy maker in this respect. It was most likely the budget constraint which led to a more prudent price policy after the EC had passed self-sufficiency for the aggregate of agricultural products at the beginnings of the 1980s (see Figure 20.4).

Constraints by non-agricultural pressure groups

Governmental interference in the markets in favour of farmers places both direct and indirect taxes on other sectors of the economy (Koester, 1991, pp. 5–17). Surprisingly, there was at least in Germany a tacit agreement between the farmers and the industrialists' unions that agricultural policy be left to the former. The industrialists may have viewed agricultural policy as unimportant, given that they were more focused on the divergence of interests within their own ranks. Some of them profited greatly from the CAP. Hence, they did not agree to a clear line of opposition to the CAP. The attitude of the industrialists' union changed in the 1980s when it became frightened of the trade repercussions caused by aggressive agricultural export subsidies. It was only then that they published a clear statement demanding a less distortive CAP. This supports the view that foreign trade constraints are most likely the main driving force for domestic policy changes.

One may wonder whether the consumers' unions could play a crucial role in constraining agricultural policy makers. There is hardly any evidence supporting the role of these interest groups; generally, they seem not to be well represented in most countries. Not being well staffed, they therefore lack the information and the power to push for policy changes.

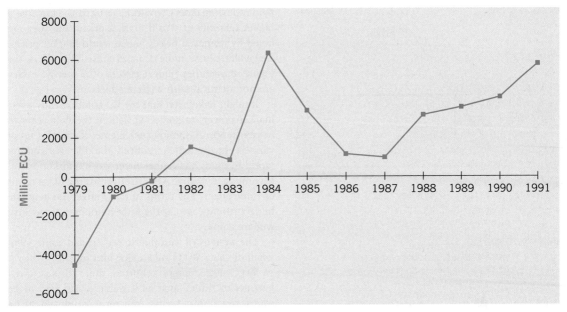

Figure 20.4 The development of the EU trading situation
Source: E U Commission (1994), p. 16. Reprinted by permission of the European Communities.

20.5 The market organizations of the CAP

The CAP has an extremely complex set of instruments and regulations, which have changed greatly since the days of its inception. Here, we concentrate on the present system, but with a flavour of the past; those interested in how it developed over the years are advised to turn to earlier editions of this book.

20.5.1 Instruments applied

From the outset, the main ingredients of the CAP were market organizations for individual agricultural products. These organizations are built on external and internal trade regulations. Farmers often believe that internal market regulations are more important for the performance of markets than external trade regulations. However, that is a fallacy. As the main objective of the market organizations is to provide a higher income for farmers, the main objective is price support. Domestic prices are higher than import or export prices. A wedge between domestic and world prices can only prevail if there are border measures in place. Hence, external trade regulations are more important for the performance of domestic markets.

Consequently, the following presentation starts with an analysis of the external trade regulations.

20.5.2 Import regulations

Variable levies and specific import tariffs

At the time of foundation, the EU was an importer of the main temperate zone agricultural products. Hence, the market organizations were set up for import situations. Originally, the EU had set threshold prices for the main agricultural products (individual grains, sugar, milk, and beef). These prices were set at the annual price negotiations; hence, these prices were politically determined. Under normal conditions, these threshold prices were far above the world market prices (cif prices, which are inclusive of cost, insurance and freight). The gap between the two prices was made up by variable levies. Variable levies are comparable to duties levied on imports, but as the levy changes with changing world prices, it becomes completely divorced from world market prices. How it functions is clarified with the help of Figure 20.5. Import prices are determined by the cif world price

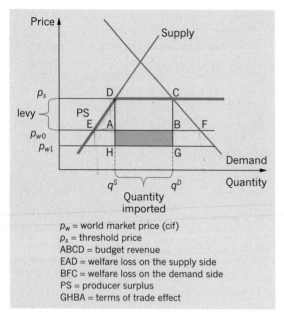

Figure 20.5 The impact of variable levies on domestic prices

plus the variable levy. The supply curve on the EU market is equal to the domestic supply curve up to the price p_s and at this price it is equal to the world market supply curve plus the levy. If it is assumed that the EU is a relatively small country which has no impact on the world market price, the supply curve faced by the EU deviates and becomes a horizontal line. The EU is assumed to be a price taker on the world market. The variable levy shifts the world supply curve upwards to the level of the threshold price. The threshold price will be the domestic price at the point of entry of the imported product. The EU has set the same threshold prices for a well-defined product for all ports of entry. These prices strongly determine domestic prices at any other location as regional prices are strongly correlated across different locations. The main difference between local prices and threshold prices are transport costs.

Figure 20.5 shows that the typical market organization at the time of setting up the schemes had positive effects for the budget. The EU could raise so-called own reserves by charging variable levies on imports. However, the scheme had also negative welfare effects. Domestic producers received incentives to increase their produced quantity, but incurred higher costs than the EU would have had to pay for imports, resulting in a welfare loss of EAD on the supply side.

Domestic consumers would have liked to consume a higher quantity at world market prices, but they are taxed by domestic prices above world market prices. The welfare loss on the demand side is BFC. Thus, the Figure shows that budget effects of a specific policy are not identical with welfare effects.

It might have been that the EU could already exert market power on some markets in the first years of her existence. Assuming such a case, the setting up of variable levies which reduced the EU demand on world markets had led to lower world market prices, generating a positive welfare effect for the EU, a terms of trade effect. The terms of trade effect did generate budget revenue and at the same amounted to positive welfare gains.

The system of variable levies existed until 1995 when the new WTO rules came into force.

WTO agreements required that all non-tariff barriers to trade, such as variable levies, had to be transformed into tariffs; the term employed being 'tariffication'. The tariff equivalents of the 1986–1990 period had to be lowered by 36% on average, but at least for 20% for individual commodities. Hence, tariff rates should not be higher than the new bound reduced tariff rate. However, as world market prices were very low in the base period, the EU has had no problems in securing the domestic price at the desired level. Anyhow, the EU managed in the last minute to get a special regulation for those grains for which there are intervention prices on the domestic market. According to this regulation the domestic threshold price is set at 155% of the domestic intervention price. The difference between the threshold price and a hypothetical cif import price (world market price) is charged on imports. The main difference on the grain market which had to be introduced was the rule concerning the threshold price. It used to be a political price which could be set annually at discretion of the Council of Ministers. The new rule sets the price in fixed relation to the intervention price and the EU had agreed not to increase the intervention price during the term of the agreement (1995/1996 to 2001/2002). Of course, the EU is free to lower the intervention price, which it did in the year 2000.

The second rule concerned the definition of the relevant world market price. Prior to the agreement, the EU considered the cif price as the relevant offer price of foreign countries at the border of the EU. This practice caused problems as imports had declined over time and, hence, it was difficult to find the representative cif price. The EU trading partners agreed in

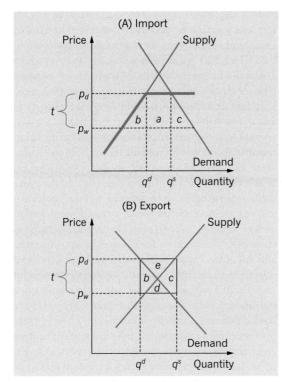

Figure 20.6 The effect of variable levies or fixed tariff rates

market price. The domestic market is therefore completely decoupled from the world market. Domestic prices are stable even if world market prices vary. If domestic supply falls short due to a bad harvest, the supply curve shifts to the left, allowing for a greater volume of imports.

If the country is an exporter of the product under consideration, the tariff or levy will not determine the domestic market price directly. However, a country cannot be an exporter with prices above p_w. Foreign supply would enter the market and drive domestic prices downward to the world market level. Panel (B) shows that a part of the tariff may become redundant. The tariff rate could be lowered without resulting in more imports. The country incurs budget expenditure equal to $(q^s - q^d) * (p_d - p_w)$, i.e. $b + d + c + e$. However, the welfare loss is equal to the triangle below the demand and supply curves, $b + d$ and $c + d$. A comparison of panels (A) and (B) clearly shows that the welfare losses of trade policies are not related to budget effects, but only to the price gap between domestic and world market prices and the price elasticities of demand and supply.

Ad valorem tariff rates

There are few agricultural products where the EU charges only an *ad valorem* tariff, e.g. for potatoes, and tropical products, or in addition to other import restrictions. *Ad valorem* tariff rates are also used to provide specific protection for EU processing industries. Concerning tropical products, the *ad valorem* tariff is higher for processed products than for the raw materials (tariff escalation) providing additional protection for the domestic processing industry. *Ad valorem* tariff rates have to be preferred to specific tariffs or variable levies if the products under consideration are heterogeneous and one levy for a set of highly differentiated products would lead to undesired distortion in trade flows. Take the case of fruit and vegetables where *ad valorem* tariff rates are applied. Even a product like cabbage is highly differentiated. If there were one specific tariff for all varieties or one levy, high quality products would enter the EU markets at a lower percentage charge than low value products. Hence, domestic producers of high quality cabbage were put at a disadvantage as compared to producers of lower quality cabbage. If the EU were to introduce alternative specific tariff rates for individual qualities, the administrative burden would be very high. Hence, it is reasonable to apply variable

the Uruguay Round to accept the representative market price in the US as the representative world market price. Adding costs for insurance and freight results in the hypothetical EU cif price. As long as this price is lower than the EU threshold price and as long as the price gap is smaller than the tariff which the EU could apply according to the agreement, the EU charges the difference between the threshold price and the cif price. Thus, the old system is almost unchanged. The effect of the regulation is clarified with the help of Figure 20.6.

The domestic price is determined for imports in panel (A). Importers can offer at prices p_w plus t, the tariff or levy. The supply curve deviates at price p_d on the domestic market if the importing country is a relatively small country. The country generates revenue equal to $(q^d - q^s) * t$ (the asterisk, throughout, standing for multiplication). However, the welfare loss of the country is equal to a plus b.

If t is a variable levy, as it used to be for most EU agricultural imports before the Uruguay Round, t varies with the world market price, leaving the domestic price completely divorced from the world

levies system or specific tariff rates only for fairly homogeneous products.

Tariff rate quotas

Tariff rate quotas are a new element in agricultural trade; they were introduced in the Uruguay Round. WTO member countries have to allow each other minimum access to their markets, amounting to 5% of consumption in the period 1986 to 1988. These imports enter the EU market at a lower tariff rate than is normally applied.

The effect of this import regulation is clarified with the help of Figure 20.6. Panel A depicts the situation of an import case. The country charges the tariff t and tariff revenue is $t * (q^d - q^S)$. If the country has to charge a lower tariff rate for within quota imports, the tariff revenue foregone is equal to $(t - t_q) * q^*$, where q^* stands for the tariff quota. Thus, the country loses revenue and enjoys a lower welfare if the tariff quotas are allocated to foreign exporters. If the quota is auctioned, the loss for the country might be minimal; private traders, whether foreign or domestic, would be willing to pay a price per unit of import quota about equal to the difference between the domestic price and the world market price. The only deviation would arise due to transaction costs. Actually, only 12% of tariff quotas are auctioned (Skully, 1999). The EU does not apply an auction system for any tariff quota.

Panel B, which is more important for the EU agricultural markets, shows the export case. It is assumed that the domestic price p_d is lower than the world market price p_w plus the tariff rate t. This is a typical EU situation. The tariff was set at the time when the EU was still an importer. Having matured to an export situation there are no imports any more. The actual tariff rate could be lowered (by the difference between $p_w + t$ and p_d) without affecting imports. There is water in the tariff rates. The EU has actually bound tariff rates which are partly redundant, i.e. tariffs can be lowered without giving rise to imports. Allowing tariff quota imports, the EU has to increase subsidies for exports as $p_d > p_w$. These additional subsidies imply a welfare loss for the EU, but only if the tariff quotas are allocated to foreign exporters.

Preferential access

It is widely agreed upon that the CAP distorts world agricultural markets. Hence, trading partners com-

plained about restricted access to EU markets. The EU response was to offer preferential access to its market. First, trade preferences were granted to some countries which had lost market access to countries which joined the EU (see Chapters 24 and 25), for example New Zealand's quota for butter exports to the United Kingdom and the USA's quota for maize exports to Spain and Portugal. In 1975 preferential access was granted to some African, Caribbean and Pacific countries (ACP countries) that had former colonial ties to some EU member countries. In the 1990s, the EU signed the so-called European Agreements, the Association Agreements, with selected Central and Eastern European countries which granted them import quotas. Recently in 2001, the EU opened her markets completely for imports from some Balkan countries and for most imports from the 49 least developed countries. In the latter case, the only restriction is for imports of bananas, rice and sugar, but only for a transition period. The effects of these agreements can be clarified with the help of Figure 20.7. The EU supply curve shifts to the right by the amount of the preferential quota or by the unrestricted imports. The EU either loses tariff revenue or has to spend additional amounts on export restitutions (see below). Hence, the welfare loss for the EU is equal to the price gap

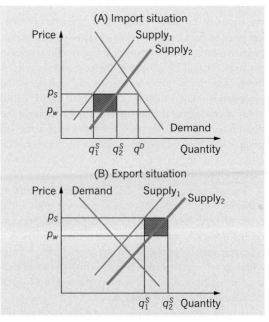

Figure 20.7 The impact of preferential access to EU markets

between domestic prices and world market prices times the quantity of preferential imports.

20.5.3 Export regulations

Until the end of the Uruguay Round in 1994, there were no real constraints on agricultural exports. GATT rules did not allow export subsidies to manufactured products. The US was instrumental in introducing the GATT waiver for agricultural exports, but GATT set the proviso that they should not be used to capture more than an 'equitable share' of world exports of the product concerned (Article XVI:3 of GATT). As it was not clear what the term 'not more than an equitable share' actually meant, countries were literally free to use export subsidies. This waiver was of utmost importance for the functioning of EU markets up to 1992. The EU developed from an importing to an exporting region for almost all temperate zone products, even with the lowering of the rate of nominal protection. In spite of declining real agricultural producer prices, the shift in the supply curve due to technological change was higher than the shift in the demand curve due to income growth. The EU was not forced to reduce prices in order to avoid surpluses at support prices as the surplus could be dumped on the world markets. The differences between domestic and world market prices were met by the EU budget. The Uruguay Round Agreement posed a significant constraint on EU policy makers. They had to agree to cut the volume of subsidized exports by 21% (based on 1986–1990) and the amount of subsidies paid by 36% (same base period). The impact of these constraints can be illustrated with the help of Figure 20.8.

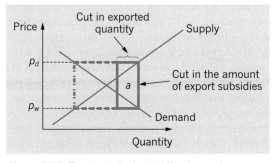

Figure 20.8 The impact of subsidized export constraints

Depending on the market situation, either quantity or expenditure constraints could become binding. So far, volume constraints have become binding on some markets. As long as EU prices are above world market prices, domestic supply has to be restricted to domestic demand plus the permitted volume of subsidized exports minus the quantity imported on minimum market access s (this is not in the figure) (tariff rate quotas).

Therefore, EU policy makers were forced to change the market regulations for some commodities; before the agreement was signed, the EU had already instituted drastic cuts in institutional grain prices of 30% (the 1992 McSharry reform, see below) and enlarged the cut by another 15% in 2000 (*Agenda 2000*, CEU, 1997a). Significant price cuts have also been instituted for beef and agreed upon for milk. A further drastic change in the market organizations was decided in June 2003.

Payments of export subsidies cause more administrative problems than charging imports. If the Commission wants to bridge the gap between the domestic prices and the competitive export prices it has to know the relevant export price. However, these prices are not quoted on a market, so instead the Commission has to collect information on prices in importing countries and take into account import charges and shipping costs (freight, insurance and harbour costs). This information is difficult to get, in particular for the many differentiated processed agricultural products. Moreover, the Commission has to know how much of the raw material had been used to produce specific processed products. Take the case of pasta. Pasta can be produced on the basis of common wheat and eggs or durum wheat. As the price gap for common wheat is smaller than that for durum wheat, the knowledge of what kind of wheat is important for quantifying the amount of export restitutions, i.e. subsidies. Another case is export of wheat flour. The Commission has to know how much wheat is needed to produce one unit of wheat flour. The information is not at all easily available; only the flour mills can provide the needed information, but it is naïve to expect them to report correct information. This may explain why the EU used to be very competitive on the international wheat flour market, where the EU share was in excess of 60% for many years. The respective share on the wheat market was not more than 16% in the 1980s.

Problems were even more pronounced on the meat market as export restitutions differed for different cuts of meat. They were the lowest for offal and high for high quality meat. Hence, there was a tendency for false declaration; indeed, the European Court of Auditors found most fraud to be in meat exports.

20.5.4 Domestic market regulations

Intervention purchases

Intervention prices are prices at which intervention agencies are obliged to buy-in unlimited amounts of a specific product like grain or limited amounts under certain conditions. These prices were introduced in order to stabilize markets. Hence, these prices, which are politically set, were supposed to be below normal market prices at the time when the market organizations were designed and first implemented. Therefore, these prices are below the threshold price at which international competitors can enter the domestic market. As long as foreign supply was needed to clear the EU grain market at a price related to the threshold price (see above) the intervention price was not relevant. Actually, buying-in took place only in some regions due to market imperfection as long as the EU was in grain deficit. However, gradually the EU matured to an exporter of grain and the intervention price could become the relevant market price if the EU did not enter the market by paying export subsidies. The situation is shown with the help of Figure 20.9. The domestic demand curve becomes completely elastic at the intervention price if private and official demand does not clear the market at prices above the intervention price. The actual market price will be above the intervention price if the government pays export subsidies. These subsidies raise domestic demand. The effect is that the domestic demand curve

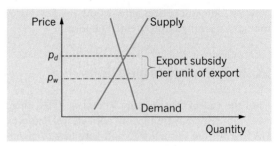

Figure 20.10 The effect of export subsidies on domestic prices

will be completely elastic at a price which is equal to the world price plus the subsidy per unit of export. It should be noted that the effect of an export subsidy on domestic prices does not depend on the quantity exported, but on the subsidy per unit of exports. Even if the EU produces a small surplus on a market, as in the case of pork with a degree of self-sufficiency of about 103, the price effect of the subsidy can be very high. Figure 20.10 clarifies this point. The volume of export is fairly small, but the gap between the domestic and world market prices is fairly high. Without any foreign trade regulations, the domestic prices would be at p_w.

Direct payments

Direct payments have become a most important element of market organizations since the McSharry Reform. These payments were originally introduced on the grain and oilseeds markets in order to compensate for the cut in institutional prices, attracting the term 'compensatory payments'. The basic idea was to offset the income loss due to the price cut, and to do this as accurately as possible, payments were linked to the area cultivated under cereals or oilseeds. Figure 20.11 depicts the effects. Grain intervention prices were reduced by 30%. Policy makers assumed that the income loss would be equal to the area $(p_I - p_{II})$ * q_0. The actual loss in income was lower since it is the negative change in producer surplus (area $p_I p_{II}CB$), hence the overcompensation was area CAB. As the payment was linked to the use of the land (it was paid per hectare of land under grain cultivation), payments were part of the gross margin earned in grain production. Hence, the area under grain production did not decline. The effect of lower prices on yields may show up after a long period of adjustment as a new set of technologies may be needed. So far yields have

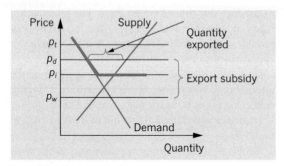

Figure 20.9 The importance of intervention prices

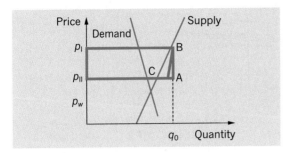

Figure 20.11 Price cuts and direct payments: the case of grains

continued to increase over time. Consequently, total grain production did not decline in spite of the drastic price cut. Due to the direct payments the supply curve became steeper below the former intervention price p_I. The supply curve may have even shifted to the right as there was overcompensation leading to an increase of profitability in grain production.

The Council had decided on a further drop in grain prices by 15% in 1999 (*Agenda 2000*, CEU, 1997b) and to reduce beef prices by 20% and dairy prices by 15%. The latter will only become effective from 2005/2006 onwards. The (falsely) calculated income losses (see the argument above) are supposed to be compensated by half. In the case of beef, payments are paid per head of animal, but in the case of dairy, payments are supposed to be linked to the reference quantity, i.e. the amount of milk a producer can achieve at high guaranteed prices.

The change from price support to direct payments had significant effects on functional income distribution, i.e. income distributed to factors of production. The price cut lowered the marginal value product of all factors of production by the same percentage. However, the direct payments were linked to the use of land in the case of grain and oilseeds production. Hence, it was a land subsidy, although conditioned on production of grain or oilseeds. The subsidy increased the marginal willingness of farmers who wanted to rent or to purchase land. Actually, the subsidy effect was stronger than the effect of the decline in the product price. The subsidy was supposed to compensate for the aggregate loss in income, i.e. the loss in labour, land and capital income. But the subsidy to compensate for the total income loss was linked to only one factor of production, namely land. Thus, it should not have come as a surprise to learn that land prices did go up after the McSharry Reform.

Set aside

The EU had already introduced a voluntary set aside programme in 1988. The father of this programme was the German Minster Kiechle. He pushed for a strategy to lower production in order to be able to raise prices. Such a policy could be in the interest of farmers were they in a closed economy or if the country had the freedom to change the external rate of protection. However, these conditions did not prevail. Kiechle seemed to have overseen that the Uruguay Round had already started in 1986 aiming at cutting the external rates of protection for agricultural products. Hence, lower domestic production would not lead to higher domestic prices, but only to reduced exports or to increased imports. It should have been clear that domestic prices in a trading economy are determined by world market prices and the external rate of protection.

Anyway, the voluntary set aside programme was not attractive for most of the EU member countries (Koester, 1989). The EU included in the 1992 reform package quasi-compulsory set aside. Farmers with above a certain size of grain production (90 tonnes) had to set aside a certain percentage of the area under grain production in order to qualify for the direct payments. The EU included this element in the reform package in order to gain acknowledgement in the GATT Round. The trading partners, in particular the US, were interested in a reduction in EU grain production. It was widely accepted that the EU grain policy depressed world market prices, hence EU production was supposed to be cut. As the EU did not want to lower prices to the world market level and as they wanted to compensate producers for the price cut, they included a production curtailing measure. The EU rightly expected that the US was not so much interested in whether the EU reduced production by liberalization through clear price cuts or through more control measures such as set aside. Thus, beginning in 1993, the EU has instituted a set aside programme which demands that grain and oilseeds producers idle a certain percentage of their arable land which was under crop and oilseed production in the past.

From an economic stance, set aside is a highly inefficient measure. Farmers are enticed into not using a scarce factor of production and get compensated for the income loss, so obviously the society at large will not get richer, but poorer. If it were nevertheless practised, that would be only to continue with the protective CAP policy.

Production quotas

The EU applies production quotas on the production of sugar, milk and tobacco. The quota on the sugar market has been set up with the organization of the regime from the onset. Production quotas are only considered as a reasonable policy alternative if

- there is a surplus on the domestic market at supported prices;
- budget outlays are high due to a high price differential between domestic and world market prices and a high exportable surplus;
- domestic production is growing, leading to even higher outlays in the future; and
- there is a bottleneck which allows controlling the produced quantities at acceptable financial costs.

The first three conditions prevail on many agricultural markets in the EU, but the bottleneck arises mainly in the selected markets where quotas have been introduced. In the case of sugar, all the sugar beets have to be processed in factories where the quantities can be checked. As to milk, at least most of it is nowadays delivered to EU dairies (over 95%), but much less so in the new EU countries. In Poland it is only about 60%.

The analysis of a quota system will focus on the milk market regime. Quotas were introduced in 1984 because surpluses on the milk market were rising and the price differential between domestic and world market prices was extremely high. The rise in milk production was not expected at the time of inception of the milk market regime. In 1967/1968 cows were mainly fed on the bases of domestically produced fodder. Hence, milk production was constrained by the domestic capacity to produce feed. However, the situation changed quickly due to some specifics of the trading regime for feed imports. The EU had agreed in GATT negotiations to apply low tariffs on imports of feed in exchange for being allowed to introduce the variable levy system for the main temperate zone products. At that time, feed (soya, tapioca and others) was not imported in sizeable quantities. However, with increased EU grain prices the willingness to pay for imported feed went up. The decline in shipping rates contributed also to booming imports of feed. A mixture of soya meal or cake and tapioca was used as a perfect substitute for grain. Thus, milk production

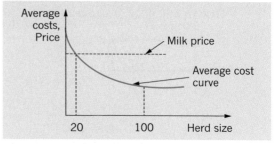

Figure 20.12 Average costs in milk production and milk prices

became less dependent on farm grown fodder and it expanded heavily. Farmers not only increased milk yield per cow from just over 3000 kg per cow in 1967 to about 5000 kg per cow in 1983, but also increased herd size, taking advantage of economies of scale in milk production. Hence, it became less feasible to support the income of milk producers through support prices. The situation is depicted in Figure 20.12. At the given milk price, most of the producers milking less than 20 cows did not make a profit since average costs were above the milk price. However, those farmers milking in excess of 20 and less than 100 cows could earn profit. Hence, there was huge incentive for increasing herd sizes for milking, almost irrespective of the amount of arable and pastureland used in the farm. Thus, milk production grew much faster than milk consumption, leading to growing exportable surpluses. EU policy makers could have lowered prices long before 1984 as the problem was already visible for many years prior to that. However, they postponed the decision as they did not dare to provoke farmers. In 1984, drastic measures were needed to correct the problem: a significant price cut by about 12% was considered as not acceptable, so the introduction of a quota system was seen as a reasonable alternative.

Policy makers and bureaucrats generally prefer a quota system to price cuts. Quotas are attractive as they do not lead to an immediate high-income loss. Bureaucrats may even value highly the new control system that has to be instituted as a consequence: the higher the bureaucratic burden, the better the prospects for job promotion. In contrast, economists generally oppose the quota systems because of misallocation of resources. An efficient farmer cannot expand production without gaining additional quotas. If they were tradable, the farmer could buy them, but the costs of expanding production would increase. Hence, structural change will be held up. Moreover, quota systems contradict the basic idea of a customs union: production cannot move to those regions and enterprises which are the most efficient ones.

Consumption subsidies

EU policy makers use different forms of subsidy. Payments for price reduction as described above are special subsidies. There are others, offered to reduce production costs, such as interest subsidies for investment or for stimulating demand. Let us examine the latter.

Consumption subsidies are most important in the milk market. Some 50% to 90% of the total annual EU demand for skimmed milk powder was so supported over the past 20 years. The respective figure for butter is 15% to 35%. Hence, without these subsidies, the exportable surplus would be much higher.

The budget effects of the subsidy schemes are difficult to assess. If the alternative would have been to get rid of the surplus by exporting a higher volume, the answer would be straightforward. If domestic demand for the subsidized product is price inelastic and world market demand for the additional EU exports is completely elastic (small country assumption), budget outlays would be higher with subsidizing EU demand. The comparison is depicted in Figure 20.13. Total revenue for producers is financed by consumers, export revenue and budget outlays. The original situation for the domestic market price p_d is shown in the figure. If the government decided to subsidize domestic consumers, the demand curve will shift to the right, increasing the demand at price p_d. This would have the same effect as lowering domestic prices, say from p_d to p_{d1}. However, consumer expenditure at price p_{d1} would be lower than at price p_d if the price elasticity of demand were smaller than 1 (in absolute terms), a condition which definitely holds for EU butter demand. Moreover, if domestic consumers expand their purchases on the domestic market, the exportable surplus would decline. Hence, revenue from sales to the world market declines. Thus, the area $a + b + c$ would be smaller than in the initial situation. Consequently, budget outlays have to be larger to cover producer revenue.

The assessment of subsidization of butter and skimmed milk powder would lead to a different result

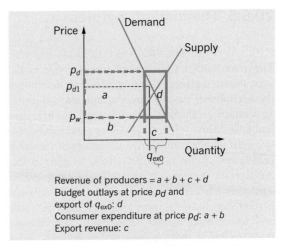

Revenue of producers = $a + b + c + d$
Budget outlays at price p_d and export of q_{ex0}: d
Consumer expenditure at price p_d: $a + b$
Export revenue: c

Figure 20.13 Budget effects of EU demand for domestic consumption as compared to export subsidization

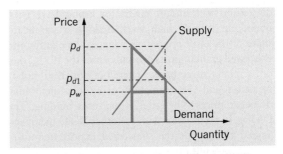

Figure 20.14 Welfare effects of consumer subsidies

were welfare effects the focus. The marginal willingness to pay at price p_d is larger than the world market price. Reducing consumer prices through subsidization creates additional welfare. The analysis is presented in Figure 20.14.

Reducing domestic prices through subsidies increases demand, the increase in the willingness to pay is equal to the bold bordered trapezoid, but the loss in revenue is only the rectangle given by the export quantity in the initial situation times the world market price. Hence, there is an overall welfare gain. Actually the welfare gain would be even higher if domestic consumers were confronted with world market prices by subsidizing the difference between producer and the world market price. This proves once more that budget effects are not related to welfare effects.

20.5.5 The market regimes

Grain market regime

The grain market regime plays a major role in EU agricultural markets. Grain production determines the agricultural income directly, but also indirectly as it affects production costs for pork, poultry, eggs and milk. Moreover, profitability of grain production is crucial for the comparative advantage of the other field crops, including fodder crops, as grain prices are a main determinant of land and lease prices. The grain market organization includes, as do most market organizations, provisions for external trade and for internal market regulations. The external trade regime is more important for domestic price formation as internal prices can only deviate from import or export parity prices if there are border measures in place, which drive a wedge between the two prices. Like all members of WTO, the EU has lost the ability to change border measures at its discretion since import tariffs for grains have been bound on a fairly high level, making a significant share of the tariff redundant. Hence, some grain and processed grain imports can only enter the EU market on a preferential basis. Therefore, internal policy measures and the regulation of exports determine domestic prices. The latter is the most binding. The EU has, in accordance with the other WTO members, agreed to: (a) cut the subsidized export quantities for all agricultural exports, classified with respect to specific groups, from the 1986 to 1990 level by 21%; (b) reduce the payments of export subsidies by 36%; and (c) allow minimum access of imports in the magnitude of at least 5% of domestic use during 1986–1988. As long as the EU produces an exportable surplus and has to pay export subsidies, i.e. if domestic prices are above export parity prices, the exportable quantity, which can be subsidized, is given by the following equation:

> Subsidized exportable surplus = Domestic production – domestic use – minimum market access – imports due to other preferential agreements

Domestic production is given by the following equation:

> Domestic production = Domestic use + subsidized exportable surplus – minimum market access – imports due to other preferential agreements

In order to comply with the export constraints, the EU has either to cut domestic production at prices above export parity or to lower domestic prices to the level of the export parity price. The EU is willing to accept the second alternative. Grain prices have been reduced in two steps, first by 30% in a 1992 decision and by another 15% as part of the Agenda 2000 Agreement of March 1999. At present, EU grain prices are still somewhat above world market prices and EU exporters have to receive export subsidies in order to be competitive on world markets.

Domestic market regulations on the grain market include intervention prices, set aside obligations with payments of premiums, and direct payments per area cultivated with grains. Intervention prices are minimum prices on the wholesale level for specified qualities of individual grains. They are the same for all grains and for all locations. These prices have become less important over time as the administration has pushed up domestic market prices above the intervention price level. This was done by paying export subsidies high enough to bridge the gap between domestic and world market prices. The profitability of producing grain is highly determined by direct payment per hectare of grain. The payments are the same for all grains, but differ with respect to regions. The differentiation was introduced because payments were supposed to compensate farmers for price cuts accurately, but the yield per hectare differs widely among regions. The payment that has been in place since 1993 was increased only once, as a further price cut was decided as part of the Agenda 2000 package. However, there is no open-end payment, instead it is limited per region. Each region received an area quota allocation. If the area planted in a region surpasses the quota, the premium per hectare planted will be reduced and the obligation for set aside will be increased for the next harvesting year. However, there is no area quota on the farm level.

Market regime for rapeseed, sunflower and soya

The market regime for rapeseed, sunflower and soya has no special border regulation. However, there is an area payment, which has been set equal to that of grains as part of the Agenda 2000 package. In contrast to grains, the domestic price for oilseeds is directly linked to import prices and hence fluctuates, making oilseeds production riskier than grain production.

Market regime for olive oil

The market regime for olive oil leads to a EU price very much determined by policy measures and more so in the case of income to producers. EU production is affected by limiting production aid to a Maximum Guaranteed Quantity (MGQ), which is supposed to equate domestic production with domestic use. The size of the production aid is supposed to provide producers with a fair income. The size of the aid is equal to the 'Production Target Price', which is set by the Council for the period 2000/2001 at Euro 1322.5/tonne, and a theoretical 'Producer Selling Price', which would provide a fair income to producers. If total production surpasses the MGQ, a proportionate cut in the level of production aid will be introduced, but for all producers. In addition, the MGQ can be reduced for the following year. External trade regulations foresee a fixed import tariff, which, for 1999/2000, is in the range of Euro/tonne 1226 to 1603. Export subsidies are paid on a tender basis to enforce the Production Target Price. The olive oil market regime is highly intransparent and has led to significant fraud, so the Commission is preparing a proposal for changing the regime.

Market regime for sugar

The market regime for sugar is one where the *internal* market is intensively regulated. There is a production quota for sugar beets and isoglucose. Farmers are confronted with a three-price scheme, a high price for production within the A-quota (the minimum price was Euro 46.72/tonne in 1999/2000), a 31% lower price for the so-called B-quota and a still lower price for the quantity, which surpasses the A- and B-quota, the so-called C-sugar. The C-sugar price might be equal to the world market price, but factories which are free to set the price may offer a blend price for B- and C-sugar. The system is considered to be largely

self-financing, as producers of A-sugar have to pay a 2% levy to finance export subsidies. However, the EU consumer actually pays for the regime as the EU sugar prices are far above world market prices. The *external trading regime* is comparable to that for cereals. Import tariffs are partly redundant, hence imports mainly enter under preferential agreements. Exports are subsidized, but the same export restrictions apply as mentioned above for cereals. Hence, the market regime has to be adjusted. The quantity produced has to be reduced in order to comply with the quantitative export constraint. In addition, the price has to be reduced if world market prices remain on the same low level as over the last years. An abolishing of the quota regime is also under discussion.

Market regime for tobacco

The market regime for tobacco is based on production quotas with producer prices being about Euro/kg 3.80 in 1999/2000. The EU has instituted quotas over the last years in order to reduce expensive export restitutions for tobacco. Import tariffs and export subsidies protect high internal prices.

Market regimes for fruits and vegetables

The market regimes for fruits and vegetables are less intensively regulated than those for temperate zone products. The EU avoids direct intervention as most of these products are only storable for short periods at high costs and in addition price incentives may stimulate production growth significantly (high price elasticity of supply). Nevertheless, producers are protected. Premiums for withdrawal are paid if representative market prices are below set buying-in prices. These premiums can be considered as the lowest market price. Withdrawal is mostly done by producer organizations. The external trading regime includes tariffs, depending on the season, and export subsidies.

20.6   Structural policy

The EU Commission had in the late 1960s already recognized that market and price policy had to be complemented by structural policy; it became obvious that market and price policy alone could not contribute to the achievements of policy objectives in the diverse EU agricultural sectors. Farm sizes differed

largely across countries and resources were not used efficiently. A simple comparison of efficiency among farms highlighted that larger farms did generally use less land, less labour and less capital per unit of output than smaller farms. However, this difference is not just related to farm size, but also to the qualification of farm managers. Thus, a small farm with a well-trained operator can be more efficient than a large farm with a less qualified manager, but with equal qualification, farm size would be crucial for the efficient use of factors. Hence, a policy directed to influence farm sizes could improve farm income and efficiency of agriculture. The first EU proposal concerning structural policy was the Mansholt Plan of 1968.[14] Dr Sicco Mansholt, who was the Agricultural Commissioner at the time, is considered the father of the first proposal. The plan, which basically relates to the guidance aspects of the CAP, proposed the following principal measures:

(i)   A first set of measures concerns the structure of agricultural production, and contains two main elements:

(a)   One group of measures, varying widely in character, must be taken to bring about an appropriate reduction in the number of persons employed in agriculture. Older people will have to be offered a supplementary annual income allowance if they agree to retire and thereby release land; younger farmers should be enabled to change over to non-farming activities; the children of farmers, finally, should be given an education which enables them to choose an occupation other than farming, if they so desire. For the two latter categories, new jobs will have to be created in many regions. These efforts at reducing manpower should be brought to bear with particular force on one group of persons within agriculture, namely, those who own their farm businesses, inasmuch as the structural reform of farms themselves . . . largely depends upon the withdrawal of a large number of these people from agriculture.

(b)   Secondly, far-reaching and co-ordinated measures should be taken with a view to the creation of agricultural (farming) enterprises of adequate economic dimensions.[15] If such enterprises are to be set up and kept running, the land they need will have to be made available to them on acceptable terms; this will require an active and appropriate agrarian policy.

(ii)   A second group of measures concerns markets, with the double purpose of improving the way they work and of adjusting supply more closely to demand:

(a)   Here a major factor will be a cautious price policy, and this will be all the more effective as the enterprises react more sensitively to the points offered by the market.

(b)   A considerable reduction of the area of cultivated land will work in the same direction.

(c)   Better information will have to be made available to all market parties (products, manufacturers and dealers), producers will have to accept stricter discipline and there will have to be some concentration of supply. Product councils and groupings of product councils will have to be set up at European level to take over certain responsibilities in this field.

(iii)   In the case of farmers who are unable to benefit from the measures described, it may prove necessary to provide personal assistance not tied either to the volume of output or to the employment of factors of production. This assistance should be payable within specified limits defined in the light of regional factors and the age of the persons concerned.

Extract from the 'Mansholt Plan', Brussels, July, 1969. Reprinted by permission of the European Communities.

The Mansholt plan rightly addressed the main problems of agriculture, not adequately functioning markets and inefficient resource use in agriculture. However, the strategy proposed to overcome the problems was questionable (see below). Anyway, the plan was widely rejected in the Union as it was considered too ambitious and inadequate: 'The proposals for reducing labour and land were particularly controversial' (Tracy, 1989, p. 267). Therefore, the Council agreed on a common agricultural structural policy in 1972 which was supposed to be less radical than the Mansholt plan. Three directives (72/159–72/161) were issued. Directive 72/159 allowed member nations to support their farmers' modernization through grants or subsidized interest rates on the condition that these farms were capable of generating income levels comparable with those of other local occupations. Directive 72/160 permitted member nations to extend lump-sum payments or annuities to farm workers aged between 55 and 65 years to lure them into leaving the industry. Directive 72/161 aimed at encouraging member countries to establish 'socio-economic guidance services' to entice farm workers to retrain and relocate. However, although the precise method of implementation (itself not mandatory) of these directives was left to the discretion of national governments, about a quarter of the necessary outlay (65% for Ireland and Italy) would be borne by the CAP guidance section. Thus, these directives were in the spirit of the Mansholt Plan.

Yet the EC expenditure on the structural aspects of the CAP remained very small. Indeed, the annual grants under all of the three directives over the decade 1975–1984 averaged no more than about 100 million ECUs (at 1986 prices) for about four million farms of less than 10 hectares in 1975.

The basic idea of the first structural policy – along the Mansholt proposal – was the distinction between farms which were considered as capable of develop-ment and those that were not. The first could be sup-ported by investment grants and interest subsidies, the second by measures to migrate out of agriculture. However, this policy was doomed to fail.

First, it is difficult to find out what farms are con-sidered as able to develop and which are not. As men-tioned above, it is true that farm size is an important determinant of efficient resource use, but it is not the only one. Second, support of profitable investment requires finding out which investment is profitable and which is not. There is hardly a bureaucracy that is able to generate the needed assessment. An investor in receipt of support may either choose the investment which (s)he had already opted for, because it is profit-able at market prices, or select those projects which are only profitable because of the aid. As there are many possibilities for manipulating profitability, farmers may be able to submit applications which sound rea-sonable for the bureaucrat, but are manipulated in order to get the aid. Striewe *et al.* (1996) found that nearly all so-called farm improvement plans looked very similar when the application for support was submitted, but four years after the investments had taken place, more than half of the farms earned a neg-ative rate of return on total capital. The variance in the income of supported farms was about the same as that for those not supported. The general message is that investment is risky by nature: nobody knows

with certainty all those factors which determine future returns. The investor will normally take the risk into account, selecting those projects where the expected return includes a risk premium. If there is financial support for specific investment projects, it is most likely that the ones selected will be riskier or have smaller private returns in the absence of support.

Moreover, the rationale for investment aid has to be questioned. The private return on agriculture could be lower than the economic return, i.e. return from the point of view of the society at large, if there were either a divergence in the marginal productivity of investment, due to external effects, or the shadow prices[16] for the products were higher than their market prices. However, shadow prices are generally lower than market prices for agricultural products in the EU, indicating a negative divergence between economic and financial returns.[17] Hence, investment aid is not suitable for dealing with policy failure.[18]

In addition, the co-financing of the investment aid by the EU and the member states can contribute to a false selection of investment projects. Take the case of milk. The shadow price for the EU as a whole is lower than the domestic market price and even lower than the world market price as the EU is a large player on the world markets. The world market price was occasionally one-third of the EU price, by about 40% in most years. Hence, the EU should promote milk production only if the investment would pay the marginal revenue received for exports. However, there were periods when the EU actually paid more for the imported feeds than it received for the processed milk produced using the imported feed. Hence, the economic return for investment in milk production was negative for the EU as a whole. Nevertheless, EU member states may have been interested in spending EU finances to support investment in milk production: if EU countries are selfish, they would not be inter-ested in what the EU received on the world market or in how much export restitution had to be paid. Instead, they may calculate the return from their point of view. Actually the shadow price for milk is much higher for an individual EU country than for the EU as a whole. The country has only to pay a small pro-portion of export restitutions, but receives the EU intervention price for additional production of milk. Hence, there is a divergence in shadow prices, and the divergence is the highest for most protected com-modities. Therefore, support of investment in milk production was more distorted than for less protected agricultural goods. If the farmer's financial rate of return (R_F) is compared with the rate of return for a member country (R_M) and for EU (R_{EU}), the following ranking can be made: $R_F > R_M > R_{EU}$. As the distortion is the highest for most protected products, the farm investment program had a built-in incentive to increase production of the highest protected products, increasing the exportable surplus even more. Thus, investment aid has contributed to the problems on the milk market which led to the introduction of the quota. Policy makers reacted to this system of incentives by exclusion of investment in surplus production. After 1984, when the quota system was instituted, investment aid was focused on milk production, in particular for building cowsheds. However, the belief that these investments would not have production effects is not well-founded. Money is, of course, fungible. If the farmers would build cowsheds anyway, some of their private money would be released for other purposes, pushing investment up.

Investment aid might be more positively assessed if it were to lower the pressure to adjust the sector and to increase farmers' income. Low income in agriculture is mainly due to wrong expectations at the time of decision to start an agricultural career and lack of sufficient factor mobility. Investment aid does not heal these market failures. In contrast, granting aid for young farmers may even raise expectations, resulting in a higher number of entrants and augmenting the sector's future income. The actual problem in agriculture is not that investment is too low (sectors with below average return tend to lower investment in order to adjust production capacities downwards), but low income for labour.

The first directives were replaced by a new ten-year structural plan in 1985. The rationale for this was the realization by then that the surpluses generated at the time did not justify a policy of trying to solve the plight of small farms through increased output, and that the slower rates of economic growth being experienced then made it more difficult for farmers to find alternative employment. Thus the new plan shied away from fundamental changes in the farm structure and put emphasis on cost reductions and quality improvement, and at the same time the aim of achieving incomes for the sector comparable with those in non-agricultural occupations was abandoned altogether. In other words, the aim was no longer to transform small farms into larger ones to enable them to obtain higher incomes, but rather to make it possible for small

farmers to survive with a reasonable quality of living. In support of the plan, an average of 420 million ECUs per annum was to be provided over the period 1985–1994 and a further annual sum of 270 million ECUs was to be made available for schemes aimed at improving agricultural marketing and processing. Despite these aspirations, total budgetary expenditure on guidance was 3.7 billion ECUs in 1996, or about 4.5% of the total budget and under 10% of total expenditure on the CAP. However, since the adoption of new proposals first made in *Agenda 2000* (CEU, 1997b), which are discussed in Section 20.5 this aspect of the CAP has been subsumed within the structural funds of the EU general budget (see Chapter 19), and given enhanced support funding.

At the end of the 1980s, new emphasis was placed on fundamental reform of the structural funds. In this reform, funds for EC structural policy were substantially increased in order to reduce the differences between individual regions, with particular attention given to least-favoured regions. In addition, the utilization of resources in the various funds (detailed in Chapter 19, Sections 19.6.1 and 19.6.2 and Chapter 20, Section 20.3.2) was to be better coordinated – and harmonized with the national activities of the individual member states (Henrichsmeyer and Witzke, 1994, p. 556). This means that the intensive interlinking between the EC, the federal government, and the federal states in agricultural structure policy increased substantially.

For the EU Structural Fund, seven targets were given priority: four so-called geographical targets and three so-called horizontal goals (see Chapters 19 and 22, Sections 19.6.2, 19.9 and 22.3.2). Responsibility for implementation of the programme lay with the federal states. The EC Commission was, however, represented in the committees that also evaluated the programme. Only coordination, communication, and evaluative functions were given to the federal government. While the federal states implemented parts of their aid programmes via the joint tasks GAK and 'improving the regional agricultural structure', the federal government participated in financing, providing 60% and 50% of the expenses, respectively (WB-BML, 1998, p. 17).

Following the Agenda 2000 reform, structural aid was streamlined; instead of seven categories of objectives, there will be only three from the year 2000 on. The agricultural structure policy will be integrated into a comprehensively organized policy of 'supporting the development of rural areas' (Thoroe, 2000, p. 196/97).

20.7   The future of the CAP

As already described, there have been specific driving forces behind the evolution of the CAP. These forces are likely to become stronger in the near future. Actually the Commission has already responded to the pressure to reform with the new *Agenda 2000* (CEU, 2000a), where new guidelines for the future CAP were stated.

The Commission had already launched a new model of European agriculture which should be based on two pillars, the traditional market and price policy, now called the first pillar, and a policy component for rural areas and the environment, termed the second pillar. The Commission had outlined the guidelines for the new model in its proposal of March 1998. The main features of this model are supposed to be:

- a competitive agricultural sector able to participate on world markets without being oversubsidized;
- a continued commitment to ensure a fair standard of living to the agricultural community, notably through stabilizing farm incomes;
- production methods in tune with consumer demands, and in harmony with the environment;
- diverse methods of production, rich on tradition, which are not just output oriented, but seek to maintain the visual amenity of our countryside, as well as the vibrant and active rural communities that generate and maintain employment;
- a simpler, more understandable agricultural and rural development policy which makes clear dividing lines between the decisions that have to be taken jointly and those that are best left in the hands of the member states; and

an agricultural and rural policy which makes clear that the expenditure it involves is justified by the services which the society expects farmers to provide. The Council had accepted this idea and included it in the *Agenda 2000* decisions. Since then the CAP has been based on the two pillars.

The new proposal submitted by the Commission in January 2003 follows this basic idea and, consequently asks for a detailed amendment of the legislation of specific market organizations. Of course, these changes will become effective only if the Council agrees. However, based on past experience, one can expect that the direction of future changes will be as envisaged by the Commission, even if the Council may ask for some modifications or delays the implementation.

20.7.1 Changes in direct payments

The present system of direct payments described above showed the main problems to be one of payments not being well targeted to the needs of agricultural operators and the other that it is less than certain that the EU can continue with these payments after the agreement in the Doha Round. The EU negotiated a waiver in the Uruguay Round based on the argument that the payments had to be used in order to compensate for the price cuts, thus to mitigate the pressure for adjustment. Trading partners agreed and classified these payments as 'blue box', indicating that a final decision had to be made in the next negotiation round. The argument for adjustment aid is not any better founded than the first price cuts of more than 10 years ago (see above). Moreover, the Commission is quite convinced that the general public may question the rationale for the payments, particularly in times of a budget crisis. Hence, the EU proposed an amendment of market organizations in January 2003 and the Council accepted a somewhat modified system in its June meeting. The agreed change in direct payments is the most important element of the proposal. For clarity, we begin by presenting the proposal and its effects, then consider the actual decision.

The proposed change had two elements. First, all payments received in the past by a claimant together with those foreseen for the reduction in milk prices, would be aggregated. Second, future payments would be based on past payments given to the farm operator irrespective of production. The new payments would be called 'Single Farm Payments'. The amount of payment an operator received would be related to the area which qualified for payments in the past and to that for pasture and fodder. The entitlement to payments would be restricted to cultivators of land and could be transferred with or without land, but in the latter case only in the form of sale. The buyer of the entitlement would have to be a farmer who cultivated land that had not been eligible for payment, i.e. land formerly used for crops originally not entitled to payments (e.g. potatoes, sugar beets and vegetables), land which had lost the entitlement due to a former transfer of the entitlement without land transfer or land which had been bought or rented without an entitlement for payments.

The new system would have implied significant changes in the effects of payments. It would have minor production consequences since the gross margin of production would not be affected by the payments. Hence, production decisions would have been largely guided by market prices. Minor production effects would have arisen as payments would have continued to have a positive effect on the incomes of farm operators, hence may have influenced the decision to continue with farming, even if overall income could have been raised by moving to another occupation. It is well known that farmer mobility is restricted; farmers do respond less to higher income incentives in other occupations, but do so to pressure to adjust if agricultural income is not sufficient to make up a reasonable living. Hence, payments, even if not linked to production or factors of production, will likely have effects on the farm structure, thus on production. Actually, the remaining production effects of the proposed system of direct payments would likely be negative. Those farmers who would have continued farming because of the payments would be those whose market income fell short of their opportunity cost. These farmers are generally sub-marginal suppliers, with below average productivity of land and animals. Were they to give up production, land would be used by more productive operators, leading to an overall increase in production.

The change in the direct payments was supposed to improve the EU position in the Doha Round. The new payments could have been classified as green as they would have no or only minor positive production effect. Hence, it should have been less difficult to dissolve the present 'blue box' payments.

The proposal highlights the Commission's reputation as the 'guardian of the Treaty' (see Chapter 3 and above). According to the allocation of competence, the Commission should defend Community interests, whereas the members of the Council of Ministers should represent the national interests. Thus, the cooperation between Commission and Council should in theory balance national with Community interests. It is therefore no surprise that the Council regularly modifies Commission proposals and also tries to secure unanimous agreement, even when majority voting is allowed by the treaties.

As expected, the Council agreed on the principles, but modified the proposal. There will be a Single Farm Payment and decoupling will become standard. However, although the system is supposed to be instituted in 2006, member countries may start somewhat later, and may even opt to decouple only up to half the national payments. Moreover, countries are free to impose a tax on the sales of the entitlements for payments. Hence, the only partially decoupled payments will still determine the use of land and the production of beef. The tax on transfers of entitlements will affect land prices since the tax influences the choice to sell the entitlement or to transfer it with land. In the latter case, no tax is imposed making this alternative more attractive. Hence, a rental contract will result in a higher rent as the owner and the tenant may share the forgone tax; a new tenant may have to pay a higher rent. Consequently, the agreed system does not shift the payments to the present tillers, which is what the Commission's proposal would have done.

The submitted changes may prove to be the most significant ever to the CAP. The pattern of agricultural grain and oilseeds production could change significantly, unless the member countries use safeguards. The latter allows them to introduce specific instruments if the new system of payments should lead to a significant change in regional production. Thus the effort to change regional production in accordance with comparative advantage is mitigated by the introduction of safeguards. Many EU farmers' regions can produce grain profitably only because of the present production-linked direct payments. Without this link, production will certainly drop significantly in both the medium and long terms. The short-term effect might be small as farmers gross margins may still be positive even if profits are too small to allow for an adequate remuneration to capital and land. However, in the long-term the use of land will change in the direction of less capital-intensive products. This will be accompanied by a significant change in farm sizes; many of the present farms will not generate a sufficient market income, hence farms will have to increase size or switch to part-time farming.

The change in the quantity and structure of production could be the most pronounced in milk. The Council has decided to lower butter intervention prices by 25% over 2004–2007 and to lower the intervention price for skimmed milk powder by 15% over the same period. Moreover, the intervention quantities for the two products will be limited to maximum quantities far below past purchases. The loss in income will be compensated by about one half through direct payment. Not many farms will be able to generate reasonable profit under these conditions. It may well be that farmers may continue with milk production for a while as gross margins are still positive, but re-investments would not be profitable. However, investment on large farms may still be profitable.

20.7.2 Emphasis on environmental effects

The new agreement asks for a restructuring of direct payments. First, farmers should only receive payments if they meet specific requirements concerning the production methods. The term used for this requirement is 'cross compliance'. Moreover, an increasing part of the present payments should be used for remunerating production that is friendly to the environment. The term used for this rescheduling of payments is 'modulation'. The Council decided that member countries may retain 25% of the amount budgeted for direct payments for the application of cross compliance. The Commission and Council strongly believe that the focus of the CAP should be changed from the first pillar, that of market and price policy, to the second, of support of rural areas and the environment. Therefore, the amount spent on direct payments will be gradually reduced in favour of money spent on environmental programmes. Modulation will become obligatory from 2005 onwards.

The decisions concerning direct payments clearly support the view that the Commission has succeeded in moving to a more rational policy. It is most likely that future changes will lead in the same direction. Consequently, the economic costs of the CAP could go down provided not too many loopholes are left for member countries to exploit. Furthermore, the agreement improves the EU's negotiating powers in the ongoing WTO round.

20.7.3 Decisions on the grain and milk market

The Council was not able to endorse the proposal concerning the grain and milk markets. The Commission had proposed a continuing liberalization of the grain market by further reducing prices, abolishing the monthly differentiation of intervention prices and by giving up rye intervention completely. The Council did not agree on a further reduction of grain prices, but accepted that intervention for rye will be given up and that monthly increments of intervention prices will be cut by half. Again, the decision indicates a further move to liberalization of the grain market.

The agreement on the milk market is outstanding. The changes in the intervention prices for butter and skimmed milk powder will likely reduce farm gate prices for milk by about 20%, a price reduction which was unthinkable only five years ago. The price decline might be even more as the quantity bought in by the intervention agency has been limited. Even if the income loss were partly compensated – by about 60% – the liberalization effect would be significant. This assessment remains valid even though the quota regime on the milk market has been extended up to the year 2014/2015. It is likely that the quota will become redundant at the reduced level of prices.

Thus, the direction of future changes seems clear: the gradual alignment of EU prices with world market prices. Indeed, the EU has no other alternative. It has signed an agreement with 49 least developed countries (LDCs) which allows them to export 'everything but arms' to the EU without any levies at the border (EBA initiative, see Chapters 24 and 25). If the EU were to continue with the present high rate of protection, in particular for milk, beef and sugar, the EU market might be flooded by imports from the LDCs. Moreover, the ongoing Doha Round will certainly require further CAP trade liberalization. Actually, the EU has submitted a proposal which contains a tariff reduction of 36% on average, a cut in export subsidies by 45% and a 55% decline in the Aggregate Measure of Support. The tabled compromise by Harbinson submitted in February 2003 demands even stronger changes in the EU trading regime.

It can be taken for granted that a further cut in tariffs and export restitutions will be part of the outcome of the Doha Round. However, it is not certain that the EU will succeed with the idea of remodelling European agriculture. There is support by some countries, particularly Japan, Norway, South Korea and Switzerland, but strong opposition by others, especially the United States and the Cairns Group. Indeed, scepticism is in order. There are strong indications that the European model of agriculture is only designed to open a new door for subsidizing farmers.

First, rural policies designed as part of the second pillar focus on agriculture, e.g. investment support for agriculture is provided in order to support rural areas. However, agriculture is not the main sector in most rural areas in the present EU. Second, it is aimed at enhancing the positive environmental effects of agriculture. However, there are policies in place which do not allow an identification of the environmental effects. These concern, for example, payments for 'best farming practices', which cannot be controlled as they are not well defined and cannot be testified. Third, it is surprising that EU member countries demand that the shift of payments from pillar 1 to pillar 2 should not lead to a change in the amount of total money a region receives from the EU. However, it should be quite clear that present regional outlays based on agricultural production patterns have no relationship to the need to create positive regional environmental effects. Anyhow, the new direction for the CAP may likely lead to further liberalization of agricultural trade, but it will most likely also lead to even a stronger regulation of farms. An auditing system has already been proposed. Even more controls than in the past will be needed in order to find out whether farmers did comply with the requirement imposed by environmental restrictions.

20.8   Conclusion

Since the prospects for change have already been discussed, the conclusion should be in the nature of an assessment of the CAP as it developed over the four decades or so since its inception. Before doing so, however, the reader needs to be reminded that the CAP support system has become rather complicated since it retains the original system for certain products while applying new methods for others and/or building them on top of the old.

Judged in terms of the need at the time of the formation of the EEC for a common policy, the CAP is obviously a success. Also, judged by its own objectives, the policy makers agree that it seems to have had several successes. However, it is questionable whether the CAP has contributed to its own objectives, let alone to its overall goal.

Any assessment of a policy cannot just focus on the development of specific variables, such as productivity or income. Instead, it has to be based on a comparison of 'with' and 'without' the CAP. The situation 'with' is easy to observe, not so the situation 'without', since one has to specify what alternative policy would have been in place (one would need a reference situation or base line; the anti monde discussed in Chapter 7). Second, the effects of this alternative policy would have to be analysed. The first point certainly contains value judgment as there is no consensus on how to specify the alternative policy; if analysts base their assessment on different reference systems, their results would necessarily differ. If, for example, agricultural policy makers claim that there is no alternative to the given policy, they implicitly assess present costs as zero.

Here, it is assumed that the alternative would have been a less protective CAP. What then would have been the effects of the CAP as per the objectives as mentioned in the Treaty and stated in Section 20.4?

1 *Effect on agricultural productivity.* Assume that there is a production function as mirrored in Figure 20.15. Given factor input F_0, production would be q_0, hence the productivity $\tan \alpha$. Reducing prices, the marginal suppliers had to leave the sector, leading to productivity $\tan \beta$. As $\tan \beta > \tan \alpha$, productivity at lower prices would have been higher. As price support reduced migration out of the sector, resulting in the survival of marginal farms, it affected productivity negatively. It should be noted that this reasoning holds even if the productivity increase in EU agriculture had been greater than in other countries and in excess of that for the industrial sectors.

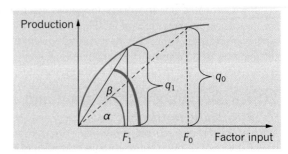

Figure 20.15 The effect of price support on productivity

2   *Effect on agricultural income.* There is no doubt
    that the total income generated in farming is
    higher with support prices than without.
    However, the important question is whether
    income per unit of factor is higher. Economists
    tend to argue that income per unit will be equal
    to the opportunity cost in the long run. Price
    support will increase income in the adjustment
    period, but after adjustment the income
    differential will be the same as at lower prices.
    Indeed, there is some evidence for this argument.
    Take the German case. Agricultural prices had
    to be lowered in 1967/1968 when the common
    prices were set. Out migration increased and
    after the adjustment, agricultural income was
    again about 60% of average income, reflecting
    preferences. Higher prices do not only increase the
    income of those who are in the sector, they also
    influence decisions to take up farming. Hence,
    employment in agriculture depends on the price
    level. Thus, one has to take into consideration the
    transfer efficiency of price support. Part of the
    income lost by those in the non-agricultural sector
    results in dead-weight losses (negative welfare
    effects); another part is transferred through the
    market mechanism to others who were not
    targeted, in particular to landlords who are the
    main winners of price support.

3   *Effect on the stability of markets.* If the CAP was
    supposed to stabilize prices, it has been a great
    success. Intervention prices helped stabilize market
    prices. However, if the CAP was supposed to
    stabilize revenue or income, it has likely failed. A
    shortfall in production due to a bad harvest might
    be compensated by higher prices in free markets.
    Actually, the revenue would be less volatile if the
    price elasticity of demand were larger than 0.5 in
    absolute terms. Taking into account the demand
    for storage and for interregional trade it is likely
    that the elasticity is larger than 0.5.

4   *The effect on food security.* High support prices
    help to increase supply under normal conditions.
    However, food security only becomes a problem
    under abnormal conditions, such as natural
    catastrophes, wars or trade conflicts. Even if a
    country is able to feed its population under
    normal conditions, it is not at all sure that it will
    have the capacity to produce enough food in
    abnormal conditions. Take for example the case
    of milk production. It was stated above that EU

farmers partly produce the milk on the basis of
imported feed. Moreover, a lot of imported energy
is needed in order to supply the market. Had
trade ties fallen apart, these requirements would
not have been met. Hence, the present production
level does not allow one to conclude that food
would have been available in emergency situations.

5   *Effect on reasonable consumer prices.* It is quite
    clear that the CAP was, right from the very
    beginning, a burden for the European consumer.

Thus, the CAP has failed badly in trying to achieve
the policy objectives set for it. Has it done better in
attempting to achieve general economic or overall
policy objectives?

Concerning general economic objectives, the answer
is clearly in the negative, given the welfare effects
identified in the analysis above. Nevertheless, one has
to accept two positive political effects. The first is that
the CAP has mitigated the adjustment process, albeit
not in the most efficient way. It has been argued that
income transfers linked to the personal income situation of farmers would have been more efficient from
the viewpoint of economics. Lack of endorsement of
this alternative may be due to its political infeasibility:
policy makers can only select those alternatives which
are acceptable to the electorate. Of course, what the
electorate would accept would depend, among other
things, on information about the alternatives and
their effects. Perhaps economists should have been
more forceful addressing both the population at large
and politicians on this alternative, but could their
academic performance match farmers' political clout?

It was shown that there is a strong path-dependency
in agricultural policy since the decisions taken at
the outset have influenced ensuing development. It is
arguable whether policy makers had an alternative at
that time. Member countries had to be convinced to
give up their national autonomy in agricultural policy
and there was only little political leeway left: it was
necessary to incorporate agriculture in the European
integration scheme. Policy makers achieved this task
at the beginning, but the evolution has not much
improved the situation. National markets are not
well integrated because of quotas for milk, sugar and
tobacco, but also because of EU expenditure constraints,
such as limits on direct payments. Nevertheless, the
Commission proposals of January 2003, decided on
by Council in June, create hope for improvement, at
least with regard to the main pillar of the CAP.

NOTES

1. A rough indication of the average levels of income for farmers, relative to the incomes of those in other occupations, can be obtained by comparing the share of agriculture in total labour force and national output. Such a comparison indicates that at the time of the inception of the EEC, average agricultural incomes in the three largest countries (France, Germany and Italy) were only about 50% of those of other occupations (Ritson, 1973, p. 96).

2. 'Agricultural incomes have risen, but in France, Germany and Italy there is little evidence that the gap in incomes between agriculture and other occupations has diminished' (Ritson, 1973).

3. That is a country which has no impact on world prices.

4. A policy failure indicates that policy decisions have reduced welfare for the society at large.

5. 'Governance is defined as the manner in which power is exercised in the management of a country's economic and social resources for development', World Bank (1992) *Governance and Development*, Washington, D.C., p. 1.

6. It should be noted that the Council does not necessarily act in the interest of the majority of farmers. A minister might possibly act in the 'perceived' interest of farmers or in the interest of some special sections of the farming population.

7. It should be noted that the main features of most countries' protectionist policies have been set into place in periods of crises for agriculture; see Petit, 1985.

8. See for example the divergence in national interest for implementing the Set-aside programme (Koester, 1989, pp. 240–248).

9. It should be noted that article 33 of the Treaty neither mentions that policy makers are supposed to achieve a specific income objective nor states that prices should be set to contribute to the achievement of the income objective.

10. Expected external costs are defined as disadvantages to an individual due to constraints imposed on the individual by collective decisions.

11. This point is discussed in more detail and empirically supported in Koester and Tangermann (1990).

12. Indeed, this observation should not be surprising for students of public choice. Western democracies have strong pressure groups which strongly resist fundamental changes.

13. The invisible transfer, due to producer prices being higher than import or export parity prices, was before the CAP reform considerably higher than the visible transfer; see Ballenger, Dunmore and Lederer (1987).

14. This refers to a series of documents, which were submitted to the Council in December 1968. The first of these was called 'Memorandum on the Reform of Agriculture in the European Community', published in the *Bulletin of the European Community*, 1969, Supplement. The series is available in one volume as Le Plan Mansholt, Brussels, July 1969.

15. The average size of holding in the United Kingdom in 1970/1971 was more than three times that in the Original Six – and if one were to include farms of less than one hectare, the difference would be more extreme. The proposal aimed at farm sizes ranging from 80 to 120 hectares for crop farms, 40 to 60 cows per dairy farm and 800 to 1000 fattened pigs.

16. The shadow price is equal to the marginal willingness to pay or the marginal revenue for the society at large from one additional unit of a product. The shadow price is equal to the world market for a small country which has the opportunity to import or to export. If the economy is relatively large, the EU case, the shadow price is equal to the marginal expenditure on one unit of imports or marginal revenue from one unit of exports. As the EU is a main exporter of most temperate zone agricultural products, the marginal shadow prices are even lower than the world market prices for most commodities.

17. The financial return is the rate of return from the point of view of the private investor. If there is a difference between the economic and private return, it is called a divergence.

18. A policy failure says that governmental interference in the markets leads to sub-optimal situations.

Chapter 21

The Common Fisheries Policy

ELLA RITCHIE AND ALI EL-AGRAA

21.1 Introduction

The case of the Common Fisheries Policy (CFP) illustrates both the potential and the limitations of EU policy. Fisheries are an inherently difficult sector to manage. Issues such as competing views on property rights and tensions between scientists, fishers and conservationists are well known in fishing communities across the world. The crisis in most major fish stocks has heightened tensions in debates over conservation and management of stocks. Key aspects of the sector such as trade, processing and ownership are becoming increasingly internationalized but this has been a difficult process in a sector where individualism and a strong sense of community runs deep. One of the challenges for fisheries' regimes is to compete effectively in the global market but at the same time to cushion communities from social costs and economic decline.

Many analysts and policy makers argued that there was a certain logic to incorporating fisheries into the EU. Most fishing activity is conducted across and beyond national territorial waters and fish take no notice of national boundaries. Fish such as mackerel, herring and cod often migrate hundreds of miles during their life cycles. They may spawn in one area, become juveniles in another and reach maturity in a third. Hence the actions of one fishing community, such as the catching of juveniles, can have quite dramatic consequences for the fishing opportunities of other communities or states. About 90% of North Sea cod, for example, spend their first year in waters off the coast of Denmark, Germany and Holland but by the time that they are three years old and ripe for catching most of them will have migrated to British territorial waters. If successful, the conservation of fish stocks could in the long run be a positive sum game for all the member states in a situation of declining resources. As Shackleton (1983) points out 'the condition seemed to exist for experts to take a

problem and produce a rational assessment of what was the common interest of the Community without vital interests blocking a settlement'.

However, an analysis of the CFP shows how difficult it is to design a policy for the management and regulation of a Common European pond and the 'problem' of the CFP is one that has bedevilled the EU since the inception of the policy in 1970. By the early 2000s, the policy had reached a crisis point in that it had failed to manage dwindling fish stocks, to respond to wider environmental concerns or to satisfy competing national interests. A number of fish stocks, including North Sea cod, were in a state of collapse and the fishing fleet had declined significantly. The policy lacked legitimacy because it imposed regulations in a highly diverse sector where there were no strong norms of obligation to a commonly accepted set of rules or institutions. There is a long chain of command from the politicians and scientists in Brussels to the fishers who are operating the policies on the high seas. One of the major problems facing the CFP is that many fishers do not comply with the detailed rules and regulations emanating from Brussels. Opinion is divided about whether the solution to this problem of non-compliance is greater uniformity and centralization or a move towards a more regionalized form of CFP which would bring the institutions closer to the stakeholders. The European Commission (hereafter, simply Commission) has itself acknowledged that one reason for non-compliance may be that the stakeholders do not feel sufficiently involved in the policy-making process. At the same time it has made strenuous efforts to try and ensure more effective methods of compliance across the EU by, for example, establishing Commission inspectors.

This chapter will begin by setting out the background to the development of the CFP. It will go on to outline the main policy objectives and nature of the policy-making process. It will then outline the recent reforms of the CFP. Finally, it assesses the institutional and governance issues associated with delivering a more effective CFP, which will be able to address the challenges of fish stock collapse and wider environmental concerns.

21.2   Background

The fisheries sector of the EU is small in terms of budget and of employment. Even when associated activities were taken into account, the sector involved no more than 1% of the entire EU economy in the early 1970s and less than 0.5% by the late 1990s. Employment in the sector has been in steep decline decreasing from 1.2 million in 1970 to 263 019 in 1995 and to an estimated 152 661 in 2002. Although fisheries are only a very tiny sector within the EU economy, the activity tends to be concentrated in peripheral regions where there is often little alternative employment. The sector as a whole is in steep decline. For example, in 2001 the value of UK landings at home and abroad was worth £423 million as compared to £661 million in 1998. The UK is the third largest EU producer of catches (13.7% of EU total), coming behind Spain, which produces the most fish, and Denmark, which catches the most. Table 21.1 gives the distribution of fish catch in 1999 between the EU member states.

About 38% of the total UK fisheries production is now by aquaculture, which is about average for the EU. Aquaculture is a growing industry worldwide and to some extent it compensates for the decline of sea fisheries. Even so, the EU as a whole imports more fish than it produces, with only Denmark, Spain and the Netherlands having positive trade balances in fishery products in 1999.

The industry and its representatives tend to be highly fragmented. In any one country fishermen are divided amongst types of fishing (long distance or inshore) and structure of ownership (individual, family, conglomerate). Modernization has been asymmetric across the EU and there is a growing gulf between artisanal fishing and the highly technological deep sea fleets. As with agriculture, the diversity of the sector adds to the difficulty of constructing an effective common policy. This has been compounded by the political salience of the issue.

The dangerous and to some extent romantic nature of the occupation, the strong sense of community and, in recent years, the linking of fishing not only to regional but also in some cases to national identity has meant that fishing interests often carry disproportionate weight within the EU.

Fisheries were included in the definition of agricultural products in the Treaty of Rome (see Chapter 20). The two industries do have much in common. Both are subject to price instability; in the case of fisheries this is because of the highly specialized human and physical capital in the industry making its short-term supply highly inelastic and also because fish has rather low price elasticity. Both have low-income elasticities for their products and both are prone to random shocks from natural causes over which there is little control. During the 1950s both sectors were made up of large numbers of small self-employed producers. Both policies are set within an international

Table 21.1 Fish Catch, 1999

Country	Percentage share of total catch
Austria	0.01
Belgium	0.53
Denmark	21.99
Finland	2.28
France	10.18
Germany	3.75
Greece	2.14
Ireland	5.05
Italy	4.63
Netherlands	8.05
Portugal	3.43
Spain	18.76
Sweden	5.50
United Kingdom	13.70

regulatory framework and face the challenges of internationalization, globalization, and increasing environmental and consumer pressure. There are, however, fundamental differences between the two sectors. Agriculture is about managing excess while fisheries is about managing scarcity. Fisheries interests are much more diffuse and poorly organized at the EU level. Finally, and most importantly, the nature of ownership of resource is much more fiercely contested in fisheries than in agriculture.

The development of the CFP followed a pattern typical for many other policy areas: authority for the policy was vested in the Treaty of Rome, general principles were laid down some years later and the detailed aspects of the policy were negotiated subsequently over many years with successive enlargements and the changing international framework acting as catalysts for policy change. In the early 1960s, fish stocks were relatively evenly spread among the six member states and there was little international regulation of fishing. By the mid-1960s, the French and Italian governments became aware that their industries were becoming increasingly uncompetitive, especially compared to the German fishing fleet, and began to put pressure on the Community to devise structural aid for their fisheries. However, the real drivers for the establishment of the CFP were changes in the international situation and the impending enlargement to include Denmark, Ireland, Norway and the UK. We will now turn to a more detailed examination of these two factors.

Historically, states had ownership over a narrow coastal strip (typically 3–4 miles) and competed for stocks on the High Seas which were deemed to be common property. This practice was workable because stocks were plentiful and 'belonged' to no one until they were caught. The increasing technical capacity of ships in the post-Second World War period and the growing awareness of threats to stocks meant that the regime of the High Seas began to be questioned. During the 1960s, there was an agreement that any vessel could fish anywhere outside a 12-mile coastal limit, which was reserved for the country whose coast bordered this zone or to states which had historically fished there. However, prompted by unilateral action by Iceland in 1970 claiming exclusive fishing rights within 50 miles of its coast, the United Nations decided in 1976 that any state could establish an Exclusive Economic Zone (EEZ) in waters up to 200 nautical miles from its coastline.

This policy (eventually ratified in 1982 under the United Nations Convention on the Law of the Sea) had dramatic implications for the EC countries, most of which had traditionally fished far from their shores in deep-sea waters. The EC responded by setting up its own EEZ in January 1977. Once the decision had been taken by the EC to set up an EEZ, policy makers had to evolve a system for distributing the stock amongst the member states (for further details see Wise, 1996).

The second factor precipitating the development of a CFP was the impending enlargement of the Community to include the fish-rich nations of Denmark, Ireland, Norway and the UK. These countries had large fishing stocks and the existing states were obviously keen to establish the principle of 'equal access' to fish rich community waters before enlargement took place. A policy was quickly hatched so that it became part of the *acquis communautaire* which the new states had to accept on joining. In 1970, an agreement set the guidelines for a common structural policy and established the right to equal conditions of access to fishing grounds. It also laid down some provisions for conservation measures and for financial aid for the restructuring of the industry. While the UK, Denmark and Ireland strenuously opposed the equal access principle, the issue was not high enough on the political agenda for it to jeopardize the long awaited and much disputed Community membership. In the end, Norway declined to join the Community, partly because it feared the effects of the equal access principle on its fisheries (see Chapter 2). The CFP did not fully come into force until 1983 when it was successfully negotiated because of the impending accession of Spain and Portugal. These two countries had larger fleets than any of the existing member states and had also lost much of their long distance fishing opportunities in the 1970s. However, pressure from the UK, France and Ireland meant that Spain and Portugal were prevented from having equal access to Community waters until 2002.

The current CFP has evolved over the years in response to a number of factors: biological (the condition of stocks), economic (the single market and trade liberalization) and political (the protection of national interests and enlargement) – see Wise (1996). The CFP and its interpretation by the European Court of Justice (ECJ) is guided by two key principles: equal access to fishing grounds within the common pond (with the exception of 6 and 12 mile coastal strips and special derogations such as the North Sea box around Shetland); and relative stability which fixed the rights of member states to access to waters. Relative stability, which is a highly contentious principle within the CFP and which, in fact, distorts the principle of equal access, is based on historic fishing patterns and special interests. For example, in 1983 the UK received an additional cod quota to compensate for the losses from the Icelandic stocks which it had traditionally fished.

The ECJ has over the years maintained the principle of non-discrimination in fisheries in that it has upheld the right of non-nationals to buy vessels (and hence a proportion of fishing quota) from other member states. Typically Spanish (and in some cases Dutch) owners have bought UK vessels thus entitling them, for example, to fish hake in Irish waters and land their catches directly into ports in NW Spain. This practice is highly controversial and states such as the UK and France have retaliated by tightening up on licence regulations. The ECJ has now stipulated that there needs to be an economic link between coastal communities and vessels which have access (through flags of convenience) to national quota by insisting that a certain percentage of fish caughtis landed in the home port. In practice, policing such complex arrangements

has, however, proved very difficult. The case of 'quota hoppers' is very interesting because it is an example of a free market principle at work within fisheries and shows the tension between supranational rules and national identities (Lesquesne, 2000b).

The main objective of the CFP until the 1990s was to manage catches so as to ensure an equitable access to supplies across member states rather than to promote the welfare of the marine system. As McCormick (2001) notes, fisheries have been viewed more as an economic good than as a natural resource. Conservation of resources was not an issue until 1983 and it is only since the mid-1990s, under conditions of severe decline in the stocks, that there has been any serious attempt to develop an ecosystem approach to stock management. This shift towards a more precautionary approach to fisheries was also influenced by the changing international agenda and the growing importance of environmental groups.

The search for equity and uniformity at the European level led to a highly complex system of rules and regulations. Superficially, the policy is marked by its centralization with a reliance on regulations rather than directives (see Chapter 3, Section 3.4). In practice however there is a great deal of diversity, unevenness of implementation and of enforcement across the member states.

21.3   Policy objectives

The CFP negotiated in 1983 gave the EU considerable leeway to prescribe detailed sets of rules for four main policy areas: market, structure, conservation and external relations.

Under the *marketing* policy, fisheries is subject to similar principles that apply to agriculture, including common marketing standards, the institution of a price support system and the establishment of producers organisations (POs). The POs play a key role in many states. For example, in the UK, the nineteen POs decide the allocation of quotas and the granting of licenses and permits. The marketing policy is commonly viewed as one of the few successful parts of the policy and has been little modified over the years. Until recently, consumer interests have not played a large part in the CFP, but since the mid-1990s there has been growing pressure on the industry to deliver fresh and wholesome fish. This is part of a changing

culture within the food industry in general but also reflects the activities of pressure groups in the area. An example of a more environmentally orientated outlook is the initiative between the multi-national Unilever and the World Wide Fund for Nature to set up the Marine Stewardship Council. This Council supports more responsible fishing by giving certification to processors who restrict their purchases to fish that are being managed sustainably. Although this has been criticized by some as a marketing gimmick, the Council has been quite successful in raising the public's awareness in campaigns such as 'Dolphin Friendly' Tuna.

Structural assistance for fishing was instituted in 1970 to 'promote harmonious and balanced development' of the industry and the 'rational use of marine resources' (Holden, 1994). Until the mid-1980s, the key aim of the structural policy was to invest in the

European fleet in order to catch more fish. However, over time the structural policy has become more flexible and more integrated with other aspects of the CFP. A growing awareness of the damage that overcapacity was having on Europe's fish stocks led in 1983 to the introduction of Multi Annual Guidance Programmes (MAGPs), designed to tie in the structural policy with the conservation policy. Increasingly, MAGPs are used to achieve effort limitation and reduction rather than fleet renewal. The targets put forward by the Commission under the MAGPs are vigorously debated, and invariably moderated upwards, by fisheries ministers, who are keen to ensure that the burden of cutback is as small as possible and is fairly distributed amongst the member states. Financial assistance for communities dependent on fisheries is now integrated into a single Financial Instrument for Fisheries Guidance, which forms part of the EU structural funds (see Chapters 19 and 22 for the sums involved, which are a very small percentage of the EU general budget). EU aid for fishing now systematically requires some form of co-funding from the member states. Financial assistance cannot be given if states have failed to meet their decommissioning targets.

The aim of *conservation policy*, which now forms the core of the CFP, is the responsible exploitation of living marine resources on a sustainable basis (Council Regulation No. 170/80 and 3760/92), taking into account its implications for the marine ecosystem and socio-economic implications for producers and consumers. There are two main policies for conservation: quotas and Total Allowable Catches (TACs); and technical instruments.

The TACs are now used as a means of conserving stocks although they were originally introduced as a means of allocating shares of available resources to the member states. The Commission bases its policy recommendations on information received from the International Council for the Exploration of the Seas (ICES). ICES scientists monitor stocks and their relative health by setting a precautionary level of spawning stock biomass (SSB – total weight of a species capable of reproducing) for each stock below which stocks should not be allowed to fall and a precautionary fishing rate above which the EU fleet should not go. Scientific evidence is often fiercely contested by fishermen on the grounds that it is out of date and is not sensitive enough to changing conditions. Fisheries science does depend on highly complex

biological and economic modelling. The interrelated life cycles of many fish (approximately 50% of fish are eaten by other fish or marine predators), the multispecies nature of most stocks and the complex nature of the ecosystem mean that predicting fish stock either through scientific data or through experiential knowledge remains fundamentally uncertain.

The advice provided by national teams reporting to ICES is assessed by ICES's Advisory Committee on Fisheries Management (ACFM) and the Commission's Scientific, Economic and Technical Fisheries Committee (STEFC). The Commission then tries to strike a balance between the advice of ICES and what is likely to be politically acceptable when it draws up proposals on quotas and TACs for the December meeting of the Council of Fisheries Ministers. Once the ministers have agreed the TACs, it is the responsibility of the member states to share out the quotas amongst their fishers and to enforce these quotas. A comparison of total allowable catches between 1998 and 2003 is given in Table 21.2.

A second element of conservation policy is technical conservation. These measures include: minimum mesh sizes; minimum landing sizes; by-catch limits; selective gear including square mesh panels and escape hatches for undersize fish; limits on length of beam and size of drift nets (as of 1 January 2003 a ban on drift nets for tuna swordfish has been in place to remove the negative impact on dolphins and other non-target species); tonnage/power regulations; and closure of fishing grounds for part of the year.

In *external relations* the Commission has the sole power to negotiate and conclude fisheries agreements with non-member states (see Chapter 24). These include reciprocal arrangements over fishing rights, access to surplus stock, access to stock in return for financial compensation, and more recently the development of joint enterprises. The EU currently has agreements in place with some 30 countries (for more details see Lesquesne, 2000a). The external policy of the EU has become much more important with the shrinking of the Community's own resource. It has recently come under heavy criticism from environmentalists and from the European Parliament (EP) because it has been seen as the exporting of the fisheries problem of the EU by exploiting the resources of developing countries. There is little co-ordination between the external aspect of the CFP and the EU's International Development policy (see Chapter 25).

Table 21.2 A comparison of total allowable catches, 1998–2003

1998

Country	Cod	Haddock	Whiting	Saithe	Plaice	Sole	Bluefin Tuna	Mackerel	Herring	Sandeel
Belgium	5 525	1 200	1 765	50	6 595	4 132	No TAC	470	7 460	No TAC
Denmark	84 754	10 330	10 430	4 020	30 690	2 245	for 1998	12 485	141 560	for 1998
Germany	38 234	4 280	1 705	10 805	5 210	1 360		20 080	137 420	
Spain	11 052	–	2 800	–	120	770		28 870	130	
France	26 242	23 060	30 820	35 250	5 355	9 080		14 740	27 740	
Greece	–	–	–	–	–	–		–	–	
Ireland	8 535	6 460	13 010	2 920	3 175	670		65 300	68 760	
Italy	–	–	–	–	–	–		–	–	
Netherlands	14 725	680	3 875	100	34 330	15 155		30 070	73 410	
Portugal	2 327	–	2 640	–	120	1 245		5 960	130	
United Kingdom	70 754	88 710	38 050	12 565	28 295	2 813		180 980	120 350	
Finland	1 931	–	–	–	–	–		–	127 220	
Sweden	34 966	930	440	550	950	55		4 230	205 600	
Not allocated	250	–	–	–	–	–		–	–	
Total EU quota	**299 325**	**135 650**	**105 535**	**66 260**	**114 840**	**37 525**		**363 185**	**909 780**	

2003

Country	Cod	Haddock	Whiting	Saithe	Plaice	Sole	Bluefin Tuna	Mackerel	Herring	Sandeel
Belgium	1 135	538	686	130	5 563	4 141	–	474	8 752	–
Denmark	30 324	4 683	2 277	6 842	29 847	895	–	28 398	118 869	938 517
Germany	18 556	2 441	429	21 719	4 383	1 074	–	20 384	73 530	–
Spain	8 951	–	2 240	–	75	611	6 383.7	28 866	41	–
France	9 301	9 795	24 962	59 960	4 817	6 967	6 298	14 943	34 317	–
Greece	245	–	–	–	–	–	473.5	–	–	–
Ireland	2 811	3 140	9 684	2 865	2 161	488	–	66 300	32 848	–
Italy	–	–	–	–	–	–	5 264.7	–	–	–
Netherlands	2 687	316	1 098	223	28 794	12 424	–	30 507	81 866	–
Portugal	3 629	–	1 360	–	75	998	752.3	5 963	41	–
United Kingdom	22 944	39 393	11 369	18 450	23 044	2 608	–	183 721	92 121	24 355
Finland	1 300	–	–	–	–	–	–	–	58 710	–
Sweden	17 301	1 205	262	1 922	1 089	11	–	4 488	87 858	–
Not allocated	100	–	–	–	–	–	59.5	–	500	31 139
Total EU quota	**119 284**	**61 511**	**54 367**	**112 111**	**98 848**	**30 217**	**19 231.7**	**384 044**	**589 453**	**994 000**

21.4 Policy process

Fisheries policy making is characterized by a multi-level system of governance ranging from the international arena, where a legal framework is set by the international fisheries regime to the European, national, regional and local levels which are responsible for the implementation and much of the monitoring of policy. At the core of this policy making process lies the supranational institutions of the EU – the EP, ECJ, Commission and Council of Ministers (see Chapter 3). The EP only has a consultative role in CFP, but its Fisheries Committee is becoming an increasingly important player in shaping policy and in liaising between fishers and the Commission. The ECJ has also continually been active in fisheries policy with landmark decisions made upholding principles of non-discrimination in the fisheries sector. Historically, the key interests in the fisheries sector have been fishers and industry representatives, but increasingly environmental groups and consumers are entering the policy terrain.

We will now turn to a brief discussion of the policy making process for fisheries. Policy initiatives come from the Fisheries Directorate General (DG XIV; now simply DG Fisheries; see Chapter 3) in the Commission which makes proposals against a background of scientific advice provided by international scientists. The Fisheries DG will typically consult with its advisory committee, regional fisheries interests, and other Directorates in the Commission. This policy process is very complicated and can be inaccessible to many fishers who are not part of an established policy community. Proposals from the Fisheries Directorate are typically watered down in the Council of Ministers where states advocate on behalf of their fishermen. Policy within the Fisheries Council is largely decided on the basis of qualified majority voting (QMV; see Chapters 3 and 27), leading to a series of trade-offs and bargains amongst the states.

The final policy emerging from the Council seldom reflects the scientists' advice because it is bargained and traded through an intense political process (see Ritchie and Zito, 1998; Payne, 2000; Lesquesne, 2000a; Holden, 1994). The example of the evolution of a policy to cope with the 2002 stock crisis illustrates this point.

When it came to advising on the TACs for 2003, the ICES and STEFC recommended a moratorium on the cod fishery and on the cod-related fisheries of whiting and haddock. In view of the likely detrimental social and economic impact, the Commission recommended to the Council a substantial reduction in cod and related TACs. The Council, at the December 2002 meeting, set the 2003 TACs for the three stocks at substantially higher levels than the Commission had recommended. The eventual decision (Council regulation (EC) No. 2341/2002 of December 2002) saw a 45% cut in the cod TAC, haddock cut by 50%, whiting by 60% and plaice by 5%. The CFP reform and the management of the stock crisis at the end of 2002 were marked by interventions from, among others, the British Prime Minister Tony Blair and the French President Jacques Chirac on behalf of their fishermen.

As mentioned above, once the policy recommendations are made they are passed on to the member states who then share out the nationally allocated quotas. Member states are also responsible for the implementation and monitoring of a large number of technical and conservation measures such as the days-at-sea regulations, tonnage and gear size regulations, minimum landing sizes and vessel capacity. Responsibility for the implementation of policy falls to a variety of national, regional and local agencies across the member states. This complexity of institutional arrangements adds to unevenness of policy implementation across the EU. One of the key difficulties in the CFP is ensuring that fishers comply with the rules. There are a number of reasons for non-compliance. Firstly, some operators ignore the regulations because adherence may be too costly (especially when profit margins are small), too complex to work out, too bureaucratic to comply with or quite simply too difficult to implement in small craft. Secondly, many regulations have technical inconsistencies. Finally, many rules are simply ignored or flouted.

There are about as many ways of flouting the rules in the CFP as there are rules to keep. Three key problems are the landing of illegal or 'black' fish, discarding fish back into the sea and the misreporting of information. 'Black' fish are landed illegally and are not reported as landings at the designated port or are landed at other ports in the EU or outside the EU where no record is taken. Landing illegal fish not only depletes the stocks but also undermines the accuracy of stock and TAC predictions which is a particularly serious problem when stocks are in decline. A second problem is the discarding of fish that are not the right size or species. This is a major problem within the CFP with estimates of 50% for some catches. Discarded fish are a waste and also a major pollutant of the marine environment. Again discarding is to some extent caused by the rigidity of some CFP rules, such as the requirement of single species landings in some areas. The final key group of problems are misrecording or misreporting of stock or misdeclared species in stocks that are legally landed in other respects. All this creates havoc with the science upon which the decisions on quota allocations are mainly based.

This brief discussion of the policy process has shown that effective collective solutions and radical policy change are inhibited by national and political interests and that the policy structure leads to short term political interests shaping policy. One of the main problems is that while the Commission is trying to effect a medium-term policy, TACs and quotas have historically been negotiated annually. Another problem is that representatives of the fishing industry have little direct role in the decision-making process (Symes, 1995). Finally, procedures and guidelines are misunderstood, ignored, circumvented, falsified or merely flouted (Cann, 1998). One of the responses of the Commission to this problem has been to put forward more controls. This has served to further alienate the fishers.

21.5   Reform of the CFP?

The CFP has in many ways been in a process of reform since 1983 with the Mediterranean enlargement of the EU where a commitment was given to review the CFP and in particular the principle of relative stability in 2002. The promised reform and re-negotiation of the CFP was to some extent deflected by the emergency measures which had to be put in place to deal with the crisis in stocks[1] and many commentators were disappointed by the limited changes proposed. For many, this was particularly disappointing given the range of interests consulted in the drawing up of the reforms.

Between 1998 and 2002 there was an unprecedented period of consultation of stakeholders and the industry by the Commission. The consultation began with 350 questionnaires being sent out to representatives and organizations involved in fishing to all EU member states. This survey revealed a great deal of dissatisfaction with the CFP and emphasized problems with the conservation policy, enforcement difficulties and issues of equity. The Commission then organized a number of regional consultations (or road shows) across all the major fisheries regions in the EU, which led to more in-depth discussion of governance and institutional questions. In March 2001, on the basis of these two consultations, the Commission launched a consultative Green Paper on the reform of the CFP, with open invitations for evidence and comment. Over 300 submissions were made from stakeholders ranging across inshore and deep-water fishermen, processors, anglers, environmentalists,

food industry and consumer organizations. Finally, the Commission held a public hearing in Brussels in June 2001, which was attended by 400 delegates from across the EU. This hearing gave particular emphasis to whether the management of the CFP should be regionalized. The polarity of views expressed ranged from an anti-regionalist perspective adopted by the Spanish contingent to a proposal for a full regionalization of decision-making powers forwarded by the British, Dutch and Swedish delegates. Other key issues discussed which elicited mixed and polarized responses were the privatization of the CFP (through the introduction of a form of individual transferable quota) and issues of enforcement and compliance.

On the basis of the numerous consultation exercises and the Green Paper, the Commission drew up a reform of the CFP which was put to the Council in December 2002. The final document inevitably represented a compromise between the different views especially on highly charged issues such as regional management. On the issue of privatization of quotas, the Commission did seem to have taken note of the majority opinion during the consultation exercise by allowing flexibility at the level of the member state. Many of the traditional areas of the policy such as relative stability and special derogations remain for the time being, although after January 2003 Spanish, Portuguese and Finnish vessels are to be allowed to fish for unallocated quota in the North Sea.

There were a number of modest changes proposed for the governance and management of the CFP but no radical reform. We will now summarize the major changes proposed in the 2002 CFP reform package:

1 Central to the reform was a longer-term approach to fisheries management. In particular proposals were put forward for a multi-annual approach to management. This policy was accompanied by a subtle shift in the roles of the Commission and the Council, with the Commission being responsible for the policy after the agreement in the first year. This does give the Commission a great deal more weight in the process of allocation.

2 There was a renewed and stricter commitment to capacity reduction and control to bring the fleet in line with available resources. The importance of linking effort limitation to catch limitation was reinforced. There is an attempt at greater coherence to the policy with new regulations being introduced to establish an emergency fund to decommission vessels to help states which need to meet recovery plan targets for effort reduction – only those states that need to reduce their efforts by 25% or more will be eligible for funding.

3 The reforms also stressed the importance of ecosystem management and the precautionary principle. The objective of the CFP was to become to 'provide for sustainable exploitation of living aquatic resources and of aquaculture in the context of sustainable development, taking account of the environmental, economic and social aspects in a balanced manner'. Chapter 1, Article 2 (1), states that in order to meet the objectives, 'the Community will apply a precautionary approach to fisheries management and will aim at . . . a progressive implementation of an ecosystem based approach to fisheries management'.

4 There was considerable discussion about increasing the role for industry and stakeholders by setting up Regional Advisory Councils (RACs). These Councils were to include fishermen and scientists, representatives of other interests such as the aquaculture sector and environmental and consumer groups who have an interest in the sea area or zone concerned, national and regional authorities from any member state may also participate and the Commission may be represented at the meetings. The Councils can only advise the Commission on policy and have no policy-making role.

5 Conservation remained the cornerstone of the CFP following the reforms:
   ● Multi-annual recovery plans for stock outside safe biological limits initially for the North Sea and west-of-Scotland cod, but to be introduced for other stocks.
   ● Establishing targets for the successful exploitation of stocks.
   ● Limiting catches, fixing the number and type of fishing vessels authorized to fish.
   ● Limiting fishing effort.
   ● Adopting technical measures (fishing gear, catches that may be retained; delimiting zones which can be fished; protection of spawning areas; minimum size of landing).
   ● Establishing incentives to promote low impact fisheries.
   ● Conducting pilot projects on different types of fishing management techniques.

6 The objective of the structural policy remains as the achievement of a 'stable and enduring balance between the capacity of fishing fleets and the fishing opportunities available to them in and outside of Community waters'. The previous support system of FIFG will be retained but aid will be concentrated on scrapping fishing vessels. The old system of MAGPs has been replaced by a simpler system which gives more authority to the member states to achieve a balance between fleet capacity and fishing opportunities. Finally, member states were to be able to provide short-term aid to industry in emergency situations.

7 Fisheries Agreements are now called 'fisheries partnership agreements' this is to denote a new focus in external relations. These will 'allow for the provision of funds for the EU partners to advance fisheries development objectives, for the transfer of technical knowledge and capital to achieve sustainable development. This policy will (supposedly) make a contribution in developing countries to food security, poverty, alleviation and sustainable development.

8 The reforms outlined a whole series of measures designed to improve enforcement of community policy. New powers have been introduced at the community level to penalize states by reducing fishing quota if there is persistent non-compliance.

Following the main body of reforms presented to the Council in December 2002 there have been a number of other reforms in the environmental area. In addition to the cuts in TACs, effort limitations in the form of days at sea have also been introduced for many cod stocks in the North Sea. Fishermen can fish between 9 and 23 days per month depending on the type of stock and the gear used, although many fishermen argue that these limitations have little meaning because the TACs are so low that they have already caught them within the first fortnight of a month.

21.6   Conclusion

The CFP reform has not marked a radical shift in the way the EU organized fisheries. However, there are signs of change. A new level of governance has been introduced. A more consultative approach is in evidence and there is more coherence in the technical aspects of the policy. The CFP is placing more emphasis on a medium-term strategic management of stocks and the discourse of ecosystem management is becoming more common.

There are still a number of problems confronting EU fisheries – declining stocks, over-capacity (which will increase with Eastern Enlargement), cumbersome rules and regulations, which are poorly implemented and competing national interests. Solving these problems will require not only further technical reform and tough conservation methods, but an improved system of governance which has the support of its major stakeholders.

NOTE

1. We are grateful to Jenny Hatchard, research associate in the School of Geography, Politics and Sociology at the University of Newcastle upon Tyne for this point.

Chapter 22

Regional policy

HARVEY ARMSTRONG

Member states of the European Community are 'anxious to ensure their harmonious development by reducing the differences existing between the various regions and the backwardness of the less favoured regions'. (Preamble to the Treaty of Rome 1958)

In order to promote its overall harmonious development, the Community shall develop and pursue its actions leading to the strengthening of its economic and social cohesion. In particular the Community shall aim at reducing disparities between the various regions and the backwardness of the less favoured regions, including rural areas. (Article 130a, Single Europe Act 1986. Reaffirmed as Article 130a of the Treaty of Union 1992 and Treaty of Nice 2001)

These two quotations, 43 years apart, illustrate the strength of the EU's commitment to regional policy; a commitment which at first sight seems curious. The EU has aspirations to become something approaching a federal system. Regional policy of the type we know in Europe is, however, rarely found in long-established federal countries such as the USA, Canada and Australia. Understanding EU regional policy requires an appreciation of the uniqueness of the European situation, with its patchwork of independent nation states moving step-by-step towards closer economic, social and political relationships.

This chapter examines EU regional policy at an important moment in the step-by-step process of European integration. The EU in 2002 finally succeeded in implementing economic and monetary union (EMU) for 12 of the 15 existing member states. Hard on the heels of this success is the looming accession after 2004 of an initial group of ten Central and Eastern European countries (CEECs), as a result of which radical changes in EU regional policy are being considered.

The chapter begins with an examination of the case for having a EU regional policy running alongside the regional policies operated by each of the member state governments. This is followed by an overview of the ways in which economic integration can affect regional disparities. Attention will subsequently be concentrated on the EU regional policy which emerged from 1989 onwards in the aftermath of the single market. This policy was strengthened and reformed after the 1992 Treaty on European Union and again in 1999. The regional policy in place during the current 2000–2006 budgetary period is, nevertheless, in large part that which was created in the great reforms of 1989. Finally, the key issues which confront EU regional policy in the immediate future will be examined. In particular, the EU's possible regional policy responses to the challenges posed by Eastern Enlargement will be considered.

22.1 The case for a EU regional policy

Regional policy has always been controversial. It is undeniably interventionist. Those who distrust the competence of governments fear that regional policy penalizes successful businesses in prosperous regions while simultaneously encouraging unsuitable economic activities in the depressed regions. To those who hold this opinion, regional disparities are the inevitable outcome of the market system – something to be tolerated until market forces such as labour migration, capital investment and expanding trade combine to automatically revitalize low-wage depressed regions.

Supporters of regional policy are much more sceptical of the ability of market forces to solve long-standing regional problems. An array of arguments is marshalled in support of an active government and EU-led regional policy. The main arguments are as follows:

1 *Equity and 'fairness'*. Regional policy is seen as a way of ensuring that all parts of society can share in the benefits of a modern, growing economy.

2 *Extra income and production*. Regional policy is portrayed as being essential if underutilized resources – particularly unemployed labour – are to be drawn into productive use.

3 *Lower inflation and faster growth*. The concentration of economic activity in a few, already prosperous regions means that during periods of economic upturn markets in regions such as London and South East England tend to quickly 'overheat'. The resulting surge in wage levels, house prices, rents, etc. sends a wave of inflationary pressure rippling across the remainder of the economy and also results in a rise in imports to meet the growing demand, thus worsening the balance of payments position. Regional policy, by spreading economic activity, eases bottlenecks in the market economy. This in turn allows the economy to enjoy lower inflation and more sustained growth over time, to the benefit of all.

4 *Fewer urban problems*. Economic activity in Europe is increasingly concentrated in the big metropolitan areas and capital cities of the member states. The quality of life in these cities is a cause of great concern. Traffic congestion, pollution, crime and overcrowding are serious problems. Regional policy offers a way of easing the pressures on the big cities by diverting part of the economic activity elsewhere.

These are powerful arguments and most are as valid now as they ever were. They do not in themselves, however, constitute a case for a *EU regional policy*. In the past they have been used to justify such policies in individual member states. In Britain, for example, the national government has had its own since 1928, a policy which has survived a succession of governments of widely differing ideologies (Armstrong and Taylor, 2000). The crucial question from a EU point of view is why a separate EU regional policy is required *in addition to* those of the individual member states. Those of the individual member states have continued alongside EU regional policy over the years since 1975 (when the European Regional Development Fund was established – see Section 22.3.1). There is no suggestion that they should be laid down in favour of a single EU regional policy.

Several distinct arguments can be advanced in support of a regional policy operated at EU level. Each argument will be considered in turn.

22.1.1 The 'vested interest' argument

The nation states of Europe are becoming increasingly integrated economies. Rapidly expanding trade links, together with much freer capital mobility and more slowly growing cross-border labour migration, are being stimulated by EU initiatives such as the single market (see Chapter 11) and monetary union (see Chapters 9 and 10). Increasingly, the economic well being of citizens of one member state depends on the prosperity of the economies of other members. The presence of disadvantaged regions experiencing low incomes and high unemployment is in the interests of no one. Put another way, the citizens of one member state have a *vested interest* in ensuring that the regional problems in *other* member states are reduced. A EU regional policy can therefore be justified as a mechanism which allows one member state to become involved in policies which stimulate economic activity in regions of other member states.

Why do citizens in a prosperous member state such as Germany have a vested interest in helping to solve regional problems in, say, Greece or Spain? They have a vested interest because the solution of regional problems elsewhere generates *spillover benefits* – benefits which spread across member state boundaries. The more integrated the EU, the bigger would be the spillover effects of one member state on another. At present they are significant, but still relatively small, and comprise:

(a) equity spillovers;
(b) efficiency spillovers;
(c) spillover of non-economic benefits.

Equity spillovers arise because there is a widely held view in the EU that the benefits of integration should be 'fairly' distributed across regions and member states. Residents in more prosperous EU member states derive utility gains from helping citizens of poorer regions and member states to improve their economic status.

In addition to the pervading desire for 'fairness', reducing regional problems in the EU also generates *efficiency spillover* gains in already prosperous regions and member states. Lower unemployment increases income and production for the EU as a whole, and also stimulates tax receipts (e.g. value added tax (VAT)) for the EU while simultaneously reducing the pressure on EU spending programmes such as social policy (see Chapter 23). A EU regional policy also has the potential to create gains for everyone in the form of lower *overall* EU inflation and easing the urban problems in the big cities at the heart of the EU.

Some of the benefits of EU regional policy are in the form of *non-economic spillover* gains. Reduced regional disparities can help in achieving greater social and political 'cohesion' in Europe. Areas which feel left out of the benefits of integration are unlikely to cooperate or to fully embrace the concept of a more united Europe. Some would go further and argue that a strong EU regional policy is vital if the EU is to survive and to progress towards a fully-fledged federal political system. If this is true, the citizens of already prosperous regions will support a EU regional policy as a means of protecting and extending the existing EU. In doing so they may also reap additional non-economic benefits in the form of extra security, the preservation of local languages and cultures and the extraordinary socio-cultural diversity for which Europe is famous.

22.1.2 The 'financial targeting' argument

The second main argument in support of a EU regional policy is concerned with the effectiveness with which regional policy is operated in Europe. Regional policies are expensive to operate and resources must be found from public sector budgets. The disadvantaged regions of the EU are not evenly distributed among the member states of the EU. Some member states carry such a burden of disadvantaged regions that they constitute depressed regions in their own right. This has traditionally been the case with some of the member states in the Mediterranean south of the EU (e.g. Greece). Enlargement of the EU after 2004 to incorporate the significantly poorer CEECs will greatly expand the number of member states of this type.

Given the inevitable pressure on public sector budgets, it is not surprising to find that it is precisely those member states with the most severe burden of regional problems which have the greatest difficulty in financing an active regional policy. Leaving regional policy wholly to the member states is not therefore effective from a EU perspective. Member states such as the UK and Germany, with fewer regional problems, have been best able to afford an active regional policy. Those with the most severe regional problems such as Greece and Portugal face chronic budget difficulties and find it hard to fund their domestic regional policies adequately.

The difficulties faced by member states in ensuring that the most disadvantaged EU regions receive the greatest volume of assistance represent a powerful case for a EU regional policy. Member states on their own are simply unable to target regional policy funds on the most disadvantaged regions. Only the EU, it can be argued, is capable of drawing resources from more prosperous parts of the EU and ensuring that they are allocated to the most heavily disadvantaged regions.

22.1.3 The coordination argument

The third argument which can be made in support of a EU regional policy concerns the advantages of a coordinated approach. The EU has immense potential to improve the effectiveness of the regional policy effort by acting as a supranational coordinating body. Regional development initiatives within the member states are offered by a bewildering array of organizations. As well as the member state governments, typically also involved are regional governments, local councils, non-elected development agencies and, increasingly, private sector organizations, community and voluntary organizations as well as an array of joint venture schemes between private and governmental bodies.

Lack of coordination can be very wasteful. Firms seeking assistance in the disadvantaged regions may be bewildered and deterred by the complexity of the types of help on offer. Different regions may compete, using regional policy subsidies as a weapon, for one another's firms or for inward investment projects of USA and other foreign firms. In addition, valuable development opportunities (e.g. cross-border transport links – see Chapter 15) may not be properly implemented as a result of coordination failures. The coordination agenda for a EU regional policy is clearly a wide one.

In exercising its supranational coordination role the EU must simultaneously attempt to link together:

1 EU regional policy with other EU policies (e.g. agricultural and social policies).

2 EU regional policy activities within a given member state with the regional policy of the member state government.

3 Member states' regional policies one with another, particularly where the member states share a common border.

4 EU regional policy, member states' regional policies and the initiatives being operated by regional and local level organizations.

This is an enormous and difficult task, but one which only the EU has the potential to perform.

22.1.4 The 'effects of integration' argument

This is the most controversial of the arguments advanced in support of a EU regional policy. EU involvement in regional policy, it is argued, is necessary to overcome the adverse regional impacts of the integration process. This argument rests upon two suppositions. The first is that economic integration, if left to its own devices, tends to cause a worsening ('divergence') of regional disparities. The second is that it is the EU, rather than the member states, which is best placed to tackle the regional problems which develop as integration proceeds. Both suppositions have been the subject of fierce debate. The effect of integration on regional disparities is an issue of immense importance and will be considered further in Section 22.2.

22.1.5 The 'effects of other EU policies' argument

A further argument frequently advanced in support of EU regional policy is that it is needed to help to mitigate the adverse regional effects of other EU policies. A number of EU policies are known to have particularly severe effects on the disadvantaged regions. VAT, for example, a major source of EU revenues, has long been known to be a regionally regressive tax (CEC, 1979c, van den Noord, 2000). Other EU policies also have their own distinctive patterns of regional effects (CEU, 1996d, CEU, 2001c). The adverse regional effects of the EU agricultural price guarantee policy – a major item in the EU budget – have been a source of particular concern. The traditional concentration of EU's Common Agricultural Policy (CAP) help on products such as cereals, milk, oilseed and beef

(products of the more prosperous northern EU farming regions) has meant that despite repeated reforms of the CAP, more prosperous northern regions continued to benefit most throughout the 1980s (CEU, 2000d). More recent evidence has shown that the McSharry reforms of 1992 have slowly ameliorated the adverse regional impacts of the common agriculture policy, but that its regional impacts remain far from favourable (CEU, 1996d).

The ideal solution, of course, to policies with adverse regional impacts such as the CAP would be to alter the nature of the policies themselves. This has been achieved already to some degree with policies such as the CAP (CEU, 2001d). Reforming a EU policy at source is, however, only possible to a limited degree and there are usually dangers to the integrity of the policy itself if it is pushed too far in a 'pro-regional' direction. The EU, therefore, has adopted a twofold approach as part of its regional policy effort. First, regular research studies are made of major EU policies to identify, and where possible rectify, policies with adverse regional effects. Second, EU regional policy initiatives are designed, wherever sensible, to mitigate the adverse regional effects of other EU policies.

22.1.6 The 'further integration' argument

This argument centres upon the incomplete nature of the EU integration process. A EU regional policy, it is argued, is necessary to ensure that the benefits of integration are more fairly spread. Only if this is done will all member states be willing to countenance further steps towards full integration. This argument too is a controversial one. Even if one accepts, post-Treaty of European Union, that economic and political union is an acceptable goal, there is little hard evidence that *regional* disparities prevent *member states* from agreeing to further integration.

The list of arguments in favour of a separate EU regional policy is a long one. The case is a strong one too. It should be noted, however, that there is no logical case here for a *complete* transfer of regional policy powers from member states to the EU. Indeed, the EU's own commitment to 'subsidiarity' – the maximum devolution of powers – requires that member states, regional and local governments and other partner organizations all have a role (see Chapters 2 and 3). The vast majority of modern types of regional policy initiatives (e.g. advice to firms, training policies) also require an active local input to be effective. The remoteness of Brussels from many of the problem regions, the lack of specialist local knowledge and experience at the centre, and the virtue of allowing variety and experimentation in regional policy all suggest that partnership and not dominance is the appropriate EU role.

22.2 The effects of integration on EU regional disparities

The implications of economic integration for EU regional disparities are still imperfectly understood. The economic processes at work are extremely complex and long lasting. The regional effects even of the creation of the original customs union have not yet been fully experienced, and the regional implications of the single market process are still really only in their early stages, even though the legislation for it was largely completed by 1992. Add to these the regional ramifications of the 1996 enlargement (which saw the accession of Austria, Finland and Sweden), together with the geographical effects of the more recent monetary union and one can see just how complex the effects of economic integration are. Each of these steps in the process of economic integration has its own very distinctive 'regional footprint' and each has set in train effects which will take decades fully to emerge. Nor will the system have time to draw breath in the decade ahead. Monetary union remains an incomplete process and further extension of the euro area, combined with a wave of new accessions in the form of the CEECs, will trigger yet more complex 'regional footprint' effects right across the EU.

An examination of the existing pattern of regional disparities in the EU reveals an array of problems which are formidable by comparison with those in other parts of the world such as the USA. Figure 22.1 shows regional GDP per capita in 2000 for the existing 15 member states (EUR 15) as well as for regions in the 10 new states scheduled to accede in 2004 (Estonia, Latvia, Lithuania, Poland, the Czech Republic, Slovakia, Hungary, Slovenia, Cyprus and Malta) and those slated to join after 2007 (Bulgaria and Romania). The GDP per capita disparities within EUR 15 are more than twice as great as those found in the USA. In 2000, GDP per capita in the richest 10% of EUR 15 regions was 2.6 times greater than that in the poorest 10%. Enlargement of the EU to include 10 more CEECs (i.e. EUR 25) would raise this ratio from 2.6 to 4.4, while the accession of Bulgaria and Romania too (i.e. EUR 27) would raise the 'top 10% to bottom 10%' ratio to 6.0 (CEU, 2003c). Figure 22.2 shows the extent of EU regional disparities using another popular indicator, the regional unemployment rate. In 2001, the best 10% of regions had an average unemployment rate of just 2.3%, compared with an average rate of 19.7% in the 10% worst performing regions – over nine times higher (CEU, 2003c).

The regional problems confronting the EU are extremely diverse as well as being severe. Prior to the current 2000–2006 regional policy budget period, the EU identified four main types of problem region. These were, respectively, 'lagging regions' (regions whose GDP per capita fell below 75% of the EUR 15 average and whose regional problems are the most severe in the EU), declining manufacturing areas, certain rural regions, and some low population sub-Arctic regions in Sweden and Finland. In addition, special EU programmes have over the years focused on border regions between member states and with the outside world, the most remote regions (e.g. Réunion, Guadeloupe, etc.), disadvantaged mining areas, areas affected by the decline of defence expenditures and so on. In other words, EU regional policy has always clearly recognized just how diverse are the *types* of regional problems faced as well as how *severe* a challenge they represent.

During the current 2000–2006 budget period a rather simpler categorization of types of regional problem has been devised, comprising 'lagging regions' and 'regions facing structural difficulties'. These two broad categories of disadvantaged regions hide within them, however, a huge array of different types of problem region. The category of 'regions facing structural difficulties' alone, for example, incorporates declining *manufacturing* areas, disadvantaged *rural* areas, certain types of *urban* areas, and areas having to restructure as a result of the decline of the *fisheries* sector. Some of the regions are suffering from problems arising from their geographical isolation from the main EU markets. Yet others suffer from economic dislocation caused by the removal of internal frontiers (disrupting their traditional trade patterns), or because they lie along the external borders of the

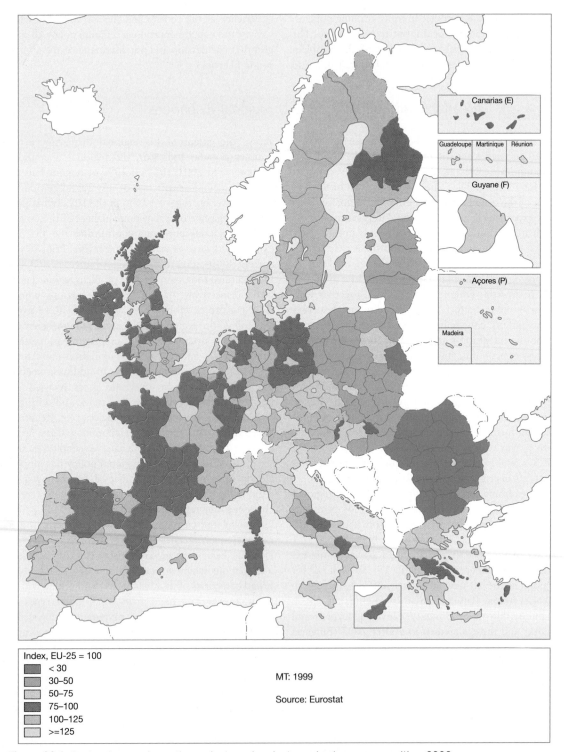

Canarias (E)

Guadeloupe | Martinique | Réunion

Guyane (F)

Açores (P)

Madeira

Index, EU-25 = 100

- < 30
- 30–50
- 50–75
- 75–100
- 100–125
- >=125

MT: 1999

Source: Eurostat

Figure 22.1 Regional gross domestic product per head, at purchasing power parities, 2000

Source: Map 1: GDP per head per region (PPS) 2000, Eurostat, © EuroGeographics Association for the administrative boundaries. Reprinted by permission of EuroGeographics.

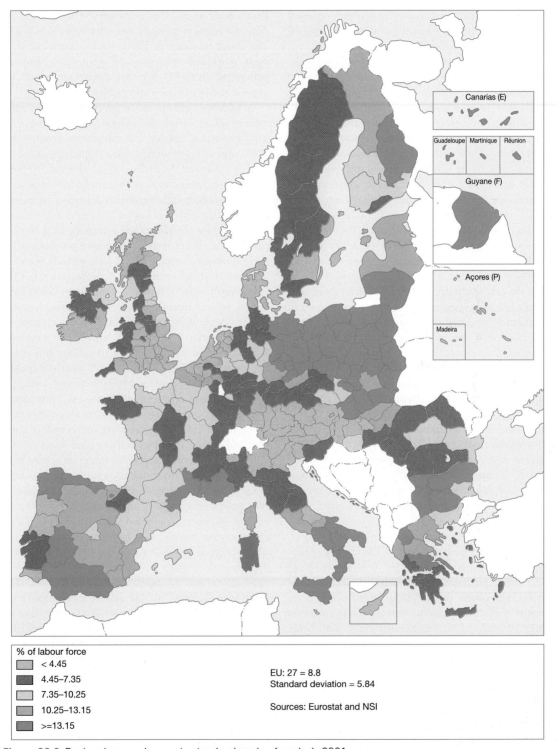

% of labour force
- □ < 4.45
- ■ 4.45–7.35
- □ 7.35–10.25
- ▨ 10.25–13.15
- ▨ >=13.15

EU: 27 = 8.8
Standard deviation = 5.84

Sources: Eurostat and NSI

Figure 22.2 Regional unemployment rates (males plus females), 2001

Source: Commission of the European Union (2003), © EuroGeographics for the administrative boundaries. Reprinted by permission of EuroGeographics.

EU. Another distinctive category of problem region is represented by the large number of island economies, many in isolated geographical locations.

Despite the great variety of EU regional problems, the overwhelming impression which one obtains from statistics such as those presented in Figures 22.1 and 22.2 is that there appears to be something of a 'core–periphery' pattern to EU regional disparities. A high proportion of the more prosperous regions lie at the geographical centre of the EU, whereas disadvantaged regions tend to be grouped around the periphery. Within the existing EUR 15 the most disadvantaged regions tend to be particularly (but by no means wholly) in the Mediterranean 'south'. Accession of the CEECs from 2004 onwards will greatly reinforce the core–periphery pattern by bringing many low-income and high-unemployment regions in along the eastern periphery (as Figures 22.1 and 22.2 show). Prior to 1995 the core–periphery pattern was even more pronounced than it appears now because Ireland (both Northern Ireland and the Republic), as well as parts of northern and western Britain, were also highly disadvantaged. As Figures 22.1 and 22.2 show, however, extremely rapid growth of both GDP and employment in Ireland (and to a lesser extent in western Britain) in the 1990s has transformed these areas so that the EU's 'western periphery' is much less pronounced than it once was. The traditional prosperous core of the EU stretches from central England to Northern Italy. There is some evidence of the emergence of a new growth belt from Northern Italy through the south of France and into North East Spain and, as we have seen, across western Britain into eastern Ireland. This does not, however, alter the overall conclusion that a 'core–periphery' situation prevails in the EU.

The 'core–periphery' nature of EU regional problems has existed for many years. It is the outcome of economic processes which predate the existence of the EU, and others that have come into existence as a result of the EU. Economic integration is a process which is progressing continuously on a worldwide scale. Improvements in transport infrastructure and transport technology have gradually reduced freight cost barriers to trade. So too have general improvements in production technology, which have had the effect of reducing the transport inputs required to assemble materials and distribute the output of manufacturing industry. Moreover, in the post-war period there has been a consensus in favour of freer trade which has led to successive international steps (e.g. WTO agreements and policies of the IMF and World Bank aimed at developing countries) designed to reduce the barriers to trade (see Chapters 24 and 25). The member states of the EU have participated in these worldwide processes of integration, and the pattern of *intra-EU* regional disparities which we observe today has been affected by them.

In addition to the broad integration processes common to all countries, the EU has acted to trigger its own distinctive 'accelerated' integration programme. The current maps of regional disparities (such as Figures 22.1 and 22.2) have been affected by these too. The regional effects of the single market process have not yet been fully experienced, partly because the complete single market has yet to be implemented and partly because the effects are extremely long term in nature. The effects of the convergence process *leading up* to monetary union in 2002 have already been felt (e.g. via pressures on member state budgets), but the longer-term regional impacts of monetary union itself are yet to be experienced. Moreover, existing regional disparities continue to be affected by the creation of the EU customs union in 1958, and by the successive widening of the customs union to include new member states in 1973 (Denmark, the UK and the Republic of Ireland), 1981 (Greece), 1986 (Spain and Portugal), 1991 (East Germany) and 1996 (Austria, Finland and Sweden). As noted earlier, the eastern enlargement process after 2004 will trigger yet another set of complex and far-reaching regional impacts.

No two rounds of economic integration ever have an identical effect on regional disparities. Each round in the integration process can be thought of as having two groups of effects: a unique regional imprint or pattern of effects, combined with a 'core–periphery' effect in common with other rounds. The creation of the original customs union, for example, involved the removal of tariffs which had previously provided most protection to *manufacturing* industries. The most severe effects of this act of integration were therefore experienced in regions most heavily dependent on manufacturing industries. The creation of a single market between 1989 and 1992 involved the removal of an array of non-tariff barriers. In this round of integration both manufacturing and service industries were affected. It is thought that a distinctive group of some 40 manufacturing sectors have been most affected by the single market, along with certain types of services such as banking and finance (CEC, 1988a; Quévit, 1995; Begg, 1995). Some regions are clearly more at risk than others, giving rise to a distinctive regional imprint. Monetary union has plunged most EUR 15 regions into a larger single currency area than before and has stripped the member states of exchange rate and monetary policy powers frequently brought to bear in the past to help disadvantaged regions. Monetary union too is therefore likely eventually to impinge more on some regions than on others (Ardy *et al.*, 2002).

While it is obvious that each round in the integration process has its own distinctive regional impact, why integration in the EU should exhibit systematic core–periphery effects as well is less clear. Evidence to date suggests that integration tends to trigger two sets of countervailing forces, one set tending to cause regional *convergence* while the other tends to bring about regional *divergence*. The existing core–periphery pattern of regional disparities suggests that at least in some periods in the past the divergence forces must have predominated. In more recent years there seems to have been something of a rough balance between divergence and convergence forces. Which set of forces will predominate in the years to come is an issue of major importance to the EU.

The forces which tend to bring about *convergence* of regional disparities within the EU are predominantly a series of automatic equilibrating processes which occur whenever a system of freely functioning markets is in operation. Free trade in goods and services will, it is argued, lead to regions specializing in the production and export of goods and services in which they have a comparative advantage. Under traditional trade theory such as the Heckscher–Ohlin model all regions benefit from this process and regional differences in wage rates and capital rentals are also eliminated (Armstrong and Taylor, 2000). The convergence effects of freer trade are reinforced by the effects of freer factor mobility. Where wage rates differ significantly between regions, there is an incentive for labour to migrate from low-wage to high-wage regions, a process which reduces regional wage inequalities. Capital investment in the meanwhile is attracted to the disadvantaged regions by the low wages and excellent labour supply available there. This too reduces regional inequalities. The combination of freer trade and large-scale factor mobility offers real hope for the convergence of regional disparities in the EU, and these processes lie at the heart of modern neoclassical 'conditional convergence' theories of regional growth which predict convergence of regional disparities (Sala-i-Martin, 1996). It is thought, however, that these processes operate only very slowly and that decades will be required before their full effects are

felt. Moreover, there are forces leading to divergence of regional disparities. It is to these that we now turn.

At the heart of the economic integration process set in motion by the EU has been a desire to achieve free trade and the free movement of labour and capital. In order to enjoy the benefits of integration (Emerson *et al.*, 1988; CEC, 1988a), it is essential that major restructuring of industry should occur. The various allocation and accumulation effects generating economic gains from integration require regions to switch production and concentrate on those goods and services for which there is a comparative advantage (Baldwin *et al.*, 1997). The greater the integration envisaged, the greater are the potential benefits, but the greater too are the restructuring implications. Painful though the restructuring process is for those involved, in principle it should be experienced by all regions. The crucial question, therefore, is why integration seems in the EU to be associated with systematic core–periphery effects. A series of different divergence forces are thought to accompany the integration process:

1 *Economies of scale.* These represent a potent source of benefit from integration. The concentration of production at larger plants can lead to great efficiency gains. Firms seeking to exploit economies of scale are likely to be attracted to regions at the geographical core of the EU. Input assembly costs are lower, and access to the whole EU market is much easier from central locations. Moreover, the core regions are already the most prosperous regions and therefore represent the strongest markets.

2 *Localization and agglomeration economies.* Localization economies arise when firms in the same industry locate close to one another (e.g. access to labour with appropriate skills, information flows, ability to subcontract work, etc.). Agglomeration economies occur when firms from many different industries locate close to one another (e.g. transport facilities, financial facilities, etc.). These 'external economies of scale' effects tend to strongly favour the core regions of the EU. Firms are drawn towards existing successful agglomerations of economic activity. The core regions of the EU contain almost all of the main financial, industrial and capital cities and are a potent magnet for new activity. The traditional 'Marshallian' localization and agglomeration economies have been incorporated in a variety of new theories which predict

industrial clustering and hence a concentration of economic activity in those regions which are fortunate to have been able to develop successful industrial clusters. Theories such as post-Fordism have stressed the advantages of clustered small firms in *new industrial districts* such as those in the 'Third Italy' within the traditional geographical 'core' of the EU (Dunford, 2000; Bagella and Becchetti, 2000). Porter's work has also highlighted the interacting sets of forces which can generate industrial clustering and the geographical concentration of economic activity (Porter, 1990), as have social capital theories of regional growth (Putnam, 1993). Within mainstream economics, new economic geography models of regional growth and some versions of endogenous growth theory also predict clustering and hence the possibility of divergent growth (Midelfart-Knarvik *et al.*, 2000).

3 *Intra-industry trade and dominant market positions.* Modern trade theory is increasingly sceptical of the ability of all regions to share equally in the growth associated with freer trade. There is evidence that intra-industry trade in similar products has shown the most rapid growth among the more prosperous core regions and member states of the EU (Neven, 1990 and Chapters 7 and 24). Regions in the Mediterranean south of the EU have fallen behind in participation in this important and fast-growing type of trade. Intra-industry trade is important because of the fast pace of expansion of this type of trade, particularly the horizontal exchange of almost identical products. By contrast, the CEECs do appear to be engaging in an increasing amount of intra-industry trade, but of the less lucrative vertical intra-industry trade category, supplying Western Europe with semi-processed inputs. Similarly, much trade in manufactured goods in the EU is now dominated by large multinational enterprises. These firms are already concentrated in the core regions of the EU and it is thought that they may exploit their ability to dominate markets in ways which disadvantage peripheral regions. Opening up peripheral regions to competition from large multinational firms could have serious effects for the smaller and less powerful firms more frequently found there.

4 *Lack of competitiveness in peripheral regions.* Research commissioned over the years by the EU (IFO, 1990; CEU, 1999c) has provided powerful evidence that many firms in the EU's peripheral regions face severe problems in meeting the competitive challenges posed by integration. The lack of competitiveness is based on a combination of factors largely outside the control of the firms themselves. These include poor location, weak infrastructure facilities (e.g. transport, telecommunications), low-skill labour forces, and local tax and financial sector problems.

5 *Selective labour migration.* The peripheral regions are also weakened, as integration proceeds, by the loss of migrants. The freeing of labour mobility stimulates migration from peripheral to core regions. Migration is highly selective. It is the young, the skilled and the economically active who migrate. Their loss is a severe blow to peripheral regions seeking to compete in an integrated EU.

6 *The loss of macro-policy powers in peripheral member states.* This is a particular problem at the present time because of monetary union. Those member states which have joined the euro have recently lost control of their exchange rates as well as other aspects of their monetary policy such as interest rates. Full monetary union has meant the complete loss of powers to try to protect a weak local economy by way of currency devaluation. Euro members have lost the power to use monetary policy to stimulate a weak local economy. Even fiscal policy is being increasingly constrained under monetary union because of the Stability and Growth Pact (SGP; see Chapter 9) and constraints on member state public sector budgets within the euro area. Peripheral member states face a future of very limited macro-policy powers. This will restrict their ability to protect their local economies.

The divergence forces set out above seem convincing and strong. There has been considerable discussion of the possibility that the divergence forces may interact and reinforce one another in such a way that *cumulative causation* occurs. This is where the loss of firms and a continuous outflow of migrants so weakens a peripheral economy that it can no longer attract new economic activities and hence goes into a downward spiral of decline. This is by no means a theoretical possibility. A number of rural regions of the EU (e.g. the west of Ireland, parts of southern Italy) have historically experienced depopulation on a large scale.

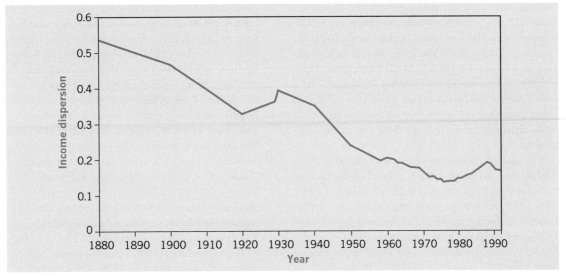

Figure 22.3 Convergence of USA state personal incomes per capita, 1880–1992
Source: From Sala-I-Martin, X. (1996). Reprinted by permission of the European Communities.

Evidence from federal countries with a long history of being fully economically integrated suggests that in the long term integration is associated with convergence of regional disparities rather than divergence, as Figure 22.3 shows for the USA (Sala-i-Martin, 1996). This evidence implies that the convergence forces at work eventually come to predominate over the divergence forces. The ensuing balance of forces results in a process of convergence which is slow (2% per annum in the USA), but is also sustained over a long period.

The evidence for convergence among EU regions is much more contested, partly because good statistics do not exist for the long periods of time necessary to check whether or not convergence is occurring. The balance of the evidence that is available suggests that cumulative causation has not occurred in the EU. Most researchers have found that prior to the mid-

1970s regional disparities in the EU had experienced quite a long period of narrowing. This was followed by a period of widening of disparities in the late 1970s and early 1980s. The EU's regional disparities, at least as far as GDP per capita figures are concerned, now seem to have stabilized in the later 1990s and perhaps to have begun very slowly narrowing again (Armstrong, 1995a, 1995b; CEU, 1999c, 2001d, 2003c). However, this evidence remains rather controversial, for some analysts have also found evidence for *divergence* among EU regions, at least for certain periods of time (Dunford, 1996; Magrini, 1999). What can be said, however, is that those spells of divergence which have been observed tend to have been recent and apparently short-lived. Economic integration does appear, on the whole, to be associated with a narrowing of regional disparities, although currently at a painfully slow rate.

22.3　EU regional policy in the period 2000–2006

22.3.1 The origins of modern EU regional policy: the reforms of 1989, 1994 and 1999

EU regional policy traces its origins to the decision in 1975 to create a European Regional Development Fund (ERDF). The policy subsequently underwent

minor reform in 1979 and 1984 (Armstrong, 1978, 1985). The current EU regional policy, however, owes most of its distinctive features to the major reform of the EU's regional policy of 1989. This reform was specifically designed to accompany the introduction of the single market and, like the single market itself, was phased in gradually between 1989 and 1992. The 1989 reform integrated a number of previously separate EU funding mechanisms, renaming them the 'structural funds'. The EU's structural funds comprise the ERDF, together with the European Social Fund (ESF), the Guidance Section of the European Agricultural Guidance and Guarantee Fund (EAGGF) and, since 1994, a Financial Instrument for Fisheries Guidance (FIFG) – see Chapter 19. The Cohesion Fund, also created in 1994, acts in many ways like one of the structural funds although it is not in fact strictly one of the structural funds.

EU regional policy continues to this day to be operated in all of its essential characteristics on the basis of the reform to the structural funds introduced in 1989. The 1989 reform package represented the most significant turning point in EU regional policy since 1975 (see CEC, 1989a, for a summary of the reforms). The 1989 reforms established the ERDF as an integral part of the EU's policy for dealing with the effects of structural changes which inevitably accompany integration. The reformed policy provided the basis for further reforms in 1994 (designed to accompany steps towards monetary union – see CEU, 1996d, for a summary) and for the rather more significant reforms in 1999 (designed to prepare the way for CEEC enlargement – see CEU, 2000c for a summary). While the 1994 and 1999 reforms were relatively minor in the sense of leaving the 1989 system largely intact, they were both accompanied by major new infusions of financial resources for the structural funds for the budget periods 1994–1999 and 2000–2006.

The outcome of the major 1989 reform package and the various amendments in the 1990s has been the creation of a comprehensive and coordinated delivery system for regional policy in the EU; one which is now very well funded by Brussels, being the second largest item in the full EU budget (after agriculture policy) – see Chapter 19.

22.3.2 EU regional policy in the 2000–2006 period

The current 2000–2006 budget period is being operated in all of its essential characteristics on the basis of the major reform to the structural funds of 1989. The structural funds have been given the task of attaining three *priority objectives* in the 2000–2006 programming period. These priority objectives are as follows, with the EU funds involved shown in parentheses:

1 Promoting the development and structural adjustment of the regions whose development is *lagging behind*, defined as having GDP per capita under 75% of the EUR 15 average (ERDF, ESF, EAGGF and FIFG). These Objective 1 regions also include two special categories of region which would not otherwise be eligible – some low population density regions in northern Finland and Sweden (which had their own particular Objective in the previous 1994–1999 programming period) and the 'most remote regions' of the EU (Guadeloupe, Réunion, Martinique, French Guiana, the Canary Islands, the Azores and Madeira). Figure 22.4 shows the current map of regions eligible for structural funds assistance. The Objective 1 regions encompass 25.4% of the EUR 15 population (down slightly on the 27.0% designated in the previous 1994–1999 period).

2 Supporting the economic and social conversion of areas facing structural difficulties (ERDF and ESF). Unlike the Objective 1 regions (which are designated by the Commission), the Objective 2 regions (see Figure 22.4) were designated by each member state, but within guidelines established by the Commission. These guidelines allow four main sub-types of Objective 2 regions to be designated. These are regions suffering *from industrial (i.e. manufacturing) decline*, certain disadvantaged *rural areas*, certain *urban areas* suffering severe economic, social and environmental problems, and *fishing communities* in decline. The Objective 2 regions encompass 18.2% of the EUR 15 population, quite a large cut from the 25.3% of the EUR 15 population designated in the 1994–1999 period.

3 Supporting the adaptation and modernisation of policies and systems of education, training and employment (ESF). Objective 3 regions are not identified on Figure 22.4. This is because Objective 3 is designed to be implemented *outside* of the Objective 1 regions. It is effectively a 'non-regional' objective, although in practice it is the disadvantaged regions which benefit the most from it. It is focused on labour market policies designed to reduce unemployment, those policies which seek to enhance access to the labour market by the socially excluded, lifelong learning and education programmes, equal opportunities schemes and policies designed to prepare communities for social and economic change.

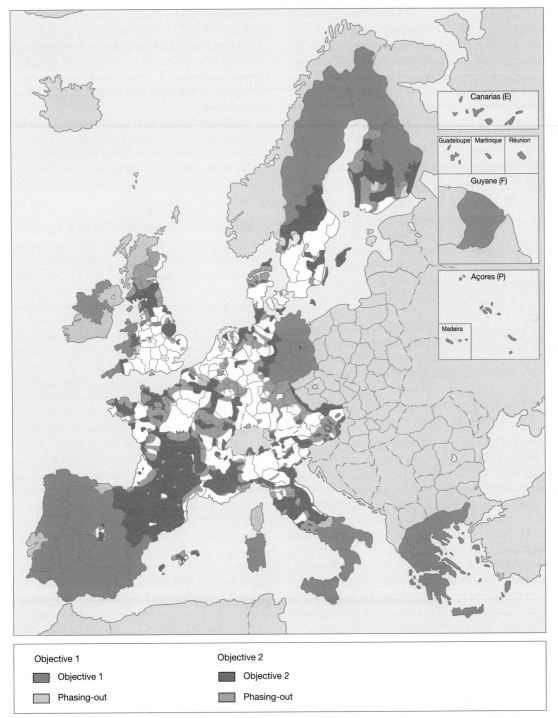

Figure 22.4 Structural funds (2000–2006): eligible regions under Priority Objectives 1 and 2, together with regions eligible for transitional assistance

Source: Map: European Union Structural Funds 2000–2006: Areas eligible under Objectives 1 and 2, EC Directorate-General Regional Policy, issued 27 October 2000, © MEGRIN for the administrative boundaries (1997), Regional and National data. Reprinted by permission of EuroGeographics.

In addition to the main programmes operated through each of the three priority objectives set out above, a portion of the structural funds (5.35% of the structural funds budget) has been held back for spending on four *Community Initiatives* (CIs). The CIs have a history stretching back to 1979 and represent programmes of assistance targeted on specific problems of a wide nature and which are thought best tackled through a pan-EU initiative. Prior to 2000 there were 13 CIs in existence, but during the 2000–2006 programming period these have been cut to just four:

1 *Interreg III*. This focuses help on cross-frontier, transnational and interregional initiatives. The internal frontier regions within the EU are the principal beneficiaries and previous generations of Interreg have proved successful in allowing regions on either side of an internal frontier (e.g. Kent and Nord-Pas-de-Calais) to take advantage of the new opportunities arising from the removal of frontier barriers.
2 *Leader+*. This initiative focuses on rural areas faced with a need to restructure their economies.
3 *Equal*. This funds transnational initiatives seeking to combat discrimination and labour market access inequalities.
4 *Urban*. This initiative focuses on the regeneration of urban neighbourhoods which are in crisis.

As Figure 22.4 shows, there are quite large swathes of territory identified on the map of eligible areas which are termed 'transitional assistance' regions. As part of the 1999 reforms to the structural funds it was decided to rein in the geographical extent of areas eligible for structural funds assistance. This was partly because some regions had prospered sufficiently to no longer need their previous degree of help (e.g. parts of eastern Ireland around Dublin). It was, however, also partly because the EU wished to have more precision than in the past in its geographical targeting of the structural funds, and partly because money needed to be freed up for enhanced *pre-accession assistance* to CEEC countries in the 2000–2006 period. It was decided that in order to avoid too sudden a removal of EU assistance, a phased withdrawal of structural funds payments would be made for de-designated areas in the 2000–2006 period and it is these areas which are shown as 'transitional assistance' regions on Figure 22.4.

Finally, during the 2000–2006 period a sum of 4% of the structural funds budget has been deliberately held back as a 'performance reserve'. These resources are to be allocated at the mid-point of the 2000–2006 programmes to those regions which have shown that they have made best use of the funds to date. A competitive element has therefore for the first time in the history of EU regional policy been added to the programmes.

The EU has deliberately concentrated the bulk of its financial assistance on the very poorest areas: in practice the Objective 1 regions. During the budget period 2000–2006 the allocations for the four structural funds, by objective, are as follows (all at 1999 prices):

Objective 1	137.06 billion euros
Objective 2	22.45 billion euros
Objective 3 (non-regional)	24.05 billion euros
Community Initiatives (CIs)	10.44 billion euros

As can be seen, Objective 1 dominates the structural funds (commanding some 70% of the total allocations), and this represents the principal mechanism by which the EU ensures that its resources are geographically concentrated on the most disadvantaged regions (a key principle of the structural funds). By contrast, Objectives 2 and 3 have been allocated only 11.5% and 12.3% respectively of the full 2000–2006 budget. Table 22.1 presents a detailed Objective and member state disaggregation of the initial indicative allocations of the 2000–2006 structural funds budget ('indicative' because actual out-turn spending may eventually differ somewhat from the initial allocations). Table 22.1 shows not only how Objective 1 funding dominates the other categories, but also how certain member states with a high proportion of Objective 1 regions fare much better than others from the structural funds. Spain, Greece, Portugal and Italy do particularly well, although had the numbers been expressed per capita of the population in each member state, Ireland too would have shown up strongly.

The structural funds are *grant-awarding* instruments, as is the Cohesion Fund. ERDF grants are essentially designed to assist industrial and infrastructure development. ESF grants are targeted on labour market initiatives such as training and mobility policies. The Guidance Section of the EAGGF and the FIFG assists a range of initiatives designed to facilitate the restructuring of the agriculture and fisheries sectors and the economic regeneration of the communities experiencing structural change.

Table 22.1 Indicative allocations, by Objective and member state for the 2000–2006 structural funds (million euros at 1999 prices)

Member state	Objective 1 Lagging regions	Objective 2 Conversion areas	Objective 3 Adaptation and modernization	Total indicative allocations
Belgium	659	433	737	1 829
Denmark	0	183	365	745
Germany	20 065	3 510	4 581	28 156
Greece	20 961	0	0	20 961
Spain	38 296	2 651	2 140	43 087
France	4 030	6 050	4 540	14 620
Ireland	3 088	0	0	3 088
Italy	22 218	2 522	3 744	28 484
Luxembourg	0	40	38	78
Netherlands	154	795	1 686	2 635
Austria	265	680	528	1 473
Portugal	19 029	0	0	19 029
Finland	944	489	403	1 836
Sweden	782	406	720	1 908
United Kingdom	6 372	4 695	4 568	15 635
Total	137 060	22 454	24 050	183 564

Notes:
1. The figures in the table for Objectives 1 and 2 include Transitional Assistance.
2. The Objective 1 figures include allocations for the Instrument for Fisheries, part of which can be spent outside Objective 1 areas. The Ireland and UK figures also include funding for a special PEACE initiative which will run 2000–2004 and the Sweden figures include funding for a special programme for coastal areas.
Source: Commission of the European Union (2000). Reprinted by permission of the European Communities.

22.3.2 Strategic planning, programming, partnership and additionality

As well as the commitment to much closer coordination of the activities of the EU's financial instruments, the regional policy which has emerged in the aftermath of the 1989 reforms places great emphasis on four further principles. These four great principles continue to underpin EU regional policy. They are the use of a system of *multi-annual programmes* of assistance, the need for a close *partnership* between all of those involved in regional policy, a commitment to *sub-sidiarity* (the retention at EU level of the minimum necessary powers) and a desire that EU money should be a genuine supplement to regional policy spending by the member states (*additionality*). None of these principles was entirely new to the 1989 reform package, but the 1989 reforms represented the first comprehensive attempt to create a regional policy 'delivery system' which would allow the principles to be achieved. The principles themselves have withstood the test of time and remain at the heart of the structural funds in the current 2000–2006 period.

The delivery of structural funds assistance through multi-annual programmes is now well entrenched. Key to the development of each programme is the drawing up of a Single Programming Document – SPD (or Community Support Framework – CSF – in some regions). These documents are effectively strategic plans for the region and are the responsibility of the regional and local partnership organizations delivering the programme, although the SPDs are subject to national and Commission involvement too. The role of the regional and local partners in the SPD is important since these partners are the ones with the local knowledge and expertise needed for effective planning. Their role also emphasizes the EU's commitment to subsidiarity in its regional policy. Each SPD contains an analysis of the strengths and weaknesses of the region, together with a development strategy and an analysis of how it is to be financed. EU structural funds can only be used in conjunction with matched funding from the member states. This whole medium-term planning process is supplemented by research and analysis of regional problems at the EU level. In particular, a system of regular periodic reports is employed to disseminate results of technical analysis of regional problems from a EU perspective (see CEU, 1999c for the most recent of these). There is also a very active programme of research on regional issues.

The multi-annual programmes first introduced in 1989 represented a major break with previous practice for EU regional policy. The original ERDF set up in 1975 awarded grants on a project-by-project basis, in much the same way as some member states' initiatives still do today (e.g. Regional Selective Assistance in the UK). From 1979 onwards, however, the EU began to experiment with a small number of programme-based initiatives. This approach has come into its own since 1989. As well as being multi-annual, programmes are essentially collaborative ventures (partnerships) between the EU, member state governments and the array of 'delivery organizations' at regional and local level involved in actually implementing the programme. A typical SPD is a group

of projects (usually hundreds in number) designed to achieve pre-designated objectives in a coordinated manner. As has already been noted, a distinctive category of programmes are the Community Initiatives (CIs). These are programmes which span the member states and are designed to tackle common problems. As their name suggests, they are initiated at the discretion of the EU rather than the member states.

The 1989 reform package and subsequent reforms in 1994 and 1999 have contained new commitments to two other long-held principles of EU regional policy – partnership and additionality. The concept of *partnership* is essential in a EU committed to the maximum devolution of power (*subsidiarity*). The reforms since 1989 have embodied ever-stronger procedures to encourage a strong dialogue between partners at all levels (i.e. EU, member state, regional and local), and an ever-wider range of types of organization has been drawn in (most recently community and voluntary organizations as well as trade unions and other 'social partners'). The SPDs, as well as the formal procedures for monitoring and evaluation of the policy, all include a requirement for close consultation with the partners.

Additionality has proved to be an exceptionally thorny issue in the EU's relationship with member state governments. Some member states have been accused of responding to increases in EU regional policy expenditures by cutting back on their own domestic regional policy budgets. The successive reforms to the structural funds since 1989 have sought to ensure that member states do not continue with this practice, although pressures on budgets in the 1990s resulting from attempts by member states to get within the EMU convergence criteria have not made the task any easier. The issue of additionality continues to be a delicate one for EU regional policy. Repeated attempts in the 1990s and again in the 2000–2006 period to use increased disclosure of funding statistics, moral persuasion and outright conflict with the members states have all proved to be only partial solutions.

22.4 Some key issues for the future

EU regional policy has shown itself to be capable of evolution and change over the years since its introduction in 1975. Some of the key issues that EU regional policy must confront in the immediate future are legacies of the past (e.g. additionality and the underfunding of the policy). Others, such as the

response of the policy to the recent achievement of monetary union and the pending eastern enlargement, are much newer issues. Each will be considered in turn, beginning with the fundamental challenge posed by eastern enlargement and the EU's initial response to this.

22.4.1 New accessions and the challenge of eastern enlargement

The EU has always found it necessary to make changes to its regional policy whenever new accessions have occurred. In most cases this has taken the form of an increase in the budget for regional policy and a re-designation of the map of the assisted areas, but without the fundamental principles of the policy itself being disturbed. This happy state of affairs has now come to an end. The reason for this is the impending accession of a series of (mostly) former Communist countries from Central and Eastern Europe. As Figures 22.1 and 22.2 have shown, these countries have much lower GDP per capita levels than most of Western Europe and also, by and large, higher unemployment rates. Many are also still within a painful period of adjustment and transition from their former Communist economic, legal and political systems towards a more Western model. This fact alone is of major importance for regional policy because it means that the institutional and governance structures in many of the acceding states make it difficult for them to effectively absorb pre-accession and structural funds money directed at them. The first wave of 10 countries (generally the more prosperous ones) pose enormous challenges for an EU which has been shaken by the cost and difficulty to date of integrating only one of the former Communist states, East Germany.

Eastern enlargement actually poses two distinctive challenges to the regional policy of the EU as described in the next two sub-sections (see Chapter 26).

The challenge to the EU budget

The EU budget is dominated by two items: the CAP and the structural funds. Between them they command the majority of the full EU budget (see Chapter 19). The economic decline in many of the CEECs which followed the collapse of Communism in the early 1990s, together with the decision to encourage them to seek early accession, triggered an enormous debate on how the challenge could be met. The main threats to the ability of the EUR 15 countries to meet the costs of enlargement were quickly identified as being via the structural funds and CAP.

The challenge to the structural funds arises from the fact that virtually all of the regions in the CEECs will be immediately eligible for the highest rates of structural funds assistance (i.e. Objective 1) under existing structural funds regulations. Figure 22.1 shows this situation vividly in that on the evidence for 2000 only a tiny handful of local areas within the CEECs would have had GDP per capita values in excess of the 75% of (EUR 25) average GDP, the critical value for Objective 1 membership (under existing 2000–2006 regulations). The challenge to the CAP budget arises from the fact that many of the CEECs, particularly some of the bigger countries such as Poland and Hungary are both large producers of agricultural products and also tend to specialize on the types of commodities (e.g. dairy products, cereals) that attract high levels of intervention by the EU.

Preliminary estimates during the 1990s of the likely additional burden on the EU budget as a result of CEEC enlargement raised the alarming prospect that the existing 15 member states of the EU would be unlikely to cope with the additional demands (Baldwin et al., 1997). Faced with estimates of this kind, the Berlin meeting of heads of state in March 1999 (European Council, 1999b) found itself with some very difficult decisions to take in setting the budget allocations for the period 2000–2006. The solution adopted, as Table 22.2 shows, was to spread the pain around. The countries seeking accession were allocated rather less money than they had hoped for, spread over a longer period. Pre-accession aid to the CEECs was set at a constant 3.12 billion euros per annum through until 2006. As Table 22.2 shows, the pre-accession aid was continued into 2000–2006 mostly in the form of the pre-existing PHARE programme, but with also 1.04 billion euros per annum in pre-accession aid from the structural funds and 0.52 billion euros per annum from CAP. As can be seen from Table 22.2, *post-accession* allocations to the new member states were scheduled to begin at a mere 6.45 billion euros per annum in 2002, but predicted to rise rapidly to 16.78 billion euros by 2006, the vast majority of which were to be in the form of Objective 1 structural funds allocations. It was argued at the 1999 Berlin Summit that the envisaged structural funds levels were pretty much the maximum that it would be safe to assume the new member states could safely absorb in such a short period of time. They do not in any sense represent the kinds of investment levels that would be necessary to solve the economic problems in the CEECs.

As the 2000–2006 period progressed, the pace of negotiation for accession of the CEECs gradually increased, culminating in the key decisions at the

Table 22.2 EU budget commitments, 2000–2006 (billion euros at 1999 prices)

	2000	2001	2002	2003	2004	2005	2006
EUR 15 – Structural funds and Cohesion Fund	32.045	31.455	30.865	30.285	29.595	29.595	29.170
EUR 15 – Agriculture policy	40.920	42.800	43.900	43.770	42.760	41.930	41.660
EUR 15 – Other internal policies	5.900	5.950	6.000	6.050	6.100	6.150	6.200
EUR 15 – External policies	4.550	4.560	4.570	4.580	4.590	4.600	4.610
Administration and reserves	5.460	5.500	5.350	5.200	5.300	5.400	5.500
Pre-accession aid: structural funds	1.040	1.040	1.040	1.040	1.040	1.040	1.040
Pre-accession aid: other	2.080	2.080	2.080	2.080	2.080	2.080	2.080
Post-accession aid: structural funds	–	–	3.750	5.830	7.920	10.000	12.080
Post-accession aid: other	–	–	2.700	3.200	3.700	4.200	4.700
Total commitments	**91.995**	**93.385**	**100.255**	**102.035**	**103.085**	**104.995**	**107.040**

Source: European Council (1999). Reprinted by permission of the European Communities.

Copenhagen Summit of December 2002 to permit a first wave of new entrants in 2004. The figures set out in Table 22.2 assumed that only six new member states would accede in the 2000–2006 period, and not the 10 which are now scheduled to enter. At the Copenhagen Summit of 2002 it was therefore decided to raise the post-accession commitments to the CEECs to 10.794 billion euros in 2004, 13.400 billion euros in 2005 and 15.966 euros in 2006 (European Council, 2002).

Where is all the extra money for the new entrants coming from? The 1999 Berlin Summit deal saw the solution lying in part in the continued economic growth in the existing EUR 15. This growth, combined with the decision to hold the EU budget at 0.45% of the combined GDP of EUR 15, has generated some of the extra funding needed. As Table 22.2 shows, however, the rest of the money is being found from cuts *in real terms* from the structural funds, from the cohesion fund and from the CAP budget in the existing EUR 15 member states. The structural funds alone in EUR 15 are scheduled to be cut from euro 32.045 billion in 2000 to euro 29.170 billion in 2006. As far as the disadvantaged regions of the existing 15 member states are concerned, therefore, the structural funds at their disposal effectively peaked in real terms

in 1999 and are now slowly declining. In a very real sense, therefore, the disadvantaged regions of the EUR 15 countries are already paying a price in the form of reduced funding in order to meet the pre-accession costs of eastern enlargement.

The Commission has sought during the current 2000–2006 programming period to preserve the fundamental features of the pre-2000 structural funds system (e.g. programming, partnership, etc.) while at the same time reining back spending in the EUR 15 countries (CEU, 1997b, 1998a). Two main changes were made between the 1994–1999 and 2000–2006 programming periods to bring this about:

1 *Reduction in the areas eligible for assistance.*
   There were six separate priority objectives during the 1994–1999 budget period. These, as was shown earlier, were cut back to only three for the 2000–2006 period. Overall, the population of EUR 15 countries eligible for either Objective 1 or 2 has fallen from 50.6% of the population to 40.4%, with the bulk of the cuts falling on former Objective 2 regions. The fact that there is transitional funding (see Figure 22.4) has undoubtedly cushioned the blow, but this help

is of a temporary nature and blow there has certainly been.

2 *Reduction in the community initiatives in the EUR 15 countries.* Community initiatives have also been radically cut back from 13 to a mere three and there has been a reduction in the CI share of the structural funds budget to 5.35%.

While the 1999 reforms to the structural funds were also used as a vehicle to try to simplify bureaucracy, and to draw in more partner organizations at the regional and local level, it is the cuts in budgets and eligible areas that are the most important feature. These have arisen directly from the need to free up resources to meet the challenge of CEEC enlargement.

The December 2002 Copenhagen Summit decisions have by no means resolved the issue of how to finance the structural funds and CAP obligations for the acceding CEECs. The key issue at the present time is how to resolve the funding dilemma in the years ahead once the 2000–2006 programming period comes to an end. A lively debate has therefore arisen on what the shape of the *post-2006* EU regional policy will look like (CEU, 2001d). This debate remains at the time of writing to be resolved, but will almost certainly result in further cuts in structural funds spending in the disadvantaged regions of EUR 15 member states to free up more money for the CEECs.

The challenge posed by the regional impact of eastern enlargement

Eastern enlargement poses a further challenge to the structural funds. As has been noted earlier, each act of economic integration tends to produce a set of broad core–periphery effects within the EU, but also a distinctive geographical pattern of losing and gaining regions. Eastern enlargement is also thought likely to have its own distinctive set of regional impacts within the EUR 15 member states. Estimates of these impacts remain rough and ready, but it is thought that it is the new entrants themselves that will gain most (up to 20% extra GDP) while the EUR 15 countries will enjoy an expansion of perhaps one-quarter of 1% on their combined GDP (Baldwin *et al.*, 1997). However, within the EUR 15 countries it is likely that it will be the relatively prosperous regions of the north of the EU (especially in Germany, France and the UK) that will gain the most from eastern enlargement, particularly in Germany (Baldwin *et al.*, 1997). The structural funds within the existing EUR 15 countries will

therefore have to cope not only with budget cuts and restricted eligible areas, but also with a new set of strains on the existing regional disparities.

22.4.2 EU regional policy and full monetary union

The attainment of the formal 'convergence conditions' for monetary union by the majority of the member states in January 1999, and the subsequent decision of 12 of the member states to push on to successful full monetary union in 2002, has important implications for EU regional policy which have yet to be confronted. EMU is effectively a further step in the long process of economic integration. As with previous rounds such as the customs union and the single market, EMU is certainly resulting in a distinctive regional imprint combined with some general core–periphery effects. Moreover, all regions are experiencing structural change as the full implications of EMU work their way through the economic system. That this would occur has been known for many years (CEC, 1990a; Emerson *et al.*, 1991).

Precisely what the regional impacts of EMU will be remains a controversial issue and one made more uncertain by the fact that some member states such as the UK have not yet decided when (if ever) they will join the eurozone. It was realized at the time of signing of the Treaty on European Union in 1992 that the step-by-step process of moving towards the attainment of the convergence criteria, and then on to the single currency, would trigger new strains within the EU and could exacerbate regional problems. These strains, it was argued, would occur immediately since the convergence criteria themselves (e.g. restraining public sector deficits) would affect the poorer regions more than the prosperous regions. This was one of the reasons which lay behind the decision to greatly increase the structural funds for the 1994–1999 budget period. The Cohesion Fund too was established in 1994 to help meet the challenges of the stage-by-stage progress towards EMU.

The effects of EMU did not, however, stop in 2002 with the introduction of the euro. The Stability and Growth Pact (SGP) continues to bring pressure to bear on member state budgets, and hence on their ability to ameliorate regional problems by way of public spending in disadvantaged regions. In the longer term it remains very unclear whether monetary union will lead to convergence or divergence in regional disparities. By accelerating the process of economic integration, monetary union should enhance the convergence forces at the heart of the neoclassical growth model. However, 'the theoretical and empirical evidence suggests that convergence can occur, but it is not inevitable' (Ardy *et al.*, 2002, p. 17). Those who take a less sanguine view of the regional impact of monetary union point to the loss of exchange rate and monetary policy powers which have been used in the past by some member states to protect their weaker regions. The eurozone is also some distance from being an optimum currency area. The inadequate nature of labour and capital mobility levels within the EU, together with the absence of the kinds of inter-state and interpersonal fiscal transfer mechanisms which exist in genuine federal states (and which cushion economic changes with adverse regional effects) remain a serious worry.

22.4.3 The issue of under-funding

Despite the great increases since 1989 in EU budget resources devoted to the structural funds, there is a serious concern that the EU regional policy remains seriously underfunded for the tasks which it has set itself. As has been noted earlier, this concern has become greatly magnified by the impending accession of the CEECs. The underfunding issue is a difficult one to examine since no one knows how much would need to be spent and over what time period for EU regional problems to be eliminated. The structural funds remain small, commanding less than half of one per cent of the combined GDP of EU member states. The experience of Britain in the 1960s, when the UK government operated a regional policy with better funding (relative to GDP) than the current EU regional policy and still failed to eliminate relatively narrow regional disparities, suggests that EU regional policy is still significantly underfunded. The fact that regional disparities even just within the existing EUR 15 member states remain stubbornly persistent and have been narrowing in the 1990s at only the slowest of paces (CEU, 2002c, 2003c) gives added credence to those who argue that regional policy is seriously underfunded.

The underfunding issue is made more serious in the EU compared with federal systems elsewhere (e.g. USA) by the inadequacies of the EU's system of *inter-*

personal and *intergovernmental* fiscal transfers. Federal countries such as Australia, Canada, Switzerland and the USA, for example, have redistributive transfer systems which eliminate a high proportion of variations in regional income differentials (O'Donnell, 1992; Fatás and Mihov, 2001). Such transfers are extremely weak within the EU where very little taxation accrues to Brussels and there would be considerable resistance by member states to a major expansion of them. As noted earlier, the weakness of the EU-level system of fiscal transfers also poses problems for the success of monetary union (see Chapter 19).

22.4.4 Additionality and subsidiarity

Despite the successive reforms of the structural funds, it is clear that additionality remains a serious problem for EU regional policy. Member states faced with domestic public sector budget problems will always be tempted to cut their local regional policy efforts as EU regional policy is expanded. Similar comments apply to subsidiarity, where some member states remain reluctant to release powers to the regional and local partners. This remains the case in the UK despite the creation of elected regional governments in Scotland, Wales and Northern Ireland. English regions still do not have elected assemblies.

22.4.5 The final division of policy powers

Perhaps the most fundamental issue that continues to face EU regional policy in the new millennium, as it did in the 1990s, is the division of regional policy responsibilities among the different tiers of government involved. The commitment to subsidiarity is useful, but does not answer the crucial question of what the final assignment of regional policy powers is to be. This is particularly important in an era of *multi-level governance* in which the powers of the member states appear to be waning. What is to be the final role for the member states? What is to be the role of the EU and the regional governments? Until this is decided, the EU will continue to find itself in a series of conflicts with the other partners in the regional policy effort.

Chapter 23 Social policies

DOREEN COLLINS AND ROBERT SALAIS

Introduction

By the time of the Treaty of Nice, the EU had acquired a broad responsibility in the social field. The central core of Community social policy is to be found in questions relating to employment, industrial health, the social costs of industry, labour mobility and the role of social spending in social affairs. Especially a more integrated approach to social issues which combines employment, social protection and economic and budgetary policy is currently being sought.

In the early years of the EC, broader issues of social welfare seemed of little relevance but the subsequent growth of its social competences has been notable. There are a number of reasons for this. Social affairs now form a large component of national public policy which, in turn, has to be fitted into a European framework and more problems have a transnational element. Community policies have also matured and as they reach into detailed areas of life, as in the equal opportunities policy, so they become more visible. In consequence, many people and organizations now recognize that their interests may be as well served by lobbying in Brussels as in the national capitals. The history of the EU also shows that the Commission, normally backed up by the European Parliament, has always believed it should play an active and positive role in social affairs and, particularly during the 1980s, it stepped up the social momentum as part of the drive to strengthen the political legitimacy of the EC in the move towards European union. It is hardly surprising that the Commission has clashed with national governments which still wish to claim credit with their citizens for their work to improve the conditions of life. Differences of view have surfaced, notably over the 'social dimension' of the single market. Here the biggest single issue has been whether the Community needs a common framework of employment law and certain rules relating to working conditions in order that the single market may work effectively. Subsequently, the

argument from Brussels has been that the EU must become 'closer to its citizens', a view that encourages an ever more important social role. The result of these pressures is that social policy now covers a wide range of individual policies with no less than five Commissioners and their Directorates having direct responsibilities for the items covered by this chapter.

The legal foundations for social policies are to be found in the Treaties of Rome (EEC), Paris (ECSC) and Rome (Euratom) as modified by subsequent developments. The Single European Act (SEA) brought changes thought necessary because of the move to the single market while the Maastricht and Amsterdam treaties both widened responsibilities and sharpened up existing ones. Some treaty provisions are clear-cut but others are of a very general nature and do not require legislation so much as political programmes, with the result that at any moment there is a wide variety of social activities which demand a different degree of commitment from member states. One consequence is the growing overlap of interest with that of national authorities which leads both to cooperation and to conflict. Although national governments remain primarily in charge in matters such as mainstream education, personal health care, the value of social security benefits and housing provision, and national sources of finance are overwhelmingly important, it is routine for ministers to attend specialist Council meetings to agree both Community policy initiatives and joint activities in these matters. It is important, however, to retain a sense of perspective. Community interest is often marginal to the main body of work carried out nationally since it derives in the first instance from economic objectives and the current emphasis upon subsidiarity suggests this division is intended to remain. An example is in education, where the EU accepts that member states are primarily responsible for fulfilling educational needs, but sees a role for a 'European dimension' through supporting language teaching, mobility of staff and students and cooperation between educational establishments in different member states.

Political rights having been covered in the TEU, discussion moved on to human and social rights. The commitment in Article 6 (EU) is to respect the European Convention on Human Rights and Fundamental Freedoms, and the possibility of suspension of membership in the case of violation has been added to the treaty. The question is still raised whether the EU should formally subscribe to it. The European Court of Justice (ECJ) has studied the question more than once, concluding that to do so would require a full-scale treaty revision (Opinion 2/94 28.3.96). There are further references to the importance of human rights in the treaties, including their significance for the common foreign and security policy. The Commission set out its views on the protection of human rights in the EU and the priorities for action in 'The European Union and human rights: from Rome to Maastricht and beyond' (COM (95) 567). It is also usual to find that contractual ties with third countries make 'respect for democratic and human rights' an essential part of the text and the Commission is particularly watchful in the case of aspiring Union entrants and the recipients of development aid. An innovation was the declaration adopted at Amsterdam noting the fact that most member states have now abolished the death penalty and that it has not been applied in any of them for many years.

If we put aside the Employment European Strategy (EES; Luxemburg, 1997), the 1990s were mainly years of consolidation, if not of relative stagnation in European social matters. The European Council in Lisbon (23–24 March 2000), followed by the Nice Council (7–10 December 2000) marked a new start. A new strategic goal was set for the Union for the next decade: 'to become the most competitive and dynamic knowledge-based economy in the world, capable of sustainable economic growth with more and better jobs and greater social cohesion' (see Chapter 13). Implementing this strategy should be achieved by improving the existing processes. More integration between social domains separated until now (for instance employment and social protection) and between economic and social policies is expected from this method. A social agenda has been established for the period 2001–2006. The ultimate goal is to modernise the European social model, by investing in people and combating social exclusion. This will offer the path to enlargement of Europe in the direction of Eastern and Southern candidate countries.

23.2   The Treaty of Rome

Although the Treaty of Rome was relatively weak on the social side it was sufficient to allow much development. First, it had general objectives of a broadly social character, such as a high level of employment and social protection and a raised standard of living. Second, it contained a recognition by member states of the need to improve living and working conditions and of their expectation that social policies would gradually align under the impact of the new system. There was agreement to collaborate in specific fields such as labour legislation, working conditions, vocational training, social security, industrial health and welfare and trade union and collective bargaining matters. Here the Commission was given the responsibility of promoting collaboration. In this way, scope for joint action was left open should the evolution of the EC require it but common policies were not considered inevitable. Third, the question of the effect of social costs on competition was raised in 1957. The sensitivity of French industry on this point led directly to the principle of equal pay for men and women. This has proved the basis for some significant policy developments. Fourth, the belief that manpower was ineffectively utilized led to the setting up of the European Social Fund (ESF), the aim of which was to help both occupational and geographical mobility. In addition, the treaty included an agreement to establish the common principles of vocational training.

The fifth item of great social significance was the adoption of the principle of the free movement of wage earners, along with rules to give it practical effect and to ensure the equal treatment of such migrants with indigenous workers. It was agreed, also, that rules would be necessary to allow the free establishment of the self-employed and for services to be provided across frontiers. These clauses have given rise to programmes of great complexity.

The free movement policy, together with its supporting policies of employment exchange collaboration, maintenance of social security rights and protection of equal working rights for migrants, was a major EC success although it owed much to the buoyant economic conditions of the time. Subsequent attempts to move the policy into the much more difficult area of social integration and social equality and to evolve a policy towards migrants from outside have been far harder to accomplish.

Sixth, special protective measures, which derive from the appropriate treaties, were set up in the coal, steel and nuclear sectors. Not only is there a special concern for health and safety matters but, in coal and steel, pioneering work was done to operate a system of cash benefits and services for workers who lost their jobs as the industries lost their pre-eminence in the economy.

23.3 The Single European Act and the Social Charter

The prime social aim of the SEA was to develop the provisions made necessary by the internal market although there were disagreements as to what these were. It also began the process of widening the concept of social policy. It made an important statement of principle in its preamble affirming the fundamental civil, political and social rights of citizens, drawing on the work of the Council of Europe for this. By doing so, it strengthened the EC's moral base and thus the hands of those who wished to see the EC play a more positive social role. A special section of the SEA supplemented the Rome Treaty. It agreed to pay special attention to better health and safety standards at work and to harmonizing standards while maintaining existing high ones. This reflected the fear that firms would be tempted to cut standards as they entered a more competitive situation. Minimum standards were to be introduced gradually by directives and passed by qualified majority voting (QMV) in the Council of Ministers. At the same time, a cautious note was sounded by stressing that the conditions in member states must be taken into account and the needs of small business considered. A dialogue between management and labour at the EC level, which might, in turn, lead to formal agreements between the two sides of industry, was to be set up.

Certain reservations about the use of QMV continued. In the social field, unanimity was still required for free movement rules, the rights and interests of employed persons and for the passing of directives which would require alteration in the methods of training for, and practice in, some professions. The treaty referred to the need for the Commission to use high standards when regulating health, safety and environmental issues and when dealing with consumer protection.

Underlying these legislative provisions were considerable uncertainties. Some member states feared that, by having EC standards imposed upon them,

their goods would be unable to compete; others feared pressure to lower their standards to meet competition from members with lower labour costs; yet others feared the import of goods, livestock and plants that would introduce new forms of disease. Denmark added a special declaration to the SEA designed to ensure it could continue with its own high standards. The United Kingdom was anxious to prevent the imposition of labour regulation which would damage the upsurge of small businesses and thought the social dialogue provisions would encourage the revitalization of trade union power which the Conservative government had been attacking at home. No solutions were found to these conflicts of interest but the SEA, by introducing clauses to satisfy everyone, made future conflict inevitable. This soon began to occur.

A new subsection introduced the concept of economic and social cohesion. Primarily concerned with regional policy and the support of the most backward Community members (see Chapter 22), it affected the use to be made of the ESF. Environmental issues were also brought under the EC umbrella for the first time (see Chapter 17).

The SEA gave a boost to the development of social policy. New initiatives to encourage language teaching, student exchanges and better vocational training and to establish health and safety norms soon began to appear and were broadly acceptable to member governments. However, the Commission was less successful in mobilizing support for proposals relating to working conditions. The opposition was led by the United Kingdom whose government disliked such formal controls over business and was suspicious of the opportunity offered by some of the proposals for the growth of trade union power. The UK government also objected to what it considered a misuse of treaty powers in that directives were being proposed under cover of the implementation of the single market when they were not really necessary for this purpose.

In consequence, they could be passed by QMV. The matter received great publicity when the Commission produced a Charter on the Fundamental Social Rights for Workers (the Social Charter) setting out the proposed actions thought necessary in consequence of the single market. There were 47 initiatives in all, many of them non-controversial and some already agreed, but others moved on to contested ground. In December 1989, the Social Charter was accepted by all governments other than the British and it became, not a legally binding document, but a statement of proposed action which the Commission subsequently used as a document to organize its work.

The ECJ is now formally empowered to ensure the respect of fundamental rights and freedoms by the European institutions. In 2000 the Charter of Fundamental Rights has been jointly proclaimed by the Council, the European Parliament and the Commission. This Charter has used the previous Social Charter as one of its sources, but has enlarged to civil, political, economic, social and societal rights. Its Preamble emphasizes the foundation of Europe on the universal values of human dignity, freedom, equality and solidarity. The Convention for the Future of Europe has recommended (in July 2003) that this Charter becomes part of the European Constitution (see Chapter 28, Section 28.3).

23.4   The development of social policy

Given the rather incoherent guidance of the early years, it is not surprising that the development of social policy was patchy. The first decade saw major steps taken to implement the policy on labour movement, a formal adoption of the equal pay policy, a narrow exploitation of the ESF and considerable study of, and research into, labour questions but there was a sense of social policy hanging fire. However, a new impetus can be detected by the end of the 1960s when hopes in Western Europe were high for social improvements and the EC benefited from this optimism. Widespread unease existing over environmental pollution, the problems of the disadvantaged, social inequalities and the increasing distance between the citizen and the services run by big bureaucracies originally developed to help the ordinary man and woman. There was a certain vacuum in social policy which enabled the EC to establish a role. The Hague conference in December 1969 agreed that the EC needed to go further in the pursuit of common economic and political goals in which a 'concerted social policy' would have a part. This line was continued by the Paris summit of 1972 which asserted the importance member states attached to vigorous action in the social field. Specifically, it referred to the need to widen participation in decision making and action to lessen inequalities and to improve the quality of life. The political momentum thus established led to the first Social Action Programme (SAP). Its hopes were, however, quickly dashed by the onset of recession and the burden of large-scale unemployment and it was this that began to dominate social concerns as the EC experienced structural changes in employment patterns, including a rapid growth in part-time and shift work, together with formidable problems of long-term and youth unemployment. A major preoccupation for the EC became the need to analyse unemployment issues, encourage cooperative action by member states and support programmes to help to overcome specific problems such as lack of training.

By the 1980s, a new momentum in the EC can be discerned, in which social policy had an important role. In 1981, the newly elected French socialist government had proposed a programme for a 'social space' for the EC and the following year the European Parliament called for a reform of the treaties and the achievement of a European union which would require a new policy for society. The entry of Greece, Portugal and Spain added another dimension by turning attention away from the urban problems of the more developed North to the importance of devoting resources to the characteristic problems of agricultural inefficiency, disguised unemployment in rural areas and lack of training for industrial work. The later entry of Austria, Sweden and Finland maintained the interest in social policy and brought the strong Scandinavian welfare tradition into the counsels of the EU.

The urge to establish the single market and the insistence that this must be accompanied by some steps towards cementing European union drove the Community towards a fresh consideration of citizens' rights. The European Council accepted two reports from the *ad hoc* Adonnino committee in 1985 which included a host of recommendations for building 'The People's Europe'. Some were new, others asked for current policies to be pursued more rigorously. Although some were implemented, others ran into difficulties.

23.5 The Treaty of Union and its perspectives

Subsequent to the passing of the SEA, controversy in social matters revolved round questions raised by the single market and, in particular, over possible extensions of European employment law. The Maastricht negotiations led to a totally unexpected result. Amended Articles 2 and 3 reiterated the social goals of the Treaty of Rome but in a broader, often more explicit, form. They now included respect for the environment, a high level of employment and social protection and the raising of the standard of living and the quality of life. Subsequent purposes included free movement of people; measures concerning the entry of people; a continuation of the ESF and the policy of cohesion; a contribution to a high level of health protection; to education and training and to the flowering of culture as well as to consumer protection and to measures in the sphere of tourism.

Most importantly, the treaty established the legal concept of Union citizenship 'to strengthen the protection of the rights and interests of the nationals of the member states'. Citizens were given the right to move and reside freely, to vote and stand as candidates in municipal and European Parliamentary elections in all member states on the same terms as nationals (each right being subject to certain limitations). Citizens, when outside the Community, received the right to diplomatic protection from the services of any member state. They may now petition both the European Parliament and the European Ombudsman. Directives are in place to give effect to these political rights and the Ombudsman has been appointed.

The novelty was that 11 (later 14) states, excluding the United Kingdom, signed an attached Protocol and Agreement, popularly known as the Social Chapter (now fully incorporated in the treaties, see below). This affirmed their wish to continue with the Social Charter and clarified the goals. Article 1 of the Agreement included 'the promotion of employment, improved living and working conditions, proper social protection, dialogue between management and labour, the development of human resources with a view to lasting high employment and the combating of exclusion'. The Agreement made explicit that the Community is competent to act in the fields of the working environment, working conditions, equality of men and women concerning opportunities and treatment at work, the social integration of excluded groups and with regard to the information and consultation of workers. It established the right of the Council to pass directives on minimum standards by the use of QMV for matters of health and safety, working conditions, information and consultation, equality at work and the integration of those outside the labour market. The Council may also act, by unanimity, on social security and protection, protection of redundant workers, the defence and representation of workers' and employers' interests, employment conditions for third country nationals, financing of measures for employment and job creation (but not the use of the ESF, which is in the main treaty). Pay, the right of association and the right to strike and impose lockouts are specifically excluded, while states may continue to provide specific advantages for women in order to equalize their working opportunities.

The Agreement introduced in decision making a role for management and unions, what has been called the European Social Dialogue. Its introduction was formally asked for at the Maastricht IGC by the European social actors (UIECE, ECPE, ETUC). First, member states may delegate to the social partners the task of implementing directives relating to the above goals; second, the Commission must consult them before submitting any formal social policy proposals; and third, the Agreement recognized that the social partners may be in a position to agree on actions themselves. In addition, they can agree to ask for the formal structures to implement agreements they have reached. Some analysts see the clauses relating to the social dialogue and the role of the social partners as very significant, arguing that they signal a new way of applying doctrines of partnership, consultation and openness and of implementing the principle of subsidiarity. The protocol was concerned with the use of the Community's institutions by the signatories to the Agreement. In 1996, the Commission argued that the social dialogue could well be promoted at sectoral level, leaving the European discussions to concentrate on strategic priorities. The more broadly these are defined, the stronger becomes the case for admitting representatives of voluntary organizations, the churches and local authorities to membership.

The effect of the Agreement on social policy was tiresome rather than significant since it was always the intention to get all members to agree if possible and only to use the Agreement as a last resort. British employers' and union organizations were represented through the European umbrella organizations, so Britain's voice was not entirely excluded. However, it is just as well that the new Labour government announced in 1997 that it was ready to accept the Agreement which thus became incorporated into the legal structure with the Amsterdam Treaty.

The Union treaty also brought changes regarding the entry of migrants. Most member states are under pressure from nationals of third countries at present and, in consequence, immigration and asylum policies are being re-examined. The Council of Ministers obtained the duty to determine the third countries whose nationals must be in possession of a visa, at first by unanimity but, from January 1996, by QMV. Emergency arrangements may be made to deal with a sudden inflow of people. Migratory movements also affect the Community role in ensuring cooperation in the fields of justice and home affairs (see Section 23.6 below).

All in all, the Union treaty gave the EU more standing in social affairs, tidied up existing policies and made explicit where the Community had arrived in the execution of its work. This, in itself, helped to avoid future arguments about the legal basis of proposals. The more significant developments in the 1990s are to be found in the broadened objectives and enhanced role of the social partners, and the launching of the European employment strategy, developments which have been consolidated through the Treaty of Amsterdam and implemented by the following European Councils. The unpopularity of the European project that surfaced during the ratification of the Maastricht Treaty heightened the belief that the EU must not only do more for the general public but be seen to be doing so. The temptation for governments to negotiate by themselves strategic compromises between national interests (and, by such, to do without the Commission) has accelerated the search for a new 'softer' European method. An open method of coordination was set up in Lisbon (2000) and incorporated into the Treaty of Nice. It intends to develop a more integrated approach of social policies, through the coordination of national policies and under the umbrella of the Broad Economic Policy Guidelines (see Chapter 10). Experimented first in employment affairs, it has vocation to extend to many other fields such as social exclusion, pension reforms, welfare reforms and so on.

This chapter now turns to examine individual policies in more detail, reflecting the fact that achieving a high level of employment and modernizing the European social model are the major preoccupation of the moment.

23.6 Free movement

An essential element of citizenship is the ability to move freely through the territory to which one belongs but, although great strides have been made, this does not apply fully in the EU and it seems generally accepted that it will be a long time before it does (see Chapter 18). The policy reflects the original economic objectives, growing out of the need to establish the free movement of workers. Piecemeal extensions have been made which have brought in more categories of people but it is not yet possible to say that free movement of persons can be taken for granted.

The 1957 provisions were primarily concerned with the mobility of unskilled labour and, in practice, were mainly of benefit to Italy. Today, matters look different. Movement within the Community takes place for many reasons. It may be a way of escaping local unemployment, of filling skill shortages, of a temporary posting from one branch of a company to another or of a firm fulfilling a contract elsewhere in the EU. Movement for non-economic reasons such as joining a breadwinner, study, holidays or the wish to live elsewhere is growing in importance.

The essential structure to ensure free movement of wage earners within the EC of six members was in place by 1968 or settled not long afterwards. The rules protected the right to move for work and to remain in a country subsequently, gave entry rights to families and elaborated a complex system for the maintenance of social security rights. They also confirmed the right to join a trade union and stand for office, the right of access to vocational training and to use the employment services. In this way, the principles of equal treatment and of ensuring non-discrimination were accepted. Broadly speaking, these rules were applied without undue difficulty. Individual cases of discrimination continue to find their way to the ECJ, eligibility to social security benefits being a particularly complex area, but, gradually, the rules have become better understood and observed.

It is necessary, of course, constantly to develop the rules as gaps are found or as the nature of migration changes. Social security for the self-employed as possibilities for movement were opened up, and rules concerning the right of families to move and to receive certain benefits soon required attention. In later years, the movement of skilled persons, managerial staff and professional people became more important. These groups can be more affected by occupational benefits than by statutory social security systems, especially for pension entitlement or by the quality of housing, availability of schools and leisure facilities and, although the EC has not become involved in all these matters, questions of transferability of occupational pension schemes, the incidence of taxation on the transfer of monies and variations in taxation methods are all ones in which it has expressed interest.

An action programme to modernize the free movement arrangements was begun in 1997, not only with the aim of rationalizing the rules but because the EU can now start from the principle of the right of free movement for EU citizens, developing the minimum number of rules for special groups as required (COM (97) 586 final). The passing of the SEA had already led to rules to establish the right to residence for students and their families during the period of education (Directive 90/366); employees and the self-employed were given the right to remain after working in a country (Directive 90/365); and other groups were covered by Directive 90/364. In all cases, the right was made subject to the possession of adequate financial resources. There is now a drive for new legal rules, means to overcome administrative difficulties and known obstacles, a more modern interpretation of eligibility of family members, as well as to cater better for third country nationals who are resident in one member state but to whom free movement rules may not apply. As part of this policy, the basic Regulation on social security (Regulation 1408/71, see OJ L28, 30.1.97 and OJ C325, 23.10.98) is progressively extended. The rules of the application of social security schemes have been clarified to ensure all persons eligible for benefits are covered (i.e. to include the non-active), to aggregate periods of entitlement, to coordinate national rules and to cover newer types of benefit, for example early retirement benefit. An extension of the Regulation is in the pipeline

(6.2.2002), aiming at ensuring equality of treatment of Community citizens and nationals of third countries legally resident in the Community, granting them comparable rights and obligations. A general Directive is proposed (23.5.2001) on the rights of citizens of the Union and their families to move and reside freely within the territory of the member states, whether or not they are pursuing a gainful activity.

Bringing vacancies and workers together was recognized as a necessity from the start but proved a tremendously difficult project. It is much affected by the efficiency of national employment services and by the existing procedures for job descriptions, methods of achieving qualifications and the content of skills expected by such qualifications. Great efforts have been made by the EC to bring some uniformity into these matters so that expectations on both sides match reasonably well. Gradually, agreed European norms are being introduced into national qualifications and into job descriptions without bringing standardization. A mechanism for matching up jobs and applicants was launched in 1994 (EURES). A web database on job vacancies and CVs covering Europe is now available for both jobseekers and employers, but still on a small scale. Handling the exchange of information between social security systems has also been greatly developed (TESS).

There are, however, still problems to overcome to ensure that workers benefit as they should from EC policies. Problems are still reported, for example concerning access to training or the application of the principle of equal opportunity while in the host country. In practice, the right to obtain work in the public sector is often restricted, for example by applying a nationality rule to areas of work which are unconnected with the exercise of public authority in any way. The tax treatment of those who live in one country and work in another or the workings of an early retirement scheme may penalize a migrant. There is also a general need for coordination between the rules for occupational and supplementary pension schemes, especially now that these are becoming more important. A start was made with Directive 98/49 to protect supplementary rights for the employed and the self-employed who are on the move by ensuring that pensions can be paid in another member state, contributions are maintained and workers properly informed of the situation. Guides are available for migrants to know their social rights when moving within the EU. Technical formalities, too, are often formidable but there are plans for a standardized EC Resident card for the automatic renewal of a residence permit, including for those whose work is interrupted by unemployment or ill health.

Free movement of the self-employed and the ability to supply services across frontiers were both written into the original treaty but were very hard to apply due to differences of standards of training, in its content and in the way services are provided in different states. Sometimes the right to supply services has been traditionally qualified by rules concerning nationality, place of origin or where qualifications were obtained, and dismantling such barriers without damage to standards is a highly technical matter. The application of rules to ensure conformity of national qualifications can take many years and in the meantime other barriers can be used to avoid letting non-nationals practise. Disputes, such as that of non-French ski instructors barred from access to work on French ski slopes, can rumble on for years.

The EC has, therefore, always been interested in the comparability, and mutual recognition, of qualifications as a necessary precondition for the mobility of working people. In 1985 the Council of Ministers agreed that the mutual recognition of qualifications must be speeded up and directions were provided on how to establish comparability (OJ C264/83; OJ C208/84). A ruling from the ECJ made it clear that many university courses could be considered as vocational training and that students from all member states must be admitted on the same terms as nationals. This ruling also helped to open up the issue of the content of professional courses. It is generally accepted, however, that it is a field of great complexity and there is a long way to go before a full transparency and understanding of qualifications is obtained.

The health sector saw some of the early work since basic training could be harmonized to a degree to allow for movement for some doctors, nurses, dentists, veterinarians, midwives and pharmacists. Other professions followed but it became necessary to adopt a general directive for the recognition of professional standards of university level and above, other than those already recognized by existing sectoral directives (Directive 89/48). This established a general right to practise, subject to the right of the state to apply limited tests to ensure competence. This was complemented by a second directive (Directive 92/51, OJ L209/92) designed to cover a wide range of education and training courses, including on-the-job training in some instances, but where specific qualifications are not laid down (CEC, 1991b).

23.7   Employment

There have been striking changes in the labour force of the EU since 1957 (see the latest issues of Eurostat *Review* and EC *Employment in Europe* (annual)). It is very much bigger as the population of working age has grown, women have come into the workplace and the EC has enlarged to become the EU. Further increases in membership are foreseen. At the same time, the employment structure has altered. One of the most dramatic changes has been in the growth of information and communications technology both as a new industry and as a business tool. Often, however, the new growth is not geographically well placed to absorb redundant workers who, in any case, would need new skills, while the jobs it offers are frequently part time or temporary, taken by women rather than men. Overall, the EU does not generate new jobs at a rate comparable with that of the USA and Japan and the European rate is inadequate to absorb the larger labour force. It is always hoped that the major economic policies of the Union, such as the single market and EMU, either directly or indirectly will create jobs but, often, taking advantage of developments means that workers must be more mobile and more highly trained than heretofore. It is obvious that there are great linguistic and cultural barriers in the EU to worker mobility and, meanwhile, there is a serious mismatch of jobs and workers which implies high unemployment rates in certain areas. European policies have paid particular attention to unemployment amongst young people, women and the long-term unemployed but there is a growing realization of the difficulties faced by older people in finding and keeping a job although they still have skills to offer. Furthermore, the changing demographic structure suggests that the EU needs to keep an open mind on the need for younger, migrant labour to replenish its labour force in the future. A great deal of time is devoted to these questions by European policy makers.

It has proved hard for states to grapple with the changes and particularly difficult for the EU to find a positive role since it operates at one remove. Nevertheless, employment is so central to the work and significance of the EU that it has found ways of developing a wide range of policies to deal with particular employment issues. In 1957, the Treaty of Rome referred to the promotion of a high level of employment and at a time of prosperity the Community could devote itself to specific tasks, such as the free movement and equal pay policies. As the pace of change accelerated and unemployment seemed composed of a number of difficult sub-issues, doubts were expressed as to whether Western Europe would ever again experience very low unemployment rates. Voices were heard – especially from the United Kingdom – suggesting that the treaty required a new goal with a definite commitment to promote employment and in 1997 a new chapter on employment was written into the Treaty of Amsterdam. This requires the Community to promote high employment through a coordinated strategy which includes training a more highly skilled workforce, a labour market more responsive to economic fluctuations (Art. 125), guidelines for member states to follow, encouragement to best practice and annual assessment of the situation. Employment considerations should, in the future, influence new policy decisions. Limited financial support is now available for experimental initiatives and the European Investment Bank (EIB) has been asked to encourage small and medium-sized businesses and new technological activities which are the main job creators. A new employment and labour market committee was created under Art. 130 (EC) and discussion with the social partners given more attention while the Employment Observatory links national organizations together in a mutual support structure and provides regular information on employment trends and on developments in national structures.

The European Employment Strategy (EES) was formally launched in November 1997 at the Luxembourg summit. But it followed several previous attempts to create some form or another of a 'European employment policy'. The first main antecedent of the EES was the White Book on *Growth, Competitiveness, and Employment* (COM (93) 700 final) directed by the Delors Commission in 1993. This first definition of a 'European employment policy' rested on four policies: an active labour market policy; the diminution of 'social charges' on labour; an industrial policy (long-term competitiveness; building of European infrastructure networks; development of new activities) and a social and democratic policy (national consensus involving the social partners). The White Book was therefore a balanced and ambitious approach, which proposed a convincing 'New Deal' for Europeans.

At the Essen summit, only the reduction of (direct and indirect) labour costs was to survive in its original form. In particular, the project of 'European networks' is abandoned. Second, the social dialogue policy remains on the agenda, but in a strange way whereby it is both enlarged (the general responsibility of the social partners in the process is renewed) and constrained as the outcome of the talks, notably on wages, is pre-determined. Last, the *employment* policy is re-dubbed *active labour market* policy (or ALMP). There was a marked policy shift, away from the traditional approach of income support for the unemployed as the main service available, to the belief that far more had to be done to match people's qualifications to the jobs of today and tomorrow. It stressed that individuals must be actively encouraged to enter, or return to, the labour market.

In the Amsterdam summit (June 1997), in order to 'keep employment firmly at the top of the political agenda of the Union', a 'separate Resolution on Growth and Employment' is adopted on top of the Resolution regarding the implementation of the Stability and Growth Pact (see Chapter 9). This resolution, apart from restating the above recipes for fighting unemployment, validates a second shift in focus, namely from 'employment' to 'employability' policies. Far from counter-balancing the restrictions imposed on growth by stage three of the EMU (see Chapter 9), the EES on the contrary limits its action into this pre-defined framework. Having abandoned the possibility to have their say on crucial economic variables such as wages, all the actors implied in the EES can only try to make labour markets work better. In the perspective of the monetary union, the stress was put on the structural reforms of the labour market.

If they can no more rely on growth to provide a sufficiency of jobs, then governments have to consider what they can do to support more labour-intensive work. Society has a significant demand for service jobs, notably in environmental improvement, child care and social services, and it may be necessary for some time to ensure some vacancies remain for unskilled workers. Since it is small and medium-sized firms that have the better record in job creation, it is worthwhile considering how to help them prosper. A main theme for the Commission has been to encourage local initiatives, employment-intensive growth, help with training and extra costs, and assist firms to overcome legal obstacles which face those that wish to take on someone who has been unemployed for some time.

A new Title VIII Employment is introduced in the Amsterdam treaty (October 1997), which makes the promotion of employment 'a matter of common concern' between member states (Art. 126). Art. 128 defines the procedure that is to be followed yearly since 1997: drawing of guidelines by the Council, acting by a qualified majority; annual reports by the member states on the measures taken to implement their employment policy in the light of the guidelines for employment; potential recommendations from the Council to member states following the examination of the national action plans (or NAPs). The EES is thus the first application of the open method of coordination. The Luxembourg process has defined 'guidelines'. These guidelines rely on four pillars: employability; the promotion of entrepreneurship; adaptability of firms and of their employees; and equal opportunities for men and women. In the National Action Plans submitted yearly by the member states, the employability pillar is quantitatively the most important. The employability guidelines are the following:

- activation of the unemployed (offering a 'New start' for every young and long-term unemployed persons and reaching a global rate of activation of 20%);
- reform of benefit and tax systems, in order to reduce poverty traps (introduced in 1999);
- reform of educational and training, through social dialogue;
- fight against discrimination and social exclusion (introduced in 2000).

In 2001, two guidelines were introduced, one to 'prevent bottlenecks' and the other to give incentives for older workers to remain in the labour force as long as possible. Emphasis has been progressively put on the local operation of labour market policies and on the involvement of social dialogue in implementation and evaluation. Last, but not least, the Lisbon summit in 2000 put stress on 'more and better jobs', which has been reformulated by the Commission as a need for 'investing in quality' both for employment and social policies (COM (01) 313 final). At the same time, quantitative targets were agreed on the raising of active participation and employment rates for the next years: increasing employment rates by the year 2010 to 70% overall, to more than 60% for women and to 50% for people aged 55–64.

In 2002, five years later, the EES has become part of a more integrated approach to European social issues. This integrated approach is all the more important as it will frame the building of social policies in Europe and, presumably, in the member states for the next years. The European Social Agenda adopted at the Nice summit of December 2000 outlined what it called the 'triangle' of mutually reinforcing policies – employment, social protection, and economic and budgetary policy. As stated by COM (2001) 362 final of 3 July 2001:

> Social protection policy must seek to ensure an adequate level of income for future pensioners, while supporting the goal of an active welfare society and without creating undue burdens for future generations or destabilising public finance . . . Structural reforms of labour markets, including effective work incentives in social protection and pension systems, should promote the goal of full employment, so as to promote the long term perspectives for pension systems . . . These reforms should support a sustained economic growth, which, in turn, should facilitate reforms and help to reconcile social and financial objectives.

The pensions reform that we will consider in the next section is exemplary of such an approach. Because only a strong interaction between the three summits of that triangle (employment, social protection, economic and budgetary policy) can guarantee the future ability of pension systems to fulfil their basic social goals.

23.8 Pensions

The future of pensions systems is a major challenge in an ageing Europe. Through different combinations of the three pillars (statutory social security, occupational and personal pension schemes), these systems currently offer an unprecedented degree of prosperity and economic independence in the EU. However, the old-age dependency ratio will start increasing rapidly in the next decade and double by the year 2050 compared to today. This is mainly the result of the post-war baby-boom generation reaching retirement age, which adds to the effects of continued low fertility rates and increases in life expectancy. As stressed by COM (2001) 362 final, although the ageing of the population is the result of positive evolutions in the patterns of health care systems and thus constitutes in itself a positive development, if no modernization is undertaken, there is an urgent need for 'safe and sustainable pensions'. Immigration can however make a significant contribution to stabilizing total employment and employment figures.

The Commission points out that achieving safe and sustainable pensions depends on policies in different areas including: social protection, employment, immigration, organisation of work and industrial relations, public finance, prudential regulation, life-long learning, equal opportunities and social inclusion. Hence it calls for an integrated approach and close coordination between policy makers in these different areas. There are a number of EU activities that are concerned with coordination. The most crucial ones are, in our view, the Broad Economic Policy Guidelines (BEPG) and the procedure of multilateral surveillance that examines the economic and budgetary implications of ageing populations. Emphasis has been put on pension reform (and, also health care systems, and care for the elderly) that 'increase the effective retirement age, stimulate higher labour supply participation, set-up and increase public pension fund reserves and possibly encourage the expansion of supplementary privately-funded pensions schemes (pillars 2 and 3)' (The 2001 BEPG, European Council of Gothenburg, June 2001). Financial sustainability of pensions systems is to be achieved, in order not to jeopardize the long-term sustainability of public finances. For the Commission, this objective requires the public spending on pensions to be maintained at a level in terms of a percentage of GDP that is compatible with the Growth and Stability Pact. Other instruments are the portability of pension rights, within the Free Movement of People (Directive 98/49 of June 1998); the proposal for a directive on the activities of institutions for occupational retirement provision (COM (2000) 507 final, 11 October 2000), the Directive 86/378/EEC of 24 July 1986 (amended Directive 96/97/EC of 20 December 1996) on the implementation of the principle of equal treatment for men and women in occupational social security schemes.

Last, but not least, this integrated approach must articulate, simultaneously, the rise of the rate of employment and the ability of pension systems to contribute to enhanced labour market flexibility. The interaction of pension systems with the tax–benefit system should be reviewed with regard to the incentives they offer for high labour force participation, in particular of women and older workers. Gradual transitions from employment to retirement should be made possible by allowing the simultaneous receipt of income from work and by making statutory retirement ages more flexible. An obstacle, at least, remains, namely the use of early retirement schemes by firms and sectors in economic difficulties to softly manage redundancies and job cuts.

As for the EES, governments have agreed to have recourse to the open method of coordination and to define common objectives and indicators. Each government had to elaborate a national strategy and to report on it by mid-2002. The first Joint Report on adequate and sustainable pensions was established by the Commission and Council in March 2003.

23.9   The European Social Fund

The principal weapon the EC possesses to combat unemployment directly is the ESF which operates through grant aid to approved schemes of vocational training and employment support (Art. 146 (EC)). It has undergone several reforms and extensions so that today it is part of a more coordinated effort to fight unemployment and to deliver a highly skilled and adaptable workforce. However, it has never been entirely clear how widely its remit should be drawn as it soon became obvious that many of the unemployed required, for example, help with social skills, child care facilities and the like. Recently, the ESF was placed squarely in the context of the employment strategy of the Amsterdam Treaty but this enables it to contribute to a number of social goals since social integration and the pursuit of equal opportunities can come through enabling people to work. Thus a variety of measures may need support. Specialized help for the long-term unemployed, assistance in developing education and training systems, the promotion of life-long learning, assistance to schemes to improve the skills of the existing workforce and to aid women's participation in the labour force are all examples of the fund's support activities. Its remit is now very wide, covering, for example, aid to help people set up in self-employment, to improve the training of teachers, to modernize employment services as well as to aid 'accompanying measures' such as child care, facilities for dependants, health care and legal assistance for those who, without such help, could not work. Although there has always been a school of thought that would like the ESF to undertake support of schemes with specific social aims, it seems clear that these must be viewed as subordinate to the main objective of helping people into employment or to move to higher skilled work. Considerable interest attaches to the question of which schemes actually receive funding, and competition is intense.

In recent years, the work has been primarily concentrated in poorer regions and countries as part of a targeted effort by all the structural funds. However, a reference to the past may help in understanding the complicated arrangements; a constant cry of reform is for simplification and clarification.

The ESF started in a limited way and primarily assisted migrants from the Italian South to move north into the industrial areas but a subsequent reform, in 1971, created a larger and more flexible fund which could be used to help with training and which gave special attention to the needs of particular groups of workers or regions. By the 1980s it was felt that the fund needed further adaptation. It began to concentrate upon work to promote the employment and training of young people under 25 years of age and, subsequently, of the long-term unemployed. By 1985, grants were also available to members of both groups wishing to set up in self-employment. Grants to special groups such as the handicapped, women workers and migrants continued, as they still do, but were no longer earmarked. Employment in small and medium-sized businesses was encouraged and special grants introduced to aid vocational guidance and placement. The most deprived regions continued to receive special aid but otherwise the fund directed its efforts to areas of persistently high unemployment and where large reconstruction projects were required.

Much of this work was formalized following the passing of the SEA. Perhaps the most important effect

was the recognition of the need to pursue economic and social cohesion as a goal which would offset the possible disadvantageous effects of the single market in some areas. A master Regulation was agreed (2052/88) which established that the European Regional Development Fund (ERDF), the European Agricultural Guidance and Guarantee Fund (EAGGF) (Guidance section) and the ESF, now known jointly as the structural funds and later joined by the Financial Instrument for Fisheries Guidance (FIFG), should coordinate their work and should work closely with the European Investment Bank (EIB) as well (see Chapter 19).

Objectives applicable to all funds were laid down. Regional definitions have recently been reduced to three (see Chapter 18). Objective (1) areas of low GDP and generally high unemployment will receive about two-thirds of structural funds monies and cover about 20% of EU population. This objective includes the very remote regions which may be sparsely populated. Objective (2) covers areas undergoing major economic and social restructuring and includes those where there are special problems, for example areas dependent upon fishing or suffering from industrial decay or rural decline. About 18% of EU population should be covered. In both Objectives (1) and (2) transitional arrangements will help those areas which will no longer be eligible. Objective (3) is concerned with the development of human resources and tackling unemployment generally and is the domain of the ESF (COM (98) 131 final, OJ C176, 9.6.98, amended COM (99) 4 final, OJ C74, 18.3.99).

The Fund has been given five broad tasks. It is to contribute to the development of active labour market policies, including the prevention of unemployment; it must promote social inclusion; it is to aid life-long learning and training to promote employability; it must help workers anticipate and respond to economic and social change and it must aid equal opportunities for men and women. It places much emphasis upon the importance of local initiatives and also provides support for back-up measures such as care and health services. While these aims are drawn up in the light of the overall employment strategy, in the past the greater part of the ESF finances was spent in the poorer regions and therefore integrated with projects falling under Objectives (1) or (2).

The budget of the ESF for the years 2000–2006 should be nearly 70 billion ECU, 35% of the structural funds monies. In most cases, its aid is limited to half the cost of an approved scheme. Of the structural funds monies, 5% is handled directly by the Commission and used to support transnational, cross-frontier and inter-regional schemes, and 1% is earmarked for a variety of innovative schemes and local projects. Here the Commission may provide total funding. It is in this area that experimental schemes, often run by voluntary organizations and working on a small scale, are to be found. The *Leader* programme is for rural areas, *Urban* for deprived city areas and *Equal* for equality promotion projects.

The search for an improved administrative structure continues. It is generally agreed that grant procedures are cumbersome and administration is opaque but successive changes seem to make little difference. The post-1988 system brought important changes with a shift towards making schemes find their place in an overall national plan which can then be approved in Brussels. The emphasis was on partnership between the Commission, member governments, local authorities and other representatives who should together formulate multi-annual programmes to their mutual satisfaction and which should give a necessary stability of finance to individual schemes. The Commission, instead of being involved in the minutiae of scheme approval, was expected to develop its monitoring, control and evaluative functions. This arrangement put far more control into the hands of the central national agency, usually a Department for Employment or its equivalent, which became a channel for the submission of applications and disbursement of grants. Administratively, this arrangement worked much more smoothly than when the Commission was involved in the detail of schemes and it can, of course, be argued that national authorities know their own needs best. One obvious danger of national control is that the Commission is less able to impose its views on how grant aid should be used. Since it tends to be forward looking and has an interest in the spread of new skills and in grasping the opportunities of technological change the Commission may clash with national representatives who are often under pressure to maintain jobs in declining industries or to support new schemes of job creation as an immediate method of reducing unemployment irrespective of long-term viability. However, great importance is currently attached to these issues, to find more effective methods of monitoring schemes and ensure financial efficiency. Current emphasis continues on the importance of partnership with regional and local authorities, economic and social partners and others, with a stress on local development initiatives. Importance is given, too, to the work of voluntary organizations, with authorities being encouraged to help them obtain a place in Community programmes. Clashes of priorities will clearly continue as not all these bodies have the same interests, the Commission has its own agenda and national governments wish to be major players in policy at home and to obtain the maximum possible share of the grants available. Evaluation and monitoring of schemes is clearly difficult for the Commission but a new monitoring committee, with a balanced male/female membership, is another innovation.

A further difficulty facing the Commission is to ensure the principle of additionality. The intention has always been that the Commission, by insisting upon matching grants from member states, ensures that more work is done than would otherwise have been the case but whether it truly does so often remains a mystery. A test of this reform will be the mid-term evaluation at the end of 2003.

The ESF has become a significant part of the EU structure, especially now that its mandate has broadened to enable it to play a role in delivering a highly skilled and adaptable workforce. It has begun, in a small way, to reach out beyond the immediate confines of work by recognizing social factors which inhibit potential workers from coming forward and thus it is beginning to play a part in the prevention of social exclusion and to reflect the view that disadvantaged people must be helped to become self-supporting.

23.10   Education and vocational training

Since the European Council of Lisbon (23–24 March 2000), the EU is facing a new challenge for the current decade: 'to become the most competitive and dynamic knowledge-based economy in the world' (see Chapter 13). This new strategic goal has put education and vocational training at the top of the political agenda (among other issues, like innovation and quality of employment).

Europe's education and training systems need to adapt both to the demands of the knowledge society and to the need for an improved level and quality of employment. They will have to offer learning and training opportunities tailored to target groups at different stages of their lives: young people, unemployed adults and those in employment who are at risk of seeing their skills overtaken by rapid change. This new approach centred on lifelong learning should have several main components: improving the quality and effectiveness of education and training systems in the EU; facilitating access for all to education and training systems; promoting new basic skills, in particular in the information technologies (e-learning), and increased transparency of qualifications.

From the start, the EEC had certain responsibilities in the field of vocational training and these have led to its gradual move into educational work. The dividing line between training and education is increasingly hard to draw since it is now believed that, in the past, educational systems were too divorced from economic reality so that many young people left school ill-prepared for the world of work. A further impetus has come from the need to reconsider the content of training in order to equip the labour force with the higher skills that industry requires. The Community, no less than its member states, is in the process of adapting to these new requirements and trying to make its services appropriate for current needs. At the same time, more attention to education and training provides an opportunity to encourage greater awareness of the EU and its objectives among the rising generation. See, for instance: COM (97) 256 final, *Teaching and Learning: towards the Learning Society* (CEC, 1995d); *Living and Working in the Information Society: People First* (COM (96) 389 final); and *Towards a Europe of Knowledge* (COM (97) 563 final); *e-Learning: Designing Tomorrow's Education* (COM (2000) 318 final); *Making a European Area of Life Long Learning a Reality* (COM (2001) 678 final); *Investing Efficiently in Education and Training: an Imperative for Europe* (COM (2002) 779 final); *The Role of the Universities in the Europe of Knowledge* (COM (2003) 58 final).

The legal base for action in the fields of education and vocational training is now in Articles 149 and 150 (EC). These refer to the Community's role in contributing to quality education while fully respecting the responsibilities of member states for educational services and their cultural and linguistic diversity. Educational action aims to develop a 'European dimension' through helping to improve language skills, increase mobility and exchanges amongst students and staff,

through work to ensure the recognition of qualifications, to promote cooperation between educational establishments and long-distance education. Similar phraseology surrounds the vocational training policy which is designed to support and supplement national efforts through encouraging adaptation to industrial changes, improved training and retraining, and facilitating access to it, and greater mobility and cooperation between instructors, training establishments and trainees.

The new drive on education and vocational training policy began in 1995. Objectives were linked to the need for a better quality of education, a spread of qualifications throughout the population and work to make national systems more comparable. Since states themselves are actively recasting educational and training systems, the Commission's role is to act as a stimulus, to help to set up schemes and to encourage their development in ways which help to cement the EU. A special interest is to foster innovation and the effective use of technology through the encouragement it can give to young people, the learning of new skills and the transfer of knowledge.

Following its White Paper of 1995 the Commission regrouped its many programmes into three main groups. Its *Youth* programme supports youth exchange schemes, short visits and voluntary participation in common projects in order to increase European awareness (see OJ C309, 9.10.98; OJ C311, 10.10.98; OJ C314, 13.10.98 for details). *Leonardo da Vinci* is concerned with vocational training. Like the *Youth* schemes it includes Norway, Iceland and Liechtenstein and is extending to cover Central and Eastern Europe, Cyprus and Malta. By 2000, there should be 31 participating countries. Placement and exchange schemes enable those in training or on university courses to obtain work placements in another member state with the aim of improving vocational training and promoting vocational skills. A particular interest is in placements in the use of information technology (Council Decision OJ L146, 11.06.99).

It was as early as the 1970s that the Commission became aware of the problem of young people leaving school inadequately prepared for work and it began to encourage schemes to provide better pre-training preparation for them. At the same time, it established the European Centre for the Development of Vocational Training (CEDEFOP), now in Thessaloniki, to encourage greater awareness of training needs and learning opportunities and to act as an information and resource centre. The Centre has a series of agreements with other European states to ensure a basic compatibility between all training developments. In similar vein, a European Foundation for Training, in Turin, maintains links with CEDEFOP and acts as a channel offering similar support to the countries of Central and Eastern Europe, the ex-Soviet states and Mongolia. One particular problem is that some states need to prepare their training systems for the hoped-for closer association with the EU and this aim requires considerable change and a great deal of effort to improve fluency in at least one EU language.

Third, the *Socrates* programme, which again includes Norway, Iceland and Liechtenstein, has responsibilities in higher education. Student exchanges figure prominently, with a special interest in language studies, joint courses and teacher exchanges. The aim is still to have 10% of the student population spending some time abroad so as to create a growing pool of graduates with EU experience for the future. A new venture is to support university courses which wish to introduce a European element into courses which are not formally joint or exchange schemes but which will, nevertheless, contain a measure of joint cooperation. A system of Course Credit Transfer is being developed which should make student mobility easier over time and this, in turn, may well lead to a greater uniformity in course content, with the benefit of making it easier for courses followed to be recognized. Recently, the *Socrates* programme has agreed to support alternative educational pathways to higher education, to promote the use of multi-media techniques and to encourage innovative schemes.

The *Comenius* programme, with similar aims, covers the secondary school years. It is based on the need to foster partnership between schools which may cooperate in language and other subject teaching; this is made easier by the growth of computer networks and fast communications. Children of migrants and itinerants have been able to benefit for many years from language and introductory courses which are now operated through *Comenius*.

Language teaching at all levels is today supported more strongly than ever with the aim of seeking proficiency in three Community languages for younger generations. This depends critically on being able to offer opportunities in other member states for language teachers and teachers in training. Improved teaching

material is always being sought and the use of open learning techniques encouraged. Support for courses in European studies in adult education is beginning.

All these schemes are now asked to support the EU broader social aims of equal opportunities and combating inequality. The *Eurydice* network exists specifically to provide information on the range of schemes, an office for educational statistics has been created and the *Iris* network handles the exchange of information on women's education.

A particular effort is being made towards Central and Eastern Europe, including the ex-Soviet states and Mongolia, to aid the reform of higher education. For the relevant states, this is believed to be a necessary preliminary to membership of, or association with, the EU. The projects are becoming more varied as different national needs are identified but it is considered important that universities, in general, should open up to outside influences. A rough division can be made between the group of states from the ex-Soviet area and Mongolia, the group preparing for membership of the EU or at least some form of pre-membership, for whom the need for change in educational and training systems is in known, although specific ways, and a third group. Their membership is a very long way off but their geographical position demands sympathy for their aspirations. These include the states of ex-Yugoslavia (other than Slovenia which falls into the second group) and Albania. Contacts with the universities of Western Europe, the provision of teaching materials and an increased mobility for students and staff are all important.

A clause in the EC Treaty decreed that the Community should contribute to the flowering of the cultures of the members. Its particular tasks are to concentrate upon encouraging cooperation between member states, improving knowledge about European culture and history and conserving the cultural heritage of European significance. As a result, the Commission has a range of initiatives relating in particular to the last-mentioned goal, and has a new framework of programmes starting in 2000. One of the most contentious issues has been the use of television and, with the increase in the number of channels, whether transmission should give some priority to European programmes. Despite efforts to make it mandatory to devote half of all viewing time to European productions it appears likely that the EU will persevere with voluntary quota systems. Financial assistance is given through 'incentive measures' to these various schemes.

For achieving this global strategy towards knowledge, the European Councils (Lisbon, March 2000; Nice, December 2000; Stockholm, March 2001; Barcelona, March 2002) call upon the member states, in line with their constitutional rules, the Council and the Commission to take the necessary steps within their areas of competence, to enhance their cooperation and to focus and report on concrete future objectives of education and training systems. A series of targets for 2010 have been agreed:

- a substantial annual increase in per capita investment in human resources;
- the number of 18- to 24-year-olds with only lower-secondary level education who are not in further education and training should be halved by 2010;
- schools and training centres, all linked to the internet, should be developed into multi-purpose local learning centres accessible to all, using the most appropriate methods to address a wide range of target groups; learning partnerships should be established between schools, training centres, firms and research facilities for their mutual benefit;

- a European framework should define the new basic skills to be provided through lifelong learning: IT skills, foreign languages, technological culture, entrepreneurship and social skills; a European diploma for basic IT skills, with decentralized certification procedures, should be established in order to promote digital literacy throughout the Union;
- to define the means for fostering the mobility of students, teachers and training and research staff both through making the best use of existing Community programmes (Socrates, Leonardo, Youth), by removing obstacles and through greater transparency in the recognition of qualifications and periods of study and training; to take steps to remove obstacles to teachers' mobility and to attract high-quality teachers.
- a common European format should be developed for curricula vitae, to be used on a voluntary basis, in order to facilitate mobility by helping the assessment of knowledge acquired, both by education and training establishments and by employers.

23.11   Consumer policy

The Maastricht Treaty gave consumer protection the status of a full policy (Article 153 (EC)). It now covers an obligation to promote the interests of consumers, ensure their protection and promote their right to information and education and to better organization to safeguard their interests. The single market raised the problem that consumers simply would not know how to judge the quality of goods bought unless minimum standards were applied, would have difficulty in obtaining redress for faulty goods or would not understand what was being offered by a service. The public has, indeed, to have full information about goods and services on offer but recent worries suggest that a good deal more needs to be done. The Consumer Committee gives direct access to the Commission for national consumer groups but consumer representation is poorly developed in the southern states and in Central and Eastern Europe. Consumer protection has now been combined with health to form a Commission portfolio. The BSE (Bovine Spongiform Encephalopathy) crisis, followed by concerns relative to foot-and-mouth disease and the spreading of genetically modified organisms has given a strong impetus to food safety ('from the farm to the fork'; see Chapter 20). The creation of an independent European Food Authority has been recommended by the White Book on Food Safety (COM (1999) 719 final).

A directive on distant selling and an improved directive on comparative and misleading advertisements were adopted in 1997 and are moving through the EU procedures. A time-share directive was adopted in 1994. The general product safety directive of 1992 was adjusted in 2001, taking into account the experience acquired from its implementation and in the light of the precautionary principle. A database on home and leisure accidents has been set up and some protection is given on the use of computer-held personal data. A multi-annual Community action plan was defined in 1999 on promoting safer use of the internet.

23.12 Working conditions and industrial relations

Collective bargaining remains a matter handled within member states and it is only gradually that industrial relations acquired a European dimension, although some of the Commission initiatives have met with fierce opposition. From the Community's point of view, three themes stand out which, in day-to-day affairs, are often tangled together. There is, first, the belief that it is important to involve employers' associations and unions in the operation of European affairs; second, that consultation, or even cross-Community negotiation, may be necessary in some cases; and third, that an integrated market may require some changes in traditional national arrangements.

The Paris and Rome treaties established certain formal structures, notably the ECSC Consultative Committee and the EEC Economic and Social Committee, to associate representatives of employers, workers and other groups with EC affairs. Subsequently, advisory committees, such as those for the ESF, were constituted with joint representation: many joint committees meet to consider the problems of a particular industry as required and a number of attempts have been made to establish a meeting place for the two sides of industry, with or without representatives of governments. However, none of these methods proved satisfactory and tension grew with the rise in unemployment. The then Commission President, Jacques Delors, was a prime mover in attempts to give the 'social dialogue' more prominence, seeing it as one way in which trade union and business opinion might be mobilized behind the process of European integration. In his view, it was essential that 'social partners' became supporters of the process of convergence toward the euro, which meant the acceptance of wage moderation and of productivity growth through new technologies and work organization.

The theme of consensus between the social partners, leading to agreed policies to improve working conditions and social security benefits, is a long-standing one in Continental systems of industrial relations but alien to the UK. The British government, particularly in the 1980s, disliked both the attempt to give the social dialogue a formal place in Community affairs and the greater legal regulation of industrial matters to which it can give rise. Nevertheless, the UK agreed that the SEA should give the Commission a duty to develop the dialogue between management and labour at European level and, with the Amsterdam Treaty, political objections have been removed. Not only is the dialogue supported but also the Commission has a duty to consult the social partners prior to any social policy initiative and, if a further development is decided upon, management and labour may handle the matter through their own procedures for agreements (Articles 138, 139 (EC)).

A recent addition to the machinery is the European Industrial Relations Observatory set up in 1997 primarily to study questions of the workplace, establish a database and keep national centres in touch with developments across the Union.

How far regulation of working conditions by the Community is made necessary on moral grounds, on economic grounds to ensure competitive fairness or simply on political grounds to meet demands from powerful interests has never been resolved. Although in recent years it has been a major bone of contention, there now exists a body of European legislation which is in process of being bedded down. It is not expected to grow a great deal during the next few years. Some of this legislation is extremely precise and detailed but some is more of an outline which member states are expected to apply themselves. This is particularly true in health and safety measures.

In the early 1970s, a particular form of job loss came through a spate of takeovers and mergers, often connected with the growth of multinational companies. Here the EC felt it could claim a particular interest and successfully passed directives on the procedures to be followed in the case of collective dismissals (now Directive 98/59 OJ L225, 12.8.98), the maintenance of employee rights when companies merged (now Directive 98/50 OJ L201, 17.7.98) and the protection of rights when a firm became insolvent (now Directive 2002/74). Subsequent attempts by the Commission to pursue higher standards of employment law proved less successful and a succession of proposals were either dropped or postponed. However, more recently, there have been signs of agreement on a number of regulatory matters. Limits on working time were the subject of a proposed directive in 1990, finally adopted in November 1993 (Directive 93/104 OJ L307/93). The directive ensures a weekly rest period of one complete day, that rules for annual holidays had to be a minimum of four weeks by 1999, the need for a break after six hours work, a maximum working day of 11 hours and night shifts with an average maximum of eight hours. Revisions have been achieved to limit the large number of exempted posts which initially included workers in transport, sea fishing and doctors in training. Managers may be exempt, apart from the annual holiday clauses, and governments can find ways of shielding some industries, including the media, agriculture and the utilities. Collective agreements may be used to modify the rules. Workers can volunteer to work for longer hours (at least until 2003) and some flexibility exists in working out the 48 hours by averaging out the hours worked over a period from four months to one year.

A proposal on the protection of pregnant women at work became law as Directive 92/85 (OJ L348/92). A directive on the provision of proof of an employment contract (Directive 91/533) was agreed but a proposal to safeguard the conditions of workers temporarily posted elsewhere in the Community dragged on until 1996 (Directive 96/71 OJ L18/97, 21.1.97). It applies to firms which post workers to another member state and to temporary employment agencies engaged in hiring out labour in another member state. Its aim is to allow workers to benefit from the working conditions operative in the state to which they are posted, subject to certain exemptions.

A long-drawn-out project has been to ensure information for, and consultation of, workers in Europe-wide firms through the setting up of works councils or their equivalent. Apart from disagreements about the substance of the proposals there have been practical difficulties about how to implement them. Real differences of national practice and interest appeared to be involved, as well as a clash between the conception of a single market as one of deregulation and free enterprise or one in which the future requires the prior agreement of the social partners and a framework of European employment law. The quarrel led to the first directive under the Social Agreement (Directive 94/45 OJ L254/94) which became operative in December 1996. It covers firms with at least 1000 employees, operating across borders and with at least 150 employees in each of two countries or more. It aims to give employees a degree of information about, and influence on, operations. This long process has resulted in Directive 2002/14/EC establishing a general framework for informing and consulting employees. Its implementation until 2007 is mainly left to national governments and to social partners. In October 2001,

a Statute for a European company with regard to the involvement of employees was supplemented by Directive 2001/86/EC.

A directive on parental leave (Directive 96/34 OJ L145/96) was also originally produced under the Social Agreement on the basis of a framework produced by the Union of Industries of the European Community, the European Centre of Public Enterprises with Public Participation and the European Trade Union Confederation and subsequently submitted to the Commission to be put up to the Council of Ministers for adoption in June 1996. Men and women are entitled to three months unpaid leave to be taken before the child's eighth birthday and to time off for urgent family reasons. It sets out minimum standards only and stresses the importance of not using the directive to level down or to indulge in discriminatory practices, makes states responsible for compliance and allows them to fix penalties for infringement. This directive is now operative in the UK (from December 1999), although in a rather limited way.

The encouragement of employee asset holding and profit sharing was done through a recommendation (COM (91) 259 final) and a directive to give better health and safety protection for part-time workers (Directive 91/383) was adopted in June 1991.

Employment difficulties are acute for the disabled and handicapped. The Council passed a recommendation in 1986 stressing the importance of providing fair opportunities for training and employment and setting out a model code of action. A proposed directive (COM (90) 588 final, amended by COM (91) 539 final) lays down rules to assist workers with motor disabilities with travel to and from work in employer-provided and public transport (see also Section 23.15).

Another long-standing issue is the question of whether European controls are needed over the conditions of part-time workers and those on temporary contracts. The Commission had long held the view that they should be employed on the same terms as full-time employees, on a *pro rata* basis including the same chances of promotion and access to the same range of benefits. The social partners began to negotiate on flexible working time and worker safety, looking at the many new forms of work now offered. This in itself is a more modern and flexible approach to a difficult subject which accepts that atypical employment has become the norm for many people and can, if handled carefully, even produce a better-balanced lifestyle as long as it can be developed without exploitation. A framework agreement on contractual rights for part-timers (whether on permanent, temporary or fixed contracts but not casual workers) was thereby reached to cover occupational pensions, paid occupational sick leave, staff discounts and paid holidays (Directive 97/81 OJ L14, 20.1.98). The control of abuse of fixed-term contracts through the repeated issue of very short-term contracts which escape the rules is also being discussed. In July 2002,

a fourth agreement was signed between the European social partners, the framework agreement on telework.

Nevertheless, the pros and cons of employment regulation by the EC continue to be hotly debated. The benefits to workers are contrasted with the possible impediment to business creation, to worker recruitment and thus to labour mobility – all of which are desirable social goals.

23.13 Health and safety

The protection of industrial health and safety stretches back to 1951 when the ECSC established a programme of research and standard setting. Special commissions were created for the steel industry and for mining, the latter including offshore oil wells, and a large number of recommendations have been issued. The Euratom treaty gave the Commission power to establish precise standards of protection in the nuclear industry while monitoring of the amount of radioactivity in the environment is carried out under Article 36. Industrial health and safety was included in the Treaty of Rome as one of the matters on which the Commission might encourage collaboration and it developed an active programme of research and recommendations as a result.

Over the years, EC interest broadened. Its span extended to include environmental pollution and issues of protection and conservation. Meanwhile, the EC edged towards a clearer role in community health with an emphasis on preventive programmes, interesting itself in questions such as the effect of modern industrial lifestyles on human welfare, the social costs of night work, the incidence of alcoholism and drug abuse and of social scourges such as cancer and Aids. The ever increasing cost of social security, of which health care forms a large part, pushed the EC into taking a greater interest in the specific question of the costs of personal health care.

Basic standards to protect both the general public and workers against ionizing radiation were published in 1980 and updated following the Chernobyl accident. An outline directive on the protection of workers against the use of dangerous substances was agreed the same year and was followed by one concerned to protect against the hazards of a major accident, this following the chemical disaster at Seveso, Italy. This directive was replaced by Directive 96/82

OJ L10/97. All such factors meant that health ministers found it advantageous to meet together and set up cooperative and joint programmes.

The drive to the internal market renewed interest in industrial health and safety standards if only because of their possible effect upon the new policy. The Act took the path of agreeing to minimum standards, to avoid placing an excessive burden on small and medium-sized businesses and accepted that no state should be forced to lower its existing standards. A framework directive was passed to cover all main sectors of activity and to set out the duties of employer and employees. This provided the context for more specialized directives dealing with particular industries. However, it remained a difficult field, in which industrial change required a faster momentum of work in order to keep pace; control and monitoring had to be made effective and the growing number of public complaints handled. It became clear, too, that interpretations differed as to what subjects should be included in terms such as 'the working environment' and 'health and safety'. The Maastricht Treaty made explicit that the EC has a duty to contribute towards ensuring a high level of health protection (Articles 3(0) and 152 (EC)) and singles out disease prevention, including drug dependence, as a main field of interest through encouraging research and information and educational programmes.

Community health problems are constantly changing and the EU, by virtue of its responsibilities in both health and the free flow of goods, necessarily takes on new subjects, as demonstrated by the question of the import of American products containing genetically modified maize and of British beef exports once bovine spongiform encephalopathy (BSE) had been identified. Such safety worries have led to the demand for an independent European Food and Public Health

Authority. The need for better data and informational programmes seems set to grow and a five-year programme for health action was established despite arguments over its financing (see COM (95) 282 final, Medium Term Action Programme for Health and Safety at Work 1996–2000).

There have been a number of cases concerned with the supply of drugs and the need to reconcile confidence in them with the maintenance of a single market. A European agency collects and analyses data on drug use while a monitoring centre analyses drug addictions. The European Agency for the Evaluation of Medicines is part of the regulatory framework. The Amsterdam Treaty has given fresh prominence to a drug action programme both in the sense of control over new, synthetic drugs and with measures to control illegal supply and drug trafficking.

Although some enthusiasts would like to see minimum standards of health care established, the EU does not have a responsibility for personal health care but it does have an effect on service provision. The free movement policies have meant the need to establish the mutual recognition of the qualifications of health professionals, some of whom now have the right to practise anywhere while others still do not. EU citizens who trained outside the EU are not normally covered although bilateral arrangements may overcome this problem. In practice, movement is on a small scale for administrative barriers abound, hidden discrimination is reported and linguistic difficulties are genuine.

The free movement of citizens policy may have a greater impact on the patients than the staff should they begin to move to obtain treatment. For some years people have been entitled to treatment if they fall ill when visiting another member state, special schemes cover some groups of workers (e.g. transport workers or students) and cross-frontier services have become acceptable although in a controlled way. There is, as yet, no explicit right for people to travel to seek help but such travel can be arranged, and there are examples of cross-frontier agreements with hospitals to supply surgery where there is pressure on beds.

Two recent cases heard by the ECJ raised the question of reimbursement from the state health insurance scheme of Luxembourg for the cost of goods and services obtained outside the home country. The Court held that prior authorization could be necessary in some circumstances but that the principles of Community law, notably the principle of the free movement of goods and the freedom to supply services, must be respected (*Kohll* and *Decker* judgment, 28 April 1998, Cases C–120/95 and C–158/96). There are other interesting questions looming, for example whether the growth of private health insurance should develop to cover care in another member state and whether a prescription issued in one country should be honoured in another. Although the legal basis for action is limited, there are considerable pressures towards seeing EU health policy expand in the future.

In its COM (2002) 118 final, 'Adapting to change in work and society', the Commission has adopted for 2002–2006 a global approach to well-being at work, taking account of changes in the world of work and the emergence of new risks, especially of a psycho-social nature. Health and safety are now viewed as essential elements in terms of the quality of work. The number of occupational accidents remains high, not far short of 5500 deaths a year in Europe. A worrying return to a rising scale of accidents has been evident since 1999, in certain member states and sectors. The candidate countries have an average frequency of occupational accidents which is well above the average for the EU, mainly because of their higher specialization in sectors which are traditionally regarded as high-risk.

Corporate social responsibility has also its role to play in those issues, with regard to the increasing trends towards outsourcing. For a large number of firms, a healthy and safe working environment is an important criterion in the choice of their subcontractors and the way they market their products. The Green Paper on corporate social responsibility (COM (2001) 366 final) stressed that health at work is one of the areas for voluntary 'good practices' on the part of firms which want to go beyond existing rules and standards.

23.14   Equal treatment of men and women

Work to improve the position of women, both socially and economically, has proved one of the most positive of EU policies. Starting from a limited legal base, the EC was able to exploit the absence of effective national policies and to become an important influence on their development. Unusually in social affairs, it had a relatively clear field which allowed it to adopt a leadership role for which its position makes it well suited.

An equal pay policy was written into the Treaty of Rome at French insistence. France already had a legal requirement for equal pay. There remained, however, a noticeable lack of enthusiasm about the enforcement of the treaty until the 1970s. Some publicity had been attracted to Article 119 (now Article 141 (EC)) by the problem of a Sabena airhostess who had lodged a complaint in Belgium concerning the inequality of her conditions of service. The question of her pay, which was less than that of a male steward, led ultimately to a consideration by the ECJ which made clear its view that the article was meant to be taken seriously and properly applied. One result was to spur the Commission to produce a directive on equal pay in 1975 (Directive 75/117 OJ L45/75). This included a definition of equal pay, to include both identical work and work of equal value, established certain controls and required an effective appeals system. It therefore provided a much stricter framework within which member states had to apply the policy.

It soon became clear, however that by itself this was a reform of limited value if women were to achieve equality at work. Apart from the need to clarify the concept of equal pay, which is gradually being done through court judgments, men and women had very different social security coverage and Directive 79/7 (OJ L6/79) required the progressive implementation of the principle of equal treatment in statutory schemes over a six-year period. There were still certain exclusions to the rules, notably for family and survivors' benefits, and member states could retain some different provisions if they wished. The most important was the right to retain different ages for retirement pensions although, in practice, this difference is slowly disappearing. Since the *Marshall* case, women have had the right to retire at the same age as men from the public sector (Case C–152/84 [1986] OJ C79). In 1986, the principle of equal treatment was extended to cover occupational schemes and provision for the self-employed (Directive 86/378 OJ L225/86 and 283/86). This directive was intended to ensure equal rights in the private sector by 1993 subject to some latitude allowed for differences in life expectancy. An important ECJ judgment in 1990 (Case C–262/88) held that occupational pensions were to be considered as part of pay and, therefore, that the rules of equal pay must apply. Different ages

for eligibility for such pensions could no longer be used, although the judgment was not retrospective. Directive 96/97 (OJ L46/97) has incorporated this rule although differences in life expectancy still affect actuarial calculations and the self-employed are not yet covered.

The Commission has been anxious, for some time, to see a new directive on social security to include benefits still outside the scope of EC directives, notably to include equal treatment for the sexes in retirement and in claiming benefits for dependants. It would also like to move the legal basis for entitlement to that of an individual's rights rather than deriving rights from the concept of dependency and this would put many women workers in a very different position from the one they hold today. Progress on these two moves is slow.

Underlying questions of pay and social security is the whole question of women's position in the labour force, which is still much less favourable than that of men. Women in practice earn less, often because they are concentrated in low skilled and low-paid work and form the bulk of part-time workers. The unemployment rate for working women is disproportionately high, partly because their work is particularly vulnerable. These factors may result in an indirect discrimination, which is much more difficult to remedy through Court rulings.

Recognition of the lack of equal opportunities to obtain work and of equality of treatment at work opened the way to a variety of EC support programmes. These have ranged from a consideration of the types of education offered to girls to the importance of effective support for the working mother through more flexible hours and the development of child care facilities and the need to encourage men to take on more household chores. Thus EC policy has, for some years, followed twin paths. On the one hand have been measures to ensure legally enforceable rights and, on the other, programmes to encourage a fuller social and working role for women. In June 2001, the European Council reached a political agreement, by unanimity, on a proposed amendment of Directive 76/207/EEC. It brings this long-standing equal opportunities directive into line with European court judgments and new Commission anti-discrimination proposals under the Amsterdam Treaty (Article 13). This amendment is a first attempt to tackle sexual harassment in Community law. It also defines the notion of indirect discrimination, encourages social partners to adopt collective agreements laying down anti-discrimination provisions. It implements the right of the woman who has given birth to return to her job, or to an equivalent post. Finally, it puts an obligation on member states to take account of the objective of equality between men and women when formulating and implementing laws and policies (the principle of gender mainstreaming has to be applied at all levels of policy making).

However, the need to pay more attention to the balance between employment and family responsibilities (or more largely to reconcile work and private life) is still receiving a modest priority. This sometimes results in paradoxical decisions. For instance, in Case *Commission* v. *French Republic* (13 March 1997), France was judged to be infringing the principle of equal treatment because of the general prohibition on night work by women in industry contained in the French Labour Code. Threatened by a daily fine, France was obliged to modify its legislation. Nevertheless, at its origin, this legislation intended to provide women with wider possibilities to reconcile family childcare and work.

Attempts to strengthen, and equalize, the position of workers taking parental leave, or leave for family reasons, were blocked for a long time but they are a useful reminder that an equal treatment policy may sometimes require more rights to be given to men. A Council recommendation on the need to develop child care facilities for working parents and for those taking courses was passed in 1992 (OJ L123/92).

The ESF has always been interested in grant-aiding schemes which help women at work and these have been important in raising the level of understanding about women's needs. Upgrading of women's opportunities through better education and more appropriate training has been encouraged; grant aid has been given to help women return to work after child rearing, to enter posts normally filled by men, to train for work using new technologies and to finance child care facilities and to give help to the female entrepreneur. In recent years, the Community Action programmes on equal opportunities for men and women have put a stress on treating equal opportunities as an objective which should run through all Community policies, and equality issues began to receive a higher profile in the Commission's work in general. Particular concerns have been to promote measures to reconcile working and family life for both men and women, to promote equality in decision making and in opportunities for education, vocational training and in the labour market. Information and research projects in culture, education and the media to raise awareness, schemes enabling the exchange of information and knowledge of good practice and a special scheme to assist in preventing violence to women have also received grant aid.

A directive on the burden of proof in sex discrimination cases before industrial tribunals is now operative and came into force in 2001 (Directive 97/80 OJ L14/98). No longer will the complainant have to carry the entire responsibility to prove a case but will be required to submit evidence of direct or indirect discrimination which the employer will then be required to rebut.

For some years, the Commission has attempted to set an example in recruiting women to posts of greater responsibility, hoping states will follow suit in their public sectors. Targets have been set for directors, heads of units and administrators in the Commission staff but the real boost to the equality goal came with the Treaty of Amsterdam. Not only did this elevate equality between men and women to a major principle, it made it necessary for all Community activities to aim at eliminating inequalities and promoting equality, made a special mention of the importance of equality in the labour market and, in maintaining the provision on equal pay, made explicit that states might pursue affirmative action in job sectors where either sex is under-represented (Articles 2, 3, 137 and 141 (EC)). The Council of Ministers has also the right to act to combat discrimination whether based on sex, racial or ethnic origin, religion or belief, disability, age or sexual orientation (Article 13 EC).

23.15 Social exclusion

The limited social responsibility of the early treaties and the emphasis upon economic integration left the EC open to the charge of weakness in social policy. Criticism mounted in the 1960s as the darker side of affluence was exposed. The marginalization of many groups, including the inhabitants of the inner cities, migrants, the elderly and disabled people, made clear that the EC itself had small scope for action to ameliorate the conditions of the most disadvantaged although it pursued active policies of encouragement to member states. The more generous wording of the Treaty of Amsterdam is meant to go some way to remedying this situation although it appears unlikely that much money will be available for supporting schemes.

An important factor in clarifying the role of the EC arose through the strain put upon social security policies as unemployment rose, the number of retired people grew rapidly, pressures on health care mounted and governments attempted to restrict social security expenditure. At the same time, schemes needed to adapt to the growth of part-time and flexible working, the changing position of women and to new health needs. A considerable study programme was launched by the Commission which included consideration of the argument that the single market would require an alignment of social security costs and benefits. Although this is not accepted as a necessary goal, the EC has accepted a recommendation (COM (91) 228 final) on the ultimate convergence of objectives and policies in view of the similarity of many of the social problems now faced by member states. At present, these include the funding of long-term care, early retirement and sustaining pension commitments. It continues to report on the trends in social security and is anxious to maintain the debate on the wider subject of social protection (COM (95) 457; COM (95) 466).

There has been some interest in the proposition that the EC should seek to establish a basic minimum resource level but this has, so far, proved impossible to define and is far from being politically acceptable. The Council of Ministers did, however, accept a recommendation in 1992 that states should provide a guarantee of basic assistance with effective administrative measures (Recommendation 92/442 OJ L245/92).

An anti-poverty programme was included in the first SAP as a result of an Irish initiative. This gave rise to interesting experiments and drew attention to the need for, and difficulties of, cross-national research. Grant aid for projects helping groups in poverty concentrated on new, and sometimes unorthodox, procedures and drew the Commission into close, direct contact with social reform movements and local authorities and associations. Innovation has been a watchword which has led to an encouragement of a multidimensional approach, the use of partnerships

to ensure effective cooperation between local actors, active participation of excluded groups themselves and transnational research, but in recent years funding has been seriously curtailed. The Amsterdam Treaty brought the aim of fighting social exclusion firmly within EU remit (Articles 13, 136, 137 (EC)) but funding is likely to remain on a very small scale.

For some years, disabled people have been a group eligible for aid from the ESF for training and, in addition, action programmes with their own modest budgets have been established. These have meant that grants were available for tasks such as access to creative activities, sport and tourism, integration in nursery schools and functional rehabilitation. An emphasis was placed on the use of new technology as an aid to integration, to independent living and to education and training and in recent years the programmes have been brought under the umbrella of the broader goal of equal opportunities and full participation in social life for all. Member states are encouraged to bring their support for the disabled into equal opportunities programmes through the use of the structural funds, mobilizing the work of non-governmental organizations (NGOs), improving access to employment opportunities and through using information technology to pursue equal opportunities.

Elderly people, too, have become a group in which the EC expresses interest. They are, of course, affected by many general EC policies, notably the extension of the free movement policy and the search for safe and sustainable pension systems (Section 23.9). Problems connected with ageing have figured in the health research programmes and a small action programme was set up to exchange knowledge, ideas and experience. At present, the Commission is very involved in setting up networks and encouraging a dialogue between itself, NGOs and independent experts. A new support programme was submitted to the Council in 1995 but ran into difficulties similar to those facing the anti-poverty programme and at present the Commission seems to be concentrating on the insertion of an 'age dimension' into other, more established programmes as a means of highlighting issues concerning the elderly.

The European struggle in favour of social inclusion took a new start thanks to a strategy adopted in the Nice Council (7–10 December 2000); a strategy formatted on the EES model (Section 23.7 above). Member states agreed that cooperation in the field of social exclusion should be based on the 'open method of coordination' (common objectives, national action plans – the NAPincs, a joint Commission/Council report). A first set of NAPincs were produced by governments in 2001. The first joint report (see the draft, Council of the European Union, 12 December 2001) identified several core challenges to be addressed (in particular through a five-year social exclusion programme): for instance, developing an inclusive labour market; guaranteeing an adequate income; guaranteeing equal access and investing in high quality public services (health, transport, social care, cultural, recreational and legal); regenerating areas of multiple deprivation. A set of social indicators to allow progress focuses on key aspects of relative monetary poverty (60 million people have been found poor or at risk of poverty in the EU) as well as on multidimensional aspects of poverty (in the areas of employment, housing, health and education).

23.16 Migration and asylum

The creation of the EEC, and more particularly the passing of subsequent treaties, progressively distinguished three groups of residents who might be on the move. Those with the nationality of a member state, those entering the EU as migrants and those resident 'third-country nationals' who wished to move within EU borders all needed their own arrangements. The first group was to be covered by the free movement policy and a brief outline of the issues relating to the second group is attempted here. The third group constitutes rather a mixed bag. It covers, for example, a non-EU spouse married to a mobile EU national and long-resident non-EU residents who wish to move to take up work elsewhere, and the EU has special rules covering these categories. Many groups will be covered, too, by the rules written into the special relationship treaties which the EU has signed, for example nationals of the EEA. The Amsterdam Treaty has now laid down the elements of an EU policy in Article 63 (EC) to which states will conform in dealing with asylum seekers, refugees and displaced persons and immigration policy but these need further elaboration.

As far as the second group is concerned, there have been two waves of concern. In the early years, it was the question of large numbers of unskilled workers entering the EU to fill job vacancies and, more recently, the flows of refugees and asylum seekers.

Although people fall into different legal categories, the reasons for movement are often similar and may present similar problems of family reunion, new working patterns, finding adequate housing and schooling as well as language difficulties. The scale of migration, from whatever source, during the 1960s brought anxieties about social integration but member states were wary about allowing the EC a competence in some of the more sensitive areas of domestic policy. As migrants came from further afield, cultural gaps became more evident and pressures on local services increased in congested urban areas. By the late 1970s, the Commission had begun to question the value of large-scale, uncontrolled migration. Stress began to be laid on the ill-effects for regions and countries losing manpower, the pressure on the urban infrastructure, the slowing down of capital development in industry and the uncertain benefits for countries of emigration. The situation became further confused as unemployment grew, member states began to ban the entry of non-EC nationals, work permits expired and many third-country migrants decided to stay in the EC illegally rather than risk the possibility they would not be allowed back when conditions improved again.

EC policy made uncertain progress at this time, with the Commission limited to encouraging states to extend to all the improvements resulting from the free movement policy. It made all migrants eligible for grants from the ESF and tried to improve the education of children through grants for induction courses, language teaching and special training for teachers. These attempts remained on a small scale and it was in any case difficult to see the lines of an effective policy when settlement policies were so different, ranging from that of the UK which received migrants from the Commonwealth expecting to stay for permanent settlement to Germany with a great influx from Turkey whose workers were originally expected only for a short while and for whom issues of family settlement were, at first, of less importance.

Current estimates suggest that there are between 12 and 14 million legally resident 'third-country nationals' in the EU. By no means all of them are in a vulnerable position; their legal rights will vary from state to state and according to country of origin. It is clear, nevertheless, that many of them are still not fully part of the society in which they now live and that problems are being inherited by the second and third generations. A variety of national policies have emerged to encourage, or insist upon, assimilation but no overall EU policy exists.

A European Migrants Forum now exists to lobby in the EU, while the Council of Ministers has set up a Consultative Committee to monitor the expression of racism and xenophobia which have seen a disturbing rise in recent years. The European Parliament, in particular, has urged the EU to take a stand against such phenomena and a number of declarations have been issued. The Amsterdam Treaty has given the EU the capacity to act against discrimination, including that based on nationality, racial or ethnic origin (Articles 12, 13 (EC)) and for some time the Commission has been urging states to provide legal protection against discrimination. Meanwhile the Justice and Internal Affairs Council, meeting in March 1996, reached agreement on legal cooperation in order to prevent infringements of national rules against public incitement and the circulation of racist literature.

New immigration on a large scale is no longer thought of as desirable and the Commission's view is that emigration needs to be controlled through cooperation with sending countries and that it will lessen if jobs can be created in the home country and, with this, Community policies can help. The EU is still likely, however, to attract better qualified migrants, people who wish to set up in business, students in training and, no doubt, other special groups and the question remains of what EU action is necessary. However this issue is becoming controversial. On the one hand, immigration could bring some ease to an ageing Europe. On the other, there is a growing threat of uncontrolled immigration from candidate countries and through them.

Now that member states have accepted that immigration is a matter of common interest, a greater rationality in rules concerning entry and movement may be expected and an interesting point was made in a Council resolution in 1996 which dealt with the factors, such as income and health, to be considered when states authorize long-term residence. It has been suggested that such residents, not holding EU citizenship, should have preference over third-country nationals when it comes to recruitment and the EP argues that such populations should have the same rights as EU citizens.

Recent moves towards common rules have also been seen in asylum policy. These have become acceptable not just because of the very large number of recent applicants whose claims are often confused but with the realization that the existence of a single market means that all states can be affected. Sudden large influxes of refugees have thrown great burdens on services in receiving states but also mean that states are now more reluctant to grant refugee status, while the long delays in processing asylum applications have led to distress and difficulty. The 1990 Dublin Convention made a single state responsible for examining an application for asylum on the basis of objective criteria (subject to the rights of other states if they are particularly affected) and allows for the exchange of information on asylum activities. In 1995 the Council agreed on a harmonized definition of a refugee, minimum guarantees for asylum procedures and a resolution on burden sharing to help with temporary problems, and these matters are now set out in treaty form. The Commission, naturally enough, would like a budget to help to co-finance schemes set up to cover the many costs for maintenance, health care, schooling and legal representation that arise as well as for integration or voluntary repatriation.

The abolition of internal border controls raises the question of the effective policing of the external frontier and no subject has required more soul searching in recent years. If the state of first entry is lax then criminal elements, terrorists and unwanted migrants gain easy access and can pass anywhere within the EU. As a forerunner of a single system, a group of neighbouring states signed the Schengen agreement in 1985, then outside the EU treaties but now incorporated within. It has created a frontier-free zone, initially for a core group of members within which people can move freely. Denmark, Iceland, Norway, the United Kingdom and Ireland are now taking part in the Schengen acquis, at least in some of its provisions which resulted in greater cooperation between the member states in this area. Any new members of the EU will be expected to accept the rules in full.

The essential elements of the system are effective controls at the external frontier and close police and judicial cooperation in criminal matters (see Articles 29–42 (EU)). The UK and Ireland are not bound by these rules since the former still wishes to operate its own border controls. However, they are entitled to 'opt in' to arrangements made under this section of the treaty and a request was made to do so on some aspects of frontier controls, police and judicial cooperation in criminal matters, anti-drug procedures and the Schengen Information system. The European Council adopted in November 2002 a framework decision on the strengthening of the penal framework to prevent the facilitation of unauthorized entry, transit and residence. Europe is also establishing minimum common standards for the reception of asylum seekers. All these efforts, that accelerated after Tampere (15–16 October 1999), intend to constitute the EU as an area of freedom, security and justice, open to immigrants who respect its citizen rules and who, legitimately, seek a long-term establishment in the EU.

23.17   An overall view

The range of topics discussed here shows how diverse the social concerns of the EU now are. At first sight, they can appear as a miscellany rather than a single coherent policy but this is inevitable given the range of modern social policy. A hard core of matters relating to employment is the bedrock of Community social policy. This core is more and more under the domination of macroeconomic imperatives and financial balance concerns. Although there is agreement that some social minimum standards are necessary to support the single market policy, there is strong disagreement between the member states on what kinds of minimum standards, at what levels should they be fixed and how they should be monitored. The Charter of Fundamental Rights, agreed at Nice (2000), that followed the Charter of Social Fundamental Rights of Workers (1989) is not yet part of the European Treaties and, as such, has no binding power on member states' legislation. In general, the member states are reluctant to yield any consistent regulatory power to the Commission in social areas.

The best way in standard setting is presumably to provide national action more with frameworks, common objectives and basic references to respect than with substantive targets. Due to the diversity of national situations and ways of thinking about policies and of implementing them, it would be an illusion that substantive European constraints could apply for all in the same way. It is undoubtedly difficult to ensure that agreements on general principles are effectively applied and do, in fact, achieve a comparable result. Often it is a case of changing attitudes, encouraging developments in similar directions and explaining current best practice; the Commission is in a favourable position to carry out such tasks. A further noticeable feature is the support it gives to research, investigations and pilot schemes which normally have cross-national elements and attempt fresh approaches to old problems.

During the 1970s, it was agreed to set up three European institutes for study and research. In 1977, CEDEFOP began work to give new impetus to a common policy of training through the harmonization of national systems and to promote new initiatives. In 1975, a Foundation for the Improvement of Living and Working Conditions was set up in Dublin. Finally, the Council agreed to support a project of the European Trades Union Confederation (ETUC) to set up a European Trades Union Institute for the study of union affairs. A more recent development has been to set up Observatories to monitor and analyse social policies and to encourage mutual understanding of national policies and cross-national networks. Observatories exist for family policies, ageing and older people, policies to combat social exclusion and employment. Recent additions are the Industrial Relations Observatory and the European Monitoring Centre for Change to work closely with the Dublin Foundation.

Many of these activities may be classified as educational and promotional. For the specialist circles that are involved they play an important part in enhancing mutual understanding. Grant aid in the social field may still be small compared with the scale of national spending but for some of the poorer countries it is very significant, for example the ESF grants for training. Even in countries where it is less important in amount, it is, nevertheless, money that governments like to have and, however grudgingly, they do adapt their activities to conform to EU ideas.

More than ever, it remains true that European social policy has developed in the shadow of economic policies. Even with the passing of the SEA it was described as a flanking policy to the introduction of the single market and the obvious need to deal with the social consequences of intended action provides a strong argument for the development of social standards. However, this view has never satisfied everybody, especially those wanting a full-blown political union and who have therefore always argued for freestanding social goals and responsibilities. The Amsterdam Treaty suggests some movement towards this view; a glance back to the early days of the ECSC shows how far social policy has come. It is now accepted that there is a European dimension in health, social security, equal pay, working conditions and other social fields even though there is always disagreement about how far policy should go.

However, since Lisbon, a more integrated approach is being sought for European social issues. The European Social Agenda at Nice outlined the 'triangle' of mutually reinforcing policies – employment, social protection and economic and budgetary policy. It is being applied to the EES and to the pension reforms. More than developing legislation, coordinating national policies is considered as a possibility to overcome political blockages: drawing guidelines; defining common benchmarking indicators; annual reports on the measures taken; potential recommendations from the Council to member states. The Commission stresses its need to be in touch with (and to involve) local and regional authorities, trade unions and employer's organizations, voluntary organizations and citizens' groups. However, the effectiveness of such a method and the type of policy trends to which it leads remain to be assessed. What is also striking is the reduction of scope to which European ambitions seem to be submitted in social issues. The outcomes in 2002 are, especially, far from the ambitious objectives fixed in 1993 by the White Book on *Growth, Competitiveness and Employment*; and objectives have been designed toward market solutions more than social solutions *per se*.

The growth of an international society is also affecting the methods of handling social policy. The EEC was originally directed to work closely with the ILO and the Council of Europe and these links are growing closer. The 1996 version of the Council of Europe's Social Charter embodies ideas also to be found in ILO conventions and bears a strong resemblance to the moves towards equal opportunities, more information for workers, greater participation in relevant decisions and protection for the elderly which are so much part of EU current interests. Contacts with Central and Eastern Europe through the Phare agreements, educational bodies and outlying agencies referred to in the text bring awareness of other social priorities and methods of approach, while developing countries often find it helpful to discuss with the Commission their plans for social security and educational development. Multilateral and bilateral cooperation are now widely practised but have grown in an *ad hoc* way which might now benefit from systematization. Discussions in recent years on international trade agreements have raised moral issues which both influence, and are influenced by, the EU and this again suggests that there is an international element in social policy today.

It is clear that the EU does not have a social policy whose *raison d'être* is large-scale resource redistribution but one that depends on many relatively small-scale programmes, framework agreements, legal rules and a multiplicity of efforts to align attitudes, share experiences and generally encourage social progress. It is increasingly difficult to envisage a EU which has developed politically without some commitment to ensure citizens a place in society, in which human rights are protected and institutions effectively democratized. The 1994 White Paper on Social Policy pinpointed the values which are shared between members and which are at the basis of EU social policy as democracy, individual rights, free collective bargaining, the market economy, equality of opportunity, welfare and solidarity. It is still struggling to determine what, in practical terms, it needs to do in order to promote these values on the grounds that member states are no longer fully competent to do so alone.

Part Six of this book deals with the external relations of the EU. Chapter 24 covers EU trade relations with its major partners and does so within the context of the Common Commercial Policy, run by the EU Commission on behalf of the entire EU member nations. Chapter 25 tackles the EU relations with the developing world in terms of both trade, aid and preferential trading arrangements.

External trade policy

MARIUS BRÜLHART AND ALAN MATTHEWS*

The external trade policy of the EU impinges on nearly one-fifth of world trade. Hence, an understanding of the principles and practice of the Union's trade policy, the Common Commercial Policy (CCP), is of vital importance to any student of the global trade environment. Ongoing research on the CCP has addressed both broad themes and detailed aspects of the Union's trade policy (Memedovic *et al.*, 1999; OECD, 2000; Messerlin, 2001). The *Trade Policy Review of the EU*, the biennial publication by the World Trade Organization (WTO), provides insight into how trade specialists view the EU and, no less important, how the EU sees its own role. A number of features of the EU's CCP make it particularly worthy of study.[1]

First, while commercial policy originally focused on tariffs and other border measures as they affected trade in goods, the scope of the policy today is much more diverse. Policies affecting trade in services and the conditions influencing foreign investment have become increasingly important. As tariffs were reduced in successive rounds of multilateral trade negotiations to near insignificance, other policy areas which fall under the general heading of regulatory issues have become increasingly relevant to international trade: intellectual property, technical standards and regulations, competition policy, labour standards and environmental policy, to mention but the most prominent. Many of these regulatory issues reach deep into the heart of domestic policy concerns, with the result that trade policy has become increasingly politicized and controversial in recent years.

Second, EU commercial policy has developed a highly complex set of trade relations with third countries, reflecting in part the way the granting of trade preferences was virtually the sole instrument of foreign policy for the EU in the past. The resulting hierarchy of preferential trading schemes has been determined by a mixture of trade, strategic and foreign policy concerns in which the conflicting interests of member states, as well as hard bargaining between the Union institutions and the member states, have played an important role. The 1990s saw a significant extension of EU regionalism. Recent policy statements suggest that the EU is now seeking consolidation rather than a further expansion of its regional trade arrangements (Lamy, 2002), but this has not prevented continuing negotiations on creating such arrangements with a number of its trading partners.

Third, EU commercial policy is increasingly shaped by the Union's obligations (and reciprocal rights) under the WTO which came into being in 1995. The purpose of the WTO is both to establish and monitor the rules for trade policy making in its members, and to encourage the liberalization of trade through successive rounds of trade negotiations to reduce tariffs and other barriers to trade in goods and services. One of its core principles is that of Most-Favoured-Nation (MFN) treatment, which means that members undertake not to discriminate in their treatment of imports originating in different members. The EU played a major role in the Uruguay Round Agreement conducted under the auspices of the General Agreement on Tariffs and Trade (GATT) and concluded in 1994 which established the WTO as well as considerably broadening its mandate. It has been to the forefront in calling for the further comprehensive round of trade negotiations which were initiated in Doha, Qatar in November 2001. There remains a continuing tension, however, between the EU's commitment to multilateral trade liberalization through the WTO and its ongoing concern with regional and bilateral agreements outside that organization.

This chapter investigates these themes in five separate sections. The first describes the pattern of

* The authors are grateful to Dermot McAleese for his permission to build on his chapter in earlier editions of this book and for his helpful comments on this chapter, and to Hansueli Bacher for valuable research assistance.

trade between the EU and the outside world. The second presents an overview of the principles and policy instruments of the CCP. The third considers EU trade policy specifically towards its main trading partners.

The fourth contains an analysis of trade policy issues which are coming to the forefront in ongoing trade negotiations. The concluding section considers the future development of the CCP.

24.1   EU trade and specialization patterns

24.1.1 The structure of EU trade

The EU constitutes the largest trading bloc in the world. Excluding intra-EU trade, exports of the Union accounted for 18.4% of world merchandise exports in 2001. The United States and Japanese shares were 15.4% and 8.5% respectively (Table 24.1; see Chapter 5 for a historical perspective).

External trade has tended to grow about twice as fast as GDP in most parts of the world, and the EU is no exception. Over the period 1990–2001, EU trade volumes increased by almost 4% annually in real terms, compared with 2% GDP growth. A useful aggregate measure of trade dependence is the ratio of exports plus imports of goods and services to GDP. For the EU this stood at 31% in 2001, considerably higher than for the US (19%) and Japan (18%).

About 41% of extra-EU trade is directed towards *developed countries*. Within the developed countries group, the United States is the largest trading partner, followed by Switzerland and Japan (Table 24.2). If intra-EU trade is added to extra-EU trade with

developed countries, we find that over three-quarters of the Union's trade is with countries of broadly similar income levels. This is a familiar empirical phenomenon worldwide, but it runs counter to the expectation that trade flows should be greatest between countries that are most different in economic structure. It has given rise to much new theorizing about the causes of trade (Krugman, 1994).

Developing countries account for nearly 40% of extra-EU trade but for only 15% of total EU trade. Generally one observes a strong asymmetry in trade relations between individual developing countries and the EU. Most developing countries rely far more on the EU as an export market than the EU does on them. For example, in 2001, 21% of India's exports went to the EU, but only 1.1% of EU exports went to India, and India's exports accounted for only 1.5% of total EU imports. African countries in general are even more dependent on the EU market. The asymmetry in bargaining positions is modified somewhat by the strategic importance of some developing country primary product exports, oil being an obvious case in point. The most dynamic element in EU-developing country trade, though, has been the growth in manufactured goods trade with Southeast Asian countries. This repeats the general pattern: as countries become more industrialized (i.e. more similar) they trade more with one another.

The commodity structure of EU trade varies greatly by geographical area (Table 24.3). Trade with developed countries consists predominantly of trade in *manufactured goods*. In 2001, these goods accounted for 87% of the Union's exports to developed countries and 82% of its imports from them. Trade with developing countries has a different composition. Primary products figure more prominently in their exports to the EU. Agricultural products comprise 13% of the total and fuels and other products a further 23%. However, the share of manufactured goods in total imports from the developing countries has grown dramatically in recent decades (up from 18% in 1980 to 64% in 2001).

Table 24.1 The EU in world merchandise trade, 2001

Exports from	Value (US$ bn)	%
European Union (excluding intra-EU trade)	874	18.4
United States	731	15.4
Japan	403	8.5
Other	2730	57.7
Total world (excluding intra-EU trade)	4738	100.0

Source: Computed from WTO *International Trade Statistics*, November 2002. Reprinted by permission of WTO

Table 24.2 EU merchandise trade by area, 2001

	Imports		Exports	
	US$ bn	%	US$ bn	%
Developed countries[a]	378.5	16.2	400.9	17.5
of which:				
United States	172.0	7.4	210.8	9.2
Switzerland	54.4	2.3	66.2	2.9
Japan	67.2	2.9	39.2	1.7
Developing countries[b]	360.8	15.4	311.8	13.6
Central and Eastern Europe[c]	136.7	5.8	137.8	6.0
Other	40.9	1.8	23.6	1.0
Extra-EU	916.9	39.2	874.1	38.1
Intra-EU	1 421.4	60.8	1 417.3	61.9
Total EU	2 338.3	100.0	2 291.4	100.0

[a] Western Europe, North America and Japan.
[b] Africa, Latin America, Middle East and Asia (excluding Japan).
[c] Central and Eastern Europe, Baltic States, Commonwealth of Independent States.
Source: Computed from Table A12 in WTO *International Trade Statistics*, 2002. Reprinted by permission of WTO

Table 24.3 Commodity composition of EU trade with major trading groups, 2001 (% shares)

	Manufactures		Agricultural products		Fuels and other products	
	Exports	Imports	Exports	Imports	Exports	Imports
Developed countries[a]	87.2	81.9	6.0	5.8	6.8	12.3
Developing countries[b]	88.5	63.9	7.3	13.3	4.2	22.8
Central and Eastern Europe[c]	89.4	64.5	7.0	6.8	3.6	28.7

[a] Western Europe (excluding intra-EU trade), North America and Japan.
[b] Latin America, Africa, Middle East and Asia (except Japan).
[c] Central and Eastern Europe, Baltic States, Commonwealth of Independent States.
Source: Computed from Table A12 in WTO *International Trade Statistics*, 2002. Reprinted by permission of WTO

The EU's *balance on extra-EU merchandise trade* has been in modest surplus since 1994. It amounted to 0.5% of GDP in 2001. So far, the Union's trade balance has not attracted much comment; this contrasts with the debates surrounding the United States deficit (4.1% of GDP) and the Japanese surplus (1.7% of GDP). Nevertheless, some bilateral trade imbalances have been perceived as troublesome, in particular the persistent deficit with Japan. The trade balance's economic importance derives from its being both a lead indicator and the largest component in the *balance of payments on current account*. This balance includes services trade and other current transactions. Trade in *commercial services*, comprising travel, transport, royalties and business services, corresponds to one-quarter of the EU's total trade with third countries.

In trying to work out the effect of a customs union such as the EU on partner and third countries, customs union theory focuses on the share of intra-union versus extra-union trade. The growth of intra-union trade could be due to either trade creation (a good thing) or trade diversion (a bad thing). As a general rule, the greater the absolute growth of extra-union trade, the less the danger of trade diversion. In the EU's case, two facts stand out. First, the share of *intra-EU trade* in total trade has risen markedly from 42% in 1961 to 61% in 2001, although the main increase in this share was recorded prior to 1990 (Brülhart and Elliot, 1998). As integration among EU members outpaced liberalization with the rest of the world, this relative expansion of intra-EU trade is in line with the predictions of theory (see Chapter 6). Second, the increase in the intra-EU trade share was accompanied by a rapid absolute growth of *extra-EU trade*. This indicates a preponderance of trade creation over trade diversion. Further analysis suggests that, with the important exception of agricultural trade, the rise in intra-EU trade has not been at the expense of non-EU countries (Sapir, 1996).

Fears of increasing trade diversion were raised in the late 1980s by the implementation of the single market. Some argued that the liberalization of the internal market would divert energies away from liberalizing external trade and give EU firms an unfair competitive edge over third-country exporters. However, *ex post* evaluation has shown that these fears of a *Fortress Europe* were unfounded. Extra-EU manufacturing imports increased their share of consumption over the period 1980–1993 from 12% to 14%. Looking specifically at developing country exporters, Buigues and Martínez Mongay (1999) found that between 1989 and 1995 the developing countries' share of EU imports increased both in absolute terms and in comparison with the United States. This increase was particularly pronounced in the sectors most affected by the single market programme (see Chapter 11). On the whole, therefore, the process of European integration does not seem to have created problems for other trading countries.

A final consideration is the *terms of trade*. This is defined as the price index of exports over the price index of imports. If, say, the price of imported oil or coffee declines, this would represent an *improvement* in the EU's terms of trade. The European consumer can consume more oil or coffee with the same nominal income and is clearly better off as a result. Likewise, a fall in pharmaceutical export prices would lead to deterioration in the EU's terms of trade. Unlike the gains from trade, the terms of trade is a zero-sum game: your loss is my gain and vice versa.

EU-wide indicators of the terms of trade are difficult to compute. We do know that the price paid for primary goods imported from developing countries has fallen over the past two decades, in some cases very steeply. African exporters have been particularly hit by declining terms of trade. Clearly, developing countries must try to diversify their exports into more profitable lines. A case on equity grounds can also be made for the EU to provide compensating aid to developing countries, given that the European consumer has been a prime beneficiary of the decline in developing country export prices.

24.1.2 Intra-industry vs inter-industry trade

Much academic interest has focused on the composition of international exchanges in terms of intra- and inter-industry trade. *Intra-industry trade* (IIT) refers to the mutual exchange among countries of similar goods. This type of trade runs against the predictions of neo-classical trade theory, according to which countries would export one set of products – those in which they have a comparative advantage, while importing an entirely different set of products – those for which the comparative advantage is held by other countries. IIT is based not on country-specific advantages, but on determinants such as consumers' taste for variety, increasing returns in production and the international dispersion of various stages in the production process of advanced industrial goods. IIT therefore typically dominates trade among diversified high-income economies.

Trade within the EU exhibits generally high shares of IIT. Brülhart and Elliott (1998) have shown that, on average, the share of IIT trade among EU countries rose from 48% to 64% over the 1961–1992 period. Given that the definition of an 'industry' in that study is very narrow (SITC 5-digit), this is strong evidence that intra-EU trade is driven by forces other than the type of comparative advantage once emphasized in the textbooks.

According to computations by the OECD (2000) for the 1970–1998 period, the IIT share of extra-EU trade has also been growing continuously. Countries with the largest and most diversified industrial bases (Germany, France and the United Kingdom) typically have the highest levels of IIT with third countries. Greece and Portugal have lower IIT levels – their extra-EU trade relations are still predominantly *inter-industry*. The proportion of IIT in the EU's trade with developed countries such as the United States is high, as one would expect, and with developing countries it is low. IIT with Japan, however, is surprisingly low, a fact often interpreted as a symptom of the impenetrability of the Japanese market to manufactured exports from the west. The EU's trade with Central and Eastern European countries (CEECs) also displays comparatively low IIT values, but for different reasons to Japan, though it has been increasing. Low IIT levels could imply that further trade liberalization with these countries might involve substantial structural adjustment costs for both parties (see Brülhart, 1998). This may explain in part the insistence on a certain minimum level of economic development being achieved by applicant countries before accession to full membership of the Union was agreed.

24.1.3 External trade and economic specialization: high-tech industries and low-skill workers

Changes in the EU's trade structure and trade policy regime have stimulated corresponding changes in the pattern of specialization of member states. The share of agricultural employment in EU total employment has fallen from 12% in 1970 to 4% in 2001 (see Chapter 20). There has been a sustained expansion of the services sector, and a fall in the share of manufacturing jobs from 33% to 20% in the same time period. Some industrial sectors were particularly hard hit. For example, since 1984, employment has shrunk significantly in iron and steel (down 36% or 184 000 jobs by 1997) and in textiles (down 44% or 776 000 jobs by 1997).

Of course, specialization pressures induced by external trade are not the only forces that shaped the observed changes in the EU's production structure. Even if the EU had existed in autarky, changes in technology, incomes, tastes and demography would have led to structural adjustment. For this reason, it is difficult to isolate and quantify the impact of external trade liberalization on observed specialization trends. However, some insights into the processes at work have been yielded by recent empirical analysis. We concentrate here on two sectors for which the role of extra-EU trade has been subject to particularly intensive debate and substantial research: *high-technology* industries and *low-skill intensive* industries. Both have been identified as losers from the EU's trade liberalization; the former due to presumed insufficient R&D efforts in the EU, the latter due to the inexorable law of comparative advantage.

Trade performance in *high-tech products* has been a source of concern to the EU for many years. The concern focuses on Europe's perceived poor performance in high-tech sectors relative to the US and Japan. One way of measuring this is by the *technology balance of payments*, i.e. the difference between exports of technology (such as international licensing contracts and technical assistance) and imports (such as purchases of foreign patents, know-how and R&D). According to OECD estimates for 1997, the EU had a deficit in technology of $4.4 billion in contrast with an American surplus of $24.3 billion (*The Economist*, 21 August 1999). Another type of indicator examines patterns in high-tech merchandise trade, such as the share of high-tech exports in total manufacturing exports, which, according to World Bank statistics for 2000, shows the EU (16%) falling well behind Japan (28%) and the United States (34%). Other trade statistics provide less conclusive results. Table 24.4 shows that the EU has negative trade balances in some key high-tech sectors such as office and telecom equipment but enjoys a surplus in others such as machinery and transport equipment. Indeed, according to the OECD (2002b), over the 1994–2000 period the EU has increased its share of the world export market in four of the five highly technology-intensive sectors analysed (aerospace, electronic goods, computers and precision instruments) and lost market share in only one (pharmaceuticals). It would therefore be wrong to claim that Europe is generally falling behind in terms of competitiveness in high-tech sectors.

The problem of high-tech industries relates to strategic positioning of the EU economy. Low-skill intensive industries give rise to a different type of concern. In the latter case, it is generally accepted that

Table 24.4 Extra-EU trade in selected products, 1980 and 2001 (US$ bn)

		Exports	Imports	Trade balance	Change in balance 1980–2001
Chemicals	1980	35.7	17.2	+18.5	
	2001	125.6	68.4	+57.2	+38.7
Machinery and transport equipment	1980	115.9	58.0	+57.9	
	2001	411.2	338.0	+73.2	+15.3
Electrical machinery	1980	11.9	5.7	+6.2	
	2001	44.9	42.1	+2.8	−3.4
Office and telecom equipment	1980	11.3	17.2	−5.9	
	2001	85.2	129.0	−43.8	−37.9
Automotive products	1980	27.5	8.2	+19.3	
	2001	86.5	44.8	+41.7	+22.4

Source: Computed form Table A12 in WTO *International Trade Statistics*, 2002. Reprinted by permission of WTO

the EU will lose market share to third countries. What is at issue is the pace of change and its effects on the incomes of *low-skill workers*, particularly against the backdrop of the EU's high *unemployment* (see Chapters 5 and 23). Some argue that the law of comparative advantage has been working to the detriment of European blue-collar workers and, in an unholy combination with institutional labour-market rigidities, has fuelled unemployment.

Trade economists have conducted numerous analyses with the aim of isolating trade-related determinants of structural change. Two concepts of structural change have been used: changes in wage differentials across industries and changes in unemployment rates. The starting hypothesis is that liberalization of trade *vis-à-vis* unskilled labour-abundant developing countries has depressed demand for unskilled labour in industrialized countries. Trade liberalization therefore either (a) contributes to the widening gap between skilled and unskilled wages, as in the United States and the UK, or (b) to rising unemployment of unskilled workers, where union power and restrictive labour-market legislation impede United States-style flexibility of wages. In the EU case, attention primarily focuses on whether increased imports from low-wage countries have exacerbated the unemployment problem.

Most available studies cover the United States or the entire OECD, rather than just the EU, and a number of different methodologies are used. Some

studies estimate average factor contents of imports and exports, and infer net effects on domestic factor demands. Other studies regress changes in factor demands over various determinants including import penetration. A majority of analyses find that trade liberalization accounts for some of the fall in demand for blue-collar workers in developed countries. However, the contribution of trade to the rise in the skill premium is at most 20%; by far the bigger culprit is trade-independent technological change (Slaughter, 1999).

A contrary conclusion was reached by Wood (1994, 1995) who argued that import penetration from the developing countries is a major cause of falling demand for low-skill workers in the OECD. He refined the standard factor-content analysis and found empirical evidence that manufactured imports of OECD countries tend to have higher low-skill labour contents than similar goods produced locally, and that imports thereby crowd out low-skill jobs in developed countries. Furthermore, he detected a tendency for OECD industry to engage in 'defensive innovation', substituting capital for low-skill labour in order to survive competition from low-wage exporters, and he pointed to the (often ignored) surge in service exports from those countries. He concluded that demand for unskilled labour relative to skilled labour in OECD countries in 1990 fell by about 20% compared to what it would have been had prohibitive barriers been imposed on trade with the developing countries. Neven and Wyplosz (1999) also found evidence of defensive innovation by EU industries in response to competition from developing countries, but the magnitude of their estimated employment and wage effects is very small.

The nature of the trade-employment link is likely to remain a controversial topic for some time. As the EU reduces its external trade barriers under WTO commitments, and as the exporting capacity of developing countries increases, the pressures for trade-induced specialization will also intensify. Underlying the empirical debate about the significance of trade liberalization for EU market adjustment there is a strong *normative* consensus against a return to protectionism. Even though trade liberalization is acknowledged to produce losers, gainers are still in the majority. The policy response suggested by economic theory is not to re-impose trade barriers to non-EU imports, but to deregulate EU markets, to subsidize employment of low-skill workers (in the short term), and to invest in education (in the long term).

24.2   The Common Commercial Policy (CCP)

In the previous section, trade flows were explained in terms of comparative costs as well as increasing returns to scale and the exchange of varieties. But trade flows are also influenced by trade policies. The EU's CCP acts both to restrict and to promote trade. This section begins with a discussion of the attempts by the EU to update its trade policy decision making to keep pace with the broadening agenda of trade policy. This is essentially a conflict between those who want to centralize trade policy at the Union level to make it more efficient and coherent, and the member states who are reluctant to lose power and influence over this useful instrument of economic (and social) policy. It then reviews the instruments available to the Union which influence trade flows. Trade policy has become less restrictive and more open under the pressure of multilateral liberalization, but considerable scope for protection remains in particular sectors (agriculture, textiles and clothing) and in the use of anti-dumping measures and regulatory barriers. The Union's series of regional and bilateral trade agreements have the objective of promoting trade, though this objective is sometimes frustrated by administrative rules. Some recent estimates of the economic impact of the EU's CCP conclude this section.

24.2.1 EU trade decision-making procedures

The key provisions of the CCP are contained in Articles 131–134 (ex Articles 110–116) of the Treaty of Rome.[2] Article 131 contains the well-known aspiration:

> By establishing a customs union between themselves member states aim to contribute, in the common interest, to the harmonious development of world trade, the progressive abolition of restrictions on international trade and the lowering of customs barriers.

The cornerstone of the CCP is Article 133. It sets out the important rule that:

> the CCP shall be based on uniform principles, particularly in regard to changes in tariff rates, the conclusion of tariff and trade agreements, the achievement of uniformity in measures towards the liberalisation of export policy and in measures to protect trade such as those to be taken in the case of dumping or subsidies.

Article 133 defines CCP coverage only with an illustrative list – mostly tariffs, antidumping or antisubsidy measures, and trade agreements. Trade in goods, including agriculture, falls unambiguously within the Community's competence. Decision making concerning trade in goods under Article 133 functions on the basis of qualified majority voting (QMV) in the Council (see Chapter 3). Subject to the Council's approval, the Commission is empowered to conduct negotiations in consultation with a special committee appointed by the Council for this purpose, the Article 133 Committee, and within the framework of such negotiating directives as the Council may issue to it. For example, the Commission negotiates on behalf of the member states in the WTO. In the cut and thrust of negotiations, the Commission may sometimes interpret its mandate in a way with which some member states may disagree, and this has been a source of tension in the past.

Multilateral trade agreements increasingly cover a wider range of topics including services, intellectual property rights, e-commerce and investment where the Community's competence to negotiate and implement trade policies is much less clear. In 1994, the European Court of Justice (ECJ) was asked to rule on the division of competences with respect to services and intellectual property rights. The Court ruled that the Community had exclusive competence with respect to cross-border trade in services but that member states retained joint competence with the Community for trade issues involving commercial presence and factor movements. As a result, the WTO Agreement was signed by representatives of both the EU Council and of the member states. In 1997, the Amsterdam Treaty modified Article 133 to grant powers to the Community to negotiate agreements on services and intellectual property, but only on the basis of unanimity. The Nice Treaty in 2001 further tilted the balance towards exclusive competence by extending majority voting to these areas (with certain exceptions such as agreements that relate to trade in cultural and audiovisual services, education, social and human health services as well as transport services which remain outside the scope of Article 133). But other areas of growing significance, such as investment issues or the traditionally contentious area of export policy, remain under the unanimity rule. Unanimity also continues to prevail in the limited instances where unanimity is required for internal decisions, such as taxation matters (see Chapters 3 and 14) – this is called the principle of 'parallelism'. The absence of QMV in these areas could make the conclusion of future trade negotiations cumbersome where the outcome is presented as a 'single undertaking' because, *de facto*, unanimity is required for the entire agenda (OECD, 2000).

24.2.2 Instruments of the CCP

The principles of the CCP are put into effect by means of *trade policy instruments* and *trade agreements*. First, we survey the principal instruments of EU trade policy, while trade agreements with non-EU countries are discussed in Section 24.2.3.

Tariffs

The most visible element of EU trade policy is the *common external tariff* (CET). More than 10 000 individual products are distinguished at the 8-digit level of the Combined Nomenclature (CN), which lists the duty rates applicable to each product. In 2002, the simple average applied EU tariff rate stood at 6.4% (WTO, 2002). Tariffs on agricultural imports were higher (16% on average); and tariffs on manufactured imports were lower (4% on average). The structure of the EU's tariff schedule is compared to those of the US and Japan in Table 24.5. These are the MFN tariffs bound in each country's schedule to the WTO. In all three countries, higher tariffs are imposed on imports of agricultural products, food, textiles and clothing. The production-weighted average tariff rate was 7.7% in the EU compared to 5.2% in the US and 3.4% in Japan. However, looking only at MFN rates does not take into account imports under preferential agreements which are particularly extensive in the case of the EU. The revenues from import duties flow into the general EU budget, after a 20% deduction retained to cover the costs of customs administration by the importing country (see Chapter 19).

Tariff averages mask substantial variation of tariff levels across individual products. For example, following the Information Technology Agreement signed in March 1997, the EU phased out remaining tariffs on most computer and telecom related goods. At the other extreme, 'sensitive' imports such as trucks, cars, clothing and footwear continue to attract high tariffs, in excess of 10% *ad valorem*. The peaks are even more pronounced in the agricultural sector. Tariffs on meat, dairy products and cereals were 28%, 38% and 39% respectively in 2002, with individual tariffs exceeding 200% in the case of some dairy products.

The restrictiveness of a tariff system depends not just on the level of tariffs but also on the degree of tariff escalation. A tariff structure is escalated when tariffs on imports of raw materials and intermediate products are lower than those on finished goods. Such escalation affords downstream activities higher effective protection than the nominal rates suggest. Under the Uruguay Round, tariff cuts were generally larger on high tariffs, so that the degree of escalation was reduced substantially. Nevertheless, significant escalation remains in textiles and clothing as well as in agricultural and food products (WTO, 2002).

Non-tariff barriers

In addition to tariffs, the EU traditionally has made significant use of various non-tariff measures to limit

Table 24.5 Production-weighted average applied MFN tariff rates[a] in selected countries, 1996 (%)

ISIC code	Industry	EU	US	Japan
1	Agriculture, forestry, fishing	10.7	7.9	5.0
2	Mining and quarrying	0.6	0.2	0.3
3	Manufacturing	7.7	5.4	3.3
31	Food, beverages and tobacco	32.5	15.9	18.9
32	Textiles and apparel	9.8	11.3	10.1
33	Wood and wood products	3.4	3.5	3.6
34	Paper and paper products	4.7	1.8	1.2
35	Chemicals, petroleum products	5.3	4.4	3.2
36	Non-metallic mineral products	3.9	4.5	1.5
37	Basic metal industries	3.6	3.7	3.0
38	Fabricated metal products	4.3	3.2	0.3
39	Other manufacturing	4.2	4.8	2.5
	Total all products	7.7	5.2	3.4

[a] The tariff averages in this table are not simple averages but are weighted by the relative importance of each product in each country's production. The data refer to 1996 and the average for each country would be scheduled for further reduction under its Uruguay Round commitments.
Source: OECD, 2000. OECD©, 2000

imports, although their importance has diminished considerably since the late 1980s as WTO rules have enforced a stricter discipline in their use. Non-tariff barriers (NTBs; see Chapters 6 and 11) include quantitative restrictions, price controls and regulatory barriers. Specific examples include import quotas, voluntary export restraints, discretionary licensing, anti-dumping duties or prohibitions for health or safety reasons.

Theory teaches that import quotas give rise to particularly severe welfare costs. Quantitative restrictions on imports are generally not permitted under WTO rules. The EU is phasing out its remaining restrictions, but they still apply to some products such as textiles, clothing, bananas, and iron and steel imports. The most important quotas are those imposed on imports of clothing and textiles under successive Multifibre Agreements and regulated by the WTO Agreement on Textiles and Clothing since 1995. Under this Agreement, the EU is committed to eliminating these quotas by 2005 in a phased fashion, but it has been criticized for back-loading the biggest steps until the very end. Quotas remain in place for imports from non-WTO countries

such as textile-related and other basic manufactures from former Soviet Union countries and Vietnam.

As visible trade barriers are dismantled, other ways of restricting imports in 'sensitive' sectors are resorted to. Frequent recourse to *anti-dumping measures* is an example of such practice. Dumping is defined as the selling in export markets below some 'normal' price. The 'normal' price of a good is commonly defined as the price prevailing in the exporter's home market. Such divergences could arise if firms export products at very low prices in order to capture markets abroad and to eliminate competition. The imposition of anti-dumping measures is permitted under WTO rules, if dumping 'causes or threatens material injury to an established industry . . . or materially retards the establishment of a domestic industry'. Complex pricing policies and adjustment for indirect cost factors leave a degree of arbitrariness in the calculation of dumping margins and 'material injury'. WTO rules also permit countries to take *countervailing action* against exports which have benefited from subsidies in the exporting country provided such exports cause or threaten to cause material injury to a domestic industry. *Safeguard clauses* under WTO provisions allow signatories to take special measures against import surges or particularly low import prices which cause material injury to domestic industries.

The EU has had frequent resort to anti-dumping measures. In 2001, the EU had the second largest number of product categories with measures in force, and only the United States had more. Over the period 1991 to 2001, the number of EU anti-dumping measures in force fluctuated between 142 and 192 and shows a slight increase over time (WTO, 2002). Anti-dumping actions take one of two forms: (a) anti-dumping duties equivalent to the dumping margin or (b) undertakings by exporting countries not to sell to the EU below an agreed price. The most affected product categories are iron and steel products, consumer electronics and chemicals. The EU rarely applies countervailing duties and, in almost all cases, the investigations concern products which are also subject to an anti-dumping investigation.

Regulatory barriers

Products imported into the EU must comply with relevant regulations, where they exist, to meet health, safety and environmental objectives. *Technical regulations* are mandatory rules laid down by the EU or the member states, while *standards* are non-mandatory rules approved by a recognized body such as a standards institute which provide an assurance of quality to consumers. Compliance is established by means of *conformity assessment procedures*. Regulations may lay down product characteristics or their related process and production methods, or they may deal with the terminology, symbols, packaging and labelling requirements applying to a product or production method. Examples include noise and emission limits for machinery, or labelling requirements such as health warnings on tobacco products or the energy consumption levels of household appliances. Such regulations raise the cost of exporting where a manufacturer has to meet a different set of standards or pay for the cost of demonstrating compliance with the importing country's rules.

The EU's use of regulations and standards must comply with its obligations under the WTO Agreement on Technical Barriers to Trade (TBT Agreement) and, for food safety and animal and plant health measures, the WTO Agreement on the Application of Sanitary and Phytosanitary Measures (SPS Agreement). These obligations generally require the EU to use international standards where they exist unless they can be shown to be inappropriate, to avoid discrimination against imported products and to avoid creating unnecessary obstacles to international trade. Between 1995 and 2001 the EU or its member states notified between 110 and 437 new regulations annually under the TBT Agreement, while additional measures were notified to the SPS Committee (WTO, 2002). Some of the more important trade disputes involving the EU have occurred around the use of regulatory import barriers such as its ban on the import of hormone treated beef, maximum aflatoxin levels in cereals, dried fruit and nuts, and its labelling requirements for genetically modified foods.

Trade rules for services

Extra-EU services trade received a multilateral legal base through the General Agreement on Trade in Services (GATS), which was negotiated during the Uruguay Round. The scope of this agreement encompasses both the right to do business across countries and the right to establish, since it also applies to services provided by foreign affiliates of multinational firms. GATS extends the non-discrimination MFN rule to all service sectors, although members can derogate from this temporarily by excluding particular sectors from their commitments (the 'negative list'). *National treatment* (i.e. equivalent treatment to that given to domestic suppliers of a service) is granted to foreign suppliers, but only in the sectors where a member makes an offer to do this by listing it in its schedule of commitments (the 'positive list').

As a result of these qualifications, the GATS provides limited coverage of service sectors, but it contained provisions for continued negotiations. Like other developed countries, the EU is an enthusiastic proponent of freer trade in services. Such is invariably the case for sectors in which countries enjoy a decided comparative advantage. Where such an advantage is less clear, e.g. in the case of audio-visual services, where Europe is a major net importer from the US, free trade is seen as posing a threat to European cultural identity. As already noted, an agreement was reached on telecommunications in 1997, according to which 69 WTO members granted each other (and most other WTO countries) national treatment in all forms of telecommunication services, thus covering over 90% of global telecommunications. The information technology agreement (ITA I) complements the services agreements while a second ITA is being prepared.

Negotiations on financial and professional services were also completed successfully, but proposals for maritime transport were blocked by the US.

The treatment of public services in the GATS has proved controversial. Whatever the merits of the debate whether the privatization or deregulation of public services might lead to an improvement or a deterioration in their quality, most people would agree that this is an issue which should be debated and decided by citizens rather than through the technocratic processes of multilateral agreements. Fears have been expressed that the GATS could require EU governments to open up the provision of public services to competition. However, the EU has included supplementary specifications in its horizontal commitments which allow subsidies to the public sector and the granting of exclusive rights to public utilities. Even in public service sectors where the EU and its member states have made market access commitments (such as private education and hospital services), they retain the right to regulate these activities with a view to achieving legitimate public objectives.

24.2.3 Regional trade agreements

The EU has developed an elaborate web of preferential trade agreements (see Chapter 1). Initially, these were mainly with neighbouring countries and former colonies, but they now extend to trans-continental agreements without these geographical or historical rationales such as those with Latin American countries. WTO rules allow the formation of regional trade agreements (RTAs) as long as trade barriers on average do not rise after integration, tariffs and NTBs are eliminated within the area on 'substantially all' intra-regional trade, and the project is notified to the WTO in time for it to determine whether these conditions are satisfied (see Chapter 5, especially the appendix on WTO Article XXIV).

The EU's penchant for regional trade agreements is apparent from Table 24.6. The most favourable treatment is given to the 121 countries that either fall into the least developed category, or are members of the Cotonou (formerly the Lomé) Agreement, or have completed bilateral trade agreements with the EU. Next come the middle income and poor countries that benefit only from non-contractual discretionary preferences offered by the EU under the terms of its Generalized System of Preferences (GSP). At the bottom of the hierarchy are countries which are members of the WTO

but not of the GSP which receive the ironically named MFN treatment. Until 1998 there were just five countries in this category (Australia, Canada, Japan, New Zealand and the United States) but they have since been joined by Hong Kong, South Korea, Singapore and Taiwan after their graduation from the GSP. However, the geographical coverage exaggerates the relative importance of trade links with preferred partners in value terms. The shares of extra-EU imports from MFN countries, from countries covered by reciprocal trade agreements and from countries benefiting from unilateral concessions are each about one-third (OECD, 2000). In fact, the share of imports entering under MFN terms may be as high as 70%, given the importance of non-dutiable imports and administrative rules which restrict the use of the preference schemes by the beneficiary countries. An example of the latter is rules of origin which determine whether a product has undergone sufficient processing to qualify as originating from a preference-receiving country. By making the rules more restrictive, the EU can disqualify many exports from receiving preferential treatment.

Why do the EU's trade partners participate in these regional trade agreements? The question is relevant, since, for many partner countries, losses from trade diversion cannot be ruled out. Their level of industrial protection remains high (average tariffs of around 30% are found in the Mediterranean countries) and, as tariffs are reduced under the RTAs, EU products could replace lower cost imports from third countries. Yet, fear of trade diversion has not deterred countries from seeking RTAs with the EU. There are three possible reasons for this. First, Europe is often their main export market and RTAs are perceived as providing much greater security of market access than a multilateral agreement. Member countries see themselves as having an inside track on policy changes that could impact on their exports. Another important attraction of RTAs is that they can act as a means of 'locking in' domestic policy reforms. RTAs bind partner governments to trade rules, outlaw the arbitrary subsidization of favoured industries and make possible better economic policy governance. The gains from this can vastly outweigh any trade diversion losses. Third, the trade aspects of RTAs are often seen as the first step in a long path towards closer integration with the EU, in some cases leading to full membership and involving major dynamic gains.

As world trade becomes more liberalized, the preferential value of RTAs will diminish. All WTO members will enjoy relative freedom of access to

Table 24.6 The EU's network of preferential trade agreements[a], 2000

Type of trade regime	Name of Agreement	Countries involved
(a) Single market	European Economic Area (EEA)	Iceland, Liechtenstein, Norway
(b) Customs Union		Turkey, Andorra, San Marino
(c) Free Trade Area		Central and East European countries, Switzerland, Israel, Cyprus, Malta, South Africa, Mexico, Chile, Croatia, FYROM, Tunisia, Morocco, Palestinian Authority, Faroe Islands
(d) Partnership and Co-operation Agreements (MFN treatment)		Russia and other former Soviet Union countries
(e) Non-reciprocal contractual preferences	First generation Mediterranean Agreements Lomé/Cotonou	Algeria, Egypt, Jordan, Lebanon, Syria African, Caribbean, Pacific countries
(f) Non-reciprocal autonomous preferences	Generalized System of Preferences (GSP) 'Western Balkans' regime	Other developing countries plus members of CIS; Albania, Bosnia, FR Yugoslavia
(g) Purely MFN treatment		Australia, Canada, Japan, New Zealand, Taiwan, Hong Kong, Singapore, United States, South Korea

[a] Negotiations on free trade areas are in progress with MERCOSUR and the Gulf Cooperation Council.
Source: Adapted from Lamy (2002) and Sapir (1998)

Europe's market. EU products might, however, suffer from discrimination created by other RTAs. To avert this danger the EU is seeking conformity across the board to WTO rules. As a result, its own RTAs are becoming less discriminatory, more insistent on reciprocity from the partner country and more broadly focused than in the past. They address regulatory issues, right of establishment, foreign investment, competition policy, financial aid and technical cooperation as well as standard tariffs and import barriers *per se*. Thus, opposition to RTAs on the grounds of their breaking the non-discrimination principle of GATT has diminished considerably over the years.

24.2.4 Estimated welfare effects of the CCP

The EU is generally perceived as having a relatively open and liberal trade policy. This perception is supported by its role as the world's single largest importer;

its relatively low tariff levels on manufactured goods; its extensive network of preferential access agreements; and the stance it has taken in pushing for further multilateral trade liberalization through the WTO. Messerlin (2001) paints a more sceptical picture by taking into account the tariff peaks in agriculture and the role of anti-dumping duties. He calculates that the average tariff-equivalent extra-EU trade barrier across agricultural and industrial sectors amounted to roughly 14% in 1990 and 12% in 2000. Using different data and estimation methods, Bouët (2002) computed an average tariff equivalent for 1999 of 9% for the EU. Bouët's estimate is somewhat lower than Messerlin's for three main reasons: he used applied tariffs rather than bound ones, he took account of anti-dumping duties only on those trade partners to whom they legally applied, and he took account of the preferential access granted by the EU under regional and bilateral agreements.

Messerlin (2001) estimated that the total cost to the EU of its remaining external trade barriers in 2000 amounted to around 7% of GDP – roughly equivalent to the national income of Spain. Again, Bouët (2002) arrived at a lower estimate, valuing the net welfare loss from the CCP at around 2.5% of EU GDP. Here, the difference is due mainly to the fact that Messerlin's estimate includes not only the traditional deadweight loss from trade restrictions, but also the tariff revenue and producer rents, which he assumed to be largely squandered. Bouët, on the other hand, followed the standard theoretical approach strictly and considered only the deadweight loss. Neither Bouët's estimates nor Messerlin's incorporate the effect of indirect trade barriers such as EU-specific technical regulations and product standards, nor do they incorporate the effects

of continuing protection in service sectors. On the other hand, their estimates make the standard assumption in calculations of this kind of full employment, an assumption whose validity may be questioned in the EU at this time.

It is no surprise, therefore, that the estimated benefits from liberalization of the CCP are also significant. Economists of the GATT (1994), for example, projected EU income in 2005 to be higher by US$164 billion in 1990 prices as a result of the Uruguay Round. When compared to an estimated total world gain of US$510 billion, this implies that the EU will obtain fully one third of the global gains. Clearly the EU is a major beneficiary of the trend towards global trade liberalization.

24.3   Trade relations with the main partners

24.3.1 Developing countries

In spite of their relative economic weakness, developing countries are a key trade partner for the EU (Table 24.4). The present pattern of trade agreements owes as much to history and proximity to the EU as to economic rationale. These trade arrangements are discussed in detail in Chapter 25 and only a very brief summary is provided here. The Mediterranean countries, for instance, are bound to the EU by many ties. Fear of excessive immigration from these areas has given the EU an added incentive to assist their economic development through strong trade preferences. Following the 1995 Barcelona Declaration, the EU and 11 Mediterranean countries agreed to form a Euro-Med free trade area by the year 2010. Also contained in this programme are pledges to abolish obstacles to trade in goods and services on a reciprocal basis. Bilateral FTAs incorporating these principles have been already signed with several Mediterranean countries (see Chapter 1).

Prior to the Barcelona programme, the Lomé Convention was the EU's most preferential agreement with developing countries. Signed in 1975, and renewed at regular intervals thereafter, it gave a group of African, Caribbean, and Pacific (ACP) countries free access to EU markets for manufactures and a substantial range of primary goods. The Lomé accords encompass more than tariff reductions. They include commodity protocols which provide preferential prices to ACP exports of bananas, sugar and beef, the relaxation of NTBs, more flexible application of safeguard clauses, rules of

origin and exemption from MFA restrictions. Trade preferences are supplemented by special aid and technical cooperation arrangements.

In spite of this preferential access, the ACP countries' export performance in the EU market has been disappointing. Their market share has been declining in most of the post-War period and accounted for only 3.4% of EU imports in 1995 (2.7% if oil is excluded). The EU therefore proposed the negotiation of regional economic partnership agreements (REPAs) with groups of the ACPs, establishing free trade areas in place of the non-reciprocal access these countries enjoyed heretofore. This move was also prompted by the criticisms made of the discriminatory nature of the EU's non-reciprocal preferences in the WTO bananas case. Getting the necessary waiver from WTO rules for these preferences was clearly going to be more difficult in the future. The Cotonou Agreement, which replaced the Lomé Convention in 2000, envisages the negotiation of REPAs over the period 2002–2008 eventually leading to duty-free access for most EU exports to ACP countries as well as for most ACP exports to the EU.

For most non-ACP developing countries the GSP dictates the degree of preferential access for their exports to the EU. Initiated in 1971 by UNCTAD, the purpose of the GSP was to help developing countries to industrialize through exports to the developed world. The GSP provides substantially weaker trade preferences than the Lomé Convention or the Cotonou Agreement. However, under the 'Everything But Arms' initiative adopted in February 2001, the EU has granted duty-free and quota-free access for all products from the 49 least developed countries under its GSP, with the exception of arms. These special arrangements for least developed countries will be maintained for an unlimited period of time and are not subject to the periodic renewal of the standard GSP scheme.

The EU's multiplicity of agreements and special arrangements with developing countries is undergoing considerable re-assessment. This issue is examined in greater depth in Chapter 25 but some general comments can be made here. First, as global trade liberalization gathers steam and trade barriers crumble, the practical usefulness of trade preferences has diminished. *Preference erosion* is likely to accelerate markedly over the next decade. This will pose special problems for the ACP countries that have enjoyed for many years advantageous access to the EU market. Second, attention is likely to focus more on issues such as the right of establishment in services markets, attraction of foreign investment, rights to tender on public sector contracts in partner countries and competition law. We will hear less about trade preferences and more about development programmes. Third, developing countries will have to provide reciprocity in future RTAs if they are to be acceptable under WTO rules. This means they will have to reduce their own import barriers as well. For some there will be a serious loss of government revenues as a result and some (small!) danger of trade diversion. While some developing country governments tend to see the reduction in tariffs as a 'concession', trade theory suggests the opposite conclusion. Properly managed, the liberalization of imports can bring considerable benefits to their economies.

24.3.2 The United States

The United States is the EU's largest trade partner, accounting for 22% of combined extra-EU imports and exports (see Table 24.2). Although trade with industrial countries is in principle governed by the rules of the WTO, this has not prevented controversy arising on many specific issues.

EU economic relations with the United States have been based on strong political and cultural ties as well as common economic interests. Yet, at times, it appears as if the two partners are locked into a state of perpetual crisis. In the past, trade wars have threatened to erupt because of disputes over issues as diverse as steel, hormone treated beef, aircraft noise,

subsidies to Airbus, genetically modified crops and bananas. The EU has complained about unilateralism in United States trade legislation, 'Buy American' restrictions, discriminatory taxes, public procurement and restrictions on non-nationals in the services industries. Some European grievances were vindicated in September 1999, when a WTO Panel confirmed that US export subsidies granted through 'Foreign Sales Corporations' and covering approximately US$250 billion worth of US exports were in violation of WTO rules and had to be abolished by October 2000. However, an arbitration panel found in 2001 that the United States' new regime was still in breach of WTO rules, and it granted permission to the EU to impose retaliatory tariffs on up to $4 billion worth of US exports. The EU launched further WTO proceedings against the US in 2002 for an increase in American protection levels against steel imports. It also complained strongly against a 2002 Farm Act that significantly raised price and income support to American agriculture. For its part, the United States feared a protectionist 'Fortress Europe' arising from the single market programme and continues to accuse the EU of unfairly subsidizing high-tech sectors such as aviation. The most acute and enduring cause of friction, however, has been trade in agricultural products, particularly concerning the EU's refusal to allow imports of hormone treated beef. Since the EU did not comply with a WTO ruling against it, the United States has imposed punitive tariffs on EU exports on a number of mostly high value added agricultural products such as Danish ham and Roquefort cheese since 1999. The United States has further objected that growing EU food surpluses are being sold at subsidized prices on third markets, thereby creating difficulties for United States exporters to these markets. The EU retorts, with increased justification since the 2002 Farm Act, that agricultural subsidies are applied on both sides of the Atlantic.

Although full-scale trade wars have threatened to break out on many occasions, the strong mutuality of interests between the United States and the EU has, on each occasion thus far, saved them from the brink. Trade relations are characterized by constant levels of minor friction rather than a deeply-set divergence of interests. Indeed, the contentious sectors in transatlantic trade are commonly estimated to account for a mere 1%–2% of total trade. There is even talk of eliminating all trade barriers, thereby creating a 'new transatlantic marketplace' of some 700 million affluent consumers.

A Transatlantic Free Trade Agreement could yield welfare gains in the range 1%–2% of GDP for Europe and 1.6%–2.8% for the United States (Boyd, 1998).

24.3.3 Japan

Trade policy towards Japan has been marked by resistance to what is perceived as excessively rapid import penetration in a narrow range of product markets. It is also marked by internal disunity within the EU. Some member states, such as the United Kingdom and Ireland, have become important hosts to Japanese investment. Naturally, these member states have tended to view sales by Japanese firms more benignly than those with a small presence of Japanese-owned production facilities. Also, countries whose domestic industries compete directly with Japanese goods tend to take a tougher line in the trade policy debate than those for which Japanese sales compete only with other imports. Thus, the high share of Japanese passenger car imports in Ireland (43%) and Denmark (34%) aroused little concern, whereas Italy and France were highly resistant to any easing on restraints on Japanese imports despite having much lower import shares (5% and 4% respectively in the mid-1990s).

The EU's persistent trade deficit with Japan has been a bone of contention. It has been attributed to the combined effects of the strong competitive performance of Japanese firms, of Japan's high savings rate and, controversially, of Japan's reluctance to open its market to EU exporters. In 2001, 7.3% of total extra-EU imports came from Japan, while the Japanese market absorbed only 4.5% of EU exports. This trade imbalance is made particularly contentious because Japanese exports tend to be highly focused on a small number of sectors (automobiles, consumer electronics).

On the basis of explicit barriers to trade, the Japanese market appears relatively open. Japan has committed itself in the Uruguay Round to a trade-weighted tariff average on industrial goods of 1.7% (weighting tariffs by production as in Table 24.5 tends to give a slightly higher figure). This is the second lowest average of all countries (surpassed only by Switzerland). However, there are important implicit barriers to imports. First, access to the Japanese market is restricted by regulatory obstacles such as the arbitrary specification of technical standards for electrical appliances and conditions for participation in the financial services market. Japanese non-acceptance of international standards and European certification procedures hamper trade in areas such as the agro-food sector, pharmaceuticals and construction. Second, the existence of tightly connected business groups ('keiretsu'), built upon interconnected manufacturers and distributors, makes it particularly difficult for European firms to sell to Japan.

The EU has exerted pressure on Japan to liberalize access to its market, albeit using a less confrontational strategy than the United States. Consultation is the keyword in EU trade diplomacy with Japan. Annual summit meetings have been held between the Japanese Prime Minister, the President of the European Council and the President of the Commission since 1991, and a permanent dialogue was established in 1993 between METI, the Japanese ministry for economics, trade and industry, and the corresponding Commission Directorate. A 'Regulatory Reform Dialogue' has been maintained since 1995 to reduce the thicket of regulations that hampers trade and foreign investment. In addition, export-enhancing schemes such as assistance for marketing in Japan and special visit and study programmes have been initiated to facilitate access to the Japanese market for European business. Notable successes in EU-Japanese trade diplomacy include the 1991 'consensus' to phase out VERs on Japanese car exports by the year 2000, Japan's agreement in February 1997 to end discriminatory taxation of imported spirits, and the Mutual Recognition Agreement of 2001 that facilitates product certification for each others' markets.

Concern over Japanese import penetration has quietened down in recent years. One reason is that the Japanese economy has proved to be weaker and more vulnerable than was believed a decade ago. Another is that despite the deficit with Japan, the EU enjoys a large overall trade surplus. Hence, to object too strenuously to Japan's surplus might give ammunition to countries which had a deficit with the EU! Third, following the major reforms of its financial sector in the late 1990s, access to Japan's market has become easier for European investors. More European companies now have a stake in good relations with Japan. Fourth, EU manufacturing companies have raised productivity by copying Japanese techniques. 'Just in time' techniques are now commonplace. Fifth, as Europeans have gained in confidence, they are more ready to acknowledge that failure to obtain market share in Japan could partly be due to their poor knowledge of the Japanese market. One piece of evidence on what has been called the 'knowledge deficit': the population of Japan is one-third of the EU but there are five times more Japanese people living in Europe than Europeans in Japan. Finally, Japanese companies are becoming more open and more prepared to engage in cooperative ventures than in the past. The Nissan–Renault merger is an exemplar of this kind of cooperation. Clearly, the EU strategy of encouraging exports to Japan and promoting investment between the two countries is superior to protectionism. One must remember that the EU consumer has gained enormously both from access to Japanese goods and from the efficiency improvements forced on European industry by exposure to Japanese competition.

24.4	Trade policy in a globalizing world

On 14 November 2001 the members of the WTO concluded the Fourth Ministerial conference with a decision to launch a new WTO round – the Doha Development Agenda – comprising both further trade liberalization and new rule making, underpinned by commitments to provide more effective special and differential treatment to developing countries. The negotiations are scheduled to last three years – until January 2005. However, the unsuccessful interim meeting in September 2003 in Cancun is likely to set this back by several years. The EU has been a leading proponent of the new round and has insisted that it should be comprehensive in scope, tackling much more than simply the 'built-in agenda' of negotiations mandated in the various Uruguay Round agreements. The EU has four stated objectives in the Doha Round: (i) to further liberalize access to markets for goods and particularly services; (ii) to strengthen coverage in the areas of investment, competition, transparency in government procurement, intellectual property and trade facilitation; (iii) to ensure that more assistance is provided to developing countries to help with their integration into the global economy; (iv) to get the WTO to focus more on issues of public concern such as the environment, animal welfare and food safety, ensuring that trade rules are compatible with the wider interests of society as a whole. A more implicit objective, but which nonetheless carries much weight in the actual negotiating process, is the EU's desire to shape WTO rules on agricultural trade to enable it to maintain support for the European model of agriculture (see Chapter 20). This section examines some of the issues at stake in this comprehensive agenda.

24.4.1 Trade and intellectual property rights

Intellectual property is an increasingly important part of international trade. Most of the value of new medicines and other high technology products lies in the research, innovation, design and testing involved. People who purchase CDs, videos, books or computer programmes are paying for the creativity and information they contain, not for the materials used to make them. Considerable value can be added even to low-technology goods such as clothing or shoes through design and the use of brand names. These 'knowledge goods', ranging from computer programmes to pop songs, and 'reputation goods' such as trademarks or appellations of origin, account for an unquantifiable but undeniably growing share of the value embodied in traded products. The nature of trade policy with respect to such knowledge and reputation goods differs radically from policy aimed at liberalizing merchandise trade, since the main concern is not to abolish obstacles to imports (as countries are generally keen to attract knowledge goods), but to safeguard owners' property rights. Negotiations on intellectual property rights therefore do not consist of bargaining on abolition of barriers, but agreements to set up minimum standards of ownership protection.

From a theoretical viewpoint, the enforcement of intellectual property rights is a double-edged sword (see Primo Braga, 1995). In the short run, protecting owners of *knowledge goods* (e.g. through patents) violates the rule that public goods, whose marginal usage cost is zero, should be free. Static efficiency considerations therefore advocate a lax implementation of such property rights, to allow maximum dissemination. In the long run, however, the generation of additional knowledge goods is costly: resources have to be invested in research and development, and this will only occur if a future pecuniary return on such an investment can be safely anticipated. A zero price of knowledge goods is therefore socially sub-optimal in a dynamic sense, because it discourages innovation.

Property rights on *reputation goods* also have their advantages and drawbacks in equity terms. Trademark protection on one hand increases the monopoly power of owners, and thereby restricts competition, but on the other hand it can increase consumer welfare by allowing product differentiation and facilitating product information.

Both sides of the theoretical argument have been advanced in multilateral negotiations on intellectual property rights. Since developed countries, including the EU, tend to be the owners and exporters of intellectual property, while developing countries are net importers, the former generally argue in favour of stricter property-right enforcement than the latter. This was particularly evident during the Uruguay Round. These negotiations culminated in the Agreement on Trade-Related Aspects of Intellectual Property Rights (the TRIPS Agreement), which, alongside the GATT and GATS, forms one of the three pillars of the WTO. TRIPS negotiations were championed mainly by the United States and the EU against much initial opposition from developing countries. Divisions surfaced again when it appeared that TRIPS protection would prevent developing countries from gaining access to generic drugs as part of their public health programmes. At Doha in November 2001, WTO ministers issued a declaration emphasizing that the TRIPS Agreement should not prevent member states from protecting public health. They confirmed the right of countries to grant compulsory licences (authorization, under certain conditions, to produce a drug or medicine without the consent of the patent holder) and to resort to parallel imports (where drugs produced by the patent holder in another country can be imported without the patent holder's approval) where appropriate. An agreement which makes it easier for poorer countries to import cheaper generics made under compulsory licensing, if they are unable to manufacture the medicines themselves, was reached in the run-up to the Fifth Ministerial meeting in Cancun in September 2003.

Under the TRIPS accord, signatories have to establish minimum standards of intellectual property right protection, implement procedures to enforce these rights and extend the traditional GATT principles of national treatment and MFN practice to intellectual property. It was agreed that 20-year patent protection should be available for all inventions, whether of products or processes, in almost all fields of technology. Copyright on literary works (including computer programmes), sound recordings and films is made available for at least 50 years. Under the agreed transition period, most countries had to take on full TRIPS obligations by 2000, while the least-developed countries may postpone application of most provisions until 2006 with the possibility of a further extension.

24.4.2 Trade and competition policy

The relationship between trade and competition policy was first raised by the US, which for many years, like the EU, claimed that Japanese corporate groups undermined market access for foreign suppliers by buying largely from each other and maintaining closed distribution chains. More recently, the EU has made the running, arguing that anti-competitive practices by businesses can have a significant impact on access to markets. It has sought rules that would require countries to introduce a national competition policy and to enforce it. It has also highlighted the need for more international cooperation to deal with questions such as international cartels and multi-jurisdictional mergers. This market access agenda is not necessarily shared by developing countries who have been more concerned about possible anti-competitive behaviour by large multinational companies at their expense. They are also unhappy at the prospect of undertaking additional commitments in an area where they have limited capacity and foresee limited gains. Reaching agreement is also made more difficult, as in the case of intellectual property rights, by theoretical disagreements as to what appropriate competition policy should be.

The EU succeeded in getting a WTO Working Group on the interaction between trade and competition policy established at the WTO ministerial meeting in Singapore in December 1996. This Group discusses the relevance of fundamental WTO principles of non-discrimination and transparency for competition policy. There is no question of trying to harmonize domestic competition laws, but even reaching agreement on a more general framework is proving difficult. The Doha Declaration set the objective of establishing a multilateral framework on competition policies, but this did not obtain the required explicit consensus at the Fifth WTO Ministerial meeting in Cancun in 2003 and thus remains as an unsettled issue on the negotiations table.

24.4.3 Trade and the environment

Environmental policy moved to a prominent position on the trade agenda during the 1990s (see Chapter 17). Up to then, virtually the only environmental concern to affect trade policy was the protection of endangered species. With the rise of ecological awareness and trans-frontier pollution problems such as ozone depletion, acid rain and global warming, trade policy came to be seen as a significant element in a country's overall environmental policy.

The main trade policy issue in this debate relates to the use of import restrictions on goods whose production creates negative trans-border environmental externalities. Economic theory suggests that in such circumstances the most efficient remedy is to apply direct environmental policy at the source of the externality (e.g. through pollution taxes, eco-subsidies or regulation; see Chapter 17). However, environmental policies are often difficult to enforce, so this first-best option may not be feasible. In that case, import restrictions may be the only practicable policy tool. The main drawback of import restrictions against polluting countries is that they provide protection to domestic producers of the importable good, and ecological arguments are therefore vulnerable to abuse by domestic protectionist lobbies. For this reason, trade measures should be temporary and accompanied by efforts to implement environmental policies in the polluting countries.

Even if the externalities are dealt with by environmental policies adopted at the source, new problems can still emerge. Environmental policies affect the competitiveness of open economies. Thus, countries with lax environmental legislation are blamed for 'ecological dumping', and import-competing industries in countries with stringent laws may lobby for protection to ensure a 'level playing field'. As before, the first-best way of ensuring a level playing field is by achieving some degree of coordination in environmental policies across countries. This does not necessarily mean that all countries must adopt exactly the same environmental regime, but it provides a powerful rationale for seeking agreement on environmental policies on a multilateral basis. Even if an agreed way of eradicating 'ecological dumping' could be found, it remains questionable if trade restrictions are the most appropriate remedy. Restricting imports can be counterproductive as it promotes the domestic activities which the environmental policy is attempting to restrain.

On another tack, some environmentalists argue that the rising volume of international trade in itself is causing serious damage to the environment. Oil leakage from tankers and pollution from increased road haulage are classical examples. They recommend reduction in trade if necessary by protection as a solution. The standard economic response would be that trade restrictions are inefficient and that policy should instead be aimed at the source of the problem (e.g. taxation of oil shipments and on the use of polluting fuels by lorries). One could agree with this while pointing out that such correct policy action may not be politically feasible. Witness, for example, the way in which the European Commission's proposals for a carbon tax have been resisted by business interests (see Chapter 17).

We conclude that trade policy is certainly not the best, and can often be an inappropriate, instrument to protect the environment. International dialogue and agreed domestic policy measures are a more efficient alternative. The main platform for such negotiations is the WTO Committee on Trade and Environment, which was established in 1995. Discussions in this committee have so far been a mere stocktaking exercise, and its report to the Singapore WTO Ministerial Conference in December 1996 contained no specific proposals. The EU, like everybody else, supports the case for multilateral environmental agreements, but the difficulty lies in getting countries to agree.

24.4.4 Trade and labour standards

The social dimension to increased international trade has received increasing attention given the concern that trade and investment flows should benefit people at large and not just international business. This has led to calls for a 'social clause' in WTO rules which would allow trade barriers to be invoked against imports from countries deemed to violate minimum labour standards. Human rights activists and moral advocates of a social clause see it as a way of promoting and enforcing core labour standards and helping to eradicate exploitative working practices. The difficulty is that trade sanctions will do little for the bulk of the labour force in developing countries which is employed in the informal sector, and could even have the opposite of the desired impact. A less well-founded argument is that lower labour standards, especially in developing countries, give them an 'unfair' competitive advantage which will either lead to 'social dumping' (the ability to sell goods abroad more cheaply analogous to 'ecological dumping'), or to the erosion of existing social standards in developed countries (the 'race to the bottom' argument) as footloose firms threaten to uproot to take advantage of laxer standards elsewhere. This version of the pauper labour argument is no less a fallacy for being restated in modern guise. Focusing only on labour costs ignores the substantially higher productivity of labour in developed countries. Developed countries are perfectly able to compete in the sectors where they have a comparative advantage.

The 1995 World Summit on Social Development in Copenhagen identified four core labour standards for the first time, and these were later confirmed by the 1998 International Labour Organization (ILO) Declaration on Fundamental Principles and Rights at Work. The four core standards are freedom of association and collective bargaining, the prevention of child labour, the elimination of forced labour, and the outlawing of discrimination. The EU is strongly committed to the protection of core labour rights, but the debate is about the appropriate role for the WTO in this task. The ILO enforcement mechanism, being limited to ratified conventions, is rather weak. Hence the attraction of using the WTO with its rules-based system and binding dispute settlement mechanism as the means to ensure compliance.

In the first WTO Ministerial Conference in Singapore in December 1996, the EU was among those which suggested that a WTO Working Party be created to look into the links between international trade and working conditions. The proposal was fiercely resisted by the developing countries, which saw it as a guise for protectionism and a cover for more restrictive trade measures. The final Declaration confirmed that the ILO was the competent body to 'set and deal' with labour standards. At the Seattle Ministerial Conference in 1999, the United States returned to the Working Party proposal while making clear that its ultimate objective was to incorporate core labour standards into all trade agreements and subject to trade sanctions. This was a major reason for the failure of the Seattle Conference.

The EU has opposed sanctions as a way of enforcing core labour standards, but it continues to insist on the necessity of showing that trade liberalization does not lead to a deterioration in working conditions. It has proposed strengthened mechanisms within the ILO to promote respect for core labour standards, a review mechanism between the WTO and the ILO, as part of which a trade angle would be linked to the reviews conducted by the ILO, and support for private sector and voluntary schemes (such as codes of conduct and ethical labelling schemes) (CEU, 2001a). It has also used social incentives under its GSP scheme to promote core labour standards by providing additional trade preferences for countries which comply with these standards and allowing for the withdrawal of preferences where beneficiary countries practice any form of slavery or forced labour.

24.5   Conclusions

An 'open' market is an elusive goal. Despite much liberalization, the EU continues to maintain strong defences against sensitive imports. Even under an optimistically liberal scenario, it will be some time before Australia and New Zealand will be able to sell agricultural produce or India textile and clothing products into the EU market without let or hindrance. However, this chapter concludes that the direction of change has leaned, and will continue to lean, towards easier access. The *Fortress Europe*, which some had feared would be erected around the single market, has happily not materialized.

The scope for further *negative integration*, in the sense of reduction of tariff and non-tariff trade barriers, is approaching exhaustion, but in its place there will be greater emphasis on *positive integration* (see Chapter 6). That means requiring governments to adapt domestic policies and institutions so as to ensure that the scope for expanded trade is not frustrated by differences in regulation, market institutions, technical standards and taxes. Linkage between trade issues and other policy areas once considered exclusively in the national domain will grow in importance over time.

Regionalism is still a strong focus of EU trade policy but its future direction is unclear. In place of the largely discretionary, non-reciprocal 'hierarchy of preferences' which has characterized EU trade arrangements until now, the EU is moving towards a Pan-European free trade area embracing all of Western and Eastern Europe, the Mediterranean countries and even sub-Saharan Africa. Some worry that this pursuit of regionalism, with its discriminatory stance against third countries, might be at the expense of the stability of the multilateral trading system. Whether regionalism is a 'building block' or a 'stumbling block' for an open multilateral system is a hotly debated topic among economists. Some argue that it risks prompting the construction of rival free trade areas centred on the Americas and Asia with the prospect that trade disputes between these rival blocs could shake the foundations of the multilateral system. The more positive view is that the EU's regional trade arrangements can act as a laboratory for rule making in some of the more contentious trade policy areas, as arguably was the case with the internal market programme, and that experience shows that the EU has pursued a policy of 'open' regionalism which is compatible with its multilateral obligations.

The precise form of the EU's future external policy will depend on several factors. First, the increasing heterogeneity among EU members is likely to increase the difficulty of reaching consensus on trade policy. This will strengthen the hand of those who call for the transfer of exclusive competence in all aspects of trade policy making to the Union, but member states will fight hard to retain as much leverage and influence as they can.

Second, the maintenance of strong economic growth remains crucial. Enthusiasm for integration gathers momentum when an economy is doing well. To some extent European integration and external liberalization are fair weather phenomena. It is also true that the process of liberalization itself tends to improve the weather! A prime concern at present is the EU's high rate of unemployment (see Chapter 23). Free trade and unemployment are uneasy, even incompatible, bedfellows. The welfare gains from increased imports do not impress the unemployed. It is remarkable how effective the Commission has been in forwarding its trade liberalization agenda. One reason may be that many EU countries have a significant balance of payments surplus; when exports exceed imports, it becomes difficult to blame unemployment on excessive imports.

Third, public support and understanding of the benefits of an open trade policy can never be taken for granted. Public opinion finds it difficult to accept that trade rules might be used to require the EU to import food it deems unhealthy, or products which might damage its environment, or that other trade rules might prevent action being taken to promote animal welfare or improved working conditions. What makes these issues difficult to handle in a WTO context is that, although they are open to abuse for protectionist purposes, they are largely driven by consumer rather than producer concerns. The EU has proposed strengthening the 'precautionary principle' in WTO rules, which would allow countries to invoke protection even where scientific opinion is divided on the likelihood of a threat to health or the environment. These concerns also explain why the EU has addressed the linkages between trade and the environment and trade and labour standards, despite the opposition from many trade partners. The EU has also highlighted the need for trade policy to contribute to sustainable development. Sustainability impact assessments are now conducted on its WTO proposals and on bilateral trade initiatives. Governments and business leaders must ensure that trade policy making remains transparent and accessible if public confidence in the process is to be maintained.

Finally, it is important to reiterate that the stakes in the debate on EU trade policy are high, particularly at a time of considerable uncertainty in the world economy and growing international tension. Estimates were given earlier (see Section 24.2.4) of the cost to the EU of its remaining protectionist barriers, but these would pale into insignificance if there were a breakdown in the multilateral system and protectionist barriers began to increase again. The danger that the resurgence of regionalism might lead to a world of competing trade blocs would be much more real if confidence in the multilateral trading system were damaged. The willingness of developing countries to pursue more open trade strategies would undoubtedly be undermined if it were felt that the industrialized countries, including the EU, no longer had the stomach for free trade. Balancing the conflicting interests of domestic lobbies, not least agriculture, as well as of the member states is an enormous challenge. EU trade policy will continue to fascinate, and to shape our futures, in the years ahead.

NOTES

1. Responsibility for trade in goods and increasingly services and the trade-related aspects of regulatory measures rests with the European Communities (EC) rather than the European Union (EU) – see Chapters 2 and 3. For ease of exposition, however, we refer to the EU's Common Commercial Policy throughout this chapter.

2. The observant reader will note that there are now only four trade articles in the Treaty where previously there were seven. The remaining three were repealed.

Chapter 25 The EU and the developing world

ALAN MATTHEWS

The EU's economic size and its role in world trade mean that it is a key player in structuring the global economic environment for developing countries (DCs) through its aid and trade policies. EU member states are the largest trading partner of DCs, providing 23% of their imports and taking 21% of their exports. The EU and its member states provide some 55% of total official development assistance (ODA) with the EU alone providing some 10% of total ODA worldwide, making it the fifth largest donor and the second largest among multilateral donors, after the World Bank (OECD, 2002a). It also has a significant indirect influence through its active participation in international organizations which attempt to manage the world economic system. The Union's development cooperation policy is comprehensive in its approach, including trade arrangements, development assistance and political dialogue. A number of useful studies have analysed the different elements of the EU's relations with developing countries and help us to better understand the dynamics behind these relationships (Cosgrove-Sacks, 1999; Grilli, 1993; Lister, 1998; McMahon, 1998; van Dijck and Faber, 2000). Important and even radical changes are currently taking place in the EU's development policy. The purpose of this chapter is to highlight these changes and to discuss their longer-term significance.

Three themes can be highlighted at the outset. First, the economic environment in which the EU's relations with DCs are played out is changing rapidly. The most striking feature of economic growth over the past three decades has been the growing differentiation in economic performance (Table 25.1). Overall differences in GDP per capita between developed countries and DCs remain large – in 2001, average income per capita was US$26 926 in the industrialized countries but only US$1204 in the low and middle-income DCs. However, for some DC regions the gap has been narrowing rapidly. This is particularly the case for the group of Asian 'Newly Industrializing

Economies' (Hong Kong, Singapore, South Korea and Taiwan) and the East Asia and Pacific region (dominated by China). These countries have pursued outward-looking development policies and have rapidly increased their share of world trade (the growth of exports from East Asia annually averaged 11.3% in the 1992–2001 period, and from China 16.0%, during a period when world trade expanded by 7%, see World Bank, 2003). The Asian financial crisis in 1997–1998 interrupted this spectacular economic performance and triggered a significant contraction of economic activity in a number of countries, although recovery in most countries of the region is now well underway.

The economic performance of Latin America and the Caribbean has been less strong. Following average 3.3% annual growth in the 1970s, the continent was devastated by the debt crisis in the 1980s which led to a 'lost decade' for development in which living standards declined. Recovery in the 1990s was weak and has been further undermined by falls in economic activity in the early years of this decade as capital flows into the region dropped sharply, reflecting investors' fears of the financial fragility of the continent in the aftermath of Argentina's default. However, its performance has still been stronger than that of either the Middle East and North Africa or Sub-Saharan Africa. In the latter sub-continent, average living standards have been contracting steadily for two decades as a result of a combination of natural disasters, slumping commodity prices, economic mismanagement, civil strife and, most recently, the AIDS epidemic. World Bank forecasts for the period to 2015 project that these differences will persist, with yearly per capita growth rates of 5.0% in East Asia and 4.1% in South Asia contrasting with 1.4% in the Middle East and North African region and 1.5% in Sub-Saharan Africa (Table 25.1). As will be seen in this chapter, the latter are the two regions on which EU development policies have a particular focus. Thus, EU development

Table 25.1 Growth of real per capita GDP by region, 1971–2015

	GDP per capita 2001 (current US dollars)	Growth (%)					
		1971–1980	1981–1990	1991–2000	2001	Estimate 2002	Forecast 2003–2015
World	5 260	1.8	1.3	1.2	-0.1	0.5	2.0
High-income countries	26 375	2.6	2.5	1.8	0.3	1.1	2.3
Industrial countries	26 926	2.6	2.5	1.8	0.4	1.1	2.3
Asian NIEs	16 195	7.2	5.9	4.7	-2.4	1.6	3.9
Low- and middle-income countries	1 204	2.6	0.7	1.6	1.4	1.5	3.4
East Asia and Pacific	956	4.6	5.6	6.4	4.5	5.4	5.4
South Asia	468	0.7	3.4	3.3	2.6	2.9	4.1
Latin America and the Caribbean	3 678	3.3	-0.9	1.6	-1.2	-2.6	2.4
Europe and Central Asia	2 101	2.5	0.7	-1.9	2.2	3.5	3.5
Middle East and North Africa	2 099	3.6	-0.6	1.0	1.3	0.6	1.4
Sub-Saharan Africa	454	0.5	-1.2	-0.4	0.5	0.1	1.5

Source: World Bank (2003), p. 201. Copyright 2003 by World Bank. Reproduced with permission of World Bank in the format Textbook via Copyright Clearance Centre

policy is required to address an increasingly disparate group of DCs, where the appropriate mixture of policy instruments is going to vary depending on the circumstances of the particular country or country grouping being considered.

Second, many of the old foundations of past EU relationships with developing countries are being swept away. These relationships were based on a mixture of trade preferences and development aid to promote trade and development in the weaker DCs, while restrictive trade measures (high protection against agricultural imports, quotas on the imports of textiles and clothing, and anti-dumping duties on the import of particularly competitive manufactured goods) and the absence of financial aid characterized EU relations with the more advanced DCs. Many DCs pursued inward-looking development strategies and were little interested in attracting private foreign investment. The liberalization of world trade and capital movements in recent years is gradually transforming these relationships.

Trade preference schemes are weakening for two separate reasons. The first is economic: trade liberalization under the auspices of GATT/WTO is reducing the value of trade preferences and the EU has been searching for new models of cooperation. The second is legal: the EU's network of discriminatory preference schemes runs counter to GATT/WTO rules on regional trade arrangements but for years the EU was able to persuade other WTO members to condone them. In the mid-1990s, it decided it would no longer seek to make an exception of these arrangements and instead would enter into WTO-compatible trade arrangements with its developing country partners. These are required to be free trade areas covering substantially all trade between the contracting parties. Thus the EU has been actively pursuing regional trade agreements with many DCs, seeking to convert its selective preferential agreements into free trade ones.

Third, EU development cooperation policy is also evolving rapidly. Private capital flows have come to dwarf the role of development aid as a source of investment capital in DCs. In the face of growing dissatisfaction with the outcome of aid programmes and growing 'aid fatigue', the search has been on to define new roles for aid and to see where it can be used most effectively. The EU has undertaken a comprehensive re-evaluation of its development cooperation policy objectives which has placed poverty alleviation at the centre. The challenge now is to follow through on that commitment. Another issue is that EU development cooperation policy has been characterized by a strong regional emphasis with particular groups of partner countries such as the African, Caribbean and Pacific (ACP) states, Asia and Latin America (ALA) countries, the Mediterranean countries and, more recently, PHARE and TACIS countries (these are the countries of Central and Eastern Europe and the Former Soviet Union, respectively; see Section 25.2.2). These regional arrangements are usually conducted within an overall framework that includes trade preferences along with development assistance and political dialogue. There is a continuing tension between those who stress the regional approach based on recognition of historical and strategic linkages with former European colonies and neighbouring countries, and those who argue for a more global approach concerned predominantly with poverty reduction.

The most long-lived and comprehensive of these regional arrangements has been the relationship with the ACP countries, originally under successive Lomé Conventions and now under the Cotonou Agreement. The Lomé Convention, originally signed in 1975, was hailed at the time as a model for a new type of development partnership between industrialized countries and DCs. Its innovations of partnership, deep trade preferences and long-term contractual aid commitments were certainly novel at the time. However, the EU's geographical priorities have been rapidly changing in the 1990s following the end of the Cold War and reflecting the changing importance of different DC regions in international trade. Priority is now given to the stability and development of neighbouring countries and to aid for countries in crisis in the regions nearest to the EU. The ACP countries are no longer as central to EU development cooperation policy as was once the case. Given that these countries remain among the poorest and least-developed in the world, these shifts and realignments have generated considerable controversy and debate.

This chapter explores the way the EU interacts with the DCs through both its trade and development cooperation policies. Section 25.1 concentrates on the trade arrangements intended to benefit DCs and Section 25.2 on the development cooperation or financial aid arrangements. Section 25.3 concludes by highlighting some of the main issues in the current debates on the EU's relations with the developing world.

25.1 Trade policy

Trade is a key mechanism for development. At the multilateral level, trade policy can contribute to ensuring a fair and equitable trading system which facilitates the integration of DCs into the international trading regime at their own pace. At the EU level, trade policy can facilitate access to EU markets by lowering trade barriers through multilateral liberalization and preferential schemes. EU trade policy can also influence the DCs' own trade policies through economic and trade cooperation agreements and by encouraging regional arrangements between themselves.

25.1.1 Developing countries in WTO

At the multilateral level, the EU supports the principle of special and differential (S&D) treatment for DCs in the application of the various WTO Agreements. S&D treatment refers to the exceptions, flexibility and extra support that DCs need in order to get the most out of WTO. The two aspects most commonly cited are the right to access (particularly preferential access to northern markets without the requirement of reciprocity) and the right to protect (specifically, the right to maintain import protection on infant industry or balance of payments grounds). More recently, given the greater complexity of the Agreements negotiated in the Uruguay Round, more emphasis has been put on granting longer transition periods and providing assistance to DCs to implement the commitments they have undertaken.

The Doha Ministerial Declaration launching the Doha Development Round of WTO trade negotiations in November 2001 recognised that S&D treatment is an integral part of WTO Agreements. It noted that many DCs were dissatisfied with the way in which S&D provisions in these Agreements had operated, and it called for a review of these provisions 'with a view to strengthening them and making them more precise, effective and operational'. The EU has made a number of proposals to address this mandate. It has proposed a joint commitment from all industrial economies and the most advanced DCs to grant tariff-free treatment by 2003 to essentially all products exported by the least developed countries (LDCs), thus replicating its own 'Everything But Arms' proposal

(see below). It also committed to support institutional capacity-building in DCs both to assist in the implementation of past commitments and in preparing for future trade negotiations. Many DCs are at considerable practical disadvantage in participating in WTO processes and negotiations, due to their lack of skilled personnel and the high cost of maintaining a delegation in Geneva (where the WTO is located) to deal with trade matters.

25.1.2 Preferential trade arrangements

EU preferential arrangements for DC exports have been of two kinds: a non-reciprocal Generalized System of Preferences (GSP) available to all DCs and special non-reciprocal preferential schemes for particular groups of countries. The two most important special schemes are the trade preferences under the Lomé Convention (now the Cotonou Agreement since 2000) with 77 ACP countries and those with the Community's neighbours in the Southern and Eastern Mediterranean. Non-reciprocity means that DCs are not required to offer similar preferential access to their markets in return for the access privileges they are granted to the EU market. The schemes differ in the extent of the products covered, their contractual basis and the size of the concessions offered. Together, they form a hierarchy of preferences with the ACP signatories to the Lomé Convention in the most preferred category, the Mediterranean countries in an intermediate category and most ALA countries in the least preferred category with GSP preferences only. Winters (2000) and McQueen (2002) provide a discussion of the motivation of the EU and its partners in entering these preferential trade arrangements.

Two controversies have always surrounded the operation of these trade preferences. The first has been legal. Preferential market access breaches the key principle of the GATT/WTO of non-discrimination, which means that all contracting parties to the GATT, and now members of the WTO, are entitled to receive most-favoured-nation (MFN) treatment. Interpreted literally, this prohibits discriminatory trade arrangements such as customs unions (CUs) or preferential trade areas (PTAs). A special clause was therefore included in the GATT (Article XXIV; see Appendix 1.1, p. 20) to permit countries to participate in CUs or free trade areas (FTAs) in which they provide reciprocal preferences to each other, provided certain conditions were met. Subsequently, an additional provision known as the Enabling Clause which granted a waiver for autonomous tariff preferences to DCs was adopted in 1971 for a ten-year period and renewed as part of the final outcome of the Tokyo Round of GATT negotiations in 1979 for an indefinite period. This legitimizes the grant of general non-reciprocal preferences to DCs, and further allows deeper preferences (further discrimination) in favour of LDCs. However, the EU's special preferential schemes are not covered by the Enabling Clause as they are not granted to all DCs nor to all LDCs, but to sub-sets of them. The EU therefore had to seek a waiver in the GATT/WTO to be able legally to offer these preferences. Following the high profile 'banana dispute' in WTO in the 1990s in which the preferential market access of ACP countries was disputed by a group of Latin American banana-exporting countries, the future of these waivers became increasingly uncertain. The EU has therefore moved to convert its preferential trade arrangements with the ACP and Mediterranean countries to free trade agreements. Not surprisingly, this insistence on reciprocity of trade concessions has been controversial, not least because of the EU's continuing reluctance or inability to offer free access in the agricultural sector because of the operation of the Common Agricultural Policy (CAP; see Chapter 20).

The second controversy surrounding the EU's preferential trading schemes has been economic and concerns the value of the preferences offered to the recipient countries. This debate runs at two levels: whether the preferences themselves have been worthwhile and whether they have had any impact in promoting the trade and development of the beneficiaries. Many economists have pointed out that the EU's GSP scheme, in particular, has been so hedged with restrictions as to nullify many of the concessions offered. The EU responded to these criticisms by considerably revising its GSP scheme in 1995 and by introducing its 'Everything But Arms' proposal in 2001 which in principle provides duty- and quota-free access for all LDC exports except for arms and ammunition. The debate on the lack of impact of these schemes is driven particularly by the poor performance of the ACP countries which has seen a dramatic fall in their share of the EU market despite having the most generous market access arrangements. The remainder of this section examines these PTAs and the changes that are taking place.

25.1.3 The Generalized System of Preferences

The EU introduced its GSP scheme in 1971. It covered all DC manufactured exports and some agricultural and food products. The list of the latter was gradually extended over time, but all products covered by a CAP regime are excluded. GSP products are divided into sensitive and non-sensitive categories. Originally, non-sensitive products were offered duty-free access while the preferences for sensitive products were characterised by quotas and ceilings, thus limiting the quantities involved. The included agricultural products enjoyed only limited tariff concessions, mainly to maintain a higher margin of preference for the EU's more preferred ACP and Mediterranean partners.

In the 1995 revision of its GSP scheme, the EU did away with quotas and replaced them with tariff preferences that vary according to the sensitivity of the products. Of a total of 10 300 products, 2 100 face zero MFN duties and of the remaining 8 200 products, approximately 7 000 are covered by the GSP (the remainder are mostly agricultural products subject to the CAP which are not covered by tariff preferences). Of these 7 000 products, 3 300 are classified as non-sensitive and 3 700 as sensitive (Panagariya, 2002).

Under the general or base GSP scheme available to all DCs (including China), the EU grants duty-free access on non-sensitive products and partial tariff preferences on sensitive products. The usual tariff preference on sensitive products is a flat 3.5 percentage points (replaced for textiles and clothing by a 20% preference margin which, on a tariff of 15%, for example, would yield a preference of 3 percentage points). For many exporters, these relatively small margins are not worth the extra paperwork involved in applying for GSP status.

The EU scheme has always provided for the 'graduation' of more competitive suppliers. This is defended by the EU on the grounds that it is intended to ensure that the preferences are targeted on those countries which genuinely need them, but it also reduces the competitive pressures on EU domestic firms. Based on certain criteria, a country may be excluded from the GSP altogether or graduated from certain products. Two criteria are applied for complete exclusion. First, the World Bank must classify the country as a high-income country for three consecutive years. Second, a development index, which measures a country's industrial development and participation in international trade relative to the EU, attains a pre-specified value. Both criteria must be satisfied (Panagariya, 2002).

Graduation from specific sectors is based on achieving a certain degree of competitiveness in the sector. Graduation may take place under one of two mechanisms: a lion's share clause and a graduation mechanism. The former applies if the EU imports of a product from a beneficiary country reach 25% of the combined imports from all beneficiary countries. The graduation mechanism is based on the specialization of the beneficiary country. A sector graduates if it reaches a certain threshold where the threshold is higher, the lower the level of development.

Additional preferences are available under social, environmental and drug trafficking clauses (the 'super GSP'). In the case of textiles and clothing, an additional 20% preference is available under these arrangements. For products receiving the flat rate preference of 3.5 percentage points under the general arrangements, the extra preference under these special arrangements is 5 percentage points. The additional incentives under the social clause are available to countries complying with so-called 'core labour standards' (see Chapter 24), while those under the environmental clause are available to countries complying with international standards on forest management (note the difference with US practice which requires countries to comply with core labour standards in order even to be eligible for GSP status under its scheme). The incentives to encourage countries to fight drug production and trafficking were initially introduced in the form of duty-free access for certain products originating in the Andean Community but were subsequently extended to some other Latin and Central American countries and, most recently, Pakistan.

LDCs always enjoyed more favourable GSP preferences than other DCs. Following the adoption of the 'Everything But Arms' (EBA) proposal in February 2001, all products from countries on the UN list of LDCs (currently 49 countries) now enter the EU market duty-free. The essential value of the EBA arrangement is that it extends duty-free access to those agricultural products which were otherwise excluded from the GSP. Apart from arms and ammunition

which are the only permanently-excluded products, transition periods have been put in place for three sensitive agricultural products, namely, bananas, rice and sugar. They will be eligible for unlimited duty-free access starting January 2006, July 2009 and September 2009, respectively. In the meantime, the limited tariff-free quotas which are currently available for rice and sugar exports from LDCs will be increased annually. Although seen as the new 'jewel in the crown' of EU trade relationships with DCs, the immediate impact of the EBA has been negligible, largely because the LDCs currently export so little in the product categories liberalized. These categories accounted for around one half of one per cent of total LDC exports to the EU in 2001 (Brenton, 2003).

The EU GSP is intended to stimulate exports from DCs in three ways. First, trade is generated as improved market access makes imported goods more attractive relative to domestically-produced alternatives; this is trade creation (see Chapter 6). Second, to the extent that DCs and industrial countries are exporting similar products, preferential tariff reductions may help to switch trade to the DC supplier; this is trade diversion (see Chapter 6). From the point of view of DCs, both effects are additive and positive. Third, the GSP may have a longer-term effect to the extent that it enhances the attraction of the preference-receiving country as a site for inward foreign direct investment (FDI) seeking to export to the EU.

Generally, analysts have had difficulty in finding a positive effect of trade preferences on exports apart from the rent transfer accompanying duty-free entry of goods (rents arise because DC exporters can benefit from the remaining tariff protection to the EU market against third countries, though this depends on the bargaining power of exporting firms in the DCs vis-à-vis the importing firms in the EU). Preference schemes appear to have little effect in stimulating new exports. Critics point to a number of flaws with GSP schemes. Non-reciprocal preferences such as those offered by the GSP lie outside the purview of WTO rules and thus can be unilaterally modified or cancelled by donor countries at any time. This uncertainty is likely to discourage investment in beneficiary countries to take advantage of these preferences, which is meant to be one of their primary rationales. The EU scheme offers minimal concessions on sensitive products (more than half of the total) which are often those in which the DCs have a comparative advantage. In the case of textile and clothing imports, quotas have been maintained on all significant suppliers under the Multi-Fibre Arrangement which is not due to be dismantled until 2005 (see Chapter 24). Tariff preferences on agricultural products have been very limited, mainly because of the difficulty in reconciling preferential access with the protection provided by the CAP but also, even in the case of tropical products which the EU does not produce itself, in order to protect the margin of preference provided to more preferred ACP and Mediterranean suppliers. The value of preferences is also reduced by restrictive rules of origin. Rules of origin are necessary to determine if a particular product originates in a preference-receiving country; rules which, if drawn too tightly, may make it difficult for firms from the exporting country to claim originating status and thus benefit from the margin of preferential access provided.

25.1.4 Relations with the ACP states

The relationship with the ACP states began in 1957, at the inception of the European Community, with the Yaoundé Conventions. This was followed by a series of five-year Lomé Conventions starting in 1975 following the accession of the United Kingdom to the EU. The fourth Lomé Convention beginning in 1990 was of 10-year duration, although with provision for a mid-term review in 1995. Since 2000 relations with ACP countries are governed by the Cotonou Agreement which was signed in 2000 and entered into force in 2003. This introduced significant changes in philosophy and instruments as compared to the Lomé Conventions. As noted earlier, the Lomé Conventions were based on a partnership model, deep trade preferences and contractual financial commitments. This section concentrates on the trade preferences provided while the aid element is examined in Section 25.2.3.

Under the Conventions, the EU offered duty- and quota-free access to exports from ACP countries, although again a major exception was exports covered by the CAP. However, more preferential treatment than to other countries was extended for CAP products. In addition, four commodity Protocols annexed to the Lomé Convention provided preferential access for a specified quantity of exports from a selected group of traditional ACP suppliers of bananas, rum, sugar and beef. This trade regime was extended under the Cotonou Agreement until the end of 2007.

From 1980 to 2000, ACP trade grew at the meagre rate of 0.7% annually, at a time when world trade grew by 6.0% annually. The ACP share in world merchandise trade, which was 7.1% in 1950, declined to 4.7% in 1980 and to only 1.7% in 2000 (UNCTAD, 2002). These trends are mirrored in the trade of ACP countries with the EU. Despite the fact that the ACP states were at the top of the EU's hierarchy of preferences with the most favourable conditions of access to the EU market, the ACP have become increasingly marginalized as EU trade partners over time; the share of ACP exports to the EU market has fallen by more than a half, from 8% in 1975 to 2.8% in 2000. However, exports to non-EU markets have grown more rapidly. The share of Africa's exports going to the EU fell from 60% in 1980 to 30% in 2000 while for the Pacific countries the share fell from 35% to 10% over the same period. Only the Caribbean countries increased their dependence on the EU market from 20% in 1980 to 30% in 2000 (UNCTAD, 2002).

These data are often used to argue that trade preferences have not worked, and indeed there is some support for this, but it is not the whole story. The importance of the trade preferences granted is often overstated. On average, 50% to 60% of ACP exports to the EU never received any preferences because they were non-dutiable, irrespective of source. Another 5% to 10% of ACP exports to the EU fell under the special import regulations of the CAP. Ultimately, only about 35% to 45% of ACP exports received preferences. These were mainly tropical beverages, whose demand is quite price inelastic and where demand is reaching saturation in the EU. Further, the margin of preference enjoyed by ACP states fell as the EU's MFN tariffs were cut under successive GATT negotiations for products such as coffee, cocoa and vegetable oils.

Trade preferences require a supply capacity to make them effective, and arguably economic mismanagement and supply side difficulties also limited ACP exports. But even with good economic management, ACP countries have been specialized in commodities whose market prospects have been poor, and where the deterioration in export prices has had a devastating effect on development efforts. It can be argued that trade preferences failed to promote necessary diversification. On the other hand, where progress in diversification was made, the products to benefit, such as textiles, fishery and horticultural products, were

those which enjoyed a substantial margin of preference over the EU's MFN and GSP tariffs. On balance,
however, ACP trade preferences have not been seen as
a success, and this was one of the factors leading to
their revision in the Cotonou Agreement in 2000.

In 1996 the Commission published a Green Paper
to promote discussion on post-Lomé relationship
with ACP states. Central to this discussion was the
nature of future trade relationships. As earlier noted,
the EU had to seek a waiver from GATT rules to permit it to offer more favourable market access to some
DCs than to others. This principle came under sustained attack during the 'banana dispute' in the WTO,
and the EU indicated right from the start of the post-
Lomé negotiations that it was not willing to seek
further waivers to defend its trade regime with the
ACP. It therefore sought new WTO-compatible trade
arrangements in the form of reciprocal free trade
arrangements with ACP states.

This shift was implemented in the Cotonou
Agreement. In future, trade relations with ACP countries will be based on reciprocal free trade agreements
which will take the form of Economic Partnership
Agreements (EPAs). EPAs will cover not only trade in
goods and agricultural products but also services, and
will also in addition address tariffs, non-tariff and
technical barriers to trade such as competition policy,
protection of intellectual property rights, sanitary and
phytosanitary measures, standardization and certification, trade and labour standards, trade and environment, food security, public procurement, etc.

The Cotonou Agreement lays out the basic principles and objectives of the new economic and trade
cooperation between the ACP and the EU, but does
not itself encompass a fully-fledged trade regime.
Negotiations started in 2002 and the new agreements
are to be completed by 2008. A further transitional
period for the implementation of the agreements can
run up to twelve years. A waiver was granted to maintain the current ACP–EU trade regime until the end of
2007 at the Fourth WTO Ministerial Conference in
Doha in November 2001.

The other novel aspect of EPAs is that the Commission intends to negotiate them with ACP countries
engaged in a regional integration process, and, in the
absence of exceptional circumstances, not with individual states. EPAs are thus intended to consolidate
regional integration initiatives within the ACP.
Possible regions to establish regional EPAs would be
the Caribbean (based on the existing CARICOM),

southern Africa (based on SADC, although this is complicated because South Africa negotiated its own free
trade agreement with the EU in March 1999), West
Africa (based on ECOWAS) and East and Central
Africa (based on COMESA). The task is complicated
by the overlapping membership and fragmented
nature of African regional groupings (see Chapter 1).

For those countries which do not feel in a position
to negotiate EPAs, alternative possibilities will be considered in 2004 'in order to provide these countries
with a new framework for trade which is equivalent
to their existing situation and in conformity with
WTO rules'. For ACP LDCs, they can benefit from the
almost-free access to the EU market through the
'Everything But Arms' proposal discussed above. For
non-LDC countries, the most likely option is the EU
GSP.

One long-run consequence may be the fragmentation of the ACP which could be divided into a number
of different groups, each with different access conditions to the EU market. These could include the LDCs
availing of EBA conditions, low- and middle-income
countries negotiating EPAs (divided in turn into separate regional groupings) and low- and middle-income
countries which do not want an EPA and which might
be offered GSP status. Whether under this new trade
framework the ACP states will be able to maintain a
unified negotiating framework is an open question.

25.1.5 Relations with the Mediterranean and the Middle East

Formal relations with the countries of the South and
East Mediterranean go back to the Treaty of Rome
which enabled France to keep, through a special protocol, its special relationships with its former colonies,
Morocco and Tunisia (Algeria was still an integral
part of France at the time). The 1973 war between
Israel and its Arab neighbours followed by the oil
embargo led to renewed efforts for improved cooperation. The first common EU policy was the Global
Mediterranean Policy (1973–1992) which involved
all the non-EU Mediterranean countries except Libya
and Albania. Bilateral cooperation agreements were
signed covering not just trade preferences but also aid
through financial protocols. The southern EU enlargement to include Spain, Portugal and Greece in the

mid-1980s reduced the benefits of trade preferences particularly to the Maghreb countries (below) given the similar export patterns of the two groups of countries. The new political climate in the early 1990s following the 1991 Gulf War and the fall of the Berlin Wall led to a renewed Mediterranean Policy (1992–1996). This increased the amount of development aid and extended trade preferences, as well as extending cooperation to issues such as human rights, the environment and the promotion of democracy.

In the mid-1990s, under pressure particularly from Spain, there was an attempt to breathe new life into the Euro–Mediterranean relationship through the *Barcelona Process* or *Euro–Mediterranean Partnership*. This was launched by the Barcelona Declaration issued following a conference of the 15 EU member states and 12 Mediterranean countries in November 1995. The 12 Mediterranean partners are Morocco, Algeria, Tunisia (Maghreb); Egypt, Israel, Jordan, the Palestinian Authority, Lebanon, Syria (Mashrek); Turkey, Cyprus and Malta. Cyprus and Malta were offered EU membership in December 2002, while Libya has observer status at certain meetings.

The main aims of the Barcelona Declaration are:

- Establishment of an area of peace and stability based on fundamental principles including respect for human rights and democracy (political and security partnership).
- Creation of an area of shared prosperity through the progressive establishment of free trade between the EU and its partners and among the partners themselves in order to create a Euro–Mediterranean FTA by 2010, accompanied by EU financial support for structural reform in the partners and to help cope with the social and economic consequences of this reform process (economic and financial partnership).
- Implementation of mutual understanding among peoples and the development of an active civil society (social and cultural partnership).

The FTA is implemented through bilateral Association Agreements between the EU and nine of the Mediterranean countries which replace the earlier cooperation agreements concluded in the 1970s. Association Agreements between the EU and Tunisia, Israel, Morocco and the Palestinian Authority have entered into force. Negotiations with Egypt were concluded in June 1999 and the Agreement signed in June 2001. Negotiations with Algeria were concluded in

December 2001 and those with Lebanon in January 2002. As a result of Turkey's association agreement, a CU with the EU entered into force on 1 January 1996.

As well as bilateral trade liberalization, the Mediterranean partners commit to implement regional free trade among themselves, but only limited progress has been made to date. In May 2001, four members of the Barcelona Process (Morocco, Tunisia, Egypt and Jordan) signed the Agadir Declaration under which they are aiming at establishing a FTA among themselves. Turkey must accede to all the EU's preferential agreements under its CU agreement with the EU.

The substance of each bilateral agreement follows broadly similar lines. For industrial products, the EU undertakes to remove immediately any remaining duties on imports from the partner country while the partner country agrees to phase out its duties, with different periods established for different goods, but with the objective of eliminating all duties on imports from EU countries within twelve years. For agricultural and fishery products, full liberalization is prevented by the EU CAP. Instead, the agreements provide for reduced duties on limited volumes of agricultural trade between the two partners. Like the Cotonou Agreement, the Euro-Med agreements go well beyond tariff reductions, and include provisions relating to intellectual property, services, technical rules and standards, public procurement, competition rules, state aids and monopolies. In these areas, the partner countries are expected to approximate their laws to those of the EU in order to facilitate trade.

The EU–Mediterranean Partnership has not yet fulfilled the high hopes held out at the time of the Barcelona Declaration. In the political background is the Arab–Israeli conflict and the Middle East Peace Process. The Madrid Peace Conference and the breakthrough at Oslo were major factors in making the Barcelona Process possible. Conversely, the cessation of the peace process has slowed down progress towards the objectives set out in the Barcelona Declaration.

25.1.6 Relations with Asia and Latin America

The remarkable growth of the East Asian economies in the 1980s and first half of the 1990s was reflected in a significant expansion of trade and investment flows between the EU and developing Asia. The EU–ASEAN

Cooperation Agreement signed in 1980 was the cornerstone of EU Asia policy for many years. ASEAN was never intended to develop into a PTA, but emphasized instead economic and development cooperation (see Chapter 1 on this and membership). It was not until 1994 that the Commission produced its first overall Asia Strategy paper (CEC, 1994c) which was subsequently updated in 2001 (CEU, 2001b). In 1996, at the initiative of Singapore's Prime Minister, a series of Asia–Europe Meetings was introduced which now provide the framework for political dialogue. The Asian partners include seven of the ten ASEAN countries, China, India, Japan and (soon) South Korea.

As was the case for Asia, EU Latin American policy was almost non-existent in the early years of the Union. The EU's attention was focused on Africa and no member state had a particular interest in Latin America. In the early 1970s, political contacts were maintained through meetings with the Group of Latin American ambassadors in Brussels and in 1971 Latin American countries became beneficiaries of the EU's GSP. Relations remained limited in the 1980s, partly because of the debt crisis which meant that European investors lost interest in the region, and partly because of differences on the Falkland War between the UK and Argentina, which led to the suspension of the Brussels dialogue.

Since the mid-1980s, however, cooperation has been intensifying. The EU membership of Spain and Portugal in 1986 with their traditional links with Latin and Central America provided the impetus for this. At the same time, however, Latin American countries were throwing off the old import-substitution model of economic development and beginning to open up their markets under the influence of the Washington consensus. The EU share of Latin American imports had been falling, which provided another reason for forging closer links. Formal institutional ties have been established since 1990 with the Rio Group, which now comprises all of Latin America as well as representatives from the Caribbean. Ministerial meetings have been held annually between the EU and the Rio Group since 1987. Political dialogue with the Central American countries began just a little earlier in 1984 with the San José Dialogue. Political relations with Mercosur (see Chapter 1) were institutionalized by a cooperation agreement in 1995 while political dialogue with the Andean Pact countries was institutionalized in the Rome Declaration in 1996. The first summit between EU, Latin American and Caribbean Heads of State was held in 1999 in Rio de Janeiro, followed by a second summit in Madrid in 2002, to develop a strategic partnership between the two regions. Conflict resolution, democratization and human rights, social progress and the reduction of inequality and the environment are among the themes emphasized in these dialogues.

Political dialogue with ALA countries has been accompanied by attempts to forge closer trade relations and by increasing flows of EU development assistance. Trade relations have been based on the GSP since 1971. During the 1970s, the Commission promoted trade agreements with a number of ALA countries but their substantive significance was small. They generally confirmed MFN reciprocal recognition while sometimes granting quotas under more favourable access terms for some ALA exports. As noted above, the Andean Pact and some Central American countries get more favourable GSP preferences in order to help them in the fight against illegal drugs. On the other hand, ALA countries have been the most frequent targets of EU anti-dumping actions (see Chapter 24), for instance in the textiles and clothing sector for which GSP preferences are already very restricted and where quantitative restrictions on imports apply.

The 1990s saw the initiation of a new phase in trade relations with Latin America with the initiation of discussions on association agreements with Mexico (which entered into force in 2000) and Chile (concluded in 2002). Discussion with Mercosur is continuing with a commitment to start the final phase of the negotiations in the second half of 2003. Negotiations on political and cooperation agreements are planned with Central America and the Andean Community to create the conditions for future arrangements similar to those with Mexico, Chile and Mercosur. No free trade agreements with Asian countries have been mooted as yet although a framework agreement exists to tackle non-tariff barriers to trade.

25.1.7 Evaluation of EU trade policy towards developing countries

The major thrust of EU trade policy towards developing countries is a move away from the autonomous preference-based and regionally discriminatory trade arrangements of the past to a more horizontal but differentiated policy emphasizing reciprocal free trade arrangements with low- and middle-income DCs and the duty- and quota-free access now offered to all LDCs under the EBA scheme. This shift has been driven partly by a realization that it would become increasingly difficult to gain WTO waivers for regionally discriminatory non-reciprocal preferential trade arrangements in the future, and partly by dissatisfaction on the part of the EU with the outcome of the previous non-reciprocal preferences. Also, the reduction in EU tariff barriers in successive rounds of trade liberalization has steadily reduced the advantages of preferential treatment. The EU argues that free trade agreements will have positive outcomes for the partner countries, through encouraging a more efficient allocation of resources and greater competition, and by creating a more attractive location for FDI. However, some potential drawbacks should be noted.

For the ACP and Mediterranean partners, entering into a free trade agreement is an asymmetric liberalization process. For manufacturing products, these countries already enjoyed duty-free access to the EU market (though in the case of the Mediterranean countries ceilings operated in the case of sensitive products such as textiles and clothing) so the main impact is the unilateral removal of trade barriers on EU exports entering partner country markets. While consumers and producers who will now have the possibility of importing cheaper intermediate products will benefit, many firms, particular small and medium-sized enterprises, may be forced to close with a consequent rise in unemployment. Also, the continued barriers to agricultural trade in the agreements, which is the sector where many of the partner countries have their comparative advantage, makes adaptation to the

required structural changes more difficult. Some fear that a consequence of this asymmetric liberalization may be trade diversion in favour of EU exports, that is, the substitution of EU imports for cheaper products currently being supplied by third countries. This would add to the economic costs of these agreements for EU partners (for estimates of the impact on the Euro–Mediterranean partners, see the studies cited in McQueen, 2002).

Proponents of these agreements therefore emphasize the likelihood of dynamic gains, particularly that the contractual nature of these agreements will lower uncertainty by locking in trade liberalization policies in the partner countries, thus helping to attract greater FDI flows. Also potentially important are the provisions to tackle non-tariff trade barriers (NTBs) thus lowering the transactions cost of trade and reducing the impact of regulatory trade barriers. Hoekman and Konan (1999) cite the case of Egypt where the trade diversion cost of an agreement limited to conventional trade barriers would generate a welfare loss of 0.14% of GDP, but could generate significant positive welfare gains of up to 5.6% of GDP if extended to tackle NTBs which they assume would occur on an MFN basis. If liberalization were extended to services trade on an MFN basis, then these authors conclude the welfare gains could even rise to 13% of GDP but this is at best a long-run objective in the Mediterranean trade agreements. For the ACP countries, a further issue which needs to be addressed is the reduction in tariff revenues as duties on EU imports are eliminated. This could curtail government spending at the same time as support for industrial restructuring and to cushion the costs of transitional unemployment is required unless other means to broaden the tax base are found.

25.2 Development cooperation

This section examines the EU's development cooperation programme referring to the provision of development aid. *Official development aid* (ODA) is defined by the OECD Development Assistance Committee (DAC) as grants or loans to DCs provided by the official sector on concessional financial terms with the promotion of economic development and welfare as the main objective. In 2000, EU ODA stood at US$4.91 billion, making the EU the third single biggest donor after the US and Japan. Net

disbursements by EU member states in 2000 were US$15.31 billion, nearly half of the total DAC volume. In addition to ODA, the EU also provides what is known as *official aid*. These are flows on aid-like terms but to countries which are not considered as DCs on the OECD list. These countries include the more advanced Central and Eastern European countries as well as Belarus, Russia and Ukraine among the New Independent States of the former Soviet Union. Such flows amounted to US$2.81 billion in

2000 compared to US$4.91 billion for ODA (OECD, 2002a).

EU development assistance policy evolved in a haphazard fashion without clear objectives or justification for many years. Its modest start was when 18 African countries, mainly ex-colonies of France and Belgium, were associated with the EU under the Yaoundé Convention (1965). UK accession to the EU raised the question of the treatment of its ex-colonies in Africa, the Caribbean and the Pacific. This led to the Lomé Convention in 1975 which over the next quarter-century determined the use of the European Development Fund (EDF) for both groups of countries. In the following year, aid resources were made available to other DCs for the first time, and in 1977 cooperation agreements were signed with neighbouring countries in the southern Mediterranean. Bilateral arrangements were subsequently made with countries in Asia and Latin America, and in the 1990s countries in Eastern Europe and central Asia gained their own regional programmes. The historical legacy of this evolution was a diffuse array of policies, budgets, administrative procedures and aid instruments. This section describes the EU ODA programme and some of the recent changes in its management, designed to make it a more efficient and effective instrument in contributing to the sustainable economic and social development of DCs.

25.2.1 EU development cooperation principles

As noted, before the Treaty of Maastricht in 1992, EU development cooperation policies had evolved piecemeal and in a fragmented fashion. The main innovation of this Treaty was to establish policy objectives for EU development cooperation and to set out how it should relate to the policies of member states. The policy objectives are stated in Article 177:

> Community policy in the sphere of development co-operation, which shall be complementary to the policies pursued by the Member States, shall foster:
> - the sustainable economic and social development of the developing countries, and more particularly the most disadvantaged among them,
> - the smooth and gradual integration of the developing countries into the world economy,

> - the campaign against poverty in the developing countries.

The Article further states that Community policy in this area shall contribute 'to the general objective of developing and consolidating democracy and the rule of law, and to that of respecting human rights and fundamental freedoms.' The emphasis on the complementary nature of Community policy implies that development aid is an area where the EU operates in parallel with the member states (in contrast to trade policy which is broadly the prerogative of the Union level alone, see Chapters 2, 3 and 24).

Article 178 establishes the important principle of policy coherence, in that it requires that 'the Community shall take account of the objectives referred to in Article 177 in the policies that it implements which are likely to affect developing countries'. Article 179 sets out that decision making should be based on qualified majority voting using the co-decision procedure (see Chapter 3). However, decisions on the EDF, an extra-budgetary arrangement designed to provide financial support to the ACP countries, are explicitly excluded from this provision and continue to be taken on the basis of unanimity.

The relationship between the EU aid programme and those of the member states is addressed in Article 180 which states:

> The Community and the Member States shall co-ordinate their policies on development co-operation and shall consult each other on their aid programmes, including in international organisations and during international conferences. They may undertake joint action. Member States shall contribute if necessary to the implementation of Community aid programmes.

The significance of this Article is that it gives the EU the legal responsibility to coordinate its own development cooperation policy and those of the member states. As noted by the OECD, this makes the EU 'a unique donor in that it plays a dual role in development, as a bilateral donor providing direct support to countries, and as a coordinating framework for EU Member States' (OECD, 2002a, p. 21).

In summary, these provisions in the Maastricht Treaty define three principles on which development cooperation policy should be based:

- *complementarity* between the development policies of the member states and the Commission;

- *coordination* between member states and the Commission in the operation of these policies;
- *coherence* of all Union policies so that they take development objectives into account.

A fourth principle was added by the Amsterdam Treaty in 1997:

- *consistency* of all external actions of the Union in the context of all external relations, including security, economic and development policies.

While the strategic focus on poverty reduction as the main development policy objective in the Treaty was welcome, this needed to be refined and made more specific for operational purposes. The diversity of the different programmes and projects supported by the EU threatened to overwhelm the institutional capacity of the Commission, both in Brussels and in the field, to manage these programmes. A more selective prioritization of what the EU should try to do was clearly desirable. These priorities were set out in the Statement on the European Community's Development Policy in November 2000 (CEU, 2000j) in the context of the Millennium Development Goals agreed by 189 countries at the UN Millennium Summit in September 2000.

In this Statement, the EU identified six priority areas for action (see box). The selection of these areas was based on where the EU could demonstrate value added and comparative advantage as compared to other donors. These are macroeconomic policies and the promotion of equitable access to social services; food security and sustainable rural development; transport; trade and development; regional integration and cooperation; and institutional capacity-building particularly for good governance and the rule of law. In addition, four cross-cutting issues were identified, namely, human rights, gender equality, protection of the environment and conflict prevention. Humanitarian assistance is an additional activity but is not a priority area for long-term development assistance (OECD, 2002a).

25.2.2 Aid volumes and trends

The EU's aid programme has continued to grow over an extended period during which many other aid donors' programmes, including those of member states, have declined. Over the past decade, net ODA disbursements by the Union grew at an average rate of 5.3% in real terms. The Union's aid programme has two distinct sources of funding: monies budgeted from the EU's own resources and contributions by member states to the EDF. Figure 25.1 shows that the growth has been largely in the budgetary contribution particularly since 1991, with EDF disbursements remaining largely static and even dipping in the mid-1990s.

A consequence of the growth in EU ODA at a time when member states' ODA has been falling is that a larger proportion of member states' ODA is now being channelled through the EU. In 1997, this figure averaged 17%, being as high as 50% for Italy but only around 5%–10% for those countries, such as Denmark, the Netherlands and Sweden, which exceed the UN target contribution of 0.7% of GNP. The Commission encouraged member states to increase their ODA contributions at the European Council meeting in Barcelona in March 2002. The combined EU members had a weighted average ratio of ODA to Gross National Income (GNI) in 2002 of 0.32%. The EU Commission target at the Barcelona Council meeting was to raise the average amount of ODA to 0.39% of GNI by 2006. This target was confirmed at the Monterrey Conference on Financing for Development in March 2002.

A feature of the EU development assistance cooperation is the importance of *geographical programmes*. These are: the Pre-Accession programme for East European Countries (PHARE); the technical assistance programme for Eastern Europe and Central Asia (TACIS); community assistance for reconstruction, development and stabilization in the Balkans (CARD); external assistance to Asia and Latin America (ALA); support to the Mediterranean and Middle East countries (MEDA); and the European Development Fund for ACP countries (EDF). Each of these programmes has its own management committee made up of the Commission and member states. There are a number of *thematic programmes* dealing with issues such as food security, poverty diseases, reproductive health, environment, NGOs, etc. Finally, the EU is the largest funding agency for *emergency and distress assistance*, much of which is channelled through ECHO, the EU's Humanitarian Aid Office. The breakdown of expenditure by type of programme and source of funding is shown in Table 25.2. This table includes official aid as well as ODA and highlights the importance of the flow of funds to the candidate

The European Union's development policy

The European Union is a major player in the development sphere. It is the source of approximately half of the public aid effort worldwide and is the main trading partner for many developing countries. This declaration expresses the Council's and the Commission's intent to reaffirm the Community's solidarity with those countries, in the framework of a partnership which respects human rights, democratic principles, the rule of law and the sound management of public affairs, and to begin the process of renewing its development policy based on the search for increased effectiveness in liaison with other international players in the development sphere, and on the involvement of its own citizens.

The principal aim of the Community's development policy is to reduce poverty with a view to its eventual eradication.

Poverty, which includes the concept of vulnerability, results from many factors. The Community is therefore determined to support poverty reduction strategies which integrate these many dimensions and are based on the analysis of constraints and opportunities in individual developing countries. These strategies must contribute to strengthening democracy, to the consolidation of peace and the prevention of conflict, to gradual integration into the world economy, to more awareness of the social and environmental aspects with a view to sustainable development, to equality between men and women and to public and private capacity-building. These aspects must be taken on board by the partner countries and included in dialogue between the State and civil society.

The Community will concentrate on six areas which have been identified on the basis of the added value of Community action and of their contribution to poverty reduction: the link between trade and development; regional integration and cooperation; support for macroeconomic policies and the promotion of equitable access to social services; transport; food security and sustainable rural development; and institutional capacity-building. Attention will consistently be given to human rights, to the environmental dimension, to equality between men and women and to good governance.

The Community's development policy concerns all developing countries. As regards the allocation of resources, the least developed countries and low-income countries will be given priority, in an approach which will take account of their efforts to reduce poverty, their needs, their performance and their capacity to absorb aid. Poverty reduction strategies will also be encouraged in middle-income countries where the proportion of poor people remains high.

The Community and its member states will coordinate their policies and programmes in order to maximize their impact. Better complementarity will be sought both within the Union and with other donors, in particular in the context of country-by-country strategies. To ensure consistency, the objectives of Community development policy will be taken into greater account in the conduct of other common policies.

The Council supports the Commission in its efforts to manage the Community's external aid more effectively. Particular roles are played by the current restructuring of the Commission's departments, by the more important place being afforded to programming, by the orientation of programmes towards results, by the development of an appraisal culture, by beginning the process of deconcentration and decentralization, and by refocusing management committee tasks towards the strategic aspects of cooperation. The simplification of the Financial Regulation and a better allocation of human resources, as requested by the Commission, must be encouraged.

This declaration on the Community's development policy is to be accompanied by a Commission action plan which will define its implementation in practice. This will be subject to constant monitoring, in particular by means of the presentation of an annual report.

Source: 'Summary' in The European Community's Development Policy, Statement by the Council and the Commission, 10 November 2000

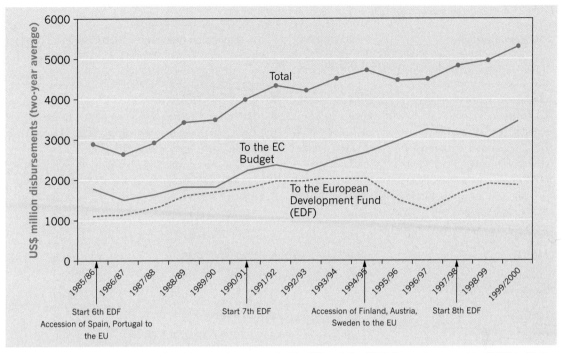

Figure 25.1 Total net ODA from the EU member states to the EC and the EDF (two-year averages (1999 prices – US$m), net disbursements)
Source: OECD (2002b). OECD©, 2002

Table 25.2 Commitments of EU funds for external relations by main instruments in 2000

Instrument	Budget		EDF	Total	%
	External Action Heading 4	**Pre-Accession Heading 7**			
Geographical programmes (ALA, MEDA, CARDS, TACIS, PHARE, ACP)	3 006.43	1 579.71	2 668.46	7 254.60	61.75
Structural adjustment	na	1 058.00	459.50	1 517.50	12.92
Community policies and initiatives	504.93	529.00	na	1 033.93	8.80
Food aid, refugees and emergencies	935.99	na	25.71	961.70	8.19
Unforeseen needs (losses from exports and debt relief)	na	na	455.16	455.16	3.87
Risk capital and interest rate subsidies	na	na	147.09	147.09	1.25
Other cooperation and pre-accession measures	377.72	na	na	377.72	3.22
Totals	4 825.07	3 166.71	3 755.93	11 747.70	100.00

Source: OECD (2002a) based on European Commission, Budget 2001 and EDF. OECD©, 2002

Table 25.3 Net disbursements of ODA to EU regional programmes

Programme/region	Total net ODA		Population (million)	ODA per head (US$)
	(current US$ m)	%		
EDF	1229	26	638	1.93
Africa	1098	24	609	1.80
Caribbean	102	2	23	4.43
Pacific	29	1	7	4.29
ALA	646	14	3606	0.17
Asia	391	8	3131	0.12
Latin America	255	5	474	0.54
South Africa	128	3	42	3.05
MEDA	688	15	225	3.06
CARDS	655	14	24	26.82
TACIS	128	3	79	1.62
PHARE	43	1	2	21.78
Sub-total	3518	75	4616	0.76
Not allocated by region	1145	24	na	na
Total	4662	100		

Source: OECD (2002b). OECD©, 2002

countries in comparison to more traditional recipients of development aid.

The distribution of ODA funds to geographical programmes is shown in Table 25.3 (note that this table does not include OA funds disbursed through PHARE and TACIS). The ACP share of EU ODA, which was nearly three-quarters in 1986/87 and still one-half in 1991/92, has now fallen to just one quarter of the total. The ALA, MEDA and CARDS programmes each have roughly equal shares with about one-quarter of the total not allocated by region.

One consequence of these shifting priorities is that, in relative terms, the emphasis of EU aid on the poorest nations has diminished. In 2000, of the total ODA which could be allocated to individual countries, 26% went to LDCs and 13% to other low-income countries (39% to all low-income countries). This proportion has declined steadily since 1996 when low-income countries received 53% of gross ODA (OECD, 2002a). This shift is due to the change in the geographical priorities for EU aid. Whereas a decade previously all

of the top 20 recipients of EU external assistance were DCs in Africa and Asia, in 1999–2000 the top ten recipients are in Eastern Europe and the Mediterranean (and five of these countries are not considered developing countries in the OECD classification). While this might be seen as *prima facie* evidence of aid diversion, Figure 25.1 suggests that the funds for Eastern Europe were new and additional, and that funding for the traditional beneficiaries has been maintained in absolute if not relative terms.

Nonetheless, the pattern of aid allocation has been criticized as reflecting EU geo-political interests rather poverty orientation. The European Parliament has called for 70% of EU aid to be allocated to low-income countries. The Commission's response is that the poverty focus of its programme cannot be evaluated solely on the categorization of the recipient countries by level of income (OECD, 2002a). There has also been criticism that there is insufficient poverty focus in the EU's sectoral allocations. The sectoral breakdown of 2000 ODA shows that 26% went on social infrastructure and services, 22% on commodity and programme aid, 17% on economic infrastructure and services, 13% on emergency assistance, 9% on productive sectors and the balance on multi-sector programmes, support to NGOs and administration. The European Parliament has been critical of the low proportion spent on social sector spending and has suggested a target of 35%. However, the allocation to social sectors is a poor indicator of poverty focus. This is better measured on a results-oriented basis rather than by targeting input categories. Also, setting pre-determined sectoral targets for EU aid runs counter to one of the other principles of the programme, that of country ownership. Recipients do not necessarily see that the EU has a comparative advantage in support-ing their social sectors, rather than providing trans-port or infrastructural aid.

25.2.3 The Lomé Conventions and the European Development Fund

As noted, the Lomé Convention was once the centre-piece of EU development policy and, despite its dimin-ished status, it is worth considering in some detail for this reason. Its successor, the Cotonou Agreement, has been concluded for 20 years, with Financial Protocols for five-year periods as before. The new agreement is distinguished from the old by its more comprehensive political dimension, its emphasis on the participation of civil society and the private sector, a strengthened focus on poverty reduction, a new framework for trade and economic cooperation, and a reform of financial cooperation.

The aid component of the Convention was traditionally divided into programmable and non-programmable allocations. The *programmable* alloca-tions were designated to individual ACP countries and regions through National and Regional Indicative Programmes. The allocation was made every five years on the basis of a formula reflecting objective criteria based on demographic, geographic and macroeconomic (GNP per capita, external debt, etc.) conditions. Once the initial envelopes were allocated, the Indicative Programmes were drawn up jointly by the recipient government and the Commission to reflect the priority areas for spending.

Non-programmable funds were generally quick-disbursing instruments and prior allocations by

country were not defined. They were granted on a case-by-case basis to whichever countries met the specified conditions. The main non-programmable resources of Lomé were support for structural adjustment, STABEX and SYSMIN, and humanitarian and rehab-ilitation assistance. The latter two were additional to the EU budget lines that existed in parallel for the same purpose.

Aid for structural adjustment took the form of general budgetary support for public expenditure as a whole or for particular sectors in ACP countries. While linked to the structural adjustment efforts of these countries, under Lomé III (1985–1990) there were no specific reform objectives either at a sectoral or macroeconomic level. This changed radically with Lomé IV (1990–1995), under which the EU only pro-vided import support to those countries which had signed up to a structural adjustment programme agreed with the World Bank or the IMF.

STABEX was introduced in Lomé I to compensate ACP countries for the shortfall in export earnings due to fluctuations in the prices or supply of non-mineral commodities, largely agricultural. The idea was to encourage economic development by stabilizing the purchasing power of export earnings. In the earlier Lomé Conventions, a few of the more advanced ACP countries were liable to have to repay these transfers, but subsequently they were all paid in the form of grants. STABEX was joined in Lomé II by SYSMIN, a scheme to help alleviate fluctuations in revenue arising from the production and sale of minerals. Funds could be requested by ACP countries which were dependent on mineral exports for a substantial part of their export earnings, if there were problems in the production of minerals or development projects were threatened by a substantial fall in export earnings. In addition, some Lomé funds are set aside for emergencies and rehabilitation. The level of funding available through each Convention and through the European Investment Bank (EIB) is shown in Table 25.4.

The volume of resources was not increased signifi-cantly under the new Agreement. The new Financial Protocol for the 9th EDF amounts to 15.2 billion euro, compared to 14.625 billion euro for Lomé IV bis (13.5 billion euro for the 9th EDF, plus 1.7 billion euro from the EIB). In addition, the remaining funds from previous EDFs (9.9 billion euro) are to be trans-ferred to EDF 9 and used in accordance with the new conditions. Because funding can only begin after the Agreement is ratified, a process which was expected to

Table 25.4 Evolution of EDF and EIB resources

	1957 Rome Treaty EDF 1	1963 Yaoundé 1 EDF 2	1969 Yaoundé 2 EDF 3	1975–1980 Lomé I EDF 4	1980–1985 Lomé II EDF 5	1985–1990 Lomé III EDF 6	1990–1995 Lomé IV EDF 7	1995–2000 Lomé V EDF 8
EDF Total	581	666	828	3 072	4 724	7 400	10 800	12 967
Grants[a]	581	620	748	2 150	2 999	4 860	7 995	9 592
Special loans	–	–	–	466	525	600	–	–
STABEX	–	–	–	377	634	925	1 500	1 800
SYSMIN	–	–	–	–	282	415	480	575
Risk capital	–	46	80	99	284	660	825	1 000
EIB own resources[b]	–	64	90	390	685	1 100	1 200	1 658
Total EDF plus EIB	581	730	918	3 462	5 409	8 500	12 000	14 625
Per capita EDF								
Current[c]	10.7	9.7	10.5	12/3	13.5	17.9	21.9	23.6
Constant[d]	62.9	50.3	41.2	31.5	22.6	24.2	24.3	23.6

[a] This includes assistance for regional cooperation, interest rate subsidies, structural adjustment assistance in Lomé IV, emergency and refugee assistance (Lomé IV) and other grants.
[b] This is a ceiling set by the board of the EIB which has never been reached.
[c] Total current value of EDF divided by associate countries' population (millions) at the beginning of each convention period.
[d] EDF totals expressed in 1997 terms; current values deflated by the EU GDP deflator index centred in the mid-year of each convention.
Source: Cox and Chapman (2000), p. 56, Table 3.4. Copyright European Communities, 2000

take two years, the Financial Protocol covers the 2000–2007 period. Although an increase in nominal terms, it represents a reduction in real terms and even more pronounced in per caput real terms, particularly if it is spread over 7 years rather than 5.

The Agreement proposes a radical revision of disbursement arrangements arising from a rationalization of the instruments of cooperation and the introduction of a system of rolling programming. In contrast to the previous Conventions, the EDF will no longer be divided into several instruments with rigid allocation systems. All EDF resources will be channelled via two instruments. One instrument will group together all non-reimbursable aid, and the other will provide risk capital and loans with a view to supporting the development of the private sector. Thus STABEX and SYSMIN have disappeared, although a new system is introduced to mitigate the losses caused by shortfalls in export earnings. The main instrument for programming grants is the *country strategy papers*. By the end of 2002 over 110 country and regional strategy papers had been prepared. These papers set out general guidelines for using the aid as well as an indicative operational programme setting out how the money will be spent.

25.2.4 Management of EU development assistance

Despite the growth in the volume of EU ODA, its management and effectiveness was severely criticized in a number of reports at the end of the 1990s. Particular attention was drawn to the following weaknesses:

- the complexity of the development cooperation system, which before the 1999 reform of the Commission under Commission President Prodi, involved five Commissioners and four Directorates General in addition to ECHO;
- the splintered framework of aid management, based around geographical programmes, meant that there was no coherent vision of aid priorities and little consistency in the weights given to the different aid elements in each geographical programme. There was a proliferation of *ad hoc* programmes, each with its own budget line, regulations and procedures which made the overall programme very inflexible;

- too much emphasis was placed on monitoring procedures and inputs and too little was placed on evaluating outputs and results. Projects and programmes rarely had performance indicators and almost no evaluations had been undertaken prior to the 1990s to document what had been achieved;
- the decision-making process was very centralized with little authority delegated to field offices. Approval of policies, regional and country strategies, individual projects and contracting was centralized in Brussels;
- staffing had not kept pace with the growth in disbursements, leading to a great reliance on external consultants for the design and implementation of projects and programmes.

A particular problem was the large and growing problem of disbursing funds which had been committed. While in 1990 outstanding commitments stood at three years annual disbursements for the EU, by 2000 this had grown to four years for EU budget funds and to six years for EDF funds (OECD, 2002a). Court of Auditors reports noted that as much as one-half of the annual budget would be committed in a rushed manner in the last month of the year. There may be good external reasons for the difficulties in drawing down funds, including the low absorption capacity of recipient country administrations, especially in ACP countries, and restrictions arising from the abuse of human rights or the breakdown of the rule of law (see below). However, internal problems, such as inadequate staff numbers to administer the programme and the large number of different budget lines and instruments, create inefficiencies and inflexibilities. Reform of the EU's aid management system was desperately needed.

The reform process was initiated when the new Commission took charge in 1999 with a restructuring of the external relations (RELEX) services. The RELEX family includes the key EU actors in foreign policy and external assistance (DG RELEX, DG DEV, DG ENLARG and DG TRADE, ECHO and now EuropeAid, see below and Appendix 3.2, p. 55, for the new designations of DGs). Under the new responsibilities, DG DEV has oversight responsibilities for the EDF programme (ACP countries) while DG RELEX has implementation responsibilities for the more politically-sensitive MEDA, CARDS and ALA programmes. DG ENLARG retains responsibility for the PHARE and TACIS programmes while ECHO manages humanitarian relief. Macro-financial assistance, including debt relief, remains the responsibility of DG ECFIN. The idea of a single External Relations Council was introduced in 2002, thus abolishing the Development Council. Development NGOS regard this as a retrograde step, fearing that development will become subordinate to foreign policy within the RELEX family.

In January 2001, EuropeAid was created to strengthen the implementation of EU development programmes worldwide and to bring consistency to programme management. EuropeAid's mission is to implement the external aid instruments of the European Commission which are funded by the EU budget and the EDF. It does not deal with pre-accession aid programmes (PHARE, ISPA and SAPARD; see Chapters 22 and 26), humanitarian activities or macro-financial assistance. It has undertaken a series of reforms to improve the efficiency and effectiveness of EU aid, including strengthening the project evaluation process and devolving project and programme management to Commission delegations in the field.

25.2.5 Strategic issues in the EU development cooperation programme

Coordination with bilateral programmes

Coordination in aid policies and programmes between the EU and member states is a legal obligation following the Maastricht Treaty, but is proving harder to achieve in practice. Policy coordination at the most basic level might include the exchange of information between donors on their current and future activities, on their experiences with project management and on their evaluation and monitoring results. At a more intensive level, it could involve agreement on development objectives or on aid strategies for individual country recipients. The EU and member states have attempted to formulate common positions in four priority sectors: food security; health and population; education and training; and poverty alleviation. However, one evaluation found only limited evidence of information exchange, with member states reluctant to share information on their activities with other donors (Cox *et al.*, 1997). It reported that a Commission study into the effect of 50 or 60 Council

resolutions had found that they had very little influence on development policy making in member states. Joint country programming would appear an obvious way for different donors to agree on common strategies, but formal common country programming among EU donors is only beginning. In the absence of significant coordination of policy priorities, coordination in operational in-country programming has also made limited progress, although there was much more information exchange in programming the 9th EDF (Lehtinen, 2003). Cox *et al.* (1997) caution that coordination at country level may often be more efficiently undertaken by multilateral agencies such as the World Bank or UNDP who can also bring non-EU donors into the picture. For example, the EU increasingly aligns its development strategies at field level with the World Bank-inspired Poverty Reduction Strategy Papers for the poorest countries involved in the Highly Indebted Poor Countries (HIPC) initiative.

Complementarity

Complementarity between the EU and member state aid programmes was another principle enunciated in the Maastricht Treaty, but no guidance was provided as to how this might be interpreted. One interpretation is that it should lead to a division of labour between donors, whether on geographical, sectoral, functional or thematic lines (Cox *et al.*, 1997). Specific aid activities would be assigned to individual donors, based on their comparative advantage, proven competence in the area, etc. Possible advantages would be the creation of economies of scale and concentration of expertise in particular agencies, a reduction in unnecessary duplication of programming, and minimizing the administrative burdens on recipient countries of having to deal with multiple donors with different objectives, reporting requirements and administrative procedures even in the same sector. But the difficulties are also obvious. Donors would have to agree on the reallocation of tasks, and Cox *et al.* (1997) argue that there is little evidence on the balance of costs and benefits either for donors or recipients. They see little advantage in trying to achieve country rationalization but recommend that the EU might try to encourage greater sectoral specialization among member state donors at country level. The sectoral priorities set out for EU aid in the 2000 Development Policy Statement can be seen as reflecting the principles of complementarity in action.

Coherence

Policy coherence was the third important principle established in the Maastricht Treaty. Coherence is the need to ensure the objectives and impacts of different EU policies and agreements do not contradict or undermine each other. The OECD (2002a) report on EU aid policy highlighted some areas where the EU faces challenges in this regard. For example, while adopting a less protectionist trade policy will benefit most developing countries, some least developed countries which currently benefit from commodity protocols under the Cotonou Agreement or from the restrictions imposed on other developing countries under the Multi-Fibre Arrangement may find themselves losing out. EU agricultural policy has frequently been attacked for its adverse effects on developing world agriculture. Agriculture is usually the sector where the least liberal concessions are offered by the EU in its free trade agreements. EU subsidized farm exports have undermined local markets to the detriment of local producers in a number of documented instances including beef exports to coastal West Africa in the late 1980s, dairy exports to Tanzania, Brazil and Jamaica and canned fruit and vegetables to South Africa. The purchase by the EU of fishing rights in the coastal waters of ACP countries to support the EU's fishing industry may have a detrimental effect on local artisanal fisheries and accelerate the decline in fish stocks. To address such problems, the EU includes a section on policy coherence in each of its country strategy papers which is intended to get the right 'policy mix' for each country. However, where policy changes are required, these will inevitably meet with resistance from the EU producer interests who benefit from them.

Conditionality

Policy conditionality has been a further contentious issue in EU development cooperation policy, not least in its relations with the ACP states. In the original formulation of the Lomé partnership model, the intention was that ACP governments would identify their own priorities and jointly manage project implementation. With the growing emphasis on structural adjustment lending and policy conditionality by the Bretton Woods institutions and diminishing confidence in governance structures in many ACP states, the EU began to take a more interventionist approach. The dilemma, of course, is that a greater role for the EU in policy formulation may lead to a loss of 'local ownership' and ACP countries accepting unrealistic commitments. Implementation of conditionality has also been a problem where different donors insist on different and possibly even contradictory policy conditions, thus overwhelming the local administration.

Another important change which has increased conditionality has been the growing concern with human rights and good governance, which we have seen was enshrined as an objective of the EU's development policy in the Maastricht Treaty. All EU trade and cooperation agreements now include provisions for political dialogue, with the EU making clear that sanctions will be imposed if human rights are breached or the rule of law overturned (McMahon, 1998). Again, the most contentious debates have taken place with the ACP states. Lomé IV and particularly Lomé IV bis which began in 1996, had already introduced some provisions in this area. In the latter agreement, human rights, democracy and the rule of law were accepted as essential elements of the agreement, a legal concept which allows cooperation to be suspended. In the negotiations on the Cotonou Agreement, the EU pushed strongly for the concept of good governance as a central part of the political dialogue, with a view particularly to targeting corruption in the administration of recipient countries. The ACP states saw this as an intrusion on their national sovereignty and were reluctant to agree to what they saw as an open-ended extension of conditionality. In the end, the final compromise put into the Cotonou Agreement does not consider good governance an essential element in the above sense, but it is designated as a fundamental element which could, in certain circumstances, trigger non-execution of contracted aid flows.

25.3   Conclusions

From an aid relationship with its ex-colonies, the EU has evolved a complex set of relationships with the DCs embracing trade preferences, development assistance and political dialogue. This chapter has summarized the main features of these relationships and how they are changing over time. For reasons of space, not all aspects of these relationships could be covered. The chapter concentrated on trade arrangements and development assistance, and nothing was said, for example, about EU humanitarian aid or food aid. Both trade and development cooperation policy have been areas of dynamic policy development in recent years. Four themes in particular stand out as shaping the EU's relations with developing countries over the next decade.

First, the forging of free trade area agreements with DCs brings the EU into uncharted territory. These agreements not only require reciprocal tariff concessions from the EU's partners, but are also much more comprehensive in their scope than anything the EU has negotiated with its DC partners until now. In some cases, these negotiations have not been easy. In the case of the trade and cooperation agreement with South Africa, for example, the EU took a hard negotiating line and the final agreement has been criticized for being less than generous to South Africa. The key unresolved problem for the EU in such negotiations concerns the status of trade in agricultural products protected by the CAP, which is very often an area where the DC partner has a comparative advantage. An agreement with Mercosur, for example, is hard to envisage unless the EU is more forthcoming on agricultural trade concessions. For the DC partners, offering concessions on services and approximating regulatory provisions with EU laws will be major economic and administrative challenges. Although the potential gains are large, they are also uncertain.

Second, the changing status of the ACP countries in the EU's development policy priorities is clearly evident. The success of this grouping in maintaining a negotiating unity, when it is bound together more by historic links to the EU than by common interests, has been remarkable. But it does look an increasingly fragile unity. The EU insistence on negotiating regional EPAs will fragment ACP countries into regional groupings, leaving EDF funding and political dialogue as the only unique parts of the EU–ACP relationship. Budgetization of the EDF has long been sought by the Commission and the European Parliament, meaning that it would be programmed as part of the EU budget process rather than remain the extra-budgetary instrument it is today. If this were to occur, a further rationale for the special status of the ACP states would be removed. This is not to argue that Africa, in particular, will not remain a central concern for EU development cooperation policy, but this may be justified more by the latter's poverty alleviation mandate than by historical sentiment.

Third, successive enlargements have had a significant influence on the orientation of EU development policy and the next enlargement is not likely to be different. UK entry in 1973 shifted the focus from Africa to Asia, while Spanish and Portuguese membership raised the profile of Latin America. The traditional aid links of the countries of Central and Eastern Europe have little in common with the regional orientation of current EU members, and they are likely to have a greater interest in cooperation with south-eastern Europe, the Caucasus and central Asia. The accession countries currently provide no more than 0.03% of their GDP on development cooperation, only one-tenth the average for OECD members. Even making a proportionate contribution to the EDF, which is financed by contributions from the member states, would imply a substantial rise in their development cooperation spending. Unless there is a prior agreement on burden-sharing, these countries may be reluctant to support further increases in the volume of aid resources.

Fourth, the internal management of EU aid policy will continue to be a matter for debate. Although great strides towards improved coordination have been made, the allocation and effectiveness of EU aid remain controversial issues. The growing emphasis on policy conditionality has introduced a much stronger political element into development policy. Strengthening its poverty focus, in line with the objectives of development policy introduced by the Treaty of Maastricht, will be one of its major tasks in the coming decade.

Enlargement, success and future of the EU

Part Seven of the book is concerned with EU enlargement, success and future, and devotes a chapter to each of the three topics. It is therefore in the nature of an overall evaluation of the success or otherwise of the EU and its future prospects; hence it serves as a conclusion to the book. In case one wonders how enlargement fits into this general picture, one would say that from the EU perspective enlargement is part of its mission and vision and from the applicants point of view it is a reflection of their confidence that the EU is their future. As the EU becomes more mature, involves more member states and encompasses more aspects of public policy, it will face a complex set of decisions about how it should organize itself for the greatest benefit. Economic analysis has a lot to contribute to that set of decisions as the three chapters explore from different directions. In the short run, however, the EU is trying to set out blueprints for the future with the Convention on the Future of Europe. This will report soon after this book goes into print. While it has aspirations to set out the next fifty years for the EU, it seems unlikely that it will be able to come up with a vision with the depth and foresight of the Treaty of Rome for the first five decades. This part thus is more an opening of a debate about the future than a conclusion.

Chapter 26

Enlargement

DAVID MAYES

The enlargement of the EU and its more effective operation as a larger unit are the key issues of the current policy agenda. The EU has agreed to admit 10 new members in 2004 – Cyprus, the Czech Republic, Estonia, Hungary, Latvia, Lithuania, Malta, Poland, Slovakia and Slovenia. Furthermore the process will continue during the present decade. Bulgaria and Romania are set to follow in the not too distant future, when they meet the entry criteria. Negotiations with Turkey are on the agenda for 2004 and Croatia and other parts of the former Yugoslavia may wish to add their names to the list. Even though there may be problems in the ratification process, the change in the nature of the EU will be considerable. It is not so much that this first step will add over 70 million more people to the EU (with over 100 million more to come when the others join) compared to the 380 million existing inhabitants but that the number of member states rises from 15 to 25. The number of faces round the table has the potential to impede the operation of many of the components of the EU if traditional formats are not changed. In the initial stages the economic impact of enlargement in absolute terms is very small – the new members will add only around 5% to EU GDP (if we take the 2001 figures as an indicator). The potential effect is however much greater as the structure of activity could change markedly if the new members converge at all rapidly to the levels prevailing among the existing members.

Enlargement is now almost entirely a matter of looking eastwards.[1] Although the previous round of enlargement ended up with rather less than expected, as only Austria, Finland and Sweden of the EFTA countries joined on 1 January 1995, there are no immediate plans to explore closer relationships with the remainder – Switzerland, Liechtenstein, Norway and Iceland. Of these, only Switzerland is not in the European Economic Area (EEA), which effectively brings them into the 'internal market', with the exception of agriculture and fishing.

Initially it appeared as if the enlargement process might be a little more spread out. The next steps were spelled out in the Amsterdam summit and in *Agenda 2000*, which was published in 1997 by the Commission (CEU, 1997b). In particular the appendices to *Agenda 2000* set out the Commission's opinion on the applications from ten Central and Eastern European countries (CEECs): Bulgaria, the Czech Republic, Estonia, Hungary, Latvia, Lithuania, Poland, Romania, Slovakia and Slovenia. The way forward for negotiation over membership was then opened for the Czech Republic, Estonia, Hungary, Poland and Slovenia – in addition to Cyprus, which was agreed earlier. The others on the list were for later consideration, as indeed was Turkey.

However, the picture changed steadily thereafter. There was considerable outcry from the second group of countries and the Luxembourg Council in 1997 went out of its way to emphasize that all the applicant countries were to be included in the enlargement process from the start, although more active negotiations were to be confined to the first six. However, in 1999, the new Prodi Commission suggested that all the applicants should be considered actively for membership and admitted when 'ready'. This procedure was approved at the Helsinki Council in December and Malta, which had renewed its application after a change in government, was added to the list, making 12 countries that could join to swell the EU to 27 members. A further surprise in 1999 was the ending of the Greek outright opposition to Turkish membership, so that discussions could advance.

When the EFTA countries were being considered for membership, there was no real question as to whether they met the appropriate criteria, with the exception of the issue of political neutrality. The question was merely whether they were willing to accept the conditions of joining, and in the case of Norway and Switzerland the answer was negative. The negotiation process was very one-sided (see Chapter 9 in Mayes (1997b) by Brewin for an exposition). Now, since there have been real concerns over whether the Union could cope with the particular applicants, it has become necessary to spell out the criteria for membership much more explicitly.[2] Thus, it is now possible to explore the full political economy of the process of enlargement much more clearly. Furthermore, as the extent of enlargement has progressed, the EU has reached the point that it has to make changes in its administrative structure and finances if it is not to find the system becoming increasingly unworkable and the cost unacceptable.

Tackling the issue of administrative and political gridlock is being addressed in a number of stages. The 2000 inter-governmental conference (IGC) started the process with extensive changes to the system and coverage of qualified majority voting and the composition of the European Parliament to incorporate all the applicant countries. This was incorporated into the Nice Treaty that came into force in 2003 (see Chapter 2). The Nice Treaty also provided an option for the European Central Bank (ECB) and Commission to make proposals on voting in the Governing Council of the ECB. The ECB opted for a system of rotating votes for groups of national central bank governors that will come into effect when the number of euro area members exceeds fifteen.

The next step is more thorough overhaul of the structure of the whole system following the suggestions of the Convention on the Future of Europe (see Chapters 2, 3 and 28) that has recently concluded. The remit was much wider than simply trying to make sure that the existing system could cope with enlargement and involved the drawing up of a constitutional blueprint on which the longer-term union could be based. These recommendations or something like them could have sweeping implications for the role of the Commission *vis-à-vis* the Council and indeed for the democratic legitimacy of the enterprise (Collignon, 2003). The proposals the Convention have made are controversial. They suggest another step on the path of integration in a detailed treaty rather than an enduring 'constitution'. They are the subject of an inter-governmental conference in 2004 that will draw up the new treaty. Unlike previous discussions, the Convention was a novel attempt to involve a wide range of the interested parties from government and parliaments at all levels and from the social partners. It is not clear what the final outcome will look like as some governments see the proposals as not looking far enough into the future of closer integration while others want to see some powers returned to the national level.

Our aim in this chapter is, however, limited. Chapter 28 deals with the main questions of the future development of the EU. We concern ourselves with four specific issues:

1 How the process of enlargement has developed over the last two decades.
2 How the widening of the EU on the present occasion has been agreed, the criteria used in choosing and their rationale.
3 The problems that the increase in size and dispersion of economic behaviour and institutions will bring – particularly for the budget, labour mobility, running the system and adapting to Economic and Monetary Union (EMU).
4 The problems that delay or exclusion may hold for those countries not in the first group of 10 new members.

These form the next four sections of this chapter. We end on a more speculative note, largely because some of the more major decisions on the future of the EU will be taken while this edition is in the process of publication and shortly thereafter.

26.1 The process of enlargement

Even from its earliest stages the European Community hoped to embrace the whole of 'Europe':

> The high contracting parties, determined to lay the foundations for an ever-closer union among the peoples of Europe, resolved to ensure the economic and social progress of their countries by common action to eliminate the barriers which divide Europe . . . and calling upon the other peoples of Europe who share their ideal to join in their efforts. (Preamble to the Treaty of Rome)

However, it took 16 years from its foundation in 1957 before the Community was first expanded in 1973, with the addition of the United Kingdom, Denmark and the Irish Republic. The delay was not because others did not want to join. The UK applied unsuccessfully in both 1963 and 1967, but it was not until the beginning of the 1970s that a set of terms could be found that was acceptable both to the UK and to all the existing members.

This problem of achieving a balance between what the applicants would like and what the existing members are prepared to concede is inevitable in such circumstances. The expansions to include Greece in 1981 and Portugal and Spain in 1986 were not without their difficulties, but the problems of the applicants were dealt with by having extended periods of transition in sensitive areas and by having explicit arrangements to assist in the structural development of disadvantaged regions, which in the case of Portugal meant the whole country. Even at that stage, it was clear that the process of enlargement presented problems for the Common Agricultural Policy (CAP; see Chapter 20), which was (and still is to a lesser extent) the major area of expenditure in the EU (see Chapter 19). Since the structure of the CAP was aimed largely at Northern European temperate products, it did not offer an easy balance of gain for the applicants and new explicit expenditures were necessary to offset this (through the structural funds).

The fourth enlargement in 1990 offered no such problems as no new treaty was required. When the former DDR joined the Federal Republic of Germany, no constitutional change was required as the eastern *Länder* were viewed as in effect being temporarily under a different administration. The questions to be resolved related to assistance with structural change and the timing of the transition periods for applying Community law. The speed of change during that period meant that there was little time to consider any wider implications. The EC was in the middle of the main phase of implementing the completion of the internal market following the Single European Act of 1986 (SEA) and was considering the steps to be taken towards EMU and forming the EEA.

Until the collapse of the former Soviet Union and the regime changes in central Europe, the remainder of EFTA – following the exit of the UK, Denmark and the Irish Republic – faced various constraints in joining the EC or indeed in developing closer relations with it. Despite negotiating entry along with the UK, Denmark and the Irish Republic, Norway had rejected membership in a referendum, and hence there was difficulty in mobilizing political enthusiasm for membership. Iceland is not only very small in population, even compared with Luxembourg, but also has been relatively slow in participating in European integration and has an economy of a very different character, dominated by fishing. Austria, Finland, Sweden and Switzerland all had concepts of neutrality built into their policy or constitutions. In the last two cases it was largely a matter of independent choice, whereas in the former it was a consequence of the construction of Europe after the Second World War. These states were therefore either unwilling or unable to contemplate membership while the Cold War continued.

Liechtenstein followed a path very similar to that of Switzerland. The changes further east led to a major reappraisal. Finland in particular was very keen to find means of strengthening itself with respect to its eastern neighbour, first because the collapse of trade with the former Soviet Union (FSU) led to a drastic cut in Finnish GDP and second because of the political instability. Finland only gained full independence from Russia in 1917 and had been forced into losing territory at the end of the Second World War.

However, economic motivation was appearing in addition to the political attractions. As it became clear that the completion of the SEA would mean a substantial step towards closer economic integration for the EC, there was an incentive, both for the EC and for EFTA, to try to deepen their relationship. Unless the EFTA countries adopted the conditions of the single market there was a danger that they could gain a substantial cost advantage through their free trade agreements with the EC. Hence the EC had a clear incentive for a closer agreement. By the same token, if the EFTA countries wanted equal access for services, a new agreement was required.[3] This led to the formation of the EEA in parallel with the Treaty on European Union in 1993.

Whereas the free trade agreements between the EFTA countries and the EC had all been bilateral, the EEA agreement was a single document which applied to all of the countries. Or rather, almost all, as Switzerland rejected membership of the EEA in a referendum in December 1992. (Liechstenstein has broken ranks with Switzerland and joined the EEA.)

One might have expected the EEA to be a very good compromise for the EFTA countries as it brought the gains of access to the single market without broaching the sensitive subject of agriculture and without the need to participate in the bureaucratic mechanisms of the EU. The Cohesion Fund which was set up to provide a transfer from the better-off parts of the EEA to the relatively disadvantaged regions was a relatively small price for the EFTA countries to pay. However, two facets of the process encouraged a different view. First, the EU was simultaneously taking another step towards integration with EMU, which might again place the EFTA countries at a disadvantage. Second, the negotiation of the EEA had not been a very happy experience for the EFTA countries (see Brewin, in Mayes, 1997b).[4] The process had been very one-sided, with the EC only being prepared to discuss variations in the timetable for transferring the relevant parts of the *acquis communitaire* into the EFTA countries' domestic law. At the last moment the European Court added to the rather one-sided nature by insisting that jurisdiction over the agreement could not be shared as originally negotiated.

Thus the EFTA countries found themselves having not just to accept most of the EEA terms as a *fait accompli* but having relatively little opportunity to influence the development of future legislation. They thus had many of the responsibilities of the EU members but without the same rights. It was not even a matter of accepting the status quo. The EU was moving on. The Maastricht Treaty made it clear that deepening was to come before further widening of the EU. There would therefore be further steps which could put the EFTA countries at a disadvantage. Furthermore, there was even the danger that some of the central European countries, such as Hungary, Poland and the Czech and Slovak Republics, might overtake them in the process of achieving membership, as the focus of interest, in Germany in particular, had clearly moved towards the east.

From the EU side, membership by the well-off EFTA countries was likely to provide few problems and could result in clear benefits in terms of increased resources to deal with the concerns of structural change. They were likely to be net contributors to the EU budget, not net recipients, and if they were to accept all the existing *acquis communitaire* there was very little downside. The market would be widened and the usual range of efficiency and dynamic gains would be available. There was therefore no need to draw up detailed rules or justifications to determine which countries were to be admitted to membership. At the same time, the CEECs were undergoing such trauma in their transition to market economies that they were clearly not in a position to cope with membership; nor indeed could the EU have coped readily had they joined.

The process of enlargement was therefore divided rapidly into two streams, without outright negotiations for membership being undertaken with the four EFTA applicants, but a range of other agreements for a slower pace of integration being concluded with the CEECs. The Visegrad countries, Hungary, Poland and the Czech and Slovak Republics, were given the fastest initial track, with separate Europe Agreements in 1993–1994, free trade agreements were concluded with the Baltic states of Estonia, Lithuania and Latvia in 1994 and new Partnership and Cooperation Agree-

ments with Russia and Ukraine in the same year. The negotiations were shorter than for any of the previous enlargements, lasting only some 13 months, and Austria, Finland and Sweden joined in January 1995 after the referendum in Norway rejected membership, just 38 000 votes swinging the result. It is interesting to note that public enthusiasm in all of the applicants was not overwhelming, implying that the popular view did not coincide with either the idea of clear economic benefits or that of obvious political imperatives.[5] Perhaps the memory of the less than enthusiastic support for EMU in France, the rejection of the Maastricht Treaty at the first poll in Denmark and the reservations of the United Kingdom helped temper the deliberation.

The negotiations themselves, which followed those on the Maastricht Treaty with a gap of only a few months,[6] were relatively straightforward, with agriculture, fisheries, energy and regional problems being the main stumbling blocks. A five-year phase-in period was agreed for the most difficult parts of the CAP, while a new Objective 6 on low population density regions (see Chapter 22) was included for the structural funds to accommodate the Nordic countries' particular regional problems. Voting within the enlarged Council caused some debate among the existing members and it is interesting to note that the member states only agreed to let the total budget for agriculture expand by 74% of the rise merited by the increase in EU GDP, a prelude for the more difficult negotiations now envisaged.[7]

The negotiations for the current enlargement have been more difficult for two main reasons. The first is the EU concern that the changes they feel necessary are actually being implemented in practice – not just legislated – and that the applicants actually have the administrative capacity to make the changes. Not only have the applicants got to make more sweeping changes even to get to the same starting-point as previous applicants but the *acquis communitaire* itself has grown in size. Conversely, the applicants themselves had worries over adjustment in sensitive areas, such as agriculture, inefficient industries from the previous regime, the social dimension requirements in terms of working conditions, etc. On previous occasions the EU has negotiated quite long transition periods but this time round it has preferred to postpone admission, as with Romania and Bulgaria, rather than have run in periods greater than five to seven years even in the most sensitive area of labour mobility.

Many of the applicants may wish to move rapidly to membership of EMU as well, especially if their currencies could be fragile or if, like Estonia, they have a currency board based on the euro. However, this was not on the table. Joining EMU requires separate consideration by the ECB and the Commission, which prepare convergence reports, and decision by the Council in the light of them. Only Sweden and Greece were considered in the reports for 2000, Greece being admitted as a result. Sweden was considered again in 2002. The new members could only be considered in 2006 after a two-year period conforming to the exchange rate fluctuation requirements of ERM2 (see Chapter 9), with the prospect of membership only as early as 2007.

26.2   Deciding on a wider membership

Deciding upon admitting other applicants on this occasion was a much more difficult task than in the case of the EFTA countries, as in the short run admitting any of them would involve net costs for the existing members. It was therefore necessary to have some criteria which would help to keep the costs and difficulties within manageable bounds. In effect these were that the applicants should be economically and politically ready, in the sense that they could meaningfully adopt the principles of the Treaty on European Union and adapt their economies within a reasonably short timetable to the full rigours of the EU market. The Copenhagen Council in June 1993 adopted three key principles to express this by stating that membership requires that the candidate country:

- has achieved stability of institutions guaranteeing democracy, the rule of law, human rights and respect for and protection of minorities;
- the existence of a functioning market economy as well as the capacity to cope with competitive pressure and market forces within the Union;
- the ability to take on the obligations of membership, including adherence to the aims of political, economic and monetary union.[8]

Agenda 2000 (CEU, 1997b) took a step forward by assessing all the 10 CEECs listed at the beginning of this chapter in a single comparative framework. It was thus possible to see not only the assessment of where the five countries first selected for negotiation lay, but where others would lie in the future. The individual country assessments were each around 120 pages in length. As negotiations have progressed so updates have been published, the most recent at the end of the negotiations in December 2002 after the Copenhagen Council agreed to press ahead with the first ten new members.

The assessments go beyond a simple listing of the measures that have been adopted into a view of how they actually operate in practice. However, they do not represent an attempt to assess the costs and benefits to either the applicants or the existing member states. While this could have been done along the lines of, say, the *European Economy* (1996) evaluation of the internal market, the outcomes would depend upon which and how many of the applicants joined at any one time. Therefore, it was probably wise to neglect the cost–benefit approach and stick to assessment of a group of indicators. One consequence, of course, is that the assessment is relatively imprecise. Jovanovic (2002) discusses what might enter the list but raises the important issue that the balance and timing of the costs of change and the reaping of benefits may be rather different on this occasion from previous enlargements. This arises simply because of the increased size of both the *acquis communitaire* and the economic gap between the starting point for the new members and the level of the existing member states. It is therefore important for both parties to ask the question of whether the development process is better advanced by extensive assistance from the EU or through actual membership. Membership imposes additional costs both literally in terms of having to make budgetary contributions but practically in terms of the extent and pace of adjustment of economic and administrative behaviour and institutions.

All of the countries involved in the accession process, whether or not deemed ready for negotiation for membership were therefore treated together under common budget headings in Part 3 of *Agenda 2000*. Bulgaria, Latvia, Lithuania, Romania and Slovakia, who were initially excluded from the fast track, were promised not just a further report by the end of 1998 but assistance with making the changes.

The criteria beyond simple income per head were taken into account in making the judgments about readiness for membership.[9] Slovakia, which had the third highest GDP per head in 1995 (after Slovenia and the Czech Republic) was not included in the first-round list, primarily because of lack of progress under the first, political, condition. Estonia, on the other hand, which had the second lowest GDP per head, was included because it has made good progress on all three fronts. With a GDP per head around a third of that prevailing in Portugal and Greece and less than a quarter of the EU average, clearly Estonia's adjustment process would be very extensive. One question mark would therefore be over the speed. The process could be long but it could also be dramatic aided in part by its close links with Finland. Estonia was also the smallest applicant at that stage with a population of only 1.5 million.[10] Table 26.1 sets out the information on the general structure of the economies that applied at the time. (This should be contrasted with Table 26.2, which reproduces the equivalent table published by the Commission at the time of the Copenhagen Council's decision to admit the first 10 new members in December 2002.) Immediately noticeable from the table is the contrast between incomes per head at current exchange rates and at purchasing power parity (PPP). This effective under-valuation of the exchange rate is a feature of the adjustment process to which we return later.

Once it is decided that an applicant meets the Copenhagen criteria, the negotiations themselves then become a matter of running through the 31 chapters of the *acquis communitaire* set out in the table in Appendix 26.1 (p. 511). In most cases on the most recent occasion it has not been necessary to agree derogations or transitional arrangements, with the clear exceptions of Environment, Employment and Social Policy, Taxation, Agriculture, and Freedom of Movement of Persons. (There have also been issues in the fields of competition, transport, fishing and energy.)

Not surprisingly, some of the recommendations over the pace of accession were controversial and some of the states relegated to the second round might have been the greatest potential gainers from membership. By 1999 the position had changed somewhat. The lead group was making steady but not necessarily uniform progress towards meeting the conditions for membership, while some of the following group made rapid advances as can be seen from Table 26.2.

The process of enlargement has been able to progress steadily thus far with few awkward discussions over where the word 'European' reaches its technical or, more likely, political limits. The decision that

Turkey counted as a European country had long been made, for instance.[11] However, from an economic point of view there is no particularly good reason why boundaries should be drawn on the basis of centuries-old decisions by geographers as to where the continents should be thought to start and end. The Russian Federation spans the Urals and, although there are various divisions in the Federation, particularly in the south, there are strong economic links across the Urals. The economic resources in Siberia are such that European Russia attaches a very strong importance to the region and drawing that particular division would make little sense to them. The Far Eastern zone is already being drawn into the Asian economy and its development will probably be strongly influenced by the other parts of Asia and the Pacific (Bollard and Mayes, 1991).

Similarly, if we look southwards, in Roman times it made more sense to think of the Mediterranean as a region – a region based on sea rather than landmass. Travel was easier by boat than by land and there was considerable economic interdependence across the region. The same line of argument can be advanced for the Baltic. As we have noted, the links between Finland and Estonia are one of the reasons why Estonia has moved to a position suitable for membership rather more quickly than many other central European countries. Similarly, Swedish banks are playing an important role in the development of the banking system in all of the Baltic States.

Most current definitions of 'Europe' therefore tend to depend on a combination of economic, political, cultural and geographic links and divisions.[12] However, it is only the eastwards definition that appears to have given the EU much of a problem. Even westwards could have included Greenland had its inhabitants decided differently. In any case, non-European parts of France and Spain already form part of the EU. Turkey poses a problem because of its size. It is more than half as large as all the CEECs considered in *Agenda 2000* and similar in size to the last two enlargements taken together. GDP per head is in the same league as that of the members of the CEECs that are not in the first round of new members (see Table 26.2). Furthermore, the very agrarian nature of Turkey, with around a half of the population still working in that sector, could pose major budgetary strains on the EU unless the basis of expenditure were altered. This is a feature also shared by Bulgaria and Romania. Calculations made by the UK Foreign and

Table 26.1 Basic data for applicant CEECs and EU member states, 1998

	Area (1000 km²)	Population (millions)	Population density (inhabitants/ km²)	GDP at current market prices			GDP at purchasing power standard			Agriculture (% of employment)
				(billion ECU)	(ECU per head)	(ECU per head as % of EU average)	(billion ECU at ppp rates)	(ECU per head at ppp rates)	(ECU per head as % of EU average)	
	1	2	3	4	5	6	7	8	9	10
Hungary	93	10.1	109	41.9	4 149	21	98.0	9 703	49	7.9
Poland	313	38.7	124	140.7	3 636	18	281.1	7 264	36	20.7
Romania	238	22.5	95	33.9	1 507	8	123.0	5 467	27	39
Slovakia	49	5.4	110	18.1	3 352	17	49.9	9 241	46	8.6
Latvia	65	2.5	38	5.7	2 280	11	13.5	5 400	27	18.3
Estonia	45	1.5	33	4.6	3 067	15	10.7	7 133	36	9.9
Lithuania	65	3.7	57	9.6	2 595	13	22.9	6 189	31	23.8[a]
Bulgaria	111	8.3	75	11.0	1 325	7	38.2	4 602	23	23.2[b]
Czech Republic	79	10.3	130	50.1	4 864	24	125.2	12 155	61	5.8
Slovenia	20	2	100	17.4	8 700	44	27.2	13 600	68	12.7
CE 10	1 078	105	97	337.0	3 547	18	796.7	7 588	38	
As % of EU 15	33	28	84	5	18		11	38		
Belgium	31	10.2	329	223.7	21 920	110	229.9	22 538	113	2.3
Denmark	43	5.3	123	155.8	28 472	143	123.4	23 277	117	3.7
Germany	357	82.1	230	1 921.8	23 282	117	1 779.4	21 686	109	3.2
Greece	132	10.6	80	108.6	10 233	52	143.0	13 569	68	20.3
Spain	506	39.4	78	520.2	12 899	65	633.3	16 088	81	8.4
France	544	58.8	108	1 297.4	21 661	109	1 214.4	20 640	104	4.5
Ireland	70	3.7	53	75.8	20 479	103	79.4	21 384	107	10.4
Italy	301	57.6	191	1 058.7	17 837	90	1 160.4	19 774	99	6.8
Luxembourg	3	0.4	133	16.4	36 428	183	14.8	34 660	174	2.5
Netherlands	42	15.7	374	349.7	21 448	108	329.8	21 009	106	3.7
Austria	84	8.1	96	188.4	23 493	118	179.6	22 224	112	6.8
Portugal	92	9.9	108	97.6	9 615	48	142.3	14 293	72	13.7
Finland	338	5.2	15	114.8	21 621	109	102.6	19 882	100	7.1
Sweden	450	8.9	20	212	22 884	115	171.3	19 343	97	2.8
United Kingdom	244	59.2	243	1 252.8	20 599	104	1 171.0	19 765	99	1.9
EU 15	3 236	375	116	7 472.6	19 868	100	7 486.8	19 906	100	5

Sources: [a] 1996; [b] 1994; Eurostat

Table 26.2 Main indicators of economic structure in 2001 (as of 3 September 2002)

	Bulgaria	Cyprus	Czech Republic	Estonia	Hungary	Latvia	Lithuania	Malta	Poland	Romania	Slovakia	Slovenia	Turkey
Population (average) (thousand)	7 915	762.3[P]	10 224	1 364	10 190[P]	2 355	3 481	394.5	38 641	22 408	5 380	1 992	68 618
GDP per head[a] PPS	6 500	18 500	13 300	9 800	11 900	7 700	8 700		9 200	5 900	11 100	16 000	5 200
Per cent of EU average	28[P]	80[P]	57[P]	42[P]	51[P]	33[P]	38[P]		40[P]	25[P]	48[P]	69[P]	22[P]
Share of agriculture[b] in: gross value added (%)	13.8[d]	3.9	4.2	5.8		4.7	7.0	2.4	3.4	14.6	4.6	3.1	12.1
employment (%)	26.7[d]	4.9	4.6	7.1	6.1	15.1	16.5	2.2	19.2	44.4	6.3	9.9	35.4
Gross fixed capital formation/GDP (%)	17.8		28.3	26.1	23.4	27.3	19.4	23.2	21.5	19.0	31.9	24.9	17.8
Gross foreign debt of the whole economy/GDP[d] (%)	77.4	74.9	26.5	26.8	44.6	45.7	25.5	179.2	23.3	21.3	33.4	27.0	47.7
Exports of goods and per cent services/GDP	55.7	46.9	71.3	90.6	60.5	44.9	50.4	87.8	29.8	33.5	75.9	60.1	33.2
Stock of foreign direct investment (million euro)	2.151		23.352[d]	2.843[d]		2.284[Pd]	2.508[d]		36.783[Pd]	5.496	2.801	3.041[Pd]	
Euro per head[a]	272		2.284	2.084		970[P]	720		952[P]	245	521	1.527[P]	
Long-term unemployment rate (%) of labour force	12.6	0.9	4.2	5.8	2.6	7.7	9.3	2.8	9.2	3.2	11.3	3.6	1.8

[P] provisional data
[a] Figures have been calculated using the population figures from National Accounts, which may differ from those used in demographic statistics.
[b] Agriculture, hunting, forestry and fishing.
[c] Total population (Maltese and foreigners).
[d] Data refer to 2000.
[e] Data refer to 1999.

Commonwealth Office in 1992 suggested that Turkey would have been a recipient on the then rules of some 12 billion ECU a year, which would have been equivalent to 15% of its GDP and 5% of the total EU budget (House of Lords, 1992). The calculations by the Commission in *Agenda 2000* for all the potential applicants and the likely cost for those which become members is an order of magnitude smaller, reaching only 19 billion ECU per year in 1997 prices by 2006. Turkey is still likely to remain on a slow path to membership even though Greek objections to the principle of Turkish membership have been withdrawn. Questions over adherence to the non-economic Copenhagen criteria remain.

The EU has, however, shown itself willing to tackle some of the hard political questions in enlargement by agreeing to the accession negotiations with Cyprus without the prior requirement of a political solution to Cyprus's continuing divisions. This presents several problems, not least the lack of recognition of a legal authority for the Turkish-speaking north. It was hoped that the accession negotiations would themselves help

to resolve some of the dispute. However, the end of the negotiation process has been reached with the issue still unresolved. Proposals by the UN to end the division are still being hotly debated and are likely to be resolved while this book is in production, with the odds at present being on continuing division. In many respects Turkey controls the decision, as its support is crucial for the north. The issue of Malta becoming a member was removed from the agenda for a while when Malta withdrew its application in early 1997. However, with an income per head similar to Spain and Portugal and 75% of its trade being with the EU it was no surprise that reactivation of the application led to successful negotiations with Malta and its inclusion in the first group new members.[13]

Since the negotiations have succeeded for the first ten new members, the point at which the fiscal and organizational issues highlighted in *Agenda 2000* have to be addressed have been reached. However, difficult questions such as the position of Russia can be put on one side for the time being as Russia advances up the ladder of closer association.[14,15]

26.3 Coping with a larger Union

There are four major economic facets related to enlargement that are worth exploring at this juncture:

1 The budgetary cost particularly related to encouraging structural adjustment and to implementing the CAP.
2 The impact on labour mobility.
3 The manageability of economic institutions.
4 The problem of achieving convergence in the context of EMU.

26.3.1 Budgetary costs

Somewhat surprisingly, *Agenda 2000* suggested that the EU would be able to absorb the budgetary consequences of enlargement reasonably readily and budgets were set out on an annual basis up to 2006 (see Chapter 19). For example, the Commission concluded (*Agenda 2000*, vol. 1, p. 74): 'Maintaining the current agricultural guideline would not pose any difficulty in covering identified agricultural expenditure needs.' Initially, this seems to be at variance with calculations about the impact of full membership by all 10 countries on the EAGGF Guarantee section of 11 billion

ECU per year by 2005 (*Agenda 2000*, vol. 2, p. 42). However, staggering membership and phasing in the introduction of the full CAP and positing structural changes in the applicant countries enables this sum to be massively reduced.

The actual agreement has turned out to be somewhat different from that planned (Table 26.3 shows the budget allocations by country and Table 26.4 the allocations by year) but the principle still applies. The total disbursements come nowhere near challenging the EU budgetary limits. Agricultural costs, including rural development, run at less than half the level of the structural measures.

Even the structural measures are an order of magnitude smaller than can be accommodated without breaking through the current 'own resources' ceiling for EU expenditure of 1.27% of EU GDP (see Chapter 19). According to the Commission's calculations, the maximum, reached in 1999, would be 1.25% with 1.22% projected for 2002–2006. These conclusions were, of course, based on a variety of assumptions and would be violated if, for example, economic growth in the existing EU 15 were slower than the 2.5% a year assumed. It was recognized that the new member

Table 26.3 The financial framework for enlargement agreed at Copenhagen – total commitment appropriations, 2004–2006[1] € millions

	Cyprus	Czech Republic	Estonia	Hungary	Latvia	Lithuania	Malta	Poland	Slovakia	Slovenia	Total
Agriculture											
– Common Agricultural Policy											**4 682**
– Rural development	66	482	134	534	291	434	24	2 543	352	250	**5 110**
Structural actions	101	2 328	618	2 847	1 036	1 366	79	11 369	1 560	405	**21 746**
Internal policies											**4 256**
of which:											
Existing policies											2 642
Institution building											380
Schengen facility	0	0	69	148	71	136	0	280	48	107	858
Nuclear safety	0	0	0	0	0	285	0	0	90	0	375
Administration											**1 673**
Special cash-flow facility	38	358	22	211	26	47	66	1 443	86	101	**2 398**
Temporary budgetary compensation	300	389	0	0	0	0	166	0	0	131	**987**
Total commitments											**40 852**

[1] Where appropriate, allocations by country are shown. For the Schengen facility, nuclear safety, special cash-flow facility and temporary budgetary compensation, these amounts are fixed. For structural actions and rural development, these amounts are indicative. Allocations by country for agricultural market measures, direct payments, existing internal policies, institution building cannot be definitively fixed at this stage.

Table 26.4 Financial package for maximum enlargement-related commitments, 2004–2006, for 10 new member states agreed at Copenhagen (€ millions, 1999 prices)

	2004	2005	2006
Heading 1 Agriculture, of which	**1 897**	**3 747**	**4 147**
a. CAP	*327*	*2 032*	*2 322*
b. Rural development	*1 570*	*1 715*	*1 825*
Heading 2 Structural actions after capping, of which	**6 070**	**6 907**	**8 770**
Structural fund	3 453	4 755	5 948
Cohesion fund	2 617	2 152	2 822
Heading 3 Internal policies and additional transitional expenditure, of which	**1 457**	**1 428**	**1 372**
Existing internal policies	846	881	916
Nuclear safety	125	125	125
Institution building	200	120	60
Schengen facility	286	302	271
Heading 5 Administration	**503**	**558**	**612**
Total (Headings 1, 2, 3 and 5)	**9 927**	**12 640**	**14 901**
	2004	**2005**	**2006**
Special cash flow facility	1 011	744	644
Temporary budgetary compensation	262	429	296
Total	**1 273**	**1 173**	**940**

states would, however, be absorbing around 30% of the structural funds by the end of the period. Reorganization of the funds would be required, with restriction in the current Objective 1 recipients and reduction in the expenditure on other Objectives (see Chapter 22). A review of the eligibility for the cohesion fund is also implied. The Commission even concluded (vol. 1, p. 84) that it would not be appropriate to reappraise the rebates to the UK until after the first further enlargement. One might question the optimistic assertion – 'The next enlargement . . . will inevitably provoke a deterioration in the budgetary positions of all the current member states. This cannot come as a surprise and should not give rise to claims for compensation.'

Practice, however, has diverged a little from the Commission proposals. When it came to deciding upon the budgetary allocations up to 2006 at the Berlin Council in mid-1999, the member states were less prepared to change than the Commission had proposed. The progress in reducing the size of the CAP was slowed and the extent of the change in the structural funds was more limited, even though several of the Objective 1 regions had successfully made the transition towards the average levels of GDP per head and unemployment of the EU as a whole. There will now be a transition period until 2006 for them. The actual budget will also be somewhat further below the permitted maximum. All of this now fits together, partly because the rate of progress of the enlargement process has been a little slower than originally envisaged. One item, which has proved difficult to negotiate, has been the expansion of the cohesion fund for the non-EU members of the EEA.

The budget agreed at the Berlin Council (see Chapter 19) gave annual figures for 2000–2006. These were on two bases – an agreed budget for the current EU 15 and an outline for the enlarged EU 21. The additional expenditure on enlargement adds a little over 15% to the EU 15 budget by 2006 or 0.16% of EU GDP. Expenditure on the EU 15 is the same in 2006 as in 2000, having peaked in 2003. The ceiling on EU spending of 1.13% of EU GDP is maintained at its starting level, which means that the Council could, if it wished, increase the budget by a further 0.14% of GDP without breaching the 1.27% ceiling. Thus it could cope with a virtual doubling of the costs of enlargement within that framework. It is a matter of relative size. Although, as shown in Table 26.4, expected spending on the 10 new members will increase by nearly 20% between 2005 and 2006 alone, this is only 0.026% of the 2000 GDP of the EU of 8.5 trillion euros. In other words it can be accommodated within a budget whose share of GDP remains unchanged at just over 1%.

26.3.2 The movement of labour

It is not at all clear that wider enlargement will not impose more substantial strains than those posed by the enlargements of 1981 and 1986, simply because of the extent of the income differentials. In the first place, it is possible that the nature of the integration will exploit inter-industry rather than intra-industry trade as has been the case until now. There may be a tendency to concentrate more labour-intensive and lower value-added activities in Central and Eastern Europe. In these circumstances, differentials between the various parts of the EU may not converge quite as fast as they otherwise would have done. The impact may be relatively complex if the development involves relocating existing activities from elsewhere in the EU. The existing member states are already experiencing high unemployment and relocation of labour-intensive activities will only serve to exacerbate the employment difficulties of change even if total real incomes rise at the higher rates hoped for in the Lisbon Council's strategy in 2000 (see Chapter 23). Member states such as Ireland that have developed rapidly on the back of relatively mobile foreign direct investment (FDI) may find that this production moves, now that wage levels are no longer low by EU standards and are much higher compared to the levels in the 10 new members.

The example of the difficulties of integrating East Germany is not a good one. For a start it occurred over a decade earlier, before any prior adjustment could take place. Second, it was decided, against the advice of the Bundesbank, to offer a very high rate of exchange for the Ost mark, thereby bringing wage levels much more rapidly into line than productivity would indicate reasonable.

An alternative scenario is that the extent of the differentials results in a degree of labour mobility that has hitherto not been too much of a concern for the EU. Substantial unemployment differentials have persisted in Europe (Mayes *et al.*, 1993, and Chapter 23), not just between member states but also within them. The economic incentives to move are not as effective as they are in the United States, for example, where the population is much more mobile. In part this is a function of history. A large proportion of families in the USA do not have roots in the same location going back more than a short period. In Europe, on the other hand, many families have lived in the same place for centuries and therefore have much stronger ties.

With very large income differentials, the incentive to move, even if only for part of the working life, may be sufficiently strong to overcome the inertia which has prevailed in Western Europe. It is noticeable in Finland, for example, where urbanization has been largely a function of the present century, that many city dwellers still have family homes in the country or have built cottages there so as to be able to return.[16] Mobility from east to west to work may therefore be substantial by comparison with the past.

However, just these same concerns were expressed when Greece, Portugal and Spain were about to join the EC (see Chassard in Mayes *et al.*, 2001). In practice not only was there no substantial inflow from the new members, but also neither was there any obvious worsening of working conditions through some form of social dumping and cut-throat competition leading to a general decline in standards. Nevertheless, the agreement that has been negotiated reflects these concerns. With the exception of Cyprus and Malta (where the income differential and populations are small) there will be a two-year period during which the existing member states can apply safeguards to protect themselves from some of the consequences of rapid migration. (Austria and Germany can apply flanking measures to protect themselves from the impact of cross-border provision of some services.) This transition period should end after five years but can last as long as seven. The new members can reciprocate and apply similar barriers. Indeed Malta has gone further

Table 26.5 Structural indictors in the accession countries, 2001

	Unemployment (%)	Participation (%)	Debt/GDP ratio (%)	Deficit/GDP (%)	Price level (%) of EU	Inflation (%)
Bulgaria	19.7	75.3	66.3	0.4	31	7.4
Cyprus	3.0	66.0	54.6	−3.0	83	2.0
Czech Rep.	8.1	71.7	23.6	−5.0	46	4.7
Estonia	12.6	63.1	4.8	0.2	47	5.8
Hungary	5.7	60.0	53.0	−4.1	46	9.2
Latvia	17.0	72.9	15.9	−1.6	54	2.5
Lithuania	13.2	67.9	23.1	−1.9	48	1.3
Malta	5.1	58.1	65.3	−7.0		2.9
Poland	18.5	76.9	38.7	−3.5	54	5.5
Romania	6.6		23.3	−3.4	39	30.3
Slovakia	19.2	70.6	43.0	−5.4	41	7.1
Slovenia	6.4	68.5	27.5	−2.5	67	8.4
Turkey	8.5	48.7	122.8	−15.1	66	54.4

Source: Based on CEU (2003c)

than this and negotiated an option for a seven-year safeguard.

With this run in period, average income differentials could have closed by more than 10 percentage points by the time the borders are as open as between the existing members states. However, it is not the average that is the appropriate measure, but the extent to which the more disadvantaged can anticipate improving their position by moving. This unfortunately could still be very considerable even in 2011. Unemployment rates in some of the accession countries are high and participation rates low (Table 26.5).

There are two obvious offsetting features to the fear of labour migration. The first is the extent to which capital moves in the opposite direction. As discussed in Chapter 18, FDI movements have up till now been relatively small compared to what one might have expected, especially after allowing for privatization and the acquisition of financial institutions. Again one might look to the example of Ireland where the very rapid take-off took well over a decade of incentives to achieve (see Hodson in Mayes *et al.*, 2001). The second is the development of social and other infrastructure, assisted by the structural and cohesion funds. The inflow will be of the order of 1% of GDP

but as a proportion of spending in the relevant area the contribution could be as much as a third. The effect will be non-trivial over a decade.

26.3.3 The manageability of economic institutions

The Commission has already recognized its own need to restructure as the EU continues with a set of institutions designed for a Community of six. Once the 10 new members join there will be 25 and 27 in 2007 if negotiations with Bulgaria and Romania conform to the expected timetable. Almost all of the new members use at least one language that will be new to the EU. They will want their stake in the running of the Union. Despite suggestions to the contrary, the expansion to 15 member states occurred without major changes except the splitting up of portfolios. The Santer Commission proposed to restructure its own procedures, with decentralization, rationalization and simplicity as the three watchwords. It suggested that it should concentrate on the core functions and hive off the others to executive agencies which can be nearer the customers. It recommended that the number of commissioners be reduced to one per member state and that the Council needs to reconsider its voting rules. However, progress was in practice more limited. The new Prodi Commission that came in during 1999 has already introduced a range of changes, reorganizing the portfolios and the structures of the directorates general. In many respects this is a response to the need to give a new face to the Commission following the forced resignation of the Santer administration, rather than just an attempt to create a body that can cope with enlargement. The intergovernmental conference (IGC; see Chapter 3) and subsequent Nice treaty succeeded in making further changes to the structure of operation of the Commission, Council, Parliament and their interaction (see Chapter 3). Nevertheless, the complexity has still grown and the changes have been more like 'more of the same' than a wholesale reform. The Commission, for example, will change to having one member per country on 1 January 2005 but it is not until the twenty-seventh member joins that they will consider having fewer members and countries and any such change will have to be agreed by unanimity. Qualified majority voting (QMV; see Chapter 3) was extended a little and the formulae changed in favour of the larger countries. It has been suggested that a structure where it is difficult to introduce change might actually be appropriate given that the EU is reaching maturity, but this does not reflect everybody's agenda.

The structure of the ECB sets a precedent whereby it is possible to operate at the highest level without one person drawn from each member state (see Chapters 3 and 9). The executive board has only six members. However, the Governing Council, the primary decision-making body, also has one from each participating country. Thus it already has 18 members, with both the Commission and the Council presidency being able to attend (and speak but not vote). There will always be a reluctance both to give up any existing powers and to give up a seat at the table. Other institutions such as the World Bank and the IMF have had to handle this problem a long time ago to prevent administrative complexities getting out of hand, but experience in such organizations is not a particularly optimistic indicator of the likelihood of a very successful reorganization. The need for rationalization, of course, applies not just to the Commission, but also to all of the institutions. The Governing Council of the ECB has made a first attempt at a solution by proposing that although all members should continue to be present and have the right to speak, only a subset should have the vote at any one time (ECB, 2003). They have proposed that the Executive Board members should have the vote all the time, whereas the National Central Bank Governors should be placed in one of three groups according to a criterion that gives a 5/6 weight to GDP and 1/6 to the balance sheet of monetary institutions. The process will start when the number of member countries exceeds 15, as that was what was thought possible under the Maastricht Treaty. Initially there will be two groups, the first having the five largest members and the second the rest. Once there are 22 member countries the second group will be divided in two with half of the total number of governors being in the second group and the remainder in the third. The three groups will have 4, 8 and 3 voting rights respectively, which the members of each group will exercise in rotation. Thus when there are 27 member states, to take the ECB's own example, the governors in each group will have voting frequencies of 80%, 57% and 38%, respectively.

This arrangement is complex and, while it has been agreed by the Council, there is time for it to be changed before it comes into operation. The net effect is that with the exception of Poland, the new members will all find themselves in the group with the lowest voting frequency and the existing members will not. It will be a very long time before GDP and financial development rises far enough to give the new members rights which bear any relation to the size of their population. The Commission picked up this point in its response to the Council on the proposal, suggesting that an equal balance between GDP and population would reflect precedent elsewhere. It also pointed out that from the point of view of monetary policy decision making, having 21 voting members is rather large (CEU, 2003b). This is already contentious. The Finnish parliament, for example, objected to the ending of the principle of one country one vote for monetary policy. Since monetary policy is aimed at the euro area as a whole and the members are all on the Governing Council in a personal capacity and not as representatives of their respective member states one might have thought that this would be the easiest area to agree a reduction in numbers. Clearly wider agreement over ECOFIN and the other bodies involved in the management of EMU is going to be a hard battle.

The Convention on the Future of Europe (see Chapters 2, 3 and 28), sitting under the Chairmanship of former French President Valery Giscard d'Estaing, has made only limited proposals but the subsequent IGC may make further progress. However, it is likely to be the actual difficulty in managing the system and the various committees that pushes the member states into action.

26.3.4 Convergence to membership of EMU

Several of the new members are almost keener to get into EMU than they are to take on various of the obligations of the *acquis communitaire*, since EMU offers them macroeconomic stabilization that might prove more difficult unaided – particularly if the difficulties of accession have been underestimated. However, early membership will impose a number of constraints, not just because they will no longer be able to use the exchange rate for adjustment and will be more tightly limited by the Stability and Growth Pact (or its successors) but because the process of more rapid real growth may pose inflationary pressures on them. These issues are dealt with in more detail in Chapter 10 but three of them are worth rehearsing here.

First of all those states with currency boards based on the euro, Bulgaria, Estonia and Lithuania, at present would experience little difference in loss of ability to manoeuvre by joining the euro zone and could expect to gain in credibility and a concurrent reduction in real interest rates. They would also get a small say in how the policy should be run.

Second, the process of adjustment is not just a matter of being able to adhere to the nominal convergence criteria for the necessary period, two years in the case of the narrow 2.25% bands of ERM2 (see Chapter 9). This has to be achievable without undue tensions and be clearly sustainable in the eyes of the market. However, as is clear from Table 26.5 most of the accession countries (excluding Turkey) are not starting with serious debt problems. Deficits are rather higher, however, with only Slovenia, Bulgaria and the Baltic States being below the 3% limit. Similarly it is also clear from Table 26.5 that inflation itself is within striking distance of the target in at least five of the

countries. It may thus not be unreasonable to suggest that at least some of the new members can reasonably hope for membership of Stage 3 of EMU, if not in 2007, then not all that long thereafter.

Lastly, it is important to note that the convergence criteria for EMU only concern some nominal magnitudes. They relate neither to GDP per head nor indeed to the price level (Tables 26.2 and 26.5, respectively). In most cases the price level could double before parity with the EU is reached. In general the price level discrepancy is a little smaller than the real GDP/head discrepancy. This suggests that although inflation above the rate in the existing members might be expected over coming years, the pressure on the real exchange rate need not be an impossible burden under euro area membership. In tradeable goods there will tend to be a substantial degree of equalization of prices across borders.

In those industries where technology is reasonably transferable, training straightforward and the capital requirements moderate, we can expect that productivity levels will rise in the new members towards the levels in the existing EU. In non-tradeables, which are principally services, prices will also tend to be equalized but the pressure will come through the labour market. There is a limit to which wages can diverge for sustained periods across the economy. While inflation in tradeables will thus tend to be fairly similar in the new and existing member states alike, inflation in nontradeables will tend to be higher as much of the cost of services is labour. This result, known as the Balassa–Samuelson effect, has been variously estimated to add perhaps around 1% a year to relative inflation rates in the new members even if the rest of the economy is well managed (Chapter 10). While budgetary and labour market problems may prove too difficult, it nevertheless appears at present as if fairly rapid movement to EMU may be possible for the new members. One problem they need to bear in mind however is that the system is deliberately structured so as to make exit difficult. While membership is a disciplining device, current decision makers have to make assumptions about the likely behaviour of their successors.

26.4   Coping without enlargement

One question which is not well addressed in the existing literature is how well the aspiring applicant countries could cope without membership of the

EU. Indeed, there might be benefits from staying out. Assuming the first 10 new members join as expected in 2004, the question applies to any delays that may be encountered by Bulgaria and Romania and to those like the components of the former Yugoslavia, who have yet to apply, Turkey, Russia, Belarus, Ukraine, Moldova and others to whom some sort of European epithet could be applied. The reason that the question is largely ignored is simply that these countries have found it very difficult to attract inward investment, whether from private sources or through governmental or inter-governmental agencies. Such investment usually requires considerable conditionality either explicitly or implicitly. The requirements for loans and project finance at the governmental or related level tend to include elements concerning fiscal and monetary prudence, the creation of market mechanisms, frameworks for property rights, etc. In the case of funds from the EU, the necessary framework is much more explicit and comprehensive. Furthermore, that framework does not usually conflict with that required by other public sector lenders or donors. There is therefore an incentive to adopt the framework irrespective of other considerations because it offers the fastest and most substantial route to achieving satisfactory structural change.

The private sector inflow, on the other hand, has a wide variety of motives (Nam and Reuter, 1992). While these will normally include an adequate infrastructure framework and some certainty about being able to enjoy the return on the investment, the same requirements for market openness may not be present, as the investor may well wish to gain from exploiting a monopoly position. In some respects, a less open and integrated market may appeal to the investor because it offers a greater certainty of maintaining cost advantages and privileged market access.

It might appear a rather short-sighted approach to permit such distortions to emerge, but the starting point is not an open market. The attraction of inward investment can be greater where there is the opportunity to buy existing incumbent firms with monopolies or near monopolies. This has been revealed very clearly in the case of New Zealand (Mayes, 1996), where inward investment over the years 1989–1995 exceeded that of the whole of the Czech Republic, Hungary, Poland and Slovakia combined, despite the fact that their combined population is about twenty times as large. New Zealand sold a large range of public sector enterprises: an airline, a railway, telecoms, steelworks, banks, insurance, a hotel chain, forestry and many more as existing enterprises. Although the New Zealand competitive framework requires that

industries be contestable (Mayes, 1997c), the practice is that the incumbents have a very strong position. Hence there is a good prospect of a strong profit stream. The domestic resources of the host country possess neither the financial capital necessary to make the investments to become internationally competitive nor the access to the necessary technological expertise and market contacts to make such investments successful.

As a result New Zealand has achieved a very rapid turnaround in just a decade, moving more swiftly into recovery than the CEECs, and experiencing a much smaller loss of GDP in the process. Of course, the circumstances are not directly comparable as the extent of distortions and lack of competitiveness were far greater in Europe. Nevertheless, there could be advantages in allowing the transformation of existing enterprises in a process of more measured transition (Mayes, 1997a) as the social costs need to be balanced against the rate of exploitation of the economic gains. Achieving this balance between 'cohesion' and competition has been a key feature governing the use of the structural funds inside the EU. There is a limit to which regional divergences are politically acceptable. Beyond that limit people vote against the process of change even though the longer-run outcome from change is clearly better, because they find the short-run costs too high.

The EU's approach as expounded in *Agenda 2000* seeks to address this point both by assistance to the countries not yet accepted for membership and by the transitional aid for those ready for membership. The irony in this arrangement is, however, that the further advanced in the process of integration a country is, then the greater assistance it receives from the EU. If, however, one were to take a view on the extent of need, then those furthest from being able to cope with membership might be thought to be those with the greatest need for assistance in the process of transformation. In part, this is a question of absorptive capacity (as the economy progresses so it is able to cope with more projects and faster structural change), but it is also a question of incentives. If less conditionality were to be attached to EU help, then the degree of transformation of the recipient economies might be lower.

Altering the process of adjustment to full membership of the EU, particularly by delaying the point at which labour mobility can be freer, may also affect the structure of the applicant economies. As discussed in Baldwin *et al.* (1995), it is not immediately clear which way a less integrated economy might develop. It will be less attractive to investors as a base for production for the whole market if there are barriers to export, but then it will need a wider range of production itself because of the same barriers. As there is a minimum time needed to establish viable firms with a higher value added product, there may be some attraction in a more measured pace of change. However, the history of 'infant industries' and related arguments for slower transition is very mixed, with considerable success stories to point to in Asia and the Pacific region and much more disastrous experiences in much of the rest of the world. It is thus not clear whether there are any clear steps, other than the process of rapid opening towards the EU model, which would diminish the risk of getting locked into a rather unattractive form of inter-industry specialization.

Phinnemore (1999) poses the question of whether the aspiring applicants to the EU might not be better advised to stop one step further back in the process and settle for association agreements as longer-term arrangements. Under such agreements it is possible for the applicants to get a wide range of benefits from trade and investment if they adopt the *acquis communitaire* and yet avoid agreements on politically difficult subjects like fishing and agriculture. The EEA is the principal example. Iceland, Liechtenstein and Norway seem satisfied with the balance. However, in many respects this involves giving up more powers than if they were full members, as they do not have any say in any new EU legislation that falls in the areas covered by their agreements. In the case of the current applicants, they all have rather more to gain from membership than the EEA members, which had no aspirations under the structural funds. They would have been net contributors rather than beneficiaries.

26.5   Concluding remarks

One cannot help but be impressed with the rate of change in the EU over the last fifteen years and with the changes proposed for the coming few years: the enlargement to include Spain and Portugal, the Single European Act, the Maastricht Treaty, the EEA, the agreements and programmes with Central and Eastern Europe, the enlargement to include Austria, Finland and Sweden, completion of Stage 3 of EMU with the founding of the ECB and the issuing of the euro and a further enlargement with 10 new members – quite possibly 12.[18] One might have expected that something or other would have collapsed along the way, particularly given some of the political difficulties with agreeing the Maastricht Treaty.

Furthermore, this major expansion of programmes has been accompanied by a substantial budgetary expansion, but not one on the scale envisaged a decade or so earlier when the MacDougall Report (CEC, 1977), for example, looked at what would be the minimum size for a budget with a more federal feel to it (see Chapter 19). For more than two decades it has been thought that the CAP would have to change markedly, but while it has indeed changed it is still the dominant area of expenditure. It is merely that the structural funds have added a second major category. It appears that the Union will be able to cope financially with the existing ceilings, despite the size of these programmes, through to 2006. The budgetary conclusions from the Berlin Council in 1999 repeat the view that enlargement can be accommodated within the existing ceiling of 1.27% of EU GDP but with somewhat less progress on agriculture and the realignment of the structural funds.

One must ask whether there is a stage at which the process will have to change its character. Taking a purely 'European' definition of the Union, the limits to size are beginning to come within the horizon for thought if not for actual long-term planning. Beyond Stage 3 of EMU the process of closer integration in other areas of economic, political and social affairs appears to be relatively slow (by comparison at least). However, it remains to be seen how much the member states will find that, for example, existing fiscal diversity is sustainable under monetary union. The temptation is always to think that the next stage in enlargement or indeed in 'deepening' the Union will be the one that triggers a more major change in the character of the institutions and the nature of the common policies and expenditures. To some extent such a change is likely within the next five years with the new enlargement, but reluctance to change thus far suggests that the member states may prefer to accept the complexities and consequent inefficiencies for rather longer. Perhaps the outcome of the

Convention on the Future of Europe and the next IGC will produce the result (some are certainly hoping that some form of European government will emerge, Collignon (2003), for example) but the Nice treaty is not a good precedent.

Any conclusion on this subject in this book is likely to be overtaken by events as many of the neces-sary decisions may be taken in the next three or four years, some within months. One might be forgiven for looking at history in a different sense and noting that grand international undertakings have a pen-chant for over-reaching themselves but the experience is not universal and can last for centuries, millennia in Asia.

Appendix 26.1 Guide to the negotiations – chapter by chapter

Chapter	
1	Free Movement of Goods
2	Freedom of Movement for Persons
3	Freedom to Provide Services
4	Free Movement of Capital
5	Company Law
6	Competition Policy
7	Agriculture
8	Fisheries
9	Transport Policy
10	Taxation
11	Economic and Monetary Union
12	Statistics
13	Employment and social policy
14	Energy
15	Industrial Policy
16	Small and Medium-sized Enterprises

Chapter	
17	Science and Research
18	Education and Training
19	Telecom and IT
20	Culture and Audiovisual Policy
21	Regional Policy and Co-ordination of Structural Instruments
22	Environment
23	Consumer Protection
24	Justice and Home Affairs
25	Customs Union
26	External Relations
27	Common Foreign and Security Policy
28	Financial Control
29	Finance and Budgetary Provisions
30	Institutions
31	Other

NOTES

1. This is not literally true in the sense of moving the eastern-most point in the European Union. Currently that is in Finland (as is the northern-most point). Of those countries under current consideration for membership, it is only Cyprus which is further east. Otherwise the Union would have to include Belarus, Russia, Turkey or Ukraine for it to stretch further eastwards. With the accession of Malta the EU will extend further southwards, although Spanish and French islands might make the claim for the boundary to be further south already.

2. The application from Turkey was not a real test either, as Turkey is so large and at such a low relat-ive income level that there was never any doubt that the Union would be unwilling to bear the cost. Similarly, Cyprus and Malta are sufficiently small that they would not pose a difficulty for the EU resources. Any grounds for decision would be largely political rather than economic.

3. Baldwin et al. (1997) show that under imperfect competition the incentive to join a grouping of similar structured economies increases as the size of the grouping increases.

4. The Austrian application for membership was made in July 1989, antedating the EEA negotia-tions, while the Swedish application was made in June 1991 before the negotiations were complete. The Finnish, Swiss and Norwegian applications were made in March, May and November of 1992, respectively.

5. The Austrian result in June was clear, with 66.4% voting in favour, and support in Finland in

October was 57%. However, the Swedish voted only 52.2% for and 46.9% against on 13 November and the outcome was in doubt right up to the end. The Norwegian vote came only a fortnight later but this time the 52.2% were against.

6. The Commission produced its favourable 'Opinions' on each of the applicants rapidly. (Norway's entry to the negotiations was officially delayed until April 1993 to allow the Opinion to be completed, although it had been involved in aspects of the negotiations earlier.)

7. Further negotiations over the CAP in June 2003 still only made limited progress, not reducing the overall level of expenditure and only partly decoupling payments from production. The subject is by no means ended and will be heavily debated by the new members.

8. The 'EFTA' group negotiations were already in progress at the time.

9. The accuracy of these GDP per head comparisons is, of course, limited but they are not so wrong as to invalidate the qualitative argument.

10. But with a land area bigger than Belgium, the Netherlands or Denmark. Malta and Cyprus are considerably smaller in size but with a relatively high income per head and hence likely to have more limited problems of adjustment. As a result, they were also part of the first group of countries to be admitted.

11. The 1964 Ankara Association Agreement with Turkey made clear that it was in principle eligible for membership. The question was merely when it would be ready. *Agenda 2000* makes it clear that Turkey will be judged on the same criteria as any other applicant. Turkey is receiving assistance from the EU to help it with the transition.

12. Sometimes the arguments over the appropriate boundary have been put in terms of the limits of the former Austro-Hungarian empire, sometimes the extent of Christianity and sometimes the limits of Catholicism (Crouch and Marquand, 1992).

13. The referendum on membership was a close call. Public and political opinions in Malta are still divided over the issue, as the history of making and withdrawing the application indicates.

14. In Mayes (1993), I described the EU as having almost a series of concentric circles of closer affiliation for countries depending upon their geographic nearness. Since 1995 the EU has had a common border with Russia. If the negotiations with all those in the next group of applicants succeed, that boundary will be increased and both Belarus and the Ukraine will then have common borders with the EU. The 'nearness' will thus continue to increase in geographic terms.

15. Interestingly enough the Italian Presidency of the Council for the second half of 2003 has suggested reopening the issue of the inclusion of Russia.

16. In part, this may be a special feature of the slow development of forests, where important proportions of rural family wealth can lie. It may take three generations to be able to reap the benefit from planting.

17. Or more if countries like Croatia with a relatively high level of income per head and market structure can satisfy the non-economic criteria for membership.

Chapter 27 Has the EU been successful?

ALI EL-AGRAA

Has the EU been successful is a question that is often being, and sometimes has to be, asked. But the question as it stands is somewhat meaningless. As we have seen, the ultimate objective of those who founded the EU was to bring about the political unity of Europe. If the question is meant to solicit an answer to this ideal, then even when all the member nations have adopted the euro, the EU would still not have arrived, so in this sense it has not been successful.

However, the EU neither started with the whole of Europe nor does it presently comprise it, although when the new enlargement following the Nice Treaty fully materializes, the EU would have largely arrived in this respect. Also, the EU has reached its present total membership of 15 in stages, through three enlargements and an accession, each one bringing with it new problems which slowed down if not frustrated the progress that had been achieved before it and complicated future development. This was compounded to by the tumultuous changes in the world economy over which the EU could not be held responsible (see below). Thus, the very fact that the EU is still here and has been able to introduce all the developments that

have been discussed in this book, are clear signs that it has been very successful indeed, i.e. survival against all odds is a true accomplishment.

It would therefore be more sensible to narrow down the question by asking whether the EU has been able to achieve the goals it set out for itself in every major treaty and in specific policy areas. With regard to the latter, an adequate answer would require a complete and exhaustive enumeration of all the conclusions reached in almost all the chapters in this book, but that would be unnecessary, due to duplication, and unwarranted, given space limitations. As to the former, one can provide general answers by looking at the aims set for the 1958–1969 transition period in the 1957 EEC Treaty of Rome, those concerning the first enlargement and EMU adopted in the Hague summit of 1969, that of the introduction of the euro in the Maastricht/Amsterdam treaties and the latest enlargement. The chapter deals with precisely these, but instead of simply enumerating aims and setting them against achievement or otherwise, they are presented in terms of the general context of the development of the EU.

27.1 The aims set for 1969

Between 1958 and 1969, the EEC transition, the original six member nations were preoccupied with the construction of the 'community' envisaged in the 1957 Treaty of Rome for the EEC. Therefore, if the question were about the EEC success at the end of 1969, then it would be about whether the EEC was able to meet the targets it set itself in the treaty.

As mentioned in Chapters 1 and 2, two of the major aims were the creation of the customs union and common market and on these, the answer is straightforward. The basic elements of the customs union (i.e. the removal of the internal tariffs, the elimination of

import quota restrictions and the creation of the common external tariffs (CETs) were established a year and a half ahead of schedule – see Tables 27.1 and 27.2. As to the common market elements, initial steps were undertaken and measures proposed to tackle the many non-tariff barriers to the free movement of goods, services and factors of production. However, laying down the rules for mobility was no guarantee of its taking place, especially in the case of labour since Europeans have a strong tendency to stay close to their birthplace. Given this proviso, one can say that by 1969 a recognizably common market existed.

Table 27.1 EC intra-area tariff reductions (%)

Acceleration of reduction	Individual reductions made on the 1 January 1957 level	Cumulative reduction
1 January 1959	10	10
1 July 1960	10	20
1 January 1961	10	30
1 January 1962	10	40
1 July 1962	10	50
1 July 1963	10	60
1 January 1965	10	70
1 January 1966	10	80
1 July 1967	5	85
1 July 1968	15	100

Source: Based on CEC (1957, p. 34)

Recall that the aims also included the creation of common policies. Because of French demands, sometimes bordering on threats, the CAP was almost fully operational by 1969. However, as Button clearly shows in Chapter 15, the common transport policy was slow to evolve. Moreover, as demonstrated in Chapters 2 and 23 the European Social Fund (ESF) and the European Investment Bank (EIB) were duly established and were fully operational at an early stage. Furthermore, as Brülhart and Matthews argue in Chapter 24, steps were taken to create a Common Commercial Policy (CCP), and, as Matthews clearly shows in Chapter 25, the original six undertook appropriate trade and aid arrangements in respect of their colonial and increasingly ex-colonial dependencies. Also, a rudimentary system of macroeconomic policy coordination was also devised (see Chapter 9). Thus, there was complete success in the case of the customs union, and variable success with regard to the common market, but given the nature of some policies, that was hardly surprising.

Table 27.2 The establishment of the CET (%)

Acceleration of adjustment	Industrial products adjustment	Cumulative adjustment	Agricultural products adjustment	Cumulative adjustment
1 January 1961	30	30		
1 January 1962			30	30
1 July 1963	30	60		
1 January 1966			30	60
1 July 1968	40	100	40	100

Source: Based on CEC (1957, p. 34)

27.2   The aims set for the period from 1969 to the early 1980s

When the transition period came to an end in 1969, it would have been possible for the original six to state that their mission had been accomplished, given that their remit was for only economic unity. However, there were several reasons why it was neither possible nor appropriate for the EU to stop there, which relate to the variable success just mentioned and to practical considerations. First, the creation of common policies in such fields as agriculture and competition required an administration to operate them. This is because

decisions regarding agricultural prices had to be taken on a seasonal or annual basis and markets had to be continuously manipulated in order that those prices should be received by farmers. And the activities of businessmen and governments had to be continuously monitored in order that factors which would otherwise prevent, restrict or distort competitive trade should be eliminated. Second, as we have just seen, although substantial progress had been made in achieving the aims covered in the previous section, when the transition period was approaching its end it had to be admitted that substantial policy gaps still remained to be filled before it could be claimed that a truly common market existed.

Be that as it may, with memories of the Second World War still fresh in people's minds and disposing of any political unity ambitions, it would have been possible for the member nations to state that, subject to the need to operate existing policies and to fill obvious policy gaps, no further economic integration or institutional development should be attempted. In fact the EU decided quite the contrary: new areas of economic policy were opened up and old ones were substantially changed.

In 1969, during the Hague summit, the original six decided that the EU should progressively transform itself into an EMU. Although important measures were subsequently introduced in order to achieve the EMU, the goal of reaching this aim eventually failed (see Chapter 9). This was due to the global economic difficulties of the early 1970s, the Nixon and Oil shocks, and to the first enlargement of the EU which brought in countries with different economic structure and problems. Nevertheless, the idea did not go away since in the late 1970s a more modest scheme was successfully introduced – the EMS. Moreover, but this overlaps with the next section, in 1989, the member nations endorsed the Delors Report, committing themselves to achieving an EMU in three stages: as we have seen (Chapter 9) the first began on 1 July 1990, the second in 1994 and the third in 1999 for the 11 member nations which passed the strict conditions specified for this purpose and which had no opt-outs, with Greece joining later in 2002. With the demise of the 1970 EMU being mainly due to the two major world shocks, one could be perfectly justified in claiming that the EEC was highly successful in meeting its EMU target.

The EMU proposal was only one of a succession of new policy initiatives during 1969–1972. Indeed, this period can be described as one of great activity. First, in 1970, the original six reached a common position on the development of a Common Fisheries Policy (CFP – see Chapter 21), although total agreement was not to be achieved until 1983. Second, at the Paris summit of 1973, agreement was reached on the development of new policies in relation to both industry and science and research (see Chapter 13). Third, the summit also envisaged a more active role for the EEC in the area of regional policy, and decided that a European Regional Development Fund (ERDF) was to be established to channel EEC resources into the development of the backward regions (see Chapter 22). Fourth, as we saw in Chapter 23, the summit also called for a new initiative in the field of social policy. Fifth, later in the 1970s, the relationship between the EU and its ex-colonial dependencies was significantly reshaped in the form of the 'Lomé Convention' (now renamed the Cotonou Agreement; see Chapters 24 and 25). Finally, there was the series of institutional developments, discussed in Chapters 2 and 3, especially the summit meetings and their formalization into the European Council.

It is obvious from all these developments that the EEC needed financial resources not only to pay for the day-to-day running of the EEC but also to feed the various funds that were established: the ESF, ERDF and, most important of all, the European Agricultural Guidance and Guarantee Fund (EAGGF). As revealed in Chapter 19, in 1970 the EEC took the important step of agreeing to introduce a system that would provide the EEC, and specifically the general budget, with its own resources, thus relieving it of the uncertainty of annual decisions regarding its finances as well as endorsing its political autonomy. Another step of great importance was the decision that the European Parliament should be elected directly by the people, not by the national parliaments. In addition, the EEC decided to grant the European Parliament significant powers over the general budget; as we saw in Chapter 3, this proved to be a very significant development. Finally, but by no means least, was the development of the political cooperation mechanism. It is important not to forget that the dedicated Europeans had always hoped that the habit of cooperation in the economic field would spill over into the political arena, i.e. into foreign policy matters. As we have seen, that has indeed happened: the political cooperation that we see today can be said to date from the Hague summit of 1969 and was formally inaugurated in 1970, and, when the Maastricht and Amsterdam treaties are fully implemented, the EU will come very close to having a common defence policy (the 1997 Amsterdam summit's qualification, stressing NATO, cannot be the permanent reality); thus it will have to have a common foreign policy on defence and security matters, the need for which has been highlighted by the vehement disagreement between the UK and Spain on one side and France and Germany on the other, regarding how to deal with Iraq. All these developments clearly show that the EEC was successful, if not in every respect or completely so.

Although there has been a series of institutional developments, the relationship between the member nations has undergone a significant change. When the member nations signed the Treaty of Rome, they opted for a Council of Ministers which could take decisions on the basis of a supranational majority voting system. However, the insistence of the French led to the 'Luxembourg compromise'. In addition, and especially after 1969, the centre of gravity of decision making within the EEC became the European Council through offering blueprints on which the Commission bases and formulates its proposals for legislation.

The method of operation of the European Council is cast in the traditional intergovernmental mould. As Swann (1988) argues, the development of inter-governmentalism might have been expected to slow down the pace of progress within the EU: the unanimity principle would always force the EU to adopt the lowest common denominator and that might mean little or even no change whatever. However, that was certainly not the case in the early 1970s: as we have seen, a number of new initiatives were launched and in the main those initiatives were designed to further the process of integration. Thus, despite the set back in terms of no progress with democratic decision making, the EEC continued to be successful.

Inter-governmentalism was still strong in the 1980s, but the performance of the inter-governmental EC of the early 1980s was markedly less dynamic than that of the early 1970s. A good deal of activity within the EU then centred around quarrels over matters such as the reform of the CAP and the general budget, especially the United Kingdom's 'unfair' contribution to it. However, settling such vital issues could hardly be deemed as lack of success since the clearing of problems should enable further progress.

To this list of achievements one should add another as well as a negative one. On the negative side is that despite developments in foreign policy cooperation, and even when the Maastricht and Amsterdam treaties are *fully* implemented, the EU would continue to lack two essential attributes of a state. These are responsibility for external affairs and defence. Thus, in spite of the serious discussions being conducted recently on these issues, as is argued in Chapter 2, the EU has a great gap in its competences, but its weight makes it highly significant in world economics and thus in world politics. The positive one is that the significant achievements of the EU during the post-1969 period made it very attractive. This attraction is demonstrated by:

1 Its first round of enlargement to include Denmark, Ireland and the United Kingdom in 1973.
2 The adhesion of Greece in 1981.
3 Its second round of enlargement to include Portugal and Spain in 1986.
4 Its third round of enlargement to include Austria, Finland and Sweden in 1995.
5 The recent acceptance of 10 new members to join in 2004 (Cyprus, the Czech Republic, Estonia, Hungary, Latvia, Lithuania, Malta, Poland, Slovenia, and Slovakia) and another two in 2007 (Bulgaria and Romania) as well as of recognizing Turkey as a candidate, after 36 years of temporizing, and stating that a change in regime will bring Croatia closer to joining.

Returning to the successes, one concrete point concerns whether the countries involved in the various enlargements have been able to negotiate their transition periods successfully or otherwise. Tables 27.3 and 27.4 give the timetable for the adjustments in the CETs and the dismantling of the internal tariffs for the three countries involved in the first enlargement: Denmark, Ireland and the United Kingdom. The tables do not cover all groups of commodities. For example, tariffs on coal imports were abolished from the day of accession, and tariffs on certain groups of commodities given in Annex III of the Treaty of Accession were abolished on 1 January 1974, etc. In the case of the CETs, those tariffs that differed by less than 15% were adjusted on 1 January 1974. Import quota restrictions were also abolished from the date of accession. Measures having equivalent effects to the import quota restrictions were eliminated by the deadline of

Table 27.3 New members' intra-tariff reductions (%)

	Individual reductions made on the 1 January 1972 level	Cumulative reduction
1 April 1973	20	20
1 January 1974	20	40
1 January 1975	20	60
1 January 1976	20	80
1 July 1977	20	100

Source: Based on *Bulletin of the European Communities*, no. 8, 1978

Table 27.4 Approaching the CET (%)[a]

	Individual adjustments made on the 1 January 1972 level	Cumulative adjustment
1 January 1974	40	40
1 January 1975	20	60
1 January 1976	20	80
1 July 1977	20	100

[a] For products which differ by more than 15% from the CET.
Source: Based on *Bulletin of the European Communities*, no. 8, 1978

1 January 1975. All three new member nations had no difficulties in achieving these changes.

In the case of Greece's membership, a five-year period was agreed for the progressive dismantling of residual customs duties on Greek imports of products originating in the EU and for the progressive alignment of Greek tariffs to the CET. Customs duties on Greek imports from the EU were to be reduced in six stages commencing on 1 January 1981, with a reduction of 10 percentage points followed by a further reduction of the same percentage points on 1 January 1982 and four annual reductions of 20 percentage points so that all customs duties on Greek intra-EU trade should have been removed by 1 January 1986. Alignment of the CET was to follow the same timetable.

Quantitative restrictions between Greece and the EU were to be abolished on adhesion, with the exception of 14 products for which Greece was authorized to maintain transitional quotas. These quotas were to be progressively increased during the five-year transitional period and to be completely eliminated by 31 December 1985. As a general rule, the minimum rate of increase for such quotas was 25% at the beginning of each year for quotas expressed in value terms and 20% at the beginning of each year for quotas expressed in volume terms. Measures having equivalent effect to quantitative restrictions were to be eliminated upon

adhesion, except for the Greek system of cash payments and import deposits which were to be phased out over three years (see *Bulletin of the European Communities*, no. 5, 1969, for these and further details).

In the case of Portugal and Spain, a ten-year transitional period was agreed. For Portugal, this is divided into two equal (five-year) stages for the majority of products and a basic seven-year period for other products, although some measures would apply for the full ten years. For Spain, there are some variations, but the essentials are basically the same.

It can be stated that Greece, Portugal and Spain have navigated their transition periods successfully. With regard to the three members joining in 1995, there is practically no transition period since they were members of EFTA, and, as we have seen, EFTA and the EU have had free trade between them in manufactured products for a very long time and now, except for Switzerland, through the arrangement now known as the EEA. Indeed, the only derogation from immediate implementation of all EU legislation is a four-year transitional period during which the new members can maintain their higher than EU health, safety and environmental standards.

So far there has been one withdrawal. The position of Greenland was renegotiated in 1984 but it remains associated under the rules of 'Overseas countries and territories'. A special agreement regulates mutual fishing interests. So this act cannot be recorded a failure, certainly not as an absolute lack of success.

Of course, one should point out that, in contrast to this rosy picture, a number of non-tariff barriers remained. However, as we have seen (Chapters 2 and 11), the aim of the 'internal market' is to abolish these either directly or indirectly via the harmonization of technical specifications which will promote the right environment for getting rid of them. All these non-tariff barriers are fully set out in Chapter 11.

Thus, the totality of all these developments over the period from 1969 to the early 1980s, clearly indicates complete success in some areas, qualified success in others and very little progress when it comes to a common defence policy and a unified foreign policy stance. However, the total picture is one of success.

27.3   The aims set for the period from the mid-1980s to the present

Without a shadow of doubt, the stars in this period must be: the 1987 SEA, which now regulates all the activities of the EU; the Maastricht Treaty, as per the

Amsterdam Treaty of June 1997, when fully implemented, with the euro being adopted by more than the 12 of the present 15 member states; the Nice Treaty when all the 10–15 nations have actually joined. As shown in Chapter 2, the SEA contains policy development which is based upon the intention of having a true single market in place by the end of 1992 with free movement of capital, labour, services and goods rather than the patchy arrangements of the past. The SEA also introduces, or strengthens, other policy fields. These include: responsibility towards the environment; the encouragement of further action to promote health and safety at work; technological R&D; work to strengthen economic and social cohesion so that weaker members may participate fully in the freer market; and cooperation in economic and monetary policy. In addition, the SEA brings foreign policy cooperation into consideration and provides it with a more effective support than it has had hitherto, including its own secretariat to be housed in the Council building in Brussels.

Institutionally, as we have seen, it was agreed that the European Council would take decisions by qualified majority voting in relation to the internal market, research, cohesion and improved working conditions and that, in such cases, the European Parliament should share in decision making. These developments were followed later by agreement regarding the control of expenditure on the CAP (which, as we have seen in Chapters 19 and 20, has been a source of heated argument for a number of years) and, most importantly, a fundamental change in the EU general budget (see Chapter 19).

Before turning to the second star, the Maastricht Treaty, recall that a three-stage timetable for EMU started on 1 July 1990 with the launching of the first phase of intensified economic cooperation during which all the member states were to submit their currencies to the exchange rate mechanism (ERM) of the EMS. The main target of this activity was the United Kingdom whose currency was not subject to the ERM discipline; the United Kingdom joined in 1991 while Margaret Thatcher was still in office, but withdrew in 1992 when the UK could not maintain the ERM parity for the pound. During the second stage, which started in 1994, the EU created the European Monetary Institute (EMI) to prepare the way for the European Central Bank which started operating on 1 January 1997. As we have seen, the Treaty allows Denmark and the United Kingdom to opt out of the final stage when the EU currency rates were to be permanently and irrevocably fixed and a single currency (the euro) floated. They exercised their option and also Sweden did likewise, for different reasons, but will conduct a referendum in September 2003.

Although the stipulated earlier (1997) floating of the single currency had to be waived and only 11 member nations adopted the euro on 1 January 1999, one can hardly be justified in claiming that the EU has not been successful recently. Apart from the achievements just mentioned, Greece adopted the euro in 2002 and the European Central Bank has been successful in its operations. Also, the British Labour government opted for participation in the 'Social Chapter' and decided to run a referendum on euro membership, possibly during 2004 if the UK passed the Chancellor of the Exchequer Gordon Brown's tests (however, on 9 June 2003 Brown declared that the tests had not been passed – see Chapter 9), and Sweden will have a referendum on the euro in September 2003 which proved unsuccessful. Moreover, membership of NATO has been extended to the Eastern European nations with the endorsement of Russia, which signed an agreement to that effect in May 1997. Finally, serious discussion is being conducted regarding the creation of a European army for defence in Europe, especially in the light of the debates leading to the Iraq war and enlargement is on schedule.

27.4 Conclusion

The main conclusion is that when one considers the major phases through which the EU has developed, each with its own aims and aspirations, one would find that the EU has been very successful indeed. This success has been not only in terms of achieving *negative* integration (see Chapter 1), but also in adopting a host of *positive* integration measures and largely succeeding in meeting them. Moreover, when the Maastricht, Amsterdam and Nice treaties have become a reality and the ten-twelve nations involved in the enlargement have successfully joined the fold, the EU would be much more than an economic union and for practically the whole of Europe, but whether it would be edging closer towards realizing the dream of its 'founding fathers', the creation of a United States of Europe, that is a matter for the future of the EU and is the subject of the final chapter.

Chapter 28 The future of the EU

ALI EL-AGRAA

This chapter is devoted to a very brief response to the often-asked question regarding where the European Union is heading to in the future. There are at least two reasons for this brevity. The first is that the book is already large. The second is that the answer is heavily dependent on the outcome of the Convention for the Future of Europe, which even if its report, expected by mid-2003, is fully endorsed by all the member nations at the end of December 2003, experience with the Maastricht and Nice treaties suggests that its ratification would take a long time to complete; thus the outcome would not be known until well after this edition has been with the reader.

To offer a meaningful answer to the question, one needs to take into consideration the views of all those concerned with and play influential roles on the drive behind European integration. Thus one must seek not only the vision of the founding fathers, but also of the recent and present EU political leaders as well as look into the draft recommendations of the Convention for a constitution for the EU. The purpose of this chapter is to do precisely that.

28.1 The vision of the founding fathers

As fully documented in Chapter 2, the founding fathers dreamed of the creation of a United States of Europe. This was because they believed that there was no other means of putting an end to the continent's woeful history of conflict, bloodshed and suffering, i.e. they saw unity as the only way to the achievement of eternal peace in an area with a long history of deep divisions and devastating wars. This call for unity was later reinforced through the need for a common defence against Soviet expansionism, orchestrated under the umbrella of the Warsaw Pact, which threatened the survival of democracy in Western Europe; hence the expansion of the 1947 Brussels Treaty Organization to form NATO in 1948, under the auspices of the United States.

The switch to emphasis on economic integration came to the fore later on, but in a reinforcing manner. There were two facets to it. The first was that, with war wounds fresh in peoples' minds during the early 1950s, it was felt that political integration was out of the question then. That is why when calling for the creation of the European Economic Community, the Benelux countries reasoned that experience gained through working together in the economic field would pave the way for political unification later on; experience clearly shown by the success of the European Coal and Steel Community, which commenced opera-

tions in 1952. The second was that Europe then, and now, stood no chance of survival against, let alone of being on a par with, the United States and Japan in terms of economic excellence and influence in world affairs without being united on both fronts. Thus, with economic unity being only a means to an end, until a single European nation became the reality, the energies of those dedicated to the founding fathers' cause would still be devoted to finding ways for doing so.

However, there are those who question the wisdom, in the modern age, of the creation of one nation for either peace purposes or for economic prosperity. With regard to peace, they argue that the ethnic-based struggles in Eastern Europe and the splitting of Czechoslovakia and Yugoslavia show that separation may be a more stable equilibrium, especially with Russia now being relatively weak and focusing on economic reform and industrial rebuilding (see, *inter alia*, Feldstein, 1997, pp. 24–26). They can appeal to reality to reinforce their argument by claiming that today there are not many of the founding fathers around and vehemently assert that their dream is not shared by the new generation of Europeans. Add to these the obsession with national sovereignty and the call for political unity goes out of the window. However, those who hold or support these views have the responsibility to provide a convincing argument as to why they believe that these newly separate independent nations are now truly peaceful and would continue to be so in the indefinite future. In other words, it is difficult to take seriously arguments which project from today's 'limited experience', even if it were true, into the indefinite future, not to mention the depressing implication that only those of the same ethnic background can achieve true unity.

As to the benefit of size for economic excellence, some argue that the experience of smaller nations such as Switzerland and Singapore is ample proof that size does not matter. That may be so, but successful individual small nations not only have no chance whatsoever in exerting any influence globally, but also, and vitally, their fortunes are heavily dependent on what happens globally.

There is therefore no need to dwell on this issue, not only because it is entirely up to the reader to decide which side represents her/his inclination, but, more importantly, also because the political vision of the founding fathers relates to the indefinite future, the road to which is inevitably not going to be smooth. It is of the essence, however, to learn about what the present EU leaders think the EU future would entail since one wants to know if their vision contradicts or lends support to, if not matches, that of the founding fathers. This is in spite of the fact that supportive policies adopted in the immediate future may not become the permanent reality since they may be negated later on by governments of opposing colours, but that would simply reinforce the point regarding lack of a smooth ride into the future.

28.2   The vision of contemporary politicians

Turning to the vision of contemporary political leaders, one needs to know their views regarding whether the opening up of the EU internal market and the full implementation of the Maastricht, Amsterdam and Nice treaties are ends in themselves or merely staging posts on the way to greater economic and political union. To concentrate attention and liven up the debate, I shall consider interchanges between the leaders of the main driving forces behind EU integration, France, Germany and the European Commission, and the largest reluctant partner, Britain. Due to space limitations, I shall concentrate on two examples of interchange, one between them before the adoption of the euro, the other recent and ongoing since these should enlighten us of general trends as well as show us if Britain is still out on a limb (see Young (1998) for excellent documentation and analysis).

28.2.1 The vision of political leaders: the 1980s and 1990s

The first example relates to the interchanges that took place between then British Prime Minister Margaret Thatcher (now Baroness Thatcher), the President of the Commission during the late 1980s, Jacques Delors, and Germany's Chancellor Helmut Kohl. During the middle of the summer of 1988, Delors predicted that

'in ten years' time 80% of economic, and perhaps social and tax, legislation will be of Community origin'. In early September of the same year, he followed this with a speech to the United Kingdom's Trade Union Congress (TUC) in which he spoke strongly of the 'social dimension' of the internal market, and called for a 'platform of guaranteed social rights', including the proposal that every worker should be covered by a collective agreement with his or her employer; a proposal which is close to the hearts of most, if not all, British trade unionists.

Later, during the same month (on 20 September), Margaret Thatcher, speaking in Bruges at the College of Europe, responded in very strong terms: 'We have not rolled back the frontiers of the state in Britain only to see them re-imposed at a European level, with a European superstate exercising a new dominance from Brussels.' Since then, she repeated similar phrases regarding the 'nightmare of an EC government' on many occasions. She did this in Luxembourg and Madrid, alongside Lake Maggiore in Italy during a summit meeting, and before the Conservative Party Conference in Brighton in the United Kingdom. Nor did she confine her attacks to broad policy issues. She also did so with regard to every single practical measure by which her fellow EU leaders sought to achieve progress within the EU. She told a somewhat bemused Italian Prime Minister (then Ciriaco De Mita) at Lake Maggiore, 'I neither want nor expect to see a

European central bank or a European currency in my lifetime or . . . for a long time afterwards.' A few years later, Baroness Thatcher declared that she regretted having signed the Maastricht Treaty, and backed William Hague for the leadership of the Conservative Party, to succeed her immediate replacement (ex-Prime Minister John Major), simply because he had vehemently announced that qualification for membership in his shadow cabinet would require unwavering commitment to ensuring that the euro would have no place in Britain. Hague's choice of Michael Portillo as Shadow Chancellor soon after the latter's return to politics was consistent with that stance since Portillo was, and continues to be, a vehement opponent of the UK adopting the euro, and actually believes in its imminent demise on the grounds that no single European currency has ever succeeded!

The first rebuttals of Margaret Thatcher's vehement utterances came not from the 'socialist' leaders of the other EC member nations at the time, such as President François Mitterand of France, Prime Minister Felipe Gonzalez of Spain or Prime Minister Andreas Papandreou of Greece. They sensibly kept their feelings to themselves, and left it to the more right-wing prime ministers, Germany's Chancellor Helmut Kohl, Italy's Ciriaco De Mita, Holland's Ruud Lubbers and Belgium's Wilfred Martens, to respond to her. The most outspoken was Chancellor Kohl, hitherto Thatcher's closest ally. He declared flatly in Brussels in November 1988 that:

1 All internal frontiers within the EC must disappear by 1992.
2 Tax harmonization is indispensable.
3 A European police force is the answer to crime and terrorism.
4 By pooling sovereignty, the EC states will gain and not lose.
5 The EC must have (in alliance with the United States) a common defence policy, leading to a European army.

He did not mention Margaret Thatcher by name, but every point he emphasized was one on which she was on record as taking the opposite view.

It should be stressed that Margaret Thatcher's stance on these matters suggested that she believed that the EU was predominantly a zero sum game: every increase in the EU sovereignty was at the expense of that of the member nations, especially of the United Kingdom. However, most of the other EU leaders had fewer illusions about what the medium-sized member countries of the EU could achieve by themselves: very little indeed. They reckoned that by 'pooling sovereignty' they would increase the range of possibilities for the EU as a whole and thus indirectly for their own countries as well. Hence, Chancellor Kohl's carefully considered remarks on this subject should have been much appreciated, particularly since Germany was not one of the smaller EU nations; indeed it is the largest country in the EU in terms of both population and GDP.

In short, it could be claimed that the other EC leaders saw Margaret Thatcher following the example of Charles de Gaulle, whose anti-EC policies in the 1960s held back the development of the EC, ironically including the admission of the United Kingdom. The comparison may have been one which Margaret Thatcher herself found flattering; would she have realized however, that de Gaulle's intransigence eventually did much to undermine French influence for a long time both within the EC and outside it? Yet despite all this, one should not forget what De Gaulle stood for; in 1967, he said: 'if a united Europe is to be built by itself and for itself without being subjected to an economic, monetary or political system that is foreign to it, if Europe is to counterbalance the immense power of the United States, then the ties and rules that hold the community together must be strengthened, not weakened'.

Although Margaret Thatcher was in a minority of one within the EC, she put herself in that position entirely by her own doing – her isolation was self-inflicted. She had been in that situation before, when she fought her long and hard battle to reduce the United Kingdom's contribution to the EC general budget, but then attracted much grudging admiration from the leaders of the other member nations. Although they objected to her tactics, they recognized that she was protecting a vital British interest and was seeking to remedy an evident injustice. However, their sympathy for the position she adopted in the late 1980s (and continues to espouse today) was non-existent. She was thought to be acting out of sheer perversity or, at least, out of nationalism of the narrowest possible kind.

So what is the message behind this interchange in terms of the vision of the EU leaders in the 1980s regarding the future of the EU? Before responding to this question, it is pertinent to ask another: why the jump from Thatcher to Hague, i.e. has Major been left out because his position towards the EU resembled that of Thatcher and Hague? The answer is that although Major did not follow closely in Thatcher's footsteps within this context, his government's downfall was partly due to a deep division within the Conservatives over the role of Britain within the EU; a division made starkly clear by the two candidates who contested the final vote for his (Major's) replacement: Kenneth Clarke, a committed pro-European, and William Hague, who as we have seen, was a devout anti-European. One can therefore claim a consistent British government attitude toward EU integration over the Thatcher period and its immediate aftermath.

Thus, the answer is that during the period under consideration, Germany and the President of the Commission, as well as the silent majority of EU nations, saw the EU as evolving beyond the commitments entered into then. In short, they envisaged the EU becoming more than an economic and monetary union with a common currency and coordinated policies on foreign affairs, defence and justice and home security. Britain took a different view and was supported by Denmark, her closest ally since the creation of EFTA in 1960, after it became clear that Britain could not go along with what the Original Six aspired for (see above and Chapter 2). However, since Britain had always seen a different role for herself from that envisaged by the 'continent', one can claim that the countries most involved with EU integration acted in a manner which suggested that the future would bring about deeper integration. Although this was not expressed in the form of concrete political unity, what is pertinent is that their vision for the next steps to be taken for further EU integration is consistent with the dream of the founding fathers.

28.2.2 The vision of the present political leaders

We now turn to the second example of interchange by considering what the present EU leaders think of how the future should be shaped for the EU.

Without a shadow of doubt, the debate was opened by Joschka Fischer, the German Foreign Minister, on 12 May 2000, in a speech delivered at Humboldt University. He began by asking his audience to allow him to 'cast aside . . . the mantle of . . . Minister'; thus to speak in a purely personal capacity. He said that 'in the coming decade, we will have to enlarge the EU to

the east and south-east, and this will, in the end, mean a doubling in the number of members. And at the same time, if we are to be able to meet this historic challenge and integrate the new member states without substantially denting the EU's capacity for action, we must put into place the last brick in the building of European integration, namely political integration' (translated into English in Joerges et al., 2000). He added that this 'finalité politique' will be preceded by the formation of a 'centre of gravity' within the Union; an 'avant garde', the driving force for the completion of political integration. With regard to the institutional arrangement, he asked for 'a constitutional treaty centred around basic human and civil rights; shared sovereignty and a clear definition of competences between European and nation-state levels of governance; a division of powers among the European institutions, including full parliamentarization and a European Parliament with two chambers, a European government and, possibly, a directly elected president, with broadly administrative powers'. With this 'division of sovereignty' between the EU institutions and the nation states, he thus distanced himself from a European superstate transcending and replacing the national democracies.

The speech has attracted a great deal of criticism and generated open hostility in some quarters where the word federation is not in the dictionary of European integration. Also, scholarly reactions have come from all and sundry, ranging from Fischer's logical inconsistency in wanting a federation where the member states remain sovereign to his not working out the path to be taken to the ultimate objective. With regard to inconsistency, Leben (in Joerges et al., 2000, p. 101) argues that classical constitutional theory recognizes only confederate and federal states; hence wonders if there can be a third type, 'a federation but not a federal state, as . . . Fischer's speech seems to suggest?' However, our concern here is with what political leaders think, so let us turn to them; those interested should turn to the excellent collection in Joerges et al. (2000).

A year later, on 30 April 2001, German Chancellor Gerhard Schröder added to Fischer's framework in the publication for the November congress for his party of Social Democrats. He called for the restructuring of the EU institutions, including the building of the European Commission into a strong executive, the transformation of the Council of the European Union into a chamber of European states and the drafting of a constitution for the EU. Singling out the weaknesses of the common agricultural and regional policies, he laid stress on greater transparency, by insisting that the member states should assume responsibility for the tasks that they can carry out more effectively than through a central administration, which is consistent with the subsidiarity principle, incorporated in the Amsterdam treaty.

On 27 June 2000, French President Jacques Chirac, in a speech delivered to the German Parliament in Berlin, called for the formation of an 'inner core of EU members' willing to push more rapidly towards further integration, thus echoing Fischer's appeal for a centre of gravity, which some would rather call a two-speed Europe. Also, he endorsed the idea of a future constitution for the EU. Some analysts saw this as support for Germany's call for EU federalism; others as politically calculated rhetoric lacking in substance. He stressed, however, that neither France nor Germany envisage the creation of a 'European super-state which would take the place of our nation states', i.e. he was advocating 'not a United States of Europe, but a Europe of united states'.

On 28 May 2001, Lionel Jospin, while still French Premier, spelled out his vision for the EU as a 'federation of nation states', but rejected the German views of federalism and distanced himself from President Jacques Chirac's idea of a 'pioneer group' to forge ahead with integration. Noting that 'federation' may appear to be a simple and coherent word, it was subject to several interpretations, and went on to reject any model based on the German federal system. He added that 'if federation means a gradual, controlled process of sharing competences, or transferring competences to the union level, then this refers to the federation of nation states coined by [ex-EU Commission President] Jacques Delors and is a concept which I fully support'. Being a dedicated socialist, he reinforced his previous suggestions that the EU should enhance its social legislation with the adoption of a social treaty, the firming up of tax harmonization and a tighter legal framework to enshrine the role of public services in the EU.

Of the EU member nations considered here, this leaves the present British government. The leader of the reformed Labour Party, some argue it is the old Conservative Party in pleasant disguise, Tony Blair, is warm towards the EU, hence he is out of step with Baroness Thatcher, not the other EU leaders. Since assuming office in 1997 he has been very sympathetic

towards the EU. In a speech in Ghent (near Bruges!) on 23 February 2000, he said that he believed that by winning the argument for economic reform in Europe, he could mould the EU agenda and in doing so simultaneously defuse much of the resentment Britons feel towards the EU. In short, he wants the UK to act from within the EU to the betterment of the EU itself and its attraction to Britons, adding that British ties with the United States have been undermined by the failure of the UK to play an active role within the EU. Later, he committed his government to the adoption of the euro, provided Britain passed his Chancellor's five tests (the 'Brown' tests) and the UK citizens endorsed adoption in a referendum afterwards. However, he remains adamant that he does not see the EU going beyond the economic field and that the alliance with the US will be strengthened; the events leading to the 2003 US–British (and alliances) war with Iraq demonstrate that.

On 6 October 2000, in his speech to the Polish Stock Exchange in Warsaw, Blair elaborated on his arguments and came up with his proposals for EU political reform, which, given its date, were obviously his response to Fischer and submission to the Convention of the Future of Europe. First, he wanted the European Council to set the agenda, which is what it actually does (see Chapter 3), but with the president of the Commission playing a part in drawing up the agenda, the Commission continuing as the guardian of the treaties and the Council having term presidencies with greater continuity. Second, he did not want to see a single document called the EU Constitution, opting for continuation of the present system of treaties, laws and precedents, i.e. to retain the British style of an unwritten constitution, and to decide on what is to be done and not done at the EU level, thus be more specific about subsidiarity. Third, have a second chamber for the European Parliament whose most important function is to review the EU's work. Fourth, streamline the Commission since with enlargement it would have 30 members, and it would become unworkable, but he indicated that there is no need to discuss this now. In short, he wanted to see the EU as a 'superpower, but not a superstate . . . an economic powerhouse through the completion of the world's biggest single market, the extension of competition, an adaptable and well educated workforce, the support for businesses large and small'. Thus, he reiterated what Chancellor Gordon Brown said on 27 June 2000. All of which amounts to saying 'no thank you' to Fischer, though the overall tone of the government is one of positive commitment to a slightly strengthened EU.

One should add that against this positive, but limited change in the British government's attitude towards the EU, the present leader of the Conservative Party, Iain Duncan Smith, holds views consistent with Thatcher's. However, the Conservative Party is not united in this respect, since it has a significant faction with very positive views of and on EU integration.

To complete the picture, one must consider the position of the current President of the European Commission, Romano Prodi, who as Italian Prime Minister during 1996–1998 can also offer a contribution from his country since on this occasion he is acting on a personal capacity. He expressed his opinions on many occasions, but no more clearly than in a speech delivered to the French National Assembly on 12 March 2003. He asked: 'What Europe do we want? What common projects are we aiming for? Just a "supermarket" or a political area that allows us to defend convictions on the world stage?' His response can be briefly captured from his statement that the Commission highlights 'the need for a Union that can "exercise the responsibilities of a world power"', that current disagreements between EU leaders about the war on Iraq 'will eventually help defend the idea on which European integration was founded' and 'when a political Union emerges, it will reap the benefit' of this approach.

Thus, not only are practically all the major players still envisaging the EU going beyond its present commitments, but also evolving into some sort of a closer political union. The debate on whether this should be 'United States of Europe' or a 'Europe of united states' does not undermine this since a federation can take different forms. Hence, the vision of most of the major EU political leaders is consistent with the substance of the dream of the founding fathers.

More on federation is in order. According to constitutional theorists, federalism fulfils two major functions. The first is a vertical separation of powers by assigning separate responsibilities to two government levels; the components and the federation are usually geographically defined, 'although "societal federalism" considers non-territorial units as components of a federation' (Börzel and Risse, 2000). The second is the integration of heterogeneous societies, but without destroying their cultural and/or political autonomy (Börzel and Risse, 2000). Implicit in both functions

is that the components and the federation have autonomous decision powers which they can exercise independently; thus, sovereignty is shared or divided, rather than being exclusively located at one level. Even without the legitimate monopoly of coercive force, the EU has acquired some fundamental federal qualities. As witnessed in this book, it possesses sovereignty rights in a wide variety of policy sectors ranging from exclusive jurisdiction in the area of EMU to far reaching regulatory competences in sectors such as consumer protection, energy, the environment, health and social security and transport, and 'increasingly penetrating even the core of traditional state responsibilities such as internal security (Schengen, Europol) and, albeit to a lesser extent, foreign and security policy' (Börzel and Risse, 2000). In most policy areas, EU law is not only superior to national law, it can also deploy direct effect giving citizens the right to litigate against their states for violating the EU laws conferred on them. This is part of a second development, which has been addressed more recently. The EU is transforming itself into a political community 'within a defined territory and with its own citizens, who are granted (some) fundamental rights by the European Treaties and the jurisdiction of the European Court of Justice . . . With the Treaties of Maastricht and Amsterdam, however, the single market has been embedded in a political union with emerging external boundaries [Article 11 of the Union treaty refers to the protection of the integrity of the Union and its external boundaries] and proper citizenship' (Börzel and Risse, 2000).

Not only has the EU developed into a political community with comprehensive regulatory powers and a proper mechanism of territorially defined exclusion and inclusion (EU citizenship), it also shares most features of what defines a federation. First, the EU is a system of governance which has at least two orders of government, each existing under its own right and exercises direct influence on the people. Second, the EU treaties allocate jurisdiction and resources to these two main orders of government. Third, there are provisions for 'shared government' in areas where the jurisdiction of the EU and member states overlap. Fourth, EU law enjoys supremacy over national law; it is the law of the land. Fifth, the composition and procedures of EU institutions are based not solely on principles of majority representation, but guarantee the representation of 'minority' views. Sixth, the European Court of Justice serves as an umpire to adjudicate conflicts between the EU institutions and the member states. Finally, the EU has a directly elected parliament (Börzel and Risse, 2000).

The EU only lacks two significant features of a federation. One is that the member states remain the 'masters' of the treaties, i.e. they have the exclusive power to amend or change the constitutive treaties of the EU. The other is that the EU has no real 'tax and spend' capacity, i.e. it has no fiscal federalism. 'Otherwise, the EU today looks like a federal system, it works in a similar manner to a federal system, so why not call it an emerging federation?' (Börzel and Risse, 2000). In short, one wonders why the word federalism frightens some EU nations so much.

28.3   The Convention for the Future of Europe

One obvious reaction to the position of the present political leaders would be that their statements summarized above should not be taken seriously since they were meant merely to set the scene for the Convention for the Future of Europe (see Chapter 2). In other words, given past experience, these positions would have to be greatly watered down if consensus is to materialize, and consensus will be needed on this occasion since a positive decision would require unanimity. This is specially so when it is being claimed that the Convention is an historic moment for the EU, just as the Philadelphia convention was for America since it will give the EU a single legal personality and provide all its institutions with a constitutional basis for their powers as well as transfer sovereignties over internal affairs (immigration, cross-border crime, drug trafficking) to EU institutions. One should add, however, that Peter Hain, British Prime Minster Tony Blair's representative on the Convention, has taken to insisting that it would be much less important than the Maastricht treaty.

It is therefore pertinent to add something on the draft constitution, submitted in early February 2003, to find out what light it sheds on the matter. Then follow this by considering the final draft, adopted in the Thessaloniki Greek summit on 20 June 2003, since doing so will shed light on the mentioned 'watering down' during negotiations. However, one should not dwell too much on the contents since the final draft itself is most likely to undergo serious change before final adoption in the Intergovernmental Conference to be held towards the end of the first half of 2004.

The first articles of the proposed new constitution for the EU, drafted by Valéry Giscard d'Estaing, Chairman of the Convention and former French President, and his 12-member 'inner praesidium', were published on 6 February 2003 (easily accessible from the EU website at **http://european-convention.eu.int**). They envisage a major role for the EU in the economy, foreign policy and even space exploration. Sixteen of its 46 articles deal with EU aims, values and powers. Article 1, on establishing an entity for the EU, states that it should be: 'A Union of European States which, while retaining their national identities, closely coordinate their policies at the European level, and *administer certain common competences on a federal basis*' (italics added). Article 3, on EU objectives, calls for, *inter alia*, the 'development of a common foreign and security policy, and a common defence policy, to defend and promote the Union's values in the wider world'. Indeed, 'the tone of the document is more federalist than expected' and, in particular, the 'Commission was pleased with the clause to allow national governments and the European Parliament to give the EU more powers' (*Financial Times*, 7 February 2003), if needed for the attainment of the objectives set by the Constitution.

These have been labelled as surprising proposals, given that the Convention was entrusted with proposing a framework and structures for the EU which is geared to changes in the world situation, the needs of EU citizens and the future development of the union. In other words, the Convention is largely meant to simplify and restructure the EU basic treaties (Giuliano Amato, one of the two Vice-Chairmen of the Convention and ex-Prime Minister of Italy, Project Syndicate/Institute for Human Science, 2002). No wonder, Britain immediately labelled the draft 'unacceptable', claiming it went further than expected towards creating a federal Europe (*Financial Times*, 7 February 2003). However, Amato responds in the same article by arguing that the 'institutional structure . . . should also reflect and help develop Europe's broader aspirations. Europe must be more than a vehicle of economic integration'. What is even more interesting is that Giscard d'Estaing, the Convention's Chairman, has proposed the streamlining of the EU foreign policy apparatus, by the creation of a single post of EU Foreign Minister (to replace the current two roles held by Javier Solana, EU foreign policy chief, and Christopher Patten, EU Commissioner in charge of external relations) as well a scrapping of the rotating six-month presidency of the European Council (*Financial Times*, 16 April 2003).

That was the draft, but how does it compare with the new draft adopted on 20 June 2003? To find out, consider its highlights:

- *Foreign Affairs*. The draft asks for the creation of a foreign minister to put together and promote a common EU foreign policy, combining the present roles of 'foreign policy representative' (Javier Solana) and commissioner in charge of EU external relations, hence EU aid funds (Chris Patten).
- *Defence*. The draft allows groups of countries to offer each other mutual military guarantees within the EU, with the final goal of 'common defence' that would eventually make the EU a military bloc.
- *Justice and Home Affairs*. The draft asks for the abolition of national vetoes on asylum and immigration and setting the EU on the path towards the 'minimum' harmonization of criminal law in areas such as the rights of individuals in criminal procedure and the rights of victims of crime.
- *The Charter of Fundamental Rights*. The draft asks that this list of EU citizens' rights take legal force, but the UK has won assurances that it would not be enforceable in national courts (the UK and Ireland are particularly concerned about workers given 'a right to strike').
- *Legal Changes*. The draft calls for the melding of the three EU treaties into one and getting rid of the current complicated three 'pillar' structure. The division and extent of EU powers is spelt out and the principle that EU law overrides national law is confirmed. For the first time, a mechanism by which a member nation could leave the EU is provided. Many of the detailed changes are in the yet to be completed part III of the final draft.
- *EU Legislation*. The draft asks that the normal EU law making procedure would be one of 'co-decision' between the European Parliament, representing the people, and the Council of the European Union (Council of Ministers),

representing the member states. If a third of national parliaments reject a proposal, the Commission would have to reconsider the text. Valéry Giscard d'Estaing also proposes a double majority in the Council to approve legislation, comprising half of the member states, representing 60% of EU population, but Spain and Portugal vigorously oppose this, preferring to stick to the QMV formula agreed in the Nice treaty.

- *Vetoes*. The draft concedes that veto rights for foreign policy and tax will broadly stay, due to the insistence of the UK and her close allies on the subjects. However, the draft proposes that member states can together decide to settle some tax issues (such as measures to tackle fraud) by majority voting. On foreign policy, a common position would have to be agreed unanimously by member states, but its detailed implementation would then be by majority voting on a proposal of the foreign minister. The draft would also pave the way for greater coordination in such areas as economic and social policy.
- *European Parliament*. The draft would see a huge increase in EP competences and would let it have the power to legislate in areas such as justice and home affairs. It would also allow it to have a say over big budget items such as expenditure on the Common Agricultural Policy and the structural funds.
- *Commission*. The draft would have the Commission 'renovated' by reducing it from the present size of 20 to 15 commissioners with full voting rights. All countries would take equal turns to sit on the Commission; a key requirement of the smaller member states. Countries not on the commission would have a non-voting representative.
- *Council President*. The draft would provide the European Council, which meets four times a year, with its first full-time president to replace the six-month rotating system. Serving two-and-a-half years, renewable once, the president would be charged with giving the EU political direction and dealing with foreign policy issues at a head of government level. However, the president's precise role is still a matter of great controversy, with many small countries fearing the new president will 'muscle in' on Commission territory.

- *Council of the European Union.* The draft's arrangements for the Council are not well defined, but the rotating chairmanship would be retained, which would be a victory for the smaller member nations. The informal Eurogroup of finance ministers whose countries use the single currency (Ecofin) would gain more formal powers over issues affecting the euro. They would be represented by a 'Mr Euro', a political figure leading the Eurogroup for up to two years.
- *Future Developments.* The draft would allow a 'bridging clause' to enable member states to abolish vetoes in the future if they agree to do so unanimously; presently, this is only possible after an Intergovernmental Conference and treaty revision. Britain has said it would oppose this furiously.

It should be apparent that the changes to the first draft have been minimal. Thus, it would seem that the pre-convention utterances were not mere political gesturing, but as already stressed, the real test is still to come since bargaining will not stop until the end of the first half of 2004.

28.4 Conclusion

Thus, the majority of European political leaders envisage a long-term future for the EU which is very consistent with the dream of the founding fathers and differs only with regard to what form it should take and how soon it should arrive there. To put it differently, economics has never been the real driving force behind European integration; it has been only a vehicle to that end.

References

Throughout this book, reference is made to numerous Communications by the Commission of the European Communities/Union to the Council. These are indicated by the official system adopted by the EC/EU, which is quite clear, for example, COM (88) 491 means Communication number 491, issued in 1988. Reference is also frequently made to the Treaties of the European Communities. Some of these are published by Her Majesty's Stationery Office (HMSO), now The Stationery Office (TSO), in the United Kingdom, but the most comprehensive set is issued by Sweet & Maxwell, which is listed here. Also listed is the Commission's Comprehensive Guide to the Maastricht Treaty (CEU, 1999d) and there is a comparative text by Euroconfidential of Belgium titled *The Rome, Maastricht & Amsterdam Treaties*. Note that in order to save space, all EC/EU publications issued by the Office of Official Publications of the EC/EU in Brussels do not have Brussels stated at the end, nor do those published in both Brussels and Luxembourg, but all those issued only in Luxembourg do.

Throughout the book, *EU Bulletin* is used to refer to the Commission of the European Communities' *Bulletin of the Economic Communities/Union* (various issues), and *OJ C, OJ L* or *OJ CL* (where L stands for legal) refer to the Commission's *Official Journal of the European Communities/Union*. Again the EC/EU's own system of referencing is clear.

Abbott, K., Keohane, R., Moravcsik, M., Slaughter, A-M. and Snidal, D. (2000) 'The concept of legalization', *International Organization*, vol. 53, issue 3.

Adedeji, A. (2002) 'History and prospects for regional integration in Africa', paper presented on 5 March at the African Development Forum III, held in Addis Ababa, Ethiopia.

Adelman, M. A. (1969) 'Comment on the "H" concentration measure as a numbers equivalent', *Review of Economics and Statistics*, vol. 51.

Agha, A. and Houghton, J. (1996) 'Designing VAT systems: some efficiency considerations', *Review of Economics and Statistics*, vol. 78.

Aiginger, K. and Pfaffermayr, M. (2000) 'The Single Market and geographic concentration in Europe', presented at EARIE Conference, Lausanne on 11 December.

Aitken, N. D. (1973) 'The effects of the EEC and EFTA on European trade: a temporal cross-section analysis', *American Economic Review*, vol. 68.

Allen, P. R. (1983) 'Cyclical imbalance in a monetary union', *Journal of Common Market Studies*, vol. 21, no. 2.

Allen, P. R. and Kenen, P. (1980) *Asset Markets, Exchange Rates and Economic Integration*, Cambridge University Press, Cambridge.

Alston, P. and Weiler, J. (1999) 'An "ever closer union" in need of a human rights policy: The EU and human rights', *European Journal of International Law*, vol. 9.

Alter, K. (1996) 'The European Court's political power', *West European Politics*, vol. 19.

Alter, K. (1998a) 'Who are the "masters of the treaty"?: European Governments and the European ECJ', *International Organization*, vol. 52.

Alter, K. (1998b) 'Explaining national court acceptance of European Court jurisprudence: a critical evaluation of theories of legal integration', in A-M. Slaughter, A. Stone Sweet and J. Weiler (eds), *The European Courts and National Courts: Doctrine and Jurisprudence*, Hart, Oxford.

Alter, K. (2000) 'The European Union's legal system and domestic policy: spillover and backlash', *International Organization*, vol. 53.

Alter, K. (2001) *Establishing the Supremacy of European Law: the Making of an International Rule of Law in Europe*, Oxford University Press.

Alter, K. and Meunier-Aitsahalia, S. (1994) 'Judicial politics in the European Community: European integration and the pathbreaking Cassis de Dijon decision', *Comparative Political Studies*, vol. 26.

Alter, K. and Vargas, K. (2000) 'Explaining variation in the use of European litigation strategies: EC Law and UK gender equality policy', *Comparative Political Studies*, vol. 36.

Alter, K., Dehousse, R. and Vanberg, G. (2002) 'Law, political science and EU legal studies: an interdisciplinary project', *European Union Politics*, vol. 3.

Amity, M. (1998) 'New trade theories and industrial location in the EU: a survey of evidence', *Oxford Review of Economic Policy*, vol. 4, no. 2.

Anderson, M. and Liefferink, D. (eds) (1997) *European Environmental Policy – The Pioneers*, Manchester University Press.

Ardy, B. (1988) 'The national incidence of the European Community budget', *Journal of Common Market Studies*, vol. 26, no. 4.

Ardy, B. (2002a) 'The EU budget and EU citizens', in S. Hatt and F. Gardner *Economics, Policies and People: a European Perspective*, Macmillan, Basingstoke.

Ardy, B. (2002b) 'The UK, the EU budget and EMU', in Ali M. El-Agraa (ed.), *The euro and Britain: Implications of Moving into the EMU*, Pearson Education.

Ardy, B., Begg, I., Schelkle, W. and Torres, F. (2002) *EMU and Its Impact on Cohesion: Policy Challenges*, European Institute, South Bank University, London.

Argyris, N. (1993) 'Regulatory reform in the electricity sector', *Oxford Review of Economic Policy*, vol. 19, no. 1.

Armstrong, H. W. (1978) 'European Economic Community regional policy: a survey and critique', *Regional Studies*, vol. 12, no. 5.

Armstrong, H. W. (1985) 'The reform of European Community regional policy', *Journal of Common Market Studies*, vol. 23.

Armstrong, H. W. (1995a) *Growth Disparities and Convergence Clubs in Regional GDP in Western Europe, USA and Australia*, Report for DG16, European Commission, Brussels.

Armstrong, H. W. (1995b) 'Convergence among regions of the European Union', *Papers in Regional Science*, vol. 40.

Armstrong, H. W. and Taylor, J. (2000) *Regional Economics and Policy*, 3rd edn, Blackwell, Oxford.

Armstrong, K. (1998) 'Legal integration: theorising the legal dimension of European integration', *Journal of Common Market Studies*, vol. 36.

Armstrong, K. and Bulmer, S. (1998) *The Governance of the Single European Market*, Manchester University Press, Manchester.

Arndt, H. W. and Garnaut, R. (1979) 'ASEAN and the industrialisation of East Asia', *Journal of Common Market Studies*, vol. 17, no. 3.

Arndt, S. W. (1968) 'On discriminatory versus non-preferential tariff policies', *Economic Journal*, vol. 78.

Arndt, S. W. (1969) 'Customs unions and the theory of tariffs', *American Economic Review*, vol. 59.

Arnold, F. (1994) *Economic Analysis of Environmental Policy and Regulation*, Wiley, New York.

Arnull, A. (1990) 'Does the ECJ have inherent jurisdiction?', *Common Market Law Review*, vol. 27.

Arnull, A. (1991) 'What shall we do on Sunday?', *European Law Review*, vol. 16.

Arnull, A. (1996) 'The European ECJ and judicial objectivity: A reply to Professor Hartley', *Law Quarterly Review*, vol. 112.

Asdrubali, P., Sorensen, B. and Yosha, O. (2002) 'Channels of interstate risk sharing: United States 1963–1990', *Quarterly Journal of Economics*, vol. 111.

Australian Society of CPAs (1998) 'Tax reform in New Zealand – the shape of things to come in Australia', *Discussion Paper*, May, cited in Cnossen 2002.

BAE Systems (2000) 'Updating and development of economic and fares data regarding the European air travel industry', *2000 Annual Report*, BAE Systems, Chorley.

Bagella, M. and Becchetti, L. (2000) *The Comparative Advantage of Industrial Districts: Theoretical and Empirical Analysis*, Physica-Verlag, Heidelberg and New York.

Bailey, S. J. (2002) *Public Sector Economics: Theory and Practice*, 2nd edition, Palgrave, Basingstoke.

Balassa, B. (1961) *The Theory of Economic Integration*, Allen & Unwin, London.

Balassa, B. (1967) 'Trade creation and trade diversion in the European Common Market', *Economic Journal*, vol. 77.

Balassa, B. (1974a) 'Trade creation and trade diversion in the European Common Market: an appraisal of the evidence', *Manchester School*, vol. 42.

Balassa, B. (1974b) *European Economic Integration*, North-Holland.

Baldwin, R. E. (1971) *Non-tariff Distortions of International Trade*, Allen & Unwin, London.

Baldwin, R. E. (1989) 'The growth effect of 1992', *Economic Policy*, no. 9.

Baldwin, R. E. (1994) *Towards an Integrated Europe*, CEPR, London.

Baldwin, R. E., Francois, J. F. and Portes, R. (1997) 'The costs and benefits of Eastern enlargement: the impact on the European Union and Central Europe', *Economic Policy: A European Forum*, vol. 24.

Baldwin, R. E., Haaparanta, P. and Kiander, J. (1995) *Expanding Membership of the European Union*, Cambridge University Press, Cambridge.

Ballenger, N., Dunmore, J. and Lederer, T. (1987) 'Trade liberalization in world farm markets', *Agriculture Information Bulletin*, vol. 516, May.

Bangermann, M. (1994) 'Information Technology in Europe: The EC Commission's View', *European Information Technology Observatory*, p. 12, EITO, Frankfurt/Main.

Barents, R. (1982) 'New developments in measures having equivalent effect: A reappraisal', *Common Market Law Review*, vol. 19.

Barnard, C. (1995) 'A European litigation strategy: The case of the Equal Opportunities Commission', in J. Shaw and G. More (eds), *New Legal Dynamics of the EU*, Clarendon, Oxford.

Barnard, C. and Sharpston, E. (1997) 'The changing face of Article 177 references', *Common Market Law Review*, vol. 34.

Barrell, R. (2001) 'The UK and EMU: choosing the regime', *National Institute Economic Review*, no. 180, April.

Barrell, R. and Pain, N. (1993) 'Trade restraints and Japanese direct investment flows', mimeo, National Institute of Economic and Social Research, London.

Barry, A. (1993) 'The European community and European government: harmonization, mobility and space', *Economy and Society*, vol. 22.

Baumol, W. J. and Oates, J. E. (1988) *The Theory of Environmental Policy*, Cambridge University Press, Cambridge, 2nd edition.

Bayliss, B. T. and El-Agraa, A. M. (1990) 'Competition and industrial policies with emphasis on competition policy', in the third edition of this book.

Bayoumi, T. and Eichengreen, B. (1996) 'Operationalising the theory of optimum currency areas', *Discussion Paper 1484*, CEPR, London.

Begg, I. (1995) 'The impact on regions of competition of the EC Single Market in financial services', in S. Hardy, M. Hart, L. Albrechts and A. Katos (eds), *An Enlarged Europe: Regions in Competition?*, Jessica Kingsley.

Begg, I. and Grimwade, N. (1998) *Paying for Europe*, Sheffield Academic Press.

Bellamy, R. and Warleigh, A. (1998) 'From an ethics of participation to an ethics of participation: Citizenship and the future of the EU', *Millennium*, vol. 27.

Benvenisti, E. (1993) 'Judicial misgivings regarding the application of international law: An analysis of attitudes of international courts', *European Journal of International Law*, vol. 4.

Berglas, E. (1983) 'The case for unilateral tariff reactions: foreign tariffs reconsidered', *American Economic Review*, vol. 73.

Berglöf, E., Eichengreen, B., Roland. G., Tabellin, G. and Wyplosz, C. (2003) *Built to Last: a Political Architecture for Europe*, CEPR, London.

Bergman, D. *et al.* (1970) *A Future for European Agriculture*, Atlantic Institute, Paris.

Bergmann, L., Brunekreeft, G., Doyle, C., von der Fehr, N.-H. M., Newbery, D. M., Pollitt, M. and Regilbeau, P. (1999) *A European Market for Electricity?*, CEPR, London; and SNS, Stockholm.

Bergstrand, J. D. (1985) 'The gravity equation in international trade: some microeconomic foundations and empirical evidence', *The Review of Economics and Statistics*, vol. 67, no. 3.

Bhagwati, J. N. (1969) *Trade, Tariffs and Growth*, Weidenfeld & Nicolson, London.

Bhagwati, J. N. (1971) 'Customs unions and welfare improvement', *Economic Journal*, vol. 81.

Bishop, W. (1981) 'Price discrimination under Article 86: Political economy in the European Court', *Modern Law Review*, vol. 44.

Bishop, S. and Walker, M. (1999) *The Economics of EC Competition Law*, Sweet & Maxwell.

Björksten, N. (1999) ', Bank of Finland Working Paper.

BLS (2003) 'Federal executive branch employment', Bureau of Labour Statistics, USA, **www.bls.gov/oes/2001/oesi3_901.htm#b00–0000**

Bode, E., Krieger-Boden, C. and Lammers, K. (1994) *Cross-border Activities, Taxation and the European Single Market*, Institut für Weltwirtschaft, Kiel, cited in Cnossen.

Boehmer-Christiansen, S. and Skea, J. (1990) *Acid Politics: Environmental and energy policies in Britain and Germany*, Pinter.

Bollard, A. E. and Mayes, D. G. (1991) 'Regionalism and the Pacific Rim', *Journal of Common Market Studies*, vol. 30.

Börzel, T. A. and Risse, T. (2000) 'Who is afraid of European federation? How to constitutionalise a multi-level governance system', in C. Joerges, Y. Mény and J. H. H. Weiler (eds).

Bouët, A. (2002) 'Commentaire sur l'article "Niveau et coût du protectionnisme européen" de Patrick A. Messerlin', *Economie Internationale*, vol. 89–90.

Bovenberg, A. L. (1994) 'Designation and origin based taxation under international capital mobility', *International Tax and Public Finance*, vol. 1, no. 3.

Bovenberg, L. and Cnossen, S. (1997) *Public Economics and the Environment in an Imperfect World*, Kluwer.

Boyd, G. (ed.) (1998) *The Struggle for World Markets: Competition and Cooperation Between NAFTA and the European Union*, Edward Elgar.

Brander, J. and Spencer, B. (1983) 'International R&D rivalry and industrial strategy', *Review of Economic Studies*, vol. 50.

Braunerhjelm, P., Faini, R., Norman, R., Ruane, F. and Seabright, P. (2000) *Integration and the Regions of Europe: How the Right Policies Can Prevent Polarization*, CEPR, London.

Brenton, P. (2003) 'Integrating the Least Developed Countries into the World trading system: the current impact of EU preferences under everything but arms', *World Bank Policy Research Working Paper 3018*, World Bank, Washington DC.

Bright, C. (1995) 'Deregulation of EC competition policy: rethinking Article 85(1)', *1994 Annual Proceedings of Fordham Corporate Law Institute*, vol. 21.

Brittan, L. (1992) *European Competition Policy: Keeping the playing field level*, CEPS.

Brooks, M. R. and Button, K. J. (1992) 'Shipping within the framework of a single European market', *Transport Review*, vol. 12.

Brown, A. J. (1961) 'Economic separatism versus a common market in developing countries', *Yorkshire Bulletin of Economic and Social Research*, vol. 13.

Brülhart, M. (1998) 'Marginal Intra-Industry Trade and Trade-Induced Adjustment: A Survey', in M. Brülhart and R. C. Hine, *Intra-Industry Trade and Adjustment: the European Experience*, Macmillan, London.

Brülhart, M. and Elliott, R. (1998) 'A survey of intra-industry trade in the European Union', in M. Brülhart and R. C. Hine, *Intra-Industry Trade and Adjustment: the European Experience*, Macmillan, London.

Buchanan, J. M. and Tullock, G. (1962) *The Calculus of Consent*, Ann Arbor.

Buckley, P. J. and Casson, M. (1976) *The Future of the Multinational Enterprise*, Macmillan, Basingstoke.

Buigues, P.-A., Ilzkovitz, F. and Lebrun, J. F. (1990) 'The impact of the internal market by industrial sector: the challenge for the member states', *The European Economy/Social Europe*, Office of Official Publications of the European Commission, Luxembourg.

Buigues, P.-A. and Martínez Mongay, C. (1999) 'Regionalism and Globalization: The LDCs and the Single European Market', in O. Memedovic *et al.* (1999) (eds), *Multilateralism and Regionalism in the Post-Uruguay Round Era: What Role for the EU?*, Kluwer, Boston.

Buiter, W., Corsetti, G. and Roubini, N. (1993) 'Excessive deficits: sense and nonsense in the Treaty of Maastricht', *Economic Policy*, vol. 16.

Burley, A.-M. and Mattli, W. (1993) 'Europe before the court: A political theory of legal integration', *International Organization*, vol. 47.

Buti, M., Eijffinger, S. and Franco, D. (2002) 'Revisiting the Stability and Growth Pact: grand design or internal adjustment?', mimeo, November.

Button, K. J. (1984) *Road Haulage Licensing and EC Transport Policy*, Gower.

Button, K. J. (1990) 'Infrastructure plans for Europe', in J. Gillund and G. Tornqvist (eds), *European Networks*, CERUM.

Button, K. J. (1992) 'The liberalization of transport services', in D. Swann (ed.), *1992 and Beyond*, Routledge.

Button, K. J. (1993) 'East–west European transport: an overview', in D. Banister and J. Berechman (eds), *Transportation in a Unified Europe: Policies Challenges*, Elsevier.

Button, K. J. (1998) 'The good, the bad and the forgettable – or lessons the US can learn from European transport policy', *Journal of Transport Geography*, vol. 6.

Button, K. J. and Gillingwater, D. (1986) *Future Transport Policy*, Croom Helm.

Button, K. J. and Keeler, T. (1993) 'The regulation of transport markets', *Economic Journal*, vol. 103.

Button, K. J. and Swann, D. (1992) 'Transatlantic lessons in aviation deregulation: EEC and US experiences', *Antitrust Bulletin*, vol. 37.

Button, K. J., Hayes, K. and Stough, R. (1998) *Flying into the Future: Air Transport Policy in the European Union*, Edward Elgar.

Byé, M. (1950) 'Unions douanières et données nationales', Economie Appliquée, vol. 3. Reprinted (1953) in translation as 'Customs unions and national interests', *International Economic Papers*, no. 3.

Bygrä, S., Hansen, C. Y., Rystad, K. and Søltoft, S. (1987) *Danish–German border Shopping and Its Price Sensitivity*, Institut for Graenseregionfroskning, Aabenraa, cited in Cnossen, 2002.

Bzdera, A. (1992) 'The ECJ of the European Community and the politics of institutional reform', *West European Politics*, vol. 15.

Callon, M. (1986) 'Some elements of a sociology of translation: domestication of the scallops and fishermen of St. Brieuc bay', in J. Law (ed.), *Power: action and belief: a new sociology of knowledge*, Routledge, London.

Callon, M. (1998) 'Introduction: The embeddedness of economic markets in economics', in M. Callon (ed.), *The Laws of the Markets*, Blackwell.

Calmfors, L. *et al.* (1997) EMU – *A Swedish Perspective Report of the Calmfors Commission*, Kluwer, Dordrecht.

Calmfors, L. and Corsetti, G. (2002) 'A better plan for loosening the Pact', *Financial Times*, 26 November.

Cann, C. (1998) 'Introduction to fisheries management viewpoint', in T. S. Gray (ed.), *The Policies of Fishing*, Macmillan, Basingstoke.

Cappelletti, M. (1987) 'Is the European ECJ "running wild"?', *European Law Review*, vol. 12.

Carraco, C. and Sinisalco, D. (eds) (1993) *The European Carbon Tax: An economic assessment*, Kluwer.

Cathie, J. (2001) *European Food Aid Policy*, Ashgate, Aldershot.

Cecchini, P. (1988) *The European Challenge 1992: The Benefits of a Single Market*, Wildwood House.

CEPII/EU Commission (1997) Volume 2 on 'Impact on Trade and Investment', *The Single Market Review*, Office of the Official Publications of the European Communities, Luxembourg and Kogan Page, London.

CEPR/European Commission (1997) Volume 3 on 'Impact on Trade and Investment', *The Single Market Review*, Office of the Official Publications of the European Communities, Luxembourg and Kogan Page, London.

Chalmers, D. (1993) 'Free movement of goods within the European Community: an unhealthy addiction to Scotch whisky?', *International and Comparative Law Quarterly*, vol. 42.

Chalmers, D. (1997a) 'Judicial preferences and the community legal order', *Modern Law Review*, vol. 60.

Chalmers, D. (1997b) 'Community trade mark courts: The renaissance of an epistemic community?', in J. Lonbay and A. Biondi (eds), *Remedies for Breach of EC Law*, John Wiley, Chichester.

Chalmers, D. (1998) 'Bureaucratic Europe: From regulating communities to securitising unions', CES, Baltimore.

Chalmers, D. (1999) 'Accounting for "Europe"', *Oxford Journal of Legal Studies*, vol. 19.

Chalmers, D. (2000a) 'Postnationalism and the quest for constitutional substitutes', *Journal of Law and Society*, vol. 27.

Chalmers, D. (2000b) 'The positioning of EU judicial politics within the United Kingdom', *Western European Politics*, vol. 23, no. 4.

Chlomoudis, C. I. and Pallis, A. A. (2002) *European Union Port Policy: the Movement Towards a Long-term Strategy*, Edward Elgar, Cheltenham.

Choi, J.-Y. and Yu, E. S. H. (1984) 'Customs unions under increasing returns to scale', *Economica*, vol. 51.

Christiansen, T. (1997) 'Reconstructing European space: From territorial politics to multilevel governance', in K. Jørgensen (ed.), *Reflective Approaches to European Governance*, Macmillan, Basingstoke.

Cnossen, S. (1987) 'Tax structure developments', in S. Cnossen (ed.), *Tax Coordination in the European Community*, Kluwer, Deventer.

Cnossen, S. (1999) 'What rate structure of Australia's VAT?', *Tax Notes International*, May 24.

Cnossen, S. (2001) 'Tax policy in the European Union', *FinanzArchiv*, vol. 58, no. 4 (58/4), Tables 8 and 9, pp. 466–558.

Cnossen, S. (2002) *Tax Policy in the European Union: a Review of Issues and Options*, Electronic documents, University of Maastricht, METEOR, www.edocs.unimaas.nl/

Cnossen, S. and Bovenberg, L. (1997) 'Company tax harmonisation in the European Union: some further thoughts on the Ruding Committee Report', in M. Blejer and T. Ter-Minassian (eds), *Macroeconomic Dimensions of Public Finance: Essays in Honour of Vito Tanzi*, Routledge, London.

Coase, R. (1937) 'The nature of the firm', *Economica*, vol. 16.

Coase, R. (1960) 'The problem of social costs', *Journal of Law and Economics*, vol. 3, October.

Cobham, D. (1996) 'Causes and effects of the European monetary crises of 1992–93', *Journal of Common Market Studies*, vol. 34.

Cockfield, Lord A. (1994) *The European Union: Creating the Single Market*, Wiley Chancery Law, London.

Coleman, D. (1985) 'Imperfect transmission of policy prices', *European Review of Agricultural Economics*, vol. 12.

Collignon, S. (2003) *The European Republic*, Kogan Page, London.

Comité intergouvernemental créé par la conférence de Messina (1956) *Rapport des chefs de délégation aux Ministres des Affaires Etrangères*, Brussels.

Commission of the European Communities (various issues) *Bulletin of the European Communities Union.* (*EU Bulletin.*)

Commission of the European Communities (various years) *Social Report.*

Commission of the European Communities (various issues and items) *Official Journal of the European Communities.*

Commission of the European Communities (three times a year) *Social Europe.* Also, Supplements.

Commission of the European Communities (annual) *Report on Social Developments.*

Commission of the European Communities (annual) *Employment in Europe.*

Commission of the European Communities (1957) *First General Report on the Activity of the Communities*, Brussels.

Commission of the European Communities (1961) *Memorandum on the General Lines of a Common Transport Policy.*

Commission of the European Communities (1963) *Report of the Fiscal and Financial Committee* (the Neumark Report).

Commission of the European Communities (1968) 'Premières Orientations pour une politique énergétique communautaire', *Communication de la Commission présenté au Conseil le 18 Décembre 1968.*

Commission of the European Communities (1970a) 'Report to the Council and the Commission on the realisation by stages of economic and monetary union in the Community', *EU Bulletin*, Supplement, no. 11 (the Werner Report).

Commission of the European Communities (1970b) *Corporation Tax and Income Tax in the European Communities* (the van den Tempel Report).

Commission of the European Communities (1970c) *Industrial Policy in the Community*, Office of Official Publications of the European Communities.

Commission of the European Communities (1972) *First Report on Competition Policy.*

Commission of the European Communities (1975) *Social Harmonization – Inland Waterways*, COM (75) 465 final.

Commission of the European Communities (1976) *Fifth Report on Competition – EEC.*

Commission of the European Communities (1977) *Report of the Study Group on the Role of Public Finance in European Integration*, 2 vols (the MacDougall Report).

Commission of the European Communities (1979a) *Eighth Report on Competition Policy.*

Commission of the European Communities (1979b) *Social Harmonization – Inland Waterways*, COM (79) 363 final.

Commission of the European Communities (1979c) *Report of Committee of Inquiry on Public Finance in the Community* (the MacDougall Report), Brussels.

Commission of the European Communities (1983) *Thirteenth Report on Competition Policy.*

Commission of the European Communities (1984) *Civil Aviation Memorandum No. 2: Progress towards the development of a Community air transport policy*, COM (84) 72.

Commission of the European Communities (1985a) *Completing the Internal Market* (White Paper from the EC Commission to the EC Council) – COM (85) 310.

Commission of the European Communities (1985b) *Fourteenth Report on Competition Policy.*

Commission of the European Communities (1985c) *Progress Towards a Common Transport Policy, Maritime Transport*, COM (85) 90 final.

Commission of the European Communities (1987a) *Sixteenth Report on Competition Policy.*

Commission of the European Communities (1987b) *European Environmental Policy*, Economic and Social Committee and Consultative Assembly.

Commission of the European Communities (1988a) *Research on the Cost of Non-Europe: Basic findings*, 16 vols (the Cecchini Report).

Commission of the European Communities (1988b) *Disharmonies in US and EC Agricultural Policy Measures.*

Commission of the European Communities (1989a) *Guide to the Reform of the Community's Structural Funds.*

Commission of the European Communities (1989b) *Council Resolution on Trans-European Networks*, COM (89) 643 final.

Commission of the European Communities (1990a) 'One market, one money: an evaluation of the potential benefits and costs of forming an economic and monetary union', *European Economy.*

Commission of the European Communities (1990b) *Second Survey of State Aids*, Office for Official Publications of the European Community.

Commission of the European Communities (1991a) *Twentieth Report on Competition Policy.*

Commission of the European Communities (1991b) *Opening up the Internal Market.*

Commission of the European Communities (1991c) *Amended Proposal for a Council Regulation (EEC) Establishing a Community Ship Register and Providing for the Flying of the Flag by Sea-going Vessels* (presented by the Commission pursuant to article 149(3) of the EEC Treaty, COM (91) 54/I final.

Commission of the European Communities (1992a) *Transport and the Environment – Towards sustainable mobility*, COM (92) 80.

Commission of the European Communities (1992b) *The Future Development of the Common Transport Policy: a Global Approach to the Construction of a Community Framework for Sustainable Mobility*, COM (92) 494 final.

Commission of the European Communities (1993) 'Stable money: sound finances', *European Economy*, no. 53.

Commission of the European Communities (1994a) *The European Report on Science and Technology Indicators*, DG XII.

Commission of the European Communities (1994b) 'EC agriculture policy for the 21st century', *European Economy*, Reports and Studies, no. 4.

Commission of the European Communities (1994c) *Towards a New Asia Strategy* COM (94) 314 final.

Commission of the European Union (1995a) *Citizens Network*, COM (95) 601.

Commission of the European Union (1995b) *High Speed Europe.*

Commission of the European Union (1995c) An Energy Policy for the European Union – White Paper of the European Commission COM (95) 682.

Commission of the European Union (1995d) *White Paper – Teaching and Learning: Towards the Learning Society*, COM (95) 590 final.

Commission of the European Union (1996a) *Energy for the Future. Renewable Sources of Energy – Green Paper for a Community Strategy*, COM (96) 576.

Commission of the European Union (1996b) *Report from the Commission on the Application of the Community Rules on Aid to the Coal Industry in 1994*, COM (96) 575.

Commission of the European Union (1996c) *Services of General Interest in Europe*, COM (96) 443.

Commission of the European Union (1996d) *First Report on Economic and Social Cohesion.*

Commission of the European Union (1996e) *First Cohesion Report*, COM (96) final.

Commission of the European Union (1996f) 'The 1996 single market review', *Commission Staff Working Paper*, SEC (96) 2378.

Commission of the European Union (1996g) 'Green paper on relations between the European Union and the ACP countries on the eve of the 21st century', CEU/DG VIII.

Commission of the European Union (1996h) *XXVth Report on Competition Policy 1995*, CEU.

Commission of the European Union (1996i) *Impact of the Third Package of Air Transport Liberalization Measures*, COM (96) 514.

Commission of the European Union (1996j) *The First Action Plan for Innovation in Europe*, COM (96) 589.

Commission of the European Union (1996k) *European Environmental Legislation*, Volumes 1–7, CEU DG XI.

Commission of the European Union (1997a) *Fifth Survey on State Aid in the European Union in the Manufacturing and Certain Other Sectors*, COM (97) 170.

Commission of the European Union (1997b) *Agenda 2000: For A Stronger and Wider Union*, Brussels, July.

Commission of the European Union (1997c) *XXVIth Report on Competition Policy 1996.*

Commission of the European Union (1997d) *Green Paper on Sea-ports and Maritime Infrastructure*, COM (97) 678 final.

Commission of the European Union (1997e) 'Notice on the definition of the relevant market for the purposes of Community competition law', OJ C372.

Commission of the European Union (1997f) 'Notice on agreements of minor importance', OJ C372.

Commission of the European Union (1997g) *The Single Market Review* (39 volumes), Luxembourg and Kogan Page, London.

Commission of the European Union (1997h) *Action Plan for the Single Market* CSE (97) 1 final, 4 June.

Commission of the European Union (1998a) *Proposed Regulations and Explanatory Memorandum Covering the Reform of the Structural Funds 2000–2006*, DG XVI.

Commission of the European Union (1998b) *Communication from the Commission to the Council and the European Parliament on Implementation and Impact of Directive 91/440/EEC on the Development of Community Railways and Access Rights for Rail Freight*, COM (98) 202 final.

Commission of the European Union (1998c) 'Financing the European Union: Commission Report on the operation of the Own Resources system', DG Budget, **www.europa.eu.int/comm/budget/ agenda2000reports_en.htm**

Commission of the European Union (1998d) *Risk Capital: A Key to Job Creation in the European Union*, SEC (1998) 552.

Commission of the European Union (1999a) *Sixteenth Annual Report on the Application of Community Law 1998*, COM (99) 301 final.

Commission of the European Union (1999b) *Mutual Recognition in the Context of the Follow-Up to the Action Plan for the Single Market*, COM (99).

Commission of the European Union (1999c) *Sixth Periodic Report on the Social and Economic Situation in the Regions in the Community*, Luxembourg.

Commission of the European Union (1999d) *The Amsterdam Treaty: a Comprehensive Guide.*

Commission of the European Union (1999e) 'Regulation 2790/1999 on the application of Article 81(3) of the Treaty to categories of vertical agreements and concerted practices', *OJ* L336.

Commission of the European Union (1999f) 'White Paper on modernisation of the rules implementing articles 85 and 86 of the EC Treaty', *OJ* C132.

Commission of the European Union (1999g) *Institutional Implications of Enlargement.*

Commission of the European Union (2000a) *Agenda 2000 – Setting the Scene for Reform,* **www.europa.eu.int/comm/agriculture/publi/ review98/08_09_ en.pdf.**

Commission of the European Union (2000b) *Working Party on the Future of the European Court System*, Luxembourg.

Commission of the European Union (2000c) *Structural Actions 2000–2006: Commentary and Regulations.*

Commission of the European Union (2000d) *The Community Budget: the Facts in Figures*, SEC (2000) 1200, Luexmbourg.

Commission of the European Union (2000e) *Second Progress Report on Economic and Social Cohesion: Unity, Solidarity, Diversity for Europe, Its People and Its Territory.*

Commission of the European Union (2000f) 'Guidelines on Vertical Restraints', *OJ* C 291, 13.10.2000, p. 1.

Commission of the European Union (2000g) 'The application of Article 81(3) of the Treaty to categories of specialisation agreements', Regulation No 2658/2000 of 29 November 2000, *OJ L 304,* 05.12.2000, p. 3.

Commission of the European Union (2000h) 'The application of Article 81(3) of the Treaty to categories of research and development agreements', Regulation No 2658/2000 of 29 November 2000, *OJ L 304,* 05.12.2000, p. 7.

Commission of the European Union (2000i) *The European Community's Development Policy*, COM (2000) 212, 26 April 2000.

Commission of the European Union (2000j) 'The European Community's development policy', Statement by the Council and Commission, 10 November.

Commission of the European Union (2001a) 'Promoting core labour standards and improving social governance in the context of globalisation', COM (2001) 416.

Commission of the European Union (2001b) 'Europe and Asia: a strategic framework for enhanced partnerships', COM (2001) 496 final.

Commission of the European Union (2001c) *Spatial Impacts of Community Policies and Costs of Non-coordination*, Study for DG-Regional Policy.

Commission of the European Union (2001d) *Electricity Liberalization Indicators in Europe*, October.

Commission of the European Union (2001e) *European Transport Policy for 2010: Time to Decide,* White Paper.

Commission of the European Union (2001f) *Reinforcing quality services in seaports: a key for European Transport Policy*, COM (2001) 35.

Commission of the European Union (2001g) *Company Taxation and the Internal Market*, COM (2001) 582 final.

Commission of the European Union (2001h) Green Paper Towards a European strategy for Security of Energy Supply. These are two documents, one of which is technical.

Commission of the European Union (2001i) *XXXth Report on Competition Policy 2000.*

Commission of the European Union (2001j) *European Economy*, Supplement A, Economic Trends, No 12 – December 2001.

Commission of the European Union (2001k) 'Commission notice on agreements of minor importance which do not appreciably restrict competition under Article 81(1) of the Treaty establishing the European Community (de minimis)', *OJ C 368,* 22.12.2001.

Commission of the European Union (2001l) 'Commission notice on the applicability of Article 81 to horizontal co-operation agreements', *OJ C 3*, 06.01.2001, p. 2.

Commission of the European Union (2002a) 'Communication from the Commission to the Council and European Parliament', ECFIN/581/02-EN rev. 3, November 21.

Commission of the European Union (2002b) 'Evaluation of the 2002 pre-accession economic programmes of candidate countries', Enlargement Papers no. 14, DG EcFin.

Commission of the European Union (2002c) *First Progress Report on Economic and Social Cohesion*, COM (2002) 46 final.

Commission of the European Union (2002d) *31st Report on Competition Policy 2001*, Luxembourg.

Commission of the European Union (2002e) 'Tableau de bord des aides d'état', COM (2002) 242 final.

Commission of the European Union (2002f) *Towards a European Research Area, Science, Technology and Innovation: Key Figures 2002*, Luxembourg.

Commission of the European Union (2002g) 'The EU Economy 2002 Review', Statistical Annexe, *European Economy*, No. 6, www.europa.eu.int/comm/economy_finance/index_en.htm

Commission of the European Union (2002h) *Financial Report 2001*, DG Budget, www.europa.eu.int/comm/budget/index_en.htm

Commission of the European Union (2002i) *Excise Duty Tables*, REF 1.015, August, DG Taxation and Customs Union, www.europa.eu.int/comm/taxation_customs/index_en.htm

Commission of the European Union (2002j) *VAT Rates Applied in the Member States of the EU*, DOC/2908/2002-EN, Situation at 1st May, DG Taxation and Customs Union, www.europa.eu.int/comm/taxation_customs/index_en.htm

Commission of the European Union (2002k) *Activities of the EU in 2000 in the Tax Field*, DOC (2003) 2101, 27 January, DG Taxation and Customs Union, www.europa.eu.int/comm/taxation_customs/index_en.htm

Commission of the European Union (2002l) 'Commission notice on immunity from fines and reduction fines in cartel cases', *OJ C 45*, 19.02.2002, pp. 3–5.

Commission of the European Union (2003a) 'Evolution of the performance of network industries providing services of general interest', Working Paper of Mr Bolkestein, Mr Solbes and Mr Byrne.

Commission of the European Union (2003b) 'Commission Opinion on the ECB recommendation on and amendments to Article 10.2 of the Statute of the ESCB', Brussels, 19 February.

Commission of the European Union (2003c) *Second Progress Report on Economic and Social Cohesion*, COM (2003) 34 final, Brussels.

Commission of the European Union (2003d) *Eurobarometer*, no. 5, Public Opinion Analysis, www.europa.eu.int/comm/public_opinion/

Commission of the European Union (2003e) 'Proposal for a Council regulation on the control of concentrations between undertaking', *OJ L 20*, 28.01.2003, pp. 4–57.

Conant, L. (2001) 'Europeanization and the courts: Variable patterns of adaptation among national judiciaries', in J. Caparaso, M. Cowles and T. Risse (eds), *Transforming Europe: Europeanization and Domestic Structural Change*, Cornell University Press, Ithaca.

Conant, L. (2002) *Justice Contained: Law and Politics in the European Union*, Cornell University Press, Ithaca.

Cooper, C. A. and Massell, B. F. (1965a) 'A new look at customs union theory', *Economic Journal*, vol. 75.

Cooper, C. A. and Massell, B. F. (1965b) 'Towards a general theory of customs unions in developing countries', *Journal of Political Economy*, vol. 73.

Corden, W. M. (1972a) 'Economies of scale and customs union theory', *Journal of Political Economy*, vol. 80.

Corden, W. M. (1972b) 'Monetary integration', *Essays in International Finance*, no. 93, Princeton University.

Corden, W. M. (1977) *Inflation, Exchange Rates and the World Economy*, Oxford University Press.

Cosgrove-Sacks, C. (ed.) (1999) *The European Union and Developing Countries: The Challenges of Globalization*, Macmillan, Basingstoke.

Cosgrove-Sacks, C. and Scappuci, G. (1999) *The European Union and Developing Countries: the Challenges of Globalisation*, Macmillan, Basingstoke.

Council of the European Communities (various years) *Review of the Council's Work*.

Court of First Instance (2002) *Statistics of the Judicial Activity of the Court of First Instance*, Luxembourg.

Cox, A., Healey, J. and Koning, A. (1997) *How European Aid Works*, Overseas Development Institute, London.

Cox, A. and Chapman, J. (2000) *The European Community External Cooperation Programmes*, European Commission.

Craig, P. (1997) 'Democracy and rule-making within the EC: An empirical and normative assessment', *European Law Journal*, vol. 3.

Craig, P. (2001) 'The jurisprudence of the Community courts reconsidered', in G. de Búrca and J. Weiler, *The European Court of Justice*, Hart, Oxford.

Crouch, C. and Marquand, D. (1992) *Towards Greater Europe: A continent without an Iron Curtain*, Basil Blackwell, Oxford.

Cruickshank, A. and Walker, W. (1981) 'Energy research development and demonstration policy in the European Communities', *Journal of Common Market Studies*, vol. 20, no. 1.

Culem, C. G. (1988) 'The locational determinants of direct investment among industrialised countries', *European Economic Review*, vol. 32.

Curzon Price, V. (1974) *The Essentials of Economic Integration*, Macmillan, Basingstoke.

Cuthbertson, K. *et al.* (1980) 'Modelling and forecasting the capital account of the balance of payments: a critique of the "Reduced Form Approach"', *National Institute Discussion Paper*, no. 37.

Daintith, T. and Hancher, K. (eds.) (1986) *Energy Strategy in Europe: the Legal Framework*, de Gruyter.

Dam, K. W. (1970) *The GATT: Law and international economic organization*, Chicago University Press.

Dashwood, A. and Johnston, A. (eds) (2001) *The Future of the European Judicial System*, Hart, Oxford.

De Búrca, G. (1992) 'Giving effect to European Community directives', *Modern Law Review*, vol. 55.

De Grauwe, P. (1975) 'Conditions for monetary integration: a geometric interpretation', *Weltwirtschaftliches Archiv*, vol. 111.

De la Fuente, A. and Domenesh, R. (2001) 'The redistributive effects of the EU budget', *Journal of Common Market Studies*, vol. 39, no. 2.

De la Mare, T. (1999) 'Article 177 in social and political perspective', in P. Craig and R. Dehousse (1998) *op. cit.*

Deaton, A. S. and Muellbauer, J. (1980) 'An almost ideal demand system', *American Economic Review*, vol. 70.

Decressin, J. and Fatás, A. (1995) 'Regional labour market dynamics in Europe', *European Economic Review*, vol. 39.

DEFRA (2002) *Directing the Flow: Priorities for Future Water Policy*, UK Department for the Environment, Food and Rural Affairs, November.

Dehousse, R. (1998) *The European Court of Justice*, Basingstoke, Macmillan.

Dehousse, R. and Weiler, J. (1990) 'The legal dimension', in W. Wallace (ed.), *The Dynamics of European Integration*, RIIA, London.

Denison, E. F. (1974) *Accounting for United States Economic Growth 1929–1969*, Brookings Institution.

Devereux, M. P. and Griffith, R. (2001) 'Summary of the Devereux and Griffith economic model and measures of effective tax rates', Annex A of European Commission 2001.

Devroe, W. (1997) 'Privatization and Community law: neutrality versus policy', *Common Market Law Review*, vol. 34.

Dezalay, Y. (1992) *Marchands de droit. La réstructuration de l'ordre juridique internationale par les multinationals du droit*, Fayard, Paris.

Domenesh, R., Maudes, A. and Varela, J. (2001) 'Fiscal flows in Europe: the redistributive effects of the EU budget', *Weltwirtschaftliches Archiv*, vol. 136, no. 4.

Dosser, D. (1973) *British Taxation and the Common Market*, Knight, London.

Downs, A. (1957) *An Economic Theory of Democracy*, New York.

Doyle, C. and Siner, M. (1999) 'Introduction: Europe's network industries: towards competition', in Lars Bergmann *et al.*, *A European Market for Electricity?*, CEPR, London; SNS, Stockholm.

Dunford, M. (1996) 'Disparities in employment, productivity and output in the EU: the roles of labour market governance and welfare regimes', *Regional Studies*, vol. 30.

Dunford, M. (2000) 'Catching up or falling behind? Economic performance and regional trajectories in the new Europe', *Economic Geography*, vol. 76, no. 2.

Dunning, J. H. (1977) 'Trade, location of economic activity and the MNE: a search for an eclectic approach', in B. Ohlin *et al.* (eds), *The International Allocation of Economic Activity*, Macmillan, Basingstoke.

ECA (see European Court of Auditors).

ECB (2001) *The Monetary Policy of the ECB*, Frankfurt, August.

ECB (2002) *Convergence Report 2002*, Frankfurt, May.

ECB (2003) 'Recommendation on an amendment to Article 10.2 of the Statute of the ECB', Frankfurt, 3 February.

EFTA Secretariat (1969) *The Effects of the EFTA on the Economies of Member States*.

EFTA Secretariat (1972) *The Trade Effects of the EFTA and the EEC 1959–1967*.

Ehlermann, C.-D. (1995) 'State aids under European Community competition law', 1994 *Annual Proceedings of the Fordham Corporate Law Institute*, vol. 21.

El-Agraa, A. M. (1979a) 'Common markets in developing countries', in J. K. Bowers (ed.), *Inflation, Development and Integration: Essays in honour of A. J. Brown*, Leeds University Press.

El-Agraa, A. M. (1979b) 'On tariff bargaining', *Bulletin of Economic Research*, vol. 31.

El-Agraa, A. M. (1979c) 'On optimum tariffs, retaliation and international cooperation', *Bulletin of Economic Research*, vol. 31.

El-Agraa, A. M. (1981) 'Tariff bargaining: a correction', *Bulletin of Economic Research*, vol. 33.

El-Agraa, A. M. (ed.) (1983a) *Britain within the European Community: The Way Forward*, Macmillan, Basingstoke.

El-Agraa, A. M. (1983b) *The Theory of International Trade*, Croom Helm, Beckenham.

El-Agraa, A. M. (1984a) 'Is membership of the EEC a disaster for the UK?', *Applied Economics*, vol. 17, no. 1.

El-Agraa, A. M. (1984b) *Trade Theory and Policy: Some Topical Issues*, Macmillan, Basingstoke.

El-Agraa, A. M. (1988a) *Japan's Trade Frictions: Realities or Misconceptions?*, Macmillan and St Martin's, New York.

El-Agraa, A. M. (ed.) (1988b) *International Economic Integration*, second edition, Macmillan and St Martin's, New York.

El-Agraa, A. M. (1989a) *The Theory and Measurement of International Economic Integration*, Macmillan and St Martin's, New York.

El-Agraa, A. M. (1989b) *International Trade*, Macmillan and St Martin's, New York.

El-Agraa, A. M. (1997) *Economic Integration Worldwide*, Macmillan and St Martin's, New York.

El-Agraa, A. M. (1999) *Regional Integration: Experience, Theory and Measurement*, Macmillan, London; Barnes and Noble, New York.

El-Agraa, A. M. (2002a) 'The UTR versus CU formation analysis and Article XXIV', *Applied Economics Letters*, no. 9.

El-Agraa, A. M. (ed.) (2002b) *The euro and Britain: Implications of Moving into the EMU*, Pearson Education, Financial Times Prentice Hall, London.

El-Agraa, A. M. (2004) 'The enigma of African integration', *Journal of Economic Integration*, vol. 19, no. 1. A simpler version can be found in 'La integración regional en Africa: un intendo de análisis' (Understanding African integration), *Tiempo De Paz*, vol. 67, November 2002.

El-Agraa, A. M. and Hu, Y.-S. (1984) 'National versus supranational interests and the problem of establishing an effective EU energy policy', *Journal of Common Market Studies*, vol. 22.

El-Agraa, A. M. and Jones, A. J. (1981) *The Theory of Customs Unions*, Philip Allan.

El-Agraa, A. M. and Jones, A. J. (2000a) 'UTR vs CU formation: the missing CET', *Journal of Economic Integration*, vol. 15, no. 2.

El-Agraa, A. M. and Jones, A. J. (2000b) 'On "CU can dominate UTR"', *Applied Economics Letters*, no. 7.

Eleftheriadis, P. (1998) 'Begging the constitutional question', *Journal of Common Market Studies*, vol. 36.

Emerson, M. (1988) 'The economics of 1992', *European Economy*, no. 35.

Emerson, M., Anjean, M., Catinat, M., Goybet, P. and Jaquemin, A. (1988) *The Economics of 1992: The EC Commission's assessment of the economic effects of completing the internal market*, Oxford University Press, Oxford.

Emerson, M., Gros, D., Italianer, A., Pisani-Ferry, J. and Reichenbach, H. (1991) *One Market, One Money: An Evaluation of the Potential Benefits and Costs of Forming an Economic and Monetary Union*, Oxford University Press, Oxford.

EMI (1998) *Convergence Report*, Frankfurt, March.

Erdmenger, J. and Stasinopoulos, D. (1988) 'The shipping policy of the European Community', *Journal of Transport Economics and Policy*, vol. 22.

European Council (1962) 'First regulation implementing Articles 85 and 86 of the Treaty', Regulation No. 17, OJ P 013, 21.02.1962, pp. 0204–0211.

European Council (1988) 'Brussels European Council', *Bulletin of the European Communities*, no. 2.

European Council (1989) 'Regulation 4064/89 on the control of concentrations between undertakings', OJ L395.

European Council (1992a) *Run-up to 2000: Declaration of the Council of 18 November*, Collection of Council Statements on Development Cooperation, vol. I, 05/92.

European Council (1992b) 'Edinburgh European Council', *Bulletin of the European Union*, no. 7.

European Council (1997) 'Regulation 1310/97 amending Regulation 4064/89 on the control of concentrations between undertakings', OJ L40.

European Council (1998) 'Regulation 994/98 on the application of Articles 92 and 93 of the Treaty to certain categories of horizontal state aid', *OJ* L142.

European Council (1999a) 'Regulation 659/1999 laying down detailed rules for the application of Article 93 of the EC Treaty', *OJ* L83.

European Council (1999b) 'Special Berlin Council 24–25 March, Conclusions of the Presidency', *Bulletin of the European Union*, no. 3.

European Council (2000) 'Council Decision of 29 September 2000 on the system of the European Communities Own Resources', *OJ L*, no. 253, 7 October.

European Council (2002) *Presidency Conclusions: Copenhagen European Council*, 12–13 December.

European Council (2003) 'The implementation of the rules on competition laid down in Articles 81 and 82 of the Treaty', Regulation No 1/2003 of 16 December 2002, *OJ L 1*, 04.01.2003, pp. 1–25.

European Court of Auditors (various) Annual Report Concerning the Financial Year, *OJ*, www.eca.eu.int/EN/reports_opinions.htm

European Court of Auditors (2001) Annual Report concerning the financial year 2000, *Official Journal C 359*, 15 December, www.eca.eu.int/EN/reports_opinions.htm

European Court of Auditors (2002) Annual Report concerning the financial year 2001, *Official Journal C 295*, 28 November, www.eca.eu.int/EN/reports_opinions.htm

European Court of Justice (1983) Commission of the European Communities v United Kingdom of Great Britain and Northern Ireland. Tax agreements applying to wine. *Case 170/78 European Court Reports*, p. 02265.

European Court of Justice (1996) *Notes for Guidance on References by National Courts*, Proceedings of the Court 34/96, Luxembourg.

European Court of Justice (2002) *Statistics of the Judicial Activity of the Court of Justice*, Luxembourg.

European Economy (1996) 'Economic evaluation of the internal market', *Reports and Studies*, no. 4.

European Environmental Agency (2000) *Environmental Taxes: Recent Developments in Tools for Integration*.

European Parliament (2001a) Task Force, Statistical Annex, November, Enlargement, www.europarl.eu.int./enlargement_new/statistics/default_en.htm

European Parliament (2001b) 'Tax coordination in the EU – the latest position', *Working Paper, ECON 128*, DG Research, www4.europa.eu.int/estudies/internet/workingpapers/econ/pdf/128_2n.pdf

European Research Group (1997) *The Legal Agenda for a Free Europe*, London.

Eurostat (annual) Basic Statistics of the Community.

Eurostat (annual) *Statistical Review*.

Eurostat (2001) *European Union Foreign Direct Investment Yearbook 2001*, Luxembourg.

Fatás, A. (1998) 'Does EMU need a fiscal federation?', *Economic Policy*, vol. 26, April.

Fatás, A. and Mihov, I. (2001) 'Government size and automatic stabilisers: international and intranational evidence', *Journal of International Economics*, vol. 55, no. 1.

Feldstein, M. B. (1997) 'The political economy of the European Economic and Monetary Union: political sources of an economic liability', *Journal of Economic Perspectives*, vol. 11.

Feldstein, M. B. (2002) 'The role of discretionary policy in a low interest rate environment', *NBER Working Paper 9203*.

Fielder, N. (1997) *Western European Integration in the 1980s: the Origins of the Single Market*, Peter Lang, Bern.

Finon, D. and Surrey, J. (1996) 'Does energy policy have a future in the European Union?', in F. McGowan, *Energy Policy in a Changing Environment*, Physica Verlag.

Fischer, P. A. (1999) *On the Economics of Immobility*, Verlag Paul Haupt.

Fitzgerald, J., Johnston, J. and Williams, J. (1988) 'An analysis of cross-border shopping', *Paper No. 137*, Economic and Social Research Institute, Dublin.

Fitzpatrick, P. (1997) 'New Europe and old stories: Mythology and legality in the EU', in P. Fitzpatrick and J. Bergeron (eds), *Europe's Other: European Law between Modernity and Postmodernity*, Ashgate, Aldershot.

Fleming, J. M. (1971) 'On exchange rate unification', *Economic Journal*, vol. 81.

Forrester, I. and Norall, C. (1984) 'The laicization of Community: self-help and the rule of reason: how competition law is and could be applied', *Common Market Law Review*, vol. 22.

Frankel, J. A. (1997) *Regional Trading Blocs in the World Trading System*, Institute for International Economics, Washington DC.

Frankel, J. A. and Rose, A. (2002) 'An estimate of the effect of common currencies on trade and income', *Quarterly Journal of Economics*, vol. 117, no. 2.

Friedman, M. (1975) *Unemployment versus Inflation? An Evaluation of the Philips Curve*, Institute of International Affairs, London.

Frohberg, K. and Weber, G. (2001) 'Ein ausblick in die zeit nach vollzogener ost-erweiterung', Institute für Agrarentwickelung in Mittel-und Osteuropa, Halle, July, cited in Swinnen, 2000.

Fujita, M. and Thisse, J.-F. (1996) 'Economics of agglomeration', *Journal of the Japanese and International Economies*, vol. 10.

Gardner, B. L. (1992) 'Changing economic perspectives on the farm problem', *Journal of Economic Literature*, vol. 30, no. 1.

Garrett, G. (1992) 'International cooperation and institutional choice: the European Community's internal market', *International Organization*, vol. 46.

Garrett, G. (1995) 'The politics of legal integration', *International Organization*, vol. 49.

Garrett, G. and Weingast, B. (1993) 'Ideas, interests and institutions: Constructing the European internal market', in J. Goldstein and R. Keohane (eds), *Ideas and Foreign Policy*, Cornell University Press, Ithaca.

Garrett, G., Keleman, R. and Schulz, H. (1998) 'The European ECJ, national governments and legal integration in the EU', *International Organization*, vol. 52.

Garrett, G. and Tsebelis, G. (1999) 'The institutional foundations of supranationalism'. at **www.sscnet.ucla.edu/polisci/faculty/tsebelis/ workpaper.html**

GATT (1994) *Market Access for Goods and Services: Overview of the Results*, Geneva.

Geddes, A. (1995) 'Immigrant and ethnic minorities and the EU's "Democratic Deficit"', *Journal of Common Market Studies*, vol. 33.

Gehrels, F. (1956–7) 'Customs unions from a single country viewpoint', *Review of Economic Studies*, vol. 24.

Gerber, D. J. (1998) *Law and Competition in Twentieth Century Europe: Protecting Prometheus*, Clarendon, Oxford.

Geroski, P. and Jacquemin, A. (1989) 'Industrial change, barriers to mobility and European industrial policy', in A. Jacquemin and A. Sapir (eds), *The European Internal Market: Trade and Competition*, Oxford University Press, Oxford.

Giannetti, M., Guiso, L., Jappelli, T. Padula, M. and Pagano, M. (2002) 'Financial market integration, corporate financing and economic growth', *European Commission Economic Paper No. 179*, Brussels.

Gibson, J. and Caldeira, G. (1995) 'The legitimacy of transnational legal institutions: compliance, support and the European Court of Justice', *American Journal of Political Science*, vol. 39 (2): 459–98.

Gibson, J. and Caldeira, G. (1998) 'Changes in the legitimacy of the European ECJ: A post-Maastricht analysis', *British Journal of Political Science*, vol. 28.

Gill, S. and Law, D. (1988) *The Global Political Economy: Perspectives, Problems and Policies*, Johns Hopkins University Press, Baltimore.

Glachant, J.-M. (1998) 'England's wholesale electricity market: could this hybrid institutional arrangement be transposed to the European Union?', *Utilities Policy*, vol. 7.

Golub, J. (1996a) 'The politics of judicial discretion: Rethinking the interaction between national courts and the ECJ', *West European Politics*, vol. 19, 360.

Golub, J. (1996b) 'Sovereignty and Subsidiarity in EU environmental policy', *European University Institute Working Paper*, RSC no. 96/2.

Gormley, L. (1994) 'Reasoning renounced? The remarkable judgment in Reck and Mithouard', *European Business Law Review*, vol. 63.

Gorter, J. and de Mooij, R. (2001) *Capital Income Taxation in Europe: Trends and Trade-Offs*, SDU Utigevers, The Hague.

Goulder, L. (1997) 'Environmental taxation and the "double dividend": a reader's guide', in L. Bovenberg and S. Cnossen (1997).

Goyder, D. (1999) *EC Competition Law*, Clarendon, Oxford.

Granovetter, M. (1985) 'Economic action and social structure: The problem of embeddedness', *American Journal of Sociology*, vol. 91.

Green, R. J. (2001) 'Markets for electricity in Europe', *Oxford Review of Economic Policy*, vol. 17, no. 3.

Green, R. J. and Newbery, D. M. (1992) 'Competition in the British electricity spot market', *Journal of Political Economy*, vol. 100, no. 5.

Greenaway, D. and Hine, R. (1991) 'Intra-industry specialisation, trade expansion and adjustment in the European economic space', *Journal of Common Maket Studies*, vol. 29. no. 6,

Grilli, E. (1993) *The European Community and the Developing Countries*, Cambridge University Press.

Gross, L. (1984) 'States as organs of international law and the problem of autointerpretation', in L. Gross (ed.), *Essays on International Law and Organisation*, Martinus Nijhoff.

Grossman, G. M. and Helpman, E. (1991) 'Trade, knowledge spillovers and growth', *European Economic Review*, vol. 35.

Grubel, H. G. and Lloyd, P. (1975) *Intra-industry Trade: the Theory and Measurement of International Trade in Differentiated Products*, Macmillan, Basingstoke.

Guruswamy, I. D., Papps, I. and Storey, D. (1983) 'The development and impact of an EC directive: the control of discharges of mercury to the aquatic environment', *Journal of Common Market Studies*, vol. 22, no. 1.

Guzzetti, L. (1995) *A Brief History of European Union Research Policy*, Commission of the European Union, DG XII (Science, Research, Development).

Haas, E. B. (1958 and 1968) *The Uniting of Europe*, Stevens.

Haberler, G. (1964) 'Integration and growth in the world economy in historical perspective', *American Economic Review*, vol. 54.

Habermas, J. (1996) *Between Facts and Norms*, Polity/Cambridge University Press, Cambridge.

Haigh, N. (1989) EEC *Environmental Policy and Britain*, Longman, Harlow, second edition.

Hancher, L. (1997) 'Slow and not so sure: Europe's long march to electricity market liberalization,' *Electricity Journal*, vol. 10, no. 9 (pp. 92–101).

Hancher, L., Ottervanger, T. and Slot, P.-J. (1999) *EC state aids*, Sweet & Maxwell, London.

Harding, C. (1992) 'Who goes to court in Europe? An analysis of litigation against the European Community', *European Law Review*, vol. 17.

Harlow, C. (1996) 'Francovich and the disobedient state', *European Law Journal*, vol. 2.

Hartley, T. (1996) 'The European Court, judicial objectivity and the constitution of the EU', *Law Quarterly Review*, vol. 112.

Hartley, T. (1999) *Constitutional Problems of the EU*, Hart, Oxford.

Hayek, F. A. (1945) 'The Use of Knowledge in Society', *American Economic Review*, vol. 35, no. 4.

Hazlewood, A. (1967) *African Integration and Disintegration*, Oxford University Press.

Hazlewood, A. (1975) *Economic Integration: the East African Experience*, Heinemann, Oxford.

Hedemann-Robinson, M. (1996) 'Third country nationals, EU citizenship, and free movement of persons: a time for bridges rather than divisions', *Yearbook of European Law*, vol. 16.

Heitger, B. and Stehn, J. (1990) 'Japanese direct investment in the EC: response to the internal market 1993?', *Journal of Common Market Studies*, vol. 29.

Helm, D. R. and McGowan, F. (1989) 'Electricity supply in Europe: lessons for the UK', in D. R. Helm, J. A. Kay and D. J. Thompson (eds), *The Market for Energy*, Oxford University Press.

Helm, D. R., Kay, J. A. and Thompson, D. J. (eds) (1989) *The Market for Energy*, Oxford University Press.

Hemming, R. and Kay, J. (1981) 'The United Kingdom', in H. Aaron (ed.), *The Value Added Tax: Lessons from Europe*, Brookings Institution, Washington DC.

Henrichsmeyer, W. and Witzke, H.-P. (1994) *Agrarpolitik*, Band 2 Bewertung Willensbildung, UTB für Wissenschaft, Eugen Ulmer Verlag, Stuttgart.

Hervey, T. (1995) 'Migrant workers and their families in the EU: the pervasive market ideology of Community law', in J. Shaw and G. More (eds), *New Legal Dynamics of EU*, Clarendon, Oxford.

Hill, C. (1997) *Convergence, Divergence and Dialectics: National Foreign Policies and the CFSP*, RSC 97/66, EUI, Florence.

Hoekman, B. and Konan, D. (1999) *Deep Integration, Non-discrimination and Euro–Mediterranean Free Trade*, Development Research Group, World Bank, Washington DC.

Hofheinz, P. and Mitchener, B. (18 March 2002) 'EU states agree to open energy markets by 2004', *Wall Street Journal Europe*.

Holden, M. (1994) *The Common Fisheries Policy*, Fishing Book News, Oxford.

House of Lords (1992) *Enlargement of the Community*, Select Committee on the European Communities, Session 1991–1992, 10th Report, HL55, HMSO.

Huizinga, H. (1994) 'International interest withholding taxation: prospects for a common European policy', *International Tax and Public Finance*, vol. 1.

IFO (1990) *An Empirical Assessment of the Factors Shaping Regional Competitiveness in Problem Regions*, study carried out for the EC Commission.

International Energy Agency (2001) *Oil Supply Security: The Emergency Response Potential of IEA Countries in 2002*, Paris.

International Energy Agency (2002) *Energy Balances of OECD Countries, 1999–2000*, Paris.

International Monetary Fund (2001) *Government Financial Statistical Yearbook 2001*, Washington, DC.

Jacqué, J-P. and Weiler, J. (1990) 'On the road to EU – A new judicial architecture: An agenda for the intergovernmental conference', *Common Market Law Review*, vol. 27.

Jeppson, T. (2002) *Environmental Regulation in a Federal System: Framing Environmental Policy in the EU*, Edward Elgar, Cheltenham.

Joerges, C. (1996) 'Taking the law seriously: On political science and the role of law in the integration process', *European Law Journal*, vol. 2.

Joerges, C., Mény, Y. and Weiler, J. H. H. (eds) (2000) *What Kind of Constitution for What Kind of Polity? Responses to Joschka Fischer*, Robert Schuman Centre for Advanced Studies, European University Institute and Harvard Law School, **www.iue.it/RSC/symposium**

Johansson, B. K. Å. *et al.* (2002) *Stabilisation Policy in the Monetary Union – a Summary of the Report*, Commission on Stabilisation Policy for Full Employment in the Event of Sweden Joining the Monetary Union, Stockholm.

Johnson, H. G. (1965a) 'Optimal trade intervention in the presence of domestic distortions', in R. E. Baldwin *et al.* (eds), *Trade, Growth and the Balance of Payments*, North-Holland.

Johnson, H. G. (1965b) 'An economic theory of protectionism, tariff bargaining and the formation of customs unions', *Journal of Political Economy*, vol. 73.

Johnson, H. G. (1973) 'Problems of European Monetary Union', in M. B. Krauss (ed.), *The Economics of Integration*, Allen & Unwin.

Johnson, H. G. (1974) 'Trade diverting customs unions: a comment', *Economic Journal*, vol. 81.

Johnston, A. (1999) 'The EC Energy Law 1999: reciprocity and the gas and electricity directives', *CEPMLP Internet Journal*, vol. 4, no. 9, **www.dundee.ac.uk/cepmlp/journal/htm1/article4-9.html**.

Johnston, A. (2001) 'Judicial reform and the Treaty of Nice', *Common Market Law Review*, vol. 38.

Jones, A. J. (1979) 'The theory of economic integration', in J. K. Bowers (ed.), *Inflation Development and Integration: Essays in honour of A. J. Brown*, Leeds University Press.

Jones, A. J. (1980) 'Domestic distortions and customs union theory', *Bulletin of Economic Research*, vol. 32.

Jones, A. J. (1983) 'Withdrawal from a customs union: a macroeconomic analysis', in A. M. El-Agraa (ed.), *Britain within the European Community: The Way Forward*, Macmillan, Chapter 5.

Jones, C. and Gonzalez-Diaz, F. E. (1992) *The EEC Merger Control Regulation*, Sweet & Maxwell, London.

Jordan, A. (1999) 'European water standards: locked in or watered down?', *Journal of Common Market Studies*, vol. 37.

Jovanovic, M. (2002) 'Eastern enlargement of the EU: topsy turvy endgame or permanent disillusion', mimeo, UN Economic Commission for Europe, November.

Kay, J. A. and King, M. A. (1996) *The British Tax System*, Oxford University Press.

Kelman, S. (1981) *What Price Incentives?*, Auburn House.

Kemp, A. G. and Stephen, L. (2001) 'Prospects for gas supply and demand and their implications with special reference to the UK', *Oxford Review of Economic Policy*, vol. 17, no. 3.

Kenen, P. (1969) 'The theory of optimum currency areas: an eclectic view', in R. A. Mundell and A. K. Swoboda, *Monetary Problems of the International Economuy*, MIT Press.

Kenny, S. (1998) 'The Members of the ECJ of the European Communities', *Columbia Journal of European Law*, vol. 5.

Klemperer, P. D. and Meyer, M. A. (1989) 'Supply function equilibria in oligopoly under uncertainty', *Econometrica*, vol. 57, no. 6.

Koester, U. (1977) 'The redistributive effects of the Common Agricultural Financial System', *Review of Agricultural Economics*, vol. 4, no. 4.

Koester, U. (1989) *International Agricultural Trade Consortium*, Washington DC.

Koester, U. (1991) 'Economy-wide costs of farm support policies in major industrialized countries', in K. Burger *et al.* (eds), *Agricultural Economics and Policy: International Challenges for the Nineties*, Amsterdam.

Koester, U. *et al.* (1988) *Disharmonies in US and EC Agricultural Policy Measures*, Brussels.

Koester, U. and Tangermann, S. (1990) 'The European Community', in F. Sanderson (ed.), *Agricultural Protectionism*, Washington DC.

Korah, V. (1997) *An Introductory Guide to EEC Competition Law and Practice*, ESC Publishing, fourth edition.

Korah, V. (1998) 'The future of vertical agreements under EC competition law', *European Competition Law Review*, vol. 19.

Korah, V. (2000) *An Introducion to EC Competition Law*, Hart, Oxford, 7th edition.

Kramer, L. (2000) *EC Environmental Law*, Sweet & Maxwell, London, 4th edition.

Krauss, M. B. (1972) 'Recent developments in customs union theory: an interpretative survey', *Journal of Economic Literature*, vol. 10.

Kreinin, M. E. (1972) 'Effects of the EEC on imports of manufactures', *Economic Journal*, vol. 82.

Kreinin, M. E. (1973) 'The static effects of EEC enlargement on trade flows', *Southern Economic Journal*, vol. 39.

Kreinin, M. E. (1979a) *International Economics: A policy approach*, Harcourt Brace Jovanovich (also subsequent editions).

Kreinin, M. E. (1979b) 'Effects of European integration on trade flows in manufacturers', *Seminar Paper No. 125*, Institute for International Economic Studies, University of Stockholm, Sweden.

Kreuger, A. O. (1974) 'The political economy of the rent-seeking society', *American Economic Review*, vol. 64.

Krugman, P. R. (1979) 'Increasing returns, monopolistic competition and international trade', *Journal of International Economics*, vol. 9.

Krugman. P. R. (1991) *Geography and Trade*. MIT Press, Cambridge, MA.

Krugman, P. R. (1990) 'Policy problems of a monetary union', in P. de Grauwe and L. Papademos (eds.), *The European Monetary System in the 1990s*, Longman, Harlow.

Krugman. P. R. (1994) *Re-Thinking International Trade*. MIT Press, Cambridge, MA.

Krugman, P. R. and Venables, A. (1990) 'Integration and competitiveness of peripheral industry', in C. Bliss and J. Braga de Macedo (eds), *Unity with Diversity in the European Community*, Cambridge University Press.

Krugman, P. R. and Venables, A. (1996) 'Integration, specialization, adjustment', *European Economic Review*, vol. 40.

Kumm, M. (1999) 'Who is the final arbiter of constitutionality in Europe?: three conceptions of the relationship between the German Federal Constitutional Court and the European ECJ', *Common Market Law Review*, vol. 36.

Ladeur, K.-H. (1997) 'Towards a legal theory of supranationality – The viability of the network concept', *European Law Journal*, vol. 3.

Laffan, B. (1997) *The Finances of the European Union*, Macmillan, Basingstoke.

Lamfalussy, A. (1963) 'Intra-European trade and the competitive position of the EEC', *Manchester Statistical Society Transactions*, March.

Lamfalussy, A. (2001) *Final Report of the Committee of Wise Men on the Regulation of European Securities Markets*, CEU, Brussels, February.

Lamy, P. (2002) 'Stepping stones or stumbling blocs? The EU's approach towards the problem of multilateralism vs regionalism in trade policy', *The World Economy*, vol. 25, no. 10.

Latour, B. (1993) *We Have Never Been Modern*, Harvester Wheatsheaf, London.

Lehtinen, T. (2003) 'The coordination of European development cooperation in the field: myth and reality', *ECDPM Discussion Paper 43*, ECDPM, Maastricht.

Lesquesne, C. (2000a) 'The Common Fisheries Policy', in H. Wallace and W. Wallace (eds), *Policy Making in the EU*, Oxford University Press.

Lesquesne, C. (2000b) 'Quota hopping: the Common Fisheries Policy between states and markets', *Journal of Common Market Studies*, vol. 38, no. 5.

Lindberg, L. N. and Scheingold, S. A. (1970) *Europe's Would-be Policy Patterns of Change in the European Community*, Prentice Hall.

Linnemann, H. (1966) *An Econometric Study of International Trade Flows*, North-Holland.

Lipgens, W. (1982) *A History of European Integration, vol. 1, 1945–47: The Formation of the European Unity Movement*, Clarendon Press, Oxford.

Lipsey, R. G. (1960) 'The theory of customs unions: a general survey', *Economic Journal*, vol. 70.

Lister, M. (1998) *European Union Development Policy*, Gower, Macmillan, Basingstoke.

Lockwood, B., de Meza, B. and Myles, G. (1994) 'When are destination and origin regimes equivalent?', *International Tax and Public Finance*, vol. 1.

Lucarelli, B. (1999) *The Origins and Evolution of the Single Market in Europe*, Aldershot, Ashgate.

Lucas, N. J. D. (1977) *Energy and the European Communities*, Europa Publications for the David Davies Memorial Institute of International Studies, London.

Lucas, R. E. (1988) 'On the mechanics of economic development', *Journal of Monetary Economics*, vol. 22.

Ludlow, P. (1982) *The Making of the European Monetary System: A case study of the politics of the European Community*, Butterworths, London.

MacCormick, N. (1993) 'Beyond the sovereign state', *Modern Law Review*, vol. 56.

MacCormick, N. (1996) 'Liberalism, nationalism and the post-sovereign state', in R. Bellamy and D. Castiglione (eds), *Constitutionalism in Transformation: European and Theoretical Perspectives*, Blackwell, Oxford.

MacCormick, N. (1999) *Questioning Sovereignty*, Oxford University Press, Oxford.

MacDougall Report (1977) see Commission of the European Communities (1977).

McCormick, J. (2001) *Environmental Politics in the EU*, Palgrave, Basingstoke.

McGowan, F. (1993) *The Struggle for Power in Europe*, RIIA.

Machlup, F. (1977) *A History of Thought on Economic Integration*, Macmillan, Basingstoke.

McKinnon, R. I. (1963) 'Optimum currency areas',

McMahon, J. (1998) *The Development Coopera-tion Policy of the EC*, Kluwer Law International, Dordrecht and London.

McManus, J. G. (1972) 'The theory of the inter-national firm', in G. Paquet (ed.), *The Multinational Firm and the National State*, Collier Macmillan, New York.

McQueen, M. (2002) 'The EU's free trade agreements with developing countries: a case of wishful thinking?', *The World Economy*, vol. 25, no. 9.

Magrini, S. (1999) 'The evolution of income dis-parities among the regions of the European Union', *Regional Science and Urban Economics*, vol. 29.

Maher, I. (1995) 'Legislative review by the EC Com-mission: Revision without radicalism', in J. Shaw and G. More (eds), *New Legal Dynamics of EU*, Oxford University Press, Oxford.

Majone, G. (1994) 'The rise of regulatory policy making in Europe and the United States', *Journal of Public Policy*, vol. 11, no. 1.

Majone, G. (1998) 'Europe's democracy deficit: The question of standards', *European Law Journal*, vol. 4.

Mancini, G. (1998) 'Europe: The case for statehood', *European Law Journal*, vol. 4.

Marer, P. and Montias, J. M. (1988) 'The Council for Mutual Economic Assistance', in A. M. El-Agraa (ed.), *International Economic Integration*, Macmillan and St Martin's, New York.

Marin, A. (1979) 'Pollution control: economists' views', *Three Banks Review*, no. 121.

Marques-Mendes, A. J. (1986) 'The contribution of the European Community to economic growth', *Journal of Common Market Studies*, vol. 24, no. 4.

Marshall. A. (1920) *Principles of Economics*, Macmillan.

Martin, S. (2001) *Industrial Organization: A Euro-pean Perspective*, Oxford University Press, Oxford.

Martin, S. and Scott, J. T. (2000) 'The nature of innovation market failure and the design of public support for private innovation', *Research Policy*, vol. 29, no. 4–5.

Mattli, W. and Slaughter, A.-M. (1998) 'Revisiting the European ECJ', *International Organization*, vol. 52.

Mayes, D. G. (1978) 'The effects of economic integra-tion on trade', *Journal of Common Market Studies*, vol. 17, no. 1.

Mayes, D. G. (1983) 'EC trade effects and factor mobility', in A. M. El-Agraa (ed.), *Britain within the European Community: The way forward*, Macmillan, Chapter 6.

Mayes, D. G. (1988) Chapter 3, in A. Bollard and M. A. Thompson (eds), *Trans-Tasman Trade and Investment*, Institute for Policy Studies, Wellington, New Zealand.

Mayes, D. G. (1993) *The External Implications of European Integration*, Harvester Wheatsheaf.

Mayes, D. G. (1996) 'The role of foreign direct invest-ment in structural change: the lessons from the New Zealand experience', in G. Csaki, G. Foti and D. Mayes (eds), *Foreign Direct Investment and Transition: The Case of the Visegrad countries*, Trends in World Eco-nomy, no. 78, Institute for World Economics, Budapest.

Mayes, D. G. (1997a) 'Competition and cohesion: lessons from New Zealand', in M. Fritsch and H. Hansen (eds), *Rules of Competition and East-West Integration*, Kluwer.

Mayes, D. G. (1997b) *The Evolution of the Single European Market*, Edward Elgar, Cheltenham.

Mayes, D. G. (1997c) 'The New Zealand experiment: using economic theory to drive policy', *Policy Options*, vol. 18, no. 7.

Mayes, D. G. (1997d) 'The problems of the quantitat-ive estimation of integration effects', in A. M. El-Agraa (ed.), *Economic Integration Worldwide*, Macmillan and St Martins, New York.

Mayes, D. G. and Begg, I. with Levitt, M. and Shipman, A. (1992) *A New Strategy for Economic and Social Cohesion after 1992*, European Parliament, Luxembourg.

Mayes, D. G., Hager, W., Knight, A. and Streeck, W. (1993) *Public Interest and Market Pressures: Prob-lems posed by Europe 1992*, Macmillan, London.

Mayes, D. G. and Virén, M. (2000) 'The exchange rate and monetary conditions in the euro area', *Weltwirtschaftliches Archiv*, vol. 136, no. 2.

Mayes, D. G., Bergman, J. and Salais, R. (2001) *Social Exclusion and European Policy*, Edward Elgar, Cheltenham.

Mayes, D. G. and Suvanto, A. (2002) 'Beyond the fringe: Finland and the choice of currency', *Journal of Public Policy*, vol. 22, no. 2.

Mayes, D. G. and Virén, M. (2002a) 'Macroeconomic factors, policies and the development of social exclu-sion', in R. Muffels, P. Tsakloglou and D. G. Mayes (eds), *Social Exclusion in European Welfare States*, Edward Elgar, Cheltenham.

Mayes, D. G. and Virén, M. (2002b) 'Policy coordina-tion and economic adjustment in EMU: will it work?', in Ali M. El-Agraa (ed.), *The euro and Britain: Implications of Moving into the EMU*.

Mayes, D. G. and Virén, M. (2002c) 'Asymmetry and the problem of aggregation in the euro area', *Empirica*, vol. 29.

Meade, J. E. (1980) *The Theory of International Trade Policy*, Oxford University Press.

Meade, J. E., Liesner, H. H. and Wells, S. J. (1962) *Case Studies in European Economic Union: The Mechanics of Integration*, Oxford University Press.

Mchta, K. and Peeperkorn, L. (1999) 'The economics of competition', in J. Faull and A. Nikpay (eds), *The EC Law of Competition*, Clarendon, Oxford.

Meij, J. (2000) 'Architects or judges? Some comments in relation to the current debate', *Common Market Law Review*, vol. 37.

Mélitz, J. (2001) 'Geography, trade and currency union', *Discussion Paper*, No. 2987, CEPR, London.

Mélitz, J. and Zumer, F. (1998) Regional redistribtion and stabilization by the Center in Canada, France, the United Kingdom and the United States: new estimates based on Panel data econometrics', *Discussion Paper*, No. 1892, CEPR, London.

Memedovic, O., Kuyvenhoven, A. and Molle, W. (eds) (1999) *Multilateralism and Regionalism in the Post-Uruguay Round Era: What Role for the EU?*, Kluwer, Boston.

Merrills, J. (1998) *International Dispute Settlement*, Cambridge University Press, Cambridge.

Messerlin, P. A. (2001) *Measuring the Costs of Protection in Europe*, Institute for International Economics, Washington, DC.

Midelfart-Knarvik, K. H., Overman, H. G., Redding, S. J. and Venables, A. J. (2000) 'The location of European industry', *Economic Paper 14*, DG for Economic and Financial Affairs, Commission of the European Union.

Mintz, J. M. (2002) 'European company tax reform: prospects for the future', *CESifo Forum*, 3/1, www.cesifo.de/

Molle, W. and Morsink, R. (1991) 'Direct investment and European integration', *European Economy*, special issue.

Monti, M. (1996) *The Single Market and Tomorrow's Europe: a Progress Report from the European Commission*, Office for Official Publications of the European Communities, Luxembourg; Kogan Page, London.

Moser, S. and Pesaresi, N. (2002) 'State guarantees to German public banks: a new step in the enforcement of state aid discipline to financial services in the Community', *Competition Policy Newsletter*, No. 2, June, pp. 1–11.

Munby, D. L. (1962) 'Fallacies of the Community's transport policy', *Journal of Transport Economics and Policy*, vol. 1.

Mundell, R. A. (1961) 'A theory of optimum currency areas', *American Economic Review*, vol. 51.

Mundell, R. A. (1964) 'Tariff preferences and the terms of trade', *Manchester School*, vol. 32.

Musgrave, R. A. (1959) *The Theory of Public Finance*, McGraw-Hill, New York.

Nam, C. and Reuter, J. (1992) *The Effect of 1992 and Associated Legislation on the Less Favoured Regions of the Community*, Office for Official Publications of the European Communities, Luxembourg.

Neill, Sir P. (1996) *The European ECJ: A Case Study in Judicial Activism*, European Policy Forum/ Frankfurter Institut, London/Frankfurt.

Neuemayer, E. (2001) 'Improvement without convergence: pressure on the environment in EU countries', *Journal of Common Market Studies*, vol. 39, no. 5.

Neven, D. J. and Wyplosz, C. (1999) 'Relative prices, trade and restructuring in European industry', in M. Dewatripont *et al.* (eds), *Trade and Jobs in Europe: Much Ado About Nothing?*, Oxford University Press, Oxford.

Neven, D. J., Nuttal, R. and Seabright, P. (1993a) *Competition and Merger Policy in the EC*, CEPR.

Neven, D. J., Nuttal, R. and Seabright, P. (1993b) *Merger in Daylight*, CEPR.

Neven, D. J., Papandropoulos, P. and Seabright, P. (1998) *Trawling for Minnows: European Competition Policy and Agreements Between Firms*, CEPR.

Neven, D. J. (1990) 'Gains and losses from 1992', *Economic Policy*, April.

Newbery, D. M. (1999a) *Privatization, Restructuring, and Regulation of Network Industries*, MIT Press, Cambridge, Massachusetts and London, England.

Newbery, D. M. (1999b) 'The UK experience: privatization with market power', Chapter 6, pp. 89–115, in Bergmann, Lars *et al.* *A European Market for Electricity?* CEPR, London; and SNS, Stockholm.

Newbery, D. M. (2001) 'Economic reform in Europe: integrating and liberalizing the market for services', *Utilities Policy*, vol. 10, pp. 85–97.

Nicholl, W. (1994) 'The battles of the European budget', *Policy Studies*, vol. 7, July.

Nicodème, G. (2001) 'Comparing effective corporation tax rates: comparisons and results', *Economic Paper No. 153*, EU Commission, DG Economic and Financial Affairs.

Nicoletti, G., Scarpetta, S. and Boylaud, O. (2000) 'Summary indicators of product market regulation with an extension of employment protection legilslation', *Working Paper No. 226*, OECD, Paris.

North, D. C. (1990) *Institutional Changes and Economic Performance*, Cambridge University Press.

Notaro, G. (2002) 'European integration and productivity: exploring the gains of the Single Market', London Eonomics, London.

Oates, W. E. (ed.) (1977) *The Political Economy of Fiscal Federalism*, Lexington Books, Toronto.

Oates, W. E. (1999) 'An essay in fiscal federalism', *Journal of Economic Literature*, vol. 37, no. 3.

Obstfeld, M. and Peri, G. (1998) 'Regional non-adjustment and fiscal policy', *Economic Policy*, vol. 26, April.

O'Donnell, R. (1992) 'Policy requirements for regional balance in economic and monetary union', in A. Hannequart (ed.), *Economic and Social Cohesion in Europe: a New Objective for Integration*, Routledge, London.

OECD (various years) *Economic Survey of Europe*, OECD, Paris.

OECD (various issues) *Geographical Distribution of Financial Flows to Aid Recipients*, OECD, Paris.

OECD (1988a) *The Newly Industrialising Countries: Challenges and opportunity for OECD industries*, OECD, Paris.

OECD (1988b) *Taxing Consumption*, OECD, Paris.

OECD (1999) *SOPEMI: Trends in International Migration: Annual Report 1999. Continuous reporting system on migration*, OECD, Paris.

OECD (2000) *The European Union's Trade Policies and their Economic Effects*, OECD, Paris.

OECD (2001) *Environmentally Related Taxes in EU Countries*, OECD, Paris.

OECD (2002a) *European Community Development Cooperation Review Series*, OECD, Paris.

OECD (2002b) *Revenue Statistics 1965–2001*, OECD, Paris.

Office of Gas and Electricity Markets (2000) *An Overview of the New Electricity Trading Arrangements V1.0*.

Ofgem (Office of Gas and Electricity Markets) (2000) *An Overview of the New Electricity Trading Arrangements V1.0*.

Ofgem (2002) *Transmission Access and Losses Under NETA*, revised proposals.

O'Keeffe, D. (1998) 'Is the spirit of Article 177 under attack? Preliminary references and admissibility', *European Law Review*, vol. 23.

Olson, M. (1982) *The Rise and Decline of Nations: Economic Growth, Stagnation and Social Rigidities*, Yale University Press, Yale.

Oort, C. J. and Maaskant, R. H. (1976) *Study of Possible Solutions for Allocating the Deficit which may Occur in a System of Charging for the Use of Infrastructure Aiming at Budgetary Equilibrium*, EEC.

Owen, N. (1983) *Economies of Scale, Competitiveness and Trade Patterns within the European Community*, Oxford University Press.

Owens, S. and Hope, C. (1989) 'Energy and the environment – the challenge of integrating European policies', *Energy Policy*, vol. 17.

Padoa-Schioppa, T. (1987) *Efficiency, Stability and Equity: A Strategy for the Evolution of the Economic System of the European Community*, Oxford University Press.

Palmer, M. and Lambert, J. (1968) *European Unity*, Allen & Unwin, London.

Panagariya, A. (2002) 'EU preferential trade arrangements and developing countires', *The World Economy*, vol. 25, no. 10.

Parry, I. (1997) 'Revenue recycling and the costs of reducing carbon emissions', *Climate Issues Brief No. 2*, Resources for the Future.

Parry, I. and Oates, W. (1998) 'Policy analysis in a second-best world', *Discussion Paper 98-48*, Resources for the Future.

Paxton, J. (1976) *The Developing Common Market*, Macmillan, Basingstoke.

Payne, D. C. (2000) 'Policy making in nested institutions: explaining the conservation failures of the EU's Common Fisheries Policy', *Journal of Common Market Studies*, vol. 38, no. 2.

Pearson, M. and Smith, S. (1991) *The European Carbon Tax*, Institute for Fiscal Studies, London.

Peeperkorn, L. (1998) 'The economics of verticals', *EC Competition Policy Newsletter*, vol. 2.

Pelkmans, J. (2001) 'Making network markets competitive', *Oxford Review of Economic Policy*, vol. 17.

Pelkmans, J. and Winters, L. A. (1988) *Europe's Domestic Market*, Routledge, London.

Perman, R., Ma, Y., McGilvray, J. and Common, M. (1999) *Natural Resource and Environmental Economics*, Financial Times, Prentice Hall, Harlow, 2nd edition.

Peterson, J. and Sharp, M. (1998) *Technology Policy in the European Union*, St Martin's Press, New York.

Petit, M. (1985) 'Determinants of agricultural policies in the United States and the European Community', *International Food Policy Research Report 51*, Washington DC.

Phelps, E. S. (1968) 'Money–wage dynamics and labour market equilibrium', *Journal of Political Economy*, vol. 76.

Phillips, A. W. (1958) 'The relation between unemployment and the rate of change of money wages in the United Kingdom', *Economica*, vol. 25.

Phinnemore, D. (1999) *Association: Stepping Stone or Alternative to EU Membership?*, Sheffield Academic Press, Sheffield.

Phlips, L. (1993) 'Basing point pricing, competition, and market integration', in H. Ohta and J.-F. Thisse (eds), *Does Economic Space Matter? Essays in Honour of Melvin L. Greenhut*, Macmillan, Basingstoke.

Phlips, L. (1995) *Competition Policy: a Game Theoretical Perspective*, Cambridge University Press.

Pisani-Ferry, J. (2002) 'Fiscal discipline and policy co-ordination in the eurozone: assessment and proposals', mimeo, Commission of the European Union.

Plötner, J. (1998) 'Report on France', in A.-M. Slaughter, A. Stone Sweet and J. Weiler (eds), *The European Courts and National Courts: Doctrine and Jurisprudence*, Hart, Oxford.

Political and Economic Planning (PEP) (1962) *Atlantic Tariffs and Trade*, Allen & Unwin.

Political and Economic Planning (PEP) (1963) 'An energy policy for the EEC', *Planning*, vol. 29.

Pollack, M. (1997) 'Delegation, agency, and agenda-setting in the European Community', *International Organization*, vol. 51.

Pollard, P. (2003) 'A look inside two central banks: the European Central Bank and the Federal Reserve', *Federal Reserve Bank of St Louis Review*, January/February.

Porter, M. (1990) *The Competitive Advantage of Nations*, Macmillan.

Posner, R. (1976) *Antitrust Law: an Economic Perspective*, University of Chicago Press, Chicago.

Press, A. and Taylor, C. (1990) *Europe and the Environment*, The Industrial Society.

Prest, A. R. (1979) 'Fiscal policy', in P. Coffey (ed.), *Economic Policies of the Common Market*, Macmillan, Basingstoke.

Prewo, W. E. (1974a) *A multinational interindustry gravity model for the European Common Market*, PhD dissertation, Johns Hopkins University.

Prewo, W. E. (1974b) 'Integration effects in the EEC', *European Economic Review*, vol. 5.

Primo Braga, C. A. (1995) 'Trade-related intellectual property issues: the Uruguay Round agreement and its economies implications', in W. Martin and L. A. Winters (eds), 'The Uruguay Round and the developing economies', *World Bank Discussion Papers*, no. 307, Washington, DC.

Public Accounts Committee (2002) *Tobacco Smuggling*, 3rd Report, Session 2002–2003, HC 143, Stationery Office, www.parliament.the-stationery-office.co.uk/pa/cmcmpubacc.htm

Putnam, R. D. (1993) *Making Democracy Work: Civic Traditions in Modern Italy*, Princeton UP.

Quévit, M. (1995) 'The regional impact of the internal market: a comparative analysis of traditional industrial regions and lagging regions', in S. Hardy, M. Hart, L. Albrechts and A. Katos (eds), *An Enlarged Europe: Regions in Competition?*, Jessica Kingsley.

Raisman Committee (1961) *East Africa: Report of the Economic and Fiscal Commission*, Cmnd 1279, Colonial Office.

Rameu, F. (2002) 'Judicial cooperation in the European courts: testing three models of judicial behaviour', *Global Jurist Frontiers*, vol. 2, issue 1.

Rasmussen, H. (1986) *On Law and Policy in the European ECJ*, Martinus Nijhoff, Dordrecht.

Rasmussen, H. (1998) *European ECJ*, GadJura, Copenhagen.

Rasmussen, H. (2000) 'Remedying the crumbling EC judicial system', *Common Market Law Review*, vol. 37.

Rawlings, R. (1993) 'The Eurolaw game: Some deductions from a saga', *Journal of Law and Society*, vol. 20.

Rehg, W. (1996) 'Translators introduction', in J. Habermas, *Between Facts and Norms*, Polity, Cambridge University Press, Cambridge.

Reich, N. (1997) 'A European constitution for citizens: Reflections on the rethinking of union and community law', *European Law Journal*, vol. 3.

Resnick, S. A. and Truman, E. M. (1975) 'An empirical examination of bilateral trade in Western Europe', *Journal of International Economics*, vol. 3.

Ritchie, E. and Zito, A. R. (1998) 'The CFP: a policy disaster', in P. Gray and P. Hart (eds), *Public Policy Disasters in Western Europe*, Routledge, London.

Ritson, C. (1973) *The Common Agricultural Policy, in The European Economic Community: Economics and agriculture*, Open University Press.

Robson, P. (1980 and 1985) *The Economics of International Integration*, Allen & Unwin.

Robson, P. (1983) *Integration, Development and Equity: Economic integration in West Africa*, Allen & Unwin.

Robson, P. (1997) 'Integration in Sub-Saharan Africa', in Ali M. El-Agraa (ed.), *Economic Integration Worldwide*, Macmillan and St Martin's Press, New York.

Rodger, B. (1999) 'The Commission's white paper on modernisation of the rules implementing articles 81 and 82 of the EC Treaty', *European Law Review*, vol. 24.

Romer, P. M. (1986) 'Increasing returns and long-run growth', *Journal of Political Economy*, vol. 94, 1002–37.

Romer, P. M. (1994) 'New goods, old theory and the welfare of trade restrictions', *Journal of Development Economics*, vol. 43.

Rose, A. K. (1999) 'One money, one market: estimating the effect of common currencies on trade', *Working Paper No. 7432*, National Bureau of Economic Research, Cambridge MA.

Ruttan, V. W. (1998) 'The new growth theory and development economics: a survey', *Journal of Development Studies*, vol. 35.

Sala-i-Martin, X. (1996) 'Regional cohesion: evidence and theories of regional growth and convergence', *European Economic Review*, vol. 40.

Sala-i-Martin, X. and Sachs, J. (1992) 'Fiscal federalism and optimum currency areas: evidence from Europe and the United States', in M. Canzoneri, V. Grilli and P. Masson, *Establishing a Central Bank: Issues in Europe and Lessons from the US*, Cambridge University Press.

Sand, I.-J. (1998) 'Understanding new forms of governance: Mutually interdependent, reflexive, destabilised and competing institutions', *European Law Journal*, vol. 4.

Sandford, C. T., Godwin, M. T. and Hardwick, P. J. (1989) *Administrative and Compliance Costs*, Fiscal Publications, Bath.

Sapir, A. (1995) 'Europe's single market: the long march to 1992', Discussion Paper, CEPR, London.

Sapir, A. (1996) 'The effects of Europe's internal market programme on production and trade: a first assessment', *Weltwirtschaftliches Archiv*, vol. 132.

Sapir, A. (1998) 'The Political Economy of EC Regionalism', *European Economic Review*, vol. 42.

Scaperlanda, A. and Balough, R. S. (1983) 'Determinants of US direct investment in the EEC revisited', *European Economic Review*, vol. 21.

Schepel, H. (1997) 'Legal pluralism in Europe', in P. Fitzpatrick and J. Bergeron (eds), *Europe's Other: European Law between Modernity and Postmodernity*, Ashgate, Aldershot.

Schepel, H. and Wesseling, R. (1997) 'The legal community: Judges, lawyers, officials and clerks in the writing of Europe', *European Law Journal*, vol. 3.

Scherer, F. M. and Ross, D. (1990) *Industrial Market Structure and Economic Performance*, Houghton Mifflin.

Schiff, M. and Winters, L. A. (1998) 'Regional integration as diplomacy', *The World bank Economic Review*, vol. 12, no. 2.

Schilling, T. (1996) 'The autonomy of the community legal order – Through the looking glass', *Harvard Journal of International Law*, vol. 37.

Scitovsky, T. (1954) 'Two concepts of external economies', *Journal of Political Economy*, vol. 62.

Scitovsky, T. (1958) *Economic Theory and Western European Integration*, Allen & Unwin, London.

Scott, J. (1998) 'Law, legitimacy and EC governance: Prospects for "Partnership"', *Journal of Common Market Studies*, vol. 36.

Scully, R. (1997) 'The European Parliament and the co-decision procedure: A reassessment', *Journal of Legislative Studies*, vol. 3.

Servan-Schreiber, J.-J. (1967) *Le Défi Américain*, Denoöl, Paris.

Shackleton, M. (1983) 'Fishing for a policy? The CFP of the Community', in H. Wallace *et al.*, *Policy Making in the European Community*, John Wiley & Sons, Chichester.

Shapiro, M. (1996) 'Codification of administrative law: The US and the EU', *European Law Journal*, vol. 2.

Shaw, J. (1996) 'EU legal studies in crisis? Towards a new dynamic', *Oxford Journal of Legal Studies*, vol. 16.

Shaw, J. (1999) 'Postnational constitutionalism in the EU', *Journal of European Public Policy*, vol. 7.

Shaw, J. and Wiener, A. (1999) 'The Paradox of the "European Polity"', *Harvard Jean Monnet Working Paper No. 10/99*.

Shibata, H. (1967) 'The theory of economic unions', in C. S. Shoup (ed.), *Fiscal Harmonisation in Common Markets*, vol. 1–2, Columbia University Press, New York.

Sinn, H.-W. (1991) 'Taxation and the cost of capital: the "old" view, the "new" and another "view"', in D. F. Bradford, *Tax Policy in the Economy, 5*, MIT Press, Cambridge MA.

Silvis, H., van Rijswijck, C. and de Kleijn, A. (2001) 'EU agricultural expenditure for various accession scenarios', Report 6.01.04, Agricultural Research Institute, The Hague, cited in Swinnen, 2002.

Skully, D. W. (1999) 'The economics of TRQ administration', *IATRC Working Paper*, no. 99–6.

Slaughter, A.-M. (1995) 'International law in a world of liberal states', *European Journal of International Law*, vol. 6.

Slaughter, A.-M. (1999) 'Globalisation and Wages', *Centre for Research on Globalisation and Labour Markets, research paper 99/5*. University of Nottingham.

Slaughter, A.-M., Stone Sweet, A. and Weiler, J. (1998) 'Prologue', in A.-M. Slaughter, A. Stone Sweet and J. Weiler (eds), *The European Courts and National Courts: Doctrine and Jurisprudence*, Hart, Oxford.

Smith, A. J. (1977) 'The Council of Mutual Economic Assistance in 1977: new economic power, new political perspectives and some old and new problems', in US Congress Joint Economic Committee, *East European Economics Post-Helsinki*.

Snyder, F. (1999a) *Global Economic Networks and Global Legal Pluralism*, EUI Working Paper Law, vol. 6, Badia Fiesolana, San Domenico.

Snyder, F. (1999b) 'Governing economic globalisation: global legal pluralism and European Law', *European Law Journal*, vol. 5.

Sodupe, K. and Benito, E. (2001) 'Pan-European energy cooperation: opportunities, limitations and security of supply to the EU', *Journal of Common Market Studies*, vol. 39, no. 1.

Solow, R. M. (1957) 'Technical change and the aggregate production function', *Review of Economics and Statistics*, vol. 39.

Stein, E. (1981) 'Lawyers, judges and the making of a transnational constitution', *American Journal of International Law*, vol. 75, no. 1.

Stone Sweet, A. and Brunell, T. (1997) 'The European Court and National Courts: A statistical analysis of preliminary references 1961–1995', *Journal of European Public Policy*, vol. 5.

Stone Sweet, A. and Brunell, T. (1998) 'Constructing a supranational constitution: Dispute resolution and governance in the European Community', *American Political Science Review*, vol. 92.

Stone Sweet, A. and Caporaso, J. (1998) 'From free trade to supranational polity: The European Court and integration', in W. Sandholtz and A. Stone Sweet (eds), *European Integration and Supranational Governance*, Oxford University Press, Oxford.

Strasser, S. (1995) 'The Development of a Strategy of Docket Control for the European ECJ and the Question of Preliminary References', Harvard Jean Monnet Working Paper, vol. 3.

Streit, M. (1991) *Theorie der Wirtschaftspolitik, WiSo-Texte*, 4. Auflage. Werner-Verlag, Dusseldorf.

Striewe, L., Loy, J.-P. and Koester, U. (1996) 'Analyse und Beurteilung der einzelbetrieblichen Investitionsförderung in Schleswig-Holstein', *Agrarwirtschaft*, vol. 45, no. 12.

Sundelius, B. and Wiklund, C. (1979) 'The Nordic Community: the ugly duckling of regional cooperation', *Journal of Common Market Studies*, vol. 18, no. 1.

Swann, D. (1973) *The Economics of the Common Market*, Penguin, London.

Swann, D. (1988) *The Economics of the Common Market*, Penguin, London, fourth edition.

Sweet & Maxwell (regularly updated) *European Community Treaties*.

Swinnen, J. (2002) 'Budgetary implications of enlargement: agriculture', *CEPS Policy Brief*, No. 22, Centre for European Policy Studies, Brussels.

Symes, D. (1995) 'The European pond: who actually manages fisheries?', *Ocean and Coastal Management*, vol. 27, no. 1.

Szyszczak, E. (1996) 'Making Europe more relevant to its citizens: Effective judicial process', *European Law Review*, vol. 21.

Tangermann, S. (1991) 'Agriculture in "International Trade Negotiations"', in K. Burger, M. de Groat, J. Post and V. Zachariasse (eds), *Agricultural Economics and Policy: International Challenges for the Nineties*, Amsterdam.

Tani, M. (2002) 'Have European become more mobile? A note on regional evolutions in the EU: 1988–1997', School of Economics and Management, University of New South Wales at the Australian Defence Force Academy.

Temple Lang, J. (1998) 'Community Antitrust law and national regulatory prodedures', *1997 Annual Proceedings of Fordham Corporate Law Institute*, vol. 24.

Teubner, G. (1997) 'Breaking frames: The global interplay of legal and social systems', *American Journal of Comparative Law*, vol. 45.

Teubner, G. (1998) 'Legal irritants: Good faith in British law or how unifying law ends up in new divergences', *Modern Law Review*, vol. 61.

Thirwall, A. P. (1979) 'The balance of payments constraint as an explanation of international growth rate differences', *Banca Nazionale del Lavoro Quarterly Review*, March.

Thirwall, A. P. (1982) 'The Harrod trade multiplier and the importance of export-led growth', *Pakistan Journal of Applied Economics*, vol. 1, Summer.

Thornton, D. L. (2002) 'Monetary policy transparency: transparent about what?', Federal Reserve Bank of St Louis Working Paper 2002-028A, November.

Thoroe, C. (2000) 'The hierarchy of agricultural policies: European Union, Federal Republic and Federal States', in S. Tangermann (ed.), *Agriculture in Germany*, DLG-Verlag, Frankfurt am Main.

Tinbergen, J. (1952) *On the Theory of Economic Policy*, North-Holland.

Tinbergen, J. (1953) *Report on Problems Raised by the Different Turnover Tax Systems Applied within the Common Market* (the Tinbergen Report), High Authority of European Coal and Steel Community.

Tinbergen, J. (1954) *International Economic Integration*, Elsevier.

Tinbergen, J. (1962) *Shaping the World Economy: Suggestions for an International Economic Policy*, Twentieth Century Fund, New York.

Tracy, M. (1989) *Government and Agriculture in Western Europe 1880–1988*, Harvester Wheatsheaf, New York.

Tridimas, T. (1996) 'The ECJ and judicial activism', *European Law Review*, vol. 19.

Trubek, D. *et al.* (1994) 'Global restructuring and the law: Studies of the internationalization of legal fields and the creation of transnational arenas', *Case Western Reserve Law Review*, vol. 44.

Truman, E. M. (1969) 'The European Economic Community: trade creation and trade diversion', *Yale Economic Essays*, Spring.

Truman, E. M. (1975) 'The effects of European economic integration on the production and trade of manufactured products', in B. Balassa (ed.), *European Economic Integration*, North-Holland.

Tsebelis, G. (1994) 'The power of the EP as a conditional agenda-setter', *American Political Science Review*, vol. 88.

Tsebelis, G. and Garrett, G. (1997) 'Agenda setting, vetoes and the EU's co-decision procedure', *Journal of Legislative Studies*, vol. 3.

Tsebelis, G. and Garrett, G. (2000) 'Legislative politics in the European Union', *European Union Politics*, vol. 1.

Tsebelis, G. and Kreppel, A. (1998) 'The history of conditional agenda-setting in European institutions', *European Journal of Political Research*, vol. 33.

Tullock, G. (1967) 'The welfare costs of tariffs, monopolies and theft', *Western Economic Journal*, vol. 5.

UK Civil Aviation Authority (1993) *Airline Competition in the Single European Market*, CAP 623, CAA.

UK Treasury (1997) UK Membership of the Single Currency: An Assessment of the Five Economic Tests. **www.hm-treasury.gov.uk**

UNCTAD (2002) *Participation of the African, Caribbean and Pacific Group of States in International Trade*, UNCTAD/DITC/TNCD/Misc., 22 August, Geneva.

Ungerer, H. *et al.* (1986) 'The European Monetary System – recent developments', *Occasional Papers*, no. 48, IMF.

United Kingdom Government (1996) *Memorandum by the British Government to the 1996 Intergovernmental Conference on the European ECJ*, Foreign and Commonwealth Office, London.

US Bureau of Economic Analysis (2003) *Regional Accounts Data*, **www.census.gov/**

US Census Bureau (2003) *State Population Estimates*, **www.bea.gov/bea/regional/data.htm**

US Department of Energy, Energy Office Administration (1997) *Electricity Reform Abroad and US Investment*, September.

Valbonesi, P. (1998) 'Privatization and EU competition policy: the case of the Italian energy sector', in Stephen Martin, editor *Competition Policies in Europe*. Elsevier Science, Amsterdam.

van den Noord, P. (2000) *The Size and Role of Automatic Stabilisers in the 1990s and Beyond*, Economics Department Report Number 230, OECD, Paris.

van der Linde, J. G. and Lefeber, R. (1988) 'IEA captures the development of European Community energy law', *Journal of World Trade*, vol. 22.

van Dijck, P. and Faber, G. (eds) (2000) *The External Economic Dimension of the European Union*, Kluwer Law International, Dordrecht and London.

Vanek, J. (1965) *General Equilibrium of International Discrimination: the Case of Customs Unions*, Harvard University Press.

Vanhalewyn, E. (1999) 'Trends and patterns in state aids', *European Economy Report and Studies: State Aid and the Single Market*, no. 3.

Verdoorn, P. J. and Schwartz, A. N. R. (1972) 'Two alternative estimates of the effects of EEC and EFTA on the pattern of trade', *European Economic Review*, vol. 3.

Vernon, R. (1966) 'International investment and international trade in the product cycle', *Quarterly Journal of Economics*, vol. 80.

Verwaal, E. and Cnossen, S. (2002) 'Europe's new border taxes', *Journal of Common Market Studies*, vol. 40, no. 2.

Viegas, J. M. and Blum, U. (1993) 'High speed railways in Europe', in D. Banister and J. Berechman (eds), *Transport in a Unified Europe*, Elsevier, Oxford.

Viner, J. (1950) *The Customs Union Issue*, Carnegie Endowment for International Peace, New York.

Volcansek, M. (1986) *Judicial Politics in Europe*, Peter Lang, Frankfurt.

von Geusau, F. A. (1975) 'In search of a policy', in F. A. von Geusau (ed.), *Energy Strategy in the European Communities*, Sijthoff.

Von Hagen, J. and Mundschenk, S. (2002) 'Fiscal and monetary policy co-ordination in EMU', *Oester-reichsche National Bank Working Paper 70*, August.

Von Thünen, J. H. (1826) *Der isoliere Staat in Beziehung auf Landwirtschaft und Nationbalök-onomie*, Perthes.

Vos, E. (1998) *Institutional Frameworks of Community Health and Safety Regulation: Committees, Agencies and Private Bodies*, Hart, Oxford.

Waddams Price, C. (1997) 'Competition and regulation in the UK gas industry', *Oxford Review of Economic Policy*, vol. 13, no. 1.

Wallace, W. (ed.) (1990) *The Dynamics of European Integration*, Pinter, London.

Walters, A. A. (1963) 'A note on economies of scale', *Review of Economics and Statistics*, November.

Wang, Z. and Winters, L. A. (1991) 'The trading potential of Eastern Europe', *CEPR Discussion Paper No. 610*, CEPR, London.

Ward, I. (1996) *A Critical Introduction to European Law*, Butterworths, London. *CEPR Discussion Paper No. 610*, CEPR, London.

WB-BML (Wissenschaftlicher Beirat beim Bundesministerium für Ernährung, Landwirtschaft und Forsten) (1998) *Integration der Landwirtschaft der Europäischen Union in die Weltagrarwirtschaft, Angewandte Wissenswchaft*, Heft 476: Bonn. www.verbraucherministerium.de/forschung/wissbeirat/gutachten/itegration_der_landwirtschaft_d,htm

Weale, A. et al. (2000) *Environmental Governance in Europe: an Ever Closer Union?*, Oxford University Press.

Weatherill, S. and Beaumont, P. (1999) *EU Law*, Penguin, Harmondsworth, 3rd edition.

Weck-Hannemann, H. and Frey, B. (1997) 'Are economic instruments as good as economists believe? Some new considerations', in Bovenberg and Cnossen (1997).

Weiler, J. (1993) 'Journey to an unknown destination: A retrospective and prospective of the European ECJ in the arena of political integration', *Journal of Common Market Studies*, vol. 31.

Weiler, J. (1994) 'A quiet revolution: The European ECJ and its interlocutors', *Comparative Political Studies*, vol. 26.

Weiler, J. (1997a) 'To be a European citizen: Eros and civilisation', *Journal of European Public Policy*, vol. 4.

Weiler, J. (1997b) 'The EU belongs to its citizens: Three immodest proposals', *European Law Review*, vol. 22.

Weiler, J. (2001) 'Epilogue: the judicial Après Nice', In G. de Búrca and J. Weiler, *The European Court of Justice*, Hart, Oxford.

Weiler, J. and Haltern, U. (1998) 'Constitutional or international? The foundations of the community legal order and the question of judicial Kompetenz-Kompetenz', in A.-M. Slaughter, A. Stone Sweet and J. Weiler (eds), *The European Courts and National Courts: Doctrine and Jurisprudence*, Hart, Oxford.

Weise, C. (2002) 'How to finance Eastern enlargement of the EU: the need to reform EU policies and the consequences for the net contributor balance', *Working Paper, No. 14*, October, European Network of Economic Policy Research Institutes, www.enepri.org

Weiss, L. W. (1971) *Case Studies in American Industry*, second edition, John Wiley & Sons, Inc., New York.

Wesseling, R. (2000) *The Modernisation of EC Antitrust Policy*, Hart.

Wessels, W. (1997) 'An ever closer fusion? A dynamic macropolitical view on integration processes', *Journal of Common Market Studies*, vol. 37.

Whitwill, M. (2000) 'European deregulation: one year on', The Uranium Institute 25th Annual Symposium. London, 30 August–1 September.

Wilhelmsson, T. (1995) 'Integration as disintegration of national law', in H. Zahle and H. Petersen (eds), *Legal Polycentricity: Consequences of Pluralism in Law*, Dartmouth, Aldershot.

Wilkinson, D. (1997) 'Towards sustainability in the EU? Steps within the European Commission towards integrating the environment into other EU policy sectors', *Environmental Politics*, vol. 6.

Williamson, J. and Bottrill, A. (1971) 'The impact of customs unions on trade in manufactures', *Oxford Economic Papers*, vol. 25, no. 3.

Wils, W. (1999) 'Notification, clearance and exemption in EC competition law: an economic analysis', *European Law Review*, vol. 24.

Winters, L. A. (1984) 'British imports of manufactures and the Common Market', *Oxford Economic Papers*, vol. 36.

Winters, L. A. (1985) 'Separability and the specification of foreign trade functions', *European Economic Review*, vol. 27.

Winters, L. A. (2000) 'EU's preferential trade agreements: objectives and outcomes', in P. van Dijck and G. Faber (eds), *The External Economic Dimension of the European Union*, Kluwer Law International, Dordrecht and London.

Wise, M. (1996) 'Regional concepts in the development of the CFP', in K. Crean and D. Symes (eds), *Fisheries Management in Crisis*, Blackwell Science, Oxford.

Wolf, M. (1983) 'The European Community's trade policy', in R. Jenkins (ed.), *Britain in the EEC*, Macmillan, Basingstoke.

Wolfram, C. D. (1999) 'Measuring market power in the British electricity spot market', *American Economic Review*, vol. 89, no. 4.

Wonnacott, G. P. and Wonnacott, R. J. (1981) 'Is unilateral tariff reduction preferable to a customs union? The curious case of the missing foreign tariffs', *American Economic Review*, vol. 71.

Wood, A. (1994) *North–South Trade, Employment, and Inequality*, Oxford University Press.

Wood, A. (1995) 'How trade hurt unskilled workers', *Journal of Economic Perspectives*, vol. 9.

World Bank (1992) *Governance and Development*.

World Bank (2003) *Global Economic Prospects of Developing Countries*, Washington DC.

WTO (2002) *Trade Policy Review: European Union 2001*, vols I and II, Geneva.

Yarrow, G. (1991) 'Vertical supply arrangements: issues and applications in the energy industries', *Oxford Review of Economic Policy*, vol. 7, no. 2.

Young, H. (1998) *This Blessed Plot: Britain and Europe from Churchill to Blair*, Macmillan.

Zürn, M. and Wolf, D. (1999) 'European Law and international regimes: The features of law beyond the nation state', *European Law Journal*, vol. 5.

Author index

Subject Index

Page numbers in *italics* indicate tables or figures